THE BIOLOGY OF BEHAVIOR AND MIND

Bruce Bridgeman
University of California–Santa Cruz

WILEY

JOHN WILEY & SONS
New York Chichester Brisbane Toronto Singapore

THE BIOLOGY OF BEHAVIOR AND MIND

cover photograph by Geoffry Gove

Library of Congress Cataloging in Publication Data:

Bridgeman, Bruce.
The biology of behavior and mind / Bruce Bridgeman.
p. cm.
Bibliography.
Includes indexes.

ISBN 0-471-87621-6
1. Psychology, Physiological. 2. Neuropsychology.
3. Brain. I. Title.
[DNLM: 1. Behavior—physiology. 2. Brain—physiology.
3. Mental Processes—physiology. 4. Psychophysiology.
WL 103 B851b]
QP360.B73 1988 87-27907
152—dc19 CIP

Printed in the United States of America

10 9 8 7 6 5 4 3 2 1

PREFACE

Physiological psychology is not an easy subject, but it is an enormously exciting one. Magnetic resonance imaging of the living brain, functional grafts to replace missing nerve cells, new chemical therapies for behavioral disorders, and other innovations are coming from the laboratories at a rapid pace. To understand and evaluate these developments, and to know a bit more about ourselves, it is necessary to learn something about the machinery of mind and brain.

The study of the brain covers many subdisciplines, at levels from single molecules to group behavior. To unify the diverse levels and approaches, this book is organized around an evolutionary perspective and an information-processing approach. Signs of one or the other theme appear on almost every page. I have tried to tell a story, rather than just reviewing the relevant experiments in each area. The evolutionary perspective shows not only what happens but why it happens. It relates human to animal studies, and it brings together disparate aspects of the narrative. I hope it also offers a historical basis and a unification with other areas of biology. Information processing is used not in the narrow sense of the information-processing models in cognitive psychology but in the broader sense of information flowing through an organism and being stored and transformed along the way. The basic concepts of both evolution and information processing are introduced in the first chapter.

TO THE STUDENT

To study how the brain works, you need some knowledge of biology, psychology, physics, and chemistry. The text provides background in these areas, but an introductory course in psychology or biology would be helpful too, as would a year of high-school chemistry or one chemistry course at the college level. You should understand the following terms before starting: atom, molecule, atomic number, atomic weight, molecular weight, bond, and charge. If you don't have this background, read the first few chapters of an introductory college-level chemistry textbook or ask a roommate or friend for information when the terms come up.

When you are reading the book, keep a bookmark at the beginning of the glossary and look up unfamiliar words. All important terms are printed in **boldface** in the text and are defined in the glossary. They are also defined in the text at their first appearance. Some other key terms are also defined in the glossary. When you come across a reference to a figure, read to the end of the sentence before examining the figure. Each figure caption begins with a brief description of the figure. Some captions also contain more advanced or specialized material as a supplement to the main text.

Each chapter begins with a chapter outline to give you an idea of where the text is going. Some of the longer or more difficult passages end with mini-summaries whose opening words are *In summary* or *In conclusion.* These mini-summaries (which do not have separate headings) wrap up a section without reviewing all its details. In addition, each chapter ends with a chapter summary. If you understand the terms and ideas in the chapter summary, you have grasped the important messages of the chapter.

Physiological psychology depends on *reductionism,* the idea that one can gain insight into the whole by studying its parts. Everyone is curious about the workings of the mind, the basis of experience, and why we perceive things the way we do. But much of our knowledge about these issues is obtained from studies of small aspects of the problem, often in animals. As you read, try to fit these studies into the bigger picture, and remember that one cannot understand the insights in the field without knowing their factual basis.

Most of all, read with an open mind. The field contains many areas of controversy, and some of its long-held ideas have been found to be false. I have tried to point these out along the way. I envy you a bit, beginning this intellectual adventure at a time when so much is known about the biology of behavior and mind—and when there is so much yet to discover.

TO THE INSTRUCTOR

One of the features of this text that differentiates it from other physiological psychology texts is more emphasis on graded potentials (Chapter 2). Graded cable properties of nerve cell membranes are introduced before the active action potential mode to let students see how information from various sources combines and interacts before it is sent elsewhere. This is the real site of information processing, as opposed to information transmission. In Chapter 3, brain organization is introduced in a phylogenetic and embryological context, beginning with the oldest structures and the most basic subdivisions. The emphasis is on topology and function rather than on topography. Sensory modalities are introduced in the order of their complexity in Chapter 4. Peripheral processes, because they are so different in each modality, are treated separately from central processes, which are similar in all modalities. The senses are also introduced in a functional way, as perceptual systems (Chapter 6) as well as anatomical entities. Many aspects of sensory systems are easier for students to grasp in the context of interactions between perception and behavior. Methods are introduced as they are needed rather than in a separate (and often dry) methods chapter. For example, a passage on anatomical methods introduces Chapter 3.

Rather than trying to decide whether to incorporate material on applications in the body of the text or to concentrate it in specialized chapters, I have done both. Applications that can be explained in a few paragraphs, such as the experimental uses of drugs to combat Alzheimer's disease (Chapter 11), are incorporated in the text; topics requiring more background, such as the biochemistry of schizophrenia (Chapter 15), are covered in separate chapters.

The first 11 chapters, the core of the book, are essential for courses in physiological psychology and neuroscience. The chapters are organized in a fairly standard sequence, with transitions between them to help students bridge the gaps. It is probably best to stick to the order in which they appear in the text, though you can skip or reverse a few chapters if students are adequately prepared for the jumps. The final 5 chapters—applications and implications—follow a less structured approach. The material in each chapter does not depend on background in the previous chapters. These chapters can be used to tailor the course to your preferred sequence and emphasis.

Two of the final 5 chapters have unique contents. The chapter on brain models and artificial intelligence (Chapter 13) speaks to an area of interest to many students, an area in which contact with the neurosciences is growing rapidly. It introduces the history and uses of brain modeling and examines intelligence and emergent processes as applied to brains. The chapter on consciousness and long-term planning (Chapter 14) provides a context for material on the prefrontal areas, as well as reviewing physiological approaches to issues of mind and body that were previously considered mostly by philosophers.

The text contains several unique pedagogical devices. Distributed coding in memory, for example, is introduced in Chapter 11 with an optical analogy, beginning with an examination of the distribution of information at the lens plane of a slide projector. This situation is, of course, familiar to students. The section goes on to introduce distributed coding and retrieval in a concrete manner. Another pedagogical device is the use of a puzzle defined in terms of formal systems (Chapter 13) to explain the difference between information processing in formal systems and intelligent information handling in humans. When students discover that the puzzle cannot be solved, they realize the extra mode of processing they possess. I have found that stories, metaphors, and examples are more useful than the most exhaustive explanation; these devices are used throughout the book.

The text has already benefited greatly from the input of many instructors of physiological psychology and similar courses. If you have suggestions or (is it possible?) corrections, please send them to me at Clark Kerr Hall, University of California, Santa Cruz, CA 95064.

ACKNOWLEDGMENTS

This book would not have been possible without a sabbatical year from the University of California, Santa Cruz, which enabled me to begin the book, and a wonderful year as a resident fellow at the Center for Interdisciplinary Studies at the University of Bielefeld, West Germany, which enabled me to finish it. My greatest debt is to my wife, Diane, who inspired me to start the project, contributed to many passages, and provided references and proofreading. The patience of my children, Natalie and Theresa, is appreciated. I also owe a debt to my mentors, J. J. Gibson, D. N. Spinelli, O.-J. Grüsser, L. W. Stark, and especially K. H. Pribram. Many of the ideas in the following pages originated with them.

A large number of colleagues and readers have provided valuable, if sometimes painful, advice. They include Rex Bierley, North Dakota State University; Dale McAdam, University of Rochester; Leo M. Chalupa, University of California–Davis; Rosemary P. Sorrentino, Brown University; Donavan E. Fleming, Brigham Young University; Paul J. Wellman, Texas A&M University; James Mitchell, Kansas State University; Aaron Ettenberg, University of California–Santa Barbara; Paschal N. Strong, University of South Florida; Peter D. Spear, University of Wisconsin; Richard King, University of North Carolina; Victor Pease, Clarkson College; and Leslie Fishel, Cleveland State University.

Special thanks go to the staff at John Wiley & Sons. I would like to acknowledge my editors, Mark Mochary, Carol Luitigens, and Warren Abraham, and John Balbalis for his contributions to the art program.

Bruce Bridgeman

CONTENTS

Part II

SENSORY AND MOTOR SYSTEMS

Part IV

APPLICATIONS AND IMPLICATIONS

Part I

BASIC PRINCIPLES

Chapter 1

ORIGINS OF PHYSIOLOGICAL PSYCHOLOGY

Physiological psychology examines the physical basis of human behavior and experience. It is fundamental to our understanding of experience and therefore of all human endeavor. But if the content of physiological psychology is so fundamental, why is the discipline so new? Curiosity about the subject is as old as humanity, yet only in the last 60 years has physiological psychology emerged as a separate area of inquiry. Most of the contents of this book are the result of an explosion of knowledge during the last 30 years. The reasons for the youth of the discipline are both philosophical and technical. The philosophical issues had to be addressed before the technical ones even arose, and philosophy continues to shape the discipline. To examine the philosophical issues, we must look at the history of ideas about the relationship of mind and body.

INTELLECTUAL HISTORY

ANCIENT ORIGINS

As with many areas of human thought, the examination of the mechanisms of mind began with the ancient Greeks. For the earliest Greeks experience was centered in the mystical soul, or "psyche," which was capable of detaching itself from the body. The soul was separate from the life force, "spirtu," and the reasoning power, "pneuma." Objective examination of these concepts was out of the question until Socrates and his pupil Plato invented philosophy in the modern sense and separated it from mysticism. For Socrates sensory experiences were not to be relied on as the basis of a philosophy; they were ephemeral and unreliable and could be tricked and deceived. Where was the certainty on which a philosophy—a system of organized knowledge—could rest? The answer was that out of sensations, but separate from them, grew an **idea**—an abstraction taken from life but more permanent and unchanging than experience. No one has ever seen a perfect triangle, but the idea can exist separate from its external representations. In modern language the abstract idea is an internal state, the stuff of psychology. In a second brilliant insight Socrates asserted that an ordering of the tumble of sensations was possible only if some innate ideas existed. Thus two of the philosophical roots of psychological psychology, **idealism** (the existence of ideas apart from external objects) and **nativism** (the reality of innate ideas), were born (Boring, 1950).

Although most of the ancient Greeks believed that the psyche was not a physical entity, a few philosophers (such as Democritus) held that the soul itself was material. This was not a new idea, even for Democritus; those whom the Greeks themselves considered to be "the ancients" all represented thought as dependent on bodily disposition (Theophrastus [ca. 300 B.C.], translated by Stratton, 1917). Equally important, the Greeks had a belief upon which science depends: that there are unchanging rules underlying the natural world.

The ancient Greeks were excellent philosophers, but they were not experimenters. They had no real idea of brain function; indeed, some thought that the brain was an organ for cooling the blood. (In this thought they were not as far off as it might seem; at rest the body loses 30 percent of its heat through the head.) It wasn't until 500 years later that others, especially the physician Galen (second century A.D.), began developing a knowledge of the correlation of brain structure with function. By examining brain-damaged neurological patients, Galen began to understand the anatomical specialization of brain functions. The idea of the immaterial soul persisted, however, and the later dominance of Christianity prevented the investigation of the divinely endowed human being until the 17th century (though some progress, notably in anatomy, was made by the Arabs in the interim).

DESCARTES AND THE MIND-BODY PROBLEM

The next major advances were made by René Descartes, a 17th-century philosopher and perhaps the world's first physiological psychologist in the modern sense. Though some of his theories today seem almost comically flawed, he contributed to both philosophy and science. The principle of **reciprocal innervation**—that muscles come in pairs with opposite actions—was among his many achievements. He also introduced the concept of **reflex** to describe quick, automatic responses.

Descartes's philosophy of mind is **dualism,** the idea that body and mind are separate entities. Descartes's dualism is very different from the implicit dualism of the Greeks; for Descartes only a person's will operates in the service of the nonphysical soul. The rest of the organism, including the control mechanisms of all the behaviors performed by animals, is purely physical and a legitimate object of scientific study. Dualism of any sort is firmly rejected by modern physiological psychologists, but in Descartes's day it represented an enormous step forward. In a single stroke Descartes snatched from under the eyes of the Grand Inquisitor three-quarters of what is now neurobiology, simply by asserting that the control of behaviors did not concern the soul. (Even so, Descartes [1665, 1972] let this part of his work be published only after his death, just to be on the safe side.) The study of the mechanisms of most behaviors, considered heresy for a thousand years, was now open to the fast-developing tools of the scientist. Serious work on brain and behavior could begin.

Cartesian (from Descartes) dualism was the predominant philosophy up to the 19th century, even though it contains a fundamental logical flaw. The doctrine asserts that biological materials obey all physical laws, being influenced only by physical forces acting on them, but the nonphysical mind can somehow influence behavior. If one can talk about one's mind, for instance, the mind must influence the brain to affect the speech machinery. For Descartes the site of this interaction was the pineal gland, chosen because of its location at the center of the head and because it is a single structure, not doubled on the left and right, as are most other structures.

Let us examine the junction of body and mind more closely. Part of the definition of a physical system is that it obeys physical laws. Therefore the mind's influence at this **interface** (point of interaction) must be a physical one, and the interface between body and mind must itself be physical. We need another interface to transfer from the nonphysical mind to the physical interface just described. But this second interface raises the same objections as the first one, and so on ad infinitum. Either matter doesn't always behave according to the laws of the physicists or the mind itself is a physical entity, an organization of matter and energy somewhere inside the brain.

Modern physiological psychology has adopted the latter alternative—that all functions of the brain, including the mind, can be described in physical terms as organizations of matter and energy. Historically, this view, known as **mechanism,** eventually triumphed over **vitalism,** the idea that there was something qualitatively different about living material. (If dualism survives, it is as a distinction between organization on one side and matter and energy on the other.) But the change did not take place until the middle of the 19th century, a period that saw the settling of most of the philosophical issues that were required to enable brain research to progress (Cranefield, 1957). Some are still discussed by philosophers, but physiological psychologists and other scientists agree, for instance, that there is a real world, that our senses bring us information about it, and that we can act on the world.

Philosophers are sometimes surprised that science is as productive as it is given that scientists are so naive philosophically. But scientists stand at the apex of a long tradition of philosophy, which gives them powerful conceptual tools to use in deciphering nature. An outgrowth of this tradition is the set of approaches and attitudes grouped together as the "scientific method." It has become a powerful way of formally bridging the gap Socrates pointed out between the unreliable senses and the permanent ideas. Because the design of our own sensory systems parallels the techniques of the scientific method in many ways, these techniques will be introduced in the chapters on sensory systems.

ORIGINS IN PSYCHOLOGY

Modern scientific disciplines have branched off from philosophy one by one for the past four centuries, beginning with astronomy and physics and continuing with the biological sciences in the 18th and 19th centuries. By the late 19th century philosophy consisted largely of doctrines about the nature of reality, experience, and behavior—areas that then branched off from philosophy to form the new science of psychology.

Progress in psychological research within philosophy led to Wilhelm Wundt's founding of the first psychological laboratory, in 1879. Wundt combined philosophical reasoning and careful **introspection**—the breaking down of one's own experience into elements analogous to the basic elements in chemistry. Wundt's students and prolific writings spread his ideas widely but also led to the development of schools of introspectionist psychology headed by rival professors. One of the great disputes of the new psychology concerned the issue of imageless thought. Wundt's school (at Leipzig) maintained that pure imageless thought was possible; E. B. Titchener's school (at Cornell University) maintained just as forcefully that thought was always accompanied by mental images and consisted of manipulations of these images (Boring, 1950). Each group produced voluminous records of introspections proving its point and contradicting the other's. Finally it became clear that neither side could win because the data—the observations—were private, subjective experiences not open to public scrutiny. That is, they were not objective, repeatable experimental results. Controversies of this sort were unresolvable. By the turn of the 20th century the whole area of introspective psychology had fallen into disrepute.

At this point, beginning about 1913, John Watson revolutionized American psychology with **behaviorism.** Watson asserted that the proper content of psychology was not experience but behavior, for only behavior could be measured objectively. It could be analyzed by finding relationships between stimuli and responses. This **stimulus-response psychology** considered the steps intervening between stimulus and response to be unmeasurable. (The standpoint is best summarized in Watson, 1920.) The promise of objectivity caused behaviorism to dominate psychology, especially in the United States, until the 1950s. But objectivity was achieved at the expense of disregarding the very problem that had gotten psychology started: the understanding of experience. Another revolution in psychology has recently brought experience back under scrutiny with powerful new objective methods, under the name of *cognitive psychology* (Neisser, 1967). Cognitive psychologists now talk of internal processes, such as memory strategies, in ways unthinkable to behaviorists. Without looking inside the brain, however, they do not have direct access to much of what is studied by physiological psychologists, who examine mental processes by looking at the structure and activity of the brain itself.

The situation of psychologists is like that of imaginary Martian behavioral scientists. Landing on earth, they discover that the dominant form of life (at least in North America and Europe) is the automobile. They study its behavior, finding relationships between pressure on the gas pedal and acceleration, between the steering wheel and the direction of travel, and so on. They can describe the behavior of the automobile in some detail; but they wil never understand how it works, and they will have no idea how to fix it when something goes wrong. For that they must open up the hood and learn about the mechanisms of the beast in terms of cyliners and pistons. Similarly, those who study humans can benefit from looking inside the brain to begin finding out how the machinery of the mind works.

ORIGINS IN PHYSIOLOGY

During the second half of the 19th century, a separate neurophysiology was developing from physiology and medicine. Neurologists codified the knowledge they had acquired from studying patients with brain damage, and they began experiments with the brains of living beings. The neurophysiological tradition culminated in the work of Sir Charles Sherrington (1906), who discovered or summarized much of what we know about reflexes today (see Chapter 7). Another important figure, the Russian physiologist I. P. Pavlov, had little respect for introspective psychologists of his day. With his famous experiments on conditioning in dogs (described in Chapter 11), he began a separate, physiologically based study of the brain mechanisms of behavior (Pavlov, 1927). Pavlov's theory was a stimulus-response scheme much like that of the behaviorists, but Pavlov was the last stimulus-response theorist in physiological psychology.

Shortly after Pavlov's major work became available in English, another psychologist, Karl Lashley (1929), indicated that the brain is not organized in a stimulus-response manner but instead shows a much more distributed processing of information (Chapter 11). The business of the brain is not a passive connecting of stimuli to responses, like a telephone switchboard. Rather it is a rich and subtle combining of sensory information with remembered experience and genetically given instructions. From these raw materials the brain generates new memories and behaviors. This process takes place in a highly integrated and densely interconnected network. In this sense physiological psychology has always been cognitive, not suffering from the limitations of the stimulus-response analysis. The task of the physiological psychologist has always been to understand the internal processes that come between stimulus and response. The stimulus-response analysis meanwhile has moved to a more microscopic level. In invertebrates it is being usefully applied to the brain-behavior relationships of sea slugs and other simple animals (Davis & Mpitsos, 1971).

THE CURRENT SYNTHESIS

In the years since World War II a new discipline has grown up from these roots. It combines the new cognitive psychology of experience with physiological psychology and neurophysiology to create a new physiological study of experience and behavior. The discipline is so new that even its name has not yet been settled; it is recognized as physiological psychology, neuroscience, biopsychology, psychobiology, and several other combinations, each with a different emphasis. It has absorbed elements of some newer disciplines, such as neurochemistry and information sciences. Thus some older disciplines that had split from philosophy at various times have recombined, with the addition of some new disciplines, to form a science with a new mission. The new discipline is still in the process of welding itself into a coherent body of knowledge; undigested chunks of some of its fields will be identifiable in parts of this book. Like psychology, the new field is part of the broad purview of biological science, the study of life and of living systems.

AN INFORMATION-FLOW APPROACH

But physiological psychology adds something more than what was contained in the roots. Just as a mechanic must look under the hood to understand the workings of an automobile, psychologists must look inside the living brain to fully understand the basis of behavior and to be able to intervene when something goes wrong. The mechanist philosophy means that physiological psychologists approach the brain in the same way that biologists would approach any other organ of the body, such as the stomach. In analyzing the functions and mechanisms of the stomach, a biologist would identify what goes in and what comes out and, most importantly, would look inside to find out what happens in between. The physiological psychologist studies what goes into the brain, what comes out of it, and what happens in between. The brain, however, processes not food but information. The incoming information consists of electrical messages from the sense organs and chemical changes in the blood; the output is the signals sent to the muscles and to some glands. What happens in between is the processing of information: recoding, storage, retrieval, and recombination. According to the mechanist philosophy, experience results as part of that processing.

In the 1940s a new language and powerful mathematical techniques were developed to deal specifically with information; they are used today to deal with information separately from whatever carries it in brains, computers, books, and other media. The new science of information—information theory—which has roots as deep as those of physiological psychology, was originated by Claude Shannon to deal with problems of analyzing transmission on telephone lines, and it developed along with the digital computer. It was formalized by Shannon, Norbert Wiener, Warren McCulloch, and others (Shannon & Weaver, 1949). The theory shows how information can be stored, retrieved, and transmitted and how information from separate sources can be combined in various ways.

MEASURING INFORMATION

The fundamental insight in the founding of the science of information was the definition of *information* itself. Shannon began by developing a formal definition, which sounds like a trivial task but turned out to be one of the great clarifications that made information theory possible. Everyone uses the word *information* to indicate something they know, but this definition doesn't help much in beginning a mathematical analysis of signals and messages. So Shannon attacked the problem from the other end—uncertainty—the state one is in before any information becomes available. Receiving information then results in a reduction of uncertainty, and the reduction of uncertainty becomes a technical definition of *information.* The unit of reduction in uncertanty is the **bit,** the deciding of a two-alternative question when each alternative is equally likely. For instance, knowing whether a person is male or female gives you exactly one bit of information.

Deciding among more than two categories requires more than one bit. Determining whether an undergraduate is a freshman, sophomore, junior, or senior, for instance, requires two choices (see Figure 1.1): one determines whether the person is a lower-division or upper-division student, and another determines whether the lower-division student is a freshman or sophomore or the upper-division student is a junior or senior. College class membership is thus a two-bit question. The procedure—repeatedly breaking the uncertainty in half with one more bit of information—can be extended to other questions.

Computers are based on **digital** devices—devices capable of assuming of two states (which can be compared to the two alternatives that define the bit). Numbers in a computer are represented as "words" made of strings of bits and are stored in

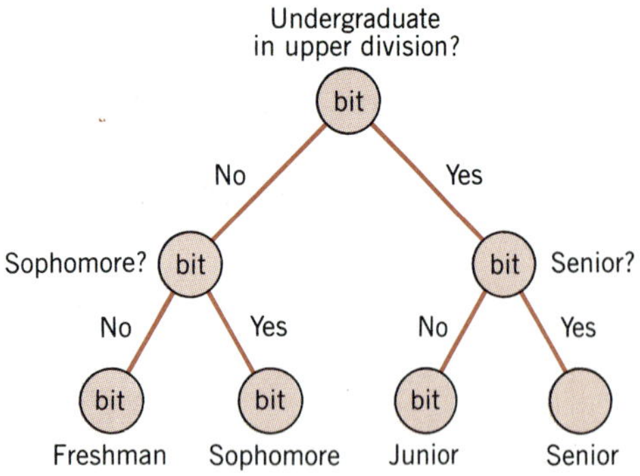

Figure 1.1 *Division of a multi-alternative problem into a series of binary choices. Each choice requires 1 bit of information. The structure is called a decision tree. In mathematical notation, one can decide among* 2^n *alternatives with* n *bits.*

memory, retrieved, and combined in that form. The organization of information in the brain is more varied and complicated. But the important point is that the concepts of information theory are independent of the particular device being analyzed. They will be used in this book to examine our own information-processing organ, the brain. Analysis in terms of bits is useful in quantifying the information flow through the retina (Chapter 4), for example, even though the retina does not use digital coding.

Analysis by bits fits well with some aspects of brain function, such as transmission of information from one part of the brain to another. Other aspects of mental life, however, are more difficult to analyze in this way. When I hear Rachmaninoff's Second Piano Concerto, I know every note, every accent, before it occurs. Therefore, listening to a familiar recording provides no new information in terms of reduction of uncertainty; the joy lies outside the analysis of information theory.

COMPUTERS AND BRAINS

The first electronic digital computers, built in the 1940s, were designed by people who had detailed knowledge of the most advanced neurophysiology of the time (including John von Neumann). They designed the basic elements of the electronic brain to imitate the functions of nerve cells as they understood them, within a system of two-state digital logic. Each computer device was either on or off, with nothing in between allowed, and the devices could communicate to turn one another on or off. This logic made computers stable and reliable. The principle worked so well that it generated the present computer revolution in an astonishingly short time. For this reason it is fortunate that the inventors of the computer completely misunderstood the functioning of nerve cells.

Contrary to the dogma of the 1940s, the brain is almost completely an **analog** machine, not a digital one (Shepherd, 1979b). Analog signals can take on not just two values but any value within their range. Each analog, or graded, signal can carry many bits of information. Information processing in brains, described in Chapter 2, is based on interactions of graded signals. Digital coding in the nervous system is used only to transmit information over long distances. Information about sensory events in the foot, for instance, travels to the spinal cord as a series of digital spikes called **action potentials;** it is broken down in the spinal cord to an analog code for determining what to do about the events.

The functions of brains and computers are also complementary. The dovetailing of brain and computer was partly intentional, for a good tool should help one do well what one cannot do alone. A large part of the complementarity of function, however, came about because it is easy to make a computer do well what brains do poorly. (The computer, however, has difficulty with some of the functions that the brain accomplishes with ease.) Computers have perfect memories, unlike people, and they can react very fast. A good computer can receive information, compare it to something in its memory, and make a simple decision in a few millionths of a second, before you or I even know there is a decision to be made.

Despite the formidable capabilities of computers, the biological computers in our heads are not obsolete, and there is no danger that they ever will be. The superiority of brains begins with the sensory and perceptual processes. Even a child can perform feats of pattern recognition, such as speech perception, far beyond the capabilities of the most sophisticated computer.

Technology is advancing rapidly, however, and we may soon lose our superiority in some tasks.

The most important advantages of humans over computers lie not in specific feats of virtuoso information processing but in deciding what information to process. Computers cannot program themselves; they do not decide what problems are to be solved. People serve a purpose in the evolutionary scheme. Sometimes they use computers to extend the power of their brains, much as they use hammers to amplify the power of their arms or telephones to enhance their communication capabilities. But they always provide the motivation for the human-machine interaction. It is this motivation (Chapter 10), derived from the motivation for survival, that makes humans and animals different from machines.

Where does the motivation for survival come from? The answer lies not in our information-processing abilities but in our history, for we are products of a long evolution in a complex biological, social, and physical world. Our brains, our emotions, our senses and behaviors are tuned by evolution to make our species successful. The process of evolution, which relates to processes described throughout this book, is the key to understanding the design of human beings.

THE EVOLUTIONARY PERSPECTIVE

One of the intellectual revolutions that made physiological psychology possible began with Charles Darwin's book *On the Origin of Species* in 1859. This book, one of the most influential works ever published, opened with the observation that most animals never contribute progeny to the next generation. They starve, are eaten by predators, fail to find a mate, or succumb to some other hazard of the natural environment (usually in infancy). Variation is found among animals in a population, however, and some of the animals do succeed in producing viable offspring. In current terminology, those who succeed are more **fit;** only *their* genes are passed on to the next generation. The process is called **natural selection.** If the **genes** (units of inheritance) of this group of fit individuals are different from those of the population as a whole, the population in the next generation will evolve. (In practice, it takes many generations to show significant change by natural selection.)

Many of Darwin's ideas were not new; his theory of evolution by natural selection supported the mechanistic philosophy that had been gaining strength for decades, and the idea that species might not be immutable was also a current one. In addition to explicitly stating his theory of evolution as a means of biological change, however, Darwin backed his ideas with such an enormous and convincing body of data that evolution by natural selection was embraced with enthusiasm by the biological community.

Darwin supplied the new mechanistic biology with a naturalistic explanation of the tremendous variety of life and its seemingly purposive design. The miracle of creation was reduced to innumerable, very small evolutionary steps over millions of years. Each step was potentially explainable according to existing laws of chemistry and physics. Nothing supernatural was needed to drive the process, and the vitalists lost one of the last underpinnings of their philosophy. The new mechanistic brain physiologists of the mid-19th century began using evolutionary theory almost immediately; in physiological optics, for instance, the great physiologist Ewald Hering was using evolutionary arguments to support his views less than a decade after the appearance of Darwin's book (Hering, 1868). Today, of course, evolution is one of the cornerstones of biology.

REACTIONS AGAINST DARWIN'S THEORY

The acceptance of Darwinian evolution by most scientists during the late 19th century is sometimes forgotten because of the protest it elicited from other quarters. That protest is not completely dead even today. The reason for the opposition was that the implications of evolution shook the world view that nearly everyone in the Western world had held for thousands of years—the idea that people were qualitatively different from animals and were outside the scheme of nature. Like the Copernican revolution, which removed the Earth from the center of the universe, the Darwinian revolution removed the human species from its unique position above nature. And the protest against Darwinism came from the same groups that had objected to Copernicanism three centuries earlier.

Evolution outraged many theologians and philosophers because it dared to address the ultimate question: Why am I here? And the answer was not a comforting one. We are here for the same reason apes and ants and ferns and fish are here—because our ancestors happened to have qualities that made them successful at reproducing. Furthermore, reproduction is the only criterion of success. Your own evolutionary fitness will be measured not by your intelligence, kindness, or other virtues but solely by the number of viable offspring you produce (see Dawkins, 1976, for a more radical interpretation). In the long run, other traits are useful only if they can influence the primary one: the raising of successful successors.

APPLYING EVOLUTION TO PHYSIOLOGICAL PSYCHOLOGY

What does all this tell us about brains and behavior? Primarily that brains are adapted to enhancing the biological fitness of their possessors. Biologists often speak, in a kind of verbal shorthand, as though useful traits were evolved purposefully, using statements such as: Fish evolved complex motor systems to coordinate their quick swimming movements. What they really mean, though, is that the fish that by chance happened to have a few more neurons in the motor parts of their brains did a little better. They survived in greater numbers and had more offspring than those that happened to have fewer neurons or less effectively organized ones. The shorthand of purposeful language will sometimes be used in this book, though the more biologically valid interpretation should always stand behind it. Similarly, when more complex or more recently evolved species are called "higher," no value judgment is implied.

One implication of the constant evolutionary pressure is that nature cannot stand still for some structure to evolve to the point of usefulness. Every change contributing to the gene pool must be immediately useful, or at least not harmful. Parts of the brain, then, evolve to serve the organism that possesses them, without looking forward to a "higher" form to come. In this continuous process, many brain areas have gone through a fascinating series of evolutionary changes, all of them serving a need for a particular organism. The mammal's auditory system, for example, evolved from the fish's lateral-line system for detecting movements in water, and much of the human's forebrain evolved from the centers serving the sense of smell in early vertebrates. In each of these changes, a **selective pressure**—a mismatch between the characteristics of the species and the demands of the environment—had to exist before the system began to evolve; otherwise animals that had begun to show chance components of the system would have had no advantage in natural selection. The first changes in an evolutionary sequence are often behavioral, putting the animal into a new environment, where the best-adapted features are different from those the animal already has. A species of fish that begins to spend part of its time on land, for instance, must evolve a whole new set of body and behavior traits. Biologists express this evolution in the maxim "form follows function," which applies to the brain as much as to any other structure.

Although Darwin provided the basis for evolutionary theory, progress did not cease with him. The application of the theory is presently being expanded through its integration with sociobiology, a new discipline that explores the biological bases of social behavior (Wilson, 1975). The combination of the new molecular genetics with evolution is another ongoing effort in which physiological psychology can play a part.

Punctuated Equilibrium

As the fossil record has become more complete, it has become clear that evolution does not progress by slow, continuous change. Instead, a species remains unchanged for millions of years and then is replaced abruptly by a different species. The time of rapid change might last many thousands of years, a brief time on the geological time scale. These observations have led to a recent refinement of evolutionary theory, which replaces Darwin's idea of continuous natural selection with the concept of **punctuated equilibrium** (Eldredge & Gould, 1973, 1977). Figure 1.2 shows how Darwin's limited data led to the idea of continuous evolution, although more complete fossil

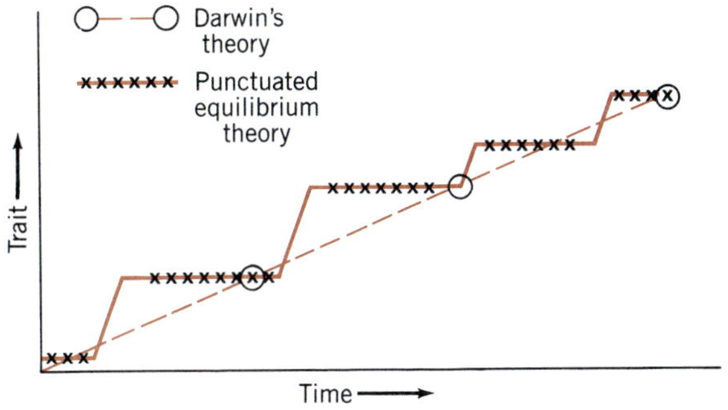

***Figure 1.2** Comparison of Darwin's theory and punctuated equilibrium theory. The trait on the vertical axis might be the size of an animal, the complexity of its brain, or some other feature. Darwin had only a few samples from the fossil record, and the data were consistent with a gradual evolution. He also was unaware of genes and the mechanisms of inheritance. Several fairly complete fossil records now available, mostly in marine organisms, show long periods of no change punctuated by brief episodes of rapid evolution. Punctuated equilibrium gives more importance to the concept of species, for some genetic mechanism must maintain the integrity of a species during periods of equilibrium. Individuals that deviate greatly from the species norms in any way are less fit than the more typical members of the population.*

records show short periods of rapid change. The punctuation is the period of rapid evolution, and the equilibrium is the subsequent period of relatively little change.

The change in outlook means that we can almost literally look backward in time by examining more ancient species; some invertebrates have existed practically unchanged over a hundred million years. By looking at such animals, we can see contemporaries of our own ancestors. Thus the punctuated equilibrium theory strengthens the comparative approach and allows us to see our own roots in other living animals. The idea also implies some mechanism that makes a species stable, so *any* deviation of an individual from the ideal of the species makes that individual less fit. The theory has now been applied to human evolution (Stanley, 1981), with the most recent (and possibly not the final) step being the emergence of *Homo sapiens* less than a half million years ago.

EVOLUTION OF NERVOUS SYSTEMS

Nervous systems have been evolving for a very long time, about a billion years (give or take a few hundred million). The structure of this long evolutionary process can give us clues to the organization of nervous systems and can help organize our inquiry. The oldest parts of the nervous system are common to all animals that have nervous systems, beginning with the coelenterates (such as the jellyfish). These are simple water-dwelling animals that have tentacles and a baglike rather than a tubelike digestive system. In the jellyfish, nerve cells are organized into a simple net, such as the one in Figure 1.3, which is very unlike the complex brain of a vertebrate animal. But the nerve cells themselves are identical to human nerve cells in many important respects. With regard to these properties of nerve cells, evolution has changed almost nothing in a billion years. The cellular building blocks of nervous systems can be considered nearly constant, even though their shape and form have changed. Thus, if we are interested in studying basic properties, it might be advantageous if we study them in simple, robust animals such as coelenterates or mollusks (for example,

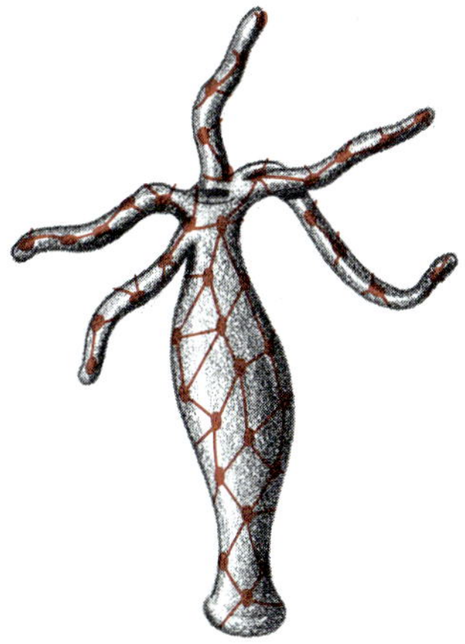

***Figure 1.3** Schematic body organization of a coelenterate (phylum Coelenterata), such as the jellyfish. Though these animals have no concentration of neurons that might be called a brain, they do have neurons that are similar in many important respects to the neurons of vertebrates.*

snails), where the investigation is technically easier. In the next chapter our investigation of brains will begin with a close look at nerve cells, or **neurons,** the building blocks of all nervous systems.

To study features of neural organization that relate to humans, we must move to the vertebrates. Even the most primitive vertebrates have a **spinal cord,** a group of neurons and fibers inside the backbone that coordinate simple movements. All spinal cords are connected in much the same way as ours; after all, the spinal cord is one of the defining features of vertebrates. Its design was frozen in evolution at a time when the vertebrates were developing. The organization is detailed in Chapter 3. Still, statements about spinal cords apply to fewer animals than statements about neurons, because the spinal cord reflects a later stage of evolution.

As the vertebrates developed further, more and more structures were added. Evolution generally progressed from the back of the brain to the front, with the most recent innovations in the cerebral cortex.

But our main interest is in people; for psychologists, the study of other animals is valid only to the degree that evolution has not significantly changed the function being studied. Physiologists are frequently interested in the functions of a particular animal and may study the same systems with quite different goals. A physiological psychologist and a physiologist may perform the same experiment, say a study of chemical messengers in the cat brain, but the physiologist is interested in the cat's feeding behaviors while the physiological psychologist is attempting to infer something about human eating patterns. It is frequently easier to examine a function in a simpler brain than to jump directly to the bewildering complexity of human brains, and the principles of evolution continually remind us to ask why a function is carried out in a certain way as well as how it works.

When we compare ourselves to other animals, we find that we have none of the obvious specializations that enable other animals to prosper. We have neither the tusks and trunk of the elephant, nor the wings of the bird, nor even the prehensile (grasping) tail of the New World monkey. Other animals run faster than we do, go longer without food, and perform many other functions better. To find the secret of our phenomenal success we must look to our unique specialization—the brain. Coupled with sharp senses and a continuous breeding cycle, it has given us the greatest range and population of any large animal, enabling us to use tools and social cooperation to overcome the disadvantages of not-so-impressive physique. We do all this through a long process of bringing up our young, using education, training, and preparation. In a word, our nature is nurture.

NATURE AND NURTURE IN HUMAN DEVELOPMENT

The Lizard

In the middle of California's Mojave Desert, black lava flows are the home of an inconspicuous lizard, no bigger than a span of the hand. The lizard is as black as the surrounding lava. A few kilometers away, in the light-colored sand of the desert, similar lizards of lighter color and more textured pattern thrive. In between, where fingers of lava stretch into the sand, other lizards display an intermediate coloring. These "side-blotched" lizards appear to be a perfect example of animals finely tuned to their environments, with selective pressures caused by predators that eat lizards of the wrong color.

But on closer inspection some facts don't fit the theory. First, the hatchling lizards in all of these areas look identical. The lava-dwelling lizards grow darker and the lizards in the lighter environment grow lighter over a period of months. Second, any animal that evolves into separate, genetically distinct populations should have a uniform color within each race. The side-blotched lizard, though, shows color variation within races. Third, a genetically distinct population should be large enough to sustain itself, but isolated outcroppings of black lava not much larger than the territory of a single lizard can be found in the Mojave, and the lizards in these areas too show a definite color-matching tendency. The lightest lizards of all, in fact, live in the white dust downwind of a desert cement plant!

All these observations lead to a startling conclusion: the side-blotched lizard is genetically equipped not to develop a specific coloration but to change its color during development to match its surroundings in which it is hatched (Norris, 1967). This humble lizard is not merely adapted to its environment but has achieved something much more powerful: it is adapted to adapt to its environment. Not only the inheritance of nature but also the conditions of nurture determine the color of the side-blotched lizard.

The Retriever

An example of animal adaptation closer to home is the case of the retriever. When a hunter shoots a bird, the hunter's faithful dog scrambles though the underbush and unerringly brings the prey back in its teeth. To a psychologist who has spent a career training rats, this seems to be a good example of an intelligent animal, the dog, learning to perform a useful function for its master.

But look more closely. Though the hunter doesn't know much about the psychology of animal training, the dog retrieves nonetheless. Retriever puppies start fetching things as soon as they can walk, and a retriever raised by humans without ever seeing another dog will retrieve for hours without obvious reward. Though some work is needed to coordinate the dog-human team, what seems to be a learned teamwork is built on a behavior pattern bred into the animal by generations of artificial selection. The dog is born to fetch.

Interaction of Environment and Heredity

The lizard and retriever examples seem distant from issues of brain and behavior, but they yield an important insight. We usually think that body characteristics are genetically given, and we consider most behavior patterns to be learned. But nature has not been so arbitrary. Most characteristics of animals and humans, whether physical or behavioral, result from an intricate interaction of environment and heredity. This is especially true of the brain, the organ that controls adaptation to the environment. We must beware of any simple statement that nature or nurture is responsible for a function, for it is the interaction of the two that controls most functions.

This interactionist approach was developed from another perspective by the Swiss psychologist Jean Piaget, who was originally trained as a biologist. In human development he found a sequence of qualitatively different stages of cognitive organization, beginning with that of the infant, who deals only with the present. Later the brain becomes capable of handling more complex situations, but the capability is not expressed until the child is challenged with observations that do not fit into a simple world scheme. The challenge results in a reorganization, an **accommodation** to the new observations. So accommodation requires two factors. First, the brain must be capable of noticing discrepancies between external facts and the internal **schema** (a way of organizing information). Second, a set of external facts must force the developmental reorganization to take place. For example, a young child concludes that a glass of water poured into a tall, thin beaker increases in volume because the water level in the beaker is higher. It is hard for us, with our more sophisticated schema, to imagine how children can think in this way, but the observation is well documented (Piaget, 1973). Children judge only sensory appearance, without taking physical properties into account. At this stage no amount of demonstrating or arguing can convince children that they are wrong. Later, when the brain is ready, children confronted again with this problem realize that volume is conserved even if appearances vary. They have advanced to a more powerful schema, which allows more effective functioning.

In most areas the interactions of heredity and environment remain to be worked out. Most of the current research about this problem in physiological psychology is in the context of the development of sensory systems, where the interactions of the two influences have proved to be more intricate than anticipated. One might expect, for instance, that the growth of neuronal connections from the retina to the brain would follow a genetically programmed course, but it is now clear that the connections are influenced by the early visual environment as well as the genes. Animals reared in unusual circumstances develop brain cells with unusual response patterns, and sometimes the animals have deficits in behavior as well. This is presently a "hot" research area, with many groups working on the puzzle and with new pieces of it being added rapidly. (The area is examined in Chapter 6.) In general, developmental processes take advantage of two sources of information, one in the inherited genes and the other in the regularities of the environment.

Environment and Heredity in Humans. Humans encounter special problems in the interaction of nature and nurture thoughout life. Most species have a long history of adaptation to a particular stable or slowly changing environment, but humans represent a relatively new species that has retained many behavior patterns from other primate species. More importantly, the environment of humans has changed far more radically than that of any other species, because humans change their environments without altering their genes.

We can assume that the human environment was about as stable as most animal environments throughout most of the history of our species. The early stone tool cultures developed very slowly, over millenia, and did not greatly alter our relationship with nature. Then, about 10,000 years ago, the Neolithic (new stone age) revolution brought farming, permanent villages, cities, writing, and all of the artifacts of civilization in rapid succession. There has been no time for significant biological evolution during this period, so our brains are essentially the same as those of the hunter-gatherers whose culture we have so thoroughly forgotten. Although we live in an urban industrial society, our brains are those of Paleolithic (old stone age) hunter-gatherers who lived in bands of not more than a few dozen people, mostly relatives. The population density of the species in Paleolithic times was low, less than one person per square kilometer, and there was little specialization of labor except by sex. Travel was by foot, communication by voice and gesture, and manufacturing by hand.

One result of the vast differences between our present world and the world in which we evolved is that our nature and our nurture sometimes come into conflict. Some of the behavior patterns that served the hunter-gatherer well are maladaptive for us. An example is our reaction to stress; one of our responses to a challenge is that our bodies pour hormones into the bloodstream to prepare us for intense physical activity. In some stressful situations, such as traffic jams and final exams, this adaptation is of no use. Other genetic capacities, once necessary for survival, are almost never expressed in modern life and become irrelevant or unnoticed remnants of the past. Our capacity to metabolize our own muscles during starvation, a sort of internal cannibalism, is an example. On a less dramatic level, some of our sensory capacities, such as our dark-adaptation ability, exceed what we use in modern environments. Except in laboratories, we almost never experience complete dark adaptation, a state that requires about 45 min of total isolation from light. Color vision disappears, depth perception is distorted, and the center of the retina becomes blind. With complete dark adaptation a human can receive useful information from reflected starlight alone, but for you and me the ability is nearly irrelevant.

A second result of our rapid environmental change is that nurture is more important than ever. We undergo a long educational process to be able to function in our complex and specialized world. But this is a challenge that our nervous systems can handle, for along with other abilities the hunter-gatherer acquired an enormous capacity to adapt. With our flexible brains and our learning ability we are able to change our environments quickly, making significant modifications in culture and life-style from one generation to the next (sometimes, it seems, from one week to the next). Like the pigmentation of the side-blotched lizard, the behavior of the human being is adapted to adapt, within limits, and is shaped by the environment. Science has become part of this adaptation process for humankind, enabling us to codify and transmit information. We do this in terms of theories about the workings of nature.

THE ROLE OF THEORY

From a distance it looks as though the business of science is collecting data. Scientists are busy from morning to night collecting, analyzing, and publishing the stuff, until the journals are packed with it. But if you ask a scientist how something works, you won't get any data in the response. If you ask about gravity, you will get algebraic functions relating gravity to mass, acceleration, and time; but no one will say, "Well, yesterday I dropped a weight from a tower, and after 1 second it was falling at 9 meters per second." Newton's laws of motion are known to every physics student, but his data have been forgotten for centuries. Scientific knowledge is expressed in theories, not data.

This means that the goal of scientific investigation is not gathering data but developing more powerful theories to understand the world. Data express events in the past and are interesting only if they can aid in the construction of theories; they are only a means to an end. Consequently, the goal of scientific endeavor is not to perform as many experiments as possible but to perform as few as possible to arrive at more powerful theories. Because experiments in physiological psychology tend to be time-consuming, expensive, and inconvenient, good neuroscientists are skilled at designing each study carefully to answer a theoretical question.

The process of science is like that of building a bridge into the unknown; the spans, made out of theories, are supported by towers, in the form of experiments. The scientist builds a theoretical span as far out as possible before engaging in the expensive and bothersome process of putting down a support. Supporting towers built without spans are useless, and towers built where the spans are already secure are a waste of effort. Sometimes new techniques, such as computer simulations, enable the bridge builder to construct longer spans without investing in experimental support, though these techniques cannot substitute for experiments.

At present, new experimental techniques are revolutionizing physiological psychology, a fact that seems at odds with the controlling role of theory. The techniques, however, are useful precisely because they enable us to ask new questions. We can develop theories where previously there were no data to be generalized into theories, or we can improve the quality of the observations supporting the theories in existing areas. The development in the last few decades of electrodes small enough to record from a single cell, for instance, has opened a whole new realm of knowledge about the coding of information in single neurons. And new anatomical techniques now being developed promise precise views of structural relationships that had been vague and confusing, or even invisible, before.

Although theories are the end product of science, it is, ironically, impossible to prove that a theory is correct! Starting with a hypothesis, which is just a theory in its early stages of development, one can design experiments that will yield results either consistent with the hypothesis or inconsistent with it. In the latter case the hypothesis can be discarded as a bad guess; but if the results are consistent, the theory still is not proved, for an indefinite number of other theories may also explain the data (Popper, 1968). Scientists deal with this problem, as with many other philosophical issues, by pragmatically sidestepping it. A theory cannot be proved, but the evidence consistent with it can become so overwhelming that it is taken as fact for all practical purposes.

To the student, science often seems to be an imposing edifice, full of arcane techniques, intricate theories, and an overwhelming quantity of facts. In a way, the edifice is an illusion. Like a cloud, it seems solid and substantial from a distance, but the closer you get to it the more its solidity seems to disappear. When you arrive at its edge, you find that it isn't at all well defined. You cannot tell what is cloud and what is just air. Similarly, a student spends years learning well-established facts and theories, approaching the edifice of scientific knowledge. Yet at the cutting edge, the state of the art, scientific investigation looks very different. It is a maze of ambiguous data, conflicting theories, and uncertain implications. Functioning in this milieu requires a tolerance for ambiguity, a willingness to work with ideas that might be correct but might also be unlucky guesses.

As a new science, physiological psychology is especially rich in uncertainties that sometimes cause confusion for students accustomed to absorbing facts. I hope this book helps students approach the cutting edge of physiological psychology with a minimum of confusion, by separating well-established principles from speculative ideas and by presenting all sides of an issue over which disputes persist.

CHAPTER SUMMARY

1. Physiological psychology is a new discipline with old roots. The ancient Greeks gave us idealism (the concept of ideas apart from sensory impressions) and nativism (the concept that some ideas are present at birth). The idea of a physical basis for thought existed among the earliest Greeks but was later lost. The second century A.D. saw the start of clinical neurology and the correlation of brain areas with specialized functions.

2. In the 17th century Descartes espoused dualism, the idea that body and mind are separate entities. This idea made possible the study of the physical aspects of brain and behavior. Dualism contains a logical flaw, however, for the site of interaction of mind and body must be a physical thing. The nonphysical mind has no way of interacting with a body that recognizes only physical laws. Two hundred years later, mechanism (the idea that all biological and psychological processes have a physical base) overcame vitalism (the notion that living material does not follow the same laws as inanimate matter).

3. The first physiological psychology was based on introspection, the examination of the contents of one's own consciousness. The method was eventually abandoned because its observations were private, subjective experiences that were not subject to public examination. Behaviorism provided an objective alternative by admitting only behavior as a valid measure in psychology. But this solution required psychology to disregard the problem that had gotten the field started: the understanding of experience. Behaviorism has been replaced by modern cognitive psychology. New cognitive methods allow indirect access to such processes as memory strategies. Physiological intervention can also address these questions.

4. Developing from physiology and medicine, neurophysiology gained a knowledge of specialized brain areas from studies of brain-damaged patients. Sherrington described the mechanisms of reflexes; Pavlov used a stimulus-response theory to explain conditioning in dogs. Lashley showed that these theories were too limited and proposed instead that the brain shows a more distributed processing of information. Modern physiological psychology combines the psychological and neurophysiological traditions, adding some newer fields such as neurochemistry and information sciences.

5. The brain can be analyzed as a manager of information flow in an organism. Information, the reduction of uncertainty, is measured in bits, the choices between two equally probable alternatives. Any signal can be analyzed in this way, even analog signals that can take on any value and are not coded in discrete pieces. Computers use a digital code; brains use analog coding for everything except transmitting messages over long distances. The computer is a tool like any other tool; the functions of brains and computers are complementary. The motivation for any tool's use comes from the human, who has evolved motivational systems.

6. Darwin's explanation of evolution by natural selection revolutionized biology. Evolution provided a mechanistic explanation for the variety of life and a natural motive force for change. Applied to the brain, evolutionary theory can help trace changes in brain structures and aid in understanding present brain organization.

7. The evolutionary idea of punctuated equilibrium holds that a species remains stable for millions of years and then is replaced abruptly by a different species in a brief burst of evolutionary change. The idea strengthens the comparative approach—the inference of mechanisms of one species from mechanisms in another—because it implies that contemporary animals of a particular species are unchanged from those living when the species originated.

8. In the evolution of the nervous system, some parts evolved early and others appeared later. Neurons developed most of their important features before brains appeared, and some structures (such

as the spinal cord) have changed little in their basic organization since they first appeared in primitive vertebrates.

9. Both bodily and behavioral characteristics develop from an interaction of genetic inheritance and environment. Human cognitive development is marked by a number of reorganizations of a child's strategies of thinking. Each reorganization requires both an environmental challenge and a brain ready to incorporate the challenge.

10. The sensory systems of animals will develop differently if the animals are raised in abnormal sensory environments. Human culture places our species in an environment that is abnormal compared to the one in which we evolved, making environment and education more important than ever in defining the human condition.

11. Science has become important in defining the physical and intellectual environment. It is based on theories; data are useful only to back up theories. Progress depends on the ability to work with conflicting theories, designing experiments to differentiate among them.

KEY TERMS

Idea
Idealism
Nativism
Reciprocal innervation
Reflex
Dualism
Interface
Mechanism
Vitalism
Introspection
Behaviorism
Stimulus-response psychology
Bit
Digital
Analog
Action potentials
Fit
Natural selection
Genes
Selective pressure
Punctuated equilibrium
Neurons
Spinal cord
Accommodation
Schema

SUGGESTED READINGS

Anderson, J. R. (1985). *Cognitive psychology and its implications* (2nd ed.). New York: Freeman.

This book looks at the computational approach to mind and brain from the perspective of cognitive psychology.

Churchland, P. M. (1984). *Matter and consciousness.* Cambridge, MA: MIT Press.

This lively and readable book goes into detail on the issues of mind and brain from the standpoint of modern philosophy. There are at least five different sorts of dualism, for example, and an equal number of materialist theories.

Eccles, J. C., & Popper, K. (1977). *The self and its brain.* New York: Springer-Verlag.

A Nobel prize–winning neurophysiologist and a philosopher exchange views on the meaning of the neurosciences. The results are often controversial but always stimulating.

Chapter 2

THE DESIGN OF THE NERVE CELL

The brain is organized into cells—the basic units of organization of life since evolution began. The information-processing cells of the brain, the *neurons,* are typical cells with all of the chemical machinery of other cells. Ten times more numerous than neurons are the **glial cells,** or **glia,** the supportive cells that surround the neurons and perform housekeeping functions for them. All cells are tiny, fluid-filled bags made of thin membranes, holding all of the biochemical machinery necessary to cell life.

This chapter will first examine the features and varieties of neurons and glia. Then it will look closely at neurons, beginning with the most ancient and general characteristics in the chain of evolution—those common to all cells. Finally, it will move to the specialized properties of neurons that enable them to process information and to communicate with one another.

NEURONS

Neurons come in all imaginable forms and sizes, from tiny local neurons barely larger than red blood cells to giants with extensions over half as long as the entire organism. Each of them has a

soma (Latin for "body") that contains the cell's nucleus and other vital **organelles**—internal structures that perform specialized tasks in the cell's life. Most also have a set of **dendrites** (Greek for "trees"), which spread out treelike from the cells, and a single **axon**—a tubular extension that carries information away from the immediate region of the cell. The dendrites and axon together are sometimes called **processes**—extensions of the cell. Figure 2.1 shows some of the many neuronal forms.

The dendrites are the most conspicuous features of most neurons, containing nearly all of the cell surface. In some cells the dendrites begin as a narrowing of the soma, then repeatedly branch to form a dense network; in others the dendrites come from several parts of the soma. The membranes that make up the dendrites are similar to the membranes of the soma; thus the dendrites can be seen as enormous extensions of the cell body.

Each neuron has only one axon. The axon may end in the immediate area of the cell body, or it may travel for vast distances (on the microscale of neuron sizes) before finally branching and terminating on other neurons or on muscles. Some axons do both, branching near their origin to send one set of endings to the area of their own dendrites and another set to a distant region.

Electrical signals are usually collected along the dendrites and on the soma of the neuron; from here they are transmitted along the axon for fur-

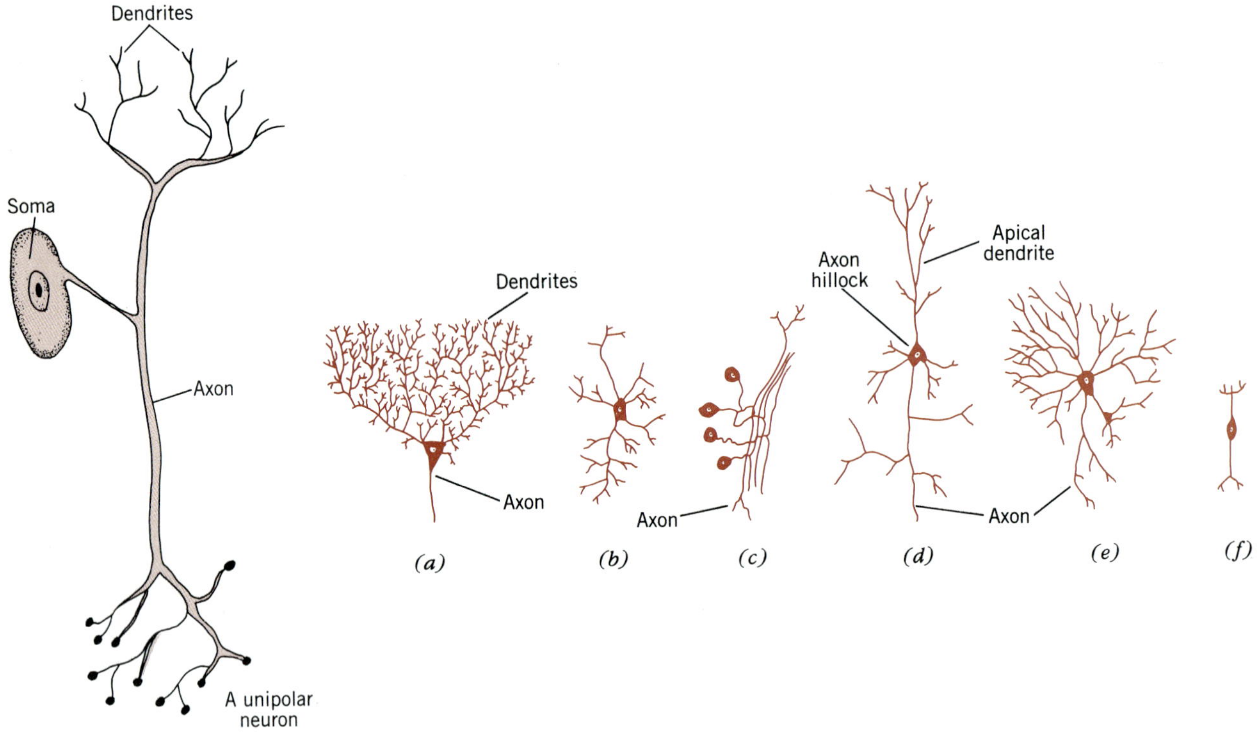

Figure 2.1 *Types of neurons.* (a) *A Purkinje cell of the cerebellum.* (b) *A spinal interneuron.* (c) *Sensory neurons extending from the skin to the spinal cord. The process that conducts impulses from skin to spinal cord extends in both directions beyond what is depicted here, and it branches extensively after entering the spinal cord.* (d) *A pyramidal cell of the cerebral cortex, the most common type of cell there.* (e) *A motor neuron in the spinal cord. The axon connnects eventually to a muscle.* (f) *A bipolar cell from the retina of the eye.*

ther processing by other neurons. There are exceptions to this general scheme, however; in some neurons, signals on the most distant dendrites are too far away from the cell body to have much effect on it. These dendrites serve mainly to link other neurons together. Some nerve cells have no dendrites, and others have unmistakable **synapses** (specialized connections with other neurons) but no axon. Most neurons have all three parts: dendrites, soma, and axon.

The distinction between dendrite and axon becomes less useful in some kinds of neurons, such as the sensory neurons that enter the spinal cord (see Figure 2.1c). The somas of these neurons form a **ganglion,** or group of cells, which is located next to the spinal cord. Each cell sends a single process out of the ganglion; the process divides and sends one branch to a sensory ending and the other into the spinal cord. By definition, the peripheral part of this long process is a dendrite and the central part (the part going into the spinal cord) is an axon. But in this case, the whole functions as an axon carrying signals in one direction and the cell body plays little role in the integration of signals.

GLIAL CELLS

About nine-tenths of the cells in the brain are not neurons but glial cells. They come in three varieties, each of which performs a set of specialized functions.

The **astroglia** (*astro* is Greek for "star") are named for their shape. These glial cells, more numerous than the neurons themselves, surround the neurons and isolate them from the **capillaries,** the smallest blood vessels of the brain. Figure 2.2 shows how some of their processes extend to wrap around capillaries while others contact the neurons. Along with the capillary walls themselves, the cells form the **blood-brain barrier,** which is really more an interface than a barrier. The astroglia absorb nutrients from the blood and transfer them to the neurons, but they block some kinds of molecules (many antibodies and drugs, for instance). (The blood-brain barrier is discussed further at the end of Chapter 3.) They also provide physical support for the neurons (there is no connective tissue in the brain) and isolate them from one another electrically to minimize

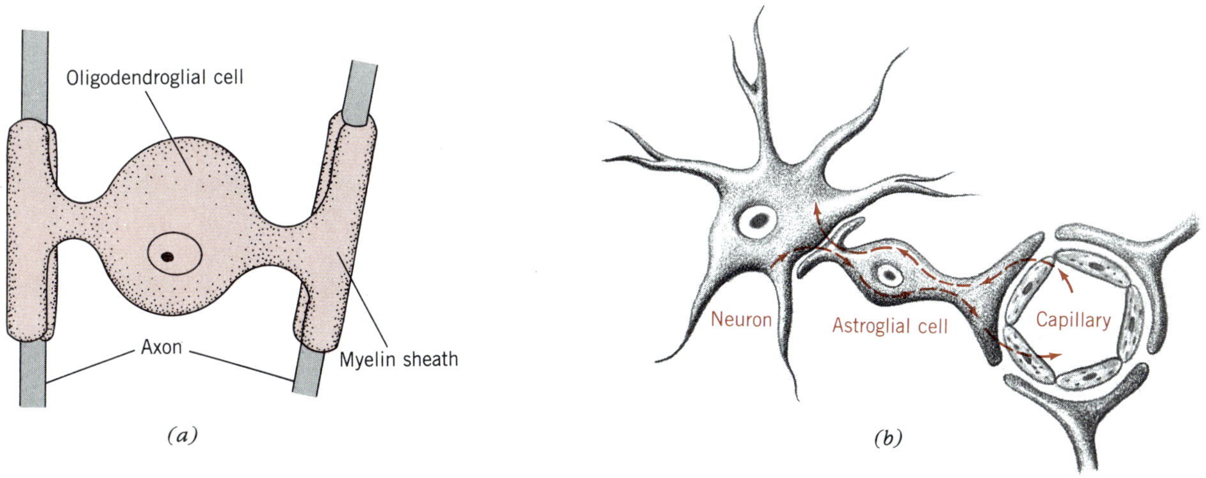

Figure 2.2 *Functions of glial cells.* (a) *Oligodendroglial cell, wrapping insulation around two axons.* (b) *Astroglial cell, transporting nutrients and waste products between a neuron and a capillary.*

"crosstalk" between nearby neurons that may be performing different functions. Some types of astroglia clean up debris in the brain, a function much like that of the white blood cells of the bloodstream. If a neuron dies of old age or is killed as a result of a head injury, a stroke (interruption of the blood supply), or an excess of alcohol or other drugs, astroglia will engulf and digest the remains of the neuron by **phagocytosis,** much as an amoeba engulfs its microscopic prey. Other astroglia will then form a dense network to fill in the space, in a process appropriately called **gliosis.** Although mature glia will divide when more of them are needed, mature neurons cannot divide (Rakic, 1985).

A second variety of glial cells—the **microglia**—are small, active cells that function as the vacuum cleaners of the brain. They move continuously among the neurons and glia, cleaning up debris. They are not fixed to one spot but wander throughout the brain with a seemingly independent existence.

Oligodendroglia—a third variety of glial cells—send out membranous processes that wrap themselves tightly around axons, forming a dense layer of spiraling membranes called **myelin.** The structure and development of myelin are shown in Figure 2.3. (The function of this wrapping, to speed long-distance communication along the axons, will be discussed later in the chapter.) Each oligodendroglial cell may wrap an arm around several axons. In the **peripheral nervous system** (outside the brain and spinal cord), the same function is performed by **Schwann cells;** each Schwann cell wraps around only one axon, however. Oligodendroglia also protect unmyelinated axons, which travel in deep notches in the bodies of glial cells (as shown in Figure 2.4).

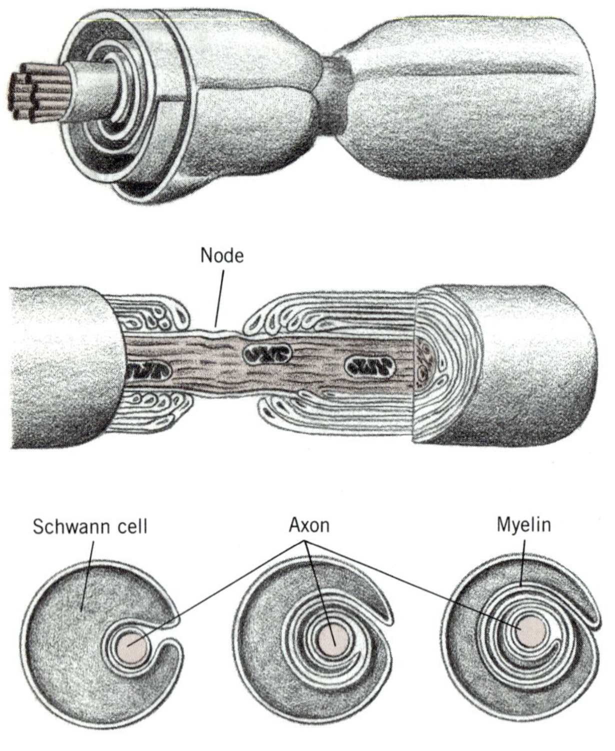

Figure 2.3 *Structure and development of myelin. A Schwann cell or oligodendroglial cell begins by forming a groove for the axon, then wraps around it several times, squeezing out the glial cell's cytoplasm as it goes. The resulting stack of membranes, facing alternately inward and outward, is made up mostly of lipids (fatlike molecules), which contain little water and are good electrical insulators.*

MEMBRANES

Neurons have all the basic biochemical equipment of other cells. What makes them unique is their

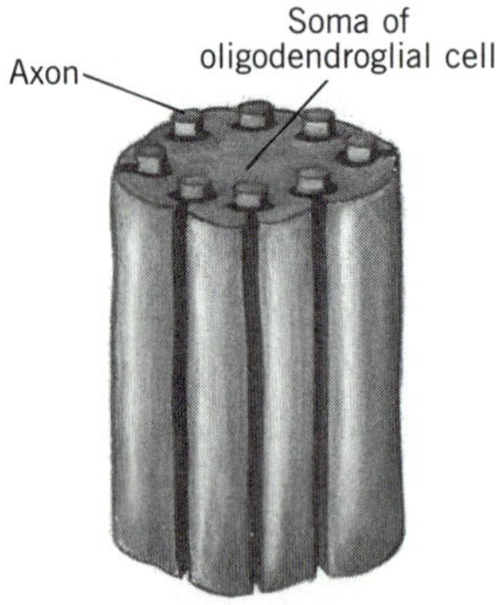

Figure 2.4 *Unmyelinated axons protected by an oligodendroglial cell. Usually, several axons are associated with a single glial cell, and a chain of glial cells protects the axons.*

capacity for rapid and specific interaction, a process that takes place on their membranes.

Design of Cell Membranes

All cells, including neurons, are enclosed in a **plasma membrane,** a two-layered structure about 90 Å (90 ten-billionths of a meter, or 90×10^{-10} m) thick. This size is beyond the resolution of the light microscope; most of what we know about membrane structure comes from electron microscope studies and indirect biochemical manipulations. The two layers of the plasma membrane consist of fatlike **lipids,** including phospholipid and cholesterol molecules. Each molecule has a **hydrophilic** (*hydro* is Greek for "water," and *philic* is Greek for "loving") head and a **hydrophobic** (*phobic* is Greek for "avoiding") tail; the tail is made of a hydrocarbon chain. Figure 2.5 shows how these molecules are organized into a surface, with the hydrophilic heads facing outward, toward the surrounding watery medium, and the hydrophobic tails pointing inward and facing one another, isolated from the water by their symmetrically opposed arrangement.

The whole system is self-organizing and stable. If purified membrane lipids are poured into water, they spontaneously assemble into small cell-like spheres (liposomes). This happens because the hydrophobic tails on the phospholipid molecules are in a lower energy state when they are not in contact with water. Only the double-layered plasma membrane can isolate them from water. The phospholipids and other molecules floating in the membrane are free to move about laterally, though; the structure has been called a two-dimensional solution (Singer & Nicholson, 1972).

Embedded in the cell membrane, giving it the complexity of a living thing, are a variety of proteins, also shown in Figure 2.5. One of their functions is to move substances across the membrane from one side to the other. They also regulate the transport of molecules through pores in the membrane. The protein inclusions are of three kinds: those exposed only to the outside of the cell, only

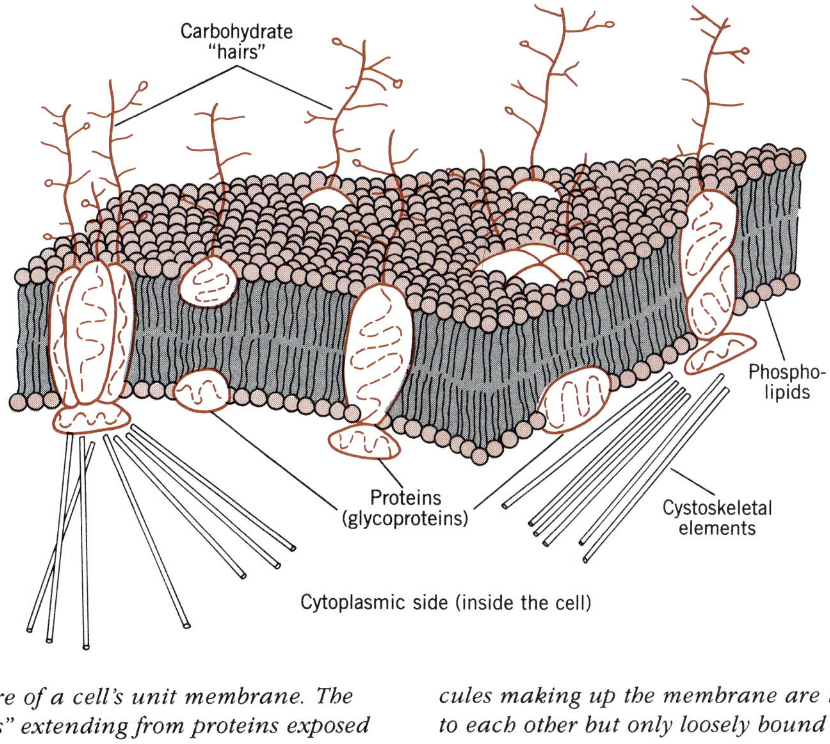

Figure 2.5 *Structure of a cell's unit membrane. The carbohydrate "hairs" extending from proteins exposed to the outside of the cell are so dense that they look like cornstalks in a field; they contact the substances that the cell absorbs. The pairs of opposed phospholipid molecules making up the membrane are tightly attached to each other but only loosely bound to neighboring phospholipids, allowing proteins in the membrane to move freely in a lateral direction. Some of the membrane proteins anchor the cytoskeleton.*

to the inside, or to both sides. Proteins exposed on only one side of the membrane are held in place by their hydrophobic inner parts and hydrophilic outer parts, as are the phospholipids surrounding them, though the proteins are much larger and more complex.

CELLULAR STRUCTURE AND FUNCTION

Most of the organelles of a cell consist of plasma membranes that resemble the cell's outer membrane but that are distinguished by their shapes and their protein constituents (see Figure 2.6). The **endoplasmic reticulum** (*endo* is Latin for "inside") is an inside extension of the cell's plasma membrane; it blends into the outside membrane in much the same way that the lungs blend into the skin. There are two kinds of endoplasmic reticulum: smooth and rough; both transport substances around the cell. The rough variety is made rough by the presence of ribosomes on its inner walls. **Ribosomes** are molecular machines directed by **ribonucleic acid (RNA)** templates derived from the cell's genes. They link together chains of **amino acids,** the building blocks of proteins. Ribosomes attached to the endoplasmic reticulum make proteins to be transported out of the cell, such as hormones; ribosomes in the cytoplasm (the internal fluid of the cell) make proteins for internal use.

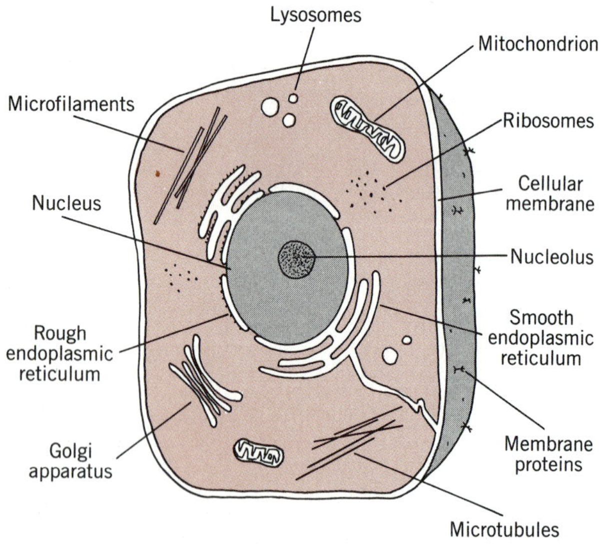

Figure 2.6 Internal structures of an animal cell. None of the organelles in a neuron is unique; all of them are also found in other body cells. The long axons and dendrites of neurons are stabilized by microfilaments and microtubules, which also aid in active transport of substances along the cell processes.

The **Golgi apparatus** (after Camillo Golgi, a 19th century neuroanatomist) manufactures membranes for use in making **vesicles,** packets of chemicals that are released from the cell. (The fate of these vesicles is reviewed later in the chapter.)

The nucleus, the master control center of the cell, is bounded by a membrane consisting of two concentric plasma membranes. It contains the cell's **deoxyribonucleic acid (DNA),** its genetic material. Communicating with the cell by pores in its membrane, the nucleus uses DNA to manufacture messenger RNA, which goes to the ribosomes, where it is made into a template for producing proteins. Some proteins provide structure, and others act as **enzymes**—molecules that facilitate chemical reactions in the cell. The nucleus also contains another structure, the **nucleolus,** which manufactures the ribosomes.

The **mitochondria** are an evolutionary mystery. They are the respiratory organs of the cell, providing energy from glucose (a simple sugar) and oxygen, but they have their own genetic material and reproduce separately when a cell divides. They are probably the descendants of simple bacterialike cells that invaded other simple cells over a billion years ago, at the start of the evolution of higher, multicelled animals and plants. Eventually they formed a **symbiosis** (cooperation) so effective and so highly integrated that it was detected only recently. It is as though we are permanently infected with these intracellular interlopers and depend on them for our lives. Mitochondria, which are especially numerous in neurons, tend to collect at places in the cell where **metabolism,** the use of energy to do the cell's work, is particularly high. Their presence is a sure sign of active energy use in a cell.

The cytoplasm in which these organelles reside is more than a chemical soup; it is highly structured by a fine network of **microtubules** and **microfilaments,** molecular-scale tubes and strands that are continually being broken down and rebuilt as the cell changes its shape and its functions (Porter, Byers & Ellisman, 1979). The living cell is like a building that is constantly being rebuilt from the inside. Yet nothing is out of place in a healthy cell; life consists of chemistry organized down to the last molecule.

From the standpoint of their unique functions, the most important parts of neurons are their membranes and the structures associated with them. They are the subject of the next section.

HOW THE NEURON WORKS: CHARGES AND IONS

The membrane processes that enable neurons to communicate and process information are electrical in nature. Understanding them requires a few definitions of electrical terms.

Electricity is carried by electrons; the difference between concentrations of electrons in two places is voltage, or **potential** (E), and is measured in **volts.** The two poles of a flashlight battery, for instance, differ by 1.5 v, with a greater density of electrons at the negative pole. Each electron has a single negative charge.

When electrons flow through a wire, their rate of flow is expressed as a current, I, measured in **amperes.** The flow of electrons is reduced if it is impeded by a resistance, R, measured in **ohms.** The relationship of the potential (E), the current (I), and the resistance (R) is expressed in Ohm's law: $E = IR$. Thus more current (I) will flow if the potential (E) is increased or if the resistance (R) is lowered. Resistance is sometimes expressed in terms of **conductance,** defined as the reciprocal of resistance ($1/R$). Its unit is the **mho** (ohm spelled backward). In biological systems the charge is usually carried out by ions rather than electrons. An **ion** is a molecule in solution with one or more extra electrons (resulting in a negative charge) or with one or more missing electrons (resulting in a positive charge).

The next two sections of the chapter will examine two kinds of potentials across neural membranes: resting potentials and graded potentials. **Resting potentials** store energy in the membrane, and **graded potentials** enable neurons to process information. Later we will see how action potentials (defined in Chapter 1) allow information to be transmitted over great distances.

RESTING POTENTIALS

Two characteristics of neurons are crucial to their functioning: the differences in ion concentrations inside and outside the cell and the resulting differences in electrical potential across the membrane—the resting potential. The two are closely related.

The differences between potential inside and outside the cell can be observed only through recordings from an electrode (a small wire insulated except at the tip) placed inside a cell. This is usually a technically difficult feat because of the microscopic size of most neurons. Since we are still examining the properties of neurons that are common to all stages of evolution, it is of great advantage to record potential differences in the largest available neurons. Many invertebrates have a small number of giant neurons, with axons up to 1 mm in diameter; inserting an electrode in such an axon, which is easily visible to the naked eye, is no more difficult than threading a needle. Hence much of our knowledge of nerve cell membranes comes from the giant axons, such as those of the squid.

As an electrode is advanced toward a giant neuron, there is no difference in potential between it and a reference electrode until the cell membrane is penetrated. At that point the electrode's potential abruptly drops to about −70 mv with respect to the outside (see Figure 2.7). This is about one-twentieth the voltage across a flashlight battery. The potential is not constant at that level but continuously undergoes small variations, as Figure 2.7 indicates.

The next step in understanding resting potentials is to measure the concentrations of ions inside and outside the neuron. This can be done directly in the squid's giant axon, which is so large that a section of it can be squeezed, like a toothpaste tube, with a roller to force out the contents of the axon. The resulting concentrations of ions are shown in Figure 2.8. Obviously, the ion con-

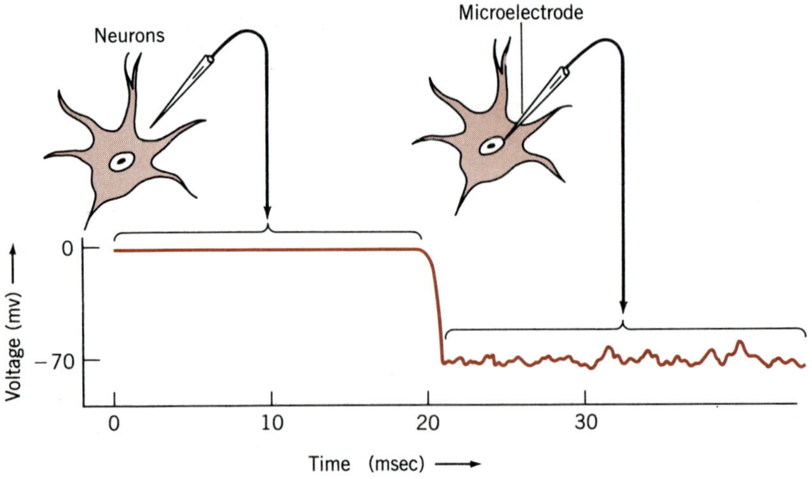

Figure 2.7 *Voltage drop across a microelectrode as it penetrates the membrane of a neuron. The graph shows the difference between the voltage at the tip of the micropipette (the micropipette is insulated except at the tip) and at the tip of a large electrode outside the cell.*

centrations inside and outside the neuron are different, with the membrane maintaining the difference in ion concentrations. For most ions there is a **concentration gradient,** a difference in concentrations, across the membrane. How do the concentration gradients bring about the resting potential?

The Nernst Equation

The electrical potential across the neuron's membrane can be calculated from the ion concentrations using the **Nernst equation.** The equation depends on the insight that the electrical charge, or potential, measures the *concentration* of electrons or ions, so the electrical charge can be viewed as a concentration in chemical terms. Thus, to describe charge, we can use the language that describes concentrations of molecules or ions in solution.

The Nernst equation states that the potential, *E,* across the membrane is predicted by five relationships:

1. *E* is related to the "ideal gas constant," *R,* from chemistry, because the motion of ions is involved.
2. *E* is also proportional to the absolute temperature, *T,* because ions move faster at higher temperatures.
3. Ions will diffuse from a region of higher concentration across the membrane to a region of lower concentration along their concentration gradient. The ions are like a swarm of flies randomly buzzing about in a jar; when the jar is opened, they are more likely to fly from the jar into the room than from the room into the jar. After a while the flies will be evenly distributed across the room. Adding a net across the middle of the room to represent the membrane does not make any difference as long as the flies can move freely through it. In the Nernst equation, this diffusion along concentration gradients means that the potential across the membrane will depend on the logarithm of the concentrations of each ion inside (*i*) and outside (*o*) the membrane ($[X_i]/[X_o]$).
4. *E* is inversely proportional to the charge, *n,* on the ion in question because one needs fewer ions to yield the same difference in charge if each ion has a greater charge.
5. Finally, *E* is inversely proportional to *F,* the **Faraday,** a unit of electrical charge.

Summarizing these five relationships in a mathematical formula, we show the Nernst equation as

$$E = \frac{RT}{nF} ln \frac{[X_o]}{[X_i]}$$

R and *F* are physical constants and *T* can also be held constant. Converting the ln into $\log_{10}$, we

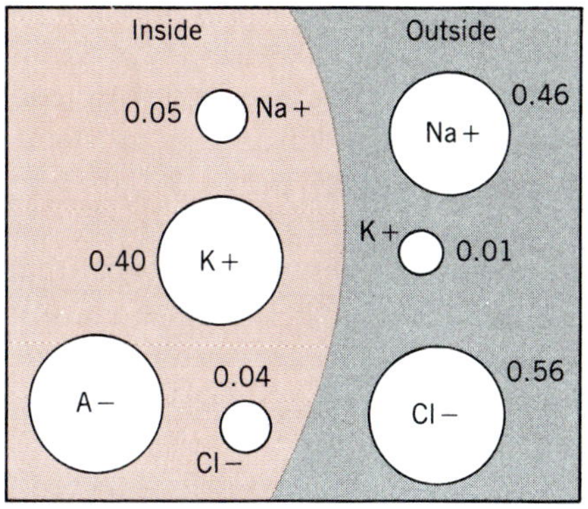

Figure 2.8 *Ion concentrations inside and outside the neuron. The size of each circle represents the concentration of ions in solution. A− represents large intracellular proteins with negative charges.*

obtain

$$E = \frac{58}{n} \log \frac{[X_o]}{[X_i]}$$

Now we can find the potentials (E) where various ions are in **equilibrium**—where ions will flow neither into nor out of a cell. We need to know only the charge of the ion and its concentration inside and outside the cell.

Applying the Nernst Equation

We can now try to predict the resting potential across the neuron's membrane—the constant −70 mv potential measured across the membrane in the absence of any biological signals—from the concentrations of ions inside and outside the cell. The concentrations of the most important ions are given in Figure 2.8. The neuron contains large, negatively charged protein molecules, labeled A^- in the figure. These molecules don't enter into the Nernst equation because they are too large to pass through the pores in the membrane. The membrane is at least semipermeable to the other ions. Using the concentrations in Figure 2.8 for chloride, Cl^-, we obtain

$$E = \frac{58}{-1} \log \frac{0.56}{0.04}$$
$$= -66.5 \text{ mv}$$

This result is close to the experimentally measured resting potential of a typical neuron. We can therefore conclude that Cl^- is in equilibrium in the neuron; Cl^- is repelled by the negative electrical potential inside the neuron, because like charges repel each other, and this repulsion results in a lower concentration of Cl^- inside the cell than outside. (The difference in electrical potential is called the **electrostatic gradient.**) But since there are more ions on the outside, it is more likely that an ion on the outside will diffuse in than it is that one on the inside will diffuse out. The two forces, electrical charge pushing the Cl^- ions out of the cell and diffusion letting them in, are in balance.

Now we can calculate the equilibrium potentials of sodium (Na^+) and potassium (K^+). Putting the charge and concentrations of the Na^+ and K^+ ions from Figure 2.8 into the Nernst equation, we obtain

For sodium:

$$E = \frac{58}{+1} \log \frac{0.46}{0.05}$$
$$= +56 \text{ mv}$$

For potassium:

$$E = \frac{58}{+1} \log \frac{0.01}{0.4}$$
$$= -93 \text{ mv}$$

The sodium ion would be in equilibrium if the membrane potential were +56 mv, not the −70 mv that it actually is. Na^+ should be pouring into the cell, following both diffusion down its lopsided concentration gradient and the electrostatic gradient attracting it to the inside. At the same time, potassium should be leaking out. What keeps them from doing just that?

First, the nerve cell membrane is much less **permeable** (selectively leaky) to Na^+ than it is to Cl^-, so diffusion is limited. There is still some permeability, however, so Na^+ should eventually reach equilibrium.

The Sodium-Potassium Pump

The second and more surprising reason for so little Na^+ inside the cell is that a microscopic "sodium-potassium pump" is actively pumping sodium out of the cell and potassium in. Potassium moves relatively more freely through the membrane, however. It diffuses back out of the membrane, following its concentration gradient, almost as soon as it is pumped in.

Why a dual pump? Wouldn't it be simpler just to pump Na^+ out of the cell, and let K^+ reach equilibrium? The answer is that it takes less energy to exchange ions, letting one in and one out, than it would to pump Na^+ out by brute force. Just as it is easier to lift a heavy load with a counterweight, the simultaneous pumping of one positive ion out and another positive ion in means that the metabolic pump is not required to change the net charge. It works mostly against the concentration gradients. The membrane potential is maintained by a kind of electrochemical trick, because the K^+ diffuses out of the cell again more quickly than the Na^+ diffuses in.

The sodium pump is more efficient at pumping Na^+ out than at pumping K^+ in; each unit of the pump transports about 200 Na^+ ions and 130 K^+ ions per second. The pump consists of a single protein molecule, or a complex of protein subunits, with a **molecular weight** of about 275,000. In other words, one pump weighs as much as 275,000 hydrogen atoms. By comparison, Na^+ has a molecular weight of 23 and K^+ of 39. Most neurons have 100 to 200 of these molecular pumps per square micron (millionth of a meter, or 10^{-6} m) of membrane surface, but near particularly active areas the density can be 10 times as high. A typical small neuron might have a million pumps (Stevens, 1979).

The amount of energy required to keep this enormous number of molecular pumps running is large; at rest, about 40 percent of the cell's metabolic energy expenditure is for pumping ions in and out. Since we know that in a highly evolved system one doesn't pay that high a price without getting something in return, we suspect that the resting potential is important for the function of the neuron.

In a larger sense we know that the resting potential cannot mean very much by itself, for it is a constant and life is lived on transients on membranes, where the biochemical processes of life take place. The study of transients on membranes is the study of life at its most fundamental level.

GRADED POTENTIALS

The secret of the resting potential is that it enables neurons to transmit and process information. It provides a baseline, a starting point. The potential can be disturbed by a sensory receptor cell, or, more commonly, by another neuron, or even by an electrophysiologist's electrode to create a graded potential. Like a drawn bow, the membrane already holds energy that can be released quickly in response to outside events. If the disturbance is a stronger negative voltage than the resting potential, the inside of the neuron becomes even more negative and is **hyperpolarized** (*hyper* is Greek for "more"). A positive potential applied inside the neuron makes it more **hypopolarized** (*hypo* is Greek for "under"), or closer to a potential of zero. The hypopolarized state is sometimes called the **depolarized** state, even though graded potentials can't change the neuron's potential to zero.

The graded disturbance is conducted along the neuron's membrane in much the same way that an electrical charge is conducted along a rather poor wire. (The nerve cell has fairly poor conductance, being made mostly of saltwater.) The electrical disturbance, the graded potential, is conducted only a few millimeters at most along the membrane. Putting current into a membrane is like pouring a few drops of water on a dry sponge; the sponge is wet right where the water was poured, but it stays dry a short distance away.

Spread in Space

The decrement of a charge from a point of electrical disturbance on the membrane is **exponential;** that is, in each unit of distance the voltage decreases by a constant fraction of its deviation from the resting potential. Figure 2.9 shows the shape of the exponential decrease (Coombs, Eccles & Fatt, 1955). If the *space constant* of a membrane is 1 mm, for instance, the voltage 1 mm away from a disturbance is 0.368 (a physical constant) times as strong as the original disturbance. At 2 mm away, the disturbance is $0.368 \times 0.368 = 0.135$ times as strong, and so on across the membrane in all directions. Clearly, processing with signals that disappear this rapidly must go on in very compact spaces, and indeed information processing in the brain takes place on a microscopic scale.

But there is more to the story of space constants in neurons. Space constants aren't really

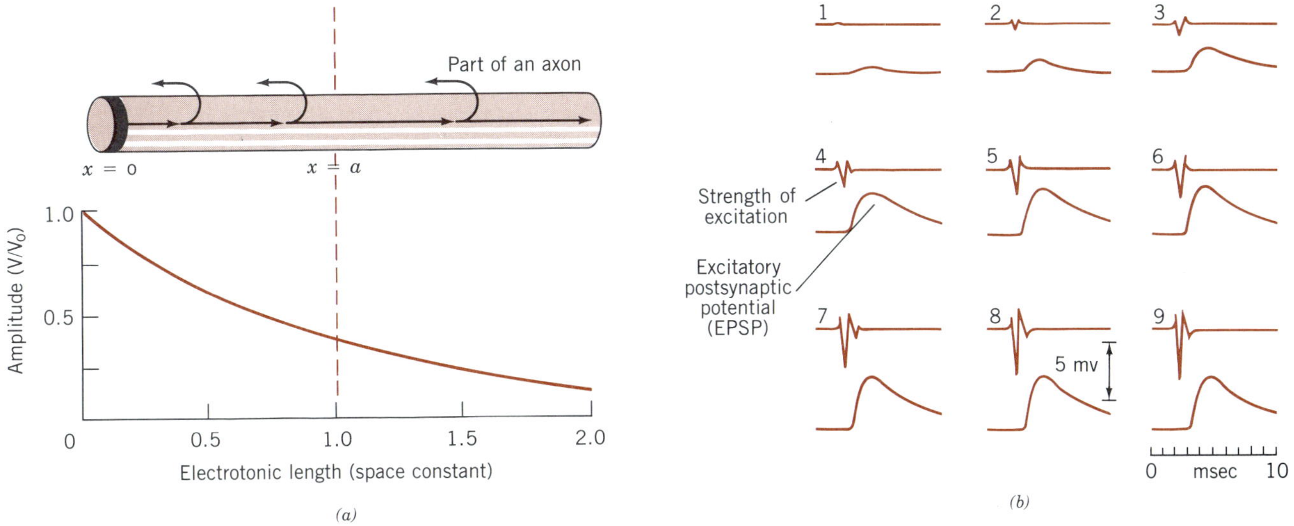

***Figure 2.9** Space and time constants.* (a) *The space constant of a typical membrane. When current is injected through the membrane at one point, it leaks back at nearby locations; the highest current is near the electrode. When a dendrite divides, its diameter decreases in such a way that the space constant does not change. Adapted from Shepherd (1974).* (b) *The time constant. The constant depends on the electrical resistance of the membrane and on the cell's capacitance—the amount of charge it can hold. In graphs 1 through 9, progressively stronger stimuli (the upper trace in each graph) are applied. The neuron's response increases in a graded fashion, but the time constant remains the same.*

constants, except at a given location; they are different on every part of the neuron, varying not only with the proteins in the membrane and the number and kinds of pores in it but also with the shape of the membrane. A space constant depends on the diameter of the dendrite, changing in each dendrite as the diameter becomes smaller. This is because the fluid inside the membrane of the dendrite conducts the electricity that enables the voltage change to spread across the membrane. In bigger dendrites there is more fluid, so bigger dendrites conduct better. As a dendrite gets thinner, its space constant gets shorter. Pushing ions through a dendrite is like pushing people through a hallway; as the hallway gets narrower, fewer people can get through at any one time. Thus the space constant varies with the diameter of the dendrites and cell body, the taper of the dendrite, and even the contents of the space outside the cell.

The disturbance just discussed is not an all-or-none affair; it can take on barely measurable values or amount to 10 mv or more. And, as we have seen, it is different at every point along the neuron's cell body and dendrites because almost everything in the cell's milieu influences it. It is this capacity for fine gradations that makes it a graded potential.

Spread in Time

As the graded potential varies in space, it also varies in time. If the electrical disturbance, or stimulus, is a brief pulse of current, the resulting graded potential takes a slightly longer time than the stimulus to decay back to the resting level. The stimulus disturbs the equilibrium ion balance of the neuron, and it takes some time for the diffusion and pumping of ions to restore the normal resting potential. In each unit of time the membrane restores itself, changing its potential by a constant fraction of its present deviation from the resting level. Therefore, it decays exponentially, like the spatial spread. The **time constant** of a typical neuron is about 4 to 10 msec, varying somewhat from cell to cell.

The interpretation of this number is similar to the interpretation of the space constant. In each 10 msec after the abrupt end of a stimulus, the neuron returns to 0.368 (36.8 percent) of its previous electrical deviation from the resting level. This means that when a stimulus is applied to a dendrite, the membrane potential is restored in a small fraction of a second, as is the case for the neuron described in Figure 2.9*b*. The time constant does not say anything about how fast a stimulus travels along the dendrite; it indicates only how fast the graded potential decays back to the resting potential at any particular place. Because the graded potential is an electrical potential, it is conducted almost instantaneously through the neuron, at a fraction of the speed of light.

By analogy, imagine pinching the middle of a tablecloth between your fingers and lifting it slightly from the table. The height of the tablecloth above the table represents the strength of the stimulus, and the amount of cloth lifted represents the space constant of Figure 2.9*a*. In fact, the diagram of Figure 2.9*a* might represent a cross section of half of the tablecloth. The speed with which the cloth falls back to the table when you let go is the time constant. Even if the tablecloth is raised and lowered gradually from the table, it begins its rise and fall at nearly the same time everywhere along its length. Similarly, the rapidity of the rise or fall of a biological signal does not limit how fast the signal is moving. As we will see later, some of the fastest rise and fall times belong to potentials that travel relatively slowly along the membrane.

In summary, the graded potential has properties that make it ideal as the information-processing medium of the brain. The potential is conducted rapidly but doesn't go very far, so the local area around the stimulus instantly "knows" that the stimulus was applied. The conduction distance and strength of the signal can be influenced by almost anything in the microenvironment, including the size and shape of the membrane carrying it, the chemical nature of the membrane, and the anatomy of the surrounding connections. All of these properties can influence information processing. The graded potential decays rapidly, but not so rapidly that biological processes cannot take place before it disappears. In a fraction of a second, however, the bioelectrical slate is wiped clean so that new processing can occur.

Interaction of Graded Potentials

Imagine the possible richness of texture in the microworld of graded potentials. These potentials can interact with each other in intricate patterns, adding together if they are both hyperpolarizing or both depolarizing, and canceling or interfering with each other if one increases the membrane voltage while the other decreases it. The influence of one graded potential on another depends on all of the properties described so far—the timing of the two potentials, their spatial separation, the diameters of the elements that support them, and the biochemical microenvironment (Stevens, 1966). In a real neuron, hundreds of graded potentials might interact simultaneously. The graded potentials interacting on a neuron's surface make the neuron a highcapacity, complex, and very compact analog microcomputer.

Seen in this way, each neuron is a tiny information-processing machine. But the neurons must communicate with one another for the results of the interactions on their membranes to contribute to the larger work of the brain. How do signals leap from one neuron to another?

INTERCELLULAR COMMUNICATION

The biological solution to the problem of how signals go from neuron to neuron is the synapse, the specialized contact point between neurons. The word was coined by Sir Charles Sherrington around the turn of the century to refer to active communication between neurons. Sherrington (1906) knew that synapses had to be the reason for the differences in response properties between a set of "upstream" neurons and the "downstream" neurons to which they were connected, and he inferred many of the information-transfer properties of synapses solely from such indirect evidence. But without the tools of modern neuroscience he could only speculate about the actual mechanism of the synapse. One of his students, Sir John

Eccles, later discovered many of the mechanisms of synaptic transmission.

In Sherrington's time two schools of thought developed about the nature of the synaptic contact between neurons. The "soups" thought the process was chemical; the "sparks" believed it to be primarily electrical. Each school had convincing, though indirect, evidence to support its case. It turned out that both schools were right; there are both chemical and electrical synapses in the central nervous system. Actually, three kinds of contacts occur between neurons; in increasing order of complexity they are ephapses, electrical synapses, and chemical synapses.

The simplest contacts between neurons, the **ephapses,** are simple juxtapositions (one neuron lies near another, with the usual extracellular space of about 200 Å between them). These contacts, seen at the upper left in Figure 2.10, are especially common in smaller branches of dendrites and axons. Because of the space between the membranes they aren't very efficient at conducting electrical signals, but they can have large effects in some systems (Korn & Faber, 1979).

ELECTRICAL SYNAPSES

More specialized contacts are **electrical synapses;** they occur when two neurons are joined by a special linking or partial fusing of their membranes. There are two varieties of electrical synapses: gap junctions and tight junctions.

Gap junctions are made by two membranes lying so close together that the distance between them is less than the thickness of the membranes themselves. The width of the gap is 20 to 40 Å. Recall that the plasma membrane has two phospholipid surfaces with a hydrophobic inner region sandwiched in the middle. If we look at the gap junction in Figure 2.11, we can count seven almost uniformly spaced layers: the three regions of one membrane, the gap of the gap junction, and the

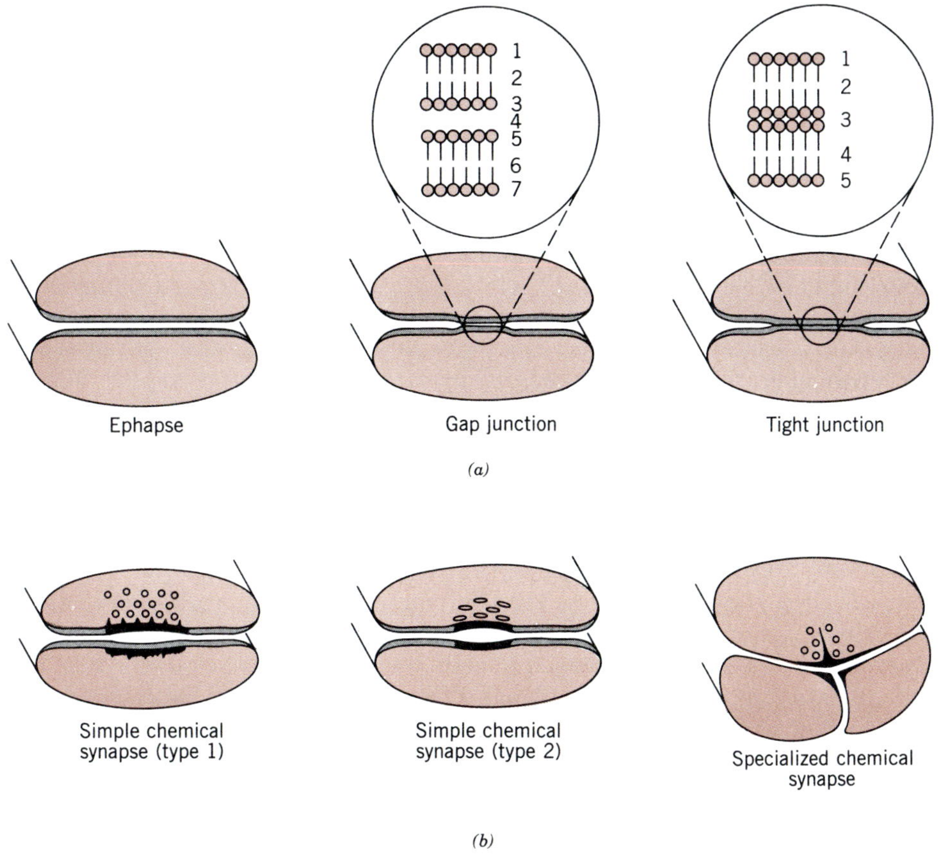

Figure 2.10 *Types of synapses.* (a) *Electrical synapses.* (b) *Chemical synapses. Type 1 is thought to be excitatory, type 2 inhibitory. The specialized synapse is a "ribbon synapse" of the retina, so named because the vesicles holding the transmitter substance are concentrated around a membranous ribbon. The presynaptic terminal is on the top in each synapse. Adapted from Shepherd (1974).*

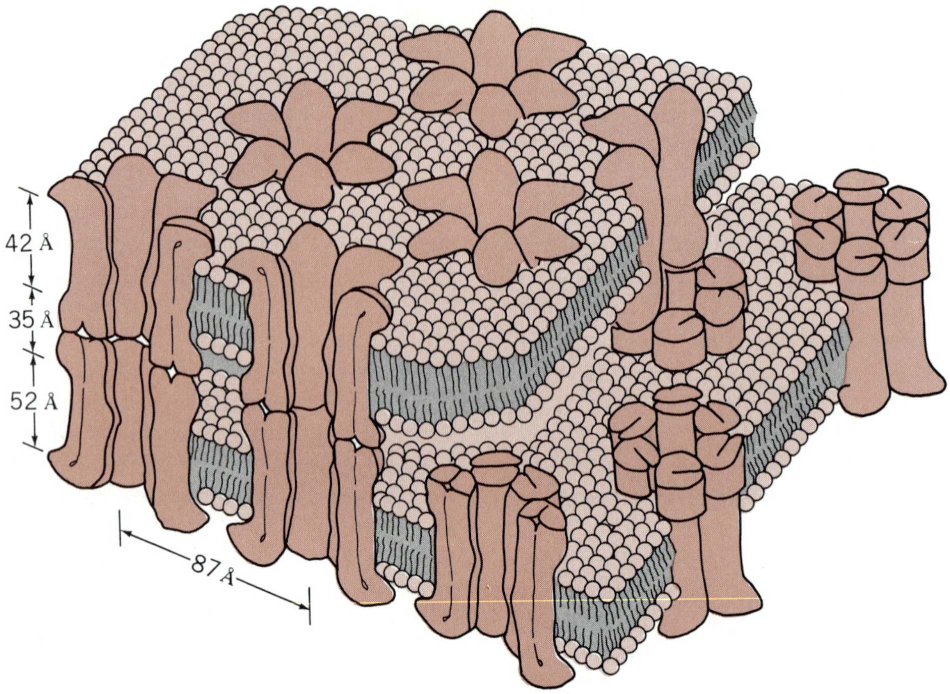

Figure 2.11 *Alignment of membrane channels in a gap junction. Adapted from Makowski et al. (1977).*

three regions of the other membrane. Physiologically, a low-resistance pathway across the gap junction facilitates transfer of the information carried by electrical charges from one neuron to the other (Reese & Brightman, 1970; Bennett, 1973).

The largest gap junctions are about 10 μm in diameter, and the smallest are only 0.1 μm across, an almost unimaginably tiny element in the neurological information-processing system. This element is about 10 times smaller than the smallest elements in manufactured microelectronic circuits.

Tight junctions are a partial fusing of the membranes of the two cells to form a five-layered complex. Figure 2.10*a* shows the five alternating hydrophilic and hydrophobic layers. The outer layers of the two membranes fuse into a single structure, so the tight junction is an actual joining of the two membranes while the cytoplasm of the two cells remains separated. Tight junctions are the only type of cell contact in which the basic membrane structure is modified.

Both gap junctions and tight junctions are formed not only by neurons but also by other types of cells. Although they function in cellular communication in neurons, the junctions may also facilitate the transfer of substances from one cell to another.

Electrical synapses have the advantage of speed; there is practically no synaptic delay in transmitting signals from cell to cell. But they have one crucial drawback; they can transmit only potentials that already exist. They cannot amplify or change the signals they transmit (though some of them can **rectify,** or transmit changes of only one sign, either positive or negative).

For the whole system to work, some way of renewing the energy of graded potentials is needed so they can continue to carry information in spite of their decrementing with space and time. These limitations are overcome by the many kinds of chemical synapses, the most complex and most varied of the three systems of communication between neurons.

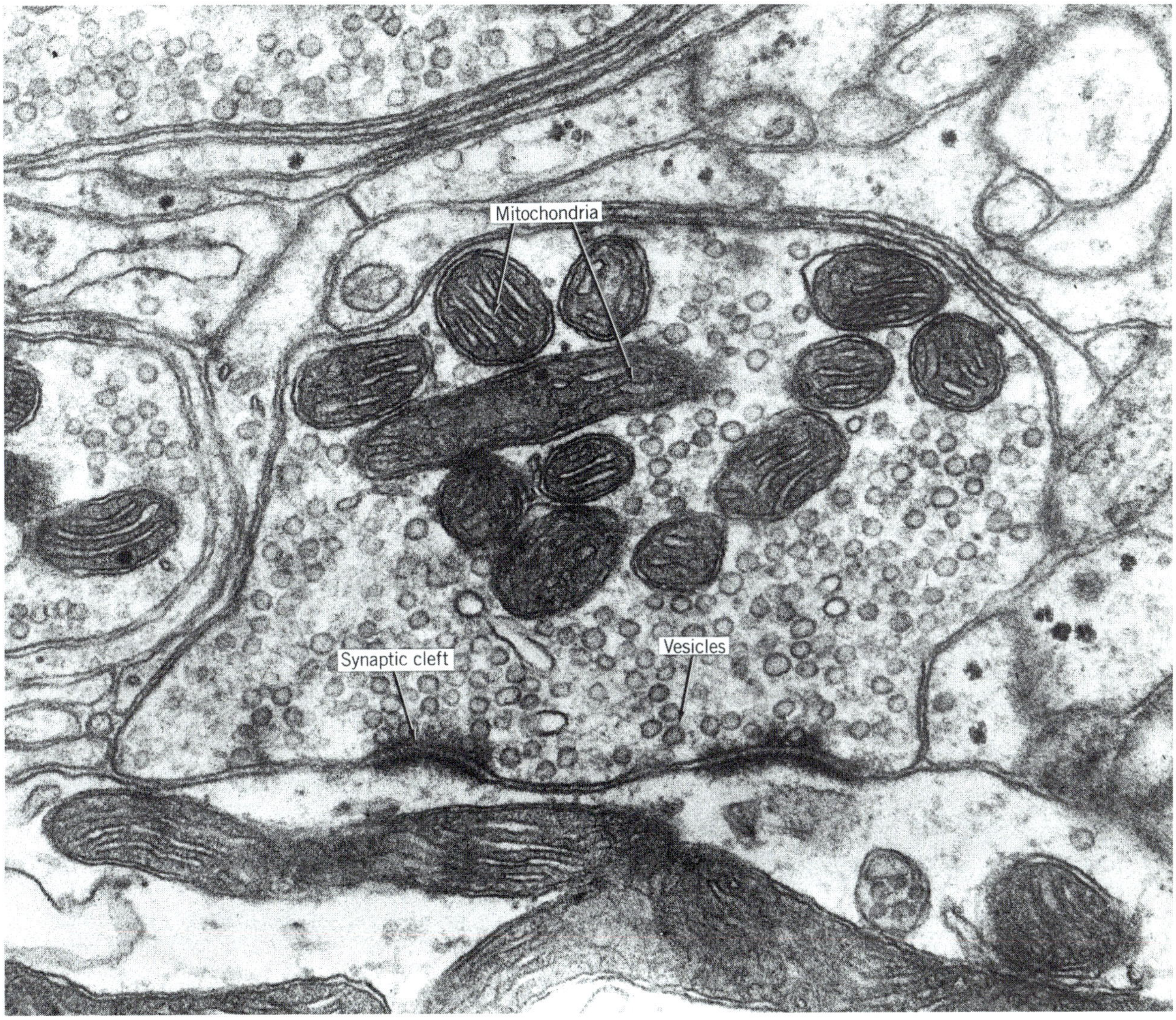

Figure 2.12 *Electron micrograph of a cross section of a chemical synapse. The small round bodies are vesicles filled with neurotransmitter. The large striped structures are mitochondria, present because synapses require large amounts of energy for normal operation. The synaptic cleft runs across the bottom part of the figure, and the thickenings of the membranes are probably the active sites of transmitter release.*

CHEMICAL SYNAPSES

Potentials are modified as they are transmitted from cell to cell by **chemical synapses.** The synapses conduct in only one direction, acting as tiny biological rectifiers. The direction of transmission establishes an asymmetry in the synapse. Information flows from the **presynaptic** (before the synapse) **membrane** across the **synaptic cleft,** or gap, to the **postsynaptic** (after the synapse) **membrane.** In Figure 2.10*b* signals flow from the top process to the bottom one. The synapses strengthen each signal and stretch it out in time, so the postsynaptic potential has a larger amplitude and a longer duration than the presynaptic potential. And most importantly, chemical synapses can either preserve the electrical sign of a po-**AChE,** the suffix *ase* indicating an enzyme), which tential or reverse it; depolarization can be changed to hyperpolarization by the chemical mediation of the synapse. An understanding of how all these things can occur will require a close look at the structure of the synapse and the events taking place during synaptic transmission.

The transmission process requires a **transduction** (change in form of energy) from electrical to chemical signals, a diffusion of the chemical transmitter substance, and a second transduction back to an electrical signal. When the information being transmitted is represented as the concentration of a chemical transmitter, it can be modified by the local biochemical environment. Chemical synapses can either excite or inhibit further long-distance transmission.

Excitatory Synapses

The structure of a typical excitatory chemical synapse, with **acetylcholine (ACh)** as the neurotransmitter, is shown in Figure 2.12. Chemical transmission will be examined using the ACh synapse as an example because it is a common type of synapse and is the most intensively studied. In addition to being present in the brain, ACh is the chief neurotransmitter in the *autonomic* part of the nervous system, the neural system outside the brain and spinal cord that controls such functions as digestion. ACh is also the neurotransmitter at the **neuromuscular junction,** the synapse between a nerve axon and a muscle fiber. (Dozens of other neurotransmitters and several more specialized types of synapses will be considered later.)

Synaptic transmission begins when the inside of the presynaptic terminal is depolarized relative to the outside. As the potential becomes less negative than normal, Ca^{++} ions begin to flow through specialized membrane channels from the synaptic cleft into the terminal. An increase in Ca^{++} concentration inside the presynaptic terminal triggers the next step, when the terminal begins to release vesicles filled with ACh. The vesicles are spheres made of the same plasma membrane that surrounds the cell. They are manufactured either locally in the terminal or in the Golgi apparatus, and they collect in the vicinity of the synapse. At the neuromuscular junction a vesicle contains 1000 to 10,000 ACh molecules. When a synapse is activated by electrical depolarization, some of the vesicles are driven to the presynaptic membrane and fuse with it, releasing their ACh into the synaptic cleft.

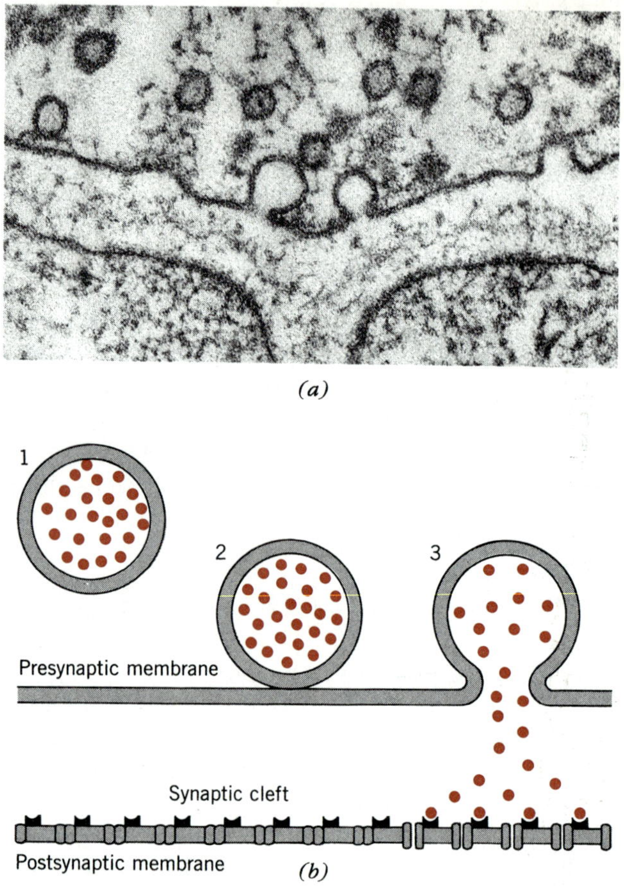

Figure 2.13 *Release of transmitter from synaptic vesicles.* (a) *ACh being released into the neuromuscular junction of a frog. The preparation was made by stimulating the motor nerve and quickly freezing the nerve-muscle system while the muscle was contracting. Vesicles are seen in several stages of merging with the presynaptic membrane.* (b) *Schematic diagram of the synaptic processes pictured in* (a). *The transmitter molecules (small spots) are free to diffuse across the synaptic cleft after the vesicle has opened to the outside of the presynaptic terminal. When they encounter receptors at the postsynaptic membrane, they cause channels to be opened.*

The vesicles move through the presynaptic terminal by a molecular mechanism similar to the mechanism of muscle contraction; each vesicle is coated with a protein, *stenin,* which interacts with another protein, *neurin,* found on microtubules running through the terminal. The proteins adhere to each other and slide along each other, an arrangement similar to the interaction of the related proteins in muscles (see Chapter 7). The initial Ca^{++} influx is a necessary step in both muscle activation and synaptic activation. As the specialized "micromuscles" inside the nerve cell move the vesicles toward the synaptic cleft, the neurin on the inside of the presynaptic membrane causes the vesicles to rupture and spill their contents into the synaptic cleft. In Figure 2.13 some vesicles have just fused with the membrane of the presynaptic terminal. The electrical signal has now been transduced into a chemical one.

Once the transmitter substance is released into the synaptic cleft, it must cross to the postsynaptic membrane, a distance of some 200 Å. No motive force transports the ACh molecules to the other side; they move solely by the process of diffusion. On the scale of everyday life, diffusion is a slow process; it takes a long time for a drop of food coloring to diffuse through a glass of water. But on the microscale of neurophysiology, diffusion takes place very quickly, because the speed of diffusion is the same as it is in our everyday experience (or slightly faster because body temperature is a bit higher than room temperature) and the distances involved are many orders of magnitude smaller (a distance one order of magnitude smaller is 10 times smaller). The system works on a scale where ordinary physical intuitions are of little use. It takes only about 50 μsec, or fifty-millionths of a second, for the ACh to reach the other side of the cleft. This time period amounts to about one-tenth of the total synaptic delay. At the postsynaptic membrane, ACh interacts with specialized receptor sites to create an **excitatory postsynaptic potential (EPSP)**—a graded potential that is a hypopolarization of the neural membrane on the postsynaptic side of the synapse.

ACh has no effect on ordinary membranes. Its action on the postsynaptic membrane is caused by receptors associated with **channels** in the membrane. The channels are not just holes in the membrane but specialized gates guarded by protein molecules. In an interaction that can be schematized with a lock-and-key structure, the transmitter opens the channel by moving a blocking molecule aside. Figure 2.14 shows an ACh molecule interacting with a channel protein. The geometry of the receptor site is still unknown; it is just a little too small to be seen with an electron microscope. The channels in the postsynaptic membrane are specialized to allow the passage of sodium and potassium ions, resulting in a partial depolarization of the membrane by the mechanism of the Nernst equation, discussed earlier. Na^+ rushes into the cell, and K^+ later leaks out. Na^+ has the stronger effect because it is further from its equilibrium concentration; the result is a net depolarization. When added to the effects at many other pores, the depolarization creates the EPSP. The chemical messenger has been transduced into an electrical depolarization on the other side of the synapse.

Recovery. Now the electrical signal, transformed by its passage across the synapse, is on its way again. But the synapse has been changed by the process and must recover. The merging of vesicles with the presynaptic membrane has increased the size of the presynaptic terminal; obviously, this process cannot go on very long, or the terminal would grow without limit. At a point on the membrane near the synaptic region, bits of membrane are pinched back into the terminal, a process called **pinocytosis** (Latin for "pinch-cell"). They become part of irregular **cisterna** (Latin for "sewers"), complexes of membrane inside the terminal, eventually to be made back into vesicles again. In nature nothing is wasted.

If the ACh remained in the synaptic cleft, it would hold the Na^+ channels open indefinitely, with disastrous consequences. If the channels were already open, no further synaptic messages could get through. Information is change, and this state of affairs would prevent changes from passing down the postsynaptic membrane. In fact, this condition, called a *depolarization block* because the information flow is blocked by the continuous depolarization of the membrane, is the mechanism of action for some of the most lethal toxins known. Fortunately, the synaptic cleft contains an enzyme, **acetylcholinesterase** (mercifully abbreviated

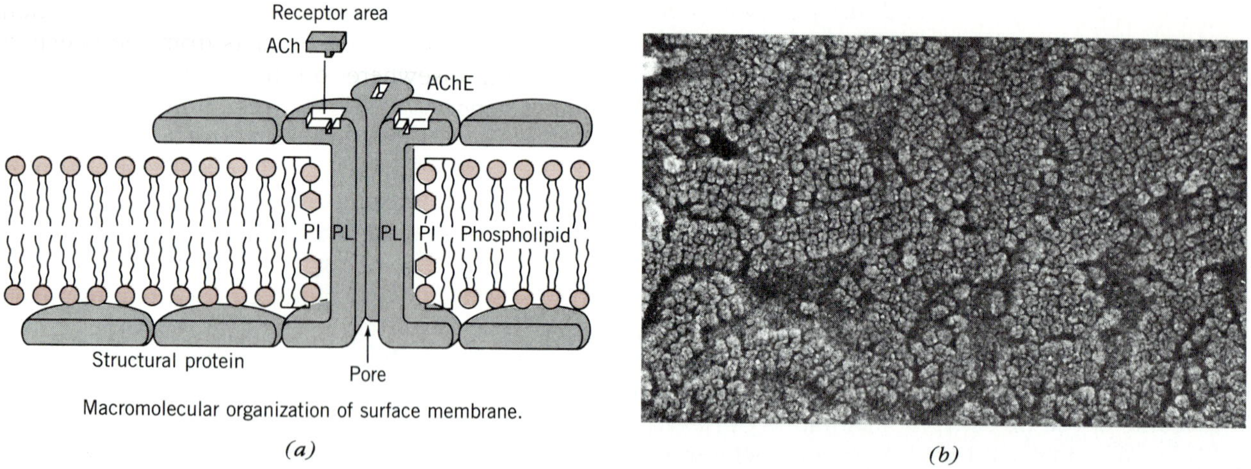

Figure 2.14 *ACh channels.* (a) *Organization of a channel complex in the membrane. Hydrophobic center sections and hydrophilic end sections of the protein molecules hold the channel in place, though it can wander laterally in the membrane.* (b) *Electron micrograph of ACh channels in a membrane. The channel is a complex of five subunits; it is 8.5 nm across, and its narrowest part is 0.8 nm in diameter.*

splits the ACh into choline and an acetate ion. Neither has any effect on the channels of the postsynaptic membrane. These two substances in turn are reabsorbed into the presynaptic terminal, to be recombined into ACh and used in the recycled vesicles. After the AChE breaks down the ACh, the channels close and the ion pumps restore the normal ion balance in the postsynaptic terminal. This process can take longer than the initial presynaptic potential, so the synapse has the effect of spreading the signal in time. The fastest presynaptic potentials rise and fall in 1 to 2 msec; the EPSP lasts at least 20 msec, and sometimes much longer.

The transformation from the incoming signal (the presynaptic depolarization) to the EPSP is an important difference between electrical and chemical synapses. Electrical synapses never change the shape of the signal, but chemical synapses always do.

Two Kinds of ACh Receptors. Postsynaptic receptors can often be identified biochemically by the drugs that bind to them. **Cholinergic receptors** (receptors using ACh as their transmitter) come in two varieties, both of them supporting depolarization and hyperpolarization of the postsynaptic membrane. One type of receptor, called **muscarinic** because it is stimulated by the drug muscarine, is found in synapses at the target organs of the autonomic subsystems (see Chapter 3). The drug atropine (belladonna) dilates the pupil of the eye by blocking these receptors; one of the results is paralysis of the muscle that constricts the iris of the eye. Muscarinic drugs have been used since ancient times to enhance the beauty of the eyes. **Nicotinic receptors** are receptors stimulated by nicotine (including that from cigarettes). They are found at the neuromuscular junction between nerves and muscles, in the spinal cord, and in parts of the autonomic subsystems. The paralyzing agent curare, a poison used in hunting by South American Indians, blocks nicotinic receptors without affecting the brain.

Inhibitory Synapses

If only excitation existed in the brain, activity would build up until most neurons were depolarized most of the time. Neural activity would be uncontrollable. To avoid this situation, the brain balances excitation with inhibition. Neural activity, then, establishes a continuous tension between excitation and inhibition. Inhibitory synapses look like excitatory ones except that they have a slightly different geometry and somewhat flattened vesicles. (At least they are flattened after preparation for the electron microscope. No one knows whether they are flattened in nature.) There are several inhibitory transmitters, **norepinephrine (NE)** being the best understood because it also occurs outside the brain, where its synapses are more accessible. Inhibitory synapses have the unique property of reversing the sign of potentials as they transmit them; depolarizations of the presynaptic membrane become hyperpolarizations on the other side. As a result they can turn excitation into inhibition, generating an **inhibitory postsynaptic potential (IPSP).** This bit of biochemical trickery is accomplished by the membrane channels which the inhibitory transmitter opens (Moore & Bloom, 1979).

The initial events in NE inhibitory synaptic transmission are similar to those in excitatory transmission at ACh synapses, except that the channels of the postsynaptic membrane are too small to admit Na^+ ions. Cl^- and K^+ ions are small enough to pass through freely, but the K^+ ions have the strongest effect on the polarity of the membrane. K^+ flows out of the cell along its concentration gradient, causing the inside to become even more negative than normal relative to the outside. The Cl^- ions, which are approximately in equilibrium, should also flow into the cell along their concentration gradient. Their flow is restricted, however, by an ingenious property of the postsynaptic membrane channels opened by NE; these channels have a negative charge and therefore repel the negative Cl^- ions from the region of the channel. Thus the K^+ hyperpolarizing effect predominates. At other inhibitory synapses the channels have positive charges and Cl^- is the active ion (Coombs, Eccles & Fatt, 1955). In both cases, depolarization on one side of the synapse has been converted into hyperpolarization on the other side; the effect lasts about 8 msec in the spinal cord but can be 100 to 200 msec in the cerebral cortex (Phillips, 1956) and other forebrain areas (Kandel & Spencer, 1961; Purpura & Cohen, 1962). This inhibition subtracts from the effects of excitation elsewhere on the postsynaptic membrane; hence it is called postsynaptic inhibition.

In Sherrington's day it was thought that all central nervous system (CNS) synapses were excitatory. Now it is estimated that about half of the synapses in the brain are inhibitory synapses using the neurotransmitters gamma-aminobutyric acid (GABA) and glycine (an amino acid) (Iverson & Bloom, 1972).

Location of Synapses

Synapses can appear practically wherever two neurons come into contact. *Axodendritic synapses* pass information from the axon of one cell to a dendrite of another. *Axosomatic synapses* pass information from the axon of one cell to the soma of another. *Axoaxonic synapses* are seen in presynaptic inhibition, which will be described later. In the more recently discovered *dendrodendritic synapses* (Rall et al., 1966; Ralston, 1971), information flows from one neuron to another in the continuous graded potential mode. The rate of transmitter release is proportional to the depolarization of the presynaptic dendrite, and it changes in a graded manner to follow the dendrite's momentary state of polarization (Graubard & Calvin, 1979). Some of these synapses work only after the graded potential differs from the resting potential by a threshold value of a few millivolts; others respond to any change, either depolarizing or hyperpolarizing. The picture in Figure 2.12 is of spinal ACh synapses, but synaptic contacts in the brain come in a tremendous variety of shapes, sizes, and forms. Figure 2.15 offers a sampling of them.

NEUROCHEMISTRY

Other Neurotransmitters

There are many neurotransmitters besides ACh and NE; the exact number is not known, but it is several dozen at least. New candidates seem to be discovered every year. The four families of transmitters are ACh, monoamines (including the cate-

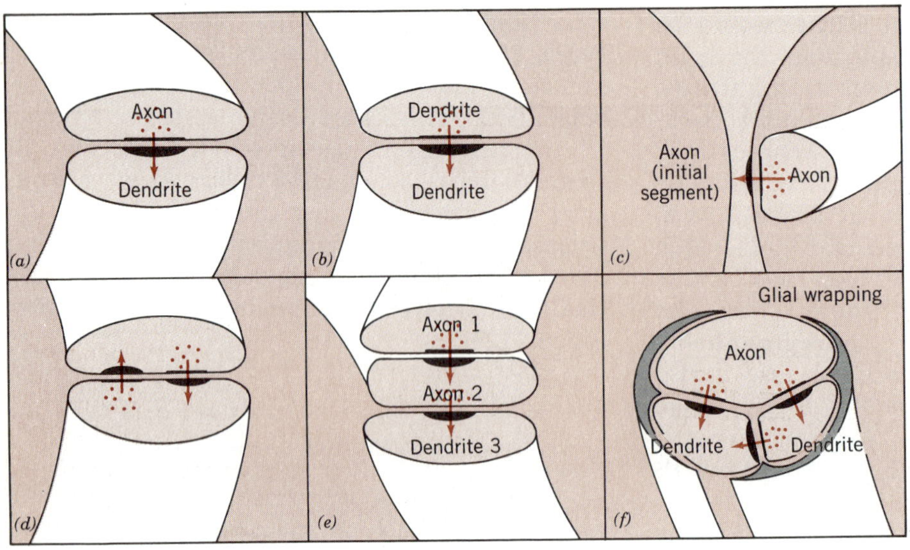

***Figure 2.15** Common types of chemical synapses.* (a) *Axodendritic.* (b) *Dendrodendritic.* (c) *Axoaxonic.* (d) *Reciprocal synapses.* (e) *Serial synapses (axoaxodendritic).* (f) *Synaptic glomerulus.* (b) *and* (d) *operate only in the graded-potential mode.* (e) *appears in more detail in the presynaptic inhibition of Figure 2.21. Adapted from Shepherd (1983).*

cholamines), amino acids, and peptides. Table 2.1 shows their actions, their locations, and some of their functions (the functions in the table are only approximations). The functions of individual transmitters will be discussed in later chapters.

All the neurotransmitters are small molecules of relatively low molecular weight, and all are water-soluble. Figure 2.16 summarizes the neurochemistry of the major transmitters. The peptide transmitters, including enkephalin, are more important than was previously thought and are now a major research area.

Table 2.1
Transmitter Actions, Locations, and Functions

Transmitter or Putative Transmitter	*Action*[a]	*Locations and Functions*
Acetylcholine (ACh)	E	Neuromuscular junctions, most CNS synapses
	I	Heart, some other synapses outside CNS
Amino acids		
Gamma-aminobutyric acid (GABA)	I	Main inhibitory transmitter throughout CNS
Glutamic acid	E	Probably main excitatory transmitter throughout CNS
Substance P	E	Pain in spinal cord, other unknown functions
Catecholamines		
Dopamine	I	Arousal, control of movement, emotion, memory
Epinephrine and norepinephrine	E, I	Widespread in CNS; arousal, wakefulness, eating, memory
Peptides		
Enkephalins	I	Pain in subcortical regions
	E	Amygdala and hippocampus (motivation?)
Beta endorphin	I, E	Vegetative functions, memory
Oxytocin	I	Related to hormone regulation

[a]E = excitatory, I = inhibitory.

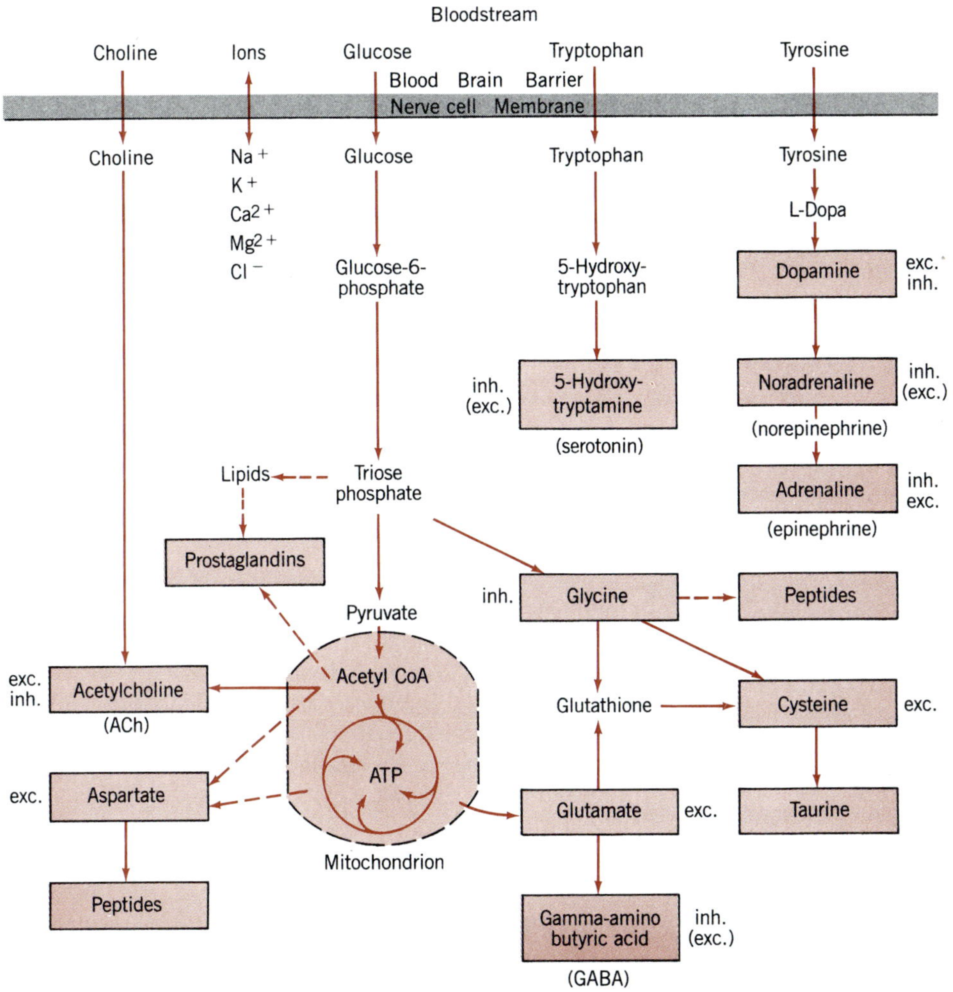

*Figure 2.16 Synthesis of the major neurotransmitters. The molecules choline, glucose (a simple sugar), tryptophan (an amino acid), and tyrosine (an amino acid) are actively transported across the blood-brain barrier. The synthesis of ACh, prostaglandins, aspartate, and glutamate uses biochemical intermediates of the Krebs cycle, the set of biochemical reactions that deliver energy to the cell. Adrenaline is named after one site of its synthesis, the adrenal glands atop the kidney (*ad- *is Latin for "toward";* renal *is Latin for "kidney"). Epinephrine is the Greek translation of the term.*

Enkephalins and Endorphins

Most neurotransmitters have been discovered by researchers isolating the chemical from brain tissue. Once a transmitter is identified, the path of synthesis, postsynaptic receptors, and other parts of the transmitter system can be investigated. The history of the enkephalins is the reverse; the receptors were discovered first, and the molecules to stimulate them were found later.

Humans have used opiate drugs to induce euphoria and deaden pain at least since the beginning of written history, but until recently it was not clear how they worked. By the early 1970s several lines of evidence pointed to internal brain receptors that were sensitive to the drugs.

First, the opiates could be effective in very small amounts. The synthetic opiate etorphine, for instance, gives rise to euphoria and deadens pain in doses as small as 0.1 mg, less than the effective dose of LSD. A drug must affect highly specific receptors to act in such small doses (Snyder, 1977).

Second, most opiates, like many other organic molecules, come in left-handed and right-handed forms. But only the left-handed *isomers* have pharmacological effects; the chemically identical right-handed isomers are ineffective.

Finally, a few small regions on the opiate molecules seem to carry the major effects. Chemists can alter other parts of the molecules without changing their influence on the brain. Small alterations on the key parts of the molecules, however, can have large effects. Opiate antagonists, such as naloxone, are similar to the opiates in their structure; yet a small dose of naloxone injected into a dying heroin addict in a hospital can almost magically revive the victim. The effectiveness of antiopiate drugs suggests that the antagonist competes with the opiates for a limited number of brain receptor sites. Using these clues as well as persistence and modern biochemical methods, Pert and Snyder (1973) isolated and described brain receptors for endogenous opiatelike substances.

Discovery of Endogenous Opiates. Once the receptors had been found, it was only a matter of time until someone discovered the natural neurotransmitters that stimulate the receptors. A scientific race to find the mystery substances began. In 1975 the race ended in a neck-and-neck finish. The first group to publish was Hughes and his associates in England; they found two morphinelike putative neurotransmitters. The chemicals were peptides, as expected, but they were surprisingly small—only five amino acids long (Hughes et al., 1975). Hughes and his associates named them **enkephalins.** The two varieties, met-enkephalin and leu-enkephalin, were named after the first amino acids on their chains, the only differences between the two peptides. Both enkephalins bound even better than morphine to the newly discovered opiate receptors. A few months later, Terenius and Wahlström (1975) in Sweden extracted a similar substance from human cerebrospinal fluid.

A wide variety of endogenous opiates have now been described, along with several different kinds of opiate receptors. The differences in the roles of the various types and their receptors are not yet clear. All the substances have similar structures and similar biochemical origins, though; they are synthesized in the brain by splitting from larger precursor molecules. The precursors, pro-opiomelanocortin, pro-enkephalin, and prodynorphin, produce beta-endorphin, enkephalins, and dynorphins (a third family of endogenous opiates), respectively. These substances have widespread and powerful effects on the brain, but proving them to be neurotransmitters will require that they pass a number of tests.

Tests for Neurotransmitters

Neurochemists have set several strict criteria for determining that a substance qualifies as a neurotransmitter. First, it must be present in adequate amounts in the presynaptic terminals. Second, enzymes to manufacture and break down the substance must be present. Third, the substance must be released by physiological stimulation, and artificial application of the substance in the appropriate amounts should mimic the natural response. Fourth, drugs that influence the various enzymatic or biophysical steps should have the appropriate effects on synthesis, storage, release, action, inactivation, and reuptake of the substance. With such a long list it is not surprising that few substances have qualified as unquestioned neurotransmitters. In fact, most of the synaptically active molecules that neurochemists encounter are called putative neurotransmitters because they have not yet met all the criteria.

Even if these stringent criteria are met, it is only likely—not proven—that the molecule is a neurotransmitter. The main value of the tests is that if a molecule flunks one of them, it can be ruled out. The reason for the elusive quality of a definite identification lies more in the philosophy of science than in the uncertainties of neuropharmacology. It is possible to disprove something by finding a counterexample or an inconsistency, but it is impossible to prove anything with complete certainty.

Anatomical Distribution of Transmitters

We can tell a lot about the function of a neurotransmitter from its distribution in the brain. New techniques enable the neurochemist to find particular neurotransmitters with radioactive tracers. One method uses a molecule that binds selectively to a particular neurotransmitter. The molecule, called a **ligand,** is labeled through the use of a radioactive element as one of its components. The labeled ligand is injected into an animal's brain, the brain is sectioned, and the radioactive areas reveal where the transmitter had existed in the living brain. The technique does not tell us, though, where the neurons using the transmitter are located. The label marks only the synapses.

The enkephalins, when they were discovered, were thought to act mainly in the brain stem and spinal cord. The ligand-labeling method has demonstrated that they are widely distributed in the CNS. Dopamine, a transmitter important in schizophrenia (see Chapter 15), was also thought to have a limited distribution. Tracing with radioactive ligands has shown that it too is widespread in the brain. Dopamine is found almost everywhere in the brain, including the cortex (Altar et al., 1985; Martres et al., 1985). The new, more widespread distribution changes our view of both dopamine and schizophrenia.

Transmitter Specialization

Why are there so many neurotransmitters? If they perform only two functions, excitation and inhibition, wouldn't it be simpler to have just two? (It certainly would be simpler for students of neurophysiology!) There are several answers, and the identification of the primary one depends more on your views about evolution than on neurophysiology. If you believe in the role of chance in evolution, a satisfactory answer might be historical accident. As the nervous system evolved, a biochemical system already developed for other functions might have begun to work as a neurotransmitter when one chemical fortuitously affected a neighboring cell. The functional role of this connection might have created an evolutionary pressure that led to the evolution of one of the many elaborate synaptic mechanisms that we now see. As different systems evolved at different times, a wide range of chemicals would have been pressed into service as neurotransmitters.

For those who have faith in the optimization of biological systems, a more satisfactory answer lies in the differences among the actions of the various neurotransmitters. Amino acids, for instance, tend to act as fast neurotransmitters; their actions last no more than a few milliseconds. Slower action is offered by the catecholamines, with time courses ranging from a few milliseconds to several seconds. Those neurotransmitters with longer-lasting effects tend to change the postsynaptic membranes more slowly. ACh, incidentally, can have either fast or slow effects, depending on the nature of the ACh receptors in the postsynaptic membrane.

The longest synaptic effects overlap in time with the actions of hormones, and indeed there is a continuity between the two. A **hormone** is a chemical that is synthesized in one part of the brain or body to have a signaling effect in another location. A neurotransmitter can be interpreted as nothing more than a fast-acting hormone with a very local effect. As various systems evolved, one can imagine, the substance with the time course of action that most closely fit the requirements of the evolving system had a selective advantage as the neurotransmitter.

In biological arguments where several interpretations are possible, it is often the case that all of them are correct. The process of evolving a neurotransmitter system probably began with whatever biochemical materials were at hand and evolved toward a matching of mechanism and function. In some of the slower peptide transmitters the process has resulted in some fairly complex chains of enzymatic action, chains borrowed from other metabolic processes.

Metabotropic Transmitters. Direct transmitters such as ACh have direct effects on receptor molecules that control channels through the neuronal membrane. Another set of transmitters, the **metabotropic transmitters,** have no direct effect on membranes. Rather, they set in motion a chain of events that eventually opens membrane channels from within the neuron. These transmitters work something like the famous Trojan horse of ancient Greece. During the Trojan war, the invading Greeks could not succeed in storming the gates of Troy. Finally, leaving a giant wooden horse as a peace offering, they abandoned the plain around the city. The seemingly victorious Trojans pulled the horse into the city and celebrated far into the night. But Greek soldiers, hidden inside the horse, emerged when all was quiet and opened the gates from the inside.

The corresponding process in the neuron begins when a metabotropic transmitter arrives in the usual way at the postsynaptic membrane. The membrane receptor combines a transmitter-specific receptor molecule exposed to the outside of the cell with an **adenyl cyclase** molecule exposed to the inside. When activated, the adenyl cyclase molecule catalyzes the conversion of **adenosine triphosphate (ATP),** the body's primary energy transfer molecule, into the related substance **cyclic adenosine monophosphate (cAMP).** The cyclic AMP in turn directs an enzyme called a **protein kinase** to attach a phosphate group to a protein in the postsynaptic membrane. This **phosphorylation** process alters the shape of the membrane protein and finally opens channels from the inside, as did the Greek soldiers in Troy. Ion flows then change the postsynaptic potential.

The metabotropic process gets its name from the use of enzyme systems involved in normal cell metabolism. Such transmitters as dopamine and norepinephrine use this mechanism. A large number of peptide transmitters use a similar biochemical route. Some cells use a variant of the ATP pathway, converting the related molecule guanosine triphosphate (GTP) into cyclic guanosine monophosphate (cGMP).

Evolution of Neurotransmitters

The peptides offer a glimpse into the chemical evolution of neurotransmitters and their functions. There are now about 40 peptide neurotransmitters, and new ones are being discovered at a rate of about 2 per year. Many peptide neurotransmitters are also hormones outside the CNS, and many of them serve as messengers in unicellular organisms and even in plants. We can see that the peptides evolved very early; the genes for producing them were pressed into service as the hormonal and nervous system became more complex. In neurons, the peptides continue to be manufactured in the soma and are carried along the axon's microtubules by **axoplasmic transport** to the synapses. The postsynaptic receptors for peptides also exist in nonneural chemical messenger systems, and similar receptors are seen in the brain (Krieger, 1983). The evolution of peptide neurotransmitters involved transferring a transmitter-receptor system to the CNS rather than structuring the system from the beginning. Many neuropeptides coexist with other neurotransmitters within the same neuron.

Probably the first neurotransmitters were the excitatory transmitter glutamic acid and the inhibitory transmitter GABA. Both occur in invertebrates, and both have direct effects on the polarization of axons even without the benefit of specialized postsynaptic receptor systems. It is easy to imagine how the postsynaptic mechanism could then evolve, even though we know that evolution cannot look forward and that each step in evolution must increase the fitness of its possessor. The production of glutamic acid and GABA is also direct; both are produced in a minor modification of the Krebs cycle, a biochemical pathway that furnishes most of the energy for the chemistry of life.

With so many neurotransmitters, and with the microstructure of the brain being such an intricate tangle, it is difficult to sort out functions and structures. Fortunately, two aspects of neurotransmitters aid the neurophysiologist in this task: vesicle size and chemical specificity of neurotransmitters. Vesicles, like chocolates, come in a variety of sizes and shapes and are stuffed with various fillings (Palay, 1967). The smallest, 200 to 400 Å in diameter, are the most common; they contain the smaller molecules, such as ACh and some amino acids. The medium-sized vesicles, 300 to 900 Å in diameter, usually contain monoamines. The largest vesicles, 1200 to 1500 Å in diameter, contain the various peptides (Shepherd, 1979b).

The second organizing aid, the chemical specificity of neurotransmitters, makes it possible to selectively stain all neurons containing a particular transmitter, thereby revealing the anatomy of that biochemical system.

The action of a transmitter depends on the nature of the postsynaptic channels it eventually opens. Some transmitters can have inhibitory effects in some places and excitatory effects in others. Again the versatile ACh is an example; it has an inhibitory influence at the heart and an excitatory influence in the synapses of the spinal cord. Further, some neurons use two different transmitters. In most cases, though, a neuron has the same action at all its synapses, so we can speak of excitatory neurons and inhibitory neurons.

The complexity and importance of neurochemistry mean that the brain is part computer and part chemical soup. Looking at one aspect or the other alone gives a partial, distorted picture of the whole. With this perspective we can return to the microworld of the junctional microstructure of the brain, where information processing takes place. The chemical synapse is the key that makes it all work, that mediates communication between cells even while it provides a point of contact between information and biochemistry.

The problem of making a thinking machine out of poorly conducting materials can now be addressed. The chemical synapse can boost activity that would otherwise die out quickly and can mediate communication among cells even though the activity is usually conducted only for fractions of a millimeter. The richness of graded interactions can now be exploited; every micron of a dendrite and every synapse can have a role in modulating information flow.

ACTION POTENTIALS

All of this processing is useless if the resulting synthesis cannot be communicated to other parts of the brain and eventually to the muscles and glands to get them to perform human behaviors. In small animals this communication is not a problem, for passive graded conduction is adequate to reach the farthest corners of the animal. A tiny marine worm only a millimeter or two long has no need of anything beyond graded potentials, and indeed graded potentials are the only ones seen in the smallest and most primitive animals with nervous systems. As animals became larger in the course of evolution, they had to develop a way of sustaining long-distance communication. But they did it with the same membranes and the same mediocre conductivities that exist in the rest of the nervous system.

The trick used to sustain long-distance communication lies in the nature of the channels in an axon. Like the channels in excitatory synapses, they cause depolarization when opened; but unlike synaptic channels, they are opened not by transmitters but by depolarization itself. At the point where the axon joins the cell body, the axon is slightly expanded into a structure called the axon hillock, where the first of the specialized axon channels are found. Here the electrical results of the graded potential interactions on the soma and dendrites of the cell are passively conducted, so that a continuously varying potential can be measured (as indeed it can be everywhere on the cell).

As long as the cell is hyperpolarized below its resting potential, or is only slightly depolarized, nothing unusual happens. But when the depolarization reaches a threshold of about −60 mv, the specialized channels of the axonal membrane open. Na^+ ions rush in along their electrostatic and concentration gradients, as Dr. Nernst would have predicted. And the depolarization of the axon decreases the resistance to Na^+ even further, so positive feedback accelerates the process. In positive feedback, a disturbance causes a greater disturbance of the same kind. The Na^+ influx is so great that in less than a millisecond the axon's local potential actually turns positive with respect to the outside, approaching the Na^+ equilibrium of +56 mv. It never quite gets there, though, because the Na^+ channels close again. Once opened, the channels close after only a fraction of a millisecond, regardless of the polarization state of the axon membrane.

The membrane is always somewhat leaky in regard to K^+ ions, and with depolarization its resistance to K^+ drops even further. K^+ pours out of the axon through its own channels, along its electrostatic and concentration gradients. The membrane potential dives back to the resting level. In many neurons it actually overshoots the resting potential level; the result is a hyperpolarization that acts like an inhibition following the dramatic events of the action potential. This happens because the excess K^+ that is always in the axon can now leak out, depressing the axon's potential even lower than the resting level until the sodium-potassium pump can restore ion concentrations. The K^+ channels open more slowly than Na^+ channels; but, as Figure 2.17 shows, they remain open until the increasing negativity of the membrane closes them again. These events complete a single action potential.

In summary, the following events take place. First, the axon's potential rises above about −60 mv, opening Na^+ channels. Na^+ rushes into the axon, further depolarizing it and turning the inside of the axon positive with respect to the outside. At about the peak of this potential the Na^+ channels close and the K^+ channels open, letting

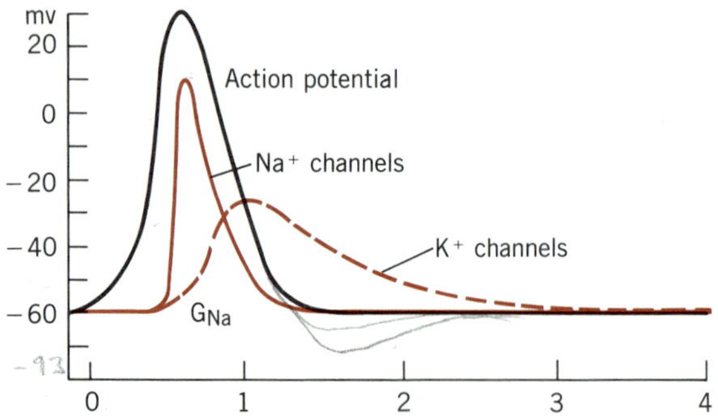

***Figure 2.17** Opening and closing of Na^+ and K^+ channels during an action potential. Na^+ channels close after a fixed duration of opening, about 0.8 msec, regardless of the polarization state of the membrane. K^+ channels are voltage-dependent, closing as the membrane resting potential is restored. Adapted from Noble (1966).*

K^+ leave the cell and restoring the negative inside voltage. The membrane overshoots its normal resting level, approaching the K^+ equilibrium potential of −93 mv; but the K^+ channels close and the sodium-potassium pump begins to restore the resting level before the potential can dip that far.

Experimental Evidence: The Voltage Clamp

By the late 1940s it was known that the action potential involved electrical events carried by ions. It was also known that Na^+ was responsible for the peak of the action potential, since the peak's amplitude was reduced if the external medium contained a reduced concentration of Na^+ (Hodgkin & Katz, 1949). The result could be predicted quantitatively with the Nernst equation. Studying these events was extraordinarily difficult because too many variables changed rapidly. An electrical event can easily be understood with Ohm's law if one characteristic changes while everything else remains constant. But *E, I,* and *R* are all changing rapidly during an action potential.

The experiments that established the steps in the generation of the action potential are a triumph of experimental design and technique, for which Hodgkin and Huxley won a Nobel Prize. They solved the problem by artificially holding the voltage constant across the membrane. An electrode was inserted inside a squid's giant axon and connected to a circuit incorporating **negative feedback,** so the voltage could be held at any desired level. In negative feedback any change in output is returned to the input with a reversed sign, tending to cancel the change. The amount of current the circuit applied to hold the voltage constant was thus a measure of the current flowing across the membrane. The technique, called a **voltage clamp,** is analogous to turning the volume knob on a radio to maintain a constant loudness; the setting of the knob reveals the amplitude of the signal coming into the radio.

In their key experiments, Hodgkin and Huxley (1952a, 1952b, 1952c) applied a step depolarization to a squid axon and measured the resulting membrane currents. After the step depolarization, there was an inward current followed by an outward current—the black line in Figure 2.18. This result is still a composite of the effects of Na^+ and K^+ ions, however. To separate the effects of the two ions, Hodgkin and Huxley repeated the experiment with the Na^+ removed from the extracellular solution. This time there was only an outward current because of the K^+ remaining in the solution. The Na^+ current could be calculated by subtracting the first curve (Na^+ and K^+) from the second curve (K^+ only). The conclusion was that the Na^+ current begins immediately and decreases spontaneously after about 0.8 msec because of the closing of Na^+ channels. The K^+ current builds more slowly and continues as long as the voltage is clamped. In the natural action potential the K^+ channels are closed by the return of the membrane to its polarized state.

Our understanding of the ion channels helps us explain the actions of some of the deadliest toxins known—for example, tetrodotoxin (TTX). This poison blocks Na^+ channels selectively, binding to the channel proteins in such a way that no ions can pass through. In the voltage clamp experiment, adding TTX to the medium around the axon changes the result from the black curve in Figure 2.18 to the I_K line, because Na^+ can no longer influence the potential. As a result the axon can no longer transmit action potentials. The puffer fish takes advantage of this fact to protect itself, producing small amounts of TTX in its ovaries. The fish is a delicacy in Japan, partly because of the

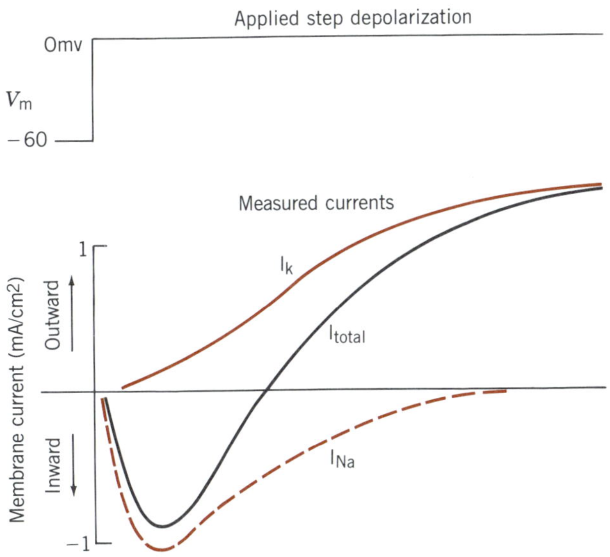

Figure 2.18 *Reactions of a squid axon membrane to an abrupt depolarization in a voltage clamp experiment.* I_K *can be measured by removing* Na^+ *from the external medium. The* Na^+ *current* I_{Na} *cannot be measured in this way because most of the* K^+ *ions are already inside the axon, where they are inaccessible. Another way to measure* I_K *directly is to block* Na^+ *channels with the potent poison tetrodotoxin, derived from the puffer fish, to block the* Na^+ *channels.* I_{Na} *can be measured directly by blocking the* K^+ *channels with the tetraethylammonium ion. The results of such experiments are in agreement with those shown here.*

adventure of eating it; if the fish is not cleaned carefully, it remains deadly. Why the puffer fish does not poison itself remains a mystery

The events revealed in the voltage clamp experiment also clarify two other characteristics of the axon, the absolute and relative refractory periods.

Refractory Periods

During the "spike" of the action potential the axon cannot be excited further. The first part of the action potential must be completed and the Na^+ channels closed again before the next spike can be initiated, no matter how strong the stimulus (just as a baseball pitcher cannot pitch another ball without a windup). In the axon this brief period of inexcitability, 1 to 2 msec in most neurons, is called the **absolute refractory period.** In the next few milliseconds after the completion of the action potential, before the K^+ channels have closed, it is more difficult than usual to excite the axon. The threshold depolarization may change from −60 mv to −50 or −40. This is the **relative refractory period,** because the axon is excitable but requires a larger stimulus than normal. All these numbers can vary greatly from one neuron to another.

The absolute and relative refractory periods impose biological limits on the frequency of action potential transmission. No neuron can respond at rates much over 1000 spikes/sec, and even this rate is possible only for a fraction of a second with very strong stimuli.

Propagation of Action Potentials

Until now we have examined only the events that take place at one location on the axon, as they would be measured with an electrode placed inside the axon at one point. Now we will consider what happens next to the point of initiation of the action potential at the axon hillock, along the axon of Figure 2.19. The change in potential is conducted to this adjacent region and causes that region's own Na^+ channels to open. Then the whole action potential chain of events takes place there as well. The channels are opened by the ionic flows of the nearby action potential and have the effect of short-circuiting the graded potentials, which otherwise would spread from the axon hillock. But the action potential caused by the opening of these channels in turn causes the opening of channels farther down the axon, and the action potential is propagated down the axon in a kind of ionic chain reaction.

This chain reaction is the secret of transmitting signals over long distances with poorly conducting materials. The action potential (unlike the graded potential) is not an ionic conduction of electricity; instead it is a traveling wave of instability moving down the axon. It is continually renewed as it passes down the axon, for its energy comes from the sodium-potassium pumps operating all along the axon. Each channel is opened by a depolariza-

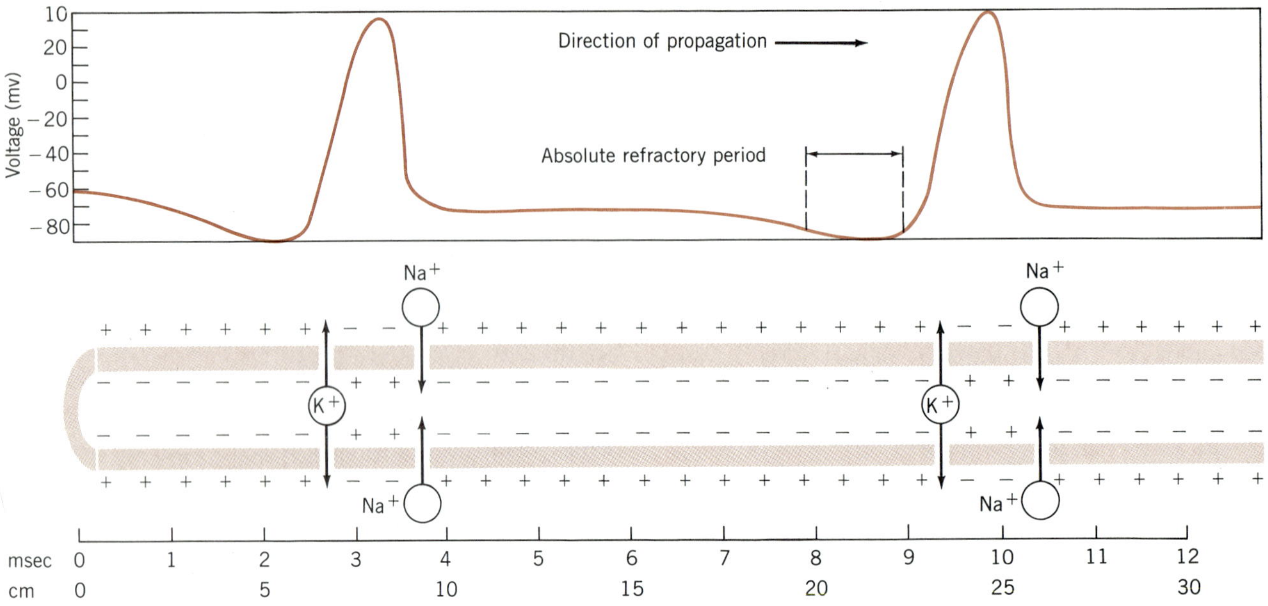

Figure 2.19 *Propagation of an action potential in an unmyelinated axon. The refractory period forces the action potential to travel in only one direction once it is initiated.*

tion caused by the opening of neighboring channels, in a self-renewing process. In terms of energy sources, the process is more like the fall of a row of dominoes than the conduction of current through a wire. Energy stored all along the axon by the pumps is released when an action potential is triggered.

To see how well this biological wire works as a conductor of signals, we can calculate the apparent resistance of an axon. Electrical resistance is found by measuring the voltage at two points on a wire and dividing the difference in the voltages by the distance between the two points. In even the best conductors there is a slight voltage drop as one moves farther from the generator or battery, and this drop defines the resistance. But the voltage at another point farther down an axon is the same as the voltage at the first point, because the potential is renewed continuously as it spreads along the membrane. The difference between the two voltages is zero. It doesn't matter how far apart the measurements are made, for zero divided by any distance is still zero, and zero is the apparent resistance of the axon. There is no conduction decrement as the action potential propagates, and no need for biological amplifiers no matter how long the axon is (it can reach several meters in a whale) or how often it divides. Occasionally some neurophysiologists talk of a "relay nucleus" in a sensory or motor pathway. This talk shouldn't be taken literally, because a signal that doesn't decrement never needs a relay station.

If action potentials are conducted without decrement, why are synapses necessary? They are needed not to renew a signal but to process it. The action potential has a major weakness as a component of an information-processing organ—it is protected against the possibility of processing information. What goes in one end of the axon is exactly what comes out the other. If an axon is constricted, the action potential may become a little smaller, but on the other side of the constriction it will be restored to its original size again. It is only at synapses, where action potentials are reconverted into graded postsynaptic potentials, that interaction with other signals can take place. The operation of the brain is a continual alteration of action potentials transmitting information and graded potentials processing it.

An axon may divide many times before it terminates; therefore, many terminals are excited by each action potential, always in the same temporal order. When the axon divides, the action potential splits, because the ionic flows and the resulting depolarizations at the dividing "Y" excite the action potentials on both branches. A single action potential at the axon hillock may become thousands as the axon repeatedly divides. In the brain, most synapses occur along the axons rather than at their ends.

But the brain pays a price for its perfectly conducting communications, and that price is in the speed of conduction. When the speed of axonal conduction was first measured, over a century ago, by Hermann von Helmholtz, the fact that conduction isn't instant caused a revolution in neurophysiology. Previously, conduction had been thought to occur at the speed of light, the speed at which current moves through a wire; but Helmholtz found the speed of conduction to be as slow as 25 m/sec in the motor axons of the forearm. This works out to 90 km/hr, about the highway cruising speed of an automobile.

Why is conduction so slow? Clearly, evolution would put a high premium on speed of conduction; it is the fast-reacting animal that gets away to reproduce. The answers seem to be that nature is doing the best it can with the materials available and that attempts to increase the speed of conduction lead to other problems. The speed of conduction is limited by the resistance to the flow of ionic current inside the axon, and the resistance in turn is governed by the diameter of the axon. The thicker the axon, the more ions are available to conduct the currents to excite the next patch of axon and the faster the whole process takes place.

If internal conduction limits the speed of propagation of the action potential, one obvious way to speed up the propagation would be to increase the diameter of the axon. This solution evolved in many invertebrates, where axons can be up to 1 mm in diameter. This is an enormous size in the microworld of synapses and membranes, and it results in a conduction speed of about 20 m/sec. There are obvious problems with such a solution, however. To achieve a conduction speed of 20 m/sec in the human optic nerve, for instance, the million or so fibers in the optic nerve would have to occupy a cable more than a meter in diameter! Because this would be unwieldy, animals that use giant axons as a device for increasing speed must limit themselves to a small number of giant axons and use them only for such important functions as escape.

The giant axon of the squid is a boon to neurophysiologists, but it is a bad solution for nature if more than a handful of messages are to be sent quickly. It is also wasteful of energy, for a large amount of ion pumping is required to support the giant axon.

Saltatory Conduction

In the process of evolving, vertebrates seem to have hit on a more effective way of increasing the speed of axonal conduction without increasing the diameter of the axons. The trick is based on the almost instantaneous transmission of graded potentials; instantaneous transmission will occur in the axon too if only the action potential can be prevented from continuously retriggering itself along the axon membrane's surface and short-circuiting the graded potential. This almost instantaneous transmission is accomplished by electrical insulation from the oligodendroglia or Schwann cells (glial cells whose only function in life is to wrap layers of membrane tightly around axons). A bit of Schwann cell membrane grows around an axon, and the cell then wraps itself again and again around the axon, leaving the layer of membranes called myelin that we saw in Figure 2.3. The membrane layers act as insulation (membranes are made up largely of lipids, or fat), preventing the action potential from taking place. Instead, the electrical pulse generated by an action potential is conducted rapidly as a graded potential inside the axon, underneath the myelin sheath. It emerges with some loss in amplitude at the other end of the Schwann cell's myelin wrapping. There, at a location called a **node of Ranvier,** there is a break only 1 μm long in the myelin (Waxman & Ritchie, 1985). Here the action potential takes place in the normal way, only to be prevented from moving farther by another myelin

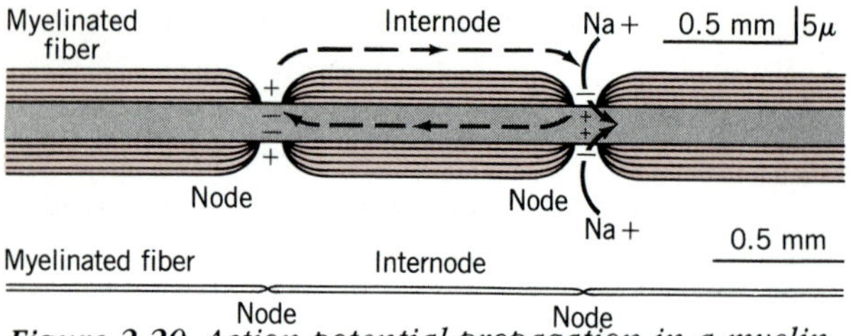

Figure 2.20 *Action potential propagation in a myelinated axon. Graded potentials (conduction of current) carry the signal quickly from one node of Ranvier to the next. Note that the vertical scale depicts the axons as thicker than they really are.*

sheath. Current flows parallel to the membrane between the nodes (see Figure 2.20), crossing only at the nodes. This is called **saltatory,** or jumping, **conduction,** because the action potential jumps from one node to the next (Tasaki, 1953).

Even with its myelin sheath, the myelinated axon is much smaller than an unmyelinated axon of the same conduction speed. By alternating the rapid but decrementing graded potential with the slow but regenerating action potential, the axon gains the advantages of each. The axon acts like a miniature submarine cable, with lengths of passive conduction interrupted by repeater amplifiers that boost the signal without changing it.

The advantage of saltatory conduction is substantial, since the fastest myelinated axons conduct impulses at about 120 m/sec. At the same time they save energy, for ions are pumped only at the nodes of Ranvier. At the nodes, the action potential appears to be caused only by the Na^+ mechanism. K^+ channels are absent at these locations (Shepherd, 1979b), but the density of Na^+ channels is 100 times greater than in an unmyelinated axon (Waxman & Ritchie, 1985).

Several demyelinating diseases show the importance of saltatory conduction to human well-being. Multiple sclerosis is the best known disease of this sort; often its first symptom is subtle visual abnormalities, including increased reaction times to visual events. Signals are not only delayed by slower conduction but often are not conducted at all because the previously myelinated axon does not have enough channels of the right kinds to support action potentials. For many nerves, demyelination is much the same as severing. Multiple sclerosis is incurable, but better knowledge of how myelin works and how the body constructs it may someday improve the picture.

Varieties of Axons

The most consistent property of neurons is their variety. The diameters of mammalian axons range from 20 μm for the largest myelinated axons to 0.2 μm for the smallest unmyelinated ones—a 100-fold difference in diameter and a 10,000-fold variation in cross-sectional area. The resting potential is not constant across or even within neurons; it tends to be lower in small processes (both axons and dendrites) than in large ones.

In the smallest axons the nature of the action potential appears to be different from that in large axons, because thin axons have only about one Na^+ channel for every micron of length (Colquhoun, Henderson & Ritchie, 1972). Action potential conduction in such an axon would be a "microsaltatory" process, with the signal moving as a graded potential five times the axon's diameter before it encountered a single Na^+ channel. This is about the lower limit of size for an action potential–conducting axon; in anything smaller, one cannot pack in enough molecules of the right kinds to support the process. These axons communicate economically, but slowly.

In large axons such as the squid giant axons, only a tiny fraction of the Na^+ ions is lost during each action potential; the axon can be removed from the squid and can conduct normal action potentials for hours with negligible changes in ion concentrations. But the smallest axons increase their intracellular Na^+ concentrations by about 10 percent with each action potential, so continuous operation of the sodium-potassium pump is essential to their function.

The effects of these differences between axons can be seen in everyday experience. When you touch a hot stove, you withdraw immediately; your withdrawal is driven by large axons. It is only later that you become aware of a burning sensation. Messages must reach the brain along 0.2 μm fibers that conduct at about 1 m/sec, a slow walk. The size of axons generally relates to the urgency of their messages; the organism must know about sharp pain right away, but a delay of a few seconds in the onset of a toothache is not critical. This is why sharp pain must be carried on large axons and toothache can arrive on small ones.

Some axons conduct only graded potentials, even though they have all of the structural characteristics of conventional axons (Zettler & Weiler, 1981). The axons are on horizontal cells in the retina, and, as you might expect, they are not very long. They reach some 800 μm (0.8 mm), about the limit for effective graded potential communication. Most axons, though, are so long that only action potentials affect the synaptic terminals. Some of these axons end in terminals that can be inhibited with a special mechanism that works only in the action potential mode.

Presynaptic Inhibition. Some axons end not on a dendrite but on another axon terminal (see axon 1 in Figure 2.21). Stimulation of these axo-axonal synapses yield a long-lasting hypopolarization (about 200 msec) on the second axon terminal (Eccles, Magni & Willis, 1962).

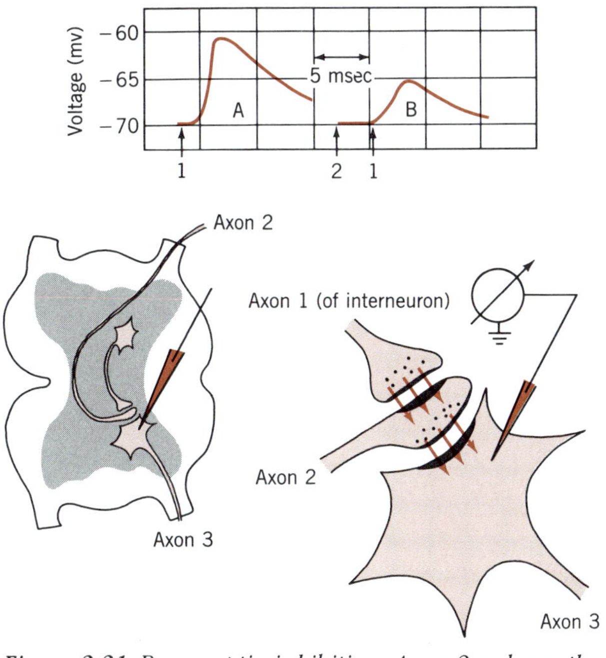

Figure 2.21 Presynaptic inhibition. Axon 2 reduces the synaptic effect of axon 1 by hypopolarizing it, without directly affecting the postsynaptic membrane of the cell giving rise to axon 3. The inset is an electrical recording of synaptic potentials without presynaptic inhibition (A) and with inhibition (B). Adapted from Schmidt (1978).

An incoming action potential in the second axon can now change the polarity of the terminal only by a smaller amount than usual; the voltage change from the already hypopolarized level is less than normal. Hence, an action potential reaching this terminal has less effect on transmitter release than it would normally. This presynaptic inhibition affects only a single source of input and can reduce the influence of that source without affecting the excitability of the postsynaptic neuron as a whole (Eccles, 1964). In the spinal cord, presynaptic inhibition probably acts to control the flow of sensory information into the CNS (Eccles, 1964). This variety of inhibition has the effect of division rather than subtraction.

Information Flow in Axons

The action potential is an all-or-none event. It either happens or it doesn't; you can't have half an action potential. In this sense the axon's information is carried digitally, a great advantage when signals are transmitted over long distances in a noisy environment. The signals generated at the axon hillock are the same as those coming out at the synaptic terminals, for the large action potentials are not affected by small variations in the axon's resting potential or its electrical environment along the way.

This does not mean that the neural code for information is digital in the same way that computers are digital. There are many possible ways to code information in nerve spikes, the most common one being a frequency code. The more spikes occurring in a given time, or the shorter the interval between two spikes, the stronger the transmitted signal. Though the spike is a digital, discontinuous event, the interspike interval is an analog, continuous quantity because it can take any value. The computer's all-or-none digital coding is based on a master digital clock that times all events. Between two ticks of the computer's clock, an event either occurs or does not occur, and the timing of an event between the ticks does not matter. The brain has no digital clock; its time relationships are analog rather than digital. The result is that the spikes themselves are all-or-none, but the coding of information in interspike intervals remains analog.

A better analogy than the computer is FM radio transmission. The FM radio signal carries its information in variations of frequency. Whenever the FM signal at the left of Figure 2.22 crosses the zero voltage level, the FM receiver generates a brief electrical spike. A second circuit then "smudges" all the spikes together. Frequent zero crossings, generating many spikes, lead to a high voltage on the bottom left curve of Figure 2.22; infrequent zero crossings yield a lower voltage. The amplitude of the incoming FM radio wave does not matter; only the timing of the zero crossings influences the radio's output. Similarly, the spikes on an axon are all of about the same amplitude, and information is coded as the durations of the intervals between spikes. Frequent spikes lead to a greater depolarization of a postsynaptic membrane (or a greater hyperpolarization if the synapse is inhibitory).

How much information can an axon carry in its trains of interspike intervals? Engineers describe information-carrying capacity in terms of **bandwidth,** a measure of the maximum density of information carried. The bandwidth of the axon is limited by its maximum spike rate, about 1 spike/msec—fast by biological standards but slow when compared to electronic devices. This limits transmission to less than 1 kHz, or 1000 cycles/sec (the unit of bandwidth). For comparison, the bandwidth of a telephone line is about 3 kHz and the bandwidth of a good stereo is 10 times greater. (This is why telephones have low fidelity.) One couldn't carry on a telephone conversation using an axon as the wire.

Because an ordinary wire has a bandwidth of several million Hertz, engineers routinely put several thousand telephone conversations on a single wire. The brain, faced with low-capacity axonal "wires," must do the opposite; the signal from any sensory system is carried not on one axon but on many thousands or even millions of axons operating in parallel, each connected to a sense organ on one end and to the brain on the other. With the principles of parallel organization and synaptic communication, we can begin to see how the brain works.

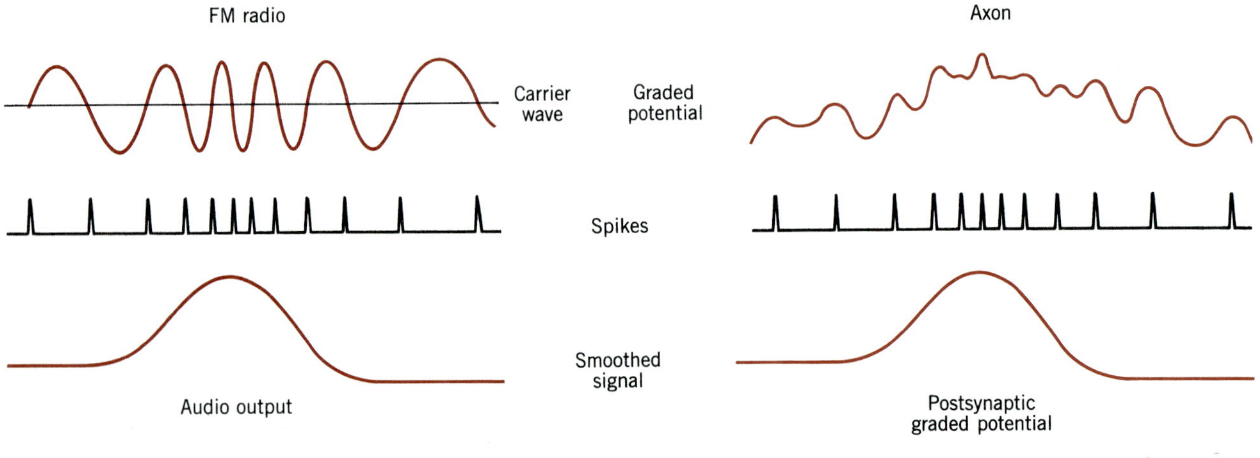

Figure 2.22 Information flow carried on an FM (frequency modulated) radio compared with flow carried by action potentials. At an intermediate stage in the process, both the FM radio and the neurons use all-or-none spikes to represent the information being transmitted. In both cases the information is defined by the time interval between two spikes. This interspike interval can take on any value; thus the interspike interval can potentially code many bits of information. In axonal transmission, however, the process is relatively imprecise, so each interspike interval carries only a few bits at best.

A UNIVERSAL NEUROANATOMY

The most important feature of brain organization is that neurons are arranged in parallel. In invertebrate nervous systems a function is sometimes carried out by one or a few neurons, but in mammals most connections are shared by thousands or millions of fibers, each with a common origin and destination. The brain begins with a layer of **receptors** arranged in parallel, taking different forms in the various senses but all providing input to the brain. These cells are connected to second-order cells, which transmit the information further. The second-order cells interact with one another (see next-to-bottom layer of Figure 2.23) before generating action potentials to send to the next layer. This communication within layers forms a basic structure for most of the nervous system; a layer of interacting cells processes information and sends it on parallel axons to the next layer. The brain consists of a series of layers of interacting cells, each with inputs from the previous layer and outputs to the next layer (Bridgeman, 1979b).

A few complications and qualifications are necessary. The axons are not strictly parallel; there is always some **convergence** (several axons converging on one cell in the next layer via branching axons) and **divergence** (one axon innervating several cells). Sometimes a group of axons skips a layer or two. Connections can also go both ways, some axons projecting forward and others projecting backward. The brain is not a hierarchy, with command neurons making decisions for the rest to follow; rather, decisions are made cooperatively. Even the simplest functions involve vast numbers of interacting neurons. Most connections between layers are excitatory.

The observation of two-way connections leads to the idea of **efferent control** (Pribram, 1971)—the influence of more central layers on layers closer to the sensory end of the network. (**Efferent** means outgoing, as in *e*xit; **afferent** means incoming, as in *a*ccess.) Afferent sensory information, for instance, can be modified by efferent signals coming back toward the receptors.

The universal neuroanatomy concept refers to a logical organization, not a physical one. In the

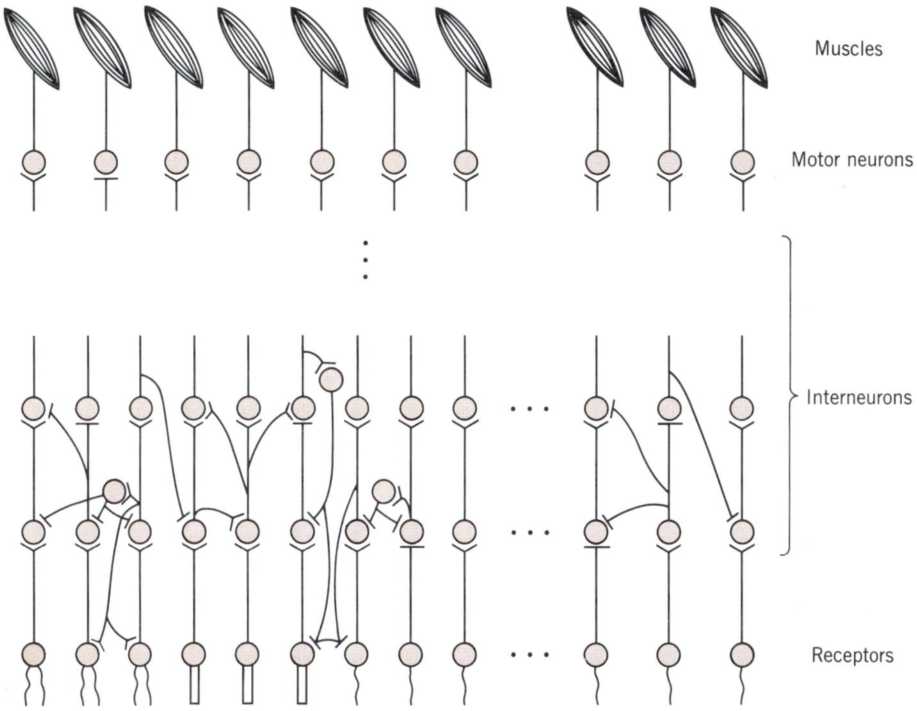

Figure 2.23 *A "universal neuroanatomy" to describe connections in nervous systems. Information is transmitted on parallel lines, and processing takes place in interactions within a layer.*

cortex, for instance, both the inputs and the outputs project from the same side. In Figure 2.23 the outputs have been flipped around to show the logical connections between cortical areas. Many brain structures are organized as *nuclei*—groups of cells with cell bodies lying close to one another and sharing common input and output locations. We can imagine spreading out the clump of nucleus cells in a layer, without changing the connections, to fit the universal neuroanatomy scheme. To picture this transformation, imagine flattening the nucleus by squeezing it, as though it were a ball of dough, into a pancake shape without breaking the surface.

The interactions within a layer are often in the graded potential mode, though action potentials are also involved. Some **local circuit neurons** have very short axons and are involved only in local interactions (Shepherd, 1979b).

An important organizing principle within layers is **lateral inhibition,** the inhibition of a neuron by its neighbors in the same layer. The interaction is reciprocal; each neuron inhibits the cells that inhibit it. Two other types of inhibition are **forward inhibition,** (the inhibition of a cell in the next layer) and **backward inhibition** (the inhibition of a cell in the previous layer). The three types of inhibition are shown in Figure 2.24.

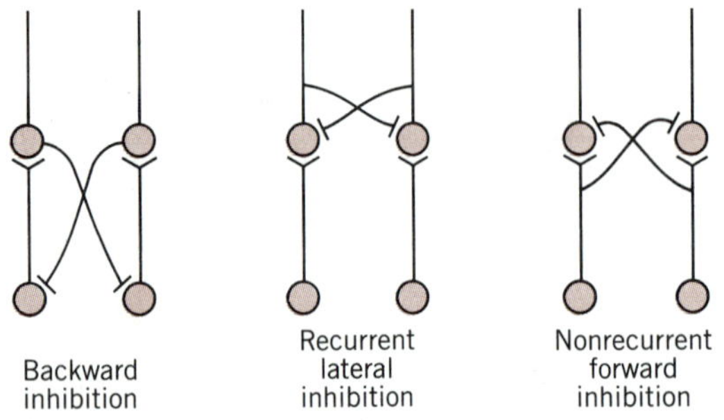

Figure 2.24 *Backward inhibition, recurrent lateral inhibition, and nonrecurrent forward inhibition. Only in lateral inhibition does a neuron directly affect its neighbors in the same layer.*

Now we can get a general impression of how the brain might work. Inputs come from the receptors on millions of parallel fibers. The resulting signals interact as graded potentials in a layer of cells, and the results are sent as action potentials to the next layer, where a state of activity is already present. The input to the next layer interacts with the existing state in the graded potential mode, and the results are sent to the next layer. Reciprocal connections between layers let the activity bounce back and forth repeatedly. Finally, the results are either stored in modifiable synapses, as memory, or arrive at the muscles reorganized as patterns of behavior.

This picture of anatomy and function is more a pedagogical device than an established fact. Many important features have been left out. But the generalizations about brain structure should help us organize the material in the following chapters.

CHAPTER SUMMARY

1. Brains are made of neurons—cells that communicate chemically or electrically with one another and with muscles. Most have dendrites to increase the area on which they can contact other cells and an axon to transmit signals. Neurons are supported and nourished by glial cells that form part of the blood-brain barrier, insulate some axons, and clean up debris.

2. The two-layered membrane surrounding each neuron has proteins embedded in it to transfer substances into and out of the cell and to give specialized properties to patches of membrane. Like other cells, neurons have an endoplasmic reticulum for internal transport, ribosomes to make proteins, a Golgi apparatus to manufacture membranes, and a nucleus to hold DNA. Mitochondria

live symbiotically within the cell, handling oxygen-based energy transfer.

3. Neuron function depends on events at membranes. Electrical events on the membrane can be calculated with the Nernst equation, which treats electrical charges in terms of chemical concentrations inside and outside the cell. For Cl^- ions the equation agrees well with the observed resting potential, but the predicted value is far too positive for Na^+ ions and too negative for K^+ ions. The discrepancy is resolved by taking into account a pump that actively moves sodium out of the cell and potassium in. The pump maintains the ion imbalance that creates the resting potential.

4. The resting potential provides a biological battery—a starting point for the graded potentials that enable neural messages to interact. Graded potentials decrease the resting value (depolarization) or increase it (hyperpolarization) by any amount within a limit determined by ion concentrations. The electrical graded potentials interact, with closer events in space or time interacting more strongly. The potentials change relatively slowly, decaying in a range from a few milliseconds to hundreds of milliseconds, but are conducted instantly. Neural information processing is largely the interaction of a huge array of graded potentials.

5. Potentials pass from one cell to another at specialized contacts called synapses. The electrical synapses—gap junctions and tight junctions—transmit signals instantaneously but cannot amplify them. Chemical synapses transmit in only one direction, change the signals as they relay them, and amplify the result. Depending on the postsynaptic channels, some chemical synapses depolarize the postsynaptic membrane and others hyperpolarize it. Vesicles in the presynaptic region fuse with the presynaptic membrane and empty their contents of neurotransmitter into the synaptic cleft, where the transmitter diffuses to the postsynaptic membrane. There, specialized channels are opened, allowing ions to flow in or out and changing the postsynaptic potential. Other processes restore the original balance.

6. The number of neurotransmitters is large and unknown; new ones are constantly being identified. Acetylcholine is a common excitatory transmitter, and norepinephrine is a common inhibitory one. Peptides, including the recently discovered enkephalins, are small chains of amino acids, the building blocks of proteins. They sometimes modify the effectiveness of another neurotransmitter without directly affecting postsynaptic potentials. Some enkephalins are involved in pain pathways, where the postsynaptic sites are sensitive to opiate drugs. Different transmitters evolved at different times, each with slightly different functions and properties.

7. Action potentials transmit the results of neural processing for long distances on axons. The action potentials are traveling waves of instability; membrane pores are opened by depolarization, causing more depolarization farther down the axon. The resulting signal has no apparent resistance because its energy is provided by the resting potential all along the membrane. Conduction is slow, from 120 m/sec to less than 1 m/sec. It speeds up in the faster fibers by jumping across insulated patches of axon, in "saltatory conduction."

8. There are many codes relating the pattern of action potentials to biological information. The action potential is a digital, all-or-none event, but most codes are analog because they are defined by continuously variable interspike intervals.

9. Brain organization can be summarized in a "universal neuroanatomy"—layers of cells connected by parallel axons. Interactions within layers complement conduction in both directions between the layers. Activity might bounce back and forth repeatedly between the first receptor layer and the final muscle layer.

KEY TERMS

Glial cells (glia)
Soma
Organelles
Dendrites
Axon
Processes
Synapses
Ganglion
Astroglia
Capillaries
Blood-brain barrier
Phagocytosis
Gliosis
Microglia
Oligodendroglia
Myelin
Peripheral nervous system
Schwann cells
Plasma membrane
Lipids
Hydrophilic
Hydrophobic
Endoplasmic reticulum
Ribosomes
Ribonucleic acid (RNA)
Amino acids
Golgi apparatus
Vesicles
Deoxyribonucleic acid (DNA)
Enzymes
Nucleolus
Mitochondria
Symbiosis
Metabolism
Microtubules
Microfilaments
Potential
Volts
Conductance
Mho
Ion
Resting potentials
Graded potentials
Concentration gradient
Nernst equation
Faraday
Equilibrium
Electrostatic gradient
Permeable
Molecular weight
Hyperpolarized
Hypopolarized
Depolarized
Exponential
Time constant
Ephapses
Electrical synapses
Gap junctions
Tight junctions
Rectify
Chemical synapses
Presynaptic membrane
Synaptic cleft
Postsynaptic membrane
Transduction
Acetylcholine (ACh)
Neuromuscular junction
Excitatory postsynaptic potential (EPSP)
Channels
Pinocytosis
Cisterna
Acetylcholinesterase (AChE)
Cholinergic receptors
Muscarinic receptors
Nicotinic receptors
Norepinephrine (NE)
Inhibitory postsynaptic potential (IPSP)
Enkephalins
Ligand
Hormones
Metabotropic transmitters
Adenyl cyclase
Adenosine triphosphate (ATP)
Cyclic adenosine monophosphate (AMP)
Protein kinase
Phosphorylation
Axoplasmic transport
Negative feedback
Voltage clamp
Absolute refractory period
Relative refractory period
Node of Ranvier
Saltatory conduction
Bandwidth
Receptors
Convergence
Divergence
Efferent control
Efferent
Afferent
Local circuit neurons
Lateral inhibition
Forward inhibition
Backward inhibition

SUGGESTED READINGS

Bullock, T. H., Orkand, R., & Grinell, A. (1977). *Introduction to nervous systems.* San Francisco: Freeman.

Emphasizing neurophsiology, this textbook includes material on invertebrate nervous systems.

Cooper, J. R., Bloom, F. E., & Roth, R. H. (1978). *The biochemical basis of neuropharmacology.* New York: Oxford University Press.

This is the authoritative book on the chemistry of neurotransmitters as well as other brain chemicals.

Kuffler, S. W., Nicholls, J. G., & Martin, A. R. (1984). *From neuron to brain.* Sunderland, MA: Sinauer Associates.

This book bears the strong imprint of Stephen Kuffler, summarizing his distinguished career. It covers areas in which he pioneered: glial cells, visual receptive fields, and the physiology of membranes and synapses.

Snyder, S. (1985, October). The molecular basis of communication between cells. *Scientific American,* 132–141.

One of the leading researchers in neuropharmacology surveys the similarities between hormones and neurotransmitters. This issue of *Scientific American,* on "the moelcules of life," includes several other valuable articles. Particularly useful for the chapter are articles on communication within the cell, the cell membrane, and the cell matrix.

Stevens, C. F. (1979). The neuron. In *The Brain* (A Scientific American Book) (pp. 15–25). San Francisco: Freeman.

The article includes spectacular electron micrographs and a thorough examination of how the neuron works.

Chapter 3

THE ANATOMICAL DESIGN OF THE BRAIN

The structure of the human brain is formidably complex. With 10^{11} neurons averaging about 10^4 synapses each (Poritsky, 1969), the total number of connections is about 10^{15}—roughly equal to the number of stars in the Milky Way galaxy. The average cubic millimeter of brain contains nearly 10^9 synapses. By comparison there are only about 2.2×10^9 sec in a lifetime.

Yet brain organization is so sophisticated that any discussion in numerical terms is misleading. This problem was demonstrated quite early to the great psychologist Karl Lashley. As a high school student he asked his biology teacher to lend him a set of microscope slides of the frog brain so he might trace the connections and learn how the frog worked. The task proved to be impossible, but even if some future Lashley succeeds in mapping all the connections, we will not be able to link the structure of the brain with its functions. For this effort, we need to work with functioning brains.

Still, our first task is to understand the physical design of the brain. Later chapters will attach functions to the various parts. The brain is structured at many scales; its components range from pieces as big as a fist to details barely visible with an electron microscope. The techniques needed to uncover these structures, which are as varied as the sizes of the structures, will be reviewed first.

We will be concerned next with the large-scale organization of the brain and with the simpler brains that appeared earlier in evolution. Many of the components of these brains serve functions that all vertebrates have in common, such as locomotion. From the more general structures we will move up to the neocortex, the largest part of the human brain.

Although all of the most important structures will be reviewed, the coverage of structure at a small scale will be selective. No attempt will be made to examine all of the thousands of identified nuclei, tracts, and regions of the brain; instead, we will be concerned with principles of organization, illustrated with examples from neuroanatomy. The anatomy of specialized systems such as the visual, auditory, and motor systems will be detailed in separate chapters on those systems.

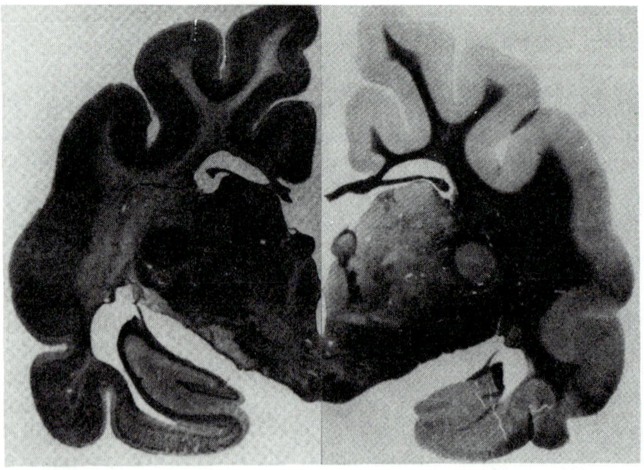

Figure 3.1 *A frontal section of a cat brain. The left side is stained with cresyl violet, a cell stain; the right side has a myelin stain (a silver stain).*

NEUROANATOMICAL TECHNIQUES

Neuroanatomists have two broad ways of approaching brain structure: histological and invasive. In **histological** (cell study) **techniques** a brain is simply removed, stained, and studied. In **invasive techniques** a researcher manipulates the brain by creating a lesion, by introducing a radioactive tracer, by changing the environment in some way, or by combining any of these methods. The resulting changes are then examined with histological methods.

HISTOLOGICAL TECHNIQUES

The neuroanatomist's problem is to remove a large and delicate brain, keeping it intact, and then to make its components visible. The first step is usually to **perfuse** an anesthetized animal with a saline solution—that is, to pump the solution from the heart through the circulatory system so the brain is cleared of blood. The saline is then replaced with **formalin,** a dilute solution of formaldehyde in water. Formalin causes proteins to form chemical bonds with adjoining proteins, creating a stiff matrix even where connective tissue is not naturally present. The process is termed **fixation,** or **denaturing,** because the proteins are no longer in their natural states. Formalin cannot be perfused directly because it would fix the proteins in the blood, blocking the arteries before the solution reached the brain.

After the brain is removed from the skull, it is embedded in paraffin, plastic, or other agents to further increase its stiffness. Sometimes it is simply frozen to temporarily harden it. Then it is sectioned by a **microtome,** a specialized knife mounted on a sliding platform to cut sections of controllable thickness. The thickness depends on the stain to be used.

In thin sections the brain is translucent, and many features cannot be differentiated. A stain is required to bring out the histological structure. Several kinds of stains are used to bring out different structures. Cell bodies are stained with methylene blue or cresyl violet, and fibers are stained with myelin stains such as hematoxylin. (The resulting cross sections are shown in Figure 3.1.)

A third kind of stain selectively acts on neuronal membranes, generally through the use of heavy metals, most commonly silver or osmium. The metal is introduced into the tissue as a soluble salt and is then reduced in place so it is deposited. A particularly useful example is the **Golgi stain** (after Camillo Golgi, a 19th century neuroanatomist), a silver stain that for unknown reasons enters only about 2 to 3 percent of neurons. These few cells, however, are stained completely, from the somas out to the finest processes. This 90 year old breakthrough enables us to see the trees by leaving most of the forest transparent; it is still providing valuable information (such as that in Figure 3.2). Golgi sections generally are cut relatively thick, 50 μm or more, to capture entire cells in one section. The sections can then be examined in three dimensions with a microscope by focusing it at various depths.

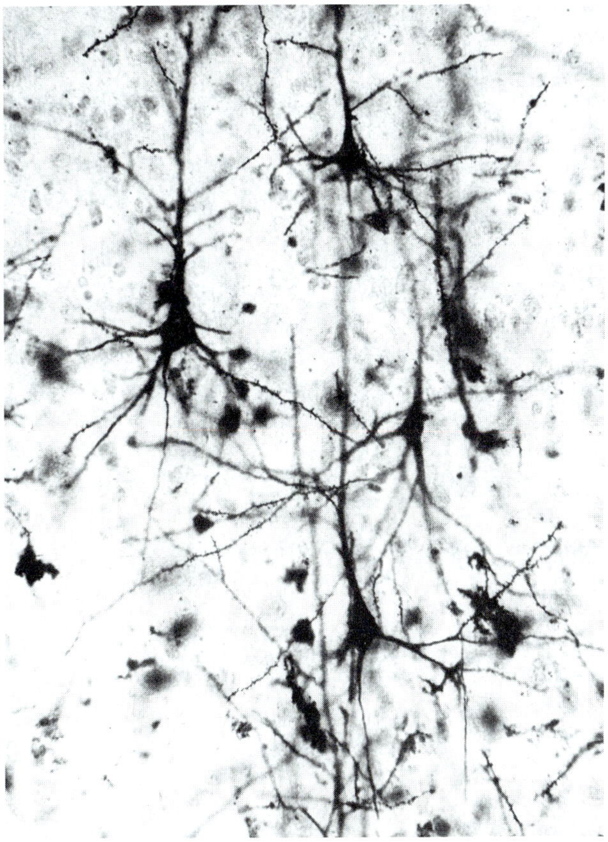

Figure 3.2 *A Golgi-stained section of cerebral cortex. If all the cells had been stained, the figure would be black. The furry appearance of the dendrites is due to thousands of dendritic spines, where synapses are located.*

Although these stains are useful for visualizing regions of the brain, they do not allow the tracing of individual pathways. The problem is not too little information but too much. Individual cells or fibers can be seen easily with the microscope, but there are so many of them that their pathways cannot be isolated from the dense tangle of fibers. Cutting thinner sections reduces the density of the **neuropil** (the mass of neural tissue) on a given section, but it compounds the problem of determining where a fiber leaving one section appears in the next. To trace connections, more specialized methods are needed; these methods involve manipulating the brain before staining it.

INVASIVE TECHNIQUES

In most invasive neuroanatomical experiments, one part of the brain is modified, and the changes that result are observed in another part. Perhaps the simplest intervention is the creation of a restricted lesion that allows the experimenter to trace the resulting degeneration of axons projecting from cells in the lesioned area.

Lesions

Several methods can be used to make lesions. If the area to be removed is near the surface, suction is a useful method. After exposing the brain, the neurosurgeon probes the target area with a hollow needle attached to a vacuum pump, literally sucking the soft brain tissue away. This method causes less damage to the blood vessels than cutting with a scalpel, and it makes possible more restricted lesions. It is the most common method used in human neurosurgery.

Where bleeding is a problem, the lesions can be made with **cautery**—that is, by burning the target tissue with a heated instrument. Cautery closes off blood vessels in the affected area but may cause unwanted damage.

Deeper in the brain, surgical lesions are impractical because they damage overlying areas. The resulting preparation would show the effects of both the intended lesion and the overlying damage. Exposing the hypothalamus to do a lesion of areas that regulate sexual behavior (see Chapter 10), for instance, would take away far more brain tissue than the hypothalamic lesion itself. In these cases, **stereotaxic** lesions can be made by lowering electrodes into the target area and passing alternating current through them at radio frequency. Like a tiny implanted microwave oven, the current generates localized heat, killing the surrounding cells.

This method depends on precise three-dimensional brain maps and standardized coordinate systems for each species of experimental animal. In the **Horsley-Clarke system,** for example, the line between the ear canals defines the "zero" level for height and the front-back dimension. The sagittal suture—the line where the left and right halves of the skull join—is the left-right centerline. With these sorts of maps and coordinates, neurosurgeons can find the right area almost every time, without ever seeing it.

More specialized lesions have been made recently by injecting toxins specific to certain classes of neurons. A toxin related to a particular neurotransmitter, for example, will kill all cells using that transmitter while leaving other cells intact. Lesions of this kind, produced by biochemical rather than geometric isolation of systems within the brain, can then be used to trace transmitter systems that are physically intermingled with one another.

After lesioning, stains that are specific for degenerating axons, such as the Nauta-Gygax stain, can be used to find the projections from the lesioned area (Nauta & Gygax, 1954). With these stains we can trace **anterograde degeneration** (*antero* is Latin for "forward") if the animal is sacrificed within about 8 days from the time of the lesion, because axons separated from the cell body die quickly.

If 6 weeks or more are allowed to pass, the anterograde degeneration is complete. The **proximal** (Latin for "near") cut axon and cell body die and degenerate. This **retrograde degeneration** (*retro* is Latin for "backward") identifies the origin rather than the target of fibers in the lesioned area. It is visualized with the Nissl stain, which selectively colors cell bodies. The stain differentiates areas of retrograde degeneration by staining the glial cells. In the process called gliosis, these cells fill the volume formerly taken up by the missing neurons. Because glial cells are much smaller than neurons, a denser staining results. The retrograde degeneration staining could be done with the Nauta-Gygax method, but the degeneration is so slow and its time course so irregular that the glial method gives more consistent results. Much of the mapping of connections within sensory systems (see Chapter 5) has been done with these techniques.

Autoradiography

Several newer methods of intervention allow remarkable precision in identifying tracts and even single cells. The techniques are now revolutionizing neuroanatomy.

One of the new techniques, **autoradiography,** enables neuroanatomists to identify the neurons metabolizing known substances. First, the substance is tagged with a **radioactive tracer**—an unstable isotope of one of the elements it normally contains. All isotopes of an element are chemically identical; they vary only in the weight of their nuclei. Radioactive carbon-14, for example, might replace the normal carbon-12 in a biological compound. This replacement produces a radioactive substance identical to the original in its chemical properties. At random times, atoms of the radioisotope decay, or split, into two other atoms and a detectable particle. Thus the location of the tagged substance can be determined. The amount of radiation is very small and does not harm the animal.

The tagged substance is injected into an animal and is absorbed by the target neurons. Then the animal is sacrificed and the brain sectioned. The radioactive section is placed on a photographic plate; after exposure, the photograph shows the areas where the tagged compound has been absorbed. Serotonerigic neurons, for example, can be labeled by injecting the animal with a tagged version of the serotonin precursor 5-HTP and later finding the target neurons by their telltale radioactivity. The technique is called autoradiography (*auto* is Latin for "self") because the radioactivity is incorporated into the tissue itself rather than being introduced during the staining process.

A particularly useful compound for autoradiography is 2-deoxyglucose (2-DG), a modified sugar. This molecule is similar enough to the nutrient glucose to be actively absorbed by metabolizing cells but not similar enough to be broken down by their metabolic processes. Like a virus, the molecule uses the cell's own metabolic machinery to perform the labeling task. Neurons showing greater activity absorb more 2-DG than less active neighboring neurons. Radioactively tagged 2-DG can be injected into the brain of an animal while it is in an environment where a particular group of cells is expected to be active. To identify visual system neurons active in the presence of vertical lines, for example, researchers expose an animal only to vertical lines for 45 min after injection of 2-DG. When the animal is then sacrificed, the radioactivity indicates the cells that were metabolically the most active during the exposure period.

The technique has resulted in some startling new discoveries about the connectivity of sensory systems (see Chapter 5). It has been extended to find differences between concentrations of brain substances by a technique called digital subtraction autoradiography, in which two autoradiographs are digitized by dividing them into small squares and assigning a numerical brightness to each square. The images are then subtracted, square by square, and the difference is displayed as an image on a computer terminal (Altar et al., 1985). Autoradiography depends on a somewhat simple assumption about information coding, however; it reveals only information that is carried by increases in total frequency of firing (frequency codes).

Recent progress in identifying and synthesizing peptide neurotransmitters and other neurochemicals is greatly expanding the applications of autoradiography and related techniques, with new methods constantly being introduced.

Single-Cell Stains

Other methods combine specific staining with lesions or microelectrode techniques. One recently developed enzyme, horseradish peroxidase (HRP), has proved particularly useful. It has the unique property of completely filling a neuron by active transport after entering it at any point, without diffusing into other cells. It can be used in several ways. If a fiber tract is cut and HRP is introduced into the wound, the HRP is carried back into the cut axons, their somas, and the corresponding dendrites by retrograde axoplasmic transport—transport through the cytoplasm of the axon. In another technique the enzyme can be injected through an intracellular micropipette. The micropipette is then removed, and anterograde transport carries the HRP out to the axon terminals. After a few days the brain is sectioned in the usual way, and the HRP is stained. An example of the great specificity and eerie beauty of the resulting micrographs is shown in Figure 3.3. Some single cell stains can be made to glow, or fluoresce, under light of an appropriate wavelength so the cell can be identified, a technique called **histofluorescence.**

ELECTRON MICROSCOPY

All of these techniques depend on the light microscope, still the neuroanatomist's most important tool. The spatial resolution (the finest discernible detail) of the light microscope, however, is limited by the wavelength of light. Internal organelles

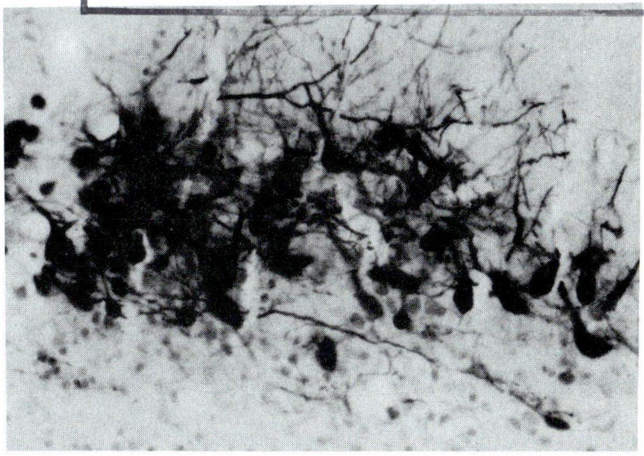

Figure 3.3 *HRP staining of an oculomotor nucleus in the brain stem, made by putting HRP on the oculomotor nerve. The HRP was carried back to the cell bodies by retrograde axoplasmic transport.*

of the cell approach the wavelengths of visible light in size, and structures such as membranes and synaptic ultrastructure are beyond the resolution of any light microscope. Better resolution requires a completely different technique—electron microscopy. Because the effective wavelength of the electron is far shorter than that of visible light, resolution can be improved greatly. With a **transmission electron microscope** a stream of electrons passes through the specimen and is focused on an image plane. There the magnified image is photographed, with results such as those in Figure 3.4. The technique is limited to thin sections of material.

A second device, the **scanning electron microscope,** uses completely different electronic optics. The specimen is scanned one point at a time, much as a scene is scanned by a television camera. The resulting image (see Figure 3.5) is less detailed than that from the transmission electron microscope but has a greater depth of field, so contoured surfaces can be examined without sectioning and painstaking reconstruction. Because of their high resolution, these devices make available hundreds of times more information about biological structure than was available previously. Neuroanatomists can now examine synaptic architecture, intracellular structure, and even some membrane characteristics.

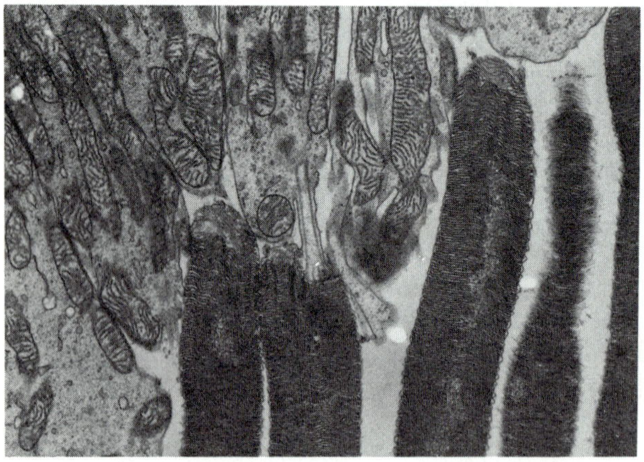

Figure 3.4 *Rods and cones (photoreceptors in the retina) in a transmission electron micrograph. The internal structures are tightly packed layers of membrane containing visual pigments.*

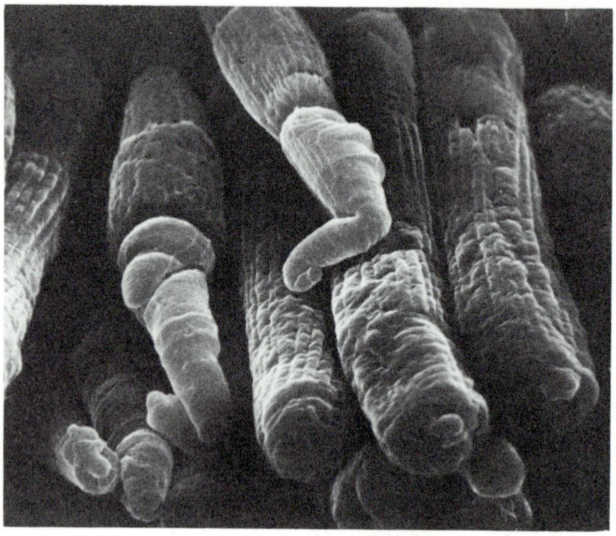

Figure 3.5 *Rods and cones in a scanning electron micrograph. The external shapes of the receptors are visible, but the internal structures are hidden. To make this type of exposure, a thin beam of electrons is focused on one point of the target image. The electrons that penetrate the target are collected by a detector on the other side of the target. The beam is then moved to an adjacent location, and electrons are collected again, forming a map of electron densities across the target.*

Electrons, however, present special problems in imaging biological materials. They radiate only in a vacuum, such as the one in television tubes, so elaborate measures are necessary to prepare specimens that will not be destroyed in the vacuum of the electron microscope's examination stage. At the energies necessary for high-resolution imaging the electrons have such great penetrating power that biological materials are transparent to them. To confront these difficulties, a highly developed art has evolved. Specimens must first be stained with heavy metals that can absorb electrons and give contrast to the image, but the staining may destroy or distort the materials under investigation.

RECORDING TECHNIQUES

An alternate way to trace connections is to infer them from electrical recordings of brain activity.

The kinds of questions that can be answered in this way depend on the kinds of electrodes used.

Gross Electrodes

Since electricity always flows in a circle, recording techniques require bringing the brain into the circle. Thus the electrophysiologist measures the difference in potential between two electrodes. If a "reference" electrode is at an inactive site, such as the earlobe, and an active electrode is in the brain, the recording is called **monopolar** (*mono* is Greek for "one"). Current flows from a neuronal generator in the brain, through the active electrode, through the experimenter's apparatus, and back to the brain via the reference electrode. This method allows activity from a wide brain area to be collected at the active electrode, but the localization of the activity is poor.

Localization is better with a **bipolar** electrode (*bi* is Greek for "two"), a pair of wires insulated except at their tips. Usually, the two tips are inserted in the brain a millimeter or so apart; in the cortex, one might be a millimeter deeper than the other. To record from active animals, the electrodes are implanted in the brain during a surgical operation and sealed in place with dental cement. A plug in the cement connects to the amplifiers, so the animal can be "plugged in" for recording. Functional pathways can be traced by stimulating at one location and recording from another. To study the direct connection from the motor cortex to the spinal cord, for instance, the experimenter stimulates the motor cortex and records from axons crossing in the medulla of the hindbrain.

These methods allow brain functions to be located with some precision. The first maps of the retina on the visual cortex, for example, were made in this way. But for the ultimate in localization we must move to smaller electrodes.

Microelectrodes

The biological unit of the brain is the single neuron; in the past few decades, electrodes have been developed that record spikes from single neurons without interference from other neurons. The tips are so small—about 1 μm in size—that they cannot be seen clearly in a light microscope. As you can imagine, they are also very fragile. The electrophysiologist determines the condition of the electrode not by inspecting it but by measuring its electrical resistance without removing it from the brain. A single cell puts out so little current that special amplifiers are needed to amplify the biological signal. Microelectrode recording was impossible before these amplifiers were developed.

Extracellular (outside the cell) recording uses metal electrodes, usually of tungsten, which are carefully advanced through brain tissue until a good spike record is found. The electrophysiologist advances blindly—without being able to see the tip of the electrode—and listens to the output of the electrode on a speaker. A burst of popping noises, amplified action potentials, signals that a neuron is nearby. The electrode tip is too small to harm the tissue; you can stick a microelectrode into your hand and let it hang there without feeling it.

Intracellular (inside the cell) recording is even more difficult. The electrodes are pipettes (thin lengths of hollow glass tubing) that are heated and pulled until the narrowed and extended tips break apart. The pipettes are filled with a conducting salt solution. The physiologist knows that a neuron has been penetrated when a drop in potential occurs (see Figure 2.7). If the electrode moves only a few microns relative to the animal, the cell is lost; in small mammalian cells, most intracellular sessions last only a few seconds or minutes. Conditions can be more stable in invertebrates, where the cells are larger and a whole ganglion can be literally pinned to the table.

Now we can look at what these and related techniques have taught us about brain structure.

UP-DOWN, FRONT-BACK, AND LEFT-RIGHT: THE THREE DIMENSIONS OF NEUROANATOMY

Roughly speaking, human brain functions can be divided along three planes. This statement does not imply that the contrasted parts are independent or antagonistic. In fact, the reverse is true, for a striking feature of brain organization is the high

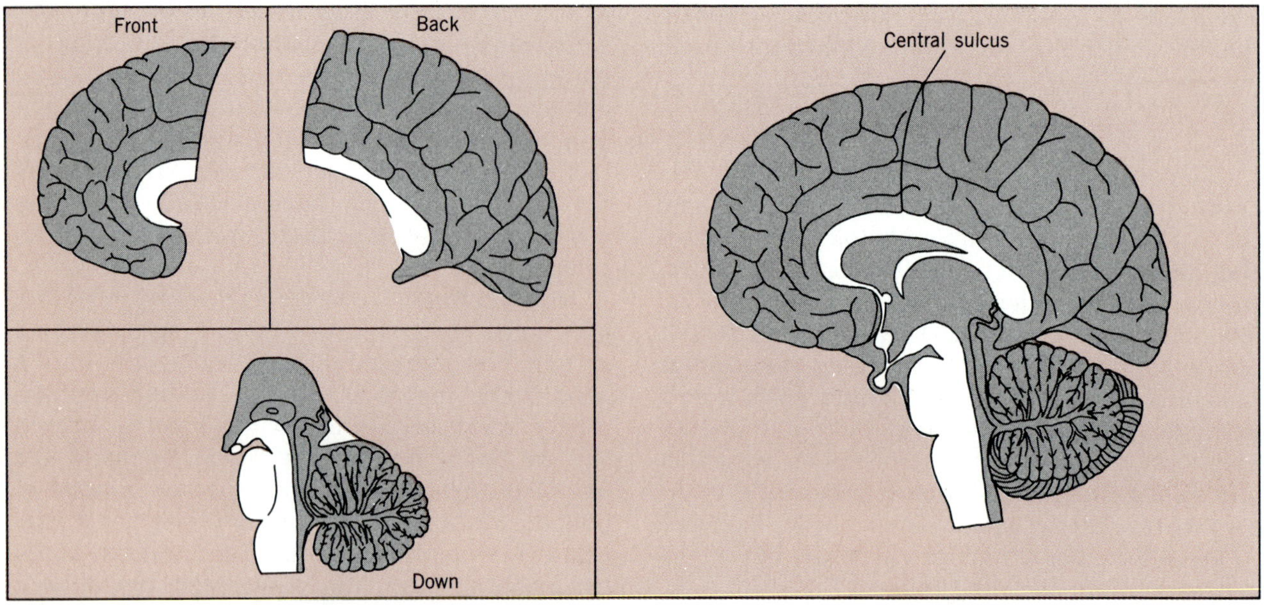

Figure 3.6 *General orientation of the human brain, divided along three dimensions. The simplest vertebrates possess only the down division in this scheme. Left-right and front-back differentiations apply only to the up division.*

degree to which the parts work together. The divisions presented here, like the division of the nervous system into central and peripheral parts, are more mnemonic devices than descriptions of independent neurological entities.

THE UP-DOWN DIMENSION

The primary division of the human brain (as shown in Figure 3.6) is into an upper part (the neocortex) and a lower part (the rest of the brain). Grouping the subcortical structures into the lower part might seem to be assigning too much to that part; this is true in terms of the variety of neurological structures found there, but in terms of sheer bulk the upper part is larger. The human cortex and its associated fiber tracts make up about three-fourths of the entire brain. The upper brain is the exclusive domain of consciousness and language—of the functions that make humans human.

In contrast, the lower brain carries out functions that all animals have in common: muscle coordination and the regulation of eating, digestion, heartrate, breathing, and other **vegetative functions**—the processes that maintain the internal environment in an optimal state (see Chapter 9). This part of the brain has changed less than the cortex in evolution, reflecting the stability of its functions, though there are important evolutionary trends in lower-brain structures. In general, a progressive substitution of cortical for subcortical processing takes place as one moves toward humans in evolution. This substitution is an example of **encephalization** (*cephalus* is Greek for "head") of functions—more and more functions being taken over by higher centers. A fish gets along fine with no cortex at all; a hamster with its cortex removed looks superficially normal but has difficulty with learning and adaptability; a human without a cortex becomes blind, deaf, dumb, and comatose.

THE FRONT-BACK DIMENSION

The two other broad neuroanatomical divisions take place within the upper brain—in the three-quarters occupied by the neocortex and its associated strucures. A division through the **central sulcus** (shown in Figure 3.6) separates the frontal lobe from the parietal, temporal, and occipital lobes.

The back, or posterior, part of the cortex contains the projection areas for the senses, in topographic maps of the sensory surfaces. In a **topographic map,** geometric relations may be distorted, but for every point on the sensory surface there is a corresponding point on the cortex. These maps are arrayed on all three lobes of the posterior cortex. A map of the skin is on the parietal lobe, a map of the ear's cochlea is on the temporal lobe, and a map of the retina is on the occipital lobe. Each sense has several topographic maps of different sizes and other characteristics. Vision has at least eight maps of the retinas (Van Essen, Newsome & Bixby, 1982), audition has at least four cochlear arrays, and the somatosensory system has at least six maps of the body (Van Essen, 1979). (Chapter 5 examines these areas in more detail.)

In addition to the topographic sensory projection areas, the posterior cortex contains specialized processing areas for each sense modality. In vision, for example, the inferotemporal cortex is concerned specifically with difficult visual discriminations (Pribram, 1960). In audition, specialized areas merge with the language-processing centers of the parietal lobe. In general, posterior areas are concerned with transforming, storing, and comparing sensory data from the outside world.

The frontal cortex, in contrast, controls the actions of the body, organizes attention and emotional behavior, and coordinates behavioral sequences. The lateral frontal areas are necessary for the long-term planning of behavior and for governing complex behaviors (see Chapter 14). The orbital frontal cortex (so named because it resides just above and beside the orbits of the eyes), together with the limbic system, helps coordinate appetitive and emotional behavior. These generalizations are very broad, however.

THE LEFT-RIGHT DIMENSION

A few decades ago, long after the fundamental distinctions between the upper and lower brain and the front and back of the cortex had been established, it seemed as though the functions of the two cortical hemispheres were nearly identical. True, it was known that damage to the left hemisphere from strokes or injuries often produced stronger disturbances in language than similar right-hemisphere damage, but this did not occur in all patients. The anatomical similarity of the two hemispheres seemed to preclude important differences between them.

Then evidence began appearing that the hemispheres were more specialized than they had seemed. One of the most important sources of new evidence was patients who had had the corpus callosum sectioned to relieve intractable epilepsy. The **corpus callosum** is a colossal bundle of nerve fibers, the largest in the body, connecting the left and right halves of the cortex. Because it connects each part of one hemisphere with the topographically corresponding part of the other, it sometimes conducts reverberations of neural firing during epileptic seizures. These reverberations eventually cause an **epileptic focus** (a region of damaged tissue) on one side to develop a **mirror focus** on the other.

The sectioning of the corpus callosum (split-brain surgery) generally diminished the epilepsy, but it brought with it some surprising side effects. The effects were not apparent on casual inspection of the patient, but they were quite dramatic when measured with the appropriate tools. The effects were first investigated by Roger Sperry (1974). Among many other results, he found that patients could verbally describe only objects appearing in their right visual fields. As Figure 3.7 shows, these fields project only to the left hemisphere of the cortex. The split-brain patients could solve pattern-matching problems only if the stimuli appeared in their left visual fields.

These examples typify the kinds of deficits found in the two hemispheres. Because language is centered mainly in the left hemisphere, the crossed visual connections send only information from the right visual field to the hemisphere with language capability. Verbal description of the stimuli can then follow. Visual information can also be processed in the other hemisphere and can be assessed through observation of nonverbal tasks, such as matching two similar objects. But the patients could not describe their visual images orally or in writing.

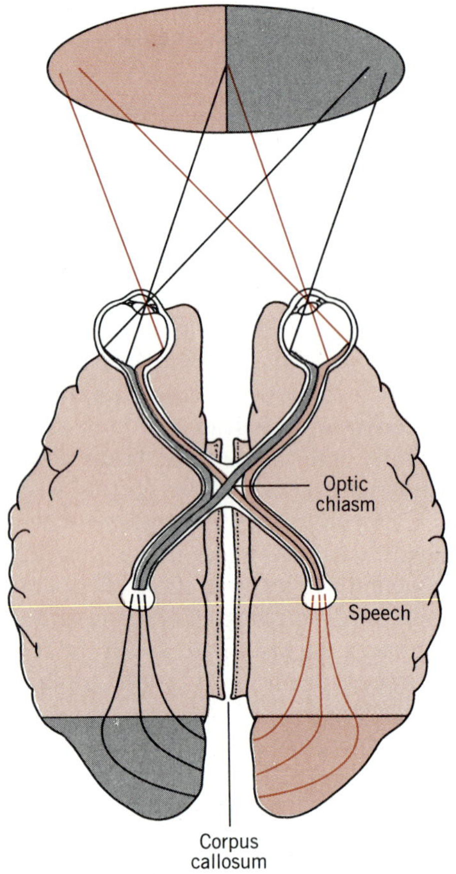

Figure 3.7 *Schematic view of visual projections in a split-brain patient. The view is from the bottom, so the severed corpus callosum appears behind the optic chiasm. The path from the nasal retina (near the nose) to the brain is crossed; the path from the temporal retina (near the temple) is uncrossed. Because the retinal image is inverted, the left half of the image in each eye goes to the right cortex and the right half to the left cortex. If stimuli are presented to a split-brain patient on only one side of the visual field, and if a small region of overlap in the center of the field is avoided, the information flow can be isolated to only one hemisphere. In animals the optic chiasm is also cut along the midline (dashed line), so each eye projects only to its ipsilateral hemisphere.*

Other tasks showed superiority of the left visual field. A patient might be shown a pattern made from a group of blocks and might be asked to create a matching pattern from another set of blocks. The patient could perform this spatial task correctly only if the information was present in the left visual field. Furthermore, the patient could solve the problem only with the left hand—the hand controlled by the right hemisphere (Sperry et al., 1969). The split-brain operation had produced two independently functioning upper brains, each with a different set of cognitive abilities.

These and similar results caused great excitement. It was soon found that the hemispheres were not quite identical even anatomically. Small differences appeared in a few areas, especially the temporal lobes, and the left hemisphere was generally a little larger than the right (Gazzaniga, 1970). Because they appear even in infants, the differences cannot be the result of environmental influences.

As a recently discovered anatomical specialization of function, the left-right distinction still requires research to be characterized fully. This is an exciting task (see Chapter 12), but the anatomical distinctions should be interpreted in the context of the many other known anatomical specializations of brain function.

With this general three-dimensional orientation to the brain, we can look more closely at brain structure in terms of evolution.

THE SPINAL CORD

The spinal cord is the oldest part of the central nervous system (CNS) in terms of both evolution and **ontogeny** (biological development of an organism). Its organization is similar in all vertebrates. In the simplest ones, it forms most of the CNS. In humans, it still performs essential functions and simplifies the tasks of higher centers. With sensory input, information processing, and motor output, the spinal cord forms a simple, semi-independent processing center with strong links to higher centers. Because of its universality among the vertebrates, it is a useful model for studying the CNS.

The spinal cord controls tasks that all vertebrates have in common, such as avoiding painful stimuli on the body and coordinating groups of muscles. Details of organization depend on the

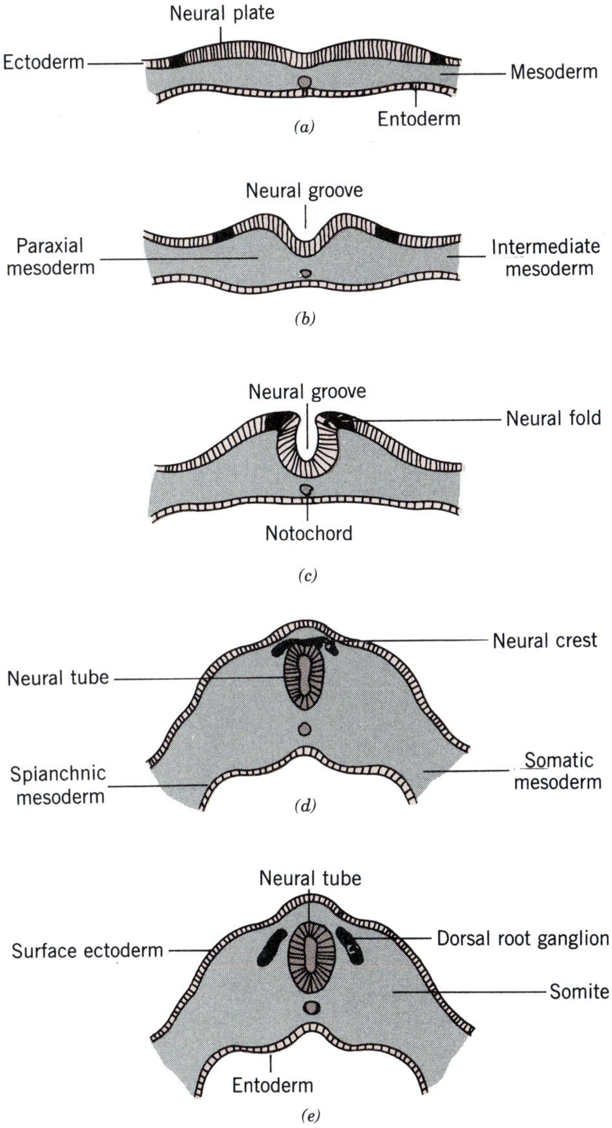

Figure 3.8 Formation of the neural tube in embryological development. The bones of the spinal column later form around the neural tube. The notochord is important in primitive vertebrates but is vestigial in mammals. The dorsal root ganglia contain cell bodies that innervate the skin. Adapted from Truex & Carpenter (1964).

body plan and environment of the animal, but the general architecture is the same.

The segmentation of the spinal cord is a consequence of the segmented organization that we have inherited from our distant ancestors—primitive segmented marine worms. The head and brain are not segmented in the same way. A current interpretation of this difference between brain and spinal cord is that vertebrates evolved by, among other things, adding a head to the basic segmented structure. Our worm ancestors were headless in more ways than one.

In human embryological development the spinal cord and brain begin as the **ectoderm,** the outer layer of the embryo. The ectoderm on the back of the embryo develops a fold that eventually pinches off to form a tube (the **neural tube** in Figure 3.8) and later develops into the spinal cord **caudally** (Latin for "toward the tail") and the brain **rostrally** (Latin for "toward the head"). (Other anatomical directions are given in Figure 3.9.) In the process the ectoderm is inverted; the

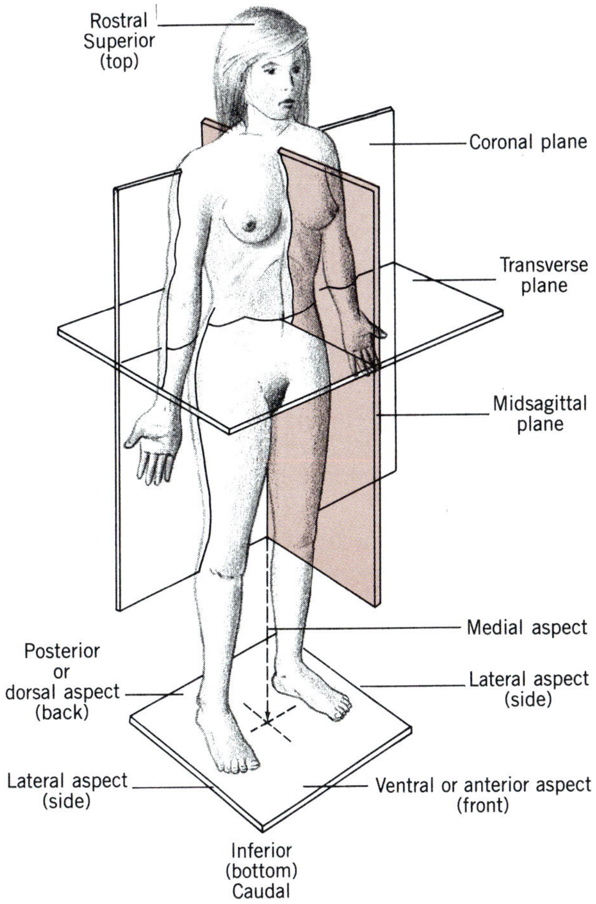

Figure 3.9 Planes of reference and some directional terms used in anatomy. The part of the spinal cord that is posterior in humans is referred to as dorsal (top), as it would be in four-footed animals.

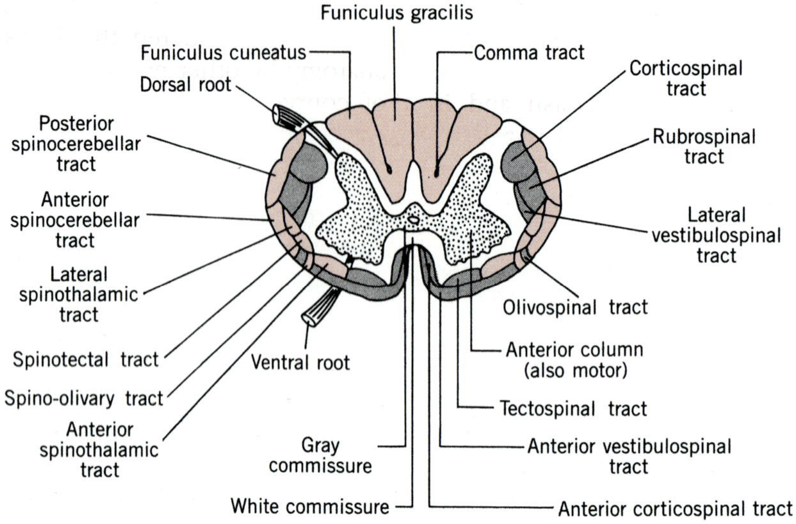

Figure 3.10 *Cross section of the spinal cord showing major fiber tracts. Ascending tracts are on the left and descending tracts on the right. Ventrally there are the anterior spinothalamic, spinocerebellar, and corticospinal tracts and the vestibulospinal and the reticulospinal tracts; dorsally there are the spinocerebellar and spinocervicothalamic tracts and the fasciculus gracilis and fasciculus cuneatus. The lateral spinothalamic, corticospinal, reticulospinal, and rubrospinal (from the red nucleus in the brain stem) tracts complete the long-distance lines. Most of the tracts have been defined by lesion and degeneration studies.*

inside of the tube contains the cells formerly on the outside of the embryo. These cells develop into the gray matter of the spinal cord, so called because it looks gray in unstained sections. The white matter surrounding it consists of myelinated fibers.

Like a large university, the spinal cord is divided into departments, or segments, all having the same basic organization. Each of its 31 segments is served by one pair of dorsal root nerves and one pair of ventral root nerves. A butterfly-shaped mass of neurons, the gray matter (shown in Figure 3.10), encloses a small hollow tube, the remains of the neural tube. It is surrounded by the white matter of tracts coursing to and from the brain. The tracts are named for their origin and destination, like subways, so it is easy to distinguish the ascending from the descending tracts (Stevens, 1966). Cerebellospinal tracts, for instance, descend from the cerebellum to the spinal cord, aiding in motor coordination. At the same time, spinocerebellar tracts ascend from the spinal cord to the cerebellum, letting the cerebellum know how it's doing. Exceptions to the naming rule are the fasciculus gracilis and the fasciculus cuneatus, which carry somatosensory information to the brain. Many of the somatosensory fibers **decussate** (cross the midline) before ascending in these tracts. Shorter spinospinal tracts surround the gray matter and carry information up and down across a few segments.

(This discussion reveals that the language of neuroanatomy is Latin, a language that has not been spoken for about 1500 years and that ceased being the international language of science about 200 years ago. Neuroanatomy is conservative. Perhaps this is just as well, since it means that the names of brain structures won't change.)

The relative amounts of gray and white matter vary according to the function of each segment. More caudal segments have less white matter, because fibers exit the cord at each segment. The cervical and lumbosacral enlargements—which serve the arms and legs, respectively—have expanded gray matter because they have more work to do. Thus each segment has a characteristic appearance based on its function and position.

In primitive vertebrates such as fish and in young human embryos, the spinal cord is as long as the spine itself. The human's spine grows faster than the cord, however. Eventually, the cord is only about two-thirds as long as the spine, and the dorsal and ventral roots extend farther and farther caudally before exiting between the appropriate vertebrae.

LOGICAL STRUCTURE OF THE SPINAL CORD

Information enters the spinal cord through the dorsal roots and exits through the ventral roots. This anatomical convenience was discovered independently by Sir Charles Bell and F. Magendie in the early 19th century and was named **Bell and Magendie's law** after them. It is one of the few examples of nature making life easier for neurophysiologists; the separation of dorsal and ventral roots makes it possible to stimulate only the input (afferent) nerves or only the output (efferent) nerves selectively.

Somatosensory neurons have their cell bodies in the **dorsal root ganglia** (shown in Figure 3.11) and have a single long process extending from sensory endings in the skin, joints, and muscles to the dorsal horn of the gray matter. In the cord, these neurons have synapses both with motor neurons, in **monosynaptic** (one-synapse) reflexes, and with interneurons, in **polysynaptic** (many-synapse) reflexes.

The brain and spinal cord are wrapped in a set of membranes that separates them from nerve cells and processes outside the membranes. The inside parts are defined as the central nervous system (abbreviated earlier as CNS); the outside parts are defined as the peripheral nervous system (PNS). The dorsal root ganglia, for instance, are part of the PNS. But information flows freely back and forth between the peripheral and central regions, so these distinctions are not barriers between functional units.

The examination of spinal reflexes could be considered either as neuroanatomy or as the study of motor and somatosensory systems because of the close relationship of structure and function in the spinal cord. In fact, much of neurophysiology could be considered the investigation of neuroanatomy by other means. Both study the structure of connections in the nervous system. (To unify the section on motor systems, a discussion of spinal reflexes is included in Chapter 7.)

THE AUTONOMIC SUBSYSTEMS

The **autonomic subsystems** control the internal organs of the body that are not normally under voluntary control. There are two subsystems: the sympathetic subsystem and the parasympathetic subsystem. They are sometimes termed the sympathetic and parasympathetic nervous systems, but the term *system* is misleading because both are part of a single integrated nervous system. A system is a group of parts that work together, functioning separately from other parts. What distinguishes the sympathetic and parasympathetic subsystems from the rest of the nervous system and from each other are anatomical, functional, and biochemical characteristics.

THE SYMPATHETIC SUBSYSTEM

Processes that prepare the organism for action, such as increasing blood flow to the skeletal muscles by opening tiny ring-shaped **sphincter muscles** around the arteries of skeletal muscles, involve the **sympathetic subsystem.** The subsystem also secretes epinephrine (adrenaline) to increase the heartrate and the blood-sugar concentration, and it dilates the pupil of the eye. (Figure 3.12 depicts these and other sympathetic functions.) Sympathetic axons also innervate hair follicles and arterioles—tiny arteries in the skin. When you are so frightened that your "hair stands on end," you are experiencing the action of the sympathetic subsystem.

Sympathetic neurons arise in the lateral part of the ventral horn of the spinal cord, in thoracic and lumbar segments at the top and bottom of the cord. Their axons pass through the ventral roots to a string of **sympathetic ganglia** (groups of cells) located laterally to the spinal cord and outside the

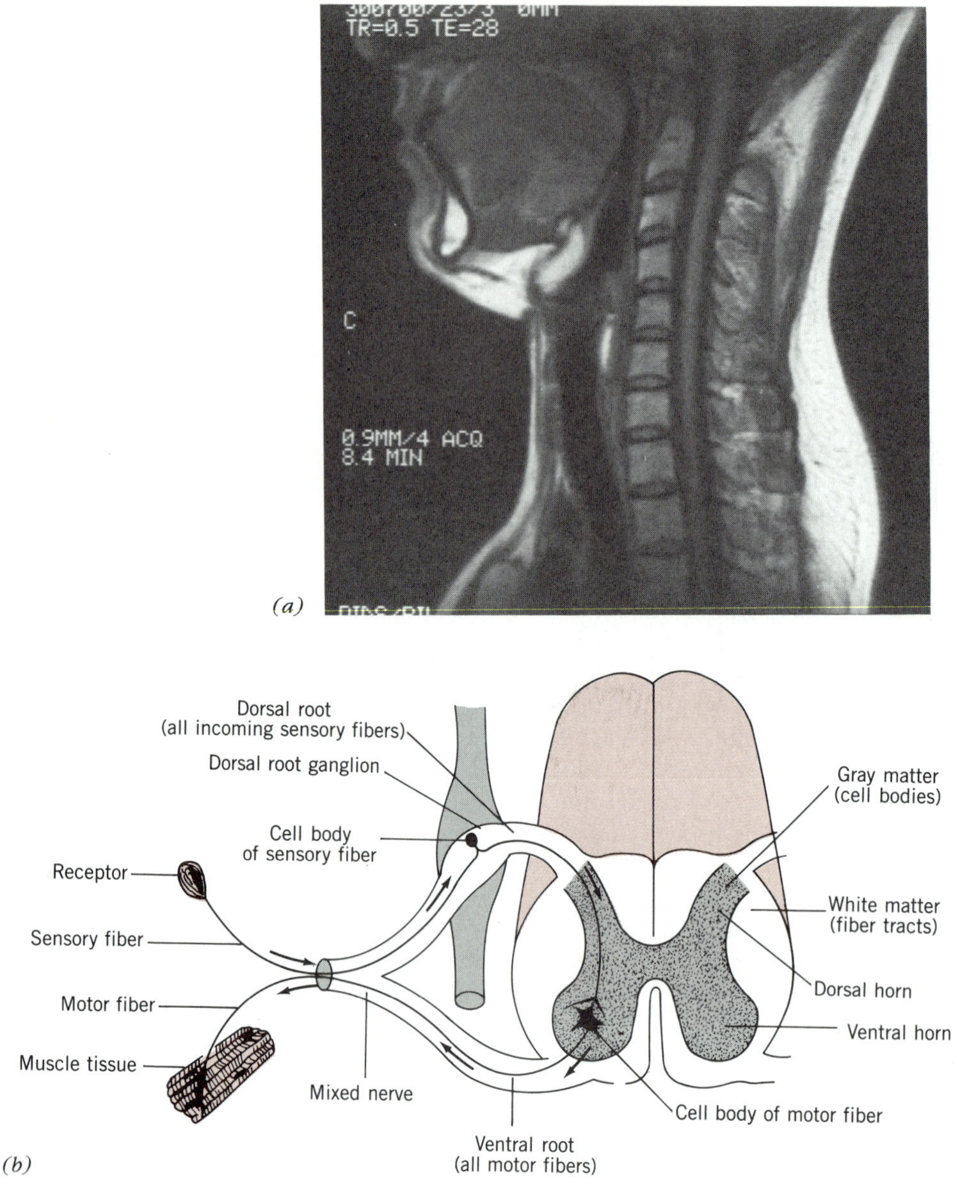

Figure 3.11 (a) *Saggital view of location of the spinal cord in a living human.* (b) *Cross section of the spinal cord, showing sensory and motor components of a monosynaptic reflex. Sensory nerves have somas in dorsal root ganglia outside the vertebral column; motor nerves have somas inside the spinal cord. Sizes of somas are greatly exaggerated. The anatomical arrangements of these reflexes are different in the head, but the logic of the connections is the same.*

vertebral column. There, some of the **preganglionic axons** (axons coming from the spinal cord) synapse with postganglionic cells sending axons to the peripheral organs. Other axons pass directly through the ganglion to organs such as the stomach and kidney. The sympathetic ganglion changes transmitters; the preganglionic neurons are **cholinergic** (secreting acetylcholine); the postganglionic neurons are noradrenergic (secreting norepinephrine)—except for the sweat-gland neurons, which continue to secrete acetylcholine. The sympathetic ganglia are linked together to form a chain that looks like a small accessory spinal cord (see the inset at the bottom left of Figure 3.12), so stimuli originating in one segment can spread to involve organs innervated from other ganglia. One pair of sympathetic ganglia accompanies each spinal cord segment. Because the ganglia are outside the vertebral column, they follow the more ancient pattern of remaining in register with the vertebrae.

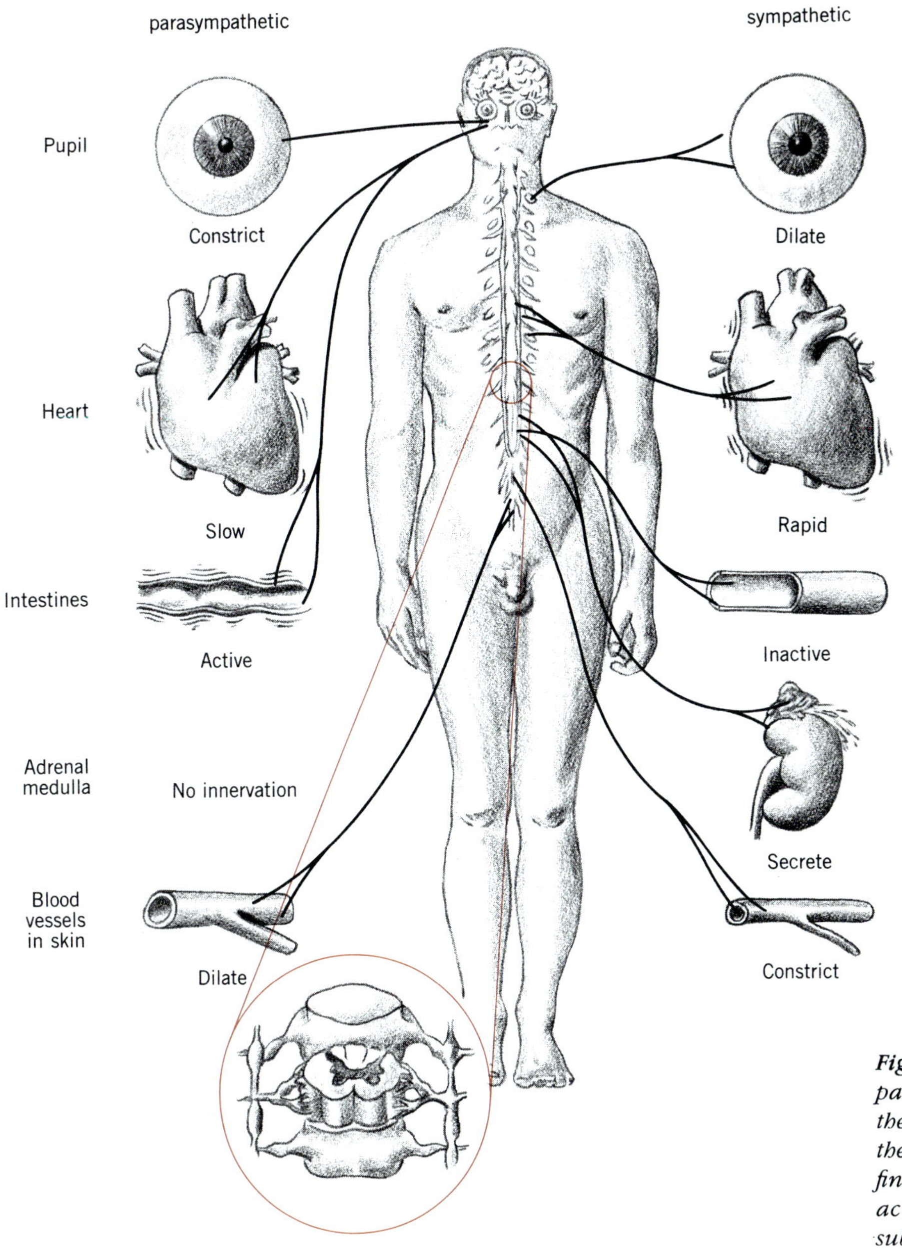

Figure 3.12 *Sympathetic and parasympathetic subsystems and their actions. Many of the fibers in the two autonomic subsystems are fine and unmyelinated, with slow actions. Both are primarily motor subsystems.*

THE PARASYMPATHETIC SUBSYSTEM

Vegetative and restorative functions are served by the **parasympathetic subsystem.** Parasympathetic motor neurons arise from the ventral horns of the caudal spinal cord or from the portion of the brain closest to the spinal cord, as shown in Figure 3.12. The spinal parasympathetic motor axons exit via the ventral roots like all the other motor neurons that innervate the body below the head; they travel to the small ganglia associated with the organs they are to innervate. Both pre- and postganglionic synapses are cholinergic.

The parasympathetic actions, which are generally antagonistic to the sympathetic actions, include salivation, digestive activity, slowing of the heartrate, and pupillary constriction. This does not mean that the sympathetic and parasympathetic subsystems work against each other, though. For instance, penile erection and increased heartrate often occur together; the first reaction issues from the parasympathetic system and the second from sympathetic innervation. Like antagonistic muscles, the two subsystems cooperate because they are coordinated from the brain.

HINDBRAIN, MIDBRAIN, AND FOREBRAIN—THE EARLIEST ENCEPHALIZATION

The CNS of primitive vertebrates, such as the lamprey, is a tubular structure consisting of the spinal cord caudally and three thickenings rostrally. The three bulges in the tube are the hindbrain, midbrain, and forebrain. The same pattern is evident in human ontogeny; the neural tube develops rostral bulges (as shown in Figure 3.13). These bulges become the three major neuroanatomical divisions. The neural tube becomes the **brain stem**—the core common to all vertebrate brains.

As the brain size of vertebrates has increased, all three brain areas have grown in size and differentiated in form. All retain a common basic organization, however, with a brain-stem core organized into nuclei and dorsal extensions organized as layered sheets of cells. The sheetlike structures are the cerebellar cortex of the hindbrain, the superior and inferior colliculi of the midbrain, and the cerebral cortex of the forebrain. The design of each will be examined later in the chapter.

The core contains tracts coursing up and down the axis of the brain stem, interspersed with nuclei made of cells sharing similar inputs and outputs. In the scheme of universal neuroanatomy (see Chapter 2), the cells of a nucleus lie in a single logical layer, even though they are gathered together physically in the brain.

Near the hollow center of the brain stem is an area with a third type of organization, a **reticular formation,** which extends through all three divisions. Many of its neurons have large axonal and dendritic trees (Scheibel & Scheibel, 1961). The reticular formation is riddled with fiber tracts so its texture is a fine feltwork of intermingled neurons and fibers. Recently, newer anatomical techniques have shown a considerable specificity of structure in this area. Previously, neuroanatomists had thought that it had largely random connections because of its tangled appearance in conventionally stained sections. Axons coursing through the brain stem often send collaterals (branches) into the reticular formation, so it receives and integrates information going to and from other parts of the brain. Many of the cells are **polymodal**—responding to stimuli in several sense modalities. The

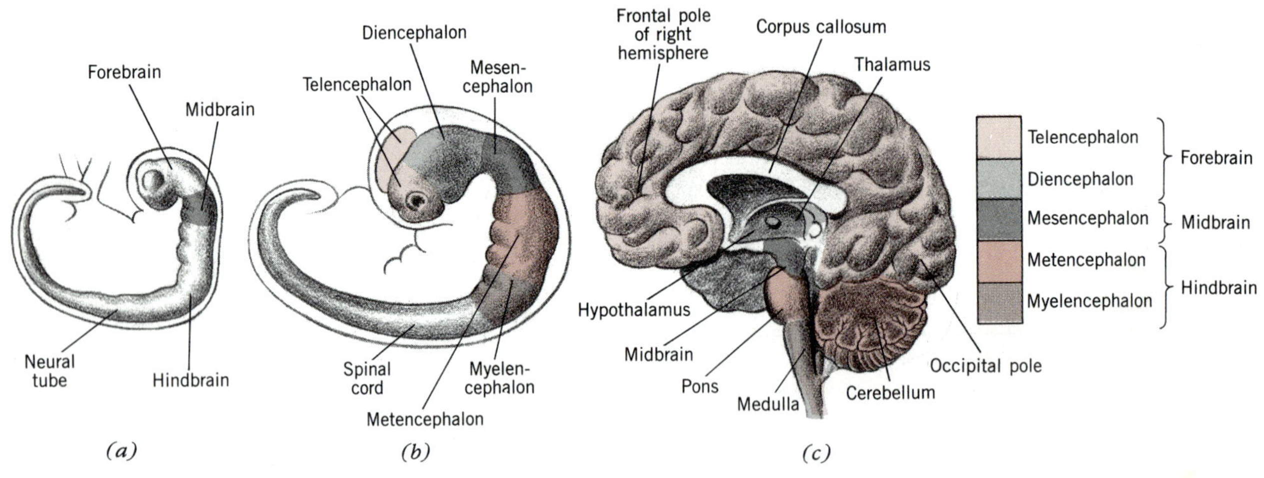

***Figure 3.13** Embryological development of segments of the brain.* (a) *A few weeks after conception.* (b) *Six weeks after conception.* (c) *Adulthood. The major divisions develop gradually from enlargements in the primitive neural tube. The brain of a lamprey, the most primitive surviving vertebrate, shows the three primary brain divisions as being nearly the same size.*

polymodal feature of these cells aids in regulating general arousal and excitability, one of the tasks of the reticular formation. The reticular formation is also a primitive center for motor coordination.

THE BRAIN STEM

Since the brain stem blends into the spinal cord and continues through the fore-, mid-, and hindbrains, it can be examined as a single structure. The brain stems of primitive vertebrates look somewhat different from those of humans, but their organization is quite similar. In the course of evolution the human brain stem underwent two bends of nearly 90 deg, changing its appearance but not its function.

The brain stem begins in the most caudal part of the hindbrain—the **myelencephalon**—with the **medulla oblongata.** Here some of the spinal cord tracts, which have been ascending ipsilaterally (*ipsi* is Greek for "same") to their origins, begin to decussate to their eventual destinations on the contralateral (*contra* is Greek for "other") side of the brain. The crossing points form the neuroanatomical landmarks shown in Figure 3.14. The **tegmentum** of the medulla—the continuation of the spinal cord gray matter—contains centers regulating respiration and cardiovascular function; excitatory and inhibitory centers are separated anatomically. We might have expected such basic vegetative functions in a phylogenetically ancient part of the brain, the part closest to the simple reflexes of the spinal cord.

Moving rostrally in Figure 3.13 to the **metencephalon**—the rostral division of the hindbrain—we find the **pons** (Latin for "bridge") and the cerebellar **peduncles** (Latin for "feet"), which give the cerebellum its input and output from the brain-stem fiber tracts. Nuclei in the tegmentum of the pons appear to be involved in sleep and in maintaining an optimum level of arousal. This area and surrounding areas have been lumped under one name, the **ascending reticular activating system (ARAS).** Recently, as the anatomy and functions of the region have become more differentiated, the term has been used less. The pons itself has a bulging appearance because of the dense fiber tract that originates in the pontine nuclei and crosses under the brain stem to rise into

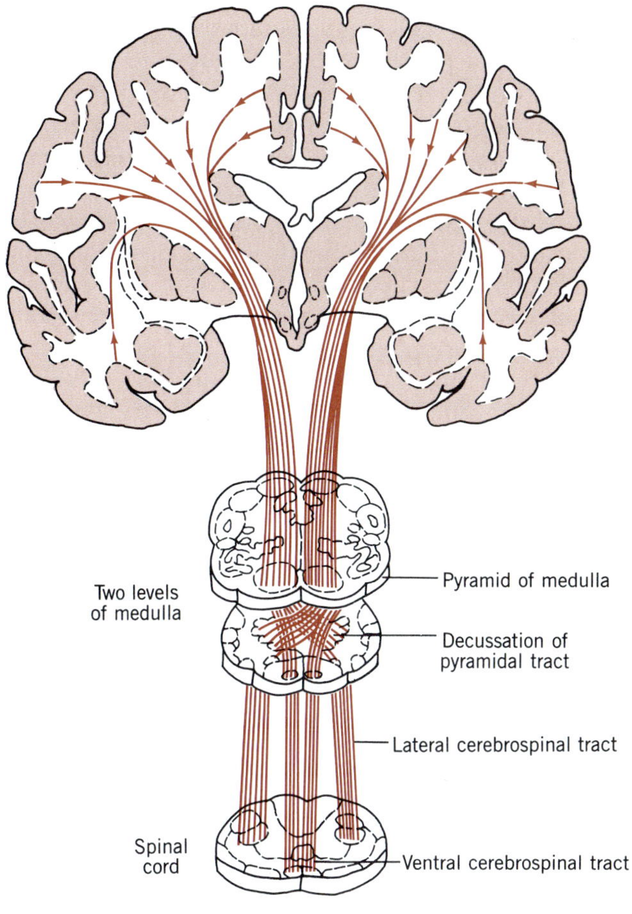

Figure 3.14 *Decussation of the pyramidal tracts in the medulla. Each tract consists of axons of cortical motor neurons, sometimes called upper motor neurons because they synapse on lower motor neurons in the spinal cord.*

the cerebellum on the opposite side (Truex & Carpenter, 1964). The pontine nuclei, in turn, receive input from the cerebral cortex, creating communication between the cerebral cortex and the cerebellum.

The hindbrain portion of the brain stem looks much the same in mammals as in primitive vertebrates. The exception is an enlargement and infolding of one of the principal synaptic links of the cerebellum with the brain stem, the **inferior olive,** in mammals. This comical but descriptive name comes from early neuroanatomists, who were keen observers but had no conception of the functions of the structures they described. (This is perhaps fortunate, for the functions of some controversial brain areas seem to change every 10 years while their appearance remains the same.)

Moving rostrally, we see that the brain stem in the **mesencephalon** (Greek for "midbrain") contains the vestibular nuclei, the first central processors of vestibular information. The mesencephalon also contains the oculomotor nuclei, structures that probably evolved out of the vestibular system. The most primitive eye movements are driven by vestibular inputs. Even in humans, there are monosynaptic links between visual and vestibular functions at this level.

In the forebrain, the brain stem merges with the thalamus and the **hypothalamus** (*hypo* is Greek for "under"); the latter is so named because it is under the thalamus. The thalamus and hypothalamus together form the **diencephalon**—a division of the forebrain at the head end of the brain stem. Parts of the thalamus near the midline and parts of the hypothalamus continue the reticular organization of the brain-stem core into the forebrain.

This completes our overview of the brain stem. We will return to the brain stem often, for it forms the core of the brain in a functional as well as a physical sense. Now we can look at the three major brain divisions—the hindbrain, the midbrain, and the forebrain—emphasizing the parts that evolved to supplement the brain stem.

THE HINDBRAIN

As one moves from the spinal cord to the hindbrain, one sees that the anatomy changes gradually from the typical spinal cord organization to the patterns of the hindbrain. The hindbrain also has functions similar to those of the spinal cord; it coordinates movements of the head in the same way that the spinal cord coordinates the body, and it mediates sensorimotor reflexes that are analogous to the spinal cord reflexes. In addition, the hindbrain controls the fine-grained coordination (small, precise adjustments) of muscle timing and activation. This coordination takes place in the **cerebellum** (Latin for "little brain").

The Cerebellum

The brain stem consists of a set of nuclei surrounded by a **cortex** (Latin for "bark") and organized as a highly structured array of neurons. In general, the cortically organized structures have changed more than the underlying tegmentum in the course of evolution. The cerebellum is an example of extensive development dorsal to a virtually unchanged brain stem. In fish, where it first appears in evolution, the cerebellum is an inconspicuous bump near the point where the spinal cord meets the brain. In mammals, it has developed into a highly folded structure, even more folded than the cerebral cortex, and has several divisions and specialized parts. It looks very different from its humble beginning in the fish. As vertebrates moved from sea to land, they began to run, hop, and jump, always requiring more information from the fast on-line computer of muscular coordination in the cerebellum.

Structure of the Cerebellar Cortex. The cerebellar cortex is remarkable in its regularity and simplicity. It contains only five cell types, always in the same anatomical relationship to one another. A look at its logical plan, as reflected in its microstructure, yields a surprise: the design is nearly identical in every creature from fish to human. The same cells are present, and they show the same patterns of connectivity. Evolution seems to have found an optimal solution to the problem of coordinating muscles quickly and effectively. The pattern has remained stable even while the specific tasks of the cerebellum have changed greatly. This is particularly remarkable because the cerebellum is capable of plasticity—of learning to do a better job with practice. We think of this plasticity as a specialization of mammals, but in the case of motor coordination it takes place partly in an ancient structure, one nearly unchanged for 100 million years.

Equally remarkable is the uniformity of the cerebellar cortex. A section anywhere in a given cerebellar cortex is indistinguishable from a section anywhere else, despite great differences in function.

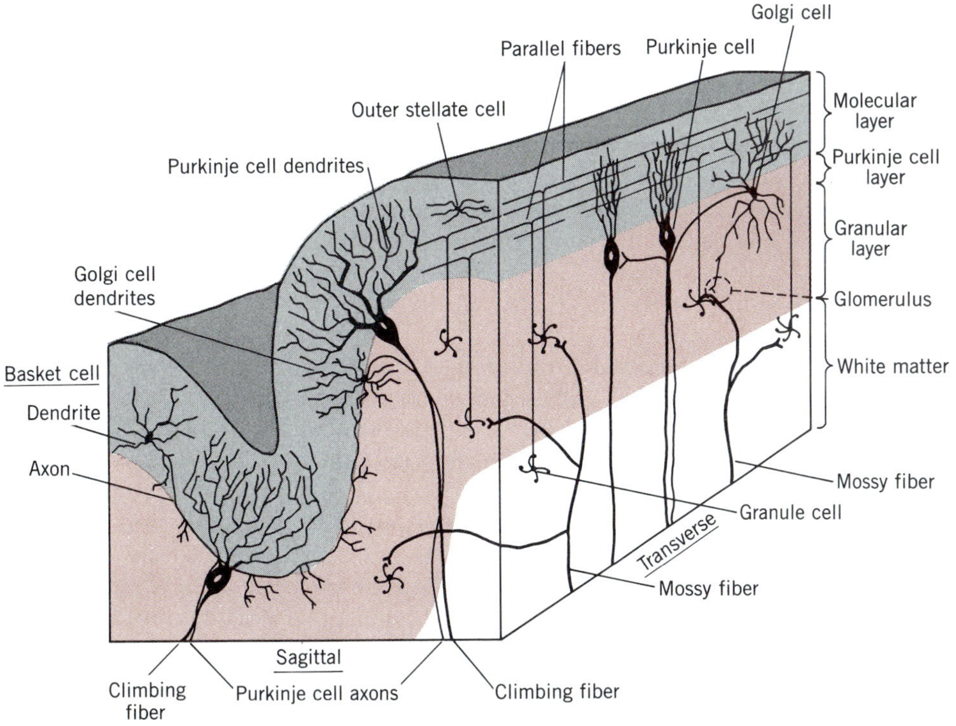

Figure 3.15 *Section of cerebellar cortex showing planes parallel and perpendicular to the folia (folds) of the cortex. The structure is similar everywhere in the cerebellum, regardless of function.*

The largest cells of the cerebellar cortex are the **Purkinje cells,** named after a 19th century Czech neuroanatomist. Each Purkinje cell has a large dendritic tree extending in only two dimensions, like the fan pattern of some tropical corals, in contrast to the usual pattern of three-dimensional dendritic trees. All the dendritic trees are arranged parallel to one another (as shown in Figure 3.15), like a vast array of closely spaced telephone poles. The Purkinje cell planes are perpendicular to the folds of the cerebellar cortex. The Purkinje cell defines the three layers of the cerebellar cortex. The outer, or **molecular, layer** at the top of Figure 3.15 consists of the dendritic trees and their connections; the second, **Purkinje, layer** of Purkinje cell bodies; and the third, **granular, layer** of efferent axons of the cells.

The enormous numbers of **granule cells** have bodies that seem no larger than granules of sand in comparison to the larger Purkinje cell bodies. In fact, it has been said that there are about 10^{11} cells in the brain, of which 10^{11} are cerebellar granule cells! This statement says something about both the tremendous number of granule cells and the imprecision of neuron counts. Each granule cell sends its axon up into the molecular layer. There, the axon divides and sends branches in opposite directions at a T-shaped junction. The branches of all granule cell axons lie precisely parallel to one another and hence are called **parallel fibers.** They also run perpendicular to the planes defined by the dendritic trees of the Purkinje cells, synapsing with several hundred of them.

Because the parallel fibers are excitatory, some inhibitory input to the Purkinje cells is needed to modulate cerebellar activity. This input is provided by **basket cells,** so called because their axons wrap around Purkinje cell bodies to literally form baskets around them, thickly covering the soma with inhibitory synapses. **Stellate** (Latin for "starlike") **cells** and **Golgi cells** (shown in Figure 3.15) provide additional inhibition.

The two inputs to the cerebellar cortex are climbing fibers and mossy fibers. Each **climbing fiber** climbs like a vine on the trellis of a single Purkinje cell, giving each Purkinje cell a "private line" (Cajal, 1911). Climbing fibers originate in the inferior olive of the brain stem (Eccles, Ito & Szentagothai, 1967), which in turn receives widespread input from the brain and spinal cord. **Mossy fibers,** in contrast, synapse only with granule cells. The fibers are called mossy because of their density of synaptic endings.

In summary, the cerebellar circuit consists of two synaptic pathways. One crosses from mossy fibers to granule cells to Purkinje cells. The other travels on a monosynaptic path, from climbing fibers to Purkinje cells. Both are modified by inhibition from within the cerebellar cortex.

The 15 million or so Purkinje cells provide the only output of this huge neuronal machine (schematized in Figure 3.16). These cells, surprisingly, are inhibitory, so the only result of the precise computations taking place in the network is the selective inhibition of other ongoing activity. This inhibition is consistent with the function of the cerebellum. Sitting astride the brain stem, with its neuronal fingers poking into messages coursing up and down, it modulates behaviors but cannot initiate them. Electrical stimulation of the cerebellum in humans never results in conscious experience, in contrast to what occurs in the neocortex and many other forebrain areas.

THE MIDBRAIN

Compared to the other brain structures, the midbrain has changed the least in the course of evolution. As the hindbrain expanded with the cerebellum and the forebrain with the cerebral cortex, the midbrain declined in relative importance. In amphibians and reptiles, the midbrain remains a prominent structure and contains the largest sensory-processing areas for vision and audition. It is also important in some specialized mammals, such as the bat, with its highly developed sonar abilities. When the very thin skull of a bat is exposed, the huge auditory centers of its midbrain are visible directly through the skull. They dominate the dorsal aspect of the brain.

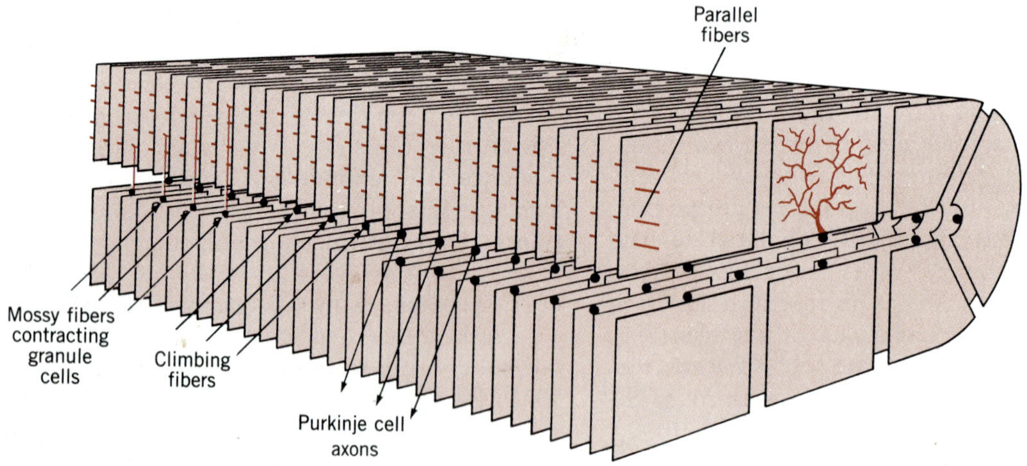

Figure 3.16 *Diagrammatic view of the functional anatomy of the cerebellar cortex, showing dendritic regions of Purkinje cells. The drawing exaggerates the regularity of the dendritic trees but not the rigor of their parallel orientation. Purkinje cell bodies are represented as block dots. Parallel fibers are the axons of the granular cells. Adapted from Braitenberg (1977).*

The Colliculi

The **superior colliculi** and **inferior colliculi** (*colliculi* is Latin for "low hills"), located on top of the midbrain, function in vision and hearing, respectively. Because each colliculus is a paired structure appearing as two bilaterally symmetrical bumps ("hills") on the brain stem, the colliculi are also known collectively as the **corpora quadrigemina** (Latin for "bodies of four twins"), or the **tectum** ("roof"), of the midbrain. Both structures are organized in several layers, and both show a gradual transformation of cell function with increasing depth from the surface of the tectum. We will use the more intensively studied superior colliculus as an example of collicular structure.

In primitive vertebrates, the optic tectum, a precursor of the mammal's superior colliculus, forms the most prominent part of the visual system. Birds, which are highly visual animals, have a huge and highly structured optic tectum. In mammals, vision becomes progressively dominated by phylogenetically newer forebrain structures. The superior colliculus still receives direct retinal input, but it serves mainly to direct eye movements and visual attention. It can also mediate the more general processing of visual space and visual orientation. The superior colliculus is also connected to the visual cortex and the frontal attention-directing cortical centers.

The colliculus is organized in alternating layers of white and gray matter, beginning with a layer of fibers. The cells of the top layers receive direct projections (fiber tracts) from the occipital cortex and the retina. They respond to visual stimuli in much the same way that other visual system cells do. The information flow proceeds in a pattern similar to that of water flowing through a coffee filter; water enters at the top and becomes more and more coffeelike as it filters down to the deep layers. In the superior colliculus, information rather than coffee is processed; the cells at the top respond only to aspects of the visual world, but those farther down relate more and more to internal oculomotor signals, until the most ventral cells show firing patterns behaviorally related to eye movements. These larger cells send their axons ventrally to oculomotor centers in the midbrain tegmentum. Thus the sensory-oriented topographic map of the retina in the dorsal colliculus is transformed into a motor-oriented map of oculomotor space in the ventral layers. The superior colliculus also receives input from the inferior colliculus and from nonspecific reticular fibers.

Although the inferior and superior colliculi are important in the evolution of cortically organized systems, in the primates they are insignificant in size compared to the greatly enlarged cerebellar cortex and especially to the cerebral cortex, the giant of them all.

THE FOREBRAIN

The forebrain carries to an extreme the general plan of nuclear brain-stem organization and sheetlike dorsal additions. In evolution, it has expanded more than the other two brain divisions because of the increasing importance of the cerebral cortex. Various other structures branch off from the original brain-stem structure to complete the forebrain.

The Thalamus

If the cortex is the director of the brain, the thalamus is the executive secretary. A group of distinct nuclei located at the head of the brain stem (as shown in Figure 3.13), the thalamus is connected with nearly all the cortical areas and has diffuse projections to the cortex as a whole. The nuclei can be divided into two broad types: extrinsic and intrinsic. The **extrinsic thalamic nuclei** link external inputs or outputs on one side with the cortex on the other. The **intrinsic thalamic nuclei** form reciprocal connections only with targeted cortical areas. Thus thalamic nuclei help define the corresponding cortical areas to which they project.

The basic design of the thalamus is simple, no more elaborate than the spinal cord. In the sensory nuclei, for example, afferent fibers from sense organs synapse directly onto **principal cells,** which in turn project axons topographically to the cortex. Each input axon connects to its own principal cell. The thalamus looks like a simple monosynaptic "relay" nucleus, but relay nuclei are not necessary in the brain because, as we saw in Chapter 2, the axons conduct without decrement. At each synapse we can expect a transformation of signals.

Imagine an organization with workers in the field (senses) reporting back to executives in the head office (CNS). If the executives don't like what they read, they tell the field workers to change their reports! It would seem that such an organization wouldn't get very far, but this is exactly how the brain relates to the senses. One of the places where sensory messages are modified to fit the current needs of the organism is in the thalamus.

One transformation comes from **intrinsic inhibitory neurons** ("intrinsic" because they send no axons out of the thalamus) mediating a lateral inhibition between principal cells. Each principal cell inhibits other principal cells through the inhibitory interneurons. In sensory thalamic nuclei, such as the visual system's **lateral geniculate nucleus** (*geniculate* is Latin for "kneelike"), or LGN, and the auditory system's **medial geniculate nucleus,** efferents from the cortex can modify the activity of the inhibitory interneurons. (These efferents are represented by the crosshatched neurons in Figure 3.17.) This modification of activity is an example of efferent control of input (Singer & Creutzfeldt, 1970). Efferents can alter the coding of cortical input because modulation of thalamic inhibitory interneurons changes the spread and strength of lateral inhibition in the thalamus (Figure 3.17). The modification is more subtle and powerful than a mere change in the intensity of incoming stimulation.

Other cortical efferents do reduce the strength of input, by presynaptic inhibition of the sensory input terminals. Still other corticothalamic efferents end on the principal cells (Guillery, 1969; Jones & Powell, 1969) and on the interneurons (Kalil & Chase, 1970). Many of these interactions take place in **synaptic glomeruli,** intricate three-dimensional structures containing specialized synaptic contacts (Szentogathai, Hamori & Tömböl, 1966).

In addition to transforming sensory input, the thalamus integrates nonspecific inputs with the specific afferent sensory signal. Retinal fibers entering the lateral geniculate nucleus, for instance, produce about the same response to light regardless of the animal's state of attention or arousal; geniculate outputs, however, depend on arousal as well as light. So what seemed to be a simple monosynaptic structure turns out to have a sophisticated design—one that mediates complex transformations of sensory input.

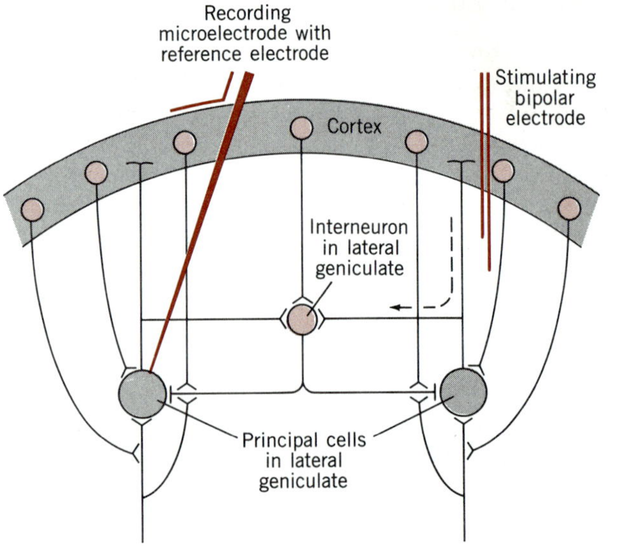

Figure 3.17 *Schematic view of the afferent and efferent connections in the lateral geniculate nucleus of the thalamus. The afferent connections go upward in the diagram, and the efferent go downward. All the connections have been verified by anatomical experiments. The basic monosynaptic pathway from retinal afferents (bottom) through the principal cells to the cortex (top) is modified by inhibitory neurons in the geniculate and by various afferent and efferent synaptic contacts. The effects of the inhibitory neurons on the flow of information through the geniculate can be explored by stimulating principal cell axons with an electrode and recording the effects with a microelectrode. Stimulation yields a brief cessation of principal cell firing as a volley of inhibition arrives, and sometimes a rebound burst of firing after the inhibition. Adapted from Bridgeman (1972).*

Other thalamic nuclei have similar designs, and all appear to play a role in modulating the state of the cortex as well as regulating its input and output. But the thalamus has only about 1 percent as many cells as the cortex. This restricts its role to modulating rather than driving the cortex. (More details are given in Chapter 5.)

The Hypothalamus

As indicated earlier, the thalamus and hypothalamus together make up the diencephalon. Though tiny, the hypothalamus is important in regulating functions associated with the "four F's" (fighting, fleeing, feeding, and sex) and in controlling the endocrine system. Specific nuclei and tracts are reviewed in Chapter 9 (homeostasis) and Chapter 10 (motivation and emotion). Examining the functions of the hypothalamus requires a look at the body's glandular systems, for many hypothalamic actions flow through the glands.

The Glands. There are two kinds of glands in the body: endocrine and exocrine. **Endocrine glands** (*endo* is Greek for "in") secrete their products into the bloodstream. **Exocrine,** or ducted, **glands** (*exo* is Greek for "out") send their products to specific locations inside or outside the body. Endocrine glands are generally under hormonal control, many of them involved in elaborate feedback systems that ultimately are controlled by hypothalamic secretions. An example is the thymus gland, which produces growth hormone and releases its products directly into the bloodstream slowly and steadily. Exocrine glands are controlled more directly by autonomic neurons. For example, the salivary glands and other digestive glands can store their products to be released quickly when needed.

Most glands help the body achieve **homeostasis**—the maintenance of ideal conditions inside the body; others are parts of systems controlling growth, sexual response, and other specialized functions. (They will be reviewed in the section on control systems, in Chapters 10 and 11.)

The Portal System. The hypothalamus is closely linked to the endocrine glands via the **portal system** (shown in Figure 3.18), a neurological organization that is intermediate between the synaptic and hormonal systems. Some hypothalamic neurons have synapses that end on blood vessels rather than on the postsynaptic membranes of other neurons; the specialized blood vessels of the portal system carry the hypothalamic control hormones less than a centimeter from the neurons to the **anterior pituitary,** an endocrine gland. There the hormones stimulate glandular secretory cells. The portal system vessels do not branch between their hypothalamic origin and their pituitary target. Thus neurosecretory cells stimulate glandular cells not by direct synaptic contact but by indirect chemical communication through the portal system's vessels.

The hypothalamic cells manufacture only tiny amounts of control hormones, amounts so small that they are difficult to detect without radioactive tracer techniques. The anterior pituitary cells in turn produce other hormones in quantities large enough to govern the entire body without excessive dilution in the general bloodstream. The portal system is involved in negative feedback control circuits governing the concentrations of hormones in the bloodstream. Sex hormones, for example, are kept in control because they inhibit the same pituitary hormones that released them.

The Limbic System

A group of interconnected forebrain structures that mediate emotional behavior as well as mediating some attentional, arousal, memory, and endocrine functions make up the **limbic system.** In addition to the anterior thalamus, already discussed, this system includes the **mammillary bodies, hippocampus, cingulate gyrus, amygdala, septum,** and associated fiber tracts. The system is a collection of cortical and nuclear structures. The cingulate gyrus, for example, blends into the neocortex but is phylogenetically older and is composed of a thinner cortex, somewhat like the hippocampus. The remaining structures are subcortical nuclei. (The anatomy and functions of the limbic system will be detailed in Chapter 10.)

The Basal Ganglia

Another group of subcortical forebrain nuclei, the **basal ganglia** are involved in controlling posture and gross motor activities and are closely connected with the cerebellum, midbrain, neocortex, and spinal cord. The basal ganglia include the **caudate** (Latin for "taillike") **nucleus,** the **globus pallidus** (Latin for "pale globe"), and the **putamen** (Latin for "pruned away"); these structures are collectively known as the **corpus striatum** be-

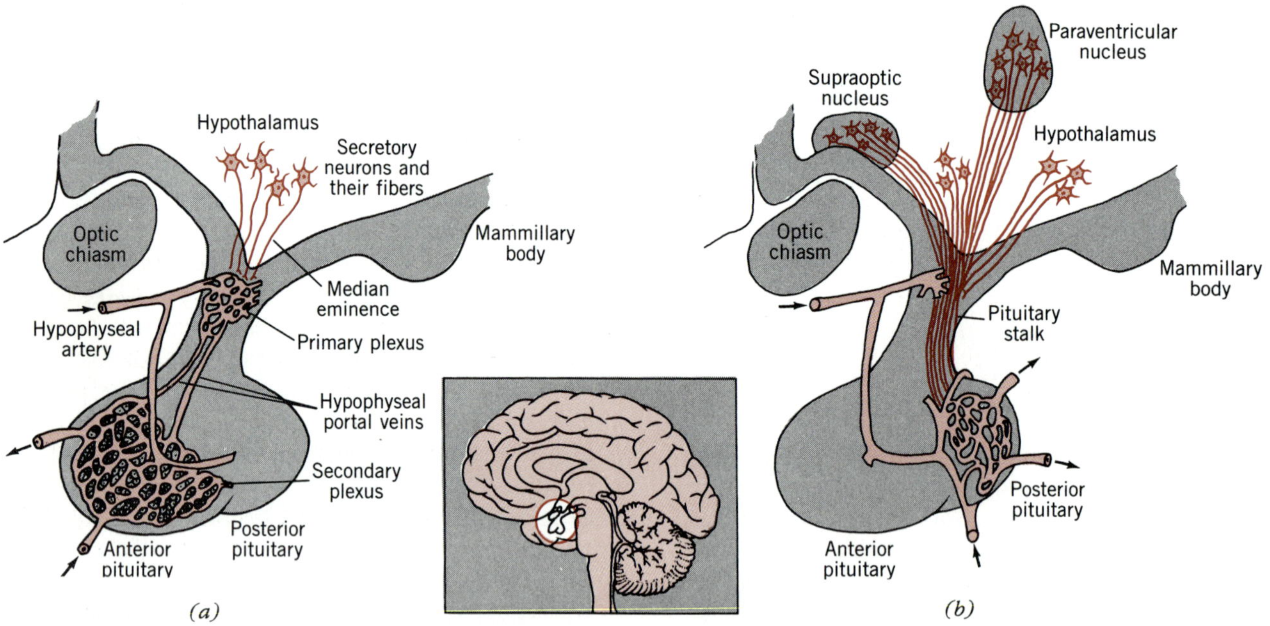

Figure 3.18 *The pituitary gland.* (a) *The portal system linking the hypothalamus with the anterior pituitary gland (also called the adenohypophysis). The pituitary acts as a biochemical amplifier, secreting relatively large amounts of hormones for the general circulation in response to small amounts of hypothalamic hormones transported in the portal system.* (b) *The posterior pituitary gland (also called the neurohypophysis), with axonal rather than circulatory information channels from the hypothalamus.*

cause fiber tracts dividing them give the assembly a striped appearance. The amygdala is sometimes included in the list, but it really belongs with the limbic system because of its functions in organizing emotional behavior.

Functional links of the caudate nucleus with the neocortex are especially close, for there is a topographic mapping of parts of the neocortex onto the caudate, and the nucleus has grown in phylogenetic development along with the cortex. The basal ganglia are also linked to motor structures of the brain stem through connections with the **substantia nigra** (Latin for "black substance") of the midbrain brain stem, so named because melanin pigment in the neurons gives this nucleus a blackish tinge. The pigment is related to the production of the neurotransmitter dopamine.

THE CEREBRAL CORTEX

The cerebral cortex began in reptiles as a streak of three-layered **archicortex** (Greek for "old cortex") atop the thalamus. In mammals, a six-layered **neocortex** (Greek for "new cortex") begins as a narrow strip of tissue and expands as animals evolve, first swelling to cover the archicortex beneath it and finally extending its folded and wrinkled surface over the entire brain while remaining closely associated with the archicortex and thalamus. In looking at a human brain from any angle, one sees mostly neocortex.

In humans the gray matter of each cortical hemisphere weighs about 250 g, and the underlying white matter is thicker and heavier (total brain weight is about 1400 g). Despite its extensive folding, each hemisphere forms a continuous sheet of neural tissue about 2200 cm^2 in area, which implies that the continuity of the tissue is important for its function. The division of the neocortex into lobes is a convenient fiction, for the sheet of gray matter is actually continuous at the deep sulci (valleys), which only appear to divide the neocortex into lobes. Even among mammals, the neocortices of various animals look very different. They range from the smooth neocortices of mice and rats, to the more folded neocortices of cats (larger in proportion to brain size than the rats') to the huge neocortices of the monkeys and apes, and finally to the neocortices of humans, the largest and most differentiated of all the primate neocortices. There are definite differences in cell size, cell density, and degree of connectivity from mouse neocortex to human neocortex, but the principles of organization are the same. The major types of cells and their connections are also similar in mice and humans (Braitenberg, 1977). Like the cerebellar cortex, the forebrain cortex has changed greatly in gross appearance but little in microstructure.

This seat of perception, intelligence, and complex behavioral organization actually has a simple cytoarchitecture (*cyto* is Latin for "cell"), with fewer cell types and synaptic layers than in the retina of a frog. Its ability to mediate complex processes stems more from its enormous capacity for integration and plasticity than from complexities of specific synaptic connectivity.

Neural Architecture of the Neocortex

The neocortex is a six-layered structure (shown in Figure 3.19). Especially unique is layer 1, at the top, for it contains almost no cell bodies. Instead, it consists of dendritic branches from most of the cells in deeper cortical layers as well as axonal branches from both local cells and more distant ones. The result is a huge, extremely fine feltwork of interlocking processes. The dominant mode of electrical interaction is graded potentials, and the fine grain of the junctional microstructure acts as a compact analog computer. In this region, cerebellar and cerebral cortices are similar; both have a top layer with a rich junctional microstructure that contains few cell bodies. Although the top layers of the two structures have a very different cytoarchitecture, both are called molecular layers because of the sparseness of cell bodies. It is as though the metabolic functions of the cell bodies have been removed spatially from the area of densest information processing, to make the most of the limited effective range of graded interactions by maximizing the density of cell processes and synapses. Layer 1 is rich in synapses of all varieties, including dendrodendritic synapses carrying graded potential interactions. Many of the processes are very fine, and they are covered with synaptic contacts. In the cortex as a whole, each axon has an average of one synapse for each micron of its length (Cragg, 1962).

Specific input to the cortex, such as topographic projections from the senses, is concentrated in layer 4; nonspecific input from such places as the reticular system is diffused through more layers and is concentrated in lower ones. Output cells, with axons leaving the cortex for subcortical destinations, are largely in layer 5.

Superimposed on the layered organization of the cortex is a **columnar organization,** with each column comprising a set of a few thousand closely linked cells reaching from the top of the cortex to the bottom (Mountcastle, 1957). The columns are roughly the size of the cortical cross sections in Figure 3.19. The cells in a column tend to have similar response properties. This system implies that most cortical interaction is vertical, so information must leave the cortex to be transmitted on U-shaped fibers to other columns if it is to undergo further cortical processing. The verticality of function can be seen dramatically in experiments where the cortex is sliced in various orientations. Crosshatching the cortex with knife cuts has no effect on function, but undercutting it has the same effect as removing the cortex completely (Pribram, Blehert & Spinelli, 1966). The intact but undercut cortex cannot communicate horizontally with other areas.

Cell Types. Only three basic types of cells compose the cortex, each coming in several variations (Braitenberg, 1977). Most important are the **pyramidal cells,** which have two distinct types of dendrites: apical and basal. An apical (from the apex) dendrite goes to layer 1; the basal dendrites cluster around the cell body (see Figure 2.1d). The axon also has two branches, one ending in a region a little below and overlapping the basal dendritic tree and the other leaving the cortex, in most cases to enter it again in layer 1 of a distant region. Pyramidal cell dendrites are covered with spines containing synaptic contacts, which may be involved in learning (see Chapter 11).

Another kind of neuron, the **Martinotti cell,** transmits signals not downward through the cortex, as the pyramidal cells do, but upward. Martinotti cell bodies are concentrated in the lower lay-

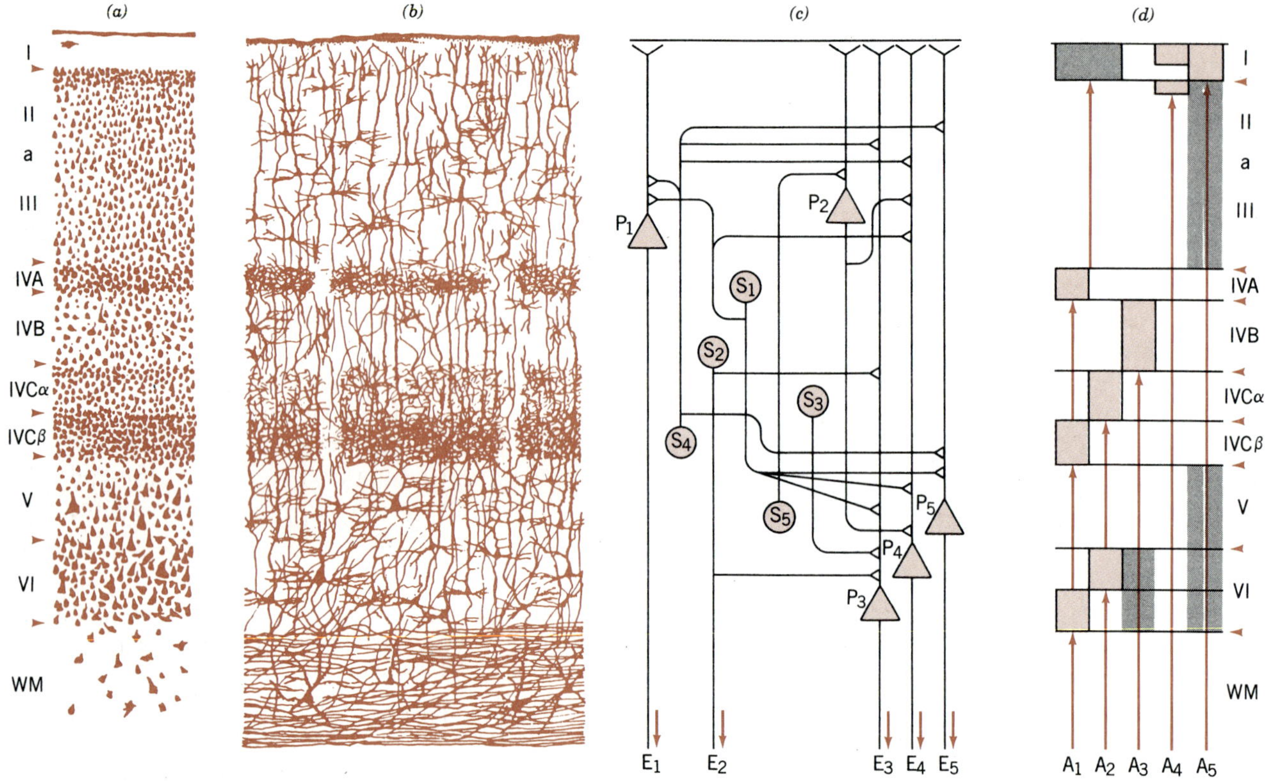

Figure 3.19 *Cross section through the cerebral neocortex.* (a) *Nissl stain for cell bodies, in visual cortex.* (b) *Golgi stain for a sample of complete neurons in the same cortex. One cortical column (center) and the sides of two other columns are visible. Layer 1 has processes but almost no cell bodies. Neuroanatomists have subdivided some of the layers; the divisions vary with the cortical area. The thickness of the layers also depends on the specialization of the cortex.* (c) *A simplified scheme of local neuronal circuits with their outputs.* (d) *The levels of five kinds of synaptic inputs. Adapted from Rakic (1981).*

ers of the cortex, sending their axons upward to divide in layer 1.

The final variety of neuron, the stellate cell, has dendrites radiating in all directions around it (hence the name). The axon also branches in the region of the cell body, so this kind of cell is involved primarily in local interactions. The stellate cells have the densest axonal trees; the pyramidal cells have the loosest and largest.

Linking Structure and Function. Using these anatomical characteristics, we can examine how the cortex might work as a neuronal machine. Although there are several theories, including some mathematical ones, and although the details of cortical function remain obscure, neuroanatomy can hint at the process. First, the cortex can be conceived of as a network of pyramidal cells, since these cells constitute 75 percent of all the cells in the cortex and more than 75 percent of the neural volume of the cortex (Braitenberg, 1977).

The basal dendritic and axonal trees of the pyramidal cells overlap extensively, putting each cell in close communication with its neighbors. The layer 1 interactions are qualitatively different, however, with each cell contacting axons from nearly all the regions of the cortex! Researchers discovered this startling fact by counting the number of U-shaped corticocortical axons and comparing it to the area of the cortex and to the spread of a large dendritic tree in a pyramidal cell, which is about 1 mm^2 in humans. There are enough of these long-distance axons for each square millimeter to receive one axon from every other square millimeter of cortex (Braitenberg, 1977). The number of these fibers dwarfs the number of fibers entering the cortex from other structures or leaving the cortex to go to other brain areas. About 99 percent of the axons leaving the gray matter will reenter it without synapsing elsewhere. The main business of the cortex is talking to itself, with relatively little input and output.

The density of U-shaped axons has been held constant throughout evolution because of its importance in cortical function (Braitenberg, 1977). In the mouse, this connecting function results in a thin layer of white matter just beneath the cortex; in humans, the same function requires huge cables of axons much thicker than the six-layered gray matter itself. Again, the function remains constant while the appearance changes, so that in each animal a pyramidal cell receives two almost equally strong inputs: one from the local region and the other from the entire cortex.

With the basic plan established, the other cells can be added to the cortical architecture. The pyramidal cells are excitatory; without modulation, they would stimulate one another into uncontrolled seizures of activity. The stellate cells, which are mainly inhibitory, may serve to modulate their firing. Because the axonal tree of a pyramidal cell tends to be below its dendritic tree, local interactions probably cascade downward in a serial manner. The distant interactions of layer 1 are more reciprocal by comparison. The upward-conducting Martinotti cells might complete the local circuit by transmitting the downward-processed information back to layer 1. Though local, the interactions probably involve the 1000 to 2000 dendritic trees that each axonal tree of a pyramidal cell intercepts. In later chapters we will examine the consequences of this structurally simple but highly interconnected network.

Specialized Cortical Areas

Although its basic organization is the same everywhere, the neocortical structure is not uniform, as it is in the cerebellar cortex. Distinct cytoarchitectural areas are based on variations in the thickness and prominence of the layers. In some cortical areas the six-layered structure is obscured and distorted. In the frontal lobe, for example, is an area called the **agranular frontal cortex,** because it lacks the small stellate cells called granule cells (not the same as the structurally distinct granule cells of the cerebellar cortex). The early 20th century neuroanatomist Korbinian Brodmann distinguished and numbered 47 cortical areas (pictured in Figure 3.20). His is the most widely used classification system; other estimates of the number of areas vary from 20 to over 200, proving that the distinctions among cortical areas are anything but clear. The motor cortex is the thickest, at about 4.5 mm, probably because it contains many large-bodied neurons with long axons; the primary visual cortex is the thinnest at about 2 mm.

There are two types of cortex: extrinsic and intrinsic. The **extrinsic cortex** receives afferents from or sends efferents to noncortical centers involved in sensory or motor functions. The **intrinsic cortex** projects only to and from other cortical areas, either directly or via thalamic nuclei. The intrinsic areas assume a larger and larger proportion of the cortex in more advanced mammals.

The former name for the intrinsic cortex was the **association cortex.** That name is a relic from the era of British associationists, the armchair psychologists of the 19th century. The associationists divided all psychological functions into sensory, motor, and association processes; when neurophysiologists discovered sensory and motor areas on the cortical surface, the anatomy seemed to match the ideas of the associationists. But most of the cortex was "silent"; stimulating it yielded neither a movement nor a perception. Because it seemed to fit neither category, it was named "association cortex" by default. The associationists assumed, without any evidence whatever, that the silent cortex performed the missing association function. The idea turned out to be inaccurate. (Later chapters will discuss how the intrinsic cortex is divided into many specialized areas connected with specific functions.)

A surprising feature of cortical organization is that sensory and motor areas are arranged not in series, as the old behaviorist theories would seem to require, but in parallel. There is no chain of

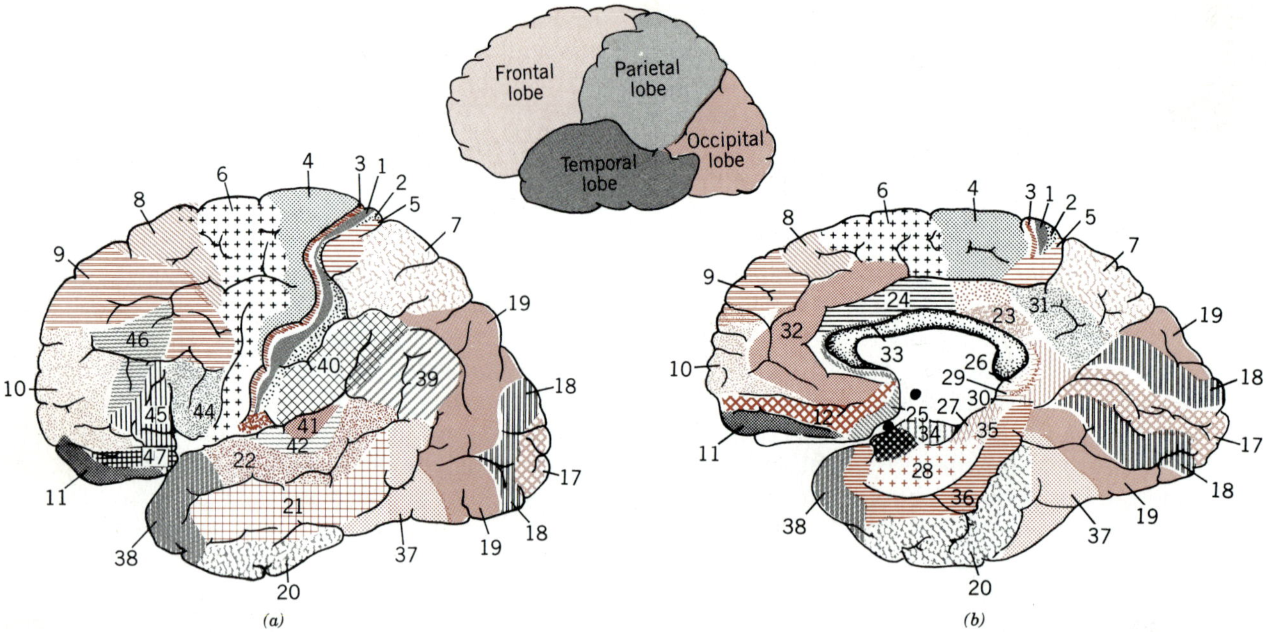

***Figure 3.20** Cytoarchitectonic areas of the cerebral cortex as defined by Brodmann (1912).* (a) *Lateral view.* (b) *Sagittal view. The numbering system is arbitrary; areas with close numbers are not necessarily similar in architecture or function. Brodmann began slicing the brain at the top and added a new number whenever a new area appeared. (This general rule got a bit tangled in the ventral and temporal regions.) Some of the areas have since been subdivided on physiological rather than anatomical grounds. Brodmann's area 19, for example, contains several distinct maps of the retina, with differing properties.*

neurons from sensory to association to motor cortex; rather there is a highly integrated reciprocal set of connections with only a tiny proportion exiting to subcortical areas. All cortical areas, no matter what their functions, are a similar logical distance from the periphery and are organized similarly.

Evolution of the Cortex

The **olfactory bulbs** of the fish were the first cortically organized structures to appear in evolution. Despite their bulbous appearance, their structure is that of a rolled-up sheet of layered cells—a true cortex. The olfactory cortex is a three-layered structure, somewhat more stereotyped in its structure than the neocortex. It shows something of the origin of the forebrain cortex in two unusual characteristics: its sensory input is uncrossed, and it enters from the top rather than the bottom.

According to current theories, the neocortex evolved as a secondary or tertiary olfactory center, becoming a six-layered structure by the addition of three more layers on the top (Truex & Carpenter, 1964). The older, lower levels handle most of the input and output; the upper ones specialize in the more recently acquired integration functions.

The old, three-layered cortex, called the **allocortex,** is in the hippocampus, tucked inside the temporal lobe. (*Hippocampus* is Greek for "seahorse"; it is so dubbed for its curving shape in human brains.) The allocortex was once thought to be part of the olfactory system, but it is now known to participate in memory and attention. Luckily, it was not originally named for its function. The hippocampus is a spirally rolled piece of allocortex; a fresh section of it looks like a jelly roll. The thin neuropil (shown in Figure 3.21) has all of its pyramidal cells concentrated in a single line, where their interactions can be densest; but activity cannot cascade from one pyramidal cell level to another, as it does in the neocortex. The cortex of the hippocampus merges smoothly with

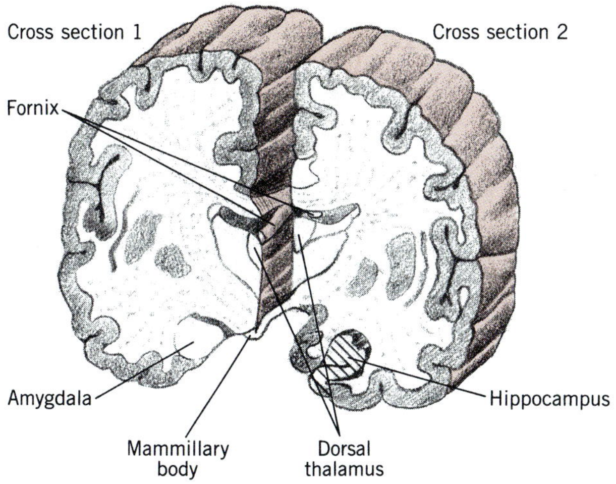

Figure 3.21 *Comparative cytoarchitecture of the hippocampus and the neocortex. Both figures are drawn from Golgi-stained material, the hippocampus by Cajal (1911) and the cortex by Lorente de No (1949). The hippocampus has all of its large pyramidal cells in a single layer; at the right the pattern breaks up as the hippocampus merges into the neocortex. Adapted from Pribram (1971).*

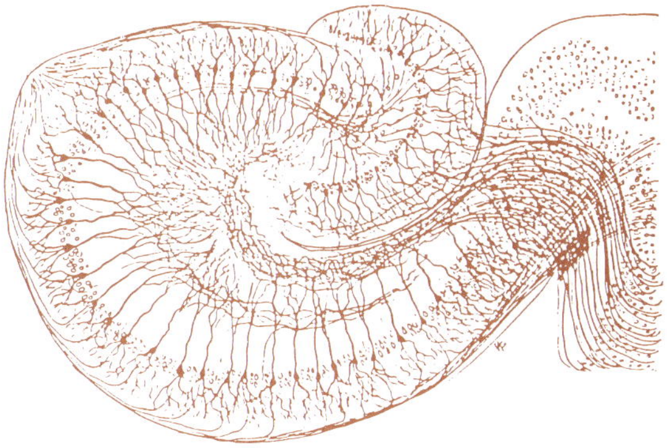

(a)

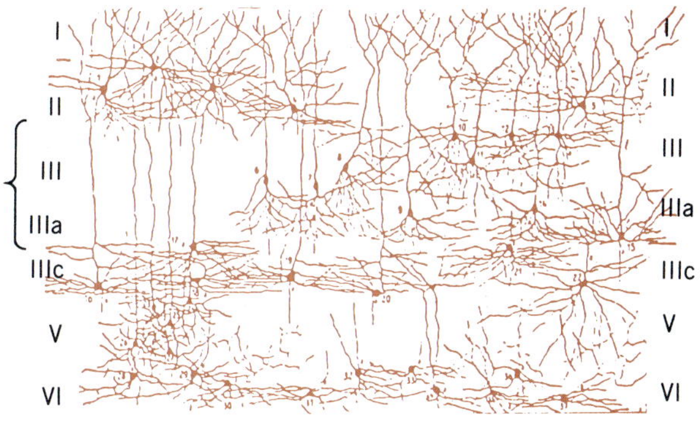

(b)

Figure 3.22 *Varieties of forebrain cortical organization, in frontal section. The archicortex of the hippocampus and the juxtallocortex of the cingulate gyrus (both crosshatched) are continuous with the neocortex in between (white). The two older structures join medially behind the corpus callosum to form the limbic lobe, a structure made from older, thinner cortex. In evolution the neocortex spread from these locations and began folding; now two-thirds of it is folded beneath the surface.*

the neocortex, undergoing a gradual change to a six-layered cortex in a transitional zone with the jawbreaker name **juxtallocortex** (Latin for "next to the allocortex") in the hippocampal gyrus (see Figure 3.22). The limbic lobe, also made of allocortex, is evolutionarily older than the neocortex overlying it.

Contrast of Function in Cortically Organized Structures

The cortex of the forebrain is both more extensive and more varied than the sheetlike arrangements in the midbrain and hindbrain. All three areas, however, share some characteristics that reveal evolutionary solutions to common problems. First, all are organized into distinct layers, with each layer specialized to perform a specific task in the overall function of the tissue. Second, the top layer of each cortex is a nearly cell-free matrix of fibers. In the cerebellum and neocortex this top layer mixes inputs from outside the cortex with the much more extensive axons and dendrites that originate in deeper cortical layers. The top layer is dense enough to permit information processing primarily in the graded-potential mode. A final characteristic of all cortical arrangements is a simple design unit (simple in comparison to the complexity of its behavioral function) endlessly repeated. As described in the universal neuroanatomy section of Chapter 2, each cortical structure occupies only a few logical layers. Each cortex contains only a handful of cell types organized in predictable patterns, and complex functions are handled by increasing the number of simple units rather than adding to their complexity.

A result of this final, and perhaps most important, feature of cortical organization is that the distance from input to output is only a few synaptic layers. This property implies that the transformations taking place in a single pass through any cortex must be simple ones.

In conclusion, cerebellar and neocortical tissues have two contrasting specializations. Information entering the cerebellar cortex makes only one pass through the system, exiting on a Purkinje cell axon to subcortical nuclei. A signal enters the cerebellar cortex, is processed, and exists within a few milliseconds, while a wave of inhibition clears the system for the next cycle (Eccles, Ito & Szentagothai, 1967). The forebrain neocortex, however, uses the simplicity of organization in an entirely different way; processing is not fast (sometimes it seems agonizingly slow), but it has access to large neural areas and enormous amounts of stored information. Incoming information passes through a small local column, then exits on cortico-cortical fibers to widespread cortical areas, where further integration takes place. The process is repeated, perhaps hundreds of times, while the signal gradually is transformed from a sensory-like code to a pattern suitable for motor output or for storage in a memory system. In sum, the neocortex uses the simplicity of basic design not for speed but for repetition of a relatively simple process.

To work successfully, all these operations must take place in a carefully controlled environment, where the metabolically sensitive neurons can function.

THE ENVIRONMENT OF THE BRAIN

The best way to characterize the brain's immediate physical surroundings is to imagine the conditions inside the skull. The CNS and associated organs are the only parts of the body completely encased in bone, which protects them from mechanical shock. The vertebral column protects the CNS against jarring during locomotion, with shock-absorbing disks between the vertebral bones. Temperature is maintained more uniformly in the brain than anywhere else in the body; during sleep, for instance, core body temperature can drop while brain temperature remains constant. In terms of the physical environment, the normal brain exists in a state of sensory deprivation.

Why must the organism invest so much metabolic energy in maintaining a constant internal environment for the brain? We can find one answer by considering what would happen if the brain were less effectively isolated from the outside: some stimuli would influence the brain twice, once through normal sensory channels and once by direct excitation of neurons. Neurons generally are sensitive to a wide variety of mechanical and chemical stimuli, though they have much higher thresholds than the specialized receptor organs. If a stimulus were to excite central neurons directly, without going through the senses, a disastrous ambiguity would result. An auditory stimulus, for instance, might excite the auditory system in the normal way but might also excite neurons involved in motor responses, generating spurious movements. Or a sharp poke might excite pain receptors and also stimulate neurons controlling sexual receptivity. Clearly, double stimulation is to be avoided wherever possible through careful insulating of the brain. The only information reaching the brain should be in the form of trains of nerve impulses and biochemical signals in the blood. The organ that experiences reality must do so only within the established channels.

THE MENINGES

Further protection for the CNS is provided by a set of three **meninges**—layers of connective tissue surrounding the brain. The meninges literally hold the brain together; because the CNS lacks internal connective tissue, a freshly excised human brain placed on a table would slump over and collapse from its own weight. Like modern materials that combine strength and protective capabilities, such as spacecraft components, the meninges have a sandwich structure of alternating hard and soft layers. The outermost layer, the **dura mater** (Latin for "hard mother"), is a thick, tough membrane surrounding the CNS and dipping into the major sulci between lobes. In neurosurgical procedures, care must be taken to cut the tough dura without

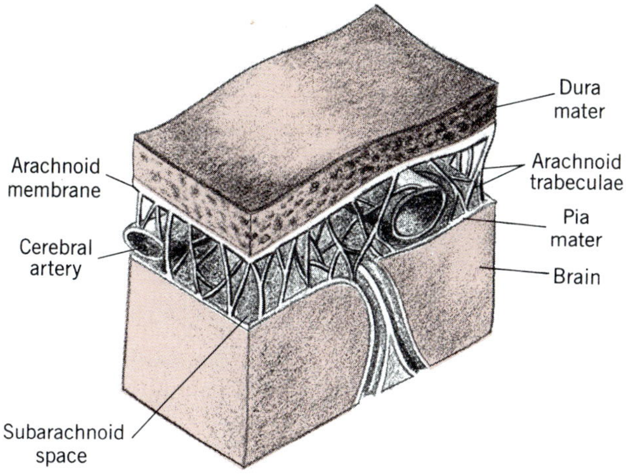

Figure 3.23 *Schematic drawing of the meninges covering the brain. The dura mater is innervated and is sensitive to pain; the underlying brain is not.*

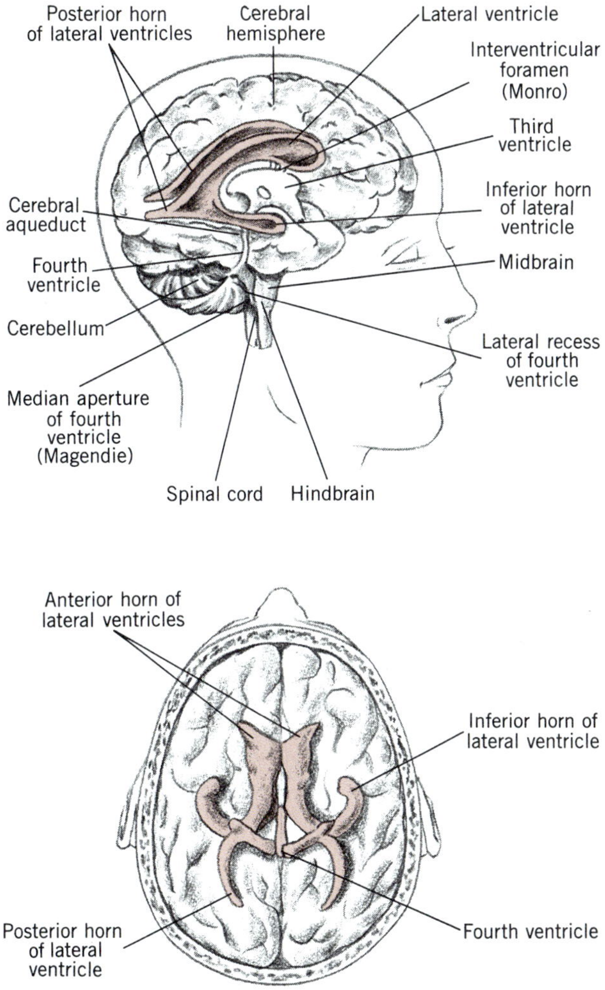

Figure 3.24 *Ventricles in lateral and superior views. The ancients believed that thinking was the circulation of air or fluids in the ventricles; Descartes had a similar theory.*

injuring the delicate neuropil underneath. By comparison with the dura mater, the two remaining layers are hardly noticeable.

The middle layer is a spongy structure named the **arachnoid** (Latin for "spiderlike") because of its spindly appendages (shown in Figure 3.23), the **arachnoid trabeculae,** which extend down from it to the next layer. Finally, the **pia mater** (Latin for "soft mother") adheres closely to the brain surface, following every sulcus and convolution.

CEREBROSPINAL FLUID

By themselves, the meninges do not provide enough support and cushioning; in addition, the CNS literally floats in cerebrospinal fluid (CSF), so most of its weight is supported by fluid displacement. CSF, which is produced in the **choroid plexus** (a vascular enlargement of the pia mater), flows slowly along a circuitous route through hollow **ventricles** (Figure 3.24 traces the route), from the curving lateral ventricles to the third and then the fourth ventricles along the midline, where more CSF is produced. The fourth ventricle is a continuation of the narrow central canal of the spinal cord, the evolutionary origin of the entire ventricle system. From the fourth ventricle, the CSF flows into the **cisterna magna** (Latin for "big tank"), and from there it spreads to the subarachnoid space among the arachnoid trabeculae, where it accumulates in the superior sagittal sinus along the top of the midline; it eventually drains back into the venous system. The superior sagittal sinus (shown in Figure 3.25) poses a technical problem for the split-brain operation; the dura incision for

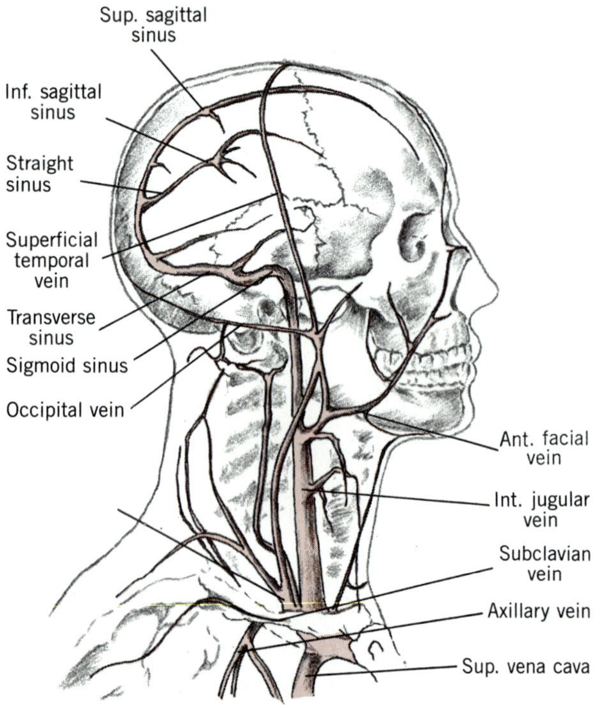

Figure 3.25 *Cerebral circulation. Location of the superior sagittal sinus and associated structures. The sinus is irregular in cross section, rather than round, as are most blood vessels.*

this operation must be off the midline to avoid damaging the sinus.

The total volume of the CSF is about 125 ml in humans, and half of it is replaced every 3 hr. Production of the fluid is continuous, regardless of the resulting pressure, and there is little feedback in the production process. Thus, if the flow of CSF is obstructed, **hydrocephalus** (Greek for "water head") results; that is, intracranial pressure increases, blocking the flow of the fluid in the cranial blood vessels, with serious consequences. In infants, whose skulls are still flexible, hydrocephalus can result in an enlarged, bulging head and permanent brain damage. Surgeons correct the condition by implanting a shunting tube to divert the flow.

THE BLOOD VESSELS

The brain lives always on the edge of metabolic disaster. Although its energy requirements are the highest of any organ, it stores no energy. In contrast with muscles, which can sharply reduce their energy requirements or use **anaerobic** (without oxygen) metabolism if necessary, neurons burn only glucose and, to a lesser extent, a few fatty acids in a high-energy oxidative biochemical cycle.

Glucose and oxygen, available only from the blood, are needed in such large quantities that a continuous blood supply is essential; a 1-sec interruption of blood flow results in a depletion of most of the available oxygen, and a 6-sec interruption causes unconsciousness. Permanent damage follows after only a few minutes.

To assure continuous brain function despite the brain's exacting metabolic requirements, the CNS blood supply is continuous, generous, and redundant. Throughout the body, the blood supply is governed by sphincter and dilator muscles in the smaller arteries and arterioles; these muscles are controlled by the sympathetic and parasympathetic subsystems. In the brain, the vessels regulate blood flow in response to the brain's needs rather than to the overall requirements of the organism. The brain always has first priority. Local increases in carbon dioxide concentration, caused by increases in metabolism, induce dilation of a region's vessels. In addition, specific neuronal pathways, transmitters, and neural networks aid in regulating blood flow and metabolism. Their actions can be either local—on restricted brain regions—or global (Reis, 1986).

Metabolic requirements remain high because the neurons are constantly active—both in waking and in sleep, and whether or not the organism is engaged in intense mental activity. Thus even the dynamics of the blood supply demonstrate that the brain is not a passive receptacle awaiting sensory inputs but instead is constantly active.

Blood reaches the brain through two major pairs of arteries: the vertebral arteries caudally and the internal carotid arteries rostrally. These arteries feed into the circle of Willis at the base of the brain (shown in Figure 3.26), a peculiar structure in the usually linear plan of the circulatory system. The arterial circle reduces the vulnerability of the system to local blockage; a stroke or other obstruction anywhere "upstream" of the circle of Willis has little effect on cerebral blood flow because blood continues to reach the brain by alternate

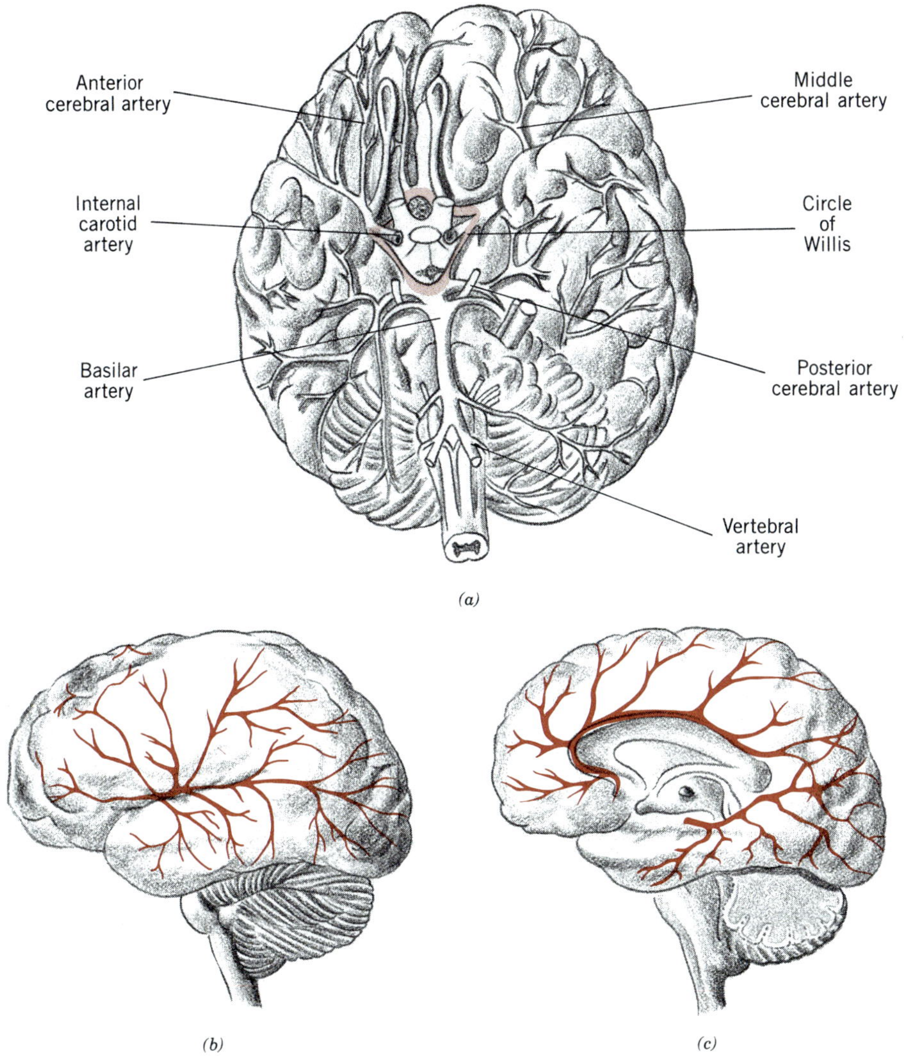

Figure 3.26 *The blood supply of the brain.* (a) *From underneath, the main arteries supplying the brain are visible.* (b) *Lateral and* (c) *medial views show the fields supplied by the posterior, middle, and anterior cerebral arteries.*

paths. Beyond this point, however, there is less redundancy of blood supply, and blockages (strokes) lead to brain damage if maintained long enough (see Chapter 16).

THE BLOOD-BRAIN BARRIER

The capillaries of the cerebrovascular system do not come into direct contact with the neurons but instead are surrounded by astrocytes—glial cells that let some substances, such as oxygen and glucose, pass from the blood to the brain while preventing many larger molecules, such as hormones and enzymes, from coming in contact with the neurons. The capillary walls and the astrocytes together constitute the blood-brain barrier, really more a selective filter than a barrier (see Figure 2.2).

The filtering action is important in maintaining the selectivity of the brain to many drugs. The drug curare, for instance, paralyzes the muscles by blocking the ACh synapses of the neuromuscular junction, but it has no effect on central ACh synapses because it does not cross the blood-brain barrier. For this reason curare and its synthetic analog, d-turbocurarin, are often used in neurophysiological research to paralyze the muscles without affecting brain function.

Just as important as the blood-brain barrier is the lack of a barrier under some conditions. The reactions of children and traumatically injured patients to drugs are often different from those of normal persons because their blood-brain barrier is less effective.

The brain's physical environment reveals an extreme example of homeostatis—a stable internal environment maintained through powerful feedback mechanisms. Against the background of physical-chemical stability is the constant play of electrochemical potentials in the axons and dendrites, as well as changes in small concentrations of hormones. The subtle changes represent the truly important environment of the brain, the information environment. The coding and processing of these potentials are the subject of the next section of the book.

CHAPTER SUMMARY

1. The brain is the most complex structure in the human body. Studying its hundred billion cells and quadrillion synaptic contacts requires special techniques. One of these techniques is staining brain sections to bring out structures such as cell bodies, fibers, and degenerating tracts. Another is making lesions and biochemical interventions to decipher brain structure. New techniques, including autoradiography (tracing radioactively labeled parts of the brain), are greatly expanding our understanding of both the physical and the biochemical design of the central nervous system. Electron microscopy, with its almost molecule-by-molecule resolution, has greatly multiplied the amount of information available about microstructure.

2. The human brain can be divided along three dimensions—up-down, front-back, and left-right. Each dimension defines a different aspect of brain function. The primary dimension, up-down, separates the cerebral cortex of the forebrain from all subcortical structures. The top three-quarters of the brain, the cortex and its associated fiber tracts, is important in perceptual processes, memory, language, and motor control. Subcortical areas specialize in vegetative functions such as control of digestion, breathing, and temperature. They also coordinate muscle action, arousal, and emotional responses. The other two dimensions subdivide the cerebral cortex. The front-back dimension, along the central sulcus, separates the posterior sensory cortex, which is concerned with the outside world, from the anterior motor and frontal areas. The latter areas are concerned more with the inside world of the organism.

3. The left-right distinction is more quantitative than qualitative. It was probably the last to evolve. Usually, the left areas emphasize sequential processing, such as language, and the right areas specialize in parallel processes, such as spatial representation.

4. The oldest part of the central nervous system, the spinal cord is a prototype for later additions. With a core of gray matter surrounded by fiber tracts, its reflexes handle much of the lower-level coordination of muscles. It also begins the processing for some branches of the somatosensory system.

5. The autonomic subsystems, sympathetic and parasympathetic, are motor systems associated with the spinal cord. The sympathetic system handles visceral responses related to preparation for action; the parasympathetic system restores and balances bodily energy. Each has a unique anatomical design and biochemistry.

6. The hindbrain is organized like the other brain regions, with a reticular core of intermingled cell bodies and fibers, a group of surrounding brain-stem nuclei, and a dorsal cortex of neurons organized in a continuous sheet. The cortex belongs to the cerebellum, a center for motor coordination, which is fine-grained in both space and time. Its highly regular and uniform structure receives information from all over the brain. It re-

fines and modulates, but cannot initiate, motor activity.

7. The smallest of the three classical brain divisions is the midbrain. It contains intermediate processing areas for visual, vestibular, and auditory information as well as oculomotor centers and other motor stations. Its cortically organized areas are the superior and inferior colliculi. The superior colliculus is visual, and the inferior is auditory.

8. The forebrain dominates the human central nervous system. Its subcortical centers perform diverse functions. The thalamus filters information going to and from the cortex. The hypothalamus coordinates hunger, thirst, emotional behavior, and temperature with both neuronal and endocrine modes of action. The limbic system is made up of a group of nuclei and cortically organized areas that are involved in the coordination of emotional responses, sexual behavior, and related functions. The basal ganglia control posture and gross motor activities in close coordination with the cerebral cortex.

9. The cerebral cortex has a simple anatomical organization, with just three basic cell types. The older cortex (archicortex) has three layers; the neocortex contains six layers, with variations among specialized cortical areas. Cortical function is organized in columns extending through the six layers. Information enters the cortex, passes through only a few synaptic layers, and exits again on corticocortical fibers to repeat the cycle. Most fibers that leave the cortex enter it again without synapsing. The corpus callosum, the largest of these tracts, connects the two hemispheres.

10. The brain is the most thoroughly protected organ in the body, both physically and biochemically. It is protected mechanically and floats in cerebrospinal fluid. It remains in constant metabolic peril, with large energy requirements and few reserves. But it has first priority on the oxygen and nutrients carried in the blood.

KEY TERMS

Histological techniques
Invasive techniques
Perfuse
Formalin
Fixation (denaturing)
Microtome
Golgi stain
Neuropil
Cautery
Stereotaxic
Horsley-Clarke system
Anterograde degeneration
Proximal
Retrograde degeneration
Autoradiography
Radioactive tracer
Histofluorescence
Transmission electron microscope
Scanning electron microscope
Monopolar
Bipolar
Extracellular
Intracellular
Vegetative functions
Encephalization
Central sulcus
Topographic map
Corpus callosum
Epileptic focus
Mirror focus
Ontogeny
Ectoderm
Neural tube
Caudally
Rostrally
Decussate
Bell and Magendie's law
Dorsal root ganglia
Monosynaptic
Polysynaptic
Autonomic subsystems
Sphincter muscles
Sympathetic subsystem
Sympathetic ganglia
Preganglionic
Cholinergic
Parasympathetic subsystem
Brain stem

Reticular formation
Polymodal cells
Myelencephalon
Medulla oblongata
Tegmentum
Metencephalon
Pons
Peduncles
Ascending reticular activating system (ARAS)
Inferior olive
Mesencephalon
Hypothalamus
Diencephalon
Cerebellum
Cortex
Purkinje cells
Molecular layer
Purkinje layer
Granular layer
Granule cells
Parallel fibers
Basket cells
Stellate cells
Golgi cells
Climbing fibers
Mossy fibers
Superior colliculi
Inferior colliculi
Corpora quadregemina
Tectum
Extrinsic thalamic nuclei
Intrinsic thalamic nuclei
Principal cells
Intrinsic inhibitory neurons
Lateral geniculate nucleus (LGN)
Medial geniculate nucleus
Synaptic glomeruli
Endocrine glands
Exocrine glands
Homeostasis
Portal system
Anterior pituitary
Limbic system
Mammillary bodies
Hippocampus
Cingulate gyrus
Amygdala
Septum
Basal ganglia
Caudate nucleus
Globus pallidus
Putamen
Corpus striatum
Substantia nigra
Archicortex
Neocortex
Columnar organization
Pyramidal cells
Martinotti cell
Agranular frontal cortex
Extrinsic cortex
Intrinsic cortex
Association cortex
Olfactory bulbs
Allocortex
Juxtallocortex
Meninges
Dura mater
Arachnoid
Arachnoid trabeculae
Pia mater
Choroid plexus
Ventricles
Cisterna magna
Hydrocephalus
Anaerobic

SUGGESTED READINGS

Braitenberg, V. (1977). *On the texture of brains.* New York: Springer-Verlag.

This engaging little book offers a fresh look at the relationship of structure and function in the cerebral cortex and cerebellum. (Most of neuroanatomy makes very dry reading.) There is also a section on the elegant anatomy of the fly's eye.

Sperry, R. (1973). The eye and the brain. In *The Nature and Nurture of Behavior* (A Scientific American Book) (pp. 5–9). San Francisco: Freeman.

This article describes Sperry's classic work on how the optic nerve of newts and frogs regenerates after the nerve is cut and the eye is rotated. Although the article is getting old, its results are still valid, and it remains a readable introduction to this branch of experimental neuroanatomy.

Stephenson, W. K. (1980). *Concepts in neurophysiology.* New York: Wiley.

Despite its title, the second half of this book reviews the basic facts of neuroanatomy in a format rich with learning aids.

Part II

SENSORY AND MOTOR SYSTEMS

Chapter 4

SENSORY SYSTEMS: TRANSDUCTION

Sensory systems take patterns of energy from the outside world and extract information useful in guiding behavior. The information generally goes through three steps before it becomes useful. First, it is transformed by nonneural processing in peripheral organs. Second, it is transduced into graded potentials. (*Transduction* is the changing of one form of energy into another.) Finally, the signals are further processed in the neural mode. Nonneural processes and transduction will be discussed in this chapter.

In the first of the three steps, energy from the outside is filtered and modified while remaining in its original form. In the ear, for instance, vibrations from the air are channeled to the eardrum, conducted through a series of bones, and transferred to a fluid while remaining in the vibrational mode. The eye focuses light with the cornea and lens, and it adjusts the intensity of the light with the pupil, before light energy is transduced into graded potentials.

Nonneural processes are closely related to the sensory receptor cells. They feed the cells energy with intensities and forms appropriate to cell function while protecting the cells from overload and from direct exposure to the outside of the body. These processes organize the energy entering a sensory system so the receptor cells encounter useful patterns of information. The patterns are more important than the energy itself; most sensory systems cannot respond to unchanging distributions of energy. This is why photographers need light meters, for instance; the human visual system can tell its owner only the pattern of light, not the amount.

After peripheral filtering, energy is transduced from its original form into specialized graded potentials, called **generator potentials.** Transduction occurs in highly specialized and sensitive receptor cells, always with several different types of receptors for each sense. A beginning of neural stimulus processing occurs at the transduction stage.

The third stage of processing is the neural mode, where the neuron's mechanisms (see Chapter 2) operate on the incoming information. In some systems, the receptor cells themselves convert generator potentials into action potentials for transmission to the CNS; in others, some processing takes place in the graded potential mode before signals are transmitted centrally. Eventually, the sensory information, transformed in the CNS, is interpreted through comparison with information stored in one of several forms of memory; then it may be used as a basis for action. This is the stage of perception, where we become aware of the information.

The first and second steps in information reception are quite different in each sense modality because of differences in the nature of the stimuli. Sound vibrations in air, for instance, require very different peripheral processing than do the chemicals of taste. But the third process, neural sensory processing, is surprisingly similar in all modalities. Each sensory system begins with a pattern of generator potentials varying in space and time and extracts from the pattern usable information about the world.

Evolution of Sensory Systems

Chemical and mechanical senses are the oldest senses phylogenetically; even the most primitive animals have them. The skin senses have the simplest peripheral anatomy, and they will be reviewed first. Vision was the next major sense to evolve, appearing independently in many groups of animals in different forms. The eyes of the squid and the octopus, for instance, appear superficially similar to those of vertebrates, but they evolved independently and differ in many ways. Hearing was the last of the human senses to evolve, originating from a system that detected patterns of water pressure in fish. Auditory receptors are disguised **mechanoreceptors,** picking up the mechanical vibrations of sound. The vestibular system is closely linked to the auditory system in anatomy and evolution and will be reviewed with it.

THE SOMATOSENSORY SYSTEM

The largest organ of the body, the skin, is richly endowed with a variety of nerve endings, which make up the **somatosensory** (body sense) **system.** The nerve endings respond to at least three kinds of stimuli: pressure (deformation of the skin), temperature, and tissue damage (resulting in the sensation of pain). Innervation (the pattern of nerve endings) is somewhat different in the **hairy skin,** which covers most of the body, and the **glabrous skin,** the especially sensitive hairless skin of such regions as the fingers, palms, and soles of the feet. Glabrous skin has a far denser innervation than hairy skin and a correspondingly finer discrimination ability. It illustrates a principle that applies to all senses: small parts of sensory surfaces are very densely innervated—at the expense of other, less densely innervated areas.

Spatial resolution is traditionally measured by a subject's reaction to the skin being touched by two sharp needle points simultaneously. The points are moved closer together in successive trials until the subject cannot distinguish the pair of points from a single point. The resulting two-point threshold varies from about a millimeter on the fingertips to several centimeters on the back. This is a static measure, however. Resolution is much better if the experimenter slides the points across the skin (Bach-y-Rita, 1972).

In some ways, hairy skin is more sensitive than glabrous skin. A fly walking on the hand, for instance, cannot be felt until it wanders into the forest of hairy skin. There the movement of hairs excites free nerve endings surrounding the base of each hair. These hairs do not keep the body warm or protect against injury, as the hairs on the head or the fur on animals does. They have only one function—to increase the sensitivity of the somatosensory system.

RECEPTOR ORGANS

Anatomically, there are two broad classes of skin receptors: free nerve endings and encapsulated end organs (Cauna, 1968). **Free nerve endings**—neural processes extending into the skin—are perhaps the simplest receptors in the body, though they are seldom completely free. In most endings a Schwann cell sheath such as the one in Figure 4.1 extends to the very tip of the sensory fiber (Cauna, 1968). The mechanism of transduction in these fibers is unknown, but it may relate to the direct opening of channels by a mechanical stretching of the membrane. The result is an inflow of Na^+ ions and the creation of a generator potential much like the graded potentials of CNS neurons. Free nerve endings are everywhere in the skin—even in the cornea of the eye. You are looking through some of them right now.

Encapsulated end organs are specialized structures associated with somatosensory nerve endings. They come in a wide variety of forms and have been divided into four main groups: Pacinian corpuscles, Meissner's corpuscles, Krause end bulbs, and Merkel's disks (Sinclair, 1967).

Pacinian corpuscles, shown in Figure 4.2, are by far the largest of the encapsulated endings, ranging from 0.5 to 4.5 mm long and 1 to 2 mm wide. They consist of a nerve ending surrounded by connective tissue layered like an onion. Embedded in glabrous skin, they are especially abundant in the hands and feet. They also serve the **kinesthetic sense** (the sense of body position) in joints, ligaments, and the walls of blood vessels. The large capsule of the Pacinian corpuscle protects the nerve ending from steady mechanical pressure, leaving it sensitive only to changes in pressure (Loewenstein & Mendelson, 1965), as revealed by the experiment in Figure 4.3.

Meissner's corpuscles, also found on hairless skin (see Figure 4.2), are smaller than Pacinian corpuscles, about 40 to 50 mm long. Each consists of one to five nerve fibers coiled in the corpuscular ending.

Krause end bulbs (see Figure 4.2) are smaller yet, consisting simply of unmyelinated fiber endings tangled like balls of yarn. They are

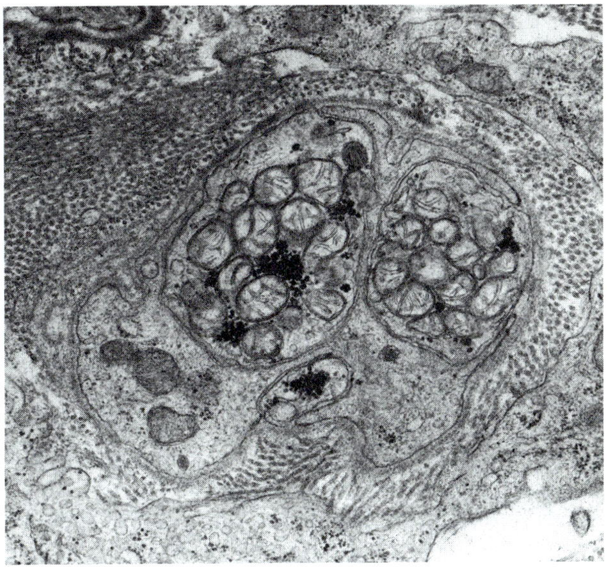

Figure 4.1 *A cross section electron micrograph of free nerve endings in the skin. The fibers run in notches in a Schwann cell, like other peripheral unmyelinated fibers, and are further protected by cells that surround the Schwann cell.*

common at junctions between mucous membranes and skin, such as the edges of the lips, eyelids, clitoris, and penis. Krause end bulbs may be analogs to the free nerve endings that surround hair follicles in hairy skin (Winkelmann, 1960). Without a hair to surround, the ending becomes just a tangle of fibers.

Merkel's disks (see Figure 4.2) consist of single flattened epithelial (skin) cells located near the terminal branches of nerve fibers called Merkel cells. Like Meissner's corpuscles, they are located in **papillae**—small bumps in the **dermis** (the inner layer of the skin) that extend into the **epidermis** (the outer layer of the skin). Studies combining electrophysiology and anatomy have established that Merkel cells are slowly adapting mechanoreceptors. Transduction is probably aided by tiny, fingerlike projections only 2 to 3 μm long fitting into invaginations (crevices) in the Merkel's disks (Iggo & Andres, 1982). A recently discovered structure, the Iggo corpuscle (Iggo & Muir, 1969), is a cluster of about 50 Merkel's disks under a dome of epidermis.

In all of these structures the molecular mechanism of transduction is unknown. There is some

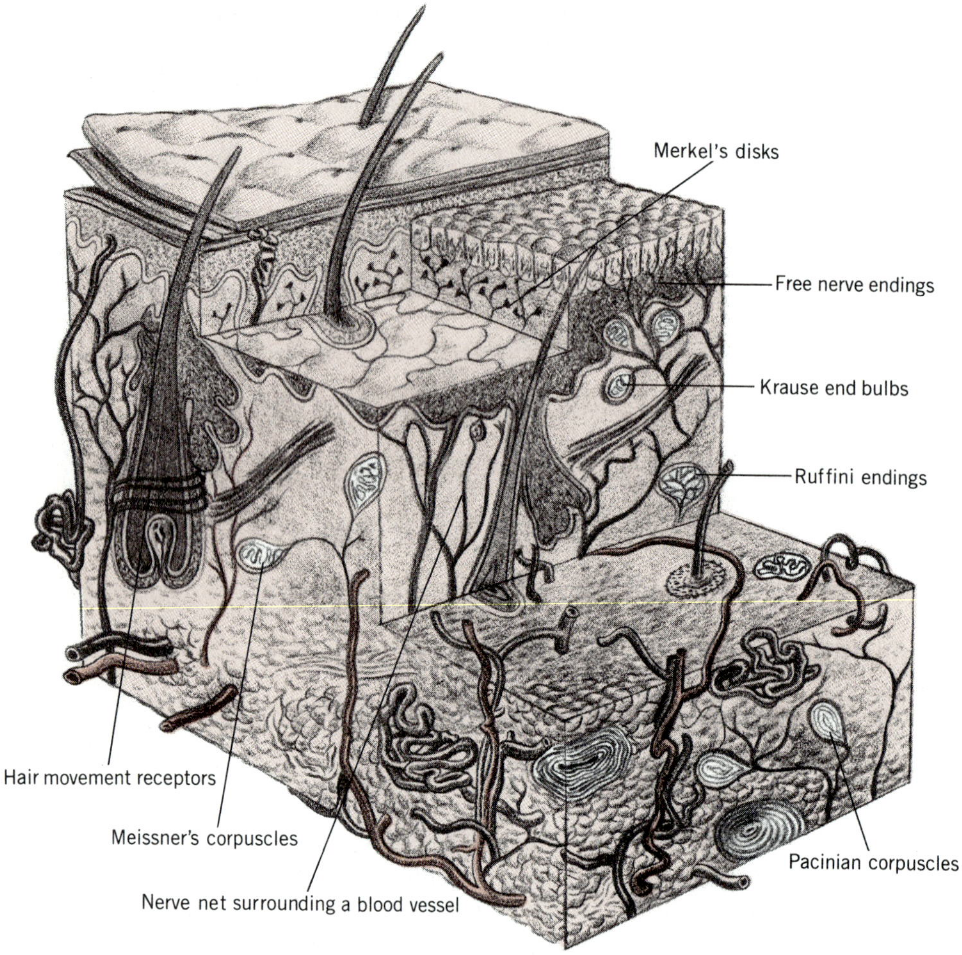

Figure 4.2 Somatosensory receptors in typical human hairy skin. The free nerve endings and Merkel's disks reach further toward the surface than the other endings; the relatively large Pacinian corpuscles are the deepest-lying structures.

recent evidence, though, that the skin itself may play a part in the transduction process, for both heat and mechanical stimulation generate electrical currents in the skin (Athenstaedt, Claussen & Schaper, 1982). The mechanical effect is called the **piezoelectric effect;** it is the same physial effect that transduces motion into electrical signals in a phonograph needle. The energy for the electrical current comes from the stimulus itself, not from biological sources. The current presumably is generated by the bending or heating of large protein molecules in the epidermis.

DISTRIBUTION OF RECEPTORS

If a patch of skin is divided into 1 mm squares and each square is tested for heat, cold, pressure, and pain, a **punctate pattern** (a distribution of points) emerges; not all squares are sensitive to all stimuli. Electrical stimulation of the skin yields the same sensations at the same points.

If we know the anatomical distribution of the varieties of free and encapsulated endings, along with the various kinds of cutaneous sensations, it should be a simple matter for us to match the receptors with the sensations. It isn't. Touch and pressure seem to be associated with the encapsulated endings, and temperature and pain are transmitted by the free endings. But even these generalizations are not always true. The cornea of the eye, for instance, has all four kinds of sensation with only free nerve endings.

Further complicating matters is the fact that many fibers respond to several types of stimuli.

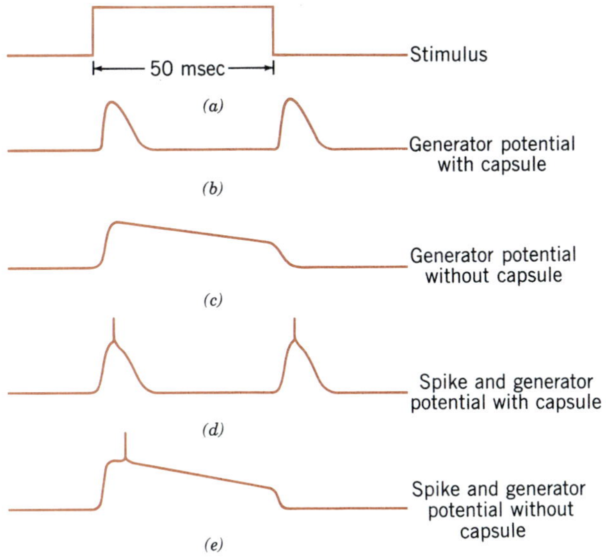

Figure 4.3 *The effect of removing a Pacinian corpuscle's outer layers on the generator potential. With the capsule removed, the ending is sensitive to steady pressure; in the normal state, with the capsule intact, it responds only to changes in pressure.* (a) *Mechanical stimulus.* (b) *and* (c) *A toxin prevents the generation of action potentials.* (d) *and* (e) *Normal conditions.*

Most mechanoreceptors are also temperature-sensitive (Sinclair, 1967), so we can decipher information about a single sensory stimulus only by looking at a group of fibers. Temperature receptors, for instance, code several kinds of sensations. Some of these receptors respond not to an absolute temperature but to the rate of warming; others respond to the rate of cooling (Hensel, 1968).

An even more serious complication is the instability of the punctate map of sensations on the skin. The points sensitive to heat, cold, pressure, and pain can be marked on the skin with ink. When they are retested the next day, however, some of the points are in different locations. These observations have caused some authorities to doubt that specific end organs can be linked with specific sensations (Uttal, 1973). There are other possible explanations, although there is no direct evidence for any of them. One possibility is that not all of the receptors are sampled by the brain at any one time. Another is that the receptors are constantly migrating in the skin because of the continual dying and replacement of the skin's epithelial cells. A verifiable explanation for the wandering map, though, remains unknown.

OLFACTION

The chemical senses—smell and taste—are also ancient in evolutionary development. Like the somatosensory system, they have a relatively simple anatomy. Not much peripheral apparatus stands between the outside world and the receptors. Olfaction is the more difficult chemical sense to study, and correspondingly less is known about it.

Olfaction developed with fish early in vertebrate evolution. Though it is poorly developed in reptiles and birds, its elaboration in early mammals led to the dominance of the forebrain. The sense of smell plays a more important role in primitive mammals than it does in primates; but it is still important for sensing food, and it may have less well understood roles in functions such as sexual receptivity.

ANATOMY OF THE OLFACTORY SYSTEM

The 50 million or so olfactory receptors are located in a small patch at the top of the nasal cavity. They occupy an area of about 2.5 cm^2 in each nostril. Each receptor is equipped with 6 to 12 tiny fingers called **cilia**—small extensions of the cell body into the nasal cavity. Figure 4.4 shows how the cilia increase the total sensory surface. The surface is 600 cm^2 in humans, an area about equal to two pages in this book.

Like the somatosensory receptor cells, the olfactory receptor cells have axons projecting directly into the CNS. The axons are among the thinnest in the body, about 0.2 μm in diameter, and therefore they conduct impulses very slowly. They do not have to carry information far, however, for the olfactory bulb of the forebrain lies directly above the receptors on the upper side of the **cribriform plate**—a thin shelf of bone (see Figure 4.5). The axons travel in small bundles through pores in the bone, never forming themselves into a single nerve tract.

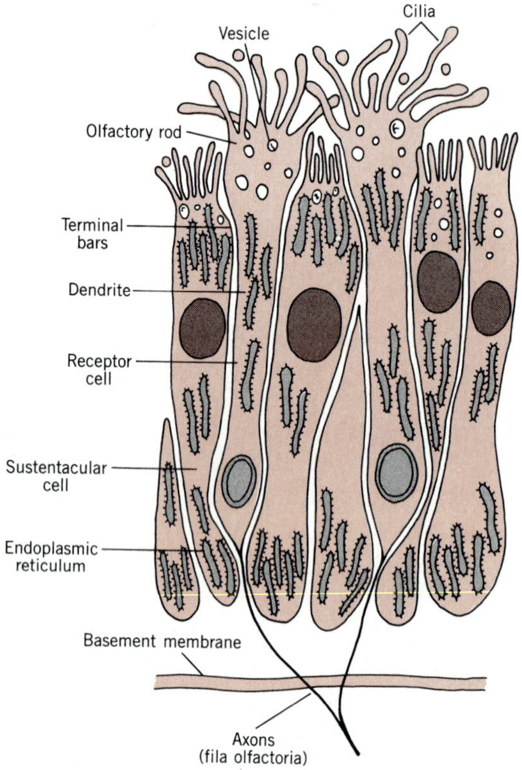

Figure 4.4 *Olfactory mucosa of a rabbit, reconstructed from electron microscope studies. The cilia on the receptors have the same basic architecture as the cilia that bacteria use for locomotion (see Figure 4.11).*

Olfactory receptors are the only neurons entering the CNS to be replaced on a regular basis throughout life. New receptors develop from **stem cells** (embryonic neurons that guide the development of other neurons) in the olfactory mucosa (see Figure 4.5), and their axons somehow find their way into the proper locations in the olfactory bulb. The process accelerates after chemical or physical injury. If the olfactory bulb is ablated (surgically removed), the persistent axons make their way right into the neocortex to form functional, if abnormal, connections (Wright & Harding, 1982).

THE PROCESS OF RECEPTION

Olfaction begins, of course, with the act of inhaling through the nose. Air is carried up to the olfactory region past the turbinate bones of Figure 4.5, which create turbulence if the air flow is from a quick sniff rather than a slow inhalation. The turbulence helps carry odorous molecules to the olfactory region. Molecules carried in the air must then be adsorbed and dissolved in the thin mucous layer over the receptors before transduction begins.

The transduction process itself is a complete mystery. In fact, much of what we know about olfactory transduction comes not from mammals but from insects. The male silkworm moth has a compelling advantage for work on chemoreception (the detection of chemicals); it can "smell" only one thing—the attractant chemical produced by the female silkworm moth. But this it does extremely well; a receptor cell can respond to a single molecule of attractant. In these admittedly specialized receptors, the attractant molecule opens membrane channels in much the same way that neurotransmitters open postsynaptic channels (Kaissling et al., 1985; Kaissling, 1986). Specialized proteins in the membrane open sodium channels when they combine with the attractant.

Several theories have been advanced to explain the more complex olfaction of mammals, but none can explain all of the data. Perhaps a combination of the existing theories will be more successful than any single one, thereby extending the idea that most sensory systems use several strategies to encode sensory signals.

The Stereochemical Theory

One idea that has found some support is the **stereochemical theory.** Amoore (1964) noted that most smells can be described by one of seven terms: camphoraceous, musky, floral, minty, ethereal, (smelling like ether), pungent, or putrid. Examining the molecules with these characteristic odors, he found that most tended to have distinctive shapes (pungent and putrid had characteristic electrical charges instead). Amoore's findings led to the idea of seven detector sites, with shapes or charges matching those of the target molecules in a microscopic lock-and-key arrangement. The evidence supporting this theory is mixed, however. Although many molecules have just the odors Amoore would have predicted, some violate the shape rules. Molecules with similar shapes, for instance, sometimes have quite different odors.

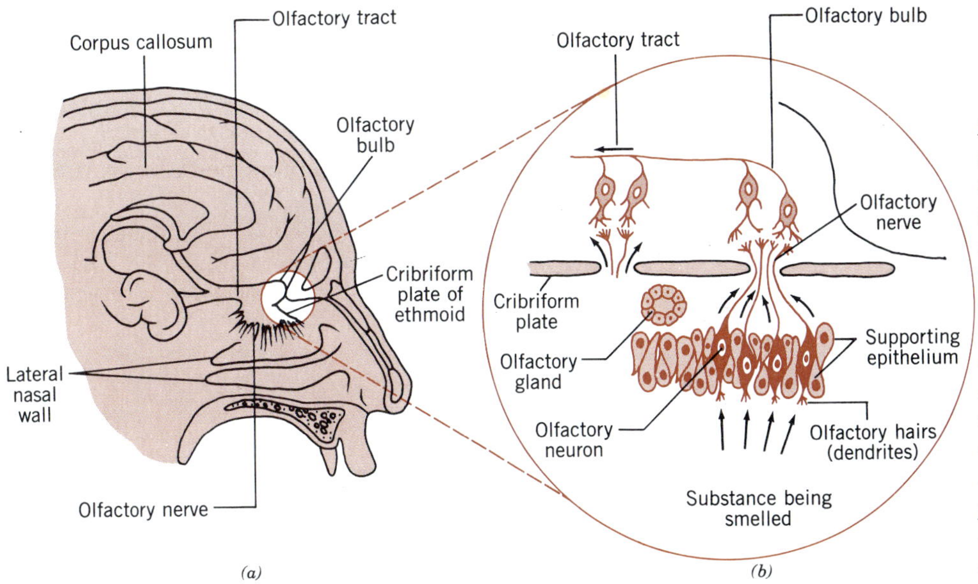

***Figure 4.5** Anatomy of the peripheral olfactory system.* (a) *The turbinate bones extend from the lateral nasal wall. The nasal passages are insensitive to olfactory stimuli except for the small patch of membrane under the olfactory bulb.* (b) *Schematic view of olfactory receptor axons passing through the cribriform plate (a part of the brain case). Sizes of cell bodies are exaggerated.*

The Chromatographic Theory

As newer theory of transduction draws an analogy between olfaction and the operation of a **gas chromatograph**—a device for detecting chemicals in a gas. In gas chromatography a sample of a gas is introduced at one end of a long tube filled with a substance that absorbs or adsorbs various chemicals. Some substances are absorbed or adsorbed right away; others travel a longer distance. After being exposed to the gas sample, the absorbing or adsorbing substance is sliced into sections, and each section is analyzed chemically. The distance traveled indicates the identity of the material.

What is the evidence that the olfactory system might operate in this way? In the frog it is possible to record electrical responses from electrodes placed in lateral branches (LB) of the olfactory nerve innervating part of the olfactory surface, and from medial branches (MB) of the olfactory nerve innervating a different part. The size of the electrical response to odor in each branch is a measure of the number of action potentials excited by that odor. Experimentally, odors can be specified quite well by their characteristic LB/MB ratios (Mozell, 1967, 1970).

Differences in the LB/MB ratios might mean either that chromatography is at work or that different parts of the olfactory mucosa have different sensitivities to specific odorants. The two alternatives were differentiated in a clever experiment: the air flow across the mucosa was reversed. If differing sensitivity is responsible for the ratios, reversing the air flow should not change anything. But if odors are determined by the distance a substance travels before being adsorbed, reversing the air flow should reverse the ratios. In fact, reversing the air flow reversed the LB/MB ratios for 16 substances under a variety of conditions; it also reversed the relative response latencies in the two branches. Similar results are found when the same experiment is done in a commercial gas chromatograph.

Although the chromatographic theory may not explain all of the subtleties of olfaction, it may at least take part in the explanation, along with such other theories as the stereochemical theory. Until the details of olfactory transduction are explained, it will be impossible to determine which theory (or theories) captures the nature of the receptors in this mysterious sense.

GUSTATION

Taste, or **gustation,** has a much simpler basis than olfaction. There are only four basic tastes: sweet, sour, salty, and bitter. Each of the four has a different pattern of receptors on the tongue, though

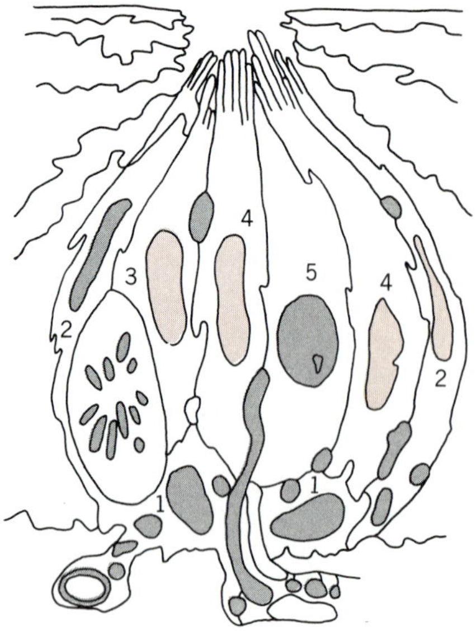

Figure 4.6 *Reconstruction of a taste bud from electron micrographs. Processes of secondary cells enter the bud from the bottom of the figure. Again, the receptors are ciliated, with an architecture similar to that of olfactory receptors.*

(a)

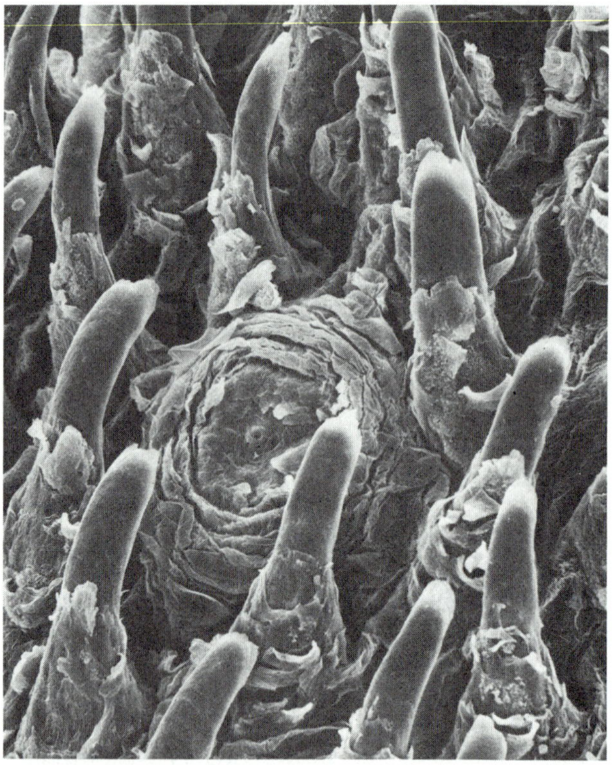

(b)

Figure 4.7 *Scanning electron micrographs of papillae on the tongue.* (a) *Dog's tongue.* (b) *Rat's tongue.*

most of the tongue is sensitive in some degree to all stimuli.

ANATOMY OF THE MOUTH

Taste buds (clusters of taste receptors) are found throughout the mouth but are concentrated on the tongue. Each looks literally like a bud opening into a specialized pore or channel on the surface of the tongue (see Figure 4.6). Many of the taste buds are organized in papillae (visible bumps on the surface of the tongue). Figure 4.7 shows some of the variety in patterns of papillae. Taste receptors are exposed to a hostile environment; they function for only about 10 days before disintegrating and being reabsorbed by the body. The short life of these receptors was determined by tagging them with a radioactive material selectively absorbed by dividing cells (Beidler, 1963). All of the radioactivity disappeared in a few days. The taste bud is in a constant state of flux, with new receptors forming on its edges and migrating toward the center as they age.

The short life of taste receptors poses a problem: how do the receptors transmit their signals centrally? It is impractical for a cell to grow a new axon in such a short time. The problem is solved with a new anatomical arrangement. A fiber from a CNS cell extends out to synapse with the receptor.

Somehow the fiber is passed along from cell to cell as older cells degenerate. The gustatory receptor is more specialized than the other receptors studied so far, for it operates solely in the graded potential mode and does not transmit its signals to the CNS. This plan is followed for taste and for vision and audition (which will be examined shortly).

Gustation uses far fewer fibers than olfaction, but the information-carrying capacity of each fiber is somewhat greater because its diameter is larger: 1 to 6 μm. A single fiber may branch to several receptors, and a receptor may supply several fibers.

THE TRANSDUCTION PROCESS IN GUSTATION

Each taste bud has many receptors, but the whole bud is most sensitive to only one of the four taste sensations. G. von Békésy (1964, 1966) showed this in some ingenious experiments. In one experiment he stimulated the tongue electrically with smaller and smaller electrodes. Large electrodes gave mixed taste sensations, but there was only one type of sensation for the smallest areas of stimulation (0.1 mm in diameter). In a second experiment Békésy sucked a papilla directly into a tiny glass tube and stimulated it with a drop of solution. Again the papilla responded with only one type of sensation.

To be tasted a substance must first be dissolved in the saliva, a step that limits taste to water-soluble molecules. (We do not taste oils, for example. The dissolved substance is then detected by unknown molecular mechanisms. The detection process may be related to the process by which postsynaptic membranes recognize specific transmitter substances. The four tastes relate to four families of chemicals.

Sourness is characteristic of acids, which implies that sour receptors are sensitive to hydrogen ions. The higher the concentration of H^+ ions (that is, the lower the pH), the sourer the taste.

Saltiness is a characteristic of chemical salts that dissociate into ions when in solution. The most common salt is, of course, table salt, NaCl, which in its ionized state (Na^+Cl^-) has one of the strongest salty flavors. Other salts of low molecular weight, such as KCl and NaBr, also taste salty, but the taste tends toward bitter as molecular weight increases. The fact that many salts share the salty taste is the basis for "salt subsititutes" used by people who must restrict their intake of Na^+ to reduce blood pressure. The salt substitutes are salts of ions other than Na^+.

The bitter and sweet tastes are more difficult to characterize chemically. Bitterness is aroused by the alkaloids—toxic plant products such as nicotine, quinine, and strychnine—and by some heavy ions. The bitter flavor seems to be nature's way of keeping us away from these harmful substances. Sweetness comes from many chemical families, including the sugars and many complex aromatic compounds with nitro groups in their molecular structure (Geldard, 1972). Many bitter and sweet chemicals have similar structures; only a minor molecular change is required for the shift from the one flavor to the other.

It would seem that the range of taste sensations is rather limited because there are only four letters in the gustatory alphabet. Indeed, much of what we think of as taste is really oflactory input while food is being chewed (see Chapter 6). The richness of taste should not be underestimated, however. By analogy, think of the richness and variety of color experiences made possible by only three kinds of color receptors.

VISION

The vertebrate visual system evolved at a time when animals had become far more complex than they were when the somatic and chemical senses were established. The visual system is more complex in two ways—the receptors are more elaborate, and there is extensive processing of light before it is transduced into graded potentials.

THE PHYSICS OF LIGHT

All objects emit electromagnetic radiation; the hotter the object, the shorter the wavelength of the radiation. Objects of near body temperature emit long-wave infrared radiation that is detected by thermal sensors in the skin. But vision takes advantage of emissions from a much hotter object—the sun. Most of the energy from the sun is radiated at wavelengths between about 380 nm and 760 nm, near the middle of the spectrum in Figure 4.8. It is

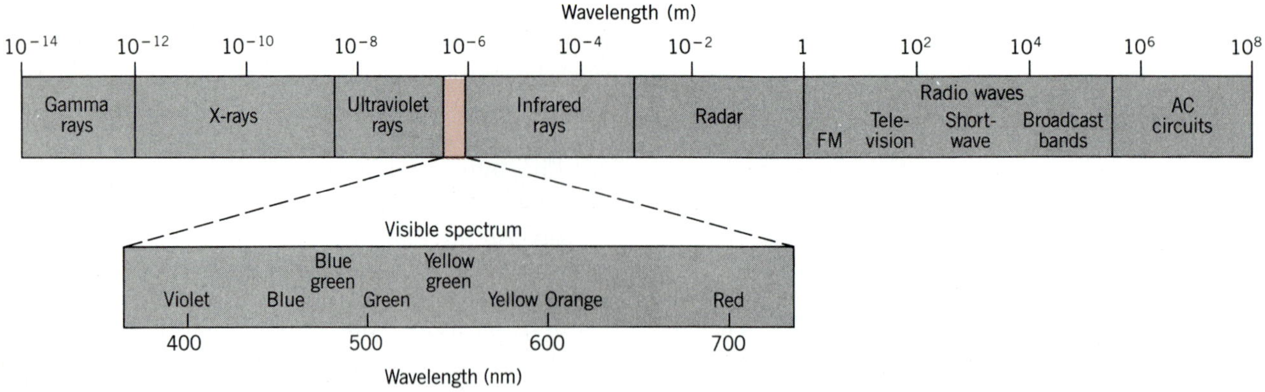

Figure 4.8 *The electromagnetic spectrum. The upper scale is logarithmic, covering a range of 22 log units. The lower scale is linear. The scales can also be thought of in terms of photons, the particles that carry the electromagnetic force. The more energy carried by a photon, the shorter the wavelength.*

here that the eye is sensitive to the radiation as light. There is also some emission at shorter wavelengths, in the ultraviolet range; many insects can see ultraviolet light, although humans cannot.

Light can also be thought of as a stream of particles, called **photons.** Photons are so small that many of their properties are more like those of waves than those of objects on a human scale. For instance, they will scatter (refract) as they pass through a very small hole.

Other sources of light stem from excitation of some materials by other forms of energy. These "cold" lights include fluorescent light and the phosphorescences of some bacteria.

The speed of light is determined by the medium through which the light is traveling. Light travels fastest in a vacuum, nearly as fast in air, and slower in water. But the speed is so great, 3×10^8 m/sec in a vacuum, that it can be considered infinite for biological purposes. If light passes from one material to another at a boundary that is not at a right angle to the path of the light, however, the change in its speed causes a change in its direction.

Light radiates from a hot object (and reflects from a cool one) in all directions, and light from all directions converges on every point in space. To extract useful information from this flood of light, an organism needs a physiological system of optics.

PHYSIOLOGICAL OPTICS

Light diverges from a luminous point; the task of physiological optics is to reconverge the light—to concentrate it on a point again when it contacts the retina. If the same thing can be done for light coming from all points, the light is focused into an image. Figure 4.9 shows the cameralike design of the eye. Light is first focused by the **cornea**—a transparent layer of living cells at the front of the eye—which does most of the necessary converging of the light.

The cornea blends into the **sclera,** the tough white outer layer of the eye. The sclera in turn is part of the dura mater protecting the CNS; thus the eye is anatomically a part of the CNS. In embryological development the retina grows out from the thalamus on a stalk that becomes the optic nerve. The sclera is not firm enough to support the eye; the eye's mechanical stiffness comes from its own internal pressure. It resembles a water balloon, which maintains its volume because of the incompressability of its contents.

The Lens

The onionlike set of protein layers that forms the lens further adjusts the focus, so objects at varying distances can be imaged sharply. But the lens must focus for objects at both long and short

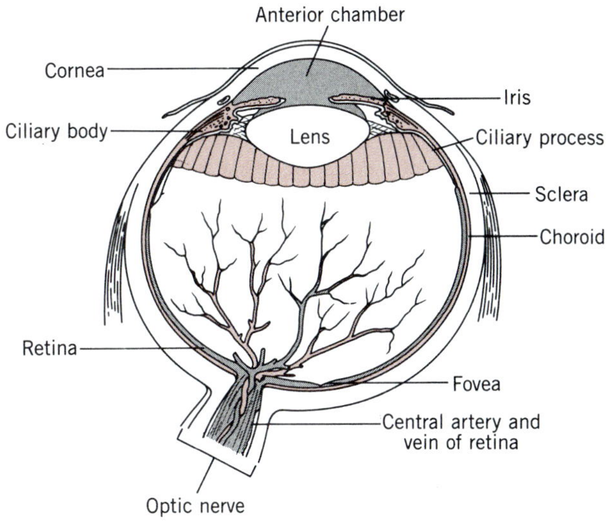

Figure 4.9 *Structure of the human eye. There are no receptors at the blind spot, where the optic nerve exits from the eye. The blind spot is not normally perceived, for two reasons. First, the blind spots of the two eyes do not coincide, so normally there are two regions of monocular vision (one for each eye). Second, the brain perceptually fills in regular textures that span the blind spot. The retina extends forward almost to the ciliary processes that function in distance accommodation.*

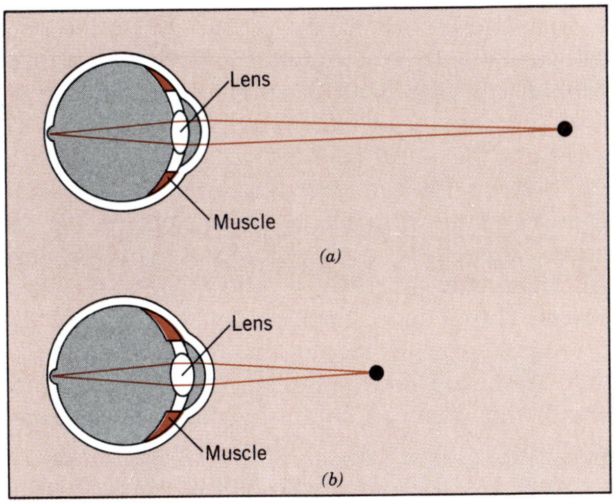

Figure 4.10 *The mechanism of focus on a visual target (accommodation) in the eye.* (a) *Far focusing.* (b) *Near focusing. There is also a longer-term accommodation; the eye grows during development if the image is blurred. This accommodation keeps the growing lens and cornea coordinated with the size of the eye and may explain why some people develop myopia (nearsightedness). In myopic people the eye is usually longer than normal.*

ranges, as illustrated in Figure 4.10. Nearby objects need a greater convergence of rays than do distant ones. The rays coming from nearby objects are diverging strongly when they reach the lens, and they must be bent more than those from distant objects (the lens must have a greater refractive power) if they are to form a sharp image on the retina. To solve the problem of varying accommodation (the varying convergence power of the eye), the lens actually changes shape; it gets flatter for distant objects and more spherical for closer objects. It is suspended on elastic fibers, the **suspensory ligaments,** which hold it taut in a flattened shape. To accommodate the eye to closer objects, a set of muscles—the **ciliary muscles**—contract to relieve tension on the suspensory ligaments. Now the lens can spring back passively into its rounded shape, refracting light more strongly.

As a person ages, the lens becomes less flexible. By the age of 50 hardly any accommodative power is left—a condition called **presbyopia** (Greek for "old eye"). At the same time, the pupil becomes slightly smaller, alleviating the condition somewhat by increasing the range of focus. The progression of presbyopia is so universal and unvarying that an optometrist can determine a person's age, give or take a few years, simply by measuring the accommodative range of the lens. In effect, one starts out in life with the optics of a Nikon and ends up with those of a box camera. Many older people wear bifocals to have two ranges of clear vision rather than one.

The Pupil

The amount of incoming light is adjusted before it is ready for transduction. Just anterior to the lens is the **iris,** a set of muscles surrounding the pupil. The fibers that are visible from outside the eye are radially arranged and enlarge the pupil when they contract. They are innervated by adrenergic neurons of the sympathetic subsystem. Another set of muscles are attached only to themselves, forming a complete loop suspended near the ends of the radial fibers. These muscles are activated by parasympathetic cholinergic neurons.

The pupil is controlled by a sophisticated neurological control system (Stark, 1968); with a feedback circuit, the control system continuously adjusts the amount of light falling on the retina. In addition, the pupil and the accommodation control systems interact. The lens is slow to react to changes in the distance of viewed objects, so the pupil helps it. If a target jumps closer, the lens accommodates and the pupil momentarily constricts. This reduces the blur on the retina while the lens completes its motion. The strategy is like that of closing the diaphragm of a camera to increase the depth of field (the range of distances over which images are in sharp focus).

The pupil helps adjust light intensity to a range where the receptors work best. But its adjustments mean that the receptors have no information about absolute light intensity. The system evolved to receive pattern information, not to detect light.

The systems of physiological optics make one more adjustment of the optical apparatus. The **extraocular** (outside the eye) **muscles** aim the camera of the eye at objects of interest. Because this system is so closely tied to higher sensory processing, it will be taken up in Chapter 6.

VISUAL RECEPTORS

In evolutionary development, visual receptors began as ciliated cells. The development of receptors from ciliated cells is a common evolutionary pattern; we have seen it already in the olfactory and gustatory systems. The visual receptors are highly evolved, and their origin would not be apparent except for the short connection between their **inner segment,** containing the cell nucleus, and their **outer segment** (closer to the outside of the eye), containing the visual pigments. Seen in cross section in Figure 4.11, these connecting links look

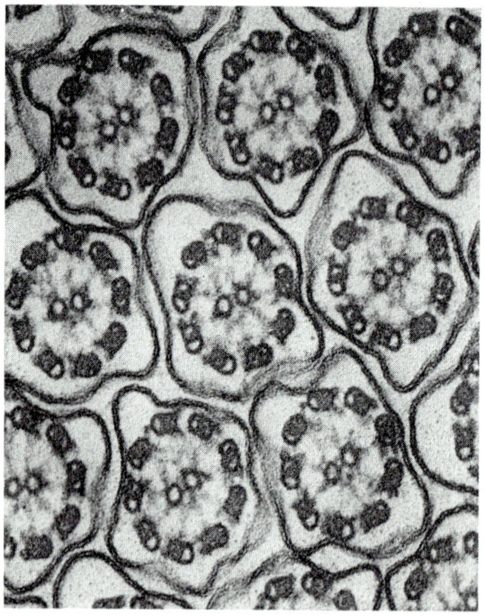

(a)

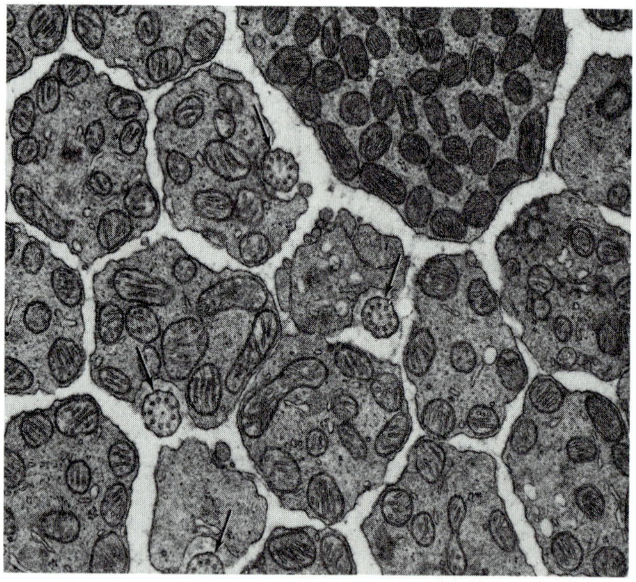

(b)

Figure 4.11 *Cilia.* (a) *Cross section of flagella (long, whiplike appendages) that give motility to* Trichonympha, *a one-celled organism that lives in the termite gut.* (b) *A cross section through the apex of the inner segments of retinal receptors, with connecting ciliary stalks (arrows). The section is cut parallel to the plane of the retina rather than across it. The receptor ciliary regions conduct graded potentials between the transducer region of the outer segment and the synaptic region of the inner segment.*

nearly identical to the cilia of other cells and even to ciliated bacteria (Cohen, 1972).

Receptors are oriented backward; their tips point away from the source of light. Their outer segments are buried in a dark **pigment epithelium,** which lines the back of the eye. This layer of cells helps provide oxygen and metabolic support for the receptors, which are among the fastest-metabolizing cells in the body. The arrangement seems peculiar because incoming light must pass through the considerable neurological machinery of the retina before entering the receptors. But this is no problem, for the retina is quite transparent.

The evolutionary advantage of the inverted retina is puzzling when viewed in humans. But the plan evolved in fish, which have much smaller eyes, though the thickness of their retinas is similar to that of ours. In these smaller eyes the retina occupies a large portion of the eye. We can speculate that an inverted retina gave an optical advantage because it placed the receptor pigments farther from the optical center of the eye.

The two kinds of receptors, **rods** and **cones,** are named for the shapes of their outer segments (see Figure 4.12). There are about 125 million rods in each retina, and they function in low-threshold night vision. There are 6.5 million cones, and they come in three varieties, each with a different visual pigment, to serve color vision. We will look at rods first because they have been more extensively studied.

Rods

The rod outer segment (so named because it is closer to the outer part of the eye) is where the transduction of light into electrical signals takes place. It is filled with a stack of several hundred disks made of cell membrane. As a result, a lot of membrane is packed into the eye; each retina contains about 1250 cm^2 of membrane in the rod outer segments alone. The area is about equal to four pages of this book. New disks are continuously formed at the base of the outer segment and migrate to the end of the rod (toward the top in Figure 4.12*b*). There they are absorbed in the pigment epithelium (Young, 1967).

Disk migration was shown with autoradiography. Rods received radioactive membrane precursors for a brief time. Later the radioactive part of the outer segment migrated outward, until the only radioactivity left was in the pigment epithelium. Thus no disk is more than a few weeks old, though the rod itself lasts a lifetime. Curiously, the

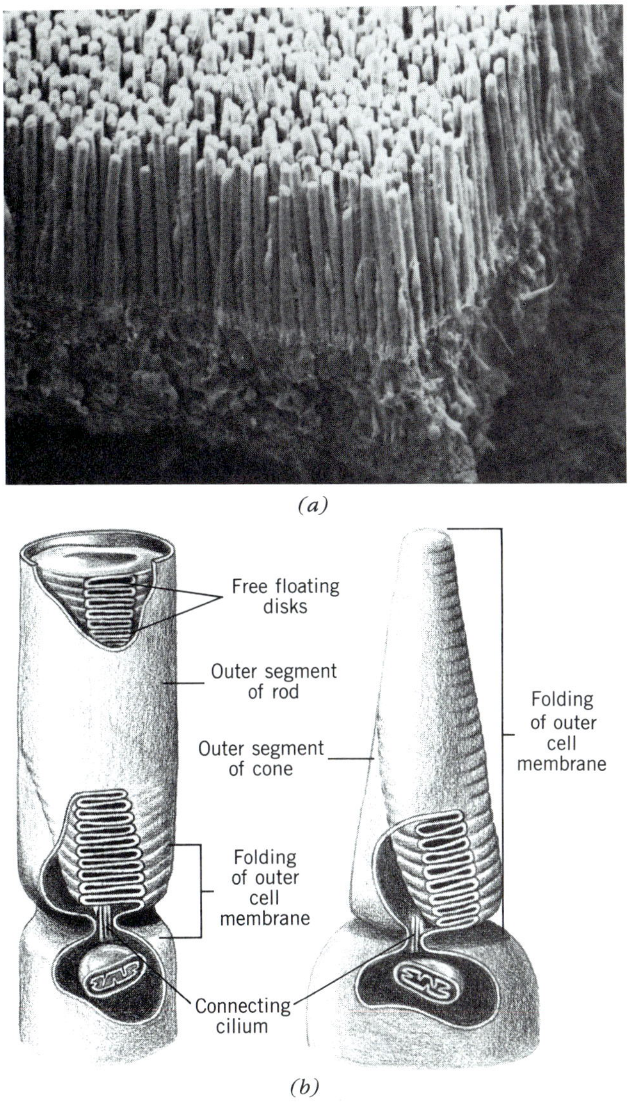

Figure 4.12 *Photoreceptor structure.* (a) *Scanning electron micrograph of the retina of a bullfrog. The cones, identifiable by their shape, are much shorter than the rods.* (b) *The membrane structures of the outer segments of rods (left) and cones (right). The receptor membranes of the rods pinch off from the outer membrane to form free-floating flattened sacs inside the structure; the cone membranes remain as invaginations of the cell's outer membrane.*

cone membrane seems to be renewed in a continuous manner, with a more uniform radioactive uptake (Young, 1969).

The visual pigment **rhodopsin,** or "visual purple," is incorporated in the structure of the rod disk membrane. Before we look at how the pigment transduces energy, we need a digression into psychophysics to determine the absolute sensitivity of the rod receptor.

The Sensitivity of Rods. How many photons are necessary for a meaningful signal to be obtained from a photoreceptor? This question was addressed in a famous study by Hecht, Schlaer, and Pirenne (1942). Their subjects saw very dim flashes after being thoroughly dark-adapted by remaining in complete darkness for 45 min. Under ideal conditions the subjects were able to detect diffuse flashes containing only a few dozen photons.

After allowing for reflection from the cornea and other surfaces of the eye, Hecht and his associates calculated that only five to eight photons reached the photoreceptors. These photons were distributed across millions of rods, so no single rod ever encountered more than one photon. The astonishing conclusion is that a single photon is enough to excite a usable synaptic message from a rod. When combined with simultaneous signals from a few other rods, this synaptic message yields a signal reliable enough to support the perception of a flash.

Methods of assessing a subject's sensitivity have progressed since Hecht's time. Sackitt (1972) asked her subjects to rate the brightness of a stimulus on a seven-point scale, from "nothing seen" to "bright." But the stimulus had one of only three values: either 0, 55 photons (dim), or 66 photons (bright). The thresholds obtained were even lower than those of Hecht, Schlaer, and Pirenne (1942); some subjects could detect a single photon of light.

We can conclude that transduction must involve an impressive biological amplification; the absorption of one photon eventually yields a synaptic transmitter release large enough that it can be distinguished from the constant release that occurs even in darkness. Also, under ideal conditions the process must be very nearly noise-free so single quantum events can be detected.

Visual Pigments in Transduction

Light is absorbed by specialized pigment molecules, so called because their ability to absorb photons gives them a color. The rhodopsin in the rods consists of two parts: **retinal,** derived from vitamin A, and **opsin,** a protein with a molecular weight of 30,000 to 40,000. Retinal contains a chain of carbon atoms that can take either of the two forms shown in Figure 4.13. All-*trans*-retinal has a straight carbon chain; 11-*cis*-retinal has a bend at the 11th carbon atom. The 11-*cis* form binds to opsin in the dark, but it is unstable. It straightens into the all-*trans* form upon absorbing a photon of light, losing its ability to bind with opsin (Wald, 1968). No chemical change occurs in the retinal; only its shape alters. The molecule breaks apart into its constituent retinal and opsin, a process called **bleaching** because the pigment suddenly loses its color. Retinal rapidly goes through several unstable intermediate forms before recombining with opsin to start the process again. In the meantime, the chemical actions of the split pigment have initiated the next steps in the transduction process. The photoreceptor is a disguised chemoreceptor, detecting the presence of breakdown products of rhodopsin.

Biochemical Events in Transduction

The result of the splitting of rhodopsin is the reduction of a **dark current.** In darkness, this current flows continuously between the depolarized outer segment and the more negative inner segment. The current flows because channels in the outer-segment membrane are open only in darkness, allowing Na^+ to flow inward. Changes in the dark current in turn change the potential in the synaptic region of the receptor, leading to the modulation of transmitter release. The dark current, then, is the visual generator potential.

There are four steps between the breakdown of visual pigment and the gating of the dark current, steps that have only recently been worked out (Stryer, 1986, 1987). The process has some remarkable similarities to the actions of metabotropic transmitters and the activation of some hormones, and it is likely that evolution has used variations on the same basic biochemical pathway for all three functions.

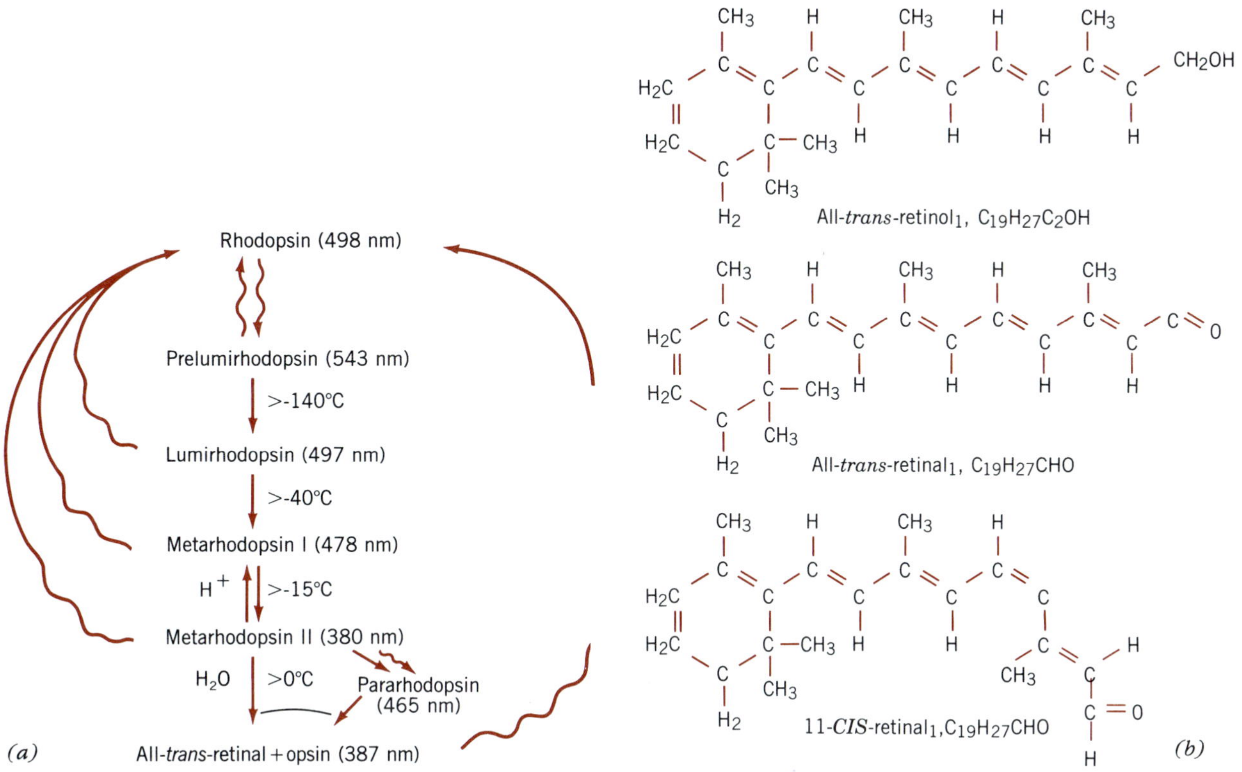

***Figure 4.13** The chemistry of rhodopsin.* (a) *The rhodopsin cycle. The numbers in parentheses are the wavelengths of peak absorption of each pigment. The temperatures are thresholds below which the next step in the reaction will not occur, so the short-lived intermediates can be preserved and studied.* (b) *Three important variants of the receptor molecule. The top molecule is a precursor in the synthesis of retinal, the middle one is the stable form of retinal, and the bottom one is the unstable form triggered to straighten upon absorbing a photon.*

First, the photon-activated rhodopsin interacts with a protein that is called transducin because of its role in visual transduction. Transducin is a three-part molecule, with its components labeled alpha, beta, and gamma. The alpha portion is normally associated with a molecule of guanosine diphosphate (GDP), an energy-transfer chemical. When transducin interacts with activated rhodopsin, its alpha portion splits off from the rest of the protein and the GDP is replaced by guanosine triphosphate (GTP), a higher-energy molecule (see Figure 4.14). Here we encounter part of the amplification process that the psychophysics demands: each rhodopsin molecule can activate about 70 transducin molecules.

In the second step of transduction the alpha transducin along with its GTP breaks down a second protein, called phosphodiesterase (PDE). This protein too has three subunits labeled alpha, beta, and gamma; the GTP-transducin complex binds to the gamma subunit, removing it from the PDE molecule. At this stage there is no amplification, for each GTP-transducin complex activates only one PDE.

The PDE, now activated by the removal of its gamma subunit, initiates a third step in transduction; it converts molecules of 3′5′ cyclic guanosine monophosphate (cyclic GMP) into 5′ GMP. This process represents a second stage of biological amplification, for every PDE molecule can convert several thousand cyclic GMP molecules into 5′ GMP.

Now the final step in transduction can occur. In darkness, cyclic GMP normally binds with the

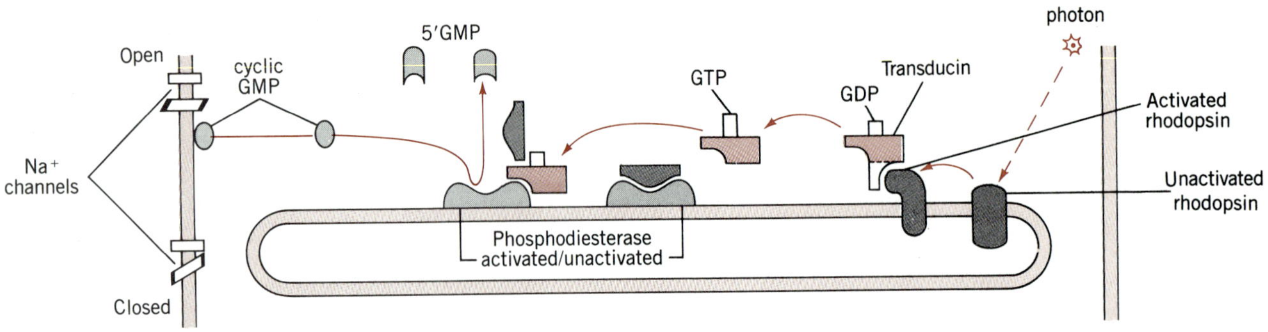

Figure 4.14 Events in transduction from photon absorption (right) to closing of Na^+ channels in a rod outer-segment membrane (left). Shapes of the proteins are schematic—the real proteins are long chains of amino acids with complex folded geometries. The membrane thickness and the size of the membrane molecules are exaggerated.

receptor membrane's Na^+ channels, holding them open to allow the dark current to flow. With so much of the receptor's cyclic GMP converted into 5′ GMP, fewer cyclic GMP molecules are available to hold open the Na^+ channels in the membrane, and many of the channels close. The dark current is reduced, and the intracellular potential at the inner segment increases, moving toward the K^+ equilibrium potential.

Light and Dark Adaptation

Until now the transduction process has been described as if the job of the photoreceptor were to detect single photons in darkness. At normal illumination levels, of course, continuous streams of photons—millions per second—arrive at the eye. As a result, most of the pigment molecules at any one time are bleached and relatively few of them are available for transduction. The result is **light adaptation**—a lowered sensitivity of the eye to light.

Pigment processes are not the only mechanisms of light adaptation. The pupil modulates light intensity before the transduction stage, and there is a neural component as well. Neural adaptation begins in the retina. (It is reviewed in Chapter 5 in the section on the peripheral retina.) A more indirect adaptation is seen in the phenomenon of interocular adaptation, where a light in one eye decreases the sensitivity to light of the other eye. Clearly, this aspect of adaptation involves afferent signals at a **binocular** level (*bi* is Greek for "two" and *ocular* is Greek for "eyes") of the visual system (the cortex).

Dark adaptation is the inverse way of defining this process. When a light-adapted eye is plunged into complete darkness, and the visual threshold is probed with small flashes, sensitivity recovers in the way shown in Figure 4.15*a*. The first part of the curve is due to the cones; the second part (after the "knee") is due to the more sensitive but more slowly adapting rods. The lowest thresholds, on the right of the graph, are reached only after a half-hour or more in complete darkness. We almost never experience them.

Along with dark adaptation comes a shift in the eye's most sensitive frequency. In a light-adapted state the eye is most sensitive to a yellowish hue (a wavelength of 550 nm), which is determined by the cone pigments (the upper curve in Figure 4.15*b*). In darkness the peak shifts to the green range (a wavelength of 510 nm) of the rod pigment (the lower curve in Figure 4.15*b*). This is the **Purkinje shift,** named after the physiologist who also discovered the cerebellar Purkinje cells. (The shift and the cells have no other relationship to each other.) The Purkinje shift explains why red fire engines are dangerous—on a dark night they can look black! The dark-adapted eye is relatively insensitive to long, red wavelengths.

Cones

Unlike rod photoreceptors, cone photoreceptors have no internal disks. Instead, their photopigments ar embedded in their extensively folded outer-segment membranes (see Figure 4.12).

The biochemistry of cones is similar to that of rods. The photopigment of cones, **iodopsin,** comes in three varieties, with the spectral sensitivities given in Figure 4.16. A single cone has only one type of pigment. Each pigment absorbs light over a broad range of wavelengths, with a peak in the red, green, or blue region of the spectrum. The spatial distribution of cones across the retina is shown in Figure 4.17; most of the cones are the equally numerous red and green types, with a scattering of blue.

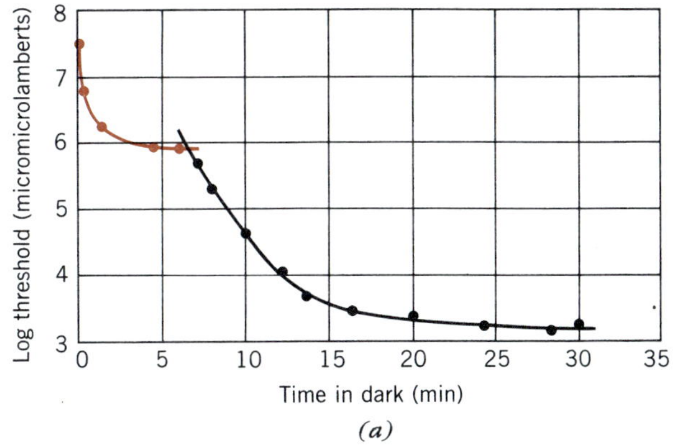

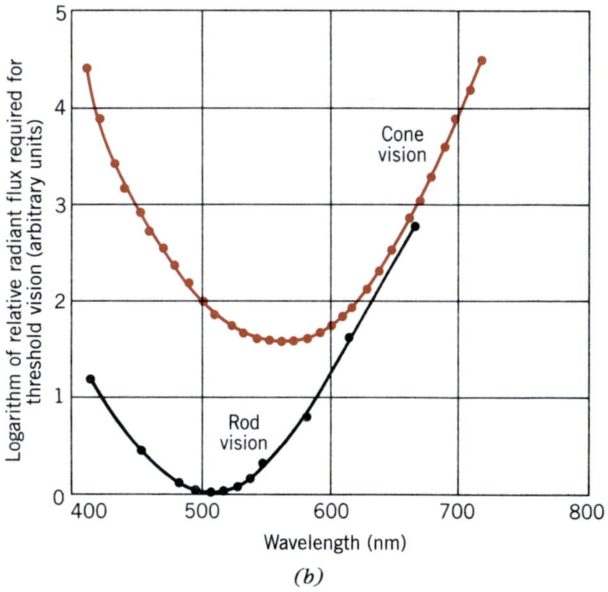

***Figure 4.15** Psychophysics of dark adaptation.* (a) *A dark-adaptation curve, showing the brightness of the dimmest flash that can be seen after a given time in complete darkness. The first section is for the cones and defines photopic* (photos *is Greek for "light") vision. The second is for the rods and defines scotopic* (scotos *is Greek for "dark") vision.* (b) *The radiant energy of the dimmest visible flash of a given wavelength tested during the cone state of adaptation (photopic, about 5 min after the start of darkness) and during the rod state of adaptation (scotopic, after about 20 min of darkness). The shift of the wavelength of the minimum effective energy is the Purkinje shift.*

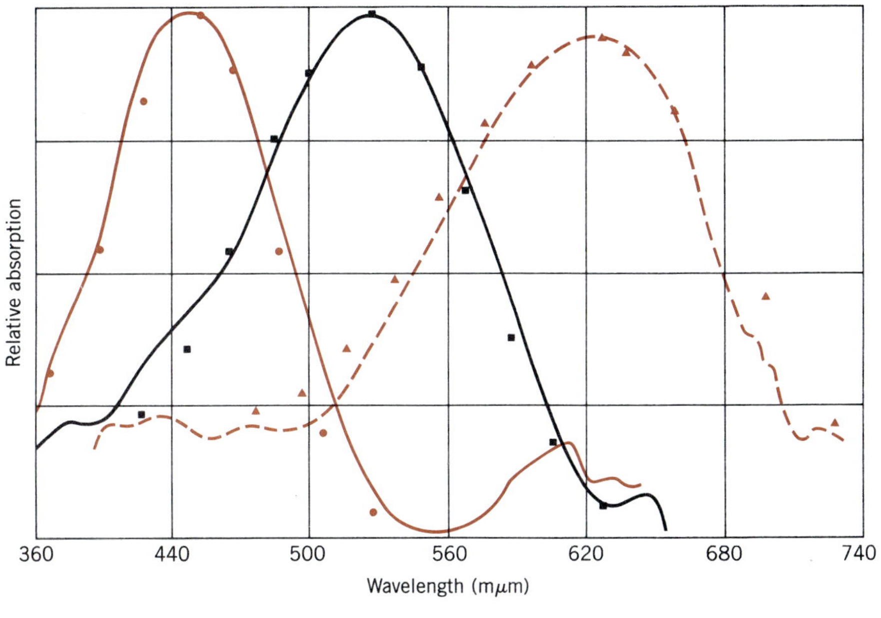

***Figure 4.16** Absorption spectra of the three cone pigments of a goldfish. The curves are found by measuring the amount of monochromatic light of various wavelengths passed through a sample of each pigment. Since the optical system, other parts of the tissue sample, and other elements also absorb light at various wavelengths, a second step is necessary to find the pigment's absorption spectrum. In the second step the spectrum is measured with brief flashes of monochromatic light in darkness, with the pigment given time to regenerate after each flash. Then the pigment is bleached by exposure to intense white light, and the spectrum is measured again. The difference between the two figures—the difference spectrum—is the measure illustrated here.*

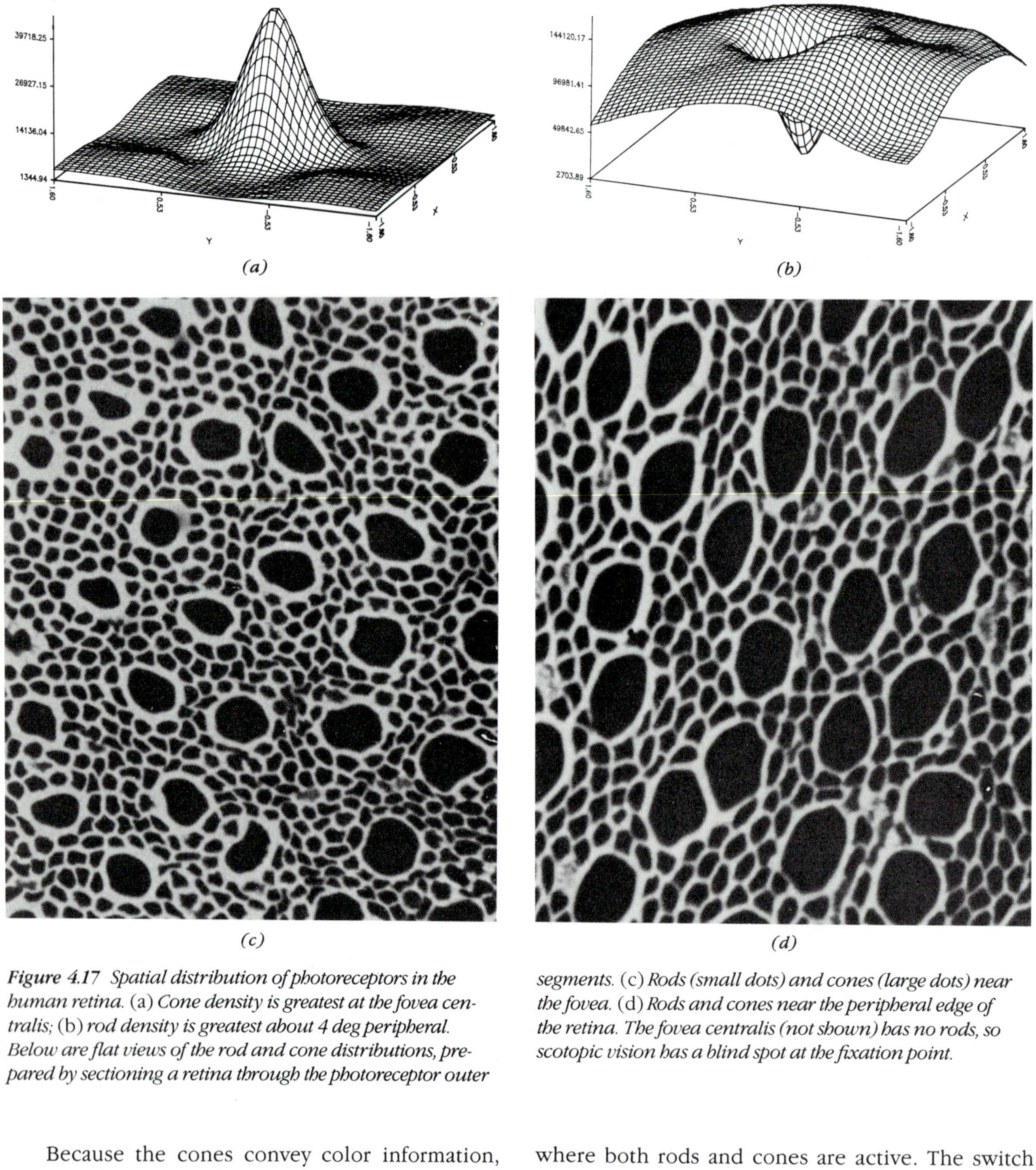

***Figure 4.17** Spatial distribution of photoreceptors in the human retina.* (a) *Cone density is greatest at the fovea centralis;* (b) *rod density is greatest about 4 deg peripheral. Below are flat views of the rod and cone distributions, prepared by sectioning a retina through the photoreceptor outer segments.* (c) *Rods (small dots) and cones (large dots) near the fovea.* (d) *Rods and cones near the peripheral edge of the retina. The fovea centralis (not shown) has no rods, so scotopic vision has a blind spot at the fixation point.*

Because the cones convey color information, you can determine when your cones are active by observing the presence of color in the visual field. Colors seem to fade in dark environments, in the **scotopic** range of light intensity, where only the rods are active. Color is seen in the bright **photopic** range. In between is a **mesopic** range, where both rods and cones are active. The switch from photopic to scotopic intensity occurs at about 10^{-2} millilamberts, about the intensity of the full moon reflected on snow. The scotopic threshold is 10,000 times lower, 10^{-6} millilamberts, about the intensity of starlight in open country.

A Review and Reinterpretation

It seems paradoxical that light leads not to depolarization of receptor synapses but to hyperpolarization of them. Light causes the release not of more transmitter but of less. This peculiar arrangement does not present a problem, because the job of the photoreceptor is not to change light into a release of transmitter but to extract information from light. As long as a change in light intensity leads to a change in the rate of neurotransmitter release, the direction of the change does not matter.

In sum, in comparing the visual system to other systems with depolarizing receptors, it makes sense to interpret the photoreceptor as a detector not of light but of darkness. In the resting state, with light present, the receptor is polarized much as any neuron is polarized. When the eye is suddenly darkened, cyclic GMP is released, opening Na^+ channels in the outer-segment membrane. The resulting Na^+ current depolarizes the receptor to about -40 mv, increasing the release of neurotransmitter. The whole process from this standpoint looks quite conventional.

AUDITION

The auditory system detects pressure waves in the air—the alternating increases and decreases in air pressure depicted in Figure 4.18. The ear of a healthy young adult human detects sounds between about 20 and 20,000 Hz. With age the peak frequency slowly decreases. Sensitivity is greatest at about 1000 to 3000 Hz. The sensitivity is less at low frequencies for a good reason. If thresholds were any lower, the ear could hear the constant rhythmic vibrations of the circulatory system. On the high end, human sensitivity isn't especially good compared to that of most other mammals. This is why we can't hear the sound made by a whistle used for calling dogs; its frequency is over 20,000 Hz, above our range but well within that of a dog.

SOUND AND THE OUTER EAR

The **pinna,** the visible outer part of the ear, channels sound into the ear canal. In mammals such as cats and bats the pinna is exquisitely mobie and occupies an area larger than that of the face. The human pinna has no functional movement and is relatively small, but it still aids in localizing sounds. To demonstrate this, you need only hold short lengths of plastic tubing in your ears and try to localize sounds with your eyes closed. (Don't try this without professional supervision.)

Localization of Sound

Two properties of sound help us localize its source. First, a sound arrives at the two ears at different times, because the speed of sound is relatively slow. Second, sounds entering the ear that is farther from the source will be less intense because they are blocked by the head (see Figure 4.19).

To study auditory localization we begin again with psychophysics. How accurately can we localize a sound source? Under ideal conditions (no echoes or background noise) a human can locate a sound with an error of about 1 deg. A little calculation shows that this corresponds to a time difference of only about 30 μsec at the two ears. It remains unknown how this locating is done in a system whose neural response latencies are hundreds of times longer than arrival-time differences, on the order of 10s of milliseconds. Localization by timing differences at the two ears works best at low sound frequencies, because at higher frequencies the waves are closer together and it becomes possible to confuse the peak of a wave in one ear with the peak of the next wave in the other.

Intensity differences are most effective as cues for localization at high frequencies. The reason for this is physical rather than biological: high-frequency sound does not bend around the head very well. At an intermediate frequency of about 3 kHz, localization is more difficult because neither cue works very well. This is just the frequency of many alarm calls in birds, ground squirrels, and other animals. The sound can be heard by the potential prey animals, but the predators have difficulty in localizing it.

Cognitive factors also influence localization. Top-down information consisting of knowledge of the auditory world can cooperate with bottom-up information from the ears. For instance, I can localize the whistling of my teakettle quite precisely

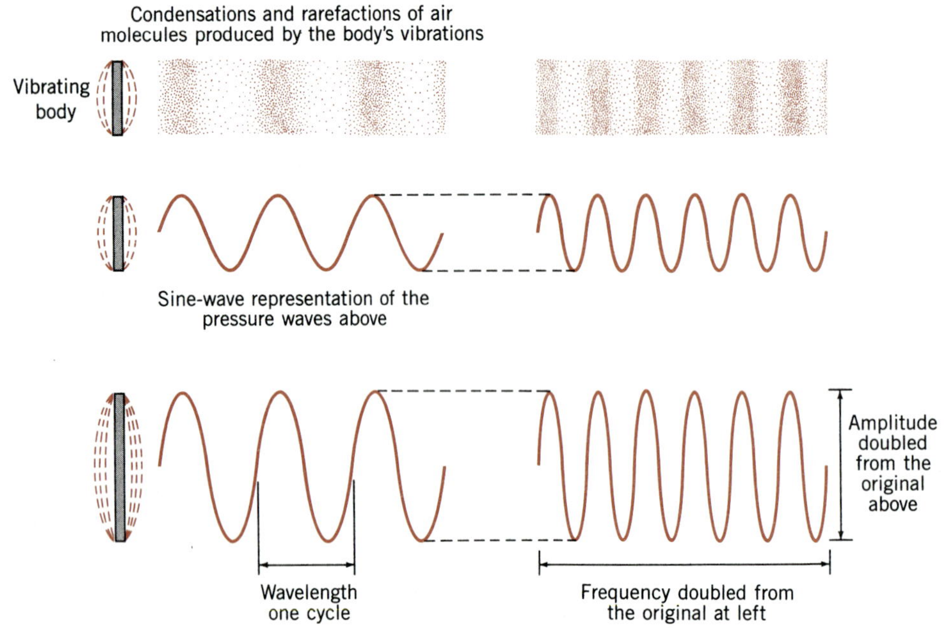

***Figure 4.18** Definitions of sound parameters. At the top a vibrating body alternately pushes and pulls on the air around it, creating waves of concentration and rarefraction that disperse from the body. Under it are three sine-wave representations of the air pressure at each distance from the source. The wavelength is the product of the period of vibration and the speed of sound. A greater amplitude of vibration yields a greater sound amplitude; a greater frequency of vibration yields a higher sound frequency.*

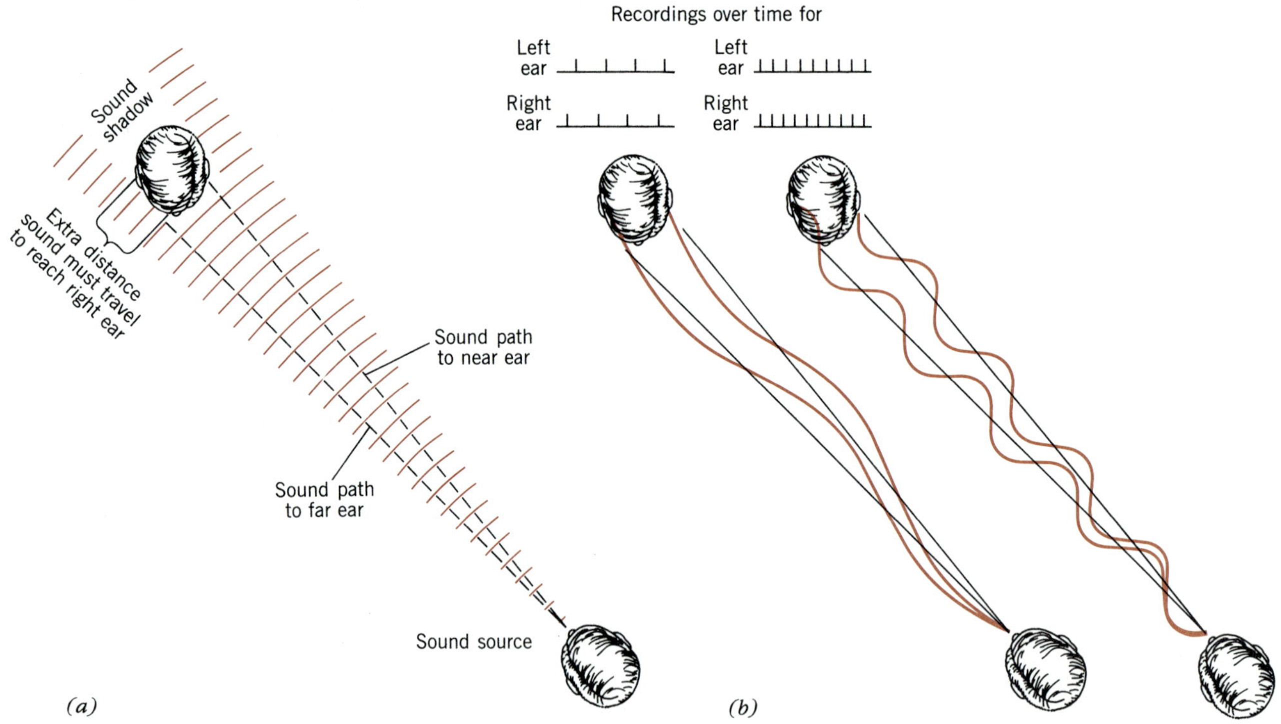

***Figure 4.19** Physical cues for sound localization.* (a) *Intensity differences as a cue. The closer ear receives a more intense sound because of its range and because the other ear is in the sound shadow of the head.* (b) *Timing (phase) differences as a cue. A pressure wave will arrive slightly earlier at the closer ear.*

even if I am in another room. Top-down information—my memory of where the stove is—provides all the information I need. In the real world of perception, where most objects are familiar, these cues cooperate with time-difference and intensity cues—and sometimes dominate them. A voice in a movie seems to come from the lips of the actors even if it comes from a speaker somewhat removed from the screen. The phenomenon is called **visual capture** because the visual stimulus captures the apparent position of the sound.

THE MIDDLE EAR

The eardrum (tympanic membrane) separates the outer and the middle ears. The **middle ear** is the air-filled cavity shown in Figure 4.20.

The auditory system developed from a system in primitive fish for detecting changes in water pressure. The transduction process still takes place in a fluid environment in the inner ear. The middle ear has evolved to transfer sound vibrations efficiently from the new air medium to the older and much denser fluid one. In reptiles this is done with a strut of cartilage between the eardrum and the **oval window,** the entrance to the **inner ear** (Wever, 1974), with the consequence that high-frequency sounds are muffled. An increase in pressure pushes on the strut and on the oval window; but before the inner ear's fluid can move, the rapid vibration of the strut pulls the oval window back again. The impedance (resistance to vibration) of the eardrum and that of the oval window are not matched.

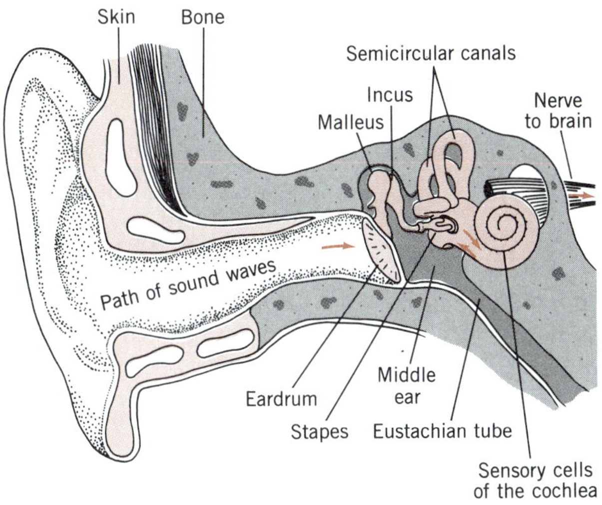

Figure 4.20 *Gross anatomy of the ear. One of the reasons for the restricted frequency sensitivity of human hearing is the physical filtering of sound waves that occurs as sound travels through the external auditory meatus between the pinna and the eardrum. The cochlea and semicircular canals (the vestibular organs) are encased in a shell of hard bone.*

The Ossicles

In the mammalian middle ear this engineering problem is solved by the **ossicles**—a subtle system of mechanical levers that reduces the amplitude of the eardrum's vibration about 20-fold, with a corresponding increase in the power of the movement. In the denser fluid medium, a small movement transmits the same energy as a much larger movement in air. The system is quite efficient, transmitting almost all of the sound energy that arrives at the tympanic membrane. The ossicles, the smallest bones in the body, evolved from parts of the jaw.

The first of the three ossicles is the **malleus** (Latin for "hammer"), which is connected to the eardrum. Next come the **incus** (Latin for "anvil") and the **stapes** (Latin for "stirrup"); the latter is fixed to the oval window. In addition to their impedance-matching function, the ossicles protect the inner ear against mechanical overload; a loud sound causes the joint between the incus and the stapes to buckle, transforming the normal in-and-out motion to a harmless rotation (Békésy & Rosenblith, 1951). Because this transformation of the auditory stimulus is mechanical rather than neural, it has no latency (time delay) and can protect even against sudden shocks. It is the first step in the process of range reduction in the auditory system, a process analogous to light adaptation in the visual system.

The Middle-Ear Muscles

Auditory vibrations are further modified by two tiny muscles, the smallest in the human body, that

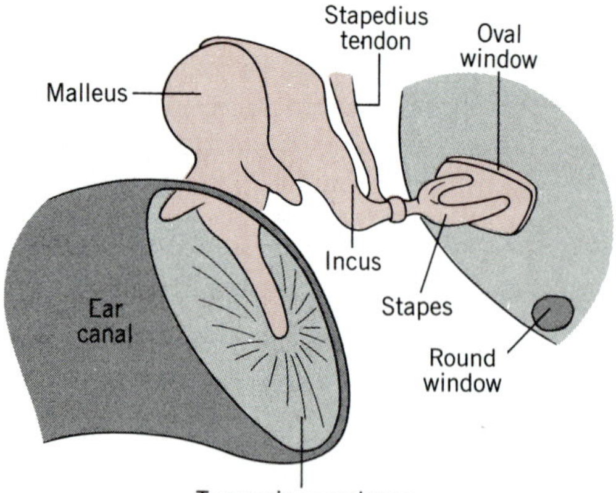

Figure 4.21 *The middle ear, showing the insertion of the stapedius tendon. The ossicles are linked together with tiny hinges of connective tissue; one of the causes of hearing loss with aging is the stiffening of these links.*

change the linkage of the ossicles (see Figure 4.21). (All muscles are attached by tendons—connective tissue that anchors the ends of the muscles.) The **tensor tympani** is attached to the malleus. As its name implies, it puts tension on the tympanic membrane when it is contracted. The even smaller **stapedius** muscle is attached to the stapes and changes the articulation between the foot of the stapes and the incus.

Both contractions stiffen the linkage between the tympanic membrane and the oval window, reducing the efficiency of sound transmission. The reflex comes into play when sound intensity reaches 80 dB (decibels) above threshold, about the volume of loud traffic (the decibel is a logarithmic unit of the sound-pressure level). Several other functions of the middle-ear muscles have been proposed (Moller, 1974); protecting the ear from the vibrations of one's own voice is one possible function.

In sum, the outer and middle ears channel vibrations, protect against loud noises, and transfer vibrations to the fluid of the inner ear. There, transduction into neural impulses takes place.

THE INNER EAR

The oval window is the entrance to the **cochlea** (*kokhlos* is Greek for "land snail"), a snail-shaped cavity in the temporal bone of the skull that contains the auditory transduction mechanism. Each human cochlea (see Figure 4.22) is about the size of a large pea. Figure 4.20 shows how the cochlea blends into the labyrinth of the vestibular system and how both share the same fluids.

Structure of the Cochlea

The design of the cochlea is seen most easily in the embryo, where it begins as the straight tube of Figure 4.23. A tough membrane, the **basilar membrane,** divides it into two parts that are joined at the tip by a tiny hole, the **helicotrema.** As embryonic development progresses, the cochlea begins to coil up until it makes about 2 1/2 turns. If the oval window were the only entrance to this bony chamber, no vibration could be transmitted to it; the **round window,** at the other end of the doubled coil, acts as a pressure relief port so the incompressible fluid can move. The motions of the round window and the oval window are reciprocal; one bulges out when the other bulges in.

The key to the function of the cochlea as an analyzer of sound is its vibration in response to pressure waves of various frequencies. Motion of the oval window changes the pressure in the fluid,

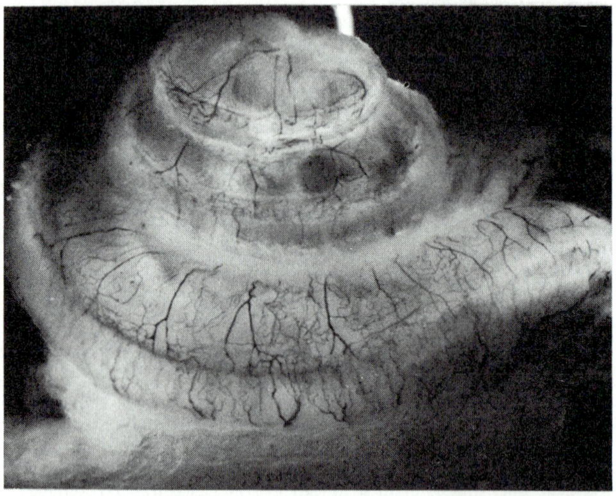

Figure 4.22 *Photo of the intact human cochlea with the surrounding bone removed. The rich vascular network of the external wall is visible.*

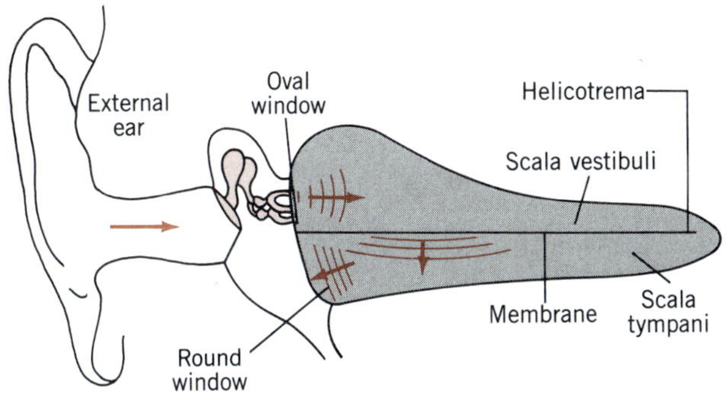

Figure 4.23 *Schematic view of the ear of an embryo, showing the helicotrema completing the fluid path from the oval window to the round window. The scala vestibuli and the scala tympani form a single fluid chamber, divided along most of its length by the basilar membrane.*

deforming the basilar membrane. High-frequency sounds with short wavelengths deform mostly the initial portion of the basilar membrane; lower frequencies with longer wavelengths deform the membrane progressively farther from the oval window. The difference in response to varying frequencies of vibration is furthered by the shape of the basilar membrane. It is narrow near the oval window and wider near the helicotrema. Consequently, the base, near the oval window, is about 100 times stiffer than the tip, near the helicotrema. The result is a rough frequency analysis; high- and low-frequency sounds have their greatest mechanical effects at different locations.

Deformation of the basilar membrane excites the **hair cells,** the transducers of the auditory system. These cells are attached to the basilar membrane, but their hairs (really cilia, as you might expect) are in contact with the **tectorial membrane** (see Figure 4.24). Bending the basilar membrane creates a shearing action on the cilia (in a horizontal direction in the figure.)

Because the cilia are only about 6 μm long, it doesn't take much shearing to stimulate the cells. At the threshold, the basilar membrane must move about 10^{-11} m to excite the hair cells (Lawrence, 1965). This is only one-tenth the diameter of a hydrogen atom! The threshold works out to a motion about the size of three hydrogen atoms at the eardrum. The cochlea is mechanically the most complex organ in the human body, with about a million moving parts (the hairs on the hair cells).

There are two kinds of hair cells, inner and outer, named for their distance from the base of the tectorial membrane. **Inner hair cells** send a strong innervation to the auditory nerve, with one nerve fiber for each cell; in contrast, many **outer hair cells** share a few nerve fibers. As a result, 95 percent of the afferent fibers in the auditory nerve come from inner hair cells, even though the outer hair cells are more numerous (Spoendlin, 1972). The inner hair cells seem to be analogous to the fovea of the retina, with much denser innervation. Intracellular recording has shown that at low frequencies the inner hair cells respond to basilar membrane velocity and the outer hair cells respond to displacement (Russel & Sellick, 1981).

Each auditory nerve contains about 29,000 fibers (Harrison & Howe, 1974), a very small number compared to the 125 million visual receptors and the 2 million optic nerve fibers. The auditory stimulus codes only one dimension—pressure—however, whereas each retina must encode both vertical and horizontal dimensions. Audition seems to need only about 1 percent as many afferent fibers as vision.

How is the bending of the cilia of the hair cells converted into neural graded potentials? The details are not known for certain, but two useful approaches exist. One emphasizes electrical events; the other stresses mechanical linkages.

Electrical Actions of the Cochlea in Transduction

A striking feature of the cochlea is that it acts as a microphone, faithfully converting vibration at the oval window into electrical signals. If an electrode made from a moistened cotton wick is gently placed on the round window, this **cochlear**

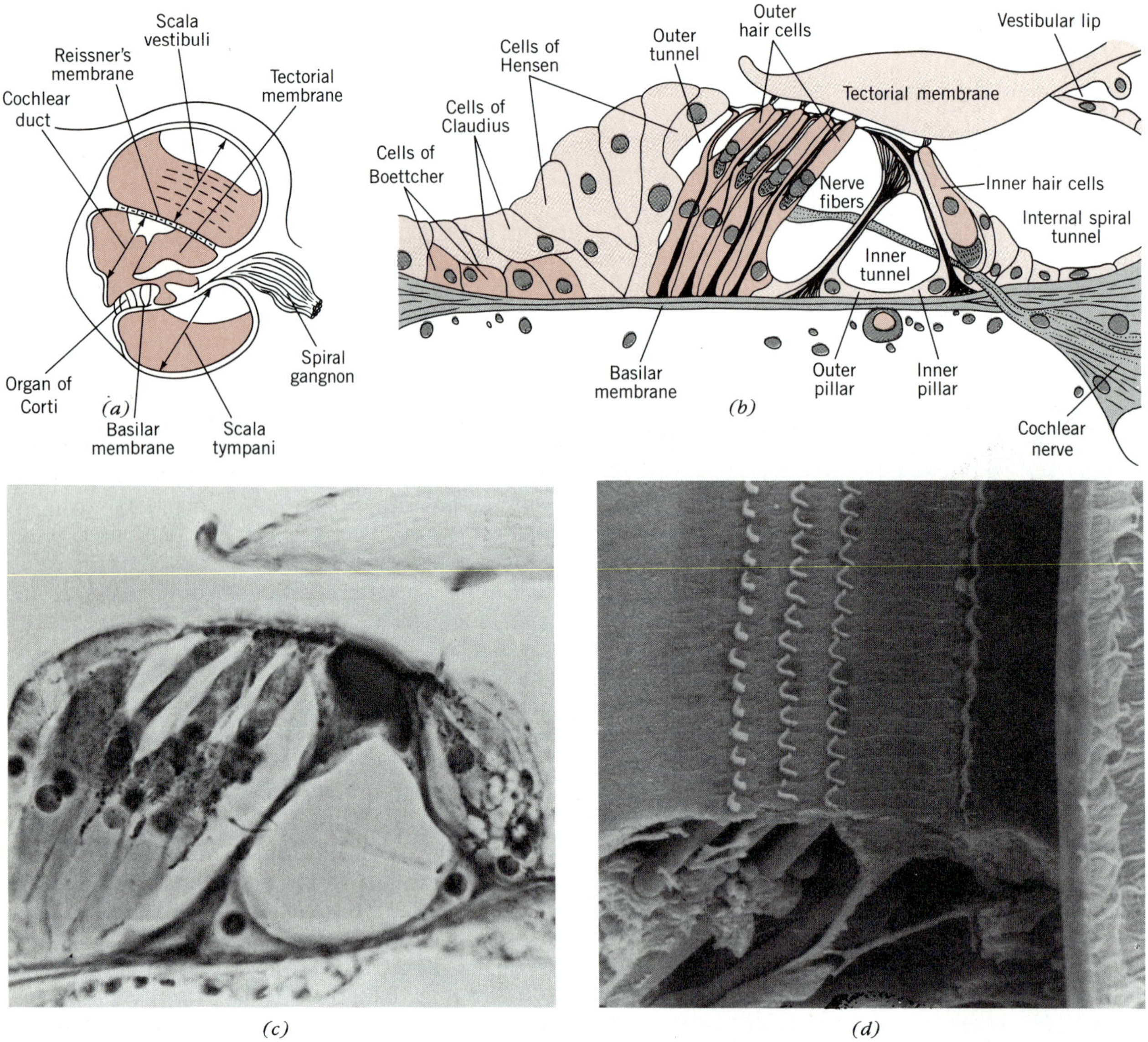

Figure 4.24 *The mechanics of auditory transduction.* (a) *Drawing of a cross section of the cochlea, showing the location of the organ of Corti, where transduction takes place.* (b) *Schematic drawing of details of the organ of Corti. As the basilar membrane moves up with sound pressure, the tectorial membrane moves to the right, stimulating the hair cells. When the basilar membrane moves down, the tectorial membrane moves to the left.* (c) *Light micrograph of a cross section of a chinchilla organ of Corti.* (d) *Scanning electron micrograph of a cross section and top view of a chinchilla organ of Corti. The tympanic lip is pulled back to expose the cilia.*

microphonic can be amplified to drive a speaker in the same manner as a conventional microphone. The cochlear microphonic has remarkable fidelity, even at high frequencies. When it was discovered, by Wever and Bray in 1930, it was the best microphone known.

The source of the cochlear microphonic can be traced to the large electrical potential differences that are maintained in the cochlea. The potential of the **endolymph** (Latin for "inner fluid") that bathes the hair cells is about +80 mv with respect to the other fluids of the inner ear (see

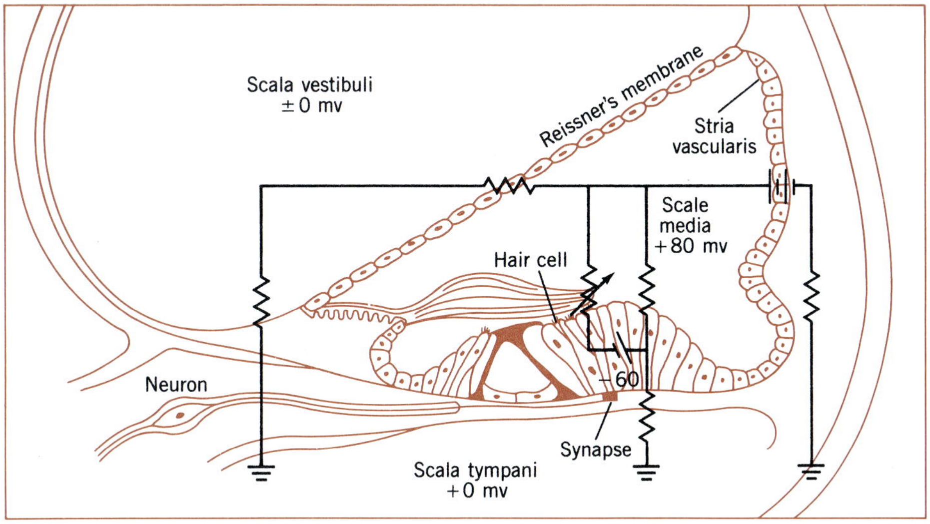

Figure 4.25 *Davis's (1965) electrical resistance microphone theory of the cochlear microphonic. The equivalent circuit is superimposed on the anatomy of the organ of Corti. The zigzag lines represent resistors; the zigzag lines with arrows, variable resistors; the triangular symbols, grounding points; the bars in the stria vascularis, the battery. The hair cell acts to gate the electrical potential difference between the inside of the cell and the scala media. The scala media has a great surplus of* K^+ *ions along with its positive potential.*

Figure 4.25). The hair cells themselves have an intracellular poential of −80 mv. The total voltage across the hair cell membrane is thus about 160 mv (Davis, 1965), probably the largest transmembrane potential in the body. Since any electrical generator requires the motion of two bodies that differ in potential, motion in this system could generate the current recorded as the cochlear microphonic. This (and other) evidence points to the hair cells as the site where the microphonic is produced. The cochlear microphonic is not the auditory generator potential, however, for it has some very nonneural qualities: it does not adapt with prolonged stimulation, it has no latency, and it continues for several hours after death.

Mechanical Site of Transduction

Where on the hair cell is mechanical action translated into a graded potential? Some theories of hair cell transduction point to the bases of the cilia as the point of action, but recent evidence implicates the tips. In a technically impressive set of experiments, Hudspeth (1982) recorded from 18 points around the tuft of cilia on a frog vestibular hair cell (see Figure 4.26). He used a micropipette electrode (a tapered hollow tube) with a tip 0.4 μm in diameter. He moved it in three dimensions under microscopic control, with an error of 2 μm on each axis. The graded potentials he recorded were greatest at the tips of the cilia, suggesting that transduction occurs there.

The latest hypothesis about transduction is based on tiny channels, one at the tip of each hair. Each one has a lid like a trap door, opened with a tiny filament attached to the neighboring, slightly longer hair. Thermal energy in surrounding molecules is continually flipping the trap door open and closed; experiments show that at rest the channel is open about 20 percent of the time (Hudspeth, 1985). When the hairs bend, the springy filament lifts up the door and allows the channel to remain open more of the time. It takes almost no energy to open the channel (Corey & Hudspeth, 1983), so thresholds can remain in the range of thermal noise. When the channel is open, K^+ ions flow into the hair and depolarize it in the usual way.

FREQUENCY CODING IN THE COCHLEA

The cochlear hair cells encode sound frequency even though the transduction process within a hair

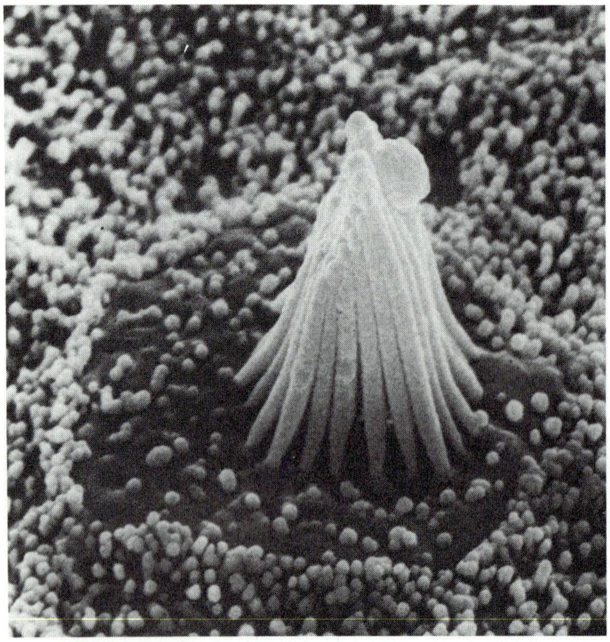

(a)

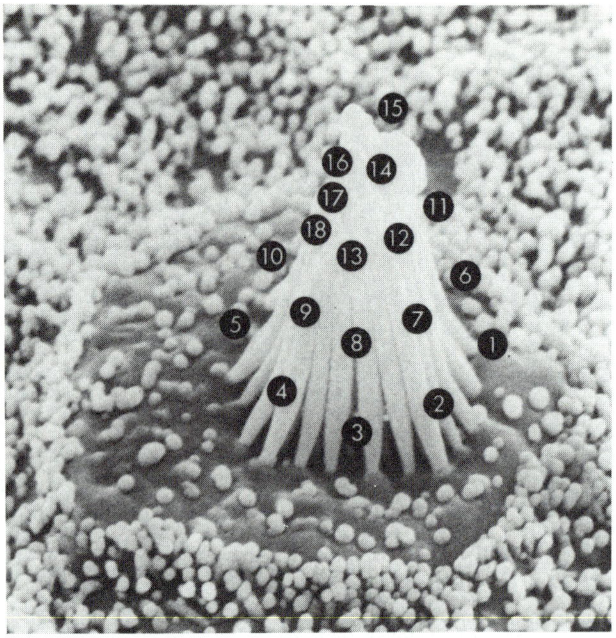

(b)

Figure 4.26 *Scanning electron micrographs of hair cells.* (a) *The apical surface of a saccular hair cell in the bullfrog. This is a vestibular cell with a direction-sensitive response, but the anatomy of the cilia is similar to that in the cochlea. The bumps are short microvilli on the surface of the hair cell. There are about 50 stereocilia (hairs) 3.5 to 8.4 μm long and a kinocilium ending in a bulbous swelling.* (b) *Locations of 18 standard recording sites. The bar at the lower left is 1 μm.*

cell is not especially selective for frequencies. The hair cells respond whenever their cilia are bent, no matter what the frequency. Selectivity for particular frequencies might be achieved either by the mechanical actions of the cochlea, so different hair cells are stimulated by different frequencies, or by the response patterns of the cells themselves. The first alternative is the place theory; the second is the telephone theory.

Place Theory

The great 19th century physiologist and physicist Hermann von Helmholtz first proposed the **place theory**—that the cochlea works somewhat like a row of tuning forks, with each sound frequency encoded in a different place. We have already seen how the cochlea is tuned to vibrate maximally in a different place for the sounds of each frequency. Can this property account for the ability to discriminate pitch? At first it seems that it cannot; the waves of vibration excited in the cochlea by sounds are very broad. For low frequencies the entire structure vibrates, from the oval window to the helicortrema. Pitch discrimination, in contrast, is very precise; in the range between 50 and 3000 Hz, humans can discriminate tones separated by only 1 to 4 Hz (Licklider, 1951).

But there is always a point of maximum vibration, and some mechanism may "sharpen" the responses of the hair cells so only the most strongly stimulated ones will report their frequency-specific messages to higher levels. The neurons at several higher levels in the auditory pathway influence one another by lateral inhibition. As a result, only the most strongly stimulated cells get their messages through. The rest are inhibited by their more active neighbors (Békésy, 1967).

A sharp peak of excitation at one point is not necessary, though, to provide the nervous system with the information that a single frequency is stimulating the cochlea. Suppose the auditory system receives signals from one of the cochlear regions shown in Figure 4.27. Since it is impossible for any vibration to create a sharper tuning curve,

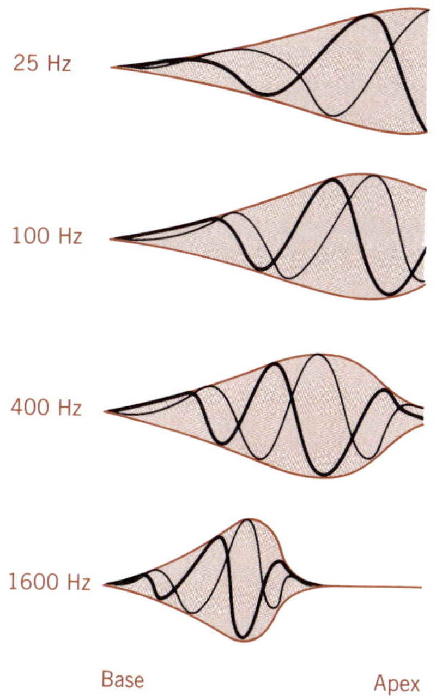

Figure 4.27 *A schematic view of the unrolled basilar membrane viewed from the perspective of Figure 4.23, vibrating in response to sounds of the frequencies indicated on the left. The traveling waves are indicated at two phases in each diagram, with the envelope describing the maximum displacement indicated in color. The vertical amplitude is greatly exaggerated. The peak displacement is closer to the base of the cochlea for the higher pitches, which have shorter wavelengths.*

the curve informs the system that only a single sound frequency is present. This illustrates an important principle: the neural signal need not look like the stimulus. Each pattern of neural activity need only correspond to a unique stimulus.

An Artificial Ear. One needs to know exactly how the cochlea works in order to design a **prosthesis,** a device to substitute for part of the body. Such a device can restore hearing in patients with certain types of deafness. The technical problems of inserting a set of electrodes into the spiraling cochlea and transferring current to them have largely been solved (Loeb, 1985). The problem of what to stimulate them with has proved more difficult. Stimulating a single bipolar electrode inside the cochlea excites a sensation with a definite pitch, but the "sound" is not a pure tone. Instead, patients describe it as something like the quacking of ducks or the banging of garbage cans.

The failure to produce pure tones from single locations along the cochlea does not disprove place theory, for the theory has always held that frequency separation is a rather rough affair. A pure tone with only one frequency will stimulate a range of hair cells in the vibrating cochlea, as Figure 4.27 shows. Conversely, a rather complex sound would be needed to create vibrations that would exactly cancel one another except at one point—the point where the electrodes are located. This is the sound heard when a single electrode is stimulated in a patient with a prosthesis.

Fourier Analysis. How does the subtle rustle of wind or the rich sonority of a human voice become encoded in patterns of hair cell synaptic activity? We already know that a rough frequency analysis occurs in the cochlea. But can complex sounds be interpreted as patterns of simple frequencies? The answer is yes. Any pattern of sound pressure can be completely described as a group of regularly repeating waves, called sine waves, added together. Each sine wave contains only one frequency of vibration.

The mathematical principle was developed early in the 19th century by a French mathematician, Charles Fourier. Figure 4.28 shows how a square wave can be constructed from superimposed sine waves. Fourier proved that one can construct any wave, no matter how complex, by adding together a series of sine waves differing in frequency (the distance between the peaks), amplitude, and phase (the way the peaks line up). The problem is that theoretically an infinite series of sine waves is often necessary, but one can get very close with a relatively small number. The example shows how a repeating wave can be constructed; but nonrepeating waves, such as isolated spikes, can also be generated with a Fourier series of sine waves. The opposite process, dissecting a complex wave into its sine components, is called **Fourier analysis.**

The theory is rigorous and elegant. But does the cochlea really work by performing a Fourier analysis of natural sound vibration patterns? There is argument about how far a frequency theory can

(a)

(b)

(c)

(d)

(e)

(f)

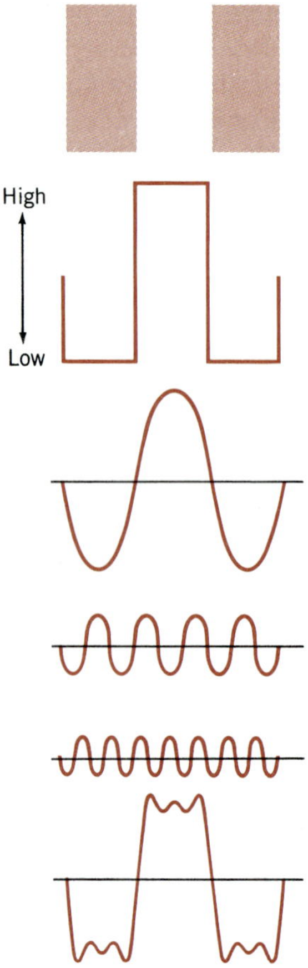

***Figure 4.28** Fourier analysis of a square wave into sine-wave components.* (a) *Part of a black and white grid.* (b) *Stimulus intensity across the grid.* (c) *First harmonic. The stimulus is broken down into a first harmonic expressing the basic periodicity of the pattern and a series of higher harmonics gradually shaping the first harmonic into a square wave.* (d) *The third harmonic, one-third amplitude. The third harmonic has three times the frequency of the first.* (e) *The fifth harmonic, one-fifth amplitude. The fifth harmonic has five times the frequency of the first.* (f) *The sum of* (c), (d), *and* (e). *The complete analysis involves an infinite series of ever-smaller sine waves of ever-higher frequency, containing all of the odd-numbered harmonics.*

be applied to hearing, for in some ways the nervous system clearly does better than is possible with Fourier analysis alone. Humans can discriminate the pitch of a tone rather well after hearing only two cycles, a feat beyond the theoretical capability of a strict Fourier analysis. Several other properties of hearing show that although frequency analysis has a place in auditory theory, it is not the whole story. The place theory does not provide sharp enough tuning to account for pitch discrimination at low frequencies. Cochlear tuning curves for nearby frequencies are practically indistinguishable, even though the frequencies themselves clearly sound different to human observers. Another theory is necessary to account for this ability.

Telephone Theory

The development of the telephone brought with it a new idea for coding pitch in the auditory system. The diaphragm of a telephone vibrates as a whole, and frequency information is coded in the frequency of the electrical signal generated, not in its location. Recordings from the neurons innervating the hair cells show that indeed the neuron's firing matches the sound pressure at low frequencies; for each peak in the sound pressure pattern, there is a spike in the neuron (see Figure 4.29). The higher the frequency, the closer the peaks and the smaller the neuron's interspike interval. The **telephone theory** is thus the theory that auditory frequencies are coded by the frequency of the firing of neurons in the auditory pathway.

This scheme works well at low frequencies, just where place theory is weakest. But at high frequencies it runs into a problem. The maximum firing frequency for neurons, about 1 kHz, is much lower than the maximum detectable frequency of about 20 kHz in humans and over 150 kHz in bats and dolphins. This problem can be overcome with Wever's (1949) **volley principle,** which relies on the fact that many neurons respond to a sensory event. At higher frequencies a given neuron can fire at the peak of a pressure wave; while it is in its refractory period, another neuron can signal the next peak, and so on. In this scheme there is no "detector" of a frequency; that information is carried only on groups of axons. The same limitation applies to higher-level neurons, so the idea of a single cell signaling a particular frequency is lost. Coding is spatially distributed, even for the simplest stimuli. Something like a volley principle probably exists in other senses as well.

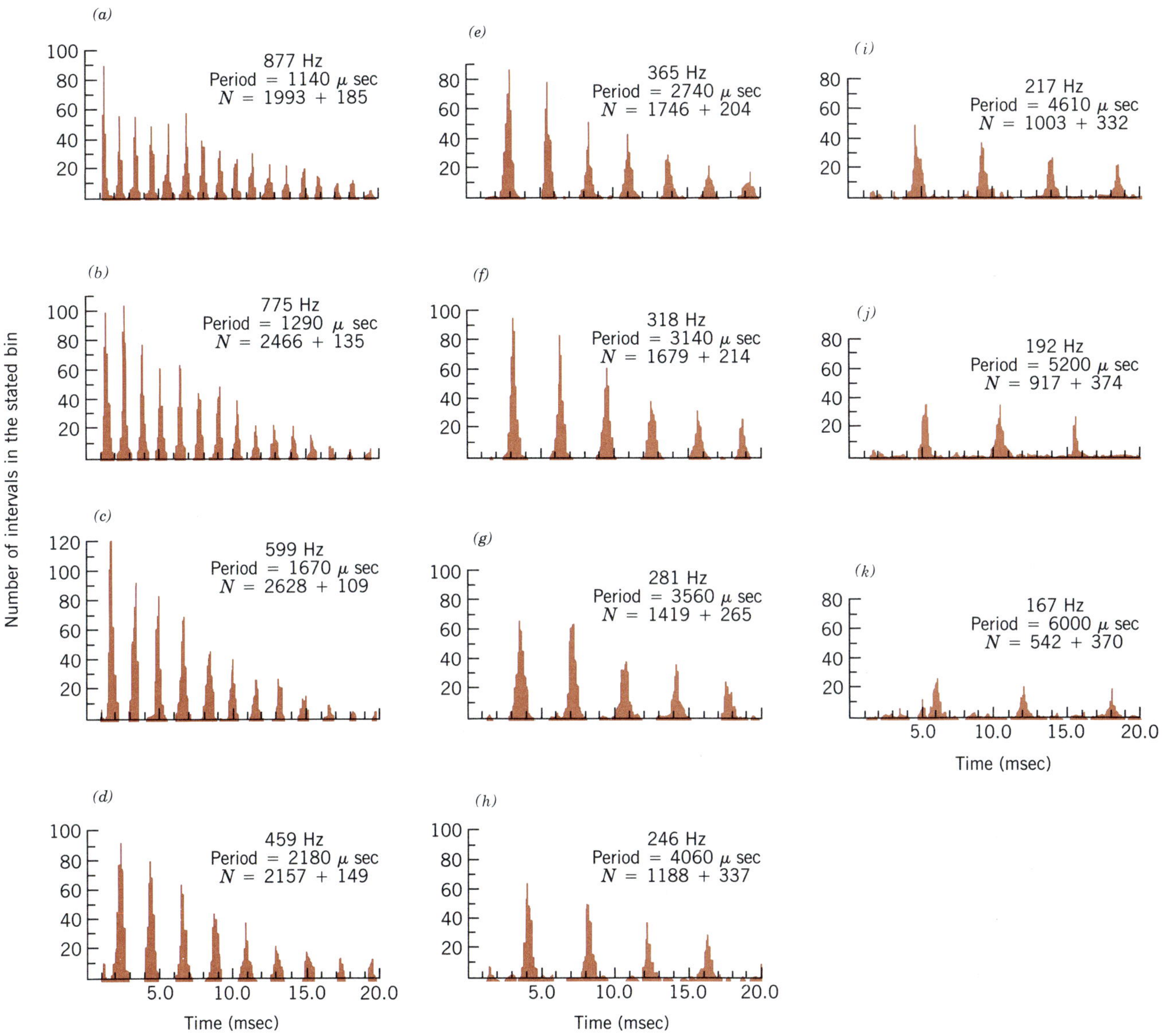

Figure 4.29 *Responses of an auditory nerve fiber of the squirrel monkey to stimuli of varying frequency. The neuron follows the sound frequency over a range of about 100 to 1000 Hz. Sine-wave stimuli (pure tones) declining from 877 Hz* (a) *to 167 Hz* (k) *show the frequency following over a broad range. From Rose et al. (1967).*

The volley principle overcomes the telephone theory's frequency limitation, but neurophysiological experiments (reviewed by Geldard, 1972) show that even the volley principle breaks down at around 4 to 5 kHz. Pitch discrimination ability abruptly begins to deteriorate above this frequency, though some discrimination remains (Licklider, 1951). It is here that location on the cochlea (place theory) is the only remaining mechanism for pitch coding, and it is at high frequencies that it works best. Thus a combination of the two theories, telephone at low frequencies and place at higher ones, fits the facts best. A compromise between two theories that seemed to be opposed turned out to be the solution.

Efferent Control

Examination of the synaptic regions of hair cells reveals a surprising organization. Each outer hair cell is contacted by two synaptic processes, one afferent and the other efferent. Thus the CNS can send information all the way back to the receptor to change its transfer properties. The efferent connection to inner hair cells ends on the afferent terminal in most cases (Iurato, 1974).

Another possible function for the outer hair cells has been discovered recently. When the cells are stimulated electrically, they get a little shorter. This changes the mechanical properties of the cochlea and probably aids in adjusting the cochlea's sensitivity to sound. Applying ACh to the synaptic zone of the outer hair cells mimics the action of the efferent fibers to these cells and contracts the cells (Brownell et al., 1985).

The efferent fibers are branches of the tract of Rasmussen, a tiny bundle of only about 500 fibers originating in the superior olive of the medulla. Their function remains to be worked out. Other senses also have efferents which in many cases synapse directly on the receptors.

THE VESTIBULAR SYSTEM

Continuing from the cochlea is a system of two sacs and three semicircular canals in an intricate arrangement appropriately termed the **labyrinth.** The sacs—the **utricle** and the **saccule**—are collectively called the **otolith organs.** They are concerned primarily with detecting the direction of gravity. The **semicircular canals** detect accelerations of the head, though there is some overlap of the functions.

The vestibular system is insensitive to constant motion. It detects only acceleration—either the constant acceleration caused by gravity or the additional accelerations induced by locomotion.

THE OTOLITH ORGANS

The oval-shaped cavities that are named otolith organs are partially lined with hair cells much like those of the auditory system. The sensitive area in the utricle is on the floor of each cavity; the sensitive area in the saccule is on the wall. The cilia of the hair cells are embedded in a gelatinous substance whose mass is increased by small crystals of inorganic calcium carbonate called otoliths (Greek for "ear stones") (see Figure 4.30). When the head is tilted, the otoliths create a shearing action on the hair cells and change the positions of the cilia.

The power of this system in controlling posture can be dramatically demonstrated in the lobster, where the vestibular organ is somewhat more accessible. The otoliths can be replaced by iron beads; when a magnet is held above the lobster, the animal turns over and happily remains on its back, convinced that down is up, until the magnet is removed.

The saccule provides information about gravitation when the head is pitched forward about 30 deg, a posture in which the utricle is relatively insensitive (Mittlestaedt, 1985). In some fish the saccule acts as part of the auditory system (Wever, 1974).

The Otoliths in Space Flight

The function of the otolith organs is transformed during space flights, when gravity is absent and there is nothing to pull on the otoliths. The organs have mass but no weight. Under this condition the utricle and saccule cannot indicate the position of the head; instead, they transduce only linear acceleration. The change from position indicator to linear accelerometer is a result of the physics of the vestibular organs.

Astronauts exposed to prolonged weightlessness eventually adapt to the changed role of the otolith organs. This is a remarkable example of the flexibility of the higher levels of the vestibular system, for such an adaptation is never necessary on Earth. But astronauts experience hours to days of space sickness before they adapt. Drugs used on earth for motion sickness relieve the symptoms somewhat. Experiments on the Spacelab orbiting

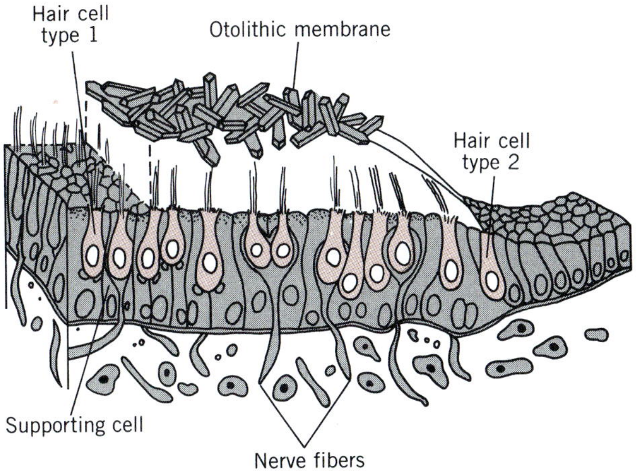

Figure 4.30 *Reconstruction of the receptor area of the utricle and saccule. A gelatinous mass surrounds the cilia of the hair cells and supports the otoliths. These dense crystals increase the mass of the system.*

satellite showed that as adaptation progressed, eye movement patterns appropriate to the new vestibular physics began to appear (Young et al., 1984).

Large individual differences exist in the speed of adaptation; some astronauts experience little discomfort, and others are incapacitated much of the time for several days. Unfortunately, tests of vestibular adaptation on Earth are of little value in predicting how severe the space sickness will be. Upon returning to Earth, the adapted astronauts experience what can be described as Earth sickness until their vestibular systems readapt to terrestrial conditions.

SEMICIRCULAR CANALS

The **vestibule,** the area where the utricle and saccule are located, also contains entries to the semicircular canals (much as a Victorian vestibule opens into its parlor). The canals lie in three orthogonal planes (see Figure 4.31), so any acceleration of the head affects at least one of them. Their principle of operation is somewhat different from that of the utricle and saccule; they rely on fluid flow rather than the movement of weights. When the head rotates, the fluid in the canals remains stationary, creating a relative motion between the fluid and the canal.

Fluid currents in the canals are transduced in the **ampulla,** a bulge near each canal's opening into the vestibule. The flow displaces the **cupula,** a gelatinous mass inside the ampulla (see Figure 4.32). Embedded in the cupula are the vestibular hair cells; cupula and hair cells together form the **crista.**

Fluid flows in the semicircular canals are difficult to observe. Steinhausen (1931) first saw them by injecting an oil droplet into a partly dissected canal in a pike. This fish has a large and relatively accessible vestibular system, but the anatomy of its canals is practically identical to the human's. When the labyrinth of the pike was rotated, the oil droplet lagged behind and moved closer to or farther from the ampulla, showing that fluid was flowing in the canal.

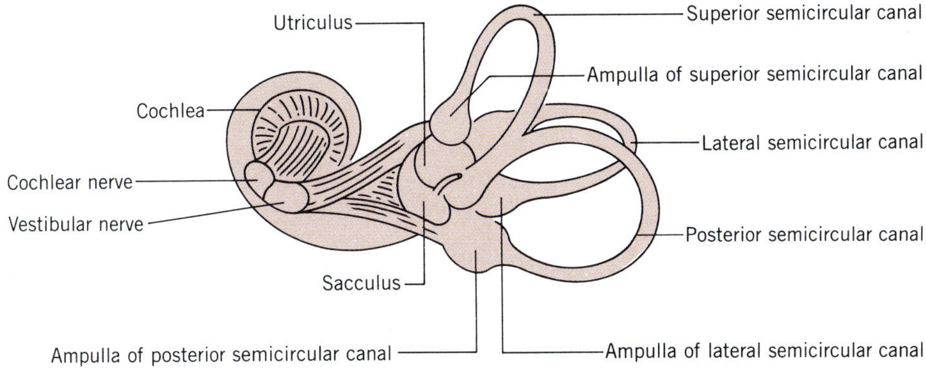

Figure 4.31 *The vestibular labyrinth and the inner ear. The planes of the three semicircular canals are not strictly horizontal, frontal, and saggital but are somewhat inclined. Most head movements stimulate all three canals to some extent.*

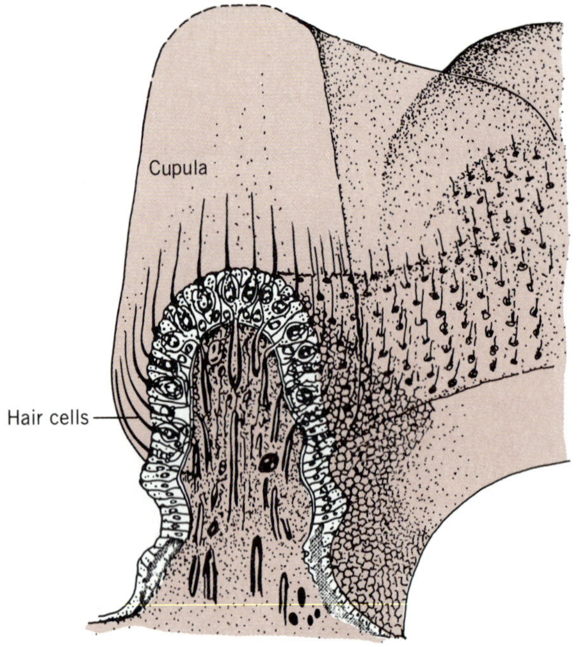

Figure 4.32 *Reconstruction of the crista ampullaris of the semicircular canals, based on light microscope studies. The cupula containing the cilia of the hair cells is a gelatinous mass similar to that in the utricle and saccule, but no otoliths are necessary because the cupula is moved by fluid flow in the canals rather than by its weight. The cupula extends vertically to intercept the fluid flow and transmit the mechanical energy to the hair cells.*

Like the cochlea, the vestibular apparatus has two types of hair cells (see Figure 4.33). Type 1 is the goblet-shaped cell on the left of the figure. It has a particularly close connection with its second-order nerve fiber, which forms a **calyx** (cup) around the entire cell body. It is easy to see how the calyx could evolve into the endings on the auditory inner hair cells. Type 2 is the cylinder-shaped cell on the right of the figure. It is not known why there are two types of vestibular hair cells.

RELATIONSHIP OF VESTIBULAR PHYSICS TO EXPERIENCE

The vestibular system is an ancient system evolutionarily, with a complicated physics but a relatively simple neural information flow. Usually the system serves us very well. When it does not, the illusions of position and motion can usually be explained in terms of the physics of the receptor organs and the transduction process.

Vestibular psychophysics begins with a paradox: we are aware of head motions, but the transducers signal only acceleration. Normally our head motions are abrupt, for we tend to alternate fixed positions with rapidly changing motion, and vision adds important information about head motion. But under special circumstances we can be seriously misled.

A subject seated on a rotatable chair in darkness feels a self-motion as the chair begins to move. But if the chair continues with a constant speed of rotation, the sensation of motion soon vanishes. At the start of the motion (see the left side of Figure 4.34) the fluid in the semicircular canals stands still when the canals (and the head) begin to rotate around it. The resulting pressure on the cristae produce a sensation of acceleration. After a few seconds the fluid begins to move, because of friction in the canals, and the sensation stops. Since the transduced acceleration is misperceived as motion, the person feels a lack of motion.

At the middle of Figure 4.34 the subject is rotating in the chair but feels no sensation of motion. If the chair is stopped, the person will begin to feel a rotation in the opposite direction (see the right side of the figure). The cause of this illusion is similar to the cause of the original feeling of movement; when the head stops, the fluid in the semicircular canals continues to rotate for a few seconds. The fluid movement gives rise to a sensation of rotation. In darkness the subject will continue to feel rotation. If the lights are turned on, the subject will experience dizziness from a mismatch between the visual and vestibular sources of information about motion.

Ballet dancers can withstand spins that would leave the rest of us hopelessly dizzy. They cannot use the obvious technique of closing their eyes, for they need vision to maintain posture and coordination. Their secret is to look at a particular point and hold the head still as long as possible. When the neck will turn no further, they execute a quick 360 deg head turn, now with the head lead-

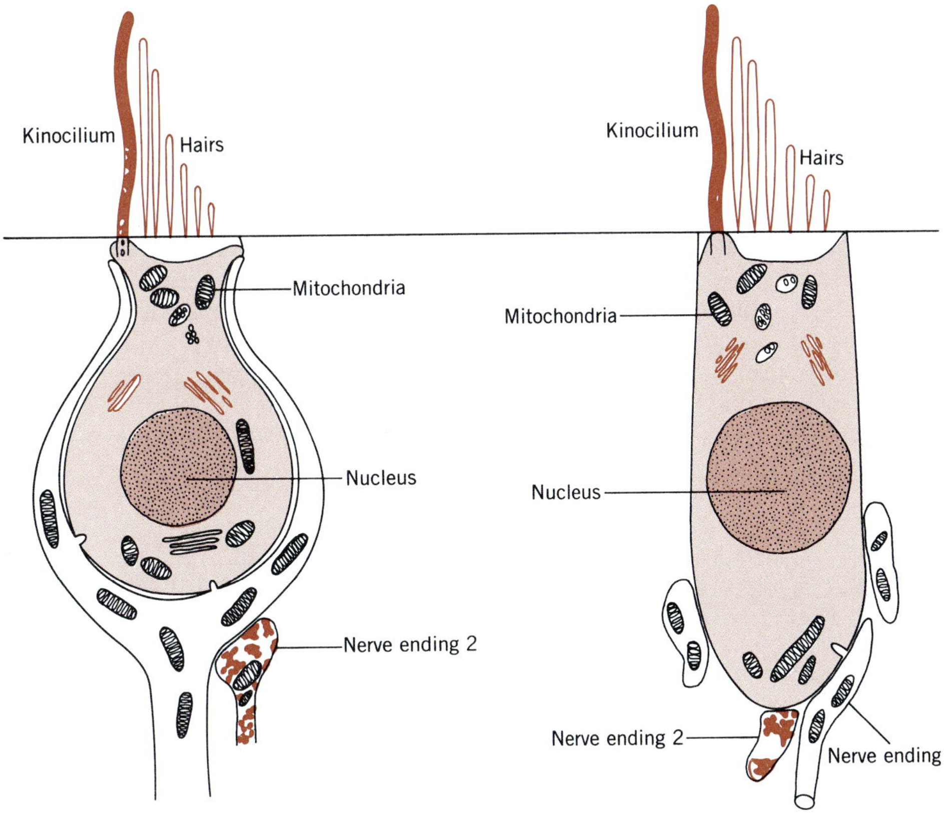

Figure 4.33 *Two types of vestibular hair cells. The mitochondria are particularly dense near the cilia.*

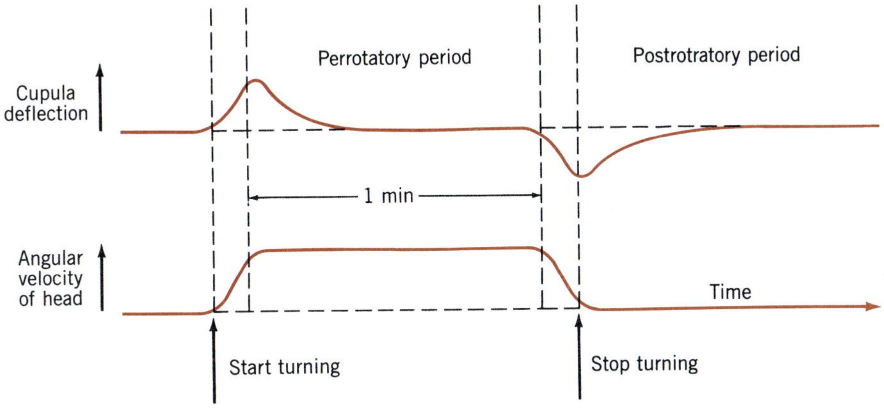

Figure 4.34 *Cupula deflection in a semicircular canal (top) caused by changes in angular velocity (bottom). The subject is accelerated in a rotating chair, which is rotated at a constant angular velocity and negatively accelerated until stopped. During constant rotation the vestibular stimulation ceases. Perception follows the vestibular stimulation rather than the actual rotation. If the subject is seated in a striped drum fixed to a surface, the perception that the stripes are moving occurs when the vestibular stimulation ceases.*

ing the body, and stabilize the head again while the body turns underneath it. In this way dancers convert a continuous spin, which would dangerously adapt the semicircular canals, into a series of alternating holds and jumps. The dancers' transducers can handle the accelerations.

You can examine the physics of this situation with a glass of water on a table. Begin slowly rotating the glass. At first, the water will rotate relative to the glass, not to the table. The water's motion may be easier to see if a toothpick is floated in the glass. Eventually, the water will rotate as fast as the glass, so there is no relative motion of the glass and the water. If you now stop rotating the glass, the water will continue to rotate. If the water were the endolymph of the vestibular system, you can see how the sensation of dizziness could arise.

Ordinarily we do not experience these vestibular illusions because we use vision to gain information about steady movement. The visual and vestibular systems are closely linked in both experience and neurology, for the afferent neurons from the hair cells synapse on neurons that receive both visual and vestibular information. After that the two are coded together. But that is the subject of the next chapter.

CHAPTER SUMMARY

1. Sensory signals undergo nonneural processing, transduction, and processing by neurons. Before transduction, signals are channeled to the receptors and sometimes are adjusted in intensity.

2. The chemical and mechanical senses were the first to evolve and have the simplest anatomy. Somatic sensation is different on hairy skin and on hairless glabrous skin. Both have a variety of end organs. Free nerve endings have no obvious anatomical receptors; they look like dendrites extending into the skin. Four kinds of encapsulated endings—Pacinian corpuscles, Meissner's corpuscles, Krause end bulbs, and Merkel's disks—are more specialized, though there is dispute about the degree of specificity. Electrical currents generated by heating or deforming the skin may participate in transduction. All somatic receptors transmit action potentials into the central nervous system.

3. Olfactory receptors are continually replaced throughout life. The method of transduction and the number of types of receptors are unknown. Two current theories are the stereochemical theory, which postulates that shapes and charges of molecules determine their odors, and the chromatographic theory, which states that the mobility of molecules is the key. Both probably have an element of truth.

4. Here there is a shift in receptor organization. The olfactory and sensorimotor receptors send axons directly into the brain; but gustatory receptors and the ones to follow produce no action potentials and are specialized for transduction into graded generator potentials. Their messages are conducted to the CNS by second-order neurons. Gustation has four types of receptors, which are found throughout the mouth area. They are replaced every few days. Sweet, sour, salty, and bitter tastes are found on separate taste buds. They can be characterized chemically, though again the mechanism of transduction is unknown.

5. Visual stimuli are extensively preprocesed before transduction. Light is focused by the cornea, adjusted in intensity by the pupil, and focused by the lens before striking the retina. The two types of receptors are the rods and the cones. Both are highly evolved ciliated cells. In the receptors, transduction takes place in an outer segment and metabolic support in an inner segment containing the cell body and synapses.

6. Rod outer segments contain stacks of membrane disks with the visual pigment molecule rhodopsin, which splits upon absorbing a photon of light. Through a series of four intermediate stages—from rhodopsin to transducin to PDE to

cyclic GMP—Na^+ channels in the rod membrane are closed, reducing the "dark current" that flows between the outer segment and the inner segment in darkness. Light adaptation takes place at the pupil, in the receptors, and in visual neurons. Cones have folded outer segment membranes instead of disks. Each has one of three kinds of pigments maximally sensitive to red, green, or blue light. Visual receptors can be conceived of as dark detectors rather than light detectors.

7. Auditory signals are filtered by the outer ear and increased in power by the bones of the middle ear, so they pass efficiently to the fluid-filled inner ear, or cochlea. The cochlea is a coiled double tube; the wall separating the two tubes, the basilar membrane, vibrates in response to sounds. High sounds vibrate only the initial portion; lower sounds affect the entire cochlea. Localization uses cues of phase differences between signals in the two ears at low frequencies and intensity differences at higher frequencies.

8. Basilar membrane motion excites the hair cells, the auditory transducers, by a shearing motion on their hairlike cilia. There is a strong electrical gradient across the hairs. Transduction may take place at their tips, where the generator potentials are largest. Audition uses two frequency codes, a place code for high frequencies (where frequency corresponds to position on the cochlea) and a telephone code at low frequencies (where neurons repeat the stimulus frequency).

9. The vestibular system has hair cells similar to the auditory hair cells. The utricle and saccule detect the direction of gravity. The three semicircular canals detect head acceleration in three different planes. The acceleration is interpreted as motion, leading to systematic illusions of motion.

KEY TERMS

Generator potentials
Mechanoreceptors
Somatosensory system
Hairy skin
Glabrous skin
Free nerve endings
Encapsulated end organs
Pacinian corpuscles
Kinesthetic sense
Meissner's corpuscles
Krause end bulbs
Merkel's disks
Papillae
Dermis
Epidermis
Piezoelectric effect
Punctate pattern
Cilia
Cribriform plate
Stem cells
Stereochemical theory
Gas chromatograph
Gustation
Photons
Cornea
Sclera
Suspensory ligaments
Ciliary muscles
Presbyopia
Iris
Extraocular muscles
Inner segment
Outer segment
Pigment epithelium
Rods
Cones
Rhodopsin
Retinal
Opsin
Bleaching
Dark current
Light adaptation
Binocular
Dark adaptation
Purkinje shift
Iodopsin
Scotopic
Photopic
Mesopic
Pinna
Visual capture
Middle ear
Ossicles
Oval window
Inner ear
Malleus
Incus
Stapes
Tensor tympani
Stapedius
Cochlea
Basilar membrane
Helicotrema
Round window
Hair cells
Tectorial membrane
Inner hair cells

Outer hair cells
Cochlear microphonic
Endolymph
Place theory
Prosthesis
Fourier analysis
Telephone theory
Volley principle
Labyrinth
Utricle
Saccule
Otolith organs
Semicircular canals
Vestibule
Ampulla
Cupula
Crista
Calyx

SUGGESTED READINGS

Dallos, P. (1981). Coohlear physiology. *Annual Review of Psychology, 32,* 153–190.

Recent progress in understanding the cochlea is reviewed in some detail.

Geldard, F. A. (1972). *The human senses* (2nd ed.) New York: Wiley.

This thorough yet readable book describes the basic anatomy, physiology, and psychology of the senses. The author has contributed a lot of the basic work to this field.

Iggo, A., & Andres, K. (1982). Morphology of cutaneous receptors. *Annual Review of Neuroscience, 5,* 1–32.

This close look at the anatomy of receptors in the skin is rich with electron micrographs.

Katsuki, Y., Norgren, R., & Sato, M. (1981). *Brain mechanisms of sensation.* New York: Wiley.

This book reviews the lower levels of sensory systems, covering all modalities.

Stryer, L. (1987, July). The molecules of visual excitation. *Scientific American,* 42–50.

This is a grand tour of the process of visual transduction, including the detective stories that brought us to an understanding of the steps involved.

Chapter 5

SENSORY INFORMATION FLOW

After nonneural processing and transduction, incoming sensory information is ready for the third step—neural coding. At this step, signals are changed from a form determined by the physiology and physics of the receptors into a form useful to the organism. Recoding occurs several times. Coding starts at the receptors as a set of adjacent but independent parts like the small ceramic pieces of mosaic artwork. Spatial and temporal integration begin immediately. The image—the faithful copy of the outside world—is lost in the process.

PROCESSING SENSORY INFORMATION

The goal of recoding is to generate sensory information, a reduction of uncertainty. But information must exist in a context: reduction of uncertainty about what? As recoding progresses in a sensory system, the answer to that question changes. The code begins as a modification of the stimulus information, emphasizing important aspects and discarding irrelevant ones. When the information reaches more central layers, the code may also reflect the expectations of the organism or the nature of the task at hand. Visual processing, for instance, begins with extraction of information about stimulus properties such as contrast and motion. Neurons in more central visual areas—in the cortex—deal with more complex tasks, such as combining inputs from the two eyes; they are also affected by the state of alertness and even by the importance of the information to the organism. As you read this, for example, you are using the shapes of the letters to get information about the meanings of the words.

READING THE SENSORY CODE

In experiments on sensory systems it is easy to be misled by signals that coexist with the code but are not part of it. The **electroencephalogram** (Greek for "electric-head-write"), or **EEG,** an electrical record from the scalp, provides an example. EEG signals are recorded with the method in Figure 5.1 and are either written with pens on an EEG machine or stored in a computer. Because the signals are recorded with electrodes so far from the neurons, the EEG reveals the ensemble activities of millions of cells. The technique is the only measure of brain physiology commonly used for humans. We have learned a lot from it, as Chapter 16 will show.

But the EEG is not a code. Though the events outside the scalp are generated by electrical field changes in neurons, the brain does not use these events in coding information. The situation is like that of trying to understand a football game by standing outside the stadium and listening to the crowd. You can learn whether things are happening and when they happen, but the shout of the crowd cannot substitute for a direct look at the game.

There seems to be only one case in which it is possible to get an accurate look at a neurological code, and that is in recording action potentials.

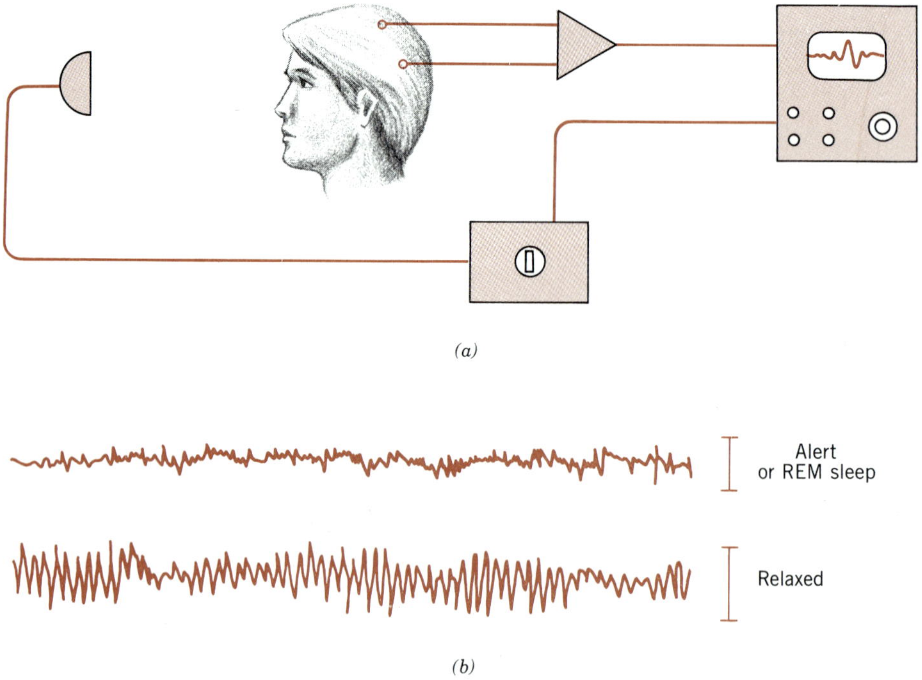

Figure 5.1 *EEG techniques.* (a) *Physical arrangement for recording a single channel of an EEG while stimulating a subject. The difference between potentials at the two electrodes is amplified and displayed.* (b) *Single-channel records of an EEG at alertness and relaxation. The amplitude becomes larger with lowered activity, implying that neurons are firing in synchrony. The EEG has very low amplitude compared to that of intracranial recordings; it is measured in microvolts, whereas extracellular microelectrode recordings register millivolts. The fastest frequencies in the EEG do not approach the spikes of action potentials; most of the power is concentrated at 8–16 Hz.*

The reason for this accuracy is the same as the reason for 'the brain's use of action potentials—they can transmit information without error. For the brain, the transmission is to the next synaptic layer, but the same principle applies to transmission into the neurophysiologist's apparatus. Since the spike is an all-or-none event, it is insensitive to the inevitable distortions that occur during the recording process. Analog events such as graded potentials are more difficult to record, because the signal at the recording site may be different from the signal affecting the synapses.

It is also possible to miss information because a code is not accessible in the method being used. A microelectrode can record accurately a message carried on a single axon. But a microelectrode might record a seemingly random sequence of spikes even though information is passing through the axon. This can happen if the information is coded in the relative amounts of firing in several neurons (a phase code). For instance, a signal might be present only if two neurons fire together. But one would never know this by recording just one neuron.

LATERAL INHIBITION

One mechanism for taking information transduced at discrete receptors and putting it into a large number of neuron channels is lateral inhibition. It might seem that inhibition would only dampen activity, but this is not necessarily the case; the action of lateral inhibition is more stabilizing than suppressing. Suppose, for instance, that cell A inhibits its neighbor, cell B. B then fires less and sends less inhibition to its neighbor, cell C, so C's activity can increase. Figure 5.2 shows a computer simulation of this process, illustrating what happens when a layer of neurons fires with a steady background rate and a group in the center is excited by an afferent input (Bridgeman, 1971). Lateral inhibition causes waves of inhibition and disinhibition to travel across the network in a series of damped oscillations. Even a localized disturbance in the network can change the firing of many cells. (Simulation is a relatively new tool in brain research. It aids in teasing out the meaning of discoveries made in animals, helping to show their implications for information processing.)

Lateral inhibition exists at all levels of sensory systems. Each neuron inhibits its neighbors by an amount proportional to its own activity. As Figure 5.3 shows, the process accentuates edges to create **Mach bands**—illusory light or dark lines where brightness gradients meet. They are named after Ernst Mach, a 19th-century German physiologist and physicist. Figure 5.4 offers two views of a Mach band. Look closely at the individual lines,

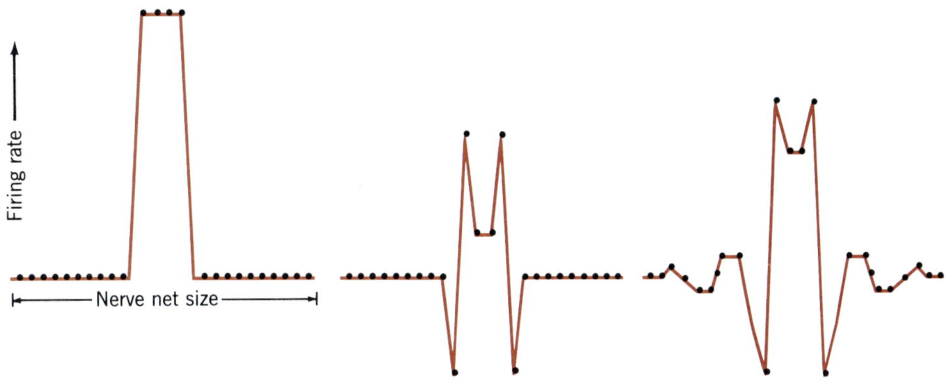

Figure 5.2 *Reverberation of activity in a lateral inhibitory nerve network following a stimulus at the center. In this simulation each neuron inhibits its three nearest neighbors on each side; the model is one-dimensional, a row of neurons rather than a surface. In the left graph the four center neurons in the network receive an excitatory input. The center graph shows the state of the network after one round of lateral inhibition. As time goes on, activity spreads further and further, until in the right graph a large number of neurons, in addition to the original four stimulated neurons, are involved in coding the stimulus.*

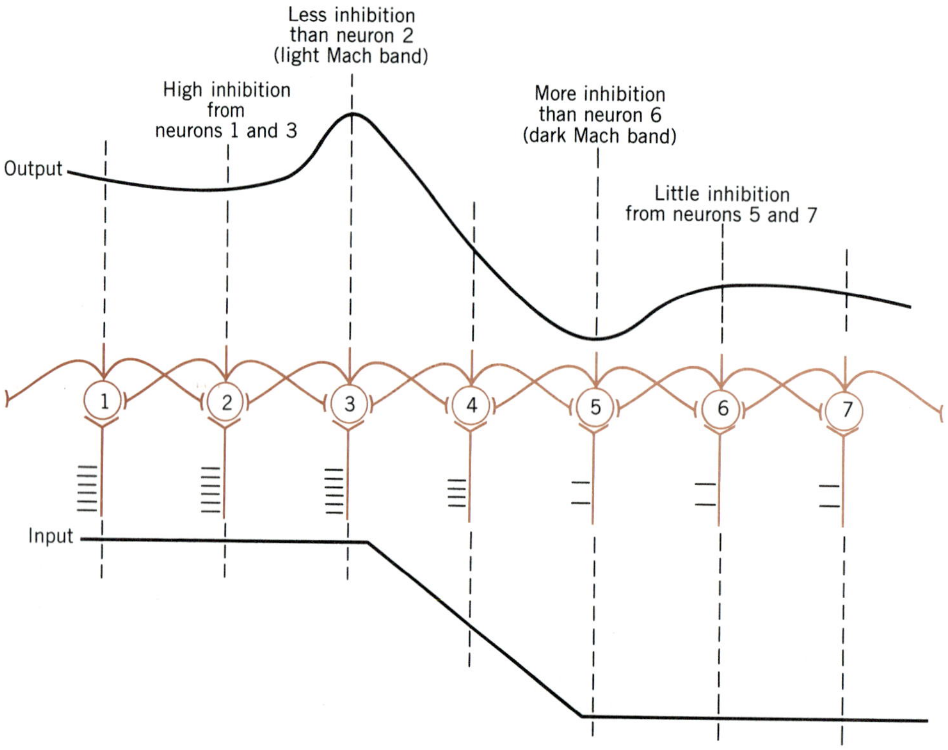

***Figure 5.3** Edge enhancement by lateral inhibition. In this diagram each neuron inhibits only its immediate neighbors on each side. The enhancement comes from neurons 3 and 5. Neuron 3 receives less inhibition from neuron 4 than its neighbors to the left receive, so its activity level is higher than that of the others. Neuron 5 gets minimum excitation but more inhibition than its neighbors to the right because of the higher activity of neuron 4. Patterns such as this have been observed experimentally in the lateral eye of the horseshoe crab,* Limulus. *From Ratliff (1965).*

and you'll see that their thickness changes in a way similar to that plotted in Figure 5.3. Then move back from the book until the lines themselves are no longer visible. The Mach bands will appear as vertical light and dark bands. Another result of lateral inhibition in perception appears in Figure 5.5. At the intersections of the light lines in the grid, a fuzzy dark spot is visible; it is a result of increased inhibition from the light areas surrounding the intersection. The only intersection missing its dark spot is the one you are looking at; lateral inhibition doesn't reach as far in the fovea.

Lest you think that all of this is removed from the needs of everyday life, the next time you are bothered by a mosquito bite, try scratching in a circle around it. Lateral inhibition will reduce the itching without irritating the bite.

With these principles of sensory information processing in mind, we can begin looking at individual modalities.

INFORMATION PROCESSING IN THE SOMATOSENSORY SYSTEM

CENTRAL PROJECTIONS

The network of somatosensory fibers appears to be quite intricate, but its logical structure is simple.

Figure 5.4 *A demonstration of Mach bands.* (a) *An exaggerated illustration of the profiles of the lines in* (b). (b) *From left to right is a region of high brightness (a narrow dark line), then a region of steadily decreasing brightness (a ramp), and finally a region of low brightness.*

Signals transduced in the skin are transmitted without synapses or other interactions directly to the CNS. Thus all peripheral sensory nerves are parallel and independent. Because the first synapses of somatosensory receptors are within the CNS, rich possibilities for neural interaction exist with the first processing of somatosensory signals. The two input pathways, the spinothalamic and lemniscal systems, remain separate all the way to the cortex (Rose & Mountcastle, 1959; Wall, 1961).

Spinothalamic Pathways

The evolutionary age of the older **spinothalamic pathway** is shown in several ways. The pathway's receptors terminate in the gray matter of the spinal cord, the oldest part of the motor system (see Figure 5.6). There they form direct sensorimotor links. And the second-order cells, those that receive synaptic inputs from the receptors, send numerous branches into the brain-stem reticular formation en route to the thalamus. In primitive vertebrates the reticular formation was an important motor coordination center, though in mammals its function has changed largely to regulation of arousal and attention.

The pathway contains smaller axons concerned with pain, temperature, and less finely localized cutaneous information. These axons are considered part of the spinothalamic system because their information is carried farther by axons of the spinothalamic tract, which is schematized in Figure 5.6. The sensory modalities are layered within the lateral spinothalamic tract; temperature fibers are dorsal, and pain fibers are more ventral. Injuries of this small tract usually affect both pain and temperature sensations. The fine fibers responsible for the sensation of bladder fullness also run through the tract (Nathan & Smith, 1951)—a good example of a poorly localized sensation. The sensation need not be conducted quickly because the state of the bladder changes only slowly.

The spinothalamic system contains about three-fourths of all somatosensory afferents, but this number exaggerates its importance because most of the fibers are small and unmyelinated. Since the fibers conduct slowly, they can carry

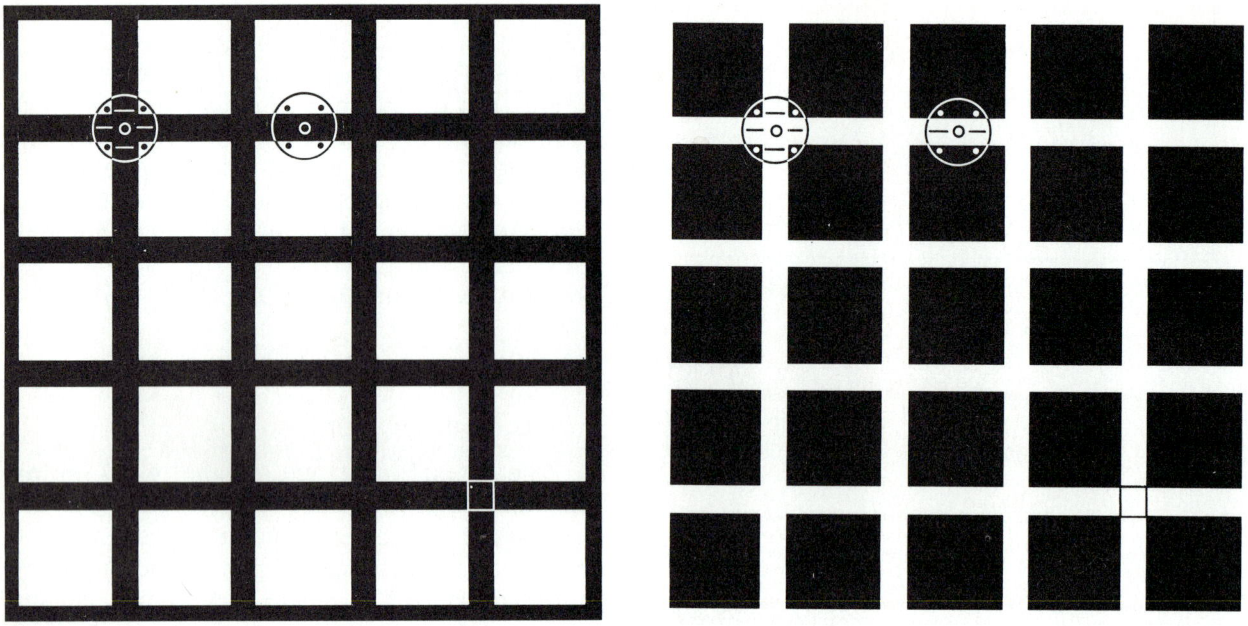

(a) *(b)*

Figure 5.5 *Hermann grids in positive and negative contrast. You can move your eyes in small steps along one of the lines between the intersections to discover the size of the foveal area, where the effect does not occur.*

fewer spikes; therefore, their bandwidth (information-carrying capacity) is lower. The axons also transmit more primitive information. Spinothalamic pain pathways, for example, are involved in gross pain sensations over a large body area rather than in sharp, localized pain (Kandel & Schwartz, 1982).

Lemniscal Pathways

"Express" service is provided by the **lemniscal pathways,** which use fast myelinated axons and impose no synapses between the transduction area and the medulla of the hindbrain. Lemniscal afferents from the toes and feet are the longest axons of the body, reaching nearly its entire length (see Figure 5.6*b*). The system consists of large, fast axons carrying high-resolution information about touch and pressure. The receptors in this system pass through the dorsal column and spinocervical tract. In the medulla, receptor axons synapse with second-order neurons. The cells thus serve a double function—transducing information into neural codes and transmitting it all the way to the hindbrain. Because the next neurons in this pathway ascend to the thalamus through the medial lemniscal tract, these neurons are considered part of the medial lemniscal system.

Proprioceptive fibers from muscle, tendon, and joint receptors follow the same course, with the addition of axon branches into the cerebellum. Because these receptors are so closely linked with the control of muscles, they will be discussed in more detail in Chapter 8.

Common Features

In both spinothalamic and lemniscal pathways, the receptor cell axons never cross the midline, though the second-order cells generally do. Because the receptor processes extend so much far-

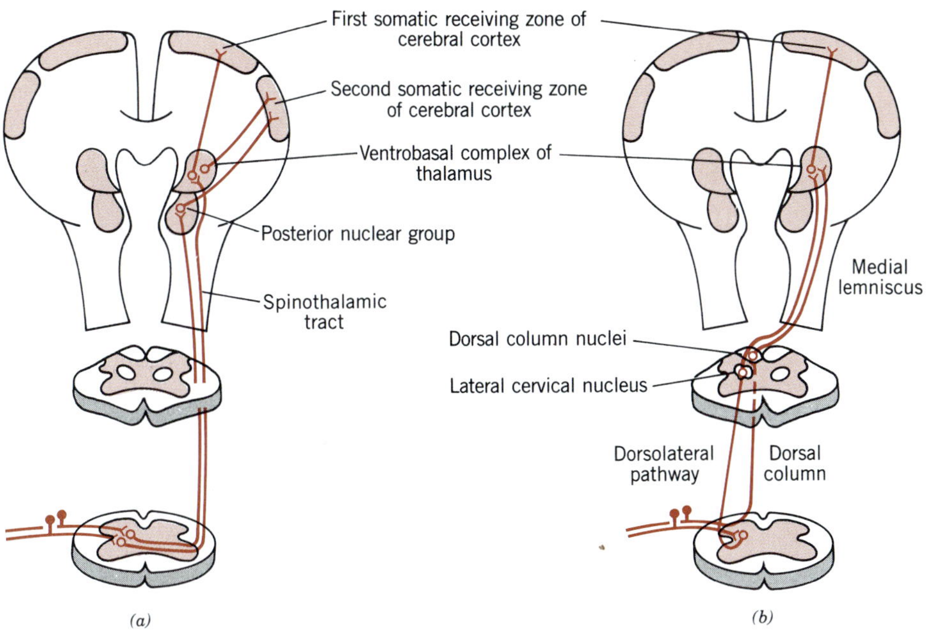

***Figure 5.6** Ascending tracts of the somatosensory system.* (a) *The spinothalamic system. The two areas of the somatosensory cortex have separate somatotopic maps of the body, but both receive thalamic afferents.* (b) *The lemniscal system, running in the dorsal columns and the dorsolateral bundle. The dorsal column fibers are added from the medial to the lateral side ascending the cord; the more medial fasciculus gracilis begins at the bottom of the cord; the more lateral fasciculus cuneatus is added closer to the brain.*

ther up the cord in the lemniscal system, this characteristic results in a curious symptom when the spinal cord is damaged on one side. Pain and temperature sensations are lost on the opposite side of the body below the level of the lesion, but position and movement sensations, spatial discrimination, and vibration sensations are lost on the same side as the lesion (Truex & Carpenter, 1964).

The two systems are also similar in that their second-order cells project in turn to the thalamus. The thalamic cells project to the somatosensory cortex. Thus in both systems the cortex is two synapses away from the receptors. In terms of the universal neuroanatomy discussed in Chapter 2, the somatosensory cortex is quite close to the periphery—closer than in most other sensory or motor systems. The flow of information to the cortex should not be thought of as following a chain of neurons, though, for there is a reorganization of the information at each level.

PERIPHERAL CODING—THE RECEPTIVE FIELD

Every somatosensory neuron has a **receptive field,** the field of skin that when stimulated will change the activity of the neuron (see Figure 5.7). Receptive fields in the spinothalamic pathway tend to be larger than those in the lemniscal pathway. For the receptor, the receptive field is the same as the area of the sensory endings. This is not the case, however, for the neurons to which the receptors project.

Second-order neurons tend to have larger receptive fields than the receptors, but they are organized differently. There is usually an excitatory region at the center of the receptive field and a larger area of surround inhibition (see Figure 5.8). Stimulating the inhibitory area on the skin reduces the response of the neuron to stimuli in the excitatory center. At the next synaptic processing layer in the receptive fields are larger yet. The surround

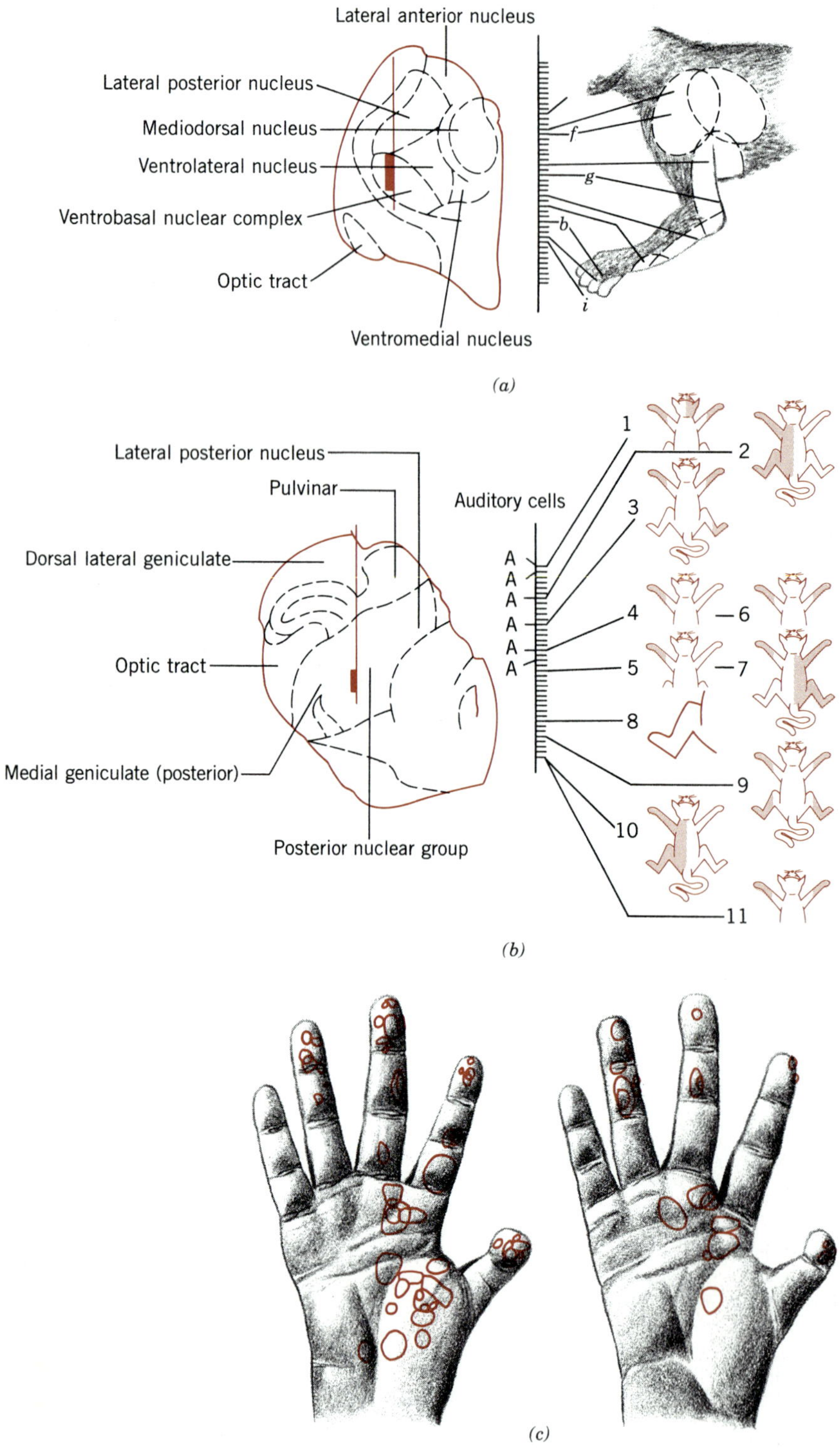

Figure 5.7 *Somatosensory thalamic nuclei.* (a) *Microelectrode penetration of the ventrobasal complex of the thalamus in the cat. The right side shows skin areas (receptive fields) on the contralateral foreleg that excite the neurons when stimulated. There is a regular topographic progression.* (b) *The left side shows penetration of the posterior nuclear group. The right side shows figures whose receptive fields are numbered in descending order. The arrangement is not topographic. Cells 1–9 respond to light touch; cells 10 and 11 require strong and destructive stimuli.* (c) *Drawings of the receptive fields of single afferent fibers on a monkey's hand.*

inhibition comes from lateral inhibition among the neurons in a single layer; each inhibits its neighbors.

The larger size of receptive fields at this stage means that they overlap more; each point on the skin is represented by a larger number of somatosensory neurons than the number of receptors at that point on the skin. Spatial information is not lost, however, because the receptive fields have differing sensitivities in different regions. Stimulation of a point on the skin is now coded in the relative activities of the several neurons having receptive fields that include the point. Suppose, for instance, that a point on the skin is in the excitatory center of a thalamic receptive field but outside the inhibitory areas of several others, as in Figure 5.8. Stimulation of that point would excite the center neuron but would not inhibit the others—a pattern that could be created only by a stimulus at that particular point. It is impossible to localize the point by looking at the activity of only one neuron, for the information is coded in several neurons at once.

The advantage of this coding scheme becomes clear if we imagine what happens when one neuron dies. The remaining neurons will still be able to represent information about stimuli on the missing neuron's receptive field. This principle of distributing information also occurs in the other senses.

CORTICAL PROCESSING

The spinothalamic and lemniscal pathways join again at the level of the somatosensory cortex. (See Figure 5.9, which shows a topographic map of the body.) A "primary" somatosensory cortex (SI) sends projections to a "secondary" cortex (SII) just anterior to the primary cortex. SI and SII are heavily connected to each other, and SII is activated by its connections from SI. SII in turn activates other somatosensory cortical areas. The primary cortex is larger than the others, and somatosensory information flows through it on the way to other cortical areas. This pattern of information flow is similar to that seen in vision; even the microanatomical details of the connections from SI to SII are similar to those in corresponding parts of the visual system, suggesting that all of the cortical sensory systems may be arranged in a similar way (Pons et al., 1987).

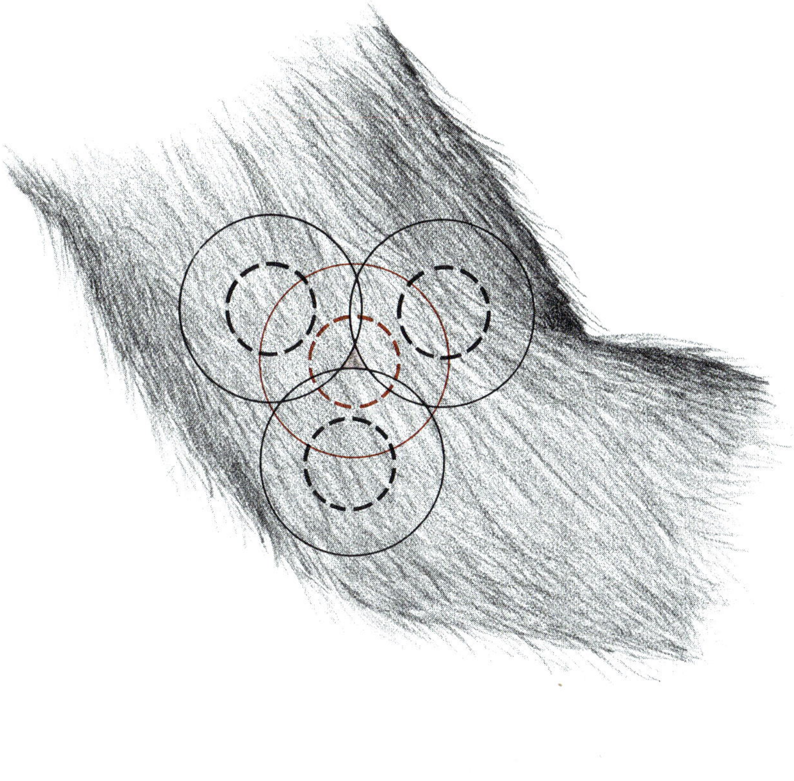

Figure 5.8 *Schematic diagram of overlapping central receptive fields projected onto the skin. If the neuron with the receptive field in the center of the figure is excited, but none of the other neurons are inhibited in their firing, then the central layer has information adequate to determine that the stimulus must have been on the small hatched area of the skin. Other combinations of activity in the four neurons specify other small areas of stimulation.*

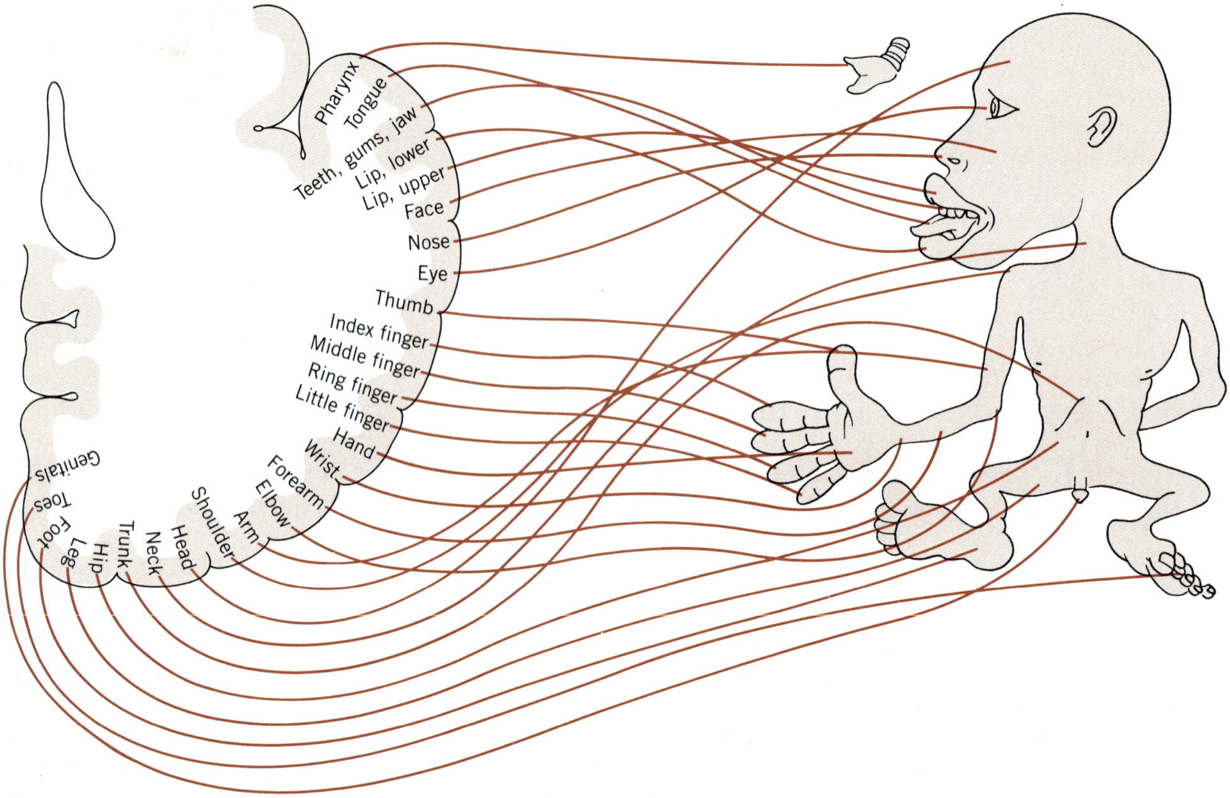

***Figure 5.9** Somatotopic projection of the body on the SI (somatosensory I) postcentral somatosensory cortex. The two-dimensional projection is squeezed into a one-dimensional representation. The exaggeration of the cortical projection area for the hands and feet is even greater than represented here.*

Columnar Organization

The topographic map on the somatosensory cortex is only an approximation; within each local region of the cortex, the organization is different. Functionally, the cortex is composed of columns of cells extending from the surface to the white matter underneath. Each neuron in a column has a similar receptive field. One column might deal mostly with pressure, another with temperature, and so on—all reporting from the same general region of skin and all intermingled (Mountcastle, 1957). This organization was discovered in microelectrode studies in which an electrode was pushed into a cortex micron by micron, under the control of a micrometerlike device. When the microelectrode rested near a neuron, the receptive field could be determined. If the electrode went into the cortex at a slant, the nature of the receptive fields recorded from successive cells remained the same for a while, then changed abruptly at the edge of a column. Columnar organization, discovered in the somatosensory cortex, exists in all sensory cortices.

The form of the topographic map depends on how and when the map is measured. It varies with the degree of anesthesia when the data are taken and with several other factors. Maps made by recording are slightly different from those made by stimulation. This imprecision has led some authors to recommend that maps such as the one in Figure 5.9 not be taken too seriously (Geldard, 1972). The map cannot be drawn without some crossing of lines; it is not just a distorted picture of the body but includes discontinuities.

Cortical Receptive Fields

In the somatosensory cortex the receptive fields show a good deal more variation than at lower levels. There is more variety in size—the range is from pinhead-sized fields to fields cover-

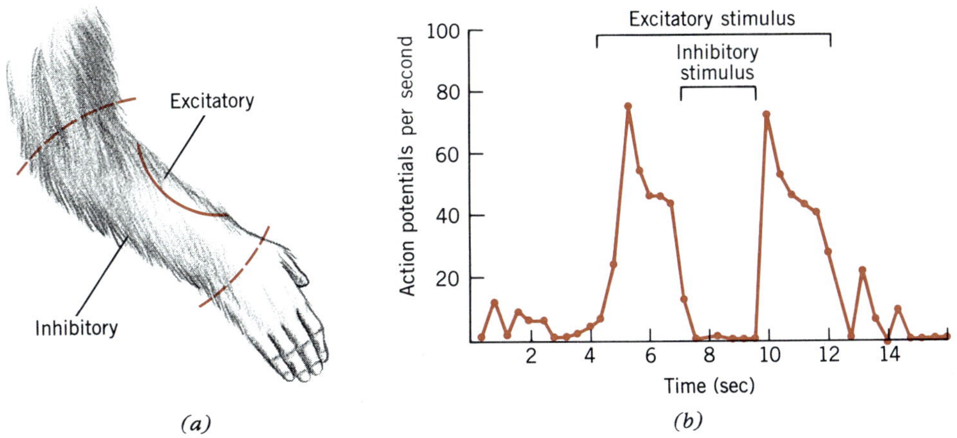

***Figure 5.10** Receptive field of a neuron in the somatosensory cortex of a monkey.* (a) *Spatial representation of excitatory and inhibitory regions.* (b) *Firing rates for tactile stimulation in the center, with suppression by another tactile stimulus applied at the same time in the inhibitory area.*

ing the whole animal—and a stronger inhibition. The receptive field of a monkey cortex neuron (shown in Figure 5.10) has a large inhibitory surround capable of completely suppressing the center response (Mountcastle & Powell, 1959). A new kind of inhibition, complementary inhibition, also appears. If two limbs receive similar excitation, the cortical response may be less than for the same stimulus on either limb alone. Such a stimulation pattern usually results from large stimuli.

Cortical receptive fields are motion-sensitive. Many neurons respond only to an object moving across the skin; they remain silent when the same object deforms the skin in the same area without moving. Other neurons respond only to vibration. We take advantage of the information-carrying capacity of these systems when we manipulate objects to identify them by touch. This activity requires close cooperation between fine motor systems and somatosensory elements (see Chapter 8), but it enables us to obtain information that is not available in a static situation. If we watch people examining the texture of a material, we see that they always move their fingertips across the sample. Roughness excites vibratory receptors only if the fingers are moving; and other properties, such as hardness and even shape, are best sensed during motion.

The complement to motion is adaptation—the reduction of feeling in the presence of steady stimulation. You literally cannot feel the shoes on your feet if the feet are not moving, because the receptors cease responding to unchanging pressure.

Somatosensory experience has a paradoxical nature. The stimuli are deformations of the skin, yet the feeling is of the object being investigated. The feeling is not referred to the skin, where the nerves are, but to the outside world. The same phenomenon is seen more dramatically in vision and hearing, where receptor activity is referred to distant events, though the receptors are inside the eye and ear.

Close examination of the skin during somatic stimulation demonstrates the contrast between cutaneous (skin) stimulation and the resulting perception. If you press your skin gently with a pencil point and observe the indentation of the surrounding skin, you see the dimple but feel only the point, even though the indentation of the skin near the pencil point is nearly as great as that directly under it. Awareness is limited to the sharp feeling of the point itself. Feeling is suppressed in the remaining area, by far the larger part of the skin affected by the pencil. Spikes flow normally from the receptors, but the pattern of stimulation prevents perception except at the sharp point.

According to Békésy (1967), the suppression of perception in such cases is due to lateral inhibition. The strongest signals (from receptors under the pencil point) get through, but the weaker signals are inhibited by the strong stimulation at the center of the dimple.

The somatosensory system works over a relatively small range of stimulus intensities. Only 2 to 3 log units separate the smallest detectable mechanical stimulation from the largest. For temperature the range is even smaller. Figure 5.11 shows a linear relationship between stimulus intensity and firing frequency (Mountcastle, 1967). The relationship holds even in human estimates of the intensity of a tactile stimulus.

INFORMATION PROCESSING IN THE OLFACTORY SYSTEM

The processing of odor information begins in the olfactory bulbs—paired structures extending on stalks (the lateral olfactory tracts) from the base of the forebrain. The olfactory bulb has a topographic organization; the **olfactory epithelium** (the tissue containing the receptors) is mapped onto the bulb, so each point on the bulb corresponds to a point on the receptor surface (Land & Shepherd, 1974).

THE OLFACTORY BULB

Like other brain structures, the olfactory bulb has a basic plan and embellishments. As Figure 5.12 shows, the bulb's input receptor axon synapses directly with the output neuron—the **mitral cell.** This contact occurs in synaptic glomeruli—specialized bundles of fine processes densely covered with synapses. Each fine receptor axon terminates in only one glomerulus, and each mitral cell enters only one glomerulus, but about 1000 receptors project to each mitral cell. A mitral cell axon sends several collaterals (branches) back into the bulb before it joins the lateral olfactory tract.

Modifying this transmission system are three kinds of **intrinsic neurons**—neurons with only local connections. **Periglomerular cells,** as their name implies, surround the glomeruli. These tiny neurons, among the smallest of the brain, connect the glomeruli to one another. Each periglomerular cell has a dendritic tree in one glomerulus and axon branches in several nearby ones. Granule cells perform a similar function, connecting the mitral cells. These neurons have no axons; they operate only with graded potentials. A third type, the short-axon cell, is only 1/200 as numerous as the granule cell and has more variable connections. These neurons interact in a microcircuit—a group of neurons that performs a transformation of information in a region small enough for graded potentials to interact.

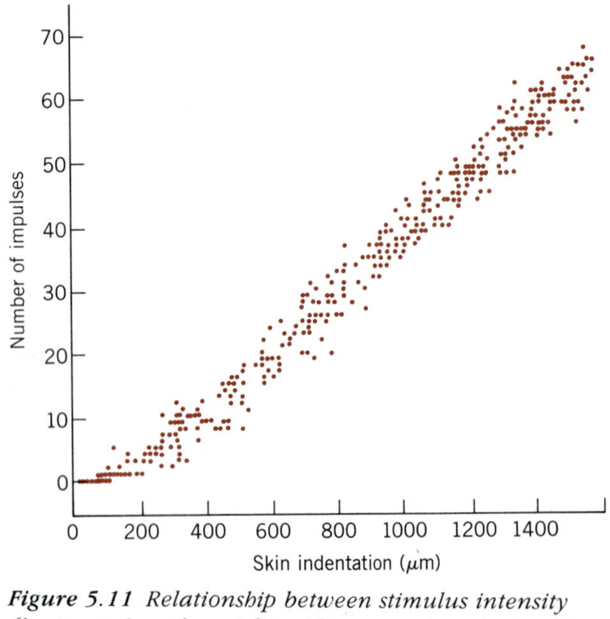

Figure 5.11 *Relationship between stimulus intensity (horizontal axis) and firing frequency (vertical axis) for a somatosensory receptor serving the base of the thumb in a monkey. There is little range restriction because the stimulus does not vary greatly from threshold to maximum.*

Transformation of Codes

The olfactory bulb recognizes olfactory input in both space and time. The olfactory receptors respond whenever an appropriate odor is present, without regard to the activities of other receptors or previous excitation. Interactions in the olfactory bulb pull an inhibitory curtain across these responses. The inhibition allows mitral cell responses to pierce through with specific information about stimulating molecules (Shepherd, 1979a). Odor stimulation generally results in localized excitation of mitral cells along with broad regions of suppression (Kauer & Moulton, 1974).

Stimulation yields a brief burst of activity followed by prolonged suppression; this gives a temporal organization to the output, but at a sacrifice in sensitivity. At near-threshold levels, sensitivity is maintained because the threshold for inhibition is higher than the threshold for excitation. Thus the inhibitory curtain is drawn back near the thresh-

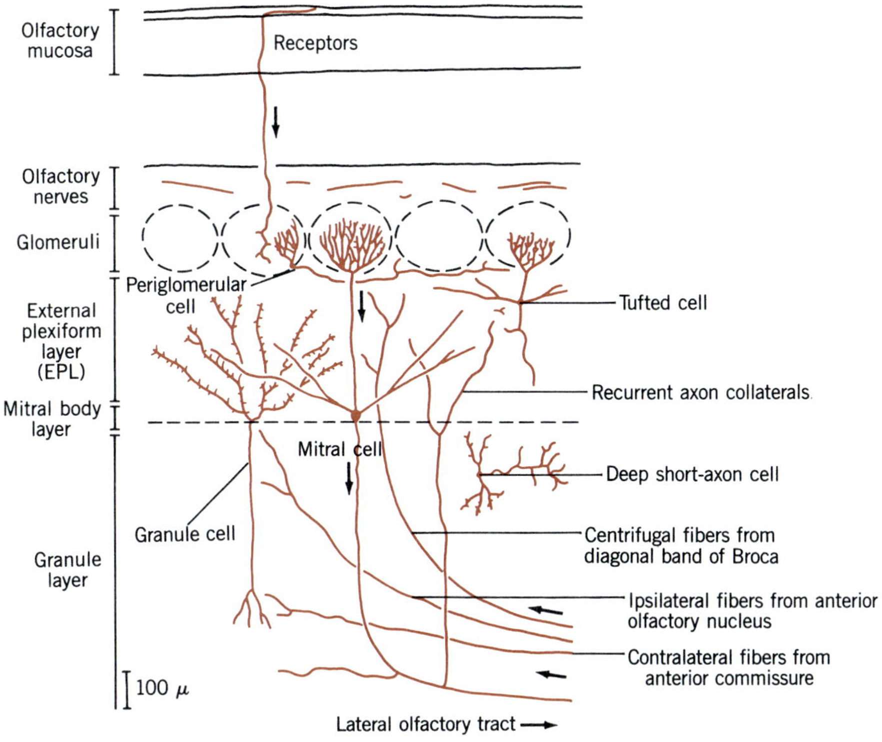

Figure 5.12 *Neural organization of the olfactory bulb. There is a regular striation, or layering, of the elements. One input is from the receptors, and three inputs are from more central layers: centrifugal fibers from the diagonal band of Broca, ipsilateral fibers from the anterior olfactory nucleus, and contralateral fibers from the anterior commissure. The neurons are: mitral cells, with primary and secondary dendrites and recurrent axon collaterals; tufted cells; periglomerular cells; deep short-axon cells; and granule cells.*

old. Weak stimuli give a prolonged weak discharge; stronger stimuli result in a sharp burst of spikes followed by inhibition from both glomerular and granule cell circuits.

The function of the olfactory bulb, then, is to punctuate the olfactory input in space and time to sharpen the definition of the neural code. By damping stronger stimuli while leaving weaker ones unchanged, inhibition also reduces the range of neural response to stimuli of differing strengths. The code is probably modified further by efferent fibers coming down the lateral olfactory tract into the bulb. Some of these fibers originate in the **contralateral** (Latin for "other side") olfactory bulb; others come from more central layers.

CENTRAL PROJECTIONS

The lateral olfactory tract sends fibers into several areas on the lateral-ventral-frontal region of the cortex (see Figure 5.13). At one time, much of what is now called the limbic system was thought to be part of the olfactory system. The old name for this region of the brain, the **rhinencephalon** (Greek for "smell brain"), still survives. The olfactory connections are now thought to be much more restricted. The primary olfactory cortex consists of the **prepyriform cortex** and the **periamygdaloid area;** both receive direct inputs from the mitral cells of the olfactory bulb. Thus olfaction is the only sense that is not relayed through the thalamus. The importance of olfaction in the evolution of the forebrain is seen in the design of the prepyriform cortex; it is made of three-layered paleocortex rather than the six-layered neocortex of the other senses. The secondary olfactory cortex is the **entorhinal area,** which receives fibers from the primary area. It is made of a three-layered archicortex and is transitional in its anatomy between archi- and neocortex.

There has been little progress in understanding the functions of these more central regions, not because we lack the physiological tools to investigate them but because we still don't know how the peripheral olfactory system analyzes odors. We can't read the neural translation of the sensory message because we don't know the letters of the olfactory alphabet. Olfactory neurons have been difficult to assign to groups, each seeming to respond to a unique combination of odors. Fortunately, the situation is not as bleak in the other senses.

INFORMATION PROCESSING IN GUSTATION

Taste fibers run along three cranial nerves—the 7th, 9th, and 10th—into the brain stem. There the various fibers converge to follow an anatomical pattern that resembles the typical auditory or somatosensory arrangement rather than the olfactory pattern. Taste fibers course from the medulla to the thalamus largely in association with the medial lemniscus of the somatosensory system. The tracts branch to the hypoglossal and salivatory nuclei to control tongue and salivation reflexes, respectively. There is a synaptic link in the **solitary nucleus** (a sensory nucleus for the taste system) of the medulla, near where the taste nerves enter the brain stem, and a thalamic center in the ventral posterior nuclei. From the ventral posterior nuclei,

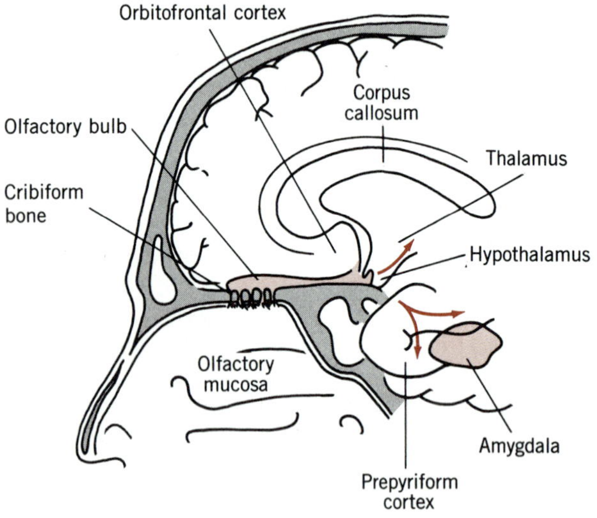

Figure 5.13 Olfactory pathways. The skull is sectioned in a saggital plane, and the left frontal lobe is sectioned in a frontal plane.

taste information runs to a gustatory cortex near the somatosensory cortex, which represents the tongue on the superior surface of the **insula,** the deep sulcus between the parietal and temporal lobes. Thus the entire gustatory path might be seen as a specialized part of the somatosensory system. A secondary gustatory cortex, analogous to the inferotemporal cortex of vision, is located nearby, in the anterior temporal lobe (Bagshaw & Pribram, 1953).

Not much progress has been made in characterizing gustatory receptive fields. We do know that each neuron responds to a number of taste qualities, so the eventual sensation is probably determined by the pattern of activities in many neurons (Bartoshuk, 1978).

INFORMATION PROCESSING IN VISION

The visual system is the best known of the sensory systems. The reasons for this are partly technical—visual stimuli are relatively easy to control, and the anatomy is accessible and well defined. Probably more important is the significance of vision in human experience. More space is devoted here to vision than to the other senses for these reasons and because many of the problems encountered in vision are common to all sensory systems.

PERIPHERAL INFORMATION PROCESSING

Anatomy of the Retina

The cytoarchitecture of the retina is particularly orderly, being constrained by the geometric regularity of optics. The basic plan (shown in Figure 5.14) is simple; there are five types of cells—three for the transmission path and two for lateral interactions.

Peripheral Retina. The photoreceptors are connected to **bipolar cells,** so named because they have two poles. One cell extends toward the

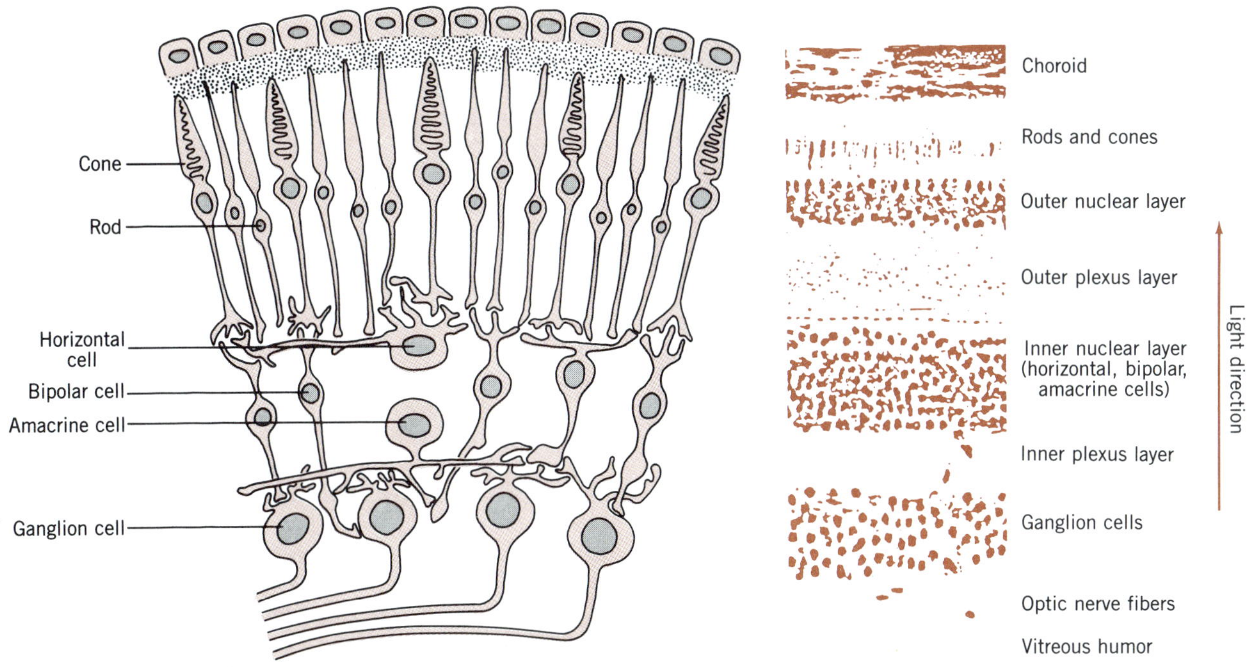

Figure 5.14 *Cross section of the retina, from a light micrograph (left) and a schematic (right). Horizontal cells were once thought to be glial cells because of their lack of long axons and action potentials, but they are now known to be true neurons.*

receptor, and another reaches forward to synapse with a ganglion cell. The ganglion cell in turn sends its axon to the **optic disc** (the light round spot in Figure 5.15), where all the axons converge to exit from the eye. The ganglion cell is the only neuron in the retina to generate a true action potential. Thus all retinal synapses operate in the graded potential mode.

Horizontally acting cells, appropriately named **horizontal cells,** act at the **outer plexiform layer** (the receptor-bipolar synaptic layer). A second set of horizontal interactions takes place on **amacrine cells**—retinal neurons that communicate between bipolar cells and ganglion cells in the **inner plexiform layer** (the bipolar-ganglion cell synaptic layer).

The receptors contact the bipolar and horizontal cells at highly specialized indentations, called **invaginations,** at the ends of their inner segments. Three processes extend into each invagination—one from a bipolar cell and two from horizontal cells—forming the complex shown in Figure 5.16. They receive input from a unique structure, the **ribbon synapse.** Its synaptic vesicles are organized around an intracellular ribbon. The function of the ribbon is unknown, but the ribbon seems to concentrate the synapse's effect in a very small area. At the other end of the bipolar cell is another ribbon synapse, contacting both an amacrine cell dendrite and a ganglion cell dendrite.

As one moves toward the periphery, one finds more and more convergence of many receptors onto each ganglion cell. Complementary to this organization is a divergence. Each receptor contacts several ganglion cells. Despite these differences, some aspects of retinal organization remain constant. Each point on the retina, for instance, is represented by the same number of ganglion cells (about 30 in the cat) regardless of its eccentricity

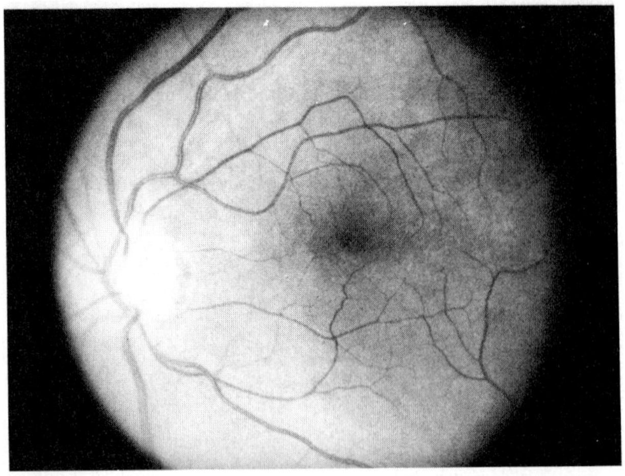

Figure 5.15 *Photograph of the human eye through an ophthalmoscope. The optic disc is at the left; it is white from the concentration of myelinated fibers. The fovea is at the center; the fine blood vessels point toward it, and no large vessels run across it. You can make the peripheral vessels visible in your own eye by shining a bright light such as a flashlight across the front of the eye, then moving the light up and down. You will see the moving shadows of the blood vessels.*

Figure 5.16 *Electron micrograph of synaptic regions of the retina.* (a) *Receptors (arrows) with ribbon synapses contacting two horizontal cell processes and a bipolar cell. The ribbon is the vertical bit of membrane surrounded by vesicles.* (b) *A serial synapse from a bipolar cell to an amacrine cell (dark arrow) and another synapse from the amacrine cell (light arrow).* (c) *A conventional synapse from a horizontal cell to a bipolar cell in the mudpuppy retina (light arrow), along with a ribbon synapse onto the ame horizontal and bipolar cells (dark arrow).* (d) *Reciprocal synapses (making a circle) between a bipolar terminal (dark arrow) and an amacrine cell (light arrow).* (e) *Triple serial synapses (light arrows, A_1 to A_4) and reciprocal synapse (A_4) in the frog retina. The frog retina is more complex than the primate retina, and its receptive fields are more specific.* (f) *Flat bipolar dendrite contacting the base of a receptor terminal in the frog retina, possibly an electrical synapse.* (g) *A gap junction (electrical synapse) between two amacrine cells in the inner plexiform layer of the rat retina.* (h) *A gap junction in the rat inner plexiform layer shown in the freeze-fracture method. The tightly packed particles, 80 to 100 Å in diameter, are characteristic of gap junctions.*

from the fovea (Fischer, 1973). It seems to be important to provide about a 30-fold redundancy everywhere on the retina.

Recently, a new and fairly rare type of ganglion cell has been discovered; it is called a **biplexiform cell** because it has dendrites in both the inner and outer plexiform layers (Mariani, 1982). It receives direct synaptic input from rods, bypassing retinal processing. The function of this straight-through path is still unknown.

Fovea. The region of the retina that has the simplest structure is the **fovea** (Latin for "pit"). Paradoxically, it is also the area of highest **acuity**—the ability to resolve fine detail. The fovea literally forms a shallow pit at the center of the retina (see Figure 5.17), where the neural layers are thinner. The center of the fovea has only cone receptors. Each connects to its own "midget" bipolar cell, which connects to a single "midget" ganglion cell, giving every receptor a "private line" to higher centers. A small area in the center of the fovea achieves even greater spatial resolution by giving up full color vision; there, the blue cones are absent (Wald, 1967).

Acuity is measured by tasks involving patterns, such as the offset of two lines in Figure 5.18*a*. This sort of acuity is sometimes called **hyperacuity** because it is so phenomenally good in the fovea; the smallest detectable offset for two lines is about 0.1 min of arc, a small fraction of the visual angle occupied by a single receptor! (One minute of arc is one-sixtieth of a degree.) More conventional acuity is measured by such tasks as detection of a gap in the C-shaped pattern of Figure 5.18*b*. Acuity falls off at different rates for different measures moving away from the fovea (Westheimer, 1982). Therefore acuity depends on the organization of visual information processing as well as the density of receptors.

The foveal plan of connectivity offers the highest acuity, but it is expensive in terms of the neu-

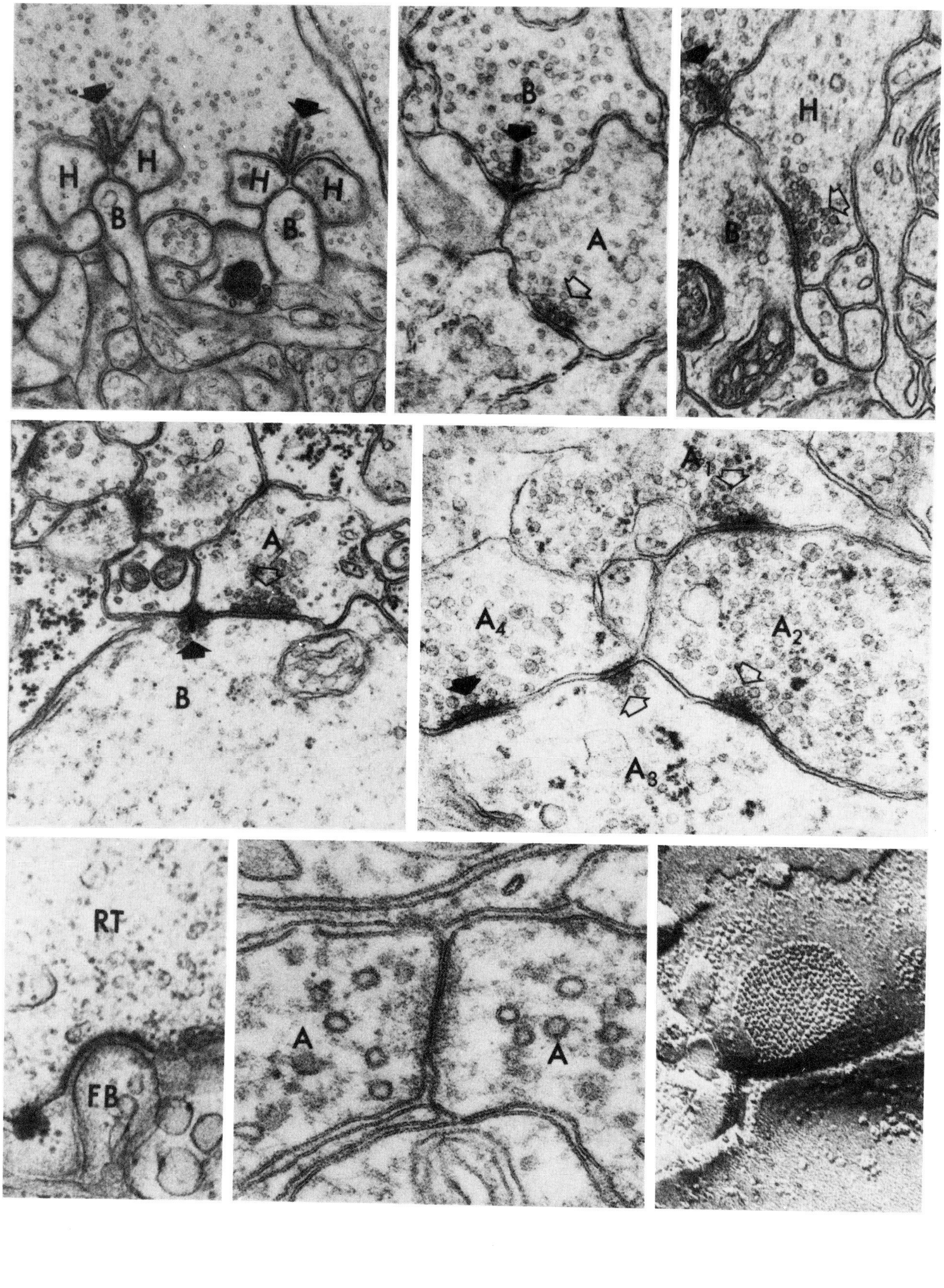
H
H
B
H
H
B
B
A
H
B
A
B
A_1
A_4
A_2
A_3
RT
FB
A
A

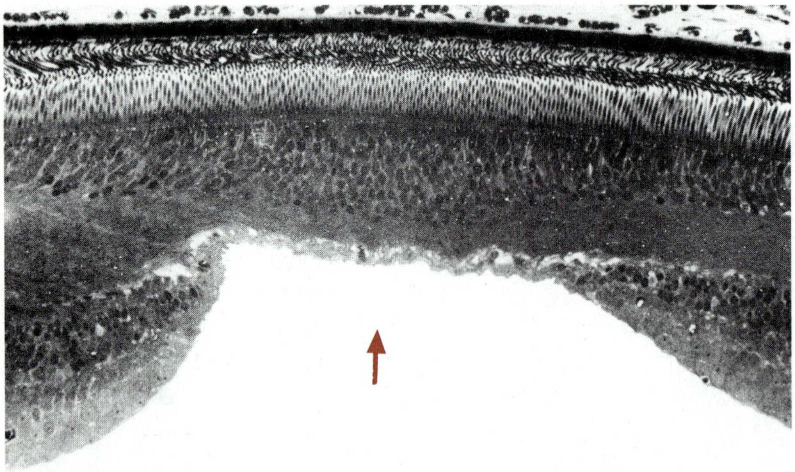

Figure 5.17 Photograph of a cross section of a monkey retina at the fovea. Light enters from below (arrow). Ganglion cell bodies are displaced laterally, away from the foveal center.

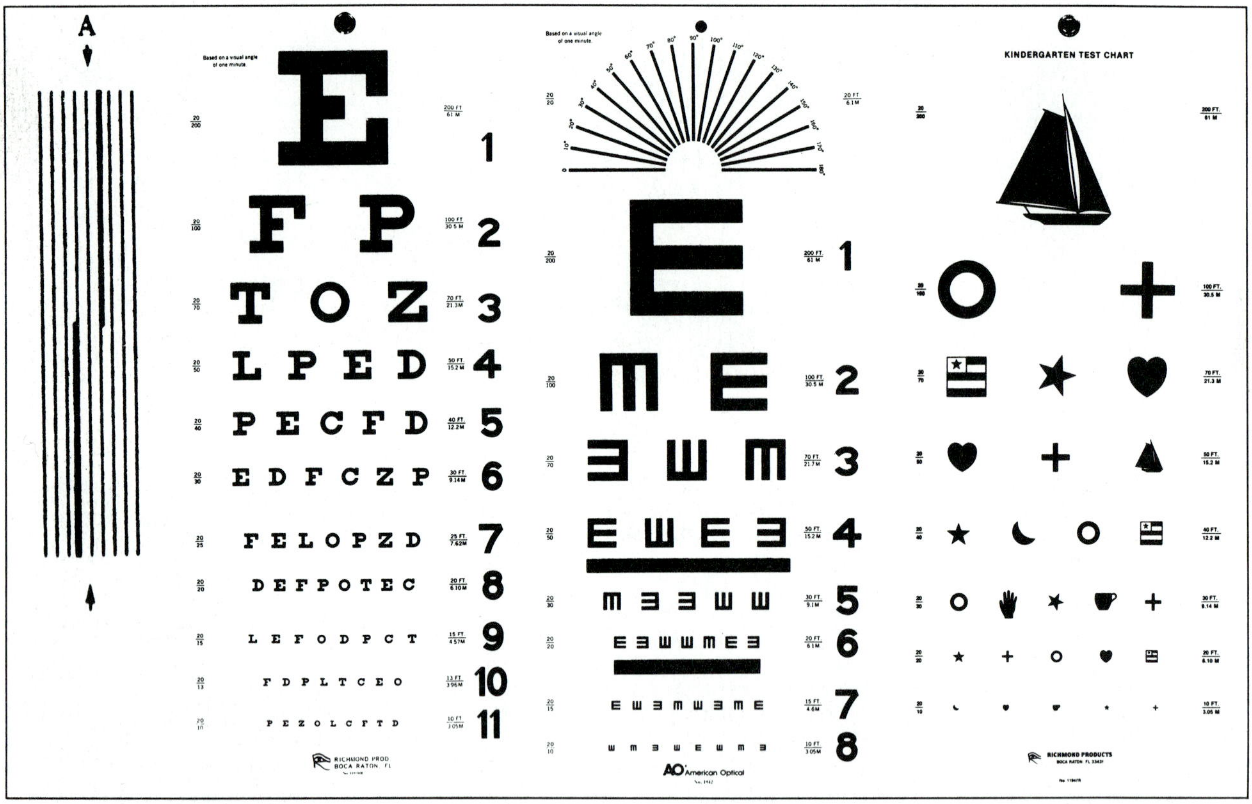

Figure 5.18 *Acuity measures.* (a) *A vernier acuity target.* (b) *Charts for testing acuity, using letters, Snellen figures, and pictures of objects. These tests measure only sensitivity to the finest detail; they do not assess sensitivity to lower spatial frequencies. (See the section on spatial frequency theory later in the chapter.)*

rological machinery required. The human fovea is about 1 deg in diameter, but one-fourth of the visual cortex is needed to process foveal information. Like the glabrous skin of the fingertips, the fovea achieves high spatial resolution while sacrificing sensitivity and requiring a disproportionate share of neurons. The difference between the fovea and the periphery, however, is not sharp. A cell-sized microscopic explorer, finding its way through the retinal neuropil, would not be able to draw a line at a periphery-fovea border. For this reason, estimates of the size of the fovea vary somewhat, depending on the criterion used.

Artists sometimes take advantage of the fovea's concentration of attention and acuity in one small region. In the painting in Figure 5.19, rich detail at the location where the eye is attracted creates an illusion of completeness even though the periphery of the painting is finished in rough strokes. The artist was making a statement about what is important in the composition, and he took advantage of foveal attention and retinal anatomy to do it.

Receptive Fields. The receptor's receptive field is just as large as the diameter of the receptor

Figure 5.19 *Manet's* Isabelle Lemannier Seated. *Only the area near the face is finished in high-acuity detail.*

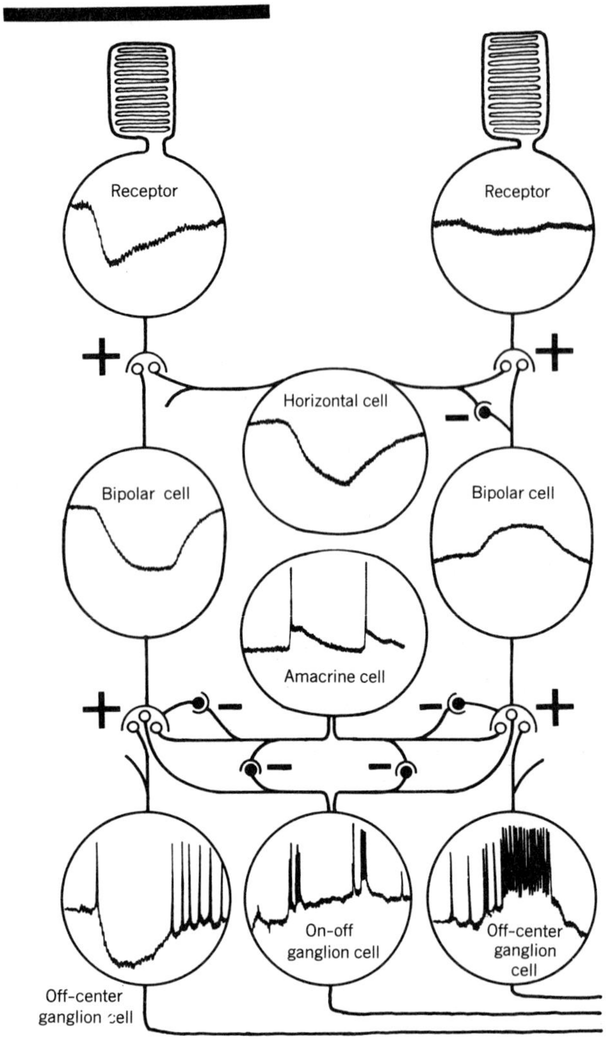

Figure 5.20 *Summary of synaptic organization of the mudpuppy retina, with intracellular recordings from each of the cell types. Light is presented to one receptor (the dark bar). Both bipolar cells have the same synaptic connections, but the illuminated one is hyperpolarized by the receptor and the other one is hypopolarized by the horizontal cell. The on-off ganglion cell receives strong inhibition from amacrine cells.*

itself. The bipolar cell has a more complex field, with a concentric surround antagonistic to the center response. The field is diagrammed in Figure 5.20. If light in the center of the receptive field hyperpolarizes the cell, light in the surround (from the right in the figure) depolarizes it. This surround is contributed by the action of the horizontal cells.

Ganglion cells also have concentric receptive fields with a stronger and more complex antagonistic surround, plotted by computer in Figure 5.21. The surround is contributed both indirectly (by horizontal cells) and directly (by amacrine cells). Each source of inhibition has a separate function. The axons of the ganglion cells form the optic nerve, running along the base of the brain, so an electrode in the optic nerve records from the retinal ganglion cells without having to penetrate the retina.

In a ground-breaking series of experiments, Kuffler (1953) measured retinal receptive fields. He projected a spot of light onto a screen while recording from a ganglion cell axon in a cat. Flashing a small spot in the center of a receptive field gave the vigorous response shown in Figure 5.21*c*. As the spot was increased in size (while the intensity was held constant), the cell responded more and more strongly, until a critical size was reached; beyond that size the firing rate decreased. The spot had grown to fill the excitatory center and began to illuminate the inhibitory surround. In other experiments Kuffler probed receptive fields with a small spot; about half the cells gave a burst when the spot came on in the center of the field (on-center cells). They also responded when a spot in the surround went off (off-surround cells). The other cells showed the reverse pattern, with off-centers and on-surrounds.

Retinal Light Adaptation. The retina must function with light intensities differing by as much as 12 log units (Werblin, 1979). That means it must detect some lights of only a few photons and other lights a trillion times brighter. The relation between light input and graded potential output is graphed in the S-shaped curves of Figure 5.22. The steeper the slope of the curve, the more the output changes in response to a given change in input. As a result, the retina can report finer gradations of intensity. But a steeper slope also means that a smaller range of intensities can be handled. The retina escapes this impasse by shifting the whole S-shaped curve sideways when the average light intensity changes. Part of the range adjust-

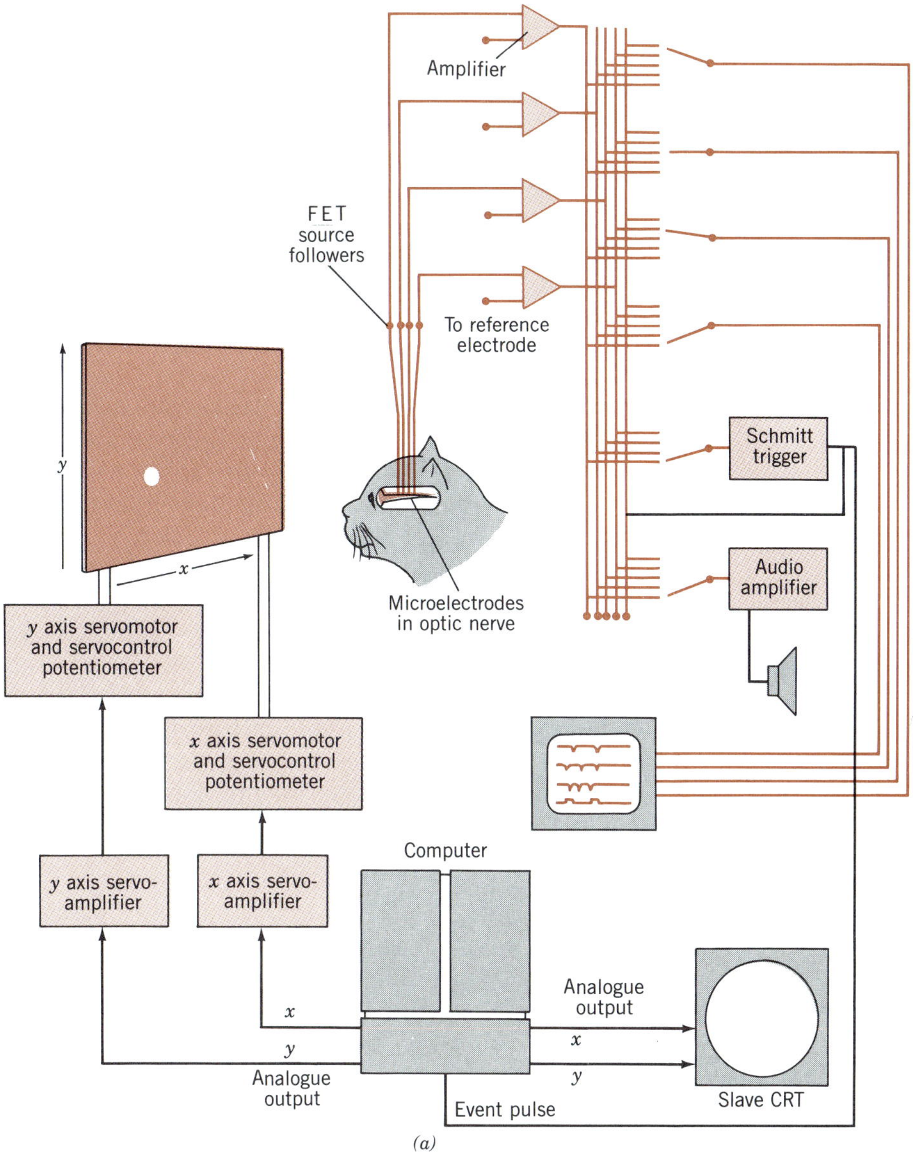

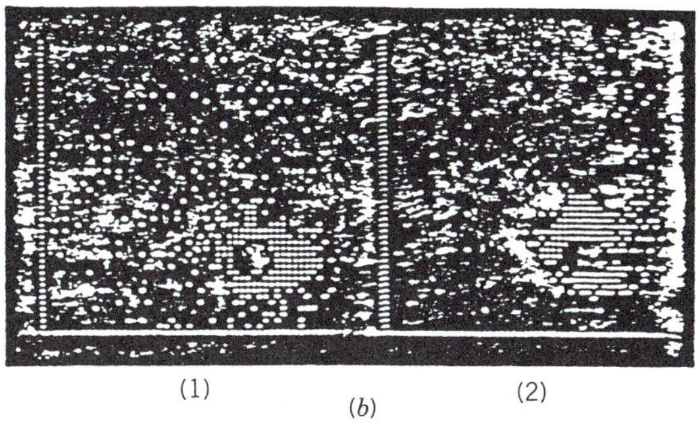

Figure 5.21 *Retinal ganglion cell receptive fields.* (a) *Method for recording from single ganglion cells. Microelectrodes penetrate through the brain to record from ganglion cell axons forming the optic nerve. The electrodes are extracellular, located near rather than within an axon. The experimenter can listen either to the spikes as they are amplified from the electrode or to a Schmitt trigger that generates a pulse only when the spike exceeds a threshold value. Signals can also be displayed on an oscilloscope and stored in a computer that moves a stimulus in front of the cat.* (b) *Off-center receptive field of a cat retinal ganglion cell recorded with the automated method. (1) Horizontal scan. (2) Vertical scan.*

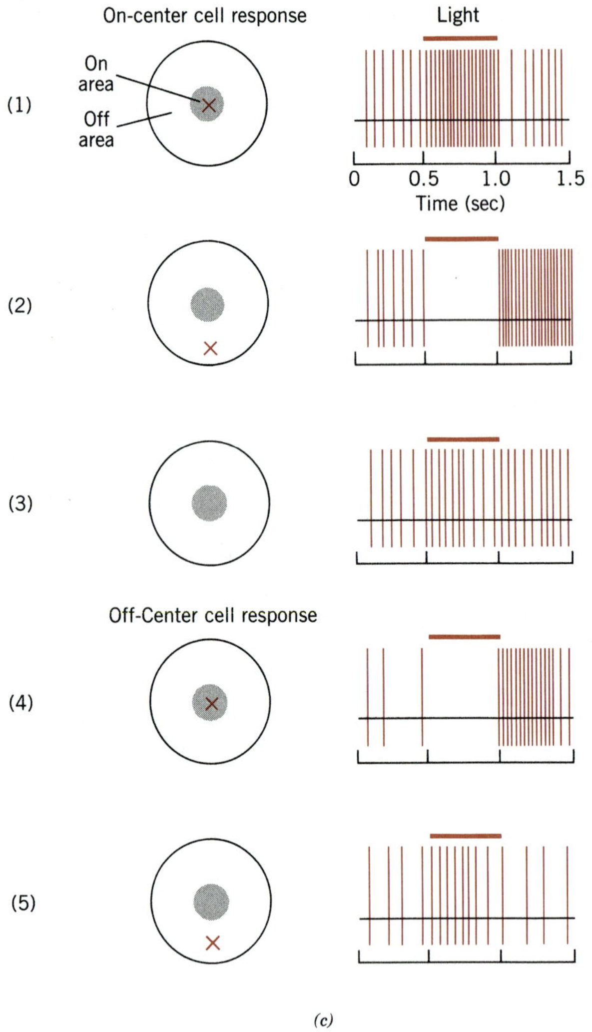

Figure 5.21 (c) *Responses of on-center and off-center ganglion cells. (1) Illumination of only the on area, with spike pattern. (2) Illumination of only the periphery. The spontaneous firing is inhibited. (3) Diffuse illumination giving little or no response. (4) Off-center cell inhibited with center light. (5) Off-center cell excited with peripheral light.*

ment is made by light adaptation in the pupil and the photoreceptors. Another part is neural and begins with the horizontal-bipolar interaction.

Each horizontal cell contributes inhibition that is proportional to the overall average light intensity in its region. The more light there is, the stronger the inhibition. The inhibition tends to keep the bipolar cell within a range where it is sensitive to changes in input from the photoreceptors (see Figure 5.22). Mechanisms designed to keep a neuron operating in its most sensitive range are common in all senses.

At the next synaptic stage, inhibition from amacrine cells has a different function. It suppresses the ganglion cells over their entire response range, damping primarily responses to change (Naka, 1977). The result is something like adjusting the contrast control on a TV set: the S-shaped response curve in Figure 5.23 moves downward.

Central Projections. The optic nerves from each eye meet at the X-shaped optic chiasm (*chi* is Greek for "X"), which is visible at the base of the brain in Figure 3.7. There the fibers from the nasal half of each retina cross the midline to join the fibers from the temporal half of the other retina. The reorganized nerve, now called the optic tract, preserves the principle of sensory inputs crossing to the opposite side of the brain. The halves of the two retinas that are exposed to the left half of the world project to the right optic tract and vice versa.

As the ganglion cell axons extend up the optic tract, a few branch to the superior colliculus and the rest enter the lateral geniculate nucleus of the thalamus.

Lateral Geniculate Nucleus

As we saw in Chapter 3, the lateral geniculate nucleus (LGN) is a monosynaptic nucleus. Retinal afferents synapse onto principal cells, whose axons go to the visual cortex. Superimposed on this simple organization are inhibitory interneurons, which carry self-inhibition and lateral inhibition. Other synapses, schematized in Figure 3.19, influence just about every imaginable point in the network. The LGN also receives projections from the brain stem. Figure 5.24 shows the elegant series of irregularly alternating layers the LGN receives from the two eyes.

Geniculate Receptive Fields. The principal cells of the LGN are similar to the retinal ganglion cells in their center-surround organization. Activity is also modified by nonvisual influences such as level of arousal. Paradoxically, to neurophysiologists, LGN responses don't seem as "clean" as

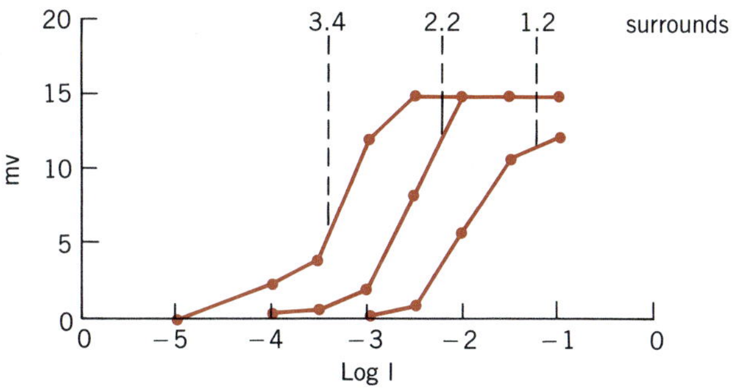

Figure 5.22 *Responses of a depolarizing bipolar cell measured at three levels of surround illumination. For each curve the background light is held constant; along the curve a small center light is increased in intensity. When the background is increased, the cell becomes less sensitive, so the same amount of contrast between background and center lights evokes about the same response.*

those from retinal ganglion cells, even though LGN neurons reflect a further stage of processing. But the brain isn't seeking clean responses; rather, it is extracting useful information from the visual image and at the same time combining it with other information.

Retinal and LGN receptive fields were compared directly in the cat by simultaneous recording from a retinal afferent fiber and from the LGN principal cell driven by that fiber (Cleland, Dubin & Levick, 1970a, 1970b). Finding a matching cell and fiber is a difficult feat even with the aid of topographic organization; it must be done "blind," by examination of the pattern of electrical activity from two microelectrodes without a view of the cells involved. Cleland and his associates found that each LGN neuron receives most or all of its excitatory input from a single retinal ganglion cell. The LGN on-center and off-surround (or vice versa) are both contributed by this ganglion cell. In addition, there is a "suppressive field" beyond the traditional receptive field surround where light onset or offset, or any movement, inhibits the cell. This additional zone probably originates from inhibition within the LGN.

X, Y, and W Cells. In both the retina and the LGN, three types of receptive fields are based on

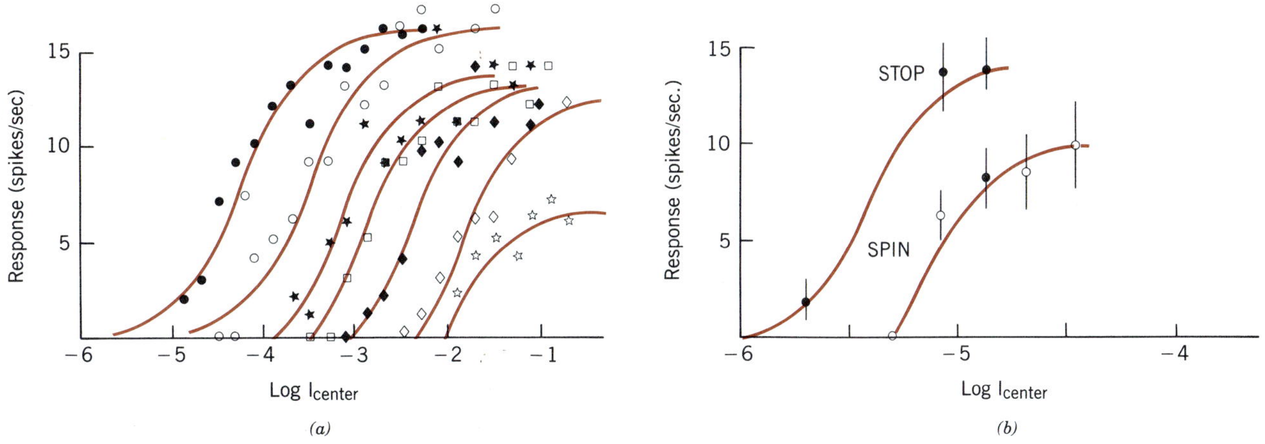

Figure 5.23 *Adaptation in retinal ganglion cells.* (a) *Responses of mudpuppy "on" ganglion cell to light of varying intensity. The experiment is similar to that in Figure 5.22, except that response is measured as firing rate instead of being graded.* (b) *Ganglion cell responses at constant background intensity, with a windmill-shaped stimulus centered on the receptive field. When the windmill is fixed (the "stop" graph), the response is similar to that in* (a)*; but when it rotates (the "spin" graph), the motion-sensitive inhibitory surrounds of the amacrine cells are activated and the ganglion cell response is compressed. Lateral interactions in the outer plexiform layer (horizontal cells) cause the sideways shift of the graphs; interactions in the inner plexiform layer (amacrine cells) shift the graphs downward.*

interactions between the center and the surround. In one type, the **X-cell,** an appropriate stimulus in the surround can completely cancel a simultaneous stimulus in the center, so the cell does not respond (Enroth-Cugell & Robson, 1966). X-cells show **linear summation**—one can predict the response of the neuron by knowing the center and the surround regions of the receptive field. **Y-cells** do not possess such linearity. Y-cells have larger receptive fields, faster axons, and shorter response latencies. X-cells also provide chromatic (color) information, whereas Y-cells transmit only luminance (intensity) information (Schiller & Malpeli, 1977). The two types of cells will appear again in the cortex section of the chapter. Enroth-Cugell and Robson (1966) originally called X-cells dull and Y-cells interesting but changed to a more neutral (and harder to remember) terminology before publication. Retinal X-cells project to LGN X-cells, and retinal Y-cells project to LGN Y-cells. X-cell axons project only to the cortex; Y-cell axons reach both the cortex and the superior colliculus.

A third type of retinal receptive field cell is the **W-cell**—a visual neuron with large, complex receptive fields. It projects to the lateral geniculate and the superior colliculus on fine, slow-conducting axons (Stone & Hoffman, 1972). Many of the W-cells are movement-sensitive.

Optic radiations are the LGN visual output. Their name comes from the principal cell axons radiating out to the much larger visual cortex.

CORTICAL INFORMATION PROCESSING

In the cortex things become more complicated. The types of receptive fields are more varied and more elaborate. There are also more neurons; over 90 percent of visual system neurons are in the cortex.

Afferent fibers from the LGN enter the cortex in Brodmann's area 17 (visible in Figure 3.21), also called the **striate cortex** because of a prominent striation (Latin for "stripe") visible in a cross section of the cortex (see Figure 5.25). The striation is in layer 4 of the six-layered cortex, at the location where afferent fibers synapse on cortical neurons. It consists of myelinated LGN fibers that run laterally before synapsing. A few afferent fibers also extend into layer 1 and arborize (branch out) there. Each fiber arborizes only within a limited zone—the region of a cortical column.

Information flows through only a few synaptic layers before leaving the striate cortex. Neurons in layer 4 have the simplest receptive fields; those above and below them have more elaborate re-

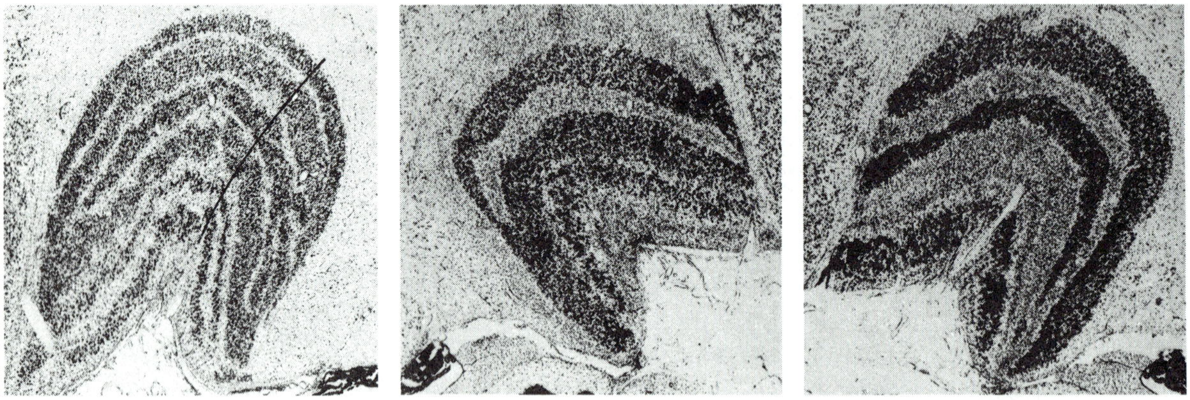

(a) *(b)* *(c)*

Figure 5.24 *Lateral geniculate nucleus (LGN) of a monkey.* (a) *LGN of a normal monkey—right eye. The six layers are in register, so any cell along the black line has a receptive field covering the same part of the visual world.* (b) *LGN of a monkey with vision in only the left eye—left LGN shown. The contralateral connections—layers 1, 4, and 6—are atrophied.* (c) *LGN of a monkey with vision in only the left eye—right LGN shown. The ipsilateral connections—layers 2, 3, and 5—are atrophied.*

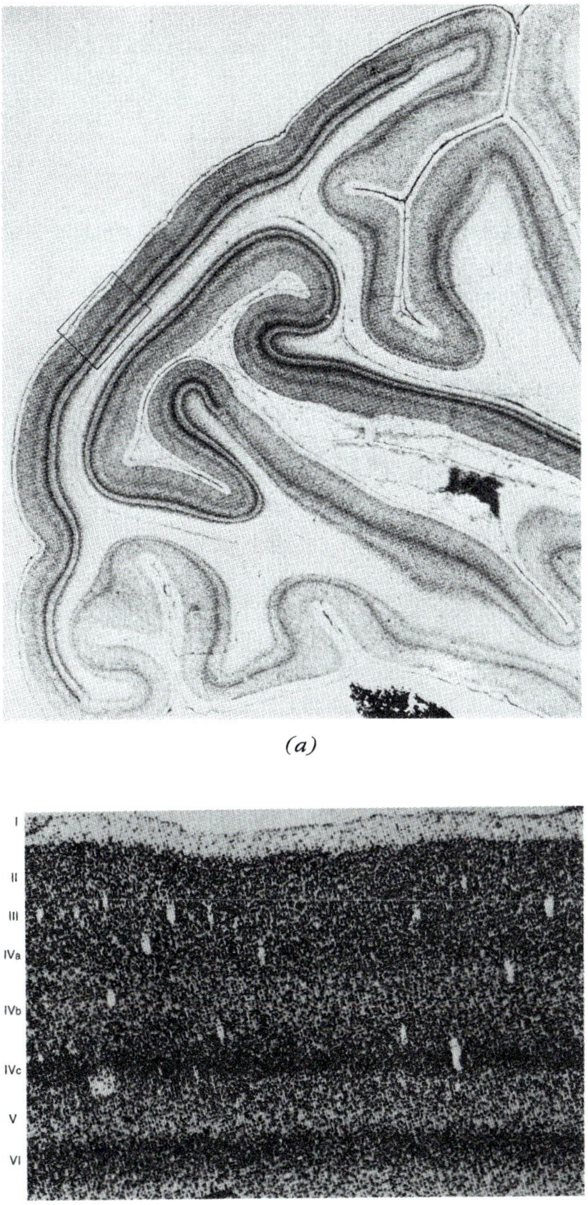

Figure 5.25 *Primary visual cortex.* (a) *Cross section of visual cortex, showing the striation (line of Gennari) of the striate cortex. The striation ends abruptly at the border of area 17 (the striate cortex), with area 18. A Nissl strain was used.* (b) *The section inside the box is enlarged, with the cortical layers numbered. The open areas are tears in the tissue, artifacts of mounting.*

sponse properties. Most of the fibers leaving the cortex are corticocortical, going to other topographic maps of the retina in areas surrounding the striate area. Other efferents link with the frontal cortex, the LGN, the superior colliculus, and other areas.

Cortical Receptive Fields

In 1959 and 1962, David Hubel and Torsten Wiesel wrote two papers that revolutionized our ideas of sensory coding in the visual cortex. Using microelectrodes to record from single cortical cells while presenting cats with simple stimuli, they found that most cells respond best to bars or edges at a particular orientation. Just above layer 4 are **simple cells**—neurons that respond best when a bar is in a specific position in the visual field. The simple receptive fields (shown in Figure 5.26*a*) are made of discrete excitatory and inhibitory patches; one can predict the responses to large targets by probing them with a point stimulus.

Above and below these layers are **complex cells** (see Figure 5.26*b*)—neurons that respond to a bar or edge anywhere within the neuron's receptive field. Hubel and Wiesel hypothesized that complex cells receive their input from simple cells, forming a cortical hierarchy or chain of receptive fields. Complex cells drive a further set of cells, called **hypercomplex cells** (see Figure 5.26*c*). These cells have the additional property that a bar must terminate in the receptive field to excite the cell.

Feature Detector Theory. A natural extension of this organization was the **feature detector theory** of visual information flow. In this theory, groups of simple cells would detect lines and edges. Further cells in the hierarchy would combine these simple features. After many steps, activity would converge on cells coding perceptually meaningful units of the visual world. If this scheme were continued at higher levels of processing, it would result in "grandmother cells"—neurons in a person's head that fired only in the presence of the person's grandmother.

This was the dominant theory of cortical visual processing until the 1970s. It made specific predictions, and several of them were soon tested.

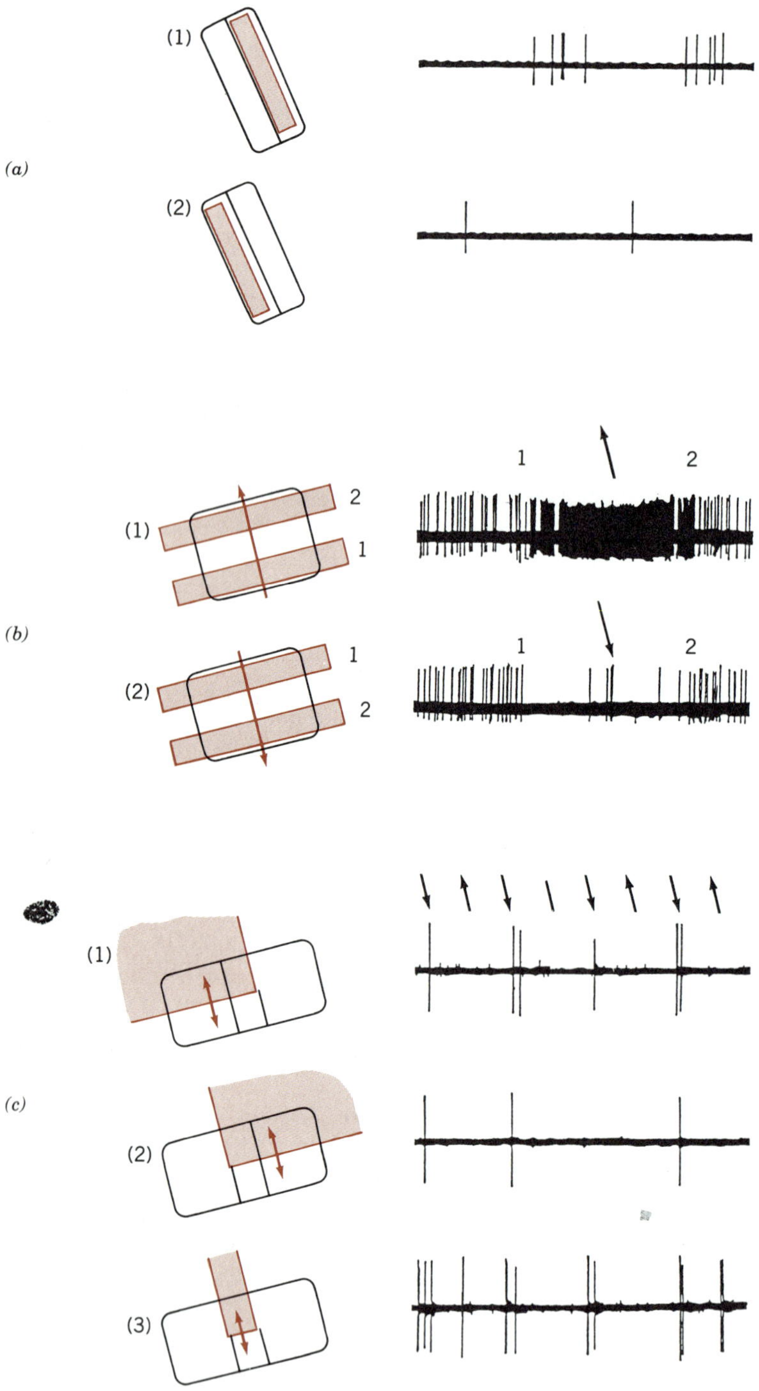

Figure 5.26 *Receptive fields.* (a) *Simple field.* (b) *Complex field.* (c) *Hypercomplex field. Arrows indicate direction of stimulus movement. Receptive fields appear in color.*

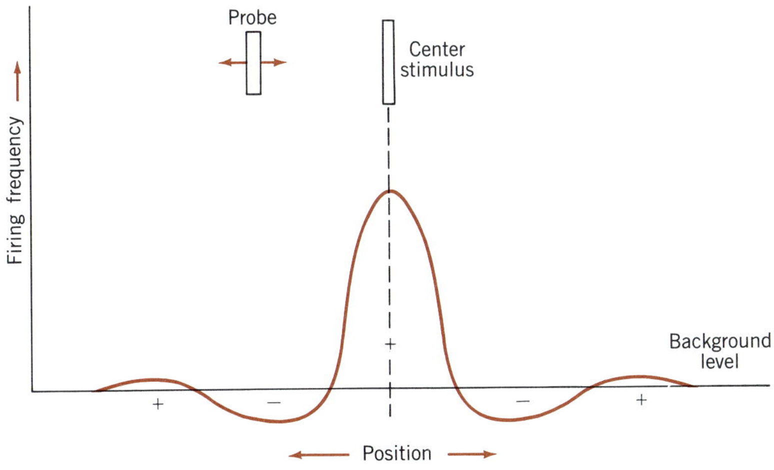

Figure 5.27 *Schematic drawing of alternating excitatory and inhibitory regions in a striate cortex receptive field. Two techniques increase the sensitivity of profile mapping. In the first, the neuron is stimulated suboptimally, with the stimulus in the receptive field center. In the second, computer averaging is used, so that many trials are summed for each position of the simultaneously presented probe. The horizontal line represents the firing rate of the cell with a center stimulus but no probe. The averaging reduces the effects of noise.*

First, the response latency of complex cells should be longer than the latency of simple cells; that is, if the simple cells feed the complex cells, the first cells in the chain must respond first. Unfortunately for the theory, this turns out not to be the case; both complex and simple cells have similar latencies. And both types have a direct input from the LGN (Hoffman & Stone, 1971). Second, any stimulus that excites a complex cell should also excite the simple cells that feed it. Some complex cells, however, respond to stimulus velocities too fast to drive the simple cells (Pettigrew, Nikara & Bishop, 1968). The hierarchical feature detector theory was in serious trouble.

Another kind of problem with the theory concerns the detectors themselves. A good detector should respond strongly to the feature being detected and not at all to everything else. Cortical cells, however, are rather broadly tuned; they respond in some degree to a wide variety of stimuli. Worse yet, later studies of cortical receptive fields, using more sensitive methods, revealed some puzzling properties. The mapping method (shown in Figure 5.27) showed that many cells had more than just an excitatory center and inhibitory surround. They also had excitatory sidebands beyond the inhibitory surround, and sometimes there was another inhibitory region beyond that (Bishop, Coombs & Henry, 1971). Why would bar and edge detectors have so many alternating excitatory and inhibitory regions?

Spatial Frequency Theory. In the early 1970s, an alternative conception of visual coding began to emerge. Figure 4.27 showed how a sound wave could be separated by Fourier analysis into a series of sine waves varying in frequency, intensity, and phase. Visual stimuli can be described in an analogous way. But the sound wave is spread out in time, and the visual scene is extended in space. For vision we will need a Fourier analysis not of time but of space.

The simplest visual stimulus in Fourier terms is not a point or a line but a sine-wave grating such as the one in Figure 5.28*a*. The only structure in this figure is a sinusoidal (sine wave–like) variation in brightness along the horizontal dimension. Only a single **spatial frequency** (repeating variation in brightness) is present. Bringing the bars closer together, as in Figure 5.28*b*, increases the spatial frequency, the number of cycles per degree of visual angle. Separating the bars decreases the spatial frequency. The simplicity of this sinusoidal pattern in Fourier terms has made it a popular stimulus in vision research. Adding several sine-wave gratings together, as in Figure 5.28*c*, can generate a variety of patterns.

This is an elegant way to analyze systems, but

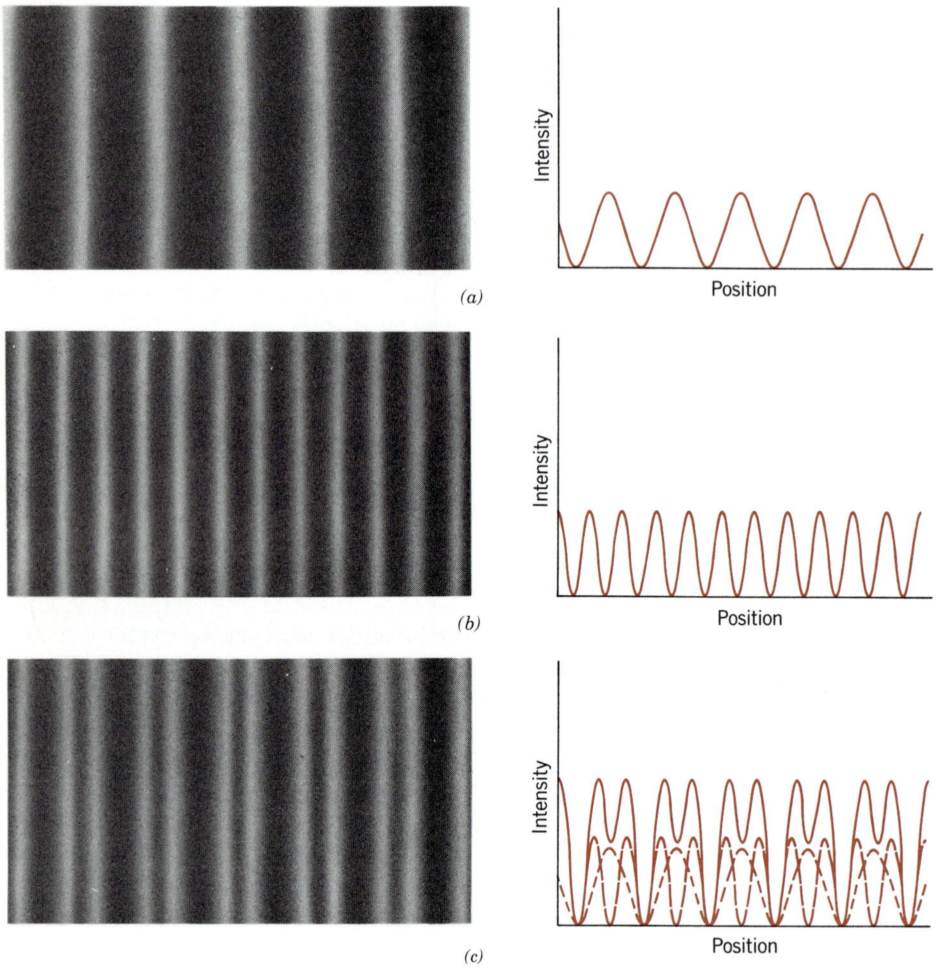

Figure 5.28 *Sine-wave gratings.* (a) *Grating with a frequency (number of cycles per degree of visual angle) of* f. (b) *Grating with a frequency of* 2f. (c) *Grating with a frequency that is the sum of the first two; the intensity at each point is the sum of the intensities at the corresponding points in the other two gratings.*

it can also be applied to real-world scenes. It is possible to break any image into Fourier components—a series of gratings of varying orientations, spatial frequencies, and phases. The first step is to break the two-dimensional retinal image into a series of one-dimensional waves, as shown in Figure 5.29. Then one can break each of the one-dimensional waves into sine waves by moving from the composite wave, such as the wave in Figure 5.28*c*, to the waves that make up the composite wave: the waves in Figures 5.28*a* and 5.28*b*.

This technique of image analysis has proved useful in describing stimuli quantitatively. Does it have anything to do with the way the brain codes visual information? Some compelling evidence now indicates that it does, though the frequency analysis in the brain is not quite what Fourier had in mind and is certainly not the only processing taking place.

Spatial Frequency Analysis in the Brain

The idea of spatial frequency analysis began with a ground-breaking paper by Campbell and Robson (1968) suggesting that the visual system might analyze a visual image by its spatial frequency components. The evidence was psychophysical. The two researchers first exposed a subject to a single sine-wave grating for a few minutes and then tested the subject's sensitivity to gratings over a wide range of spatial frequencies. Figure 5.30*b* shows that sensitivity was reduced near the exposed frequency. A grating near that frequency needed a higher contrast than normal to be visi-

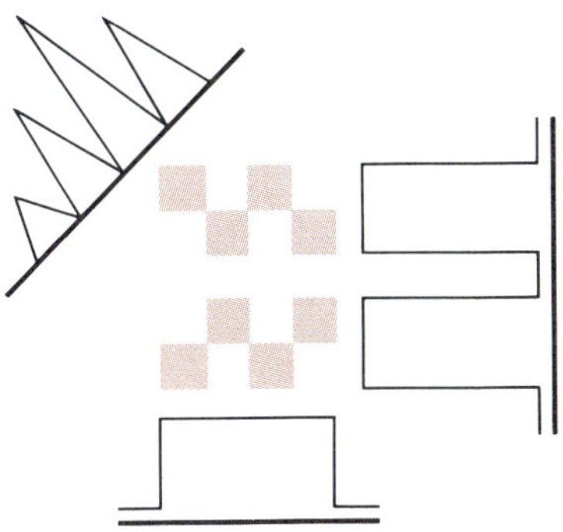

Figure 5.29 *Resolving a two-dimensional image into a series of one-dimensional profiles. The profiles (graphs) above each heavy line show the amount of the pattern present in the corresponding part of the image. Repeating this process for a large number of profiles at different angles can completely specify the contents of the image. This is a purely physical analysis. According to the spatial frequency theory, elongated receptive fields in the cortex might perform a similar analysis of the image.*

ble. The width of the area of reduced sensitivity was about one **octave** (one doubling of spatial frequency). A similar adaptation experiment is illustrated in Figure 5.31. It is difficult to explain the phenomenon in terms of feature detectors.

The spatial frequency scheme has been tested by researchers recording spikes from single cells while exposing an animal to gratings. But one must do more than this. One must also show that the results are more compatible with neural spatial frequency analysis than with the feature detector theory. We know that cells in the striate cortex are

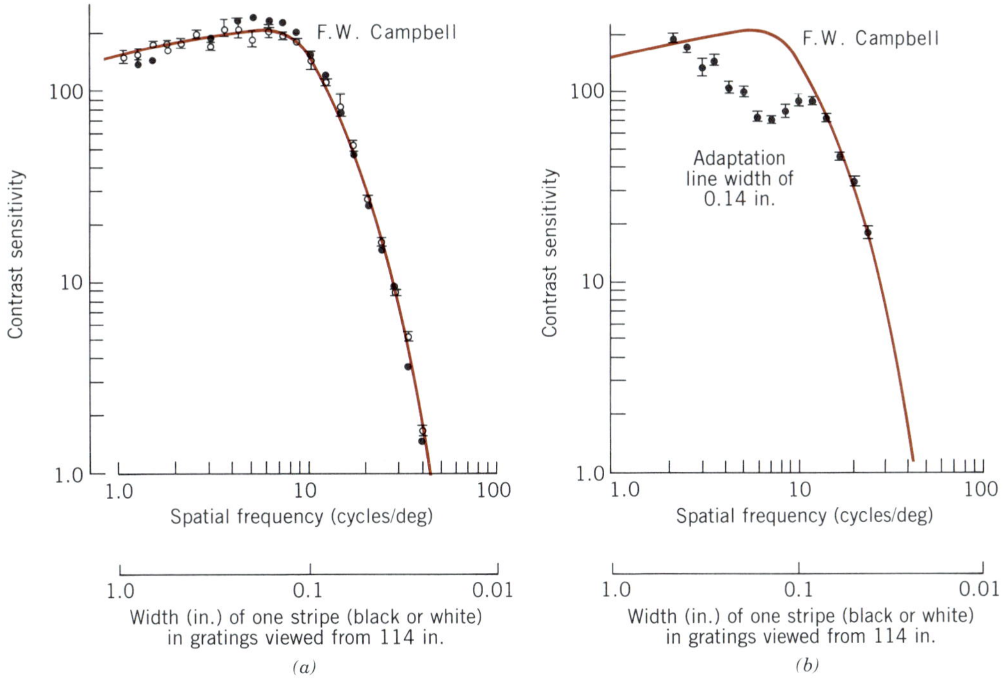

Figure 5.30 *Modulation transfer functions (MTF).* (a) *Sensitivity of a normal human visual system to varying spatial frequencies.* (b) *MTF of the same subject after adaptation to a grating with the spatial frequency indicated by the arrow.*

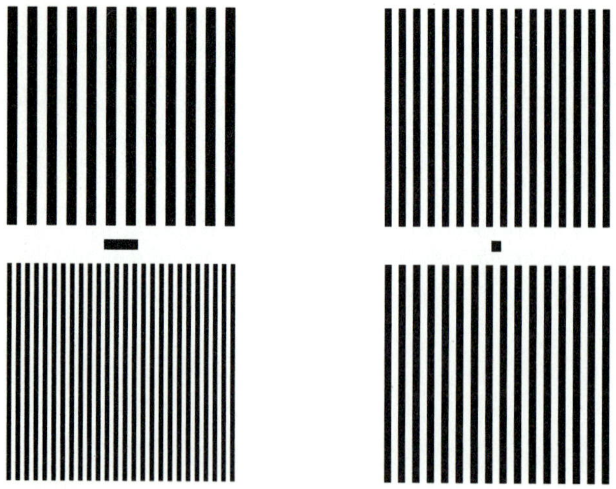

Figure 5.31 Spatial frequency adaptation. First look at the horizontal bar between the gratings on the left side of the figure for about a minute (you may move your eyes along the bar). Then look at the small square between the gratings on the right; the top grating will appear finer than the bottom one. Adapted from Blakemore & Sutton (1969).

quite specific about the gratings they will respond to (Schiller, Finlay & Volman, 1976). If a grating is about an octave away from the optimum spatial frequency for that cell, the response will be reduced by about half. Tuning the same cells for single bars is not nearly as exact (Albrecht, DeValois & Thorell, 1980), for each cell will respond to a wide range of bar widths. The range can be predicted from the spatial frequency sensitivity of the cell. In short, the cells are good detectors of sine-wave gratings but poor detectors of bars.

Another piece of evidence for neurons as approximate spatial frequency filters is that they are tuned by lateral inhibition from cells sensitive to neighboring spatial frequencies (Tootell, Silverman & DeValois, 1981). A cell gives a brisk response to its optimum frequency but is inhibited if a grating at a nearby frequency (higher or lower) is added. Again, this result is difficult to interpret in feature detector terms. The sharpening of spatial frequency tuning in the cortex is analogous to spatial sharpening in the retina and LGN.

Simple cells in the cortex correspond to the X-cells of the retina and LGN by showing linear summation of stimuli on their receptive fields (DeValois, Albrecht & Thorell, 1982). This can be demonstrated in two experiments. First, it is always possible to find a position where a flashed grating will produce no response from a simple cell because excitation and inhibition balance exactly. Figure 5.32*a* shows such a "null" response at the 0 deg and 180 deg positions. Second, a grating can drift across the receptive field. A simple cell shows a large change in firing as the bright bars of the grating alternately cross the excitatory and inhibitory regions. Complex cells (see Figure 5.32*b*) increase their firing for a grating of the right spatial frequency and orientation at any position in the receptive field. They have no null point. Another way of describing this property is to say that the complex cell, like the Y-cell of the retina and LGN, is insensitive to the phase of a grating and is excited at any phase.

A powerful way to plot receptive fields is used in Figure 5.33. Spatial frequency is represented as distance from the center of the plot, and the orientation of a stimulating grating is shown as an angle. LGN cells exhibit little orientation preference and show up as circles concentric with the center of the plot. Cortical cells, with oriented receptive fields, are sensitive to restricted regions in both orientation and spatial frequency. They appear as small, distinct regions in the figure.

Although there is now fairly wide agreement on the data, their interpretation is still controversial because the spatial frequency conception contradicts the detector theory. Neurons can be thought of as "detecting" sine-wave gratings, but we don't see many of these gratings except in vision laboratories. An alternative coding scheme is a piece-by-piece analysis of the visual field by spatial frequency and orientation. With this scheme, many cells are needed to code even the simplest stimulus.

In sum, spatial frequency coding breaks a visual image into many sine-wave gratings. Sharp detail and broad structure are coded separately. In the process, the code distributes information across a large number of cells. Coding a single point of light, for example, requires a great assembly of neurons responding to differing orientations and spatial frequencies, all overlapping the location of the point.

Application to Visual Illusions. Spatial frequency analysis has been used to tackle some old puzzles in vision research. For over a century geometric illusions have been powerful demonstrations that vision is more than the transmission of a retinal image into the head, but the effects have never been explained. To apply spatial frequency theory to these patterns, we begin by assuming that judgments about the gross features of a pattern, such as its size, are made on the basis of the lowest spatial frequency components, or "blobs." By filtering out the high frequencies of the images, we can make these blobs visible (see Figure 5.34). In some cases, the "illusory" characteristic turns out to be present in the low spatial frequencies. In the Müller-Lyer illusion, for example, the

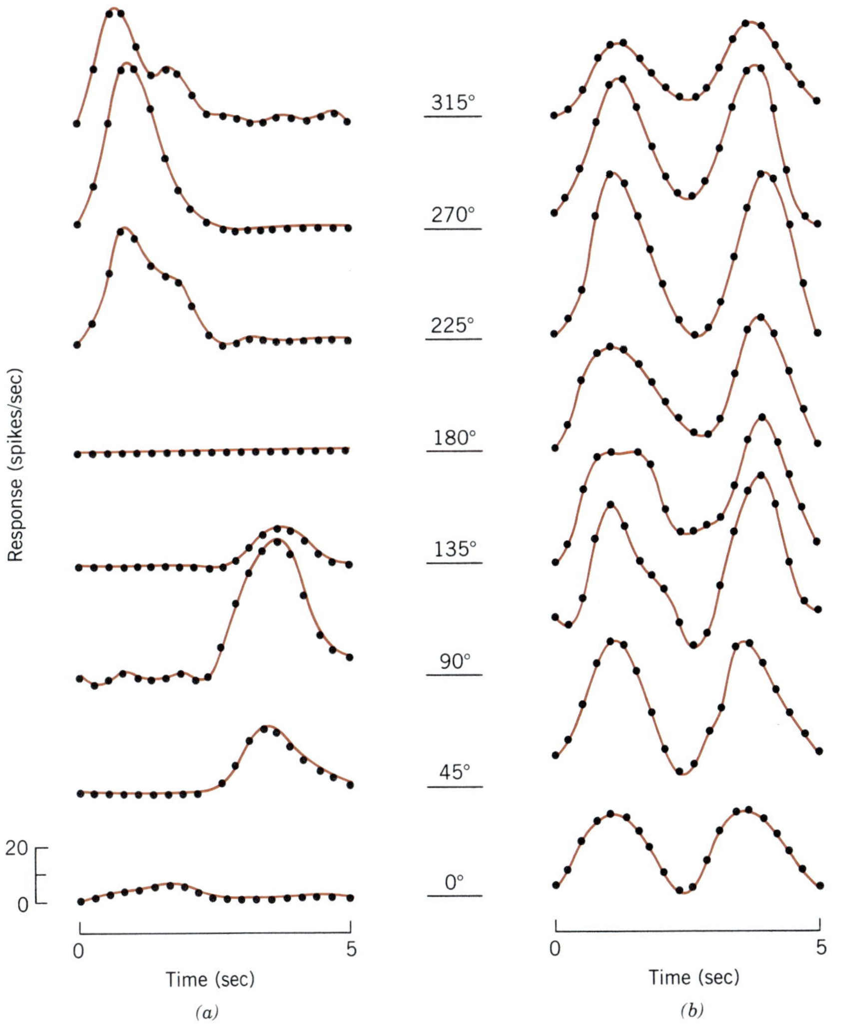

Figure 5.32 *Responses of a simple cell and a complex cell to a counterphase modulated grating. The grating (not illustrated) starts as a uniform field, gradually increases in contrast until it reaches a maximum, decreases to a uniform field, and increases in contrast again, with dark bars where the bright bars were previously. The stimulus looks like two superimposed gratings simultaneously drifting in opposite directions. Degree marks show the position of the counterphase modulated grating with respect to the receptive field.* (a) *Simple cell, showing cancellation at 0 and 180 deg.* (b) *Complex cell, showing frequency doubling (peak response at both positive and negative peaks of the counterphase grating) at all positions.*

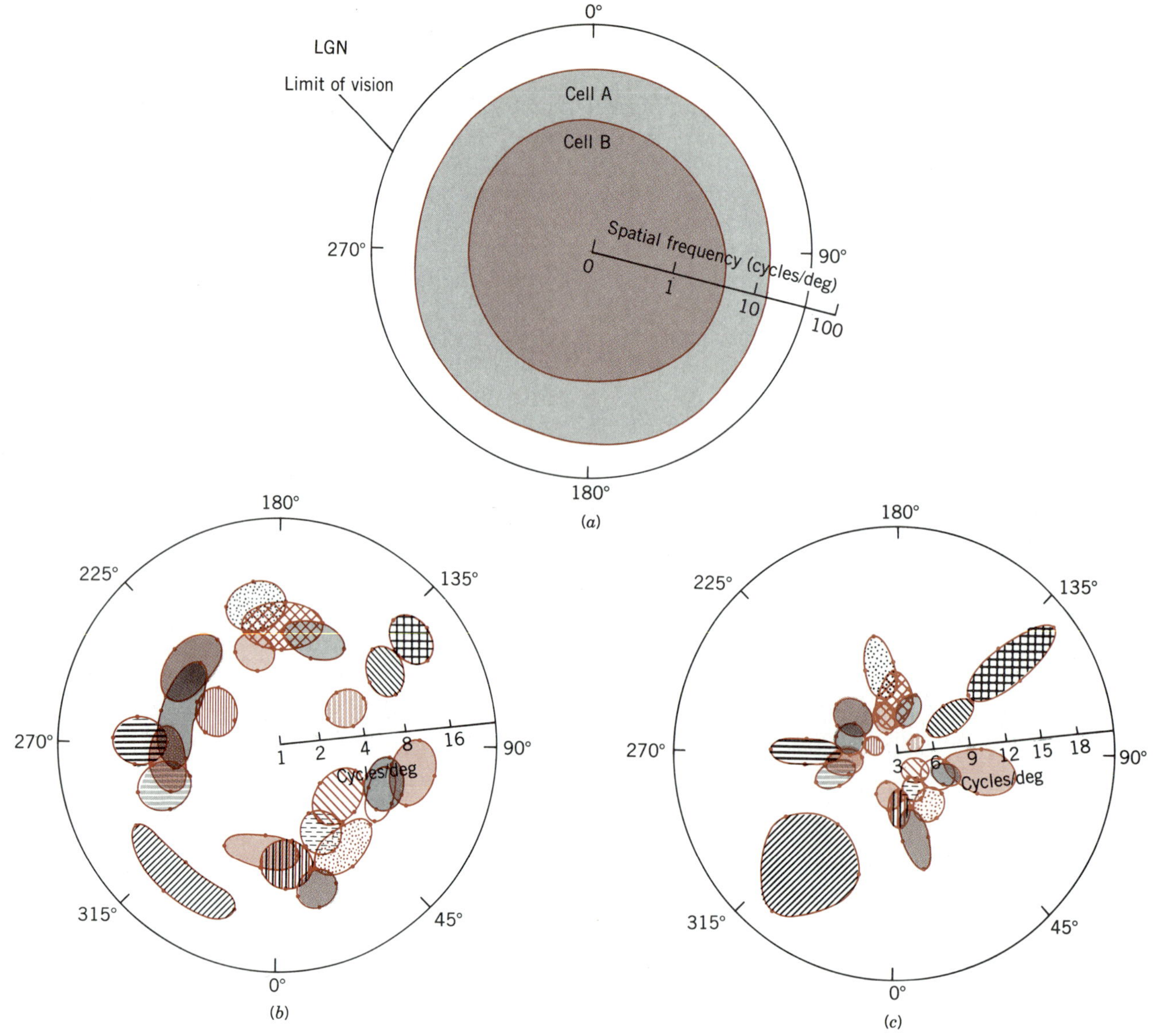

***Figure 5.33** A two-dimensional polar plot of spatial frequency and orientation sensitivity.* (a) *Two LGN cells.* (b) *Striate cortex, 1 deg from fovea, log scale of spatial frequency.* (c) *Same as* (b), *but linear scale.*

fundamental frequency describing the length of the line on the bottom really is higher (expressing a shorter line) than the fundamental frequency describing the figure with the out-facing arrows at the top. The Gestalt grouping of dots placed close together expresses a component of the image present in the low spatial frequencies (Ginsburg, 1984). According to this idea, the grouping is not a cognitive process (an organization imposed on something that is not objectively there). Rather, it is a result of spatial frequency filtering.

Fourierlike analysis has also been used to predict the conditions necessary to abolish a geometric illusion. To my knowledge, it is the only theory to be successful in doing this. A spatial frequency explanation of the Poggendorff illusion is shown in Figure 5.35. The component needed to describe the vertical and the diagonal lines in the region where they approach each other lies between the true positions of the two lines. A low spatial frequency receptive field would get the strongest signal when it is positioned where both lines stimulate it. At low spatial frequencies, the two lines near the angle cannot be resolved. A low spatial frequency field represents both of them at once and bends inward when the oblique line nears

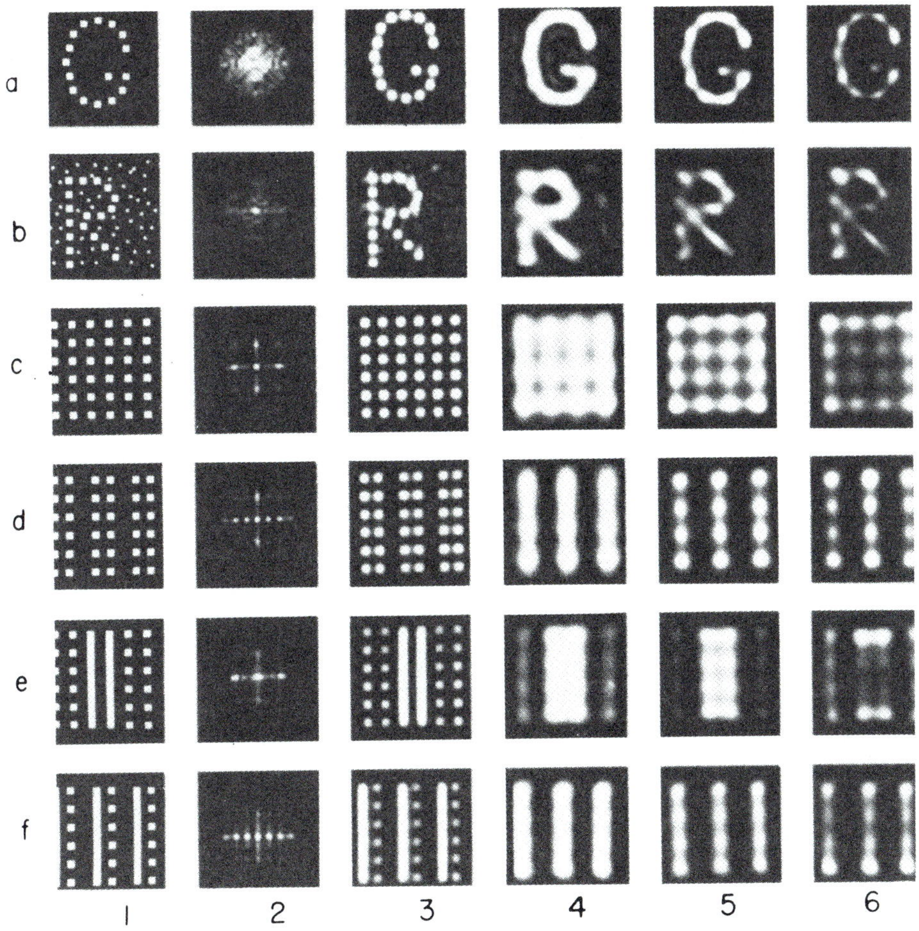

Figure 5.34 *Some geometric illusions and their low spatial frequency components. Column 1: Geometric illusions. Column 2: The power spectrum of each illusion, plotting the orientation of each spatial frequency component on radial axes, the spatial frequency as distance from the center, and the power at each location as brightness. The spectra are weighted according to the human MTF. Column 3: The Fourier transforms remodulated back into conventional X–Y plots. Column 4: Only the lowest spatial frequencies (near the center of the plots in column 2) are used. In this column the components correspond to the illusions in column 1. Row a: The Müller-Lyer illusion. Row b: The Müller-Lyer illusion without lines. Row c: The Poggendorff illusion. Row d: The Ponzo figure. Because of the computer digitization necessary to do the transforms, the illusions are best viewed at arm's length.*

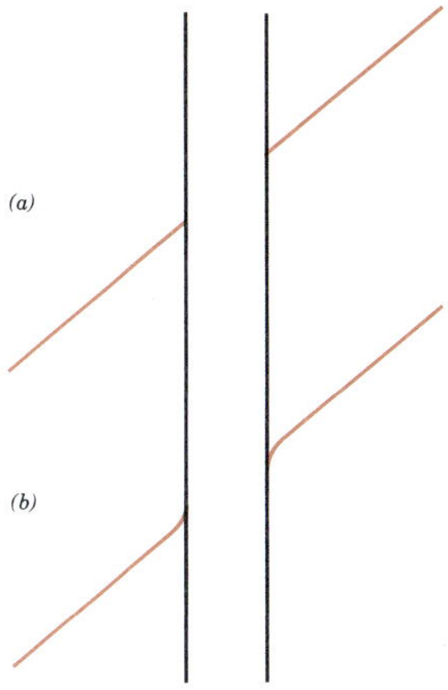

Figure 5.35 *Cancellation of the Poggendorff illusion. The apparent offset of the diagonal in* (a) *is canceled by small curves moving the low spatial frequency components into alignment in* (b).

one of the parallel lines. The result is that the lines do not seem to meet because the low spatial frequency components really don't meet. To make them meet it is necessary only to add a slight bend to the cross-line in Figure 5.35*b*. This straightens out the low spatial frequency component, and the illusion magically disappears.

Columns

Early neuroanatomists, examining the dense tangle of neural fibers in the cortex, thought that much of the organization of the cortex was random. Microelectrode studies have since shown its unexpectedly precise anatomical structure. Neurons with similar receptive field orientations are arranged in vertical columns reaching from the bottom of the cortex to the top (Hubel, Wiesel & Stryker, 1978). Figure 5.36 shows columns of cells sensitive to particular spatial frequencies (Tootell, Silverman & DeValois, 1981).

Superimposed on this structure is an array of larger ocular dominance columns—columns receiving input from one eye alternating with columns receiving input from the other. The arrangement in Figure 5.37 is more one of parallel slabs of cortex than of round columns. The ocular dominance columns appear most strongly in layer 4; in the other layers, most cells are binocular. All of this organization is superimposed on the topographic map of the retina, showing that the map itself is an approximation. It is accurate on a large scale; but on a small scale, adjacent regions represent different properties rather than different retinal locations.

The relationship of large- and small-scale organization of monkey striate cortex is shown in Figure 5.38. A pattern of rays and concentric rings (top) was shown to one eye of the monkey while 2-deoxyglucose was administered to label active neurons (Tootell et al., 1982). The pattern consisted of irregular flickering patches to excite all of the neurons driven by the eye. The lines on the cortex (bottom) are the areas where the 2-deoxyglucose was absorbed, indicating active cells. They are dashed rather than solid because only the ocular dominance columns for the exposed eye are darkened. The spatial map is revealed in stunning detail.

In summary, one can conceive of the visual cortex being composed of about 3000 modules, each about 1 mm^2 in extent and containing columns for all of the information about a retinal region. Fine detail is processed by neurons with high spatial frequency receptive fields, grosser detail by neurons with low spatial frequency fields, and intermediate levels of detail by intermediate band-pass receptive fields. All orientations are represented at each spatial frequency, and neurons driven primarily by each eye are included. Each neuron represents some value of each of these properties. The neurons in the module also contain a complete range of receptive field coding for color.

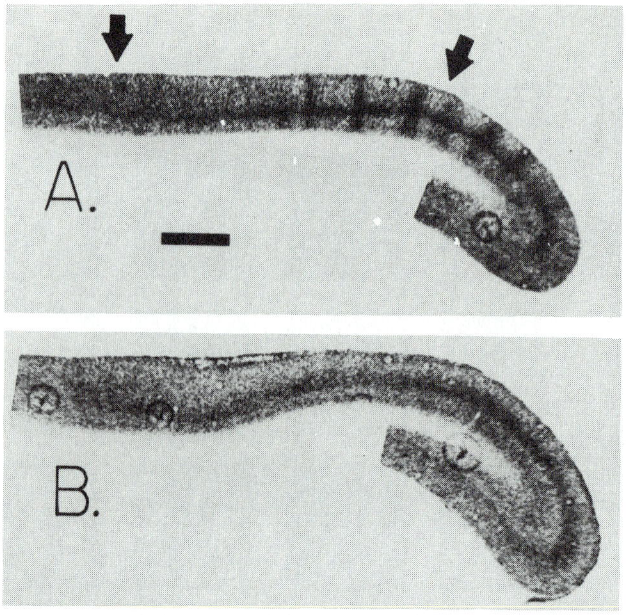

Figure 5.36 *Spatial frequency columns in a cross section of cat striate cortex. Two cats were injected with 2-deoxyglucose (2-DG). Then cat A viewed a 2 cycle/deg grating presented at various orientations and cat B saw multiple spatial frequencies. Autoradiographs show columnar segregation only in cat A. The bar is 2 mm. Adapted from Tootell, Silverman & DeValois (1981).*

Color

Mechanisms of color have been investigated for over 150 years; the first progress in this area came from psychophysical research. The evidence was from color mixing experiments in which spectral colors (colors sampled from the spectrum) were projected together on a screen. To create the impression of any spectral color by a mix of the projected lights, only three projectors were needed. This phenomenon led to Thomas Young's proposal in 1802 that there were three kinds of visual receptors, each sensitive to a different color. In 1867 Helmholtz elaborated this idea into what is now called the trichromatic (Latin for "three-color"), or Young-Helmholtz, theory.

A second set of observations was more psychological in nature. One can easily imagine a bluish

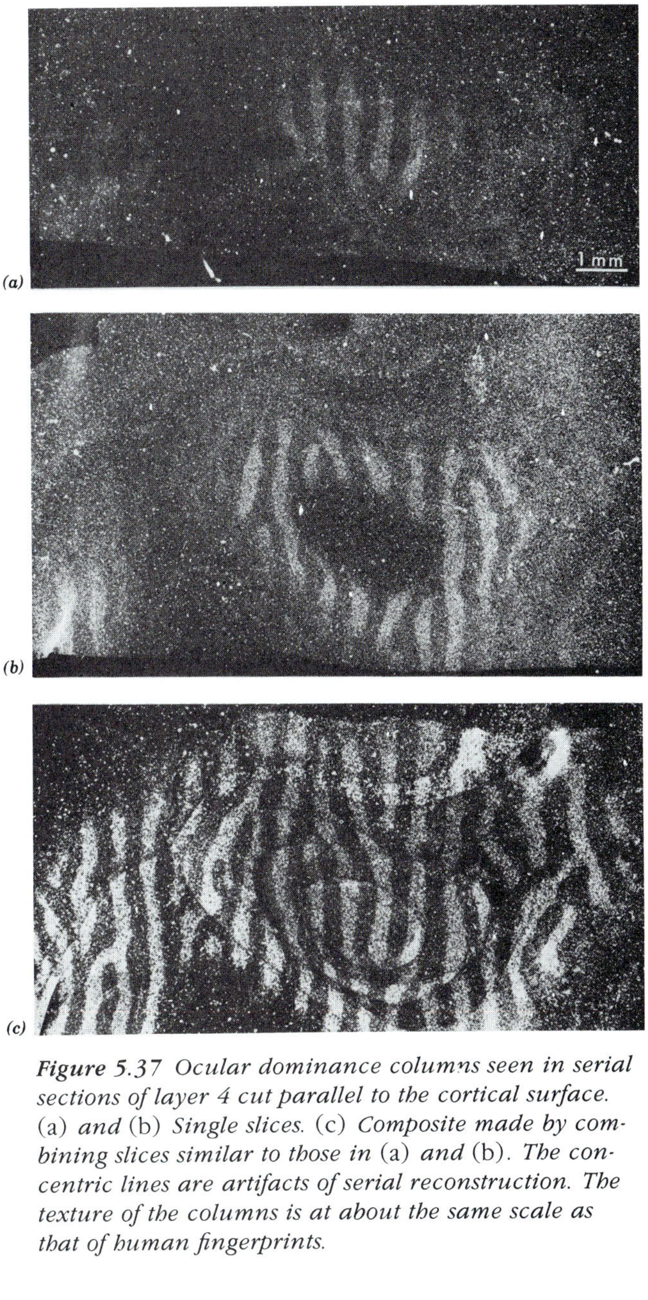

***Figure** 5.37 Ocular dominance columns seen in serial sections of layer 4 cut parallel to the cortical surface.* (a) *and* (b) *Single slices.* (c) *Composite made by combining slices similar to those in* (a) *and* (b). *The concentric lines are artifacts of serial reconstruction. The texture of the columns is at about the same scale as that of human fingerprints.*

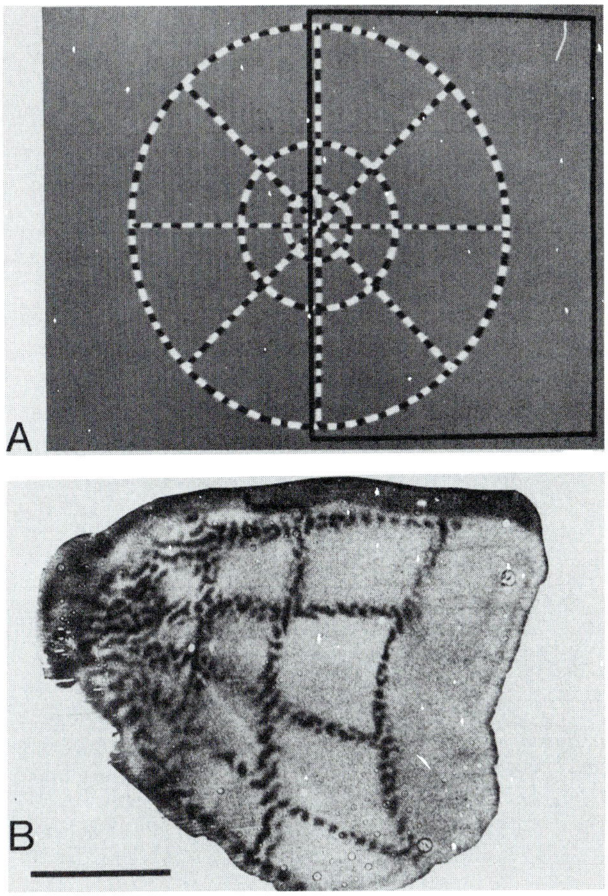

***Figure** 5.38 Geometry of the projection of the retina on the striate cortex of a macaque monkey.* (a) *The pattern to which the monkey was exposed.* (b) *Autoradiograph of a flat mount made by slowly flattening the curved cortex. The photograph is not retouched. The second and fourth lines, representing the diagonal rays in the exposure pattern, are slightly shorter than the other lines, suggesting a neural basis for the lower sensitivity of monkeys and humans to diagonal orientations than to vertical and horizontal orientations.*

green or a reddish yellow, but there is no greenish red or yellowish blue. These "complementary colors" form the basis for the Hering (1920) theory of two opponent pairs of colors. Black-white luminance contrast yields a third opponent pair.

Battles raged for decades between proponents of the two theories. It turned out that both were right—the trichromatic theorists about the receptors and the opponent theorists about higher levels. A cone receptor has one of three pigments, as measured in isolated cones (Marks, Dobelle & MacNichol, 1964), following the trichromatic scheme. But in the retinal bipolar cells receiving signals from the cones, color information is al-

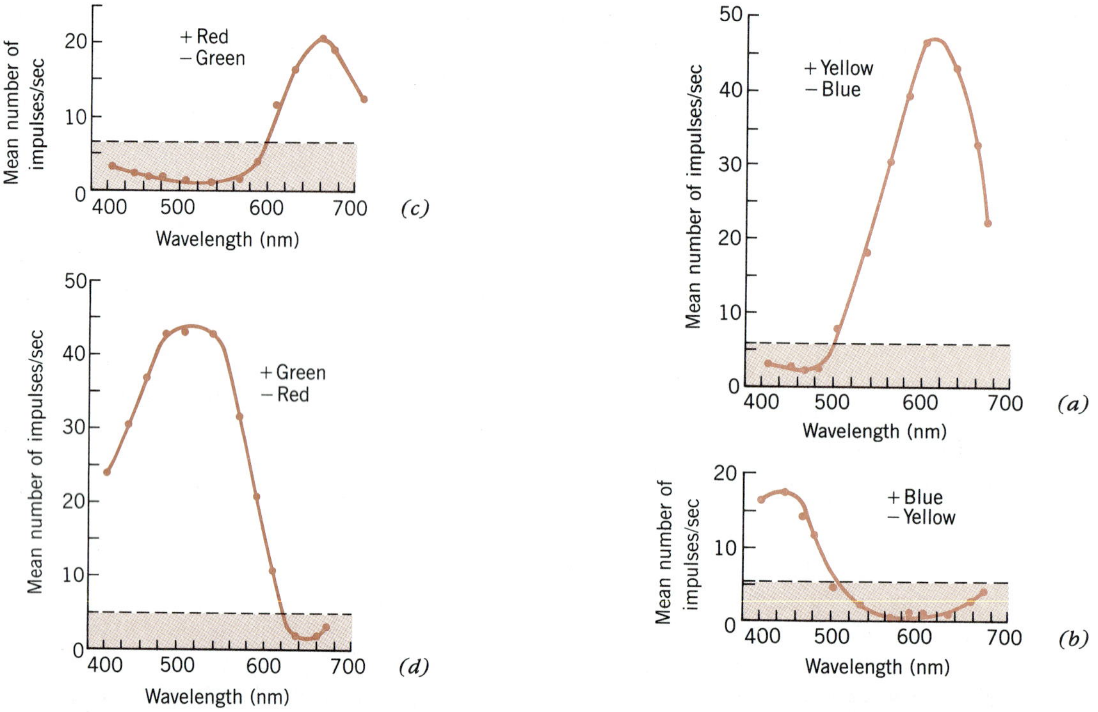

***Figure 5.39** Opponent process organization in principal cells of the moneky LGN.* (a), (b), (c), *and* (d) *are different classes of neurons. The yellow response is a summation of red and green inputs. The blue effects are smaller than the red, green, and yellow effects because of the smaller number of blue receptors. Each plot is made by stimulating the monkey with monochromatic light at a series of wavelengths, while recording from a single LGN neuron. The "+" means "excited by"; the "−" means "inhibited by."*

ready reorganized into an opponent code. A landmark paper by DeValois, Abramov, and Jacobs (1966) showed opponent organization in the monkey LGN, with cells excited by red and inhibited by green or vice versa. Other cells gave opposite responses to yellow and blue. Figure 5.39 shows the resulting scheme.

In the striate cortex the picture is more complicated. About 10 percent of the cells give vigorous responses to particular spectral hues, but most seem insensitive to wavelength when probed with patches of colored light (Hubel & Wiesel, 1968; Spinelli, Pribram & Bridgeman, 1970). When color is added to grating stimuli, though, most cortical cells show specific color responses. Gratings can be made of color stripes rather than luminance stripes; for instance, red and green regions of equal brightness can be alternated. Such patterns, called **chromatic gratings,** have no brightness differences. But they still drive most cells in the striate cortex if the gratings have the right color balance, spatial frequency, and orientation, and they drift across the receptive field (Thorell, DeValois & Albrecht, 1984). Color and form are coded in the same cells, an example of the **multiplexing** of sensory information; that is, several messages are carried by the same neuron.

A recently described class of color cells is the double-opponent cells, found only in the cortex. A double-opponent cell might have a center excited by red and inhibited by green. At the same time, the cell's surround will be excited by green and inhibited by red. Again, despite its highly structured color responses, the cell will not respond much to a large uniform patch of color. You can see the perceptual results of this organization in yourself by holding a large patch of uniform color, such as the cover of a book, near your eyes. No matter how intense the color, it will fade in a few seconds because your cortical neurons are insensitive to it. Patches of color and brightness are defined only at their borders.

Complications beyond the Classical Receptive Field

Until 1964 it seemed that each neuron in the visual system reported from a restricted region of visual space. There was a center and a surround, and in the cortex there might be several on- and off-regions. Then McIlwain (1964) discovered the **periphery effect**—that large, moving stimuli very distant from the receptive field center could modulate the activities of retinal and LGN neurons. There is a story that the effect was discovered when someone opened a laboratory door during single-cell recording and inadvertently stimulated the cell. Be that as it may, the observation changed ideas about the messages carried by single neurons. McIlwain's periphery effect extended 60 to 90 deg from the receptive field center. This is an enormous range, compared to the few degrees where the same receptive fields will respond to small spots. Later, Ikeda and Wright (1972) showed that the periphery effect is not an artifact; in the retina it is carried on horizontal cells.

The periphery effect is not an activation but a modulation of activity already excited by stimuli in the classical receptive field. Yet, in the real world, where texture is everywhere, we can expect most cells to be stimulated to some degree and none to be stimulated optimally. So the periphery effect should affect most cells. Since the area of the visual field over which the effect takes place is thousands of times greater than the area of the center and surround, we can conclude that under some conditions much of a cell's change in firing comes not from the center but from the periphery effect. Mysteriously, though, there seemed to be no sign of the effect at the cortex.

It took a more highly organized stimulus to reveal a cortical effect. Discovered by Krueger, when he was still a student, the cortical **shift effect** was found by the rapid shifting of a large grating. The region of the screen covering the cell's receptive field was left blank (Krueger & Fischer, 1973; Fischer & Krueger, 1974). The grating shift elicited a brief burst of firing if a stimulus was also projected on the receptive field center to increase the cell's ongoing activity. So again the effect modulated firing rather than exciting the cell alone. There is also a psychophysical analog to the shift effect; Breitmeyer named it the far-out jerk effect because it comes from jerking a grating far from a test spot, as in Figure 5.40. Near the time of the jerk, a spot of light flashed in a blank area in the grating is less likely to be perceived (Breitmeyer & Valberg, 1979). These studies emphasize the idea that cells have the job of integrating information, not reporting on particular areas of the world.

Information Flow in Striate Cortex

Up to now we have been looking at responses of the visual system when the animal is passive. No behavior or memory is expected. The animal couldn't care less what sorts of bars or gratings the experimenter is waving around. The stimuli have information content from the neurophysiologist's standpoint, but not from the animal's standpoint. What we have been measuring, then, is the signals

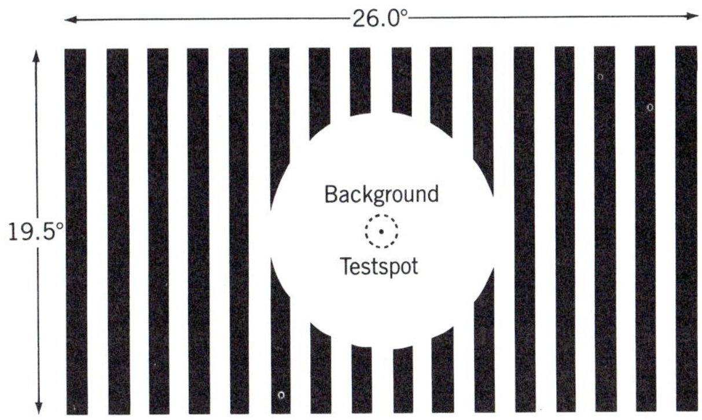

Figure 5.40 *The far-out jerk effect. The small dot in the center is the subject's fixation point. The test spot is flashed within the dotted circle, far from the grating. A similar stimulus is used to test for the shift effect in single cortical neurons.*

that are left over when no information is flowing through the system. The studies so far have told us much about anatomy and physiology but little about psychology. How can we investigate the visual system while it is working? First, we should record from awake animals that exhibit some behavior. Second, we should have the animals perform a visual task, since information must flow from a stimulus to a response. Third, we should place our electrodes where we can expect to intercept the information flow.

One study that met these requirements involved recording from cortical neurons. A monkey was given apple juice for choosing the brighter of two briefly flashed disks. One of the disks was projected on a neuron's receptive field. If the monkey was about to choose correctly, the neuron fired briefly. This was the receptive field response. The firing was followed by an even larger burst of firing, never seen in immobilized animals. If the behavioral choice was about to be incorrect, the second burst was missing (Bridgeman, 1980b, 1982). All of this occurred before the behavioral response took place.

In summary, the visual cortex does more than just represent a retinal image. It combines visual information with memory and participates in the decision-making process. This process continues in areas beyond the striate cortex.

Other Visual Areas

The striate cortex is the largest of the maps of the retina, but other visual areas cover even more cortex. Not much is known yet about the other areas, and much of what we do know is fragmentary.

Surrounding area 17 are two belts of cortex with additional maps, areas 18 and 19. Area 19 was once thought to be a single topographic map, but now it is known to have about a half-dozen separate maps marching in a regular progression down the side of the cortex. These maps contain a high proportion of complex receptive fields (Hubel & Wiesel, 1965b), and many of the cells respond vigorously to color. But their contribution to normal vision is unknown. In fact, monkeys seem to have normal vision and normal visual discrimination abilities after the removal of both area 18 and area 19. They can do two-alternative discriminations, for instance, receiving a reward for pressing a red panel rather than a green one or pressing a panel with a + rather than an x on it. Areas 18 and 19 seem to be recent additions to the mammalian system. In the cat they receive inputs directly from the LGN, but in the monkey and human their visual input comes only from the striate cortex.

The **inferotemporal (IT) cortex,** well developed only in primates, is another mystery area. At first it seemed that removing this area created blindness; without it, monkeys were helpless at performing visual discriminations. At Yerkes Primate Center in Florida, Karl Pribram (1971) had to carry such a monkey and its cage about a mile from the monkey "hotel" to the "school." One hot day, after weeks of unsuccessful training, Pribram sat down to rest with the monkey beside him. The monkey reached out of the cage, caught a gnat, and ate it. Pribram grabbed for a gnat and missed. The monkey caught another gnat, and the man missed again. Clearly, this monkey wasn't blind! It turned out that the monkey, and others like it, had considerable visual ability. Removing the IT cortex has no effect on visual acuity, depth perception, or other attributes of the visual image. And an IT-lesioned monkey can still do simple visual discriminations. A deficit appears only for difficult visual discriminations such as distinguishing "3" from "8."

Receptive fields in the IT cortex tend to be large, and they always include the fixation point. They are excited even by small and unimpressive stimuli somewhere in the field, if those stimuli have meaning for the animal (Gross, Bender & Rocha-Miranda, 1969). Recently, IT cells have been found with quite specific response properties. Some respond selectively to an object of a particular degree of complexity, regardless of its position in the receptive field (Desimone et al., 1982). Others respond only to faces presented in the receptive field (Desimone et al., 1984). For evidence that faces are processed in specialized ways, see Figure 5.41.

The prelunate area is another area that is attracting attention. It is located anterior to areas 18 and 19, and in the monkey some of its cells seem to be related to decisions about eye movements and visual tracking. While a monkey is learning a

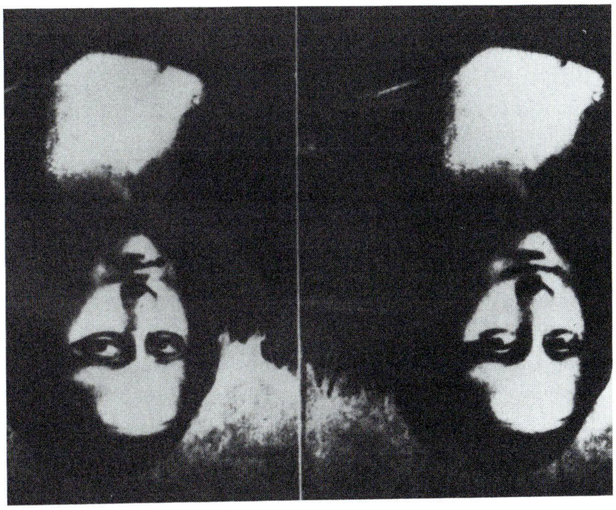

Figure 5.41 *Demonstration that facial features are perceived correctly only when the face is right side up.*

tracking task, these cells fire between the time of the stimulus movement and the time of the resulting eye movement. As the monkey improves at the task, the cells cease responding to the stimuli and the behavioral response comes more quickly. The cells are active only during learning (Fischer & Boch, 1982).

EFFERENT CONTROL

The brain controls visual input at several levels. We have already seen how higher levels control the processing of light before it is transduced, by controlling the pupil and lens.

Visual input is also controlled at a neural level. Like most nerve tracts, the optic nerve tracts contain fibers running in both directions. Some of the information carried on the efferent fibers is of a general sensory nature; it includes both auditory and somatic signals (Spinelli, Pribram & Weingarten, 1965; Spinelli & Weingarten, 1966). We know that the fibers are efferent because the signals are abolished when the optic nerve is cut between the recording site and the brain.

Some of these signals change the size of ganglion cell receptive fields when the cortex is stimulated (Spinelli & Pribram, 1967). The change in receptive field size reflects a modification of the code representing sensory information. Perhaps the change reflects the organism using different aspects of visual information.

Other, more specific changes in receptive field organization have been found more recently (Marrocco, 1986). Cortical stimulation can change the sensitivity of LGN receptive fields, or it can change just the center or surround parts of the fields. Thus not only the stimulus world affects sensory systems; even at the retina and LGN, the requirements of the task modify the system's functioning. At higher levels, attention changes the functioning of sensory systems even more strongly (see Chapter 10).

The anatomical basis of these effects is still not completely worked out. Cragg (1962) has found efferent nerve terminals ending on amacrine cells, and Dowling (1979) has identified what he calls an interplexiform cell—an inverted amacrine cell that sends fibers back into the outer plexiform layer as well as connecting with ganglion cells in a more conventional fashion. It is not known whether this local feedback neuron is part of a long-distance efferent pathway.

A SECOND VISUAL SYSTEM

Most of the discussion of vision has concerned the **geniculostriate** (lateral geniculate and striate cortex) visual system and its many supplementary cortical areas. Another visual system, much older in evolution, is centered in the superior colliculus of the midbrain. This system receives its own independent retinal input. It can function even if the geniculostriate system is removed (Schneider, 1969). Trevarthen (1968) has named it the **ambient visual system,** emphasizing its use of the entire visual field to determine the relationship of the organism with visual space. The geniculostriate system is the focal system in Trevarthen's terms, emphasizing its concentration on visual attention and on pattern recognition functions. In humans the ambient system probably extends beyond the midbrain to the cortex to include some parietal visual-motor areas (Mishkin, Ungerleider & Macko, 1983).

Evidence for the ambient system's function in humans comes from studies of **blindsight**—the ability of humans with large lesions in the striate cortex to use vision for basic spatial orientation. Such people have large **scotomas**—areas of the visual field where they have no visual experience—just as normal people have a small scotoma on the blind spot of the retina. Nevertheless, blindsighted people can point to a target in the blind part of their visual field (Weiskrantz et al., 1974). They can even improve this ability with practice (Bridgeman & Staggs, 1982). They can also direct eye movements to a target in the blind field (Zihl, 1980). While performing these tasks, they may protest that they are guessing, because they can't see anything in the blind field. Presumably, subcortical visual centers enable them to do these tasks.

These examples show that we have a lot to learn about the physiology of visual information flow. We don't yet know what many of the visual areas do or how their functions fit together to provide the experience of a single powerful and flexible visual system.

INFORMATION PROCESSING IN AUDITION

Auditory coding is simpler than visual coding in principle because the auditory stimulus can be described with two dimensions instead of three. Also, audition carries much less information than vision. The anatomy of the auditory system, however, is more complicated.

ASCENDING PATHWAYS

The path from the cochlea to the auditory cortex is shown in Figure 5.42. Fibers from the **spiral ganglion**—a group of cell bodies inside the cochlea—form the eighth cranial nerve. They branch to two parts of the **cochlear nucleus**—the site of the first synapse in the auditory pathway in the medulla. From the ventral cochlear nucleus they connect to the **superior olivary complex**, where the first **binaural** (from the two ears) interactions take place. The dorsal part sends projections, some direct and some indirect, to the inferior colliculus, so named because it is just inferior to the superior colliculus. In contrast to the situation in vision, it is common for part of an auditory tract to skip a synapse and project directly to the next layer, complicating the description. The two paths rejoin at the inferior colliculus, and all of the ascending fibers synapse at the **medial geniculate** of the thalamus (sure enough, just medial to vision's lateral geniculate) before reaching the cortex. Along the way, the system sends fibers into the cerebellum and the brain-stem reticular formation.

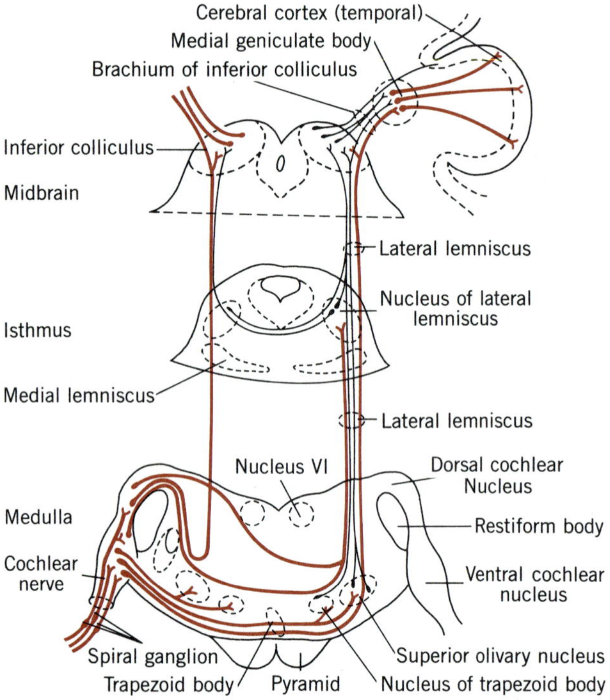

Figure 5.42 *Anatomy of auditory pathways. Auditory connections flow from the hindbrain through the midbrain to the forebrain. Though cortical representation is bilateral, most fibers cross to the opposite side in the brain stem. The auditory system's lateral lemniscus is unrelated to the medial lemniscus of the somatosensory system. Some of the secondary and higher-order fibers branch medially to enter the reticular formation, where they may mediate reflex closing of the eyes and turning of the head toward a loud noise. Efferent fibers are not shown.*

AUDITORY CORTEX

Because each synapse implies information processing, a large amount of combining and recoding of auditory information takes place before signals reach the cortex. But they do so rather quickly; potentials can be recorded at the cortex with a latency of about 20 msec, less than the striate cortex latency. The spontaneous activity is very high throughout the subcortical auditory pathways, implying that some information is carried as modifications of sustained firing.

The pattern arriving at the auditory cortex is a **tonotopic** (arranged by frequency) map of the cochlea; each cochlea is represented on both sides of the brain. Here, information about location and pattern in the auditory input is unraveled. The temporal cortex contains several tonotopic maps, each heavily interconnected with the others. When the one-dimensional map of the cochlea is laid out on the two-dimensional cortex, one dimension represents sound frequency and the other is used to code sound intensity. In the ectosylvian gyrus of the dog, recordings from gross electrodes show that location along the length of the auditory cortex corresponds to frequency and location across the gyrus corresponds to intensity. Each region responds most strongly to a tone of a particular frequency and intensity (Tunturi, 1952). Tones of the wrong frequency or intensity, whether louder or softer, cause weaker responses.

Central Processing of Location

The cortical machinery for auditory localization should have an auditory map of space. But the many auditory areas are organized by frequency, with maps of the unrolled cochlea. There is some eivdence for a spatiotopic map of auditory space in an unexpected place: the striate visual cortex. Many striate cortex neurons also have auditory receptive fields (Spinelli, Star & Barrett, 1968). The cells are relatively unselective for auditory features such as frequency, but they respond only to sounds coming from a particular location. The visual and auditory maps coincide (Morrell, 1972). Perhaps the "visual" cortex could be better conceived as the cortex that maps immediate surrounding space. Like the visual system, the auditory system seems to separate anatomically the "where" from the "what." Auditory coding in the striate cortex remains controversial; more work will be needed to characterize the interactions.

Central Processing of Pattern

The tonotopic pattern on the auditory cortex implies that the rough frequency analysis performed at the cochlea is carried through to the highest levels. In fact, the frequency tuning is sharpened going up the auditory pathway, probably by lateral inhibition (Békésy, 1967). We can find the "tuning curve" of a cell in the auditory system by measuring its response to pure sine-wave tones of varying frequencies. Then, for each stimulating frequency, we can plot the stimulus strength necessary to elicit a minimum response from the cell. Compare the resulting **tuning curves** in Figure 5.43; the response sharpens at higher anatomical levels; that is, the tuning curves become narrower and the cells respond to a narrower range of frequencies (Katsuki, 1961). The tuning curve at lower levels follows the motion of the basilar membrane rather closely (Khanna & Leonard, 1982). Higher levels show a more restricted frequency range, especially a sharpening at the low end of the tuning curve. The auditory sharpening of temporal frequency tuning at higher levels is comparable to the sharpening of spatial frequency shown in Figure 5.33.

The tuning curves never become as narrow as the best discrimination ability. As we saw in Chapter 4, the best frequency discrimination is about 1 to 4 Hz; the sharpest tuning curves in Figure 5.43 are nearly 100 times wider. Clearly, discrimination of pitch is based on the activities of combinations of cells. Like the visual system, where three broadly tuned color channels produce all the subtleties of color, the broadly tuned auditory neurons support our exceedingly fine pitch discrimination abilities.

But frequency is a physical attribute, and pitch is a sensory experience. Perceived pitch depends not only on frequency but also on such other factors as intensity, duration, musical training, and the harmonic structure of a sound (its temporal frequency components).

Many auditory neurons respond to more complex aspects of sounds. The onset and offset of a

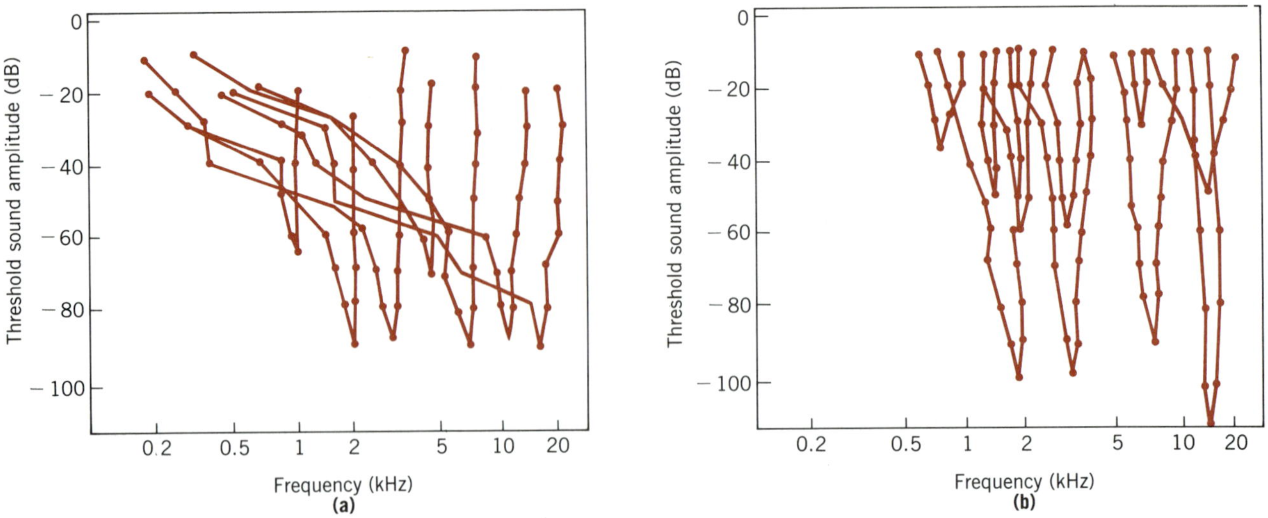

Figure 5.43 *Tuning curves in auditory neurons.* (a) *Auditory nerve.* (b) *Inferior colliculus. Both are log-log plots. The unit of sound pressure on the vertical axis is the decibel (dB), based on the bel, a logarithmic unit. One bel is a 10-fold increase in sound pressure, and a decibel is an increase of one-tenth of a bel.*

sound are particularly important behaviorally, and there is a corresponding set of neuronal responses in the inferior colliculus. The neurons respond selectively to sound onset, sound offset, or both. Others exhibit a sustained response or the intermediate pattern shown in Figure 5.44 (Watanabe & Katsuki, 1974). These five types of response properties are separate from the auditory system's frequency analysis. At the cortical level, many neurons do not respond to pure tones (Webster & Aitkin, 1975). Some are driven by increases or decreases in frequency—an example of frequency modulation (Whitfield & Evans, 1965). In the cat, the auditory cortex does not appear to be necessary for simple frequency and intensity discriminations. But a cat with auditory cortex lesions cannot distinguish different sequences of auditory events, such as two minimelodies made up of the same

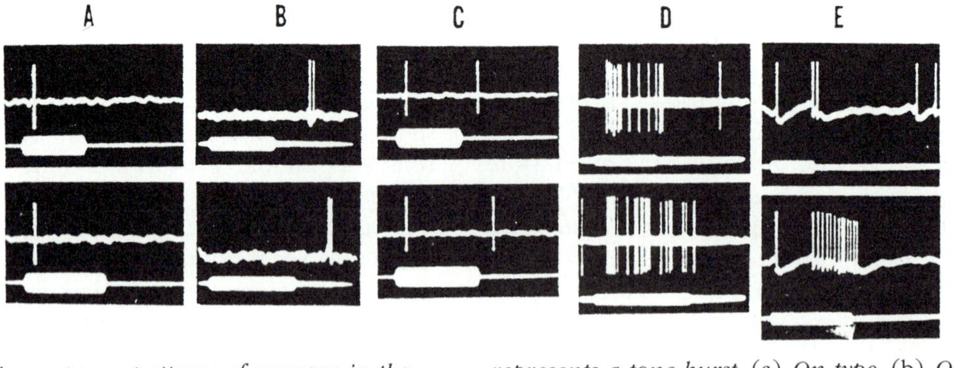

Figure 5.44 *Five response patterns of neurons in the inferior colliculus. The upper trace in each figure is a single cell recorded from a microelectrode; the lower trace is the stimulus, where the widening of the trace represents a tone burst.* (a) *On type.* (b) *Off type.* (c) *On-off type.* (d) *Sustained type.* (e) *Intermediate type. Adapted from Watanabe & Katsuki (1974).*

three tones in different orders (Diamond & Neff, 1957).

We know from the visual system that detection of specific features of the environment can work in only a limited way. The detector scheme, however, is seen in particularly important auditory patterns, such as the species-specific vocalizations of the monkey. Squirrel monkeys have a small number of distinct calls, and some cortical neurons are triggered by particular cells (Funkenstein, et al., 1971).

Efferent Control

Like vision, hearing controls its input both before and after the transduction stage. We have already reviewed the role of the middle ear muscles in modifying the conduction of vibration to the oval window of the cochlea and the mechanical changes in the cochlea itself.

Efferents arrive at the receptors from the tract of Rasmussen, a tiny bundle of about 500 fibers in each ear coming from the superior olive (Smith & Rasmussen, 1963). Its function is probably related to an animal's ability to extract signals from noise, for this ability is impaired when the tract is cut (Dewson, 1968). Electrophysiological studies suggest that the tract may adjust the sensitivity of the hair cells to match the intensity of the input, a sort of automatic gain control like that on a tape recorder. The system helps the auditory pathway handle the enormous intensity range of audible sounds. Between the auditory threshold and the sound pain threshold the range is about 120 dB, or 12 log units.

Physiologists are still speculating about the mechanism for adjusting sensitivity, but one possibility is a recently discovered mechanical action of outer hair cells. These cells shorten slightly when electric current or ACh is applied, stiffening parts of the cochlear structure (Brownell et al., 1985). There are also efferents at other levels of the system from the cortex down.

This ends the survey of the physiology of sensory systems. Their application to the perceptual activities of the organism is the subject of the next chapter.

CHAPTER SUMMARY

1. Once sensory signals are transduced into the neural mode, all senses have a similar task. They transform inputs from receptors into information meaningful to the organism. Neurophysiologists have access to only a distorted and incomplete version of this information.

2. Lateral inhibition exists in many sensory structures. It helps in adaptation, compressing the wide range of stimulus intensities into a narrower range of neuronal responses, and it increases contrast. Lateral inhibition also distributes information more widely in a sensory network.

3. Somatosensory signals reach the brain along two paths—an older spinothalamic path and a newer, faster lemniscal path. Each neuron has a receptive field, the field of skin to which that neuron is receptive. Higher-order neurons have larger central neural machinery. Bipolar cell receptive fields have an antagonistic enter and surround, and ganglion cells have a stronger surround. Half have an on-center, where light excites the cell, and half have an off-center. Horizontal cells and amacrine cells provide inhibition to adapt the retina to existing light levels. Efferent control can change the size of receptive fields.

6. Retinal ganglion cells project to the lateral geniculate nucleus (LGN), a monosynaptic station with more lateral inhibition and added input from nonvisual areas. Both the retina and the LGN have X-cells, where excitation and inhibition add together, and Y-cells, which are excited by contours in any position on the receptive field.

7. Most cortical neurons have elongated receptive fields. They respond best to patches of sine-

and more highly organized receptive fields. Many of these neurons are inhibited by stimuli in an area surrounding the excitatory center. The somatosensory cortex is organized in columns, and many cells respond only to specialized properties such as a particular direction of motion or frequency of vibration. All show adaptation, responding only to changes in stimulation. The somatotopic map of the body on the cortex is only an approximation; it is discontinuous and does not apply on a cell-by-cell microscopic scale.

4. The olfactory bulbs were an evolutionary prototype for the neocortex. They have monosynaptic pathways from olfactory input to mitral cell output, with other neurons modifying the activity. Inhibition in the bulb sharpens the output by surrounding it with suppression and reduces the range of signals by damping the stronger ones. Detailed knowledge of coding at more central levels awaits an understanding of the olfactory alphabet—the categories by which odors are analyzed. Similarly, not much is known about central processing in the gustatory system, which follows the somatosensory system in its central anatomy.

5. The retina is a two-synapse pathway with lateral interactions at each synapse. Receptors project to bipolar cells, modulated by horizontal cells; the bipolar cells then drive ganglion cells, modulated by amacrine cells. Only the ganglion cells have action potentials. The simplest structure is at the fovea, where visual acuity is highest. There, each receptor has its own bipolar cell and ganglion cell. The rod-free fovea trades high acuity and color vision for lower sensitivity and a large investment in wave gratings, and are inhibited by gratings of the wrong spatial frequency or orientation. Simple cells correspond to X-cells because they have alternating excitatory and inhibitory areas; complex cells show nonlinear summation like that of Y-cells. Spatial frequency effects contribute to some, but not all, visual illusions. The visual cortex is arranged in columns for orientation, spatial frequency, and ocular dominance. Color is coded in two ways, with three primary colors in the receptors and three opponent processes (red-green, blue-yellow, and black-white) centrally.

8. Beyond the classical receptive field, neurons are sensitive to large moving stimuli covering large parts of the visual field. In active situations where information flows through cortex the responses are even more complex, depending on information content from the animal's standpoint as well as stimulus properties. Other areas are specialized for such tasks as visual discrimination and the control of visual search. A second visual system, based in the superior colliculus, handles the body's relationship to immediate visual space.

9. Auditory processing involves more synaptic layers than visual processing but uses the same organizational principles. Auditory cortical areas are arranged by frequency and intensity; auditory space is probably coded in the visual cortex. Many auditory neurons are sensitive not only to frequency but also to onset, offset, change in frequency, and other complex patterns. In monkeys, some auditory cortex neurons respond to species-specific calls. Audition also has efferent control all the way to the receptor level.

KEY TERMS

Electroencephalogram (EEG)
Mach bands
Spinothalamic pathway
Lemniscal pathways
Receptive field
Olfactory epithelium
Mitral cell
Intrinsic neurons
Periglomerular cell
Contralateral
Rhinencephalon
Prepyriform cortex
Periamygdaloid area
Entorhinal area
Solitary nucleus
Insula
Bipolar cell
Optic disk

Horizontal cell
Outer plexiform layer
Amacrine cell
Inner plexiform layer
Invaginations
Ribbon synapse
Biplexiform cell
Fovea
Acuity
Hyperacuity
X-cell
Linear summation
Y-cell
W-cell
Optic radiations
Striate cortex
Simple cell
Complex cell
Hypercomplex cell
Feature detector theory
Spatial frequency
Octave
Chromatic grating
Multiplexing
Periphery effect
Shift effect
Inferotemporal (IT) cortex
Geniculostriate
Ambient visual system
Blindsight
Scotoma
Spiral ganglion
Cochlear nucleus
Superior olivary complex
Binaural
Medial geniculate
Tonotopic
Tuning curve

SUGGESTED READINGS

Békésy, G. von. (1967). *Sensory inhibition.* Princeton, NJ: Princeton University Press.

Written over two decades ago, this volume is still a delightful and informative account of the author's Nobel-prize winning experiments on sensory coding, mostly in the auditory and somatosensory systems.

Gregory, R. L. (1978). *Eye and brain* (2nd ed.). New York: McGraw-Hill.

With an engaging and readable style, Gregory traces vision from the physics of light to visual illusions, answering along the way such questions as why the pupil always looks black.

Uttal, W. R. (1973). *The psychobiology of sensory coding.* New York: Harper & Row.

This book reviews coding in all of the senses, maintaining a clear distinction between the codes and the physical mechanisms and making a real attempt to compare codes in the various input pathways.

Chapter 6

THE ACT OF PERCEIVING

Up to now we have viewed sensory systems as though the organisms they belonged to were passive, waiting for things to happen to them. In the real world, though, we get most of our information by active investigation. Much of our behavior (such as the act of reading this book) is directed toward gathering information. This is the act of perception. As a result, much of the neural machinery essential for perception is in parts of the brain that we don't think of as sensory. Examples are motor systems that orient receptors and motivational systems that activate investigations of the world.

The development of perceptual systems also depends on active interaction with the environment. Thus we can make a distinction between passive sensory systems and active perceptual systems. In this chapter we will look first at motor systems in the service of perception and then at the interaction of development and perception.

THE CONCEPT OF PERCEPTUAL SYSTEMS

Aristotle named the five senses: sight, hearing, touch, taste, and smell. Yet in the previous chapters we encountered not five types of receptors but dozens. We also found vestibular and kinesthetic senses that don't even appear in the classical list of senses.

In addition, our sensory experience fails to mirror the anatomy of the sensory systems. We pride ourselves on a complex and subtle sense of taste, for instance; yet, if the olfactory cavities are blocked, foods taste flat and discriminations are difficult. A potato and an apple become indistinguishable. Much of what we experience as taste turns out to be mediated by the olfactory anatomy. The pleasures and distinctions of fine wines, for instance, are almost entirely a matter of odor (though not-so-fine wines may betray themselves by true sour or bitter flavors). So don't let anyone tell you that wine preference is a matter of taste.

Other seemingly unified experiences are compounded of signals from many types of receptors. The experience of wetness, for example, is a combination of temperature and pressure. The fact that one cannot distinguish among the many types of receptors by introspection shows the tenuous link between receptors and experience. The nature of the receptors must be examined with physiology and anatomy as well as with psychology.

Physiologically, it would seem that Aristotle's list of five senses is hopelessly obsolete, yet the idea persists. Why? The answer might be that though there are many types of receptors, there are only five modes of sensory attention: the activities of looking, listening, touching, tasting, and smelling. Perception is something you do.

When we use these systems, we are generally aware of external events rather than physiological processes. Perception involves information about the outside world, not about the status of the receptors. When I perceive a flower, I am aware of the smell and look and feel of the flower, not of olfactory, visual, and tactile sensations. Gibson (1966) calls *sensations* the experiences resulting from energy falling on receptors and *perceptions* the pickup of information from the environment. They are separate phenomena, and perceptions need not be based on conscious, analyzable sensations. The senses evolved to provide information about the world, not about themselves.

All of the perceptual systems can direct the body in the pickup of information. Touching uses the whole body to investigate objects, employing muscle systems that are also used in locomotion and other activities. Smelling and tasting also use multipurpose muscle systems, making it difficult to isolate their contributions to perception. Listening can use the uniquely sensory middle-ear muscles, but they are poorly understood. In any case, they play only a minor role in the hearing process. Seeing, however, requires a specialized system of **extraocular muscles,** whose only role is in the service of vision. Therefore the oculomotor system can best inform us about the interaction of perception and behavior. It is also an elegant example of a neurological control system, because its inputs and outputs can be isolated.

THE OCULOMOTOR SYSTEM—A NEUROLOGICAL CONTROL SYSTEM

The arrangement of the extraocular muscles of humans is shown in Figure 6.1. We will look first at those of the shark, which exhibit the basic vertebrate pattern, and then at those of humans.

SHARKS AND HUMANS COMPARED

In the shark each extraocular muscle has a simple job. There are six muscles, arranged in three opposing pairs. Two muscles pull the eye up and down; two turn it right and left; and two rotate it like a wheel, with the line of sight as the axle. The eyes point in opposite directions, one from each side of the head. The muscles serve to compensate for the shark's locomotion; as the shark moves, the eyes track the visual world so it remains stationary on the retina. When the eye has tracked about as far as it can go, it snaps back in a quick movement called a **saccade** (French for "jerk") and begins tracking again.

In both sharks and humans the oculomotor system also uses vestibular signals to reduce image movement on the retina. The advantage of vestibular input is that it works with very short latency. Compensation can continue in darkness, so the eyes are stabilized as soon as light is available after an occlusion. The compensation in the vertical direction is called the "doll reflex" because in humans the eyes roll downward, like those of a doll, when the head tilts back.

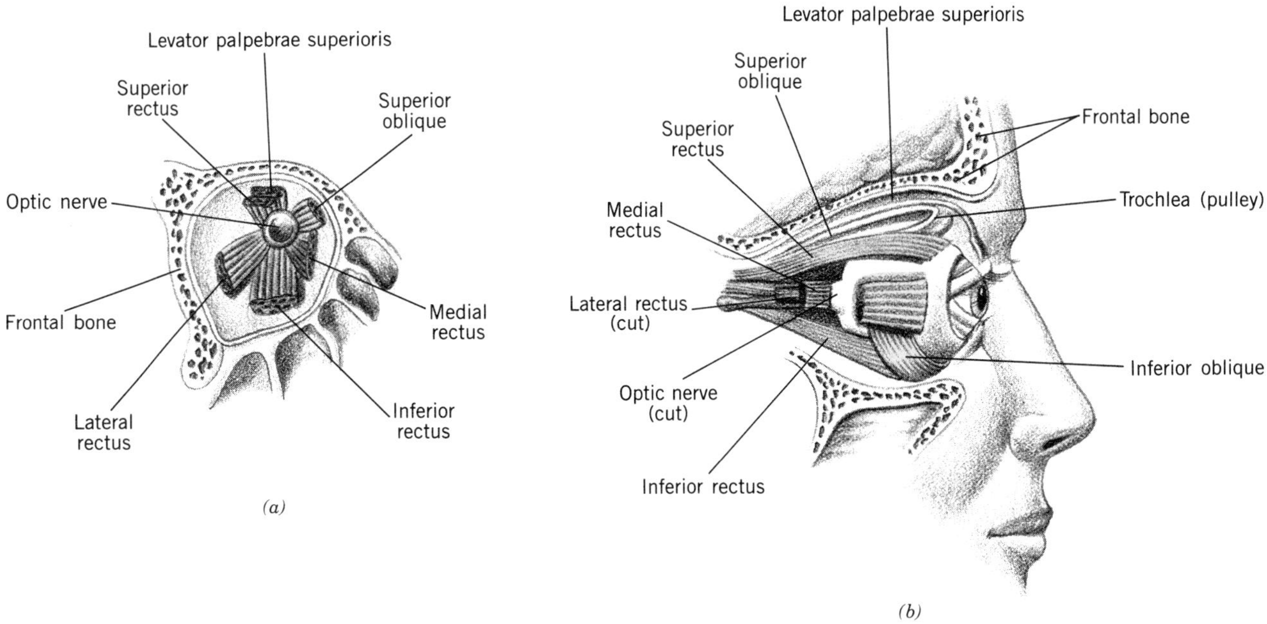

Figure 6.1 *The human extraocular muscles. Each muscle attaches to the eye along a broad line rather than at a point, so a pull on the muscle will have about the same mechanical effect regardless of where the eye is pointed when the contraction begins. The muscles are innervated by three different cranial nerves: the lateral rectus from the sixth nerve, the superior oblique from the fourth nerve, and the rest from the third nerve.* (a) *Origin of the muscles, in frontal section.* (b) *Lateral view.*

The system even predicts image motions, by monitoring motor commands sent to the neck muscles. When the head turns, the eyes begin compensating movements with no latency. The system cannot be very accurate because, like the vestibular reflex, it is a feedforward system. It predicts retinal image motions rather than measuring them. The predictions are never completely accurate, but, together with visual tracking, they reduce errors. You can demonstrate the effectiveness of this system in yourself by turning your head back and forth while looking at a word on this page. You will continue to be able to read the word. If you generate the same retinal movement by rapidly moving the book, the word will be blurred, because visual pursuit begins only after a latency of over 100 msec.

Humans have the same six muscles as sharks, but the arrangement and functions of the muscles are more subtle and flexible. During evolution the orbits (eye sockets) moved to the front of the head, so we have binocular vision. The three dimensions of space are built into our eye movement control system. We can consider our two eyes a single organ, handled by a single neurological control system (Hering, 1868). It controls the point of sight, where the lines of sight from the two eyes intersect.

In addition to left-right and up-down movements of the eyes, which have separate control systems, the point of sight is moved toward the body by the two medial eye muscles. The two lateral muscles move the point of sight farther away. These **convergence movements** (motions of both eyes toward the nose) and **divergence movements** (motions of both eyes away from the nose) have their own control system. Thus each direction of visual space is represented by a pair of eye muscles operating in various combinations. Rectangular coordinates were not invented by mathematicians; they were there all along in the oculomotor control system.

THE OCULOMOTOR SYSTEM IN PERCEPTION

The human's oculomotor system, like the shark's, provides a stable platform so the retinas can receive visual information. The shark accomplishes this by alternating saccades with slow movements that compensate for locomotion. Humans do the same, with two complications introduced by the presence of a fovea. First, pursuit eye movements track an object of interest, regardless of the motion of the rest of the image. Second, exploratory saccades move the fovea from one part of the visual world to another.

Pursuit Eye Movements

A feedback built into the oculomotor control system keeps the image on the fovea stable. If the image begins to drift, the extraocular muscles move the eye to stop the drift and restore the image to its original location on the fovea. This system is involuntary and cannot be turned off. The movements are called **pursuit eye movements** because the eyes pursue the foveal image.

The pursuit system takes over when the eye tracks an object that is moving relative to its background. The resulting situation seems paradoxical. Pursuit prevents the image from moving on the fovea while the background drifts across the peripheral retina. Yet we perceive just the opposite; the fixated object seems to move while the background remains stable. When we track a moving train, for example, the background moves on the retina and the train doesn't. Yet we perceive the train as moving and the tracks as standing still.

If this were the complete description of the oculomotor system, life would be uninteresting indeed. Once pursuit locked vision onto a single object, we would be stuck there forever. Fortunately, a second eye movement system breaks the feedback loop by jumping the eye to a new position.

Saccadic Eye Movements

Saccadic eye movements are important because they are by far the most frequent of all human behaviors. They are time-optimal; that is, the eye moves as fast as is physically possible (Clark & Stark, 1975). The saccade is an oculomotor sprint to a new fixation point, with no concern for vision during the movement. Indeed, visual sensitivity to flashes of light is suppressed during and just before each saccade (Volkman et al., 1978). But the visual image does not change in brightness from one fixation to the next; rather, it changes in position. We would expect the perception of displacements of the world to be suppressed during saccades.

If a target jumps during a saccade, as in Figure 6.2, the target must move about 25 percent as far as the eye does to be detectable (Mack, 1970; Bridgeman, Hendry & Stark, 1975). Standing behind a subject in such an experiment, one can see the target plainly jumping about; yet the subject sees no movement. The perceptual system seems to assume that any small movement of the entire visual world during a saccade is due to the eye movement.

Image displacements during saccades are not suppressed in the second, motor-oriented visual system (introduced in Chapter 5). The experimenter can isolate the second system from perception by having subjects point to a target without being able to see their own pointing hands; thus no visual feedback will enter their perception. If the target movement is masked during the saccade, the subjects still will point to the true position (Bridgeman et al., 1979). Information about displacement is actively removed from perception, where it would only be a distraction.

A saccadic eye movement is **ballistic,** in the sense that once started, it cannot be stopped. Starting a saccade is like throwing a ball; once the ball leaves your hand, its path cannot be altered. If you begin a saccade and then change your mind, the movement must be completed anyway.

At the start of a saccade, the agonist eye muscles (the ones pulling on the globe) receive a pulse of innervation that activates them to their maximum extent. The duration of the pulse depends on the size of the intended movement. About halfway through the movement, the innervation drops back to the level required to hold the eye in the new position (Bahill & Stark, 1975). This is the pulse-step pattern of innervation. For large saccades, there is a braking pulse in the antagonists near the end of the movement.

The strategy of the oculomotor system in driving a saccade is like an automobile driver's strat-

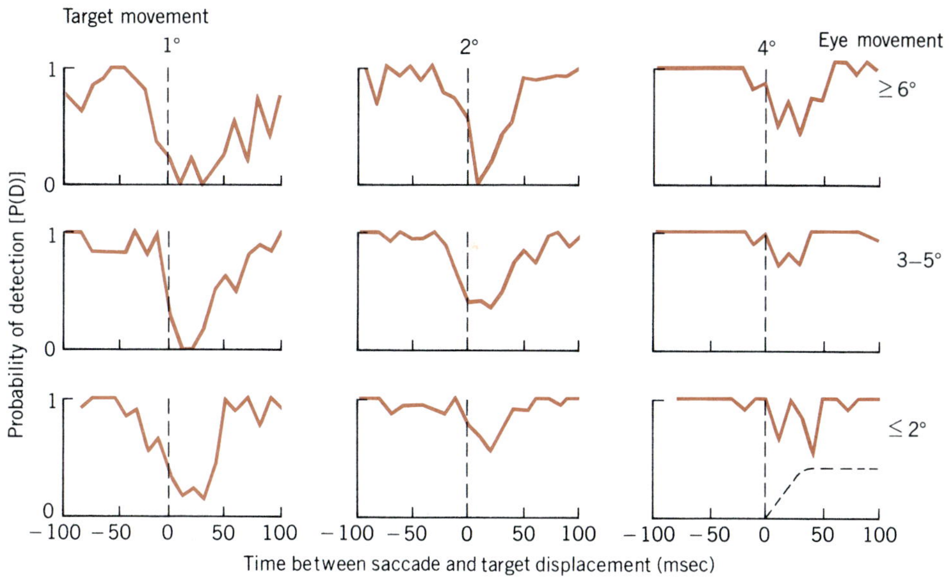

Figure 6.2 *Saccadic suppression of displacement. Each graph shows the probability of detecting the abrupt jump of a large projected pattern, 14 deg wide × 10 deg high. Larger eye movements are shown in the upper graphs, and larger target jumps are shown in the rightmost graphs. The graphs for the 2-deg target displacement condition (center column) are smoother than the rest because twice as many trials were collected for this condition. A 6-deg saccade is shown schematically in the lower right-hand graph (dashed line) to indicate its onset and duration. Graphs along the right-slanting diagonals are similar, showing that the ratio of eye movement to target movement is the determining factor in the amount of suppression found. The three graphs in the upper left-hand corner show no detections of target displacements in 42 trials when the target was displaced 10 msec after the eye began to move.*

egy in entering a crowded freeway. To reach cruising speed as quickly as possible, the driver presses the gas pedal to the floor. The faster the driver wants to go, the longer the pedal stays on the floor. This is the pulse of the pulse-step strategy. When cruising speed is reached, the driver lets back on the pedal to maintain a steady speed. This corresponds to the step of innervation.

NEURAL MECHANISMS OF EYE MOVEMENT GENERATION

Differences between pursuit and saccadic movements are also seen in the neural machinery that drives them (Robinson, 1981).

Pursuit Mechanisms

Smooth pursuit begins about 100 msec after a target begins to move; if about 55 msec are lost in peripheral visual processing and another 25 msec in the motor system, only 20 msec remain to organize the pursuit movement. In response to this time pressure, the strategy of the pursuit system is to pursue first and ask questions later.

Cells directly related to pursuit are found in the **flocculus,** a phylogenetically old part of the cerebellum. Some Purkinje cells there fire in proportion to the velocity of gaze in space (the speed of eye motion relative to the visual world); their discharge rates are the sum of eye velocity in the head and head velocity in space. Such cells seem necessary to control pursuit; removing the cerebellum of monkeys abolishes pursuit (Westheimer & Blair, 1973). The gaze Purkinje cells project to the brain stem by unknown pathways, probably through the paramedian pontine reticular formation (PPRF), shown in Figure 6.3.

The only cortical neurons yet discovered that are concerned exclusively with pursuit are in the

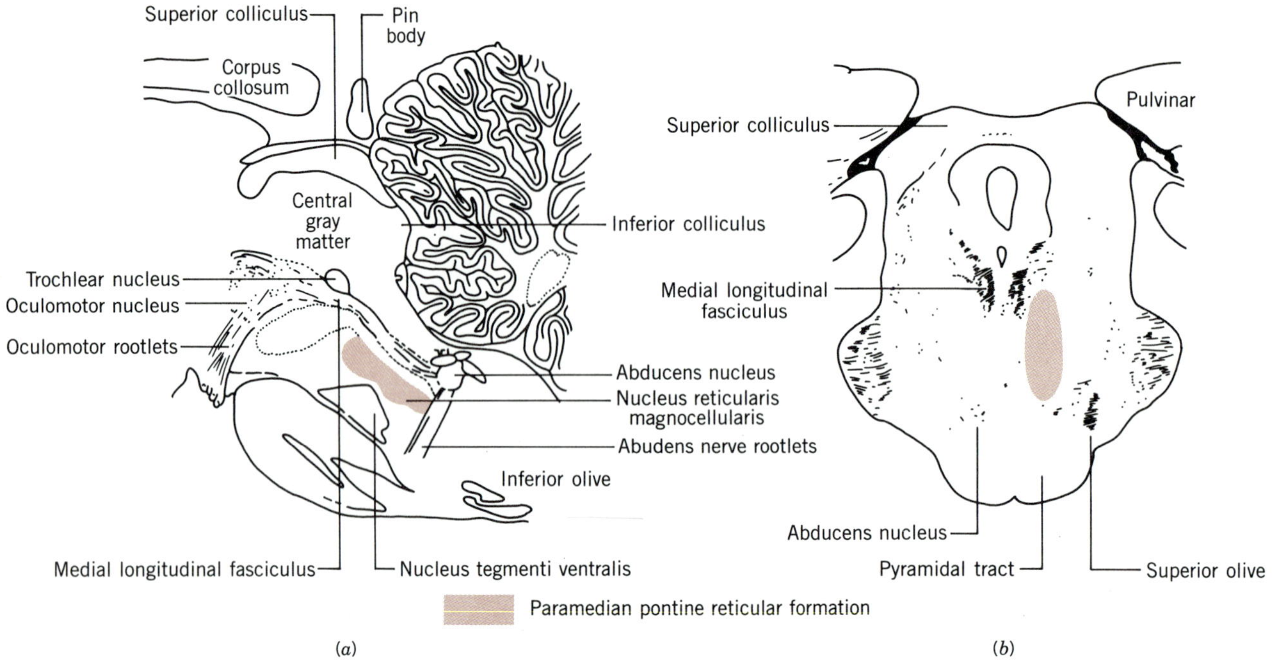

***Figure 6.3** Location of the paramedian pontine reticular formation (PPRF) in the mesencephalic brain stem.* (a) *Sagittal section.* (b) *Frontal section. The fourth nerve nucleus is just anterior to the plane of the section, and the sixth nerve nucleus is just posterior.*

parietal lobe (Lynch et al., 1977). These neurons were discovered in monkeys that were trained to track a moving target while the experimenters recorded from single neurons. The cells fire when a monkey tracks a moving target. The discharge rate depends on the target's direction but not on its speed. This dependence would be expected of neurons concerned more with initiation of pursuit than with its feedback control. Once the neurons get the system going, pursuit seems to be controlled mainly in the hindbrain. Not much is known about the anatomical connections between cortical and hindbrain pursuit mechanisms.

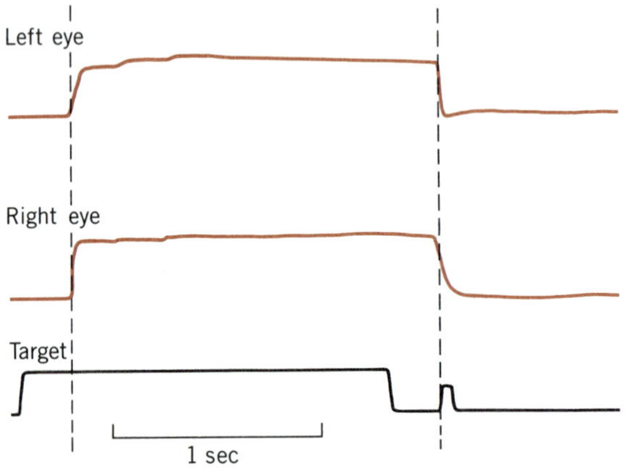

***Figure 6.4** The microstructure of saccadic eye movements. Leftward movements are shown by upward deflections. The left eye undershoots when going leftward (first saccade) and overshoots when going rightward (second saccade). The right eye is more accurate in both directions. The eye ignores the second, smaller step on the right side of the "target" trace. Adapted from Bahill et al. (1976).*

Saccadic Mechanisms

Errors in saccades reveal how the saccadic control mechanism works (Bahill, Clark & Stark, 1975). Figure 6.4 shows some common inaccuracies in normal saccades. We are unaware of these events in our own eyes, even though they occur thousands of times each day. They are examples of the rather small role that consciousness plays in our mental life, a theme to be taken up again in Chapter 14.

The first electrophysiological sign of the organization of a new saccade is in long-lead burst neurons in the PPRF. These cells begin firing 100 to 150 msec before a saccade, in what Robinson (1981) calls a "ragged, low-frequency preamble" followed by a burst before, during, or after the saccade. Long-lead neurons seem to encode the distance the eye must travel rather than the initial or final eye position. In other words, they function in retinal coordinates.

In regard to similar cells in the superior colliculus, Sparks and Pollack (1977) have captured the single-cell signs of a monkey making a decision and changing its mind. They trained monkeys to execute a saccade when a small visual target was jumped from point A to point B. Long-lead burst neurons gave the usual ragged discharge followed by a sharp burst. Now the researchers moved the target from A to B and then jumped it from B to C before the monkey had a chance to execute the A-B saccade. Sometimes the monkey would cancel the A-B movement and look directly to C. In these cases, long-lead neurons active for the A-B direction would give a preamble but no burst, as though the plan to make the A-B saccade were being formulated and then discarded.

Medium-lead burst cells (shown in Figure 6.5) generate the pulse of the pulse-step control signal. These neurons excite the motor neurons monosynaptically. Each of them fires only before saccades with components in a particular direction. Once the pulse is delivered, a tonic innervation must hold the eye in the new position. As diagrammed in the figure, the innervation comes from tonic cells in the PPRF.

Initiation of Eye Movements

Normally, the only conscious decisions involved in oculomotor behavior are those of whether and when to initiate saccades. Even this is often automatic, without the owner of the saccadic system thinking about its behavior. Accordingly, two separate systems can initiate saccades, one in the midbrain (superior colliculus) and the other in the frontal lobe—in the frontal eye fields of Brodmann's area 8. For a long time it was thought that area 8 neurons played little role in initiating

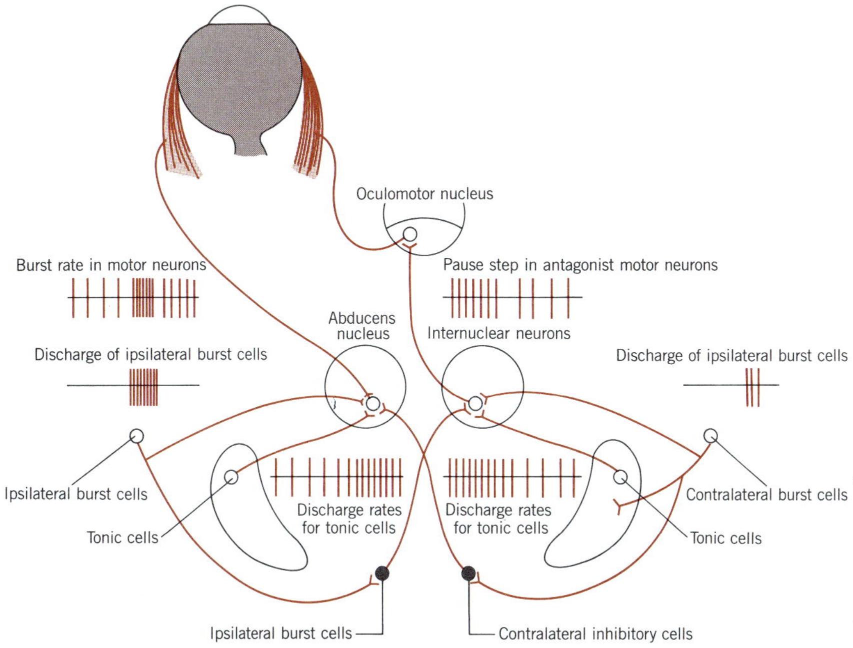

Figure 6.5 *Robinson's (1981) model of saccade generation. In the diagram the system is executing a saccade to the left. The lateral rectus is the agonist, and the medial rectus is the antagonist. Filled circles are inhibitory neurons; open circles are excitatory neurons. On the agonist side the motor neuron totals the bursts from the ipsilateral burst cells and the tonic cells. The motor neuron is inhibited by the contralateral burst cells. On the antagonist side the same ipsilateral burst cell inserts a pause in the motorneuron innervation through an inhibitory interneuron.*

saccades, for most of them fired only after the beginning of a saccade. The recordings that provided this information were made when the animal was only casually looking around the laboratory. But when a monkey initiates a deliberate saccade to obtain a reward, things look very different. Many cells in the posterior part of area 8 fire just after the change in the visual stimulus but before the saccade (Goldberg & Bushnell, 1979).

All of this machinery is designed to steady the image on the fovea for as much time as possible. The next section will answer the questions: what does the visual system do with that image, and how does it decide where to fixate next?

SCANPATHS

When you come upon a new visual scene, your eyes jump first to the area of greatest interest—the area where the density of information is greatest. Then they jump to a spot determined by information content, distance, and your own interests. A series of jumps generates a **scanpath**—a pattern of fixational eye movements (Noton & Stark, 1971).

The scanpath is the meeting point of oculomotor physiology and cognitive psychology. Decisions about where to move the eye next are made with great rapidity (up to five decisions per second) and usually without awareness of the decision process, yet they involve a sophisticated use of information The separation of figure and background is important in guiding the scanpath, as Figure 6.6 shows; in this rather difficult image, subjects scan the image widely before they identify it. After the face is found, the scanpath narrows to the areas that are generally the most informative within faces. For images that can be interpreted in several ways, the scanpath depends on the interpretation of the moment (Stark & Ellis, 1981).

After the identity of the scene is established, higher-level questions govern visual scanning patterns. Yarbus (1967) showed subjects a painting while asking them questions about the people in it; the scanpaths (illustrated in Figure 6.7) depended on the nature of the question being asked. Subjects always scanned the most information-rich regions of the painting, but the definition of what provided the most information changed with the question being asked.

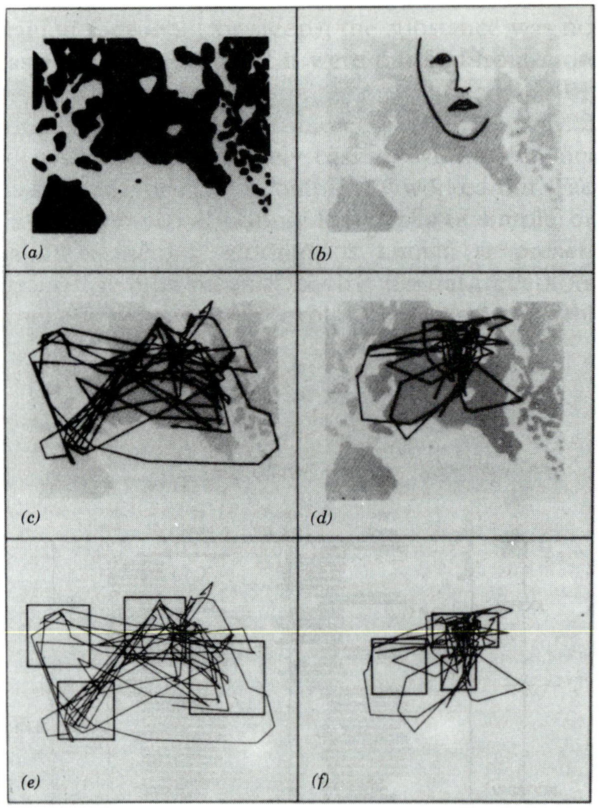

Figure 6.6 *Change in scanpath after recognition of a figure.* (a) *A hidden face.* (b) *Same face shown in outline. Before identifying the figure in* (a), *subjects generate scanpaths such as that in* (c). *After identification the eye shifts to scanpaths such as that in* (d), *even though the image has not changed. This shows the influence of top-down, internally generated information in driving exploratory behavior. The last two images show fixation regions* (e) *before identification and* (f) *after identification.*

Even between exploratory saccades, the eye is never still. Another family of eye movements appears during attempts to hold fixation steady.

Eye Movements during Fixation

Fixating eyes continue to generate three kinds of eye movements: fast, very small oscillations of a few seconds of arc; drifts at a few minutes of arc per second; and **microsaccades**—small jumps of a quarter degree or less that occur one to two

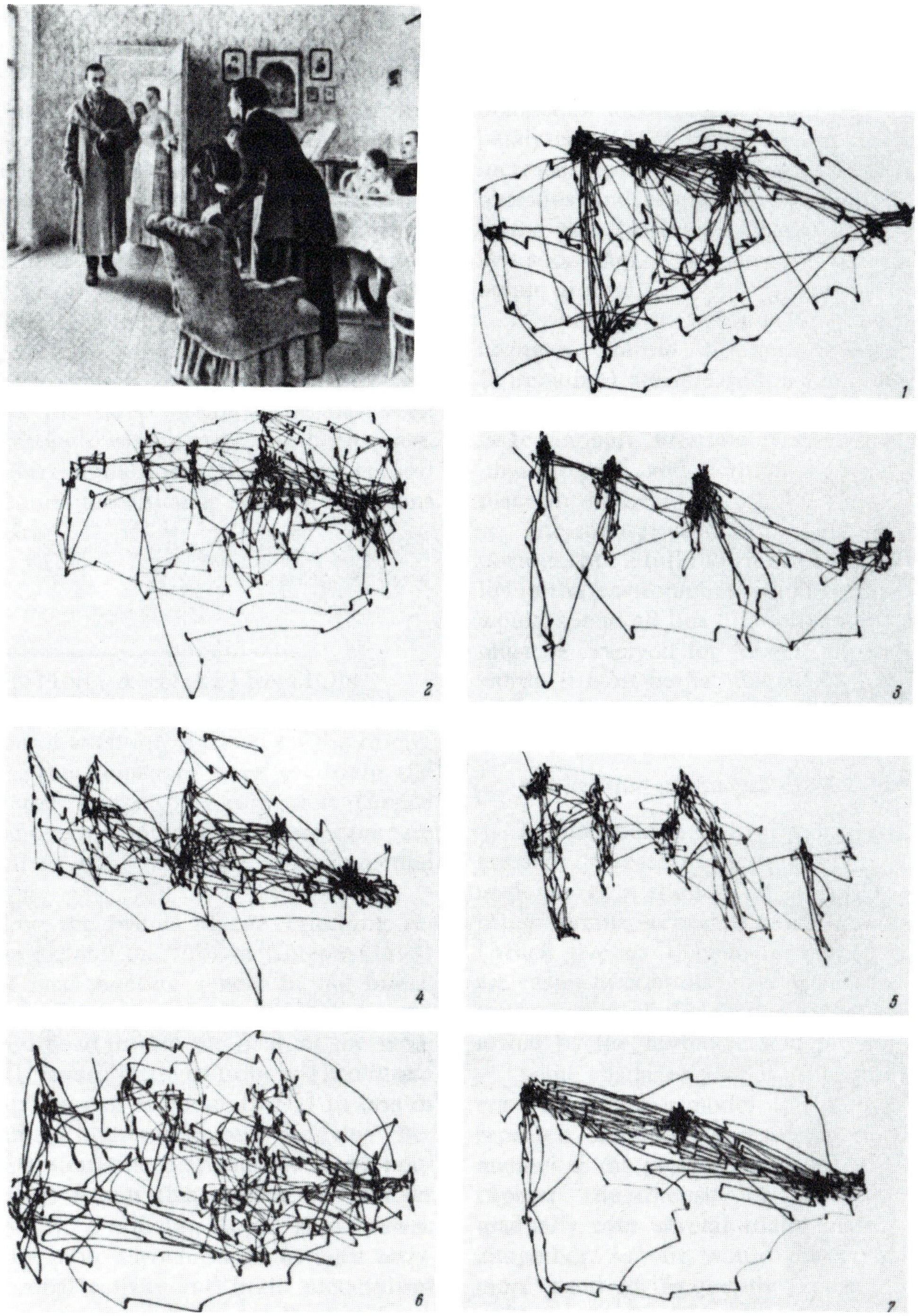

Figure 6.7 *Scanpaths following a series of questions about the painting at the top. (1) Free examination. (2) Subject asked to estimate the material circumstances of the family. (3) Subject asked the ages of the people. (4) Subject asked what the family had been doing before the arrival of the "unexpected visitor." (5) Subject asked what clothes were worn by the people. (6) Subject asked the positions of the people and objects. (7) Subject asked to estimate how long the "unexpected visitor" had been away.*

times a second. One can best see the function of the movements by getting rid of them; if all retinal motion is prevented, the image disappears in a few seconds (Gerrits, Stassen & von Erning, 1984).

Microsaccades do not aid in high-acuity tasks such as rifle-shooting and needle-threading (Winterson & Collewijn, 1976), and they are not needed for observing high-acuity events (Bridgeman & Palca, 1980). In fact, microsaccades decrease in number just when high acuity is needed most. A recent hypothesis holds that microsaccades maintain vision in the retinal periphery, so the image does not become stabilized and disappear. Since these jumps need not be very frequent, drifts can maintain foveal vision between microsaccades (Gerrits, Stassen & von Erning, 1984).

ACTIVE PERCEPTION IN THE SOMATOSENSORY SYSTEM

Information samples are also integrated in other senses. The somatosensory system, for instance, receives a sequence of deformations of the skin while you explore an object tactually. Exploring a chair in the dark, you feel only small samples of the chair at any one time. Yet you perceive a constant, whole object. Again, the information from successive samples is stored in a form of perceptual memory to synthesize a perception of the sensory world.

Researchers have investigated the physiology of this process in awake monkeys by training the monkeys to explore a texture with their fingers. While the monkeys were exploring, neurons were recorded in areas 1 and 3b of the postcentral somatosensory cortex. Neural discharges were influenced by both the finger movement and the characteristics of the spatial pattern. Because the receptive field patterns of the neurons vary widely (see Figure 6.8), spatial features of the surface are represented only by responses of a population of cells. The responses of individual cells are ambiguous (Darian-Smith, Sugitani & Heywood, 1982). As was the case in vision, these neurons do not function as detectors of particular patterns.

In all perceptual systems, much of what we think of as perceptual information comes from top-down hypotheses—assumptions about the nature of the environment. The combining of a top-down schema in the brain with bottom-up information from the senses might make a good definition of perception. In other words, perception is the combining of sensory signals with meaning.

Unfortunately, almost nothing is known about the physiological basis of such processes, so the story must end here. But active interaction with the environment also plays a part in the development of the perceptual systems themselves, and here knowledge is increasing rapidly.

TUNING THE BRAIN TO ITS ENVIRONMENT

In the early 1950s there was great excitement in biology as the genetic code was being cracked. It seemed that it would soon be possible to follow the process of development step by step, practically molecule by molecule, until the construction of an organism was understood. When the molecular alphabet of the genes was finally worked out and the amount of information in the genes was calculated, biologists received an unpleasant surprise. The information in the genes wasn't enough to specify the construction of even a brain, let alone an entire organism! The problem was worse in higher organisms, for complexity seemed to increase faster than the genes' information capacity.

Eventually, the puzzle was solved in several ways. First, it wasn't necessary to have a separate gene to code each neuron or each synapse; using more economical coding schemes, nature could specify a large network by laying down only the rules by which the network would grow. Painting in broad strokes, the genes could control the general structure without determining all the details. (Other solutions will appear later in the chapter.)

EMBRYONIC DEVELOPMENT

A new specialty has grown up to study the problems of development: **neuroembryology.** Several principles of brain growth have emerged; they are economical ways to grow a nervous system. One principle is that embryonic neurons are equipped to find their way along chemical or electrical gra-

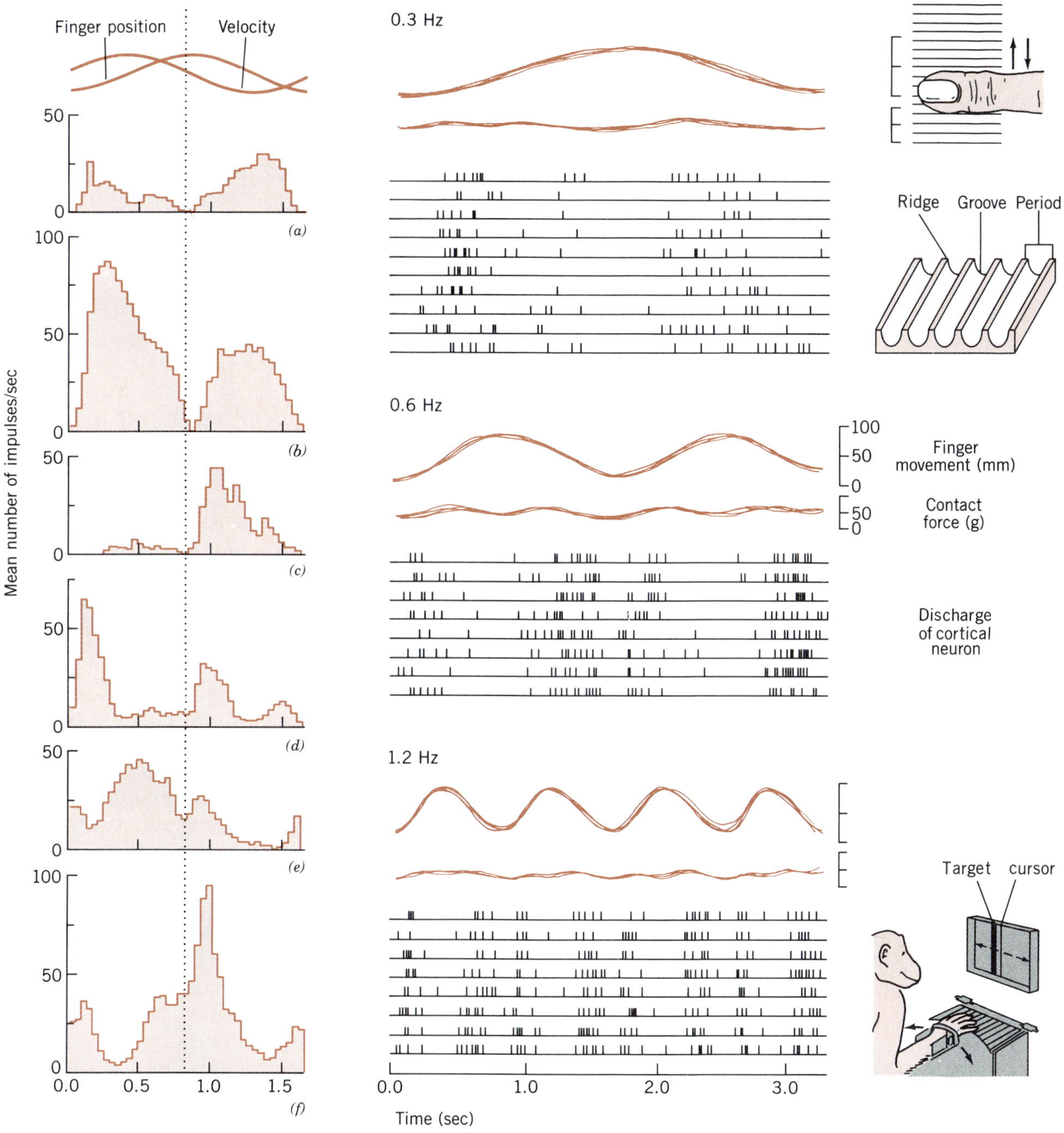

Figure 6.8 *Discharges of neurons in the somatosensory cortex when a monkey rubs the fingers of the contralateral hand across a ridged surface. The monkey was trained to make sinusoidal finger movements of the appropriate frequency, amplitude, and pressure. The left column shows histograms summing over 100 trials from this neuron* (a) *and from five other neurons (*b *through* f*). Differences are evident in firing patterns among the neurons. The center column illustrates the discharge of a single neuron in cortical area 3b. In each block of data the frequency is the monkey-generated movement frequency. The upper traces are finger positions on the grating, the next traces are finger pressure, and the following traces are single-cell spikes, each line representing one trial.*

dients when their processes are developing. A growing axon develops a **growth cone**—a set of fingerlike endings on its growing tip that seem to sense the local environment and guide the elongation of the axon behind the cone. The growth cone moves and waves as it pushes its way to its destination. A target tissue, such as the cortex, may send out chemical signals to help the axons find their way. If the target tissue is removed, the axons get lost.

The first neurons to innervate a developing nerve tract are called pioneer cells; they need genetic information that tells them where to go. Later axons growing along the tract need only be informed by the genes that they should follow the paths of the other axons.

An example of higher-level economy in providing genetic information comes from ingenious studies on three-eyed frogs (Law & Constantine-Paton, 1981; Constantine-Paton & Law, 1982). The frog would seem an unpromising subject for studies of binocular interaction, for each of its eyes normally projects to a monocular optic tectum on the opposite side. These frogs, however, were implanted as embryos with an eye primordium (the bit of tissue that eventually develops into an eye) from another frog embryo. Some of the primordia matured into normal eyes, usually located on the top of the head. These eyes sent axons into one or both optic tecta, where they competed for space with the axons from the natural eyes. Anatomical analysis showed striped ocular dominance columns similar to those seen in cats and monkeys.

This result shows that the striped pattern is due not to a "stripe" gene but to some more basic property of neural development. The pattern develops from the application of two basic structure-building rules. First, the axons from the two eyes are ordered by a rough chemical gradient in the tectum, each eye attempting to fill the entire tectum. Axons from a natural eye and the third eye, still randomly mixed, thus project to the proper regions of the tectum. Second, local interactions within the tectum sort out the axons by maintaining as neighbors only axons arising from cells that started out as neighbors in one of the retinas. The only pattern that can simultaneously optimize both the gradient and the local-clumping processes is a series of stripes.

The implications of these solutions to the problem of genetic guidance of development are profound. If synaptic connections are specified in only a general way, theorists concluded, the details must be at least partly random. Earlier work had led to an effort to investigate information flow in randomly connected networks and to study self-organizing systems (Minsky & Papert, 1969). The capabilities of these systems turned out to be very limited, however; another solution was needed.

A second idea was more successful at resolving the puzzle of inadequate genetic capacity. It was that there is another source of information available to construct organisms—one that is less easily measured but just as real as the genetic source. The hidden source is the information available in the regularities of the environment. This information comes into the brain through the sensory systems, which interact with the environment to tune themselves to it.

The world is full of environmental regularities that can be used to help build an organism. Gravity always pulls downward, light appears in a 24-hr cycle, and so on. Beyond these basic regularities are others that can tune a perceptual system, such as the rules of geometric optics. Turning the head or eyes to the right results in a retinal image transfer to the left, and moving forward generates a highly structured flow field (see Figure 6.9). Other transformations in the visual world specify moving, rotating, or looming objects.

If these regularities of the sensory world could be combined with genetic information to construct a perceptual system, the system could escape the information limitations imposed by genetics. At the same time, it could be fine-tuned to peculiarities of the environment in which it found itself. An organism living in a visual world particularly rich in horizontal and vertical contours, for instance, could develop greater sensitivity to these stimuli. Like the side-blotched lizard of Chapter 1, it would be adapted to adapt. What is the evidence that such tuning to the environment takes place?

ENVIRONMENTAL INFLUENCES ON VISUAL DEVELOPMENT

The tuning of sensory systems to the environment is a relatively late development in evolution; it appears first in mammals. The evidence against environmental adaptation in lower animals comes from

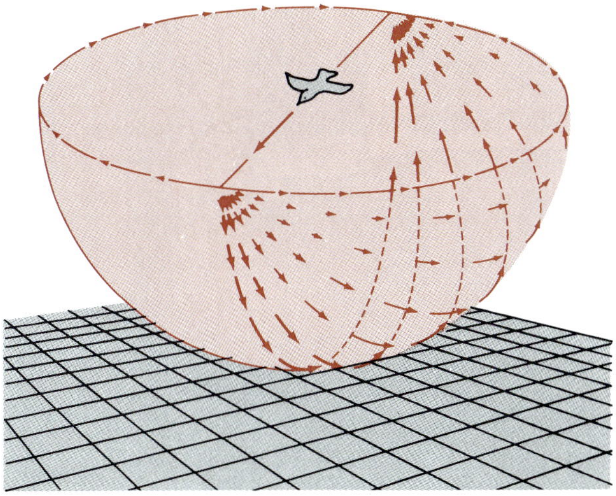

Figure 6.9 *The flow field of the optic array during locomotion. The arrows are vectors representing the speed of the image motion on the corresponding point of the bird's retina. The direction of travel is the point from which the motion vectors diverge. In the real world the vectors would also be proportional to the distance of objects from the eye.*

experiments in which sensory input is rearranged, either by surgery or by changes in an animal's environment. A frog whose eyes have been surgically inverted, for instance, will snap at flies on the wrong side of the visual field. If a fly is on the left, the frog will snap on the right, and vice versa. The frog never learns from its mistakes and will starve even in a room full of buzzing flies. The frog must be force-fed if it is to stay alive.

The situation is similar in young chicks, which will peck accurately at small objects from a few minutes after hatching. The accuracy appears to be wired in. If a chick is fitted with tiny prism goggles to displace the visual world, it will consistently peck to one side of the target (Hess, 1956). Again, no learning or adaptation to the prisms takes place. In both the frog and the chick, visuomotor coordination takes place in the optic tectum, a phylogenetically ancient midbrain structure analogous to the superior colliculus of mammals. These experiments show that the tectum lacks the developmental plasticity available to animals that rely on the neocortex.

Development follows a different course in young kittens. Here, active interaction with the environment seems to be necessary for the establishment of effective sensorimotor coordination. Merely restraining a kitten's actions and finding impaired development would not prove the point, for impaired mobility might retard development by restricting sensory input. Held and Hein (1963) exposed two kittens to nearly identical sensory stimulation while giving only one of them sensorimotor feedback, using the ingenious gondola arrangement in Figure 6.10. Eight pairs of kittens were dark-reared (reared in darkness) until they were strong enough to move in the apparatus, at about 8 to 12 weeks of age.

After the exposure period, the active kittens showed normal behavior in several visually guided tasks. They blinked at an approaching object, they reached out their paws when carried toward a surface, and they avoided walking over the edges of tables. The passive kittens showed none of these behaviors. At first they appeared to be blind. They developed normal coordination, however, after a few days in the light. These experiments have been criticized because the passive kittens learned more than Held and Hein had intended; they discovered that none of their actions had any consequences for perception or locomotion. Later, they had to unlearn this before they could begin to learn normal coordination. Regardless of the outcome of the criticism, the experiments establish the importance of the environment in calibrating the sensorimotor function of young animals. Further work has been done on the mechanisms of this environmental influence.

Development of Receptive Fields

The first work on the interaction of environment and development was based on clinical observations. Children are sometimes born with cataracts clouding the lenses of their eyes. If the cataracts are not surgically removed within a year after birth, vision never becomes normal. This is true even after the optics of the eyes are fully corrected.

The phenomenon was studied physiologically in kittens. The cat is a good animal for visual development studies because it is born visually immature; its eyes do not open until about 10 days after birth. Its later development is fast enough

Figure 6.10 *Apparatus for equalizing visual and vestibular experience in two kittens while giving only one of them visuomotor feedback. The active kitten moves freely about; the littermate in the gondola undergoes the same motions without locomotion. The kittens stayed in this apparatus about 3 hr a day for an average of 10 days.*

that studies can be completed in weeks rather than years. Neurons recorded from the striate cortex just before the time of normal eye opening show "sloppy" receptive fields. The fields are large, are not particularly sensitive, and have a wide tuning for orientation and spatial frequency; the neurons often fire with long latencies. The inhibition that is so prominent in adult cats is irregular in kittens.

Researchers can restrict visual environments during development by rearing kittens in darkness or by sewing their eyelids shut so they get only a small amount of light (prolonged dark-rearing leads to retinal degeneration). The kittens can then be exposed to normal environments after varying periods of deprivation. Those deprived for less than about 12 weeks quickly develop normal visual abilities, and their cortical neurons have normal receptive fields. Those deprived for longer periods show impairment in their behavior. Many of their cortical neurons show abnormal receptive fields or none at all. If the cats are deprived of light over a long period, they appear to be blind (Hubel & Wiesel, 1965a; Wiesel & Hubel, 1965).

The interval during which vision can still be restored is called the **critical period.** It is defined as the time during development when the environment can affect visual organization. The cat's critical period lasts about 12 weeks, the human's about a year.

Binocular Effects

The mechanisms that normally sharpen the receptive fields of cortical neurons have been investigated further with more subtle conditions of deprivation. One such condition is monocular (rather than binocular) deprivation—limiting vision in only one eye. Binocular neurons are the most common in normal striate cortex. But a monocularly deprived cat or monkey has almost no binocular neurons; most of these neurons are driven only by the exposed eye (see Figure 6.11). This means that cortical neurons normally innervated primarily by the deprived eye are being driven instead by the exposed eye, as though axons from the left and right lateral geniculate nuclei were competing for access to synaptic sites. The competition hypothesis has been supported by autoradiographical mapping of ocular dominance columns of a monkey. In normal monkeys, both eyes have columns (actually cortical slabs) of equal thickness; the eyes of deprived monkeys show thicker columns for the exposed eye (see Figure 6.12) (Hubel, Wiesel & LeVay, 1977).

These exciting results opened up the possibility that the mechanisms of tuning by the environment could be probed with ever more specific environmental manipulations. The race for better "environmental surgery" was on.

One of the first such manipulations was to give both eyes of a kitten visual experience, but not at the same time. One eye would be patched on odd-numbered days and the other on even-numbered days. The result was that neurons from both eyes drove neurons in the striate cortex, but hardly any cells received equal input from both eyes. Most of the cells responded to stimuli from one eye or the other, but not from both. A normally binocular cortex had been made monocular by the kitten's alternate monocular experience.

A more subtle deprivation is to misalign one eye of the cat rather than closing it. The condition is known clinically as **strabismus.** The deviated eye always sees patterns, but the patterns in the two eyes do not match. The resulting pattern of ocular dominance (see Figure 6.13) shows that, again, most neurons became monocular. As you might guess, binocular vision is poor in these cats (Wiesel & Hubel, 1965).

Surgical realignment of the eyes is a permanent measure. Can binocular vision recover if the eyes are misaligned temporarily during development? The eyes can be temporarily misaligned with prisms worn over the eyes. When young mon-

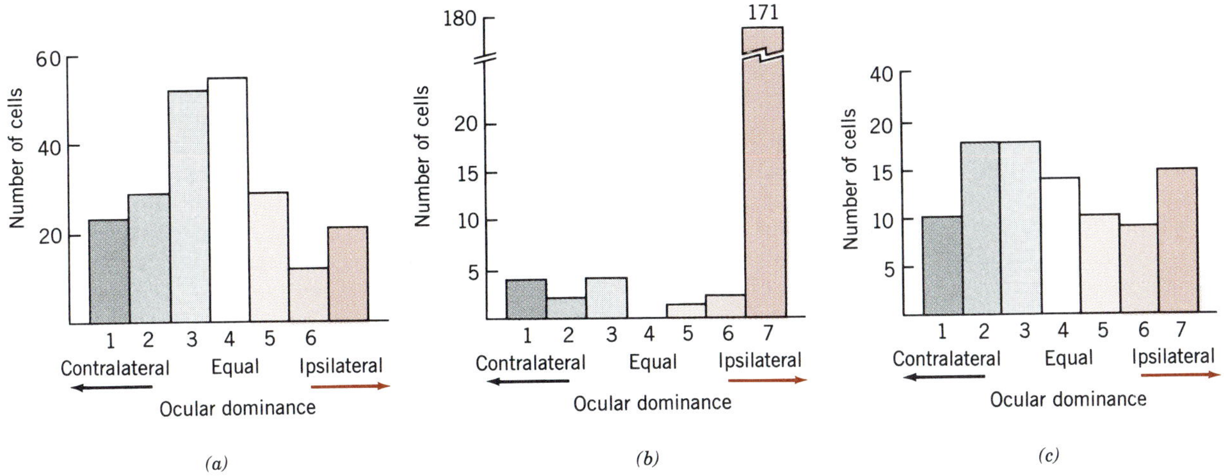

Figure 6.11 *Plots of the number of cells showing various degrees of ocular dominance. A "1" indicates that the cell is driven by contralateral stimuli but that stimuli from the ipsilateral eye have no effect. A "7" means that only inputs from the ipsilateral eye are effective. A "4" means equal influence from the two eyes. The other numbers indicate intermediate amounts of bias. (This qualitative scale has been quantified as the ipsilateral/contralateral ratio in other research.)* (a) *Normal. The most frequent category is equal innervation from the two eyes, with a slight contralateral bias.* (b) *Monocular deprivation through the early critical period. Most neurons are driven by only one eye after monocular deprivation.* (c) *Binocular deprivation. A much flatter than normal ocular dominance histogram results from binocular deprivation.*

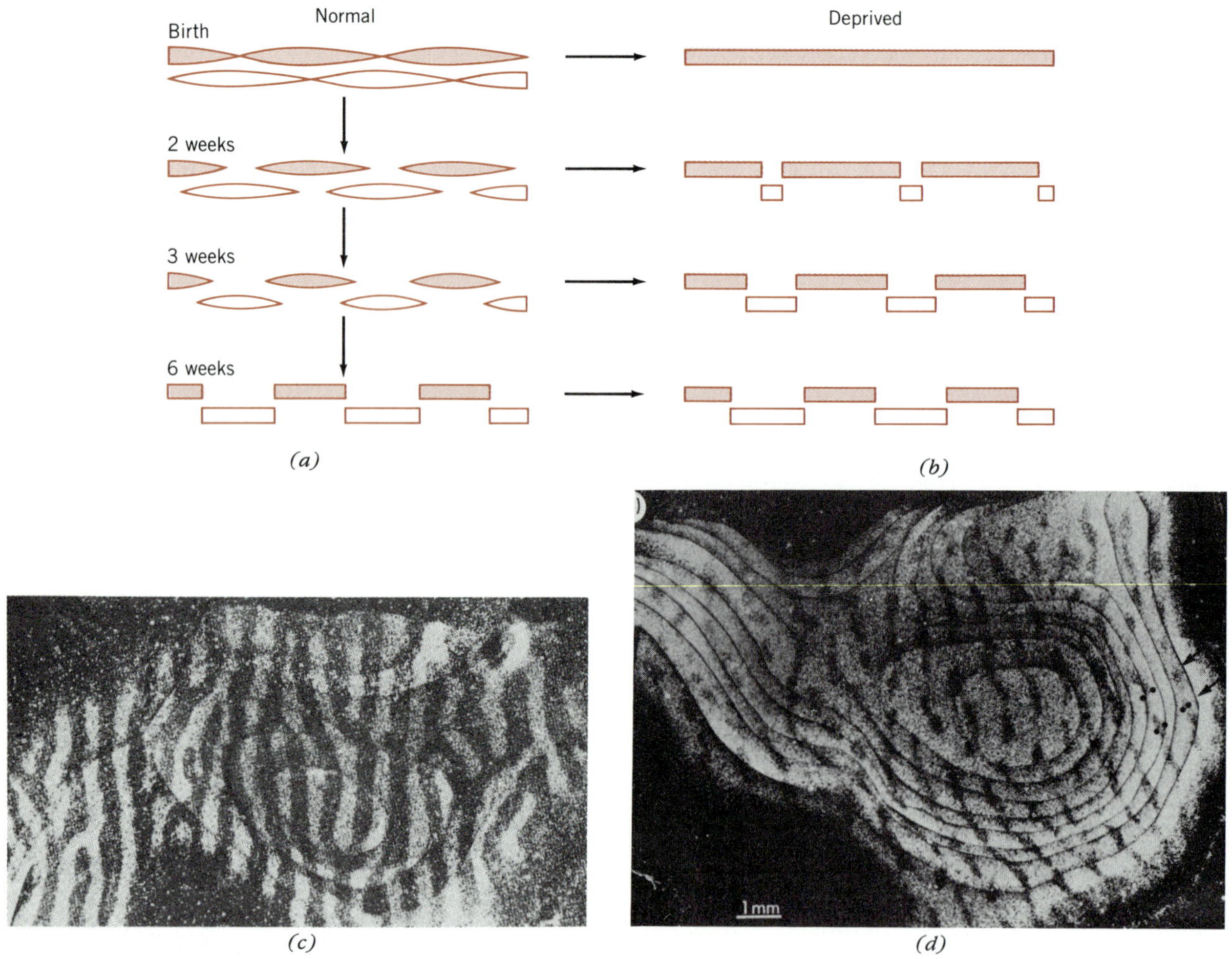

Figure 6.12 *Development of ocular dominance columns.* (a) *Schematic view. In the normal animal (left), gross biases in eye dominance sharpen to well-defined columns in a few weeks. If monocular deprivation begins at birth, only monocular neurons develop (top right).* (b) *If monocular deprivation begins later, the other eye takes over some of the neurons.* (c) *Autoradiogram of normal monkey striate cortex.* (d) *Autoradiogram of striate cortex of monkey whose right eye was closed from 2 weeks to 18 months of age. When the animal reached adulthood, the left eye was injected with a radioactive amino acid and an audioradiogram of the left striate cortex was prepared. Columns from the undeprived eye were wider than in control monkeys. Adapted from Hubel, Wiesel & LeVay (1977).*

keys wore prisms during the second month of life, they became **stereoblind**—unable to use binocular cues for depth perception. Recordings from the cortex showed that even as adults, the monkeys had abnormally few binocular neurons in both area 17 (V1) and area 18 (V2) (Crawford et al., 1984). So the answer is no; abnormal correlation between the images in the two eyes has permanent effects if it occurs during the critical period.

Nature performs a similar experiment on humans born with an extraocular muscle imbalance. Once the critical period is past, it is too late to restore normal function. The strabismus can be corrected surgically so the two eyes will see corre-

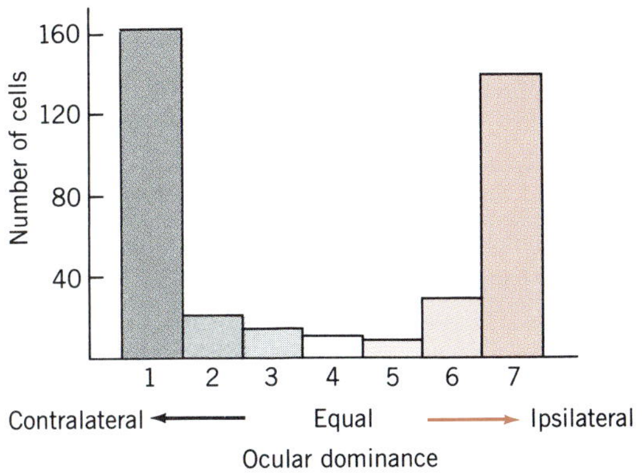

***Figure 6.13** Ocular dominance histogram of an animal raised through the critical period with strabismus artificially induced by the cutting of one of the extraocular muscles. Most of the cells in the striate cortex have become monocular.*

sponding images. But binocular depth perception remains poor even if the acuity in each eye is normal (Schor, Bridgeman & Tyler, 1983).

It now appears that the competition among incoming axons for access to synaptic sites on neurons in the visual cortex gives the more active axons the advantage in establishing connectivity (Spear, Langsetmo & Smith, 1980; Spear & Tong, 1980; Tong & Spear, 1980). Because excitation normally is equal from the two eyes, most neurons become binocular. The competition process continues throughout early development but becomes frozen in the adult animal, so later changes in exposure have no effect on the neurons.

Stimulus-Specific Receptive Fields

In 1970 Helmut Hirsch, then a graduate student at Stanford University, began studying kittens that were deprived of vision in all line orientations but one. After much effort, Hirsch was able to raise kittens through the critical period with the ingenious masks shown in Figure 6.14.

Hirsch's plan was to test the kittens' behavior to see whether the kittens responded differently to the exposed orientation in discrimination tasks. Just before behavioral testing was to begin, Nico Spinelli suggested that he and Hirsch record from the cortical neurons first. Spinelli, Robert Phelps, and I had been recording from single neurons with an automated system (Figure 5.21).

Our preparations for recording the receptive fields of the first kitten began at 8:00 A.M. We used methods typical for such studies. We anesthetized the kitten, inserted a breathing tube down its throat, and exposed its brain. We injected a long-lasting local anesthetic at all incisions and pressure points and began an infusion of a synthetic curare to paralyze the animal. Then we waited for all signs of the anesthetic to wear off before beginning microelectrode recording. When we recorded from the first neurons, the receptive fields we mapped were disappointing; they were large and diffuse, revealing no specific patterns.

About 10:00 P.M. we mapped yet another field and saw a large streak running most of the way across our 25 × 25 deg screen. At first we thought it must be an artifact. Perhaps the cell had put out a long spontaneous burst of firing, as can happen when an electrode damages a cell membrane, or

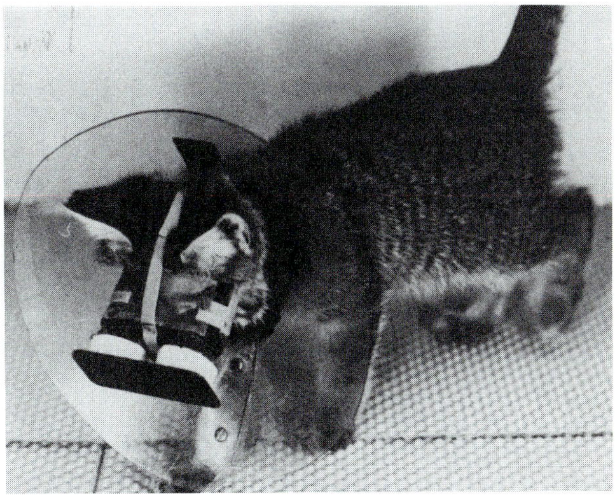

***Figure 6.14** Masks for exposing a kitten to only a single stimulus during development. At the end of the mask a plate blocks direct visual stimulation. Behind it is a circular plastic diffuser, then a slide of the desired image. Between the slide and the eye is a lens to place the pattern at optical infinity. The mask is worn a few hours a day; for the rest of the time the animal is dark-reared with its mother. The cats see a pattern of vertical stripes in one eye and horizontal stripes in the other.*

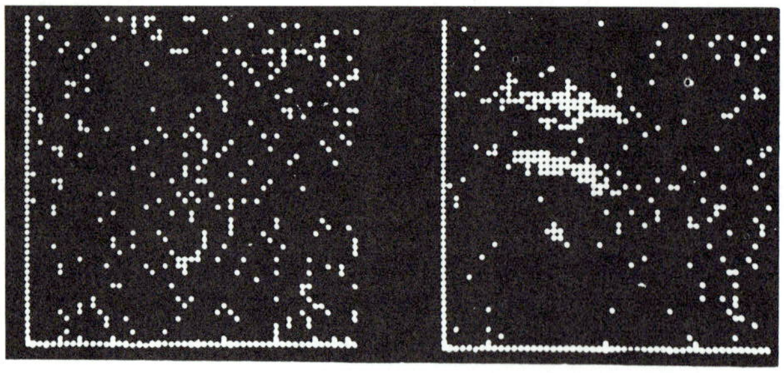

(a) (b)

Figure 6.15 *Receptive fields of a kitten raised wearing the mask shown in Figure 6.14. Each square represents the 25 × 25 deg recording area. A small spot at the lower left corner moved across the screen and back, then moved upward 0.5 deg. The process was repeated 50 times. A spot was generated whenever the neuron fired.* (a) *Map of left eye, showing a large receptive field.* (b) *Map of right eye, showing only background activity. This kitten's mask had vertical stripes in the left eye and horizontal stripes in the right eye.*

perhaps something had gone wrong with the display apparatus. We checked the animal; everything seemed in order. We mapped the receptive field again, this time with scans running at right angles to the original ones. The same streak appeared, larger than any receptive field we had ever seen. (See the vertical streak in Figure 6.15*a* and the horizontal one in Figure 6.15*b*.) We looked at one another, astonished; this was real!

We mapped the neuron with the left eye covered, then the right. The field was monocular, a rarity in the layer of cat cortex we were recording. We didn't know whether its orientation matched the exposed orientation for that eye, for Hirsch had not brought his records along. Later that night we recorded several other such fields; all were vertical or horizontal, all were monocular, and all were huge.

After working with several more cats, we confirmed that the receptive fields nearly always matched the orientation of the stripes in the corresponding eye. Rather than selectively depriving the cat of some receptive field orientations, the masks had fundamentally reorganized the structure of the visual cortex. About one-third of the cells turned out to have the monocularly oriented characteristic. And the large size of the fields implied that they were tuned to the very large stripes in the mask (Hirsch & Spinelli, 1970).

Later, Spinelli and Jensen (1979) described a few cortical neurons with even more specific receptive fields. The parallel sensitive areas shown in Figure 6.15 appeared at the same spacing as in the previous exposure pattern. Could such cells be related to memory of the stimulus?

When Hirsch and Spinelli (1970) published their results, a team of researchers in Cambridge, England, saw the report and rushed their own, similar findings into print (Blakemore & Cooper, 1970). They had used a quite different technique; their cats, raised in long striped tubes (see Figure 6.16), saw only one orientation. The receptive fields were normal except that most of them were

Figure 6.16 *Apparatus for exposing a kitten to only a single line orientation during development. The kitten was free to turn its head, so lines that were always vertical in space could take on any orientation on the retina. A wide collar prevented the kitten from seeing its own paws and body. When not in the apparatus, the kitten was dark-reared.*

oriented near the exposed orientation. Behaviorally, the tube-reared cats exhibited apparent blindness to contours at right angles to their exposure. Cats raised in horizontally striped tubes bumped into table legs; those raised in vertically striped tubes walked off the edges of tables. (The physiological result has proved controversial; replication has succeeded twice (Mize & Murphy, 1973; Turkel, Gijsders & Pritchard, 1975) but failed once (Stryker & Sherk, 1975).)

Relating Behavior to Receptive Fields

When Hirsch completed his dissertation, the visual abilities of his cats were nearly normal (Hirsch, 1972). They could distinguish vertical from oblique lines nearly as well as normal cats. Why were the mask-reared cats almost normal and the tube-reared cats, with much less drastic cortical changes, impaired?

To answer this question, we must look at the information flow from the cats' visual world in each experiment. The mask-reared cats received retinal images that were unrelated to events in the real world. There was no reduction in uncertainty and thus no information in the images. In terms of information, these cats should act like deprived cats. The tube-reared cats, in contrast, continued to receive visual information from their abnormal world. When they moved their heads, the motion of the image gave visual information about the head movement. There was an abnormal distribution of orientations of the stimuli giving this information, though, so the cats adapted to an abnormal world.

Another reason for the difference has to do with the critical period. The mask-reared cats were removed from the deprivation situation just before the end of the critical period. They could therefore develop some normal functioning, though many of their receptive fields remained changed for years (Spinelli et al., 1972). The tube-reared cats were deprived well beyond the critical period and therefore could not recover when brought into a normal environment. The end of the critical period is not abrupt, though, and some kinds of changes can occur later than others. Some researchers call the period a "critical comma" to avoid the impression of abruptness and finality.

Cortical Plasticity. Once the results came out, other kinds of plasticity (change caused by the environment) were found in the cortex. Pettigrew and Freeman (1973) looked for a highly abnormal stimulus, raising "planetarium cats" in a visual world consisting only of points of light in the dome-shaped cover of their cage. In these cats, a small point of light could excite a cortical cell anywhere in a large area of the visual field. The resulting receptive fields were qualitatively different from anything seen in normal cats, again reflecting the exposure conditions.

The area remains controversial. Some researchers maintain that receptive fields are not modified by experience but require stimulation to maintain their innate organization and to develop normally (Stryker et al., 1978).

These studies showed the enormous flexibility of receptive fields in the visual cortex, but they did not reveal how the system eventually "freezes" a certain organization. Spinelli, Jensen, and Standish (1979) were able to obtain renewed sensitivity to environmental surgery long after the end of the usual critical period by injecting the drug colchicine into the cortex of adult cats. The drug may disorganize the synaptic patterns that already exist. Then the environment can influence the development of new ones. Kasamatsu and Pettigrew (1979) have lengthened the critical period with drugs that stimulate the norepinephrine systems in the cortex; their work implies that norepinephrine maintains plasticity in young animals. The drugs in both studies were infused directly into the cortex.

Later work has tracked down more of the mechanism; it implicates postsynaptic beta-adrenergic receptors on cortical neurons. In one experiment, the cortex of a 6 to 7 week old kitten was continuously perfused with a beta-adrenergic blocker for a week, while one eyelid was sutured shut. Ordinarily, this would result in a cortex full of monocular neurons. But the blocker prevented the plasticity that would otherwise be expected—many normal binocular neurons could still be recorded from the perfused cortex (Shirokawa & Kasamatsu, 1984).

These studies show that manipulations of the noradrenergic system can change neuronal plasticity. Do such influences affect animals in real life? To test this question, the noradrenergic neurons of the locus coeruleus in normal adult cats were stimulated electrically while the cats were given brief exposure to monocular stimuli. Otherwise, the cats were housed in the dark. After a week, recordings showed a lower than normal proportion of binocular cells. Thus plasticity had been restored to the striate cortex without direct intervention in that cortex. The effect was clearly noradrenergic, since the plasticity could be prevented if the cortex were perfused beforehand with the catecholamine-related neurotoxin 6-hydroxydopamine (Kasamatsu et al., 1983). At this point the investigation of developmental plasticity merges with the more general investigation of plasticity and learning (see Chapter 11).

CONCLUSION

The last three chapters have traced signals from the environment through preprocessing, transduction, and conduction to the brain. At every stage, there was a selection of information and a transformation into forms useful to the organism. Absolute energy levels were discarded almost immediately in favor of the maximum range of neural response to the signals at hand; and later, more subtle transformations took place. Finally, there was a comparison of incoming signals with remembered information. The conclusion is that perception is the process of making sense of sensation.

At every stage there was efferent control of the information flow, with the signals adjusted to suit the higher layers. Sensory information was processed in many separate cortical and subcortical centers, connected both in parallel and in series. At this stage efferent control expands to involve behaviors of the whole organism, moving around in the world to find or create the desired environment. The focus shifts to the motor system.

CHAPTER SUMMARY

1. Sensory systems actively interact with behavior, experience, and development to produce perception. Much of our behavior, in the service of perception, involves active investigation of the world.

2. The five senses correspond not to anatomy but to modes of sensory attention: the activities of looking, listening, touching, tasting, and smelling. These are the five perceptual systems. The various receptors of a modality contribute to unified perceptions within that modality.

3. The oculomotor system is appropriate for looking at the active process of perception, because it functions only in sensory activities and because its inputs and outputs can be isolated. The six muscles that move each eye are arranged in three pairs of antagonists, organized around the three planes of Cartesian space. The two eyes constitute a single coordinated organ of sight.

4. Slow eye movements hold the retinal image stable, and saccades jump the image to another position. A phylogenetically older slow movement system is based on the retinal image as a whole, and a newer one tracks only the image on the fovea. The older system is closely linked to vestibular input. Saccades jump the eye as fast as possible to a new position. During saccades, vision is suppressed. The speed of a saccade depends only on its size; and once initiated, it cannot be stopped. Saccades and pursuits alternate in visual exploration. The two movements are generated by differ-

ent brain-stem control systems, and the pulse and step of the saccade are developed by separate groups of neurons. Mismatches between the pulse and step can change saccade trajectories, an example of the influence of brain-stem controllers on observable human behavior.

5. People viewing scenes generate scanpaths—sequences of eye movements unique to the individual and to the pattern being viewed. Scanpaths also depend on the top-down interpretation of the image and on the question the observer is asking. During fixation, three kinds of eye movements occur: tremors, drifts, and microsaccades. The movements prevent the retinal image from becoming stabilized and fading. Active scanning occurs in all perceptual systems and creates a sequential as well as a parallel flow of information.

6. In mammals, active processes also contribute to the development of sensory systems. Raising animals without visuomotor feedback impairs their visuomotor coordination later in life. Visual receptive fields develop abnormally in abnormal environments, which demonstrates that the system uses both genetic and environmental information for normal development. To be effective, environmental information must be available within a critical period after birth. Closing one eye of a kitten during this period has a much stronger effect than closing both eyes; monocular deprivation results in mostly monocular visual receptive fields controlled by the exposed eye. A similar defect results from misaligning one eye, which simulates strabismus in humans. If alternate eyes are closed on alternate days, the kitten will develop monocular receptive fields for both eyes.

7. Cats raised with masks that expose vertical stripes to one eye and horizontal to the other show corresponding receptive fields—fields that are larger than normal, monocular, and with orientations matching the exposed eye. These cats receive no abnormal information about the world, however. More precisely, they receive no real-world information at all; the stimulus on the retina is not contingent on visual events.

8. Cats raised in vertical tubes painted with vertical or horizontal stripes, in contrast, receive information from abnormal visual worlds and develop normal receptive fields; but all of their receptive fields have orientations near the exposed orientation. These cats have more severe behavioral problems. Other abnormal rearing conditions, such as the "planetarium" condition, in which only spots of light are visible, result in correspondingly abnormal cortical receptive fields.

9. The opening and closing of the critical period can be manipulated biochemically, extending the period or even reopening it in adults. The techniques involve cortical adrenergic receptors.

KEY TERMS

Extraocular muscles
Saccade
Convergence movements
Divergence movements
Pursuit eye movements
Ballistic
Flocculus
Scanpath
Microsaccades
Neuroembryology
Growth cone
Critical period
Strabismus
Stereoblind

SUGGESTED READINGS

Gibson, J. J. (1966). *The senses considered as perceptual systems.* Boston: Houghton Mifflin.

Gibson is a radical within psychology, insisting that sensations are unimportant and that the structure of the perceptual world is the key to understanding how perception works. He is weak on physiology but strong on the active role of the organism in perception.

Movshon, J. A., & Van Sluyters, R. (1984). Visual neural development. *Annual Review of Neuroscience, 7,* 477–522.

Two active researchers review recent work on the influences of environmental manipulations on the organization of the developing visual system.

Robinson, D. A. (1981). Control of eye movements. In J. Brookhart & V. B. Mountcastle, Eds., *Handbook of Physiology: Sec. 1. The Nervous System: Vol. 2. Motor Control.* Bethesda, MD: American Physiological Society.

This is a neuron-by-neuron examination of the physiology of the eye movement control system. Some parts are technical or mathematical, but the article includes everything known about the topic. There is also a thorough bibliography.

Chapter 7

MUSCLES AND MOTOR ORGANIZATION

Physiological psychology depends on reductionism—the assumption that a whole can be better understood by studying its parts. With this assumption, an appropriate place to begin analyzing behavior is with the muscles and the motor neurons innervating them. Sherrington (1906) called motor neurons the "final common path," where all the efforts of the nervous system, whatever their sources, are transformed into action.

Reflecting the dominance of muscles in life, about 70 percent of the human body's weight is muscle; the figure is slightly higher in males than in females. All behavior is expressed through muscles and glands. The purpose of the central nervous system is to control them, and they in turn make interaction with the world possible. We will begin at the molecular level of structure and build up to the level of skilled acts.

TYPES OF MUSCLES

The same contractile mechanism is used by all three types of muscles: striated, smooth, and cardiac (see Figure 7.1). That is, all three work in the same way at the molecular level. Most of the voluntarily activated muscles of the body are **striated muscles,** named for their prominent striations, which are visible under a microscope. All of the muscles that are attached to the skeleton are striated, as are some muscles that are not attached (facial muscles, for example). Striated muscles are organized in bands of parallel muscle fibers. In embryological development, each fiber starts as a group of cells; the cells later fuse to form a fiber with several nuclei. Despite the presence of many nuclear masters, the muscle fiber functions as though it were a single cell.

Most striated muscles are subject to both voluntary and involuntary control. Arm muscles, for instance, are involved in purposeful actions such as writing, in involuntary shivering, and in movement reflexes controlled at the spinal level, such as withdrawing from a hot stove.

Striated muscle is a very old evolutionary invention; its organization is practically identical in the insect (Figure 7.2) and in the human, though there are some differences in the details (Hoyle, 1983). The structure probably evolved before the common ancestors of flies and humans diverged. (We don't know the common ancestor that first had modern-looking striated muscles.)

Smooth muscles are less parallel in their organization. They function in involuntary activities such as digestion. They are also found where tension must be held for long periods, such as at the urinary sphincter. Their fibers contract more slowly than striated muscle fibers following motor neuron activation and release more slowly when motor neuron firing stops. After a motor neuron trigger, many smooth muscles tend to undergo sustained rhythmic contraction. Smooth muscle fibers seem less specialized than striated muscle

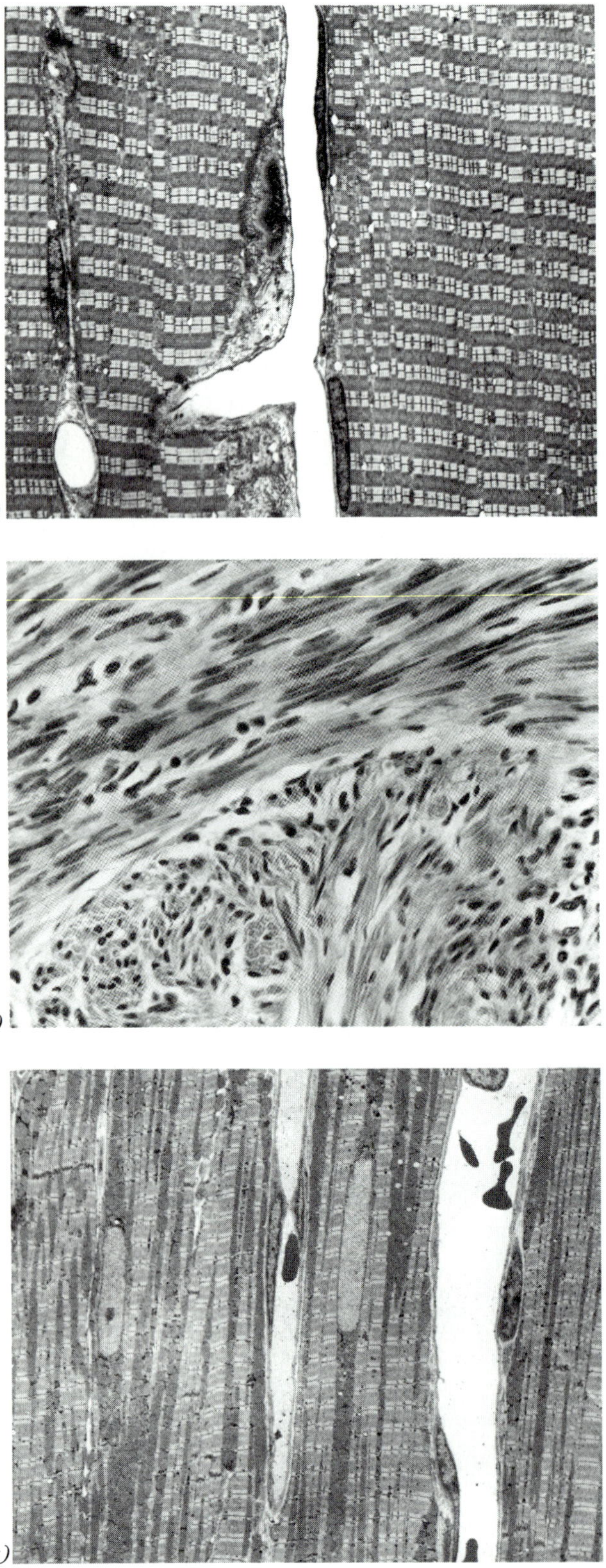

Figure 7.1 *Three kinds of muscle tissue.* (a) *Striated muscle, named for the prominent striations created when the molecular constituents of the muscle fibers line up in register. The openings are spaces for blood vessels.* (b) *Smooth muscle, less tightly organized and able to contract for a long time.* (c) *Cardiac muscle, found only in the heart.*

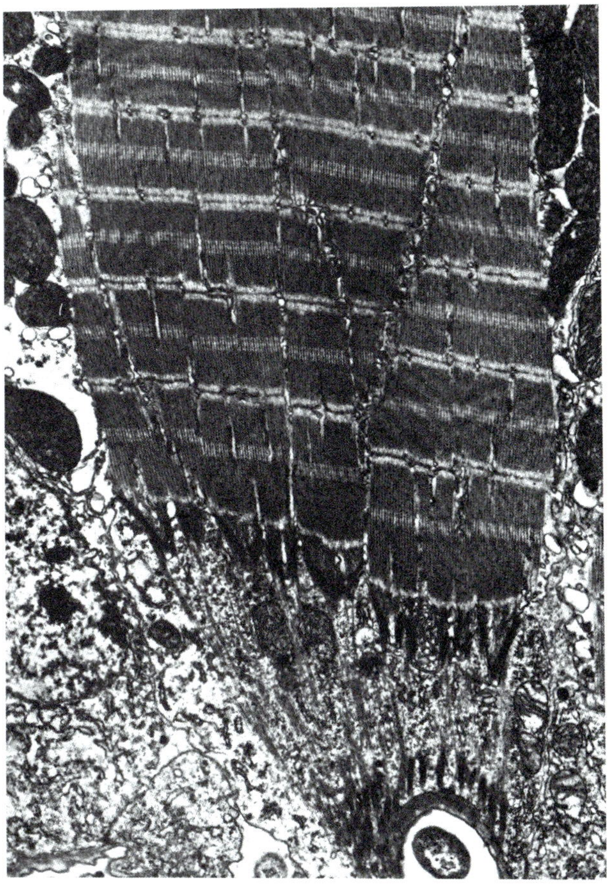

Figure 7.2 Antenna muscle cell of copepod Doropygus *The muscle contracts only a small percent of its length in normal use. The rounded bodies at the sides are mitochondria, supplying metabolic energy to the muscle.*

fibers. Each fiber has only one nucleus, and the fiber's loosely organized contractile elements are concentrated toward the ends of the fiber. Smooth muscles probably came earlier in evolutionary development than striated muscles.

Cardiac muscle is intermediate between smooth and striated muscle. As the name implies, cardiac muscle exists only in the heart. It contracts rhythmically even without innervation, each beat spreading from a **pacemaker region** of muscle fibers—a region of the heart where cells spontaneously change polarization, generating activity that causes the heart to beat. The cardiac muscle fibers in this region have unstable membranes that slowly depolarize until they reach a threshold and initiate a contraction, even without nervous system control. (So it is true that the connection between the heart and the brain is rather tenuous.)

THE CONTRACTILE MECHANISM

Muscle structure and function are related at every level from the atomic to the organismic. The working part of a muscle consists of alternating thick and thin protein filaments arranged in the parallel bands of Figure 7.3 (which shows striated muscle, the easiest to see because all the filaments are lined up). Each thick filament in the figure is a bundle of several hundred molecules of **myosin**—a protein that, with actin, makes up the contractile part of muscle. Myosin has a "head" protruding at one end. The heads come in clusters of three, evenly spaced around the bundle. These clusters in turn are staggered; each complete repeating unit of the bundle contains six heads.

The thin filaments are made of a complex of proteins, the **actin complex.** The entire highly structured bundle of proteins is often simply called actin (see Figure 7.3).

Muscles contract when the myosin filaments slide across the actin complex, shortening the structure (Huxley, 1973). The process is triggered by an action potential at the neuromuscular junction. The depolarization of the postsynaptic membrane causes an influx of Ca^{++} ions, as in chemical synaptic transmission. Ca^{++} binds to the troponin part of the actin complex. Then a myosin head, together with a molecule of adenosine triphosphate (ATP), binds to the actin (Weber & Murray, 1973). (ATP is the molecule that fuels most of the energy-consuming reactions in the body.)

According to the sliding-filament idea, this binding should stiffen the muscle, because the myosin heads become cross-bridges that link the muscle proteins into a single structure. Muscle viscosity, measured by the resistance to precisely controlled tugs on a muscle tendon, does indeed increase during a brief delay before contraction begins (Cecchi, Griffiths & Taylor, 1982).

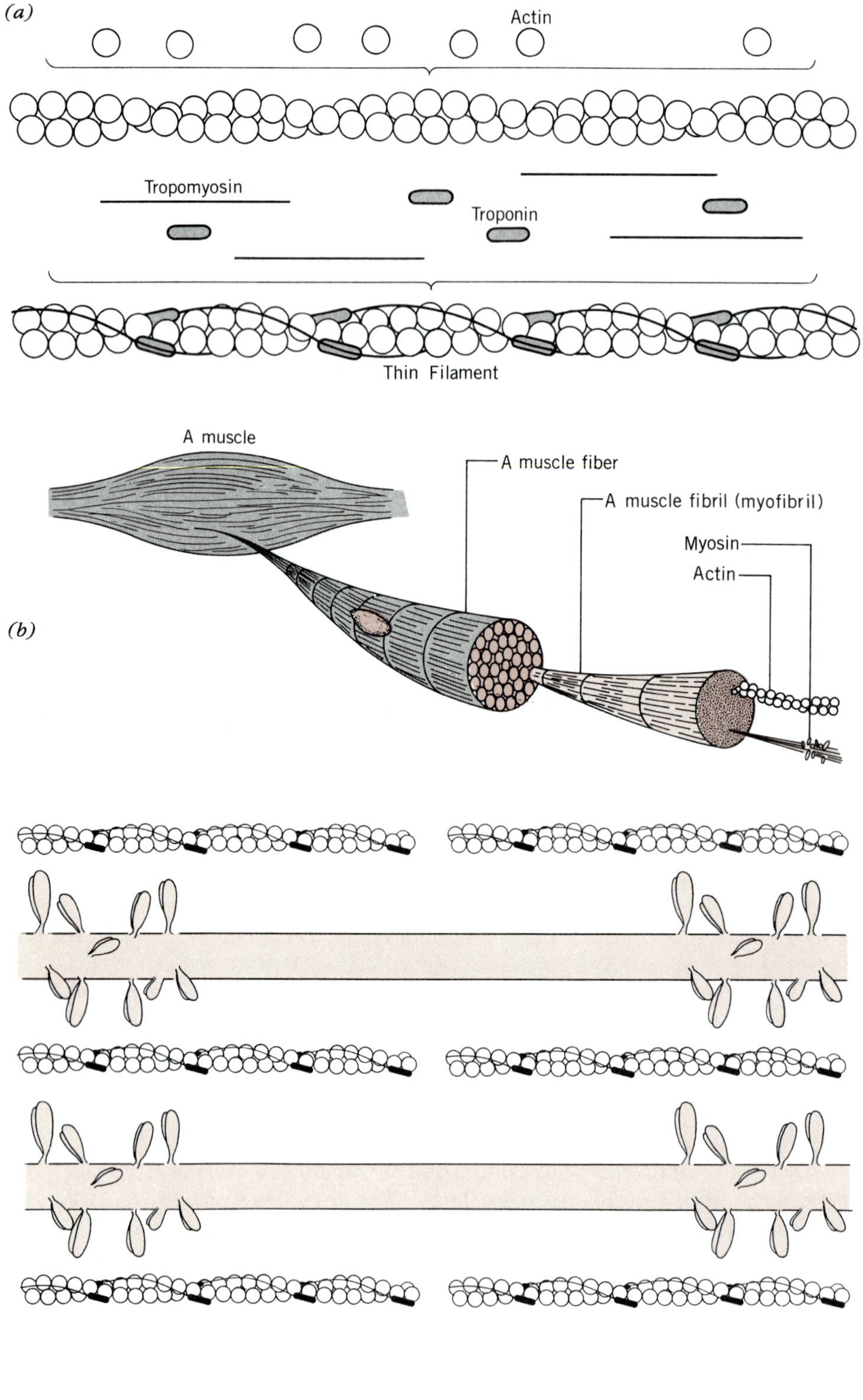

***Figure** 7.3 Molecular structure of striated muscle.* (a) *Structure of the thin filament. Though the structure is highly regular, the actin filament can stretch and bend slightly without breaking because of the elasticity of the molecular bonds.* (b) *Actin (thin filaments) and myosin (thick filaments) arranged in a muscle. At any one time, most of the myosin heads are not engaged on the actin complex.* (c) *Cross section of a muscle from a rabbit. Differing densities of individual fibers come from cutting the muscle at different points. See* (b).

The myosin head bends after it links to the actin. It slides itself along the actin filament, converting the ATP to adenosine diphosphate (ADP) and phosphate in the process. The energy in one of ATP's three phosphate bonds is released, powering the contraction. Enzymes quickly remove Ca^{++} from the region so the process can be repeated. The details of this process are still obscure, as seems generally to be the case in biology at the most microscopic level.

The microscopic "step" of the myosin moving along the actin filament is about 10 nm long and takes 1 msec. It is an all-or-none digital process; it either occurs in full or does not occur at all. The step is so small, however, that its digital nature is never seen in the action of the muscle as a whole. Muscle contraction, then, is the scampering of millions of tiny molecular feet across the nearest actin fibers—or, to follow the accepted terminology, the scampering of millions of tiny heads.

Actin and myosin filaments are organized into units called **sarcomeres,** each about 2.2 μm long. Each sarcomere contains a complete muscle contractile unit. Actin strands are connected at **Z-lines** (*zwischen* is German for "between")—protein structures that anchor the contractile mechanism to the muscle; myosin is held in place only by its cross-bridges. Within a sarcomere the strands act in parallel, increasing the strength of the muscle. Successive sarcomeres are linked end to end in series to increase the length and speed of the muscle's contraction. The string of sarcomeres constitutes a muscle fiber. Each muscle consists of many fibers linked in parallel and held in place by tough tendons of connective tissue; the tendons fasten the body of the muscle to the places (usually bones, near joints) where the muscle exerts its force.

ATP for the contractile mechanism is normally provided by oxidative reactions in the mitochondria, where ADP combines with sugars from foods to make new ATP. But when a muscle is working hard, it requires enormous quantities of energy, and normal oxidative mechanisms cannot keep up. When this occurs, ATP is synthesized along another metabolic route. **Glycogen** (chains of glucose molecules, called animal sugar, stored in the muscles) is converted into lactic acid by an anaerobic process—a process that does not require oxygen.

The lactic acid must be removed from the muscle to be metabolized in the liver, or it will poison the muscle. During heavy exercise it cannot be removed fast enough; its buildup causes muscle pain of the sort experienced by long-distance runners. The muscles are telling the body that they are near metabolic exhaustion and that it is time to stop. After a race, a runner must pant to pay back the oxygen debt incurred by the anaerobic metabolism, thereby restoring the muscle chemistry to its normal state. The advantage of this alternate pathway is clear—it allows the organism to produce great bursts of energy by living on borrowed time.

IMPLICATIONS OF CONTRACTION FOR MUSCLE BEHAVIOR

The molecular organization of muscle determines many of its large-scale properties. First, the strength of a muscle depends on the number of cross-bridges connecting actin and myosin filaments. More cross-bridges mean more contractile power. The muscle is weaker when it is stretched out because most of the myosin heads cannot engage actin filaments. When the muscle is fully contracted, the actins from opposite ends of the sarcomere begin to run into one another. The muscle works best in a small range of intermediate lengths. (See length-tension relationships in Figure 7.4.)

To take advantage of the greater strength of muscles at intermediate extensions, most striated muscles are attached to the skeleton in such a way that they contract by only a small fraction of their total length. The physiology of the muscles and the anatomy of the skeletal system are thus tuned to each other. The design of bicycles also takes advantage of the muscle length-tension relationship; maximum power is needed not when the legs are fully flexed or fully extended but only in between.

The flexor muscles at most joints are organized in such a way that small changes in muscle length result in large movements. The physics of the arrangement is that of the second-class lever at the top right of Figure 7.5. The fulcrum (point of rotation) is at one end of the lever, and the load is at the other end. Force is applied between the ful-

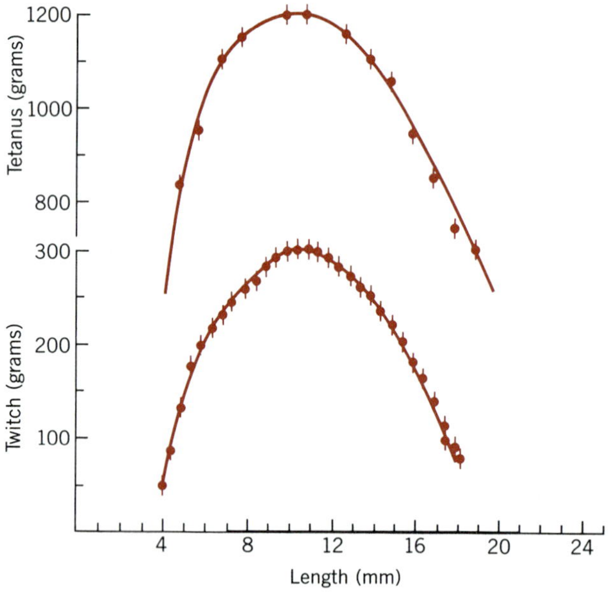

Figure 7.4 *Length-tension diagram for tetanus (upper curve) and twitch (lower curve) in the flexor hallucis longus muscle of the cat. Power is maximal at a muscle length of about 11 mm, decreasing above and below that length.*

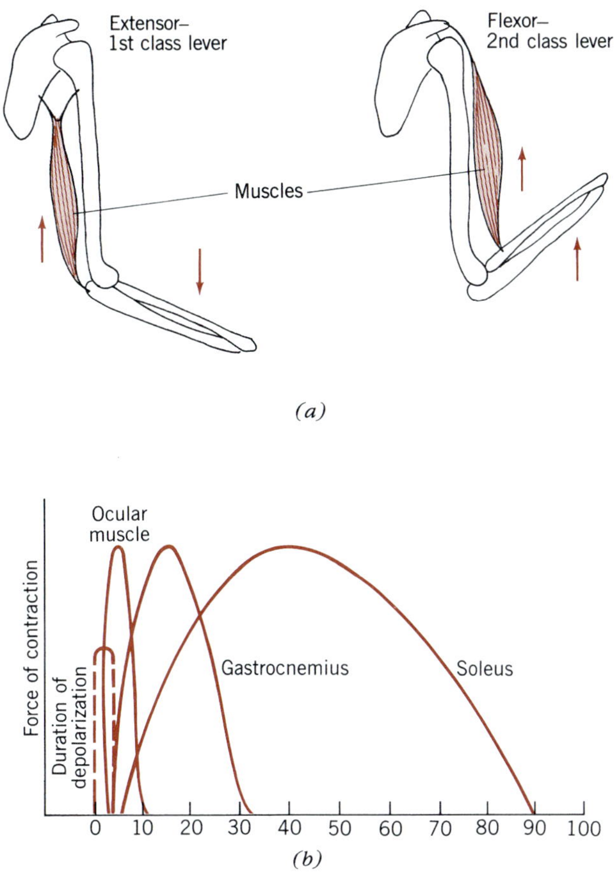

***Figure** 7.5* (a) *Muscle physiology. Lever arrangements of flexors and extensors.* (b) *Twitch duration following a single depolarizing pulse in three muscles. The ocular muscle is the fastest in the body; the soleus, in the leg, is among the slowest. Contraction time, the rising portion of the curve, is always faster than relaxation time, the falling portion of the curve. Slower muscles have a longer latent period before contraction begins.*

crum and the load, so a short pull near a joint (such as the elbow) results in a large movement at an extremity (such as the hand).

The extensor muscles are usually first-class levers, at the top left of Figure 7.5—machines with the fulcrum in the middle. A pull on one side of a joint is converted into a movement in the opposite direction on the other side of the joint. Mechanically the extensors and flexors are organized into pairs of antagonists, each balancing the other's opposite effects. Since the human is both a mechanical and a logical machine, antagonistic innervations match the antagonistic mechanical arrangements. Levers are used further to enable the muscles, which can only contract, to power a body that can stretch, bend, and twist in the marvelously complex patterns of human movement.

Another implication of the molecular contraction mechanism is a limitation on the speed of contraction. The myosin heads can "walk," but they cannot "run." Activities requiring a very quick motion, such as the jump of a flea or the snap of human fingers, involve the quick release of mechanically stored energy. The flea, for example, stores energy in springlike parts of the legs before a jump.

Fast and Slow Muscles

The speed of each muscle is adapted to its function in the body. The fastest muscles (for example, the extraocular muscles in Figure 7.5*b*) reach the peak of their contraction very quickly after an excitatory spike. Slower muscles, such as the locomotor muscles in the legs, reach their peaks more slowly and have a longer duration of contraction. In this way the muscles are specialized for faster or slower jobs.

Even within a single striated muscle, different fibers are specialized for different functions. Slow-twitch fibers are rich in **myoglobin,** a protein related to oxidative energy-transfer mechanisms; the color of myoglobin, like that of its relative hemoglobin (in the blood), is red. Thus slow-twitch fibers have a red color.

Fast-twitch fibers do their work in short bursts, borrowing energy from anaerobic reactions; they have a whitish color and little myoglobin. In humans the two kinds of fibers are mixed, giving most muscles a red tinge. But in some more specialized muscles, such as a chicken's flight muscles, the paleness of "white meat" reveals fast-twitch fibers.

As the muscle is contracted more strongly, more of the axons innervating the muscle begin to fire and the firing frequency of the axons increases. At higher stimulation frequencies the fiber contracts continuously, a state called **tetanus.**

Faster muscles reach tetanus only at higher stimulation frequencies.

The specialization of each muscle's dynamic properties simplifies the information flow through the CNS. The larger muscles in humans, such as the leg muscles used in walking, have a high concentration of slow-twitch fibers; they can contract on their own for several hundredths of a second without further attention. Faster contraction would give them no advantage because their loads are heavy and the limbs cannot move quickly in any case. Fast muscles require more neural machinery because their contractions die quickly without continuous innervation, but they allow precise control over the dynamics of movement. The contractions summate in time, so a train of action potentials results in a stronger contraction than a single spike (see Figure 7.6).

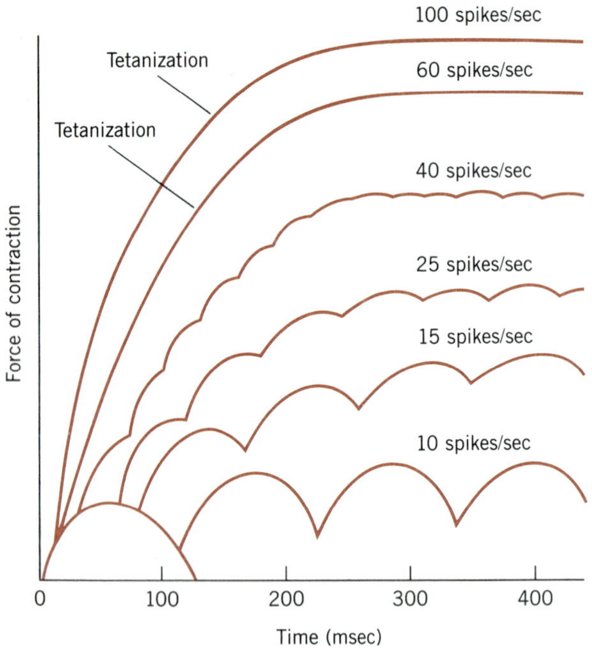

***Figure 7.6** Wave summation and tetanization. Frequently repeated stimuli summate to develop a more powerful contraction than does an individual twitch. Each of the muscles in Figure 7.5 would have a set of curves like this one at a different time scale.*

THE NEUROMUSCULAR JUNCTION

Muscles are controlled by nerves at specialized and greatly enlarged synapses—the neuromuscular junctions (see Figure 7.7). Much of the early work on the chemistry and mechanism of synapses was actually done on neuromuscular junctions because of their large size and accessibility. Neuromuscular junctions differ from conventional synapses in that a single spike always elicits an action potential and a contraction—a single "twitch." Thus the all-or-none property of muscle contraction extends to the level of the single fiber.

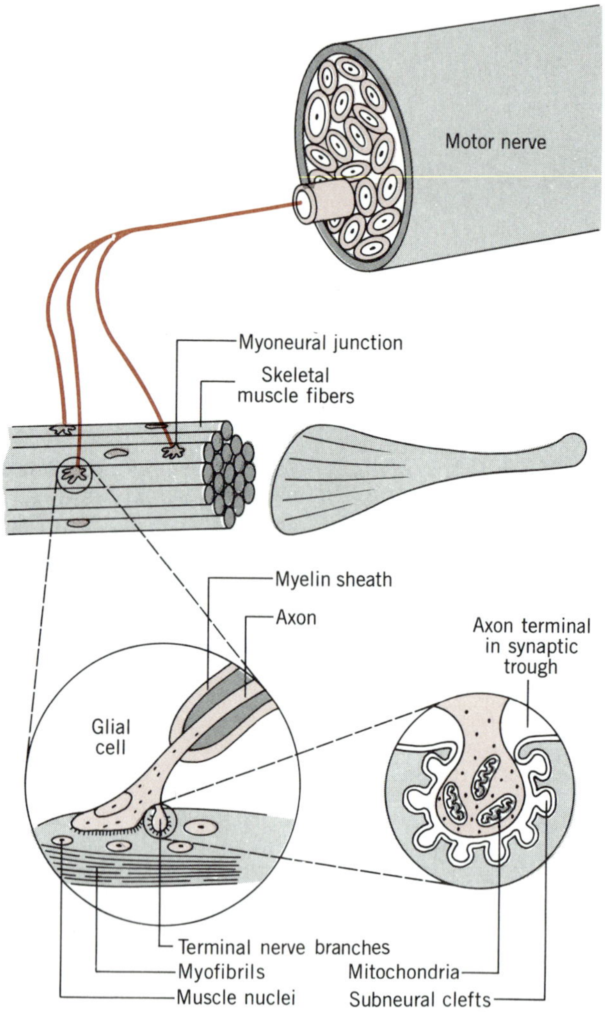

***Figure 7.7** The neuromuscular junction, a specialized synapse. A motor axon terminates in a cluster of invaginated neuromuscular junctions in several muscle fibers.*

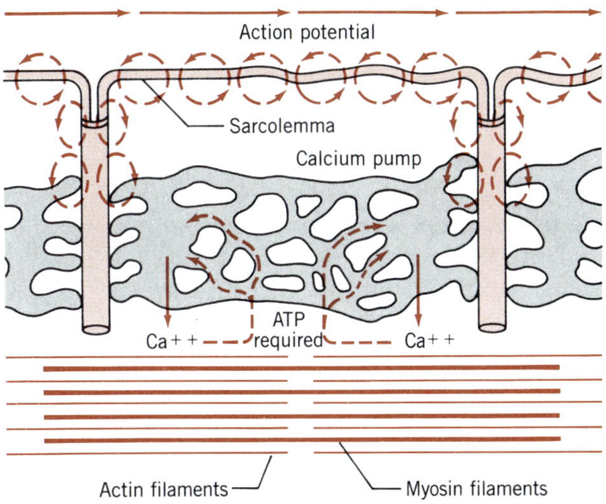

Figure 7.8 *Flow of calcium ions during muscle contraction. Ca^{++} is actively removed from the intracellular space of the fiber by a pump that requires metabolic energy. The sarcolemma is the cell body of the muscle fiber.*

The presynaptic processes contact the muscle along extensive invaginations in the muscle structure, using ACh as the neurotransmitter to elicit an action potential in the fibers. This is a particularly dramatic event, as a contraction follows the course of the action potential along the fiber. The action potential can be seen directly with a microscope in this way. A muscle action potential involves the inflow of Na^+ ions and the outflow of K^+ ions in the same manner as axonal action potentials, as well as an influx of Ca^{++} ions that triggers the contraction. The action potential and the Ca^{++} are conducted into the muscle fiber by the T-shaped structures shown in Figure 7.8. Ca^{++} remains inside the fiber for only a millisecond or so before being pumped back out by a Ca^{++} pump in the muscle fiber membrane.

The warmup period that benefits athletes has a partly molecular explanation. The first contraction of a muscle that has not been activated for some time is weaker than subsequent contractions, because the Ca^{++} pump has been working for a long time. Little intracellular Ca^{++} is left in the muscle fibers; therefore, fewer myosin heads bind to actin and the resulting contraction is weaker.

Subsequent activations result in stronger and stronger contractions, a phenomenon called **treppe** (*treppen* is German for "stairs") because the contraction spikes look like a staircase (see the voltage plot of Figure 7.9). The molecular mechanism involves Ca^{++} binding at the actin-myosin cross-bridges (Ridgway, Gordon & Martyn, 1983). Treppe does not violate the all-or-none rule of striated muscle contraction; the contraction of a fiber still either occurs or does not occur, but a single action potential leads to a stronger contraction when the muscle is warmed up. This aspect of the warmup, then, has nothing to do with temperature or even available energy; it involves only ion concentrations.

Innervation Patterns

Motor axons always divide to innervate several fibers. The number of fibers innervated determines the limits of fine control of the muscle. The ratio of axons to fibers, the **innervation ratio,** varies from one to three in the extraocular muscles to one to several hundred in the large muscles of the leg. The innervation ratio is fixed for a given muscle, so improvements in skilled movements are limited by it. This is why we play a violin with the fingertips and cannot play it with the knees.

In some invertebrates, both excitatory and inhibitory synapses end directly on the muscle fiber and can affect muscle contraction. Vertebrates, however, have only excitatory neuromuscular junctions; a muscle can be relaxed only by the elimination of activity in the motor neuron. In the vertebrates the last transformation of information has been moved back from the muscle to the motor neuron itself. The remainder of the system (motor

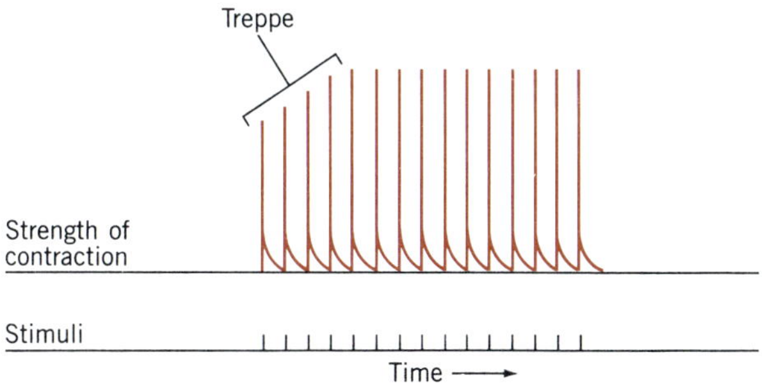

Figure 7.9 *Treppe, the "staircase effect" in a chain of muscle stimuli. The muscle's first contraction after a long rest period may be only half as great as it is 30 to 50 twitches later.*

axon, neuromuscular junction, and muscle) acts as a unit, called the **muscle unit.** The control of vertebrate muscles is strictly within the CNS, but it involves intimate feedback from the muscles themselves.

Load-Sharing

The system as it has been described would encounter problems in the real world, because each muscle fiber and each motor neuron has a slightly different threshold. The muscle fibers unfortunate enough to be innervated by low-threshold motor neurons should be almost constantly innervated and therefore should quickly become exhausted, while muscle fibers with high-threshold motor neurons should hardly ever be activated.

Evolution has solved this problem by sharing the load among the motor neurons; this is done by means of **recurrent collaterals**—motor axon branches that eventually affect the neurons from which they originated (see Figure 7.10). The recurrent collaterals end locally on small interneurons, called **Renshaw cells** after their discoverer Renshaw. These cells are activated whenever the motor axon fires. They are inhibitory cells that induce long-lasting (up to 500 msec) inhibitory postsynaptic potentials (IPSPs) on the somas of the same motor neurons that originally excited them. This negative feedback circuit tends to turn the ventral horn motor neurons off soon after they are activated, so they fire in bursts. Because a more active motor neuron receives more inhibition, the Renshaw cell recurrent pathway protects the cell against becoming too active. This process is called both self-inhibition and Renshaw inhibition.

Renshaw cells also inhibit other nearby motor neurons, an example of lateral inhibition. But it is still true that stronger motor neuron excitation yields more firing, for the recurrent pathway is not as strong as the excitatory input. The average excitation to the motor neuron (input) is always stronger than the Renshaw recurrent inhibition (output). If we define the system's **gain** as the output divided by the input, we can say that the gain of the recurrent collaterals is less than 1; that is, the output is less than the input. A similar mechanism assures load-sharing for smooth muscles.

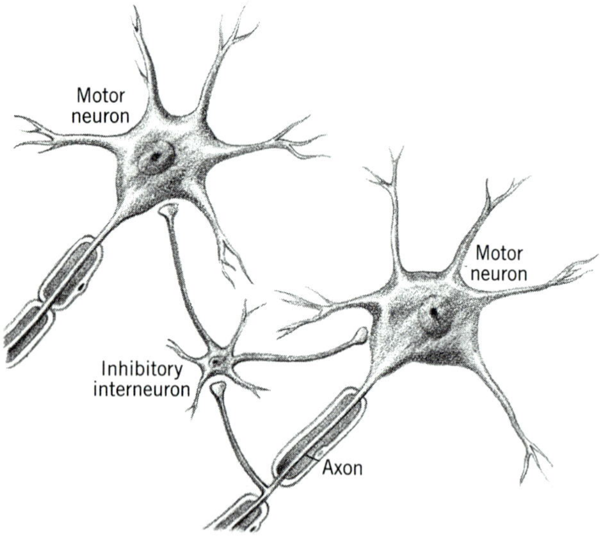

Figure 7.10 Negative feedback by recurrent collaterals. The inhibitory cell is a Renshaw cell. Though Renshaw inhibition can briefly silence a motor neuron, the inhibition on the average is less than the motor neuron's excitatory input. This is an example of monosynaptic feedback.

MUSCLE CONTROL

The system as described so far is adequate to contract a muscle, but it cannot execute movements. By analogy, we have the gas pedal, but we need steering and feedback about the results of the movement to be able to control the system usefully. The steering and feedback in the motor system come from sensory endings on the tendons and in the muscles.

MUSCLE RECEPTORS AND THE STRETCH REFLEX

The simplest reflex in the body, the **stretch reflex,** is seen when you pull gently on a muscle; it pulls back, as if resisting the stretch. This miniature tug of war is the basis of higher-lever motor control. It is easy to observe in a human or other animal under conditions in which there is no interference from the brain; for instance, if one pulls gently on the slightly flexed leg of a relaxed, reclining cat or human infant, the leg will pull back. This reflex exists for all skeletal muscles, serving to maintain posture and aid in the continual resistance against gravity. To see its importance, picture the extensor muscles of your legs as you walk with your knees slightly bent. As your body's weight falls on a leg, the knees bend and the extensors stretch, causing the stretch reflex to activate the muscles and prevent the leg from collapsing. This happens automatically and unavoidably, so higher centers controlling walking will have a simpler job; they do not have to adjust muscle tension as the load on the leg increases.

The stretch reflex depends on receptors sensitive to muscle length. Striated muscles contain two types of fibers: extrafusal and intrafusal. **Extrafusal fibers** do the work of contracting; the smaller **intrafusal fibers** function only in control. The term *fusal (fusus* is Latin for "spindle") refers to the shape of the intrafusal fibers. These fibers, also called muscle spindles, contain two types of receptors. Each is concentrated in the nuclear bag region at the center of the spindle (see Figure 7.11).

Annulospiral (primary) endings spiral around the center of the nuclear bag, and "flower spray" (secondary) endings branch into its ends. Annulospiral endings signal a change in muscle length with a burst of firing and then settle down to a reduced firing rate; thus they are dynamic (phasic) receptors. Flower spray endings are static (tonic), responding more slowly but maintaining their discharge (Granit, 1977).

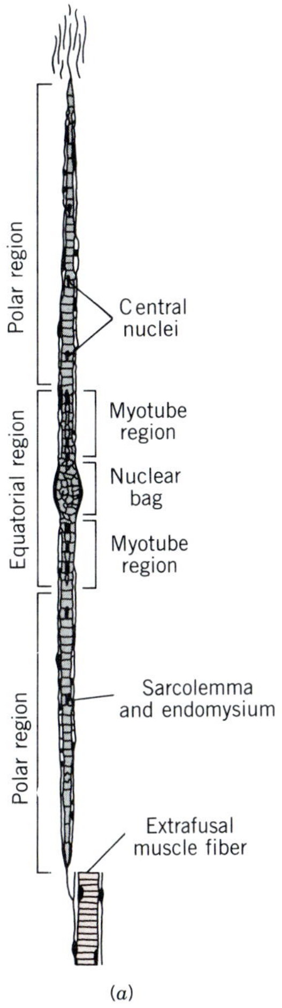

***Figure 7.11** Annulospiral and "flower spray" endings in a rabbit intrafusal muscle fiber. The swelling in the nuclear bag region at the middle of the fiber is exaggerated.*

Application of the Stretch Reflex

How do these receptors function in controlling muscle actions? Suppose you are holding your arm out horizontally and a weight is dropped on it, as in Figure 7.12. Your arm will drop slightly, lengthening the biceps muscle and with it the intrafusal fibers. The annulospiral endings will respond quickly with a burst of firing. Their axons lead back into the spinal cord, where they have monosynaptic excitatory synapses with the motor neurons of the biceps muscle. The motor neurons activate the muscle, contracting the extrafusal fibers and lifting the load. Then the feedback from the flower spray endings adds a tonic excitation to the motor neurons, holding the arm in the proper position. The receptors are part of a negative feedback loop controlling muscle length.

This local feedback system has two advantages over control from the brain. First, it is fast; the monosynaptic reflex is the fastest of all the body's responses, because it crosses only one synapse. The latency of contraction in this stretch reflex is about 50 msec, not much slower than the activation delay of the muscle itself and a good deal faster than the fastest processing times involving

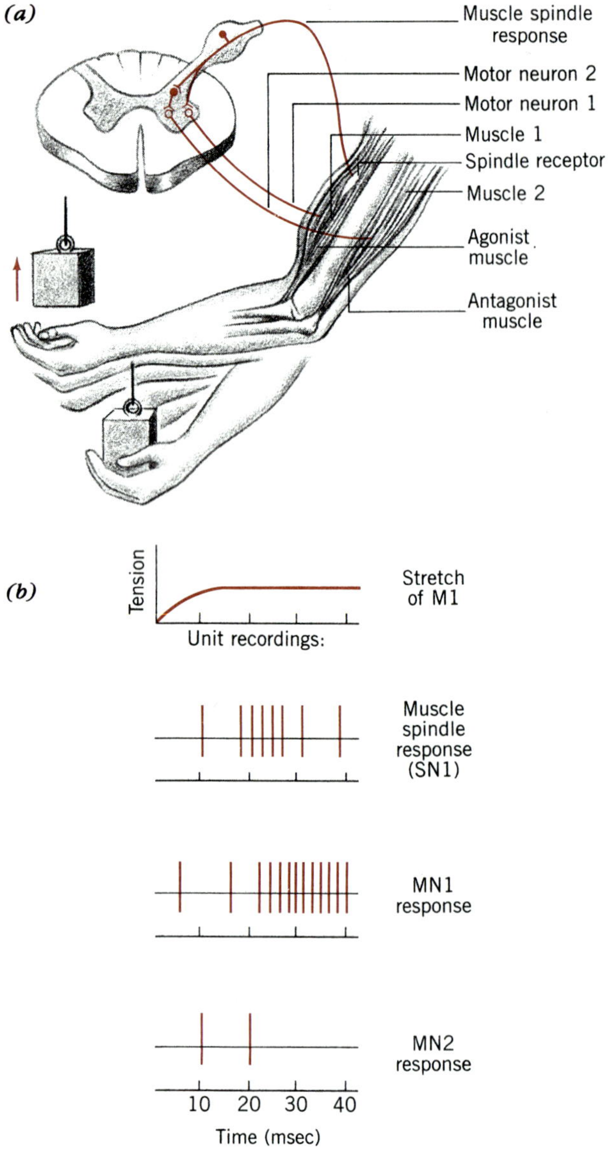

Figure 7.12 *Function of the stretch reflex in load compensation.* (a) *The muscle spindle receptors excite the alpha motor neurons, contracting the agonist; the antagonist motor neuron is inhibited by a feedforward path.* (b) *Typical changes in nerve firing.*

higher centers. Speed is important here because events in the real world can happen quickly; if you had to wait until command signals returned from the brain, you would drop the weight. Second, the correction for changes in load at the spinal level simplifies the brain's task in controlling the muscles. Higher centers can be concerned with actions; they need not perform all the calculations necessary to maintain position as loads vary. (We will examine the role of the stretch reflex in maintaining posture later in the chapter.)

Tendon Reflexes

Tendons contain stretch receptors called **Golgi tendon organs,** which detect the tension on muscles. These receptors are in series with the muscles, whereas the intrafusal fibers are in parallel with them. Some of the Golgi tendon organs have rather high thresholds and serve as safety devices for the muscles. Many skeletal muscles are strong enough to tear themselves apart if all the fibers are in tetanus simultaneously; signals from the Golgi tendon organs and other receptors prevent this occurrence by inhibiting the motor neurons, providing a biological negative feedback. The higher the tension on the muscle (and therefore on the tendon), the greater the inhibitory effect. The inhibition is carried by interneurons which link the tendon organs with the motor neurons of the same muscle (see Figure 7.13), using the inhibitory neurotransmitter glycine to produce IPSPs. This reflex is called the clasp-knife reflex because the muscle first resists pulling (thanks to the stretch reflex), then suddenly is released like an unfolding pocket knife blade when the tension is increased. Lower-threshold tendon afferents tell the brain how hard the muscle is pulling.

The clasp-knife reflex is polysynaptic (whereas the stretch reflex is monosynaptic). It works through spinal cord interneurons interposed between the sensory input and the motor neurons. Recent recordings from these interneurons suggest that much of the clasp-knife reflex comes not from Golgi tendon organs but from still-unidentified receptors in the muscle that signal changes in muscle force (Cleland, Rymer & Edwards, 1982).

The Gamma Efferent System

This section will begin with a mystery and end with a description of a sophisticated neurological control system. The mystery first arose in experi-

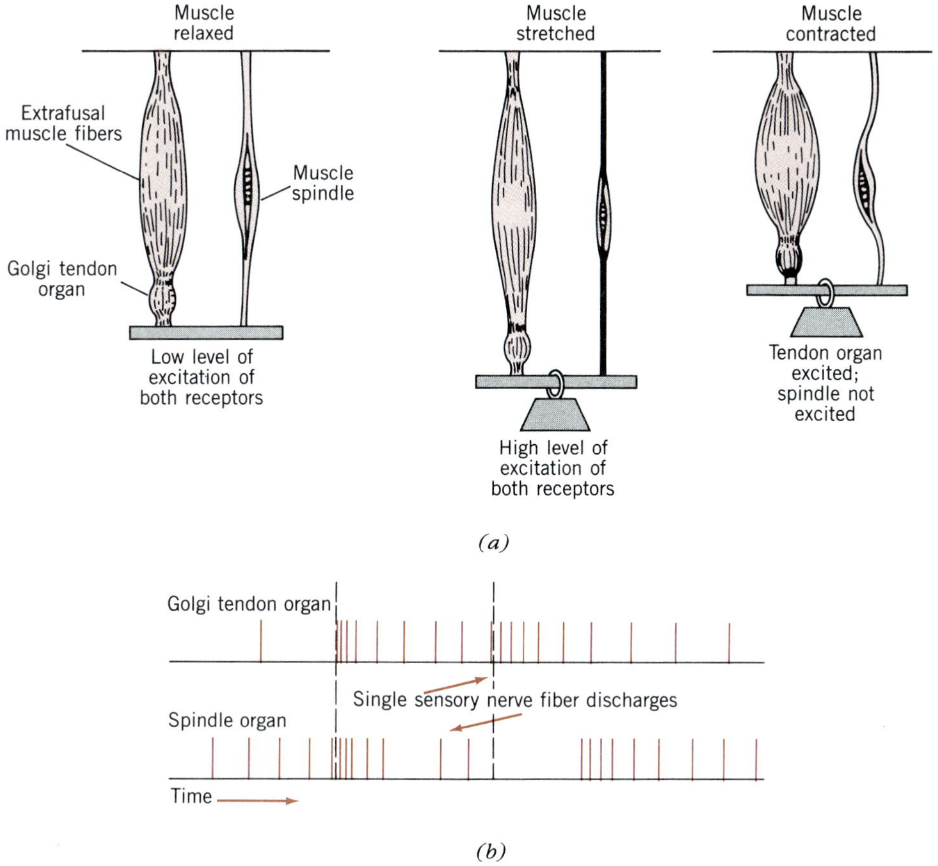

Figure 7.13 Contrasting responses of spindle receptors and Golgi tendon organs. (a) *Schematic arrangement of intrafusal fibers, extrafusal fibers, and tendon organs. The intrafusal fibers are in parallel with the extrafusal fibers; the tendon organs are in series.* (b) *Responses of Golgi tendon organ axons and spindle organ axons to muscle stretch. The Golgi tendon organ axons respond only to tension on the muscle, whether the tension is achieved actively or passively. The spindle organ axons, in contrast, respond to the length of the muscle rather than to the degree of contractile effort.*

ments in which motor nerves were stimulated (Granit, 1977). The largest axons, called **alpha fibers** because of their large size, behaved in a straightforward way: each stimulation with an electrode elicited an action potential and resulted in a twitch of a motor unit (the group of muscle fibers innervated by a single axon). But a group of smaller fibers, called **gamma fibers** because of their smaller diameters (see Figure 7.14), had no apparent function. They were definitely efferent, exiting from cell bodies in the ventral horn of the spinal cord and entering the muscles; but no muscle contraction resulted when they were stimulated. Rather, they somehow induced the alpha motor neurons to fire, and the extrafusal fibers in turn contracted the muscle.

The mystery was solved with the discovery that the intrafusal muscle fibers could contract in the same manner as the extrafusal fibers, but they were so small and weak that the contraction had no mechanical effect on the muscle as a whole. The sole purpose of the contraction was to stimulate the annulospiral endings and the flower spray endings in the fibers, biasing them in a manner analogous to adaptation in other sensory systems. The intrafusal fibers are contractile mainly on their ends; their central part is specialized for sensory reception and does not contract.

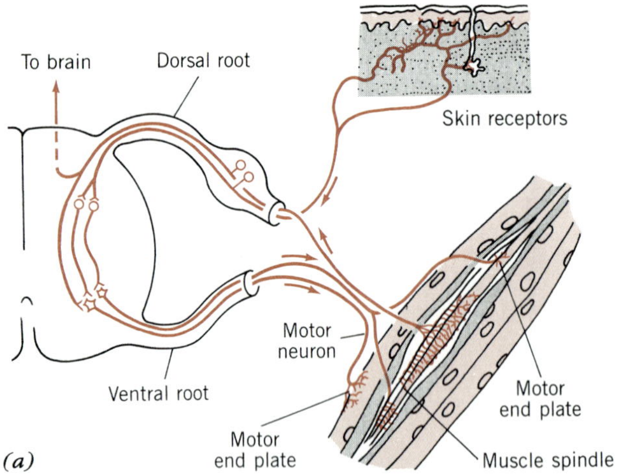

(a)

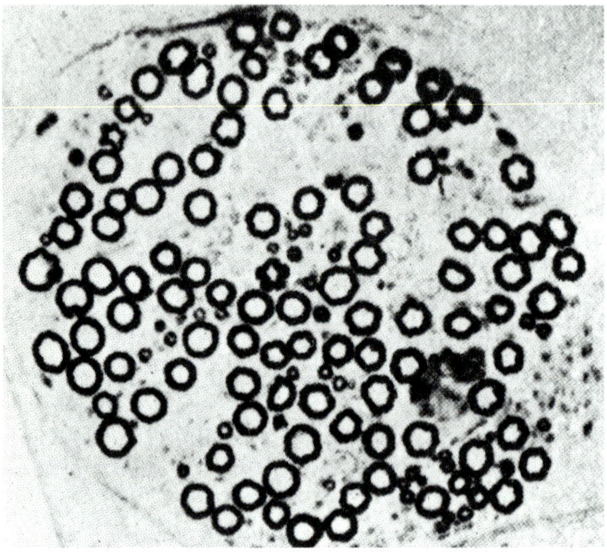

(b)

Figure 7.14 *Muscle contraction initiated by the gamma system.* (a) *Alpha and gamma fiber innervation are initiated in parallel by the skin receptor axons. The mechanical feedback from the gamma system modulates the contraction while a copy of the gamma receptor activity is sent on a branching axon to the brain.* (b) *Cross section of a deafferented motor nerve in the cat. Only the efferent (motor) fibers remain. The large fibers are alpha motor neuron axons; the small fibers are gamma axons. Blank regions are locations of degenerated gamma-afferent fibers.*

We know that the intrafusal fibers contract upon gamma stimulation because Boyd (1966) observed the contractions directly under the microscope. Looking at isolated cat spindles that were anchored at both ends, he saw the ends of the fiber contract to stretch the middle part, extending the coils of the annulospiral ending.

To examine the effects of intrafusal fiber contraction, consider the train of events in Figure 7.14*a*. The gamma efferents contract the fiber, causing its sensory endings to fire just as if the muscle had been lengthened. The endings respond only to the local conditions; they know nothing about the source of their stimulation. The extrafusal afferent spindle axons project their signals back to the alpha motor neurons via the stretch reflex, and the muscle contracts.

What is the advantage of starting muscle contraction in this roundabout way? It is certainly slower than direct excitation of the alpha motor neurons, but it has the crucial property of taking the state of the muscle into account. If the muscle is already fully shortened, for instance, the gamma efferent innervation will have little effect. If your elbow is already bent as far as it will go, it would be a waste of effort to activate the biceps muscle.

In practice, the motor system frequently innervates alpha and gamma efferents together, a strategy called coactivation (Granit, 1977). Again, the automobile analogy can show the usefulness of this strategy. In getting on to the freeway, one presses the gas pedal and looks for an opening in the traffic. Pressing the pedal corresponds to alpha innervation—getting the process started as quickly as possible. Looking for an opening involves feedback but requires more time. In the muscle, coactivation offers the advantages of speed and control.

Frequently, the alpha system leads the gamma system, for it contains larger, faster-conducting axons and receives its innervation earlier. As gamma control comes in, however, alpha innervation must decrease so the two systems do not fight each other. Valbo (1971) showed this by putting small needle electrodes into his own peripheral nerves to record the muscle spindle afferents and the muscle's own electrical activity (with the **electromyogram** (Greek for "electric-muscle-write"), or **EMG.** The muscle always began contracting before the muscle spindle afferents fired, showing that the alpha system started the contraction.

The principle of gamma feedback control is similar to that of warming a room by turning up the thermostat rather than starting the furnace directly. The thermostat, like the gamma system, is based on feedback from the environment and takes care of itself once it is set. Flipping the "on" switch on the furnace would be like activating the muscles with the alpha motor neurons.

To refine the control system even further, each muscle has two kinds of intrafusal fibers: "bag" fibers with a membranous bulge in the middle and thinner "chain" fibers with a straight profile. The bag fibers contract slowly and give a sustained stimulus to their receptors; the chain fibers contract more quickly and transiently. In this way the system gains more control over the dynamics of contraction. The strategy is analogous to that of the visual system's simple cells giving a transient response and complex cells giving a more sustained response. Both the visual system and the motor system can respond quickly while maintaining sensitivity to ongoing stimuli.

We can see the importance of the muscle receptors by examining what happens when the afferents from the muscle receptors are cut. This is done most conveniently at the dorsal roots, taking advantage of Bell and Magendie's law (see Chapter 3). The operation cuts the axons coming from the muscle receptors but leaves both the alpha and the gamma motor systems intact. The experiment is a more thorough version of what happens when one of your limbs goes to sleep from a cutoff of circulation. Sherrington (1906) found that deafferentation causes paralysis, even when the efferent motor neurons to the muscles are normal. More recently, Taub and Berman (1968) have shown that a monkey will learn to use a deafferented limb if forced to. If both forelimbs are deafferented, for instance, the monkey will learn to use them in a coordinated way over a few months, and even a single deafferented limb will become functional if use of the other is restricted.

FUNCTIONS OF THE STRETCH REFLEX

The stretch reflex is the first of many examples of cooperative control—lower-level and higher-level centers working together to divide the job of controlling complex activities. Higher-level centers can adjust muscle activation by biasing the gamma loop, letting that system control the movement. This example shows the close relationship of the sensory and motor systems, for motor control is accomplished here by efferent control of the local environment near a set of receptors.

The gamma reflex introduces feedback from the load itself to control the strength of the contraction; the outside world becomes part of the feedback control loop. A heavier weight induces more rapid firing in the intrafusal receptors, causing more excitatory postsynaptic potentials (EPSPs) in the alpha motor neurons. As a result, the efferent axons in the ventral root fire faster to contract the muscle more strongly. When the load lightens, the process is reversed.

The continual alternation of these processes induces a slight oscillation in the movement, a characteristic of feedback systems that is also seen in postural control. It is impossible to remain totally still, for the stretch reflex transforms even static conditions into feedback-controlled dynamic states. You can prove this to yourself by holding a book on your fully outstretched palm—the book jiggles slightly as postural reflexes adjust the arm muscles.

Reinterpreting the Reflex

These observations have led to a fundamental reinterpretation of the reflex concept. The reflex is now seen not simply as a contraction (a re-flexion, as its name implies) but as an operation carried out on a sensorimotor control system. It can be viewed as an example of the test-operate-test-exit (TOTE) process that applies widely to neurological and psychological control systems (Miller, Galanter & Pribram, 1960). According to the TOTE concept (see Figure 7.15), input is compared to the current state of the system (in this case the muscle) to see whether the desired state of affairs exists. This is the "test" phase. If the comparison fails, an operation is performed to change that state and the test is started again. The process continues until the test succeeds. In this case the operation is the activation of alpha motor neurons. The test takes place in the intrafusal fibers; if they have been relaxed by extrafusal contraction, the

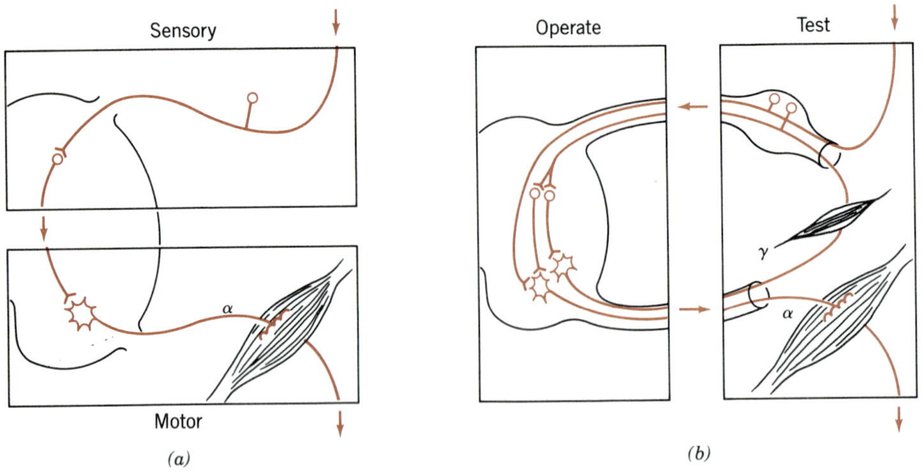

Figure 7.15 *Two concepts of spinal control.* (a) *Traditional feedforward concept of a reflex.* (b) *Test-operate-test-exit (TOTE) feedback concept. The gamma system performs a test on the state of the contraction, completing a feedback loop that has both neural and mechanical components.*

action is complete. The result is (if you will pardon the expression) not a knee-jerk response but a matching process. Figure 7.16 shows the organization of the feedback and feedforward aspects of muscle control.

The stretch reflex described here is simpler than stretch reflexes seen in nature, because real events never occur in isolation. Many muscles and many fibers in each muscle participate simultaneously in each action. Each muscle spindle afferent diverges to innervate many motor neurons, and fibers from many sensory axons converge on each motor neuron. At the same time, the higher centers are informed of the action by axon branches that ascend in the dorsal columns of the spinal cord. The rest of the chapter reviews the role of these centers in controlling behavior.

ORGANIZATION OF THE MOTOR SYSTEM

ACTS VERSUS MOVEMENTS

Movements are defined in terms of an organism; they involve particular muscles and joints. Acts, in contrast, refer to results in the outside world. Flexing my finger is a movement, but pressing a key on my typewriter is an act. If I pressed the key with my nose, the movement would be different but the act would be the same. At the highest levels of control, the motor system deals with acts, not movements.

The organization is partly hierarchical, with the higher centers controlling behavior by activating spinal reflexes. But a cooperative specialization of functions exists at the higher levels. Motor regions are closely coordinated with one another, and they generally exchange information before a motor act is initiated.

SPINAL REFLEXES—A COOPERATIVE HIERARCHY

Reciprocal Inhibition

The stretch reflex contains a paradox. It arises because most muscles are organized in antagonistic pairs, so one muscle must stretch while the other contracts. When the biceps muscle in the arm contracts, the triceps, which normally extends the arm, is stretched. The triceps ought to respond with a contraction through its own stretch reflex. But both muscles would then be pulling simultaneously in opposite directions, and the movement would get nowhere.

The problem is solved by turning off the stretch reflex in a muscle when its antagonist contracts. This is **reciprocal inhibition,** the process in which one muscle of a pair is activated while its antagonist is inhibited. Reciprocal inhibition cannot be based on feedback, because feedback would be too slow. It could not begin until after signals from the agonist muscle had inhibited the

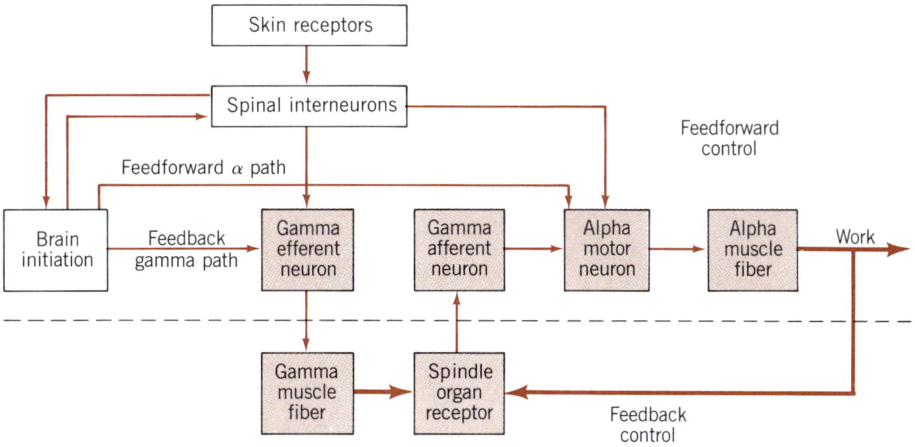

***Figure** 7.16 Alpha and gamma control of muscles. Part of this control system is shown anatomically in Figure 7.14. The tinted boxes are part of the alpha system; the shaded boxes are part of the gamma system. The heavy lines connecting the boxes represent mechanical work, the light lines represent communication through axons, and the dashed line represents the division between feedforward and feedback control.*

motor neurons of the antagonist. In the meantime, both muscles would be active simultaneously.

To avoid this inefficient situation, the antagonist is inhibited by a feedforward pathway. A muscle spindle afferent activates its agonist motor neuron and excites inhibitory interneurons to inhibit firing in the antagonist's motor neurons (see Figure 7.17). With this mechanism, the activation of the agonist and the inhibition of the antagonist begin almost simultaneously. The initiation of antagonist inhibition from the muscle spindle afferent also means that the inhibition is closely tied to the stretch reflex. One cannot operate without the other.

Of course, the muscle used as the antagonist sometimes functions as the agonist, having an inhibitory connection to the other muscle through its stretch reflex. This is why the inhibition is

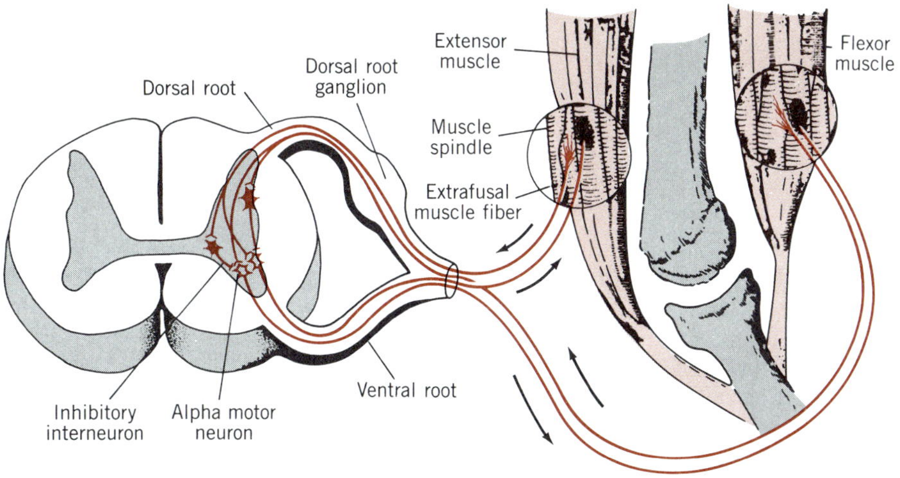

***Figure** 7.17 Forward inhibition of an antagonist's alpha motor neurons by the agonist spindle organs. The spinal cord is shown much larger than its true scale. A single spinal cord afferent axon splits to both excite the agonist motor neuron and inhibit the antagonist motor neuron.*

called reciprocal (Descartes, [1665], 1972). Again, there is convergence and divergence, so no pathway acts in isolation; hundreds of muscle units and their motor neurons are affected in parallel, but the basic path is a two-synapse connection. Mechanically, a muscle may have several antagonists. Examples are the neck and shoulder muscles, where movement in many directions is possible. The corresponding neural control includes weaker inhibitory connections to motor neurons of muscles that are only approximately in mechanical opposition.

The reciprocal inhibition of muscles has a practical result. You can often relieve a muscle cramp by strongly activating the antagonist to the cramped muscle, so the cramped muscle's motor neurons are inhibited by antagonistic inhibition. This is a way of using higher centers (your intention to relieve the cramping) to take advantage of spinal cord organization in governing behavior. You can relieve a cramp in the gastrocnemius muscle, which stretches your ankle, for instance, by pulling your foot upward. Forcing the same movement to occur passively, by pulling on your foot with your hands, will have no effect. You cannot relax the cramp by direct voluntary control; you must do it by taking advantage of an involuntary system. In fact, the most common mode of higher control of the muscles is to play on the reflexes themselves, not on the motor neurons. Higher centers make the reflexes do much of the actual organization of motor neuron firing.

The logical structure of the spinal cord can be expressed in terms of the universal neuroanatomy of Chapter 2. We need only rotate the dorsal and ventral roots until they are at opposite ends of a stack of processing layers, as in Figure 7.18. Incoming signals synapse at least once (for monosynaptic reflexes) on the way from the dorsal to the ventral root axons. Recurrent inhibition operates within a layer to modify the activity of cells in the same layer.

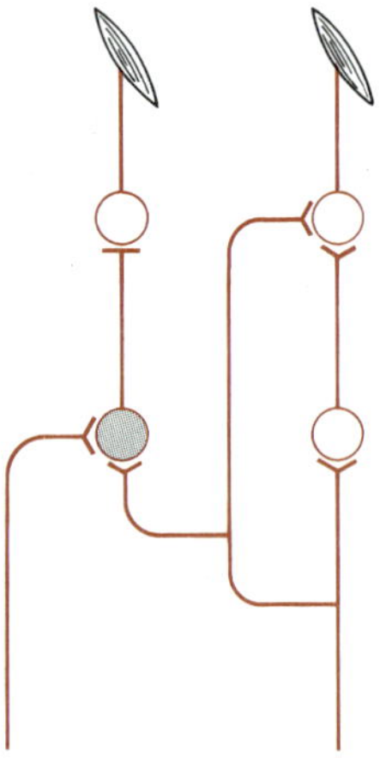

***Figure** 7.18 Logical structure of the connections in the spinal cord. The minimal, monosynaptic connection has only one logical layer. Antagonist inhibition goes through two layers, and other reflexes mediated by a single inhibitory interneuron also use two layers.*

Other Polysynaptic Reflexes

Many polysynaptic reflexes contribute to smooth coordination of the muscles. Sherrington (1906) is the best source of information about these reflexes. The following descriptions rest largely on his observations.

The **crossed-extensor reflex** is a crossed reflex, activating extensors on one side when flexors are excited on the other side. This is accomplished by interneurons crossing the centerline of the spinal cord within the gray matter. The reflex facilitates walking in humans by helping to extend one leg when the other is flexed.

Related reflexes connect all the limbs to coordinate four-legged walking, even in humans. You can experience the effectiveness of these reflexes by crawling on all fours; though you are only dimly aware of the movements needed, all of your limbs move in the right direction at the right time. These reflexes are similar to the reflexes that control normal locomotion in four-footed animals; since there is no selective pressure against them, they remain in humans. Sherrington (1906) demonstrated the self-organizing nature of the polysynaptic reflexes with a simple experiment. After sectioning a cat's spinal cord, he struck the cut end with a hammer and obtained four-footed "walking" movements. The mechanical blow directly stimulated many of the cut axons, and the reflexes organized the behavior.

Other polysynaptic pathways originate in the

skin. Probably the simplest is the pain withdrawal reflex, which everyone has experienced on touching a hot stove or a flame. The reflex works only on the flexor muscles, affecting several of them simultaneously. Here, extreme speed is essential to avoid tissue damage. The speed of the movement is enhanced by spinally mediated antagonist inhibition. Only after the withdrawal is completed does one feel the burning sensation, which was transmitted to the brain on small, slow-conducting axons.

Some seemingly complicated behaviors, such as scratching a point of irritation on the skin, are controlled not only in the brain but also independently in the spinal cord. The location of the scratch reflex can be demonstrated in an animal whose connection between brain and spinal cord has been severed. Such an animal cannot stand or walk because the higher-level commands are lacking. But when the animal's skin is stimulated, a limb will rise as if by magic to make a regularly repeated scratch on the area. Clearly this involves an impressive amount of neural computation; the most appropriate limb must be selected and moved to the right place before scratching can commence. The scratching itself involves at least two neural oscillators—one for motion along the skin and another for up-and-down motion—and includes a way to stop the whole process.

All of this takes place in the prewired neuropil of the spinal cord gray matter, without benefit of learning or experience. Most of the spinal reflexes work about as well in newborns as in adults. This does not mean that there is no room for plasticity in the spinal cord, however. If a spinal nerve is cut, the tissue normally serving the missing input will shift to represent the other, still intact axons. If function is restored, the neurons will shift back to their original roles.

BRAIN-STEM MOTOR STRUCTURES

The oldest parts of the brain mediate three kinds of motor functions: cephalic continuation of spinal functions, specialized control centers, and tonic (steady-state) control from the reticular formation.

Distributed throughout the brain stem are a series of cranial nerve nuclei, which do for the head what the spinal cord does for the body. Containing the motor neurons for muscles of the head, the cranial nerves mediate the stretch reflex and more complex reflexes. Most of the cranial nerves have both sensory and motor fibers (see Figure 7.19).

The medulla contains several centers for controlling such vital functions as respiration and heartbeat. This is one of the few brain areas where even a small lesion can lead to death within seconds; therefore, human neurological patients are not a good source of information about these areas. Related areas coordinate "vegetative" functions such as digestion. These areas are quite old phylogenetically and show little evolutionary change.

The reticular formation is particularly important in gamma motor system control. It determines the set points of the gamma servo control loops in the muscles and spinal cord. Tonic effects on spinal reflexes are divided anatomically into two regions: a rostral region that facilitates flexor reflexes and a caudal region that facilitates extensor reflexes. If a cat's brain stem is sectioned between these two regions, only the caudal one can affect the body; the result is a tonic extensor rigidity. More exactly, the facilitation is of the antigravity muscles, not the extensors. Similar damage to the human brain stem produces the posture shown in Figure 7.20, with extension in the legs and flexion in the arms. Patients with neurological diseases who suffer from a lack of inhibition of this area walk with a stiff-legged gait; typically, they hold their hands near their shoulders, their wrists and fingers curled and their elbows tucked into the body. The activity of many of the fibers in the reticulospinal tract is modulated by cutaneous pressure, suggesting that these fibers aid in postural control (Wolstoncroft, 1964).

More rostrally, at the midbrain, the brain stem contains motor nuclei for the oculomotor system. These nuclei are closely tied to the overlying superior colliculus as well as the cerebellum. This region of the brain stem and the area just behind it contain neuronal machines that calculate the control signals needed to generate saccadic eye movements (see Chapter 6).

Beyond this level, three structures—the basal ganglia, the cerebellum, and the neocortex—con-

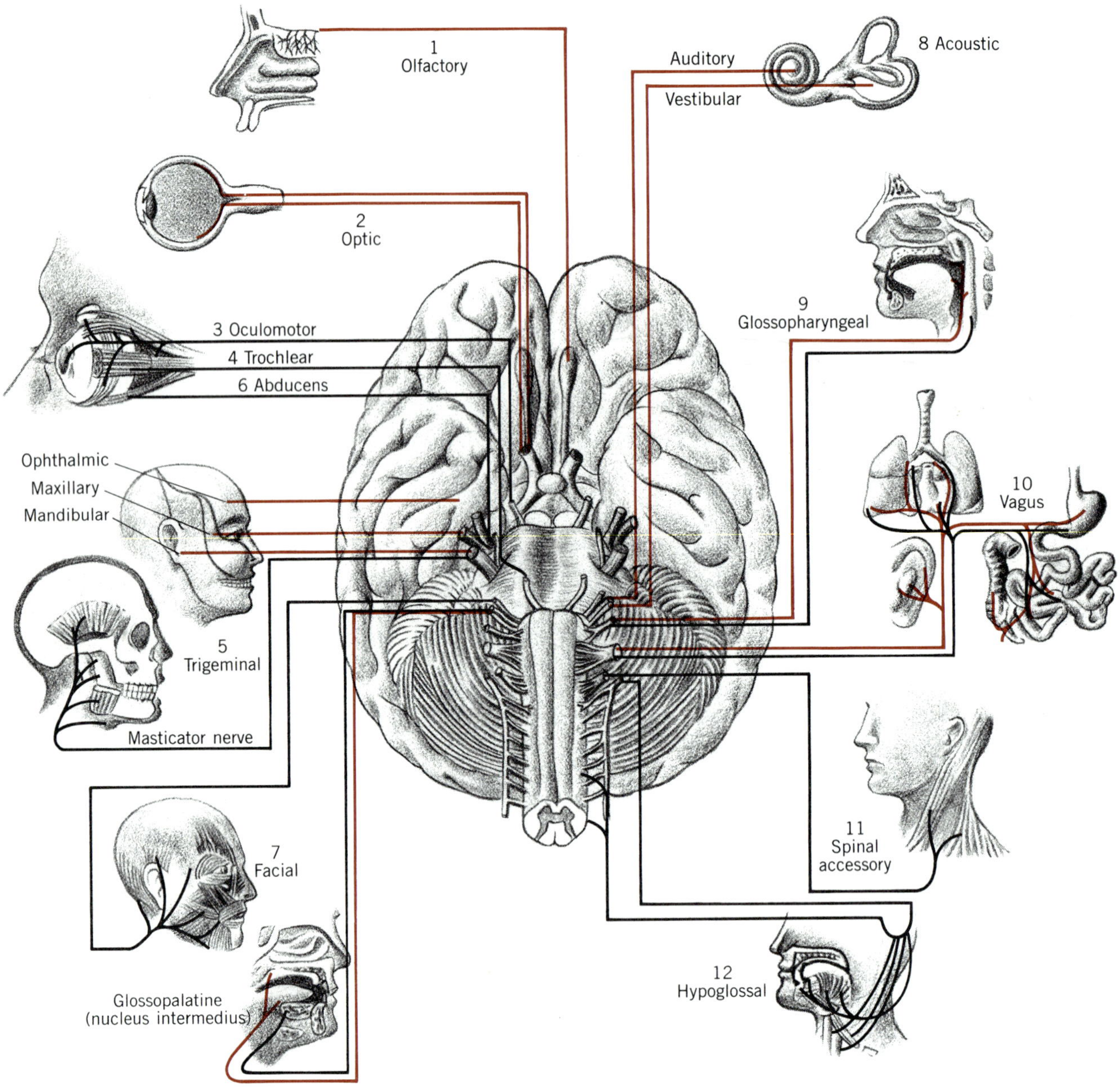

***Figure** 7.19 The 12 cranial nerves. Each nerve is paired, with one rootlet on each side. In the head the nervous system loses its segmented character, so each cranial nerve has a distinctive anatomy. The first (olfactory) and second (optic) nerves are not really peripheral nerves but extensions of the CNS within the dura.*

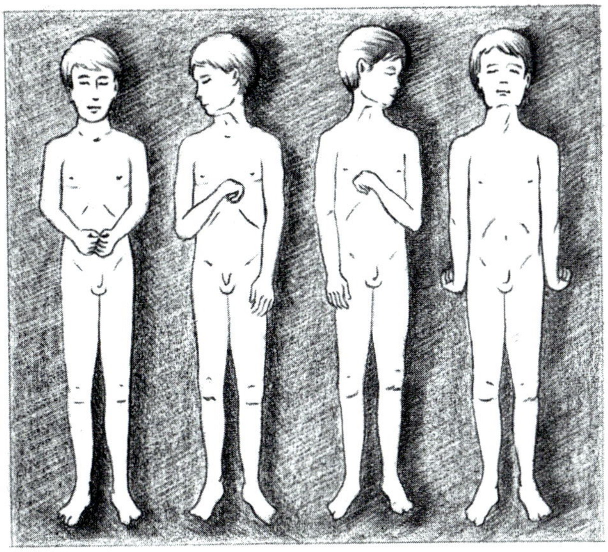

Figure 7.20 *Human decorticate rigidity. The patient is lying supine, and the limbs move as the examiner rotates and elevates the head.*

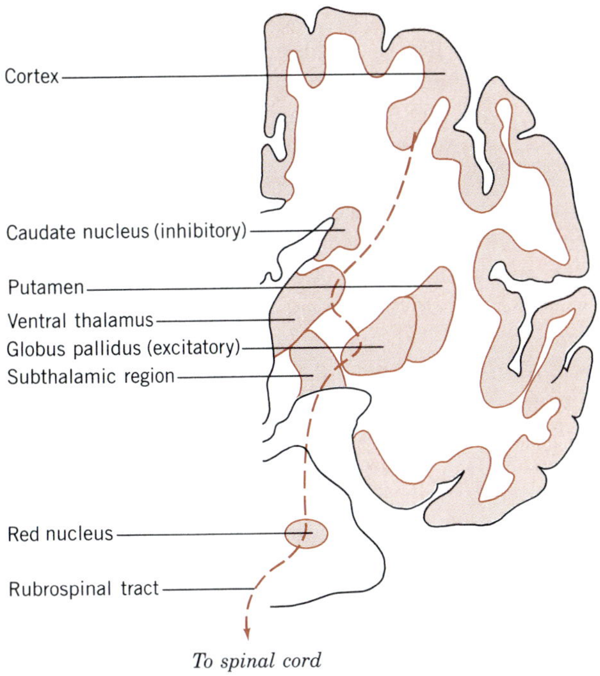

Figure 7.21 *The principal connections of the basal ganglia. Slow "ramp" movements can be generated by looping activity between the basal ganglia and the cortex. Most of the descending output of the system goes through the red nucleus.*

tribute specialized components to the organization of motor acts. The cooperative conception of motor organization described here will follow that of Kornhuber (1974), currently the dominant conception of central motor organization.

BASAL GANGLIA—SLOW MOVEMENTS

Structure and Evolution of Basal Ganglia

The basal ganglia are well situated to control motor activity. They receive input from nearly the whole cortex and send output to the motor cortex as well as to brain-stem motor structures. The main connections are shown in Figure 7.21. The oldest of the basal ganglia, the globus pallidus, is pale because of the many myelinated fibers coursing through it; it is the output for all of the basal ganglia. The globus pallidus is also called the paleostriatum (Latin for "old striped body") and the pallidum (Latin for "palid body").

During evolution, newer structures were added "upstream" of the globus pallidus, sending their output into and through it. These structures include the putamen and the caudate nucleus, collectively called the **neostriatum** (Latin for "new striped body"). The putamen and caudate nucleus may be the same structure with two lobes, for they are continuations of each other and have essentially the same cytological structure (Truex & Carpenter, 1964).

Function of Basal Ganglia

The basal ganglia are involved in generating slow ramp movements where a signal of a smoothly changing magnitude is needed. Common postural adjustments, such as standing and sitting, use ramp signals that are included in basal ganglia functions. Evidence of this comes from studies of patients with basal ganglia damage; one of their symptoms is spontaneous, uncontrollable movements, called **dyskinesias** (Greek for "disturbed movements"). Dyskinesia is a side effect of several antischizophrenic drugs.

Researchers have studied the motor functions of the basal ganglia in awake monkeys by recording from single cells while the monkeys perform motor acts. In these studies, the brain is exposed surgically and a cap with fittings for a microelectrode drive is implanted in the skull. The monkey is then allowed to recover before recording begins. Recordings from neurons in the basal ganglia show discharges at the onset of many movements, demonstrating that the neurons either participate in the initiation of the movements or are informed of the process. One of the basal ganglia, the putamen, shows discharges during slow movements but not during rapid movements of the same limbs (DeLong, 1974). Recordings from the **red nucleus** of the mesencephalon, a brain-stem center closely related to the basal ganglia, describe a similar pattern (Kohlerman, Gibson & Houk, 1982). Neurons there are best activated by what Kohlerman and his associates call a "twister," which is similar to the throttle on a motorcycle; it requires finely coordinated wrist and finger movements. Discharges begin consistently about 70 msec before muscle activation. Figure 7.22 shows how the duration of a discharge corresponds to the duration of a movement.

Parkinson's Disease

The most common disturbance of the basal ganglia is **Parkinson's disease,** a neurological disorder that appears mostly in the elderly. Parkinson's patients have a stooped posture, a blank and masklike facial expression, a shuffling gait, and a resting tremor that usually appears as a shaking of the arms when at rest. More severely affected patients have difficulty in initiating or halting activities such as walking.

All of these problems are a result of deficits in postural adjustments and ramp movements normally controlled by the basal ganglia. The shuffling gait is an adaptation to the disease; since the controlled slow movements of walking cannot be generated, the patient instead walks with saccadic steps generated by the cerebellum (Kornhuber, 1974). These steps must be small to remain controllable, because there is no feedback control.

Parkinson's disease is a handicap, but it does not prevent some kinds of productive work. One Parkinson's victim was a surgeon; he would shuffle into the operating room, his hands trembling, as his staff prepared the patient. Hunching over the patient, he would ask for the scalpel. Holding the scalpel in his trembling hand, he would reach out to begin the operation—and make a smooth, precise incision. After that, the operation would proceed without incident. The surgeon was able to function because fine voluntary movements, coordinated by the cortex, remained intact.

The biochemical cause of Parkinson's disease has recently been traced to an abnormality in the fibers that enter the basal ganglia from the substantia nigra, using dopamine as their neurotransmitter. The fibers function poorly because of an inadequate synthesis of dopamine. Many Parkinson's patients are helped by the administration of **L-dopa,** a precursor of dopamine. L-dopa crosses the blood-brain barrier to stimulate dopaminergic neurons in the substantia nigra.

A new chapter in the understanding of this disease began with the appearance of a young man at the emergency room of a California hospital in 1982. Though only in his twenties, he had a masklike facial expression, could not speak, and could barely move. The case was finally diagnosed as one of the most severe cases of Parkinsonism ever seen. In the next weeks, three more patients appeared with similar symptoms. The cause turned out to be MPTP (1-methyl-4-phenyl-1,2,5,6–tetrahydropyridine), sold on the streets as part of a "synthetic heroin" (Langston et al., 1983). Given to mice, MPTP caused Parkinson symptoms and provided an animal model for work on the disease. In these animals, grafts of adrenal medulla into the striatum alleviated the symptoms, probably by facilitating growth of dopamine neurons and fibers (Bohn et al., 1987). Use of the technique in humans is still experimental.

The basal ganglia have a role in controlling all parts of the body except the eyes. Slow eye movements are possible, but they are not controlled internally. Rather, the external stimulus itself creates the ramp and the oculomotor system only corrects errors. We can track slow-moving objects with our eyes, but the same movements are impossible in the absence of objects to follow. The ramp need not be generated in the brain, for the appropriate ramp generator exists in the outside world.

THE CEREBELLUM—FAST MOVEMENTS AND COORDINATION

The anatomy of the cerebellar cortex was reviewed in Chapter 3. Functionally, the most striking as-

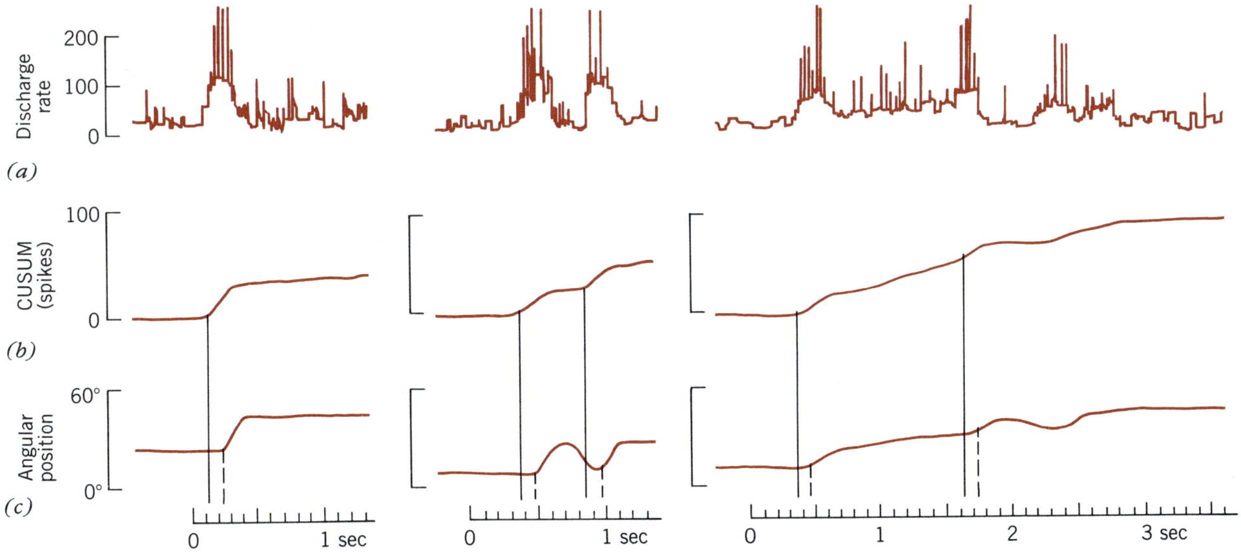

***Figure 7.22** Correlation of single-cell discharges in the red nucleus with angular position of a monkey's response. The monkey's task was to impose precise movements on a rotatable handle (a twister).* (a) *Response to a step on the twister.* (b) *and* (c) *Responses to ramps. The top row shows the instantaneous firing rate. The middle row shows an integration of the firing rate (CUSUM, or cumulative sum) generated by raising the line each time the cell fires. The bottom row records the angular position of the twister.*

pect of the cerebellum is its great speed. Incoming information passes through only one or two synapses before the first output becomes available, and the cerebellum is cleared and ready to accept new input in only 30 msec (Eccles, Ito & Szentagothai, 1967). At this speed, cerebellar circuits can go through almost seven complete cycles in the time between two ticks of a watch.

As the cerebellum evolved, it acquired new parts with new functions, without changing its basic cytoarchitecture. The oldest part, appropriately named the **archicerebellum** (*archi* is Latin for "old"), is closely linked with the vestibular system and helps maintain balance. You can feel it in action when you stand on one foot; occasional quick adjustments of the ankle prevent you from falling. You are unaware of the size or timing of these adjustments. Another of the older components is the **paleocerebellum** (*paleo* is Greek for "old"), which helps manage muscle tone. Each of these motor regions is organized as a **homunculus** (Greek for "little man"), a small map of the body on the surface of the cerebellar cortex.

The **neocerebellum,** by far the largest part of the human cerebellum, is specialized for the coordination of ballistic movements. An understanding of how these movements might be organized in the cerebellum requires a further look at cerebellar anatomy.

Relationship of Cerebellar Structure and Function

Clearly, something about the regular geometry of the cerebellar cortex is important to its function. The whole assembly is a three-dimensional formal garden on a microscopic scale. Researchers can explore the structural symmetries of the cerebellar cortex by sectioning it vertically and comparing the sections at various orientations. The orientation makes a big difference in the appearance of the sections (as Figure 3.16 showed) because of the parallel arrangement of the Purkinje cell dendritic trees and the parallel fibers. In the cerebellar cortex, both the geometric plan and the topological design are important. Sections at various orientations in other cortically organized structures, however, are indistinguishable. In these other brain structures, topography seems less critical than the logic of the connections.

Other unique features of cerebellar design also suggest the importance of the physical layout; for instance, the cerebellar cortex is the only brain cortex that continues across the midline. An imaginary microbe crawling through the cerebellar neuropil would not know when it had crossed from one side to the other. In an examination of a microscopic section of the cerebellar cortex, the midline would be undetectable; there is no discontinuity at the crossing line from left to right. The continuous structure, called the **vermis** (Latin for "worm"), is a worm-shaped piece of archicerebellum that curves around the entire cerebellum straddling the midline.

Further, the folds in the cerebellar cortex are neatly arranged parallel to the parallel fibers. In contrast, the haphazard folds of the cerebral cortex vary widely from one individual to the next. The thickness of the cerebellar cortex remains quite constant from one animal to the next despite huge variations in its area. This is evidence that thickness is another crucial property; once the structure of the system had been settled, early in vertebrate evolution, it was maintained with little change.

These peculiarities of cerebellar cortex anatomy might be consequences of the unique task of the cerebellar cortex: the fast coordination of finely graded muscle actions. The cerebellum is important in skilled and graceful performances that require the precise timing of many muscles.

The key to the puzzle of cerebellar structure probably lies in the parallel fiber and Purkinje cell dendritic tree arrangement. The whole structure appears to convert time into space (Braitenberg & Atwood, 1958), as time delays become recoded in distance along the parallel fibers. The conduction of an action potential to the end of a parallel fiber involves a delay of a few milliseconds, so communication along a parallel fiber from one Purkinje cell to the next requires about 100 μsec. The two-dimensional structure of the Purkinje cell dendritic arborization prevents this delay from becoming blurred in time as the parallel fiber passes through the dendritic field, and the precise perpendicular arrangement of parallel fibers and Purkinje arborizations assures a maximum precision of timing. At this point, one can speculate on the functions of the cerebellar circuits in defining the precise timing of events (a pleasure that will be left to the reader).

Cerebellar Damage

The functions of the neocerebellum are revealed in patients with neurological damage to that area. Like patients with basal ganglia damage, these people too have a tremor—but an action tremor rather than a resting one. Patients appear normal when they are sitting quietly; they exhibit good posture and an alert look. As soon as they reach for something, though, the deficit appears. Typically, the patients will overreach, pull back too far, and oscillate for a while before homing in on the target. This symptom, called **ataxia,** is also revealed in difficulty with maintaining balance while walking. Ataxia appears in eye movement patterns too (Selhorst et al., 1976a). Patients have difficulty fixating a target because their eyes move too far in saccades; therefore, they must concentrate on each movement to execute it successfully.

Other symptoms of cerebellar damage include two types of speech disorders: slurring words together and breaking them into explosive bursts. Some lesions lead to a peculiar kind of **nystagmus** (repetitive eye movement); patients execute alternating saccades that are normal in their dynamics but have no purpose (Selhorst et al., 1976b). Each symptom results from a lesion in a different part of the cerebellum.

Contrast these movements with the grace and fluidity of movement in athletes and dancers. A ballet dancer trains for years, tuning the fast cerebellar circuits to perfection. When we enjoy the beauty of the dancing, it is primarily the cerebellum we are admiring; the muscles just do their duty slavishly. The cerebellum can fashion beautifully coordinated movements from gross action commands, but it cannot initiate actions; that function is carried out in the forebrain.

MOTOR CORTICES—THE IMAGE OF ACHIEVEMENT

Though motor functions are present in widespread areas of the cortex, they are concentrated in the classical motor cortex, just anterior to the somatosensory cortex. This area was among the first cortical areas to be discovered, because of the dramatic effects of stimulating it. Probably the first systematic stimulation studies were done by Fritsch and Hitzig (1870), who began, at night, in their apartment, stimulating the cortices of dogs. Then, during the Franco-Prussian war of 1871, they directly stimulated the exposed brains of wounded soldiers at battlefield hospitals. They found a regular relationship between the location stimulated and the movement of a part of the body. Stimulation yielded movement only in the small part of the cortex now known as the motor cortex; the motor homunculus (see Figure 7.23) looked similar to the sensory homunculus just behind it. The movements were generally smooth and coordinated, not the jerks one obtains from stimulating the muscles or their nerves. These studies led to the idea of the motor cortex being the executive that directs voluntary movement.

But there are at least two problems with the idea. First, subjects in stimulation studies never report an urge to move the affected body part. The movement happens by itself, as if the subject were observing it rather than performing it. This suggests that the motor cortex serves in executing movements but not in initiating them.

Second, even early neurophysiologists noted the paradox that we have already encountered in the somatosensory cortex: stimulation of the same place does not always result in the same movement. The homunculus seems to squirm about a bit on the surface of the cortex. The actual body movement produced depends on the present state of the motor system, the body's posture, the alertness of the subject, and some unknown factors. Further, damage to the motor cortex does not result in paralysis. Patients with unilateral damage can move smoothly and effortlessly on the intact side ipsilateral to the damage, but they must painstakingly think out each move on the contralateral side. It seems that something other than simple movement is coded in the motor cortex. How could these disturbing observations fit into the conventional conception of motor cortex function?

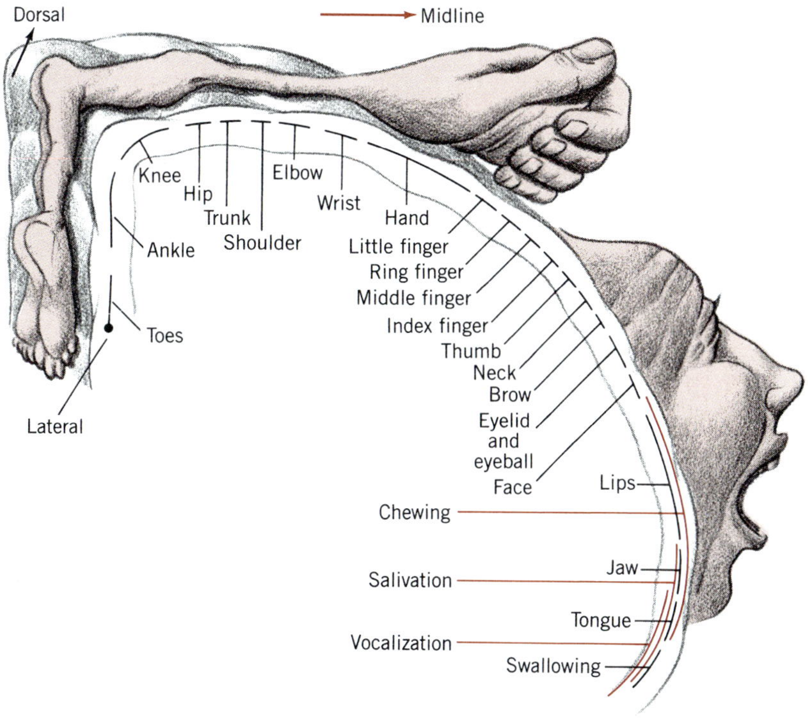

Figure 7.23 The homunculus on the motor cortex. Its topographic organization is similar to that of the sensory homunculus. Several other topographically organized motor areas are not illustrated.

Distributed Control

The idea of the precentral motor cortex being a master control center has now been rejected in favor of a more distributed view of motor control: that a large area of the cortex participates in the initiation of movements. Some of the studies that led to this new interpretation involved recording brain potentials from the scalps of humans while the humans performed voluntary motor activities (Kornhuber & Deecke, 1965). The instructions in these experiments were important; the subjects were told to lift a finger from a switch at a time they determined, but at irregular rather than rhythmic intervals. The switch release was then used as an event marker in averaging many trials. Figure 7.24 shows the slow change in electrical potential found over a wide area of both sides of the cortex; the change began as much as 800 msec before the movement started.

This event, the *Bereitschaftspotential* (German for "readiness potential"), was largest over precentral and parietal areas. (Widespread direct current, or DC, shifts—changes in steady voltage—such as these indicate a change in cortical excitability, a biasing of function. When the surface of the cortex becomes negative, the cortex is more excitable; it is easier for neurons to fire.) Then, about 50 msec before the switch was released, the area of potential change suddenly contracted to the motor cortex, to the finger area on the side contralateral to the motion. This was the motor potential itself.

Evidence from the *Bereitschaftspotential* is consistent with clinical experience. Patients with large bilateral lesions outside the primary sensory areas often show *apraxia*—the loss of the ability to perform skilled, aimed movements even though there is no paralysis. Patients afflicted with such lesions sometimes want to perform a voluntary action but can't get it started.

From these studies and others, Kornhuber (1974) concluded that the motor cortex is not the master initiator of voluntary movement. Rather, it performs a sophisticated somatosensory regulation of movement sequences that require close cooperation of the sensory and motor systems. Kornhuber found seven other pieces of evidence for this conclusion:

1. Somatic afferents form the largest sensory input

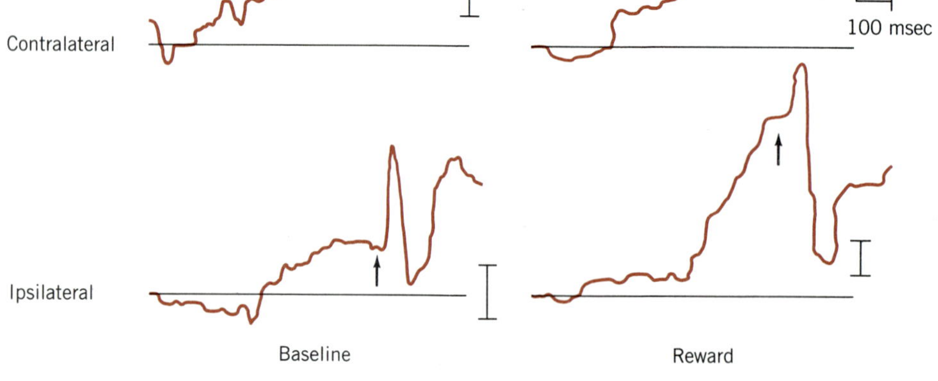

Figure 7.24 *A* Bereitschaftspotential *obtained from one subject. Recording is from the scalp, between an electrode near the vertex and a neutral reference. Using a convention of the older neurological literature, negative is up.* Contralateral *and* ipsilateral *refer to the position of the finger. The arrows represent the times of occurrence of the motor responses. The DC shift of the* Bereitschaftspotential *is a long-lasting deviation of the record from the baseline.*

to the motor cortex. (Vestibular afferents are next.)

2. The somatosensory and vestibular cortices are adjacent to the motor cortex.
3. These areas have the only direct corticocortical connections to the motor cortex.
4. There is a close quantitative correspondence between sensory and motor homunculi.
5. The only responses lost after removal of the motor cortex are those requiring somatic-motor coordination.
6. Eye movements, the only movements unrelated to somatic regulation, are not influenced by the motor cortex.
7. Conversely, finger movements—the movements that depend most on somatic feedback—are the most heavily corticalized.

These lines of evidence point to the motor cortex as a place where somatic and motor programs are coordinated. We can interpret the motor cortex as being not so much a driver of motor neurons as a sensory cortex for planned sequences of movements. The results of complex interactions throughout the cortex converge at the motor cortex for packaging and export to the muscles. The relationship of the somatosensory cortex and motor cortex might be similar to that of the primary and secondary visual cortex, for instance, in that the secondary area elaborates information flowing from the first. This may be the key to transforming actions into movements. If the motor cortex holds an image of the planned achievement (Pribram, 1971), close feedback relationships will be necessary to ensure that the intended action is being carried out.

Since the publication of the Pribram and the Kornhuber theories, in the early 1970s, other evidence consistent with their general conception has appeared. Sir John Eccles (1973) investigated the view of motor control as a distributed process. He found that the cortex, basal ganglia, and cerebellum show extended rhythmical activity before the initiation of a motor action. During the period of the *Bereitschaftspotential,* these areas "talk" to one another as though agreeing on the role of each in the upcoming action.

Another way to examine the function of the motor cortex is to stimulate it and record the results of the stimulation with electrodes. This method too shows a closer relationship between the precentral cortex and the somatosensory system than the old motor cortex theory predicted. The motor cortex turns out to be responsive to cutaneous stimuli, and the sensory and motor homunculi match; if stimulation of a cortical location results in the movement of a particular body part, stimulation of that body part yields a maximal electrical response in the cortex at the same location (Rosen & Asanuma, 1972). This provides a direct, topographic motor-cutaneous feedback.

Single-unit microelectrode studies of the precentral motor cortex lead to the same conclusion. The area is organized in much the same way as a sensory cortex; its cells respond to hair, touch, pressure, and joint stimuli (Welt et al., 1967). About three-fourths of the neurons have local receptive fields, and the rest have wide, or labile (changeable), fields. This organization is superimposed on a topographically uniform array of columns with a diameter of 0.1 to 0.4 mm.

The response of a neuron before and during movement in various directions can be measured to obtain a motor field that is similar to the receptive field of sensory neurons. Each neuron responds best to movement in an optimal direction but also responds to a rather large range of movements in other directions. During a movement, many neurons with different optimal directions are activated. When the activities of these neurons are added together, though, they indicate precisely the direction of the movement. In this way movement is coded in a population of neurons, not in any particular cell (Georgopoulos, Schwartz & Kettner, 1986).

In addition there is a second, supplementary motor area on the medial surface of the frontal lobe, just rostral to the primary motor area; the second area has a smaller homunculus. The word *supplementary* implies a subservient role for the area, but there is no evidence of subservience in the area. The second area appears to be connected in parallel with the primary motor area (Truex & Carpenter, 1964). The role of the area in humans remains a mystery; unilateral ablations produce no permanent deficits, either in posture or in the capacity to initiate movement (Penfield &

Rasmussen, 1950; Penfield & Welch, 1951). The area is consistently activated during motor activity, though.

Reflecting the variety of ways in which the motor cortex influences motor activity, outputs of the motor cortex include both indirect, polysynaptic extrapyramidal pathways and a direct "hot line" to the spinal motor neurons in the pyramidal system. (The pyramidal system will be discussed shortly.)

The Extrapyramidal System

The naming of the **extrapyramidal system** occurred by default. This is unfortunate, because the system constitutes the entire motor system in primitive vertebrates. It contains the majority of motor machinery even in primates. The extrapyramidal system consists of motor structures that are not part of the **pyramidal system**—the direct corticospinal neurons that run through the pyramids of the medulla. The motor cortex is considered part of both systems because it is closely linked with each of them. The extrapyramidal system is the older system evolutionarily, functioning to create the postural background on which other motor systems base their actions. This function is largely the responsibility of the basal ganglia, which are part of the extrapyramidal system. The system can also play a more active role, as shown by skilled movements that can occur after pyramidal tract sectioning (cutting).

The extrapyramidal system is tangled in both anatomy and nomenclature. It consists of the basal ganglia, along with motor portions of the thalamus and brain stem (see Figure 7.25). There is also an extrapyramidal motor pathway from the cortex to the spinal cord via the thalamus.

The Pyramidal System

The human pyramidal system was named after the pyramid-shaped motor tracts that are easily visible as they decussate (cross) on the ventral side of the medulla (see Figure 7.26). The system consists of a bundle of about 1 million fibers that originate from cell bodies in the cortex and descend all the way to the spinal motor neurons without synapsing. Everything else in the motor

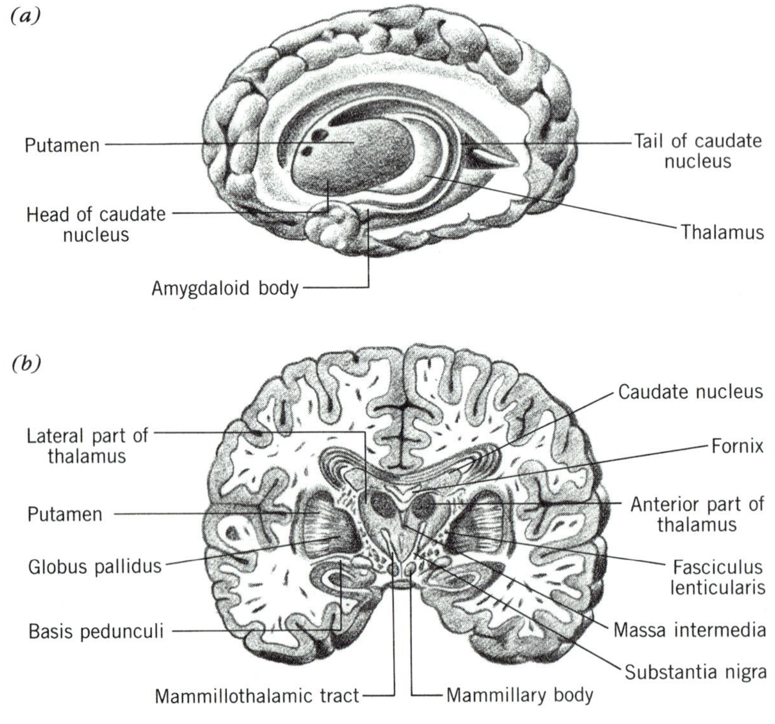

Figure 7.25 Major parts of the extrapyramidal motor system. (a) *Cutaway drawing with the cortex on one side removed.* (b) *Frontal section at the level of the vertical line in the cutaway. The rolled structure at the inferior medial end of the cortex is the hippocampus.*

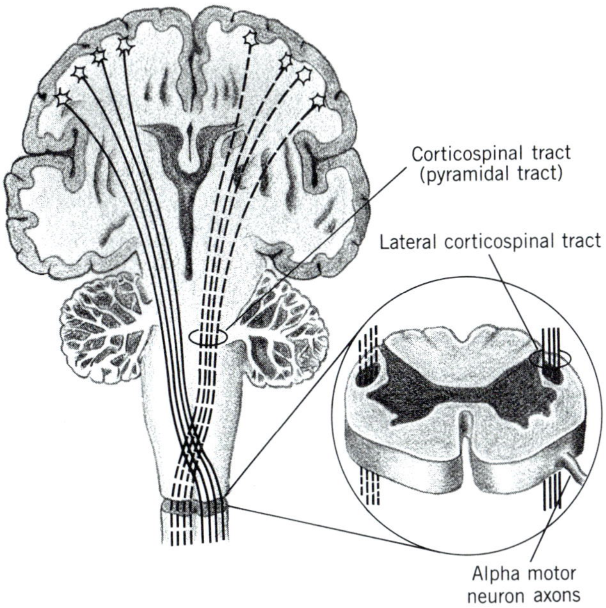

Figure 7.26 *Major parts of the pyramidal motor system. The corticospinal tract also makes extensive interconnections with subcortical motor nuclei. The tract consists mostly of large myelinated axons.*

system is extrapyramidal. The pyramidal system is the express train of the motor system, with large, fast myelinated fibers offering nonstop service directly to the last station on the final common path to the muscles. Some of the tract originates in the axons of the Betz cells—large pyramidal cells in the lower layers of the cortex. (The pyramidal cells are named for the shape of their somas and are not necessarily related to the pyramidal tracts.)

About two-thirds of the fibers originate not from motor cortex but from widespread areas of the cortex. They converge as they descend through the brain stem to cross at the pyramids of the medulla. About 20 percent of the fibers come from the postcentral somatosensory cortex. Part of the tract goes to the motor neurons of the cranial nerve nuclei (which correspond to the spinal neurons that serve the body). The spinal branch of the system is appropriately called the corticospinal tract.

The widespread origins of the pyramidal tracts justify the word *cortices* in the title of this section. Many parts of the cortex participate directly in the control of movement and action.

Function of the Pyramidal System. We can look at the effects of pyramidal sectioning in monkeys to infer the role of the pyramidal system in humans. The results are not as dramatic as one might expect; after a few weeks of recovery, posture and gross motor activity are normal. The only lasting deficits are limited to fine movements of the fingers and longer latencies with faster "fatigue." Pyramidal sectioned monkeys also have difficulty releasing things from the hands, though they can open the hands when climbing.

It is interesting to compare this set of deficits with the abilities of small children. Toddlers also have limited ability in fine finger coordination and seem to fatigue quickly, though the same muscles work long and hard in crawling and climbing. My infant daughter can grasp a cup and drink from it, but she often seems incapable of releasing it; instead she waves it around until something else catches her interest and the cup drops. Since myelination comes relatively late to the pyramidal tracts, the condition of the one-year-old might be seen as a natural experiment in extrapyramidal motor control.

Evolution of the Pyramidal System. Another way of understanding the role of the pyramidal tracts is to examine their evolutionary history. The pyramidal system is a relatively new system, first seen in mammals, and its tracts are more direct in primates than in other species. Even in the cat, pyramidal fibers terminate on spinal interneurons, whereas in primates they extend all the way to the motor neurons. Thus the cortex gains direct control over the muscles. The pyramidal tracts are no more prominent in humans than in other primates, though.

Using the differences in pyramidal anatomy in various mammalian species, Heffner and Masterson (1975) searched for correlates of dexterity. They found the depth of penetration of pyramidal fibers to be important; the farther down the spinal cord the fibers reached, the greater the animal's dexterity. Also helpful was ventral penetration of the fibers into spinal gray matter, toward the motor

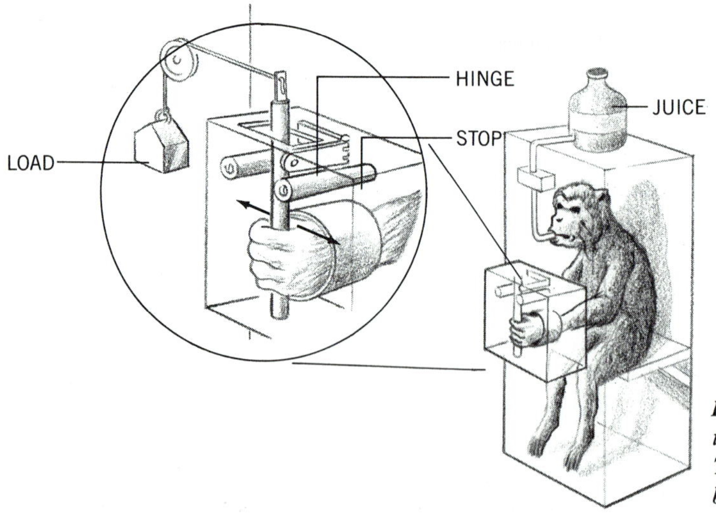

Figure 7.27 *Apparatus for determining the role of the motor cortex in motor activity (Evarts, 1968). The handle can move in only one dimension, but the resistance to movement can be changed by changing the weight at the left (inset).*

neurons. Other factors, such as the number and diameter of the fibers, did not make much difference. (A cow has more pyramidal fibers than does a rhesus monkey.) These data are consistent with the idea that the pyramidal system functions in fine coordination of the fingers and has other jobs as well.

Pyramidal Tract Activity during Movement. The most direct way to assess pyramidal function is to record from the neurons of the tract during various kinds of motor activity. This requires use of the implanted microelectrodes described earlier. Before the implantation surgery, monkeys were trained to move a lever to a stop, in the apparatus shown in Figure 7.27. Flexion and extension of the wrist were the only ways to move the lever. The monkeys were rewarded with grape juice for movements of the correct speed.

The first problem was to determine whether the cortical neurons under the microelectrode were part of the corticospinal tract. To find the right neurons, the experimenters looked for **antidromic responses** (action potentials conducted on axons in the direction opposite the normal physiological direction). They used the experimental scheme illustrated in Figure 7.28. Before recording began, they implanted stimulating electrodes in the pyramids of the medulla. If a cortical neuron responds to stimulation here with a short and constant latency, the cell's axon is being stimulated antidromically without an intervening synapse (Figure 7.28).

During the experiments, the monkeys' levers were loaded with various weights. This meant that the monkeys had to vary the force needed to perform the required movements. The frequency of firing in pyramidal tract neurons varied with the force of the movement but was less closely related to its extent. Most neurons consistently fired before the movement began, as Figure 7.29 shows. This pattern would be expected for a system involved in initiating movement (Evarts, 1968).

Most importantly, the neurons firing before the movement acted more vigorously if the resistance was expected to be large. The motor cortex anticipated the load, and the pyramidal neurons fired accordingly. The neural response corresponded to the amount of effort needed rather than to the amount of the resulting movement. Thus a form of motor memory was seen in these cells. The pattern was the reverse in the postcentral somatosensory area, where most neurons fired only after the start of the movement.

In later experiments, Evarts (1974) again demonstrated the special relationship between the motor cortex and the somatosensory system. Monkeys were trained to move the handle as quickly as possible after either a visual signal or a small movement of the handle. Visually triggered wrist move-

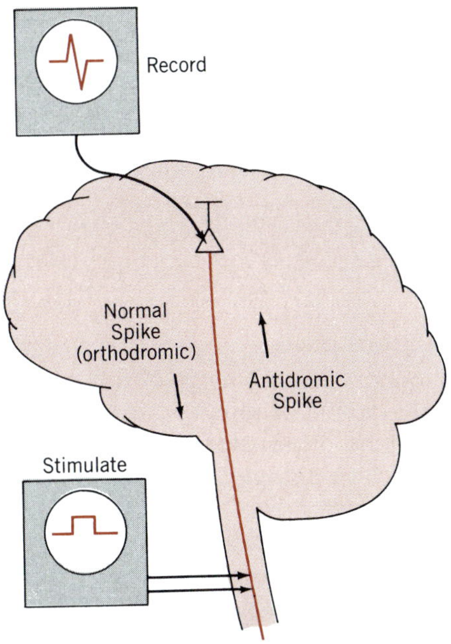

Figure 7.28 *Method for determining whether a cortical neuron sends an axon into the corticospinal (pyramidal) tract. Normal action potentials begin at the axon hillock and travel downward (orthodromic) in the diagram. An action potential initiated by electrical stimulation in the medulla travels in the direction opposite that of the natural one (antidromic), to be recorded by a microelectrode near the cortical cell. The latency is short because no synaptic transmission is involved. If the neuron generates an action potential near the time that the stimulation occurs, the orthodromic and antidromic action potentials will obliterate each other and no antidromic action potential will be recorded.*

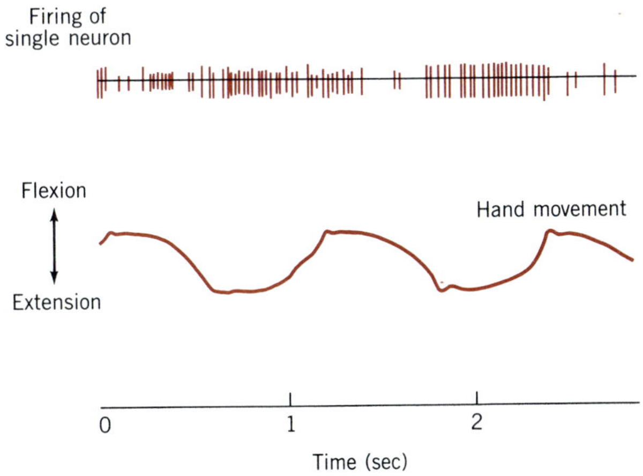

Figure 7.29 *Activity of a single pyramidal system neuron in the motor cortex during voluntary movement. Neurons beginning activity after the movement begins show a firing pattern similar to that of neurons beginning activity before the movement.*

ments had a latency of about 100 msec from visual stimulus to pyramidal activation; movements triggered by a perturbation of the handle had latencies as short as 25 msec. Further, activity in the postcentral region began before the response to the tactile stimulus but after the response to the visual stimulus. In the visual case, the activity was probably due to the sensory effects of the monkeys' motor responses. Quick response was possible in the tactile task because the sensory signals came directly to the postcentral somatosensory cortex. This cortex is in a good position to control movement; it is closely connected to the precentral motor cortex (as we have seen), and it is rich in neurons whose axons enter the pyramidal tract directly.

CONCLUSION—DISTRIBUTED MOTOR CONTROL

The command center of the motor system has slipped through our fingers. Just as there was no locus where higher sensory information converged, there is no master location where motor signals originate. The precentral cortex is only one of a number of specialized motor centers performing part of the task of organizing behavior. At the highest level, the lateral frontal cortex, in cooperation with other areas, governs the long-term organization of behavior and the setting of priorities (the evidence is in Chapter 16).

Specific acts originate in widespread areas of more posterior cortices, which have direct access to the pyramidal tracts. The acts are read into an image of achievement in the motor cortex—a set of goals that can be checked against cutaneous and muscular feedback. Simpler motor-tactile control of the same sort occurs in parallel in the red nucleus and the reticular formation, both of which

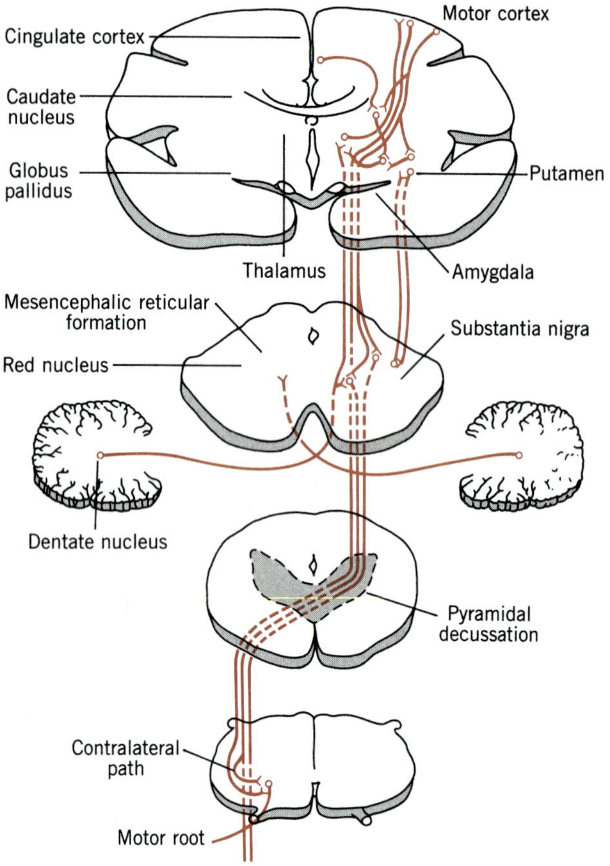

***Figure** 7.30 Summary of the main connections in the motor system, both extrapyramidal and pyramidal. Activity correlated with a voluntary movement can begin in the system several hundred milliseconds before the start of the movement; activity can also occur in brain areas not usually thought of as motor areas.*

receive input from the cerebellum and basal ganglia. The basal ganglia contribute slow ramp movements of variable speed and extent, and the neocerebellum generates the fast ballistic components needed for predictive control. Brain-stem and spinal mechanisms provide postural backgrounds and relieve the more rostral levels of the need to keep track of the details of muscle unit activation. The exception is the direct control of the motor cortex over highly skilled finger movements. The neural control of behavior consists largely of effects on receptor functions, both at the muscle level (with the gamma control loop) and at higher levels (with the close relationship between the somatosensory and motor systems). The anatomy is summarized in Figure 7.30.

In investigating the motor system, we have found that there is no such thing; most areas of the brain contribute to control of the muscles, and many of those areas participate in other functions as well. Just as earlier chapters traced sensory systems until the thread of the information flow was lost in the breadth of the cortex, this chapter has traced the source of motor organization from the opposite end of the stimulus-response pair. With both processes traced, we have not yet found a well-defined meeting point, for the large-scale integrations necessary to control behavior cannot be defined in strictly sensory or motor terms. It is time to attack the control systems directly.

CHAPTER SUMMARY

1. All behavior is expressed as muscle contractions and glandular secretions, collectively called the "final common path" of the nervous system. There are three kinds of muscle: striated, smooth, and cardiac. Striated muscle includes all skeletal muscles and most voluntarily activated muscles. Smooth muscle powers the viscera and other internal organs with slow but sustained contractions. Cardiac muscle is found only in the heart.

2. The contractile parts of muscles are made of actin and myosin—proteins that slide against each

other when the muscle contracts. Calcium ions enter the muscle fiber and cause molecular heads on the myosin filaments to attach to the actin strands and then bend, shortening the muscle. Most striated muscles can contract either with oxygen, using aerobic metabolism, or in an inefficient but high-capacity anaerobic mode that converts nutrients to poisons, which must later be removed. The fibers are specialized for either fast or slow contraction.

3. Muscles are innervated with specialized, enlarged cholinergic synapses—the neuromuscular junctions. These junctions invade deep furrows in the muscles, causing an action potential and a resulting contraction in a muscle fiber each time they fire. Each axon of a motor neuron innervates several fibers, the number depending on the fineness of control over the muscle. Inhibition briefly turns off each motor neuron following firing, so both low-threshold and high-threshold neurons contribute to contractions.

4. Muscles contain two kinds of fibers—extrafusal fibers to do the work of contraction and intrafusal fibers to detect muscle length. Sensory endings in the intrafusal fibers are of two types—one with a fast, phasic response and the other with a slower, tonic response. They send axons to excite extrafusal motor neurons in the spinal cord, contracting the muscle when it is passively stretched. This stretch reflex compensates for changes in load on the muscle. Tendon receptors detect muscle tension, inhibiting the motor neurons when tension becomes dangerously great.

5. The intrafusal fibers can contract through innervation of smaller gamma motor axons, biasing the responsiveness of the intrafusal sensory endings. In this way innervation from the brain to the gamma system can control muscle length; muscle tension is adjusted at the spinal level. With this arrangement the stretch reflex operates as a feedback check on muscle tension rather than as an inflexible contractor.

6. Motor structures organize muscle movements into acts defined in terms of their effects on the environment. Organization is hierarchical at the lower levels but largely cooperative at the highest level. Most muscles are organized in antagonistic pairs; while one is active, the other is inhibited by spinal feedforward circuits. At the spinal level, reciprocal organizations mediate such functions as withdrawal from pain, coordination of the limbs, and even scratching. These systems utilize direct neural connections among the motor neuron pools being coordinated.

7. The brain stem controls vegetative functions such as respiration, digestion, and heart modulation. A series of cranial nerves serve the head in the same way that spinal nerves serve the body. The reticular formation is involved in controlling the gamma motor system, adjusting set points for the gamma servo control loops in the muscles. Thus the tenseness or readiness of the muscles to respond is regulated.

8. The basal ganglia are subcortical forebrain nuclei reciprocally connected to both the cortex and the brain-stem motor structures. They generate slow ramp movements, with continuous variation of movement under feedback control, and they help regulate the spinal reflexes that mediate such activities as walking and controlling posture. Parkinson's disease, a disturbance of the basal ganglia, results in poorly controlled ramp movements and a resting tremor, which disappears when the cortex takes over motor control. L-dopa, a precursor of dopamine that crosses the blood-brain barrier, often relieves the symptoms by facilitating the dopaminergic neurons of the red nucleus.

9. Fast motor control requires the cerebellum, which is specialized for generating ballistic movements. The evolutionarily older parts of the cerebellum are related to vestibular action and to muscle tone; the larger, newer part coordinates voluntary movements. The system is a fast on-line computer, calculating muscle commands needed to execute a movement even while the movement is occurring. The cerebellum completes its functions within 30 msec. Saccadic eye movements, because they are ballistic, are good examples of movements coordinated by cerebellar circuits.

10. The old idea of the precentral motor cortex

as the master controller of the motor system is no longer accepted. Before a voluntary movement, electrical potentials appear in wide areas of the cortex, concentrating on the motor cortex shortly before the act commences. The precentral cortex helps coordinate the somatosensory and motor systems. It holds an image of achievement generated elsewhere and compares it with the progress in an act.

11. Most of the motor system is included in the extrapyramidal system, which mediates nearly all movements, including many skilled movements. The system includes a pathway from the cortex to the spinal cord via the thalamus. The pyramidal system consists of fibers from the cortex that descend directly to the spinal motor neurons. About a third of the fibers originate in the precentral motor cortex. The system controls movements requiring great dexterity. Thus there is no "highest" center of the motor system; rather, there is a distributed control by many brain areas.

KEY TERMS

Striated muscle
Smooth muscle
Cardiac muscle
Pacemaker region
Myosin
Actin complex
Sarcomere
Z-lines
Glycogen
Myoglobin
Tetanus
Treppe
Innervation ratio
Muscle unit
Recurrent collaterals
Renshaw cells
Gain
Stretch reflex
Extrafusal fiber
Intrafusal fiber
Golgi tendon organ
Alpha fibers
Gamma fiber
Electromyogram (EMG)
Reciprocal inhibition
Crossed-extensor reflex
Neostriatum
Dyskinesia
Red nucleus
Parkinson's disease
L-dopa
Archicerebellum
Paleocerebellum
Homunculus
Neocerebellum
Vermis
Nystagmus
Extrapyramidal system
Pyramidal system
Antidromic responses

SUGGESTED READINGS

Brooks, V. B. (1986). *The neural basis of motor control.* New York: Oxford University Press.

This book is a synthesis of physiology, neuroanatomy, kinesiology, and the psychology of motor control at the level of an advanced textbook. Throughout the book, the author considers questions of adaptation, motor learning, and guidance by the limbic system.

Cohen, C. (1975, November). The protein switch in muscle contraction. *Scientific American,* 36–45.

The role of calcium ions in initiating the interaction of action and myosin is described at the level of molecular interactions. The regulatory proteins troponin and tropomyosin play central roles.

Hoyle, G. (1983). *Muscles and their neural control.* New York: Wiley.

A strong point of this book is its wealth of micrographs demonstrating the great variety of muscles and neuromuscular control systems.

Kornhuber, H. (1974). Cerebral cortex, cerebellum, and basal ganglia: An introduction to their motor functions. In F. O. Schmitt & F. G. Worden, Eds., *The Neurosciences: Third Study Program* (pp. 267–280). Cambridge, MA: MIT Press.

This article introduces the idea that has since become the dominant interpretation of motor control and reviews the evidence for it.

Miller, G. A., Galanter, E., & Pribram, K. H. (1960). *Plans and the structure of behavior.* New York: Holt, Rinehart & Winston.

This was a seminal book in psychology, calling for a change in the analysis of organisms from a stimulus-response model to a feedback model. Reflexes and motor behavior, among other psychological functions, are reinterpreted in terms of feedback mechanisms.

Part III

CONTROL SYSTEMS

Chapter 8

HOMEOSTASIS

In studying control systems, we will first look at neurological systems engaged in the feedback control of internal body states. The goal of these systems is homeostasis, the maintenance of a stable internal environment. The term applies to systems dealing with temperature, water balance, nutrient balance, and several other functions. It is only against a homeostatic background that other, more active systems can function, and many of an animal's activities are motivated by homeostatic needs. Though the goal of these systems is simple, the strategies and mechanisms used are often surprisingly complex. Predictive feedforward control, feedback control, and several interacting levels of processing are required. The systems usually start with information from internal receptors.

Core Brain Receptors

In embryological development the brain stem originates from the ectoderm, on the outside of the embryo (see Figure 3.9). Later, the entire surface of the ectoderm becomes innervated with sensory endings. On the skin, these endings develop into the somatosensory system. In the remnant of ectodermal surface left on the inside of the brain stem, they become receptors tuned to the internal environment. Thus some outside receptors sense skin temperature, and the corresponding inside receptors are the sensors for the core brain temperature regulation mechanisms. Similarly, other receptors sense blood sugar (glucose) levels and osmotic pressure to control hunger and thirst. Still others sense blood carbon dioxide indirectly, by assessing the pH of the blood.

Some core brain receptors have become more specialized in the course of evolution. They detect not the chemical substances that might appear on the outside of the body, but those that occur only on the inside of the body. One example is the chemoreceptors that are sensitive to sex hormones, such as testosterone and estrogen, in the blood. Generally, the core brain receptors line the fourth ventricle—the rostral extension of the hollow core of the spinal cord. In the forebrain they are in the hypothalamus. Here again the principle of anatomical separation of antagonistic centers is preserved for such states as hunger and satiation.

TEMPERATURE BALANCE

Temperature control is a particularly good example of homeostasis, because it involves only a single, well-defined parameter and because the evolution of the human temperature control system is relatively clear (Satinoff, 1978). Before animals emerged from the sea, there was no reason to regulate internal temperature. The temperature of the surrounding water was nearly constant night and day, and it would have taken extraordinary amounts of energy to try to increase the internal body temperature while countering the very effective transfer of heat to the water. The only temperature-regulating creatures now inhabiting the sea are the whales and porpoises that returned there after a long period of evolutionary adaptation to land.

The first amphibians to colonize the land encountered both the problem of temperature regulation and opportunities to solve it. The problem arose because temperatures on land vary a good deal more than those in the sea. In most climates an animal without some form of regulation would be alternately baked and frozen. The solution came from the fact that air is a good insulator, so animals could keep their temperature more constant than that of the environment. Cold air will cool an animal, but it will not drain so much heat that the animal cannot warm itself.

ECTOTHERMS

The behavioral adaptations of the amphibians make them **ectotherms** (*ecto* is Greek for "external," and *therm* is Greek for "temperature"). They are not cold-blooded, but they adjust their temperatures as best they can by finding an appropriate microenvironment.

The best-developed ectotherms are the reptiles. In terms of temperature regulation they are largely solar-powered animals, taking advantage of sunlight or of places warmed by sunlight to gain heat. A desert lizard, for instance, is too cold to be active in the early morning. Its movements are stiff and its reactions slow. It must sit in the sun for a while, as in Figure 8.1, absorbing enough heat to raise its internal temperature into the range where it can actively go about its business. As the desert heats up, the lizard prefers to orient into the sun, minimizing the amount of body surface exposed to the warming rays. Later it seeks shady spots. Temperatures differ by a surprising amount between areas only a few meters apart, and the reptile cannot remain long in spots that are too hot or too cold. In extremely hot climates the lizard may have to seek refuge by burying itself in cooler sand, remaining active only in early morning and late afternoon when temperatures are tolerable. Reptiles prefer an internal temperature of about 37° C, the same temperature that birds and mammals maintain.

Many reptiles also have other means for adjusting temperature. One of them is the ability to modify the insulating capacity of the skin through peripheral vasomotor changes. The reptile can open blood vessels in the skin to heat or cool itself and close them to insulate the body. This ability may have evolved because of an entirely different problem faced by the early amphibians—precursors of the reptiles. Amphibians have poorly

***Figure 8.1** Behavioral regulation of temperature in a lizard. It is thought that the large size attained by some dinosaurs may have resulted in a body heat sink large enough that the animal could maintain a stable internal temperature near the average daily temperature, losing heat at night and gaining it during the day.*

developed lungs; they rely on vessels close to their moist skins to exchange gases directly with the environment. Vasoconstrictors and vasodilators in the skin vessels help regulate the process. In reptiles, with their thicker, more impermeable skins, this mechanism serves temperature regulation by coming under the control of thermoreceptors in the hypothalamus and other brain areas (Cowles, 1958). As the reptiles evolved, an existing system acquired a new function.

The reptilian solution to the problem of thermoregulation is an economical one. Since the energy for maintaining temperature comes from outside, the reptile need not consume food that will be burned in maintaining body temperature. Consequently, a reptile can survive on about one-eighth of the food needed by a bird or mammal of the same size.

The problem with this system is that in many environments it doesn't work very well. Frequently, there is not enough energy in the environment to warm the reptile up to a working temperature, and the animal must remain in a state of **torpor** (inactivity because of low body temperature). The reptile's enzyme systems—its biochemical machines of life—must be adapted to keep the animal alive even at low temperatures. As a result, they don't work as efficiently as a mammal's more specialized enzyme systems at higher body temperatures. Mammals and birds have solved these problems, but at a cost.

ENDOTHERMS

For mammals and birds, a more effective temperature control system evolved. These animals, the **endotherms** (*endo* is Greek for "internal"), regulate their own metabolic rates to create heat internally. A far more precise and consistent degree of temperature regulation is the result, and the endotherms take advantage of it. Their specialized enzyme systems are very effective but work only in a narrow range around their **set point**—the internal temperature standard that homeostatic heating and cooling mechanisms strive to maintain. The core body temperature in most endotherms is allowed to vary by only a few tenths of a degree. This small range around the set point is the **neutral zone;** as long as temperature remains within this zone, the animal makes no efforts at heating or cooling.

As a result of their temperature regulating abilities, mammals and birds are capable of higher sustained rates of metabolic output; that is, they can remain more active and for longer periods than reptiles can. Most vertebrates can sustain a metabolic output about 10 times their resting rates (their metabolic rates during rest), so endotherms, with their higher resting rates, can also achieve higher peak outputs. Reptiles can "sprint" at high energy rates for a few seconds or minutes, but they must do it with anaerobic metabolism in the muscles, borrowing energy from a forced inactivity during recovery. In a long-distance chase, an endotherm will always catch an ectotherm.

Endotherms retain all of the thermoregulatory behaviors of ectotherms. They use environmental energy for heat when needed and lose energy to the environment when they are too warm. Their metabolic regulation resembles that of a furnace added to a solar-heated house.

A thermostat analogy describes the feedback systems that enable endotherms to achieve precise temperature control. The analogy is a good one, but it is limited because the thermoregulation of animals is far more sophisticated than the thermoregulation of homes. For the house model of thermoregulation to be more realistic, the house would have to interact with the outside environment in a more sophisticated way. Feedback mechanisms might open the shutters on south-facing windows on sunny days to let solar energy heat the inside. Other feedback mechanisms might close the shutters on hot days for cooling and might even open the windows when the inside of the house is too hot and the outside is cooler.

Like the animal's thermostat, the house's thermostat has a neutral zone, in which no effort at heating or cooling is necessary (see Figure 8.2). In regions above and below that zone, active thermoregulation is initiated. But to approach the complexity of the endotherm's thermoregulation, the house would need feedforward as well as feedback systems. Feedforward control works on the anticipation of future temperature changes. For instance, the house can be equipped with a device that turns on the furnace whenever the front door is open and the outside temperature is cold. In-

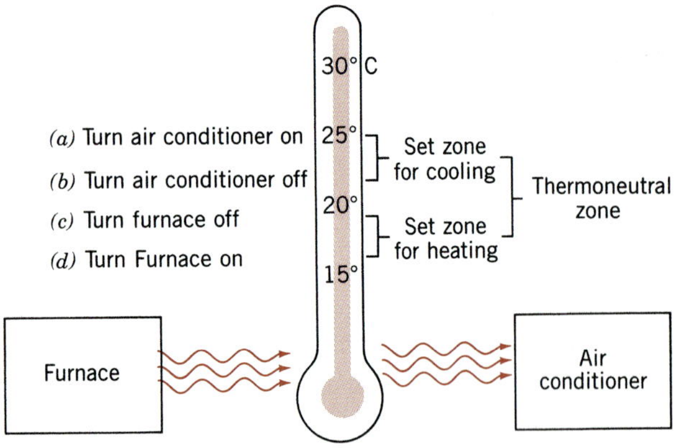

Figure 8.2 *Feedback regulation of a furnace and air conditioner by a temperature sensor. When the temperature is in the thermoneutral zone, neither heating nor cooling is activated. A hysteresis (nonlinear response) is built into the system. When the temperature is dropping, the furnace is not turned on until the lowest level* (d) *is reached; but when the temperature is rising, the furnace stays on until the higher level* (c) *is attained. If* (c) *and* (d) *were the same temperature, the furnace would be turned on and off too frequently. A similar hysteresis occurs at higher temperatures for the air conditioner.*

stead of waiting for the house to cool, this system could prevent a temperature drop. Gadgets to adjust the furnace need not be linked together except to share a common set point so they won't work against each other. In animals, behavioral heat regulation can be driven by peripheral receptors alone; animals leave very hot or very cold environments before the core body temperature begins to change.

Control Mechanisms

As in the well-equipped house, temperature regulation in endotherms involves many mechanisms and many controllers. The master controller is in the anterior hypothalamus. The **preoptic area**—the area anterior to the optic chiasm (and having nothing to do with vision)—is just rostral to the anterior hypothalamus. The preoptic area governs both heat production and heat conservation (Satinoff & Henderson, 1977). Experimentally, heating an animal's preoptic area with tiny implanted thermocouples causes the animal to pant or sweat even if the body is cool. Cooling the area induces shivering, an increase in heart rate, and peripheral vasoconstriction— regardless of body temperature. The goal of thermoregulation, then, is to keep thermoreceptors in the hypothalamus warm! (This is an oversimplification, but a useful one.)

Though local hypothalamic temperature changes evoke both behavioral and autonomic responses, lesion studies have shown that the two types of regulation are separated anatomically. Rats with small lateral hypothalamic lesions showed normal activity and motivation and could regulate their temperatures metabolically. But for many weeks after the lesions were made, they would not press a bar to get heat (Satinoff & Shan, 1971; Van Zoeren & Stricker, 1977). Rats with preoptic lesions learned to turn on heat lamps and cooling fans appropriately, even though they had no autonomic control over temperature. They would have faced certain death without their behavioral responses (Lipton, 1968).

The brain stem contains phylogenetically older temperature control centers that have come under hypothalamic control in endotherms but that can still function independently if their connections with the hypothalamus are severed. Roberts and Mooney (1974) could elicit three separate heat-loss strategies in rats by heating various locations in the diencephalon (forebrain) and mesencephalon (midbrain). They passed high-frequency current through electrodes, gently heating the surrounding tissue. (The principle is similar to that used in microwave ovens.) Stimulated at certain locations, the rats would groom themselves, cooling themselves with their saliva. Stimulated at other locations, they would move about actively; and at still other locations, they would lie quietly in a sprawled position. The responses were not due to accidental stimulation of cells other than thermal detectors; when the same cells were stimulated electrically without heat, completely different behaviors, such as rolling and eye closing, appeared.

Other thermoregulatory centers are located in the spinal cord. But their neutral zone is so large (2° to 3° C) that an animal would die if they were the only control centers. In intact animals, these centers control thermoregulatory responses only at times of extreme thermal stress. The characteristics of the three thermoregulatory centers (the hypothalamus, the brain stem, and the spinal cord) are shown in Figure 8.3. Because the hypothalamus has the narrowest neutral zone, it controls thermoregulation under normal conditions.

The biochemical control of temperature involves endorphins, for endorphins injected directly into the hypothalamus induce the lowering of body temperature (Martin & Bacino, 1978). To show that the temperature response is a result of the injection mimicking normal receptor activity (rather than of some toxic or other pathological response of the organism to the drug), researchers administered the opiate antagonist naloxone to rats. Normal thermoregulatory responses to heat and cold stress were disrupted (Holaday et al., 1978). The relationship of endorphins and temperature control is not surprising, for endorphins are important in mediating pain, and the pain and temperature senses are closely related in anatomy and embryology. Pain and temperature fibers ascend together in the spinal cord and brain stem.

Fever

When bacteria or viruses invade the body, the internal temperature sometimes rises several degrees above the ideal set point of 37° C. Is this a result of the disease or of the body's response to it? Recent evidence indicates that the temperature elevation is part of the body's active bacteria- and virus-fighting system working with the immune system to repel the invaders.

Elevated temperature is toxic to animal cells and to many enzyme systems, but it is even more toxic to bacteria. Bacteria that infect rabbits, for instance, grow poorly with a combination of high temperature and low iron concentration (iron concentration in the blood is reduced during fever) (Kluger & Rothenburg, 1979).

The high-temperature defense is not limited to endotherms. During infections, ectothermic animals such as baby rabbits (whose metabolic thermoregulation function has not yet developed) and even iguanas will seek a higher-temperature environment if one is available (Bernheim & Kluger, 1976).

A fever begins when small proteins known as **pyrogens** (*pyro* is Greek for "fire," and *gen* is Greek for "to make") are given off by bacteria. The pyrogens affect the temperature-regulating centers of the anterior hypothalamus and preoptic area, raising the set point. The bacteria aren't committing suicide, though; the proteins are by-products of normal bacterial metabolism that the hypothalamus uses to detect infection.

When the set point suddenly increases, warm-

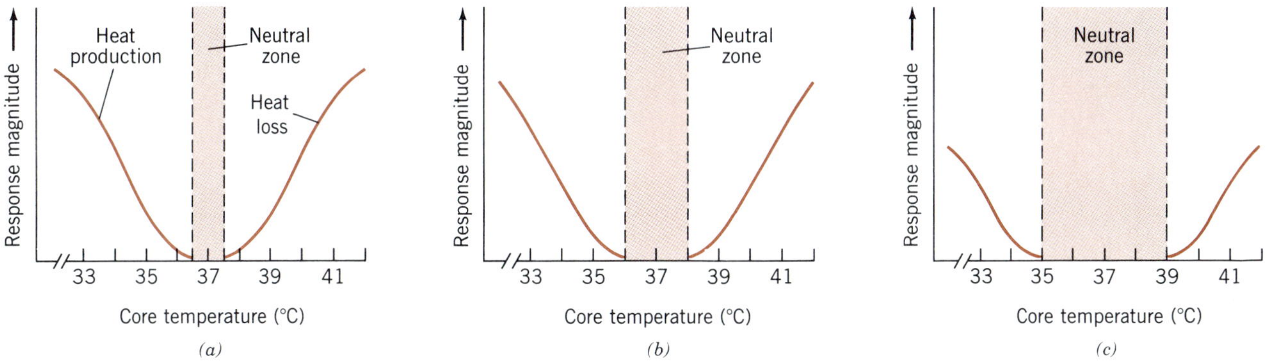

***Figure 8.3** Temperature ranges of three thermoregulatory regions.* (a) *Hypothalamus.* (b) *Brain stem.* (c) *Spinal cord. Each graph shows the amount of energy expended for thermoregulation at a given temperature. The neutral zone, where no energy is required, is at the center of each graph. Normally, hypothalamic control prevents body temperature from deviating from the neutral zones of the brain stem and spinal cord.*

ing behaviors and metabolic mechanisms are abruptly mobilized. When we are fighting off infections, we have "chills" even though our bodies are warmer than usual. Later, when the bacteria are defeated and the fever breaks, we feel hot, feverish, and sweaty until the body core temperature returns to normal. During the fever we risk convulsions and delirium from impaired CNS functioning, but the effects of unchecked bacteria are even more serious. This natural experiment shows the importance of precise temperature regulation to normal functioning in endotherms.

Strategies of Thermoregulation

Because endotherms use much of their energy to maintain body temperature, it is important that they manage heat as efficiently as possible. The problem is more acute for the young of any species, whose body surface to volume ratios are higher. Figure 8.4 shows how a growing animal's surface increases in proportion to the square of its length, whereas its weight increases with the cube of its length. Heat loss varies with surface area, and metabolic heat production varies with volume.

Heating. Rat pups limit their energy use by remaining ectothermic for some days after birth; they are heated by their mother, who periodically visits them (Alberts, 1978). Between maternal visits they remain warm by huddling together, staying in a tighter clump if the temperature is colder. Human babies cannot use this strategy; instead, they are endothermic from a few hours after birth and are richly endowed with brown fat, a specialized tissue that is metabolized for heat production. The chubby little cheeks and chubby little arms of the human baby are vital to its survival; they are the deposits of brown fat. This fat is so specialized for heat production that it cannot be metabolized to provide food; an infant can starve and still be unable to break down its brown fat reserves.

Other animals use a wide variety of strategies to keep warm or cool. The arctic fox, for instance, with its thick fur, is an insulation specialist, to the delight of fur hunters and the misfortune of the fox. The shrew keeps warm solely by virtue of its enormous metabolic output, even though it is small (with a high surface to volume ratio) and nearly hairless. Shrews eat almost constantly to maintain their high activity rates. A few animals conserve heat through their sheer bulk. The elephant has almost no hair because it has almost no need for heat conservation in its tropical environment. The only endotherms that spend all their lives in the sea, the whales, have responded to the heat-transfer properties of water by developing a huge bulk and thick insulating blubber.

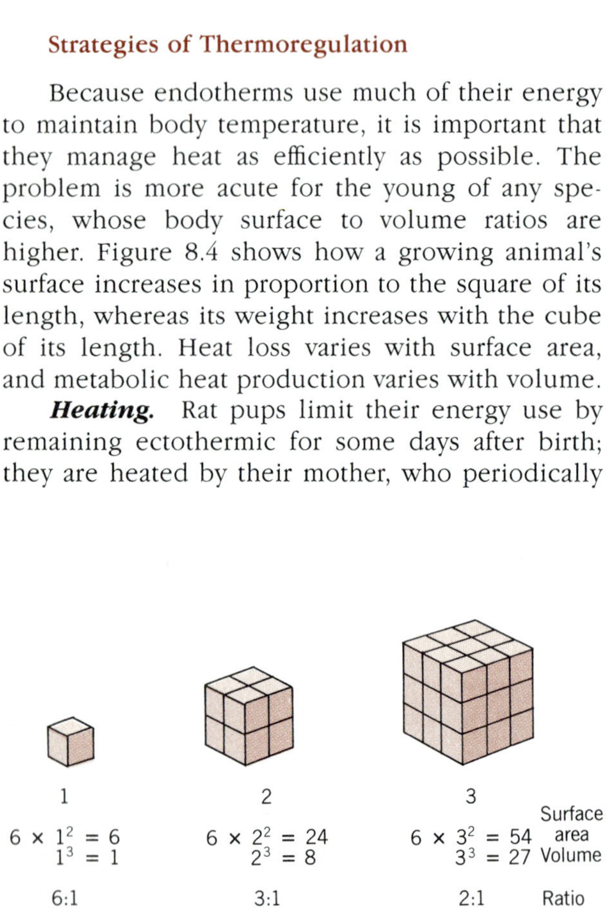

Figure 8.4 *Change in surface to volume ratio as an animal increases in size. For a cube-shaped (six-sided) animal, surface = length × width × 6. Volume = length × width × depth. Another way to change the surface to volume ratio is to change the shape. Several animal families have species in both tropical and cold climates; the cold-dwelling species are more compact than the tropical ones.*

Cooling. When cooling rather than heating is necessary, all animals act like ectotherms. Because animals do not reduce their basal metabolic rates for cooling, they can use only behavioral means to lose heat. Specialized heat-loss mechanisms sometimes concentrate on cooling the brain even at the expense of other body parts. This is the case with the rete mirabile (Latin for "net miraculous")—the brain heat exchanger colorfully named by Galen in the second century A.D. (see Figure 8.5). The rete mirabile bathes the finely branched cerebral arteries in cooler venous blood coming from the nasal surfaces (Baker, 1979). On a hot day this brain cooler can keep a dog active, while the rabbit it is chasing, without much of a cooler, dies from overheating of the brain.

But the most sophisticated thermoregulation for both heating and cooling comes from human behavior. Our clothing is a successful thermoreg-

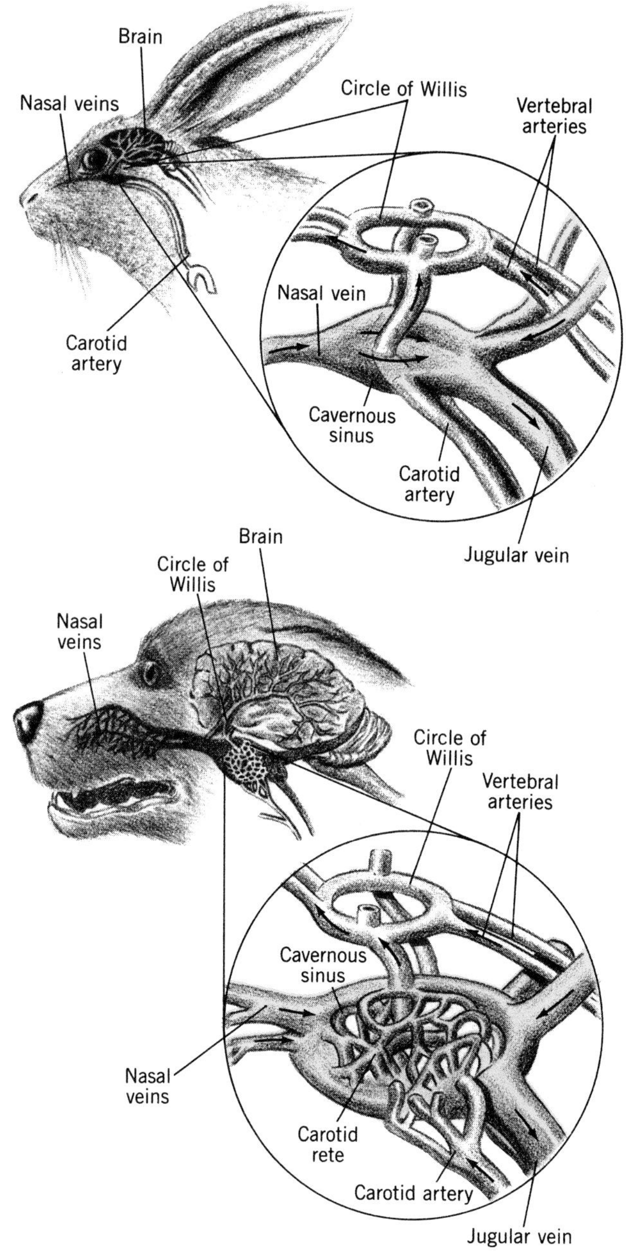

Figure 8.5 *The simple rete mirabile of the rabbit and the more elaborate one of the dog. Blood in the nasal veins is cooled by the evaporation of fluids in the nearby nasal mucosa and cools arterial blood moving from the heart to the circle of Willis. The two kinds of blood do not mix. A similar heat exchanger conserves heat in arctic birds by cooling arterial blood going into the legs and warming venous blood returning from the legs.*

ulatory device, enabling us to live in an enormous variety of climates. It minimizes the thermal demands on metabolism and remains flexible enough to be changed quickly, unlike fur or feathers, when we move from one environment to another. Regulation of internal temperature by clothing is usually a feedforward process: you button your coat before going out in the cold. Of course, the house and its thermostat, with its feedback control, are also aspects of human thermoregulation, built by humans to maintain thermoneutral temperatures regardless of the climate. The house and its occupant are linked in thermoregulation (see Figure 8.6). Thus the house is more than a metaphor; it is part of the human thermoregulatory system. Its external feedback adds to our internal feedback systems in an extension of the hierarchy of control. Since these higher-level thermoregulatory strategies are governed by cortical mechanisms, perhaps there is some truth to the tongue-in-cheek assertion that the function of the cortex is to keep the hypothalamus warm.

FLUID BALANCE

As was the case with temperature, the earliest creatures had no problem with fluid balance. Living in primitive seas, their internal fluids matched the external salt content and osmotic pressure of the sea. Water could flow freely between them and their environment. In higher organisms, especially land animals, the problem becomes more complicated. Land animals must carry their primitive sea with them. Replenishment is not always available; and if it is, the organism must decide when and how much to drink. We will see that these decisions, like those for thermoregulation, involve both feedback and feedforward mechanisms.

Water balance is also interesting because it shows the limitations of introspection in understanding body and brain processes. Who could guess from analyzing feelings that there are two kinds of thirst, driven by different physiological needs and controlled by different neural and hormonal systems? To see why thirst needs two

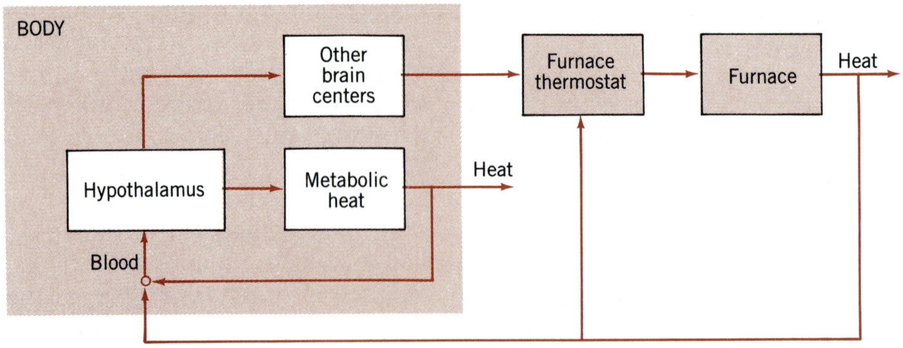

Figure 8.6 *Feedback control loops in indoor thermoregulation. The small loop within the "body" box is the natural homeostasis. The loop on the right, going from the furnace to the thermostat, is an automatic control system that is independent of moment-to-moment human intervention. The two loops are linked into a single large thermoregulatory loop by furnace heat reaching the human at the bottom of the diagram and by human adjustment of the thermostat at the top. Similar diagrams might be drawn for clothing and other human thermoregulatory systems.*

control systems will require a digression into physiology.

FLUID COMPARTMENTS IN THE BODY

We think of most of our body fluid as being blood, because of the dramatic result of cutting the skin (one experiment I don't advise). In fact, however, only about 7 percent of the body's fluid is blood plasma; two-thirds is intracellular, and the rest fills the interstitial (extracellular) spaces between the cells (see Figure 8.7).

The body maintains a homeostatic balance among the three fluid compartments, which is controlled partly by passive forces and partly by hormones directed by the CNS. Interaction between the circulatory and the interstitial compart-

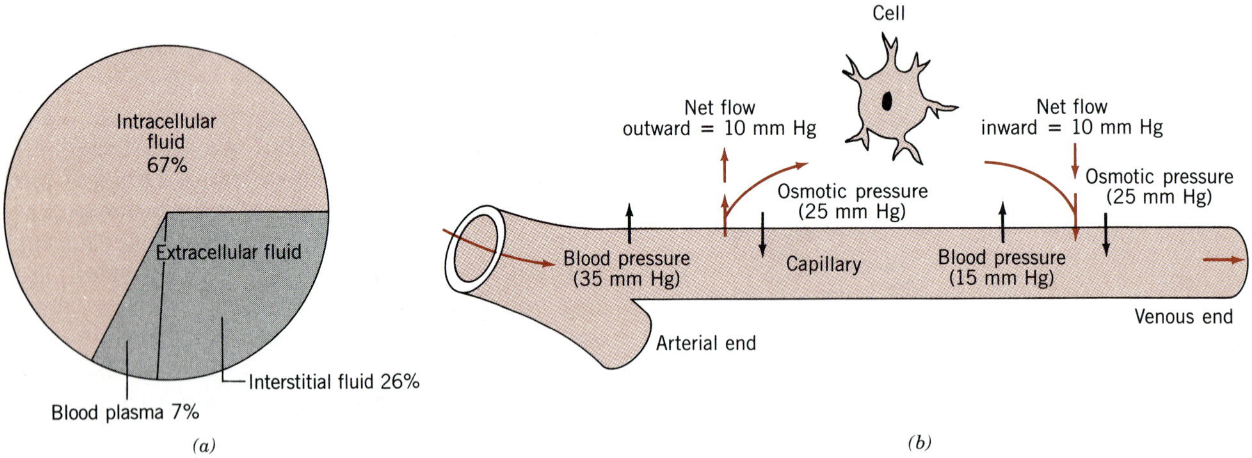

Figure 8.7 *Body fluid balance.* (a) *Percentage volume of the three fluid compartments of the body.* (b) *Interactions between the fluid compartments. Osmotic pressure, based on the difference in concentrations of dissolved matter in the blood and in the interstitial fluid, remains nearly constant because only a small proportion of the water in the blood leaves the capillaries. Blood pressure decreases from left to right in the figure because of the high resistance of the narrow capillary to blood flow.*

ments takes place at the capillaries, where vessel walls become very thin and permeable to water. Blood cells and the larger proteins of the plasma cannot pass through the capillary walls. The presence of proteins means that the concentration of water is slightly lower in the capillaries than in the interstitial spaces. Water will tend to flow from the region of its higher concentration (outside the vessels) to the region of its lower concentration (inside the vessels). The concentration difference is called the **osmotic gradient,** and the tendency of water to diffuse to a region of lower concentration is an **osmotic pressure.**

In blood vessels, the inward osmotic pressure is countered by blood pressure from the heart. At the arterial end of a capillary (see the left side of Figure 8.7*b*), the outward blood pressure exceeds the inward osmotic pressure. Fluid flows from the blood into the interstitial space. By the time the blood reaches the venous end of the capillary (see the right side of Figure 8.7*b*), the pressure has been reduced by the resistance of the capillary until the inward osmotic pressure exceeds the blood pressure. Here fluid enters the vessel again, establishing a microcirculation of fluid. The osmotic pressure remains the same, but the blood pressure decreases as it goes from left to right in Figure 8.7*b*.

Since water passes freely through cell membranes, the interstitial fluid and the intracellular fluid remain in osmotic balance. Changes in the concentration of dissolved matter in the interstitial fluid are countered by changes in cellular volume until equilibrium is restored. Thus the three fluid compartments of the body (blood, extracellular space, and intracellular space) are closely related.

Now we can look at the two kinds of thirst. Dehydration inside cells leads to cell shrinkage and osmotic thirst, and reduction of fluid volume in the blood and interstitial compartments leads to volumetric thirst.

INTRACELLULAR FLUID AND OSMOTIC THIRST

The body is always losing water. There is evaporation from the sweat glands (to cool the skin), urine production in the kidneys, evaporation from the lungs, and saliva and other digestive juices entering the digestive tract—which is topologically outside the body (from inside the gut, you can get to the outside without crossing any membrane). All of these processes except urine production increase the concentration of salts in the body's fluids, for although water leaves the body, most dissolved salts stay behind. Frequently, we make things worse by eating salty foods, further increasing the need to take in water for restoring osmotic balance.

Regulation of the body's salt balance is a fairly direct process, involving physical rather than hormonal mechanisms. The first step in investigating salt regulation took place in the 1930s. Gilman and his associates injected solutions of controlled osmotic strength into the bodies of dogs. The solutions were **hypertonic** (*hyper* is Greek for "over," and *tonic* is Greek for "steady")—having a greater osmotic strength than the body fluids. (Any NaCl solution with a concentration greater than 0.87 percent is hypertonic.) The injections of hypertonic saline induced drinking in the dogs, but injections of urea at the same osmotic strength led to only half as much drinking (Gilman, 1937).

Analysis of these results can reveal both the stimulus for osmotic thirst and the location of the receptors. Na^+ crosses easily between the blood and the interstitial fluid, but it cannot enter cells (recall the Na^+ pump of Chapter 2). Therefore, Na^+ in the interstitial fluid draws water out of the cells by osmosis, and cell shrinkage results, producing thirst. This explains how the hypertonic saline had its effect.

The situation is different with urea because the cell membrane is permeable to it. The osmotic pressures of the intracellular and interstitial fluids rise together following a urea injection, remaining in balance. The fact that urea induces some thirst is attributable to its failure to cross the blood-brain barrier. (As a waste product of protein metabolism, urea is excluded from the brain. See Reed & Woodbury, 1962.) The urea in the body draws water from the brain by osmosis, slowly dehydrating the receptor cells there.

Osmotic Receptors. Further localization of the osmotic receptors, by lesion studies and by direct application of hypertonic NaCl solutions, showed them to be located in the hypothalamus. There are two sets of anatomically separated receptors, each controlling a different physiological response to osmotic stress.

The receptors can be stimulated through a **cannula,** a hollow needle implanted in a target area of the brain during surgical anesthesia. The cannula is fastened to the skull with screws and a bit of acrylic cement. After the animal recovers from the anesthetic, a small amount of hypertonic NaCl solution can be injected through the cannula. The amount injected is so small that it has effects only in the immediate region of the cannula. A long series of cannulation studies has shown that most of the sites that cause drinking are located in the preoptic area of the hypothalamus, near the midline (Peck & Blass, 1975).

The second set of receptors controls water retention by the kidneys. Activation of these receptors leads indirectly to the secretion of **antidiuretic hormone (ADH),** also called **vasopressin,** in the posterior pituitary gland. This hormone passes into the bloodstream, stimulating the kidneys to produce more concentrated urine. The kidneys function by filtering blood to produce plasma, much like the capillaries, and then reabsorbing water and other useful constituents, leaving waste products behind. ADH increases the reuptake of water before the concentrated plasma is passed to the bladder as urine.

The receptors governing ADH secretion are in a tiny and obscure part of the hypothalamus called the **nucleus circularis,** which consists of a group of only about 275 neurons on each side of the brain; it is one of the smallest functional units found in any vertebrate brain. The cells lie in a rich capillary bed. A surrounding tight tube of heavily myelinated fibers (see Figure 8.8) isolates them from the general interstitial brain space (Hatton, 1976). Electrical stimulation of the nucleus circularis produces water retention.

EXTRACELLULAR FLUID AND VOLUMETRIC THIRST

Blood volume must be carefully regulated, for an adequate supply of venous blood is necessary to passively fill the left atrium of the heart—the first chamber of the heart encountered by blood returning from the body. The job of the left atrium is to fill the left ventricle—the powerful muscle that squirts the blood through the lungs. Without a blood flow to prime the pump of the heart, cardiac efficiency is impaired. This impairment can lead to further decreases in ventricular filling and ultimately to a positive feedback cycle ending in heart failure and death. Extensive bleeding from hemor-

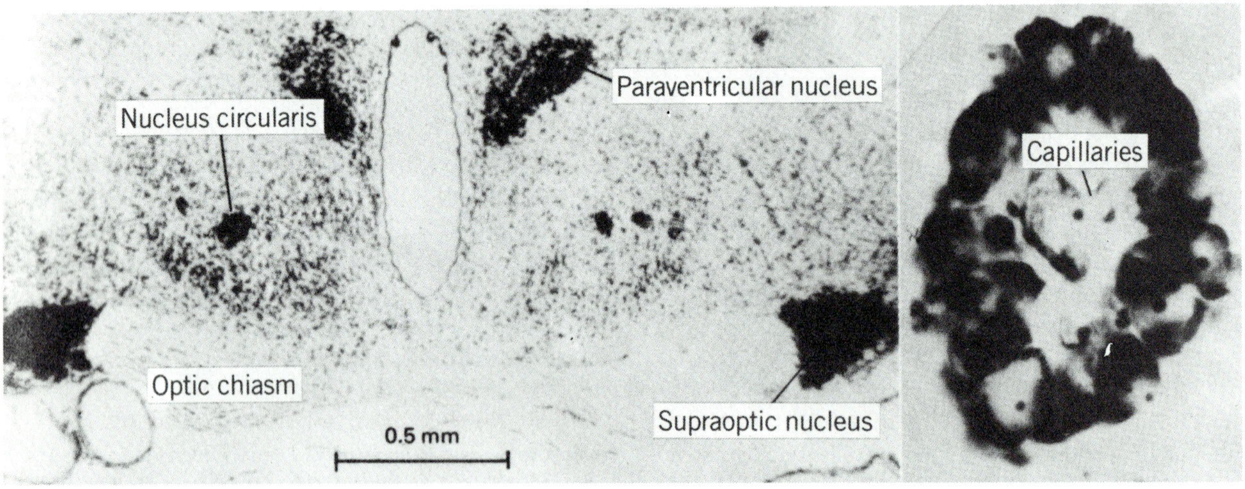

Figure 8.8 *The anatomy of the nucleus circularis in the hypothalamus. Myelin is stained dark in this preparation.*

rhage or external injury requires quick restorative action to keep the heart functioning. On a less dramatic scale, the action of the kidneys can reduce blood volume to dangerous levels under some conditions.

The response to blood-volume stress begins at **baroreceptors** (pressure receptors) in the veins and the left atrium, which initiate a complex series of hormonal and neural events. Muscles in the walls of the veins contract to reduce the volume of the circulatory system, and ADH is secreted in the posterior pituitary to minimize reduction in blood volume from urine production.

Another set of hormonal responses was seemingly well understood by the early 1970s. Now, however, the story is more complicated and the mechanisms are less understood.

Hormonal Control. Let us look first at the hormonal events triggered by **hypovolemia** (*hypo* is Greek for "under," and *volemia* is Greek for "volume"). Baroreceptors cause the kidneys to release the hormone **renin** through a still-unknown neural pathway, and the kidneys themselves produce renin in a direct response to hypovolemia. Renin in turn initiates the synthesis of **angiotensin I** (*angio* is Greek for "blood vessel," and *tensin* is Greek for "tension" or "pressure"). Angiotensin I is then converted to angiotensin II through a minor biochemical change. Angiotensin II, a small polypeptide of only eight amino acids, and raises blood pressure and constricts the veins. All of this occurs in the body, outside the brain. When angiotensin II is injected into water-satiated rats, they start drinking. Furthermore, very small amounts of the hormone are effective in eliciting the drinking response when the hormone is injected through a cannula into the preoptic area of the hypothalamus (Epstein, Fitzsimons & Rolls, 1970). This line of research initially led to the reasonable conclusion that angiotensin II combated hypovolemia in two complementary ways—by increasing blood pressure and by initiating drinking.

Two difficulties with this conception arose almost immediately, however. First, angiotensin II does not cross the blood-brain barrier readily (Volicer & Loew, 1971), and it does not penetrate the choroid plexus into the cerebrospinal fluid. Thus it seemed unlikely that it could serve directly as a neural signal. Second, quantitative studies suggested that under normal physiological conditions not enough angiotensin II is produced to induce drinking (Abraham, Denton & Weisinger, 1976; Stricker, 1977, 1978). One researcher claimed that the only function of angiotensin II is to increase blood pressure (Stricker, 1978).

Several studies have attempted to resolve these discrepancies, though some unsolved problems remain. It appears that the researchers using cannulas (Epstein, Fitzsimons & Rolls, 1970) were able to obtain their effects because many of their cannulae passed through the ventricles on the way to the hypothalamus. The hormone then leaked back along the paths of the cannulae into the ventricles. Angiotensin II has strong effects when it is infused directly into the ventricles. (As Figure 3.8 showed, the ventricles begin in embryology on the outside of the body, so we would expect receptors to line the ventricle walls.) Normally, these regions receive angiotensin II from the blood, not from the cerebrospinal fluid in the ventricles; the regions are folded inside the brain but remain outside the blood-brain barrier (Rolls & Rolls, 1982).

One likely location for the angiotensin II receptors is a nucleus called the **subfornical organ,** so named because it sits just below the fornix along the ventricle wall. Injections of angiotensin II into the subfornical organ stimulate drinking even at very low doses, about 10^{-14} moles (Mangiapane & Simpson, 1980). Furthermore, lesions of the organ abolish the normal drinking response to injections of intravenous angiotensin II, and local application of an angiotensin II antagonist has the same effect (Simpson, Epstein & Camardo, 1978).

Other structures lining the ventricle walls may also contain angiotensin II receptors. A series of ingenious studies using cold-cream plugs to mask parts of the ventricular system concluded that the active site was the **organum vasculosum** (Latin for "vascular organ") of the lamina terminalis, at the anterior end of the third ventricle (Johnson & Buggy, 1977). The conclusion was reinforced by studies using radioactive labels (Swanson, Kucharczyk & Mogenson, 1978). Even if the hormone was injected through a cannula in another site, it affected drinking only when radioactivity leaked into the anterior part of the third ventricle.

Another view in this controversy is that the

preoptic area of the hypothalamus is a site for the angiotensin II receptors. Again, minute doses of the hormone injected through a cannula induce drinking (Richardson & Mogenson, 1981). However, radioactive markers injected through the same cannula do not enter the ventricles, making one suspect that angiotensin II from inside the brain excites this region.

Angiotensin II is not the only hormone implicated in volumetric thirst. Another negative feedback pathway is based on small peptide hormones called **atriopeptins,** which are released from the atriums of the heart when they are stretched. Atriopeptins suppress the release of another hormone, **arginine-vasopressin,** in the pituitary. Arginine-vasopressin in turn stimulates atriopeptin release, so reduced levels of arginine-vasopressin mean that fewer atriopeptins will be released. During hypovolemia, a lowered release of atriopeptins would allow arginine-vasopressin levels to grow. This feedback loop is linked to the angiotensin II loop by the ability of angiotensin II to stimulate the release of atriopeptins (Manning et al., 1985).

In conclusion, there may be several receptor areas for volumetric drinking. The apparent discrepancies between the studies may arise because the areas are connected to one another in unknown ways and are redundant; thus, when one is removed, others take over (Rolls & Rolls, 1982). This makes life safer for the organism but more dangerous for the neurophysiological theorist.

INITIATION OF DRINKING

Preoptic stimulation can elicit prodigious amounts of drinking, but it is difficult to evaluate the relative roles of osmotic and volumetric thirst in initiating the drinking. The two systems can be separated experimentally because the stimulus for volumetric thirst originates in the body, whereas the stimulus for osmotic thirst is initiated from receptors in the brain. If the two compartments can be manipulated independently in an intact animal, the two kinds of thirst can be separated.

Ramsay, Rolls, and Wood (1977) did this in dogs by injecting fluids into either the carotid arteries (leading to the brain) or the jugular veins (leading away from it). They first deprived the dogs of water, which caused both hypertonicity and reduction in blood volume. Then they infused pure water into the carotid arteries until the osmotic pressure of the cerebral plasma had returned to predeprivation levels. They controlled brain osmotic pressure by monitoring the salt concentration in the jugular vein, using the method shown in Figure 8.9. The dogs reduced their water consumption by 75 percent. The researchers measured volumetric thirst by depriving the dogs again and then injecting enough isotonic saline into the jugular veins to restore the plasma volume to normal levels; they determined the volume by sampling blood from a vein in the leg. Because the body is larger than the head, this test required more fluid than the first one. This time drinking was reduced by only one-quarter, showing that osmotic mechanisms are more important than volumetric mechanisms in controlling drinking. The results were confirmed in later injections using a small number of monkeys (Rolls, Wood & Rolls, 1980). (It is becoming increasingly popular for researchers to do the main body of their work with subprimates and to check the results with primates.)

Drinking has several functions in addition to its role in fluid balance. Thermoregulation, for in-

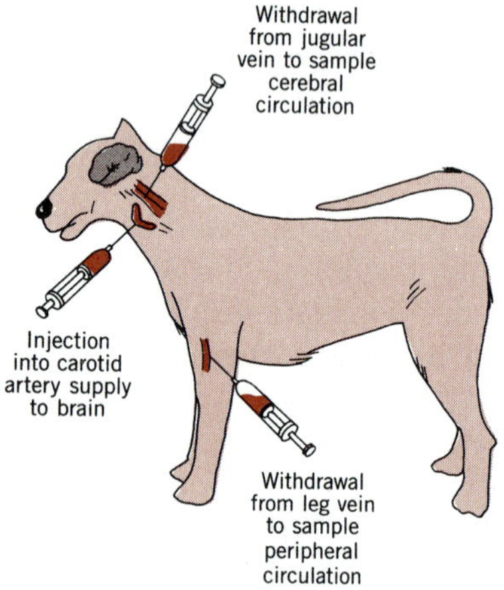

Figure 8.9 *Independent manipulation of osmotic and volumetric thirst. For osmotic regulation, fluid is injected into a carotid artery supplying the brain, and the results are sampled at a jugular vein. For volumetric regulation, fluid is injected into a jugular vein, and the results are sampled at a vein in the leg.*

stance, stimulates drinking on hot days, especially if a cold beverage is available. And even rats and monkeys will drink more if a little sweetener has been added to their water. Both rats and people will also increase their fluid intake if several flavors are available.

Psychological Influences. The physiological stimuli controlling water intake can be separated from the motivations for drinking. Osmotic pressure may be a powerful stimulus for drinking, but we don't line up at the water fountain when we feel that our osmosis is out of balance. Rather, we drink because water tastes good and we are thirsty. Research on humans has shown that they rate water as tasting more pleasant after mild deprivation and that its palatability decreases as subjects approach satiety (Cabanac, 1971).The hypothalamic detectors gain access to the behavior of the whole organism through motivational systems.

Mention the control of drinking to an average person and he won't think of water. Ironically, drinking alcoholic beverages can lead to dehydration even though most of the volume of these beverages is water. This occurs because alcohol interferes with the ability of the kidneys to actively reabsorb plasma filtered from the blood, leading to excessive fluid loss. When the concentration of alcohol is about the level in beer, the water intake just about matches the loss from the kidneys. Beyond that concentration, the body dehydrates.

CESSATION OF DRINKING

The control of drinking is more complex than the simple ingesting of fluid when water is low, for most animals drink much faster than their bodies can use fluids. A dog can drink a day's supply in two or three minutes, and a human can drink about two-thirds of the daily requirement in that time. Drinking must stop when enough water has been ingested, though restoration of water balance in the body can take an hour (Rolls, Wood & Rolls, 1980). A feedforward mechanism is required to limit drinking, because feedback from osmotic or volumetric receptors would be too slow. Drinking is a bit like filling a bucket just to the top with a hose. If you don't want to spill any water, you must start turning off the faucet before the bucket is full.

The feedforward mechanisms of satiation, like the feedback controls of thirst, can be analyzed by separating pathways anatomically. Rats can be surgically altered to bring the esophagus outside the body so no water enters the stomach. They will drink about four times as much as normal before stopping for a rest and will take that amount frequently (Blass & Hall, 1976). When their stomachs are artificially filled with water, they stop drinking.

In the monkey, drinking is controlled further by osmoreceptors in the first segment of the small intestine. Water injected there makes animals stop drinking even if they are deprived, but isotonic saline has no effect (Rolls, Wood & Rolls, 1980). The control is based on osmotic pressure rather than volume. Ordinarily, water would not be released into the intestine until the stomach is nearly full, and food would increase the osmolarity of the intestine rather than decreasing it. Osmoreceptors in this region provide a reliable control for water consumption, in cooperation with digestive mechanisms located literally "upstream."

Different diets require different amounts of water. Rats learn to adjust their intake to a particular diet, drinking just enough with a meal to provide the water that will be needed to digest it. When switched from a carbohydrate-rich diet, requiring little extra water, to a protein-rich diet, rats change their habits to ingest about one and a half times as much water. At first they drink the extra water after each meal, when osmotic thirst drives the system; but after a few days they return to drinking most of their water with their meals (Fitzsimons & LeMagnen, 1969). These mechanisms go beyond classical osmotic and volumetric stimuli. Complex learning supplements the hypothalamic mechanisms to achieve a well-coordinated schedule of water intake.

NUTRIENT BALANCE

Eating is a more complex activity than drinking or regulating temperature because the body requires not just an optimum level of a single entity but a balance among many—and with complicated interactions among them. We will look first at what the eating system does and then at how it is controlled.

Humans require 22 of the 64 amino acids (we synthesize the rest) as well as carbohydrates, fats, and an unknown number of vitamins and minerals. To obtain these nutrients we will eat just about anything; we are near the extreme among animals in the variety of foods consumed. We are also extreme in the capability of our digestive systems to handle different foods. Some Eskimo groups, for instance, eat mostly meat and fat because vegetables are an unobtainable luxury for most of the year. In contrast, millions of people in India are strict vegetarians. Most of us are between these extremes, eating a wide variety of foods.

Our ancestors probably had even more varied diets than we do, for groups that move from a nomadic life into agriculture generally simplify their diets at the same time. The only other animal with a comparable range of food sources is the chimpanzee; in the wild, it recognizes several hundred plant and animal foods. The ability to eat a wide variety of foods is a characteristic we share with chimpanzees on our branch of the primate evolutionary tree. Because this characteristic also complicates the control of food intake, this section will begin by examining the control of feeding in a simpler animal.

FEEDING IN SPECIALISTS

Eating behavior in the fly is relatively simple and well understood, and the system controlling it has been worked out practically neuron by neuron (Dethier, 1976). A food-deprived fly becomes more active, moving about until it happens to encounter a fluid that tastes or smells like food. This stimulus causes the fly to lower its proboscis—a long, thin feeding tube—into the fluid and to suck the fluid directly into its digestive tract. As the fly feeds, its sensory receptors adapt to the taste of the meal; if they stop firing completely, feeding ceases. They will fire again in response to food of a different kind, encouraging diversity of diet. The cessation of feeding involves negative feedback from mechanoreceptors in the gut; when the gut is full, the feeding reflexes are turned off, even if the peripheral receptors are still firing. If the nerve from the gut is severed (a triumph of microsurgery), the fly will eat until it literally bursts.

This simple feeding system has several features in common with the human system, including the separation of mechanisms for beginning and ending a meal. The fly also shows "specific hunger," the tendency to consume more of a food when the body's supply of it is low. In the female fly this happens around the time of egg-laying, when more protein is consumed. The switch to more protein-rich foods is again done indirectly, by a shift in the relative sensitivity of the receptors. By becoming less sensitive to salty solutions, the fly is less likely to reject salty but usually protein-rich food sources (for example, dung piles).

HUNGER AND SATIETY CENTERS?

Theorizing about the regulation of food and water intake began with emphasis on such peripheral factors as dryness in the throat for thirst and stomach contractions for hunger (Cannon, 1929). But why should the throat feel dry, and what causes the stomach to contract? Further, why should blood taken from starving dogs and injected into satiated dogs cause the latter to eat (Luckhardt & Carlson, 1915)? Attempts to answer these questions led researchers to the CNS.

Early experiments by Klüver and Bucy (1939) showed that bilateral removal of the entire temporal lobe in monkeys leads to a host of symptoms (named the Klüver-Bucy syndrome after the two researchers). Among the symptoms are obesity and a tendency to put almost anything, edible or not, into the mouth. No laboratory nut or bolt was safe around a Klüver-Bucy monkey. Lesions of the amygdala, a structure just under the temporal pole, produce some of the same symptoms (Pribram & Bagshaw, 1953). But eating is difficult to measure in monkeys; they store food in cheek pouches and throw it about when sated. The rat is a more convenient animal for quantitative studies of eating. It is also a good model for human control systems, because both rats and humans are omnivores.

Pribram (1971) relates the story of how the studies of monkeys were followed up at Yale. Bal Anand, a visitor from India, and Professor John Brobeck made stereotaxic lesions in rat amyg-

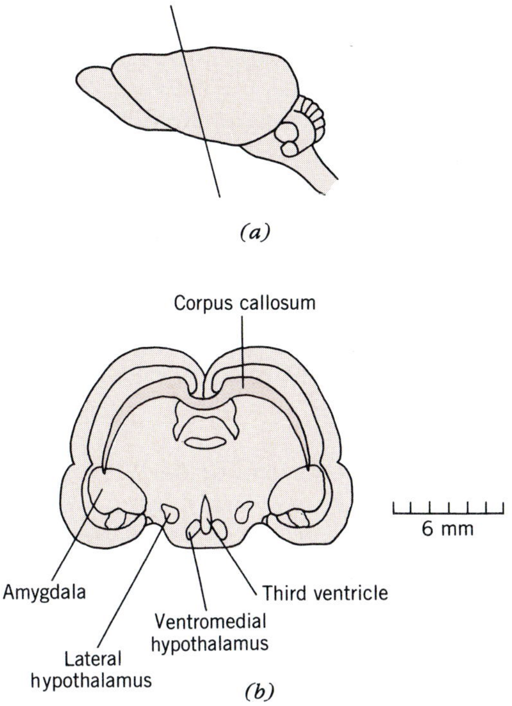

Figure 8.10 *Areas of the rat diencephalon involved in the control of eating.* (a) *Rat brain, showing the location of the frontal section illustrated in* (b). (b) *Frontal section through the hypothalamus.*

dalas with electric current (see Figure 8.10), and Pribram, using other rats, removed the structure surgically. To determine whether the expected eating disturbance was due to a change in the sensation of taste, they gave the rats a choice of a fatty mash or a mixture of sawdust and axle grease; the mixture resembled the mash but tasted awful. They also offered both bitter- and sweet-flavored water.

The results were disastrous. Over half of Pribram's rats died not after the surgery but before it—from eating too much axle grease and sawdust and drinking too much bitter water. Though the survivors returned to drinking bitter water and eating axle grease and sawdust after the amygdalectomy, Pribram did not feel like carrying the experiment to its predictable end.

Anand and Brobeck fared even worse, or so it seemed at first. Almost all of their rats died after the stereotaxic surgery—not from the effects of surgery but because they stopped eating and drinking altogether. Almost a year after the start of the project, it looked as though nothing conclusive would be found. But when Anand did an anatomical reconstruction of his rats' lesions, there was a surprise. The lesioning electrodes had gone more medially than intended and had missed the amygdala altogether. Instead, Anand and Brobeck had lesioned an area lateral to the hypothalamus and discovered the lateral hypothalamic (LH) feeding center (Anand & Brobeck, 1951), which presumably controlled the initiation of feeding.

The discovery of this center complemented the earlier finding of a "satiety center"—lesions in the ventromedial hypothalamus (VHM) led to obesity in rats (Hetherington & Ranson, 1940). Thus a neat picture emerged—of one center controlling the initiation of feeding and another the cessation of feeding, with each inhibiting the other. This simple model was not to last for long, however.

Lateral Hypothalamus. If the LH were really the initiator of eating, lesions of it should result in total and permanent cessation of eating. But LH-lesioned rats will recover if they are helped through their **anorexic** (Greek for "noneating") period by being fed through a stomach tube (Teitelbaum & Stellar, 1954). The recovery takes several weeks, and eating begins before drinking. At first, the animals show behavioral lethargy and sensory neglect, ignoring stimuli normal rats would react to; later, they retain only eating-related deficits (being finicky about food and not eating enough). Eventually, the rats stabilize at a lower than normal weight, but they maintain (defend) that weight with feedback mechanisms in the same way that normal rats maintain a higher weight (see Figure 8.11).

There is a problem with the lesions, though, because the LH is peculiar. It has relatively few cells and is crisscrossed with fiber tracts. Are the lesion results caused by the removal of the neurons or by the cutting of the axons of passage? The question has been answered by researchers who created a biochemical lesion, removing the neurons without harming the fibers coursing among them. The neurons were poisoned with kainic

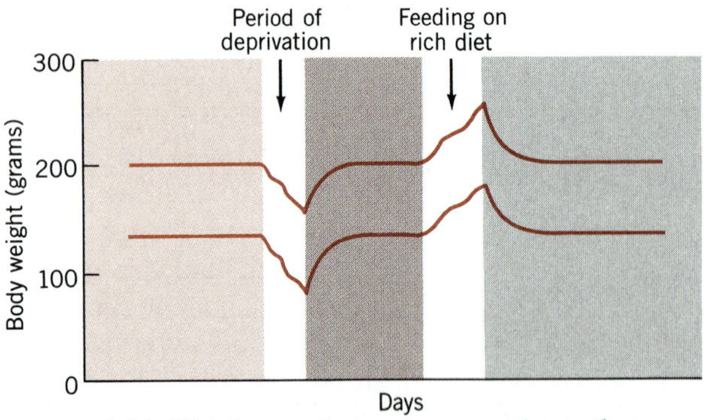

Figure 8.11 *Weight regulation in normal rats (top graph) and in rats that have fully recovered from bilateral lesions of the lateral hypothalamus (bottom graph). Both groups respond to deprivation or dietary change in the same way, with feedback control of weight levels.*

acid, a neurotoxin that kills cell somas without harming axons passing nearby. The researchers injected about 1 μg of kainic acid bilaterally into the LH; the result was a cessation of both eating and drinking, without the general behavioral lethargy brought about by electrolytic lesions (Grossman et al., 1978). The effect lasted for only about a week, though, making one suspect that other centers take over control of eating and drinking in the absence of the LH.

During periods of total food deprivation, both normal rats and recovered LH-lesioned rats lose weight at about the same rate. When food is restored, they gain weight in parallel until they reach their predeprivation levels. If only rich food is available (eggnog does well), both groups gain weight, only to lose it again with a normal diet (Keesey, 1980). The precision of weight control in LH-lesioned animals is as good as that in controls, but the set point of the lesioned animals is lower.

Ventromedial Hypothalamus. VMH-lesioned rats show different kinds of feeding abnormalities, all of them inconsistent with the idea of the VMH as a satiety center. These animals do not eat continuously; instead, they gorge themselves until they reach an excessive weight, which they then maintain. After force-feeding, they lose weight until they reach their original degree of obesity; and after deprivation, they regain their predeprivation weight.

The VMH syndrome is not just a change in the set point, though; it is a disturbance of normal feedbacks. A VMH-lesioned rat fed a rich diet will stabilize at the high weight shown in Figure 8.12. On a diet of bitter-tasting chow (adulterated with quinine) or in a situation where it must work hard to obtain food, a VMH-lesioned rat will weigh less than a normal one (Sclafani, Springer & Kluge, 1976). Thus the weight gain associated with VMH lesions may result more from excessive sensitivity to environmental variables than from a change in the set point. Perhaps the environmental variables seem more important because either the set point mechanism itself or the internal receptors have been damaged.

Another interpretation of the VMH syndrome is that the rats are constantly in an **absorptive phase** of metabolism. Normal organisms alternate between absorbing nutrients from the intestine, in the absorptive phase, and mobilizing body nutrient reserves in the **fasting phase.** VMH lesions increase the conversion of glucose into fat, normally a function of the absorptive phase. This process continues even when no food is being digested. Consequently, blood glucose levels fall quickly between meals; fatty tissue fails to act as a buffer to even out nutrient availability. The VHM-lesioned animal eats not to gain weight but to maintain an adequate supply of blood glucose (Friedman & Stricker, 1976).

Other studies have shown that when lesions are strictly limited to the VMH, obesity is not obtained (Gold, 1973). The weight disturbances found in these studies seem to be due instead to damage to the nearby **ventral noradrenergic bundle,** a small group of fibers extending from the midbrain into the forebrain. Lesions or knife cuts sectioning this fiber bundle do produce obesity. But how can one prove that these new lesions did not disturb yet another nearby group of cells?

The question was answered with a technique that takes advantage of the bilateral symmetry of the brain; the bundle was sectioned at different levels on the two sides. If these sections gave the same result as bilaterally symmetrical lesions, then only the interruption of the fibers could be causing the obesity. Indeed, a section of the ventral noradrenergic bundle near the VMH, coupled with a more posterior lesion of the bundle at the

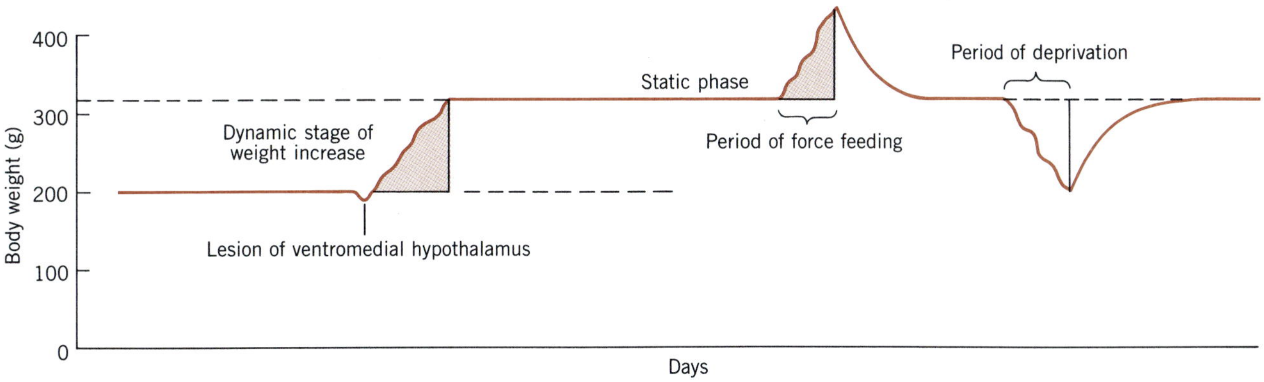

Figure 8.12 *Weight control in rats with ventromedial hypothalamic lesions. The slight initial dip in weight after surgery is a side effect of the anesthesia. The rat "defends" a high weight, returning to the same weight after force-feeding or deprivation.*

midbrain level on the opposite side, produced the effect even though no group of cells was lesioned on both sides (Kapatos & Gold, 1973). The ventral noradrenergic bundle ends in the region of the paraventricular nuclei of the hypothalamus, where we would expect to find receptors. (Recall that receptors for internal states are generally arranged along the ventricles.) Other areas of the dorsolateral tegmentum are probably also involved in this pathway. (Nature seldom divides functions as neatly as we would like.)

Other Receptors. The brain is an unlikely place to look for nutrient receptors, because its nutrient supply is maintained even at the expense of the rest of the body (see Chapter 2). A more reasonable location for such receptors is the liver, the master control organ for the blood. Among its dozens of functions, the liver directs the conversion of fats into directly usable nutrients and the conversion of nutrients into fats. It also manages the sugar balance of the blood and stores some sugars.

The liver is closely connected to the brain. Infusions of glucose into the blood supply of the liver affect the firing rates of afferent fibers from the liver (Niijima, 1969). Like the sensory systems examined in Chapter 5, the nutrient sensory system in the liver also receives centrifugal influences from the brain (Frohman, 1971). Hunger, then, may originate in signals sent from the liver when it has mobilized all of its readily available energy reserves (Friedman & Stricker, 1976).

Control of Nutrient Intake

Humans and other animals face a difficult information-processing task in determining when, how much, and what to consume. The problem arises because a meal is completed long before its physiological results begin to be felt. Feedback from glucose receptors in the brain or from other sources will be of no help, because the receptors will not receive the metabolic results of the meal until it is too late to modify feeding. Lack of feedback means that the brain must estimate the nutritional value of ingested food by less reliable, feedforward means. These include such sensory qualities as the taste, smell, and texture of food; they also include such internally monitored qualities as a meal's bulk. Habits, including the customary time of eating and the preferred diet, are also part of this feedforward process. They vary widely from culture to culture, of course.

For a look at higher-level control of feeding, we must return to the amygdala. Further investigation of the amygdala with the lesion technique has led to a differentiation of two antagonistic subdivisions: a **basolateral group** of nuclei and a phylogenetically older **corticomedial group.** Basolateral lesions cause **hyperphagia** (*hyper* is Greek for "over," and *phagia* is Greek for "eating"); corticomedial lesions cause **aphagia** (Greek for "non-eating") (Thompson, 1980). With larger lesions of the amygdala, the basolateral effect is dominant, reflecting the earlier results of Pribram and of Klüver and Bucy. As one would expect, if this area governs the hypothalamic centers, the basolateral division sends fibers to inhibit neurons in the LH and excite the VMH. The corticomedial amygdala inhibits the same VMH cells. The amygdala's effects are not mediated entirely through the hypothalamus, however, for lesions of both the LH and the VMH fail to eliminate amygdalar hyperphagia (Morgane & Kosman, 1960).

These deficits are accompanied in amygdala-lesioned humans by a dissociation of emotional affect (emotional responses) from behavior. Pribram (1971) describes a patient who had gained a great amount of weight following amygdalar surgery. This person did not describe an overpowering hunger and was indifferent when offered food by the doctor. But when the interview ended and the dining room doors were opened, the patient pushed everyone else aside, grabbed food with both hands, and began to eat voraciously. Called back to the examining room, the patient expressed no greater hunger than before. The link between eating and affect had been broken. We will encounter other examples of such dissociations between attitudes and behavior in the section on emotions in Chapter 9.

Most obesity, though, is caused not by amygdalar lesions or even by hormonal abnormalities but by factors less directly related to normal feedback systems. Obesity problems tend to be located in the elaborate feedforward systems that govern eating. An example in the rat is obesity brought on by the stress of a mild tail pinch, not even at a painful level, administered twice a day. This treatment caused a 129 percent increase in caloric intake (Rowland & Antelman, 1976). The relationship between stress and overeating may be mediated by the stress-induced release of dopamine.

In summary, the neural control of eating has turned out to be a complicated business. It depends on a variety of influences, having no master command center. The history of the field includes several false starts and misinterpretations. The flow of information about nutrition begins with receptors in the region where the hypothalamus comes in contact with the ventricles. The lateral and ventromedial hypothalamic areas are involved in establishing a set point for normal weight, using both receptors and higher-level controls as inputs. Higher-level centers include the corticomedial amygdala, related to the stimulation of eating, and the newer basolateral amygdala, which inhibits ingestion. The amygdala serves as a point of contact between eating behaviors and the motivational and emotional systems, including the neocortex, that control them. Stress and other environmental influences can also modify eating behaviors.

Initiation of Feeding

Many animals must eat whenever food is available and their stomachs have space for it. Most humans and carnivores, however, rely on other cues, both external and internal, to initiate feeding.

Imagine what feeding behavior would look like if internal receptors directly controlled the process. Soon after the absorptive phase was over and the fasting phase began, receptors would begin to weakly signal nutrient needs and eating would begin. Eating would soon cease, however, because the need state would not be very great and receptor activity would be minimal. With this sort of control system we would be perpetually snacking, never having substantial meals. Clearly, the habit of fasting between large meals requires a more elaborate link between receptors and behavior.

The control process begins with the receptors themselves. To study the process, a single neuron in the LH and VMH can be stimulated chemically through a micropipette. Single-unit electrical recordings are then made through the same pipette. The injection of a few nanoliters of glucose inhibits about a sixth of the LH neurons and excites a third of the VMH neurons (Oomura, 1976). Thus the LH and VMH neurons function as receptors. **Insulin** (the hormone controlling sugar metabolism in the body, but not in the brain) and free fatty acids have opposite effects, as shown in Figure 8.13*b*. Free fatty acids in the bloodstream may indicate that the body is breaking down stores of lipids. Thus either low glucose or mobilization of stored reserves can indicate deprivation to the

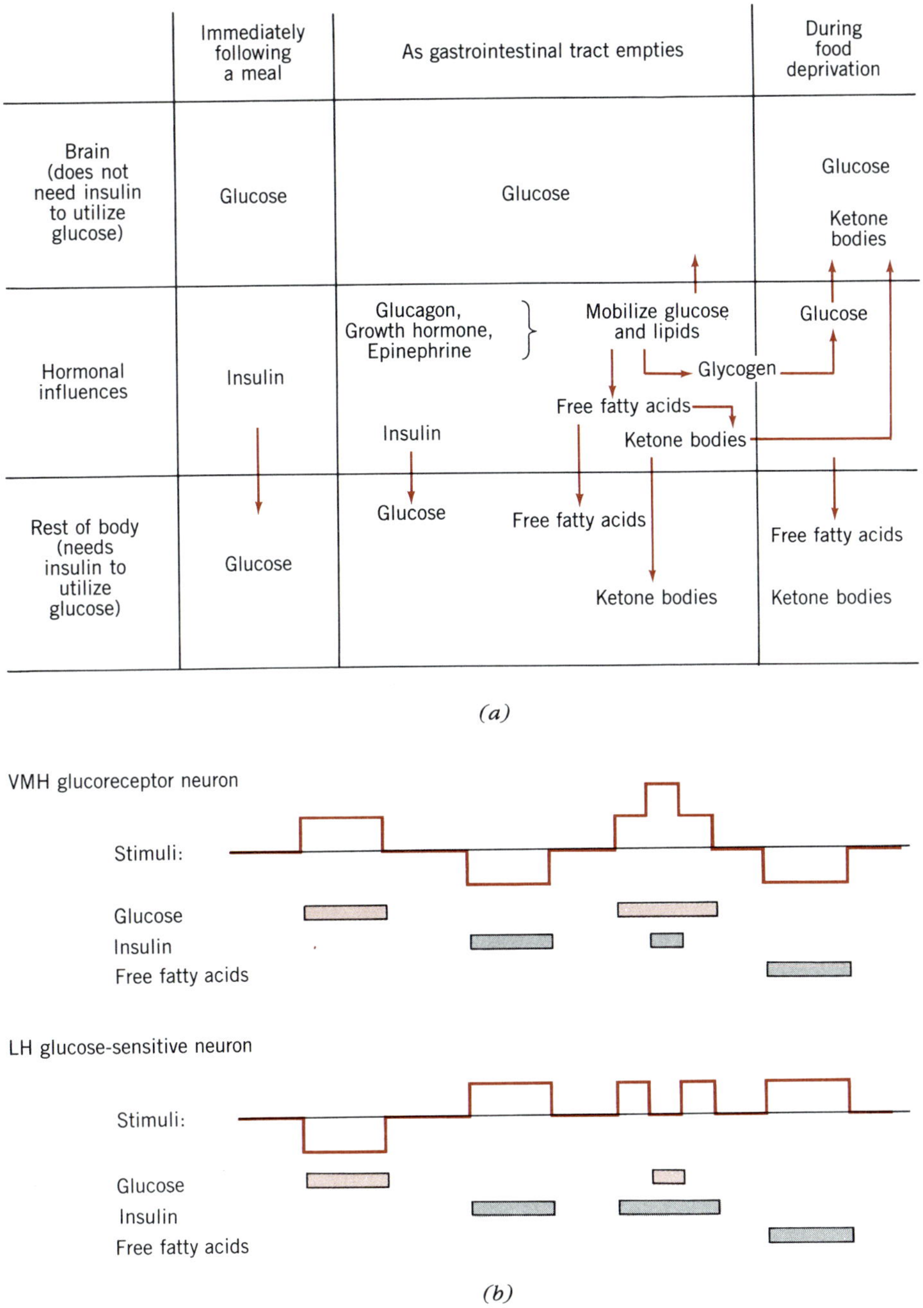

Figure 8.13 *Chemistry of digestion.* (a) *Flow of hormones and nutrients during and following digestion of a meal.* (b) *Responses of VMH and LH neurons to glucose, insulin, and free fatty acids. Effects at the two locations are generally opposites of each other. Based on results of Oomura (1976).*

brain. These direct and indirect indications of food need are like the detecting of a fire either by seeing the flames or by noting the presence of fire fighters and hoses.

There is some evidence that hypothalamic glucose receptors sense the difference between blood glucose concentrations in the arteries and in the veins: the A-V difference. The A-V difference is a measure of the rate of glucose uptake, and it correlates with perceived satiety in humans (Mayer, 1953). As the arterial concentration of glucose decreases, the cells can no longer efficiently extract it. The remaining glucose stays in the blood, reaching the venous circulation system at nearly the same concentration as in the arterial system.

This property of the receptors might explain why a diabetic person feels hungry even when the blood glucose level is high. The body cannot metabolize glucose without adequate supplies of insulin, so the A-V difference remains low, as Figure 8.14 indicates. A low A-V difference, in turn, normally indicates that the body is running out of fuel. So the diabetic's brain receives information consistent with glucose deprivation even though there is excess glucose in the blood.

How are the signals from the glucose receptors translated into the alternating pattern of meals and fasting? Part of the answer seems to be that a conditioned release of insulin just before a meal actually leads to abrupt changes in the A-V difference, converting a learned expectation into a physical deprivation state. Rats accustomed to eating one meal per day at a fixed time show a conditioned insulin release and a consequent lowering of blood glucose a few minutes before their meal (Woods et al., 1977). Insulin release can occur in humans even when they look at food, but only at mealtimes (Rodin, 1981). One can imagine that

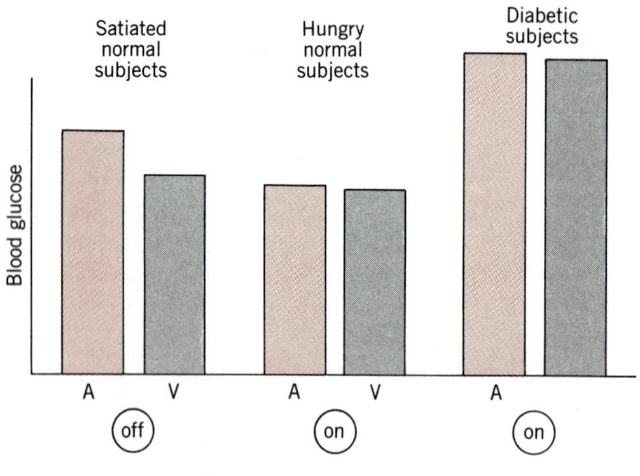

Figure 8.14 *Differences between arterial and venous glucose concentrations in normal and diabetic subjects. The A-V difference is large only in satiated normal subjects; a low A-V difference signals hunger, independently of the absolute blood glucose levels.*

bakery windows are a response to this human reaction.

Some hypothalamic neurons have been found to have firing patterns consistent with these characteristics of the feeding system. About 13 precent of the neurons in the monkey hypothalamus respond to the taste or sight of food, but only if the monkey is hungry. This response is a result of learning and is greatest for the most preferred foods. There is also a projection from the responding neurons to the cerebral cortex (Rolls, 1982), evidence that the hypothalamus is not the initiator of feeding behaviors. Instead, it is an organizing center for widespread activity that can be triggered by visual, tactile, or other sensory activity as well as by central receptors.

Termination of Feeding

The start of a meal involves positive feedback (the appetizer effect), for eating is steady and the hunger that one experiences can even increase at the start of a meal. But eventually the meal must terminate, and it must do so before the ingested food begins to influence the blood chemistry. Some of the cues that terminate meals are social or cultural; it is embarrassing to continue eating when everyone else is leaving the table. There is also the feeling that the stomach is full. But the most important termination signals are biochemical.

A Satiety Hormone? One possible satiety hormone is **cholecystokinin (CCK),** a substance released by the initial segment of the small intestine when it receives food from the stomach. CCK initiates further steps in digestion and has various effects on the brain. Intraperitoneal injections (injections into the abdominal cavity) of CCK suppress feeding in rats, cats, and dogs (Gibbs, Young & Smith, 1973; Mueller & Hsiao, 1978). The hormone is found in the cerebral cortex, but its concentration there is lower in genetically obese mice than in normal litter mates (Straus & Yalow, 1979).

Despite this daunting array of circumstantial evidence for CCK as a satiety hormone, there are doubts about its role. Animals may stop eating when given CCK because it is aversive. The aversion was discovered in experiments where rats were allowed to choose freely between two flavored-water solutions. When the hormone was paired with one of the two solutions, rats avoided the one associated with CCK but continued to drink the other (Deutsch & Hardy, 1977). In humans, CCK injections are reported to be unpleasant (Sturdevant & Goetz, 1976). Furthermore, CCK administered in amounts normally found in the body failed to cause satiety (Deutsch, 1978). Larger amounts suppress feeding even in rats with lesions of the supposed satiety center in the ventromedial hypothalamus (Kulkosky et al., 1976). In sum, there seems to be good evidence both for and against CCK as a negative feedback hormone for eating.

A possible solution to this dilemma has been hypothesized. CCK no longer induces satiety when the stomach branch of the vagus nerve is cut; there is also evidence that the critical fibers are afferent nerves from the stomach (Smith et al., 1981). Thus intraperitoneal injections of CCK may cause satiety by affecting vagal afferents, which implies that the same effect would occur on the natural release of CCK. According to this idea, CCK's effect is peripheral, and the neural hormone remains to be identified.

Contrary evidence has appeared, though, showing that CCK also has a central effect. Indeed, CCK is a neurotransmitter in the sympathetic ganglion that serves the colon (Schumann & Kreulen, 1986). The hormone is widely distributed in the CNS, as is shown by studies of the binding of radioactively tagged CCK to brain tissue (Zarbin et al., 1983).

Several effects of CCK are opposite to those of endogenous opiates such as beta-endorphin, suggesting that the two substances might have opposing effects on CNS homeostatic functions. The hypothesis that CCK and endorphins are antagonists was tested using one of the endorphins' most dramatic properties, the reduction of pain (Faris et al., 1983). CCK antagonized opiate-induced analgesia without affecting non-opiate-induced analgesia. This might explain why CCK injections are unpleasant. If CCK and opiates are antagonists in pain, they may act as antagonists in the control of appetite as well.

It is clear by now that CCK plays an important role in the termination of feeding, but the exact role and the mechanisms are yet to be determined. The conflicting interpretations might be resolved with the idea that satiety itself may be aversive, as in the stuffed, queasy feeling the one gets after too much Thanksgiving dinner.

Amphetamine. Evidence for another possible neural satiety hormone has come from an unexpected source, as a by-product of work with amphetamine. In addition to its well-known psychological effects, this stimulant causes stereotyped motor activity at high doses. It also induces hyperthermia, anorexia, and constriction of blood vessels. While studying motor activity, investigators at the National Institutes of Health noticed a strong binding of amphetamine to neurons in the hypothalamus (Paul, Hulihan-Giblin & Skolnik, 1982). They detected the binding by homogenizing various parts of rat brains in a blender and incubating the mixture with radioactively labeled amphetamine. After 20 min, they rinsed away the radioactive amphetamine. Amphetamine bound to brain receptors remained, and its radiation was measured.

Why would amphetamine bind to the hypothalamus, a structure unrelated to motor activity? Paul, Hulihan-Giblin, and Skolnik (1982) reasoned that the hypothalamic binding might be related not to amphetamine's motor effects but to its anorexic "side effect." The team postponed their investigation of motor control to track down this new phenomenon—the specific binding of a drug that suppresses appetite. To look at the appetite effect more closely, they examined a number of other phenylethylamine derivatives (chemical relatives of amphetamine) for the strength of hypothalamic binding. They compared the resulting values to both the stimulant and the anorexia effects of the drugs; the results are shown in Figure 8.15. Clearly, hypothalamic binding is related to the anorexic effect but not to the stimulant effect. This is strong evidence that the hypothalamic binding is due to receptors for an appetite-suppressing hormone structurally related to the phenylethylamine derivatives.

It is safe to assume that the amphetamine binding sites did not evolve in anticipation of the future human use of amphetamine. The binding sites must function with some as yet undiscovered

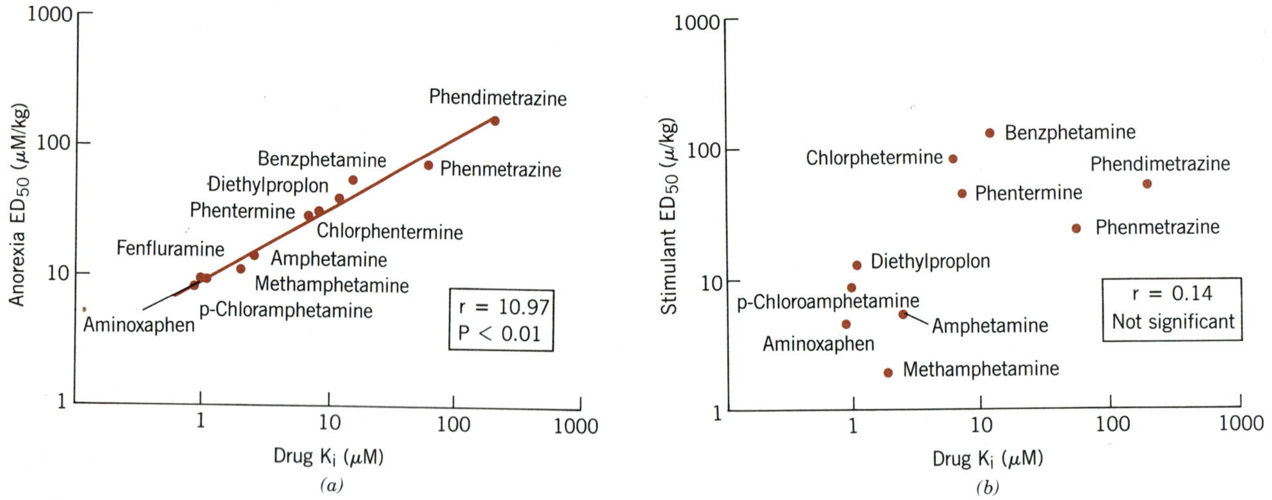

Figure 8.15 *Effectiveness of various phenylethylamine derivatives in causing behavioral anorexia and stimulation in rats.* (a) *Anorexia ED_{50} is the average dose of the drug needed to cause a 50 percent decrease in food intake.* (b) *Stimulant ED_{50} represents the average dose of the drug needed to cause a 50 percent increase in the response rate in a continuous avoidance paradigm. Thus, for both* (a) *and* (b), *a low ED_{50} represents a strong effect on behavior. K_i is a measure of the strength of binding to hypothalamic receptors. Binding is highly correlated with anorexia but unrelated to stimulant effectiveness.*

endogenous hormone or neurotransmitter that suppresses appetite. Alternatively, amphetamine might modulate the release, reuptake, or response of other neurotransmitters involved in the hypothalamic regulation of appetite (Paul, Hulihan-Giblin & Skolnik, 1982).

In addition to the effects outlined here, amphetamine influences motivations, emotions, and feelings. The homeostatic functions reviewed in this chapter are related to motivation and emotion on anatomical, pharmacological, and psychological levels.

CHAPTER SUMMARY

1. Homeostasis is the maintenance of a stable internal environment. Animals expend energy to achieve homeostasis. The process is governed by systems using both feedback and feedforward control. The brain contains many independent homeostatic systems governing various functions.

2. Temperature regulation began with the evolution of ectotherms, land animals that use environmental energy to obtain heat. The process is controlled by hypothalamic, brain-stem, and spinal mechanisms. This strategy is economical, requiring little food, but prevents ectotherms from occupying many environments.

3. The endotherms—mammals and birds—use metabolic energy to maintain a constant internal temperature. Control is more precise, enabling endotherms to use more efficient enzyme systems to catalyze biological reactions; but endotherms

require more food energy. Both heating and cooling are used to maintain temperature; metabolic processes are added to the behavioral strategies of the ectotherms. Control is centered in several areas in and near the preoptic area of the hypothalamus, where separate systems mediate metabolic and behavioral thermoregulation. Fever is a thermoregulatory response to infection, killing bacteria with heat.

4. Animal species have varied specializations in heat control, such as insulation, high metabolic activity, and bulk. Humans specialize in elaborate learned feedforward behaviors, including clothing and houses.

5. There are two types of thirst: osmotic and volumetric. Osmotic thirst controls intracellular water balance, and volumetric thirst controls extracellular fluid volume. Osmotic thirst is triggered by receptor cells in the preoptic area near the midline; another set of receptors in the nucleus circularis directs the production of antidiuretic hormone (ADH) to increase water uptake in the kidneys. Volumetric thirst is triggered by baroreceptors in the circulatory system, stimulating production of ADH and of angiotensin, a hormone that may stimulate thirst through receptors in the lamina terminalis. Osmotic thirst is ordinarily the more effective of the two mechanisms in regulating drinking. Cessation of drinking is influenced by feedforward mechanisms, by intestinal receptors, and by the effects of learning.

6. Humans obtain nutrients from a great variety of foods. The lateral hypothalamus (LH) seems to govern hunger, and the ventromedial hypothalamus (VMH) governs satiation; obesity occurs when the VMH is removed. But LH-lesioned rats eventually stabilize at a lower weight, and VMH-lesioned animals become obese only if palatable food is easily available. When food is hard to get, VMH-lesioned rats become thinner than normals. The VHM lesion interferes with the weight set point, making environmental control relatively more important. The lesion also increases the conversion of glucose into fat. VMH effects may arise from the lesioning of the ventral noradrenergic bundle leading to receptors in the paraventricular nuclei. Hypothalamic centers are controlled in turn by the amygdala and other forebrain regions.

7. Initiation of eating is related to receptors detecting the difference between arterial and venous glucose concentrations, and these are influenced by conditioned insulin release. Psychological factors are also important. Single hypothalamic neurons reflect all of these complex influences. Satiation normally is signaled directly by the stomach and indirectly by hormones. Cholecystokinin (CCK) appears to participate in a local control mechanism in the intestines, and amphetamine-like transmitters modulate hunger in the brain.

KEY TERMS

Ectotherms
Torpor
Endotherms
Set point
Neutral zone
Preoptic area
Pyrogens
Osmotic gradient
Osmotic pressure
Hypertonic
Cannula
Antidiuretic hormone (ADH)
Vasopressin
Nucleus circularis
Baroreceptors
Hypovolemia
Renin
Angiotensin I
Subfornical organ

Organum vasculosum
Atriopeptins
Arginine-vasopressin
Anorexic
Absorptive phase
Fasting phase
Ventral noradrenergic bundle
Basolateral group
Corticomedial group
Hyperphagia
Aphagia
Insulin
Cholecystokinin (CCK)

SUGGESTED READINGS

Friedman, M., & Stricker, E. (1976). The physiological psychology of hunger: A physiological perspective. *Psychological Review, 83,* 409–431.

The evidence for peripheral receptors, especially in the liver, is analyzed.

Rolls, B., & Rolls, E. (1982). *Thirst.* London: Cambridge University Press.

This compactly written little book summarizes most of what is known about the physiology of thirst, emphasizing neurological control systems.

Satinoff, E. (1978). Neural organization and evolution of thermal regulation in mammals. *Science, 201,* 16–22.

Satinoff describes three thermoregulatory systems in mammals and their possible origins in evolution.

Chapter 9

MOTIVATION AND EMOTION

Chapter 1 suggested that motivation makes animals fundamentally different from machines. All organisms must do certain things to survive and reproduce in their environments; built-in motivational systems assure that these things are done. All animals, for instance, must find food, water, and shelter; avoid danger; and reproduce. Motivational systems facilitate the behaviors that accomplish these goals. In addition, most higher animals must meet a variety of other challenges. They must explore and possibly defend a territory, learn social behaviors, and interact with group members.

In this chapter we will move beyond homeostasis to consider active intervention in the world. The strong feelings that accompany many of our activities result from the operation of the neurological machinery that organizes the activities. The brain's motivational systems operate at many levels, from simple reflexes to complex patterns of behavior. At the lowest level, for example, spinal reflexes withdraw your hand from a hot stove (see Chapter 7), minimizing damage from a danger in the environment. The long-term "motivation" for this act is evolutionary; animals that possess the behavior are more likely to survive than those that do not. The immediate mechanism, the well-understood spinal reflex, is so direct that it is difficult to think of the behavior as motivated.

What happens next, however, reveals that the quick withdrawal is only the first of a series of actions that deal with the environmental challenge. After your hand is withdrawn from the stove, you begin to feel a sharp pain, followed by a more diffuse, gradual pain carried on small unmyelinated fibers. You seek relief by cooling the hand with water, bandaging it, or applying other first aid. Perhaps you cry out, which may unintentionally summon the assistance of others. Finally, the experience motivates learning; you will be more cautious around the stove the next time!

Another motivated behavior organized at several levels is sex. Copulatory reflexes organized in the caudal spinal cord are a necessary part of the system, but they do not begin to express the variety of emotions and behaviors associated with sex. Broadly defined, these behaviors involve any activity that increases sexual fitness, including activities that increase one's attractiveness to the opposite sex. Education might be part of this process for some people. And part of that education in turn is the act of reading this book.

Motivational systems include both behaviors and subjective feelings. Unfortunately, however, only the behaviors can be studied with objective methods. Though this chapter must deal mainly with behaviors and their physiological mechanisms, we should remember that feelings and emotions are important parts of the systems. They may, for example, link the physiological systems with the consciousness needed to organize various motivational needs into priorities for action. (Chapter 14 will take up this issue again.)

"DRIVES" AND MOTIVATION

Motivation has been analyzed traditionally in terms of **drives**—postulated activators of behavior that are inbuilt and that affect behavior under the appropriate circumstances. Eating, for instance, is a behavior explained by a hunger drive, and drinking is a behavior explained by a thirst drive. It is easy to see why there are quotation marks in the title of this section: the term *drive* explains nothing. It only restates the problem in slightly different language. Unless independent evidence for a drive is defined at some level other than behavioral description, the definition of *drive* is circular; we postulate a drive to explain a behavior and then use the same behavior to explain the drive.

At one time it was thought that the circle could be broken because drive-reducing stimuli were a special class of environmental events. A stimulus that reduced hunger, for instance, was qualitatively different from ordinary perceptions of events in the outside world. Most stimuli provide information but don't reduce drives. A series of clever experiments, though, showed this hypothesis to be false (Premack, 1959). Food-deprived rats earned food by running in activity wheels attached to their cages. Later, the same rats were deprived of activity by being housed in small cages, and they consumed food to be allowed access to the activity wheels. Food deprivation made food a reinforcer, and activity deprivation made activity a reinforcer. Thus the drive-reducing stimulus lost its special status, and the circularity of the *drive* concept was worse than ever.

The only way out of this circle is to find evidence at another level to support the assumed cause of the behavior. We will examine anatomical, biochemical, and physiological evidence for the existence of inherited motivational systems that are built into the structure of the brain. Emotion results from the activation of these motivational systems. But the term *motivation* might suffer the same circularity of definition as *drive* unless some independent evidence can be found for the organization of motivational systems in the brain. There is now a wealth of such evidence, from anatomy, neurochemistry, and electrical recording. One of the most dramatic and effective techniques for the physiological study of motivation has been self-stimulation, a method that allows direct access to the brain's motivational systems.

ELECTRICAL SELF-STIMULATION

We can assume that during rewarded behavior the performance of the behavior leads to the registering of a reward state somewhere in the brain. This brain reward center in turn should activate the animal to continue the activity. The study of rewards and motivation would benefit from the ability to address reward centers directly, bypassing the sensory channels that normally stand between the central mechanisms and the real world. The finding that animals will perform behaviors solely for the reward of brief stimulation of a part of the brain opened the way for physiological study of these mechanisms. The method was discovered by accident.

At McGill University in the early 1950s, James Olds and his graduate student Peter Milner were studying arousal by the reticular formation. They attempted to implant electrodes in this area, but they missed; in one animal the electrodes apparently wound up in the hypothalamus (we will never know for sure—this animal's brain was lost). Here the story diverges into two versions. The first is that the relatively primitive recording amplifiers of the time leaked a little current back into the recording electrodes, stimulating the target tissue. The other is that the investigators tried brief stimulations through the electrodes, with unexpected results. In any case, Olds and Milner were surprised to find the animal returning to the place where it had been when the current was applied, as though coming back for more (Olds, 1973). Realizing the importance of this behavior, they immediately dropped the arousal work and began a famous series of studies that defined the phenomenon of self-stimulation.

The first step was to control the relationship between behavior and stimulation. The perfect apparatus for this step already existed—the "Skinner box," a training apparatus developed by B. F. Skinner for the behavioral study of reinforcement (see Figure 9.1). Placed into a Skinner box, rats with surgically implanted stimulating electrodes would press a bar to the point of exhaustion (Olds & Milner, 1954) for the reward of only a brief pulse of electrical brain stimulation. This work opened the new study of self-stimulation.

DIFFERENTIATION OF SELF-STIMULATION SITES

The obvious next steps were to define the brain site responsible for the effect and to determine how this site reinforces behavior. The brain site was easy to find (a little too easy for those who believe in sharp anatomical localizations of func tions). As Figure 9.2 reveals, large regions of the subcortical forebrain support self-stimulation, though with varying degrees of enthusiasm on the animal's part.

The strongest and most reliable effects were found when the electrodes were implanted in the **medial forebrain bundle (MFB).** This group of fibers runs along the axis of the brain stem (see Figure 9.3). Part of its course is through the lateral hypothalamus, as it links subcortical forebrain centers with more caudal regions. The MFB is so general that it is not very helpful in the study of motivation. Anatomically, it is like a tree trunk, concentrating fibers from a wide region of the brain stem (roots) and dispersing them to another wide region of the limbic forebrain (branches). Perhaps it is because of this anatomical concentration of fibers that self-stimulation in the MFB is so effective. A localized stimulus can drive a large number of fibers.

Decades of self-stimulation work have shown that there are several motivational systems. Researchers have sorted out the systems by noting the effectiveness of self-stimulation sites when animals are in various motivational states. Many self-stimulation sites, for instance, overlap with those that control eating and drinking; an animal with electrodes in a feeding center will self-stimulate more when hungry. This result shows the relationship between self-stimulation and normal reward systems. Motivation appears to be controlled by a group of loosely associated sites, mostly in and near the hypothalamus, rather than by a master reinforcement center.

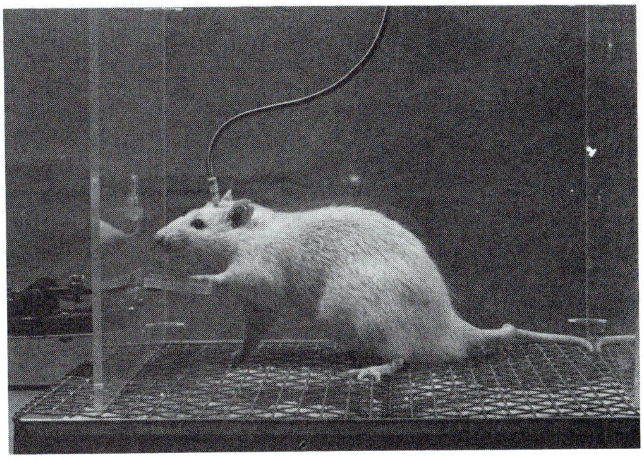

Figure 9.1 *Rat in a Skinner box pressing a bar to obtain electrical stimulation. The stimulation consists of 0.5 sec of bipolar pulses delivered at 60 Hz. Stimulation usually is done with a rapid alternation between positive and negative polarity, because sustained current of a particular polarity can cause ions to migrate toward or away from the electrode, with toxic results.*

Comparing Natural and Electrical Rewards

Several observations of what appeared to be different rules for self-stimulation than for normal reinforcement cast doubt on the validity of self-stimulation as a model for normal motivation. When normal reinforcements, such as food and water, are withdrawn, animals usually press the bar in a Skinner box many times, but with diminishing frequency, before they give up. The phenomenon,

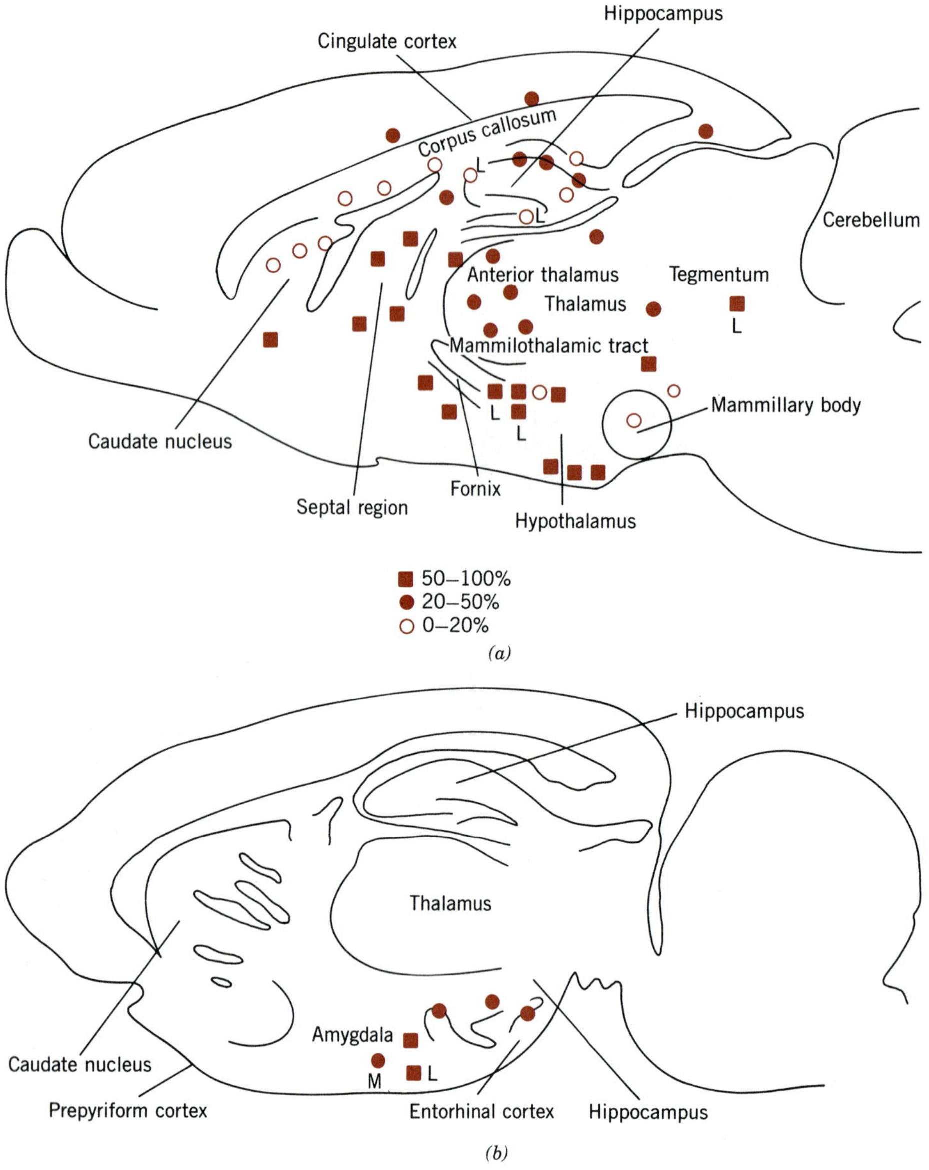

Figure 9.2 *Reward centers in rat brain.* (a) *Sagittal section near the midline, showing loci that support self-stimulation.* (b) *Sagittal section 2 to 3 mm more lateral. A few loci are outside these planes. The letter* M *indicates centers medial to the plane shown; the letter* L *indicates more lateral centers. Adapted from Sheer (1961).*

called **extinction,** is the repression of a response after repeated presentation of the conditioned stimulus without the unconditioned stimulus. Like a jilted lover repeatedly telephoning a former sweetheart, the rat eventually accepts the fact that no more reinforcement is forthcoming. But animals show faster extinction with self-stimulation; behavioral responses cease almost as soon as the electricity is disconnected.

Extinction is no longer the problem it had seemed to be, however; when food, water, and electrical reinforcement are directly compared under controlled conditions, the difference disappears (Olds & Fobes, 1981). An explanation for the earlier discrepancy might be that electrical stimulation has a "clean" all-or-none property, whereas the smells and feels of material rewards may remain for a while. When experimenters compensate for these differences, the extinction under the two kinds of reward is comparable.

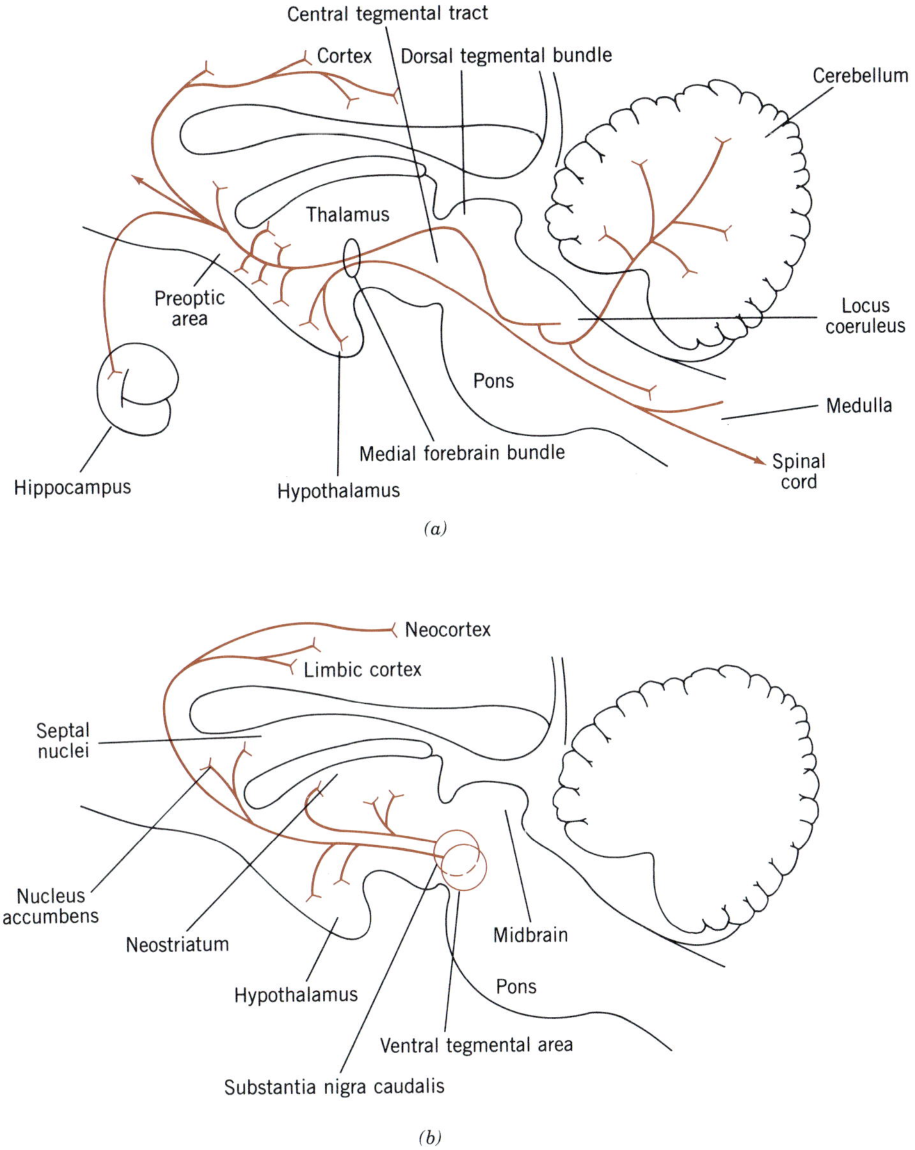

Figure 9.3 *The principal catecholaminergic neurons in the CNS.* (a) *Noradrenergic pathways.* (b) *Dopaminergic pathways. The substantia nigra caudalis (located laterally) and the ventral tegmental area are the origins of two major dopaminergic systems. The ventral tegmental area system, called the mesolimbic system after its terminations, is involved in arousal and attention, and may be involved in schizophrenia (see Chapter 16).*

Another peculiar feature of electrical self-stimulation is that animals seem to forget about it overnight. A few jolts of current, however, will get them going again. This **priming effect** may be due to the fact that self-stimulated animals are not deprived before testing. Motivational centers normally influence behavior only when the animal is in a state of deprivation, but with self-stimulation the access is direct and rewarding regardless of the animal's physical needs.

Does natural reinforcement have this property too under the right conditions? It does, if the reinforcer is one that is effective even when an animal is satiated. Rats will do anything for chocolate milk and will drink it even if they have just had their fill of normal rat chow. Thus chocolate milk is parallel to electrical stimulation in that deprivation is not necessary to obtain performance. Panksepp and Trowill (1967), in experimenting with natural reinforcement, squirted the milk directly into the animals' mouths to make the reward immediate, like self-stimulation, and not dependent on the animals' further behavior. Under this condition, the animals did show priming; when placed into the experimental chamber, they would seem to have forgotten the task until given a few "free" squirts of milk to get them going again. They also reached extinction three times faster than hungry rats. Again, natural reinforcement had properties similar to self-stimulation if the conditions were made similar.

Some sites in the brain seem to be the opposite of reward centers; when stimulated at these sites, animals will work to turn off the stimulation. Some of these areas create truly aversive feelings—pain centers, for instance. Others, however, are paradoxically the same areas that support self-stimulation. Both cats and rats will work to turn a stimulus on and work further to turn the same stimulus off (Bower & Miller, 1958; Roberts, 1958). This ambivalent effect is found for most of the sites that support self-stimulation (Valenstein & Valenstein, 1964). If you think such patterns are foreign to human experience, consider whether you would like to experience orgasm and then consider how you would feel if the orgasm went on forever. This observation implies a delayed aversive effect in motivational systems, so no single reward system can dominate behavior.

Self-Stimulation and Drive Reduction

We have seen that self-stimulation is effective even in an animal that has no need for such obvious reinforcements as food and water (Panksepp & Trowill, 1967). But this does not imply that self-stimulation is unrelated to drives, for we are directly stimulating centers that ordinarily are activated only when deprivation states exist. Further, some motivating feelings, such as sexual ones, may produce an overt behavior only in an appropriate environment (the presence of the opposite sex). Thus it is difficult to prove a relationship between self-stimulation and the reduction of an independently identifiable drive. But counterexamples, where self-stimulation is obtained in sites that increase drive, should be able to separate motivation (revealed by self-stimulation) from drive reduction.

It seemed at first that any electrode that would elicit eating when stimulated would also support a high rate of self-stimulation. A closer examination, using smaller electrodes which presumably had more specific effects, found a more flexible relationship between ingestion and self-stimulation (Olds, Allan & Briese, 1971). Some electrodes in and near the hypothalamus elicited eating, some elicited drinking, and some elicited self-stimulation. Others elicited all three behaviors, and still others suppressed eating and drinking.

To see why a stimulus that seems to increase drive can be reinforcing, we must look more closely at the relationship between "drives" and the activation of behavior. A state of deprivation, such as intense hunger or thirst, is certainly aversive, but the act of relieving it is not. Most of us enjoy eating, drinking, and other drive-induced activities, for the obvious reason that our ancestors survived because they enjoyed the same things. Here the word *enjoy* implies the activation of a motivational system. To get the maximum amount of enjoyment, people do the things that assure their survival.

But people enjoy eating most when there is some degree of deprivation, so the drive and the consumption can interact. Brain stimulation in centers associated with feeding may provide the reinforcing signal that normally occurs only with the combination of deprivation and its resolution. Electrical stimulation provides a sort of false alarm, a signal that a need is being resolved even if it is not. Again, this can happen only because our stimulation method bypasses the normal sensorimotor access to these organizing centers. The hypothalamic neurons we encountered in Chapter 8 (Rolls, 1982), which fire in the presence of food only if an animal is hungry, can be electrically stimulated even when the animal is satiated.

In conclusion, behavior is driven by pleasure as well as by aversive stimuli or their threat. Healthy environments give us a wealth of sights, sounds, and smells that we find pleasant; we tend to stay in those environments even without identifiable drives. The concept of motivational systems allows us to escape some of the narrowness implied by the old concept of behavior controlled by drives connected to need reduction. Taking full advantage of these systems requires integration beyond the level of the hypothalamus. Biochemistry will suggest connections between the motivational systems of the hypothalamus and other parts of the forebrain.

THE BIOCHEMISTRY OF MOTIVATION

The emphasis in work on motivational systems has recently shifted to the biochemistry of their neurotransmitters. It is now possible to separate the systems with histofluorescence techniques that selectively mark neurons containing a particular family of neurotransmitters. Drugs can selectively block or facilitate individual systems. These techniques promise to unravel the somewhat tangled neuroanatomy of self-stimulation.

Histofluorescence showed a striking relationship between self-stimulation sites and catecholaminergic neurons—norepinephrine (noradrenaline) and dopamine (see Figure 9.3). These neurons seemed natural candidates for the biochemical substrate of self-stimulation. Another observation leading to this conclusion was the strong facilitation of self-stimulation by amphetamine, a catecholamine agonist. But was the effect truly a catecholamine facilitation, or was it merely a result of amphetamine's well-known stimulation of general arousal? The question was answered by investigating the influence of amphetamine on electrical current thresholds for self-stimulation.

To measure the self-stimulation threshold, researchers trained rats to press two levers. One lever triggered brain stimulation but gave a weaker pulse with each successive press. The other gave no pulse itself but restored the weakened pulse of the other lever to its original strength. To get the maximum amount of reinforcement a rat would have to press the first lever until stimulation was near the threshold, then press the other lever (Stein & Ray, 1960). Rats given amphetamine pressed the first lever more times before resetting the level, thereby showing that the drug made them sensitive to lower current levels. The amphetamine effect was not due to general arousal.

A later experiment, with no response required, yielded similar results (Poschel & Ninteman, 1966). Rats received "free" brain stimulation in one compartment of a two-compartment cage and nothing in the other. Stimulating current was set to a level such that the rats spent only slightly more time in the stimulation compartment. When they were then given amphetamine, the rats spent most of their time in the stimulation compartment, which indicated that they were now more sensitive to the stimulation.

These studies made it clear that catecholamines are somehow involved in motivational systems; the matching of self-stimulation sites and catecholamines was more than coincidence. But which of the catecholamines was involved? The first to be studied was noradrenaline, because it was known that the locus coeruleus, a noradrenergic nucleus in the dorsal pons, would support self-stimulation (Stein, 1964, 1968). This turned out to be a false direction, however. In several brain areas, blockage of norepinephrine synthesis failed to influence either self-stimulation behavior or the effect of amphetamine on that behavior. In some studies, researchers depleted noradrenergic synapses by injecting 6-hydroxydopamine, a drug toxic to catecholaminergic neurons, directly into the brain (Phillips, Van der Kooy & Fibiger, 1977; Clavier, Fibiger & Phillips, 1976). Other investigators obtained similar results using different pharmacological techniques (Lippa et al., 1973; Cooper, Konkol & Breese, 1978).

Dopamine, the other catecholamine neurotransmitter, has fared better, with good evidence from several anatomical areas that it plays a central role in motivational systems. In the lateral hypothalamus, for instance, self-stimulation was blocked with intracranial injections of sprioperidol, a blocker of postsynaptic dopamine receptors (Mora et al., 1975). Similar effects also occur with other dopamine receptor–blocking agents, such as pimozide and haloperidol (reviewed by Fibiger, 1978), so the results cannot be attributed to side effects of the blocker.

But we know from Chapter 7 that dopamine is involved in the generation of motor activity. How can we prove that suppression of self-stimulation is not just a motor effect? By investigating the effect of dopamine blockers on extinction. If the blockers affect reward, the administration of a blocker should result in an extinction curve similar to that found after withdrawal of electrical reinforcement. A motor effect, in contrast, should reduce bar pressing even at the start of the extinction trials. Blocking dopamine synapses with pimozide, Fouriezos and Wise (1976) found a normal extinction curve—evidence that the dopamine effect was specific to reward mechanisms.

Though these studies show that the dopamine effect goes beyond interference with motor behavior, they do not prove that dopamine specifically interferes with reward. The reasons for this demonstrate the interaction of experimental designs and conclusions. After the dopamine-blocking results were obtained, other researchers looked carefully at the designs of the studies and found that learning and behavior had not been separated. When animals are required to learn a discrimination, for instance, dopamine inhibitors reduce the number of responses but do not change the rate of learning (Anisman, 1982; Tombaugh, 1982).

It seems that dopamine is part of the story, but not all of it; perhaps the neurotransmitter is involved in connecting stimuli with responses, without reducing the effects of rewards in general. The debate on the role of dopaminergic systems in reward continues, as new experiments add exceptions to the rules found so far. Everyone agrees, though, that dopamine is not the only neurotransmitter in the central control of reward. Opiates are also involved under some conditions (Wise, 1982).

Dopamine has not provided an answer, but at least it has given us a starting point for investigating the biochemistry of reward. Further investigation of the dopamine system may reveal further aspects of the problem. Dopaminergic neurons project to such areas as the caudate nucleus, septal region, prefrontal cortex, and limbic cortex, as well as to the hypothalamus. These areas contain the systems that control and coordinate the motivational systems. The problem of determining the activators of behavior persists, but the label changes from *motivations* to *emotions*.

EMOTION—LIMBIC AND CORTICAL SYSTEMS

We often think of emotions as weaknesses and of strength as a lack of emotion. Yet the emotional systems must have evolved to perform some function; they must do something for us that isn't done by other neurological systems. We might think of emotions as points of contact between the higher-level organization of behavior and the lower-level motivational systems. If a necessary function isn't being performed, an emotion can intervene to galvanize further action.

It seems presumptuous to include such a personal, subjective experience as emotion in a book about the scientific bases of behavior. It is doubtful that subtle twinges of regret or vague feelings of sympathy will ever be understood through scientific analysis. But other emotions, such as rage, fear, and euphoria, have powerful influences on behavior and deserve our attention.

EARLY THEORIES

The earliest physiological theories of emotion followed the ideas of Galen, whose four "humors," or body secretions—sanguine, choleric, phlegmatic, and melancholic—were believed to determine emotions. Thoughts circulated in the ventricles of the brain, and emotions in the vascular system. Remains of this conception continue in our language: "She broke my heart." "He makes my blood boil." Theories of emotion have gradually shifted away from the humoral view and toward the dominance of neurological processes (Pribram, 1981).

The first modern theory of emotions was the **James-Lange theory,** which added the brain to the emotional mechanism. Because William James is perhaps the best writer that science has ever produced, it is best to describe the theory in his terms:

> Supposing the cortex to contain parts, liable to be excited by changes in each special sense-organ, in each portion of the skin, in each muscle, each joint, and each viscus, and to contain absolutely nothing else, we still have a scheme capable of representing the process of the emotions. An object falls on a sense-organ, affects a cortical part, and is perceived; or else the latter, excited inwardly, gives rise to an idea of the same object. Quick as a flash, the reflex currents pass down through their preordained channels, alter the condition of the muscle, skin, and viscus; and these alterations, per-

ceived, like the original object, in as many portions of the cortex, combine with it in consciousness and transform it from an object-simply-apprehended into an object-emotionally-felt. No new principles have to be invoked. (James, 1893, 472–474)

Thus emotion was seen as the result of the perception of one's own body states, such as the knot of fear in the stomach and the feeling of hair standing on end.

The James-Lange theory contains an element of truth, but it has fatal flaws. Cannon (1929) pointed them out: the viscera respond too slowly to be responsible for emotional feelings, artificial visceral stimulation does not induce emotion, and the emotions show far more variety than the simple body changes. Cannon explained the visceral responses as reactions of the sympathetic division of the autonomic system to a sudden threatening condition. The alternative **Cannon-Bard theory** emphasized the role of the thalamus and hypothalamus in organizing emotional states. There is some truth in this idea also, though again more is involved than just these areas.

A broader theory, first outlined by Papez (pronounced papes) in 1937 and later elaborated by MacLean (1949, 1958), invoked a circulation of activity in a part of the limbic system now called the **Papez circuit** (see Figure 9.4). The concept does not require a literal circling of action potentials through the limbic forebrain but rather identifies closely related structures in the initiation and control of emotional states. At last it seemed that the "visceral brain" had been found, and that the same brain region governed emotions. But again the idea was too limited. Even as the theory was being published, evidence that the viscera could be controlled by the cerebral cortex appeared (Kaada, Pribram & Epstein, 1949; Wall & Pribram, 1950). Further, ablation and stimulation of limbic areas also affects problem solving and memory in ways unrelated to emotions (see Chapter 11).

We must finally conclude that emotional reactions are not a class apart but are integrated with the brain's job of organizing responses to challenges of the environment. *Emotional* is not an insult but a description of a mode of activation of motivational systems. Visceral activation is sometimes (but not always) part of the preparation for action. A look at the cerebral organization of emotional systems will show how they connect cognitive processes on one side with visceral and motivational systems on the other.

ORGANIZATION OF THE EMOTIONAL SYSTEMS

Physiologically, emotions have been studied with traditional stimulation and ablation techniques

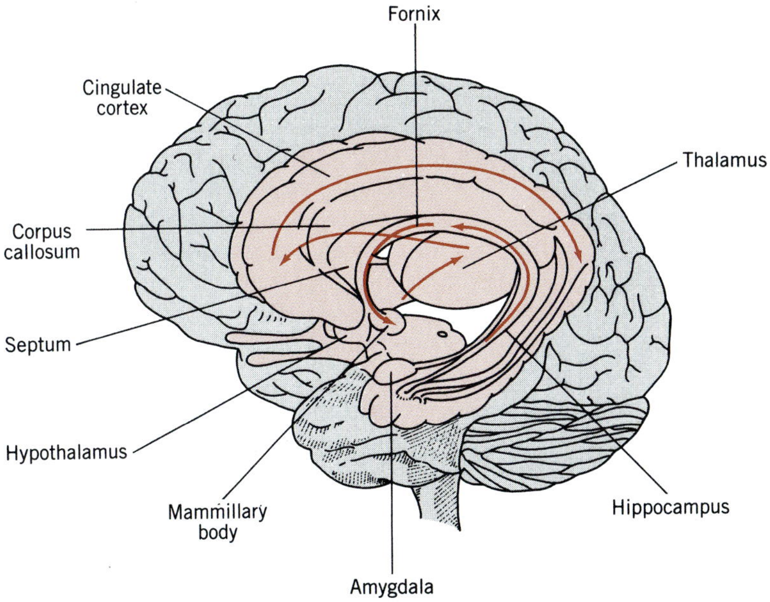

Figure 9.4 *The Papez circuit in the limbic forebrain. The circuit is a set of conceptually linked functions. A literal circling of activity has never been observed here.*

and more recently with biochemical methods. One of the earliest and most drastic experiments in this area was the removal of the entire cerebral cortex in cats (Bard, 1934). These animals gave exaggerated responses to almost any stimulus: a touch, a loud sound, a puff of air. On being stimulated, a cat would assume the arched-back "Halloween cat" posture and would hiss, growl, claw, and bite. Despite all this unpleasantness, a nearby observer usually would not be hurt; the attack was not directed toward a particular outside target but rather was a set of internal responses displayed nonspecifically. Bard named the syndrome **sham rage.** Because it could no longer be elicited if the hypothalamus was also damaged, Bard concluded that the expression of rage was coordinated in the hypothalamus. The organization of aggressive responses, however, lay elsewhere.

Aggression

Later researchers worked with subdivisions of Bard's huge lesions, finding components of the sham rage syndrome. Using localized electrical stimulation in awake, unrestrained animals, Delgado (1969a, 1969b) found sham rage–like responses following stimulation of the anterior and medial hypothalamus. In contrast, ferocious directed attacks on other cats followed lateral hypothalamic stimulation.

Stimulation outside the hypothalamus revealed different kinds of aggressive behavior with different contributions of emotion. The experiments started with cats that ordinarily do not attack mice. When stimulated in the medial forebrain bundle, the cats executed quiet and very effective attacks on mice, usually killing them on the first bite. Stimulation in the periventricular gray area elicited more dramatic but less effective responses: hissing, piloerection (erection of the hairs of the fur), and other signs of aggression, accompanied by biting and pawing at the mouse. But usually the victim escaped (Chi & Flynn, 1971). This kind of attack behavior was accentuated by amphetamine and reduced by the tranquilizer chlordiazepoxide (Horovitz et al., 1966; Panksepp, 1971).

These experiments differentiated two kinds of aggression. The quiet-biting attack defines predatory aggression, which perhaps shouldn't qualify as aggression because it shows none of the social signs usually associated with aggressive behavior. Rather, it is part of the predatory cat's normal feeding behavior (Glickman, 1977). The stimulation that elicited this behavior was in an area involved in feeding; the area also supports self-stimulation. The second, more emotional form of aggression was stimulated from the central gray areas usually associated with pain systems. Some authorities go beyond this differentiation to identify as many as seven separate kinds of aggression (Moyer, 1976). It is no accident that we are in familiar anatomical territory here; emotions are channeled through the same structures that govern motivational systems.

Control of Emotions

With brain stimulation we can activate emotional systems at will and perhaps answer an old question in psychology: how are the emotions normally released? Traditionally, there are two alternatives. The first, a "hydraulic" theory usually identified with Freud, supposes that emotions build up inside us. Without release, they eventually will be triggered by even the most trivial event. The second theory insists that strong releasing stimuli must be present to elicit an emotional response; without the trigger, an emotion is never expressed.

Physiological evidence points toward the second theory. One example occurs in experiments where brain stimulation in a monkey leads to attacks on smaller, more submissive monkeys (Delgado, 1969a). If only larger monkeys are present, the stimulated monkey appears agitated and vocalizes but does not threaten or attack. Apparently, at least in this experiment, expression of emotion is keyed to social or environmental conditions, even when the emotion is activated directly by electrical stimulation.

Other studies of monkeys have shown the importance of the limbic system, especially the amygdala (see Figure 9.4), in controlling aggression and other emotions. But the effect is more in how animals interpret information than in the direct expression of aggressive behavior.

When exposed to a new situation, normal monkeys (and people) show a set of **orienting responses**—groups of behaviors and physiological reactions that include both sensory acts and less obvious physiological responses. Among them are changes in heart rate, respiration, and the conductivity of the skin (the **galvanic skin response,** or **GSR**). After a few exposures to the novel situation, these responses are **habituated,** or progressively decreased in intensity.

Lesions of the Amygdala. Following bilateral removal of its amygdalas, a monkey continues to orient behaviorally. But it fails to habituate, acting as though the situation were continually new (Bagshaw & Coppock, 1968). One would expect that the physiological components of orienting would also fail to be habituated. Here, though, we encounter a surprise; the amygdalectomized monkey shows no physiological signs of orienting! In the normal animal, changes in GSR, heart rate, and breathing apparently accompany neural reorganizations that enable the animal to register the experience in memory (Pribram, 1971). The registration process fails in the amygdalectomized animal. Behavioral orienting continues, however; the body tries to load novel information into a missing system. We will look more closely at this situation in Chapter 11.

The failure of the amygdala to control emotional systems has drastic consequences in the ability of monkeys to handle social aggression. This was shown in a series of experiments on a group of rhesus monkeys living in a social colony (Rosvold, Mirsky & Pribram, 1954; Pribram, 1962). Animals in social colonies quickly form dominance hierarchies; the dominant, or "alpha," male is usually found near the center of the group; he shows aggression toward the other monkeys but is not attacked himself. The experimenters did an amygdalectomy on the dominant monkey, Dave. After he recovered, he was reintroduced to the group, with the results shown in Figure 9.5. Dave immediately tumbled to the bottom of the hierarchy. More precisely, he failed to react appropriately to social and aggressive signs from the other monkeys. An amygdalectomized monkey can always be spotted in a group cage because he wanders about, almost independent of the other monkeys, like an animal of another species.

Next, the experimenters amygdalectomized the new alpha male, Zeke; he too lost his position. But the third monkey, Riva, remained on top following his lesion. The explanation for Riva's continued dominance was not in Riva's own behavior but in the personality of Herby, the new number 2 monkey, who was rather placid. No one remaining below Riva offered a serious challenge.

Minor differences in the extent and locus of the lesions did not correlate with the differences in the behavioral results. Thus it is not only the neurologies of the individuals but also the social situations that determine the behavioral effects of a control system. This is an example of how the cortical mechanisms of long-term behavioral control interact with emotional systems to govern social behavior.

You may have noticed that all the monkeys in the experiment were males. Males were used because most female primates show little aggressive behavior toward members of their own species, except when defending infants. A similar sex difference exists in humans, though human aggressive behavior is more influenced by learning and socialization. One reason for the sex difference in aggression is not personality but biochemistry; the male steroid hormone **testosterone** is one of several hormones that has a strong influence on emotional behavior.

Biochemical Influences on Emotion

The study of emotions has come full circle. It started with Galen's humors, and the current emphasis has been shifting to biochemical and hormonal influences on emotional behavior. The difference is that the current work emphasizes biochemical influences on the brain; the hormones modulate the activities of emotional and motivational systems, but the chemicals are not the emotions.

Some emotional states seem to have a direct link with specific neurotransmitter systems. There is some evidence that anxiety is closely related to brain receptors for **benzodiazepines**—molecules similar to the inhibitory neurotransmitter gamma-aminobutyric acid (GABA) but larger and more complex. In rhesus monkeys, the infusion of ethyl beta-carboline-3-carboxylate (beta-CCE), a compound with a high affinity for the benzodiazepine

Figure 9.5 *Social dominance hierarchies in a group of male rhesus monkeys following repeated amygdalectomy of the dominant monkey.* (a) *Before surgery was begun.* (b) *After Dave, the dominant animal, received a bilateral amygdalectomy.* (c) *After both Dave and Zeke were amygdalectomized.* (d) *After Riva was also amygdalectomized. The failure of Riva to drop in the hierarchy was explained in later experiments by the nonaggressive nature of Herby, the new number 2 monkey. Adapted from Koch (1962).*

receptor sites, induces all of the behavioral, autonomic, and pharmacological effects of anxiety (Ninan et al., 1982). Animals receiving this compound struggled, defecated and urinated, picked and scratched at themselves, and had penile erections. They also had elevated heart rates and increases in blood epinephrine (adrenaline). The effects were prevented if a benzodiazepine receptor antagonist, RO 15–1788, was given along with the beta-CCE. Thus the preliminary indications are that anxiety is a more unified emotional system than orienting or aggression, with internal and external signs driven by the same neurotransmitter systems.

The animals given beta-CCE also showed frequent distress vocalization, a behavior that one researcher has assigned to another emotional system. Specifically, Panksepp (1982) has proposed the existence of a "panic" system in the hypothalamus and limbic forebrain, based on stimulation studies in the rat. The system's primary role is a social one—to inform other animals of the distress. The panic system may involve opioid sites, for there are similarities between the neurochemical dynamics of opiate addiction and social dependence (Panksepp, 1982). Further, behavioral signs of panic are elicited by stimulation of opioid-rich sites, including the dorsomedial thalamus, the ventral septum, and the preoptic areas. The system seems to be particularly active in young animals, including human babies, for whom distress vocalizations are, at first, the only way to communicate dangers and needs.

These examples show that the physiology of emotional systems and their relationships to one another are far from worked out. The most thoroughly investigated system to date, aggression, may indicate where work on other systems will lead.

The Biochemistry of Aggression. It has been known for a long time that the castration of males reduces their violent and aggressive behavior. In castrated mice, aggressive behavior is restored by injections of **androgens**—male sex hormones—in a dose-related manner (the larger the dose of androgens, the more aggressive behavior). Figure 9.6 shows that it is the concentration of sex

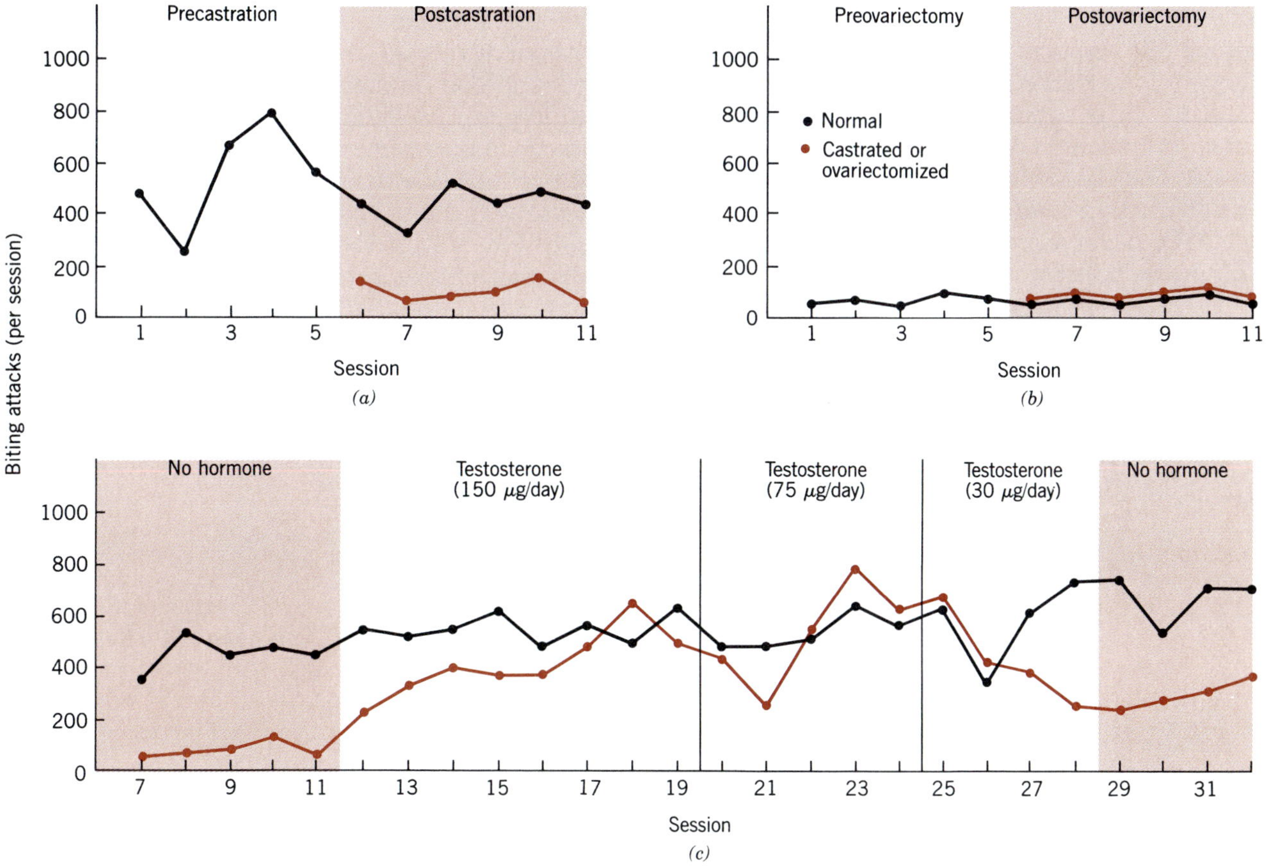

Figure 9.6 *Behavioral effects of castration and testosterone replacement therapy in mice. Aggression is measured by the number of biting attacks on an inanimate object introduced into the home cage.* (a) *Male behavior before and after castration.* (b) *Female behavior before and after removal of ovaries. Females show little attack behavior either before or after.* (c) *Effects of hormone replacement on attack behavior of castrated males. Adapted from Wagner et al. (1980).*

hormones in the blood—not some other effect of castration—that causes the reduction in aggression (Wagner, Beauving & Hutchinson, 1980). Similar effects are seen in humans, though the ethics of experimentation in this area make it necessary to restrict the subjects of study. In some countries, castration is a punishment for repeated sex crimes; it results in the disappearance of both heterosexual and homosexual aggressive attacks (Sturup, 1961; Laschet, 1973). When testosterone injections are given to the castrated men, violent behavior reappears (Hawke, 1950).

Testosterone is not the only hormone influencing aggression. Removing the adrenal glands of mice reduces aggressiveness (Harding & Leshner, 1972), but injecting **corticosterone,** an adrenal cortex hormone, restores the behavior (Walker & Leshner, 1972). This does not mean that corticosterone is responsible for aggressive behavior, however. As Figure 9.7 shows, the hormone participates in a negative feedback loop involving other hormones. Glucocorticoids, including corticosterone, cause the hypothalamus to reduce the production of **adrenocorticotropic hormone (ACTH)** in the anterior pituitary. Reducing ACTH in turn reduces the production of glucocorticoids in the normal animal. But it also reduces the production of testosterone, branching from the feedback loop at the bottom of Figure 9.7. Thus the feedback loop regulating glucocorticoids has a feedforward branch involving testosterone.

It is difficult to analyze a feedback loop experimentally because events in one part of the loop influence events in other parts. To study the system, one must open the loop. This was done on rats for the ACTH negative feedback loop by a combination of adrenalectomy to open the glucocorticoid branch and castration to open the testosterone branch (Leshner et al., 1973); the result is shown in Figure 9.8. Next, the animals were given replacement therapy with corticosterone and testosterone to create an open-loop preparation with normal hormone levels. The experimenter, rather than the hypothalamic feedback, controlled the hormone levels. ACTH could no longer drive the feedback loop through the missing adrenal cortex. But despite this change, the ACTH injections still reduced aggressiveness. Thus the reduction in aggression was due to the ACTH itself. Replacement therapy with a glucocorticoid alone did not restore aggression; testosterone was always necessary to induce aggressive behavior.

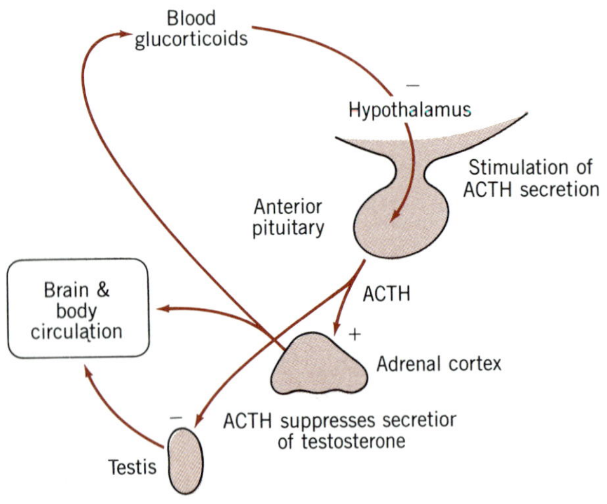

Figure 9.7 *Indirect feedback control of testosterone production in males. A feedback path through the hypothalamus and the circulatory system has a branch that governs testosterone synthesis in the testes.*

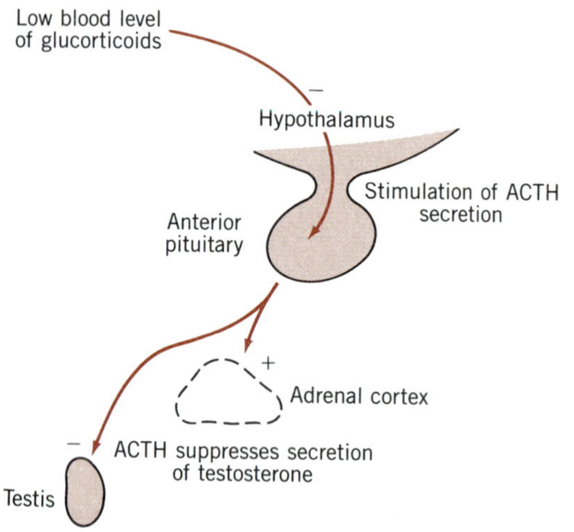

Figure 9.8 *An open-loop preparation for studying mechanisms governing testosterone production. The feedback loop is opened by removal of the adrenal cortex.*

In sum, several hormones can influence aggression in mice; glucocorticoids increase it and ACTH reduces it. But testosterone is always necessary for aggression to occur, at least in rodents. Though some testosterone is found in both sexes, it is also the primary male sex hormone, providing a strong link between aggression and the regulation of another important control system—sex.

THE NEUROLOGY OF SEX

Chances are good that you turned to this section of the book (or were tempted to) before it came up in the regular order of subject headings. The reason for your curiosity is clear from an evolutionary viewpoint—you come from a long and unbroken line of people who have reproduced successfully. Since sexual fitness provides a final common path through which all other attributes are passed on, it is no wonder that we have inherited such a powerful motivational and emotional system connected with it.

It is said that the two sexes are entirely identical, except that they are completely different! The differences begin to appear early in intrauterine development.

DEVELOPMENT OF SEX DIFFERENCES

Embryological development begins with a fertilized egg containing either an XX sex chromosome pair (female) or any XY pair (male). The sex of the embryo makes no difference in its development until about the seventh week, after the other major organ systems have already developed. At this stage the embryo has the beginnings of two reproductive systems: The **Wolffian ducts,** which can develop into a male system, and the **Müllerian ducts,** which can become a female system. At this point the gonads of an XY embryo begin to produce male hormones, stimulating the development of the Wolffian system and causing regression of the embryonic Müllerian system (see Figure 9.9*b* and 9.9*d*). Without these hormones the system develops into the female form (see Figure 9.9*c* and 9.9*e*). Female development is the default condition and will occur even if no gonads are present. One can say that every human becomes a female unless something happens to produce a male.

Once the testes have differentiated, they release androgens that induce the development of male external genitalia. The glans develops into a penis, and the fetal labiosacral swelling becomes the scrotum. The testes begin their descent from their original location beside the kidneys. While these changes are occurring, the mother's body is flooded with estrogen from the pregnancy. Yet this female sex hormone doesn't affect the embryo's development. The embryo is protected from its mother's hormones by alpha-feto protein, a substance that prevents estrogen from crossing the embryo's blood-brain barrier.

Without hormonal influences, the gonads remain in their original locations to develop into ovaries, the glans becomes the clitoris, and the labiosacral swelling differentiates into the **labia majora** (Latin for "large lips") surrounding the vaginal opening.

Abnormal Sexual Differentiation. The organization of sexual development is revealed in cases where it goes awry. If a genetic female (with XX chromosomes) is exposed to high enough levels of androgen at the sensitive time in development, she will develop a male body and behaviors. Only her (his?) sterility will reveal the abnormality. If androgen levels are intermediate, however, the embryo will differentiate to a form intermediate between the normal male and female forms. This can occur because the adrenal glands of both sexes produce some androgens, and if either the fetus or the mother produces too much during the critical period, some masculinization will occur. The result is a person with external genitalia intermediate between the two normal forms.

The reverse abnormality can also occur. If the tissues of a genetic male (with XY chromosomes) are insensitive to androgens, he will develop the female body form shown in Figure 9.10, even if the testes were formed normally (Money & Ehrhardt, 1972). Such a person also shows little pubic hair; in both males and females, its growth is caused by androgens secreted at the time of puberty. Of course, the androgen-insensitive male is also sterile.

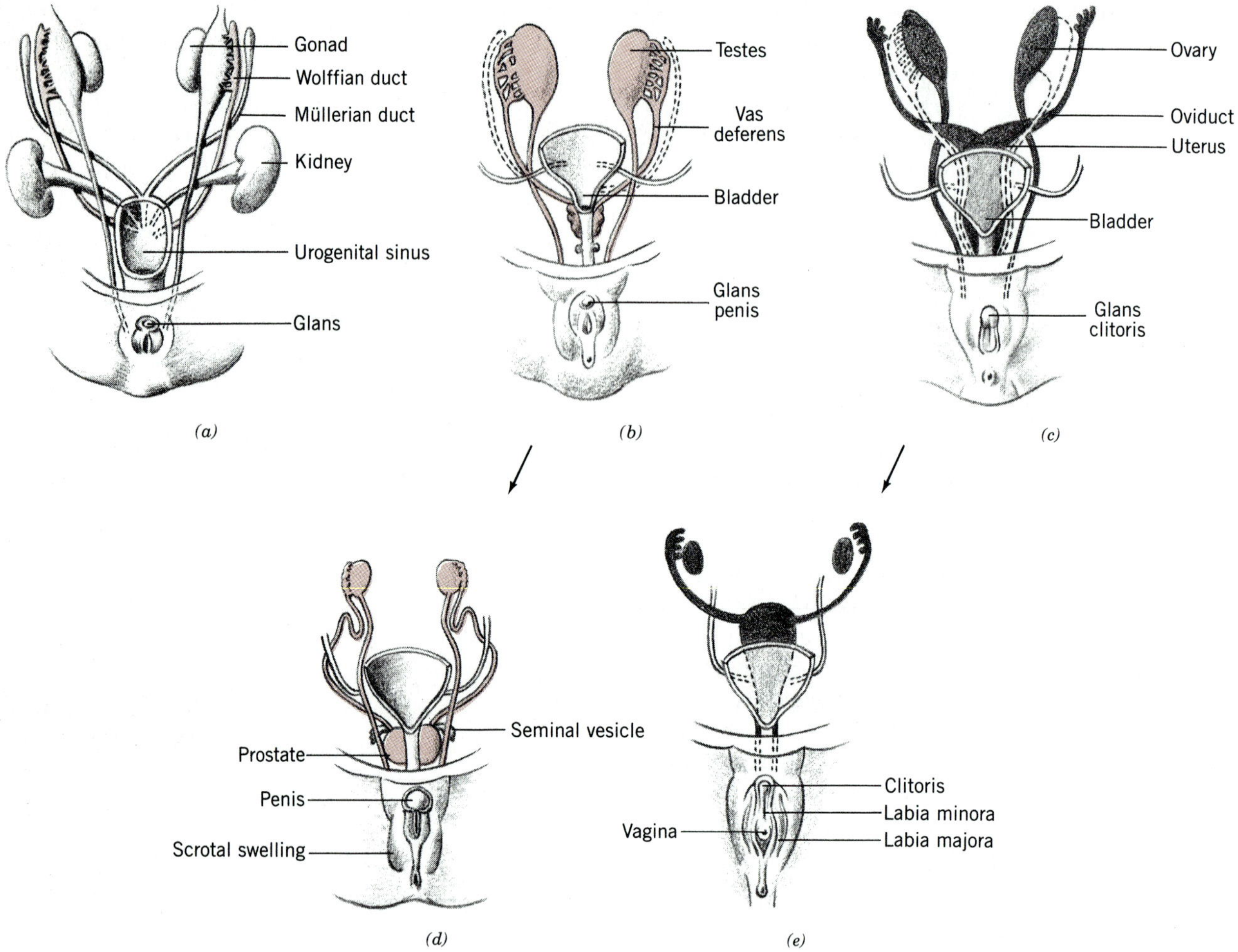

Figure 9.9 *The embryonic development of male and female reproductive systems. Both systems appear in each early embryo; hormones then cause the development of one and the regression of the other. The male testes remain inside the body, descending into the scrotum near the time of birth.* (a) *Six weeks, undifferentiated.* (b) *Eight weeks, male.* (c) *Eight weeks, female.* (d) *Fifteen weeks, male.* (e) *Fifteen weeks, female.*

These abnormalities reveal a surprising characteristic of the inheritance of sex-specific traits: all of the genes controlling normal male development are present in each female of the species, and all the female characteristics are coded in each male. The only critical male body characteristic carried by the Y chromosome is the genetic "switch" that produces hormones in the fetus. Other male traits can be induced artificially in females by the injection of androgens.

All of this would be of only tangential importance to the subject of this book if it were not for the fact that most sex hormones also affect the CNS. Male and female brains develop according to the same rules as male and female bodies.

MALE AND FEMALE BRAINS

At one time it was thought that boys and girls were similar in both body and behavior until the changes of puberty, except for the genitalia. Differences in behavior or personality were attributed to socialization. Recent evidence, however, shows that the brains of the sexes are different from birth. In the anterior hypothalamus, the sensibly named sexually dimorphic nuclei of the preoptic

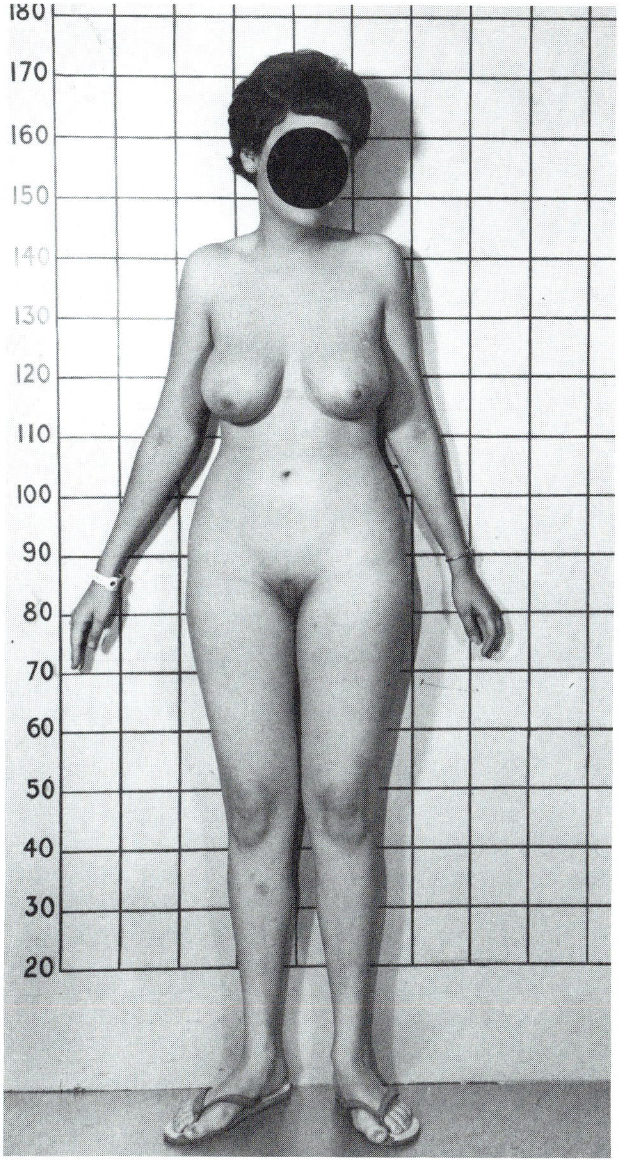

Figure 9.10 *A female body form in a person with XY (male) genes. The development of female body features is a result of insensitivity to testosterone; the lack of pubic hair results from insensitivity to another androgen, androstenedione. From Money & Erhardt (1972).*

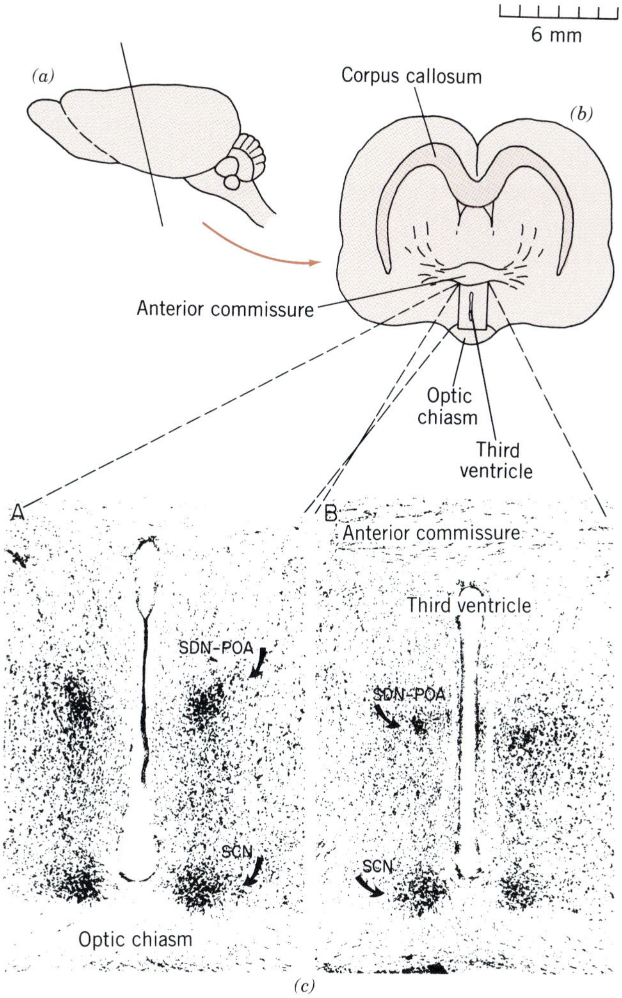

Figure 9.11 *The sexually dimorphic nucleus of the preoptic area in the rat.* (a) *Lateral view of rat brain, showing plane of frontal section.* (b) *Frontal section of rat brain, with rectangle showing hypothalamus (enlarged in* [c]*).* (c) *Sexually dimorphic nucleus in normal male rat (left) and normal female rat (right). For comparison, the more ventral suprachiasmatic nucleus is about the same size in both sexes.*

area (SDN-POA) are 8 times larger in male rats than in females, as Figure 9.11 shows (Gorski et al., 1978). In humans, the difference is less extreme; the region is about 2.5 times larger in adult males than in females. (The amount is based on examinations of brains from people who died at the ages of 10 to 93—Swabb & Fliers, 1985.) In monkeys the difference is more subtle; the preoptic area is about the same size in both sexes, but in males it has more extensive dendritic branching (Ayoub, Greenough & Juraska, 1983). The observations were of juvenile monkeys, so differences in levels of circulating hormones could not bias the results. The sexually dimorphic nuclei are in a region of the hypothalamus where androgen-sensitive neurons are found, and their size can be altered by androgen treatments in newborns. The function of the area, though, remains unknown in both rats and humans.

Sex differences in the human corpus callosum were mentioned in Chapter 3 and are shown here in Figure 9.12. Females have a larger splenium—the caudal part of the commissure connecting the hemispheres. The functional implications of this difference are still a matter for speculation. The smaller male splenium might mean, for instance, that males have a higher degree of functional independence between their hemispheres.

Biochemical Differences

The most important differences between male and female brains are not anatomical but biochemical. The brain reorganization induced by fetal androgens cannot be reversed by more androgens later in life. Thus the same principles that applied to body development also apply to the development of sexual behavior.

In humans the critical period for hormonal influence on later behavior is before birth, but in rats it is after birth and therefore easier to study. Female rats exposed to androgens shortly after birth show no immediate changes but fail to demonstrate normal female sexual behavior as adults, even if injected with female hormones. If the rats are given androgens at maturity, they display typical male mounting behavior (Levine, 1966). With males the experiment is a little more complicated, because the testes will produce a male animal no matter what is injected early in life or in adulthood. But castrated males can be feminized by estrogens at maturity and show typical female sexual behavior.

Female Hormones. At puberty, human females begin a hormone cycle that continues throughout reproductive life, with interruptions during pregnancy and lactation. Directed by the hypothalamus, the cycle is a circular series of events, each triggered by the one before. It begins when the hypothalamus directs the anterior pituitary to secrete **follicle-stimulating hormone (FSH),** which controls the production of estrogen and progesterone. The follicles—small clumps of epithelial cells surrounding the ova (Latin for "eggs")—respond by growing and releasing **estrogens.** The estrogens complete the first loop of the feedback cycle (see Figure 9.13) by influencing the hypothalamus. In response to the estrogens, the hypothalamus directs the anterior pituitary to produce **luteinizing hormone (LH)**—a sex hormone that influences hormonal secretions in the gonads of both sexes—causing one of the follicles to release an egg. The remainder of the follicle transforms itself into a **corpus luteum** (Latin for "yellow body"), a temporary endocrine gland that produces progesterone for a few days before decaying. Figure 9.14 shows the physical appearance of the structures at various stages in the cycle.

Progesterone, another female hormone, has two kinds of effects; it prepares the uterine lining for implantation of the egg in the event of fertilization, and it inhibits the hypothalamus from triggering the next surge of FSH. For this reason, progesterone is an ingredient in many birth control

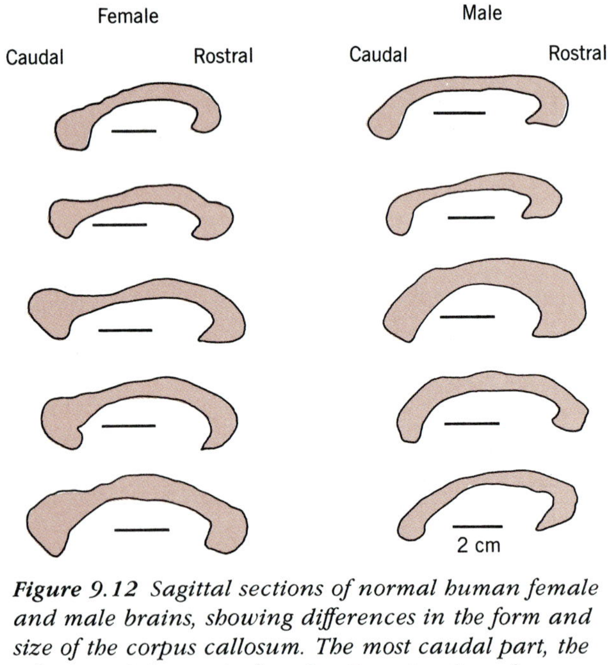

Figure 9.12 Sagittal sections of normal human female and male brains, showing differences in the form and size of the corpus callosum. The most caudal part, the splenium, is larger in females. Examination of many brains shows that the difference is consistent and is not a result of chance variation in the examples illustrated.

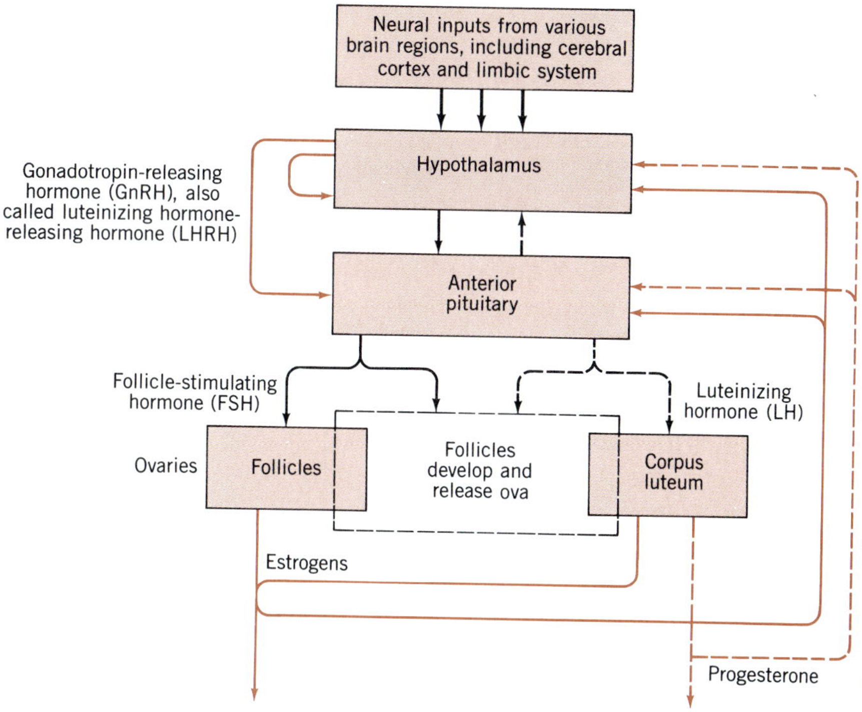

Figure 9.13 *Neural regulation of ovarian function. All hypothalamic influences are indirect, through a second hormone acting at the anterior pituitary. Estrogens promote the development of female reproductive organs and of female secondary sex characteristics (body form, breasts, etc.) while progesterone prepares the uterus for pregnancy and the breasts for lactation.*

pills. As the corpus luteum decays, progesterone decreases and the hypothalamus initiates another cycle. Because two passes through hypothalamic control centers are made in each menstrual cycle, the hormonal events constitute a double oscillator (two oscillating cycles linked to each other).

Male Hormones. In males, hormone levels do not cycle regularly. Androgen levels can increase, primarily in response to stress, but the trigger is outside rather than inside the body. The hypothalamus triggers puberty by releasing a master control hormone, **gonadotropin-releasing hormone (GnRH),** inducing the anterior pituitary to manufacture LH and FSH. These hormones stimulate the production of testosterone in the testes, and the testosterone suppresses production of the hypothalamic and pituitary hormones to provide a feedback control of testosterone levels. A large amount of gonadal hormone has a relatively small feedback effect in males, so the levels remain stable.

Hormonal activities prepare for the climactic event of sexuality—fertilization. This event requires appropriate sexual behavior on many levels.

SEXUAL BEHAVIOR

Relatively early in evolution, long before primitive animals left the sea, sexual behavior became necessary. Sexual union was usually a simple matter, for in a watery medium it was necessary only for eggs and sperm to be released at approximately the same time and place; the sperm could swim to the eggs on their own. The gathering of animals and the synchronization of **gamete** (sex cell) release were accomplished largely by chemical mediators.

When animals moved to land, they continued to require water for fertilization to occur. As they became more independent of wet environments, however, a new adaptation—internal fertilization—became necessary. It was spectacularly successful. It not only allowed the gametes to remain in a watery medium, but it protected them better than they were before. Its disadvantage was that

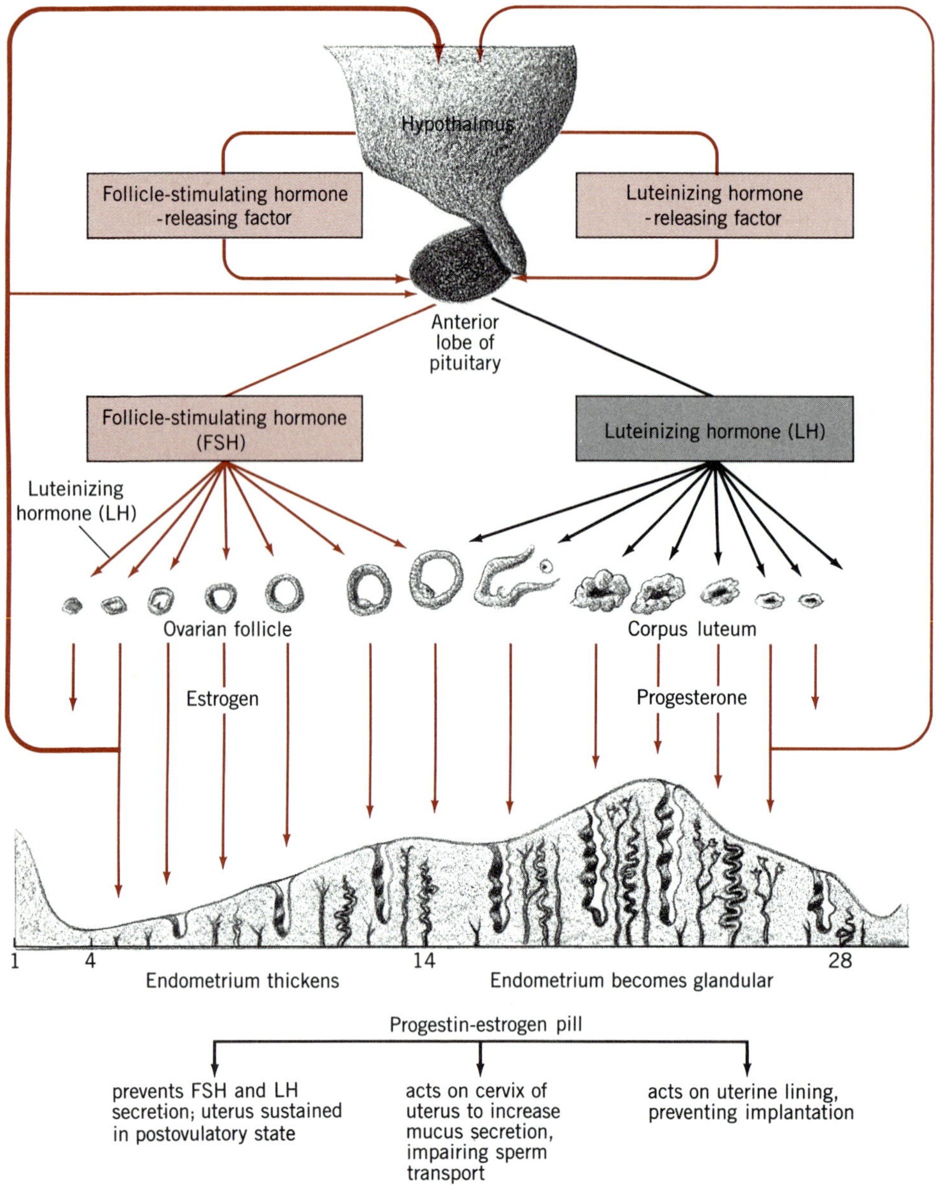

***Figure 9.14** Uterine changes in the female reproductive cycle. The uterine lining thickens and then sloughs off (menstruation) with each cycle of about 28 days. Birth control pills take advantage of the fact that pregnant women do not become pregnant again until after delivery; the pills simulate the hormonal conditions of early pregnancy.*

it required more complex sexual behaviors, both for finding mates and for copulation. Internal fertilization required not only vaginas and penises but brains.

Male and Female Reproductive Behavior

Many sexual behaviors in both sexes are coordinated at brain-stem and spinal levels. In male humans, erection and ejaculation are mediated by autonomic reactions; other components, such as pelvic thrusting, originate in skeletal nerve centers of the spinal cord. In male dogs, all of these responses can be elicited by stimulation of different parts of the penis if the spinal cord is severed from the brain (Hart, 1978). In intact male dogs, the brain modulates these spinal reflexes, so they occur only in the presence of a bitch (a female dog) in heat. Male animals, however, will be sexually unresponsive if the SDN-POA is damaged. Lesions of this area abolish copulatory behavior (Hart, 1973; Hart, 1974). However, the nucleus contains receptor sites for testosterone. If testosterone is administered locally to the SDN-POA of castrated animals, it restores sexual response.

Many female sexual reflexes are also coordinated at low levels. In spinally sectioned female dogs and cats, tactile stimulation causes the hindquarters to arch to one side and the tail to move to the side (Hart, 1978). These are components of copulatory behavior in normal animals.

In humans, sexual responses include the elaborate behaviors and physiological actions summarized in Table 9.1. Surprisingly, many of them have been discovered only recently (Masters & Johnson, 1971). The fact that many of these responses were unknown for so long shows how automatic they are. It also shows the reluctance of researchers to investigate emotion-charged topics such as human sexual intercourse.

Complex Sexual Behaviors

All of us are aware that sexual behavior involves far more than has been reviewed so far. For both sexes, arousal depends more on learned cues than on the olfactory cues dominant in nonprimates, and there is enormous variety in the stimuli and behaviors that lead to arousal. Hormones, though, remain a powerful influence even in humans.

Female Sexual Behavior. Sexual interest for women begins with the production of both estrogens and androgens at puberty. Thereafter, sexuality is maintained despite the regular menstrual oscillation of hormonal levels, though sexual activity in other animals generally occurs only near the time of ovulation. The stage of the menstrual cycle may have a small effect on the frequency of sexual intercourse (reviewed by Bancroft, 1978), though the variability is great.

Androgens are produced by the adrenal cortex in both males and females. They are also produced by the ovaries, because testosterone and other androgens are biochemical precursors of estrogens. Hence women's blood testosterone levels are about one-tenth those of men. There is some evidence that testosterone can increase sexual interest in women who complain of lack of sexual responsiveness; tranquilizers, though they relaxed such women, had no effect on sexual interest (Bancroft & Sakkebaek, 1979). A study of women using oral contraceptives, however, showed no increase in sexual interest from testosterone. (Possibly the synthetic progesterone used in these contraceptives can itself alter sexual responsiveness.) Thus the data are sketchy on this point. But even if testosterone does turn out to enhance female sexuality, it won't make a good aphrodisiac (sex stimulant). It must be injected to be effective, and it wouldn't work on everyone. Also, its masculinizing side effects with prolonged use would be unacceptable.

Menopause is the cessation of the menstrual cycle in women. The hypothalamus continues secreting FSH but receives no negative feedback from the follicles. As a result, FSH levels increase, causing reductions in estrogen and progesterone levels. Subsequently, changes in the vaginal lining and in mood occur in many women, but sexual interest is usually maintained.

Male Sexual Behavior. Learning, context, and hormones strongly influence male sexual behavior. Decortication generally has a greater effect on sexual performance in male animals than in females, perhaps because in most species more complex behavior is required of males during intercourse.

The need for cortical flexibility involves not only copulation itself but also the choosing of appropriate sex partners. Normally, a male must recover for some time after copulation; but if a new partner becomes available, the male experiences a resurgence of sexual ability. This phenomenon, known as the "Coolidge effect," has a clear advantage for the evolutionary fitness of the male animal. The effect is said to have been named after an incident that occurred when president Calvin Coolidge and his wife were visiting a farm. Mrs. Coolidge asked whether the unceasing sexual activity in a flock of hens was due to a single rooster, and the farmer replied that it was. She remarked, "You might point that out to Mr. Coolidge." The president then asked whether the rooster approached a different hen each time, and when told that

Table 9.1
Sexual Response Cycle—Pelvic Viscera

Male	*Female*
Excitement Phase	
Penile erection (3 to 8 sec)	Vaginal lubrication (5 to 15 sec)
$\uparrow\downarrow$ as phase is prolonged	$\uparrow\downarrow$ as phase is prolonged
Thickening, flattening, and elevation of scrotal integument	Thickening of vaginal walls, flattening and elevation of major labia
$\uparrow\downarrow$ as phase is prolonged	$\uparrow\downarrow$ as phase is prolonged
Moderate testicular elevation and size increase	Expansion of inner $\frac{2}{3}$ vaginal barrel and elevation of cervix and corpus
$\uparrow\downarrow$ as phase is prolonged	$\uparrow\downarrow$ as phase is prolonged
Plateau Phase	
Increase in penile coronal circumference and testicular tumescence ($\frac{1}{2}$ to 1 $\times$ enlarged)	Orgasmic platform in outer $\frac{1}{3}$ of vagina
Full testicular elevation and rotation (30 to 35 deg)	Full inner $\frac{2}{3}$ vaginal expansion, uterine and cervical elevation
Purple cast to corona of penis (inconsistent, even if orgasm is to ensue)	"Sex-skin" discoloration of minor labia (constant, if orgasm is to ensue)
Mucoidlike emission (Cowper's gland)	Mucoidlike emission (Bartholin's gland)
Orgasmic Phase	
Ejaculation	Pelvic Response
1. Contraction of accessory organs of reproduction a. Vas deferens b. Seminal vesicles c. Ejaculatory duct d. Prostate	1. Contractions of uterus from fundus toward lower uterine segment
2. Relaxation of external bladder sphincter	2. Minimal relaxation of external cervical os (nullipara)
3. Contractions of penile urethra $\frac{8}{10}$ sec for 2 to 3 contractions (slowing thereafter for 2 to 4 more contractions)	3. Contraction of orgasmic platform $\frac{8}{10}$ sec for 4 to 8 contractions (slowing thereafter for 2 to 4 more contractions)
4. External rectal sphincter contractions (2 to 4 contractions at $\frac{8}{10}$-sec intervals)	4. External rectal sphincter contractions (2 to 4 contractions at $\frac{8}{10}$-sec intervals) External urethral sphincter contractions (2 to 3 contractions at irregular intervals to 10 to 15%)
Resolution Phase	
1. Refractory period with rapid loss of pelvic vasocongestion	1. Ready return to orgasm with retarded loss of pelvic vasocongestion
2. Loss of penile erection in primary (rapid) and secondary (slow) stages	2. Loss of "sex-skin" color and orgasmic platform in primary (rapid) stage Remainder of pelvic vasocongestion as secondary (slow) stage

Sexual Response Cycle—General Body Reactions

Excitement Phase	
Nipple erection (30%)	Nipple erection Sex-tension flush (25%)
Plateau Phase	
Sex-tension flush (25%) Carpopedal spasm Generalized skeletal muscle tension Hyperventilation Tachycardia (100 to 160/min)	Sex-tension flush (75%) Carpopedal spasm Generalized skeletal muscle tension Hyperventilation Tachycardia (100 to 160/min)
Orgasmic Phase	
Specific skeletal muscle contractions Hyperventilation Tachycardia (100 to 180/min)	Specific skeletal muscle contractions Hyperventilation Tachycardia (110 to 180/min)
Resolution Phase	
Sweating reaction (30 to 40%) Hyperventilation Tachycardia (150 to 180/min)	Sweating reaction (30 to 40%) Hyperventilation Tachycardia (150 to 180/min)

Source: Adapted from Masters & Johnson (1971).

he did, said, "You might point that out to Mrs. Coolidge."

Although castration results in an eventual loss of sexual interest, treating normal males with additional testosterone usually does not increase sexual activity. The reason for this seeming contradiction is the "ceiling effect"—most males already produce more than enough testosterone to keep themselves at a maximum level of sexual interest. Additional testosterone has an effect only in males with low natural testosterone levels who complain of a lack of sexual responsiveness. Given testosterone supplements, most of these men rapidly recover sexual responsiveness (Davidson, Camargo & Smith, 1979). Because of the strong effects of beliefs and attitudes on sexual performance, it is important to note that this study was done double-blind; neither the patients nor their doctors knew whether testosterone or a placebo was being given.

Homosexuality. Why are some males, and a smaller number of females, attracted primarily to members of the same sex? There are two ways to explain this phenomenon, which is found in all cultures, despite sometimes violent suppression of it. One explanation is that homosexuality provides benefits for a group of humans by freeing some of its members from child-rearing activities. Though homosexuality clearly does not enhance an individual's evolutionary fitness, it may give an advantage to heterosexual relatives.

Another explanation, on a different level, is that homosexuality may be an unavoidable aberration in biological development. If that is the case, we must look to embryological development to find its causes, for we know that hormones do not change sexual preference in adults. Administering androgens to adult females or estrogens to adult males causes secondary physical changes but not same-sex attraction. Further, it is uncertain whether testosterone levels are any different in male homosexuals than they are in male heterosexuals. Some studies find lower levels in homosexuals, some find the same levels, and still others find higher levels (Bancroft, 1978).

Early exposure to abnormal levels of hormones associated with the opposite sex may cause irreversible changes in the brain, leading to changes in adult sexual preferences and behaviors. The evidence is diverse but indirect. When female rats have many brothers in the same litter, testosterone produced by the embryonic brothers may leak into the embryonic female in the uterus. These females are more likely to exhibit male mounting and other male sexual behaviors; the effect is weaker in females with fewer brothers (Clemens, 1971).

Some human females have been unintentionally androgenized with hormones given to their mothers to prevent miscarriage. Understandably, these drugs are no longer used. Also, some girls whose adrenal glands secreted large amounts of androgens exhibited at birth clitoral enlargement and some labial fusion, which were corrected surgically. During childhood, the girls described themselves as "tomboys," preferring male to female playmates and choosing toy trucks and guns instead of dolls (Money & Ehrhardt, 1972). A follow-up study of the girls showed no evidence of homosexuality, though other studies indicate possible increases in bisexuality (Erhardt & Meyer-Bahlburg, 1979). The results may simply reflect an overall increase in sexual behavior, with bisexual activity increasing along with heterosexual activity.

Complementary effects are found in males exposed to estrogens before birth. At one time, diabetic mothers were given synthetic estrogens to prevent miscarriage. Their sons at age 16 were less aggressive and assertive than normal, and they were less skilled at athletics (Yalon, Green & Fisk, 1973). There was great variability, however, and the effects were statistically weak. In an experiment simulating more natural conditions, Ward (1972) stressed pregnant rats with a bright light. The stress increased the mothers' production of steroid hormones, presumably suppressing androgen production in their embryonic sons. The offspring had abnormally small external genitalia and at maturity showed deficient sexual behavior. They were also more sensitive to estrogen treatment than normal males, responding with more female sexual behavior than usual.

Though there is no consistent evidence that hormone levels differ in homosexual and heterosexual males, there may be a difference in the sensitivity of homosexual males to sex hormones. One recent study found that male homosexuals are intermediate between male and female heterosexuals in their hormonal response to an injected estrogen preparation (Gladue, Green & Hellman, 1984). Women showed an initial decrease in LH levels, followed by a strong increase; heterosexual men showed only the decrease. Homosexual men showed a decrease followed by a slight increase. The injections lowered testosterone levels in homosexual men more strongly than in heterosexual men, even though baseline testosterone levels were the same in both groups. The women showed no change in their testosterone levels. Whether the hormone responsiveness causes changes in sexual preference, or whether some other factor affects both hormone responsiveness and behavior, remains to be seen.

In conclusion, the evidence for a biological basis of homosexuality is sketchy for both males and females. One reason for the weakness of the evidence is that many environmental factors are at least as important as early hormonal exposure in determining adult sexual patterns. Genetic males can assume the opposite sex role if they are raised consistently as females, and they will typically be attracted to males later in life (Money & Ehrhardt, 1972). The same flexibility applies to genetic females. Even in hormonally influenced behaviors, experience is crucial. Experiments on the role of early experience in human sexual behavior range from difficult to unethical; information on the issue must come from other primates.

An Animal Model of Experience and Socialization

At the University of Wisconsin, Harry Harlow and his associates wished to raise healthier rhesus monkeys. They hit upon the idea of raising the baby monkeys in separate cages, keeping them warm and providing them with bottled formula from nipples.

The effort failed miserably. Most of the monkeys died within a few weeks of birth, though they were kept much cleaner than is possible in messy group cages. Harlow then threw in the towel, and that was the answer; survival rates improved considerably when a scrap of terrycloth was left in the

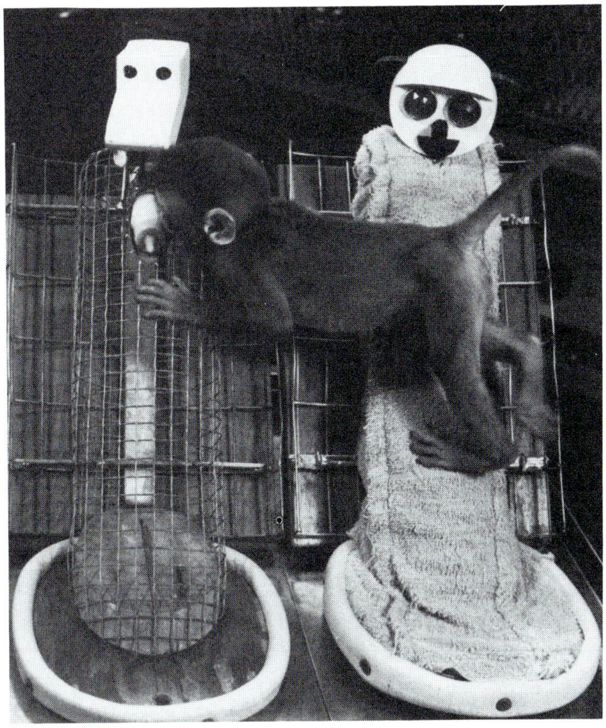

Figure 9.15 Behavior of a surrogate-reared rhesus monkey. Though food is provided only on the wire "mother," the infant spends most of its time clinging to the cloth mother. The behavior shows that food reinforcement does not play a strong role in establishing the mother-infant bond.

cage. Like a human infant, the baby monkey became attached to the cloth and would scream if anyone tried to remove it. Harlow came to suspect that monkeys had an unlearned need for contact with a soft body. To make a firm conclusion from these qualitative observations, he initiated studies comparing cloth and wire "surrogate mothers" (see Figure 9.15). He separated food reinforcement and contact comfort by providing a nipple only on the wire mother. As expected, the baby monkey visited the wire mother only for feeding. It spent most of its time near the cloth mother. At times of stress it would jump up and cling to the cloth mother (Harlow & Zimmerman, 1958). In this way, infant monkeys could be raised to maturity.

When these monkeys grew up and began interacting with other monkeys, however, Harlow received another nasty surprise. The results of trying to breed these animals were "frighteningly unsuccessful." The monkeys were hopeless at courtship and reproductive behavior. Many seemed willing but couldn't figure out what to do. Their activity looked more like the play of normal juveniles. Giving them further social experience didn't help much, for many of the monkeys, especially those reared with only a wire mother, were vicious and aggressive. Lack of early social experience had permanently handicapped these monkeys, both socially and sexually (Harlow, 1962).

Harlow pressed on. Faced with the monkeys' social failure at sexual behavior, he studied a few surrogate-reared females who had managed to become pregnant (mostly by experienced group-reared males). Of 38 first-time mothers, 5 killed their infants. A sixth infant was removed after the

Figure 9.16 Infant abuse by a monkey reared under the method shown in Figure 9.15. The mother is not punishing the infant in an effort to improve its behavior but is rejecting what she seems to interpret as an annoyance.

mother seriously maimed it. Most of the other infants survived despite the brutal abuse and neglect they suffered (see Figure 9.16). Maternal behavior may be inborn in many species, but in monkeys (and even more in humans) early social experience is crucial in developing the appropriate skills and attitudes. The experience need not even include contact with adults; monkeys raised in groups of peers were far from normal, but they were more-or-less successful at assuming adult sex roles and behaviors. The experiments yielded another important lesson: the whole research program was a series of failures, but from each failure emerged an important new aspect of primate behavior.

Harlow's surrogate-reared monkeys showed one other frightening characteristic; many of them were viciously self-destructive. They injured themselves so seriously that the males had to have their long canine teeth removed to prevent them from killing themselves. Clearly, these monkeys also had a pathological response to pain.

PAIN

The painfulness of a stimulus depends as much on the context as on the stimulus itself. In the dentist's chair, many people find the slightest touch painful, even if the dentist is only shaking their hand. The expectation of pain potentiates the experience. In other situations, people seem extraordinarily insensitive to pain. Soldiers in battle, for instance, can suffer horrible wounds without realizing that they have been hurt. Later, when the life-or-death emergency is over, unbearable pain begins even though the major tissue damage is long over.

These experiences demonstrate the major difference between perception and pain: the act of touching or looking informs, but pain motivates. The reaction to pain must be internal, a resetting of behavioral priorities. Pain thus depends on behavioral context as well as tissue damage, so other priorities (such as the stress of battle) can modify the experience of pain.

THE ANATOMY OF PAIN

Physiologically, pain is associated with the potential for tissue damage. Free nerve endings probably are stimulated by still-unidentified chemical messengers that are released when tissue is damaged. From here pain is transmitted in two systems—one consisting of large, fast-conducting myelinated fibers and the other of unmyelinated fibers. Both ascend in the spinothalamic tract (see Figure 9.17). Collateral axons branch to the reticular core of the brain, so pain is also transmitted by a spinoreticulothalamic pathway. Many of the fibers end on the small reticular cells of the periaqueductal gray matter, near the receptors for other internal homeostats. Stimulation of the large fibers gives rise to bright, sharply localized pain—a pricking or stabbing; the small fibers are responsible for aching, burning, and less clearly localized pain.

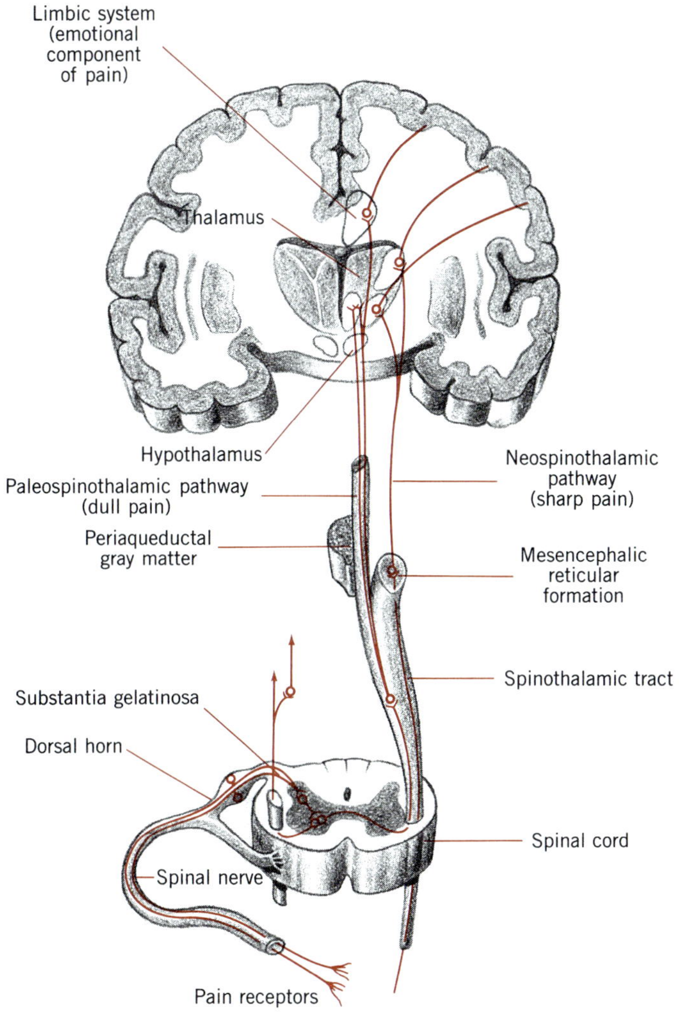

Figure 9.17 *Two afferent systems for somatosensory pain. Opiates are involved with the phylogenetically older paleospinothalamic pathway; opiate receptors are concentrated in the substantia gelatinosa and the central thalamus.*

It is sometimes said that pain pathways end in the thalamus, but our ability to localize painful stimuli and to react to them implies a cortical involvement. In fact, the pathways continue to the amygdala and frontal cortex. Pain and temperature fibers run together throughout this path (Pribram, 1981), and there is evidence that the two senses may be functionally related. In humans, brain stimulations that deaden pain are accompanied by the feeling of cold (Richardson & Akil, 1974). The folk medicine remedy of ice packs for pain turns out to have a physiological basis.

The sensations associated with dull aches emphasize the motivating role of pain over its informing role. Localization is sometimes so poor that we have little idea exactly what structures are causing the problem. Localizing a toothache to a particular tooth is often difficult and the source of visceral pain is often seriously mislocalized. The pain from the starving cardiac muscles in a heart attack, for example, is often felt in the left shoulder or left arm.

If we think of pain as motivating the sufferer to do something about the condition, it is easier to understand why pain systems could evolve with such gross errors in localization. Before the appearance of modern medicine, exact localization of visceral pain was pointless because nothing specific could be done about it anyway. The pain served to force the sufferer to cease activity, to stay out of danger, and to seek whatever help was available.

An extreme form of mislocalization is the phantom limb phenomenon: amputees sometimes report episodes of feeling or even pain in an amputated limb. The problem may persist for years and is not relieved by local anesthesia of the nerves in the stump. The pain centers appear to reorganize themselves in a pathological way to support the pain sensation independent of peripheral stimulation. Lesions in the spinothalamic tract sometimes provide relief; but if the condition has gone on too long, even this is ineffective and thalamic lesions are necessary. When even thalamic lesions don't work, pain-killing drugs are the only alternative.

Efferent Pathways. Efferent control is particularly important for pain, since top-down influences are so crucial for determining the perceived intensity of the stimulus. Fibers from the periaqueductal gray matter terminate in the nucleus raphe magnus, where descending fibers of the dorsolateral columns originate (see Figure 9.18). Through spinal interneurons, the signals arrive both presynaptically and postsynaptically on afferent pain neurons, where the transmitters are enkephalins (Ruda, 1982).

Before enkephalins were discovered, the feedback control of pain had been elaborated into a gate control theory (Melzack & Wall, 1965). In this theory, small neurons in the **substantia gelatinosa** of the spinal cord gate (filter) the passage of pain signals into the brain. Though the theory as originally proposed is now thought to be incorrect in some of its details (Liebeskind & Paul, 1977), it is still useful in emphasizing the importance of efferent control on pain perception. The efferent pathway is partly responsible for the extraordinary flexibility of the response to pain, but it is not the only modulator of painful feelings.

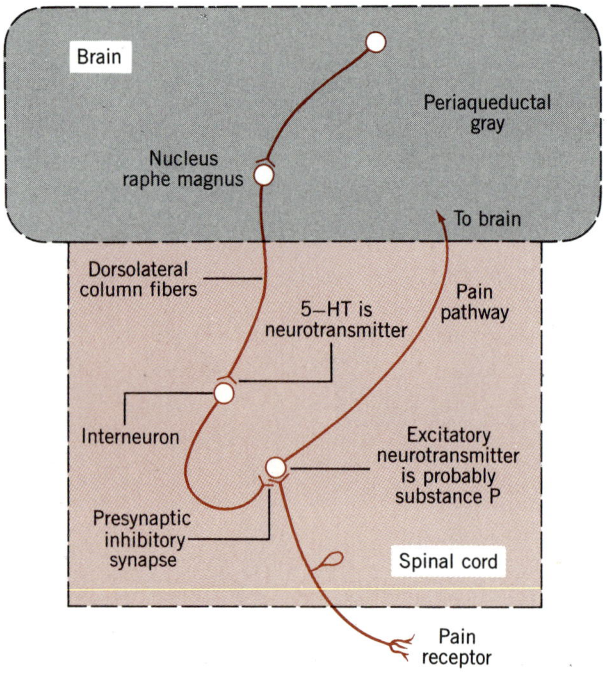

Figure 9.18 Efferent control of painful somatic stimulation. This pathway mediates opiate-induced analgesia.

THE PSYCHOPHARMACOLOGY OF PAIN

Since ancient times, humans have sought to relieve pain through drugs. One of the oldest pain relievers, and still among the most effective, is opium. Refined into morphine, it is commonly used in hospitals despite one serious drawback—it is strongly addictive. The effectiveness of morphine led to a search for brain receptor sites (see the section on enkephalins and endorphins in Chapter 2) where naturally occurring opiates might govern pain transmission. The discovery of enkephalins opened research on biochemical techniques, and there is already substantial evidence of the role of enkephalins in pain perception. There are sensitive assays for their presence in brain and body fluids, and the opiate antagonist naloxone can be used to cancel the effects of endorphins.

The role of enkephalins in the perception of pain can be investigated in natural and artificial situations where pain sensitivity is reduced or enhanced to see whether corresponding changes in enkephalin levels take place. The analgesia created by electrical stimulation of the periaqueductal gray increases enkephalin levels (Hosobuchi et al., 1979), and the stimulation analgesia is blocked by the simultaneous infusion of naloxone.

Enkephalin levels frequently rise in situations where natural analgesia is found. They increase during childbirth and during sexual intercourse. The effect of stimulation on analgesia in women is very specific; pain thresholds, measured on a finger, increase for stimulation of the anterior vaginal wall but not for stimulation of the posterior wall or the clitoris. Analgesia is greater for pleasurable self-stimulation than for simple pressure (Whipple & Komisaruk, 1985). These effects might be mediated partly through the arousal aspects of these situations.

Enkephalin-based analgesia can even extend to some social situations. For instance, mice repeatedly subjected to defeat in aggressive encounters with other mice show opioid analgesia (Miczek, Thompson & Shuster, 1982). Analgesia in this study was measured with a standard technique: focusing radiant heat on the tail and measuring the latency of the mouse's tail flick when the heat became uncomfortable. (In this way analgesia can be measured without inflicting unnecessary pain on the animals.) Analgesia was measured before and after defeat in a male-male social encounter; defeat was guaranteed by introducing a strange mouse into another mouse's home cage. The strength of the attack was measured in bites. The defeated mouse ended the encounter by assuming a characteristic posture (see Figure 9.19). Analgesia was blocked by the opiate antagonist naloxone, and repeated defeat led to morphine tolerance; the increase in morphine needed to produce a given degree of analgesia increased as much as tolerance induced by a 75 mg morphine pellet. Thus the natural opiates released by the defeat had a pharmacological effect similar to that of morphine.

Figure 9.19 *Defeated mouse in a characteristic posture. At this stage the mouse will not counterattack if further attacked, but it is protected by endogenous opiates.*

Acupuncture, an ancient method of reducing pain, is based on electrical and mechanical stimulation of the skin with small needles. Traditional acupuncture points, however, have no obvious connection with the physiological structures found upon dissection. Perhaps acupuncture analgesia is related to distraction of attention and to a placebo effect—an effect caused by the belief of the patient in the effectiveness of the procedure. There is a report, though, that naloxone blocks acupuncture analgesia, implying that the procedure induces the release of enkephalins in the brain (Mayer et al., 1976).

Does this mean that we should go back and examine the acupuncture points more closely? Not necessarily, for the placebo effect itself is related to enkephalins. Many of a group of human patients given a sugar pill and told that it was a pain reliever experienced some relief, but those given the same pill and the same advice along with naloxone got no relief (Levine et al., 1979).

Not all analgesia is induced by opiates, however. Most stress-induced analgesia, for example, is not reversible by naloxone and seems to be produced by other mechanisms. Rats subjected to inescapable shock show analgesia measured by the tail-flick test, and naloxone does not reduce the effect (Maier, Drugen & Grou, 1979). Control rats given escapable shock do not develop analgesia. Apparently, pain sensations are maintained when the signals continue to serve a useful role in controlling behavior.

A similar conclusion comes from a study of signaled versus nonsignaled foot shock. Ordinarily, animals prefer a warning buzzer before a shock, but naloxone eliminates the preference (Fanselow, 1979). In experiments like these, an animal is tested in a two-compartment cage. In one cage the animal receives shock after a warning buzzer, and in the other there is no buzzer. Normal animals spend most of their time in the first compartment. It seems that the buzzer leads to a conditioned release of enkephalins, which induce the analgesia.

Though the results of these two studies agree on the role of pain in active avoidance, they differ on the role of enkephalins in the process. The exact conditions in which opiate versus nonopiate analgesia occur remain to be defined.

Opiates affect more than just pain modulation, being widely dispersed throughout the brain (Khachaturian et al., 1983). Indeed, morphine is named after Morpheus, the Greek god of sleep. Perhaps the sleep-inducing property of the opiates, both natural and artificial, compliments their analgesic function; sleep may be an alternate way of forcing an injured animal to remain inactive. Motivational and emotional systems influence the level of arousal and in turn are influenced by arousal. This is the subject of the next chapter.

CHAPTER SUMMARY

1. Motivation activates behavior at many levels, from spinal reflexes to complex long-term behavior patterns. The concept of internal drives cannot explain motivated behavior, for if a drive is defined for each behavior, the concept becomes circular. The circle is broken by physiological experiments independently describing the drives; an example is electrical self-stimulation.

2. Animals will work to obtain stimulation through electrodes anywhere in a large region of the subcortical forebrain; they will also work to have the same stimulation turned off. Many of the sites are related to natural rewards such as eating, drinking, and sex, for they are less effective when an animal is satiated by the relevant reward. Electrical reinforcement has the same properties as physiological reinforcement under conditions where the two are made comparable, suggesting that the stimulation bypasses normal sensory channels and motivational filters to activate reward systems directly. Some self-stimulation sites are related to drive reduction, and others actually increase drives; we enjoy and will work for the opportunity to reduce a drive. The implication is that normal behavior is driven by pleasure as well as by pain or the threat of pain.

3. Biochemical studies have implicated the catecholamines, especially dopamine, in motivational systems. Self-stimulation can be blocked with intracranial dopamine injections; blocking dopamine receptors yields an extinction curve.

4. Emotion was first considered to be a humoral function, then a visceral function, and finally a neurological system based in the limbic forebrain. Emotions are now seen as part of an integrated motivational capacity, with both cortical and limbic components. Early experiments identified hypothalamic contributions to the emotion of rage, which was later differentiated into anatomically distinct components.

5. The control of emotions probably relies on environmental information. The coordination of aggressive behavior involves the amygdala but also

depends on the social situation and the behaviors of other animals. Anxiety is linked with brain benzodiazepines (related to the more popular tranquilizers); aggression requires the male hormone testosterone and is increased by glucocorticoids and decreased by ACTH.

6. Sexual differentiation begins in the uterus, where testosterone induces male development. Male and female brains also are differentiated, especially in their responsiveness to sex hormones. At puberty, female brains begin sexual cycling directed by the hypothalamus, and males produce testosterone continuously. Along with growth comes changes in attitudes and behaviors toward the opposite sex, dependent on hormones but greatly elaborated by learning. Sexual interest is increased by testosterone and other androgens in both sexes, though female interest can continue beyond menopause without further hormonal input. Changes in early hormonal inputs may lead to changes in later sexual behavior, though learning remains crucially important in humans of both sexes. Even in monkeys, rearing in isolation leads to permanent deficits in sexual and reproductive behavior as well as in socialization.

7. The senses provide information, and pain provides motivation for immediate behavior. The perception of pain depends on a combination of tissue damage, motivational state, expectation, and arousal. There are two pain systems—a fast neospinothalamic path that transmits sharp pain and a slower, phylogenetically older, paleospinothalamic path carrying dull aches. The pathways send branches to the periaqueductal gray in the brain stem, then continue to the thalamus and finally to the amygdala and frontal cortex. Localization in the paleospinothalamic system is often poor, especially for visceral pain. Efferent control of the pain system, originating from the periaqueductal gray matter, modulates feelings of pain.

8. Enkephalins are neurotransmitters in the pain pathways that provide analgesia when injected into pain centers. Many painful situations lead to an increase in brain enkephalins, though there are some exceptions. The presence of enkephalin-based natural analgesia is tested by giving the opiate antagonist naloxone, which antagonizes analgesia in acupuncture and in the placebo effect but not in stress-induced analgesia.

KEY TERMS

Drives
Medial forebrain bundle (MFB)
Extinction
Priming effect
James-Lange theory
Cannon-Bard theory
Papez circuit
Sham rage
Orienting responses
Galvanic skin response (GSR)
Habituation
Testosterone
Benzodiazepines
Androgens
Corticosterone
Adrenocorticotropic hormone (ACTH)
Wolffian ducts
Müllerian ducts
Labia majora
Follicle-stimulating hormone (FSH)
Estrogens
Luteinizing hormone (LH)
Progesterone
Corpus luteum
Gonadotropin-releasing hormone (GnRH)
Gamete
Substantia gelatinosa

SUGGESTED READINGS

Buck, R. (1976). *Human motivation and emotion.* New York: Wiley.

This book is a broad introduction to the psychological literature on motivation and emotion, emphasizing human studies and animal experiments with direct application to humans. A physiological orientation is maintained throughout.

Olds, M. E., & Fobes, J. (1981). The central basis of motivation: Intracranial self-stimulation studies. *Annual Review of Psychology, 32,* 523–574.

Appetitive and electrical rewards are compared in this review of the self-stimulation literature.

Pribram, K. H. (1981). Emotions. In S. Filskov & T. Boll, Eds., *Handbook of Clinical Neuropsychology.* New York: Wiley.

The history of ideas about emotions and the major modern approaches are reviewed; extensive discussions of the assumptions behind the approaches are included.

Chapter 10

SLEEP, AROUSAL, AND ATTENTION

It is obvious that humans and other animals have daily rhythms of activity, but it is less obvious why this should be so. We spend about a third of our lives asleep, consuming metabolic energy but producing nothing, and everyone knows that we are more efficient at some times of the day than others. What advantage do we gain from these rhythms, for which we pay so high a price?

BIORHYTHMS

Several hypotheses address the functions of **circadian** (*circa* is Latin for "around", and *dia* is Latin for "day") **rhythms.** The first is based on the idea that environments change greatly during each daily cycle and that most animals are best adapted to a single environment. An animal that thrives in a hot, brilliantly lit desert, for instance, will do poorly in the cold, dark habitat of the night. To find food most efficiently, the animal should restrict its activity to the day. At night it should conserve energy and avoid danger by remaining inactive. Thus energy conservation and predator avoidance are two possible reasons that animals might show circadian rhythms.

Other hypotheses about circadian rhythms include the possibility that restorative functions and growth increase during rest. There is even the possibility that memories are consolidated during sleep. To evaluate these ideas, we must look at the physiological mechanisms of circadian activity cycles.

PHYSIOLOGY OF THE BIOLOGICAL CLOCK

If future human space travelers ever contact intelligent beings but find direct communication impossible, the aliens will still be able to determine the period of rotation of the earthlings' home planet about its axis. The 24-hr rhythm is so deeply rooted in our physiology that even in space we will be obliged to follow it. In almost all animals, circadian rhythms continue even in the absence of external cues. Experiments in humans, for instance, have often taken place in deep caves, where temperature and light levels are constant. The subjects in the experiments continue to sleep, wake, and eat in cycles of about 24 hr (see Figure 10.1).

Attempts to enforce a cycle time of much more or less than 24 hr have met with failure. In one of the earliest of such experiments (performed in 1938 and reported in Kleitman, 1963), two volunteers lived for a month in an isolated part of Kentucky's Mammoth Cave. They attempted to maintain a 28-hr day, with 19 hr of activity and 9 hr of sleep per cycle. One subject managed to adjust both his wakefulness and his temperature cycles to the 28-hr schedule, though he always became sleepy before the new bedtime and experienced difficulty waking up. The other subject, Kleitman himself, managed to sleep at the right time; but his temperature cycles continued to follow a 24-hr pattern, and his feelings of sleepiness coincided with the temperature rhythm.

This study and others like it reveal several characteristics of circadian rhythms. First, they are **endogenous** (*endo* is Greek for "within," and *gen* is Greek for "to create")—driven by an internal clock rather than by external events (Pittendrigh, 1974). Both humans and animals can function on light cycles deviating by less than about 2 hr from the 24-hr normal day. But they cannot adapt to longer or shorter cycles (Webb & Agnew, 1975). Second, there are many endogenous circadian rhythms, each separate but normally synchronized with the others. They include sleep and temperature cycles as well as over 100 more obscure rhythms (Dement, 1974), such as those in urine production and in the secretion of several hormones.

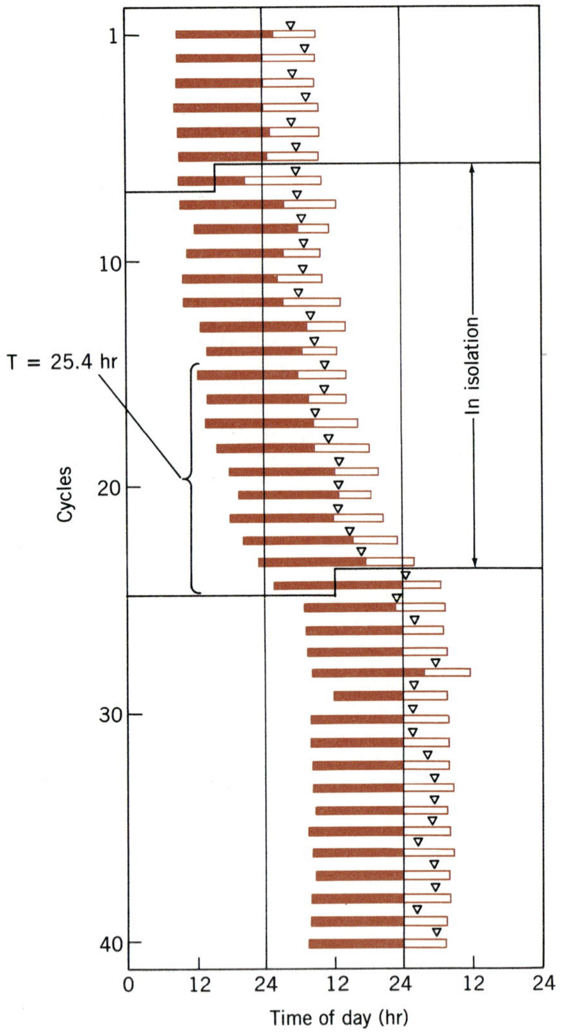

Figure 10.1 *Entrained and free-running circadian rhythms in a male human subject, from experiments conducted in a cave in Andechs, West Germany. Each horizontal bar represents one cycle of waking (dark) and sleep (light). Each successive cycle starts on a new line. Open triangles show the time of minimal body temperature in each cycle. "T" is the length of the artificial day. Adapted from Aschoff (1969).*

The circadian clock is remarkably resistant to interference; in ectotherms it is unaffected by wide swings in metabolic rates. Even in endotherms it runs continuously despite such activities as lengthy hibernation. Its time-keeping is not disturbed by food and water deprivation, x-rays, tranquilizers, alcohol, anesthesia, anoxia (oxygen deprivation), long periods of forced activity or inactivity, removal of the endocrine glands, or brain damage (except to the hypothalamus) (Richter, 1965). Figure 10.2 shows how electroconvul-

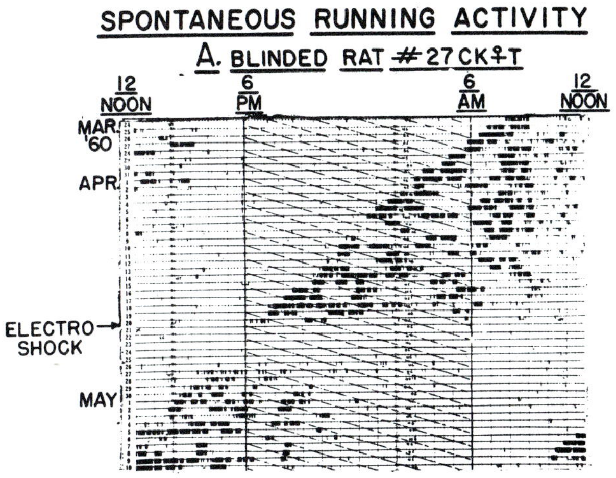

Figure 10.2 Interruption of circadian rhythm by electroconvulsive shock. The clock remains running while the rat is in a coma and directs activity on the previous schedule after recovery. Adapted from Richter (1975).

sive shock puts a rat into a coma for several days and how, at recovery, the clock picks up on schedule. The only metabolic intervention that has been successful in significantly resetting the clock is feeding the animal heavy water (D_2O) instead of normal water (H_2O) (Richter, 1970). Heavy water is identical chemically to normal water; its only distinguishing feature is that its molecular weight is 20 instead of 18. Why this should affect the clock is unknown.

RESETTING THE BIOLOGICAL CLOCK

Despite its phenomenal stability, the biological clock always seems to run a little fast or slow, usually by a few minutes per day (as Figure 10.1 showed). The combined characteristics of stability and inaccuracy pose a puzzling question for students of biological rhythms: why should nature go to such great lengths to metabolically protect a clock—and then build in an inaccuracy? It seems to be important to have a clock that is reliable but only approximately correct.

Part of the answer to the question is that under normal environmental conditions the clock is reset every day, usually by light. During the daily cycle, the master clock governs variations in many physiological functions without environmental feedback, receiving a resetting signal once each day. The signal is called a **zeitgeber** (*zeit* is German for "time," and *geber* is German for "giver"). If light is not available, a variety of other environmental signals can serve as the resetting signal. The zeitgeber need not be a natural day; just a brief flash of light every 24 hr can synchronize rats' circadian rhythms (Aschoff, 1979).

Anatomy of the Clock. Most orders of vertebrates have three eyes: the two on the sides of the head and a third, "pineal" eye consisting of photoreceptors located in the **pineal organ,** shown in Figure 10.3. Buried beneath the brain, the pineal organ is of no use in pattern recognition or spatial orientation; it functions only as a receptor for the zeitgeber (Menaker, 1974). Enough light penetrates the small heads of these vertebrates to stimulate the photoreceptors directly. Of course, no lens or other optic apparatus is necessary.

Mammals have no such receptors. Instead, a small group of fibers leaves the primary optic tract from the retina, just after the optic chiasm, projecting to the hypothalamus. This **retinohypothalamic tract** carries a mammalian zeitgeber. When the tract is cut, light no longer influences circadian rhythms (Moore, 1974).

Now that its input has been located, we can track down the clock itself. Located in the **suprachiasmatic nucleus** of the hypothalamus (located just above the optic chiasm), it is a group of about 10,000 small neurons tightly packed together and extensively connected to one another. There is no obvious hierarchical structure in the nucleus. The structure suggests instead that the timing mechanism, whatever it is, exists in each cell independently. Accuracy may be improved by linking the cellular pacemakers together.

Hormonal Control of the Clock. The clock in the suprachiasmatic nucleus has both neural and biochemical outputs. Biochemical signals are sent indirectly to the various organs via the pineal body, which secretes a daily dose of the hormone melatonin. This melatonin trigger comes not directly from an external zeitgeber but from the master clock in the suprachiasmatic nucleus. Melato-

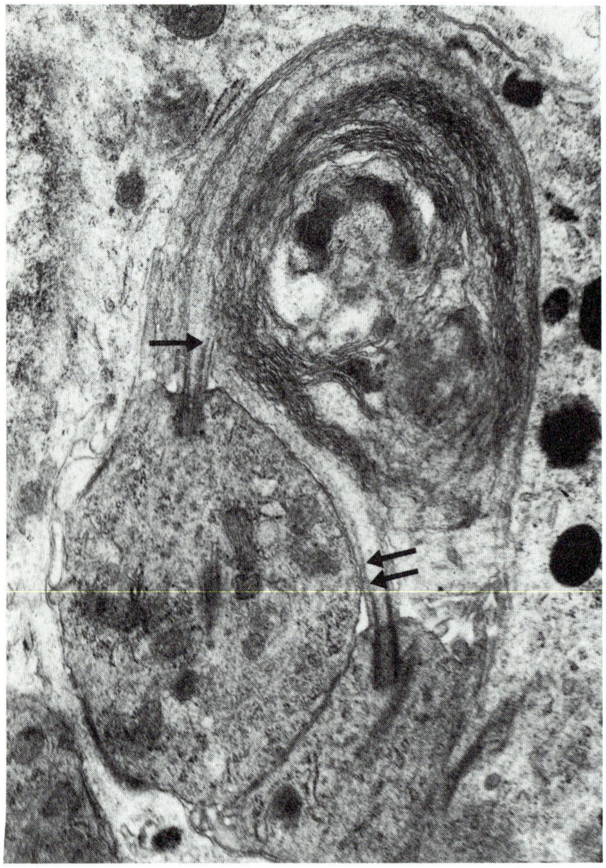

Figure 10.3 *Part of the pineal organ of the pigeon, showing structures that resemble the outer segments of retinal photoreceptors. These cells have an inner segment rich in mitochondria and granular endoplasmic reticulum. A cilium (single and double arrows) links the segments. From Menaker (1974).*

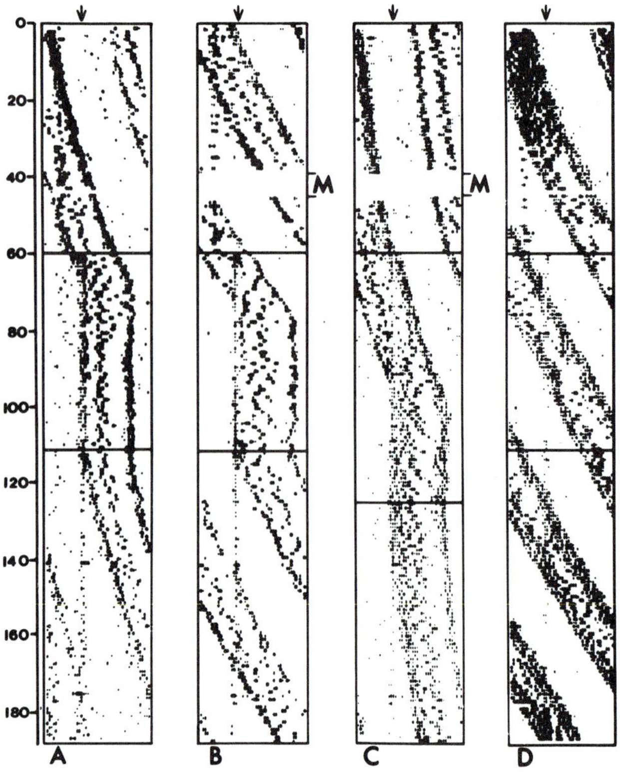

Figure 10.4 *Entrainment of the circadian rhythm by daily injections of melatonin. Three rats (A, B, and C) received melatonin, and a fourth (D) received injections of a control solution. Solid horizontal lines divide the records into preinjection (top), injection (middle), and postinjection (bottom). Arrows indicate the time of daily injections in the injection stage. M indicates missing data. Entrainment occurs only when the injection comes into synchrony with the endogenous rhythm. Adapted from Redman, Armstrong & Ng (1983).*

nin, in turn, synchronizes many organs and glands controlling circadian functions. If rats are kept in constant dim light, their circadian rhythms begin free-running—cycling at their endogenous rate. These rats can be entrained to (synchronized to follow) a 24-hr activity cycle with daily injections of melatonin. Control injections of saline solution have no effect, as Figure 10.4 shows.

The entrainment is not always immediate, and its timing suggests an answer to the second part of the question of why the endogenous circadian rhythm is slightly more or less than a day. Melatonin has an effect only if injected at certain times during the cycle. If daily injections are not given during this critical period, the animal will continue free-running. If the circadian clock's period were precisely 24 hr, and the animal somehow became desynchronized (for instance by east-west migration or by exposure to an arctic summer or winter), the clock and the zeitgeber might never communicate with each other. The potential zeitgeber might always come at a time when the clock was insensitive to the resetting stimulus. A slight bias in the endogenous period—a slight deviation from 24 hr—is necessary to bring things back into synchronization.

Endogenous melatonin concentrations peak at night in both nocturnal and diurnal species. A pulse of pineal melatonin signals the beginning of daily activity in rats, for instance, whereas it coincides with the beginning of rest in starlings. This hormonal pulse corresponds to an increase in the metabolic activity of neurons in the suprachiasmatic nucleus during the day, as revealed by the 2-deoxyglucose autoradiography technique in Figure 10.5. The technique is similar to that described in Chapter 5. Labeling of the nucleus is greater during the day, before the peak of melatonin release. More radioactively tagged 2-deoxyglucose is absorbed then (Schwartz & Gainer, 1977). We can conclude that the organization of the biological clock remains constant as new species evolve. New circadian rhythms evolve not by altering the clock but by altering the responses of the target organs to the clock's signals.

Bright light can quickly reset the circadian clock in humans by resetting the melatonin pulse

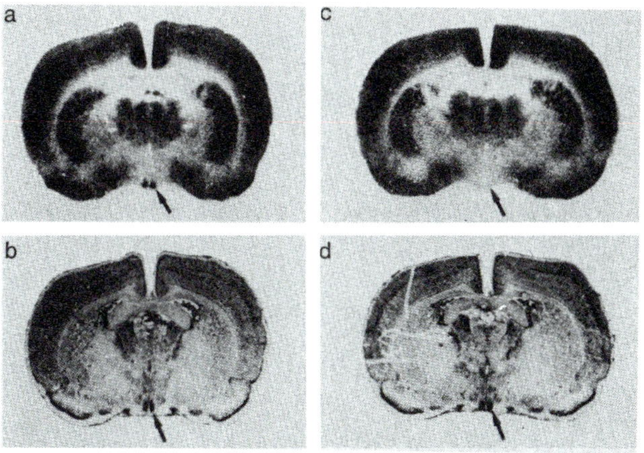

Figure 10.5 *Circadian rhythms in glucose utilization by the suprachiasmatic nucleus in rats. Rats are injected with 2-deoxyglucose (2-DG) either during the day, as in* (a) *and* (b), *or at night, as in* (c) *and* (d). (a) *and* (c) *are autoradiographs showing more metabolic activity (darker areas) during the day.* (b) *and* (d) *are Nissl-stained sections adjacent to the autoradiographs. The data indicate greater glucose utilization during the day.*

(Czeisler et al., 1986), but only if the subject has an endogenous rhythm of less than 24 hr. The human rhythm is usually a bit more than 24 hr, but it shortens with age. Bright light for several hours a day is also effective as a therapy for some kinds of depression, especially depression that becomes worse in winter.

Other Clocks. The suprachiasmatic nuclei are not the only organs with an endogenous circadian rhythm. The adrenal cortex, for instance, shows circadian rhythms of corticosterone production for as long as 10 days after it is removed and cultured in a glass dish (Andrews, 1971; Menaker, 1974). The mechanism is rather sophisticated, for like the hypothalamic clock it is temperature compensated. Its zeitgeber appears to be a daily pulse of ACTH. Like the zeitgeber of the master melatonin controller, the ACTH pulse is effective only at certain phases of the circadian oscillation. This example shows how control of circadian rhythms is like homeostatic temperature control: several control centers are normally governed by a master center but are capable of independent function. Neural output from the suprachiasmatic nucleus also shows this property, for interruption of different output tracts affects different functions.

Unfortunately, little is known about the physiological mechanism of the biological clock itself. We know a good deal, however, about one of the most dramatic events in the circadian cycle: sleep.

SLEEP

Until the mid-20th century the physiologist and the person on the street thought of sleep in much the same way: it was a period of inactivity, perhaps of restoration. There was no behavior and nothing much to study during sleep. The exception was dreams, which science had stripped of their supernatural implications without substituting another function. Sleep research was (I can't resist the pun) a sleepy backwater of physiology.

The situation changed abruptly in 1952, when Nathaniel Kleitman assigned to a student the job of investigating the slow, rolling eye movements that occur after a subject falls asleep. A subject was fitted with electrooculogram (*EOG*) electrodes (*electro* is Greek for "electric," *oculo* for "eye," and *gram* for "write") to detect the tiny currents the eyes generate when they move. With this technique, eye movements could be recorded during sleep. William Dement, in his book *Some Must Watch while Some Must Sleep* (1974), relates the story of what happened next. The student, Eugene Aserinsky, was shocked to see spectacular deviations on his eye-movement monitor an hour or so after the first sleep onset. It was not until he observed the movements directly through the closed lids of his sleeping subjects that he was convinced of the reality of the bouts of rapid eye movements occurring during this supposedly restful state (Aserinsky & Kleitman, 1955). Dement, then a sophomore medical student in the same laboratory, noted an extensive set of physiological changes that occurred along with the eye movements, defining a state he named rapid-eye-movement, or REM, sleep (Dement & Kleitman, 1957a). These breakthroughs rapidly led to a subsequent explosion of sleep research; the physiology of the state has turned out to be varied and complex.

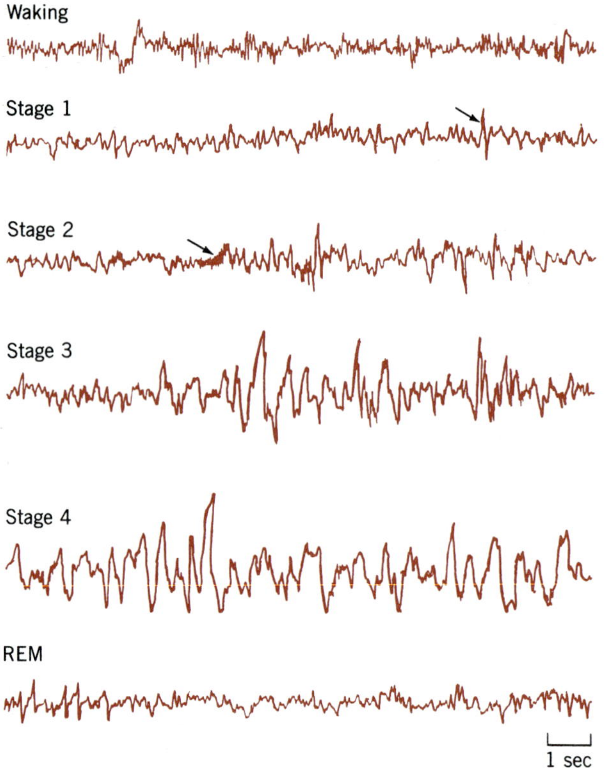

Figure 10.6 EEG during waking and five sleep stages. The arrow in stage 1 indicates a "vertex spike," largest when recorded from the vertex (top) of the scalp, that is characteristic of this stage. The arrow in stage 2 points out an episode of sleep spindles that help define this stage. The record is made with pens that sweep in an arc, so the large waves of stages 3 and 4 seem to tilt to the right. Adapted from Brazier (1960).

STAGES OF SLEEP

Slow-Wave Sleep

Sleep begins with a relaxation that gradually slips into a state characterized by slower, more irregular brain waves than are seen in waking. (Figure 10.6 summarizes the changes). In **stage 1 sleep,** the lightest sleep, the **alpha rhythm** disappears. This rhythm, a brain wave at about 10 Hz, defines relaxed wakefulness. The heart rate slows, muscle tension is reduced, and body temperature begins to drop. At first, the drop in body temperature is more rapid than simple heat loss would allow; active cooling mechanisms such as sweating cool the body rapidly, lowering the metabolic rate as quickly as possible. If awakened while still in stage 1, many subjects would deny having been asleep, though they would have been unresponsive to mild stimulation. It is at this stage that one sees the slow, uncoordinated rolling of the eyes that Aserinsky had set out to study.

After a few minutes, the subject will usually pass into **stage 2 sleep,** characterized by **sleep spindles**—groups of spikes in the EEG recordings that consist of bursts of 12 to 16 Hz waves that last for a second or two. The threshold of arousal rises further.

Next, the subject goes into **stage 3 sleep,** defined in the EEG by spindles and large, very slow waves at 1 to 2 Hz. The heart rate, respiration, and metabolic rate all continue to decrease as muscle tension drops further.

Finally, the subject reaches **stage 4 sleep,** the deepest sleep. Metabolism is slowest and arousal thresholds are the highest of any stage of slow-wave sleep. If awakened during stage 4 sleep, a subject feels groggy and disoriented. The EEG at this stage is a continuous train of slow waves, with fewer of the sleep spindles that characterized stages 2 and 3. These stages are collectively called **slow-wave sleep** because of the prominent slow waves in the EEG.

REM Sleep

After about half an hour at stage 4, a rapid ascent through the sleep stages begins; and about 1 to 1.5 hr after sleep onset, the EEG pattern suddenly shifts to a low-amplitude, high-frequency pattern, as if the subject had suddenly awakened. Yet the sleeper remains difficult to arouse, and the muscles suddenly become paralyzed. This is the onset of REM sleep. Over a period of a few seconds the desynchronized EEG pattern appears, eye movements begin, and a number of physiological changes occur. Heart rate and breathing become more rapid and irregular; penile erection occurs in men, and vaginal blood flow increases in women. Despite these signs of arousal, the muscles are flaccid except for an occasional twitch. Arousal thresholds are higher than at any other stage of sleep. For this reason, REM has been called **paradoxical sleep;** it has some characteristics of wakefulness and some of deep relaxation. We might speculate that the paralysis makes it safe for the brain to become aroused.

The most striking behavioral change in REM sleep is the body paralysis; except for the eyes, the body is effectively isolated from the brain. Physiologically, there are two ways to prevent body movement. The brain can either withhold excitatory impulses from motor neurons or actively inhibit the motor neurons. To determine which was occurring, it was necessary to record from inside spinal motor neurons to see whether they were receiving IPSPs from the brain during sleep. The experiment is technically difficult, for recordings must be made when animals are in as normal a state as possible; yet a movement of only a few microns between the microelectrode and the cell can lead to damage or loss of the neuron. Recently, these recordings have been made successfully (Glenn, Foutz & Dement, 1978), with the finding that neurons are actively inhibited. IPSPs are prominent in the intracellular records, preventing the neurons from firing and overwhelming the EPSPs that are also seen during REM sleep. The brain is not withholding excitation from the muscles; instead, it is actively inhibiting the motor systems.

The need for REM sleep is separate from the need for sleep in general, as studies of REM deprivation show. A sleeping subject can be awakened every time the EEG shows signs of transition into REM. Arousal becomes more difficult as REM deprivation builds up; at first, a buzzer in the sleep lab is adequate, but later the subject must be shaken violently to be aroused (Dement, 1960).

When finally allowed to sleep uninterrupted, REM-deprived subjects show a rebound effect; they have much more REM sleep than usual, and the first REM episode of the night starts sooner. The excess of REM sleep during recovery never matches the amount lost during deprivation, though. Control subjects awakened at the same times as the experimental subjects have neither REM deprivation nor rebound. The rebound phenomenon might reflect the body's making up for lost REM sleep, or it might merely be a by-product of resetting the REM rhythm.

Electrophysiological changes in REM sleep are not limited to the cortex. Recordings in animals have shown trains of spikes that originate in the pons and are conducted via the lateral geniculate nucleus to the occipital cortex (Brooks & Bizzi, 1963). These pons-geniculate-occipital (*PGO*) spikes occur spontaneously only during REM sleep in normal cats, but during REM deprivation they begin to appear in slow-wave sleep and even during waking (Dement et al., 1969). Their function is unknown, but animals seem to have a need for a fixed number of PGO spikes in each circadian cycle; if they can't get them during REM sleep, the spikes appear at other times.

PGO spikes may be signs of intense brain activity or attention. The spikes never appear in recordings from the brains of cats sitting quietly in a laboratory. But they have been observed as part of an orienting response during wakefulness, even if the animal is in darkness and vision is inactive (Morrison, 1983). To obtain nonvisual orienting, cats in darkness were exposed to the odor of tuna fish.

Dreaming. REM sleep is also dream sleep; subjects awakened during the REM stage almost invariably report vivid dreams, whereas those awakened during slow-wave sleep seldom do. This observation does not mean that all dreaming occurs during REM sleep, and it is now almost certain that some dreams occur in other sleep stages. Toward the end of a night of sleep, the distinction between dream reports from REM sleep and from slow-wave sleep begins to break down, but for most of the night REM dreams are the most common and the most vivid.

Although dreams are maddeningly subjective as subjects of experimental inquiry, some techniques have been successful in revealing characteristics of these mysterious experiences. For instance, we can ask whether the subjective impression of time in a dream matches the actual duration of the dream. Because dreaming often starts along with a REM episode, Dement and Kleitman (1957b) awakened subjects after varying durations of REM sleep and asked them to relate their dreams. As predicted, later awakenings resulted in longer dream reports, but the effect peaked after about 15 min of REM sleep. Awakenings after longer intervals than this all led to about the same length of dream report. Dement and Kleitman concluded that the dreams seemed to occupy about as much time as it would have taken to act them out in real life, but memory of the dreams stretched back only about 15 min. Sometimes an external sound is incorporated into a dream; the ringing of an alarm clock might become a telephone ringing in your dream palace. Experiments show that these sounds, too, become inserted into dreams at about the intervals one would expect from the duration of corresponding events during waking.

A further step toward relating the content of dreams to the physiology of sleep would be to relate the scanpaths of eye movements to the contents of dreams. Early studies reported such a relationship, but later results have been mixed. Some researchers find a relationship between eye-movement patterns and reported dream experiences, but others find none (Moskowitz & Berger, 1969). Interpreting such studies is difficult. How strong must a relationship between dream reports and eye movements be to have significance?

Another way of examining the relationship between dreams and scanpaths is to look not at the scanpaths but at the movements themselves. If the REM-sleep eye movements are exploratory movements driven by visual imagery, they should have the characteristics of normal waking eye movements: the saccades, pursuit tracking, or vergence movements described in Chapter 6. These are specialized control systems, permitting only a few kinds of movements. Saccades must fall on the saccadic main sequence (see Figure 10.7), with a fixed peak velocity for each amplitude of movement. But pursuit movements cannot exceed a velocity of about 80 deg/sec. Convergence and divergence are even slower. These restrictions create a "forbidden zone," where neither saccades nor pursuits can exist. (See the graph of amplitude versus peak velocity in Figure 10.8.)

To learn whether sleep REMs are exploratory, one need only look in the forbidden zone of large eye movements too fast to be pursuits but too slow to be saccades. Unfortunately, this is not as easy as it sounds. The EOG usually used in sleep studies

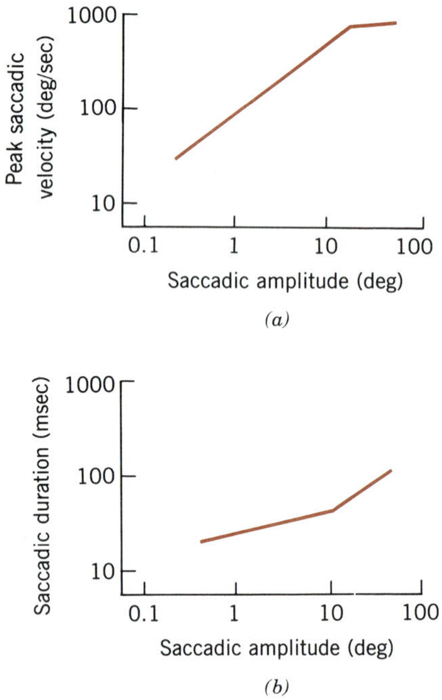

***Figure 10.7** A saccadic main sequence for saccadic eye movements recorded during waking. A saccade of a given size always has the same peak velocity* (a) *and duration* (b) *in a given individual. Adapted from Bahill, Clark & Stark (1975).*

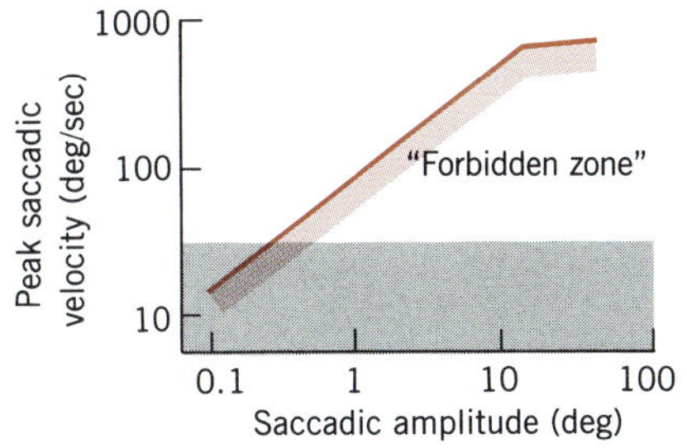

Figure 10.8 *Dynamic limits of saccadic eye movements (upper region) and pursuit movements (lower region). During waking, conjugate eye movements do not occur in the space between the two regions at amplitudes greater than about 2 deg. Sleep REMs, however, can fall in this region; they are neither saccades nor pursuits.*

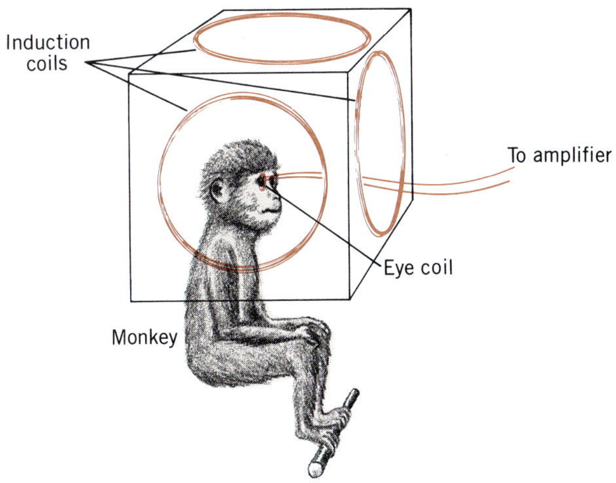

Figure 10.9 *The "search coil" method of monitoring eye movements in a monkey. The three large coils induce currents in a single small coil attached to the eye. Each of the coils receives alternating current in a different phase (timing of the peaks), so the relative strengths of induced current at the three phases can be decoded from the induced signal in the search coil. The technique allows the recording of eye movements from closed eyes in darkness.*

to measure eye movements cannot measure ocular dynamics with the necessary precision, and most other methods require the eyes to be open. One technique, however, fulfills all the requirements. The procedure is to sew a small coil of fine wire into the sclera surrounding the cornea of a monkey's eye, leading the two ends of the wire out to a recording apparatus. Using the same principle as that of a conventional transformer, researchers can induce alternating currents in this coil with three huge induction coils surrounding the monkey in each plane (see Figure 10.9). Eye movements can be recorded quite accurately, whether the eyes are closed or open.

Sleep studies with implanted search coils (Fuchs & Ron, 1968) showed that many so-called REMs fell into the forbidden zone, which implies that the movements had random dynamics and were not related to visual exploration. The cat also has REMs inconsistent with visual exploration, for all of the movements are in the same plane (Dement, 1974). The eye movements of REM sleep are not continuous; they occur in bursts of a few minutes' duration. A typical burst in humans begins with slow movements, continues with more rapid movements up to saccadic velocity (recall that the oculomotor system cannot generate movements faster than saccades), and concludes with slow movements (Gabersek & Ghiloni, 1970). All of these observations contradict the idea that REMs are exploratory saccades.

Do dreams help organisms review the experiences of the day? If this were their main function, we should see less REM in organisms with fewer experiences. REM sleep is seen even in unborn fetuses, however. Shortly before birth, infants spend most of their time in this state (Birnholz, 1981). If they are dreaming, it is difficult to imagine what they dream about.

If dreams review or consolidate the day's experiences, we should be able to manipulate the amount of eye movement allowed during the day and find a corresponding change in sleep REMs that night. In fact, the opposite occurs—people induced to make smaller eye movements during the day made larger ones at night (Herman & Roffwarg, 1983). In these experiments, subjects wore goggles that were opaque except for a 5-deg aperture. Mounted in the aperture were fish-eye lenses that gave the subjects a 30-deg field of view. The subjects wore these goggles for several days at a time; and, as one might expect, they made smaller eye movements than normal. At night, however, their REMs (shown in Figure 10.10) compensated by becoming larger. In a similar vein, but manipulating frequency rather than amplitude of saccades, Berger (1968) trained monkeys to make fewer eye movements during the day. He found an increased REM frequency in sleep. These phenomena are reminiscent of the rebound following REM deprivation. Perhaps the system needs a certain amount of oculomotor activity each day.

FUNCTIONS OF SLEEP

At one time, the function of sleep seemed obvious. But new knowledge of the activity and complexity of sleep called into question the old rest-and-repair idea, and several observations deepened the puzzle. Paradoxically, the effects of too much sleep were found to be as detrimental as the symptoms of sleep deprivation (Taub & Berger, 1969). Furthermore, humans who habitually get very little sleep suffer fewer ill effects than had been expected.

If a biological function is truly necessary for survival, as eating and breathing are, we expect to find that every member of a species must perform the function. Sleep does not follow this rule; a few individuals remain healthy while sleeping very little. Professor B. Q. Morgan, for instance, regularly slept less than 4 hr a night (Dement, 1974). Morgan slept a conventional 6 to 8 hr a night until he went to Germany on a fellowship at the age of 23. One night he went to bed at his customary 10:00 P.M. and awoke without warning at 2:00 A.M., unable to get back to sleep. The next night the same thing happened, so he lit his candle and resumed his studies. The pattern continued for the rest of his life, enabling him to be enormously productive without feeling sleepy during the day. Morgan was quite pleased about his unexpected change in sleep requirements. (I am a little envious myself.) At the age of 80 he volunteered to sleep in Dr. Dement's sleep laboratory at Stanford for five consecutive nights. He was followed by Dement's assistants during the intervening days. His reports of sleep time and of waking health and energy were verified; the young student assistants had to work in shifts to keep up with him.

The record for a documented case of brief sleep is held by a 70 year old woman (recorded by Meddis, 1979). EEG records showed that she slept an average of about 1 hr a night—and on some nights did not sleep at all.

Although observations on a tiny, nonrandom sample usually cannot be used to draw inferences about the entire human population, these counterexamples are enough to show that the human organism does not require 6 to 8 hr of sleep per night to remain healthy. The examples do not reveal the function of sleep, but they do limit the possible hypotheses. They seem to thoroughly discredit the rest-and-repair theory, and they make it hard to believe that memory consolidation or some other vital cognitive function requires sleep. What is left?

Sleep as Energy Conservation

One way of studying the functions of sleep is to look at its evolution, comparing changes in

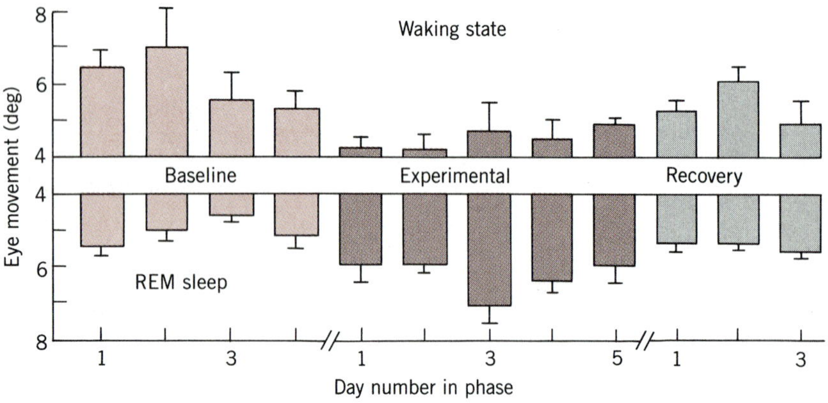

Figure 10.10 Eye movement amplitude during waking and REM sleep in three subjects. Waking values were obtained during 20-min samples of controlled activity. Episodes of REM sleep interrupted by body movements or brief arousal were eliminated. The lines remain about the same length throughout, but more of the eye movement occurs in the REM phase during waking deprivation.

sleep with changes in physiology. Sleep appears to be exclusive to mammals and birds, and slow-wave sleep appears to have evolved along with endothermy (Walker & Berger, 1980). If we define *sleep* as an increase in sensory thresholds, a relaxed posture, and a slow, high-amplitude EEG, we find that reptiles do not show true sleep even though they generally are active only during the day. (EEG signs are difficult to interpret, because mammalian EEG recordings are made largely from the neocortex, and reptiles have no neocortex.) Because they are ectotherms, reptiles do not need sleep to remain inactive at night; torpor is forced on them by the unavoidable drop in body temperature. Endotherms, according to this theory, need sleep because their high body temperatures would otherwise keep them active in environments to which they are not adapted.

REM sleep in this view is an extreme form of energy conservation. Not only are the muscles flaccid, using the minimum possible amount of energy, but there is no metabolic temperature regulation. Animals in REM sleep are temporary ectotherms (Parmeggiani & Rabini, 1967; Heller & Glotzbach, 1977). In most animals, the reduction in body metabolism exceeds the REM increase in brain metabolism, resulting in a net decrease in energy consumption as the animal passes from slow-wave sleep into REM sleep. Humans, with their large brains, are an exception, for the brain effect predominates and overall metabolism rises slightly (Brebbia & Altschuler, 1965; Haskell et al., 1981). Although we do not know the function of REM sleep, the high activity of the brain during this paralyzed state has the result of protecting the brain from dangerous degrees of cooling.

Evolutionary evidence points to REM as the last type of sleep to evolve. The most primitive of existing mammals, the egg-laying spiny anteater (echidna), shows slow-wave sleep but no REM sleep. Though endothermic, the spiny anteater regulates its temperature at only 30 to 32 deg, compared to the 37 deg of placental mammals (Schmidt-Nielson, Dawson & Crawford, 1966), and it has a correspondingly low metabolic rate. This temperature is near the lower limit for endothermic functioning. Perhaps the anteater cannot afford the luxury of interrupting thermoregulation in REM sleep.

Hibernation, an extreme form of inactivity and energy savings, is a state that seems to merge with slow-wave sleep in its regulatory and EEG patterns. Recordings during entire bouts of hibernation in alpine ground squirrels (Walker et al., 1977) reveal dramatic drops in brain temperature, but the animals remain endothermic in that they continue to respond metabolically to added cold stress. At a brain temperature of 25 deg, REM sleep disappears, leading to the conclusion that REM sleep appears only at high, typically mammalian brain temperatures even though it is accompanied by inhibition of temperature regulation. This may explain why the small animals in Figure 10.11 have short but frequent episodes of REM, and the larger animals have longer and less frequent episodes. If the small animals cool off more quickly, they must come out of REM sleep sooner to maintain an adequate body temperature.

If energy conservation is the principal function of sleep, then we should expect to see something similar in birds. Mammals and birds evolved separately from reptiles and developed endothermy independently. But both groups have the problem of conserving energy when they are inactive. In fact, birds show a condition very much like mammalian sleep, and some birds change their sleep patterns when energy is short. Several species of hummingbirds reduce their temperature overnight in a brief hibernationlike torpor when their energy reserves are depleted (Lasiewski, 1964). The much larger dove shows the same pattern when deprived of food (Walker et al., 1981)—and, indeed, is similar to ground squirrels and pocket mice in this characteristic. This is an example of **convergent evolution**—two animal groups independently arriving at similar solutions to a problem. Thus the evidence from birds supports the concept of sleep as an energy conservation mechanism.

Influences on Sleep Time. If sleep is an energy conservation process, several predictions can be made about when animals can be expected to sleep. In addition to the obvious night sleep for diurnal animals and day sleep for nocturnal ones, most animals (and humans) sleep more when outside temperatures are warm, after eating large meals, and during pregnancy (Dement, 1974).

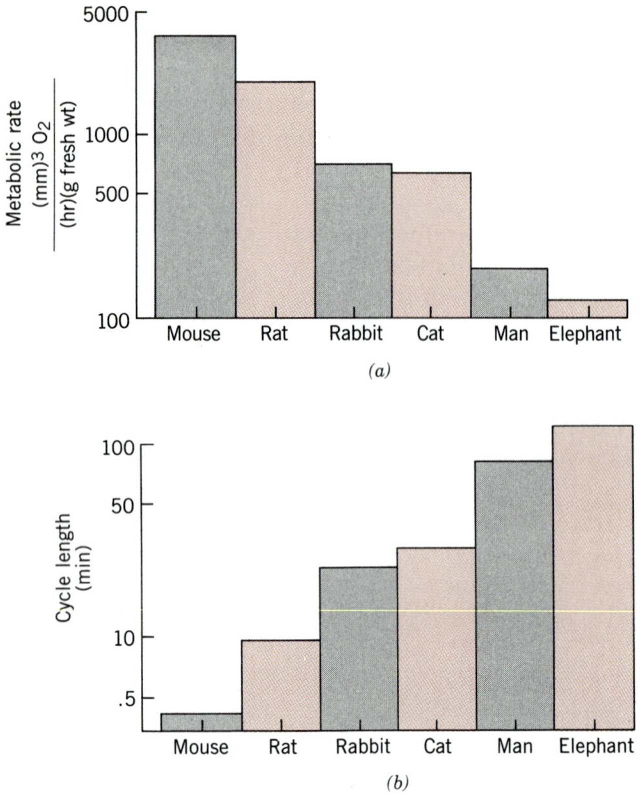

Figure 10.11 *Relationship between basal metabolic rate and size and between length of REM cycle and size for six mammals.* (a) *Metabolic rate.* (b) *REM cycle. The vertical axis is logarithmically scaled in both graphs.*

Children and the suckling young of other mammals sleep more than adults. Other conditions can have an even stronger influence; there are reports that Eskimos sleep twice as much in the arctic winter as in the summer.

Sleep and Memory

Questions about the relationship of sleep and memory had originally been asked in the context of the rest-and-repair hypothesis, for sleep was thought to function in reviewing the day's activities (perhaps unconsciously). Now that we know sleep to be an active process with several stages driven by neurological control systems, the relationship between sleep and memory must be reexamined. Two possibilities are that learning may take place during sleep and that sleep may function in strengthening or consolidating memories.

Sleep Learning. Effortless learning has been an elusive goal of humankind ever since Euclid reluctantly informed the king of Egypt that there is no royal road to knowledge. Claims of learning by listening to tapes played while one is asleep have attracted attention, but controlled tests of sleep learning have been disappointing. Such tests require continuous EEG recording from the sleeping subjects during a learning exposure, for unmonitored subjects may be awake even though they are lying quietly in the dark. After a number of false starts, the evidence became clear; if subjects remain asleep, even simple verbal learning is impossible (Tani & Yoshii, 1970).

Memory Consolidation. Data are less conclusive on the role of sleep in consolidating memories. Typical experiments in this area involve subjects learning some material, then attempting to recall it following a fixed period of sleep. A control group learns similar material for recall after the same delay spent awake (Ekstrand et al., 1977). Unfortunately, any difference between sleep and waking cannot be separated from two other effects. The control group will suffer from sleep deprivation (if the learning is done in the evening) or from being at a different phase in the circadian rhythm than the experimental group (if the control group learns in the morning). Furthermore, when awake, the subjects must do something, and that activity might interfere with retention. For instance, suppose that half of a group of subjects completes a learning task, stays awake for 4 hr, and is then tested for retention. The other half learns and then sleeps for 4 hr. How do we know that differences between the groups are not the result of a disruption of normal biorhythms in the awake group or the lack of interference from subsequent experience in the sleep group? There seems to be no way to design experiments to avoid this dilemma.

Because REM sleep is such an active state, it is a good candidate for some role in memory consolidation. Studies in both humans and animals have shown memory impairment as a result of REM-sleep deprivation (McGrath & Cohen, 1978; Rideout, 1979). REM-sleep deprivation in mice has been automated by placing each mouse on a small island made by inverting a flower pot in a pan of cold water. The mouse sleeps normally in the slow-wave state, its head held out of the water by muscle tension. As soon as REM sleep starts, muscle tension disappears and the mouse's head dips into the water. The mouse abruptly wakes up, and the sleep cycle starts again. Eventually, the mouse learns to awaken before REM paralysis begins, so it never gets wet. Under these conditions, REM sleep–deprived mice were slower to learn a complex maze than nondeprived mice (Rideout, 1979).

There are several complications in interpreting this experiment, in addition to the general problems with the sleep memory studies already described. First, the flower-pot animals are under considerable stress, a factor that may inhibit learning quite independently from REM-sleep deprivation. Second, some mice who failed to sleep at all on the flower pots showed no maze-learning deficit. This does not necessarily mean that total sleep deprivation protects mice from the effects of REM-sleep deprivation, for the nonsleeping mice are a self-selected sample. Perhaps something different about mice that cannot sleep on flower pots makes them better maze runners, or perhaps by avoiding sleep these mice also avoid stress.

Many of the methodological pitfalls of active intervention experiments can be avoided by training animals to perform a task and observing any changes in subsequent sleep patterns. Here again, REM sleep is implicated in memory. REM sleep in rats is longer on nights following maze learning; the increase is greatest when performance on the task is improving most quickly (Luchero, 1970; Bloch, 1976), which suggests that more REM sleep is required to consolidate the new memories. The evidence is only circumstantial, though, and observations such as these cannot prove a causal relationship between memory and REM sleep.

Even if there were convincing evidence that REM sleep facilitated memory consolidation, it would not mean that consolidation was the purpose of sleep. This function could have become attached to sleep after the pattern had already evolved for other reasons.

As an analogy to such a development, consider the relationship of heart rate and respiration. The heart rate decreases when thoracic pressure is high (Hrushesky et al., 1984). You can demonstrate this by feeling your pulse, then taking a deep breath and holding it while monitoring your heart rate. If you are normal, your heart will slow down a bit while you are holding your breath and speed up again when you release the air. The energy-conserving value of this reflex is clear: the heart can do a greater share of its task when it is working against a smaller back pressure. But the lungs did not develop to modulate the heart; the two merely adapted to each other's presence. Similarly, REM sleep may not have developed to facilitate memory consolidation but may have adapted to the need for consolidation. The examples of people who sleep very little show that at least some humans can consolidate memories quite well with very little REM sleep.

PHYSIOLOGY OF SLEEP

When sleep was conceived of as a passive state, there was no need to look for a sleep mechanism; sleep was what happened when activation ceased. But the many stages and properties of sleep now demand a neurological machine to govern them. Because sleep is a phylogenetically new development, appearing fully developed only in mammals

neuro

and birds, we would expect to see sleep controlled from newer areas of the brain. Surprisingly, though, most of the areas that have been implicated in sleep are located in the brain stem near areas that control arousal and attention in more primitive animals.

Physiology of Slow-Wave Sleep

The first steps in elucidating the control of sleep were made by mistake, before slow-wave and REM sleep had been differentiated. While looking for connections from the vermis of the cerebellum to the cerebral cortex, Moruzzi and Magoun (1949) discovered that stimulation of the midbrain and hindbrain parts of the reticular formation would awaken a sleeping animal or increase alertness in one already awake. The stimulation was followed by desynchronization of the EEG. This discovery was the birth of the ascending reticular activating system (ARAS), really a complex of activating systems in the reticular core of the brain stem.

Merely stimulating a cat's brain and obtaining arousal does not prove that the stimulated area is an arousal control center. (I could bang on your thumb with a hammer and obtain instant arousal without proving that the thumb is an arousal center.) The reticular formation has polysensory inputs, so electrical stimulation might induce the sensation of bells ringing and lights flashing, for instance, and these in turn would rouse the cat.

To demonstrate that the ARAS was an arousal control center rather than an alternate sensory pathway required two additional experiments. The first used surgery to sever the brain stem at the level of the superior colliculus; the surgery was termed the **cerveau isolé** preparation (*cerveau* is French for "brain," and *isolé* is French for "isolated") (Bremer, 1935). The operation separated the ARAS from the anterior parts of the brain; the result was prolonged sleep and a synchronized EEG.

The sleep might come either from an effect on the ARAS or from the operation's restriction of sensory input. These alternatives were distinguished in a second experiment—the cutting of all the sensory pathways. The result was an unresponsive animal but one that continued to have a circadian rhythm of synchronized and desynchronized EEGs (Lindsley et al., 1950). The experiments seemed to reveal a straightforward mechanism for sleep: when the ARAS was active, the animal was aroused; and when it wasn't active, the animal was asleep.

This simple story was soon to become more complicated. It turned out that the *cerveau isolé* animals recovered in a few days—sleeping at night and staying awake during the day (Villablanca, 1965)—though there was more sleep than normal. This observation implies that the ARAS is not the only structure controlling sleep.

The following analysis of sleep and arousal centers follows and extends the theory of Michel Jouvet (1972, 1974), who considers sleep to be controlled by a number of centers distinct in anatomy and biochemistry.

Arousal Centers. Two brain-stem areas, each with its own neurotransmitter, function in arousal. They are the locus coeruleus and the substantia nigra. The **locus coeruleus** is a noradrenergic center in the dorsal pons that yields arousal when stimulated electrically. It is a good example of a small region with connections to a broad efferent network (Ashton-Jones et al., 1986). The area is near the reticular formation (see Figure 10.12) and, in fact, may be the area that Moruzzi and Magoun (1949) stimulated when they were aiming at the reticular formation. Lesions of the locus coeruleus result in hypersomnia (excess sleep), with both slow-wave and REM sleep increasing greatly (Jones, Bobillier & Jouvet, 1969).

The second arousal system is located in the *substantia nigra,* a center also involved in motor coordination and postural muscle tone (see Chapter 3). Substantia nigra lesions in cats create a comatose state with slow waves in the EEG; in some cats, the condition is permanent (Jouvet, 1972). These lesions also interrupt fibers of the ventral nonadrenergic bundle.

The substantia nigra neurons use the catecholamine neurotransmitter dopamine, a substance that has effects on many neurological functions. Dopamine is necessary to obtain the arousing effects of mild stress (a tail-pinch in a rat, for instance); from here one can speculate about the role of dopaminergic systems in the relationship between stress and sleep. Dopamine receptors may be a pathway by which amphetamine and co-

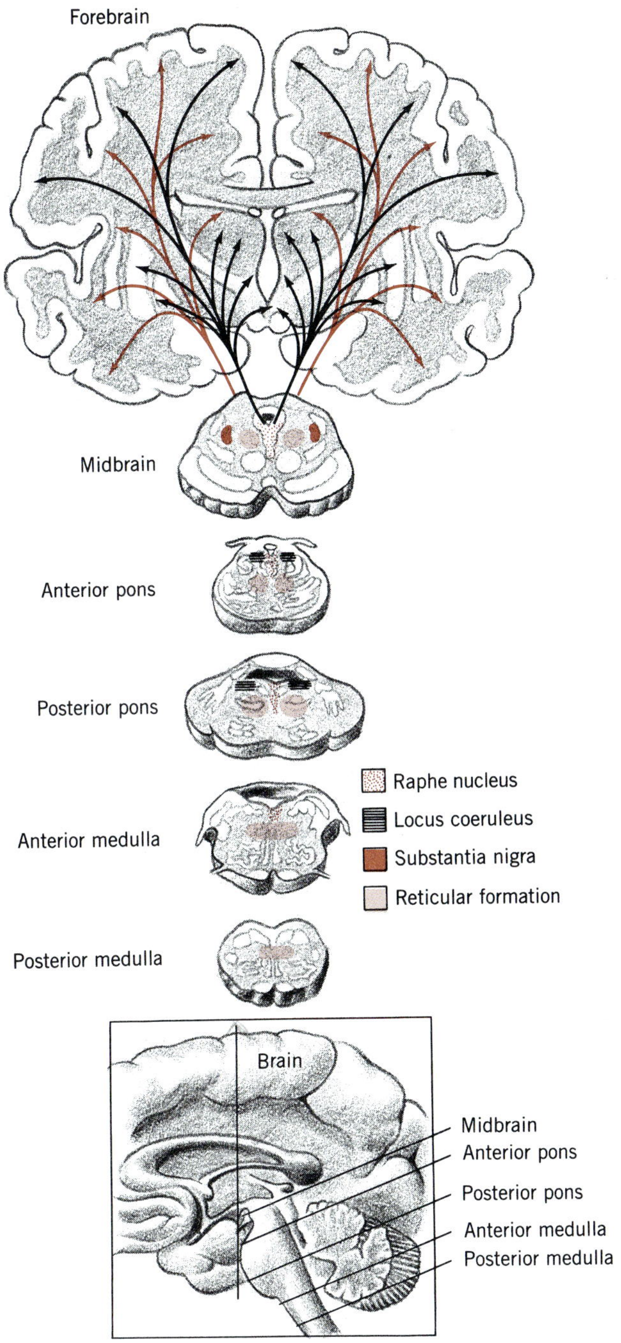

Figure 10.12 *Anatomy of the locus coeruleus and the median raphe in humans. The structures extend from the anterior medulla into the midbrain.*

caine, powerful catecholamine agonists, have their effects on sleep. Tempting and plausible as they are, however, these speculations remain to be proved.

One difficulty with the substantia nigra hypothesis is its lack of generality. The somnolence effect is not found in rats; activity increases instead of decreasing when the rat's substantia nigra is lesioned (Simpson & Iverson, 1971).

Sleep Centers. The most important candidate for brain-stem control of sleep is the median **raphe** (Greek for "seam," pronounced rā'-fē). Aptly named, this complex of midbrain and hindbrain nuclei lies on the seam between the two halves of the brain stem (see Figure 10.13). It is as if a vertically oriented sheet of cardboard had been slipped into the middle of the brain stem. This anatomy makes the raphe difficult to analyze; one cannot stimulate or ablate very much of it without affecting other, more lateral structures.

Large lesions of the raphe in cats lead to total insomnia for several days (Jouvet & Renault, 1966), followed by the gradual return of a few hours of sleep per day. The amount of insomnia is related to the size of the lesion, larger lesions allowing less sleep. The lesions also reduce the brain's level of **serotonin,** the neurotransmitter secreted by the raphe neurons, so the amount of serotonin remaining is correlated with the amount of sleep.

This observation leads to the hypothesis that serotonin, from serotonergic neurons in the raphe, is the normal trigger for sleep. The hypothesis was tested by researchers who manipulated brain serotonin levels and monitored the resulting amounts of sleep. In one test, they reduced the amount of serotonin by interfering with its synthesis. Normally, the transmitter is produced when the amino acid tryptophan is hydroxylated by the enzyme tryptophan hydroxylase, producing 5-hydroxytryptophan (5-HTP), which in turn changes into 5-HT (serotonin). The synthetic drug **parachlorophenylalanine (PCPA)** blocks tryptophan hydroxylase, thereby reducing serotonin synthesis. As predicted, the result of the interference was insomnia (Jouvet, 1968). To be sure that the PCPA was causing insomnia by inhibiting serotonin, not by some other pathway, PCPA-treated cats were given 5-HTP as well as PCPA. Since 5-HTP appears

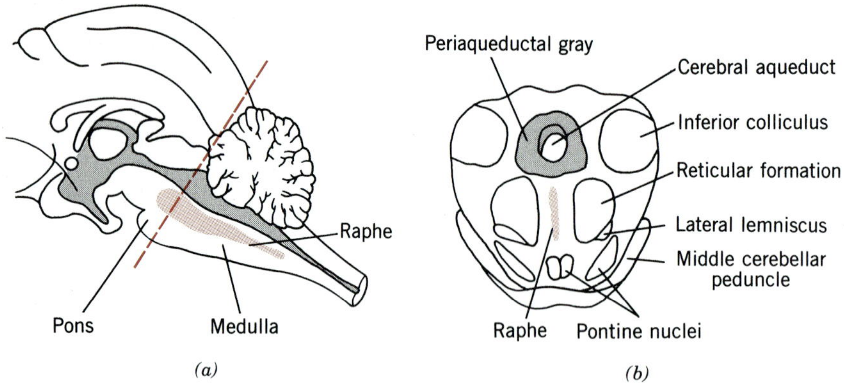

Figure 10.13 *The median raphe in the rat.* (a) *Sagittal section.* (b) *Transverse section.*

after the PCPA-poisoned step in serotonin synthesis, it should allow serotonin to build up despite the presence of PCPA. Indeed, sleep was restored when both drugs were given together.

Knowledge of this bit of biochemistry allows us to evaluate the folk remedy of drinking a glass of warm milk before bedtime to promote sleep. Milk is rich in tryptophan, allowing more sleep-inducing serotonin to be produced in the brain.

Like the homeostatic mechanisms in Chapter 8, sleep seems to have multiple controls at every stage, for both the raphe lesion results and the PCPA effect wear off after a time. This does not negate the original results, but it suggests that an alternative mechanism begins to control sleep when the primary one is rendered ineffective. The resulting sleep is not normal, however; without the action of serotonergic neurons, the phasic events of REM sleep—muscle twitches, PGO spikes, and rapid eye movements, for example—begin to intrude into slow-wave sleep and eventually into wakefulness (Hendriksen, Dement & Barchas, 1974). The PCPA cats seem to have hallucinations and sudden attacks of bizarre behavior.

Electrical stimulation of the raphe has yielded inconsistent results, sometimes inducing sleep and sometimes arousal. It is difficult to isolate stimulation to the raphe, though; other structures may have been involved. More generally, one cannot prove that a given brain area performs a given function by stimulating the area, because the function will appear only if the stimulation closely imitates the natural pattern of activation of the area. A simple frequency code is usually the only one that can be imitated with stimulation.

A second slow-wave sleep center is located in the nucleus of the solitary tract. This nucleus, in the medulla, also processes information from digestion and the sense of taste and is linked to the reticular formation. Cooling the solitary tract in a sleeping cat, thereby creating a temporary lesion, results in arousal; stimulating it yields the EEG synchrony shown in Figure 10.14. The center may be involved in the sleep-inducing effects of a large meal, suggesting a function of sleep separate from the nocturnal mechanism linked to the biological

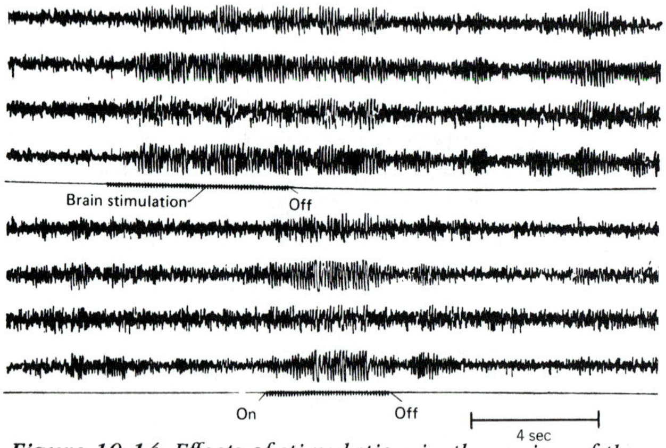

Figure 10.14 *Effects of stimulation in the region of the nucleus of the solitary tract. The electrical stimulus is an alternating current delivered through depth electrodes. EEG synchrony, indicating drowsiness, begins with a latency of about 1 sec and continues for several seconds after the stimulation is terminated.*

clock. This is another example of multiple control of a behavioral system.

Still another control center for slow-wave sleep is located in the forebrain, just rostral to the hypothalamus and near the suprachiasmatic nucleus, which controls circadian rhythms. Lesions of this area, the preoptic-basal forebrain region, in rats produce total insomnia (Nauta, 1946). In cats the effect is weaker, yielding only a transient insomnia that lasts a few weeks (McGinty & Sterman, 1968).

As one would expect of a sleep control area, electrical stimulation of the preoptic-basal forebrain region was shown to put animals to sleep (Sterman & Clemente, 1962). Applied to unanesthetized, freely moving animals with permanently implanted electrodes, the stimulation produced the cortical slow waves shown in Figure 10.15, usually followed within half a minute by an orderly settling down to sleep. The electrical activation stimulated sleep but did not force abrupt sleep, as narcolepsy does (see the next section of the chapter). Later, Clemente, Sterman, and Wyrwicka (1963) were able to use electrical stimulation of the region to condition animals to go to sleep upon the presentation of a tone. The stimulation functioned as a sort of reverse alarm clock. A 30-sec tone was sounded; 10 sec after its start, basal forebrain stimulation began. After a few pairings of tone and stimulation, the cat would show EEG and behavioral signs of entering sleep before the stimulation began.

The preoptic region is appropriately connected for controlling sleep, with inhibitory influences on the ARAS (Bremer, 1970). The inhibitory connections are reciprocal, for reticular forma-

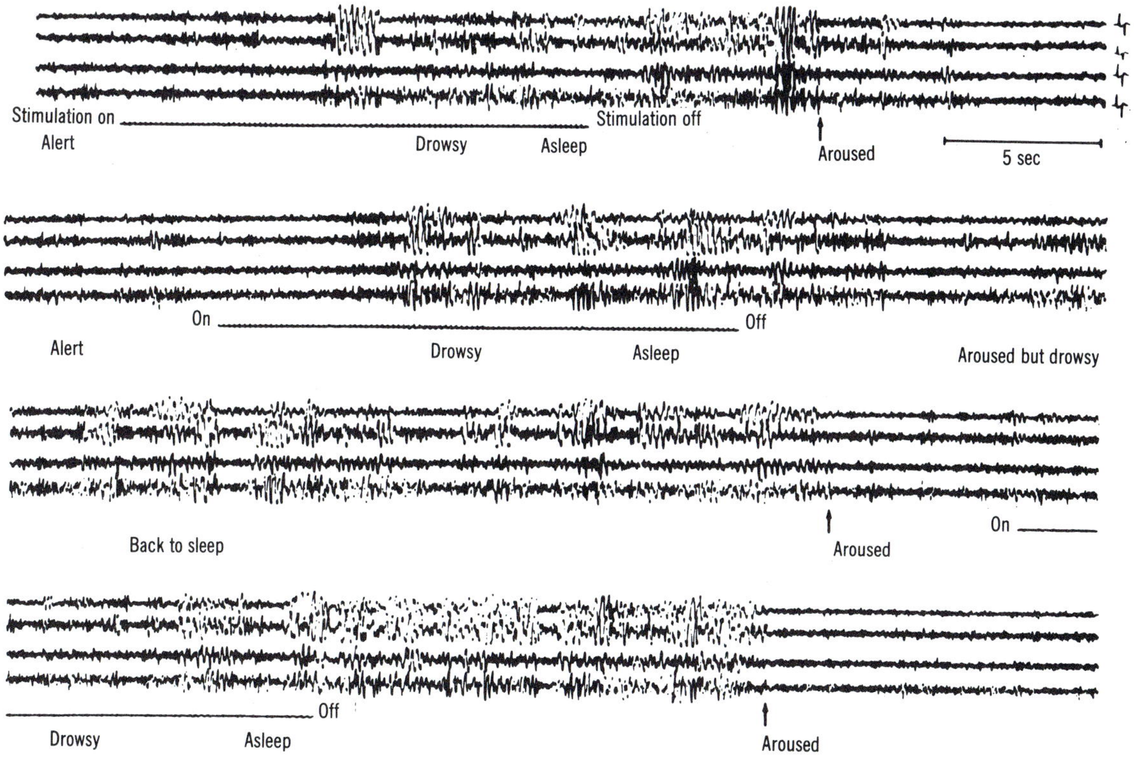

Figure 10.15 *Effects of stimulation in the basal forebrain region. Sleep signs in the EEG recording follow the onset of electrical stimulation by about 10 sec, implying that activity in the region organizes sleep behaviors rather than causing them directly.*

tion stimulation has produced electrophysiological signs of inhibition in the area (Bremer, 1975).

The preoptic area may be involved in the link between warmth and sleepiness, for it is also a thermoregulatory center (see Chapter 8). Warming the area with tiny thermocouples implanted in the brain stimulates thermoreceptors and elicits drowsiness and slow waves on the EEG (Roberts & Robinson, 1969). As appealing as the sleep-from-warmth hypothesis may be, it is still possible that these effects are mediated by indirect relationships among areas that are anatomically intermingled but functionally distinct.

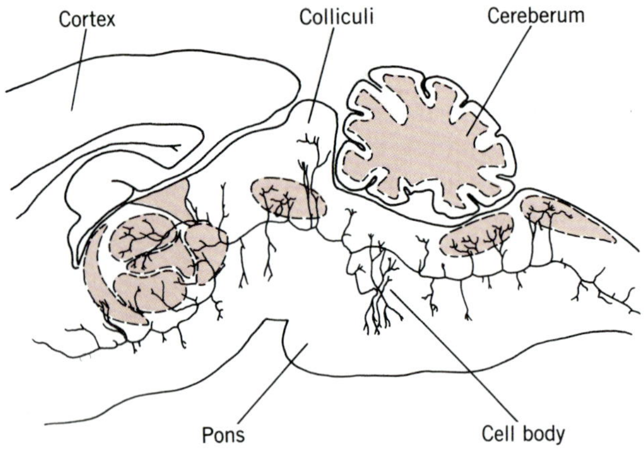

Figure 10.16 *The axonal arborizations of a single FTG neuron. Activation of the neuron at the axon hillock will result in transmission of signals to all of the terminal arborizations, always in the same temporal order. "R" is the cell body location. Adapted from Brazier (1960).*

Physiology of REM Sleep

In Jouvet's scheme, REM sleep is triggered indirectly by the serotonergic neurons of the caudal raphe. These neurons maintain slow-wave sleep by releasing serotonin at their terminals in the locus coeruleus. As slow-wave sleep continues, serotonin levels decrease. The reduction in serotonin levels triggers the locus coeruleus to initiate a cycle of REM sleep.

The characteristics of REM sleep are controlled by several anatomically distinct regions. The caudal locus coeruleus inhibits the actions of the skeletal muscles, and the medial locus coeruleus stimulates the oculomotor nuclei. The stimulation occurs through a set of gigantocellular tegmental field (FTG—the abbreviation of the term in Latin) neurons (see Figure 10.16), which, as their name implies, have very wide-spreading axonal trees in the brain stem. The 300 FTG neurons have synapses in the region of 9 million reticular formation neurons (Scheibel & Scheibel, 1961), an anatomical design that is effective in mediating widespread but nonspecific effects. These neurons are also the starting point for the PGO spikes of REM sleep (Laurent, Cespuglio & Jouvet, 1974). In the rat and the cat, FTG neurons are even more active during waking than during REM sleep (Siegel & McGinty, 1977). The activity implies that the region helps regulate phasic motor activity but does not initiate REM sleep. The fact that motor areas are active during the paralyzed state of REM is another of the paradoxes of sleep.

Several kinds of brain-stem lesions and sections can prevent the inhibition of action of skeletal muscles during REM sleep while leaving the other signs of REM sleep intact. The release from paralysis was discovered by Jouvet (1972), who created small lesions in the caudal part of the pontine reticular formation of cats. Instead of going into motor **atonia** (*a* is Greek for "without," and *tonia* is Greek for "tone") at the onset of REM sleep, lesioned cats stood up and appeared to act out their dreams; they seemed to attack unknown enemies, play with an absent mouse, or show signs of aggression or fright. Despite this activity, the animals remained unresponsive to visual and auditory stimuli. Like normal cats, they remained exothermic during REM sleep (Morrison, 1983). The analysis of behavior during REM sleep became a new tool for exploring the mechanisms of REM.

Further investigation of the release from REM atonia has revealed mechanisms both of REM sleep and of the motor system itself. The release can also be obtained through small lesions in tracts connecting the locus coeruleus with the reticular formation (Morrison, 1983). Small lesions in the most dorsal part of these tracts give only a partial release from atonia; the cats can lift their heads and use their forelimbs, but they cannot walk during REM sleep. Larger lesions extending deeper into the brain stem give a more complete release (Hendricks, Morrison & Mann, 1982). This observation suggests a topographic organization of the brain-stem motor center, much like the organization of other motor systems (see Chapter 7).

Some other characteristics of these animals suggest that they are doing more than just acting out dreams. When awake, the lesioned cats have normal muscle tone and posture but are more active than normal. They constantly run about the laboratory to investigate inconsequential things. Formal measures of locomotor activity confirm the observation.

This work has led to the proposal that a "locomotion center" in the caudal brain stem controls spinal reflexes. The center is inhibited by a lateral locomotor strip extending from the medulla into the pons. Although the anatomical organization of the center is not yet understood, it is clear that lesions of this lateral locomotor area strengthen the effects of REM sleep without atonia.

Research on motor mechanisms in REM sleep has yielded one additional observation—a paradoxical association between heightened arousal and reduced motor activity. REM sleep is a period of intense brain activity, yet the muscles are flaccid. A similar state sometimes occurs briefly during arousal in the waking state as well. Hesitation and a weak feeling in the knees are common experiences in emergency situations such as fights or impending auto accidents, though the feeling normally lasts only seconds.

Disorders of Sleep

Narcolepsy. Another link between behavioral arousal and momentary motor inactivity is seen during orienting. Part of the orienting response is a cessation of ongoing activity; even breathing is momentarily interrupted. The motor inhibition is slightly different from that seen in REM sleep, for muscle tone remains while action is prevented.

An extreme form of this reaction is **narcolepsy**—a sleep disorder whose victims can lapse suddenly from wakefulness into the paralysis of REM sleep. The attacks generally occur at times of emotional arousal, such as might accompany laughter or anger. The syndrome is especially awkward during sexual intercourse. An abnormally low threshold for the link between arousal and brain-stem motor inhibition might contribute to narcolepsy. Indeed, the night sleep of narcoleptics begins with paralysis and a normal REM period (Dement, 1974). The disorder has been treated with the dopamine agonists amphetamine and methylphenidate, drugs that interfere with REM sleep.

Insomnia and Barbiturates. Almost everyone has been bothered by insomnia (difficulty in sleeping) at one time or another. Usually, the problem disappears without treatment, but many people are forced to resort to medication to deal with it. Most people suffering episodes of insomnia are given barbiturates—powerful CNS depressants with biochemical actions unrelated to the mechanisms of sleep. At first, the drugs are effective, as sleep follows a period of drug-induced unconsciousness. After a few days to a few weeks, though, tolerance to the drugs develops and the patient (or the doctor) may increase the dose to restore sleep. This cycle may continue several times, but the patient never concludes that the drug is causing the problem because withdrawal makes the insomnia even worse and often leads to nightmares. These are the classic signs of addiction.

All-night recordings of these patients have shown that the sleeping medications actually interfere with normal sleep. Patients spend very little time in stage 3, stage 4, or REM sleep, so they suffer many of the effects of sleep deprivation even if they spend most of the night unconscious. Nightmares upon withdrawal of the medication result from normal REM rebound. Since most of these patients are physiologically normal, and since most started taking medication during a transient episode of insomnia, the best treatment is gradual withdrawal of all sleep medication. Because the sleeping pills are the problem, getting rid of them is the solution.

Chronic Insomnias. Some insomnia does not involve lack of sleep. All-night sleep recordings may reveal normal amounts and patterns of sleep despite patients' reports of sleeplessness at night and fatigue during the day. Some patients dream about the last thing they were doing during the day—lying awake in bed. It is difficult to convince them that they really were sleeping, for the tests that Descartes devised to distinguish dreaming from waking, such as continuity with ordinary experience, do not apply. In other cases there is no obvious explanation of the pseudo-insomnia. Clearly, sleep medications can only make this problem worse.

Other cases of insomnia are more difficult and have been discovered only recently. In 1972, shortly after the Stanford Sleep Disorders Clinic was founded, William Dement and Christian Guilleminault recorded the sleep of a patient who had complained of insomnia for 30 years (reported in Dement, 1974). They were astonished to find that the patient's breathing stopped as soon as sleep began. They too held their breaths until, 100 sec after sleep onset, the patient awoke, gasped for air, and returned to another episode of sleep without breathing. Anoxia had caused the respiratory centers to arouse the patient; and as soon as a few breaths had been taken and blood gases had returned to normal, the patient's sleep resumed. Patients with this disorder, now called **sleep apnea,** can either breathe or sleep, but cannot do both simultaneously. The pattern was seen earlier in patients complaining of too much sleep (Gastaut et al., 1968); apparently those patients did not remember their frequent awakenings.

According to Dement (1974), the mechanism of the disorder may involve the collapse of the throat because of exaggerated muscle relaxation as the patient enters slow-wave sleep. At present, there is no cure, though the drastic measure of surgically inserting a tube in the throat provides relief.

The search for effective sleeping remedies is an old one; the first recorded use of drugs is the Greeks' use of morphine as a sleeping aid. Although we now know that opiates and barbiturates can cause more problems than they solve, more satisfactory drugs have been difficult to find.

A sleep-promoting factor has recently been isolated from human urine, suggesting that we still have a lot to learn about the biochemistry of slow-wave sleep. When the substance is infused into a rabbit's brain at the tiny dose of 5 picomoles (trillionths of a mole) per kilogram of body weight, it induces a 50 percent increase in slow-wave sleep (Krueger, Pappenheimer & Karnovsky, 1982). Named **factor S** (for sleep), the substance was not easy to obtain; 30 μg of it were purified from more than 4.5 tons of human urine. Its structure is fairly simple, though; it has a molecular weight of 922, so it should be relatively easy to synthesize once its structure has been completely worked out. Factor S is composed of only four types of simple organic molecules. Nothing is known at present about its biosynthesis or its natural receptors; when they have been explored, the story of the

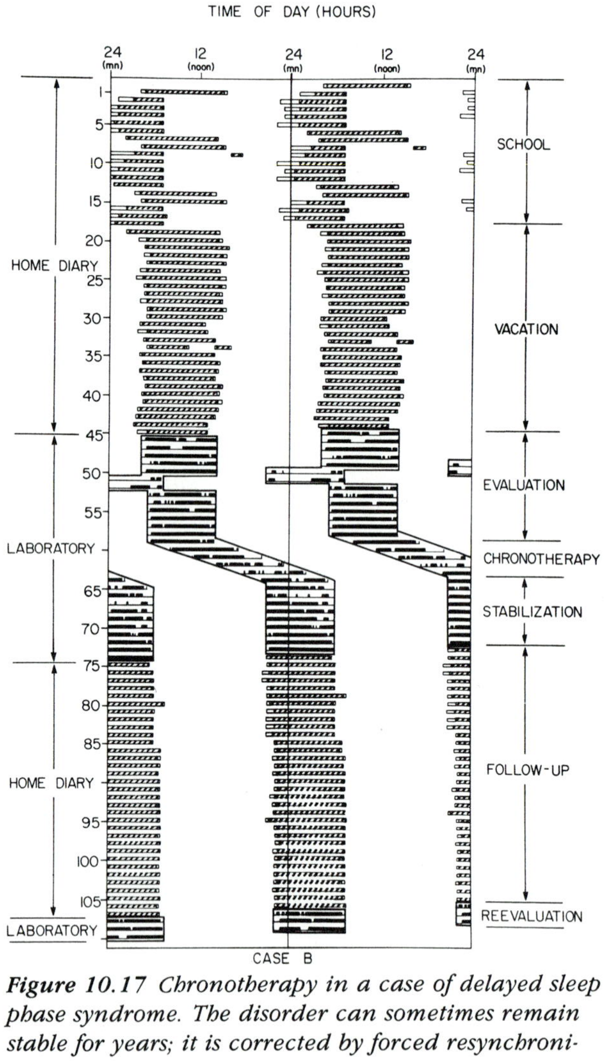

***Figure 10.17** Chronotherapy in a case of delayed sleep phase syndrome. The disorder can sometimes remain stable for years; it is corrected by forced resynchronization. Because the normal endogenous rhythm is slightly longer than a day, the phase is retarded rather than advanced. From Czeisler et al. (1981).*

biochemistry of sleep may look quite different. In the meantime, tryptophan (in warm milk) is as effective a sleep aid as any, and it is a good deal safer than most.

Another sleep problem occurs not in the amount of sleep but in its timing. Some people seem to suffer from "jet lag" even when they haven't gone anywhere; their disorder is called **delayed sleep phase syndrome** (Weitzman et al., 1981). The patient has difficulty both in getting to sleep and in waking up. The cure (illustrated in Figure 10.17) is to force a delay of 3 hr in each night's sleep until the patient is in phase with normal circadian rhythms (Czeisler et al., 1981).

Until now, the sleep-waking cycle has been described as though waking were a uniform state. This is an oversimplification, of course; arousal level and attention to particular events and actions continually vary.

ORIENTING AND ATTENTION

The regulation of attention is based on the orienting response. The behaviors serve to orient the receptors to the source of information (hence the name), and other internal processes prepare the organism to deal with the environmental challenge.

To examine the events of the orienting response, let us expand on William James's (1893) example of a man meeting a bear in the forest. The first behavioral sign of orienting is a turning of the eyes and head toward the bear. At the same time, the EEG pattern changes from a relaxed one (mainly of alpha waves at about 10 Hz) to one of lower-amplitude, higher-frequency activity. Because the EEG sums the activities of many neurons, the change means that neurons no longer fire in synchrony, producing large, slow waves. Rather, they are more asynchronous in their activity. Total neuronal activity and brain metabolism can increase even as the peak amplitude of the brain wave decreases. The heart at first slows dramatically (it "skips a beat") to interfere as little as possible with acute hearing. Then it speeds up to prepare for action. Even breathing is momentarily suspended, generally after a quick inhalation. The inhalation increases the oxygen supply during the suspension, so nothing interferes with the senses. This is the gasp of surprise. All other body movement ceases momentarily, perhaps using the same brain-stem locomotor inhibitory system as in the paralysis of REM sleep. Blood flow to the head increases at the expense of blood flow to the extremities, and changes in the electrical resistance of the skin (galvanic skin response, or GSR) follow soon after. GSR is used as a measure of autonomic arousal.

Orienting is accompanied by biochemical changes. Steroid hormones and epinephrine (adrenaline) are released, leading to the "knot in the stomach" feeling if the release is sudden and large enough. Presumably, the same behavioral, physiological, and hormonal changes are taking place in the bear.

The survival value of the orienting response is obvious, but a full-blown orienting to every stimulus in the environment would be unwarranted; we would spend all our time orienting. The response must be reserved for "novel" situations. In other words, it must be habituated.

Habituation of the Orienting Response

As indicated in Chapter 9, habituation is a progressive decrease in the intensity of the orienting response as a stimulus is repeated. Experiments using simple repeated stimuli, such as tones (which give less dramatic orienting than bears but are easier to control), have shown that the behavioral aspects of the response disappear first, followed by the hormonal and physiological signs.

Some characteristics of habituation are consistent with a passive model, in which sensitivity to a repeated stimulus decreases in much the same manner as the process of adaptation in sensory receptors. The intensity of the response declines gradually over several trials, finally disappearing altogether. As one would expect, habituation is more rapid for frequently repeated stimuli. The orienting response recovers if the stimulus is withheld for a sufficient time. There is also a generalization gradient in most cases; stimuli similar to the habituated one generate a smaller response.

Other properties of orienting violate the assumptions of this simple model. Strong stimuli, for instance, generate less habituation than weak ones, and very intense stimuli may cause increased response (sensitization) rather than habituation. An irregular stimulus rhythm yields slower habituation than a steady rate, even if the stimulus properties and the average rate of presentation are the same.

The strongest evidence for the inadequacy of the adaptation model came from E. N. Sokolov (1960) of Moscow University. Sokolov measured brain waves and GSR in subjects exposed to a tone repeated until habituation was complete, with no remaining EEG desynchronization or autonomic signs of arousal. At this point, presenting a more intense tone would have led to an orienting response. But Sokolov instead presented a weaker tone. The adaptation model would predict a weaker response, but a clear orienting—a dishabituation—was obtained instead, as Figure 10.18 shows. After rehabituation to the original tone, Sokolov presented a shorter tone and again obtained dishabituation at the time when the tone unexpectedly ceased. The same thing happened with a longer tone; no orienting occurred until the duration of the tone began to exceed that of the habituated stimulus. Then, a sudden orienting response occurred.

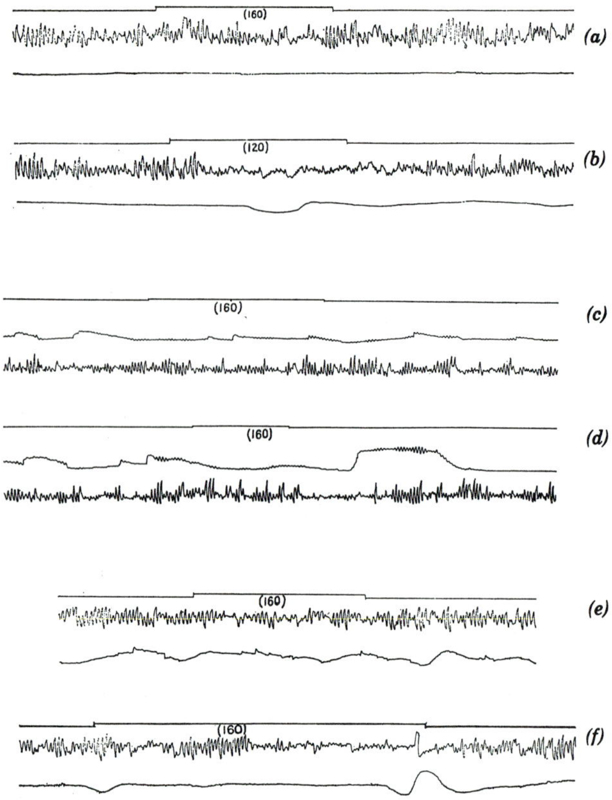

Figure 10.18 *Dishabituation to changes in a habituated stimulus. The stimulus has an intensity arbitrarily set at 160.* (a) *No response after habituation.* (b) *Dishabituation (orienting) with stimulus intensity lowered to 120.* (c) *Rehabituation.* (d) *Orienting to a reduced stimulus duration.* (e) *Rehabituation.* (f) *Orienting to an unexpected increase in stimulus duration. GSR is delayed because of the sluggishness of the autonomic system. Adapted from Sokolov (1960).*

Pribram (1971) calls this the "Bowery-el phenomenon" after an elevated railway line that once ran in New York City, right next to the third-floor apartments of Bowery residents. The residents became habituated to the presence of the trains; every few moments, conversation would cease in midsentence as a train roared by, to continue as if nothing had happened when the train passed. Finally, the elevated line was replaced by a subway. At about that time the police began to get calls late at night complaining about some vague disturbance that had aroused the callers from sleep. Investigations revealed no prowlers and no unusual events. The calls came at the times when the trains had formerly rumbled past; the disturbance was not a noise but the absence of one.

These phenomena imply that more is happening in habituation than meets the eye (or the ear). Habituation occurs not to a particular stimulus energy but to the entire pattern of the stimulation. Orienting reappears if any aspect of the pattern changes. A new theory was needed. Sokolov (1960) proposed that habituation occurs not in the sensory channels but in the process of matching sensory input against an internal model of the stimulus. If the model matches the stimulus, no orienting occurs. But if there is a mismatch—if the stimulus is too loud, too soft, too long, too short, or different in any other way—orienting reappears and habituation begins anew.

This theory of active habituation assumes that we hold a model of the environment inside our heads and that we continuously check it against sensory input. If all stimuli find matches in the neurological model of the world, internal processes go on undisturbed; but orienting occurs if anything unusual happens.

Even verbal messages can change the internal model. Hagbarth and Kugelberg (1958) habituated subjects to a weak electrical shock on the skin and then told them that the next stimulus would be painful. The internal model changed and orienting reappeared, even though the shock they presented was actually of the same strength as the habituated one.

Habituation of the orienting response can also be measured as the amplitude of an evoked response—an electrical wave recorded in the cortex as a result of sensory stimulation. After a long train of stimuli, the evoked response diminishes in amplitude. But if the train is interrupted, a cortical response is evoked at the time the stimulus was expected. This "missing stimulus" potential can arise only from the top-down expectation of a bottom-up external event. It is a direct electrical measure of expectation.

In sum, we are habituated to a wealth of stimuli around us. The clothing on our backs, everyday sights and sounds, even the drone of the professor in front of a class can be ignored completely. Orienting occurs only when something new appears, when cognitive effort is likely to be rewarded. Arousal is a product of uncertainty, defined not only by the stimulus but also by the individual's past experience. Each individual's unique set of experiences results in a unique set of arousing conditions, as new perceptions continually sift through the filter of past experiences that help define a unique personality.

But we can do more than orient; we can also direct attention by internal plans and priorities, independent of the demands of the environment. This is the active process of selective attention.

SELECTIVE ATTENTION

PARIETAL AREAS

Two regions of the parietal lobe (illustrated in Figure 3.21) are particularly active in attentional processes. They are the inferior region, which is related to self-perception, and the posterior region, which is related to the perception of surrounding objects.

Inferior Parietal Cortex

Like many other aspects of brain function, the earliest information about the neurology of attention came from cases of brain injury. Deficits in selective attention are associated with unilateral damage to the cortex of the inferior parietal lobe. Patients with such damage suffer from the syndrome of **unilateral neglect;** they generally ignore everything on the side contralateral to the lesion (see Figure 10.19). When asked to draw a clock, for example, a patient may draw all the numbers on one side of the face. A flower will be drawn with leaves and petals on only one side (Heilman & Valenstein, 1979).

The deficit also extends to self-perception. In severe cases of unilateral neglect, patients will dress only one side of the body, shave on only one side, and even deny ownership of the arm contralateral to the side of the damage. The problem does not seem to be perceptual, though, for visual fields and sensory thresholds are normal. Patients often deny that anything is wrong. They typically become angry when someone points out that they

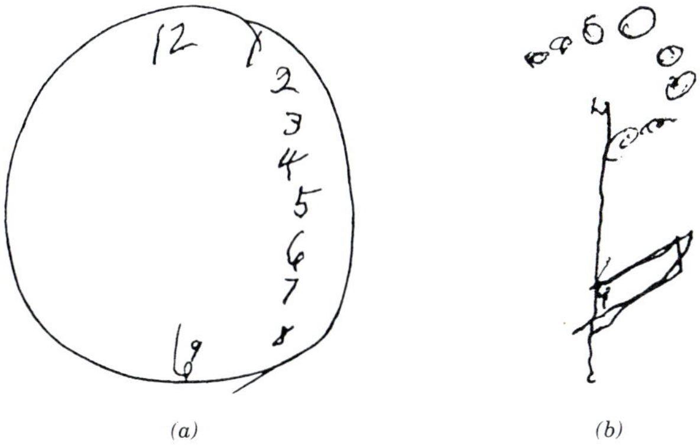

Figure 10.19 *Unilateral neglect syndrome of inferior parietal cortex.* (a) *A drawing of a clock face begins with the correct placement of landmarks 12 and 6, but the remaining numbers are concentrated on the right side (ipsilateral to the lesion).* (b) *A flower is similarly distorted. Adapted from Heilman & Valenstein (1985).*

are only half-dressed; and they insist that they do not belong in the hospital, being perfectly capable of carrying out their usual activities.

The unilateral neglect syndrome has been characterized in several ways. Since the effects usually (but not always) arise from a lesion of the right hemisphere, they may be related to the right hemisphere function of representing spatial information. This function can also be characterized as selective attention. The inferior parietal region is well placed anatomically to mediate attention (Melusam et al., 1977) because it has reciprocal connections with polymodal cortical sensory areas, the cingulate cortex of the limbic system, and frontal regions, including the frontal eye fields (Brodmann's area 8). (The inferior parietal region is discussed further in Chapter 14.)

Posterior Parietal Cortex

At the single-cell level in rhesus monkeys, many neurons of the posterior parietal cortex are influenced not only by a visual stimulus but also by attention to a visual task (Lynch et al., 1977). Studying these neurons requires recording from awake monkeys in which hardware has been implanted to hold micromanipulators. At recording time, a tube above the cortex is opened and the micromanipulator with attached microelectrode is fastened to the implanted apparatus. Eye movements are monitored at the same time; the monkey is trained to fixate a small point of light anywhere in the visual field by being given a reward of a few drops of juice after a few seconds of fixation. Success at the fixation task defines the state of attentive fixation. Control recordings are made when the animal is awake and looking about but not attending to anything particular. Posterior parietal neurons respond only weakly to visual stimulation if the animal is merely looking about, but they give strong bursts of firing during attentive visual fixation (Lynch, 1980).

Attention and Spatial Orientation

Later studies using this technique have revealed that the majority of the posterior parietal neurons respond best not only when the monkey is attentive and when a stimulus is on a particular part of the retina but also when the eyes are oriented in a certain direction relative to the head. There are two patterns of response. One type of neuron responds best when the monkey is looking in a particular direction (see Figure 10.20), and another type smoothly increases its firing as the monkey makes a smooth pursuit eye movement across the screen (Andersen & Mountcastle, 1983). Some of the neurons fire only when the animal is visually attentive, when it is looking in a particular direction, and when a visual target is in a particular location. These neurons, then, respond only when an object of interest is present at a particular location relative to the head. Thus the neurons as a group solve one aspect of the problem of position constancy: the perception that objects in the environment remain stable despite movements of the eyes. The animal is free to attend to events in the world without being concerned about the relationships between the receptors and the stimuli.

These studies reveal a close link between attention and sensory systems, emphasizing the interaction of perception and active exploration that was discussed in Chapter 6. On a single-cell level, Chapter 5 reviewed changes in receptive fields in the striate cortex and superior colliculus—both sensory areas of the brain—as the information content of stimuli was varied. These changes can also be considered in terms of attention. Mechanisms of attention may relate to the efferent control described for each sense modality in Chapter 5. To see in detail how attention affects the sensory channels, we can look further at efferent control.

FRONTAL AND INFEROTEMPORAL AREAS

Information processing in sensory systems is not a passive, unchanging process. Instead, selective attention tailors the processing to the current needs of the animal. Moment-to-moment changes in sensory processing are difficult to measure, but one sign of the changes is based on the time it takes to process sensory signals. During that time, sensory channels are less sensitive to new input. This can be seen in the contrast between sensory evoked potentials in anesthetized versus awake animals. An anesthetized animal shows a brief, "clean" evoked potential that is highly repeatable and dies out quickly. The signal disappears before process-

(a)

(b)

(c)

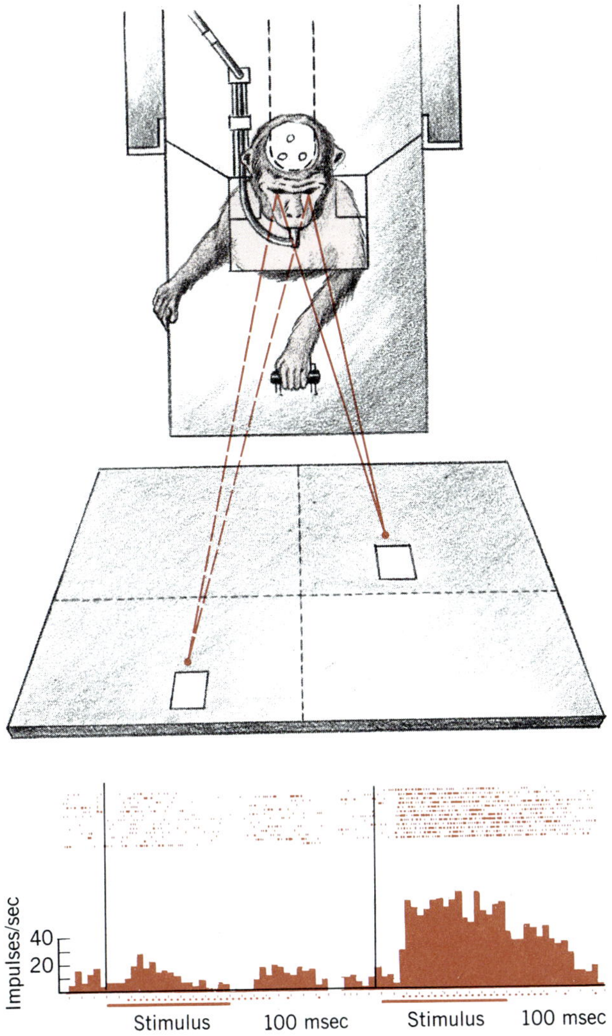

Figure 10.20 *Parietal neuron recording.* (a) *Experimental arrangement for measuring the effect of gaze angle on responses of a parietal visual neuron. With the head fixed, the monkey fixated a small light placed at a series of positions on the screen. At each fixation position a 6 × 6 deg square was flashed 10 deg above the fixation point. Thus the retinal position of the stimulus was always the same. Fixations were randomized in position.* (b) *Impulse replicas for two fixation positions. Each line represents a single trial, and each mark is a single firing of the neuron.* (c) *Histograms summarizing the data shown in* (b). *The neuron fires most when the monkey's gaze is to the left—solid fixation lines in* (a). *Adapted from Andersen & Mountcastle (1983).*

ing is completed. The potential from an awake animal is more variable and contains late activity, up to several hundred milliseconds after the stimulus. We also know that evoked potentials recorded from the human scalp contain more prominent late components when the stimuli require a response than when they are simply being passively observed. Figure 10.21 shows that the late potentials are more variable than the early ones. They change not only with stimuli but also with attention and task requirements. From such observations we can surmise that later activity is evoked only when processing continues beyond the arrival of stimulation at the cortex.

To find the source and the function of this variation, one must first have a measure for the amount of time a stimulus uses to pass through a sensory channel. One way to obtain such a measure is to stimulate the channel twice; if the time between the stimuli is larger than the time required to process a stimulus, then the neural response to the two stimuli will be the same. If the second stimulus arrives before the processing of the first is completed, the response to the second stimulus will be smaller. This **recovery function** is the gradual recovery of the neural response to the second of a pair of brief stimuli as the stimuli are presented further and further apart in time. Recorded with bipolar electrodes implanted in the visual cortex, the response to the second of a pair of flashes is about two-thirds of the response to the first if the flashes are 25 msec apart, recovering to an asymptote with about 150 msec between flashes (Spinelli & Pribram, 1966, 1967).

We know from Chapter 5 that the inferotemporal (IT) cortex is involved in visual discriminations. Indeed, stimulation there during double-flash presentations lengthens the recovery function, as Figure 10.22 shows. The frontal cortex, in contrast, is part of the "front brain" (see Chapter 3), usually associated with internal processes as opposed to sensory processing. Stimulation there shortens the recovery function. One can interpret this result by assuming that the primary sensory cortex is ready sooner for new input, because it is not doing an extensive evaluation of the stimulus.

Here research hit a snag. Spinelli and Pribram had difficulty in replicating their original finding

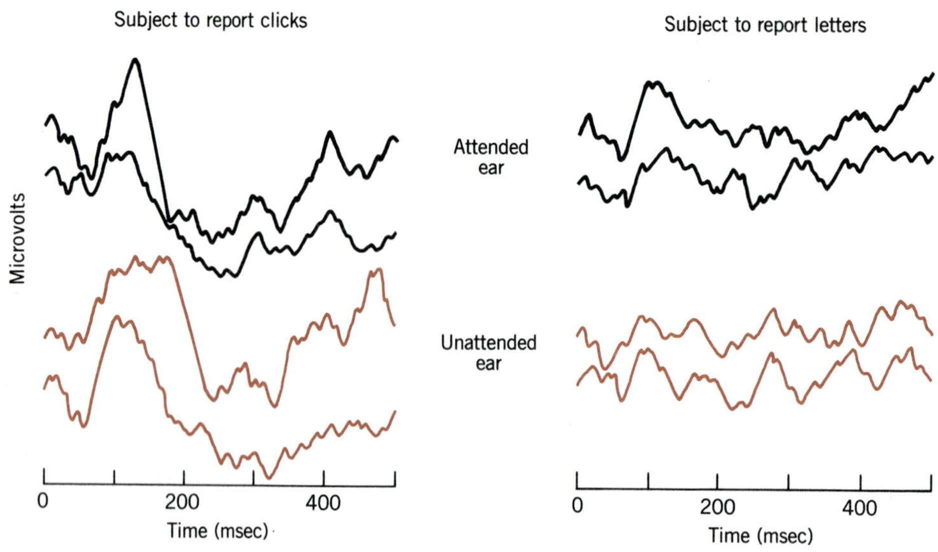

***Figure 10.21** Enhanced evoked potentials with attention. The subject hears both a letter and a click. The records show averages of 50 trials synchronized with the clicks. Responses are greater and longer-lasting when the subject is instructed to report the clicks than when the subject reports the letters. Adapted from Smith et al. (1970).*

of longer recovery functions with IT stimulation. They resolved the dilemma by discovering that the amplitude of the evoked response was larger when the monkey was attentive (Gerbrandt, Spinelli & Pribram, 1970). If the monkey was confined in a closed testing box, the response was small. With the box open, the monkey would look actively about and the cortical response to lateral geniculate nucleus (LGN) stimulation would be large; but IT stimulation would not increase it further. Only when the monkey was bored would IT stimulation affect the striate cortex response. It is as if IT stimulation imitates the effects of attention, slowing recovery functions and increasing the amplitude of evoked activity in the striate cortex. In the original experiments, Spinelli and Pribram had run so many trials that both monkeys and experimenters had become severely bored, allowing the attention enhancing effects of IT stimulation to appear.

The neuronal mechanism of these effects remains unknown, but we have some hints about it from computer simulations. Efferent signals might increase or decrease the strength of lateral inhibition at the striate cortex or lower levels. A change in lateral inhibition could bias the coding process without preventing sensory signals from getting through (Bridgeman, 1978). Further evidence supporting the role of lateral inhibition is that IT stimulation reduces the size of the LGN receptive field center (see Figure 10.23*b*). Frontal stimulation, in contrast, increases background activity and reduces the inhibitory surround of the receptive field (see Figure 10.23*c*). These results can be summarized with the hypothesis that the frontal cortex decreases lateral inhibition in the LGN, and the IT cortex increases it.

Lateral inhibition might be responsible for a property of the striate cortex: its reduced background activity with visual attention. Attentive visual fixation can be assured by having a monkey track a moving spot for a juice reward. During tracking, background activity is reduced in most visual cortex cells and dramatic inhibition occurs in some of them (Bridgeman, 1973).

What is the usefulness of these changes for the animal? In single cells of cat striate cortex, activity decreases when the cat expects a rewarded stimulus. This allows the neural response to the rewarded stimulus to stand out more clearly

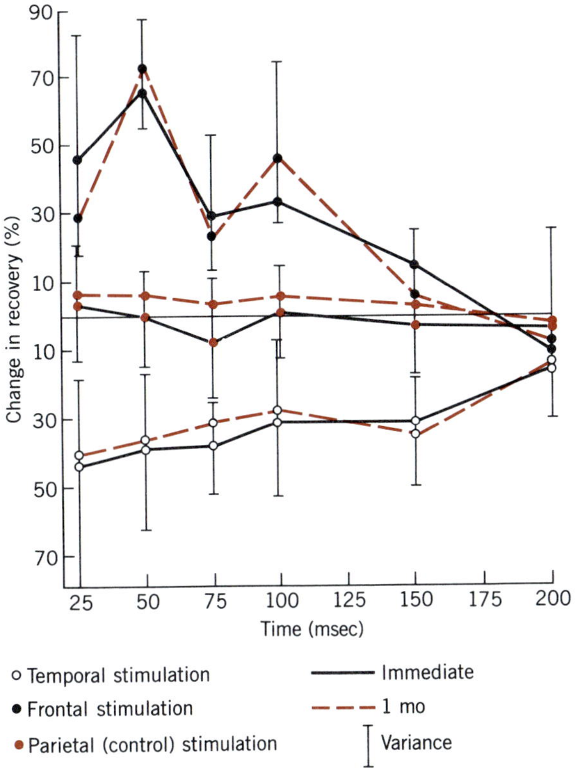

Figure 10.22 *Amplitude of evoked response to the second of a pair of stimuli, changed by stimulation of the temporal lobe, frontal lobe, or parietal lobe. The vertical axis is a comparison of evoked response magnitude during the experimental stimulation to magnitude before any stimulation was begun. The horizontal axis represents the time delay between the first and second stimuli. Temporal stimulation lengthens recovery, frontal stimulation shortens it, and parietal (control) stimulation has no effect. Adapted from Pribram (1971).*

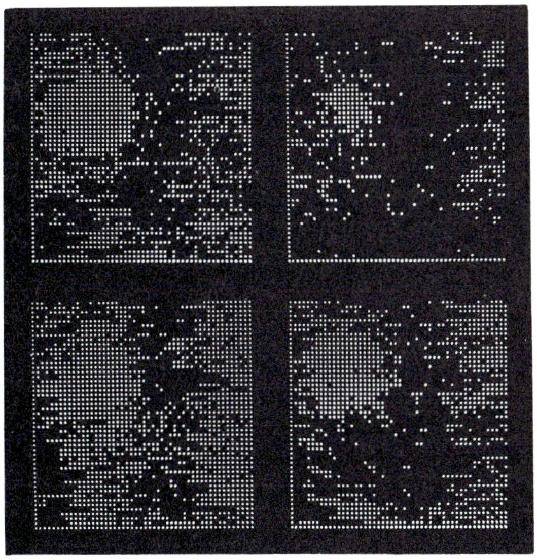

Figure 10.23 *Change in maps of visual receptive fields in the LGN during cortical stimulation.* (a) *Normal LGN receptive field, plotted automatically by the method of Figure 5.16.* (b) *The same receptive field mapped during inferior temporal cortex (temporal lobe) stimulation. The field has contracted.* (c) *Map made during stimulation of frontal cortex. Background has increased.* (d) *Unstimulated control, 55 min after* (a) *was recorded. Adapted from Pribram (1971).*

(Bridgeman & Artim, 1983). Thus attention is accompanied by continual changes in "background" activity, changing the canvas on which the events of mental life are painted.

But attention means more than simply increasing or decreasing sensitivity to stimulation. It can also mean attending to a particular aspect of a stimulus—to either the melodic line or the orchestral texture of a symphony, for example. Neurophysiologists have investigated selective attention by training monkeys to respond to stimuli that differ on two dimensions: form and color (Rothblat & Pribram, 1972). First, the monkeys learned to respond to red rather than green. They were rewarded whenever they pressed a panel containing a red stimulus, regardless of its shape. Then the task was reversed, so the monkeys received a reward only when they responded to a green stimulus. Up to this point, the monkeys responded only to color, regardless of the form of the stimuli. The hard part for the monkeys was a switch from color to form discrimination while the stimuli remained physically identical. Although it took many trials, eventually the monkeys learned to respond to form ("hit the squares") rather than to color ("hit the green"). The physical stimuli remained the same, but their meaning changed. The change in meaning was reflected first at bipolar electrodes implanted in the IT cortex, (see Figure

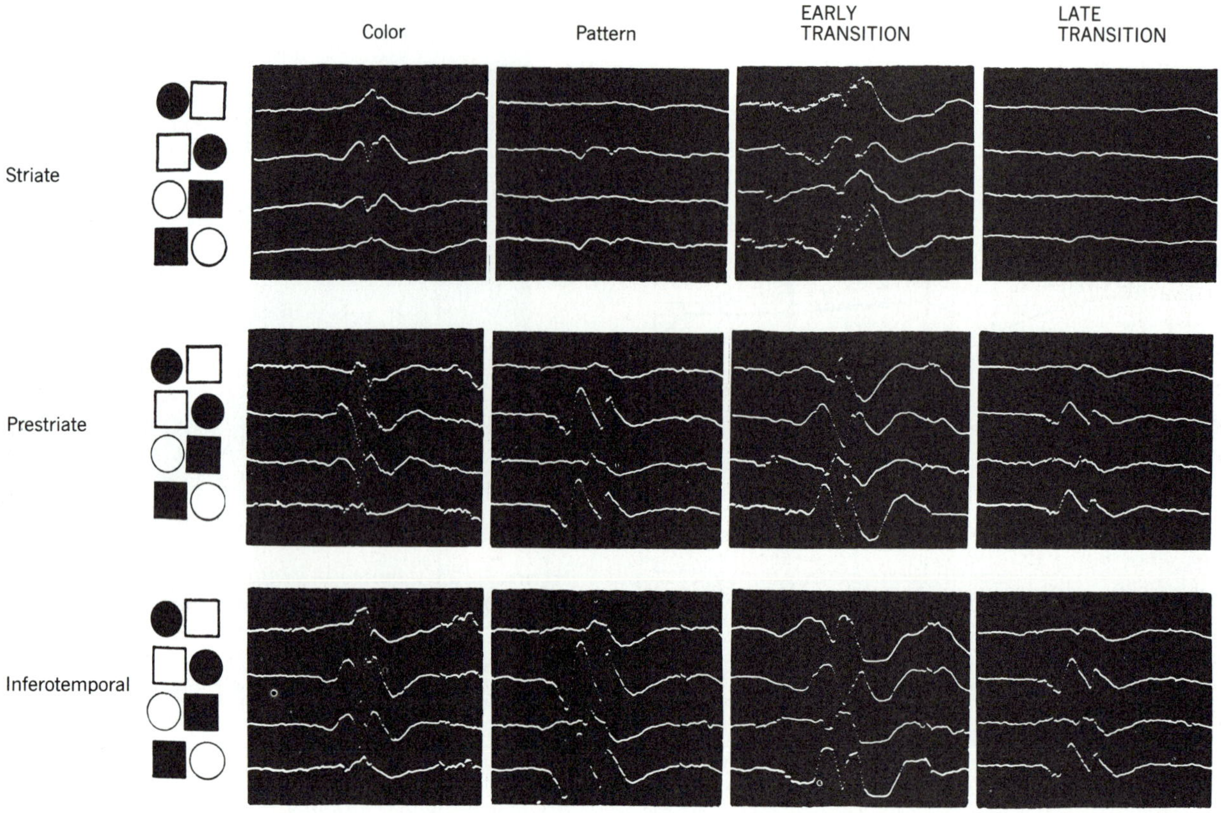

Figure 10.24 *Change in intracortically recorded potential during discrimination training and shift from color to pattern discrimination. Rewards determined whether the monkeys were to attend to pattern or color. Each wave form shows 250 msec before the behavioral response and 250 msec after it. In the first column, the animal is responding on the basis of the color of the stimuli, regardless of their pattern. In the three other columns, the reward is based only on pattern. Activity in all regions increases as the animal begins the transition to pattern discrimination. Reliable differences in wave form based on pattern appear first in the inferotemporal leads (early transition) and are seen later in the striate cortex. Adapted from Pribram (1971).*

10.24) and later appeared at the striate cortex as well.

Again, the differences in evoked potentials were a result of the animal's internal state—specifically of its top-down interpretation of what is important about the stimuli. The source of these differences involves the neurobiology of learning and memory, the subject of the next chapter.

CHAPTER SUMMARY

1. Biorhythms are prominent features of almost all animals and plants. They continue to free-run with slightly more or less than 24-hr cycles even without environmental influences. Efforts to change the period by more than about 2 hr have usually failed. The biological circadian clock is remarkably resistant to potentially disruptive influences but always runs a little fast or slow, requiring a daily zeitgeber signal for calibration. The offset from 24-hr rhythms may serve to bring the several subunits of an organism's clock back into synchronization following a disruption.

2. The vertebrate clock is located in the suprachiasmatic nucleus at the anterior medial edge of the hypothalamus. The light zeitgeber comes from a third pineal "eye" in lower vertebrates and from a small group of retinohypothalamic fibers in mammals. The suprachiasmatic output triggers a surge of the hormone melatonin each evening, synchronizing body activities and the semiautonomous clocks of other organs, such as the adrenal cortex.

3. Formerly interpreted as a period of inactivity, sleep has several distinct stages and a regular temporal structure. Slow-wave sleep, named after its characteristic brain wave, goes through four stages before the first episode of REM, or paradoxical, sleep. REM sleep shows brain waves similar to those of the waking state, but the body is paralyzed and arousal is difficult. Eye movements occur in brief episodes throughout a REM-sleep period. REM-sleep deprivation leads to increased REM sleep during a rebound period, and the PGO spikes characteristic of REM begin to appear more frequently at other times.

4. Dreams take about as long as the experiences they contain, but the eye movements of REM sleep are not exploratory eye movements elicited by dream imagery. They have dynamics that do not match any waking eye movements, and increasing or decreasing the amount of eye movement during waking causes a compensatory adjustment during sleep.

5. For some people, very little sleep is needed for a normal life. Sleep might serve to conserve energy, and, in fact, it uses less energy than quiet wakefulness; hibernation merges into sleep and may just be a more extreme form of energy saving. Learning does not occur during sleep, but it is possible that memory consolidation is aided by sleep. A causal relationship between sleep and learning has yet to be established.

6. Sleep is controlled by a complex of brainstem centers—the reticular activating system being the first discovered. The locus coeruleus and the substantia nigra (the latter of which is dopaminergic) probably mediate arousal from slow-wave sleep; the median raphe (which is serotonergic) facilitates sleep. The nucleus of the solitary tract may initiate sleep following large meals. Other sleep-inducing regions are found in the preoptic-basal forebrain region, which is also a thermoregulatory center. Facets of REM sleep are controlled by several regions, including the caudal locus coeruleus (which controls muscle inhibition) and parts of the reticular formation.

7. Some cases of insomnia are made worse by adaptation to sleep medications; others are caused by a failure to breathe during sleep. Disturbances in circadian rhythms also lead to sleep complaints.

8. The orienting response to novel or particularly informative stimulation includes behavioral and autonomic components. Both are habituated, but reappear if any aspect of the situation changes, implying that habituation is a matching process between external stimulation and an internal model.

9. Attention is mediated by large regions of the forebrain, including parietal regions, where lesions lead to sensory neglect. Single neurons there are activated only when an animal has reason to be interested in the stimuli presented. One mechanism of attention changes is efferent control of cortical inputs, which changes the transformations of sensory input according to the organism's

needs. Posterior intrinsic areas of the cortex change their activity according to the aspects of a stimulus that are most relevant for current behavior, so both stimuli and expectations influence them.

KEY TERMS

Circadian rhythms
Endogenous
Zeitgeber
Pineal organ
Retinohypothalamic tract
Suprachiasmatic nucleus
Stage 1 sleep
Alpha rhythm
Stage 2 sleep
Sleep spindles
Stage 3 sleep
Stage 4 sleep
Slow-wave sleep
Paradoxical (REM) sleep
Convergent evolution
Cerveau isolé
Locus coeruleus
Raphe
Serotonin
Parachlorophenylalanine (PCPA)
Atonia
Narcolepsy
Sleep apnea
Factor S
Delayed sleep phase syndrome
Unilateral neglect
Recovery function

SUGGESTED READINGS

Dement, W. C. (1974). *Some must watch while some must sleep.* San Francisco: Freeman.

An informal, compelling account of some of the major discoveries about sleep in the past few decades, emphasizing Dement's own work.

Mesulam, M. (1983). The functional anatomy and hemispheric specialization for directed attention. *Trends in Neurosciences, 6,* 384–387.

This is an account of the three major cortical components in attention-directing networks—the posterior parietal cortex, the frontal eye fields and surrounding region, and the cingulate cortex. Observations in humans suggest that the right hemisphere is specialized for the processes of directed attention.

Morrison, A. R. (1983, April). A window on the sleeping brain. *Scientific American,* 94–103.

This is an account of the author's discovery of the brain-stem motor areas that mediate the paralysis of REM sleep. Investigations of the behavior of cats with the inhibitory centers ablated reveal some of the mechanisms of REM sleep.

Chapter 11

MEMORY

The physiological basis of memory is one of the central puzzles of physiological psychology. David Krech (1973), who spent a lifetime studying it, said, "Memory is a big and rich and awesome phenomenon" (p. 245). If the mechanisms of memory were known, this chapter would simply describe the processes. Since they are not known, the chapter will sort through tentative hypotheses and fragmentary data. There are many hypotheses, and there will probably turn out to be many mechanisms. Some initial definitions and distinctions will help clarify the problems.

DEFINING LEARNING AND MEMORY

Though learning and memory are basic to human experience and brain function, psychologists paradoxically have found the terms difficult to define. Textbooks on learning often devote several paragraphs to the definition of *memory,* starting with such vague phrases as "a relatively permanent change in behavior that occurs as the result of prior experience." There follow long lists of things that memory isn't, such as maturation, disease, and physical injury. This definition hasn't gotten us very far.

We can do better by focusing on the memory itself rather than on the resulting behaviors and by admitting the presence of a brain that stores information. **Memory** then becomes information stored in the brain as a result of sensory experience, and **learning** is the acquisition of new memories. The word *information* is used in its technical sense, as a reduction of uncertainty, and therefore can exist only in a context: reduction of uncertainty about what? Fundamental to the idea of memories is that they relate to one another, to brain organization, and to the sensory world.

The definition of *memory* excludes information from the genes, making possible a dichotomy between the two great influences on behavior: memory (which is changeable within a lifetime but exists uniquely within an individual) and genetics (which spans generations but is unchangeable within an individual's lifetime). As we have seen in previous chapters, perceptions and actions involve intimate interplay between these two sources of information.

CODES VERSUS MECHANISMS

There are two aspects to the memory problem: the code that represents information and the mechanism that physically preserves it. The two aspects are independent. As an example of the distinction between codes and mechanisms, consider the words in this book. They are written for the most part in the English language, which is a code for representing information. Alternative codes would be the German language, the French language, or any other set of conventions that relate visual or auditory symbols to ideas and events. Each code contains both a set of words (the units of meaning) and a set of conventions about the units that can make them up. The conventions define, for instance, the group of shapes that will be accepted as the written letter *a*.

The mechanism used in this book is letters printed on paper. As I write this paragraph, though, the letters are appearing through a different mechanism, as luminous patterns on a computer terminal screen. But the code remains the same. The code, the English language, could be equally well represented with other mechanisms. Code and mechanism are independent because I could communicate in, say, the English or the German code, with ink or electrons or speech as the mechanism.

The problems in applying the distinction between code and mechanism to memory research come in attempts to understand one aspect without knowing much about the other. Research on mechanisms of memory, for instance, cannot get very far without knowledge of what is being remembered—the code in which the information is represented. The meanings stored with a particular mechanism cannot be read unless the code is known, even if somehow the mechanism has been unraveled. If you don't know Morse code, you can't distinguish the message "I love you" from random dots and dashes.

These problems have led to a division between specialists working primarily on codes and those working primarily on mechanisms. Difficulties arise because workers specializing in one aspect of the problem often assume the existence of a trivial or idealized solution to the other aspect. Those interested in codes often assume that the mechanism is perfect, even if the appropriate codes haven't yet been found. Investigators of mechanisms often assume that the code is trivial. In neurophysiology, for instance, it is often considered enough to show that a synapse activated more frequently will transmit signals more efficiently. Biological codes are far more complex.

Both psychology and clinical experience indicate that there are two kinds of knowledge—declarative and procedural—and that they use different mechanisms and probably different codes.

DECLARATIVE VERSUS PROCEDURAL KNOWLEDGE

A brain-damaged patient sits down to learn a task that a neurologist presents to him. The patient is to read material that he can see only through a mirror arrangement (see Figure 11.1). At first, the patient reads very slowly, taking the time to deci-

Backward writing is often used in tests of memory because it is unfamiliar.

Figure 11.1 *An example of mirror writing.*

pher each letter; but after some practice, the reading pace improves considerably. In fact, the patient learns to read mirror-image writing about as fast as normal subjects do. The next day, when the patient is asked to perform the mirror-reading task again, he declares that he has never seen the apparatus or the experimenter. The patient has **amnesia**—a loss of memory (*a* is Greek for "not," and *mnemnos* is Greek for "memory").

At this point, one might conclude that the patient has only short-term memory and that nothing remains from the previous day's experience. After the task has been reexplained, however, the patient sits down and begins mirror-reading as skillfully as he had the day before. When asked about the source of this skill, the patient informs the neurologist that the task isn't really very difficult and that anyone could do as well.

The patient is the famous N.A. (Cohen & Squire, 1980), who became amnesic in 1960 following an encounter with a fencing foil. (We will return to this patient and similar ones later.)

N.A. has amnesia for **declarative knowledge,** the sort of memory that can be put into words; but he retains the ability to acquire and use **procedural knowledge,** the memory for rules and procedures. Procedural learning modifies existing schemata, or ways of going about solving a problem (Rumelhart, 1981). The declarative-procedural distinction has also been characterized as knowing *that* versus knowing *how* and as memory with record versus memory without record.

The distinction between declarative and procedural knowledge will be needed in the comparative study of animal and human learning. Humans are often tested on declarative knowledge, such as learning a list of words or identifying movie stars. Learning in animals, in contrast, is often measured in terms of procedural knowledge—in tasks such as running a maze or avoiding a compartment associated with shock. Keeping the distinction in mind will help clarify apparent differences between the neurological organization of animal and human memory.

Another useful way to divide rules from instances is to distinguish semantic from episodic memory. **Semantic** (rulelike) **memory** tells us that Sacramento is the capital of California. The knowledge can be put into words, and it expresses an enduring characteristic of the world. Knowing of your trip to Sacramento last week would require **episodic memory**—memory for a particular episode in your life.

RECALL, RECOGNITION, AND SAVINGS

Suppose you are asked to learn a list of words, say English words and their Swahili translations. An hour later you are given the English list and are asked to reproduce the Swahili words. This is a test of **recall**—the ability to retrieve items from memory. A month later you might not be able to recall any of the words. This does not mean that all memory of them has disappeared, for you would probably do better than chance at distinguishing the correct translations from incorrect ones. Less information is needed in memory to perform this **recognition** task; only one bit is required to say yes or no to a translation presented to you.

Recognition is a more sensitive measure than recall. A year later, however, even the recognition test might fail, yielding random performance (assuming that you have had no contact with Swahili in the meantime). But something might still remain in memory. You would probably relearn the original list faster than you could learn a similar list of new words. This measure, called **savings,** is the most sensitive of all.

Even if a lesion wiped out recall, the more sensitive recognition or savings measures might reveal some memory. Also important for the physiology of memory is the relationship between consciousness and the three measures of memory. Recall is accompanied by awareness that the memory is preserved, but recognition usually includes awareness only if the sample materials are present. Savings never involves a realization that memory is still present, even while the faster relearning is taking place.

CODES

Like many other aspects of neuroscience, the study of the physiological coding of memory received its first data from clinical observations. Memory is protected against erasure caused by injury; brain damage never seems to remove particular memories, no matter what the lesion. In the extreme case, the patient who loses half of his brain does not go home to recognize only half of his family. But when a computer loses half of its memory, some information is utterly destroyed and other information remains intact. Humans and animals suffer a different kind of loss; rather than losing particular events, nearly everything becomes a little more vague.

Some large lesions may remove specific kinds of memories, such as the memory for certain kinds of words, but the loss is always of a class of material rather than individual items.

DISTRIBUTED CODING

These observations were formalized by Karl Lashley (1929, 1950) in a landmark series of experiments testing the effects of various ablations on rats' memory for mazes. Lashley's goal was to find the **engram,** the physical substrate of memory. Large lesions were successful in abolishing whole classes of memories: removal of the entire visual cortex, for instance, removed visual memory as well.

Smaller lesions, in contrast, were singularly unsuccessful. Lashley could, for instance, ablate one-third of the visual cortex and find no effect on memory. The rats ran the mazes with the same number of errors as a sham-operated control group (a group whose cortexes were exposed but not removed, to assure that the secondary effects of the operation did not cause behavioral changes). Ablating a different third of the visual cortex in another group of rats had the same negative result. This should lead to the conclusion that the memory resides in the final third of the visual cortex. But, as you have probably guessed, the final third gave negative results also. This result held for Lashley's easiest maze. The more difficult the maze, or the greater the amount of cortex ablated, the greater the deficit (see Figure 11.2).

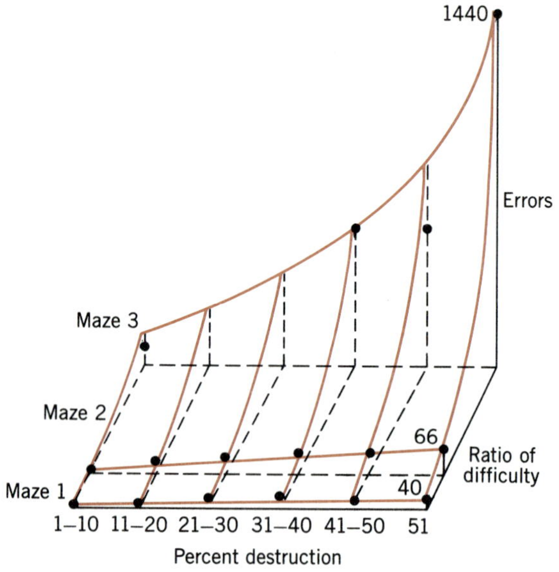

Figure 11.2 *Mass action in the rat cortex. Mazes 1, 2, and 3 are in increasing order of difficulty. The first two mazes show a "floor effect"; the tasks are so easy that even extensive brain damage has little effect. Adapted from Lashley (1929).*

These and similar results led Lashley to the principle of **mass action:** that the quantity of remaining cortex rather than its location determined the amount of remaining memory. The corollary to this principle is **equipotentiality:** that within a cortical area one region is as good as another at storing information. The principles are generalizations, accurate only within limits. They apply to specialized cortical regions, not to the brain as a whole. Subsequent work has shown that although memory is widespread, it is not homogeneously distributed. These results challenged the then-dominant *connectionist* idea of memory: that the association cortex connects ideas in the way that a telephone switchboard connects telephones.

Compared to the enormous effort devoted to unraveling the mechanisms of memory, relatively little work has been done on codes since Lashley's time. One reason for this neglect is that distributed codes are generally inaccessible to the most powerful techniques of neuroscience. If a memory engram is distributed among a thousand or a million neurons, a microelectrode recording from any one of them will reveal only a thousandth or a millionth of the information stored. Similarly, newer anatomical techniques, such as 2-DG autoradiography (see Chapter 3), can detect only frequency codes—where information is carried on axons by a change in average firing frequency. A distributed memory engram may remain invisible to these techniques.

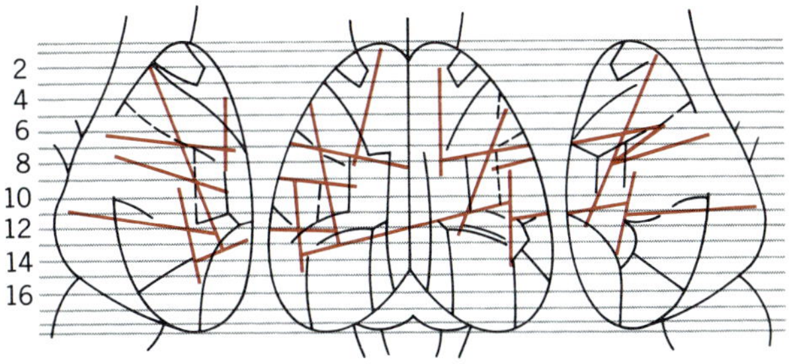

Figure 11.3 *Incisions in rat brains having no effect on performance in a maze. One knife cut was made in each rat brain.*

Classical Conditioning and Connectionist Theories of Coding

The idea that each memory is stored in a widely distributed code can be contrasted with the connectionist (or switchboard) theory, which was a direct extension of Pavlov's theory of **classical conditioning.** Let us take as an example one of Pavlov's dogs, which is repeatedly given meat powder about 1 sec after the ringing of a bell. Without any learning, the dog salivates after the meat powder is presented. The salivation is an **unconditioned response (UR),** and the meat is an **unconditioned stimulus (US).** After several pairings of bell and meat, the dog learns to salivate at the sound of the bell (which is a **conditioned stimulus,** or **CS**), before the food appears. The early salivation is a **conditioned response (CR).** Pavlov theorized that a neural connection was formed between the cortical area representing the CS and that representing the UR, so neural activity traveling along the chain would mediate a behavioral CR.

Extensive experimental work since Pavlov's time, much of it performed in Russia, has failed to find this connection. Lashley himself tested memory in rats after making extensive knife cuts through the cortex, presumably cutting any possible Pavlovian connections. The cuts, shown in Figure 11.3, had absolutely no effect on memory.

Statistical Theories of Coding

Other data have pointed to a statistical rather than a switchboard conception of memory storage. According to the statistical idea, each neuron participates to a small degree in many memories. The situation can be viewed as a large number of neurons voting rather than a small number commanding.

If memory coding is a statistical process, it should occur in a large number of neurons. We might probe it by measuring evoked potentials with pairs of implanted wire electrodes that summate activity from large pools of neurons. The problem is that we don't know what to look for. What is the evoked potential for the memory of a square or a face? E. R. John (1967, 1973) attacked this problem by conditioning animals with flickering light (the CS), a type of stimulus that can be traced using evoked-potential techniques. By looking for brain activity at the stimulated frequency, he could label the evoked potentials and identify them wherever they appeared.

The first step in John's experiments was to record the activity evoked from a large number of brain areas in a cat by a strobe of, for instance, 6 Hz. The hungry cat was then trained to approach a feeding tube and press a lever (a CR) to obtain a reward that was available only when the strobe was flashing. This type of conditioning is called **instrumental conditioning,** because the animal is instrumental in obtaining the reward. The result was that after conditioning the flash elicited activity from many brain regions, including the midbrain reticular formation and the hippocampus (see Figure 11.4). Even the visual cortex showed stimulus-correlated activity only after conditioning, because the sensory cortex extracts information rather than just relaying images (see Chapter 5). After overtraining (further practice after reaching the training criterion), the evoked electrical activity shrank back to a smaller set of areas, different from those activated before conditioning began.

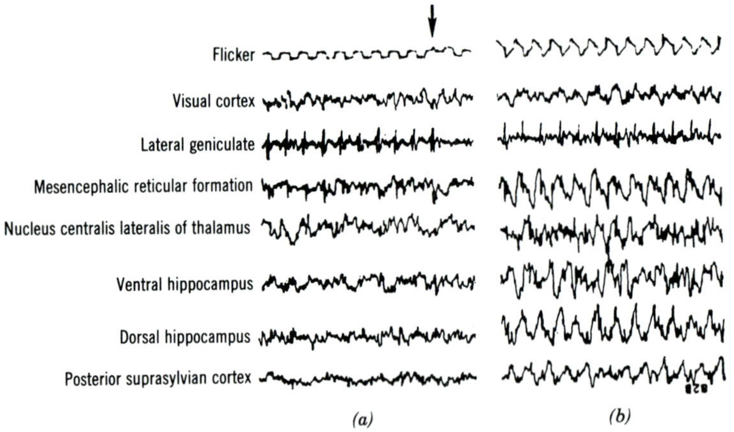

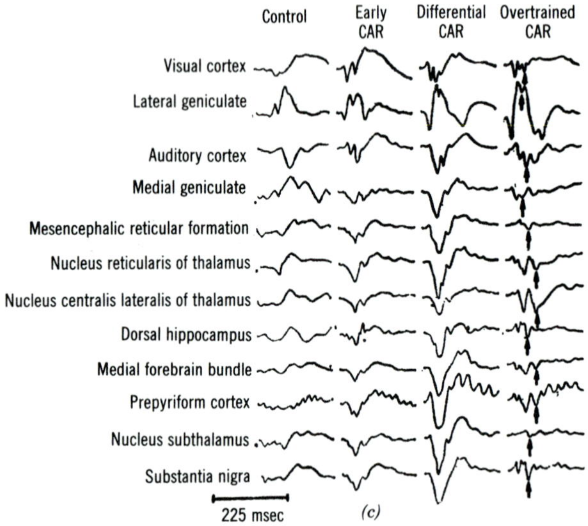

Figure 11.4 *Brain potentials recorded in a cat during conditioning.* (a) *Response before a 6 Hz flicker became a cue.* (b) *Response after the same flicker became a cue not to press the lever in a frequency discrimination. The cat responded correctly by not pressing the lever.* (c) *Development of visual evoked responses. Control was recorded from a naive cat. Early conditioned avoidance response (CAR) was just after establishing a simple avoidance. Differential CAR was just after establishing an approach to one flicker frequency and an avoidance of another frequency. Discrimination training enhanced the response amplitude and the similarity between traces from different areas. Overtrained CAR was after many months of practice on the differential task. Arrows show components that are smaller or absent when the animal fails to perform.*

The widespread activity suggests that large regions of the brain participate in the learning process. But other interpretations are also possible. Perhaps the conditioning procedure merely increased arousal, releasing neural responses that are normally inhibited. To control for this possibility, John taught his cats a second task. The strobe was now set to flash at a different rate, say 10 Hz, a few seconds before a floor grid was electrified. The cats responded by jumping over a low barrier to a safe cage. They learned to jump before the shock began, performing a **conditioned avoidance response (CAR).** Electrophysiological results were as before: widespread brain areas showed stimulus-evoked rhythms during conditioning.

Next John made things more complicated for his cats. He presented generalization trials with a strobe flash at the intermediate rate of 8 Hz. The cats had two alternatives. They could interpret the 8 Hz rate either as a distorted version of the first strobe rate (and perform a CR) or as the second rate (and perform a CAR). In the evoked responses to the generalization trials, some of the electrodes showed an **exogenous** (outside) **rhythm;** they were driven by the 8 Hz stimulating frequency. Other electrodes revealed an **endogenous** (inside) **rhythm** at one of the original training frequencies. The endogenous rhythm in Figure 11.5 was not present in the stimulus; it existed only in the cat's memory of previous trials. It is an electrophysiological sign of a memory. Thus the widespread stimulus-evoked activity of the learning situation is more than just an expansion of sensory

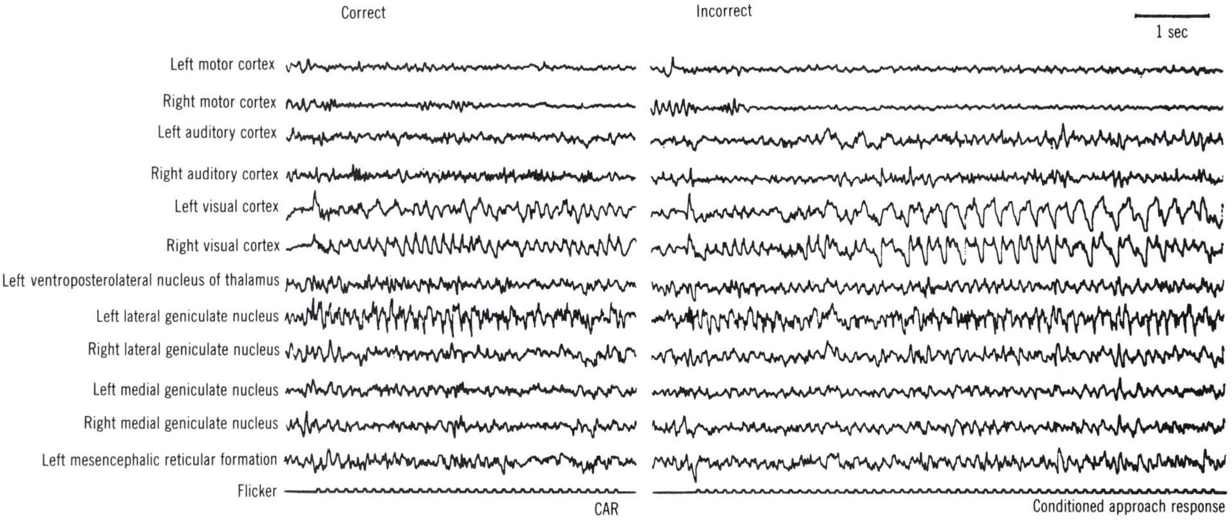

Figure 11.5 *Contrast of electrical activity preceding a correct response and an incorrect response. The behavioral response occurs at the end of each record. The cat sees a 7.7 Hz flicker. In the correct trial, many brain areas repeat that flicker frequency; in the incorrect one, some areas show an endogenous rhythm matching the discriminative stimulus of 3.1 Hz. This is particularly clear in the visual cortex. All records are bipolar.*

coding with increased arousal; it has something to do with establishing a specific memory.

Endogenous rhythms appeared in widespread brain areas, including the visual cortex, sometimes thought of as fairly peripheral in the sensory processing scheme. Even at this stage, only two synapses from the retina, memory is already influencing the pattern of evoked activity.

With data from the CR-CAR experiment it is possible to quantify the concept of equipotentiality of memory in the cat brain (Bartlett & John, 1973). The endogenous contribution can be plotted against the exogenous contribution. The result is a measure of the relative roles of sensory and memory processes in various brain areas. As Figure 11.6 shows, the representation of an experience is distributed in many brain regions. This technique cannot prove that information is permanently stored in areas showing high endogenous activity. It shows only that endogenous information appears in these areas during recognition. Cortical, limbic, and brain-stem regions participate in the readout process.

A newer technique, double-labeled autoradiography, offers a closer look at areas uniquely involved in memory (John et al., 1986). The 2-deoxyglucose (2-DG) technique can measure brain activity in various areas during learning. The technique controls for two different kinds of influences in addition to memory. The first influence is the general metabolic changes caused by being in the testing situation. The changes result from alerting, motor activity, and eating. The second influence is the difference between unlearned and learned cues in guiding behavior.

To control for general changes, split-brain cats were trained in a two-choice pattern discrimination. Cues given to one eye then entered only one hemisphere. The difference between the naive hemisphere, where only general changes take

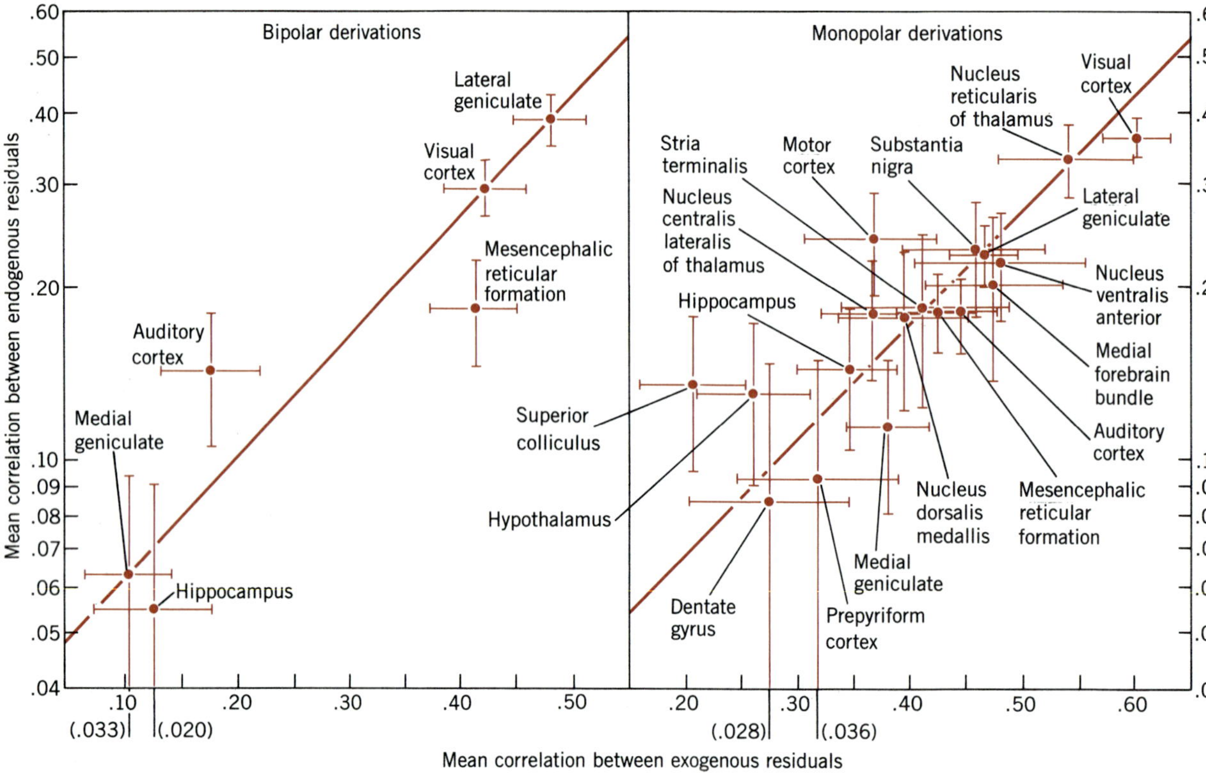

Figure 11.6 Correlations between the exogenous residuals and endogenous residuals in various brain areas. Each point plots two correlations, one exogenous and one endogenous. The amount of endogenous activity observed is strongly related to the amount of exogenous activity in the same brain region.

place, and the trained hemisphere, where both general and memory-specific changes are present, reveals brain activity specific to learning.

To test for the difference between learned cues and unlearned cues, cats worked under two conditions. In the first, they performed the discrimination and were given a radioactive form of 2-DG with a long half-life (a long period of radioactivity). In the second condition, in new trials, the cats chose between two identical patterns and were rewarded for either choice. During these trials they were given another form of 2-DG—one with a shorter half-life. They were doing all of the information processing necessary for successful discrimination except for the learned discrimination itself.

After the cats had run these two sets of trials, the autoradiography captured the brain concentrations of both forms of 2-DG. When the short half-life version had decayed, the autoradiography was done again. This time only the long half-life version affected the autoradiographs. The difference between the first and second autoradiographs showed the brain's uptake of the short half-life 2-DG.

The conclusion from these rather complicated experiments was that a wide variety of brain regions showed changes specific to memory. The regions included most cortical areas, the limbic system, parts of the cerebellum, and the thalamus. The implication is that an enormous number of neurons, between 5 million and 100 million out of the 2 billion in the cat brain, participate in even this simple memory. To look more closely at what changes take place, we must record from single neurons with microelectrodes.

Coding in Single Neurons

Many investigators have recorded from single cells during or after conditioning. Though methods and behavioral tasks vary widely, the studies agree that between 5 and 70 percent of neurons change their response properties during conditioning. This very large number has some clear implications for memory-coding schemes.

Let us begin with the low estimate of 5 percent. If memory were organized in a "filing card" scheme in which each card was kept anatomically separate from all the others, the animals in these studies could encode a maximum of 20 items. Clearly, this is not the case; each cell must participate in many memories.

At first glance, such statistical skulduggery seems impossible, but in fact overlapping storage is common in physical systems. An example occurs in the information passing through an ordinary optical lens.

MODELS OF DISTRIBUTED CODING

A model of memory coding should be consistent with several characteristics of memory storage. First, it should distribute information in such a way that single memories cannot be erased by removal of part of the physical substrate of the memory system. This is the analog of the resistance of natural memories to erasure by lesions. Distribution of memory makes necessary a second characteristic—that many memories be intermingled to overlap in the same substrate. But it must still be possible to store and retrieve each memory independently. Third, memories should be encoded and decoded in relation to one another rather than to some external filing scheme. Memories have no Library of Congress numbers, no indexes, no labels. Instead, they have an intrinsic self-reference system. We retrieve memories by recalling related events or categories, hooking memories to one another in a great self-supporting web. Each memory is content-addressable.

We might still accommodate distribution and overlap in a modified connectionist theory by postulating that memory modules coding a single memory are repeated over and over in different anatomical areas. This code would be redundant and wasteful, however. At present there is no evidence in favor of it, and the difficulty of eliciting memories by punctate stimulation (stimulation at one point) argues against it. As we will see, there are more sophisticated ways of distributing information in a neural system.

The content-addressable characteristic of memory reveals itself when we encounter a friend on the street. We instantly recognize the person's face and remember a host of other things connected with the person. We make no long search through large memory banks; our recognition is immediate, as though no search had taken place.

These three properties of memory—distribution, overlap, and content-addressability—are shared by a family of optical information storage schemes. (Incidentally, the computer memory coding analogy fails on all three counts.) Distribution and overlap occur at some stage in practically all optical systems; we will use a familiar one—a slide projector—as an example.

Information Flow in a Slide Projector

Figure 11.7 shows the optical path of light from a light source through a slide and a lens to a projection screen. At the slide and again at the screen the information contained in the light is organized in a discrete, point-by-point fashion. Each bit of information is spatially separated from the other bits. In the lens plane, however, the coding is fundamentally different. From each point on the slide, the light radiates to every point on the lens. Thus information from each point on the slide is coded across the entire lens, and each point on the lens receives light from every point on the slide, so the conditions of distribution and overlap apply.

We can see one implication of this coding scheme by placing an occluding object such as a pencil in the light path. If the pencil is just in front of the screen, it will cast a shadow that obliterates information coded in that area of the image. Information represented elsewhere is unaffected. Held just in front of the projector's lens, however, the pencil obliterates nothing. Here, the lens has not yet had a great effect on the distribution of information in the light. The whole projected image becomes a little dimmer (like memory following a lesion), but no particular pieces are lost.

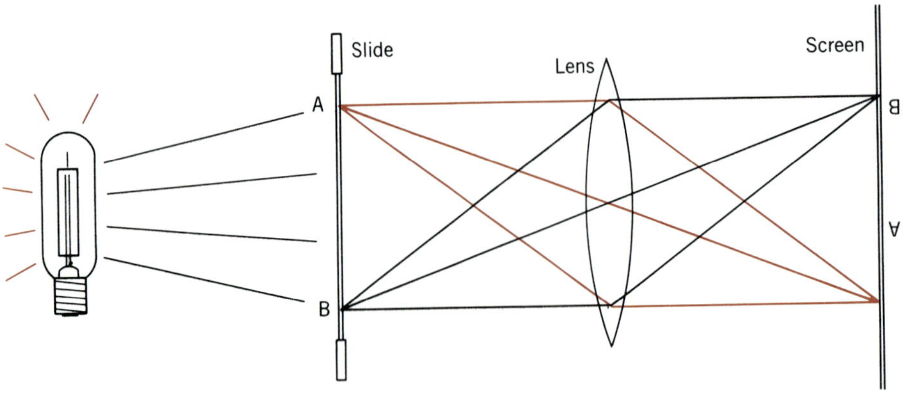

Figure 11.7 *Paths of selected light rays through the optical system of a simplified slide projector. An object occluding part of the lens will occlude some rays but will not occlude all the rays originating from any one point on the slide.*

The distribution-of-information effect can be seen without a slide projector, for the information in the light entering your own eye is coded in the same way. Hold a wire by both ends (a straightened paper clip will do) and move it very close to one eye while closing the other; no part of the visible world will be occluded. More generally, light is distributed in this way whenever it radiates from an extended region onto a plane without benefit of a lens.

The photons of light arriving at the projector's lens are sorted out according to their angles of arrival and their locations on the lens surface. There is no storage of the information and no possibility of combining information from various sources.

Information Storage in a Hologram

To store the distributed information at the lens plane of the slide projector, we need a way to "freeze" the incoming signals without confusing them. Such a method was invented by Dennis Gabor (1949) in an attempt to increase the resolution of the electron microscope. He named it the **hologram** (*holo* is Greek for "whole," and *gram* is Greek for "write"). Despite its potential usefulness, the hologram did not become practical or widely known until lasers became available, in the mid-1960s.

Encoding. The hologram is a way of storing the light advancing from an object. The technique takes advantage of a unique property of light emitted by a laser: the light is coherent, with all of its wave fronts lined up in register with one another.

To make a hologram, one passes light through a half-silvered mirror so half of it is reflected to a photographic plate and half is transmitted to an object (say a round ball). The coherent light reflected from the object carries information about the object. The image (see Figure 11.8) is stored by the interference pattern set up between the reference beam reflected from the half-silvered mirror and the light reflected from the object.

Since there are no lenses in this system, information is distributed across the hologram in the same way it is spread across the lens of the slide projector. Like biological memory, the information is spatially distributed. To see how the system supports another kind of overlap of information and how it codes memory in a content-addressable form, we must look at the decoding process.

Decoding. Once exposed, the hologram is developed and a positive transparency is made in the conventional manner. When the transparency is illuminated with the reference beam (see Figure 11.9), the object magically reappears to an observer looking through the hologram. During encoding, the reference beam and the object create the hologram; at decoding, the reference beam and the hologram yield the object.

Since the hologram codes both the direction and the phase of the incoming light, all of the information that the light had carried from the scene is present on the film. The third dimension is not lost, as it is in a conventional photograph; objects

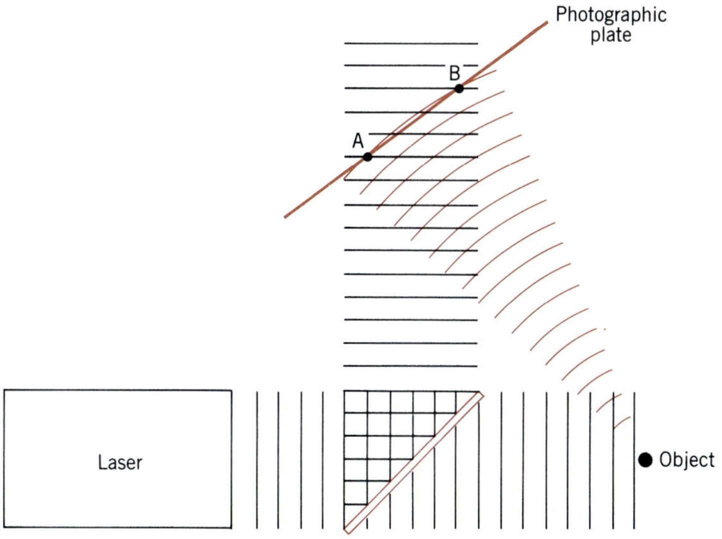

Figure 11.8 *Constructing one type of hologram. The peak of a wave from the reference beam intersects the peak of a wave from the object at point A on the hologram, creating a dark spot on the developed film. The waves at point B interfere with each other, a peak from the object coinciding with a trough from the reference beam. The two waves are out of phase with each other. No energy intercepts the film at this point, and the film is left transparent. Other points on the film give intermediate results, each being darkened in proportion to the phase relations between the reference beam and the object beam at that point. In real life the waves intersect the hologram plane at the speed of light; but since the light is coherent, the phase relationships at each point remain constant. An instant later, for example, the peaks at point A will have moved on and two troughs will intersect at the point.*

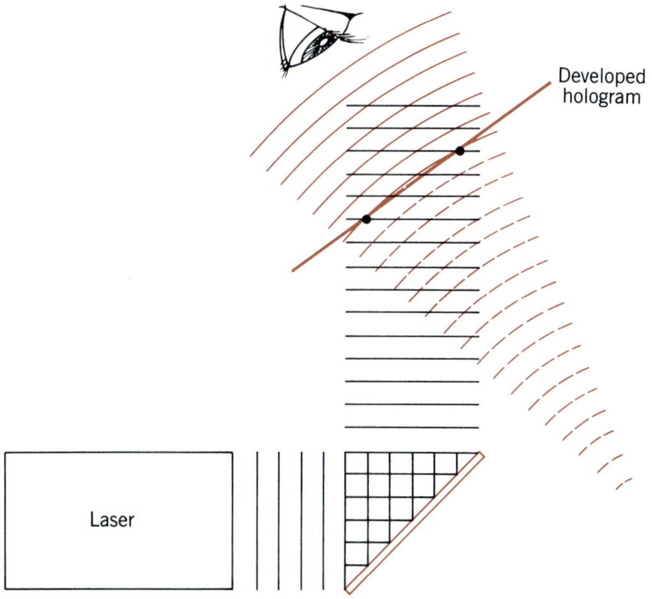

Figure 11.9 *Looking at a hologram. Because the light rays are reconstructed, not imaged, the observer looks through the transparency rather than at it.*

occluded from one angle can be seen by looking through the hologram from another angle.

This completes the review of the basic construction and reading of holograms. Their similarities to properties of memory coding are several. First, the hologram can be cut in half with scissors and each half handed to an observer; each observer would be able to see the entire scene that was originally recorded. The experience with a half-hologram is like the experience of looking into a room through only half a window. This is the analog to Lashley's lesion experiments.

Second, to extend the parallel with biological memory, it is necessary to code many memories simultaneously on the same substrate. This is done in several ways. An obvious one is to present not just one object but a group of objects in the image; each will, of course, be recorded throughout the extent of the holographic plate. A more interesting strategy for **multiplexing**—recording several separate signals in the same substrate—is to change the frequency of the reference beam. Now a new object can be encoded at the same angle as the previous one, without interacting very much with the original object. The new reference beam creates interference fringes that are statistically independent of the original ones, so each signal at one frequency looks like a bit of random noise at the other frequency. In this way, many signals can be represented independently.

Content-Addressable Memory. The hologram is an interaction of two beams, or two sources of information. In our example we used a plane mirror as one of the sources. Let us now replace it with another object—for instance, a cube. The hologram now encodes the interference pattern set up between light from two objects. To see the ball that appeared in Figure 11.9, we would reflect light from the cube instead of the mirror. But the encoding scheme is symmetrical, with both objects illuminated in parallel, so we can also recover the image of the cube by reflecting light from the ball. Such images are called **ghost images,** but there is nothing ghostly about them; they are just as real as any other images.

If either object is used to construct the reference beam, the other object appears immediately to the observer. There is no search for the information, for it is present everywhere. Recovering information is a matter of finding the right reference object and frequency rather than the right location; the memory is content-addressable. In a more complicated hologram, more than two objects can interact.

Distributed Models of Memory

The parallels between the properties of holograms and of memory are suggestive, but they do not explain how a distributed coding scheme might be applied to biological memory. We are quite certain that there are no lasers in the head and no photographic plates. The hologram, though, is a mathematical reality as much as a physical arrangement, and similar mathematics can be applied to biological memory coding. We need only a substrate capable of storing the information and ways of encoding and decoding it.

The mathematics of holograms is Fourier analysis, which we examined in Chapter 5. The hologram itself is little more than a Fourier transform of the sensory image (Arbib, 1972). Since holographic coding is defined mathematically, we need only a neurological machine that can perform the necessary mathematical transformations; we have no need for lasers in the head. Several hypotheses about the neural hologram in memory exist (Arbib, 1972; Pribram, Nuwer & Baron, 1974; Westlake, 1970), as do related ideas such as autocorrelation (Uttal, 1975) and correlogram (Willshaw, Buneman & Longuet-Higgins, 1969) hypotheses. All are somewhat speculative, but they provide concrete alternatives to the old connectionist ideas.

A more recent set of models uses schemes of distributed coding purely as mathematical ideas. No attempt is made to relate the codes to particular brain structures. This movement is called *new connectionism* in psychology.

Some of these models consider memory a vector—a way of representing several numbers simultaneously. To code three quantities simultaneously, for instance, one can imagine a point within a box. The point's height, horizontal position, and depth in the box represent the three numbers. The models, called matrix models, emphasize parallel organization rather than a network of connections or associations. Their advantage is that their structure does not become more complex as the amount to be remembered increases (Hinton & Anderson, 1981).

Two models apply hologramlike mathematics to human memory. Murdoch (1982) uses convolution as an encoding mechanism; each new chunk of information is combined with the information already in memory. Retrieval is a process of correlation, matching a memory cue with the contents of the memory. Eich (1982) has simulated a similar model on a computer. The program, called CHARM (Composite Holographic Associative Recall Model), predicts about a dozen characteristics of human verbal learning. In particular, it can model the ease of learning material that is similar to previously learned material and the difficulty of learning material that contradicts what has been learned earlier. CHARM makes several predictions about errors in recall that the old connectionist theories do not predict. It also predicts some results that seem counterintuitive but are well-verified experimentally.

In a direct comparison of correlation models and matrix models of distributed memory, Pike (1984) concludes that matrix models have a better ratio of signal to noise in recalled information and the simulations of the models are also more successful at recalling things in the correct serial order. Deciding which of many matrix hypotheses is the most plausible will be aided by knowledge of the physical mechanisms of memory.

MEMORY MECHANISMS OF INVERTEBRATES

The physical basis of memory has proved to be extraordinarily difficult to isolate. The reason lies partly in the distributed nature of most memory and partly in the difficulty of proving that a change in brain biochemistry or anatomy is due to learning, not to fatigue, normal repair processes, exercise, and so on. Thus it is necessary to retreat to the simplest forms of memory in the simplest organisms, where recent progress has been rapid.

MECHANISMS OF HABITUATION IN SEA SLUGS

There are several advantages to performing neurophysiological experiments with simple invertebrates. Their nervous systems are very small, often consisting of only a few dozen or a few hundred neurons instead of billions. In mollusks, for example, the neurons are generally large, easy to find, and consistent from animal to animal. A neuron identified and recorded in one animal can be investigated further through its counterpart in the next animal. Invertebrate neurophysiologists give the neurons names and numbers for identification. The nervous systems of invertebrates are hardy, surviving for hours after being dissected from the body and placed in glass dishes. Slugs, for example, have no bones, so there is no skull to penetrate.

The disadvantage of work with simple animals is that the applicability of their behavior to the human condition may be limited. Nonetheless, neurophysiologists have learned from work on axons and synapses that the basic building blocks are conserved through evolution. And as we saw in Chapter 1, the phylogenetically ancient structures are similar in mammals and in primitive invertebrates. If behavioral plasticity, like axons and chemical synapses, is basic to all animals, perhaps the anatomical and biochemical mechanisms of plasticity will also be similar.

Habituation Behaviors

The study of habituation in the marine gastropod mollusk *Aplysia* began with a thorough analysis of the animal's behavior. The important behavior for the study is the mollusk's gill-withdrawal reflex. *Aplysia* has a dorsal gill protected only by a light mantle shelf and has a siphon that pumps water over the gill as the animal crawls along the sea floor (see Figure 11.10). If something touches the mantle or the siphon, the animal retracts its gill fully under the mantle. This is the response that habituates. It has been studied electrically and biochemically by Eric Kandel (1976, 1979) and his associates.

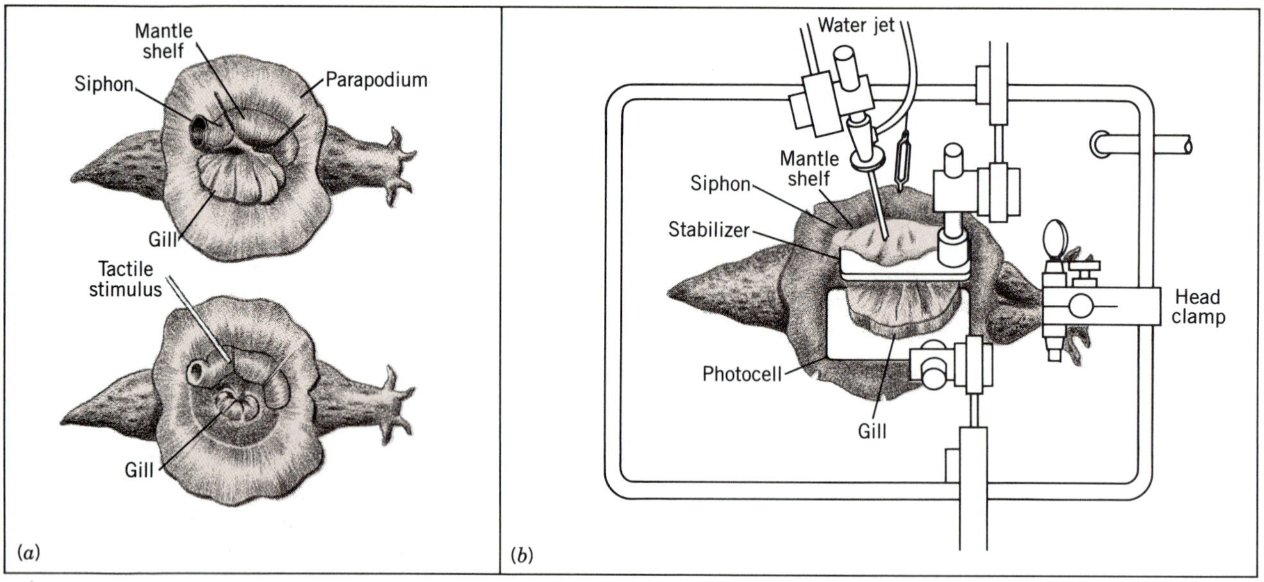

Figure 11.10 *Recording from* Aplysia *during conditioning.* (a) *Appearance and gill-withdrawal behavior of the marine gastropod* Aplysia. (b) *Preparation for behavioral measurement. A jet of water stimulates contraction, exposing the photocell to light to yield a measure of gill contraction.*

Gill-withdrawal habituation shares many properties with more complex habituations. Some of these properties restrict the possibilities for physiological mechanisms of the behavior. Habituation is specific to particular locations on the mantle; following habituation, a touch on another part of the mantle or siphon still yields a vigorous response. Since the habituated animal is still capable of performing the withdrawal, we know without doing any neurophysiological study that the reduction in response cannot be due to fatigue in the muscles or adaptation at the neuromuscular junction. Like vertebrate habituation, the effect is temporary; responsiveness is restored after an interval of no stimulation. Therefore the change is not structural. There is also a sensitization effect: a painful stimulus to the animal's head potentiates the withdrawal reflex.

Neuronal Mechanisms

Electrophysiology. The circuit that controls gill withdrawal is shown in Figure 11.11. The relevant neurons are in the abdominal ganglion, a group of a few hundred neurons on the ventral side of the animal. Besides a group of sensory neurons, the circuit consists of exactly nine cells: six motor neurons and three interneurons. The anatomy shows some similarities to that mediating the spinal reflexes of vertebrates: a direct pathway supplemented by polysynaptic routes. To study the gill-withdrawal pathways, Kandel's group usually removed the abdominal ganglion together with the siphon, mantle, gill, and sensory and motor nerves.

Several possible sites of plasticity are indicated in Figure 11.11. A series of experiments proved that the receptors did not adapt; sensory signals were the same in a habituated animal as in a responsive one. Approaching the reflex from the motor end, the researchers found that the motor neurons did decrease their firing rates as habituation progressed. The change had to be somewhere in between, at the synapse between the receptor and the motor neurons.

The researchers found plasticity in the presynaptic terminals, where the magnitude (but not the number) of EPSPs decreased with habituation.

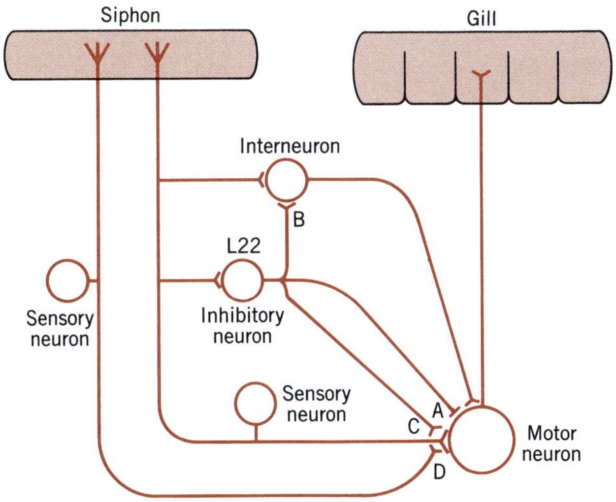

***Figure 11.11** Anatomy of gill control in* Aplysia. *Possible locations of plastic synapses are the motor neuron* (A), *an excitatory interneuron* (B), *terminals from a sensory interneuron* (C), *and a different, direct sensory pathway* (D).

Since the interneurons contributed relatively little to the reflex, this must be the principal site of habituation. Sensitization occurred at the same locus; spikes from receptors in the head excited interneuron L22. This neuron in turn activated a terminal attached to the presynaptic terminal of the monosynaptic sensory-motor synapse. To study the system in more detail requires a switch to biochemical methods.

Biochemistry. Theoreticians have concentrated on the synapses of the sensory neuron with the motor neuron. The membrane of this terminal has three kinds of gated channels, for Na^+, K^+, and Ca^{++}. In the control condition, shown in Figure 11.12, most of the K^+ channels are open, tending to inhibit the Ca^{++} channels and drive Ca^{++} from the terminal. Since both K^+ and Ca^{++} are positive ions, they repel each other. As we know from Chapter 2, Ca^{++} is necessary to initiate the binding of synaptic vesicles to the presynaptic membrane at the first step of synaptic transmission. During habituation, the increased number of impulses decreases the number of open Ca^{++} channels, reducing the binding of vesicles to the presynaptic membrane. The presynaptic potentials are the same as they were before habituation, but fewer quanta of transmitter are released with each one. The transmitter is not exhausted, but it is not released effectively (Klein & Kandel, 1980).

Sensitization affects the same Ca^{++} mechanism by a different route. The interneuron L29, probably using serotonin as the neurotransmitter, causes release of the secondary transmitter cyclic AMP (cAMP) within the terminal (see Figure 11.13). The cAMP closes the K^+ channels and allows the Ca^{++} channels to open, increasing the intracellular Ca^{++} concentration. Efficient synaptic transmission can resume.

Some of the steps in this process are still hypothetical, but as a complete theory of a mechanism of normal behavioral plasticity it represents a significant step forward. There is still a long way to go before comparable systems for vertebrates are understood. The first problem is that of coding. *Aplysia* does not have the luxury of a distributed code and therefore cannot transform information very much before storing it. Second, the "habitua-

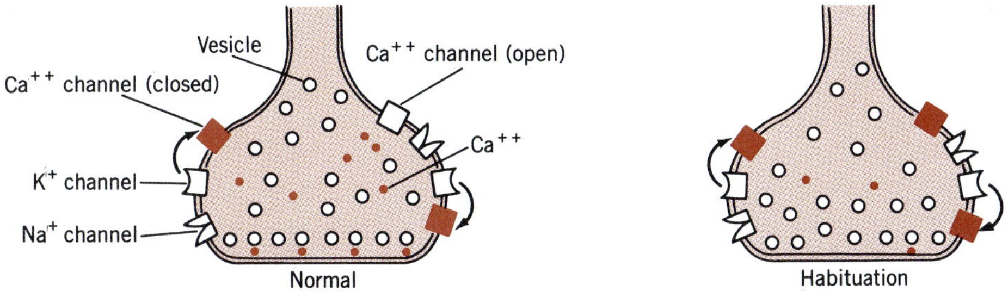

***Figure 11.12** Channels active in habituation of presynaptic terminals. Open channels are shown in white, closed channels in color. The control condition shows the state of the synapse before any behavioral manipulations. Adapted from Klein & Kandel (1980).*

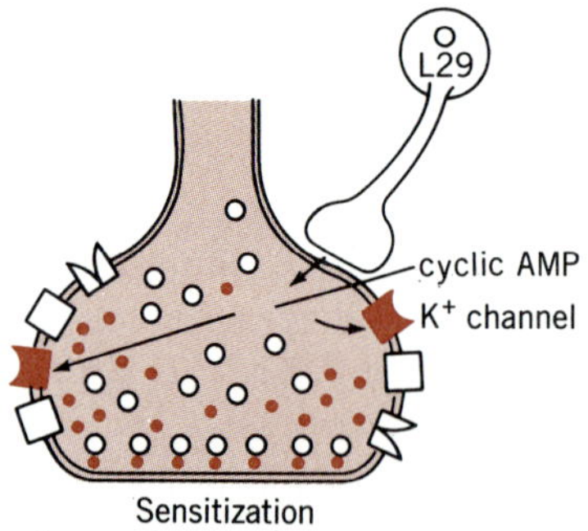

Figure 11.13 *Channels active in sensitization. The second messenger cAMP (cyclic AMP) closes the K^+ channels from inside the terminal. L29 is the name of a specific neuron. Adapted from Klein & Kandel (1980).*

tion" of this animal cannot have the behavioral complexity of the human habituation described by Sokolov (1960), where stimuli of unexpected amplitude or duration restore a habituated orienting response (see Chapter 10).

Mechanisms similar to those responsible for habituation and sensitization have recently been implicated in more complex forms of learning that involve associations between stimuli and responses. Classical conditioning in *Aplysia* includes stimulus generalization, extinction of responses that no longer are rewarded, and faster relearning following extinction (Hawkins et al., 1983). Mechanisms of associative learning have been thoroughly worked out in the marine sea snail *Hermissenda.*

CLASSICAL CONDITIONING IN THE SEA SNAIL

Plasticity in the invertebrate *Hermissenda* also involves modulation of intracellular Ca^{++} (Alkon, 1983). The animals approach light during the daylight portion of their light-dark cycle but can be trained to slow their approach if their statocyst (a primitive version of the vertebrate saccule and utricle) is stimulated in the presence of light. In nature this form of plasticity is useful in keeping the animals away from the ocean's surface during storms, when turbulence might be dangerous.

Alkon (1983) trained the snails by penning them in the ends of glass tubes and then spinning them on a turntable in the presence of light (see Figure 11.14). After conditioning, he tested the snails by freeing them to crawl toward the light (at the center of the figure); trained snails crawled more slowly than untrained ones. Control groups included one group given both light and rotation, but not paired with each other (a pseudoconditioning control). Five other groups received light and/or rotation in various combinations. Habituation and sensitization were ruled out, for practice alone did not change the snails' behavior. Only the conditioned animals slowed their crawl rates.

Anatomical analysis showed that the snail's eye contains a grand total of five photoreceptors, two defined by their anatomical connections as type A and three as type B. An eye this simple cannot do much more than detect the direction of light. The photoreceptors inhibit motor activity. Conditioning is mediated by statocyst hair cells (the snail's vestibular receptors) modifying the type B photoreceptors through an existing inhibitory channel. Since photoreceptors of invertebrates are depolarized by light (not hyperpolarized, as vertebrate photoreceptors are), their electrical resistance is reduced in light. This reduces the effect of simultaneous inhibition from the hair cell neurons, increasing the responsiveness of the photoreceptors to light and ultimately inhibiting motor activity.

The plasticity turns out to be in the photoreceptors, but the changes are found in the cell body and axon, not at the synapses. Activity increases intracellular Ca^{++}, activating calcium-dependent enzymes that attach a phosphate group to membrane proteins regulating the flow of Ca^{++} and K^+ ions (Alkon, 1984). After training, the enhancement effect persists in the photoreceptor because the phosphorylated membrane proteins persist.

Again, the learning in this system is coded in a very different way from that of vertebrates. But mechanisms at the most microscopic level may be similar, for vertebrate membrane channels and synapses are also modulated by calcium. Perhaps the usefulness of invertebrate preparations in studying axons and synapses will be extended to plasticity—at least at the microscopic levels, where the two kinds of nervous systems have a lot in common.

Neither of the invertebrate systems described here is an example of the most sophisticated kinds of learning. The marine slugs and snails are not

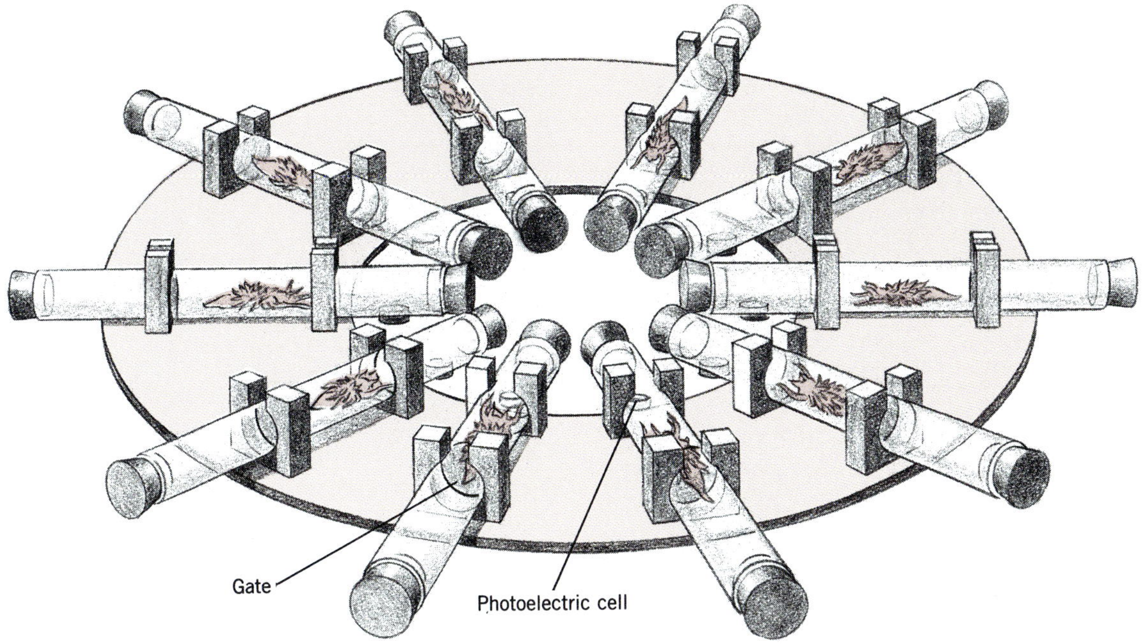

Figure 11.14 *Training apparatus to inhibit the light-approach response. Before training, researchers find each snail's phototactic response to light by measuring the time needed by the snail to cross a photocell in the tube. Training consists of rotating the turntable while a bright light is on and the snails are confined to the outer ends of the tubes. In a pseudoconditioning control experiment, other snails are subjected to light and rotation at random times. Sensitization controls consist of presenting rotation alone or light alone. In a true conditioning, only the animals receiving the paired light and rotation will show behavioral changes.*

learning something truly novel, such as the name of the latest winner of the World Cup soccer championship or the total of 12 × 12, but are only modifying existing connections. The mechanisms studied so far are procedural learning of a primitive sort, centered on single cells or synapses and coded in the same way as an existing reflex. For complex vertebrate brains, activity in a particular cell cannot be uniquely interpreted (John, 1972). We have seen that each vertebrate neuron, each synapse, must participate in coding many memories.

MEMORY MECHANISMS OF VERTEBRATES

Researchers have approached the study of vertebrate memory mechanisms in several ways; among the approaches have been biochemical, anatomical, and electrophysiological studies. This section will review engram hypotheses and their experimental support.

THE DNA/RNA HYPOTHESIS

The cracking of the genetic code in the 1940s and 1950s was an exciting time for biology. DNA was found to contain a biological mechanism for storing enormous quantities of information accurately and permanently. Inherited information is stored in long molecular chains, the double helix of DNA. The machinery of the cell can copy the information onto chains of RNA and then read the chains according to a simple four-letter code to manufacture proteins. If the method worked so well for genetic information, researchers wondered, was environmental information stored in the same way? There is generous redundancy in the genetic code, and unused DNA in every cell could be used for other purposes.

If memory were held in altered DNA or RNA, it might be possible to extract the genetic material from a trained "donor" animal and inject it in a naive "receiver" animal to transfer the learning. James McConnell (1962) and colleagues tried an even simpler procedure, using the flatworm *Planaria,* which is cannibalistic if given the chance. These flatworms have the added advantage that, unlike rats, their memory can be localized when they are cut in two. Each half regenerates a smaller version of the missing half and can be tested separately. McConnell classically conditioned the flatworms to contract upon the presentation of a light. A dish full of swimming flatworms was illuminated, and a second later an electric current was passed through the water. The flatworms' UCR was to curl up in a protective posture. Eventually the worms would curl up at the presentation of the light alone. When trained worms were chopped up and fed to naive ones, the memory was transferred (though weakly) to the new animals.

McConnell and his colleagues ran into difficulty getting this revolutionary work accepted by scientific journals. Their controls were deemed inadequate and their statistics unconvincing. Faced with a situation of this sort, a researcher has three alternatives: go back and repeat the experiments more carefully, forget the whole thing, or establish a new journal. McConnell and his colleagues chose the third alternative, and thus was born the *Worm Runner's Digest.*

The *Digest* brought instant fame, but its title contained the fatal flaw in the paradigm: worm runners (i.e., humans) digest differently than worms. The primitive *Planaria* ingest whole sections and cells of other worms, not differentiating between the ingested tissue and their own. Thus any memory mechanism, no matter what its nature, could be transferred to the recipient worms. Also, other researchers had difficulty replicating the experiments and even conditioning the worms. *Planaria* are no longer used for memory research.

Another approach to memory storage in macromolecules was pioneered by Hydén (1965). He compared the RNA of trained rats to that of naive control rats. The rats were trained to run up an inclined wire to a food platform (see Figure 11.15). RNA concentrations in the vestibular nuclei rose following the learning, and the ratios of the four molecules making up the genetic language were changed. This indicated that the RNA produced after learning was different from that manufactured during the cells' normal functioning. The RNA effects disappeared by 24 to 48 hr after the learning session, however, even though the learning persisted. Furthermore, the effects of physical activity may have changed the metabolism of the vestibular nuclei independently of the neural information storage. These results are important in interpreting the mechanisms of memory consolidation (reviewed in the next section of the chapter) but do not make a convincing case for memory coding directly in RNA.

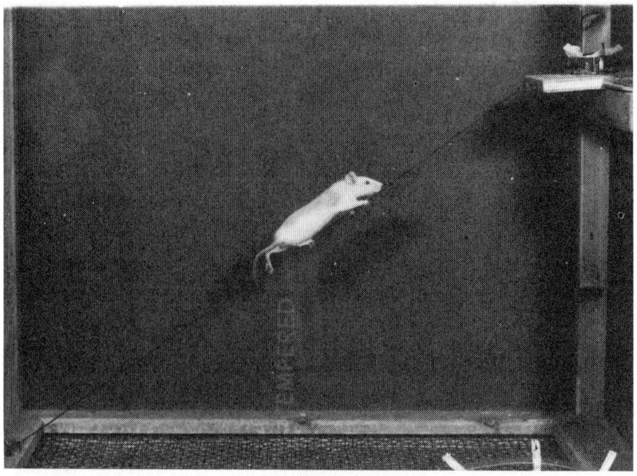

Figure 11.15 *Experimental apparatus used by Hydén (1965) to train rats to climb a wire to reach food. Training started out with a low platform and a short wire; the platform was gradually raised as the rat learned the task.*

The history of the search for chemical memory transfer holds some lessons for the relationship between mechanism and code. Was it really plausible in the first place that each memory could be coded in a different macromolecule and that the molecular structure could somehow be related to the nature of the experience? How could such memories be modified, related to one another, and used as tools for thought? The relationship between code and mechanism had been glossed over. The work did show, however, that normal metabolic processes are active in laying down the engram. Though specific macromolecules probably do not relate to specific memories, the process of modifying the brain to store a memory involves the production of proteins.

THE CONSOLIDATION HYPOTHESIS

The ancients knew that a head injury could sometimes result in the loss of memory for events that occurred shortly before the accident, even though older memories remained intact. In time, memory would gradually recover, with the oldest memories returning first. For a few hours or days the injured person would usually find it difficult to remember new experiences for more than a few minutes. There seems to be something different about memories that have been stored for only a short time; their engrams are labile, more vulnerable to disruption than older memories. Different memories seem to be held by different mechanisms.

The theoretical development of this area came not from clinical neurology but from an unexpected source—the behavioral study of verbal learning that had been developing in Germany in the late 19th century. Students of verbal learning had noted a similar volatility of more recently learned material. In 1900, Müller and Pilzecker proposed the **perseveration-consolidation hypothesis** to account for the phenomenon. According to this idea, new experiences enter labile memory, where they perseverate (remain active) but are easily disrupted. Gradually, the information is transferred to, or consolidated into, a memory that is permanent and resistant to disruption. The American psychologist McDougall (1901) soon applied the perseveration-consolidation hypothesis to the **retrograde** (backward-acting) **amnesia** that occurs after head injuries.

Mechanisms of Consolidation

In its modern form, the perseveration-consolidation hypothesis usually involves some form of reverberating circuit that holds the short-term memory for an experience (Hebb, 1949). This actively coded memory is then gradually consolidated into a different mechanism (and probably a different code as well), involving a change in some aspect of neuronal structure. The labile short-term memory need not literally be stored in loops of circulating activity. More consistent with cortical architecture is a repeated transfer of the information from one cortical area to another, perhaps reciprocally.

Signals reverberating between one region and another are not the only possible mechanism for short-term information storage. It is likely that the hippocampus is centrally involved in the transfer of short-term memory to long-term storage. Hippocampal synapses show reversible changes that last for many hours after electrical stimulation at rates that might be expected from natural synaptic sources (Bliss & Lømo, 1973). In the dentate gyrus of the hippocampal formation, trains of stimuli a few seconds long at rates of up to 100 per second result in postsynaptic responses up to 1.5 times the control magnitude. The enhancement (shown in Figure 11.16) is called **long-term potentiation (LTP).** Potentiation by electrical stimulation also increases the rate of learning in a subsequent conditioning task (Berger, 1984).

The mechanism of this potentiation is not certain, but changes have been seen in the spines on dendrites in the dentate gyrus after potentiation. These **dendritic spines** have synaptic contacts at their tips and often form most of the synaptic input to a neuron. The necks of the spines appear to be enlarged after potentiation (Fifkova & van Harreveld, 1977), resulting in an increase of the effect of a synapse on graded potentials within the neuron. The enlarged neck offers less electrical resistance than the normal one.

The consolidation hypothesis was difficult to follow up in behavioral experiments, for retrograde amnesia could occur without any localized brain injury. Furthermore, one couldn't move the phenomenon to the laboratory by systematically hitting people on the head with baseball bats.

Discovery of a New Technique. Again help came from an unexpected quarter, this time from psychiatrists who had begun using **electroconvulsive shock (ECS)** to treat some forms of depression. The technique was introduced by the Italian psychiatrist Cerletti (Cerletti & Bini, 1938), who noted that pigs in the local slaughterhouse were rendered more manageable by a shock across the temples. He tried this treatment on a schizo-

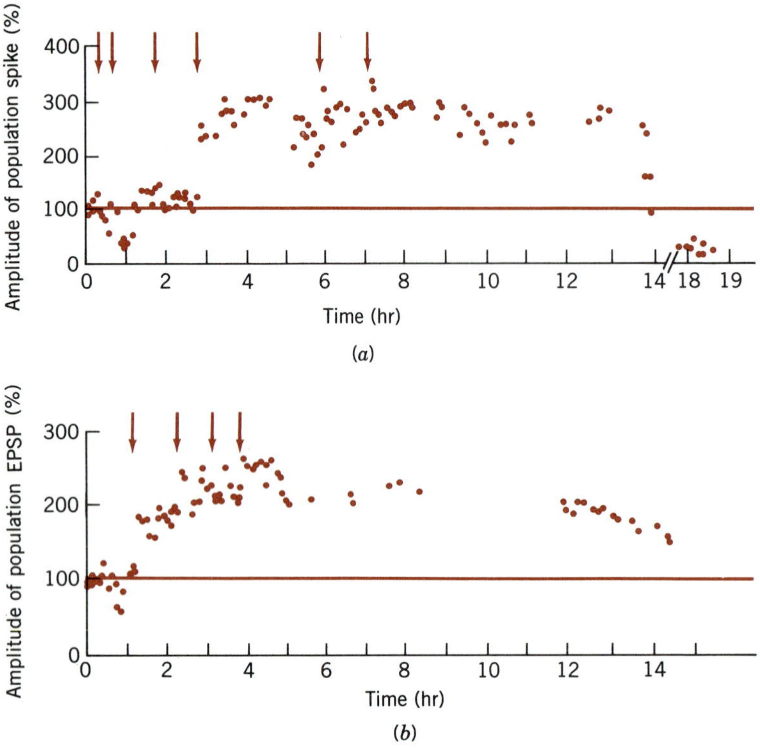

***Figure 11.16** Potentiation of synapses in the dentate gyrus of the hippocampal formation following electrical stimulation of entorhinal input. Each arrow shows the time of a 10-sec interval of stimulation at 15 pulses/sec for 10 sec. Double arrows show 3 sec of stimulation at 100 pulses/sec. The population is the summated responses of many neurons acting together.* (a) *Amplitude of population spike.* (b) *Amplitude of EPSP in another experiment. Adapted from Cotman & McGaugh (1980).*

phrenic patient who hadn't spoken a coherent sentence in years. The first shock was too weak to produce unconsciousness; but when Cerletti announced that he would try again, the patient exclaimed, "Not another one—it's deadly!" Encouraged by this success, the psychiatrist immediately increased the current and obtained a full-blown **grand mal epileptic seizure**—a seizure involving loss of consciousness and convulsions of the whole body. (Epilepsy is discussed in detail in Chapter 16.) When the patient had fully regained consciousness, he was asked what had happened to him; he calmly replied, "I don't know. Maybe I was asleep."

This case was enough to make ECS an enormously popular therapeutic technique. It soon became clear, however, that the procedure produced more than a simple retrograde amnesia and relief from depression. Repeated ECS treatments also led to an impairment in the ability to encode new memories and to other generalized memory encoding deficits (which we will examine later in the chapter). At this point World War II intervened, and laboratory work on ECS was not begun until after the war (Duncan, 1949; Gerard, 1949).

Experimental Paradigms for Consolidation Research

The amnesic effects of ECS in humans led directly to the application of ECS to the study of memory mechanisms in animals. The general paradigm for such studies is to teach animals a specific task, then apply ECS at varying times after the learning to determine how long memory remains labile. The first step in bringing ECS into the laboratory was to find a task that could allow the time of learning to be precisely determined. Psychologists had known for generations, however, that learning in the various conditioning paradigms was gradual and required many trials. Fortunately, the people beginning ECS research didn't know this, and they rapidly invented paradigms that enabled laboratory rats to learn in a single trial. One such paradigm is **active avoidance**—a conditioning paradigm in which an animal must perform a behavior to avoid an aversive stimulus. In one active avoidance procedure the floor of a rat's cage is suddenly electrified. To avoid foot shock, the rat must run to a safe compartment. The moment of escape is the moment that the required information becomes available to the animal. Rats generally learn in one trial; on the next trial they quickly run to the safe compartment.

Unfortunately, the ability to run is reduced by drug treatments in some experiments. An animal may fail to move just because it feels sick, and in the active avoidance paradigm this would be mistakenly interpreted as amnesia. A methodologically safer technique for such situations is **passive avoidance**—avoidance of a shock by not performing a behavior. In one passive avoidance procedure a rat or mouse is placed on a platform in the center of a cage with an electrified grid floor. The first thing any self-respecting rat will do in this situation is head for the nearest corner. But upon stepping down from the platform, the rat receives a shock, jumps back to the platform, and remains there. Again the moment of learning is determined, but this time an experimental amnesia-inducing drug will be interpreted as failing to produce amnesia if the rat is too sick to step down. The danger of false positive results is reduced.

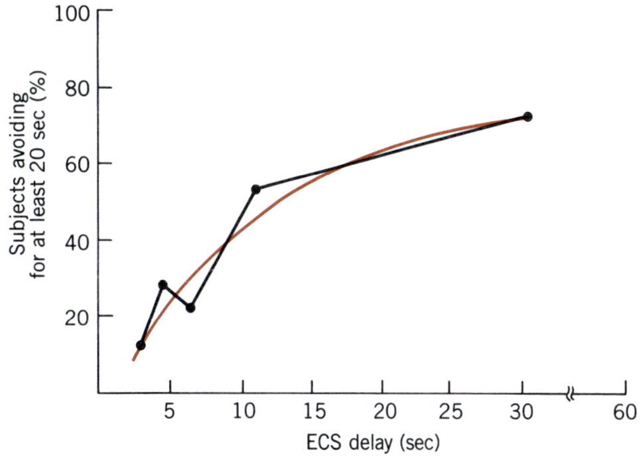

Figure 11.17 Consolidation curve for a passive avoidance task. The study required many animals because each one yielded only 1 bit of information: whether the 20 sec of avoidance was achieved. Adapted from Chorover & Schiller (1965).

ECS Tests of Consolidation

Armed with these techniques, several laboratories began investigating the effects of ECS on learning. First, researchers trained a group of rats on an active or passive avoidance task. To construct a consolidation curve, some of the rats received ECS immediately after the learning experience and others received ECS after varying delays. The animals were tested 24 hr later to determine whether they had retained the learning. In Chorover and Schiller's (1965) laboratory, ECS produced amnesia when applied immediately after learning but lost its effectiveness a few seconds after the task was learned (see Figure 11.17). The way seemed clear to quantifying consolidation and, from there, to examining its mechanisms.

This promise did not last long, however, once other laboratories began ECS consolidation studies of their own. All obtained consolidation curves similar in shape to that of Figure 11.17, but the horizontal axis might be in minutes or hours instead of seconds. It appeared that consolidation was not a fixed process with stable latencies, like sensory transduction or axonal transmission. It varied greatly with the intensity of the ECS, the positioning of the electrodes, the criterion for learning, the difficulty of the task, and so on.

Questions about Consolidation. These inconsistencies made consolidation seem more complex than had been supposed, but Müller and Pilzecker's (1900) hypothesis was still intact in principle. Additional results, however, soon called the whole concept into question, for the amnesia caused by ECS turned out not to be permanent. If the animals were retested days or weeks after the original learning, the memory often returned, at least partially. If the ECS had erased memory while it was still in a labile form, the engram should have been gone forever. Apparently, though, the ECS had delayed consolidation but had not prevented it. The memory had been preserved in a form that could be recoded but not recalled at the time of the 24-hr test.

The one clear statement we can still make after these contradictory results is that memory is labile at the time of learning. Is the engram labile because it is new or only because it is currently controlling the animal's behavior? One hypothesis was that a memory is more susceptible to disruption when it is active, just as a book is more susceptible to the effects of rain when it is open. To test this hypothesis, researchers trained rats with the usual passive avoidance of foot shock paradigm, but this time they gave one group an additional and unavoidable foot shock several hours after learning and just before an ECS treatment (Lewis, Misanin & Miller, 1968). The memory should have been consolidated by that time, rendering the "reminder" foot shock ineffective. The reminder foot shock, however, gave the subsequent ECS the power to create amnesia for the task; the memory had been made labile again.

These paradoxical and surprising results might be seen as casting doubt on the whole consolidation hypothesis or as reflecting the inadequacy of ECS as a probe of the transition from short-term labile storage to long-term stable memory. Other brain insults (causes of stress), such as anesthesia, cooling, and, of course, mechanical trauma, have similar effects to ECS, but none of them tell us much about the nature of the engram that we did not already know from clinical observations of brain injury. They are not specific enough to provide the "magic bullet" needed to probe consolidation. Perhaps probes that are more related to the consolidation processes themselves can be found.

Protein Synthesis

Since long-term memory is stable and difficult to disrupt, we can safely assume that it involves structural changes in the brain. These changes must involve RNA synthesis and subsequent protein synthesis at some stage, whether in the production of enzyme proteins that direct cell building or in the formation of new membrane channels or other structural proteins. This reasoning is distinct from that leading to the hypothesis of memory-specific macromolecules and the chemical transfer of memory, for there need not be a correspondence between particular chemical structures and particular experiences. Memories can be coded in microanatomical changes; they need not be coded in the chemistry of the proteins themselves. The important thing is where the proteins are, not what they are.

Amnesia in Mice. Even while the ECS laboratories were running into ambiguities and inconsistences, other laboratories were beginning to study the role of protein synthesis in memory. The inhibition of protein synthesis first became possible with the introduction of new antibiotics in the early 1960s. The first of these antibiotics, **puromycin,** blocked synthesis by stopping the synthesis of proteins at the ribosomes (see Figure 11.18). The ribosomes read messenger RNA chains on one side and turn out the amino acid chains that are proteins on the other. The amino acids are carried to a ribosome by **transfer RNA**—a short piece of RNA that hooks on to a specific amino acid drifting about in the cytoplasm. The structure of puromycin is similar to that of a combination of transfer RNA and the amino acid phenylalanine, so the ribosome incorporates puromycin instead of phenylalanine into the growing protein. At this point, synthesis stops, and the protein is never completed.

It seemed for a while that puromycin could interfere with consolidation in an experimentally useful way and that it remained only to work out the anatomical locations and the timing of the process (Flexner, Flexner & Stellar, 1963). But again complications arose, for puromycin was not as clean as would be desired. Effective doses proved to be toxic; mice fell sick following the injections, and many of them died during or shortly after the experiments. It may be that partially formed puromycin-tailed proteins are toxic to cells. Puromycin also causes abnormal spiking discharges in the hippocampus, an effect that could well cause amnesia independent of the drug's effects on protein synthesis (Cohen, Ervin & Barondes, 1966). The anticonvulsant drug Dilantin (diphenylhydantoin) prevented the discharges and also prevented amnesia. It looked as though the "magic bullet" was yet to be found.

Experimenters then turned to other protein synthesis inhibitors, including the drugs **cycloheximide** and **acetoxycycloheximide** (see Figure 11.18). The first of these drugs proved to be toxic at dosages necessary to prevent about 90 per-

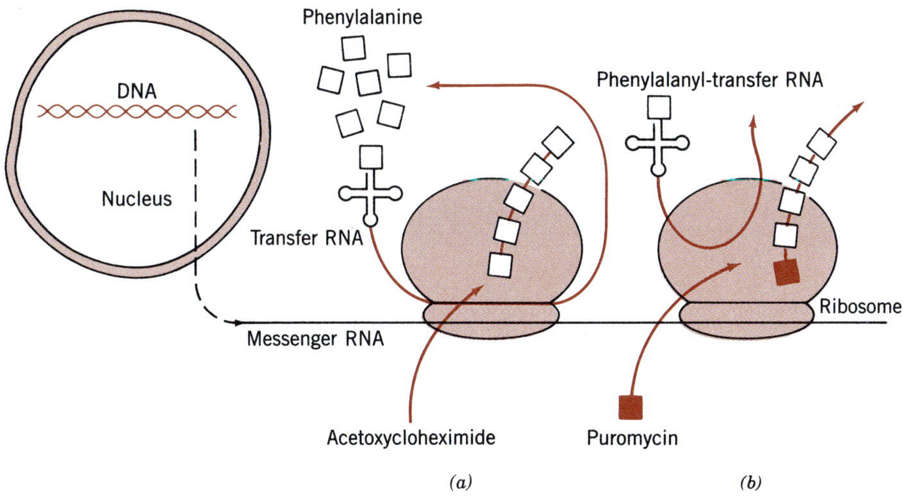

Figure 11.18 *Mechanisms of antibiotics in blocking protein synthesis.* (a) *Puromycin is taken into the protein chain by the ribosome, producing protein fragments that contain the antibiotic.* (b) *Acetoxycyclohexamide interferes with the bonding mechanism that links amino acids in the ribosome.*

cent of protein synthesis, and even high doses could overcome only weak memories. If mice were overtrained (trained further after learning to a criterion), there was no amnesia (Barondes & Cohen, 1967). The second drug fared even worse. It failed to induce amnesia even though it was more effective than puromycin at inhibiting protein synthesis. Each of these drugs inhibits protein synthesis in a different way, however, and it is possible that their differing effects on memory relate to their differing biochemical effects. At present, no hypothesis about memory formation can account for all of the results.

Amnesia in Fish. Agranoff (1967) obtained more consistent results with a more primitive vertebrate, the goldfish. For biochemical behavioral studies, these animals have several advantages over mammals: they require very little space and care, they are economical, and they won't jump out of the experimenter's hands and scurry to the nearest inaccessible corner. Furthermore, the fish can easily be trained in the active avoidance task of swimming over a barrier to avoid a shock (see Figure 11.19). The task takes advantage of goldfish ecology. First, the fish avoid swimming in shallow areas, so they seldom cross the barrier spontaneously. Second, the fish are phototaxic (Greek for "light-seeking"). If they are trained to avoid light, the behavior exists in spite of the phototaxis, not because of it.

Agranoff trained the fish by illuminating the occupied part of the training tank for 20 sec, then introducing an electric current in that part for the next 20 sec. The fish could escape the shock by swimming over the barrier after the shock began, or they could avoid it by swimming over during the 20-sec warning interval. The whole procedure was automated, including the photocell detection of the fish as they swam over the barrier.

Following training, the researchers injected the fish with an antibiotic, using the technique shown in Figure 11.20. The syringe pierced both the skin and the skull, penetrating a carefully calibrated distance to inject the antibiotic into the space between the meninges and the brain surface. The procedure effectively inhibited protein synthesis. After injecting the puromycin, the researchers injected radioactively tagged leucine into the body. Since leucine is an amino acid, it should label the brain with radioactivity if any proteins are being made there. But little labeling was found.

With these procedures, both puromycin and acetoxycycloheximide were effective in preventing consolidation when they were injected immediately after training (see Figure 11.21). One observation was puzzling, however. Puromycin injected 30 min after training allowed consolidation of more than half of the memory during that period, and injection immediately after training caused amnesia; yet the training session lasted 40 min. If some consolidation can be completed in 30 min,

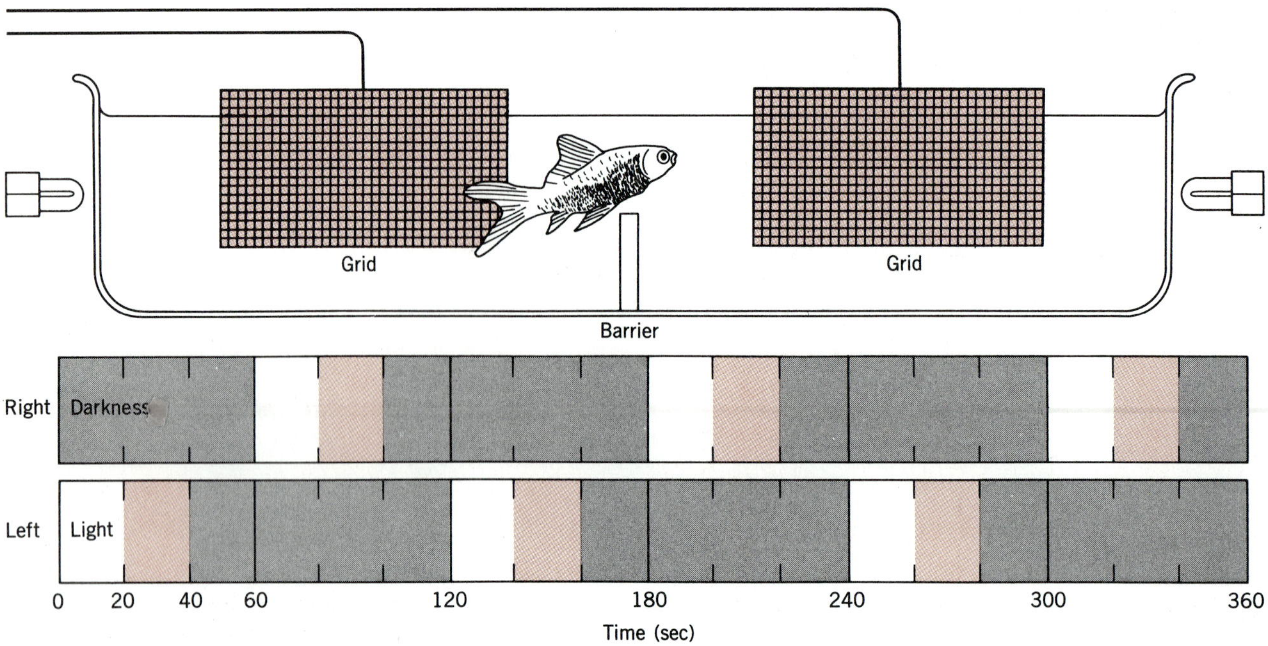

Figure 11.19 *Apparatus for automated active avoidance conditioning in the goldfish. After 20 sec with the light on, a shock is given through the grid on the lighted side of the tank. The process is then repeated on the other side of the tank, so the fish need not be repositioned between trials.*

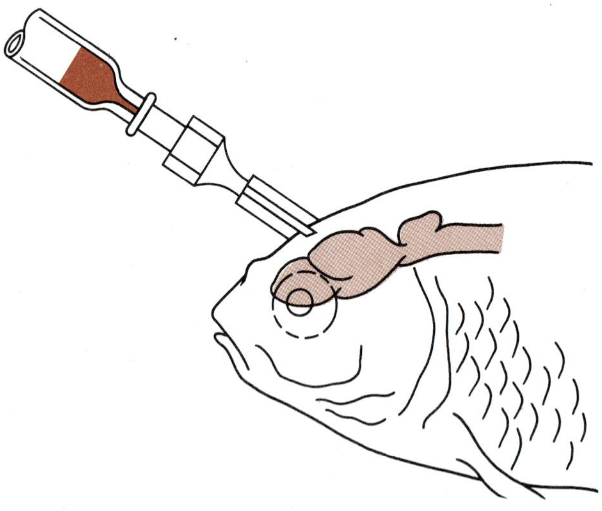

Figure 11.20 *Method of injecting antibiotic into goldfish brain without surgery. Following injection, the fish was able to swim normally.*

why didn't the first 10 min of training escape the effects of amnesia?

The key variable turned out to be the transfer of the fish to their home cages after training. Further testing showed that as long as the fish remained in the testing tank, memory remained susceptible to disruption by protein synthesis inhibitors. Thus consolidation depends not only on time but also on the behavioral context. It is more than an inflexible biochemical sequence of events; it can be influenced by cognitive variables even in a fish. Consolidation apparently does not begin until the animal is convinced that all the relevant information has been gathered. How this unconscious decision is made, and on what basis, remains a mystery.

Why did acetoxycycloheximide prove effective in the fish but not in the mouse? Perhaps additional memory mechanisms exist in the mouse, and perhaps these mechanisms continue to work even in the presence of the drug. We will not be

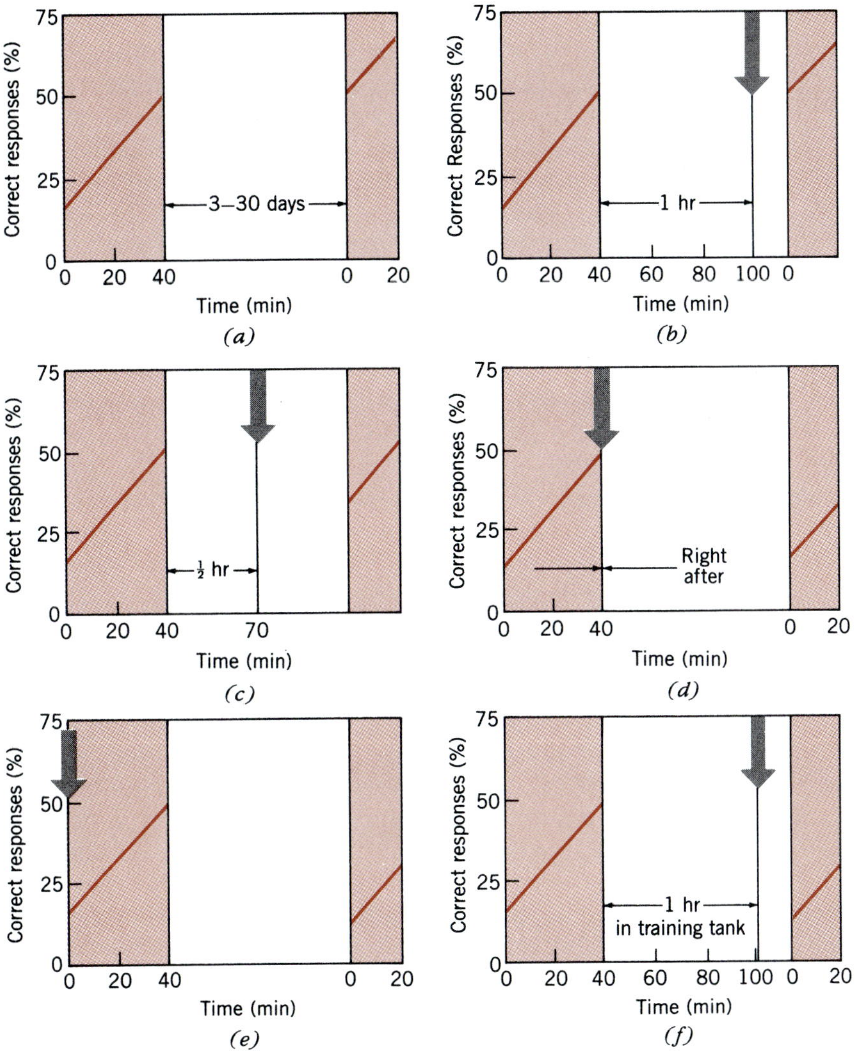

Figure 11.21 *Schematic results of consolidation following puromycin injection.* (a) *Learning in a normal fish. A pause of up to 30 days during the conditioning trials does not affect the rate of improvement or the level of performance after the pause.* (b) *Injection 1 hr after interruption of conditioning has no effect.* (c) *Injection 0.5 hr after interruption of conditioning cuts performance to half that of the control level.* (d) *Injection immediately after 20 trials erases all memory of the task. A consolidation curve can be constructed from the last three panels.* (e) *Injection immediately prior to the start of conditioning has no effect on performance, but it lowers performance to beginning levels after a 3-day pause. The injection interferes with long-term memory but not with immediate memory.* (f) *If the fish waits for 1 hr in the training tank instead of the home tank, the injection is still effective; compare with the 1-hr delay in* (b).

certain of this, however, until we understand the substrates of memory in both species.

Complications. Some of the problems with earlier inhibitors in mammals have been overcome with Bennett's introduction of another antibiotic, **anisomycin** (Flood et al., 1973). This drug is safer than the others, leaving the animals in good health. Because of its safety, anisomycin can be injected repeatedly and can be given subcutaneously (under the skin) to avoid the traumatic effects of intracerebral injection. Consolidation experiments have shown that more highly trained mice can hold a memory longer in short-term storage. The memory shown at the right of Figure 11.22 could survive up to 4 hr of protein synthesis inhibition but could still be obliterated by 6 hr of inhibition. Again it seems that consolidation is not a simple process, like some kind of mental epoxy hardening. It depends on the animal's certainty about environmental contingencies.

The area remains controversial; some reports indicate that a variety of substances can antagonize the amnesic effects of protein synthesis inhibitors (reviewed by Dunn, 1980). When these substances are injected along with the inhibitor, they allow memory to be consolidated even though protein synthesis remains inhibited. The antagonists include such diverse chemicals as stimulants (such as nicotine, caffeine, and strychnine), the cate-

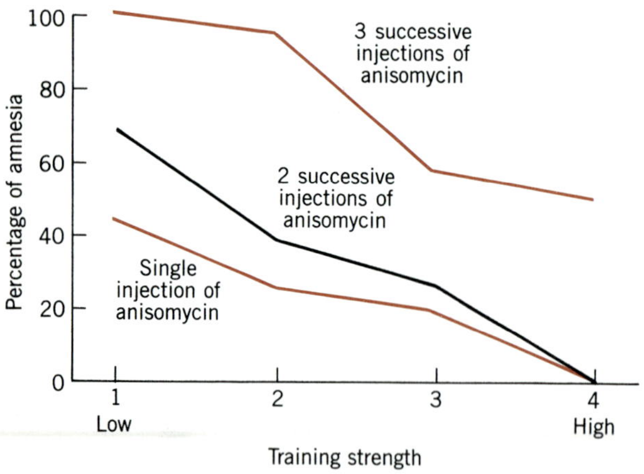

Figure 11.22 *Interaction of dose and strength of training in anisomycin-induced amnesia for a passive avoidance task. Injections were given 2 hr apart. Amnesia was greater when training was weaker and when protein synthesis was inhibited for a longer time. Adapted from Flood et al. (1973).*

cholamine agonists (such as amphetamine, L-dopa, and imipramine), several hormones, and even enkephalins.

Despite the contradictory evidence, it seems inescapable that protein synthesis is necessary at some stage in the formation of the engram. Whether that fact can be used as a lever to pry open the Pandora's box of memory remains to be seen. Other biochemical effects on memory, however, do provide clues about the engram and have practical consequences. Many drugs enhance or interfere with memory consolidation or retrieval. Since the drugs come in chemically related families, they will be examined in chemical groups.

Cholinergic Drugs

The consolidation process may involve ACh receptors, for stimulation of neuronal ACh receptors induces rapid transcription of genes in a process that requires influx of extracellular Ca^{++} ions (Greenberg, Ziff & Greene, 1986). Further, the cholinergic agonists **physostigmine** and **arecholine** (substances that enhance ACh action) improve the formation of long-term memory in adult humans (Davis et al., 1978; Sitaram, Weingartner & Gillin, 1978). Since memory might be enhanced by a placebo effect—subjects working harder because they anticipate beneficial effects of the injections—these studies compared experimental subjects with control subjects given injections of saline solution.

It is tempting to search for methods of improving the memory of normal people, creating intellectual super beings. The results in these studies indicate that the task may not be easy. Since the subjects most improved by the drugs are those who showed the poorest learning in undrugged control trials, one could say that the drugs move the poor learners toward the levels already achieved by the more successful ones. It seems that nature has set the levels of most brain chemicals at or near optimal levels, so artificially changing the levels in normal subjects nearly always degrades some aspect of performance.

It is still possible that some nonspecific arousing effect of the drugs created the memory improvement, though. If I offered you $1000 to remember a telephone number for an hour, I would find a strong effect of cash on memory. The effect would relate to motivation or arousal rather than to physiological memory mechanisms. Confirmatory evidence comes from the converse experiment. The ACh antagonist **scopolamine** interferes with long-term memory without affecting immediate memory (Drachman & Leavitt, 1974). In the past this drug was used as a pseudo-anesthetic during childbirth, so the mother could assist with the delivery but subsequently forget the whole experience. In this way, thousands of women have been deprived of what would otherwise be one of the most memorable experiences of a lifetime.

Another way to increase ACh activity is to inhibit cholinesterase, the enzyme that breaks down ACh at synapses. This process enhances the recall of old, fairly weak memories in rats, as one would expect; but, paradoxically, it interferes with the recall of new, strong memories (Deutsch, 1973). Again, memory improvement under some conditions is paid for by memory loss under other conditions. Deutsch explains this result by assuming that ACh activity is deficient at synapses coding the older memory, so inhibiting its breakdown aids recall. But newer memories, with stronger

ACh activity, suffer from a depolarization block. Memory works best not when ACh levels are as high as possible but when they are optimal for synaptic transmission, according to this hypothesis.

ACh Deficits in Brain Pathology. Senility is one of the most feared and devastating diseases of aging. One of its first symptoms is a loss of the ability to form new long-term memories, even though short-term memory and recall of older memories remain intact. In other words, there is a specific deficit in consolidation. Since the disorder affects only about 5 to 15 percent of the aged, and since some people are affected relatively early in life, senile degeneration is now interpreted as a specific syndrome: **Alzheimer's disease.** It is not an inevitable result of aging.

Coyle, Price, and DeLong (1983) investigated the biochemistry of Alzheimer's disease by comparing the brains of affected individuals at autopsy to age-matched individuals who died of unrelated causes. They assessed ACh activity in life by measuring levels of **choline acetyltransferase,** the enzyme that combines with choline to synthesize ACh. The enzyme remains stable in the brain for many hours after death. In diseased brains, the level was 60 to 90 percent lower than in undiseased brains. Changes were greatest in the hippocampus and neocortex, especially frontal and temporal regions. Most of the ACh terminals in the cortex, however, do not originate from cortical neurons. They project from a region that centers around the diencephalic nucleus near the preoptic area called the **nucleus basalis of Meynert** and that includes the **diagonal band of Broca** (many of the nuclei in this region are named after eminent 19th century neuroanatomists) and the **medial septal nucleus** (see Figure 11.23).

Many individuals with Down's syndrome suffer a deterioration of their already limited cognitive abilities, beginning at 30 to 35 years of age. They too show a reduction of choline acetyltransferase, as well as reduced neural populations in the nucleus basalis.

Tracking down the mechanism of Alzheimer's disease further, scientists examined these nuclei in deceased victims. Three-quarters of the cells in the region were missing, though adjacent regions in the globus pallidus and the hypothalamus appeared nearly normal. The brain tissue was also strewn with plaques and tangles of twisted axons.

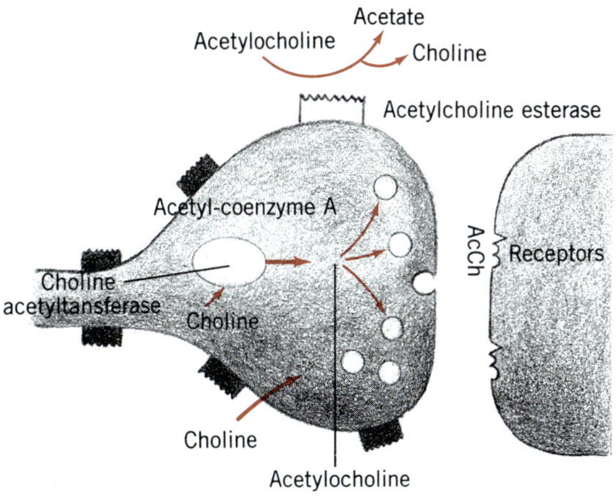

(*a*)

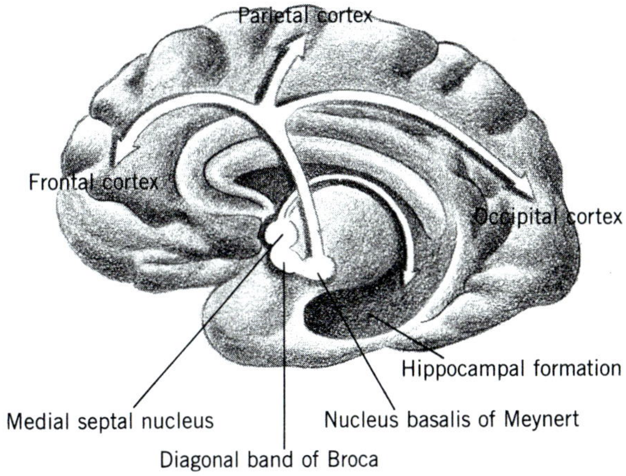

(*b*)

Figure 11.23 *Plasticity in the cholinergic system.* (a) *Schematic biochemical events in a cholinergic terminal. ACh is synthesized in the terminal from choline and acetyl-coenzyme A, catalyzed by the enzyme choline acetyltransferase. The postsynaptic action of ACh is terminated by acetylcholinesterase, which breaks down the ACh before its constituents are reabsorbed into the terminal.* (b) *Cholinergic pathways in cortex.*

The brain does not passively let these changes

happen. There is recent evidence that it fights back, sprouting axon fibers in the molecular layer of the hippocampus (Geddes et al., 1985). This is evidence of anatomical plasticity even in the brains of older people.

Now that the anatomy and biochemistry of Alzheimer's disease are beginning to be understood, attempts have been made to aid patients with drugs that potentiate cholinergic neurotransmission, in the same way that L-dopa helps Parkinson's patients. The results to date have been disappointing. A possible explanation for the difference in the effectiveness of treatment of the two diseases may lie in the nature of the damaged transmitter systems themselves. Cholinergic fibers are topographically distributed and are very active, with firing rates specifically related to behavior. Dopaminergic neurons, in contrast, fire at low rates and show no correlations with specific aspects of movement or behavior. The tonic modulatory system of dopamine seems more amenable to pharmacological treatment than the more active and specific cholinergic system. Nevertheless, advances in the understanding of Alzheimer's disease give hope for the future.

Catecholamines

Dopamine and its metabolic products epinephrine and norepinephrine—the catecholamines—typically have slow synaptic effects that modulate postsynaptic actions. Thus they are good candidates for modulating the synaptic activity involved in plasticity. The strongest test of this hypothesis is to inject catecholamines after training, so the drugs can influence only memory formation, not the training itself. Indeed, memory formation in mice is enhanced by injections of catecholamines immediately after learning trials (Haycock, van Buskirk & McGaugh, 1977) (see Figure 11.24). The injections are made either directly into the cerebral ventricles or subcutaneously.

If artificially added catecholamines enhance memory, then drugs that enhance natural catecholamine synthesis should have the same effect. Confirming this conjecture, McGaugh (1973) injected amphetamine into rats after learning trials and found memory enhancement. How can one show that the enhancement is due to amphetamine's effect on catecholamine synthesis, not to its other general effects? One method is to inject amphetamine along with another drug that interferes with catecholamine synthesis—a drug that blocks amphetamine's catecholaminergic effects without changing its direct effects. Such a drug is **alpha-methyl-p-tyrosine (alpha-MPT),** a blocker of dopamine synthesis. Giving both amphetamine and alpha-MPT together blocks the memory enhancement effect. The enhancement can be restored by giving L-dopa, the precursor of dopamine (Fulginiti, Molina & Orsingher, 1976).

These examples show how behavioral neurochemists have become skilled at titrating memory

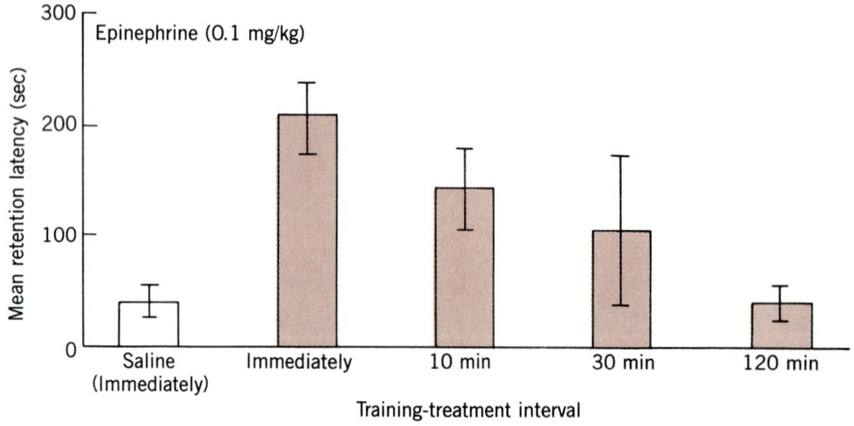

Figure 11.24 Effect of small epinephrine injections on memory in a passive avoidance task. Injection immediately or 10 min after training gives a significant increase in latency to stepping from a platform to an electrified grid. The latency increase reveals enhanced memory for the shock received during training.

capacity up and down with various combinations of pharmacological interventions. Another method for adjusting memory strength to a point where it is maximally sensitive to enhancement or inhibition by other drugs is to give anisomycin 15 min before training, to prevent protein synthesis during and shortly after training. Other drugs are then administered after a delay (Bennett, Rosenzweig & Flood, 1979). Under these conditions, amphetamine given after training causes a release of norepinephrine that restores memory without restoring protein synthesis (see Figure 11.25). Only after a time delay does amphetamine lose its beneficial effect on memory. Since amphetamine cannot restore protein synthesis, one can infer that one of the crucial functions of protein synthesis under normal conditions is to enable neurons involved in memory to manufacture enzymes involved in synthesizing norepinephrine.

Norepinephrine may provide a biochemical link between the learning of adults and the more extensive behavioral and neurological plasticity of young animals during the critical periods for sensory influences on development. As we saw in Chapter 6, norepinephrine is essential for the flexibility of the kitten cortex during the critical period, and the cortex regains its developmental flexibility if norepinephrine is infused in adult cats for extended periods.

More generally, the catecholamines can link the biochemistry of memory with motivational processes that enhance learning. Like catecholamine injections, electrical stimulation of the reticular formation can increase alertness and enhance learning. Furthermore, steroid hormones associated with motivation and stress, such as ACTH, enhance memory retention when administered after training (Flood et al., 1977).

Endorphins

The endorphins play a central role in motivational systems, and they influence memory. Morphine impairs memory in rats even if it is given after training, and the opiate antagonist naloxone enhances memory (Jensen et al., 1978). The effect is not a general influence on arousal, but is anatomically specific—naloxone also facilitates memory when it is injected directly into the amygdala in very small quantities (Gallagher & Kapp, 1978).

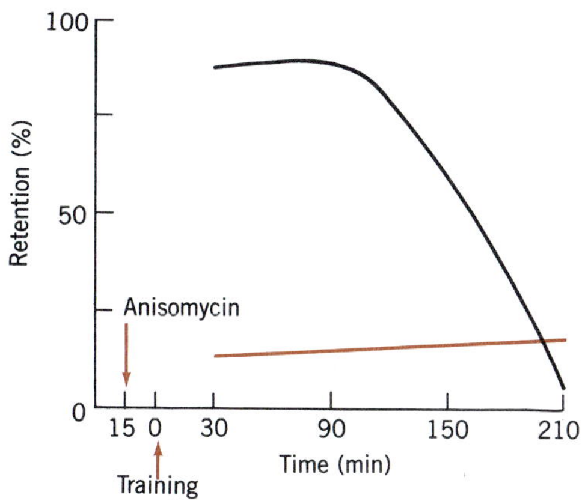

Figure 11.25 *Release from anisomycin-induced amnesia with amphetamine. The top curve shows the effects when animals receive anisomycin followed by amphetamine. The amphetamine is injected at the time given on the horizontal axis. The bottom curve shows the effects when animals receive only anisomycin.*

In conclusion, the effects of the catecholamines and endorphins indicate a close connection between the biochemistry of motivation and the biochemistry of memory. Each relies on several distinct brain biochemical systems. Apparently, the connection between motivation and memory is an old and inseparable one in evolution. Taken together, the studies implicate several brain areas in memory consolidation. In order of importance these areas are the hippocampus and amygdala, other limbic areas, parts of the medial thalamus, and the neocortex. A closer look at these areas involves a combination of behavioral testing and lesions in both humans and other animals.

ANATOMY OF STORAGE AND RETRIEVAL

If the distribution of engrams thwarted attempts to link memories with specific macromolecules, perhaps the same distribution could be used to advantage in looking for changes in widespread brain regions following learning. To be successful, such an approach must expose the experimental animals to extensive learning, for the contribution of any single memory (if there is such a thing in isolation) must be very small.

Effects of Enriched Experience

In a long series of studies, an interdisciplinary group at the University of California at Berkeley has investigated the effects of rearing animals in an enriched environment. After weaning, littermate rats were assigned to either normal colony cages (one to a cage—the impoverished condition); to the same cages with 3 animals per cage (the standard condition); or to cages with 10 to 12 animals and a variety of "toys" that were changed daily (the enriched condition). The rats were raised in these conditions for 80 days. Initially, the experimenters measured cortical area and concentrations of brain acetylcholinesterase (AChE), the enzyme that breaks down ACh, because at that time it was difficult to assay ACh directly. We now know that AChE is also present in some neurons that do not use ACh (Coyle, Price & DeLong, 1983). Still, the enhancement of cholinergic systems should increase brain AChE.

AChE showed greater increases in the enriched condition than in the impoverished one (Rosenzweig, Krech & Bennett, 1961), but initially there seemed to be no effects on anatomy. Then an undergraduate assistant, assigned the tedious job of counting square millimeters on rat brains, had the labor-saving idea of weighing the cortex instead of measuring its area.

The cortex of enriched rats turned out to be heavier and thicker than that of impoverished rats, even though the areas were the same (Rosenzweig et al., 1962). Later it was found that 30 days was enough to obtain maximal effects on a variety of brain measures. As Figure 11.26 shows, the cortex was enlarged while the rest of the brain was not. The occipital cortex changed most (Rosenzweig & Bennett, 1978). These studies cannot point to specific mechanisms because the definition of what is learned remains vague. And they do not speak to memory codes at all. They do show that experience can affect both quantitative neuronanatomy and brain biochemistry.

Could these results be due to influences other than learning? Rosenzweig and his colleagues ran control procedures to exclude the effects of handling, locomotor activity, and body weight. Active involvement rather than sensory stimulation was necessary, for rats that only observed the enriched environment were not different from the control group. To assess the possibility that enrichment might have affected maturation, the experiments were repeated with rats raised in the standard colony and exposed to either the enriched or the impoverished condition as adults. Brain effects were smaller but in the same pattern as the original groups.

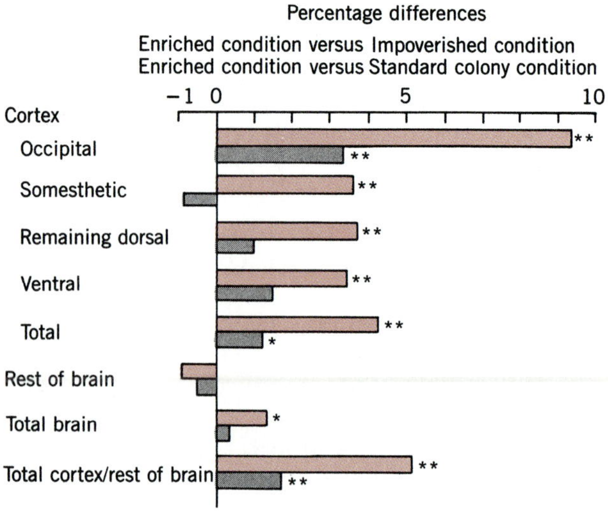

*$p < 0.01$. ** $p < 0.001$

Figure 11.26 *Effect of enriched experience on weights of various brain areas. Eighty-seven rats were assigned to each condition at 25 days of age and were differentially exposed for 30 days. Differences are consistent but rather small, less than 10 percent even for the largest changes. Adapted from Rosenzweig & Bennett (1978).*

Unfortunately it is impossible to separate completely the effects of growth from the effects of plasticity in these experiments, for rats continue to grow throughout life, though at a slower rate after sexual maturity. To separate growth from plasticity, it would be useful to have a (very expensive) replication of these studies in cats or primates.

Effects of Conditioning

There is some evidence from cats that gross anatomical changes correlating with experience do occur, but only in immature animals. Four-week-old kittens were trained to flex a foreleg to avoid a mild shock (Spinelli & Jensen, 1979). The kittens also wore goggles similar to those in Figure 6.10 and saw a pattern of horizontal stripes in one eye during the shocks. A pattern of vertical stripes was presented to the other eye when the leg was retracted. The horizontal stripes became a "danger" signal. Kittens learned quickly to hold up their forelegs; they were shocked only 5 percent of the time. The kittens were trained for only 8 min per day, spending the rest of their time in a normally illuminated environment.

Effects on both visual and somatosensory areas were extensive. We know from other developmental studies that if one eye receives more visual exposure than the other, the more exposed eye comes to dominate the neurons of the visual cortex. In these cats, the opposite occurred; more cells responded to the danger signal (horizontal stripes in some cats and vertical in others) than to the safety signal, even though each cat received a cumulative total of only 10 to 29 min of exposure to the danger signal. Apparently, it is the information value of the stimulus, not simply the duration of exposure, that induces receptive field development. As we would expect from Chapter 6, most of the neurons were monocular.

In the somatosensory cortex, the homunculus (see Figure 5.6) was greatly distorted, with the representation of the shocked foreleg being three to four times its normal size (see Figure 11.27). Furthermore, 75 percent of the cells in that representation were polysensory, responding also to visual stimuli—compared to 30 percent in the corresponding cortex of the other side.

Anatomical effects included increases in the number and complexity of dendrites in the somatosensory cortex representing the enlarged foreleg projection (Spinelli, Jensen & DiPrisco, 1980), a finding similar to that of the Berkeley rat-raising group. Golgi-Cox-stained sections in Figure 11.28 show the greater density of connections.

The cat result that is most important for interpreting the Berkeley studies came from the study of an older kitten, which began training at 11 weeks of age (still not fully grown). This cat readily learned the foreleg withdrawal but showed none of the electrophysiological changes found in the younger kittens. The result brings to mind the "critical periods" during development, when environmental exposure can alter the structure of sensory systems (see Chapter 6). It also hints at something more—a difference between the sorts of plasticity possible in young brains and older brains.

A "Superplasticity" in Young Brains?

Only in growing, developing brains can sensory inputs compete for cortical machinery on the basis of the information they convey. Once growth is complete, this "superplasticity" continues only on a smaller scale, within the already established pattern.

We can see reflections of this change in the development of human abilities. If you are more than 12 years old as you read this book, for instance, you will never be able to speak a foreign language like a native unless the language is already familiar. Similarly, musicians know that no amount of study of the piano or violin can make you a virtuoso if you do not already play. Most world-class players begin playing before the age of seven. After 12, it is too late; these skills are lost to your brain. In looking for mechanisms of memory, we must consider the differences between the changes that can take place in any member of a species and those available only to the young.

These speculative ideas may help expand the meaning of the adult's loss of organizational plasticity. First, we can ask how the distorted somatosensory and motor homunculi develop in normal brains and how the fovea comes to dominate the striate cortex. Certainly, some of the distortion is genetic, for it is seen in newborn animals; but the distorted patterns might be reinforced by the greater density of information arriving from lips and fingertips and from the densely packed foveal cones. Thus a positive feedback would develop in the normal young animal, generating information-processing structures where they were needed most. The newborn cortex is like wet clay, roughly formed but still workable, before being fired hard by maturation and experience.

Second, we can ask why the change in modes of plasticity must occur. Surely we would be more powerful creatures cognitively if we retained the childlike superplasticity throughout life. Certainly, I would like to speak Italian like a native and to

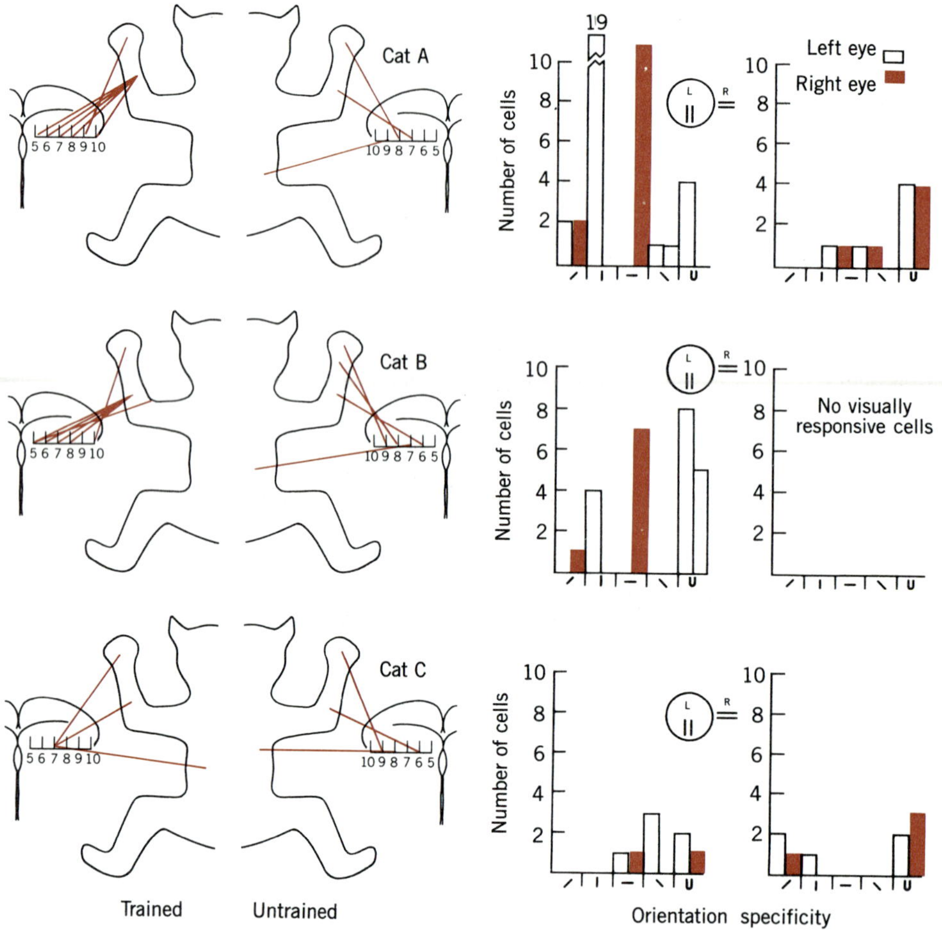

Figure 11.27 *Expanded foreleg projection onto somatosensory cortex. Each row gives data for one cat. The lines from the cortical maps to the body outline show cortical projections from corresponding parts of the body; the sheaf of lines from the trained side of cats A and B (but not C) shows an enlarged foreleg representation at the site of the conditioning stimulus. The histograms indicate the orientation specificity of single neurons in the somatosensory cortex. The angles of oriented lines used are shown on the horizontal axis. The left histograms describe the trained side and the right histograms the untrained side; 75 percent of the neurons on the trained side are polysensory, and 30 percent on the untrained side are polysensory.*

master the piano. But children may pay a price for their ultraplasticity in the necessity to use simpler schemata for viewing and interpreting the world. Perhaps it is not a coincidence that a child reaches the highest stage of cognitive development, the stage of formal operations (Piaget, 1973), at about the time that flexibility for language learning, musical skills, and even the ability to recover from brain lesions begins to wane. Physiological evidence for these changes comes from an EEG measure that shows growth spurts in the left hemisphere but not the right at 2 to 4 years of age, when the child reaches the stage of concrete operations and can perform elementary reasoning tasks. Another, smaller growth spurt occurs at 12 to 15 years of age, again only in the left hemisphere, at the beginning of the stage of formal operations (Thatcher, Walker & Giudice, 1987).

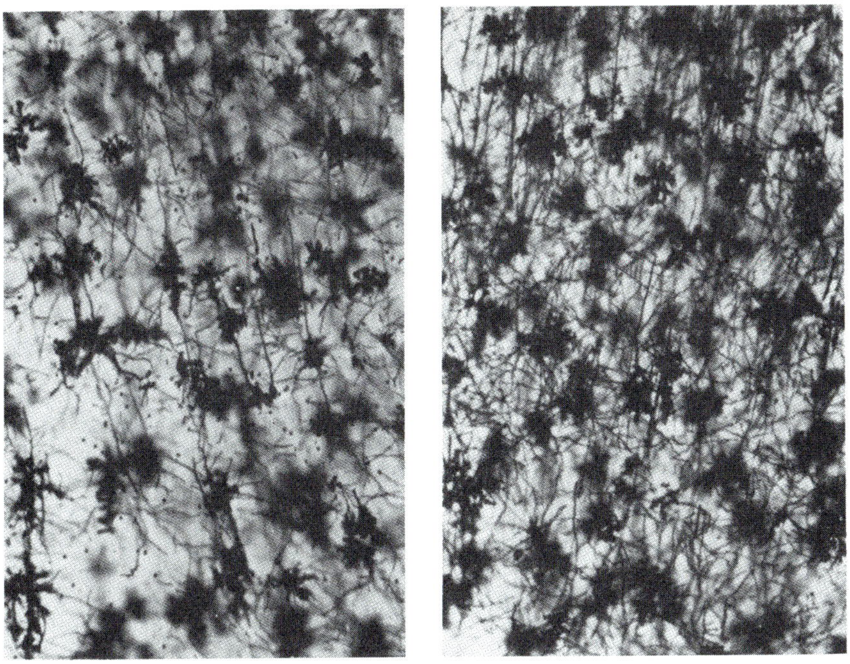

(a) *(b)*

Figure 11.28 *Golgi-Cox stains.* (a) *Control (untrained) somatosensory cortex.* (b) *Trained somatosensory cortex.*

HUMAN AMNESIA

Human lesions resulting in anterograde amnesia have been one of the richest sources of information about systems involved in laying down new engrams. **Anterograde amnesia** is the inability to form new memories, even though memories consolidated before the lesion causing the amnesia may remain intact. Even before we do any neuropsychological analysis of these patients, we know that their deficits are not due to the removal of a retrieval mechanism, for they are able to recall older memories.

Anterograde amnesia comes in two varieties, with different anatomical bases and somewhat different behavioral symptoms (Squire, 1982). One is based on damage to the hippocampus and amygdala (bitemporal amnesia) the other on pathology of the diencephalon (diencephalic amnesia).

Bitemporal Amnesia

Most of what we know about human **bitemporal amnesia**—amnesia resulting from damage to the hippocampus and amygdala under the temporal lobe—comes from a handful of patients who have anterograde amnesia caused by neurosurgical operations. The syndrome was discovered following an operation performed in an attempt to relieve a severe case of epilepsy that did not respond to drug treatment. A young man began having epileptic seizures at the age of 16. The epilepsy worsened, until at age 27 he was having several *grand mal* seizures a day and could not work. After the epileptic focus was localized to the medial temporal region, neurosurgeon Herbert Scoville performed a bilateral removal of the uncus, hippocampal gyrus, the anterior two-thirds of the hippocampus, and amygdala. The operation had been performed previously on two psychotic patients, without severe effects on memory, though the lesions had been smaller. But the results were disastrous for this patient, the now-famous H.M. Though his epilepsy was largely relieved, he could no longer form long-term memories (Scoville & Milner, 1957). There was also some retrograde amnesia for events up to 3 yr before the operation.

H.M. has been the subject of extensive neuropsychological testing by Brenda Milner and associates (Milner, 1965). He is perhaps the most thoroughly studied neurological patient in history. Though his long-term memory deficit is profound, he remains alert and cooperative and has a better than average IQ. (This says something about both the nature of the deficit and the limitations of IQ tests.) The anterograde amnesia is complete for verbal tasks and extends to some nonverbal tasks as well. For instance, H.M. could not reduce his errors in a 28-choice maze even after 215 trials. His digit span (the number of digits that can be repeated immediately without error) was within the normal range, at 6 digits, but he could not extend the span by a single digit even after 25 trials on the same 7-digit list (Drachman & Arbit, 1966). Normal subjects, in contrast, can lengthen their digit spans up to about 20 digits in 15 trials.

On some other tasks, such as tracing a figure seen through a mirror (shown in Figure 11.29), the patient learned at a normal rate even though he denied ever having seen the apparatus on successive days.

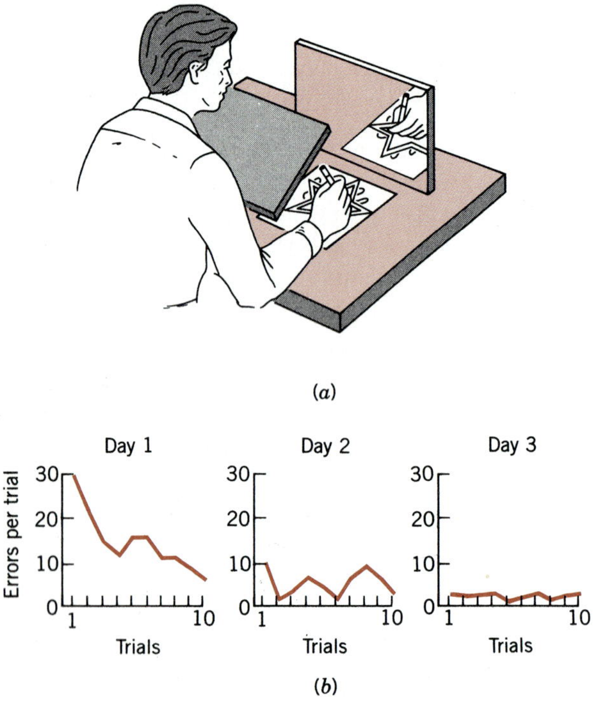

Figure 11.29 Mirror-tracing task. (a) *Performance of patient H. M. on mirror-tracing task. The hand and the traced figure are visible only through a mirror.* (b) *This test of procedural memory showed improvement both within days (short-term memory) and between days (long-term memory). Tests of declarative memory in this patient showed amnesia. Adapted from Milner (1965).*

H.M. was aware that he had a memory problem because he could not remember events of the past few decades or even the past few hours. The deficit separated him even from himself, as he eloquently pointed out: "Every day is alone in itself, whatever enjoyment I've had, and whatever sorrow I've had.... You see, at this moment everything looks clear to me, but what happened just before? That's what worries me. It's like waking from a dream. I just don't remember" (Milner, 1970, p. 37).

Several other brain pathologies have since been recognized to include bitemporal amnesia. Among them are some postencephalitic pathologies, vascular disease, anoxia (to which the hippocampus is particularly susceptible), and degenerative diseases (Horel, 1978). In such cases, it is more difficult to isolate the memory-related lesions from other brain damage and from nonspecific effects of the diseases. Damage to both hippocampus and amygdala, incidentally, makes the amnesia worse; lesions of either structure alone have less effect on memory. One patient, however, showed significant anterograde amnesia even though damage was limited to the pyramidal cells in the CA1 field of the hippocampus. This field is the first half-turn of the spiral of hippocampal cortex, and it seems to be particularly important for memory. The patient died 5 years after the onset of his amnesia. The autopsy showed that the damage was bilateral and that all of the pyramidal cells were missing from this region (Squire, 1986).

Another important source of data on bitemporal amnesia is the many cases of amnesia resulting from ECS treatments prescribed for depressive illness. Because the therapy is a scheduled event, pre- and post-tests can be given, making each patient his or her own control. The amnesia increases somewhat after each treatment in a series and cumulates across treatments (Squire, 1982). By 1 hr after treatment, amnesia is the only major remaining side effect of the ECS. Symptoms are similar to those in patient H.M., though there is a gradual partial recovery of the ability to form new memories. Damage to the hippocampus is particularly likely in ECS because of the fragile blood

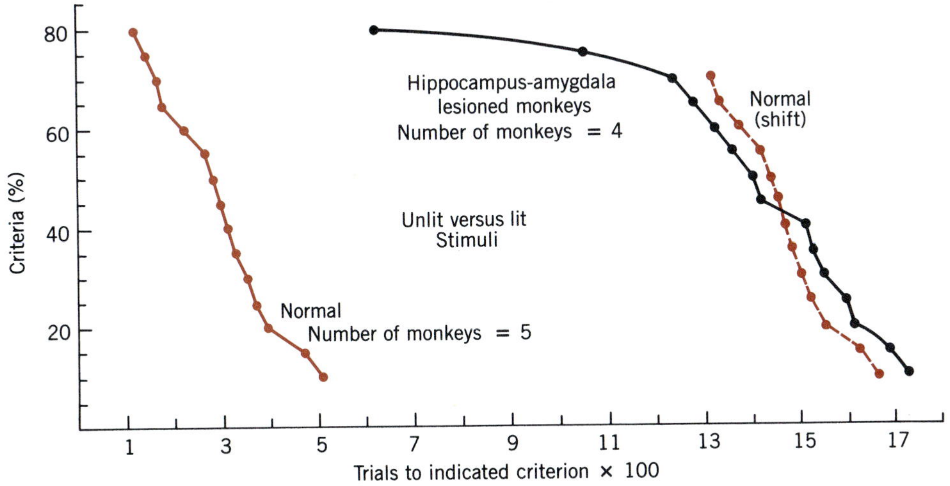

***Figure 11.30** Discrimination training in normal monkeys and in hippocampus-amygdala lesioned monkeys. The monkeys are doing an easy discrimination, pressing lit panels rather than unlit ones. The normal (shift) curve is the curve for normal animals shifted across the abscissa to be superimposed on the hippocampus-amygdala lesion learning curve. The slopes of the two curves are about the same. Adapted from Pribram, Douglas & Pribram (1969).*

supply of the area and its proneness to seizures.

Animal Models. To investigate this syndrome further, an animal model was needed so lesions could be controlled and electrical recording performed. As happens so often in memory research, however, the results of hippocampal and amygdalar lesions in animals were not as straightforward as had been anticipated. Inexplicably, monkeys seemed to have remarkably robust memory encoding systems, resisting even the effects of large lesions. For instance, monkeys with bilateral lesions of the amygdala and hippocampus were able to learn to perform visual discriminations (Pribram, Douglas & Pribram, 1969) and other tasks as well (Douglas, 1967; Isaacson, 1972). Discrimination learning was far from normal; the monkeys tended to get stuck at the random response level for a long time. But as Figure 11.30 shows, once they moved away from that level, their learning was as fast as that of the control monkeys. According to Pribram, Douglas, and Pribram (1969), the deficit was not so much in learning as in forming and maintaining hypotheses. As a result, the animals had particular difficulty with reversals, where the rewarded stimulus became unrewarded and vice versa (Kimble, 1968).

The learning curves of the lesioned monkeys were similar to those of retarded humans, suggesting an alternative interpretation—that there was an attention deficit in both cases. In seeming contrast to humans with lesions, monkeys with hippocampus-amygdala lesions had more difficulty with behavioral flexibility than with memory.

It now seems that an explanation of these differences, which have puzzled neuroscientists for nearly three decades, is at hand. Several technical and conceptual problems have contributed to the confusion: one of them involves the distinction between declarative and procedural knowledge. Looking back, the resolution of the problem seems obvious, but at the time the idea that different kinds of memory could follow different rules and be encoded by different mechanisms was a missing piece to the puzzle.

The discrepancy between animal and human results was finally resolved with a task that showed amnesia both in monkeys and in bitemporal amnesic humans. The task involves a delayed non-matching to sample. A human or monkey is briefly shown two objects; after a delay, one of the objects is paired with a novel object. The human or monkey is rewarded for picking the novel object. Monkeys with hippocampal and amygdalar lesions fail if the delay is more than 8 sec (see Figure 11.31), and patient H.M. is impaired on a similar task

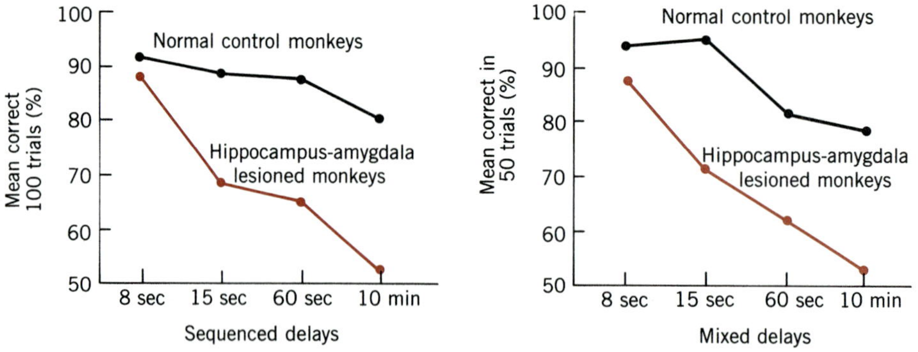

Figure 11.31 *Performance of normal control monkeys and hippocampus-amygdala lesioned monkeys on delayed nonmatching to sample. In the right graph, delays are arranged in a mixed order from trial to trial. The horizontal axis, giving the duration of the delay between the sample figure and the match figures, is not linear.*

(Zola-Morgan, Squire & Mishkin, 1982). The controversy and its resolution are examples of the close relationship between code and mechanism; studying either requires some knowledge about the other.

Diencephalic Amnesia

Knowledge of **diencephalic amnesia** comes largely from thousands of patients who have never seen a neurosurgeon but instead have inflicted major brain lesions upon themselves. The patients are severe alcoholics, victims of the **Korsakoff syndrome** (named after the Russian neurologist who described the syndrome in 1887). After years of alcoholism, brain pathology develops as a result of thiamine (vitamin B_1) deficiency; since alcoholics get most of their calories from alcohol, they don't ingest enough thiamine. Furthermore, alcohol interferes with thiamine absorption. Following an acute period, when all cognitive functions are minimal, the hospitalized Korsakoff patient recovers—but retains anterograde amnesia, general confusion, and flatness of emotion. Unlike bitemporal amnesics, Korsakoff patients frequently deny their deficit. They confabulate (make up) memories when they must recall a forgotten fact. They do gain some knowledge of their problem, though; hospitalized Korsakoff patients are willing to play poker with one another, but they refuse to play with members of the hospital staff.

non-Korsakoff patients?

A diencephalic amnesic in better condition than Korsakoff patients was the patient N.A., whom we met at the beginning of the chapter. He is cooperative and has a postlesion IQ of 124. This is the patient who sustained a fencing injury; CAT scans (see Figure 11.32) showed damage in the left dorsomedial thalamic nucleus (Squire & Moore, 1979). As we would expect from a lesion on the left side of the brain, N.A.'s language functions were particularly affected.

Though N.A.'s injury would implicate the dorsomedial thalamus in the diencephalic syndrome, studies of Korsakoff patients are less conclusive. Unfortunately, few of these patients have had both the thorough memory tests and the extensive brain autopsy necessary to decide the issue. Some patients seem to have damage mainly to the mammillary bodies, some to the dorsomedial thalamus, and many to both. Most of the brains have been examined only with gross dissection, and it is possible that the deficits are based on microanatomy or biochemistry. Another possibility is that the important damage in the mammillary body area is a sectioning of tracts connecting the temporal and frontal cortex in that region.

Distinguishing between Bitemporal and Diencephalic

The defining distinction between bitemporal and diencephalic amnesia is the rate of forgetting

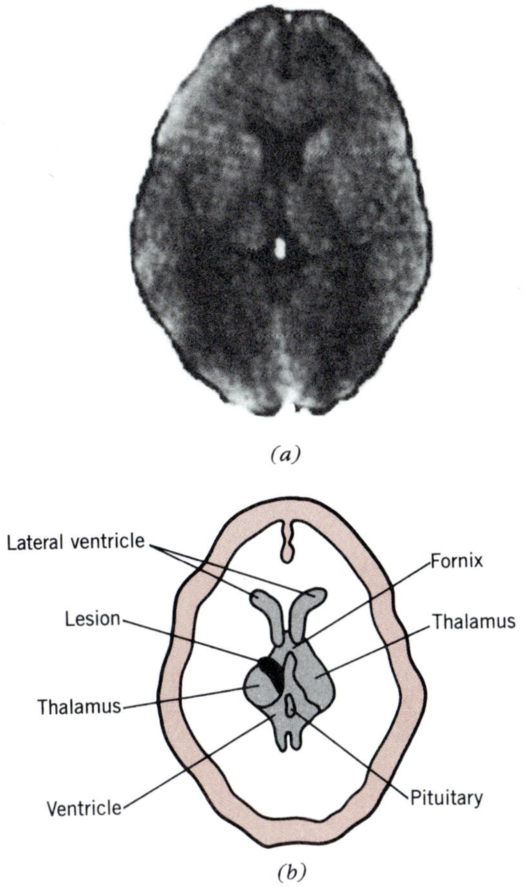

Figure 11.32 *Computerized axial tomogram (CAT scan) of the brain-damaged patient N.A.* (a) *The x-ray technique shows the anatomy of a single horizontal slice through the brain (the technique is described in Chapter 16). Recent evidence based on magnetic resonance imaging indicates that N.A.'s left diencephalic lesion is larger than was suggested by CT scan (Squire, Amaral, Zola-Morgan, Kritchevsky, and Press, 1987).* (b) *The diagram shows the site of the lesion. Adapted from Squire & Moore (1979).*

of new material (Lhermitte & Signoret, 1972; Huppert & Piercy, 1978, 1979). The difficulty in designing appropriate tests was to find tasks that all the amnesics could perform at some level and to equate the initial levels of learning before allowing forgetting to take place. For learning, patients viewed 120 pictures on slides. To equate learning at 10 min after exposure, Korsakoff patients viewed the slides 4 to 8 times longer than normal controls. H.M. viewed them 15 times longer.

Recognition was tested 1 and 7 days after learning by researchers who randomly mixed 40 of the old slides with 40 new ones and then asked patients whether each slide was old or new. Normal humans do phenomenally well at this task. After several weeks, they recognize nearly all the pictures, even if the exposure is increased to 1000 or more slides. Korsakoff patients showed a normal rate of forgetting for the material they were able to learn, whereas H.M. had an abnormally rapid forgetting rate despite his longer initial exposure to the materials.

There was a nagging possibility that the severer the amnesia, the faster the forgetting rate. A second set of experiments ruled out that possibility with the lucky coincidence that the diencephalic patient N.A., some diencephalic San Diego Korsakoff patients, and bitemporal ECS patients all achieved a similar retention level 10 min after learning (with the same exposure times). The next day, N.A. and the Korsakoff patients showed normal forgetting rates, but the ECS patients forgot at an abnormally rapid rate. Thus there seem to be two different kinds of amnesia, one characterized by rapid forgetting and the other by normal forgetting but difficulty in encoding memories (Squire, 1986).

CONDITIONING IN THE HIPPOCAMPUS

Once the hippocampus was identified as a key site for memory processing, researchers could record from single hippocampal neurons during learning to look more closely at the mechanisms of establishing memory. Richard F. Thompson and colleagues have done this by examining classical conditioning in the rabbit (Berger & Thompson, 1978; Patterson, Berger & Thompson, 1979). First, the animals heard a brief CS tone, about 250 msec before receiving the US—a puff of air in the eye. The UR was an eyeblink, and the CR was an eyeblink after the onset of the tone but before the puff. The eyeblink was chosen because all the variables could be quantitatively controlled or measured and the animals could perform the behavior while being restrained for microelectrode recording. Furthermore, rabbits will sit still without anesthesia during the conditioning.

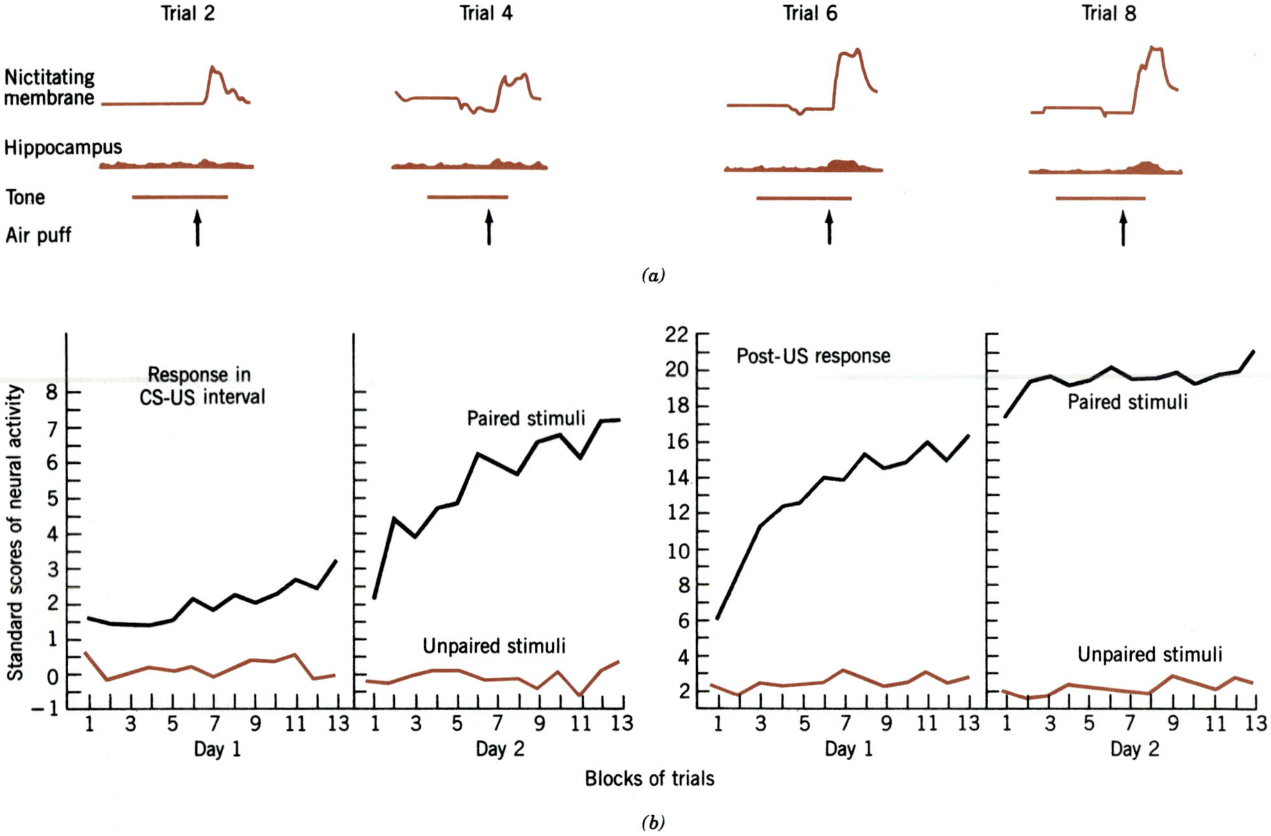

***Figure 11.33** Conditioning in the hippocampus.* (a) *Responses in the hippocampus and the nictitating membrane during early conditioning trials. The nictitating membrane response comes after the air puff, and the hippocampal single-unit response gradually builds.* (b) *Further enhancement of the hippocampal response during 2 days of training. The lower curve (unpaired stimuli) is a pseudoconditioning control. Adapted from Berger & Thompson (1978).*

In order to validate this paradigm as a measure of hippocampal function, the researchers ablated the hippocampus bilaterally in the rabbits; conditioning was no longer possible (Weisz, Solomon & Thompson, 1980). A slight change in the paradigm, however, makes the conditioning invulnerable to lesions of either the hippocampus or its principal input in the rabbit, the medial septum (Lockhart & Moore, 1975). The change in the paradigm was to sound the tone continuously until the CR was performed (delayed conditioning), rather than terminating it before the CR began (trace conditioning). Delayed conditioning is easier to learn. In trace conditioning, the animal must briefly hold the CS in memory before the CR behavior begins. According to the principle of mass action, the delayed conditioning task should require less neural tissue.

The conditioned behavior is not really a blink but a retraction of the eye back into the orbit, accomplished by an extraocular muscle appropriately called the retractor bulbi. When this happens, a whitish membrane, the nictitating membrane, passively extends over the eye. The nictitating membrane is sometimes visible in sleepy cats, sliding over the eye from the nasal side. Humans lack this entire system, one of several indications that cats are superior to humans!

Before conditioning, the rabbit hippocampal neurons were unresponsive to the CS. After a few trials, they began to fire at a relatively constant interval of 25 to 35 msec before the response, which

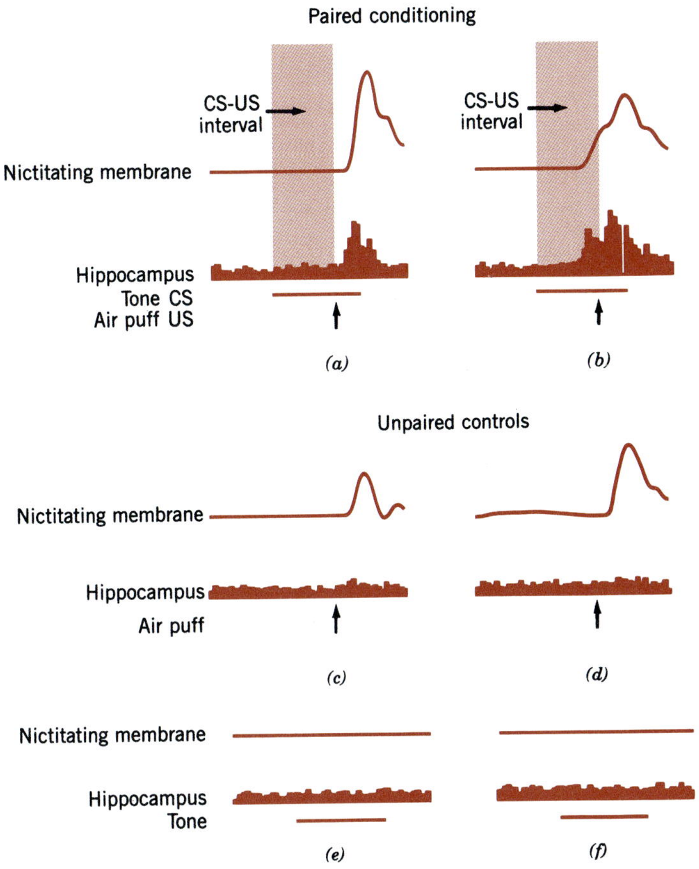

Figure 11.34 *Contrast of nictitating membrane and hippocampal responses before and after conditioning. The width of each bar in the histograms is 15 msec. The tone (CS) duration is 350 msec. The vertical arrows point to the time of the air puff. The two responses begin after the air puff at the first conditioning trials* (a) *but before the air puff after conditioning* (b), *successfully protecting the eye from the puff. Again, pseudoconditioning controls* (c, d, e, *and* f) *show no hippocampal activity, though there is a vigorous reflex response of the nictitating membrane after the puff* (c *and* d). *Adapted from Berger & Thompson (1978).*

is graphed in Figure 11.33. When the nictitating membrane response began to appear as a CR before the air puff, it would precede the puff on some trials and follow it on others. The improvement in performance (shown in Figure 11.34) was a matter of increasing the proportion of trials with an all-or-none CR, not of gradually reducing the latency of the behavior.

During conditioning, a correlation developed between hippocampal unit activity and behavior (see Figure 11.35). The correlation might have originated elsewhere, however, and been transmitted to the hippocampus. To investigate this possibility, researchers recorded neurons in the medial septum (the source of input fibers to the hippocampus) and the lateral septum (the destination of hippocampal output fibers). The medial septum units responded to both the CS and the US from the beginning, and the lateral septum units reflected the hippocampal pattern. The hippocampus was the first location in the chain where plasticity was observed.

A pseudoconditioning control, where tones and air puffs are present at the same frequency as during conditioning but not correlated with each other, yielded no change in the hippocampal responses. The conditioning pattern was similar in the cat, except that the units had some response to tones and air puffs right from the start (Patterson, Berger & Thompson, 1979).

Discovering the physical bases of the plastic changes in these neurons is a job for the future. But a strong hypothesis about the mechanism of hippocampal plasticity already exists.

A Specific Memory Mechanism

A change in hippocampal synapses that seems

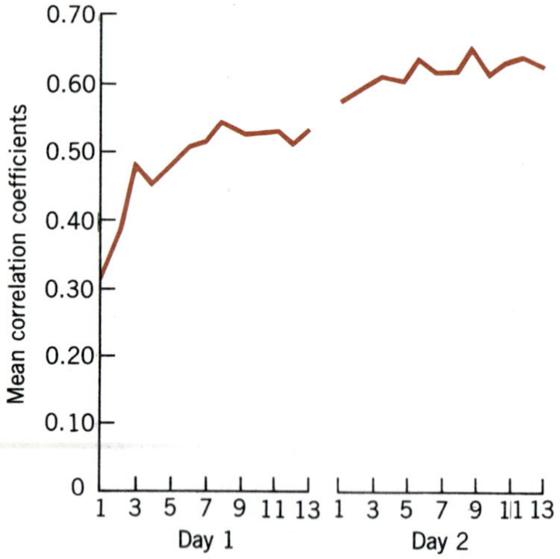

Figure 11.35 *Correlation between nictating membrane and hippocampal activity across blocks of conditioning trials. The latency from hippocampal single-unit activity to nictitating membrane motion settled to a consistent 40 msec after training, so correlations could be best estimated by shifting the hippocampal curve 40 msec. The activity in the nictitating membrane and shifted hippocampal records was only slightly correlated at the start but became tightly coupled as conditioning progressed; by the end of training the correlation reached .82.*

to be related to behavioral plasticity is the long-term potentiation (LTP) that we first saw in Figure 11.16. LTP has several of the characteristics needed for the job; it is triggered by brief physiological events, seems to be strengthened by repetition, and under some circumstances can persist indefinitely. Since the inputs in Figure 11.16 form a monosynaptic connection to the hippocampal pyramidal cell outputs, the synapse where the plasticity occurs can be located. Further work with this synapse has led to a specific hypothesis about the mechanism of plasticity (Lynch & Baudry, 1984). There is good physiological evidence to back up every step in the process.

The neurotransmitter at this plastic synapse is probably glutamic acid. Experiments using slices of the hippocampus showed that high-frequency stimulation of the synapse increases the binding of glutamate to the synaptic membrane. But the binding occurs only if calcium is present, suggesting a trigger for the process. According to Lynch & Baudry's hypothesis, then, bursts of firing cause a transient increase of Ca^{++} in the hippocampal dendritic spines. This activates **calpain,** a calcium-dependent enzyme that splits proteins apart.

The split protein turned out to be **fodrin,** a structural protein that maintains the shape and receptor structure of the presynaptic spine membrane. Breaking up part of the fodrin network produces structural and chemical changes in the region of the postsynaptic membrane, exposing previously occluded glutamate receptors in the membrane. Stronger or repeated bursts of input firing produce more widespread rearrangement of fodrin, possibly leading to the structural changes that have been observed in the hippocampal dendritic spines. The structural changes might become permanent, changing the transfer characteristics of the hippocampal pathway.

There is a good deal of evidence supporting the hypothesis. Glutamate binding to hippocampal membranes increases in rabbits trained in air-puff conditioning. No changes are found in pseudoconditioning control animals. Similarly, glutamate binding increases in rats exposed to an enriched environment for 2 weeks. And drugs that inhibit calpain activity also interfere with learning.

The mechanism might participate in some forms of plasticity but not others. It is specific to the telencephalon, for calcium has virtually no effect in uncovering glutamate receptors in the brain stem or the cerebellum. And again, the hypothesis speaks only to the mechanism, not to the code of memory.

CONDITIONING IN THE CEREBELLUM

If delayed conditioning can occur without the hippocampus, where and how is this conditioning mediated? Using the delayed conditioning of the nictitating membrane, McCormick and Thompson (1984) found the crucial site in an unexpected place—the cerebellar nuclei. A lesion of about 1 mm^3 in the region of the dentate and interpositus nuclei below the cerebellar cortex abolished the conditioned response. The lesion's effect was not due to interruption of pathways to the cerebellar cortex, for lesions of nearly the whole cerebellar cortex had only minor effects on the response. Cerebellar cortex was not necessary for producing the response in trained rabbits, but it probably participates in control of the amplitude and time course of the response.

Single-unit recordings from the dentate-interpositus region showed the development of cell firing in response to the air puff. Onset latency varied widely, with firing in some neurons preceding the conditioned response by 40 to 60 msec and other neurons becoming active only after the behavioral response began. Stimulating the area with electrical current resulted in nictitating membrane responses, showing that the nuclei are involved in motor control of the membrane. Lesions in other nearby regions abolished similar conditioned responses from other parts of the rabbit's body.

These results reveal a surprising specificity in the location of a learned response (Thompson, 1986), in contrast to the more distributed plasticity of the cerebral neocortex. The difference in specificity may parallel the difference in the modes of information processing in the cerebellum and neocortex. The cerebellum has a one-pass, rapid processing system, whereas the neocortex does repeated iterations of processing carried by corticocortical fibers. Repeated iterations would spread information, and presumably plasticity with it, whereas the cerebellar in-and-out processing would require a more localized plasticity. The differences in the anatomy of learning might reflect differences in the initial encoding process.

APPLICATIONS TO NEUROLOGY

Curing Amnesia with Brain Transplants

Clinical and experimental brain lesions result in incurable learning deficits, because the brain cannot regrow lost tissue. But rapid progress is being made in the technique of transplanting brain tissue from one animal to another, and it has recently become possible to make transplants that become functional in repairing a learning deficit.

The breakthroughs in this area have been the use of fetal brains as sources for donor tissue and the implantation of donor tissue from the same brain area as that of the recipient. Fetal brains are used because their axons are still actively growing outward and making new synaptic connections. But the fetal tissue is already committed to particular functions. It will continue to perform those functions if transplanted to a homologous location.

A useful model for impairment of learning abilities is the aged rat. Rats of advanced age (21 to 23 months is very old for a rat), tested in a water maze, do rather poorly. Neurons obtained from the septal area of rat fetuses were injected as a cell suspension into the hippocampal formation of the aged rats. When the animals were tested after 2.5 to 3 months, they performed better than age-matched controls but not as well as young rats. Histology showed that the injected cell suspension had sent cholinergic fibers into the hippocampus (see Figure 11.36). The new fibers apparently "rejuvenated" the aged hippocampus, enabling the rats to perform the task (Gage et al., 1984). In another experiment, rats lesioned in the medial frontal cortex showed deficits in spatial alternation but were improved with grafts of fetal frontal tissue (Labbe et al., 1983). Cerebellar cortex implanted in the same location had no effect on performance.

Though these experiments have not yet been attempted in humans, and a lot of research must be done before that is possible, the technique holds promise for the future treatment of amnesics.

Normal Humans

If the memory deficit in amnesic, brain-damaged humans and animals is due to an encoding failure (Warrington & Weiskrantz, 1974), it should be possible to simulate the syndrome in normal humans by preventing normal encoding. One way to prevent encoding is to present subjects with a task that requires attention to some nonsemantic (unrelated to meaning) aspect of a list of words, such as determining whether a word shares any of its vowels with the preceding word

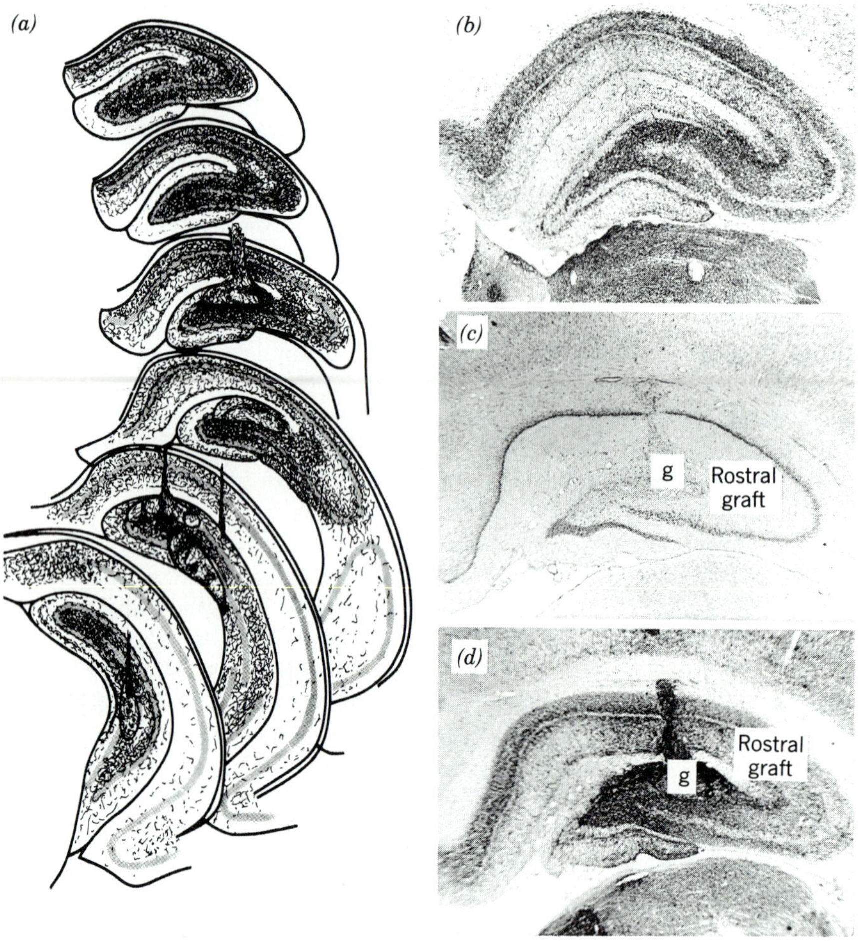

Figure 11.36 *Brain grafts of fetal septal tissue into the hippocampal formation of aged rats. Fetal cells are injected as a suspension and organize themselves into a layer along the hippocampal cortex, sending fibers into the hippocampus. Other cells remain along the path of the injection (the top of each section).* (a) *Summary of six equally spaced sections.* (b) *Photomicrograph of AChE-positive fiber plexus from graft.* (c) *Hippocampal section, cresyl violet stain.* (d) *AChE-stained section adjacent to* (c).

in a list—the words being presented one at a time (Graf, Mandler & Haden, 1982). Being required to remember the vowels in the words, the subjects are effectively prevented from encoding them semantically.

Subjects given this task behave like amnesic patients; on a subsequent recall test, few words are remembered. This is hardly surprising, considering the task the subjects were given. But another parallel between the normal subjects' performance and that of amnesics suggests that one concomitant of amnesia is a failure to encode meaning. In a recognition test where amnesic subjects are asked to complete each word after being given the first three letters, they do as well as normal controls who had learned the list simply by reading the words. Brain-damaged amnesics also succeed at this recognition task, which is easier than recall (mass action again?).

This experiment indicates that a crucial component of human memory is the appropriate coding of sensory information. Without it, subjects behave as though the memory-recording apparatus had been removed. The result is a reminder that memory does not function like a tape recorder, blindly laying down sensations; rather, interpreting and remembering are inseparable, part of the same process of digesting information. The experiment also shows that further progress in understanding human memory requires the investigation of another uniquely human characteristic: language.

CHAPTER SUMMARY

1. Memory is information stored in the brain as a result of sensory experience, and learning is the acquisition of new memories. Memories are stored according to codes—systems of symbols that carry meaning. Mechanisms are physiological substrates that carry codes. Declarative knowledge of things that can be described is distinct from procedural knowledge of rules and procedures, and each shows different characteristics in memory. Recall is the least sensitive measure of memory; recognition of material previously presented is more sensitive; and savings upon relearning the same material is the most sensitive.

2. Memory is coded in a distributed manner; each memory is stored with many others in a region of the brain rather than in a particular location. The destruction of any small region yields only slight disturbances, but they apply to many memories. Memory distribution is shown in experiments using flash frequencies to tag stimuli. There is widespread brain activity at the relevant frequency during learning, even outside the classical sensory areas. Following the learning of a second task at a different flash frequency, generalization trials show endogenous records at one of the original frequencies before a decision is made.

3. An optical analogy aids in thinking about distributed coding: information at the lens plane of a slide projector is coded in a distributed fashion. The information can be stored by the creation of an interference pattern between the coherent light bouncing from an object and the light reflected from a mirror. The resulting pattern, a hologram, has distributed coding and the capacity for multiple encoding in the same locations. If a second object is used instead of the mirror to create the hologram, either can be decoded by presenting the other—a model for associative memory coded by context and requiring no serial search for recall. The brain may support a mathematical analog of the hologram.

4. Mechanisms of memory have been investigated in invertebrates, where calcium channels are involved in both habituation and classical conditioning. These examples of plasticity are modifications of existing anatomical connections. With vertebrates, the hypothesis that memory is coded in macromolecules (RNA or proteins) has been discredited, though protein synthesis is required for learning to occur.

5. Enriched experience, presumably leading to increases in learning, leads to greater cortical weight and increases in cholinergic enzyme systems. In cats, specific training has enlarged topographic sensory maps in the cortex, but only for young animals. Similarly, young animals have more plasticity in their learning capacities than adults do.

6. The consolidation hypothesis, that memories begin in a labile active state and gradually are recoded into a permanent structural state, began with the observation of retrograde amnesia in brain-injured patients. Retrograde amnesia from electroconvulsive shock was transferred from the clinic to the laboratory. Consolidation times, measured as the maximum delays between learning and shock that still give amnesia, vary widely from one laboratory to another. Animals given a "reminder" of the learning are put into a labile state again. Furthermore, the amnesia is not permanent.

7. Consolidation seems to require protein synthesis, for protein synthesis inhibition delays consolidation and brain RNA required to direct protein synthesis is changed during consolidation. But the process is not a passive biochemical action, for it does not begin until the animal has left the training environment. Many methodological questions remain in this area.

8. Both cholinergic and catecholaminergic drugs, when injected after learning, can influence consolidation, with agonists facilitating memory and antagonists inhibiting it. Endorphins, in contrast, seem to retard memory.

9. Lesions in human patients can cause two kinds of amnesia. The first is bitemporal amnesia, which involves the hippocampus and amygdala and is defined by difficulty in encoding declarative memories and an abnormally rapid forgetting rate. It is seen in patients with limbic lesions and in ECS patients. The second amnesia is diencephalic amnesia, which involves the dorsomedial thalamic nucleus and possibly the mammillary bodies. Learning is difficult, but the rate of forgetting material once learned is normal. This type of amnesia is seen in a few lesioned patients and in Korsakoff's syndrome.

10. Conditioning can be observed in single cells of the hippocampus and cerebellum. Neurons feeding the hippocampal cells show no plasticity, whereas those fed from the hippocampus reflect the hippocampal pattern.

11. Transplants of neurons into the hippocampus promise to improve memory where it is deficient. Amnesia can be imitated in normal humans by preventing them from using their most powerful encoding techniques. This emphasizes the active and interactive nature of memory.

KEY TERMS

Memory
Learning
Amnesia
Declarative knowledge
Procedural knowledge
Semantic memory
Episodic memory
Recall
Recognition
Savings
Engram
Mass action
Equipotentiality
Classical conditioning
Unconditioned response (UR)
Unconditioned stimulus (US)
Conditioned stimulus (CS)
Conditioned response (CR)
Instrumental conditioning
Conditioned avoidance response
Exogenous rhythm
Endogenous rhythm
Hologram
Ghost images
Perseveration-consolidation hypothesis
Retrograde amnesia
Long-term potentiation (LTP)
Dendritic spines
Electroconvulsive shock (ECS)
Grand mal epileptic seizure
Active avoidance
Passive avoidance
Puromycin
Transfer RNA
Cycloheximide
Acetoxycycloheximide
Anisomycin
Physostigmine
Arecholine
Scopolamine
Alzheimer's disease
Choline acetyltransferase
Nucleus basalis of Meynert
Diagonal band of Broca
Medial septal nucleus
Alpha-methyl-p-tyrosine (alpha-MPT)
Anterograde amnesia
Bitemporal amnesia
Diencephalic amnesia
Korsakoff syndrome
Calpain
Fodrin

SUGGESTED READINGS

Butters, N., & Squire, L. R. (1984). *The neuropsychology of Memory.* New York: Guilford Press.

This review covers mostly human memory impairment, emphasizing the authors' own work and describing clinical material.

Kandel, E. R. (1979). Small systems of neurons. In *The Brain* (A Scientific American Book) (pp. 29–38). San Francisco: Freeman.

This article is a lucid description of the nervous systems of some small invertebrates, their neurophysiology, and some mechanisms of plasticity.

McGaugh, J. L. (1983). Hormonal influences on memory. *Annual Review of Psychology, 34,* 297–324.

This is an authoritative and readable account of the actions of a number of hormones and related substances in facilitating and blocking memory.

Thompson, R. F., Berger, T. W., & Madden, J. (1983). Cellular processes of learning and memory in the mammalian CNS. *Annual Review of Neuroscience, 6,* 447–492.

This is a look at memory mechanisms at the most microscopic level, mostly using microelectrode techniques in awake animals.

Part IV

APPLICATIONS AND IMPLICATIONS

Chapter 12

THE NEUROLOGY OF LANGUAGE

Language is a new communication system built largely of old parts. Though it is a uniquely human system, it did not spring from nothing with the evolution of **Homo sapiens;** its roots reveal characteristics both of language itself and of the neurological systems supporting communicative functions.

EVOLUTION OF LANGUAGE

The evolution of language will always be a mystery—words leave no fossils. We can infer a good deal about its origins, though, from indirect sources such as the cognitive and communicative abilities of primates, the structure of language itself, and the development of language in children.

Even the evolutionary age of language is a matter of controversy. It is known that nonhuman primates, and even human infants, do not have vocal tracts adequate for the production of a variety of speech sounds. Thus speech is physically impossible for them. The analysis of the vocal tracts in early humans suggests that the right size and shape developed only about 50,000 years ago (Lieberman, 1979). A vocal tract capable of language production and a brain capable of using it must have evolved together, so we would not expect to see one without the other. But inferring the talents of a vocal tract from incomplete fossil bones is a risky business, and the conclusion that language capability developed 50,000 years ago has been vigorously disputed.

COMMUNICATION IN NONHUMAN PRIMATES

The communication systems of nonhuman primates are simple by human standards. Though they might include gestures and postures, there are at most a few dozen different calls, compared with the thousands of words available to every human. Though monkeys have a great variety of communicative sounds, their communication is limited largely to the expression of their internal states. For instance, calls might express alarm, social threat, territoriality, or other emotional conditions; but monkeys are incapable of asking whether a large fruit tree is still bearing or where a fellow monkey received a nasty bruise.

Primate systems of social calls generally lack the capacity to refer to time and place, and the calls are not combined into a grammar. Each call refers to only one state, so the number of messages cannot exceed the number of calls. Like the hypothetical feature detector neurons in sensory systems (see Chapter 5), this scheme leads to inefficient coding. Human speech, in contrast, combines a few dozen sounds to form thousands of words and uses the thousands of words to form limitless sentences. Like the internal neural codes, human language codes take advantage of the power of combinations to carry a great many messages with a small number of elements.

Researchers at the Max-Planck Institute for Psychiatry in Munich have extensively studied the vocal behavior of squirrel monkeys living in troops in large group cages (Ploog, 1981). Radio-controlled stimulation of the limbic system and related structures in these monkeys elicits vocalization, whereas cortical stimulation has little effect. This reflects the emotional nature of most monkey vocalizations. The perception of calls by squirrel monkeys (as opposed to the production of calls) seems to depend more on cortical mechanisms, for auditory neurons in the temporal lobe respond selectively to particular calls.

The limbic "language" is retained in humans as cries, sighs, gasps, and other such exclamations; but we would not confuse these sounds with true language or try to build a language from them. Only in humans does vocalization have a dual purpose: expressing both emotional and symbolic meaning.

Studies of nonhuman vocal behavior rely on the correlation of brain events with behaviors and do not show causality. Stimulation of other areas of the brain may also yield vocalizations, and noncortical neurons might also be involved in sensing species-specific calls. The issue of brain localization of monkey communication centers can be decided with ablation studies. When the superior temporal gyrus is ablated, macaque monkeys lose the ability to discriminate between two of their "coo" vocalizations (Heffner & Heffner, 1984). The deficit is associated with the loss of the left auditory cortex; lesions on the right side have no effect, and bilateral lesions of the areas corresponding to those responsible for language perception in humans produce no deficit. Though the effect is lateralized, the right auditory cortex quickly learns to do the discrimination if the left is removed.

Sign Language in Chimpanzees

Studies using observational and stimulation methods show what nonhuman primates ordinarily do, but they do not probe the limits of their communicative abilities. Humans, after all, go through a long period of cultural exposure as well as maturation before speech begins to appear. Attempts to overcome this restriction by raising chimpanzees in a human environment have been unsuccessful—not because the chimps could not adapt to human ways but because speech simply did not appear. An attempt by Hayes and Hayes (see Hayes, 1951), who raised a female chimp, Viki, like a child in their own home for several years, resulted in an animal who behaved in many ways like a human child. Viki's motor development was a bit faster than that of a human, as was her cognitive development for the first year or so. But her spoken language amounted only to the word *cup,* uttered indistinctly under strong motivation. (Like squirrel monkeys, chimps do not vocalize spontaneously except in emotional situations.) A few other words were even less clear.

When Allen and Beatrice Gardner of the University of Nevada viewed a film of Viki performing this linguistic feat, they noted that the animal was gesturing frantically while trying to obtain the cup at the dinner table. Knowing the importance of gesture in wild chimpanzee communications, they reasoned that chimps might be more successful with a gestural language than a spoken one. The language they chose was American Sign Language (Ameslan), used by many deaf people in North America as their only language. They named the young chimp in their project Washoe, after the county in which the University of Nevada is located.

The Gardners had spectacular success at teaching Washoe to communicate. The chimp readily learned Ameslan signs (see Figure 12.1), both from instruction and from observation of her caretakers signing to each other (Gardner & Gardner, 1969). Washoe would sign during games as well as in serious situations; one of her first signs was *tickle.* She developed a vocabulary of several hun-

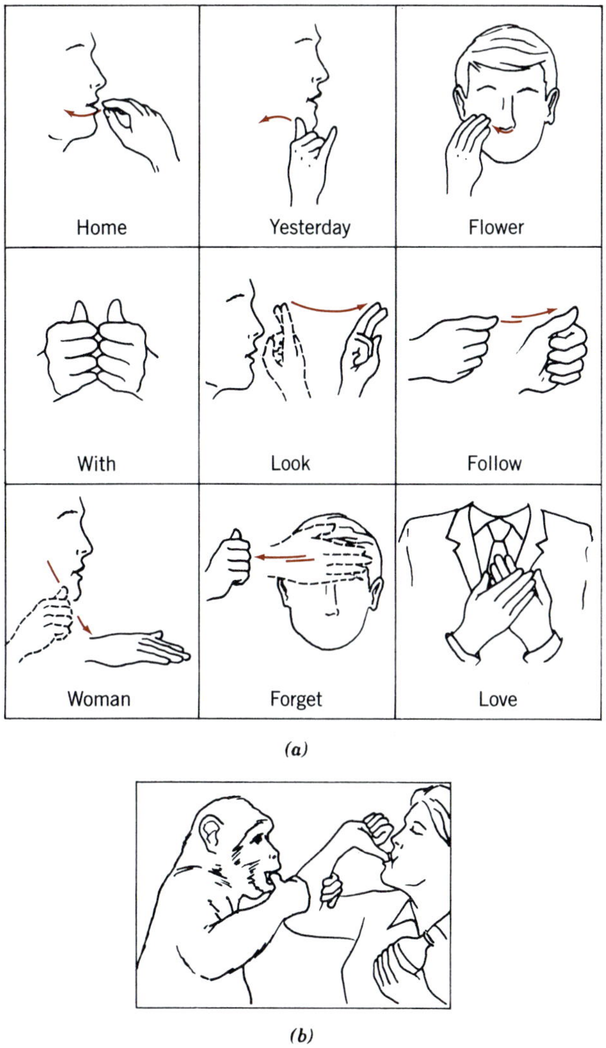

Figure 12.1 *Sign language in the chimpanzee.* (a) *Some signs of Ameslan. Washoe learned each of these signs.* (b) *Washoe making the sign for "drink" in imitation of a caretaker. Based on photos taken in December 1967, when Washoe was 2.5 yr old.*

dred signs, learning nearly as fast as a signing human child. More significantly, Washoe combined signs in novel ways, creating a primitive grammar (Gardner & Gardner, 1975). After learning the sign for *more* while being tickled, for example, she signed for *more sweet* at mealtime; she also produced other novel combinations, such as *listen dog.* These combinations are parallel to the two-word **slot grammar** used by 1 and 2 yr old children all over the world; in slot grammar, utterances are limited to two words and don't follow adult grammatical relationships. The two words fit into "slots" in the closed grammatical system; no further modifications are allowed. The example of *more sweet* also shows nominalization—using an adjective as a noun—even though it had never been used that way by Washoe's caretakers. This is another characteristic of human language. Later, Washoe used more elaborate grammatical forms, though she never became as fluent as deaf human children.

The success of Washoe at learning sign language that could be understood by deaf "speakers" of Ameslan created a sensation. Linguists were forced to define language more carefully to be sure that Ameslan could be considered a legitimate language. Philosophers began to reconsider the differentiation of humans and animals, and psycholinguists rushed to repeat and extend the finding that Washoe could use sign language.

At Stanford University, Penny Patterson raised an infant gorilla, Koko, with sign language, finding many of the signing abilities that had been seen in Washoe. Premack and Premack (1972) taught chimpanzees to string together symbols on a magnetic board to identify objects, ask for things, and so on. With extensive training, the animals could form short novel sentences with appropriate meaning, and they mastered logical relations such as "larger" and "brighter." The chimpanzee Lana at the Yerkes Primate Center learned "Yerkish," a computer-based language, with keys on a large console functioning as words (Rumbaugh, 1977). Again, the chimpanzee developed the ability to use some grammatical relationships and to generate novel strings of symbols. These methods are less labor-intensive than teaching Ameslan because parts of the procedures can be automated, and they are less prone to unconscious prompting by the experimenter. But Lana lacked the extensive learning by observation and the natural social interaction of real language learning.

Challenge and Response. The next attempt at teaching sign language to a chimpanzee led to a strong attack on the language capabilities of Washoe and the other language-using chimps. Herbert Terrace, a former student of the behavioral psychologist B. F. Skinner, taught sign language to a chimpanzee named Nim Chimpsky (after the linguist Noam Chomsky). In Nim, Terrace found important differences between chimpanzee and human use of signs. According to him, nearly all sign use was in imitation of signs used shortly before in interactions with a trainer or caretaker, and grammatical strings were imitations of other grammatical strings, with perhaps a substitution here and there (Terrace, 1979). In his analysis of films of Washoe and other chimps, Terrace claimed that those animals too signed mainly by rote imitation, usually without the experimenter being aware of the imitative nature of the signing.

The Gardners responded to these challenges with reminders of the differences between their training methods and Terrace's. Washoe had been raised in as naturalistic a situation as possible, with spoken language among caretakers forbidden. Terrace's training, in contrast, was restricted to formal structured sessions more in accord with the tradition of conditioning experiments. The experimental animals were caged and had little human contact outside the conditioning sessions. The same applied to Premack's chimps.

Under these circumstances, the Gardners argued, it is not surprising that chimps respond in limited, imitative ways. If you teach an animal to use language by rote, it will use language by rote. Terrace also claimed that the "talking" chimps seldom or never made spontaneous statements without some prompting or questioning by humans. But Washoe frequently initiated signing by making requests, and the Gardners have evidence of Washoe making signs when she was by herself, filmed with a hidden camera. Signing when alone occurred fairly early in Washoe's training, when she was still in diapers, and may correspond to the "egocentric" speech of young humans. Patterson's gorilla, Koko, has also been filmed signing to herself—while looking at pictures in a magazine.

The controversy has not been resolved, but already chimpanzee language studies have made several contributions. First, they have forced linguists to be more careful about their definitions. When do signs and combinations of signs really become language? Some grammarians are arriving at definitions that sound like those of the cognitive development stages of Piaget. The important features, they say, are not the surface structure of speech (sentence length, for example) but the underlying mental operations. These include reversibility, reference to objects not present, and communication of meaning by grammatical structure. By some of the more restrictive definitions, much of the speech of human toddlers would not qualify as true language.

Second, the studies have forced a reconsideration of the role of humans in nature. At about the same time that Washoe was learning Ameslan, DNA studies were showing that humans are more closely related to chimpanzees than to any other primate; the two species share over 96 percent of their genes. Chimpanzees share more genetic material with humans than with other living apes. Humans and chimps have proved to be about as closely related genetically as are, for instance, horses and donkeys. It is not surprising, in retrospect, that many of the human's much-prized cognitive and communicative abilities should be seen in other forms in the chimpanzee. It is clear, though, that 96 percent of the genes do not control 96 percent of the behavior, for a small genetic difference gives humans a large advantage in communication.

It is also clear that the great apes, with brains about a third as large as ours and lacking some of our linguistic specializations, will never reach the more complex and subtle aspects of human language. Their language deals with the here and now, for instance. The apes seem unable to handle references to events already past or to possibilities not yet realized. In this respect, the nonhuman Ameslan dialects are similar to the speech of young children: it does not seem to be connected to long-term declarative memory on one hand or to planning on the other.

Language of Other Animals

Animals other than apes are also being investigated for their communicative use of signs. Rhesus monkeys can understand human spoken words, and, of course, dogs can also respond to isolated commands. Even chinchillas can discriminate words (Kuhl & Miller, 1975), though ordinarily they don't respond differentially to them outside a conditioning situation.

The most surprising report of language processing in nonprimates concerns a parrot that has been trained to recognize and choose objects on the basis of spoken words. The bird can vocalize the words in the correct context (Pepperberg, 1983). It also uses short phrases appropriately—for instance, to ask for a break during a training session. The parrot demonstrates that there is nothing special about the relationship between the neocortex and some aspects of language use, for in birds the striatum rather than the cortex is the forebrain structure that underwent extensive development.

Bird Brains and Birdsong. Among the most complex communicative sounds made by any animals are the songs of birds. Some songs are simple, repeating a single basic unit. Others are more complex, showing regional "dialects" and changes over time. The songs are so rapid and so densely textured that human students of birds must play the songs back at one-quarter speed to hear all of the transitions. The communicative functions of birdsong are quite specialized, however. The songs nearly always announce territoriality, availability of mates, or dominance; and they are sung only by males.

For some birds, the song is controlled by a stereotyped genetic program that is not modified by auditory experience or the lack of it. Ring doves, for example, will sing the same song whether they are deafened early in life, reared in isolation, or reared normally (Nottebohm, 1980). Other birds, however, are more like primates in that early experience is important in developing an adult song. Even experience in the nest, a year or more before singing begins, is vital in shaping the songs of many birds. Sparrows follow this pattern. They have an innate song that develops even in isolation but is normally shaped by exposure to other songs into a more complex and distinctive pattern. An early-deafened bird will generate only an indistinct screech, very unlike any normal song (Marler & Tamura, 1964).

Birdsong is especially important in the comparative neurophysiology of language because a good deal is known about the physiology of song generation. First, there are strong similarities in the anatomy of bird and human vocal control. The muscles of the bird's vocal apparatus, the **syrinx,** are controlled by the left and right hypoglossal nerves. Sectioning the right hypoglossal nerve produces hardly any change in the song, but sectioning the left nerve silences the song. According to Nottebohm (1977), birds whose left nerve has been sectioned look like tiny actors in silent movies.

The neural control mechanisms of birds are also lateralized. Lesions in the left striatum yield unstable, abnormal songs; right striatum lesions have little effect (Nottebohm, 1980). In this respect, birds are similar to humans; their left hemisphere is specialized for language.

Another aspect of neural control of birdsong, however, is very different from the human situation. Birds sing only seasonally, and the brain regions responsible for generating the song increase greatly in size each year under the control of testosterone. Female birds given testosterone injections can sing, once the corresponding areas of their brains have grown. Even more surprisingly, the annual growth of the song-controlling areas appears to involve the creation of new neurons (Paton & Nottebohm, 1984), an exception to the rule that no neurons are produced in adult brains. After the singing season, the neurons die.

STRUCTURE OF LANGUAGE

Though human languages seem endlessly varied, they in fact have a good deal in common. Language variation is a valuable tool for understanding the human organism, for it marks the range of plasticity in human systems involved in language. The universal structures, or design features, of all languages define the properties of the built-in neurological systems that support them. In identifying some of these design features (Hockett, 1972), we also identify features of the neurological systems dealing with language.

Beginning with speech production at the lowest level, language is a string of speech sounds, or **phonemes** (see Figure 12.2). The phonemes are

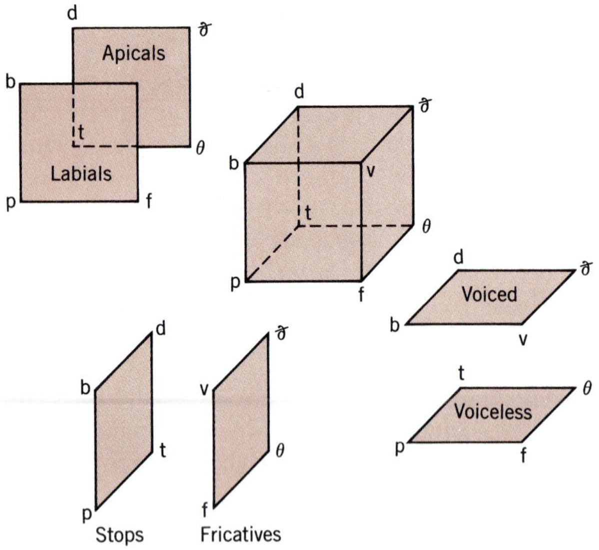

*Figure 12.2 Eight English consonants divided into three distinctive binary features. Labials (*labia *is Latin for "lips") are produced by bringing the lips together; apicals (*apex *is Latin for "top") are made with the tongue forward in the mouth. Fricatives are made by the friction of air between the teeth and either the lips or the tongue. Each phoneme is defined by all three dimensions. Adapted from Brown (1965).*

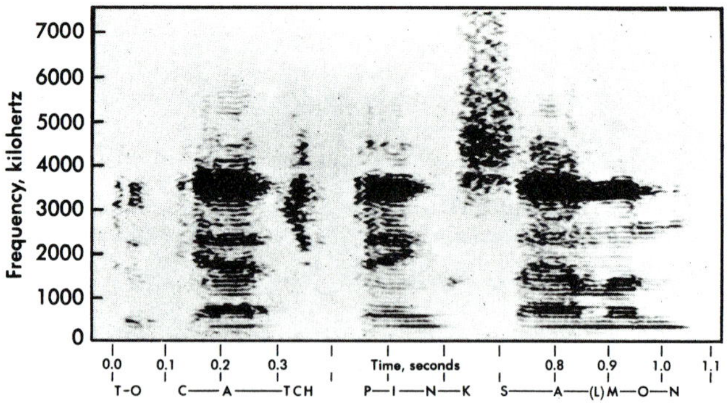

Figure 12.3 A sound spectrogram. Three dimensions are plotted: sound frequency on the vertical axis, time on the horizontal axis, and intensity of sound in the darkness of the color. A pure sine-wave tone would be represented as a sharp horizontal line. Speech sounds tend to be organized into formants—components with a distinct frequency range and duration. The two [a] phonemes here, for instance, have a similar distribution of formants.

single sounds such as [f], [e], [t], and [θ] (pronounced [th]). The phonemes carry no meaning in themselves; they are semantically empty. Each natural language (any language used by some human group) makes use of a set of between 15 and about 85 phonemes. English falls near the middle of the range, with 45. The number is probably small so that each phoneme can be easily distinguished from all of the others (Brown, 1965).

Even at this level, we encounter a paradox originating from the prodigious rate at which humans speak. The normal rate is about 10 phonemes per second in all languages, and it can reach 25 to 30 per second in short bursts (Lieberman, 1982). But the human vocal tract simply cannot produce separate auditory gestures at those rates. How does the system nevertheless manage to generate phonemes so rapidly? The answer is contained in a second paradox: when we look at records of human speech, as in Figure 12.3, the phonemes aren't there! Instead of a series of discrete, easily discriminable units of language, we find only a seemingly smooth set of sound transitions punctuated by breaks that appear to be different for each word and each speaker. Though phoneme production usually follows a set of rules, no consistent pattern specifies each phoneme.

The two paradoxes can be solved by combining them: in normal speech the phonemes are not produced in isolation but are spread throughout a speech sequence (Liberman, 1974). In other words, information about several phonemes can be transmitted simultaneously. Somehow the linguistic receiving apparatus unpacks the intermingled signals (see Figure 12.4). We perceive the string of discrete phonemes that was intended by the speaker but that was intermingled in the auditory communication channel. The external human code of speech turns out to have surprising similarities to the internal codes encountered in the

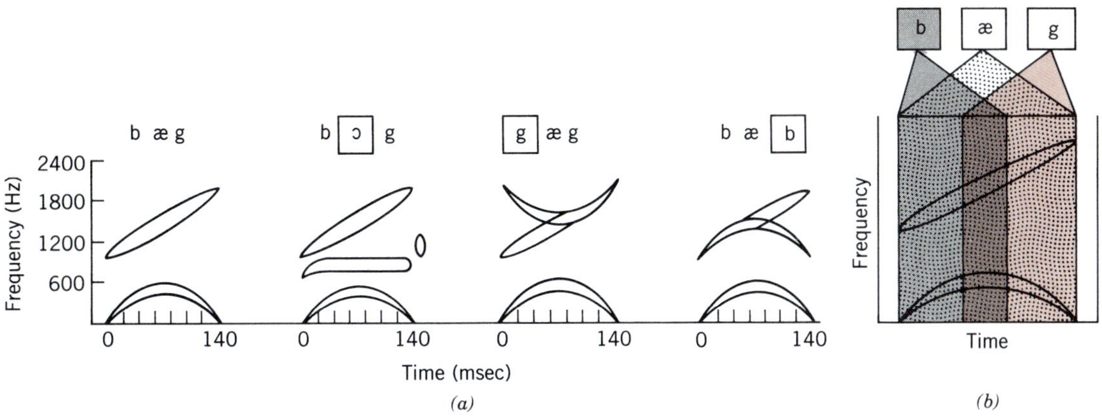

Figure 12.4 *Components of sound spectrograms.* (a) *Schematic sound spectrograms for four English consonant-vowel-consonant (CVC) sequences, showing the differences between spectrograms for each sequence and the previous sequence (dashed lines).* (b) *The regions of the spectrogram that are modified for the initial consonant, vowel, and final consonant, respectively. The regions coding the consonants overlap in the middle, and the vowel is coded throughout the sequence. You can hear the overlap in your own speech by comparing the position of the center of your tongue when you say [kee] versus [ko]. The second [k] is further back in the mouth, though we think of the two consonants as the same. Adapted from Liberman (1974).*

sensory systems, with multiplexing and distribution of information in the time dimension.

The overlap of phonemes does not stop even at word boundaries. Figure 12.5 shows a sound spectrogram for the words *gray ship,* a sequence that includes a stop (a brief silence) in the middle. By changing the length of this stop and the following phoneme artificially (Repp et al., 1978), they could change subjects' perception of the term from *gray ship* to *great ship, gray chip,* or *great chip* (a tongue-twister-writer's dream) (see Figure 12.6).

Speech in unfamiliar languages usually sounds faster than speech in a familiar one, even though phonemes are produced at about the same rate in

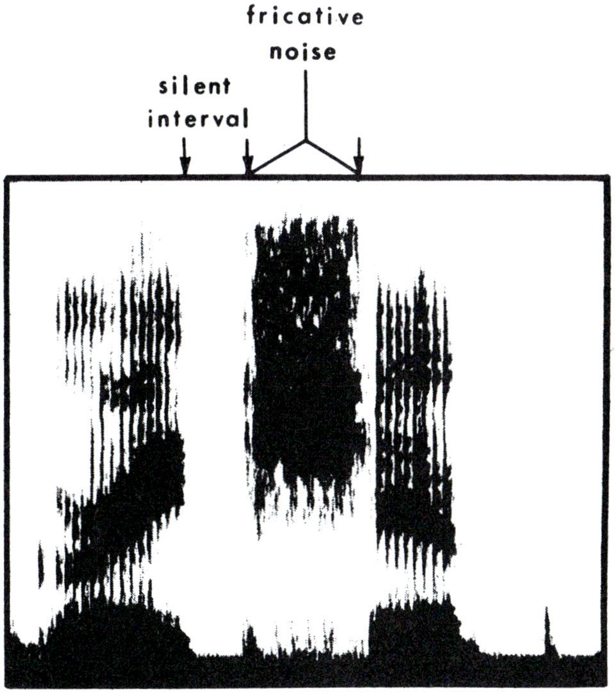

Figure 12.5 *Spectrogram of the words* gray ship. *The fricative noise is heard as [sh]. The duration of the silent interval influences the perception of both the last phoneme of the first word and the first phoneme of the second word. From Repp et al. (1978).*

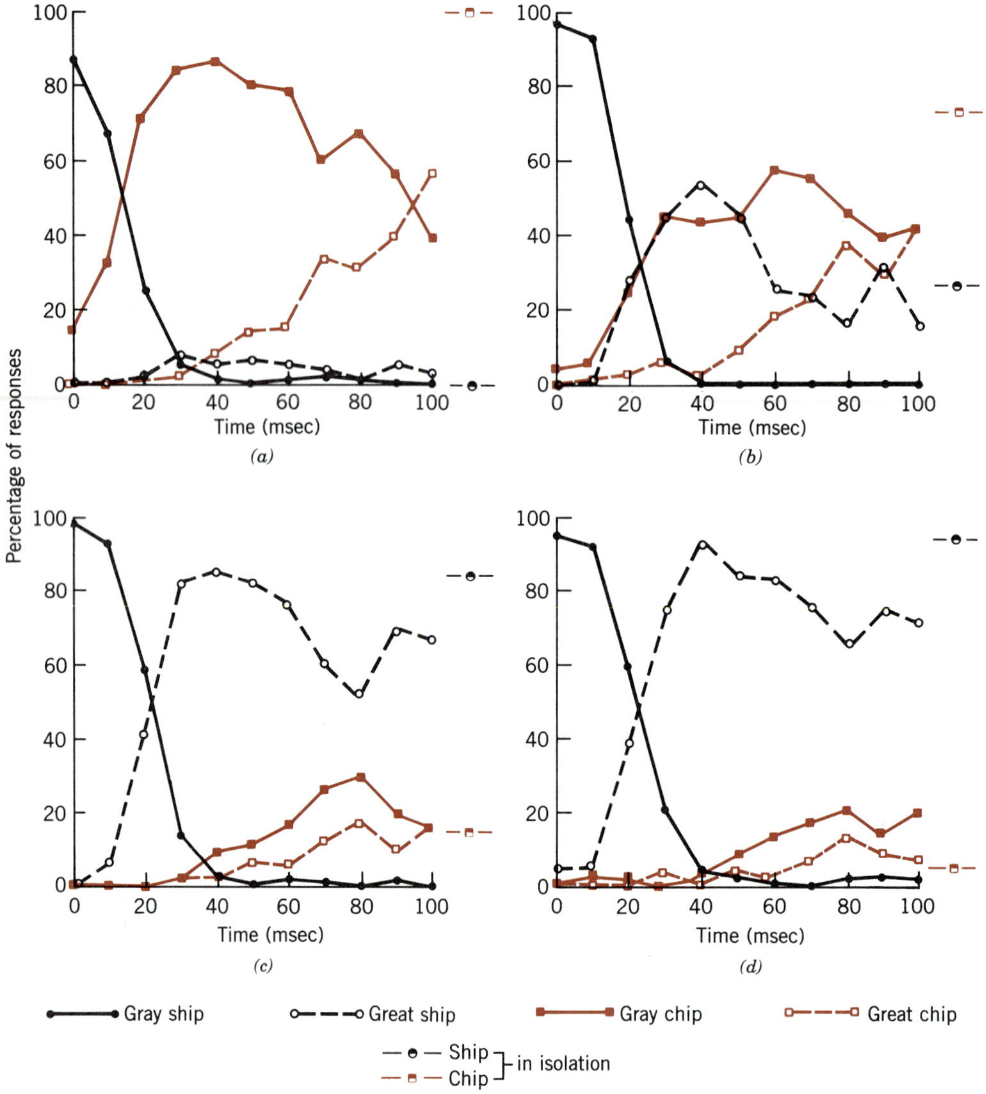

Figure 12.6 *The effect of the duration of silence on the perception of* gray ship *and similar phrases. Each graph represents one duration of the fricative noise. Psychophysical data are taken from native speakers of English.* (a) *Noise duration is 62 msec.* (b) *Noise duration is 102 msec.* (c) *Noise duration is 142 msec.* (d) *Noise duration is 182 msec. Adapted from Repp et al. (1978).*

all of them. The difference probably appears because of the ways in which we interpret familiar languages, breaking the speech train into larger units and grammatical constructions rather than trying to follow the individual phonemes. By "chunking" smaller units into larger ones, we code more efficiently and reduce the short-term memory capacity needed to interpret speech (Miller, 1956). Thus higher-level information processing can have effects that seem to be perceptual. The effects are referred to the outside world even though the differences lie in us.

Grammars

All languages have a **grammar,** a set of rules by which words may be combined to impart meanings; and grammars themselves follow universal rules despite their diversity. All grammars, for instance, distinguish among subject, verb, and object; all have ways of differentiating past, present, and future; and all have sentence and pluralization rules.

Each language has two grammars. One is the type formalized by grammarians and learned (usually unwillingly) by grammar school students, and the other is the type internalized in the brains of users of the language. I remember feeling resentment at having to learn English grammar rules in elementary school when I could already speak grammatically without them. It was a pleasant surprise to find out in college that the grammar I had learned was only one of several possible English grammars, imposed after the fact on an existing language. A grammar is a theory, intended to order existing data. The data are the utterances of native speakers of the language. Typically, a formal grammar will fail to describe some utterances and at the same time will generate some strings of words that native speakers find uninterpretable.

The distinction between the two grammars, internal and external, becomes particularly vivid when one learns a second language. One laboriously studies grammatical rules for the new language—and sometimes actually uses them for writing or for very hesitant speaking. True fluency, however, seems not to appear until the formal rules are forgotten. They are gradually replaced by an unconscious internal grammar, a neurological organization that generates grammatical utterances and analyzes the speech of others with rules that are impossible to fully externalize. Grammar uses procedural memory, as unconscious as the learning that occurs in the cerebellum when one starts riding a bicycle; the skill develops, but the learned rules are difficult to articulate.

The internal grammar also contains rules that generally are not learned in elementary school because they are applied almost without error by native speakers. Most speakers are unaware of the existence of such rules and will deny their existence until shown an example. One example, a standard English modifier order, is given in Table 12.1. It is entertaining to make up a lengthy string of modifiers (such as "the first two big old red barns") and to see the string fit unerringly into the prescribed order rules.

Languages vary greatly in their **surface structures**—the strings of words that speakers produce. But their **deep structures**—the logical relationships that underlie the sentences—are similar in all languages. It appears that the human language machine can handle certain kinds of deep structures and invents surface structures to express them.

Is Speech Special?

The brain-voice-ear-brain channel of speech communication is not made up entirely of old parts, but has a biology of its own. The perception of speech sounds, for example, seems different from the perception of nonspeech. The classic experiment in this area involves the discrimination of speech sounds along a continuum that crosses a phoneme boundary; continuously delaying the voice onset in the syllable [ba], for example, can slowly transform it into [pa]. Figure 12.7 shows that people perceive small differences in voice onset better near the phoneme boundaries and fail to perceive equally large differences in voice onset time when that difference would not be critical for distinguishing one phoneme from another. The change in thresholds cannot be explained by inborn differences in auditory sensitivity at the boundaries, though, for different languages put the boundaries in different places.

Other evidence for the uniqueness of speech processing involves **dichotic listening**—hearing different sound patterns in each ear. If different consonants are presented to each ear, the result is not a combination of the sounds. Most people perceive the sound entering the right ear; that sound goes mainly to the left hemisphere, where the speech centers are located.

If a segment of speech is divided, with some of the information coming into each ear, the speech sounds remain intelligible. But a speech transition, such as the transition in Figure 12.8 that distinguishes [da] from [ga], can be presented in isolation without a vowel. The subject hears only a

Table 12.1
Sequential Order of Modifiers in English Noun Phrases

Particles	Possessive	Ordinal Number	Cardinal Number	Characteristic	Size	Shape	Temperature and Humidity	Age	Color	Origin	Noun	Head Noun
the							*cool*		*blue*	*Aegean*		*sea*
a												
this	*train's*	*first*	*four*								*passenger*	*cars*
that	*boy's*		*three*	*unusual*				*young*	*grey*	*Persian*		*cats*
those												
some												
many												
any				*remarkably*			*hot, damp*			*tropical*		*climate*
your												
his					*short*	*stocky*						*frame*
her												
their												
our												
my	*son's*			*witty*			*warm*		*colorful*			*personality*

Source: Brown (1965).

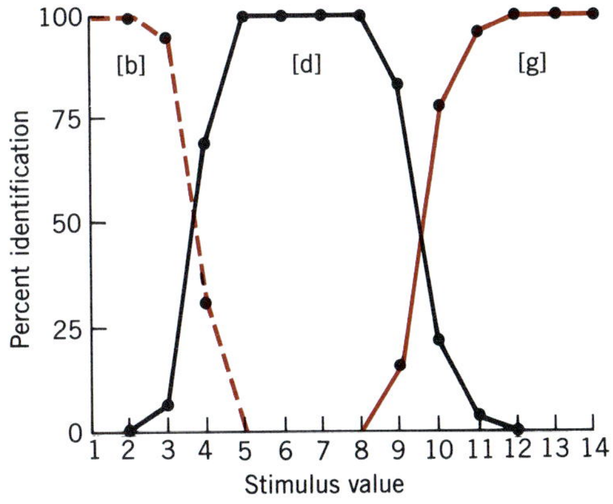

Figure 12.7 *Perceived consonants as voice onset is delayed in a segment of computer-synthesized speech. Data from one subject are shown here. Most people hear a clear [ba] when voice onset is early, then switch abruptly to [da] and later to [ga] as voice onset is delayed. In categorical perception, differences of timing within the domain of a judged consonant are not perceived; for example, stimulus values 5 and 7 would be indistinguishable even though the switch from 3 to 5 would result in a clear phoneme change. δ is the sound [zh]; θ is the sound [th]. Adapted from Brown (1965).*

short chirp (Liberman, 1982). In language, the chirp is integrated into a phoneme. The change in sound frequency remains unperceived.

Another school of thought holds that the special nature of speech is much more limited than had been believed. Categorical perception across phoneme boundaries, after all, is a quantitative difference, not a sudden jump. The greater sensitivity at the boundaries may be the result of learning, like any other perceptual learning (Massaro & Cohen, 1983). A source of evidence in the controversy about whether phoneme perception is categorical or continuous is reading. This skill has appeared so recently in evolution that there is certainly no unique language processor connected with it, at least on the perceptual end. Here one sees many of the properties that seem to make phoneme perception special, including integration of multiple cues for visual recognition of letters and syllables (Massaro, 1979).

The resolution of this controversy, like many others, will probably lie in a combination of the two approaches. Some areas in which speech seems special, such as the perception of combined features, may turn out to be general capabilities of perceptual systems. Other, higher-level functions, such as the generation of utterances quickly and fluently by grammatical rules, may turn out to have

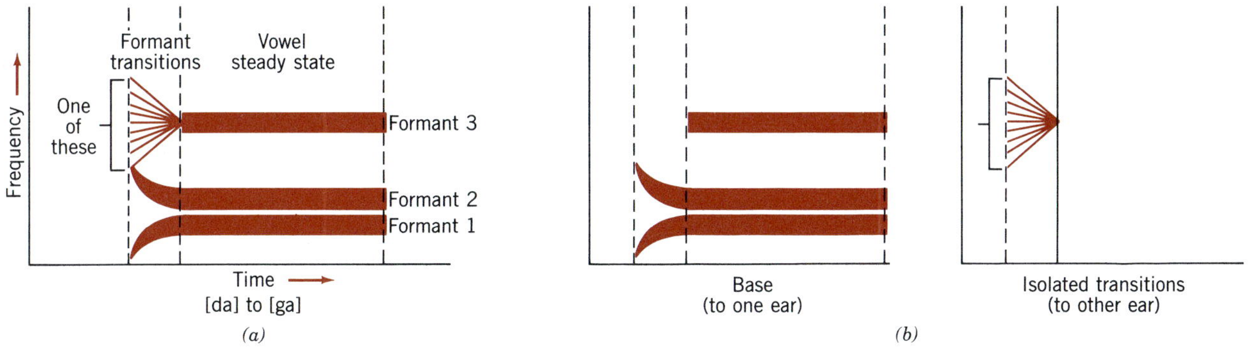

Figure 12.8 *An experiment in which a sound spectrogram like those in Figure 12.4 is artificially divided and parts of it are presented separately to the two ears (dichotic listening). The only difference in the spectrograms is the change of sound frequency with time in the first part of formant 3.* (a) *Normal (binaural) presentation.* (b) *Duplex-producing (dichotic) presentation. When presented with the base spectrogram (left), the formant completes the percept of [da] or [ga]. If one of the alternative formants is presented in isolation (right), only a rapidly ascending, steady, or rapidly descending tone is heard.*

specialized neurological processors. On this point we have additional evidence.

LANGUAGE DEVELOPMENT IN CHILDREN

Robert MacLeod once said that in studying language one should start not with phonemes but with babies. The advice applies also to the study of the neural basis of language, for language is a good example of an interaction between inherited neural structures and experience. Every normal human learns a language, yet humans raised in isolation do not talk. Both experience and the neural structures competent to take advantage of the experience are necessary.

An infant begins life with a good start on the primate limbic sounds such as cries and gasps. It develops the ability to communicate quite effectively with gestures, grunts, and squeals long before the first word appears at about 1 yr of age. At this stage the temptation is great to hypothesize that human language arose from systems of gestures; in fact, children learning sign language as their first language begin signing before hearing children begin speaking.

The first word appears as part of a **holophrase**—a combination of conditions including gestures, context, and verbal output. The child works hard on the first unintelligible approximations to words with no obvious reinforcement. Attempts to find reinforcement explanations for language learning (e.g., Skinner, 1957) have been unsuccessful. Too much must happen before any reinforceable speech is generated to sustain a reward-oriented motivation. Rather, the practice of speech seems to require a positive motivational system (like those of Chapter 10), with rewards for the very act of trying out language.

The child soon begins using a two-word slot grammar. The grammar of these phrases bears little similarity to adult language. It is the same in all languages studied so far, including English, Japanese, Korean, Finnish, German and Russian (Brown, 1973). It seems to come from within the child rather than from the adult linguistic community. Examples of children's constructions at this stage are shown in Table 12.2.

Even before this stage, children show evidence of internalizing grammatical rules. Since the use of correct forms in short fragments of speech might be merely rote imitation, evidence for rules must come from incorrect forms. English is maddeningly rich in irregular verbs and varieties of pluralizations. The child who says "two foots" or "I goed" is applying rules deduced from other examples. All children learn the complexities of grammar in about the same order, though the timing of the steps varies widely from child to child (Table 12.3). The process is not complete until after puberty.

Table 12.2
Semantic Relations in Two-Word Sentences

Semantic Relation	*Form*[a]	*Example*
1. Nomination	that + N	*that book*
2. Notice	hi + N	*hi belt*
3. Recurrence	more + N, 'nother + N	*more milk*
4. Nonexistence	allgone + N, no more + N	*allgone rattle*
5. Attributive	Adj + N	*big train*
6. Possessive	N + N	*mommy lunch*
7. Locative	N + N	*sweater chair*
8. Locative	V + N	*walk street*
9. Agent-action	N + V	*Eve read*
10. Agent-object	N + N	*mommy sock*
11. Action-object	V + N	*put book*

Source: Adapted from Brown (1970).
[a]Adj = adjective; V = verb; N = noun.

Table 12.3
The Acquisition of Six Grammatical Morphemes

Morpheme	*Order of Acquisition*	*Transformations*	*Semantic Dimensions*
Present progressive	1	Progressive affix	Temporary duration
On	2.5	Preposition segment	Support
In	2.5	Preposition segment	Containment
Plural	4	Noun suffix, nominal agreement, article	Number
Past irregular	5	Verb agreement	Earlierness
Possessive	6	(Not given in source)	Possession

Source: Adapted from Brown (1973).

Grammatical rule learning is, of course, heavily influenced by the parent language and to some degree is specific to the peculiarities of that language. An experiment in which children were raised with a **lexicon** (a vocabulary of words) but without an adult grammar would tell us more about the basic grammar of children.

Grammar in Creole Languages

It would be highly unethical for linguists to remove a group of children from contact with natural languages to see what sort of grammar would appear. This removal has occurred several times, however, in the history of colonialism. The British, Americans, French, Dutch, Spanish, and Portuguese all established labor-intensive agricultural colonies and imported labor from distant ethnic groups. The new workers found themselves uprooted from their cultures, with employers and fellow workers speaking incomprehensible languages. The response of these immigrants was to develop pidgin language, a linguistic hodgepodge that is unique to each speaker and gener-

Table 12.4
Examples of Pidgin and of Hawaiian Creole English

Pidgin	*Hawaiian Creole English*
Building—high place—wall part—time—nowtime—and then—now temperature every time give you.	Get one [There is an] electric sign high up on da wall of da building show you what time an temperature get [it is] right now.
Now days, ah, house, ah, inside, washi clothes machine get, no? Before time, ah, no more, see? And then pipe no more, water pipe no more.	Those days bin get [there were] no more washing machine, no more pipe water like get [there is] inside house nowadays, ah?
No, the men, ah—pau [finished] work—they go, make garden. Plant this, ah, cabbage, like that. Plant potato, like that. And then—all that one—all right, sit down. Make lilly bit story.	When work pau [is finished] da guys they stay go make [are going to make] garden for plant potato an' cabbage an' after little while they go sit down talk story ["shoot the breeze"].
Good, this one. Kaukau [food] any kind this one. Pilipin island no good. No more money.	Hawaii more better than Philippines, over here get [there is] plenty kaukau [food], over there no can, bra [brother], you no more money for buy kaukau [food], 'a'swhy [that's why].

Source: Bickerton (1983).

Table 12.5
Verb Conjugation in Various Creole Languages

	Nonstative Verbs			*Stative Verbs*		
Verb Form	*Hawaiian Creole*	*Haitian Creole*	*Sranan*	*Hawaiian Creole*	*Haitian Creole*	*Sranan*
Base form ("he walked"; "he loves")	He walk	Li maché	A waka	He love	Li rêmê	A lobi
Anterior ("he had walked"; he loved")	He bin walk	Li té maché	A ben waka	He bin love	Li tê rêmê	A ben lobi
Irreal ("he will/would walk"; "he will/would love")	He go walk	L'av(a) maché	A sa waka	He go love	L'av(a) rêmê	A sa lobi
Nonpunctual ("he is/was walking")	He stay walk	L'ap maché	A e waka	—	—	—
Anterior + irreal ("he would have walked"; "he would have loved")	He bin go walk	Li t'av(a) maché	A ben sa waka	He bin go love	Li t'av(a) rêmê	A ben sa lobi
Anterior + non-punctual ("he was/had been walking")	He bin stay walk	Li t'ap maché	A ben e waka	—	—	—
Irreal + nonpunctual ("he will/would be walking")	He go say walk	L'av ap maché	A sa e waka	—	—	—
Anterior + irreal + nonpunctual ("he would have been walking")	He bin go stay walk	Li t'av ap maché	A ben sa e waka			

Source: Bickerton (1983).

ally fails to represent many of the subtler aspects of natural language grammars.

The children of the immigrants do not speak pidgin dialects. Instead they speak a language with some very peculiar characteristics (Bickerton, 1983). It is uniform throughout the linguistic group, regardless of the ethnicity of the speaker's family, and it functions according to set grammatical rules. Furthermore, it arises in a single generation, without models or instruction. Such languages are called "creole" by linguists. (See Table 12.4 for examples of pidgin and Hawaiian Creole English).

Even more astonishing, isolated creole languages all over the world have virtually the same grammar (see Table 12.5), whether their lexicon is borrowed mostly from English, French, Portuguese, or other languages. The grammar is not a subset of that found in natural languages but is a complete system that can include distinctions and forms not found in the parent language. For instance, English does not require a speaker to differentiate purposes that have been accomplished from those that have not. "John went to Honolulu to see Mary" does not specify whether John and Mary actually met. But a creole speaker must choose between "John bin go Honolulu *go* see Mary," if John saw Mary, and "John bin go Honolulu *for* see Mary," if John missed Mary or if the speaker does not know what happened.

According to Bickerton (1981, 1983), the children have made up the new language themselves. The creole constructions, in this view, represent a default condition for human grammar, the form that appears when no contradictory forms are present. The constructions are built into the language areas of the brain, a grammar given by the genes rather than by a culture. Thus the creoles present a priceless opportunity to look directly into the grammatical mind of the young child. Furthermore, the constructions of creole languages bear an uncanny resemblance to the grammatical productions of 2 to 4 year old children in natural linguistic communities (see Table 12.6).

Children find learning the constructions that their language and the creole base have in common to be nearly effortless, whereas constructions contradictory to the creole are more difficult and are generally learned later. The English suffix *ing*, for instance, is learned very early. It expresses duration in sentences such as "I reading bookie." One would expect it to be overgeneralized, just as the suffix *s* is used to make *foots* and *sheeps,* but it is not. Children almost never produce "I liking daddy"; the difference between stative verbs such as *like* and nonstative verbs such as *read* seems to be realized instinctively. The marker for duration is present in all creole languages—for instance, as the word *stay* in Table 12.5. Incidentally, this example also shows that the neurological grammar

Table 12.6

Examples of Child Language versus English Creole Languages

Child Language	*English Creole Languages*
Where I can put it?	Where I can put om? (Hawaii)
Daddy throw the nother rock.	Daddy t'row one neda rock' tone. (Jamaica)
I go full Angela bucket.	I go full Angela bucket. (Guyana)
Lookit a boy play ball.	Luku one boy a play ball. (Jamaica)
Nobody don't like me.	Nobody no like me. (Guyana)
I no like do that.	I no like do that. (Hawaii)
Johnny big more than me.	Johnny big more than me. (Jamaica)
Let Daddy get pen write it.	Make Daddy get pen write am. (Guyana)
I more better than Johnny.	I more better than Johnny. (Hawaii)

Source: Bickerton (1983).

is more sophisticated than most people's formal grammar—the latter being the one that they can explain and analyze.

The new theory hypothesizes that creole languages reflect an earlier state in the social evolution of languages, before layers of custom and usage had built up around the biologically given form (Bickerton, 1984). Previously, Chomsky (1965, 1980) had proposed the idea of an inborn grammatical machine in a different form: a universal human grammar might make available a wide range of grammatical models from which the child could pick and choose. Studies of the speed with which children acquire these complex logical systems, at an age when they can't do much else intellectually, tended to confirm the idea of a universal grammar (Lenneberg, 1967). The new idea emphasizes instead that young children begin with a single grammatical model built into the neurology of the brain's language areas. Then they gradually mold it into the shape of a natural language.

The hypothesis is certainly controversial, and it promises to stimulate debate for years to come. One of its values lies in its recognition of the importance of biological mechanisms of language—mechanisms that can be studied by other means.

ANATOMY OF LANGUAGE

The study of the physiological basis of language offers two challenges. The first, and perhaps the more difficult, is to determine what is to be analyzed. What is language behavior, and how much of it is reflected in brain structures? The second challenge is to relate brain structures and mechanisms to the resulting communicative behaviors.

Since language can be studied only in humans, less is known about its anatomy and physiology than is known about other systems. Most of the universal attributes of language do not show up in the currently known anatomy. The Roman physician Galen knew that language was usually represented on the left side of the brain. No one knew much more than that about the neurology and anatomy of language until well into the 19th century.

BROCA'S APHASIA

In 1861 Pierre-Paul Broca described a patient who had great difficulty in producing speech, though the patient's understanding of the spoken word was less affected. Speech is slow and deliberate in victims of **Broca's aphasia** (*a* is Greek for "without," and *phasia* is Greek for "speaking"), as though the patient must think out each word; and grammatical errors are frequent. Verbs and more abstract words are affected more than nouns; in severe cases, the patient is rendered mute. Goodglass (1976, p. 278) gives an example of speech in a Broca's patient who was asked about a dental appointment: "Yes . . . Monday . . . Dad and Dick . . . Wednesday nine o'clock . . . ten o'clock . . . doctors . . . and . . . teeth."

Broca's original patients had suffered strokes involving the middle cerebral artery, which supplies blood to a broad region around the Sylvian fissure (see Figure 3.26). Broca had learned in medical school that language and other uniquely human traits were functions of the frontal lobes. His teachers in turn had derived their doctrine from the phrenologists, who had noted that humans have both a high forehead and linguistic ability. Without further evidence, they assumed that the two were associated. Broca noticed that the only place that his aphasic patients' lesions overlapped the frontal lobe was in the lobe's posterior inferior region (see Figure 12.9). Thus **Broca's area** was born (Pribram, 1971). The designation of the area survived because it made neurological sense as well—lying adjacent to the primary motor cortex that controls the lips and face.

Broadening Broca's Area

Subsequent evidence for the language role of Broca's area came from stimulation studies (Penfield & Roberts, 1959). Textbooks often claim that electrical stimulation of the area can lead to the arrest of ongoing speech. The actual area in which stimulation has this result, however, is much broader than Broca's speech area (see the dots in Figure 12.10). It includes a wide swath on the anterior side of the Sylvian fissure and large parts of the parieto-temporal region (Ojemann, 1983). Sometimes stimulation results in hesitation, slurring, distortion, or repetition of speech (Roberts,

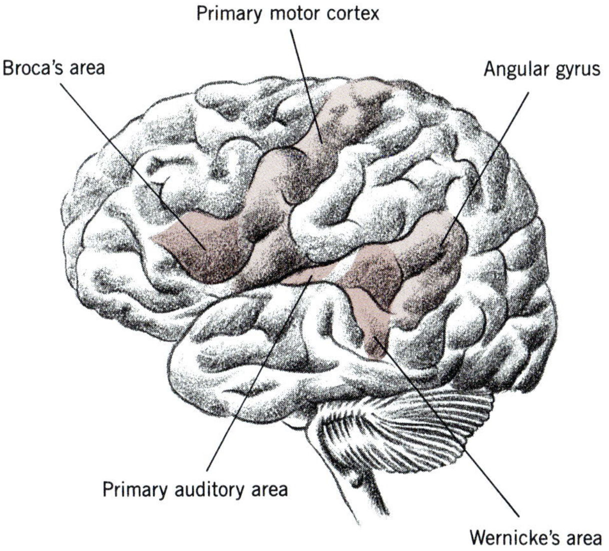

Figure 12.9 Language areas on the left hemisphere of a normal human cerebral cortex. Speech regions surround the primary auditory and motor areas.

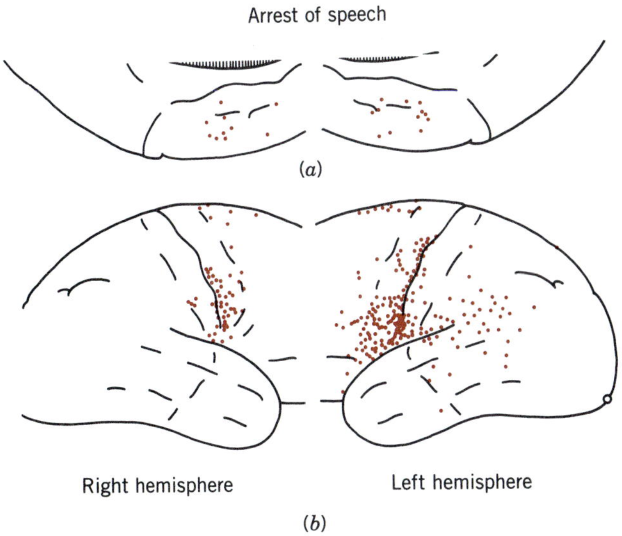

***Figure 12.10** Regions of the cortex where arrest, hesitation, slurring, distortion, or repetition of speech are obtained upon electrical stimulation.* (a) *Medial sides of hemispheres, shown inverted.* (b) *Lateral sides of hemispheres (schematic). Effects are found in the motor cortex extending forward to Broca's area and in the supplementary motor areas on the medial surface of both hemispheres. Adapted from Roberts (1961).*

1961). A good many points in the right hemisphere have the same properties, suggesting that lateralization is not total; both hemispheres participate in language functions. In any case, the classical Broca's area certainly doesn't stand out in Figure 12.10.

The application of the CAT scan to aphasia has made it possible to correlate lesions with symptoms in living patients. Figure 12.11 shows the stroke-induced lesion of a patient whom Kertesz (1982) considers to have a classic Broca's aphasia. A sample of the patient's speech is shown in Table 12.7. The lesion in this patient clearly involves Broca's area in the left hemisphere. But, like the

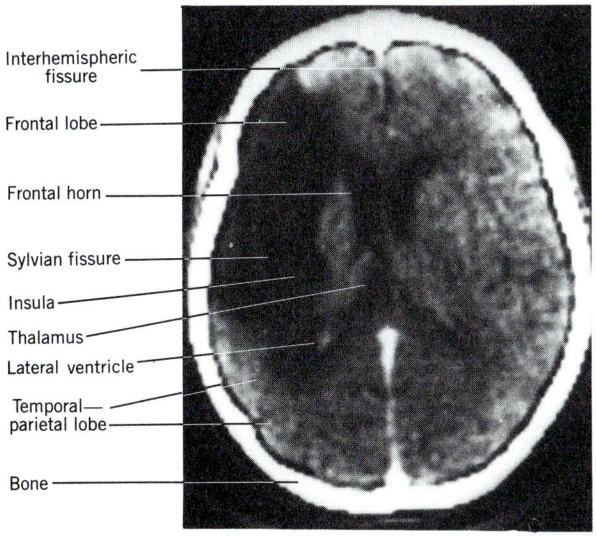

***Figure 12.11** CAT scan of brain of patient with Broca's aphasia. This x-ray technique, described in Chapter 16, permits detailed examination of a single horizontal section through the living brain. The view here is from above. The ventricles are the dark areas visible most clearly on the right side; the lesion is the additional darkening on the anterior and middle left regions. The ventricles are enlarged on the side of the lesion.*

Table 12.7
Speech of Patient with Broca's Aphasia

Mrs. D. N.—transcript of the interview, 4 years poststroke:

E	How are you feeling?
DN	I–I'm fine.
E	Have I ever tested you before?
DN	No–two, three.
E	What is your full name?
DN	Oh dear.–Henry–oh----[correct, but the name for sake of privacy, is omitted].
E	And your full address?
DN	Oh dear. Um. Aah. Oh! No–oh. Oh dear. very–there–were–there ave. [**veri ðeɚwɚðeɚ**] ave–devershеr avenyer [**dɛvɚ ʃɚævɚnjɚ**]. (Correct address. Devonshire.)
E	What kind of work did you do before you became ill?
DN	Oh. I–I–um. Um–oh dear. I–I–dun know. I don't–want–to.
E	Can you tell me what you did for a living? Did you work? Did you have a job?
DN	Oh yes–I–I–um–um. The–the–say [se]—si [**sɪ**] selum [**sɛlʌm**] dum–nogglewife [**nɔgɚlwaɪf**]. Oh dear.
E	Can you tell me why you're in the hospital, or What happened?
DN	Oh–y–yes. M–My h–husband is going to–the–the–the–the–um–um–oh. He was–oh.
E	He had an operation?
DN	Ya–uh–uh. And so
E	You went back to St. Mary's?
DN	Ya. Uh–huh.
E	Look at the picture and tell me what you see going on in the picture.
DN	Oh dear. Um–oh dear. That–oh good–um. Oh, isn't that good i [ɪ] There and there and there and there and there.
E	Ya, can you tell me what they're called?
DN	Waving and uh–the–oh dear–and the kite and boy and– and eeth [**ið**]. uh–barking and a–a lil boy and a bigs [**bɪgs**] thing in uh–in the–Oh dear he's dreeging [**drigɪŋ**] in the uh. Oh dear–I can't say it but he's–ray [**re**]. And a man and–woman–do no–no–uh–uh sawst [**sɔst**] all a people–one–two–three and four and–and oh–the–oh boy–good and–oh waitingull [**wetngʌl**] but no I–oh!

Source: Kertesz (1982).

lesions of other aphasic patients, it includes more posterior areas as well.

There is no evidence that lesions restricted to Broca's area result in permanent language disturbances; rather, lesions producing aphasia seem to be centered along the junction between the parietal and temporal lobes (see Figure 12.12). Lesions reaching anteriorly into Broca's area yield an expressive aphasia; those reaching more posteriorly result in a receptive aphasia, first described by Carl Wernicke in 1886.

WERNICKE'S APHASIA

Patients afflicted with **Wernicke's aphasia** at first seem better off than those with Broca's, for their speech has normal fluency and rhythm. Listening to a receptive aphasic who speaks a language different from your own, you would have difficulty recognizing that anything is wrong. The only problem is that the speech doesn't make sense. Usually, short phrases and segments seem to hang together, especially common ones such as "I don't think so" and "never mind." But in the larger context, the words go nowhere. They have a fascinating similarity to the rhetoric of some politicians.

It is as though the speech of receptive and expressive aphasics breaks down at different levels. The expressive aphasic has difficulty at the level of phoneme and word; the receptive aphasic has a deficit at the **semantic** level—the level of meaning. There is almost always some expressive difficulty, though, suggesting that speech recognition and production are not totally separated (Blumstein, 1981). And all groups of aphasics have some

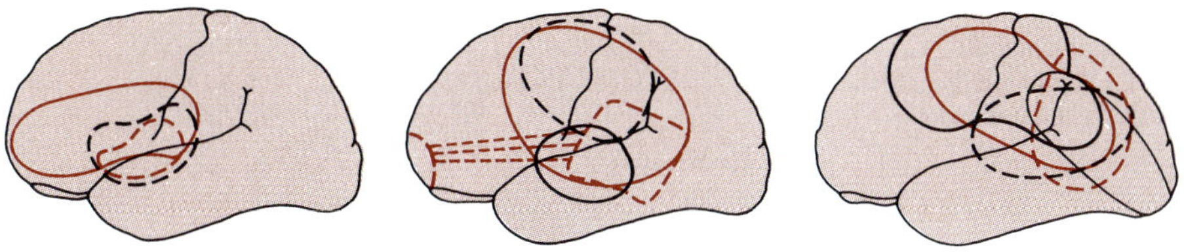

Figure 12.12 *Composite drawings of lesions resulting in marked aphasia, all in the left hemisphere.*

trouble in articulation. The errors usually differ from the correct form by a single distinctive feature.

Table 12.8 offers a sample of the speech of a 74 year old woman with Wernicke's aphasia, and Figure 12.13 shows a CAT scan of her lesion. The region identified by Wernicke as crucial for the understanding and production of meaningful language lies in the superior part of the posterior temporal lobe, adjacent to both the primary and secondary auditory cortex (see Figure 12.9).

The key problem of the receptive aphasic is understanding speech. Patients with expressive aphasia can often follow even elaborate commands if the required responses are nonverbal. Receptive aphasics, in contrast, have difficulty getting the commands straight. The pattern of deficits implies that the transformation from semantic to production levels is handled by the same cortex that transforms speech to semantics in speech understanding. Alternatively, the two transformations may take place in closely intermingled regions.

Specificity of Function

Receptive aphasics display a wide variety of symptoms. Some find it difficult to name objects but have no other language disability; this is often the residual deficit of a stroke victim who has recovered or relearned most functions. Other receptive aphasics have difficulty with sentence structure but can name objects readily. Still others mix up the syllables within words but create grammatically correct sentences and name objects reasonably well (Luria, 1964). Less common syndromes involve such characteristics as loss of the ability to write or to read, without other symptoms. Some patients can read concrete nouns but not more abstract words.

The existence of such specific deficits implies that a great specification of function occurs within the language regions. The organization of these regions may be slightly different in each individual, so similar lesions yield different patterns of symptoms.

In accord with both of these conclusions, stimulation studies have shown an intermingling of language functions. Combining careful psychological procedures with electrical stimulation of the exposed cortex during operations in awake humans, Ojemann and Mateer (1979) found sites connected only with the naming of objects. Other sites yielded repeating or deficits in verbal short-term memory or language production. The regions

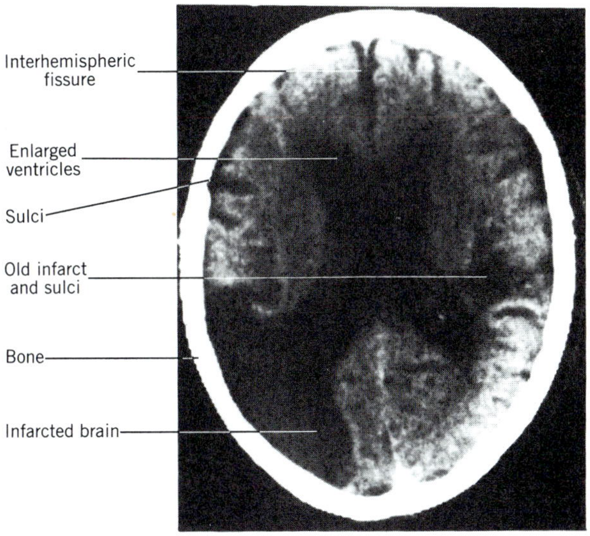

Figure 12.13 *CAT scan of brain of patient with Wernicke's aphasia, view from above. The scan was made 1 year after a stroke. Ventricles are enlarged on the lesioned side, and there is both cortical and subcortical damage.*

Table 12.8
Speech of Patient with Wernicke's Aphasia

Mrs. J. A.—transcript of the first interview, 2 weeks poststroke:

E How are you today, Mrs. A.?

JA Yes.

E Have I ever tested you before?

JA No, I mean I haven't.

E Can you tell me what your name is?

JA No, I don't I–right I'm right now here.

E What is your address?

JA I cud [**kʌd**] if I can help these this like you know–to make it. We are seeing for him. That is my father.

E What kind of work did you do before you came into the hospital?

JA Never, now Mista Oyge [**ɔɪdʒ**] I wanna tell you this happened when happened when he rent. His–his kell [**kɛl**] come down here and is–he got ren [**rɛn**] something. It happened. In these [**ðis**] ropiers [**ropiɚz**] were with him for hi–is friend–like was. And it just happened so I don't know, he did not bring around anything. And he did not pay it. And he roden [**rodɛn**] all o these arranjen [**ɚrendʒən**] from the pedis [**pɛdɪs**] on from iss [**ɪs**] pescid [**pɛskɪd**]. In these floors now and so. He hasn't had em round here.

E Can you tell me a little bit about why you are in the hospital?

JA No, I don't think I have. . . . No, I haven't.

E Can you tell me what you see going on in the picture? [A drawing of children flying a kite]

JA No, I can uh take him.–uh. I haven't read [**rid**] 'em anybody to right in there. That's the little girl here.

E Anything else? What do you see over here?

JA No. [pause] I really had pays [**pez**] too. Inste van gup [**ɪnstɛ væn gʌp**]. Here ee [**i**] little boy being read, too. There he's being there on the ceiling there.

Source: Kertesz (1982).

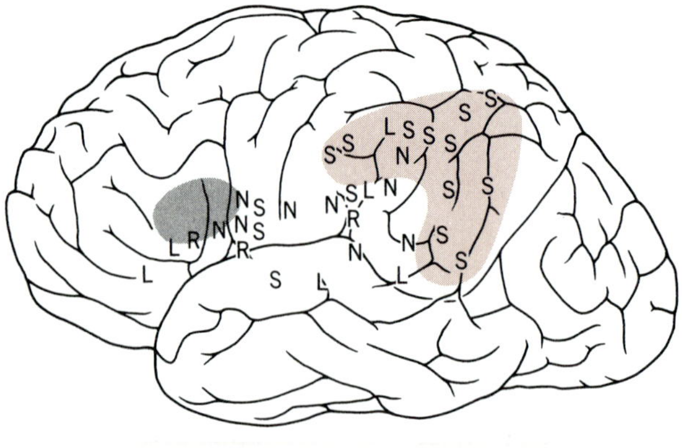

L = Language
N = Naming
R = Repeating movements
S = Short-term memory

Figure 12.14 *Results of electrical stimulation in language areas. Deficits appear at all labeled areas. A short-term memory system (brown region) is located immediately posterior to the regions involved in language production and understanding. The dark gray area shows the final motor path for speech.*

concerned are shown in Figure 12.14. The arrest of speech was accompanied by a temporary facial paralysis.

Observations of bilingual patients reveal a plasticity of language areas (Ojemann, 1983). In one woman, stimulation at some sites interfered only with naming things in English and other sites affected only naming in Greek (the patient's second language).

OTHER APHASIAS

Conduction Aphasia

A rare but distinct type of aphasia has been identified with the severing of corticocortical connections between Wernicke's and Broca's areas, without significant damage to either area. This **conduction aphasia** is an example of one of Geschwind's (1965, 1975) disconnection syndromes. Geschwind proposes that language information passes from Wernicke's area to Broca's area and surrounding regions through the **arcuate fasciculus,** a bundle of corticocortical fibers coursing from the temporal regions to the frontal lobe. As one might predict, patients with conduction aphasia have difficulty repeating words given by an examiner, because verbal information cannot pass through the arcuate fasciculus to the speech production regions. Comprehension is usually good because of an intact Wernicke's area, and commands to perform nonverbal acts can be carried out accurately. Patients are aware of their mistakes and often try to correct them (Blumstein, 1981).

Conduction aphasics show an unexpected ability to identify and repeat numbers; in fact, they visibly relax when a neurological examination moves into number-related tasks. Geschwind proposes that number ability is preserved because of strong, specific visual and somatosensory images connected with numbers, so information can travel indirectly from understanding to production centers. This hypothesis does not explain how equally vivid images of concrete nouns do not save these words from confusion. Perhaps patients can gain access to a different code for written numbers, the nonphonetic code "1, 2, . . ." rather than the phonetic "one, two, . . ." In this way they could escape dependence on phonetically based language centers.

Aphasia and Dyslexia

The invention of a phonetic system of writing was a great advance in civilization because it meant that people no longer had to learn very much in order to be able to write. A spoken vocabulary could be combined with a system for recording speech sounds on paper, phoneme by phoneme, without the need to know a different symbol for each word. Once the phonetic alphabet was learned, writing could rely on the oral speech machinery already developed (except in perverse languages, such as English, that have irregular spellings). In Western languages, only numbers are represented nonphonetically. Thus both reading and writing, even when they occur without an auditory context, remain closely tied to the auditory mode of language organization. As a result Wernicke's aphasia is often accompanied by **dyslexia** (*dys* is Greek for "difficult," and *lex* is Greek for "read").

Evidence confirming this interpretation comes from cultures in which writing is pictographic rather than phonetic. Unlike Westerners, the Chinese must learn to write each word separately. They spend 10 hours a day, 6 days a week in school for many years doing it. All this effort does provide an advantage, however, for Chinese patients with receptive aphasia retain the ability to write accurately (Luria, 1970b). The oral and the written lexicon appear to be stored separately in the brain and to be organized differently.

Japanese aphasics are a particularly useful source of information on the differences between phonetic and pictographic coding, for the Japanese write with four separate systems—three phonetic and one pictographic. Each Japanese student learns the Roman phonetic alphabet, two Japanese phonetic systems called *kana,* and enough Chineselike *kanji* symbols to represent a few thousand common words. The Chinese symbols act as a kind of shorthand in Japanese writing and are intermingled with the phonetic scripts in normal written discourse. Thus each Japanese aphasic can act as her or his own control, with both phonetic and pictographic organizations present in the same brain. Japanese studies of aphasic patients (Sasanuma, 1975) confirm that left temporal lobe lesions interfere with *kana* writing. Other lesions, presumably in the intrinsic visual cortex, interfere with the ability to produce *kanji* symbols.

The difference in coding for phonetic and pictographic information has been applied to children who have dyslexia without any obvious brain damage. Dyslexic children who had severe reading disabilities but were not retarded were taught to associate English words with Chinese characters (Rozin, Poritsky & Sotski, 1971). They learned quickly, acquiring about 30 characters and the ability to combine them into sentences with 2.5 to 5.5 hr of individual tutoring. As a control, the experimenters tutored the children in reading alphabetic words; predictably, they had no success. Thus the dyslexia was not due to poor teaching or lack of attention. In their final examination these children were able to read the sentences shown in Figure 12.15, despite their previous failures with phonetic material. If these children had been Chinese, it is likely that their deficits would never have been discovered. This work has not been replicated, and it remains controversial; but it points out the contrast between phonetic and symbolic coding systems.

Another group of patients who do not suffer dyslexia with receptive aphasia is the deaf. Deaf readers must learn to read without phonics, of course. As a result, they must code written words much like Chinese characters. They never learn to read as well as average hearing readers. The words

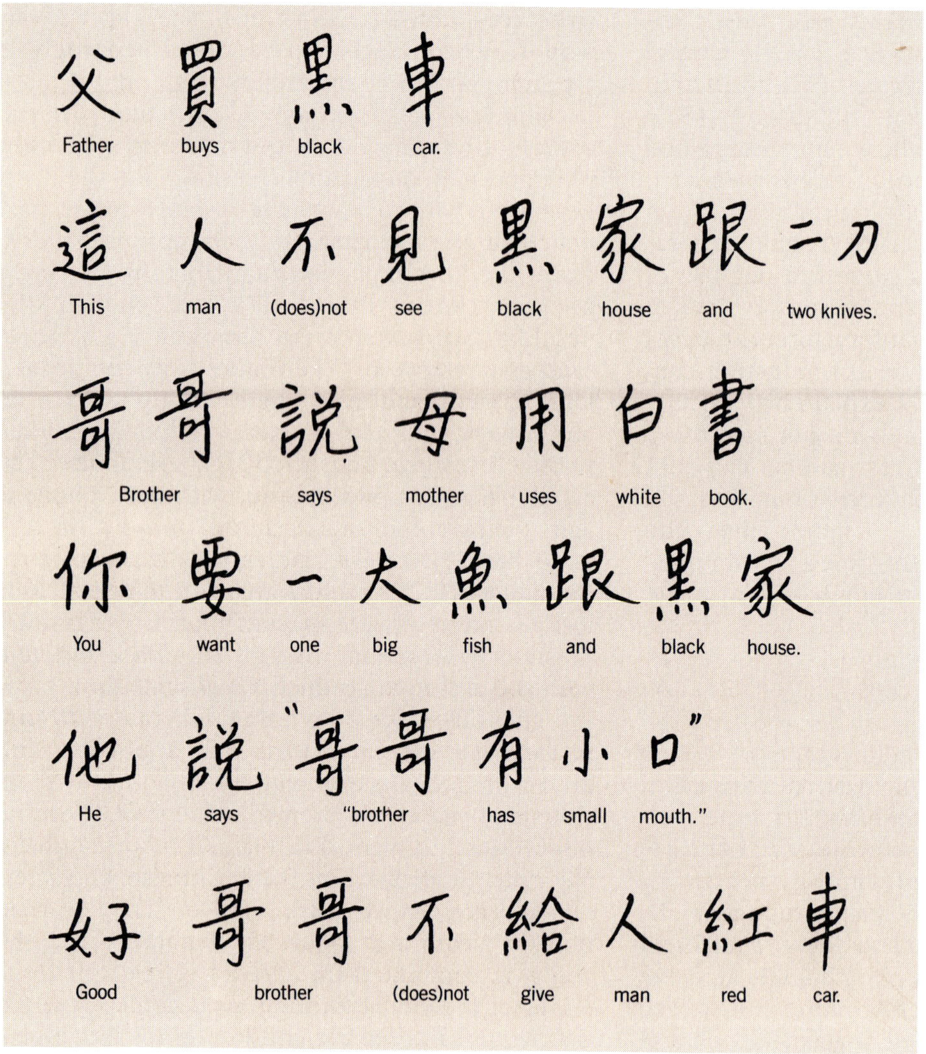

Figure 12.15 *The final examination for dyslexics who had been taught to read a few Chinese characters. Subjects were shown only the Chinese characters and were asked to give the English translations orally. From Rozin, Poritsky & Satski (1971).*

are elements unto themselves—unified symbols for their referents rather than phonetic reminders.

LATERALITY AND LANGUAGE

An epileptic patient, a candidate for temporal lobe surgery, sits in a neurologist's office. He is asked to raise both hands and to begin talking while the neurologist injects a solution into an artery in the neck. Suddenly the right arm drops while the left stays in the air. Speech is slurred for a second or two, then stops, as the patient looks about the room with a puzzled air.

The patient has just undergone the **Wada test** (Wada & Rasmussen, 1960), a vivid demonstration of the laterality of language processing in the human cortex. The injection was into the left carotid artery, and the fluid contained sodium amytal, a short-acting barbiturate anesthetic. Most of the anesthetic remained on the left side as it passed into the brain and briefly anesthetized the speech areas on the left side. The arms were raised as a control, to assure that the anesthetic had an effect in the event that the injection did not interrupt speech. The arm fell because of interference with the left motor cortex. Since the patient's epilepsy was centered on the right side, the surgeon could proceed with the knowledge that vital language areas would not be lesioned by mistake.

Broca, Wernicke, and their contemporaries understood that language areas were usually on the left side of the brain, but they knew little of what happened in the homologous areas of the right. It didn't seem plausible that the right hemisphere would just lie there, absorbing metabolic energy and serving as neurological insurance against brain damage in children. Except for language, though, brain areas and functions seemed symmetrical on the left and right. Sensory and motor systems, for example, were equally represented on the two sides.

Evidence from patients in whom the corpus callosum had been split only added to the mystery. Sectioning this enormous bundle of axons, the largest fiber bundle in the body, seemed to have no effect at all on measures of intelligence, sensory acuity, or other functions. One neurophysiologist wryly suggested that perhaps the corpus callosum served to hold the two halves of the brain together.

In the 1950s Roger Sperry attacked the problem by separating the input to the two isolated hemispheres; he found evidence that the corpus callosum has functions after all. In one series of experiments he surgically severed both it and the optic chiasm of cats along the midline, so that cats became **hemianopic** (*hemi* is Greek for "half," *an* is Greek for "without," and *opic* is Greek for "eye"). Recall that each eye projects its axons only to the ipsilateral hemisphere under these conditions, according to the scheme of Figure 3.7 (Sperry, Stamm & Miner, 1956). The cats could then be taught a visual discrimination, say receiving a reward for pressing a panel marked "*" but not "+," while one eye was covered. The information would be recorded only in the hemisphere on the same side as the exposed eye. The contingencies could be reversed, rewarding "+" but not "*," when the patch was switched to the other eye, so the two hemispheres learned opposite tasks.

The information remained isolated in the two sides. Split-chiasm cats would happily perform one task with one eye exposed and the opposite task with the other eye exposed, without interference. From experiments like these, the "two minds in one head" idea was born.

Language in Split-Brain Patients. The experiments progressed further when Sperry began collaborating with Joseph Bogen, a neurosurgeon who had proposed that some cases of epilepsy could be alleviated by severing the corpus callosum. Many epileptic seizures progress from an epileptic focus on one side of the brain through the callosum to a mirror focus on the other side. The positive feedback from one side to the other might be eliminated by a split-brain operation. The technique would be attempted only on severely ill patients, those for whom drugs and less drastic treatments were inadequate.

The application of the split-stimulation tests to the split-brain patients resulted in findings that eventually won Sperry a Nobel prize. First he confirmed that the left hemisphere controlled language, for objects seen only by the right hemisphere could not be described in speech. The relationship was weakened or reversed for about half of the left-handers. The "silent" right hemisphere could match objects, but speech came from the left hemisphere, which often made up stories about the behavior being controlled by the right. A picture of a spoon could be projected to the right visual cortex, for example, and the subject could find a spoon from among a group of objects hidden behind a baffle (see Figure 12.16) even though the object could not be named. The subject would succeed, however, only if the left hand (controlled by the right hemisphere) did the tactile searching. If the picture of a spoon appeared in the right visual field (projecting to the left hemisphere) and the word *fork* appeared in the left field, the subject would say he or she was searching for a spoon but would produce a fork. In these experiments, input was restricted to one hemisphere by exposing only one side of the visual fields (see Figure 3.7), since the optic chiasm was not split.

The early studies showed all language func-

Figure 12.16 *Experimental arrangement for testing split-chiasm humans. Visual stimuli are presented tachistoscopically (in brief flashes) to one or the other half field to lateralize the input. The subject is instructed to fixate the point in the center of the screen. In animal experiments the crossed part of the chiasm is split along with the corpus callosum, so only the ipsilateral paths remain. Inputs are lateralized regardless of the animal's gaze position.*

tions, including both speech and reading, to be firmly entrenched in the left hemisphere. Split-brain patients quickly learned to hold a book in the right hand, for the nonreading right hemisphere (controlling the left hand) would put the book down if there were no interesting pictures to look at. A few years after the first split-brain operations, the Sperry group's conception of language processing was shaken when two of the patients began to develop right-hemisphere language. The ability of the right was never as great as the fluent behavior of the left, being limited to a small vocabulary, but even simple grammar could come from the right side. The left hemisphere continued to dominate language when both were free to respond, as in the examples of Figure 12.17.

As the size of the patient population increased, it became clear that the early patients were not representative. A new East Coast group of patients has been added to Sperry's original California group. Little language ability has been found in their right hemispheres. The issue remains controversial, with Sperry's colleague Michael Gazzaniga (1983) maintaining that cases of right-hemisphere language are due to early damage to speech areas in the affected patients. Another colleague, Eran Zaidel (1983), maintains just as stoutly that some right-hemisphere language ability is the rule rather than the exception.

Evolution of Left-Right Differences

In the process of evolution some characteristics of an organism become so central to its organization that they are shared by all members of the species. The genetic code ensures their presence in all individuals through multiple and redundant coding in the organism's genes. These characteristics are called **canalized traits** (Waddington, 1960, 1968); examples for humans are the presence of two arms and legs and a spinal cord. Other traits can be represented by several alternatives, corresponding to several **alleles** (varieties) of the same set of genes. Eye color and hair curliness are examples of noncanalized traits that show variation across individuals. Applying this idea to

Figure 12.17 *Right-hemisphere behavior rationalized by the left hemisphere language centers in a split-callosum patient. The command in the first panel of each row is given in the apparatus shown in Figure 12.16, with the subject fixating on the center of the screen. The left hemisphere is unable to explain the behaviors it controls.*

neuroanatomy, we find that the up-down and the front-back aspects of neurological organization (see Chapter 3) are canalized in humans, but the left-right distinction is not.

Several characteristics of the left-right dichotomy show that it is not canalized. First, it is not present in everyone. In some left-handed people, the left hemisphere specializes in sequential processes such as speech, and the right does simultaneous processing, just as in right-handers. In others, the specialization is reversed. In still others, the specialization is not strongly developed on either side but seems to be shared more equally. There is also a sex difference: males generally have stronger lateralization than females, especially in visuospatial functions (Harris, 1978). Recently, an anatomical correlate of this difference has been found; the splenium—the posterior part of the corpus callosum that carries fibers from the peristriate (nonprimary visual), parietal, and superior temporal areas—is consistently larger in females than in males (deLacoste-Utamsing & Holloway, 1982). The implication is that there is less interhemispheric communication in the more highly lateralized male brain.

Second, the left-right specialization is established very late in maturation. Though there are signs of lateralization even in infancy, hemispheric specialization seems to develop with the appearance of language and is not fully established until about 12 years of age. If the cortex of one hemisphere is damaged before this age, the other can often take over its functions. Thus a young child can recover language following left-hemisphere injury even though recovery would be incomplete in an older person.

Third, the distinctions between the two hemispheres are a matter of degree. Both hemispheres normally participate in language functions, for instance, with the left participating more. This is to be expected because the corpus callosum connects corresponding parts of the two hemispheres. (The anterior commissure, a more ventral tract, connects the temporal lobes.)

Finally, the specialization has evolved very recently. Though there are subtle signs of it in other primates, it is fully developed only in humans, along with the appearance of language.

Two Minds in One Head?

The difference between left and right specialization is a fascinating one and lends itself to generalizations about dominant versus nondominant hemispheres, rational versus intuitive thought, and even yin versus yang. Though such metapohors have generated great interest, we must remember that there is no direct evidence for them. The related idea that there may be two "minds" in one head is a similarly appealing one, but it applies mostly to split-brain patients, not to normal humans.

In the intact human, of course, the corpus callosum immediately makes information from one side available to the other. Information cannot be isolated in a single hemisphere. Indeed, blood flow studies have shown increases in metabolic activity in both hemispheres during linguistic tasks, though the increases are greater in the language hemisphere. There is no question of competition between the hemispheres (any more than there is about competition between, for instance, the parietal lobe and the temporal lobe). Instead, there is cooperation fostered by heavily interconnected parts. The concept of the cortex as a giant mixing machine contradicts the idea of competition in normal brains; the effects seen in split brains are examples of disconnection syndromes. The brain must reorganize itself somewhat to function in the severed state.

The split-brain studies have also shed light on the issue of consciousness, or self-awareness, for the patients feel that they have little control over the activities of the right hemisphere. (Fortunately, this gives them little difficulty except in the experimental situation, where sensory inputs are lateralized.) Consciousness and language seem to have something to do with each other; at least that is what the speaking left hemisphere tells us. But that is a subject for another chapter.

CHAPTER SUMMARY

1. Human language probably began with the appearance of modern humans. The neurological machinery of human language has many parts in common with that of other primates. Monkeys and apes have extensive systems of calls and cries, but their utterances usually reflect the animals' emotional states. They are not combined into a grammar but are coordinated in the limbic system, along with other emotional responses.

2. Chimpanzees and gorillas can be trained to use gestural codes that include grammar and the generation of novel utterances. Though apes in some projects are limited to conditioned responses, others show many characteristics of language. Other animals also have the limited ability to understanding single words of human language.

3. Birdsong constitutes a complex signaling code. In many species, experience and practice are important in developing an adult song. Song-generating areas of the male bird expand each year by adding neurons that last for only a season.

4. Human languages have universal features in their deep structures that help define the design features of the human neurological system involved in producing and understanding language. All languages have a limited set of elementary speech sounds, the phonemes. Grammar combines words into sentences and longer utterances. The formal grammars of linguists are incomplete models of the internal grammars that set the rules for constructing utterances.

5. Parts of the human speech apparatus are unique; the evidence is that we are the only speaking animals. Much of the perceptual apparatus, though, is the same as that used for perceiving nonlinguistic stimuli. Categorical perception at phoneme boundaries follows rules similar to those of perception in other contexts.

6. Gestures and emotional utterances precede the first word at about 1 year of age. The rewards for early attempts at speech are negligible, suggesting that intrinsic motivation propels the child's first efforts. Single-word utterances give way to a 2 word slot grammar unlike adult grammar but common to children in all language groups. As children gradually acquire adult grammar, they make mistakes that reveal efforts to internalize grammatical rules.

7. In some colonial environments, children were given a lexicon but no consistent grammatical models. These children developed creole languages that have similar grammars no matter what the parent languages. Young children in every language context spontaneously produce creolelike grammatical constructions. The creole grammars give an insight into the neurologically built-in grammatical system and suggest that natural languages modify the creole grammar rather than selecting from many grammatical possibilities.

8. Broca's aphasia affects primarily speech production and is based on lesions in the parieto-temporal area that extend frontally. Similar lesions with a more posterior extent result in Wernicke's aphasia, a deficit in understanding speech and producing meaningful utterances. Conduction aphasia results from severing the arcuate fasciculus linking the anterior and posterior language areas. It appears especially in such tasks as repeating what another person has said, though comprehension is good. A related deficit in readers of a phonetic script is dyslexia, which often appears with Wernicke's aphasia. Readers of nonphonetic scripts are handicapped by lesions in different brain areas.

9. The Wada test—injecting an anesthetic into one side of the brain—measures the laterality of language. Language areas are concentrated on the left side in most right-handers. The right side specializes in spatial tasks. Split-brain patients show an isolation of language understanding on one side. The issue of whether language is completely lateralized remains controversial.

KEY TERMS

Slot grammar
Syrinx
Phonemes
Grammar
Surface structures
Deep structures
Dichotic listening
Holophrase
Lexicon
Broca's aphasia
Broca's area
Wernicke's aphasia
Semantic level
Conduction aphasia
Arcuate fasciculus
Dyslexia
Wada test
Hemianopic
Canalized traits
Alleles

SUGGESTED READINGS

Arbib, M. A., Caplan, D., & Marshall, J. C. (Eds.). (1982). *Neural models of language processes.* New York: Academic Press.

A number of leading authors review their work on language. The book contains many valuable illustrations of brain lesions in language-impaired patients, along with their cognitive deficits.

Bickerton, D. (1983, July). Creole languages. *Scientific American,* 116–122.

A hypothesis that creole languages represent a primitive built-in human grammar is developed on the basis of Hawaiian creole. The fascinating cultural history of creole language development is also reviewed.

Damasio, A. R., & Geschwind, N. (1984). The neural basis of language. *Annual Review of Neuroscience, 7,* 127–148.

This is a thorough summary of recent work on neural mechanisms of language, including studies using electrical stimulation and modern medical imaging techniques.

Chapter 13

BRAIN MODELS AND ARTIFICIAL INTELLIGENCE

Brain models are mathematical descriptions of neurological processes, and **artificial intelligence (AI)** is the performance of intelligent tasks by machines. What is a chapter on these subjects doing in a book about biological mechanisms of behavior? The question was answered for me at a conference intended to bring together psychologists and computer scientists. Psychologists at the time were engaged in furious controversies about the possible role of Fourierlike spatial frequency analysis in the visual system (see Chapter 5).

The computer people, in the meantime, were building systems that had to detect a pattern from the world, transform it into a useful form, make a decision about it, and perform a behavior based on that decision. A robot, for example, might find a piece of machinery, identify it, and turn it upright. Sometimes a Fourier transform of the input was convenient right at the beginning of processing to make the mathematics more tractable. From the perspective of the computer scientists, the psychologists had barely begun to make a dent in the real stuff of what intelligent behavior involves. The computer scientists had out-psychologized the psychologists.

This episode demonstrates the value of efforts in artificial intelligence and model building to brain researchers: when one must develop a workable system requiring a chain of events from transduction to behavior, one gains an understanding of how information processing occurs in the real world. As noted in Chapter 1, the computer and the brain solve computation problems in fundamentally different ways. Yet, in some cases, the tasks they do can be made similar. Then the process of instructing a machine to do a task can force us to become aware of aspects of the task that we had taken for granted. We must define the problem precisely and expose hidden assumptions and prejudices. Thus AI offers a way of approaching problems of higher-level organization.

An example of the influence of computational thinking in psychology is the role of memory in cognition. Computers have shown us the crucial role of memory in all aspects of information processing. They have also demonstrated the usefulness of having several kinds of specialized memories.

Workers in AI generally do not care whether their machines use the same principles as the brain; they are interested only in getting the job done. Their contribution to physiological psychology is to define problems and suggest possible solutions. Efforts by psychologists to produce mathematical models of brain processes and to test them on computers are more constrained by neurological data but usually do not model every aspect of organization from sensory to motor. A look at the beginnings of these efforts shows that the interchange between modeling and physiology has been productive for a long time.

Figure 13.1 *Mechanical figures, the first automata. Photo by B. Bridgeman.*

HISTORY OF BRAIN MODELS

In the 17th century, Descartes (1665 [1972]) thought of the minds of animals as more sophisticated versions of the mechanical figures that danced in European clock towers at each hour (see Figure 13.1). These figures had behaviors, sometimes quite complex ones, driven by springs or weights and controlled by ingenious mechanical arrangements of levers, cams, and gears. The figures were **automata**—devices that perform a task without human intervention. When the mechanical animation was done well, the figures were compellingly lifelike. But the resemblance was only superficial, for the movements were stereotyped and inflexible. If the bell were removed from a clock tower, for instance, the bell-ringing figure would pull out his hammer anyway and swing mightily at the place the bell had been.

The mechanical figures were missing an essential ingredient of intelligent behavior: they had no senses, no information about the state of the world, no feedback correcting their behaviors. Their control systems were strictly feedforward devices. They performed a programmed sequence of actions regardless of the environment, much like a human sneeze or swallow. An intelligent device must employ feedback, modifying behaviors according to the present situation and adjusting for the effects of previous behaviors in accomplishing a goal.

The next advance started out as a mathematical exercise: what is the minimum level of machine needed to compute any function that is computable? British mathematician Alan Turing (1936) came up with a startling answer. His first big advance was to simplify and define the problem. Pointing out that any sequence of symbols can be represented as a series of dots and blanks on a tape, he reduced the problem to the ability to change any given string of dots and spaces into any other string. The tape was divided into a sequence of discrete locations, each of which could contain only a dot or a blank; no intermediate values were allowed. This is an example of digital coding.

The necessary machine turned out to be very simple; it consisted of a mechanism to read and move the tape and a device for making and erasing marks on it in response to what was written there. Turing proved mathematically that the system could in principle compute any function. (I say "in principle" because some problems required an infinitely long tape or an infinite number of steps. These are minor problems to mathematicians.)

The machine had intelligence of a sort; it could sense its limited tape environment and change its tape-writing behaviors on the basis of what it found on the tapes. From that time on, digital coding was secure as the preferred way to represent information in automata. The device was a computer of a sort, with its stored and modifiable program written on the tape, but no Turing machine was ever built; the whole effort was an intellectual exercise.

After the Turing machine, it was much simpler to evaluate the computational abilities of a new device. One needed only to show that the device could **stimulate** (act like) a Turing machine to prove that it could compute any function. This was to simplify the next step: combining neurology with computational theory.

THE MCCULLOCH-PITTS NEURON

Exploiting the parallel between humans and machines, neurophysiologist Warren McCulloch and mathematician Walter Pitts explored the computational capabilities of neurons as they were then understood. In a pioneering paper, "A Logical Calculus of the Ideas Immanent in Nervous Activity" (1943), the two proved that arrangements of neurons could simulate a Turing machine.

As usual, simplifying assumptions were necessary to make the idea work. In order to analyze nerve networks, McCulloch and Pitts grouped all neural events into discrete time bins. Neurons were conceived of as simple summing junctions; the location of a connection on a neuron didn't matter. Inputs had integer values; they didn't change with frequency of stimulation. If the input to a neuron during a given time bin equaled or exceeded a threshold value, the neuron "fired" and sent excitations to its terminals in the next time bin, as in Figure 13.2. All of these assumptions are contradictory to the properties of neurons reviewed in Chapter 2, but all are simplifications of the physiological conditions. Thus anything that the stripped-down theoretical neurons could do would be no problem for real ones. Using these simplified neurons, McCulloch and Pitts demonstrated a number of networks that had useful properties—for instance, short-term memory.

It didn't take long for a minor academic discipline to arise around the McCulloch-Pitts neuron. Theoreticians designed nerve networks to perform brainlike tasks such as pattern recognition, stimulus generalization, and generation of fixed motor sequences. But the model-making was, in the end,

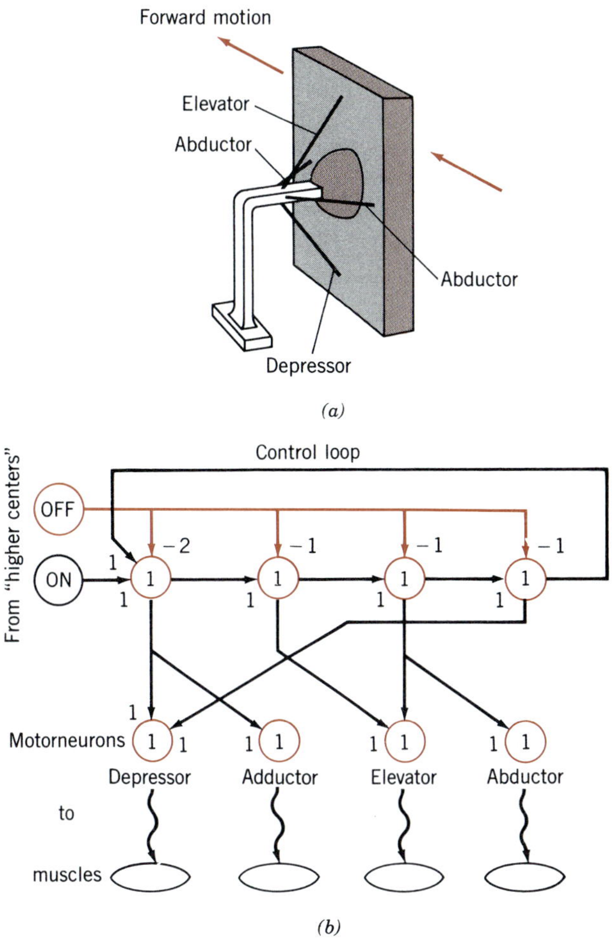

Figure 13.2 *A robot-controlled leg.* (a) *Mechanics of the leg.* (b) *A simple network of McCulloch-Pitts "neurons" to control the leg. They have perfect spatial summation on their dendritic trees, instantaneous integration of inputs, digital thresholds, and fixed axonal conduction delays.*

an empty exercise, for it was already known that any property could be built into a network. If one can build a Turing machine, then one can compute any function that is computable. After that, actually designing a network is little more than a game.

Other problems also appeared in the modeling efforts. The most serious was that many of the models, when scaled up to imitate human capacities, needed unrealistically large numbers of neurons. Even relatively simple simulated functions often required more neurons than the entire brain contains. Most of the networks required more precise connectivity than is commonly found in brains. The models would break down if only a few key connections were out of place. Specifying exactly the connections of a large model sometimes required more information than the genes could provide in assembling a brain (see Chapter 6).

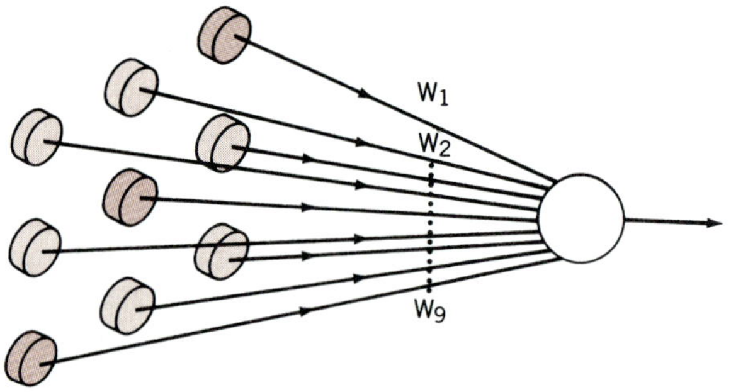

Figure 13.3 *A simple perceptron. The receptors and the output neuron have the same properties as McCulloch-Pitts neurons. "W" stands for weights of connections.*

SELF-ORGANIZING SYSTEMS

The problem of capacity led some researchers to the opposite extreme—exploring the capabilities of self-organizing systems. Beginning with randomly connected networks, they applied fixed rules to modify the connections to more useful patterns.

A class of randomly connected machines was given the optimistic name **perceptrons.** The machines received intensive analysis. A perceptron consists of a single layer of receptors connected to an output neuron by synapses of variable weights (see Figure 13.3). During training, the weights are changed to optimize pattern recognition. Later, more complex multilayer and cross-coupled perceptrons (whose neurons in a layer were connected to one another) were analyzed (Rosenblatt, 1960; Minsky & Pappert, 1976). The perceptrons, though, turned out not to have very interesting properties. A perceptron could be taught to recognize a triangle easily enough, for instance, but it would have to start all over to recognize the same triangle inverted.

None of these attempts at brain modeling made real efforts to analyze the conditions occurring within real brains. The construction of a biological nerve network is not deterministic, but neither is it random. Rather, it seems to be a kind of messy, flexible determinism, governed by organizing principles but not completely specified by them.

From this point, most efforts at modeling biological systems have gone in the direction of the models reviewed in Chapter 11. Researchers now place less emphasis on synapse-by-synapse connections and more emphasis on the logic behind the models—the **algorithms** (mathematically specified strategies) used to perform tasks. One influence of AI on the neurosciences has been the realization of the usefulness of an algorithm level between functions (such as pattern recognition) and mechanisms (such as visual receptive fields). The algorithm level defines how a structure goes about reaching its computational goal.

Another group of researchers have carried this strategy even further. They ignore the brain's way of solving problems altogether and concentrate instead on algorithms that are particularly suited to the most powerful and flexible information-processing machines available: computers. This is the new science of AI.

COMPUTER-BASED INTELLIGENT SYSTEMS

The first challenge in designing an intelligent system was to define intelligence. This has proved a difficult job, and a completely satisfactory definition is still lacking. The definition created by Alfred Binet, the founder of modern intelligence testing (Binet & Simon, 1908), is still quoted by psychologists. For Binet, **intelligence** is the ability to take and maintain a direction without becoming distracted, to adapt means to ends, and to criticize one's own attempts at problem solution. A definition this general does not get us far in defining precisely what an intelligent machine should do (and one of the values of AI has been to point out the vagueness of such definitions).

A useful alternative to a definition—the Turing test—has set a standard for attempts at producing intelligent machines. If you were to administer the **Turing test,** you would work in a room containing nothing but two identical computer terminals. One would be connected to a computer, and the other would be connected to another terminal, operated by a human being (as in Figure 13.4). If you cannot discover which terminal is linked to the computer and which to the human, the machine has passed the test (Turing, 1950). The test does not define what intelligent behavior is, but it provides a framework for thinking about the requirements of machine intelligence.

LANGUAGE TRANSLATION

One of the first problems to attract computer scientists was translating one natural language into another. The problem seemed simple enough; one needed only to store a dictionary of word translations from one language to the other and add a few grammatical rules. The repetitive process of looking up words and translating them one after the other was perfectly suited to the speed and accuracy of the computer.

The results of translation projects ranged from disappointing to disastrous. First, the translation of grammar turned out to be more difficult than had been anticipated. The problem was never solved satisfactorily. Even when grammatical sentences were produced, other, even tougher problems arose. To test the programs, a useful technique is to translate a sentence from English to Russian, for instance, and then translate it back into English again. Even if the retranslation does not emerge word for word as it went in, the general thought should be preserved. In one exercise, the computer was asked to translate "The spirit is willing, but the flesh is weak." The response came back: "The vodka is strong, but the meat is rotten."

This example shows the central problem of translation programs; they can translate words and even transform grammar, but they cannot handle meaning. Speakers of natural languages work in a rich context of meaning, sorting out ambiguous phrases and selecting among alternative meanings of a word. Without this context, the programs cannot translate effectively. Using language requires understanding it.

It became clear that building humanlike understanding into translation programs was beyond the capabilities of programmers. After the failure of translation projects, artificial intelligence retreated to the simpler synthetic world of games.

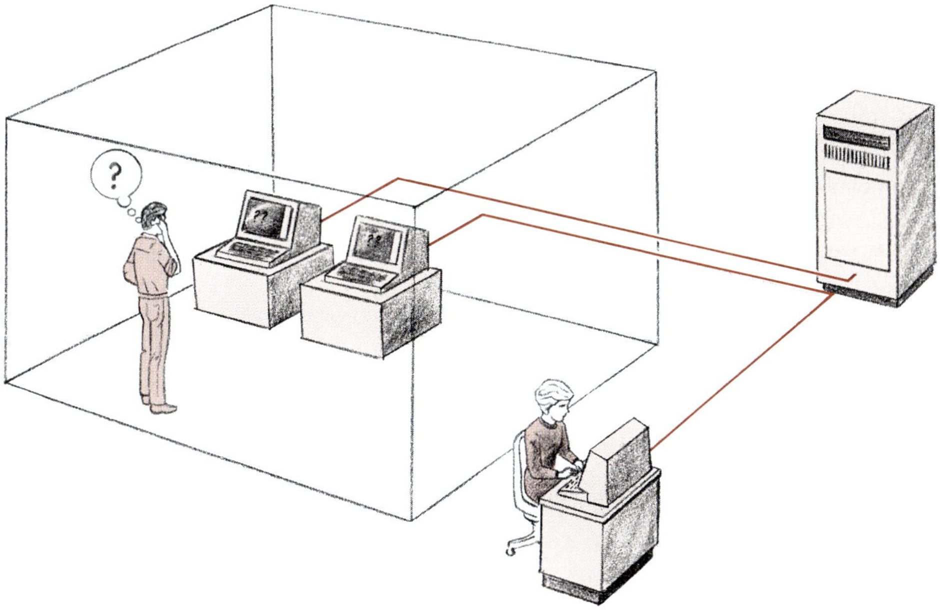

Figure 13.4 Physical layout for the Turing test. The person administering the test does not know which terminal is connected to the human.

GAME PLAYING

It is difficult to design a machine that deals intelligently with the complexities and ambiguities of the real world. Thus efforts at AI in computers (actually in computer programs) began with the simplified environments of games such as checkers and backgammon. Philosophers and psychologists agreed that checkers was certainly a game of the mind and that any program playing a passable game of checkers with a human would have to be considered intelligent.

It wasn't long before such programs were written, but the occasion did not result in a triumph for the advocates of AI. Critics did not examine the results. Instead they concentrated on the algorithms by which the programs defeated their human opponents. The programs were merely lists of rules, applied inflexibly, with no hint of understanding of the game or even of what humans would call a reasonable strategy. There was none of the sense of effortlessness, of instantaneous clarification that comes from human introspection about thinking. The programs proceeded blindly, just as a thermostat adjusts room temperature without having any conception of human comfort.

Since the games could be won with simple algorithms, it became clear that checkers and backgammon were rather stupid games after all. Indeed, the world champion backgammon player is now a program. To demonstrate the real power of reasoning, critics argued, would require a more complex game, such as chess.

Chess Programs

Playing chess requires enormous computational power because of the large number of possible moves to be considered during a game. In midgame an average of 35 moves is possible, and the opponent can respond to each of them with 35 more moves. Thus considering a single move and response exhaustively requires analyzing about 35^2, or 1225, positions. After only 3 moves and responses, there are more than 1.8×10^9 combinations (Waltz, 1982). The alternatives can be viewed as a tree (see Figure 13.5).

Even the fastest computers cannot look very far ahead in a game under these conditions, though they can examine many more moves than a human. Sometimes the speed of the computer can be a disadvantage. One early program, in a game with a human, registered a rather common opening by the human (king's pawn → king 4). The machine raced ahead dozens of moves, considered the alternatives—and promptly resigned.

The fastest computers can examine about 160,000 positions per second. Yet human players, able to examine only a few moves per minute, sometimes come up with combinations that look ahead five or six moves. The human, considering about 100 board positions per move, can sometimes outplay a program that considers 29 million positions. How does the human do it?

One answer is that human chess players don't search trees; instead, they pick a goal, such as capturing a particular piece, and work backward to find ways to reach the goal. Experience will tell human players their opponent's most dangerous moves, so the moves can be countered. Humans bring to the game a knowledge base that they use to reduce the search to the most promising areas. It is extensive use of experience, rather than quick computation, that enables humans to excel at chess.

Computers reach the same goal (finding an effective move) with a very different strategy. Early programs attempted to use rules to prune the search tree, reducing the number of moves to be considered by halting searching in unpromising directions. But the time taken to decide whether a direction was promising was excessive, and the brute-force method of Figure 13.5 turned out to be more successful in practice. Faster programs could be made by considering more positions with simpler rules. Again, once the algorithms were known, the chess programs did not seem "intelligent" after all.

Differences between Human and Machine Chess Players. Why should brains and computers solve chess problems in such different ways, given that both of them are glorified Turing machines? Those who prefer computational theory approaches might answer in terms of the different organizations of the two types of information-processing machines. The human content-addressable memory is a big advantage in looking for solutions to problems that are similar to those encountered before but novel in their details. More knowledge about a particular environment can be added with-

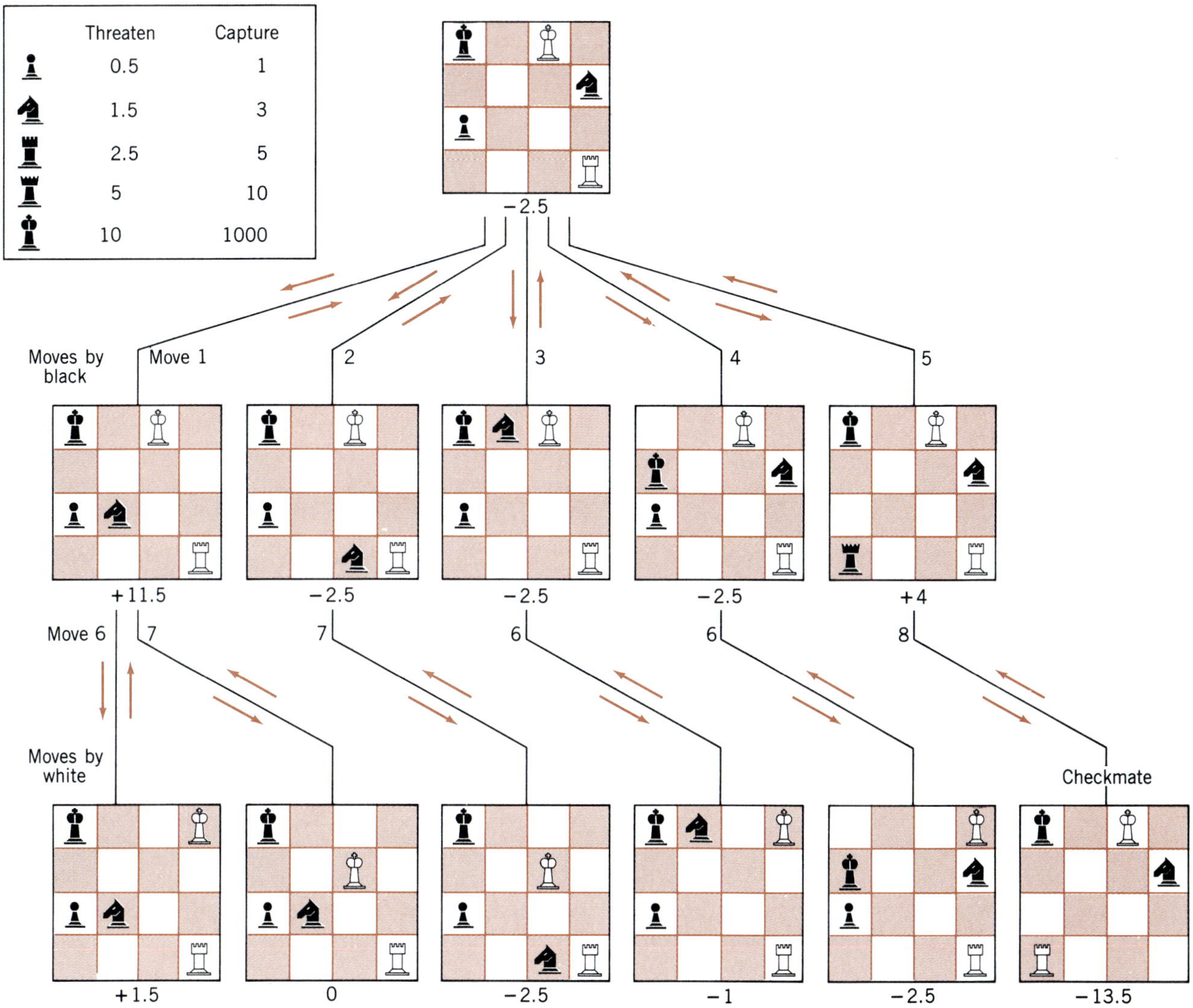

Figure 13.5 *A "tree" of alternative moves on a simplified chessboard. The characteristics of the tree are determined only by the rules of chess. Chess-playing computer programs construct similar trees internally to generate future moves. In this "tree," the computer is playing black. Numbers below each board summarize the program's evaluation of the corresponding position. Adapted from Waltz (1982), Freeman Publishing Co.*

out complicating retrieval, because memories can be retrieved without search (see Chapter 11). A richer knowledge base serves to link concepts into a more tightly interconnected web, both more powerful and more accessible.

Computers, in contrast, must rely on fast implementation of fixed algorithms. A larger memory means a longer search. Information that is similar in meaning but different in surface structure (the sequence of symbols) cannot be brought to bear easily. There have been a few efforts to allow chess programs to learn and improve with practice, but they have been limited to the memorizing of particular combinations or the changing of the numerical values assigned to particular pieces or positions.

Those who prefer evolutionary analyses of brain function might differentiate computer algorithms from human ones on a more fundamental level. Humans seem to revel not in performing computations but in avoiding them, in finding more efficient and effective ways to solve problems. We are always seeking to improve by applying past knowledge to present situations, finding shortcuts and alternative methods. Computers cannot (yet!) cope with such flexibility. Perhaps this is why the best chess players are still human.

Attempts to program AI systems to use knowledge more productively have been restricted to two kinds of programs. One builds detailed knowledge of a simplified world into the programs; the other assembles and formalizes knowledge gleaned from experts in a given specialization. These programs have shown the unexpected importance of an extensive knowledge base for generating intelligent behavior. Intelligence is not just clever manipulation; it also requires a base of facts to manipulate.

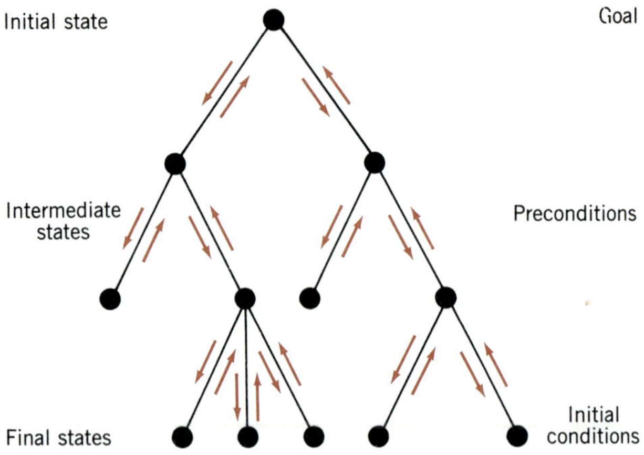

***Figure 13.6** An inverted tree structure for finding the intermediate steps necessary to solve a problem in a blocks world. Control passes from higher nodes to lower ones to generate a plan of sequential actions.*

UNDERSTANDING A BLOCKS WORLD

Educating a human to function intelligently in the real world requires many years of learning about the world through interactive exploration. The education process has been simulated in AI by giving a computer reasonably complete information about a simplified world consisting of a few blocks on a table. A program then uses that information to manipulate the blocks in order to attain predefined goals. The planning of operations from initial state to goal is organized as the search of an inverted tree, with initial conditions on the bottom and the goal on the top (see Figure 13.6). Simple English-language phrases are attached to each operation, resulting in a blocks-world conversation that appears surprisingly intelligent, if a bit single-minded (see Figure 13.7).

Later adventures in the blocks world have resulted in programs that learn to improve their performance in a limited way. A program solves a blocks problem and then stores the solution in memory. The program might then solve a more difficult problem by finding that the stored solution applies to part of the new problem. The experienced program can solve problems faster than the naive one, but it does not solve them any more cleverly.

Probably the most important contribution of the blocks world has been to reveal the importance of a knowledge base, a "common sense," in performing even simple tasks. The knowledge base is the central feature of another class of AI efforts—constructing expert systems to apply the knowledge of human experts.

EXPERT SYSTEMS

Many jobs performed by humans consist of applying knowledge gained by experience or training—knowledge that is common to the people working in a particular job or profession. By codifying the knowledge that has been accumulated in a profession, programmers can automate some aspects of the job. Many of the **expert systems** are surprisingly compact. A program that locates a brain lesion, when given neurological signs from a patient, can run on a microcomputer. The seemingly esoteric neuroanatomical skills learned by medical students turn out to involve straightforward reasoning, once all the facts are assembled. And to aid in assembling the facts, the programs will ask for more information or request specific tests that

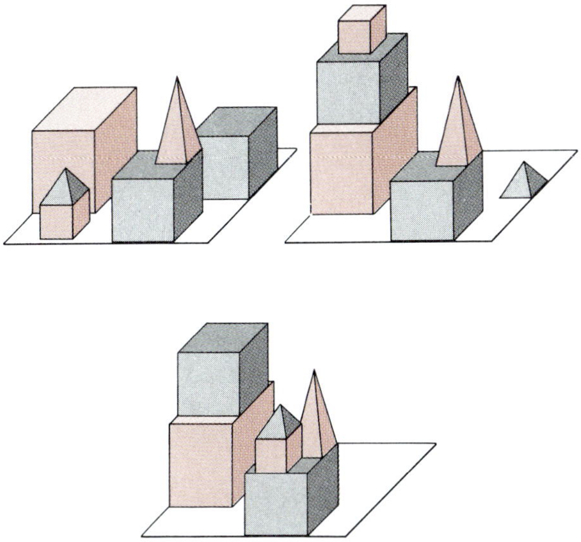

Will you please stack up both of the red blocks and either a grey cube or a pyramid?
OK.
Which cube is sitting on the table?
The large grey one which supports the red pyramid.
Put a small cube onto the grey cube which supports a pyramid.
OK.
Put the littlest pyramid on top of it.
OK.
How many things are on top of grey cubes?
I'm not sure what you mean by "on top of" in the phrase "on top of grey cubes."
Do you mean:
1—Directly on the surface
2—Anywhere on top of?
2
Three of them.
Had you touched any pyramid before you put the grey one on the little cube?
Yes, the grey one.
When did you pick it up?
While I was stacking up the red cube, a large red block and a large grey cube.
Why?
To get rid of it.
Why did you do that?
To clear off the red cube.
Why did you clear off that cube?
To put it on a large grey cube.
Why did you do that?
To stack up the red cube, a large red block and a large grey cube.
Why did you do that?
Because you asked me to.

Figure 13.7 *A conversation generated by the SHRDLU blocks-moving computer program. The program does not attempt to do realistic language processing; the grammar consists of stringing fixed phrases together.*

are necessary to complete a diagnosis. The anatomy of the brain is not built into the programs; instead, they combine discrete neurological clues in predetermined ways. For instance, if such a program is given the symptoms of vomiting and vertigo (difficulty with balance), it will suspect brainstem damage and ask about other symptoms, such as oculomotor abnormalities, to try to determine the extent of the lesion.

A final example shows both the promise and the dangers of the expert systems approach. By about 1970 AI had progressed to the point where a program could respond to simple natural-language commands typed into a console. The programs recognized the parts of speech and stored some simple grammatical forms. Meaning was coded by storing groups of related words together.

To demonstrate these limited language-understanding strategies, both Joseph Weizenbaum (1966) and Ken Colby wrote programs simulating a conversation between a psychiatrist and a patient. (Actually, the programs simulate clinical psychologists, because they can't prescribe drug therapy.) Originally, the automated psychiatrists were written almost as afterthoughts, to explore language-processing strategies.

When the programs are started, the psychiatrist begins the therapy with an innocuous comment such as: "Good morning. What seems to be troubling you?" The "patient" then types in a comment or complaint. The psychiatrist-program, by recognizing key words or phrases in the reply, generates a further comment, leading to the sample conversation that appears in Table 13.1. If the name of an important person such as "mother," "brother," or "god" comes up more than one or two times, for example, the program might generate a phrase such as "You need to think through your relationship with your [mother, brother, god]." If the response of the patient was unintelligible, containing none of the recognized words or phrases, the computer might answer "I see," or "Could you elaborate on that?"

Clearly, such a "conversation" has little to do with the conversations we hold with other humans. The authors of the programs make no pretense that their electronic psychiatrists understand the conversations. Rather, the programs take advantage of superficial aspects of the situation to maintain an illusion of understanding. The popularity of the programs, however, has been enormous from the start. Weizenbaum was surprised to see his colleagues pouring their souls out to the computer. Some people even felt more comfortable confessing their troubles to the computer than to a human psychiatrist. The fact that the

Table 13.1
A Sample Conversation between a Human and the "Psychiatrist" Program ELIZA

Men are all alike.

In what way

They're always bugging us about something or other.

Can you think of a specific example

Well, my boyfriend made me come here.

Your boyfriend made you come here

He says I'm depressed much of the time.

I am sorry to hear that you are depressed

It's true. I am unhappy.

Do you think coming here will help you not to be unhappy

I need some help, that much seems certain.

What would it mean to you if you got some help

Perhaps I could learn to get along with my mother.

Tell me more about your family

My mother takes care of me.

Who else in your family takes care of you

My father.

Your father

You are like my father in some ways.

What resemblance do you see

You are not very aggressive but I think you don't want me to notice that.

What makes you think I am not very aggressive

You don't argue with me.

Why do you think I don't argue with you

You are afraid of me.

Does it please you to think I am afraid of you

My father is afraid of everybody.

What else comes to mind when you think of your father

Bullies.

Does that have anything to do with the fact that your boyfriend made you come here

Source: Adapted from Weizenbaum (1966).

computer didn't really understand the conversation failed to dissuade people from valuing conversations with it.

The success of the psychiatrist programs says something important about either psychiatry or the nature of human intelligence. Critical for our purposes is the human's interpretation of the conversation. Since the human patients read more into the conversation than is actually there, the program is providing a structure for the patient's own thinking rather than doing any thinking on its own. This brings up a crucial issue: can a computer program be made to understand its world in the way a human does? To address this issue, we will have to look more closely at both computers and intelligence.

IS ARTIFICIAL INTELLIGENCE INTELLIGENT?

INTELLIGENCE AND COMMON SENSE

Recently, AI has approached intelligence directly with programs that use a database of "common sense" to simulate the role of experience in understanding. An example is a program that can answer simple questions about particular types of stories (Shank & Abelson, 1977). The program has an interpreter to decode some forms of English sentences, and it stores a script describing the normal sequence of events that occurs when a person eats at a restaurant (enters, sits down, gets menu, and so on). The program then receives a story about an incident at a restaurant. For example: "A man went into a restaurant and ordered a hamburger. The hamburger he received was burnt to a crisp, and the man stormed out of the restaurant angrily, without paying for the hamburger or leaving a tip." If you heard this story and were then asked whether the man ate the hamburger, you would probably answer no, showing your understanding by inferring an event not explicitly mentioned in the story. Similarly, the program can answer questions about implied events, as long as they occur in stories about restaurants. Within this limited domain, it comes close to passing the Turing test.

But does the program understand anything about restaurants? Searle (1980) thinks not and gives the following scenario as proof. Suppose you are locked in a room like the one in Figure 13.8 and you are given a large batch of Chinese script (you don't know any Chinese). Suppose further that you are given a second batch of Chinese script along with a set of rules for relating the first batch to the second. Next you are given a third batch of Chinese script together with some instructions enabling you to correlate elements of the third batch with those of the first two batches. These rules instruct you to give back certain Chinese characters in response to certain sorts of characters given in the third batch.

Unknown to you, the people who are giving you all of these symbols call the first batch a "script," the second a "story," and third "questions." If the people giving you the information are sufficiently clever, and if you follow the rules, a speaker of Chinese might conclude that your locked room contains someone who understands Chinese. Yet you don't understand anything about the stories you are processing, and you are unlikely to learn anything about them as long as you are locked in your room.

Figure 13.8 *An isolated person receiving questions and stories in Chinese and creating meaningful answers to the questions without understanding anything about the subject matter. Single neurons within brains work in a similar information environment, transforming inputs into outputs without regard to the information content of the problem.*

Clearly, adequate experience could have made it possible for you to understand the stories in the common meaning of the term. If similar scripts, stories, and questions are passed to you in English, you will understand what is going on even if your behaviors in English and Chinese are indistinguishable from outside the room. In English you are an intelligent human; in Chinese you are an AI device. Paradoxically, you can pass the Turing test without knowing anything about the situation.

Can such a person in a room, or an indefinitely large group of people locked in rooms and passing strings of characters to one another, ever understand what is going on and become conscious? The answer seems to be an obvious no until we consider the information environments of single neurons (Bridgeman, 1980a). Locked in their bags of membrane, they receive nothing but chemicals and electrical potentials and generate nothing but other chemicals and potentials. As individuals they know only local events, and are no more conscious than the corresponding electrical circuits (a situation schematized on the front cover). Yet the human brain becomes conscious. Or does it?

INTELLIGENCE AND INTROSPECTION

The example of the human (or the neuron) locked in a room shows that intelligence and consciousness cannot be attributed to too low a level of neurological organization. Rather, both are **emergent phenomena,** appearing as characteristics describing a large organized group of units but not belonging to any one of them. An intelligent machine such as the brain, moreover, has properties that are not duplicated in computer programs. A puzzle developed by Hofstadter (1979) is useful in illustrating one of these properties. To get the point, you must try to solve the puzzle.

The puzzle introduces the idea of **formal systems**—sets of symbols generated and manipulated by explicit rules. Starting with the string of letters

MI, you must try to generate the string MU by applying the following four rules to the string. Two of the rules allow you to lengthen the string:

Rule 1: If you possess a string whose last letter is I, you can add on a U at the end.

Rule 2: If you have M*x*, you can add M*xx* to your collection.
Two examples follow: From MI, you can get MIU (rule 1). From MIU, you can get MIUIU (rule 2). The remaining two rules shorten the string.

Rule 3: If III occurs in one of your strings, you can insert a U in place of the III.

Rule 4: If UU occurs inside one of your strings, you can drop it.
For example: From MIIII, you can get MUI or MIU (rule 3). From MUUII, you can get MII (rule 4).

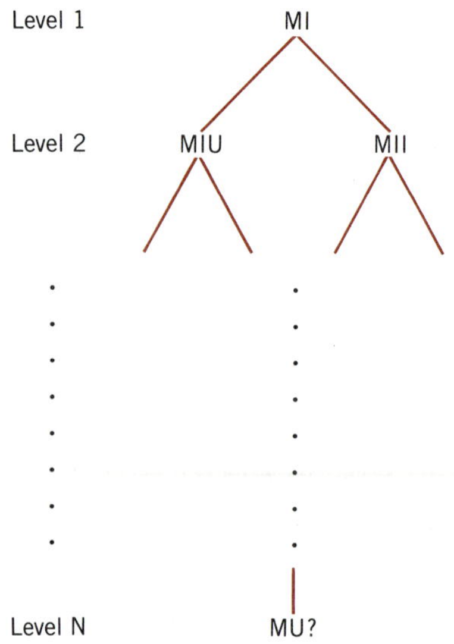

***Figure 13.9** A tree structure for solving the MU puzzle. In a computer solution, all efforts at problem solving must occur within this structure.*

Now go ahead and try to solve the puzzle. Write down in Figure 13.9 the strings you generate with the four rules and new strings generated from the ones you make.

A computer would try to solve this problem by creating a tree structure, first generating two main branches of the MU "trunk," MIU and MII, and going on from there to generate all possible strings of characters. The tree would rapidly become very large. It might be "pruned" according to specific formal rules if it seemed that the strings generated in a particular branch were moving further from the solution than the original string. In principle, however, there is nothing to prevent such a program from working on the problem forever. A human, in contrast, constructs a few strings and sits back to examine the pattern of results. This is where real intelligence comes in, different from the sort shown in AI. The human removes himself from the four rules of the formal system and begins to work outside the system.

The essential and unique characteristics of human intelligence, then, lie not in our ability to manipulate symbols but in our ability to change the rules—to examine systems from different perspectives and to step outside them. This ability is reminiscent of Binet's definition of intelligence near the beginning of this chapter. Our flexibility comes from our history as organisms, evolving to solve problems in the real world by whatever means are necessary. To manage this flexibility we have acquired monitoring systems to guide our behavior and thinking—systems that go by the name "consciousness."

CHAPTER SUMMARY

1. Artificial intelligence can be useful to physiological psychologists in defining problems and in uncovering assumptions and prejudices. The earliest models of living things—mechanical figures—lacked feedback, an essential ingredient of intelligent behavior. More formal approaches to computational theory, beginning with the Turing machine, established that a very simple machine could compute any function that is computable. The machine consisted of a digitally coded tape and a device to move the tape, read it, and write on it.

2. The idea of digital coding was applied to brains by McCulloch and Pitts, whose idealized digital neurons could be put together into nerve networks to perform various neurological functions. Modeling with these neurons showed that mechanistic models of brain processes could be built, but the models often required too many neurons and too precise a connectivity.

3. Subsequent efforts at artificial intelligence have moved away from neurons. They concentrate instead on practical value and on the Turing test, making machine responses indistinguishable from human ones within a restricted domain. Early attempts at translating natural language failed because the programs did not encode the meaning necessary to decide among possible translations.

4. Programs for playing games such as checkers and chess have concentrated on investigating all possible moves and responses rather than on the human strategy of using experience and investigating only a few alternatives. The differences in successful strategies may reflect differences in the structures of human and computer memory.

5. Learning from experience has been demonstrated in a group of programs that function in a highly restricted world of blocks. The programs divide a task into a hierarchy of smaller tasks. A knowledge base has been important in giving these programs a "commonsense" ability to manipulate blocks.

6. A practical application of artificial intelligence has appeared with expert systems—programs that perform parts of the jobs of human specialists. Such programs are already widespread in business. More sophisticated programs performing the jobs of professionals are less developed. Some tasks, such as finding brain lesions from neurological signs, have proved surprisingly straightforward. Simulations of a psychiatrist-patient interaction have shown that simple algorithms can imitate human speech in a restricted world, without the programs understanding the conversation.

7. More direct approaches to understanding have again emphasized a database in a restricted domain. The operations of the programs can be explained in terms of formal logic, without reference to the outside world, so their degree of "understanding" is problematic. Individual neurons in brains suffer from the same restrictions of information input and output, yet the ensemble of neurons becomes conscious. Thus intelligence is an emergent phenomenon, arising out of the organization of a large number of elements.

8. Human intelligence differs from machine intelligence by the human's ability to step outside formal rules, applying previous experience to approach a problem in a novel way.

KEY TERMS

Brain model
Artificial intelligence (AI)
Automata
Simulate
Perceptron
Algorithm
Intelligence
Turing test
Expert system
Emergent phenomena
Formal system

SUGGESTED READINGS

Arbib, M. A. (1972). *The Metaphysical Brain.* New York: Wiley.

This book introduces cybernetics as artificial intelligence and brain theory. It also ties neurophysiology and computer science together, with numerous flowcharts to clarify the logical arguments.

Hofstadter, D. (1979). *Gödel, Escher, Bach: An eternal golden braid.* New York: Basic Books.

Hofstadter introduces the normally dry concept of formal systems with a fascinating mixture of Bach fugues, Gödel's undermining of mathematics, and Escher's mathematics-based art. Anyone at all interested in mathematics, artificial intelligence, or baroque music should read this book.

Waltz, D. L. (1982, October). Artificial intelligence. *Scientific American,* 118–133.

Several computer programs are reviewed in a relatively nontechnical way. Among them are programs for resolving three-dimensional structure in line drawings and others for analyzing concepts.

Chapter 14

CONSCIOUSNESS AND HIGH-LEVEL CONTROL

In the scheme of evolution, every major structure and behavioral trait must have a purpose. Nothing remains for long if it does not confer some advantage to the organism. How, then, did consciousness evolve? What is the source of the irresistible feeling in each of us that there is someone inside us looking out through our eyes and listening through our ears?

We know that a complex system such as consciousness must have evolved over a very long time. So the first question to address must be the adaptive value of the phenomenon. We must consider the puzzle of consciousness like any other neurological system, examining its functions and mechanisms in the context of useful interactions with the environment. We will find that consciousness and other high-level control systems serve to organize long-term sequences of behavior—sequences that require many steps and take advantage of past experience.

FUNCTIONS OF CONSCIOUSNESS

Some activities, such as withdrawing the hand from a hot stove, occur without consciousness. (The consciousness in this case comes after the behavior.) Walking and chewing gum can continue without higher-level control. Other activities require conscious intervention. Here are four types of mental activity that seem to be accompanied by internal experiences: (1) planning, (2) executing plans, (3) directing attention, and (4) retrieving long-term declarative memories. The types of activities, based loosely on the work of Shallice (1972, 1978) and Norman and Shallice (1980), are given more as a way of organizing empirical data than as a complete theory of consciousness.

Planning. Behavioral schemata—plans for executing particular acts—must be set up in advance so actions can proceed toward preexisting goals. These plans must be organized separately from motor activity, to be held until the appropriate time for their execution. The results of actions can then be checked against the goals as the behavior proceeds. This process assures that the behavior will continue to remain appropriate. Hammering a nail, for instance, will be more effective if the carpenter checks after each blow to see whether the nail is flush, using the scheme in Figure 14.1. On a larger scale, an activity such as earning a B.A. degree requires a good deal more planning. One must set up a schema with a hierarchy of subordinate parts. To earn the degree you must complete a major; to do that you must take physiological psychology; to pass physiological psychology you must study this book; to do that you must read the following sentence. In this way the long-term planning function allows you to break large goals into smaller parts. Feedback from the environment guides the execution of each step. An internal record of the entire process, and your current place in it, is necessary to make the system work.

Executing Plans. Because some of the behavioral schemata require a long time for their completion, and because several goals are sometimes being pursued simultaneously, there must be a way of ordering the schemata and evaluating the priority of each schema. The priorities will change with the circumstances. The goal of eating, for instance, is not important just after a meal, but it will consume all of your attention if you haven't eaten for 3 days. Thus priorities can be assigned both for inborn homeostatic motivations such as hunger and thirst and for learned activities such as earning a B.A.

In principle, the process of ordering schemata is no different from the process of ordering behavioral acts, except that the raw materials are the schemata themselves rather than motor patterns. Thus we might expect some of the same neurological machinery to organize both the action schemata and the priorities.

Assigning priorities for action involves suppressing some behavioral schemata in favor of others; earning the B.A. sometimes must yield to more immediate goals, such as eating. Thus the system must store unfinished schemata for reactivation at a later time. Simpler schemata, such as walking and chewing gum, can be executed simultaneously. Others, such as eating and earning a B.A., must be alternated in time, with a priority assigned to each. The regulation of behavior in humans must clearly involve hundreds of schemata. Each schema gains control of the motor system at different times, according to the needs and circumstances of the individual.

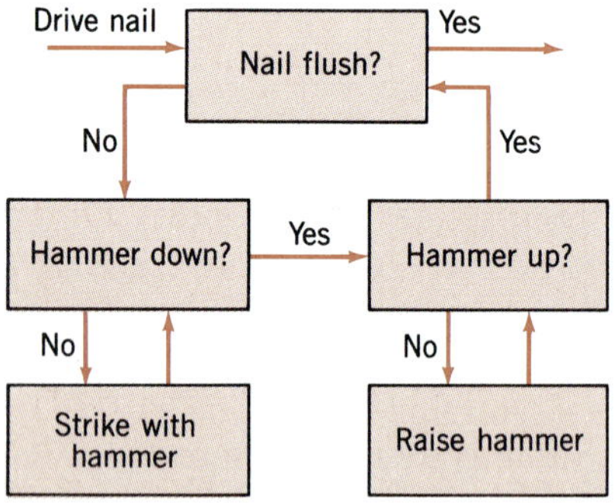

Figure 14.1 Feedback control of nail hammering. Control flows around the loop once for each blow, exiting when the nail is flush. The organization is hierarchical and can be extended to further layers for more complex tasks. Compare to the TOTE organization of Figure 7.15. The scheme requires storage of the question "Is the nail flush?" even when the question is not being asked.

Directing Attention. Behavior is influenced not only by internal schemata but also by events in the sensory world. Sometimes the environment places such a great demand on cognitive resources that attention is diverted automatically, as in the case of William James's man meeting a bear in the forest. When this happens, other active schemata must be suspended as the orienting response (and perhaps resulting actions) dominates behavior.

Since the individual generally does only one thing (or a few simple and compatible things) at a time, the direction of attention must be linked to the system that organizes behavioral priorities. Attention becomes a way of quickly reorganizing priorities according to the needs of the moment. We might call this outside-in attention because the outside world demands the brain's sensory and motor capabilities. Attention can also be controlled by internal schemata—for instance, when one is searching for a particular event in the world (such as one's name in a newspaper). This can be called inside-out attention because the motivation for shifting activities comes from inside (Wundt, 1910). In both cases, it is necessary to control selective attention through the system that determines the behavior currently being elaborated.

Retrieving Long-Term Declarative Memories. The system that performs long-term planning for the individual and sets priorities for action is the only system that can make use of long-term memories for events. The usefulness of memories, after all, is in predicting the future. The individual works on the assumption that the future can be predicted from the past and uses memory to aid in constructing action schemata, to assign priorities to them, and to direct attention. Memories concerning events in the sensory world might be coded and organized in much the same way as memories concerning the stored action programs. They might be retrieved by the same master system.

This completes the enumeration of neurological functions that require a master control process. Norman and Shallice (1980, pp. 21–22) list five characteristics of tasks that appear to require what they call "deliberate attentional resources":

(a) they involve planning or decision-making,
(b) they involve components of trouble shooting,
(c) they are ill-learned or contain novel sequences of actions,
(d) they are judged to be dangerous or technically difficult,
(e) they require overcoming a strong habitual response or resisting temptation.

If these are the functions of conscious control, where does the feeling of consciousness itself—the irresistible introspection that there is an "I" inside the head—come in? Perhaps the "I" is a necessary consequence of a neurological control system capable of performing the functions listed here. It may result from the temporal integration of behaviors and schemata.

Empirical evidence bearing on the concept of consciousness comes from the same sources that have shed light on other neurological functions: anatomical techniques, lesioned animals, neurological patients, and electrical recording.

PLANNING OF BEHAVIOR

Strong correspondences exist between the functions of our hypothesized central organizing system and prefrontal neocortex (Luria, 1966; Norman & Shallice, 1980), though other areas are certainly also involved. The functions of prefrontal cortex are closely tied to the establishment and organization of plans. These are functions (1) and (2) at the opening of the chapter.

The prefrontal neocortex is the only major brain area we have not yet examined, and it is a large one. It occupies 29 percent of the total cortex in humans (see Figure 14.2) and a smaller but still impressive proportion in other mammals: 17 percent in chimpanzees, 11.5 percent in gibbons and macaque monkeys, 7 percent in dogs, and 3.5 percent in cats (Brodmann, 1912). Though there are anatomical differences between the prefrontal regions in humans and in other animals (Passingham, 1973), the removal of those areas has qualitatively similar effects across species. As one would expect, the deficits after removal are generally more severe and persistent in the animals with a larger prefrontal cortex.

ANATOMY OF THE PREFRONTAL CORTEX

The prefrontal cortex is an anterior intrinsic cortex. We can best summarize its role by comparing it with posterior intrinsic cortex, including, for example, inferotemporal (IT) cortex. Posterior intrinsic cortex organizes and elaborates sensory inputs. Prefrontal cortex has the complementary role of organizing outputs—of coordinating sequences of behavior. The word *prefrontal* seems to be a contradiction in terms; it refers to the part of the frontal lobe anterior to the classical motor cortex.

The anatomy of the prefrontal cortex is well suited to its functions. The region is heavily con-

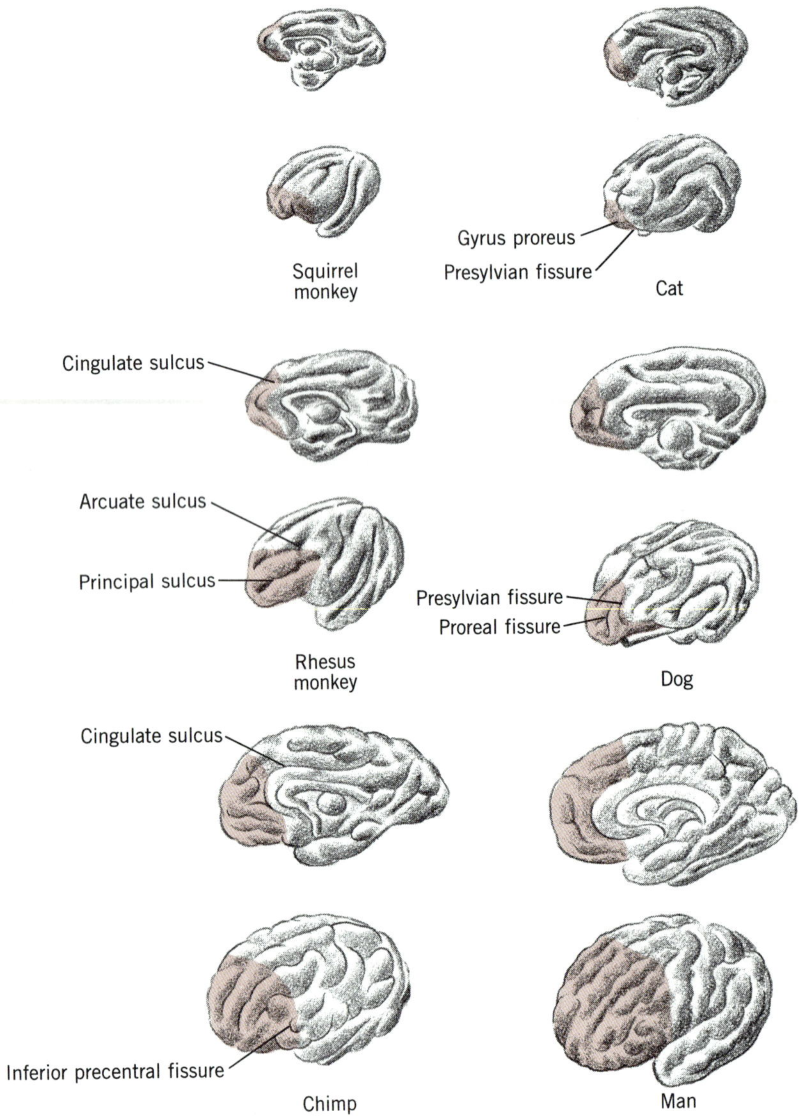

Figure 14.2 *Prefrontal cortex relative to total cortex in various mammalian species. Adapted from Brown (1965).*

nected both to the more posterior sensory-related intrinsic cortex and to several subcortical areas. The subcortical areas include the limbic system, caudate nucleus, and basal ganglia. There are also reciprocal connections between the entire prefrontal cortex and the mediodorsal nucleus of the thalamus. In fact, the thalamic connection (see Figure 14.3) is one of the best defining attributes of the prefrontal cortex. In human evolution, the mediodorsal nucleus has grown in relative size along with the prefrontal cortex.

The prefrontal cortex has three subdivisions: frontal eye fields, lateral frontal cortex, and orbital frontal cortex. Area 8, the *frontal eye fields,* was discussed in Chapter 6. This area is linked to the more posterior visual areas and to the superior colliculus, and it is strongly related to the direction of spatial attention. The **lateral frontal cortex** has several specialized regions of its own. It deals especially with planning and priority-setting functions. The **orbital frontal cortex** has emotional and motivational functions and is linked

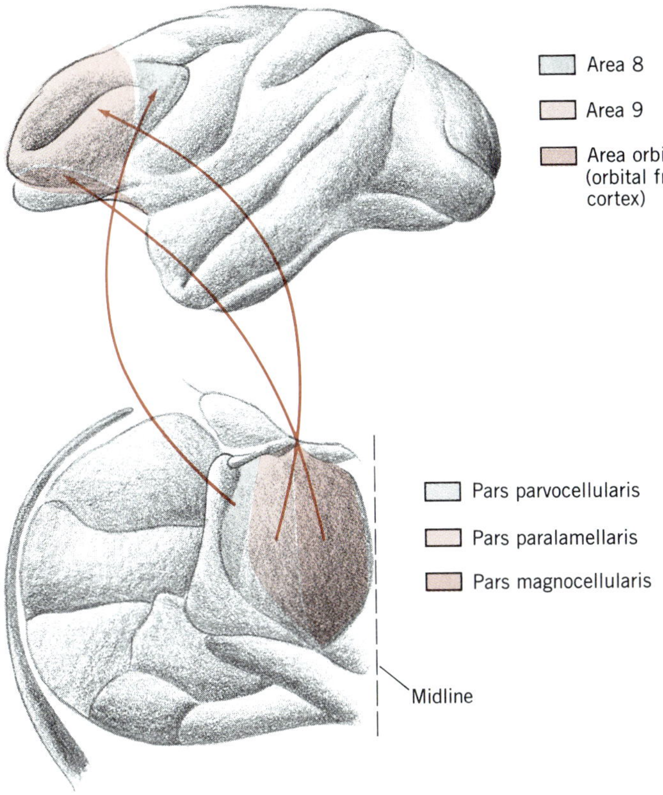

Figure 14.3 Thalamic connections of the prefrontal cortex with the mediodorsal nucleus. The precentral motor cortex, also in the frontal lobe, connects to other thalamic nuclei. Adapted from Akert (1964).

anatomically with the limbic system. It is named after its position; it surrounds the orbits of the eyes on the medial and inferior parts of the frontal lobe. Now we will look at the roles of these areas in the four functions of consciousness.

CREATING PLANS

The first evidence for the role of the prefrontal cortex in long-term regulation of behavior came from clinical observations of lesioned patients. Typically, these patients are "stimulus-bound"; they can deal with whatever happens to be in the environment, but they are also trapped by that environment. A frontally lesioned patient going to get a coat to go outside, for instance, might be found half an hour later reading instead because a magazine happened to be lying in view. When asked about this, the patient will remember that getting the coat was the original goal but typically will be unconcerned that the goal was neglected.

Perhaps the most celebrated early example of frontal damage is the case of Phineas Gage. A construction worker, he sustained damage to his frontal cortex as a result of an accident in a stone quarry. While he was tamping gunpowder with a long iron rod, the powder exploded and the rod shot obliquely through his face from below, exiting at the top of the head. The first miraculous circumstance following the accident was that the victim survived; the second was that his deficit was carefully described (J. Harlow, 1868). Changes in his behavior were so marked that his co-workers commented after the accident that he was "no longer Gage." Previously a conscientious family man, he began to use excessive profanity and to show vacillation, capriciousness, poor planning, and uncontrolled impulsivity. His family left him, and he began drinking.

Although incidents such as this one are informative about the general nature of brain processes in the area affected, they are not precise enough to serve as a basis for theories of function. The closest thing we have to a histological reconstruction of Gage's lesion is shown in Figure 14.4. Better-documented cases come from nonhuman primates and from war injuries. Each war since the Franco-Prussian war of 1870–1871 has yielded a rich source of frontal head traumas.

Primate Studies—Delayed Response

Lesion Studies. Clinical observations were formalized in a series of experiments on primates with lesions of prefrontal cortex. Jacobsen (1936) found that prefrontally lesioned chimpanzees have particular difficulty with tasks requiring a delayed response.

In these tests, shown in Figure 14.5, the animal sits before two food wells. Both are covered so their contents cannot be seen. The experimenter places a reward such as a peanut or a raisin in one of the wells. The lesioned animal has no trouble picking the treat out of the correct well. Now the experimenter baits one of the wells and pulls down a screen between the chimpanzee and the well. The animal must wait until the screen is raised again before it can claim the reward. A normal chimpanzee has no difficulty with such tasks, but the frontally lesioned animal chooses at random.

At first, the animal seems to have a memory deficit, but other tests show that memory is intact. A prefrontally lesioned monkey has no difficulty in performing a discrimination learned before the operation and can even learn new discriminations, though at a slower rate than normal (Harlow & Dagnon, 1943; Harlow & Settlage, 1948). If a monkey is always rewarded with a peanut placed under a cigar box but not under an ashtray, for instance, it soon learns to look under the cigar box. If the stimuli to be discriminated are presented one at a time instead of simultaneously, however, the monkey has serious difficulties (Ettlinger & Wegener, 1958; Iverson, 1967). The problem is not with memory but with the temporal organization of events; the animal cannot assemble events taking place at different times and places into a meaningful whole.

To further investigate this deficit, researchers gave monkeys more than two alternatives to choose from. One object always had a peanut under it; the others were unrewarded. The monkeys were allowed to investigate only one object per trial. Monkeys with temporal lobe lesions had difficulty in searching, requiring many trials before

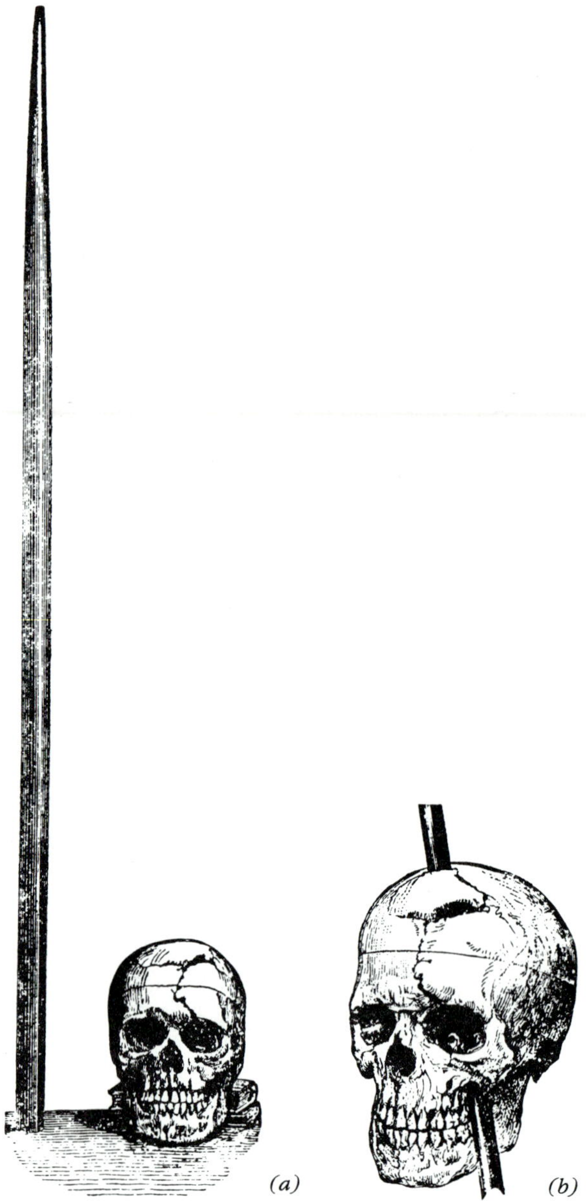

Figure 14.4 *The skull injury of Phineas Gage and the bar that passed through his brain.* (a) *The skull and bar.* (b) *The bar as it passed through the skull. The possibility of additional subcortical damage cannot be excluded.*

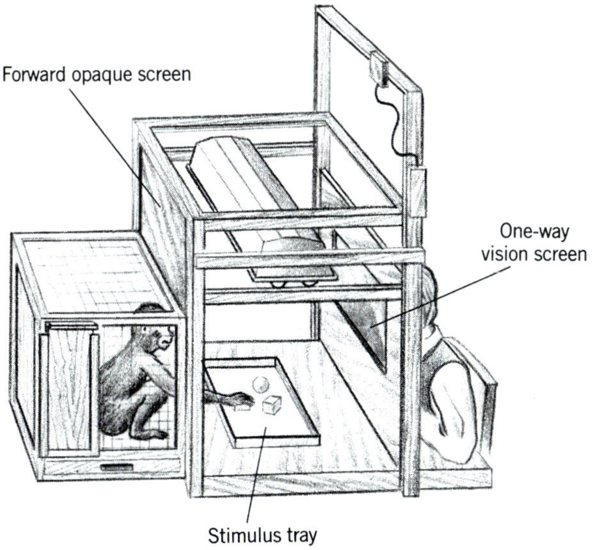

Figure 14.5 *The Wisconsin General Testing Apparatus (WGTA), used in early tests of delayed response in monkeys and chimpanzees. The opaque screen was lowered during the tests. The procedure is now automated and computer-controlled, with the animal pressing panels to respond. Adapted from Pribram (1971).*

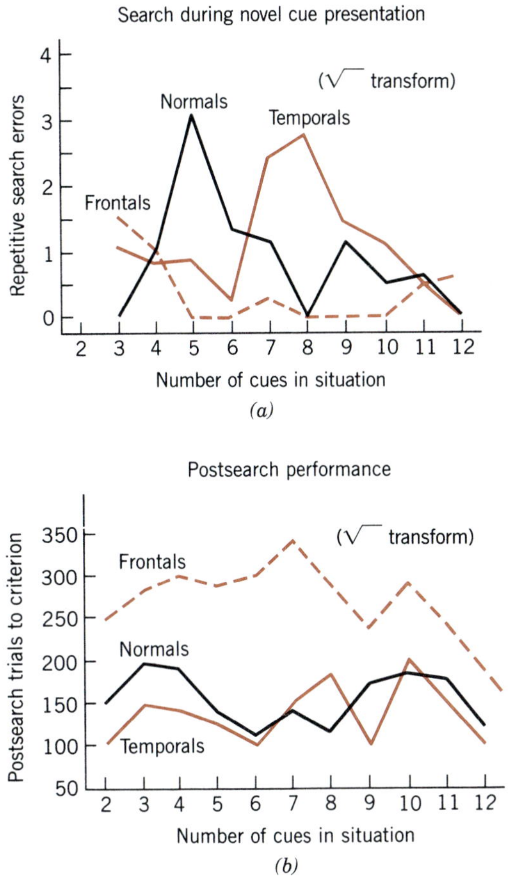

Figure 14.6 *Performance of prefrontally lesioned monkeys, inferotemporally lesioned monkeys, and normal monkeys in tasks involving choices among multiple objects.* (a) *Repetitive errors in search trials—those coming before the first correct response to a novel object. Normal and inferotemporal monkeys show peaks indicating confusion between novel and familiar cues. Prefrontal monkeys are not confused.* (b) *Number of trials to criterion following first correct response. Prefrontal monkeys have difficulty sticking with the correct solution once the cue for it has been discovered; inferotemporal monkeys do as well as normals at this stage. Adapted from Pribram (1971).*

happening upon the rewarded object. Prefrontally lesioned monkeys, in contrast, had no difficulty with the search; instead, they seemed incapable of sticking to the successful choice once it was discovered (Pribram, 1967). Figure 14.6 shows their behavior. The temporal animals behaved like normals once the sensory problem had been solved, but the prefrontal animals continued to make errors. They were capable of receiving and interpreting information coming in through the senses but were unable to make use of that information in a behavioral schema. For a closer look at the function of the prefrontal cortex during delayed-response tasks, we can examine the activity of single neurons.

Single Neurons. Neurons might be active during the cue (stimulus-related coding), the delay (memory), or the response (motor-related activity). Prefrontal neurons show all of these patterns (see Figure 14.7). The majority of them fire during the entire delay interval, as in Figure 14.8, even if the delay lasts 1 min or more (Fuster & Alexander, 1971; Fuster, 1980). Mock trials without a cue stimulus do not cause the sustained discharge; nor do presentations of the cue to a naive animal.

Are the cells preparing the motor system for a forthcoming response, or are they holding a short-term memory? There is evidence that both hypoth-

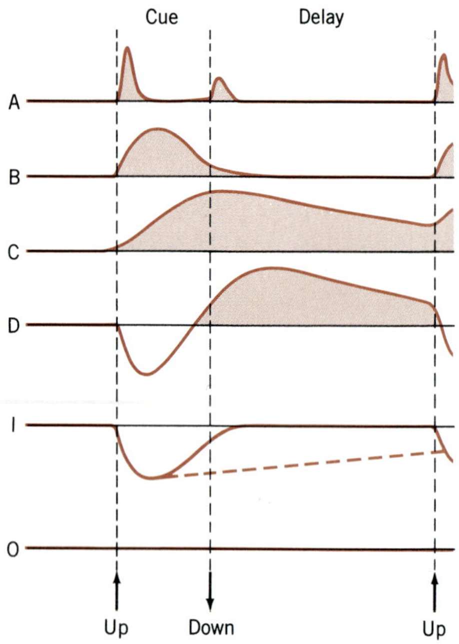

Figure 14.7 *Single-unit firing patterns in monkey prefrontal cortex during delayed-response trial. A screen goes up (first arrow) to reveal a correct test object during a cue period. Then it comes down (second arrow) for a delay period of about 18 sec. Finally, the screen goes up again (third arrow), and the monkey can choose the correct object. Deviations from spontaneous activity are shown by the heavy solid line in each pattern. Adapted from Fuster (1973).*

eses are correct. To decide this question, monkeys were trained on two different tasks. In a spatial delayed-response task, the cue and response were at the same location; in a conditional-position discrimination, a cue in one place required a delayed response in another place. In some neurons, sustained discharge depended on the cue's location; in others, it depended on the location of the motor response (Niki & Watanabe, 1976a, 1976b).

In summary, during the delayed-response task, prefrontal neurons appear to be involved in sensory attention, short-term memory, and motor set (preparation for a motor response). Some neurons participate in more than one of these functions. This is another example of multiplexing in single cells, a principle that we encountered in the discussions of sensory systems in Chapter 5 and memory coding in Chapter 11.

Human Prefrontal Lesions

The ability to organize events into a meaningful whole would seem to be central to the information-processing abilities that support consciousness. This makes it useful to study human patients with prefrontal lesions. Unfortunately, such patients are numerous; many of their lesions were made intentionally, for reasons to be detailed in the next chapter.

Regardless of the source of the prefrontal injury, these patients share a number of symptoms (Fuster, 1980). They have a severe handicap in planning, finding it difficult not only to formulate new plans but also to execute them (Luria, 1966). Carrying out plans requires establishing future goals and then updating and retaining information in order to attain them. This degree of internal organization appears to be impossible for prefrontally lesioned patients.

These patients also perceive the world in an excessively concrete way. Both perception and thinking are constricted in scope and complexity (Goldstein, 1944). The disability is not absolute, however, for the patients can abstract some simple concepts and situations—though they seem to lack the inclination to exert the mental effort needed to carry through their plans. They lose control of their behavior (as in the example of the patient who neglected to retrieve his coat). They live in the here and now, able to perform routine or practiced tasks but unable to handle new challenges from the environment.

The deficit also appears in the production of language; Broca's area, after all, is at the posterior edge of the lateral frontal cortex. Many lateral prefrontal lesions reduce the amount of spontaneous speech, and restrict the amount and range of narrative expression (Luria, 1970b). Sentences are reduced in length and complexity, as would be expected from a deficit in planning and in the ability to establish internal temporal order. The lesions in these cases generally include the cortex just anterior to Broca's area, in the left hemisphere.

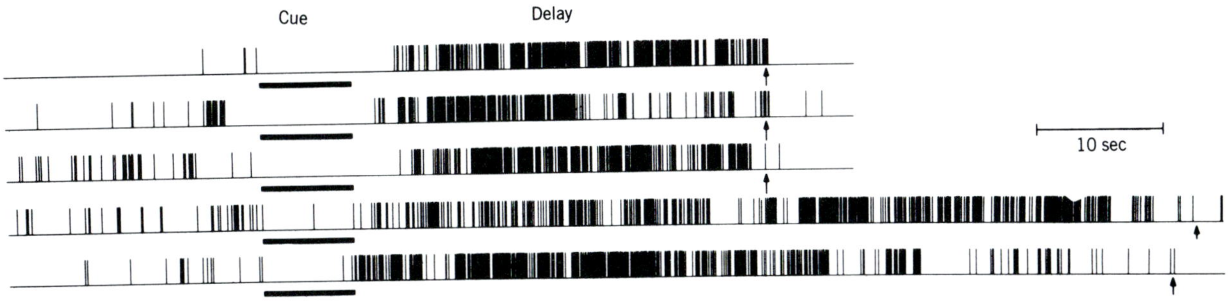

Figure 14.8 *Single-unit activity in prefrontal cortex during five delayed-response trials, in the experimental design shown in Figure 14.7. The arrow marks the end of the delay in each trial. This is a type D unit in the scheme of Figure 14.7.*

ORGANIZING GOALS AND PRIORITIES

In addition to forming behavioral schemata and allowing them to be carried out, the prefrontal cortex organizes the internal world and manages the schemata themselves (function 2 at the chapter opening). This characteristic can be tested with an indirect form of the delayed-reaction task: an animal works to receive a token (such as a poker chip) and later is given an opportunity to use the token to obtain a food reward. The token has no value in itself; it is only a symbol of a future value.

A Token World

Living in a token environment, chimpanzees learn to work for tokens, and eventually the tokens assume a value in themselves. The chimps hoard them and even attempt to steal them from one another (see Figure 14.9). Some have been known to exchange them for sexual favors.

The situation is different when a prefrontally lesioned chimpanzee is introduced to the token world. Though the animal has the physical and sensory abilities needed to earn tokens, it does not work for them (Jacobsen, Wolfe & Jackson, 1935). It fails to make the token a symbol of things of value, to impose an internal organization on intrinsically worthless objects. Thus we can conclude that the prefrontal cortex is necessary to enable the animal to organize the token world in terms of future values.

With humans the situation is more complex. Prefrontally damaged humans can sometimes value tokens, but usually they don't bother. Again, the frontal deficit has its contact with cognitive processes through motivation.

The token as symbol has been carried a step further by Premack and Premack (1972), who trained the chimpanzee Sarah to arrange tokens in strings to construct grammatical sentences. Here meaning is carried not by a single token but by an organized sequence of tokens. By extension, we can think of human words as tokens signifying meanings in the outside world. The tokens have become internal organizations rather than pieces of plastic, but their function is similar.

Delayed Alternation Controversy

Another example of prefrontal cortex imposing order on the world comes from still another variant of the delayed-response task. Here a monkey has two identical panels to press. Normal monkeys can learn an alternation, where first a response on the left panel and then a response on the right panel yields a reward. To the monkey the task looks like this, with a 5-sec delay after each trial:

LRLRLRLRLR . . .

Prefrontally lesioned monkeys, however, fail to learn the task.

At first it was thought that the deficit was in short-term memory, that the animals could not remember what had happened on the previous trial. Pribram and Tubbs (1967) thought otherwise and arranged the alternation a bit differently. Instead of requiring the monkey to respond every 5 sec,

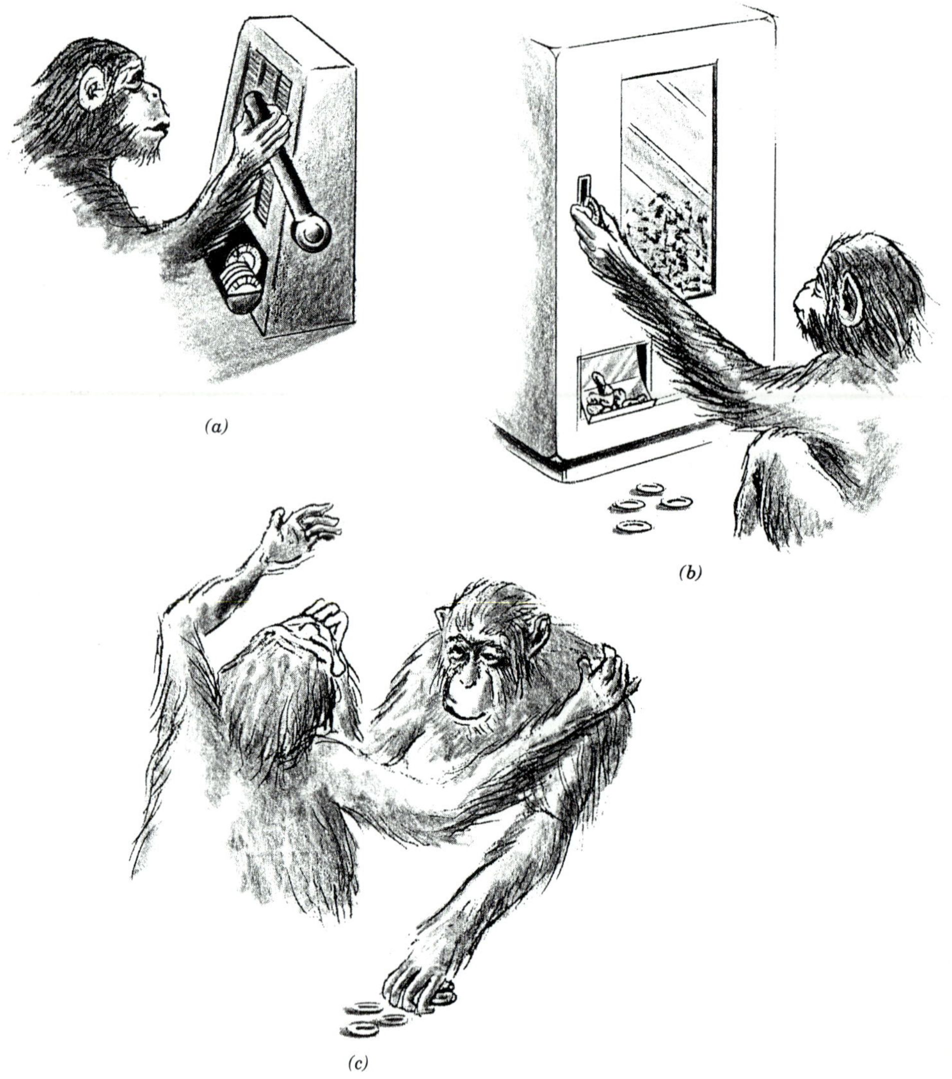

***Figure 14.9** Chimpanzees in a token economy.* (a) *The chimps work to obtain tokens.* (b) *They use the tokens to obtain food in a vending machine.* (c) *Once the tokens acquire a value of their own, the chimps try to steal them from one another. Adapted from Pribram (1971).*

alternating left and right, they lengthened one of the intervals to 15 sec. A monkey's-eye view looks like this:

LR LR LR LR . . .

If memory deficits were responsible for the failure in alternation, this change should make performance even worse, because the average delay is longer than it was before. But the lesioned monkeys were able to do the modified task. The monkeys' problem was not in the delay itself but in ordering the schemata for response. When the order was imposed from the outside, by the use of a different delay interval for each response, the animals could do the task. The differences in timing imposed an external order on the task, compensating for the missing ability to impose an internal order.

This interpretation has been criticized in recent experiments, in which the short-delay-right and long-delay-left trials were not alternated but presented in random order (Rosenkilde, Rosvold & Mishkin, 1981), like this:

R LRRR L LR LR L L LR . . .

Prefrontally lesioned monkeys could perform this task, showing that they had learned not an ordered alternation but simply a time discrimination. A long delay meant "go left;" a short one meant "go right." The Pribram and Tubbs result could be interpreted in the same way. The time discrimination task, though, can be performed without consideration of the context of other trials; each trial presents an independent problem that can be solved in isolation. No ordering of schemata is necessary.

Perhaps the monkeys in the recent experiments were not lesioned properly, so the crucial bit of prefrontal cortex was spared. To test that possibility, Rosenkilde and his colleagues had the same animals do a standard delayed-alternation task; as expected, the animals failed to learn the task.

But the Pribram group did not give up. They tried another variation on the experiment, reasoning that if the animals had learned a temporal discrimination, it should be difficult for them to reverse the discrimination. A reversal changes the structure from

LR LR LR LR

to

RL RL RL RL . . .

To do a reversal, the monkeys would have to unlearn an already mastered temporal discrimination and learn the opposite one. If the animals were using the difference in intertrial delays only to parse or organize the trials, however, a daily reversal should hardly be noticed. This, in fact, is what happened. The animals did not perform quite as well on reversals as on nonreversals, but they still did far better than on trials without parsing (Pribram et al., 1977). According to this interpretation, the lateral frontal lesions should actually aid in the reversal, because the animals do not establish a context that then needs to be reversed.

Perhaps the two sides in this controversy are not as far apart as they seem, for both sets of results can be interpreted in a consistent framework. If temporal discrimination is more difficult to learn than parsed alternation, animals might learn the alternation when the task is structured with alternating L–R pairs. They would learn temporal discrimination only if this structure is not available. Clearly, more study is necessary to determine the precise mechanisms responsible for performance in these tasks.

Specializations of the Prefrontal Cortex

Impairment in delayed-response learning does not require lesions of the entire lateral prefrontal cortex; only the cortex in the **sulcus principalis** (see Figure 14.10) need be lesioned (Gross & Weiskrantz, 1964; Goldman & Rosvold, 1970). After this specialization was discovered, the crucial area was tracked down to a surprisingly small bit of tissue lining the middle third of the sulcus principalis (Butters et al., 1971; Butters, Rosen & Stein, 1973). Monkeys with ablations in the inferior prefrontal region have difficulties with both spatial tasks and nonspatial reversals.

Removal of the **arcuate sulcus** (roughly Brodmann's area 8) does not reliably impair any of the delay tasks (Rosenkilde, Rosvold & Mishkin, 1981). Instead it affects visual search. The orbital cortex, in contrast, seems to mediate not search but choice. Orbitally lesioned animals tend to **perseverate**—to stick with a particular choice long after it is no longer appropriate (Mishkin, 1964). In alternation tasks, for instance, the animal may stick with left choices even though none of them after the first is rewarded. In the next session, it may perseverate on right choices. This behavior is similar to that seen after hippocampal or septal lesions. Indeed, the orbital frontal cortex is closely connected to hippocampus and limbic system. Thus it is possible to subdivide frontal cortex into a number of areas with different functions (as in Figure 14.11), though the principle of mass action still applies in the prefrontal regions (Fuster, 1980).

ATTENTION

Consciousness and attention are closely related. In fact, the word *mind* came into English as a verb relating to attention, as in "Jane, mind the teacher" (Ryle, 1949). Since *attention* can be defined in terms of the activation of schemata performed in function 2 (organizing goals and priorities), we can expect the neurological mechanisms control-

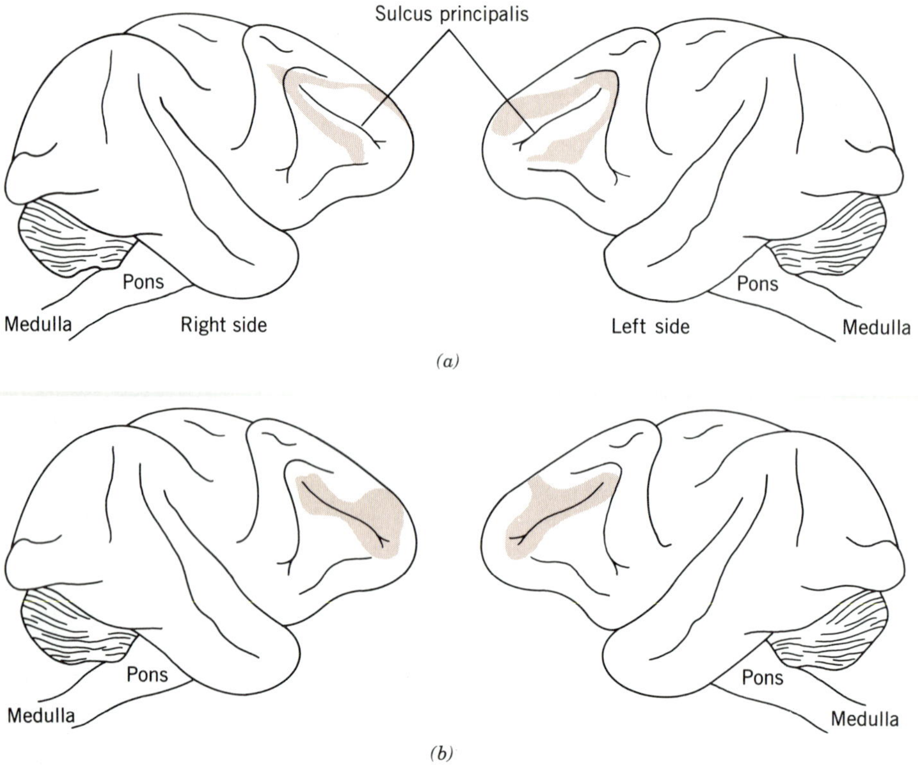

Figure 14.10 Schematic drawings of lesions in two regions of the prefrontal cortex of a rhesus monkey. (a) *Lesions surrounding the sulcus principalis but sparing the sulcus itself. These have no effect on delayed-response learning.* (b) *Lesions of the sulcus principalis that impair delayed-response learning. Adapted from Warren & Akert (1964).*

ling attention to be related to those producing and managing behavioral schemata. The same prefrontal systems that are concerned with schemata might also be involved in attention. Some areas seem particularly closely related to attention-directing functions.

Deficits in the directing of attention are not limited to prefrontally damaged patients. Chapter 10 reviewed the role of the posterior parietal areas in focal attention. In these areas, single neurons respond only when a stimulus is about to trigger a behavioral reaction. Lesions there lead to sensory neglect. And the cases of blindsight in Chapter 6 show a condition in which lesions of the primary visual cortex dissociate the use of visual information from conscious visual experience. Subjects can respond behaviorally without being aware of stimuli in their visual fields. Another important aspect of attentional control, though, centers on the frontal eye fields.

Frontal Eye Fields and Attention

Early studies of the frontal eye fields (area 8) found that unilateral lesions resulted in deviation of the eyes and head toward the side of the lesion. There was also forced circling toward the lesion and neglect of stimuli in the opposite visual field (Kennard, 1939; Latto & Cowey, 1971). More recently, these deficits have been linked to the intentional component of orienting responses (Watson, Miller & Heilman, 1978). Thus a better name for the region would be "frontal attention fields," though we will stick with the traditional name.

Damage to the frontal eye fields does not eliminate saccadic eye movements; rather, the deficit is in the use of eye movements for effective search and exploration—the results of selective attention. Eye movement control is shared between area 8 and the superior colliculus. Ablation of the superior colliculus results in only a transient deficit in

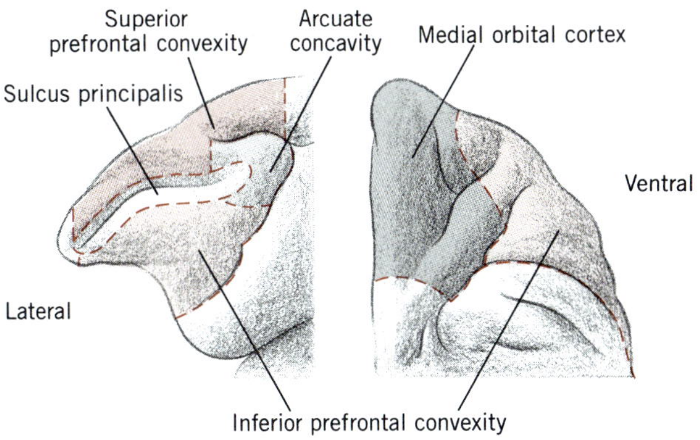

Figure 14.11 *Specialized regions in the prefrontal cortex of a rhesus monkey. Adapted from Rosenkilde (1979).*

eye movements; eventually, the only sign of the lesion is an increased latency of saccade onset. Similarly, area 8 lesions merely reduce the overall frequency of saccadic eye movements (Latto & Cowey, 1971). Apparently, both areas have separate access to brain-stem oculomotor control centers. In addition, the two areas are heavily connected to each other (Lynch & Graybiel, 1983). But lesioning both areas together leads to total and permanent loss of saccadic eye movements (Schiller, True & Conway, 1980). Other eye movements, such as pursuit, are still possible. This result shows that all saccadic control flows through one center or the other.

Despite their parallel access to the oculomotor system, the two areas are not redundant. Collicular neurons respond best to events and are topographically arranged to register their locations; thus they are well equipped to organize responses of orientation. Schlag and Schlag-Rey (1983) speculate, however, that frontal eye field neurons are specialized for orienting that has an internal rather than an external trigger. This kind of orienting requires pattern analysis, recognition of objects, evaluation of their significance, and, finally, target selection.

Area 8 is involved particularly in motor components of visual attention, for lesioning impairs performance of tasks requiring visual search (Latto, 1978). Lesioned cats can no longer visually attend to a region that they know will contain an informative stimulus (Schlag-Rey & Lindsley, 1970). Electrical stimulation of the area yields complementary results, for one obtains more than just eye movements. Many of the reactions resemble fragments of the orienting responses discussed in Chapter 10. Examples are pupil dilation and movements of the head (Wagman & Mehler, 1972).

Single Neurons. In most of area 8 there are two kinds of neurons. One type fires only during voluntary saccades and is unresponsive during involuntary saccades, such as the return phase of optokinetic nystagmus (the tracking movements made automatically when the head is rotating—see Chapter 6). The other type fires continuously during smooth pursuit or during orienting in a given direction (Bizzi, 1968; Bizzi & Schiller, 1970). Other neurons in the banks of the arcuate sulcus begin firing before saccades.

Some area 8 cells have visual receptive fields, usually large movement-sensitive ones (Mohler, Goldberg & Wurtz, 1973; Wurtz & Mohler, 1976a), so we cannot think of the region as purely motor. Rather, it seems to be both sensory and motor at the same time. According to one influential interpretation, it is the place where corollary discharges—the signals generated along with movements to inform the brain of the intended movement—are integrated with perception (Teuber, 1964, 1972). The idea would mean that the frontal eye fields, and perhaps the prefrontal cortex in general, have the function of anticipating events and preparing the animal without interrupting stability and continuity (Fuster, 1980).

Global Electrophysiological Measures of Attention

Signs of an anticipatory role for the prefrontal cortex can also be recorded as potentials from the scalp. Because it is easier to control attention in humans than in other primates, much of the work on the electrophysiology of attention has been done with humans. The limitations of scalp recording are less serious in studies of attention than in studies of such other functions as sensory processing, because attention generally seems to generate widespread and long-lasting changes in cortical potentials. Evoked-potential techniques are ideal for recording these changes.

Vertex Potentials. Attention does not seem to influence the earliest evoked potentials—those arising from peripheral events and from the arrival of sensory signals at the primary sensory cortex. The first potential that is modified by attention is the **vertex potential**—really a series of electrical potentials that are largest over the vertex of the scalp (the top center portion of the head). Figure 14.12 shows an enhancement of the N_1 component of this potential in an auditory attention task. The subject must attend to a tone of a particular frequency. The component is called N_1 because it is the first prominent negative component in the evoked potential. Enhancement occurs between about 80 and 130 msec following the stimulus.

Changes in vertex potentials do not occur in all attention experiments; there are at least two special requirements. First, the attended and the irrelevant stimuli must be distinguished by some simple physical cue, such as the location of a visual stimulus or the pitch of an auditory one. These differences can be interpreted as differences in location on a cortical map of a sensory surface, such as the visual cortex for the retina or the auditory cortex for the cochlea.

Second, the task must be made challenging for the subject. Usually this is done by presenting the stimuli at a rapid pace or by requiring difficult discriminations, such as very small differences in pitch (Hillyard & Picton, 1979). The spatial origin of vertex potentials is controversial; Hillyard and Picton (1979) conclude that they arise from fronto-central intrinsic cortex.

P300 Waves. A second wave influenced by attention is the P3 or P300 wave, which also appears only when particular demands are placed on the subject. The wave is called P3 because it is the third major positive wave and P300 because, coincidentally, it occurs about 300 msec after stimulus onset. It is largest when a relatively infrequent stimulus is presented in a context of more frequent ones. Also, the subject must make some motor or cognitive response to the stimulus. For example, the subject might be asked to press a button after an infrequently presented red flash

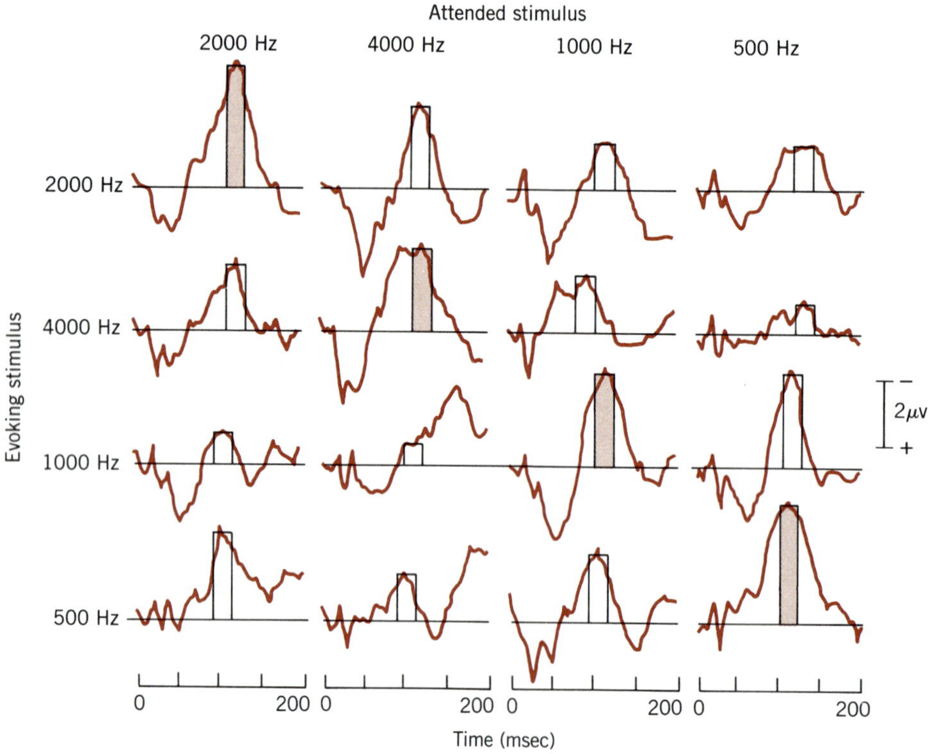

Figure 14.12 *Auditory vertex potentials elicited by a random sequence of tone pips. Each has a different frequency and a different spatial location. In each experimental condition (each column), subjects attended to one of the frequency/location combinations. When the attended frequency was given, the N_1 component was enhanced (shaded bars). Adapted from Hillyard & Picton (1979).*

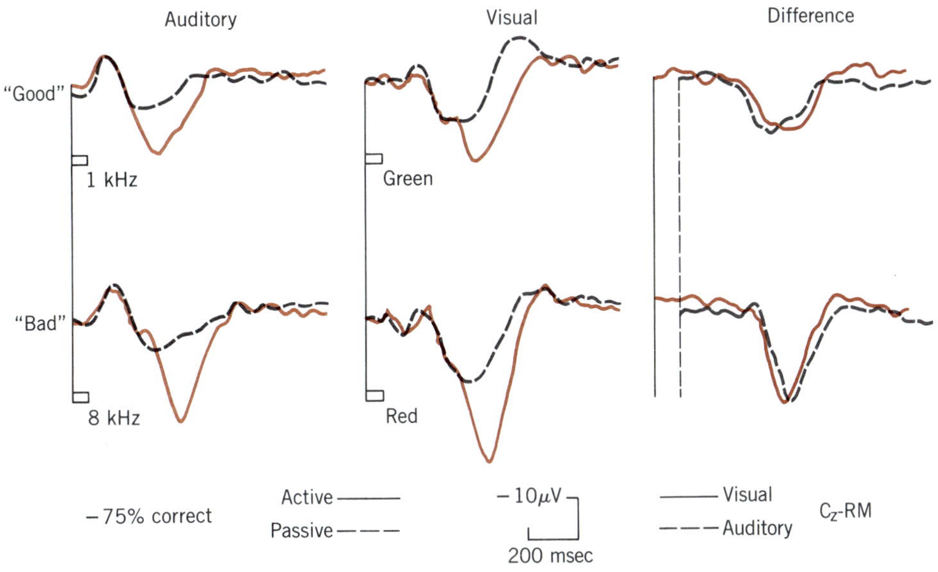

Figure 14.13 *P300 waves elicited by auditory and visual stimuli. In the auditory condition the subject reported the presence or absence of a near-threshold auditory signal and received a 1 kHz tone for a "good" judgment and an 8 kHz tone for a "bad" judgment. In the visual condition the feedback was a faint green light for "good" and a faint red light for "bad." In the passive conditions the subject fixated on the visual feedback area but ignored all stimuli. The right column shows the difference between active and passive conditions for each modality. Visual wave forms are advanced by 80 msec to cancel latency differences between audition and vision. Adapted from Hillyard & Picton (1979).*

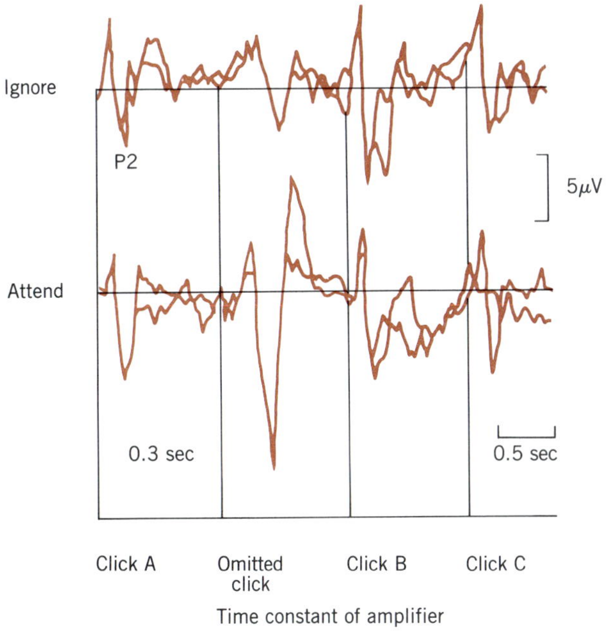

Figure 14.14 *Evoked response to an omitted click in an ongoing series of clicks. In both ignore and attend conditions, two separate averaged traces are superimposed to show the reproducibility of the result. The enhanced P300 appears only when the subject attends to the clicks. Recordings are from vertex to mastoid (near ears), negative up. Adapted from Hillyard & Picton (1979).*

mixed in with many trials of green flashes. To separate the P300 from motor potentials, the subject might have to count the number of red flashes in a block of trials consisting mostly of green flashes.

The P300 is independent of sensory modality. It depends more on meaning (defined from the subject's standpoint) than on the physical characteristics of the stimulus (Ritter & Vaughan, 1969). It is elicited equally well by visual, auditory, and somatic stimuli (Figure 14.13). P300s can even be elicited by a missing stimulus—one that is expected but not present (see Chapter 11), if the other requirements for the wave are met (Picton et al., 1974). The experiment involving an omitted stimulus certainly shows that the P300 is endogenous (see Figure 14.14)! The recent discovery of P300 waves in monkeys (Arthur & Starr, 1984) brings the promise that the neural basis of the waves can be explained.

The P300 wave can be long-lasting relative to earlier stimulus-bound potentials. But it is still restricted in time compared to the third kind of attention-related evoked potential, which can last many seconds.

The CNV. Suppose you are asked to press a button as quickly as possible after a light flashes, and suppose further that a warning tone comes on a few seconds before each flash. Between the warning tone and the flash a surface-negative potential will develop over frontal areas of the cortex, ending abruptly with the motor act. This is the **contingent negative variation (CNV),** a long-lasting steady potential occurring when an event is expected to involve an action or a decision. Because the DC amplifiers necessary to record steady potentials were not practical until recently, it was only in 1964 that the CNV was discovered (Walter, 1964).

The CNV has at least two components. One, developing over the central area just before movement, is the *Bereitschaftspotential* of Chapter 8. It is associated with the motor act itself. The other is slower, also negative, and more frontal in its distribution (Borda, 1970; Järvilehto & Fruhstorfer, 1970). It appears in delayed-response and delayed–matching to sample tasks and does not necessarily require a motor response.

The similarity between tasks evoking a CNV and those classically used to test for the function of the prefrontal cortex did not escape researchers in this area. In fact, CNVs are seen in monkeys over the prefrontal cortex when the monkeys perform a delayed-response task (Stamm & Rosen, 1975).

The CNV may also be related to another of the hypothesized functions of consciousness—the memory function. Of course, a CNV cannot appear in a naive subject, for something must be anticipated for the negativity to appear (see Figure 14.15). A delayed response may be learned more quickly if trials are given only when there are spontaneous surface-negative potentials in the prefrontal region (Sandrew, Stamm & Rosen, 1977). Thus the CNV and spontaneous changes in DC polarity have an effect similar to that of artificial surface-negative polarization of the cortex: both accelerate the learning process. This line of research, then, leads to a picture of continually changing potentials biasing regions of the cortex, sometimes potentiating and sometimes inhibiting ongoing activity. Selective attention would result from particular patterns of DC shifts.

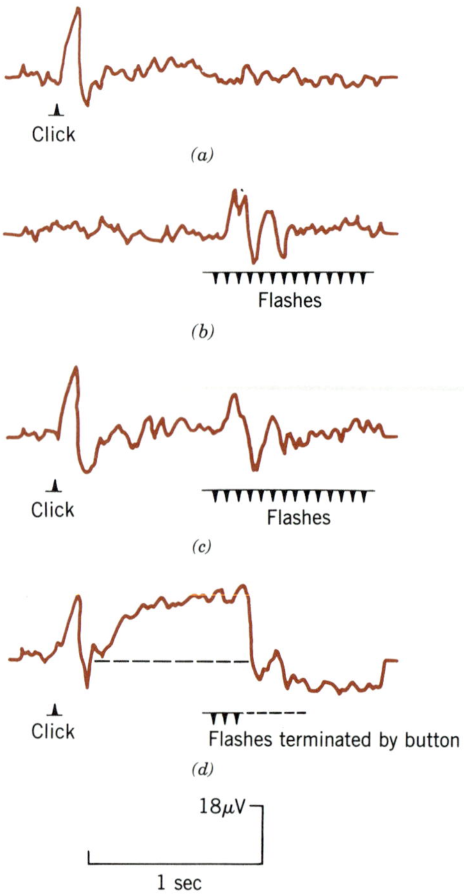

Figure 14.15 *CNV from the frontal region of a human brain.* (a), (b), *and* (c). *Responses to auditory and visual stimuli before conditioning.* (d) *Response of subject instructed to press a button when the flashes begin; the click serves as a warning that the flashes are about to appear. Negative up. Adapted from Walter et al. (1964).*

Electrical Stimulation and Recording

Another way to study the electrophysiology of consciousness is with electrical brain stimulation in conscious humans, to measure the relationship between stimulation and awareness. The relationship has not proved to be a simple one, even in the primary sensory cortex.

Somatosensory Thresholds. We can first ask what sort of stimulus it takes to gain access to conscious processing—to force an alteration in ongoing behavioral schemata. The first researchers to examine this question recorded from the scalp during stimulation of the skin. The threshold for evoked potentials seemed to correspond reasonably well with the threshold for conscious sensation (Shagass & Schwartz, 1961). This was an intuitively satisfactory state of affairs, and the matter was not investigated further for some time.

Then, Libet and his associates (1967) noted that scalp potentials are reduced in amplitude because the recording point is distant from the brain. This is especially true for the earliest components of the evoked response, which are the most localized on the cortical surface. To accurately measure the correspondence between cortical response and conscious sensation, the recordings should be made directly from the cortical surface. Such recordings can be done during brain surgery for other neurological problems. The skin can then be stimulated while evoked responses are measured from the exposed somatosensory cortex.

The minimal electrical stimulus needed for conscious reporting in this case is larger than the stimulus needed to elicit an electrically evoked response to direct cortical stimulation. Figure 14.16 shows a range of stimulation intensity in which the neurons clearly respond but no sensation is reported. We must conclude that at least some of the activity of the sensory cortex is unconscious.

Cortical Stimulation. An even more surprising result came from further experiments in direct electrical stimulation of somatosensory cortex. A single electrical pulse to the cortex could not be perceived at any reasonable current strength, although a train of pulses was perceived. The train had to be quite long, 0.5 to 0.6 sec in most subjects, before the subjects reported the stimulation (see Figure 14.17). At the same time, cortical electrical responses were recorded from a nearby electrode. The figure shows that each pulse of the train was adequate to evoke firing in nearby neurons (Libet, 1973).

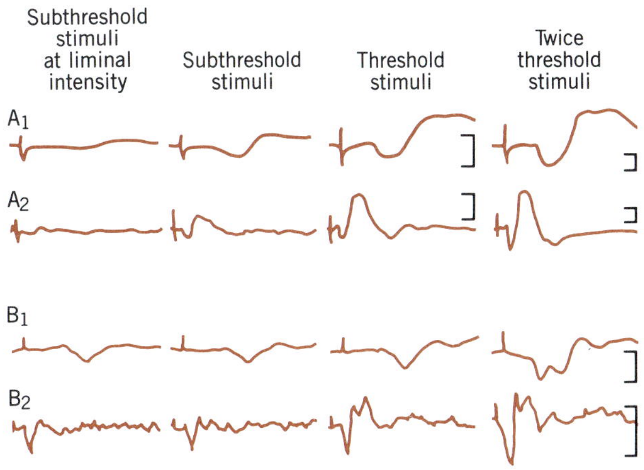

Figure 14.16 *Averaged evoked potentials recorded from the exposed somatosensory cortex in patients with Parkinson's disease. Some of the 500 stimuli in the threshold stimuli column were not felt. Subthreshold stimuli are weaker stimuli, and subthreshold stimuli at liminal intensity are still weaker. All stimuli are reported in the twice threshold stimuli column. A and B are separate subjects. The stimulus artifact is made visible at the start of each trace. Adapted from Libet et al. (1967).*

This result had a disturbing implication: if we do not report conscious sensation until the cortex has been stimulated for half a second, how does consciousness remain in "real time"? Clearly, we do not live half a second behind events in the outside world. There are two answers to the question.

First, stimulation of the skin, unlike stimulation of the cortex, does yield an immediate conscious report to even the briefest stimulus. Presumably, the afferent signal has been preprocessed by subcortical centers to have a form immediately recognizable by the cortex. The coding of the direct electrical stimulation, in contrast, is inappropriate for conscious perception. Perhaps the electrically evoked signal must travel down to the thalamus and then return to the cortex on sensory fiber tracts before perception takes place, although even that would take much less than 0.5 sec. It seems that a lot of neural processing is necessary before the results of this unnatural stimulus can

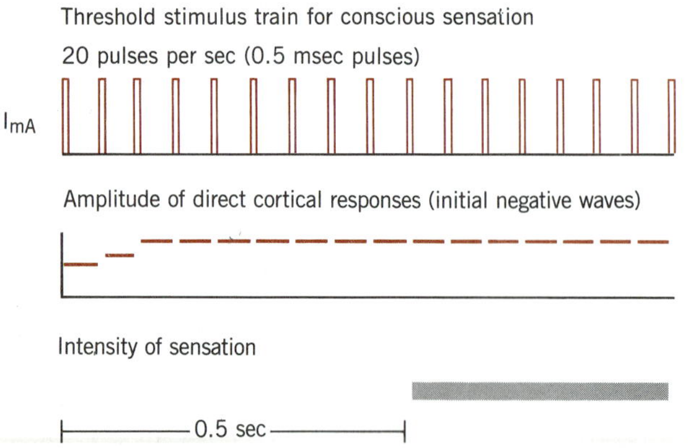

Figure 14.17 Schematic results of electrical stimulation of the somatosensory cortex (postcentral gyrus) in awake humans. The direct cortical responses are measured from electrodes nearby. The subjective sensation begins about 500 msec after the start of electrical stimulation and about 400 msec after the evoked responses to each pulse have reached their maximal value. The subjective intensity remains constant while the stimulus train continues. I_{mA} *is current in milliamps. Adapted from Libet (1964).*

enter consciousness. The nature of this processing remains unknown.

The second answer to the puzzle of the 0.5-sec delay came from experiments where the subject compared the apparent time of onset of the cortical stimulus to the onset of other, more natural stimuli. In these experiments the time of onset coincided with the time of the natural stimuli. Somehow, the timing of the cortical stimulus train was referred back to the first pulse of the train, even though conscious sensation was delayed (Libet, 1973). Clearly, extensive cortical processing must occur before conscious processes become involved in evaluating even the simplest stimulus. Another example of this processing comes from neurological patients who are unable to recognize faces.

Face Recognition. A rare but fascinating syndrome is the inability to recognize faces, although other perceptual abilities remain nearly unaffected. The deficit, called **prosopagnosia,** is caused by damage to the visual system beyond the primary visual cortex. Patients are unable to recognize either familiar faces, such as those of family members, or the faces of people they have met since the onset of the problem. Sacks (1987) describes a prosopagnosiz patient, a professor of music, who is unable to recognize his pupils or even his wife except by their voices and movements. In the neurologist's office, he mistook his wife's head for his hat. With his undiminished musical talent, his adaptation to his handicap makes a curious and moving story.

The patients are not totally without information about faces, though. They still show autonomic signs of orienting when they view photographs of familiar faces (Tranel & Damasio, 1985). The orienting is measured by changes in the galvanic skin response (GSR) of the hand. Thus some processing of the faces is going on, enough for some brain areas to be informed about face identity. Yet the patients remain unable to use this processing to guide behavior. For further insight into conscious processing, we can turn from perception to behavior.

Hyperactivity

A common result of lateral prefrontal lesions in primates is **hyperactivity** (Fuster, 1980), which is often defined as continual pacing or repetitive movements. These symptoms led early researchers to conclude that the prefrontal cortex normally operates by inhibiting motor activity. This view fitted in with the old idea that the frontal lobes harbored our most noble ideas. In this conception, culture, and therefore the frontal lobes, inhibited instinctive urges.

Examined more closely, however, hyperactivity is seen not simply as an increase in movement, for it changes with the level of stimulation in the environment. Hyperactivity can be suppressed if the lesioned animals are placed in the dark or if their sensory stimulation is otherwise reduced (Gross, 1963). Conversely, added stimulation increases hyperactivity (French & Harlow, 1955; Gross, 1963). The externally driven nature of activity in the lesioned animals may relate to the animals' distractability—their overreaction to stimuli that are irrelevant to ongoing behavior (Klüver, 1933; Konorski & Lawicka, 1964; Grueninger & Pribram,

1969). Thus hyperactivity can be reduced to hyperreactivity (Fuster, 1980). Behavioral orienting in lesioned animals seems to continue long after normal animals would have become habituated. The control of activity or reactivity by the frontal cortex may be a recent development in evolution, for it is seen in apes and rhesus monkeys but not in carnivores or squirrel monkeys (New World monkeys with a smooth cortex) (Warren, 1964).

Paradoxically, the animal's difficulty with behavioral habituation is accompanied by a reduction in the autonomic components of the orienting response (Kimble, Bagshaw & Pribram, 1965; Zernicki, 1972). If this sounds like the deficit in amygdala lesions (Chapter 10), the resemblance is more than coincidental, because the limbic areas and the frontal cortex are closely connected.

Under some conditions, the hyperactivity of these animals can be more apparent than real; the actual amount of movement generally is not as elevated as casual observation would imply. One is struck by the activity of a continually pacing animal, whereas the varied activities of a normal animal look more reasonable, even if the total amount of movement is the same in both animals. Just as unfamiliar foreign languages seem to be spoken very rapidly, the meaningless movements of hyperactivity seem excessive because we do not parse them into meaningful chunks. One is reminded of the movements of so-called hyperkinetic children.

Biochemistry of Attention

Hyperkinesis. Children who are *hyperkinetic* (Greek for "overactive") not only are overactive but are extremely distractable. They can never settle down to concentrate on a task, and this leads to difficulties when they start school. The treatment for hyperkinesis is not harsh discipline or sedatives; surprisingly, the most effective regimen is regular doses of amphetamine, methylphenidate, or other dopamine agonists! Though these drugs are potent stimulants in normal adults, they seem to calm hyperkinetic children to the point where they can function normally.

The effectiveness of the treatment leads to the hypothesis that attention is mediated by forebrain catecholaminergic systems. (Recall that the catecholamines include dopamine and norepinephrine.) The prefrontal cortex is a likely participant in these systems, via the dopaminergic pathways from the ventral tegmental area to the nucleus accumbens, olfactory tubercule, and prefrontal cortex.

A simpler explanation of hyperkinesis is based on the observation that most young children become hyperactive when they are tired. They dash about the house and can't concentrate on anything, until finally they fall asleep. Perhaps hyperkinetic children are simply tired most of the time. A dose of amphetamine wakes them up to the point where they function normally. Whatever the reason, these children reveal a close connection between attention and dopaminergic systems.

Schizophrenia. Another approach to the attention problem comes from schizophrenia, which can be characterized as a disturbance of selective attention. The schizophrenic is troubled not so much by lack of attentional abilities as by lack of control of attention. The victim seems to attend sometimes to everything and sometimes to nothing. A particularly articulate victim of the disease, upon recovery, described her disturbance in this way:

> The mind must have a filter which functions without our conscious thought, sorting stimuli and allowing only those which are relevant to the situation in hand to disturb consciousness. And this filter must be working at maximum efficiency at all times, particularly when we require a high degree of concentration. What had happened . . . was a breakdown in the filter, and a hodge-podge of unrelated stimuli were distracting me from things which should have had my undivided attention. (McDonald, 1960, p. 218)

Schizophrenia is controlled in many patients with dopamine antagonists. A dominant current hypothesis is that the disease affects dopamine receptors. Schizophrenics may have too many dopamine receptors, potentiating dopamine's post synaptic effects (Owen et al., 1978). This hypothesis is examined further in Chapter 15.

Although we cannot conclude that attention is

simply a function of catecholamine activity, we know where to look in future studies of attentional mechanisms. Again the control of a neurological function has turned out not to be purely logical (like the interactions of McCulloch-Pitts neurons) or purely chemical. Rather, it is something in between, affected both by the anatomy of connections and by the biochemistry of synapses.

Cortex versus Reticular Formation in Attention

The distinction between arousal and selective attention roughly parallels the distinction between brain-stem reticular formation and the prefrontal areas in regulating attention. Reticular control adjusts attentional level as a whole, and forebrain mechanisms act as modulators. The forebrain mechanisms concentrate sensory and motor resources on particular aspects of the environment at the expense of other aspects. The conscious functions of attention, though, reside with the forebrain mechanisms. The evidence for this assertion comes from split-brain studies, one of the richest sources of information about the neurology of consciousness

Split-Brain Studies. The functions of the hemispheres, reviewed in Chapters 3 and 12, can be made independent by the split-brain operation, though, of course, the brain-stem structures remain intact. Functions controlled by the reticular formation, such as waking and arousal, affect both hemispheres equally. The various aspects of consciousness, in contrast, become independent. According to Sperry (1974, p. 7):

> We can now demonstrate with appropriate tests a whole array of distinct impairments that are most simply summarized by saying that the left and right hemispheres, following their disconnection, function independently in most conscious mental activities. Each hemisphere, that is, has its own private sensations, perceptions, thoughts, and ideas all of which are cut off from the corresponding experiences in the opposite hemisphere.

In other words, Sperry concludes that systems using conscious control do not extend to the brain stem. They reside solely in the forebrain. Split-brain patients sometimes have the feeling that there is another "I," a stranger, living in the right hemisphere.

Emotions, in contrast, tend to spread easily from one hemisphere to the other (Sperry, 1974). An offensive odor or an embarrassing photo presented to one hemisphere may present vascular changes (recall James's theory of emotions), changes in facial expressions, or other clues to the uninformed hemisphere. In this way, many of the functions of emotional expression remain unified when the cortex is divided.

Mechanisms of orientation and attention also tend to bring hemispheric activity into unified focus, perhaps because one hemisphere can observe the motor activity elicited by orienting or problem-solving behavior in the other hemisphere. This observation does not weaken the separated consciousness and separated attention hypothesis, for the interference between the two hemispheres can be largely nullified with practice under the right conditions (Gazzaniga, 1970). To the degree that attention requires access to cortical mechanisms governing the planning of ongoing behaviors, its functions will be divided in the split-brain patient.

MEMORY AND CONSCIOUSNESS

A common test for the presence of consciousness and selective attention in the real world is through memory: "Johnny, were you paying attention? What was the teacher saying?" In this example, memory is used as a criterion for conscious processing. Since a chapter has already been devoted to memory, it remains only to link memory with conscious processing.

Only the contents of memory are available to consciousness; the process of recovering a memory is not conscious. The retrieval process need not interfere with ongoing behavior, and therefore there is no need for high-level attentional intervention in retrieval. It is only when a memory proves difficult to retrieve that conscious intervention is necessary. This might occur if other long-term memories must be recovered and applied to the problem of reconstructing a less accessible memory. In trying to recall the name of my third-grade teacher, for instance, I find it helpful to recall other events in my childhood so my content-addressing mechanism (see Chapter 11) can be activated.

Conscious Effort in Retrieval. Recall strategies have been investigated with the tip-of-the-tongue phenomenon (Brown & McNeill, 1966). William James (1893, p. 251) describes the phenomenon in his vivid way:

> Suppose we try to recall a forgotten name. The state of our consciousness is peculiar. There is a gap therein; but no mere gap. It is a gap that is intensely active. A sort of wraith of the name is in it, beckoning us in a given direction, making us at moments tingle with the sense of our closeness and then letting us sink back without the longed-for term. If wrong names are proposed to us, this singularly definite gap acts immediately so as to negate them. They do not fit into its mold. And the gap of one word does not feel like the gap of another.

Brown and McNeill (1966) studied James's gap by reading to students definitions of infrequent words such as *apse, nepotism, cloaca, ambergris,* and *sampan.* In most cases, students either guessed the word immediately or had no idea what it was. But in about 13 percent of the cases the tip-of-the-tongue phenomenon was elicited. Brown and McNeill describe the feeling as a mild torment, something like the brink of a sneeze. When the word was found, the subjects' relief was considerable.

It turned out that the subjects often knew some characteristics of the elusive word, such as number of syllables or syllabic stress. They could frequently identify patterns similar in sound or meaning to the target word, all before the word was successfully retrieved. Because memory is content-addressable, conscious strategies were necessary to search meanings and recall the words.

Delayed Response and Object Constancy. Memory and frontal functions are also linked through the delayed-response task described in Figure 14.5, for which an animal had to remember the position or identity of a cue during a forced delay in order to receive a reward. What is the usefulness of such a talent in the real world? One application appears in Piaget's (1973) concept of **object constancy**—that objects in the real world retain their identity despite momentary disappearances and transformations. Object constancy in turn requires an ability to process objects in relation to their contexts. This is one of the hallmarks of prefrontal function.

The object-constancy tests of Piaget were "monkified" by showing a monkey a grape, then hiding it under one of three inverted baskets (see Figure 14.18). The baskets were then moved and exchanged in shell-game fashion before the monkey had a chance to retrieve the grape. Figure 14.18*b* shows that normal monkeys performed the task easily, but prefrontally lesioned animals searched randomly (Anderson et al., 1976). Once the grape had disappeared beneath a basket, the prefrontal monkeys could no longer keep track of its hidden movements. Again, prefrontal cortex was necessary to impose order on the sensory world.

In summary, a set of neurological functions manages long-term behavior in higher mammals. The functions are associated with consciousness, attention, planning, and long-term episodic memory, all of which are aspects of this behavioral control system. They set priorities for behavior, using past experience as a guide, and monitor the animals' progress toward goals. They enable an animal to escape from the needs of the moment, looking beyond the here and now to sustained and powerful interactions with a larger environment.

ALTERED STATES OF CONSCIOUSNESS

Having examined a theoretical framework for normal consciousness, we can seek further experimental techniques for testing the theory. One strategy is to increase the variability of the phenomenon in question as much as possible. Then we can inquire about the sources and consequences of the variability. Altered states of consciousness promise to offer insights into consciousness because they provide the needed variability.

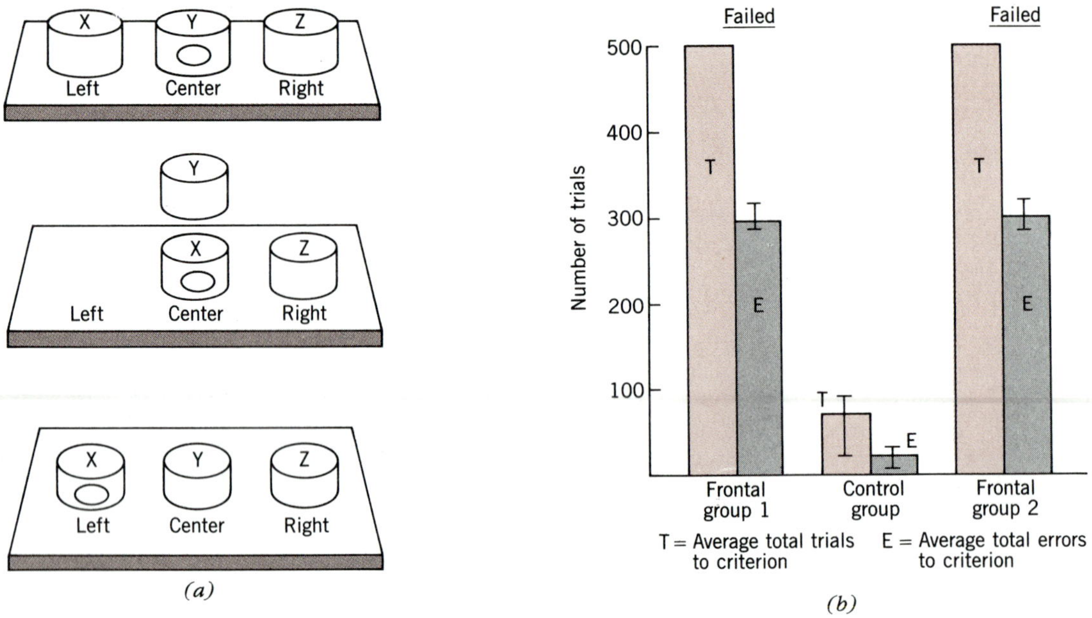

***Figure 14.18** A shell game modified for monkeys and played on an apparatus similar to the WGTA (Figure 14.5).* (a) *The monkey sees the experimenter place a grape under basket Y. Then Y is lifted, basket X is placed over the grape, and basket X and the grape are slid over to the left position while the now-empty basket Y is replaced in the center. In other trials, other baskets were manipulated similarly.* (b) *Trials and errors before criterion performance was reached on the basket task. Training was terminated if a monkey had not reached the criterion within 500 trials. Frontal groups 1 and 2 had similar lesions but were run successively. Adapted from Anderson et al. (1976).*

HYPNOSIS

If you immerse your hand in ice water and leave it there for a few minutes, you will feel no pain, if you have been adequately **hypnotized** (*hypnos* is Greek for "sleep")—put into a state of increased suggestability—beforehand. This is not a magician's stage trick but a repeatable laboratory phenomenon (Hilgard, 1969).

Hypnotic analgesia is not a simple blocking of afferent impulses, like the analgesia induced by local anesthetics. Something in the brain still senses the pain, but the pain does not get through to consciousness. Hilgard (1973) has demonstrated this with results like those in Figure 14.19. Pain was present, but it was less severe and less distressing than it would be normally. The response to pain under hypnosis seems suspiciously like that reported by human subjects with prefrontal lobotomies; they say that they still feel the pain, but they are not particularly bothered by it. Could the relationship be more than a coincidence? In the context of the theory of consciousness outlined in this chapter, we might think of hypnosis as a substitution of outside control for internal control over behavioral schemata. The hypnotized subject transfers executive control to the hypnotist.

It is possible to interpret hypnosis not as a change in the way the brain works but simply as highly motivated role-playing. The subject attempts to produce what the experimenter expects. Even with this interpretation, the extent of change that can be achieved in perception and memory is impressive.

Keep in mind the functions of consciousness in planning, attention, and memory while you read the following list of characteristics of the hypnotic state (Hilgard, Atkinson & Atkinson, 1979, p. 178):

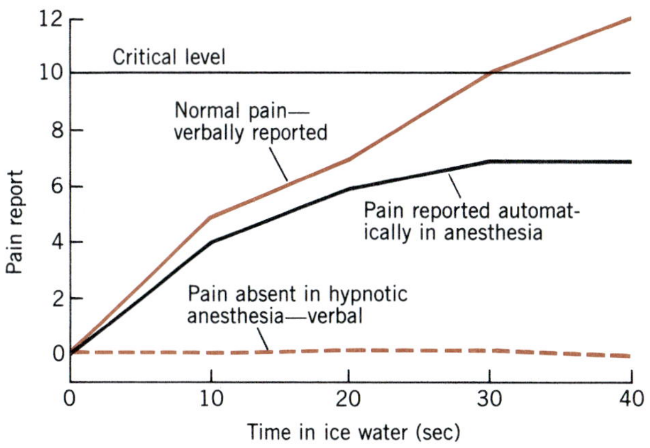

Figure 14.19 *Verbal pain reports in normal control condition, in hypnotic anesthesia condition by "automatic" writing, and in hypnotic anesthesia. Data from a single subject. Adapted from Hilgard et al. (1979).*

1. The subject ceases to make plans.
2. Attention is redistributed.
3. Reality testing is reduced and reality distortion accepted.
4. Suggestibility is increased.
5. The hypnotized subject readily enacts unusual roles.
6. Posthypnotic amnesia is often present.

So it seems that hypnosis may not be as closely related to sleep as its name implies and as was thought when the technique was developed in the 19th century. But another alteration of consciousness is more closely related to sleep than was first thought.

MEDITATION

The goal in hypnotism is to have behavioral schemata directed by an outside agent; the goal in meditation is not to have them at all. Most meditation exercises can be interpreted as methods of freeing the mind of plans, of executing no schemata, and of simply being. For example, the meditator might devote great attention to a meaningless stimulus—a mantra. (Fortunately, the process is not perfect, and people do terminate meditation sessions spontaneously.) Experiments in India have shown that yoga masters maintain extensive control over body processes normally thought to be involuntary (see Figure 14.20). They can reduce their heart rates and metabolic rates far below those found in normal sleep, for example (Wenger, Bagchi & Anand, 1961). Their brain waves resemble those of deep anesthesia more than those of sleep.

The more popular sorts of meditation, as practiced in the West, have a less impressive record. EEG recordings from meditating subjects have not revealed a unique state of consciousness. Rather, most meditators fall into a stage of light sleep,

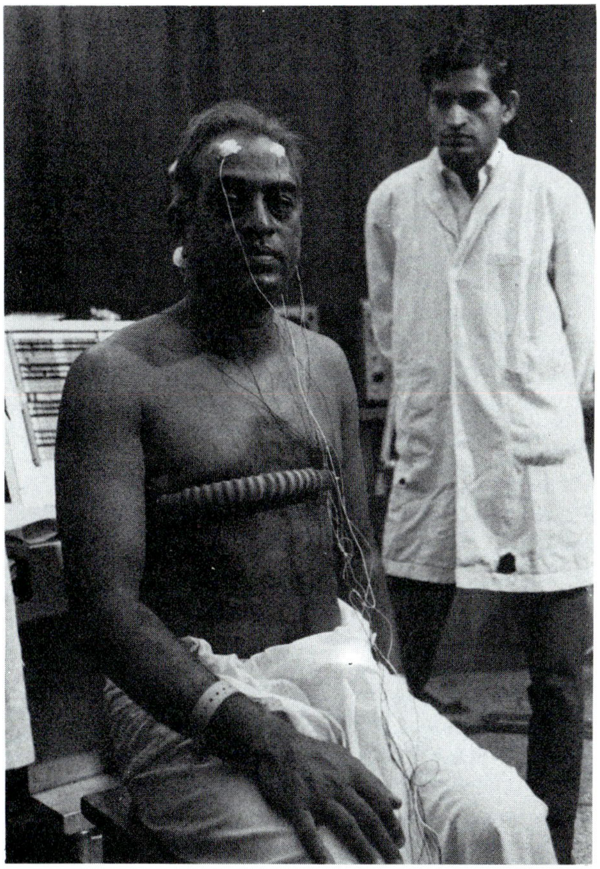

Figure 14.20 *Ramanand Yogi fitted with transducers and EEG electrodes, preparing to reduce his oxygen needs while sealed in an airtight box.*

easily distinguished by the EEG signs shown in Chapter 10, for part of the session (Younger, Adriance & Berger, 1975; Pagano et al., 1976). For most people, meditation as a natural drug is not as effective as other psychoactive drugs.

PSYCHOACTIVE DRUG STATES

Psychoactive drugs reveal a close relationship between motivation and consciousness, for most of them affect both. They also demonstrate that consciousness is a brain process like any other neurological process. It can be biased by some of the same drugs that influence neurotransmitter systems.

Biochemistry of Psychoactive Drugs. In both structure and mode of action, most psychoactive drugs are chemically similar to neurotransmitters. The potent hallucinogen mescaline, derived from the peyote cactus, is similar in structure to norepinephrine, and STP is similar to mescaline. Both affect noradrenergic synapses. Cocaine prevents reuptake of norepinephrine into the presynaptic terminals, interfering with further transmission. Figure 14.21 illustrates the similarities in chemical structures of several neurotransmitters and psychoactive drugs.

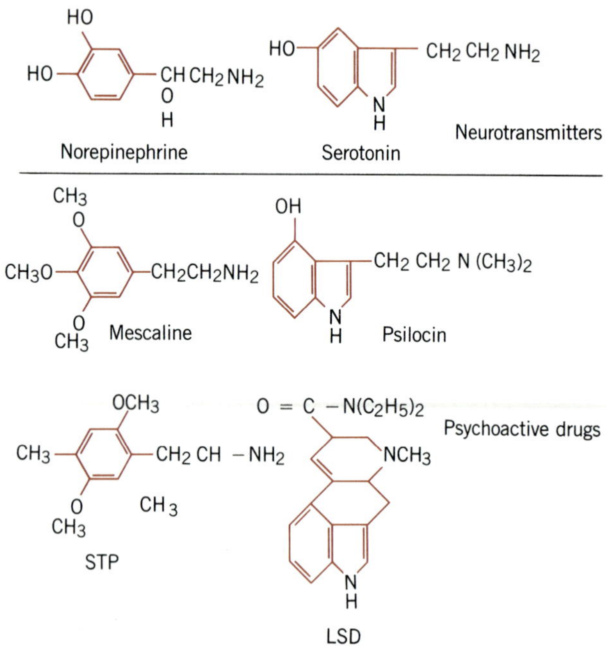

Figure 14.21 Structural similarity of four psychoactive drugs to neurotransmitters. The drugs probably affect the receptor sites normally responsive to the neurotransmitters but have different affinities and time courses of action.

Psilocibin and LSD are molecular expansions of the serotonin molecule. LSD was first synthesized by Swiss biochemist Albert Hoffman, who intended to produce a new psychoactive drug with therapeutic value. He got more than he bargained for. LSD has potent effects on both perception and state of consciousness as well as at least three distinct pharmacological effects. Each is presumptively associated with a different effect on consciousness. LSD blocks serotonergic synapses for a few hours, causing hallucinations; decreases the number of postsynaptic serotonin receptors for a few days, causing hallucinatory flashbacks (Jacobs & Trulson, 1979); and interacts with dopaminergic synapses, causing psychotic symptoms.

The opiates, morphine and heroin, and their biochemical similarity to the brain's enkephalins have already been discussed in Chapter 2. Some of the effects of endogenous opiates may be indirect, through the action of the sometimes addictive drug alcohol (ethanol). Experiments with tissue cultures show that ethanol inhibits the binding of opiates to their specialized postsynaptic receptors. After long-term exposure, the cells respond by increasing the number of opiate-binding sites, an effect that is reversible when the ethanol is withdrawn. The tissue culture effects can be compared with clinical intoxication, tolerance, and withdrawal (Charness, Gordon & Diamond, 1983) and may explain the addictive effects of this relatively simple molecule. Mercifully, low doses of alcohol have negligible effects on the receptors.

Drugs and Mental Illness. Some aspects of mental illness can be looked on not as disturbances of the rational machine but as drug-induced altered states of consciousness. The drugs are not taken voluntarily but are produced internally. Alternatively, the mentally ill person may react abnormally to normal amounts of endogenous psychoactive substances. Therapy includes other drugs to restore the biochemical balance and return the patient to a functioning, if not always normal, state.

The drugs are not cures, though. They only alter an abnormal biochemical balance without addressing the cause of the abnormality. Some of them have serious side effects when taken for long periods. Diagnosis is still a difficult problem, and treatment must also include insight into the patient's psychological condition, as part of a program of psychotherapy.

CHAPTER SUMMARY

1. Consciousness is a neurological system like any other, with four functions that confer advantages on an organism. First is long-term planning—the ability to formulate plans (schemata) for future action and to hold them separate from ongoing behavior. Second is organizing priorities—holding several schemata in mind and acting on them according to present needs. Third is directing attention. One kind of attention is driven internally by a schema; another is driven by outside events. Fourth is retrieving long-term declarative memories. These memories are useful only to produce new schemata, assign priorities, or direct attention. Consciousness comes into play whenever a task is particularly novel, difficult, or dangerous. The "I" inside the head can be thought of as a necessary result of the operation of this neurological system.

2. There is a relation between some functions of consciousness and the prefrontal region, though one cannot say that consciousness is located there. Prefrontal cortex consists of the frontal lobe anterior to the primary motor cortex. Alternatively, it can be defined as the region of the cortex that projects to and from the mediodorsal nucleus of the thalamus. It has three parts: frontal eye fields, linked to visual areas and the superior colliculus; lateral frontal cortex, involved in organizing schemata; and orbital frontal cortex, linked to the limbic system and organizing emotional and motivational functions.

3. Prefrontal lesions, especially of lateral prefrontal cortex, lead to a lack of long-term planning. The deficit is seen in tasks requiring delayed response. Memory is intact, but monkeys cannot use environmental information to organize temporal sequences of behavior. Single neurons in the prefrontal cortex are involved both in preparing forthcoming motor responses and in holding short-term memory. Humans with prefrontal lesions have deficits in planning, remaining stimulus-bound. They view the world with excessive concreteness, and the amount and complexity of their language are reduced.

4. Organizing goals and priorities is necessary to live in a world where tokens can take on value by being exchanged for food or other rewards. Prefrontally lesioned chimpanzees will not work to earn tokens. Prefrontally lesioned monkeys perform poorly at left-right alternation but succeed if a delay is interposed between each left-right pair, so that the experimenter rather than the monkey parses the information. Alternatively, the monkeys might be learning a temporal discrimination, tested with randomly occurring left and right trials with a delay preceding each right-going trial.

5. Lesions in restricted areas of prefrontal cortex reveal anatomical specializations. Delayed-response deficits occur with lesions of the sulcus principalis, and inferior prefrontal lesions yield difficulty with both spatial and nonspatial tasks. The arcuate sulcus is concerned with visual search. The orbital cortex is related to choice, lesions there resulting in perseveration.

6. Attention is controlled in both parietal and frontal cortex. Lesions in the frontal eye fields yield difficulty with visual search and with the di-

rection of saccadic eye movements by internal schemata. Neurons there burst before or after the start of an eye movement. Some fire continuously during orienting in a particular direction. Many of the neurons have visual receptive fields as well, showing that prefrontal regions have sensory as well as motor functions.

7. Correlates of attention in humans are measured with evoked potentials. The earliest such potential following a stimulus is a vertex potential that is larger when a subject is actively attending. A second potential, the P300 wave, is independent of sensory modality. It appears when the subject must process a relatively infrequent event, even if no overt response is required. The contingent negative variation (CNV) is a surface-negative DC shift that appears during delayed-response tasks. It consists of a motor potential preceded by a slower and more frontal wave. Together, the attention-related potentials leave a picture of a cortex regulated by localized, continually shifting DC potentials.

8. Electrical stimulation of the cortex shows that conscious experience can arise from almost any cortical area. The firing of cortical neurons is not enough, for stimulation adequate to excite nearby neurons does not necessarily evoke a conscious experience. Direct cortical stimulation must continue for about 0.5 sec before conscious sensation results, but that sensation is referred back in time to the onset of stimulation. The delay shows that the stimulation was being processed, though not consciously, and that an activity must follow particular patterns before it can enter consciousness.

9. Motor abnormalities with prefrontal lesions are often defined as hyperactivity. But motor activity is reactive—driven by outside stimulation rather than inside schemata. Hyperkinesis in human children includes high activity and difficulty in concentration. It has been linked with low dopaminergic activity and may be linked through dopaminergic systems to sleep and arousal mechanisms. Schizophrenics also have attentional difficulties, which can be controlled with dopamine antagonists. Both syndromes point to the role of catecholamines in attention. Split-brain studies show that attentional activities related to consciousness reside in the forebrain, whereas overall arousal comes from subcortical regions.

10. Memory is available to consciousness as information, not as the process of memory access itself. The tip-of-the-tongue phenomenon shows that many characteristics of forgotten material can be brought into consciousness before the material itself is recalled. In primates the prefrontal cortex aids in establishing object constancy; memory imposes order on sensations from the environment.

11. A hypnotized subject acts as though the job of manipulating behavioral schemata has been transferred from the prefrontal regions to the hypnotist. The subject exhibits many of the characteristics of a patient with a prefrontal lobotomy, ceasing to make plans and showing disturbed attention, personality, and memory. Meditation shows that with practice, some humans can control neurological systems that were thought to be inaccessible to consciousness. More casual meditation often resembles relaxation or light sleep.

12. Psychoactive drugs show the close relationship of motivation and consciousness. Most of them are chemically related to the neurotransmitters. Some forms of mental illness can be interpreted as biochemical abnormalities induced not by drugs from the outside but by psychoactive chemicals produced endogenously.

KEY TERMS

Lateral frontal cortex
Orbital frontal cortex
Sulcus principalis
Arcuate sulcus
Perseverate
Vertex potential
Contingent negative variation (CNV)
Prosopagnosia
Hyperactivity
Object constancy
Hypnotism

SUGGESTED READINGS

Fuster, J. M. (1980). *The prefrontal cortex.* New York: Raven Press.

This compact volume reviews the structure and functions of prefrontal regions, emphasizing the work of the author and his colleagues.

Pope, K., & Singer, J. E. (Eds.). (1978). *The flow of conscious experience.* New York: Plenum Press.

A variety of philosophers and psychologists contribute their interpretations of the role of consciousness in life, and some suggest possible brain mechanisms.

LeDoux, J., & Hirst, W. (Eds.). (1986). *Mind and Brain: Dialogues in Cognitive Neuroscience.* Cambridge: Cambridge University Press.

Neuroscientists and cognitive psychologists exchange information and views on perception, attention, memory, and emotion in an interactive format.

Chapter 15

APPLICATIONS I: BEHAVIOR

Until now, this book has been concerned mostly with basic research. But the neurosciences also have an important influence on society, both in changing our view of ourselves and in making possible interventions in brain processes. We have seen how the close parallels between the brains of humans and of other animals emphasize that the human species is part of nature, not above it.

On a more practical level, interventions in brain processes have been motivated both by the need to treat mental illness and neurological disease and by the desire to mold behaviors. Some of those behaviors stem from neurological abnormalities, and others are more problematic; but for many years neurosurgeons have attempted to change behavior through surgery.

PSYCHOSURGERY

Psychosurgery can be differentiated from other neurosurgery by its goals. **Neurosurgery** addresses brain diseases such as tumors and circulatory problems; **psychosurgery** attempts to change behavior by ablating or stimulating brain regions. By this definition, the split-brain procedure, for instance, would be classified as neurosurgery. Its motivation is to relieve a well-defined neurological abnormality (epilepsy); the surgery's behavioral consequences are largely unwanted. (Another definition claims that it is neurosurgery if you approve of it and psychosurgery if you don't!)

ABLATION

The practice of psychosurgery requires three controversial assumptions. First, one must assume that particular behavioral functions are controlled by well-defined areas that have no other important functions. Second, one must assume a match between the function of a particular area and the behavioral problem manifested in a patient. Finally, one must assume that no other significant brain damage will result from the surgery.

As we have seen in previous chapters, the first

assumption is usually false. Most neurological functions are controlled at many interacting levels, and most brain areas participate in many functions. The ventromedial nucleus of the hypothalamus, for instance, has a role in controlling food intake. But many other brain centers also participate in controlling feeding and weight, and the ventromedial nucleus also participates in other functions. The idea of anatomical separation of functions, in short, cannot be reduced to a set of independent centers controlling definable behavioral functions.

Similarly, there is little evidence for the second assumption. Psychosurgery is often proposed because of the similarity of symptoms from lesioned animals and from a small group of psychiatric patients. But often the overlap is small, and the other consequences of the operation are significant. A case in point is **prefrontal lobotomy**—the isolation of the prefrontal cortex.

Prefrontal Lobotomy

Largely by historical accident, some of the first attempts at psychosurgery dealt with the prefrontal region of the cortex. Valenstein (1973) relates that the practice of removing parts of the frontal lobe began with an incidental remark by Jacobsen that one of his prefrontally lesioned chimpanzees seemed tamer and more manageable than before the lesioning. (Tameness was probably a result of orbital frontal damage.) The remark was made at the Second International Neurology Congress in 1935. At the end of Jacobsen's presentation, Dr. Egas Moniz, a neuropsychiatrist, rose from the audience and asked whether prefrontal lobectomy (removal of the lobe) might relieve anxiety states in human psychiatric patients. Both Jacobsen and his professor, John Fulton, were a little shocked by the suggestion. But Moniz (1936) persisted with this idea and soon began performing prefrontal lobectomies in an effort to make psychiatric patients calmer and more cooperative. The first attempts seemed to meet with success, according to Moniz. The procedure soon became popular.

Always looking for more efficient procedures, neurosurgeons began merely undercutting the cortex (performing lobotomies) to sever the fiber tracts that connect the prefrontal areas with the rest of the brain. This procedure required only two small incisions in the temples; a knife called a leucotome was inserted in the incisions and swung liberally back and forth. The operation, called a leukotomy, was simpler than lobectomy and contributed further to the popularity of the procedure. Eventually the operation was simplified still further; the leukotomes were inserted through the orbits of the eyes, to avoid disfiguring scars, and swung back and forth laterally while the patient was "anesthetized" with ECS (Freeman and Watts, 1950). Leukotomy became an office procedure and could be enormously profitable. Over 40,000 patients were treated in one variation or another in the United States alone.

The operation turned out to be more profitable for the physician than for the patient. It was later discovered that lobotomized patients suffered from all of the deficits found in prefrontally lesioned monkeys. The results were devastating for mental life. The predictable impulsivity, the inability to carry through plans, and the other symptoms outlined in Chapter 14 emerged. At present, prefrontal leukotomy is practically never performed.

It is easy to fault early neurosurgeons for their enthusiasm for lobotomy, but we should remember that the physician has a more urgent job than the researcher. When a patient appears at the doorstep with a malady, the physician must find a treatment immediately. The illness will not wait until researchers develop improved methods. When lobotomy was popular, there were no antipsychotic drugs. The surgery truly may have improved some of the patients who had been in grievously disturbed states, whatever the sacrifice in potential mental life.

Subcortical Interventions

Other aspects of social behavior have also been treated with psychosurgery. Lesions have been attempted in a wide variety of brain sites, including the cingulate cortex, the amygdala, and various parts of the hypothalamus. The treatments address an equally wide variety of deviant behaviors; only a few examples will be given here. One example is the attempt to reduce uncontrolled displays of violence and aggression by lesions in the temporal lobe. We have seen in previous chapters that lesions of the amygdala and associated structures in monkeys can result in tameness and lack of aggression. Furthermore, some neurologists have identified unprovoked outbursts of aggressive behavior with temporal lobe epilepsy. The patient often has an epileptic **aura,** or warning, before an attack, and epileptic activity can be recorded from the temporal region by an EEG.

Stereotaxic amygdalectomy (see Figure 15.1) was one of the first psychosurgical procedures to be attempted after the introduction of prefrontal lobotomy (Narabayashi, 1972). At first, only patients with temporal lobe epilepsy and psychomotor seizures were candidates for amygdalectomy. Later, other patients with destructive behavior, especially if it was "associated with various degrees of feeble-mindedness," were operated on too (Narabayashi et al., 1963).

Here is a case history that Valenstein (1973, p. 12) believes is typical of the Narabayashi results:

> This 7-year-old boy had been diagnosed as having symptomatic epilepsy with right spastic hemiplegia and imbecility. . . . When he reached the age of five, he began to have convulsions once or twice a week, such attacks lasting approximately one hour. . . . Following the second operation (the bilateral operation was done in two stages), however, the change in behavior was so complete, the patient had become so obedient and cooperative that it was almost impossible to imagine that it was the same child who had been so wild and uncontrollable preoperatively. The electroencephalogram no longer revealed spike discharges on either side.

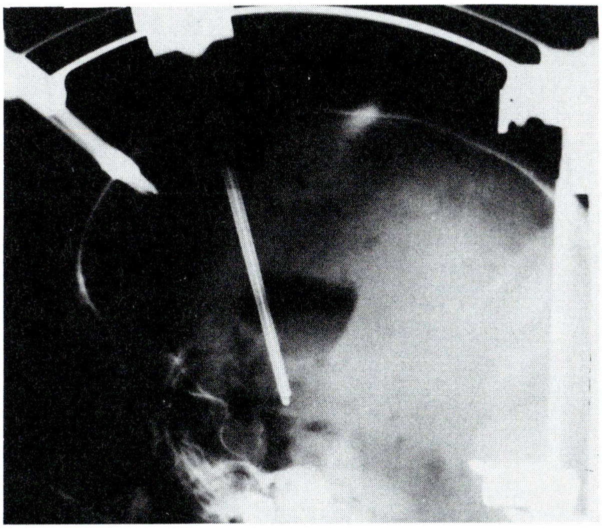

Figure 15.1 An x-ray showing a lateral view of the head with electrodes inserted into the left and right amygdalas for a stereotaxic amygdalectomy. The dark area in the center is the lateral ventricle. It serves as a guide for locating the electrodes.

The evaluation of results is based on such case reports rather than on formal testing or standardized procedures, so it is difficult to compare these procedures with others. Also, neurosurgeons are not trained in behavioral observation and may miss important behavioral problems. (These are common problems in the clinical literature.) The Narabayashi group did not report any of the control-system disruptions that we would expect from the results of primate experiments involving amygdala lesions. Other groups doing amygdalectomies in humans have reported increases in sexual libido, appetite for food, and body weight. One such group, headed by V. Balasubramaniam in India, used the following scale for evaluating the results of the surgery (Balasubramaniam & Ramamurthi, 1970):

A. There is no need of any drug. Patient is able to mingle easily with others.
B. Very much docile and given to occasional outburst only.
C. Manageable when given drugs, though not leading a useful life.
D. Transient improvement but relapses.
E. No change.
F. Died.

I will leave it to the reader to discover the methodological flaw in this scale. (*Hint:* How does one code a patient who gets worse?)

Another set of lesions of the amygdala and nearby temporal areas has been carried out by Mark and Ervin (1970). They describe a "dyscontrol syndrome" marked by occasional outbursts of violent behavior, including assault and murder. Mark and Ervin cite many cases of violence caused by the syndrome, a form of temporal lobe epilepsy. They imply that much of the violence in our society may be due to the disorder. Their group uses depth electrodes to localize abnormalities in the brain sites and to create radio frequency lesions. Again, the number of patients is small and there is no objective measure of the results. Furthermore, the fact that other societies are far less violent than ours makes one doubt that a disease such as epilepsy could be responsible for our society's violence.

One other effort at psychosurgery brings ethical problems into particularly sharp focus. The program began when a group of West German physicians saw a film by Schreiner and Kling (1953) demonstrating hypersexuality in amygdalectomized male cats and monkeys. The animals would mount anything that moved, male or female (see Figure 15.2). Sometimes they would even mount inanimate objects. Since later lesions by Kling in the ventromedial nucleus of the hypothalamus (VMH) eliminated the hypersexuality, the group decided to perform lesions of the VMH in men who had a compulsive desire for homosexual relations with younger men or boys. Over a 10-year period, about 20 patients were treated. (It must be said in the group's favor that the lesions were unilateral.) The operation eliminated the homosexual urges in most cases, but it probably accomplished this by reducing the sex drive in general. There is no evidence that the operations produced a change in sexual orientation (Valenstein, 1973).

Despite the disappointing results of psychosurgery, it still has a powerful hold on the popular imagination. Further, science fiction accounts of human brain stimulation sometimes depict the subjects, or victims, hopelessly addicted to self-stimulation, to the exclusion of all other activities. The reality is somewhat less dramatic and more reassuring about the stability of human motivational systems.

MIND CONTROL THROUGH BRAIN STIMULATION

We saw in Chapter 8 the powerful influence of brain stimulation on motivational systems, where it is possible to bypass the usual environmental stimulation of the systems and gain direct access to the control centers. A dramatic demonstration of the power of brain stimulation to control behavior is José Delgado's ability to stop a charging bull with electrical stimulation (see Figure 15.3). A particularly aggressive breed of bull was used. The intruder into the animal's territory was armed only with a radio transmitter. The bull was diverted with a radio-controlled brain stimulator developed by Delgado (1969b); the electrodes were in the caudate nucleus.

But something is strange about the situation. Why should the stimulation be in the caudate nucleus? This nucleus is one of the basal ganglia, which are usually concerned with motor control; they are not in a region that modulates aggression. A closer examination of the behavior suggests that it is not aggression that is being controlled. Rather, the stimulation forces the animal to circle so it can no longer charge (Valenstein, 1973). Following the stimulation, the animal seems relatively tame; Valenstein interprets this tameness as confusion induced by disorganization of the motor system.

The effects of brain stimulation are not as straightforward as they had seemed. When we move to human beings, the effects are more complex yet.

Human Stimulation

Because electrodes are implanted in human brains only for therapeutic reasons, they seldom reach likely sites for electrical self-stimulation. Two particularly informative cases of human self-stimulation were reported by Robert Heath (1963). The patients were equipped with portable stimulators that could be used outside the hospital setting. The stimulators also recorded the frequency of use for each electrode.

One subject, suffering from narcolepsy, received implants in several areas expected to induce arousal. Stimulation of the mesencephalic tegmentum was alerting but was so aversive that the patient ingeniously modified a hairpin to prevent the button from being pressed. Stimulation of the septal region was the most rewarding of all the sites. It gave a "good" feeling as though building

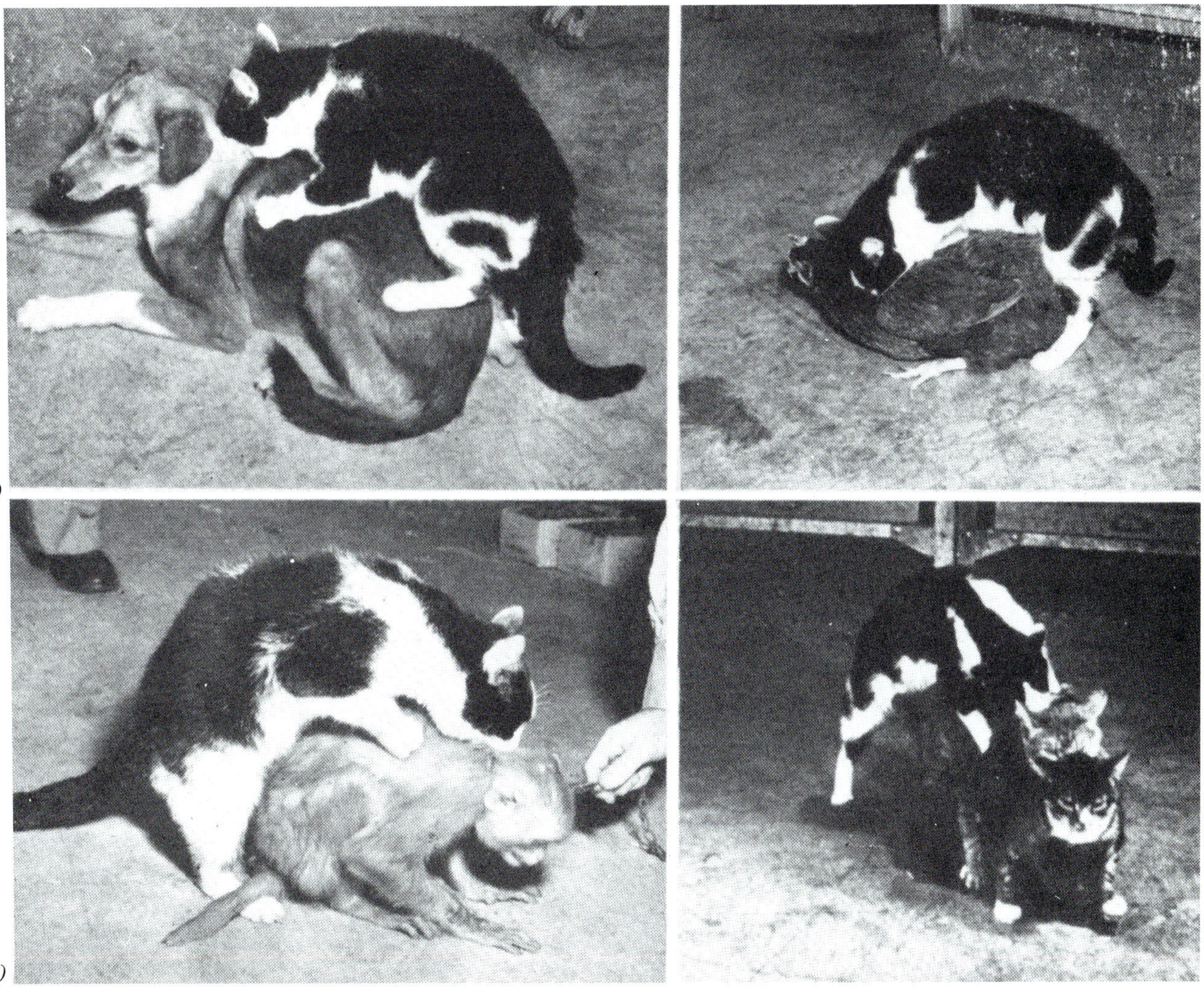

(a) *(b)* *(c)* *(d)*

Figure 15.2 *Hypersexuality in a male cat following bilateral lesions in the temporal lobe. The cat attempts copulation, including characteristic neck bites, with* (a) *a dog,* (b) *a chicken, and* (c) *a monkey.* (d) *Four male cats attempt tandem copulation.*

up to sexual orgasm. It also alerted the patient, thereby combating the narcolepsy.

Sometimes narcoleptic sleep came on so suddenly that the patient did not have time to press the button. Recognizing this, fellow patients and friends would push the button for him, enabling him to work as a nightclub entertainer with the portable stimulator.

Heath's epileptic subject received implants in a greater variety of brain regions and showed a variety of subjective responses when stimulated (see Table 15.1). Some of the stimulated sites yielded feelings of euphoria or sexual arousal. But the highest rate of self-stimulation did not result from any of these feelings. Instead, the most frequently activated electrode produced irritability. The subject reported that he was almost able to recall a memory during this stimulation, but he could not quite grasp it. The frequent self-stimulations were an effort to bring this elusive memory into clear focus. The feeling must have been something like the tip-of-the-tongue phenomenon reviewed in

Figure 15.3 Radio-controlled brain stimulation stopping a charging bull. The animal in full charge is stopped by caudate nucleus stimulation and shows stereotyped behavior. After several stimulations there is a lasting inhibition of charging.

Chapter 14. The electrode in the centromedian thalamus evoking this feeling was near the location where Squire (1982) later described the snydrome of diencephalic amnesia on the basis of patient N.A. and Korsakoff patients (see Figure 11.35).

The importance of this result for the issue of mind control is that the patients did not become slaves to the stimulation, even though the electrodes were implanted in some of the sites expected to yield the most potent self-stimulation behavior. They did not self-stimulate until they dropped, nor did they lose interest in other events around them. The electrode yielding the highest stimulation rates was not a short-cut to euphoria but was related to the motivation to continue a memory retrieval process once begun. Thus the fears of those envisioning a future dictator controlling a population with implanted electrodes are not likely to be realized.

Limitations of Stimulation

Mind control by brain stimulation has a limited future for other reasons too. First, and most obvious, any group that would submit to the implantation process probably wouldn't need added control anyway. Second, there are easier ways to gain access to human motivational systems. To force a human to do almost anything, one need only withhold food for a while, for instance, and then offer food as a reward for the desired behavior. The political technology for controlling whole peoples with a combination of positive and negative contingencies was already well developed in Nazi Germany. Physiological psychology has little to offer in addition to the powerful techniques of social control known in the 1930s and 1940s.

Other limitations on brain stimulation are technical. Mark and Ervin (1970, pp. 106–107), for instance, describe a patient who reported "going wild" and "losing control" as a result of medial amygdalar stimulation. A site only 3 mm more lateral yielded hyperrelaxation and detachment—"just like an injection of Demerol." When such small electrode movements generate such large differences in affect, one must be very careful in placing and maintaining the electrodes. Further-

Table 15.1
Intracranial Self-Stimulation in Humans: Reward Sites

Region Stimulated	*Average/Hr*	*Subjective Response*
Left centromedian	488.8	Partial memory recall; anger and frustration
Right posterior septal	394.9	"Feeling great"; sexual thoughts; elimination of bad thoughts
Left caudate	373.0	Cool taste; "like it OK"
Mesencephalic tegmentum	280.0	Drunk feeling; "happy button"; elimination of bad thoughts
Anterior amygdala	257.9	Indifferent feeling; somewhat pleasant but not intense
Posterior amygdala	224.0	Moderately rewarding; increase of current requested

Source: Heath (1963).

more, the experience of clinicians is that the most important motivation for their subjects comes from a desire to please the doctor, not to gain instant nirvana. Valenstein (1973) cites reports from two laboratories that patients will continue to "self-stimulate" at about their usual rate after the power is turned off.

The effects of intracranial stimulation also vary widely with the environment, even when electrode location and parameters of stimulation remain constant. Remember that the stimulation bears little relationship to the coding of natural stimuli on bundles of afferent axons. All neurons near the electrode are stimulated, whether excitatory or inhibitory, afferent or efferent. Under these conditions it is often surprising that the stimulation has any effects at all. In the cortex it usually has no effect, possibly for this reason.

In conclusion, electrical stimulation offers a fascinating glimpse into the internal brain organization of humans but gives little threat of misuse by political forces and is of only limited usefulness in clinical medicine. More naturalistic behavior control techniques are extremely powerful, however (Campbell, 1983; Trivers, 1983). Biochemical interventions have generally proved more effective than psychosurgery, especially in the treatment of mental illness.

MENTAL ILLNESSES

Humans enjoy the advantages of large and complex brains, but we have also inherited a dark side of intelligence—the increased risk of mental illness. Becuase of the social and personal costs of mental illness, the problem is one of the major challenges for the neurosciences.

One of the first questions we must ask in investigating the problem is: What causes mental illnesses, and what are relative contributions of environment and heredity? This is a controversial topic, especially among mental health professionals. Many of them have been trained almost exclusively to think of treating behaviors and environmental influences. There is mounting evidence, though, that many mental illnesses have a strong genetic component. Some sceintists see a danger that the emphasis on genetic contributions to mental illness may lead to fatalism—to the idea that since the disease is in a person's genes, there is no help for the mentally ill person. Sometimes quite the opposite is true, however; the discovery of a genetic mechanism can lead to an effective treatment for a mental disorder.

PHENYLKETONURIA—A TREATABLE FORM OF MENTAL RETARDATION

A case in point is a form of progressive mental retardation called **phenylketonuria (PKU).** The disease in not a mental illness, in the sense of an aberration of behavior, but a developmental disorder with mental consequences. It is a useful example because its origin is well understood.

Victims of PKU are normal at birth but suffer progressive mental retardation that begins in infancy. The disease is a result of faulty metabolism of the essential amino acid phenylalanine, due to the absence of the enzyme phenylalanine hydroxylase. (The biochemistry of the disorder is summarized in Figure 15.4.) Without the enzyme, undigested phenylalanine accumulates in the blood, sometimes up to 100 times the normal level, and metabolic derivatives such as phenylpyruvic acid are formed (Gardner, 1983). Some of the derivatives are toxic to brain metabolism and cause irreversible brain damage. Figure 15.5 shows a child with PKU.

The syndrome is caused by a defect in a gene directing the synthesis of phenylalanine hydroxylase. Normally, one inherits a copy of this gene from both parents, but the copy from one parent may be defective. In that case, no symptoms of PKU will appear, because the gene from the other parent can direct production of the enzyme. But the individual is a carrier of the defective gene. (The individual is **heterozygous** [*hetero* is Greek for "different"] because two different forms of the gene are present.) The defective gene is **recessive,** because the syndrome is seen only if the gene is inherited from both parents. Even then, the chance of having a PKU child is only 25 percent; each parent has a 50 percent chance of passing the defective gene to the child, and the gene must be inherited from both parents for the syndrome to' appear.

This discovery of the metabolic defect and its genetic basis led directly to a treatment for the

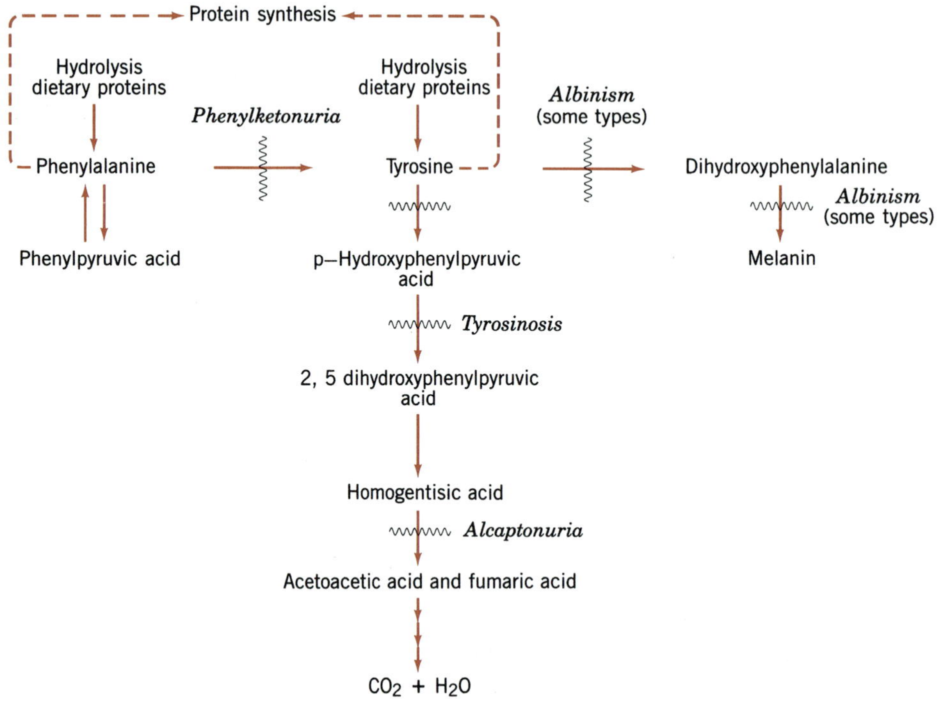

***Figure 15.4** Metabolic pathways for phenylalanine, with enzyme deficiencies leading to phenylketonuria and several other syndromes. Alcaptonuria is a blackening and hardening of cartilage. Tyrosinosis is an inability to degrade the amino acid tyrosine. Albinism is a lack of skin pigments.*

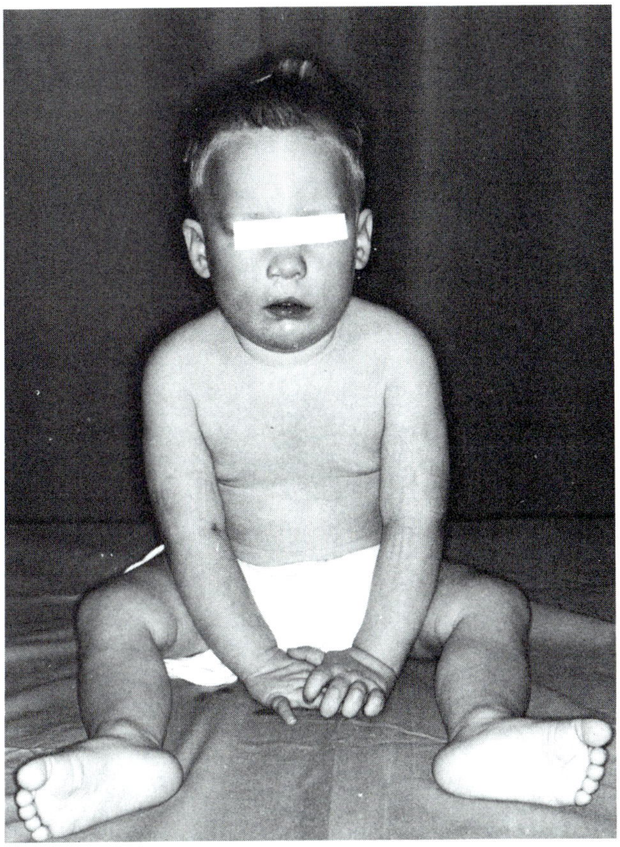

Figure 15.5 *Typical appearance of a child with phenylketonuria. The child's mental state is normal at birth but deteriorates during infancy to severe retardation as toxic metabolic by-products accumulate. Other features are fair hair and skin, eczema, blue eyes, and agitated and restless behavior. Early diagnosis is possible with a urine test or a blood test.*

disease. If PKU is diagnosed in infancy, the mental retardation can be avoided with a carefully controlled diet. The diet must contain enough phenylalanine to allow the synthesis of body proteins, for the body cannot produce the amino acid. But there must not be enough to allow a buildup of the abnormal and toxic phenylalanine derivatives. Successful treatment of PKU is one of the dramatic achievements of the modern synthesis of genetics and biochemistry. It is not a cure, however. The defective gene remains in the population, and all children of PKU victims will either be carriers or have PKU themselves.

In the case of PKU, treatment followed the understanding of the genetics and biochemistry of the disease. Mental illnesses are more complicated, however, and the progression of research into them is not as orderly. In the next disease to be discussed, the major breakthrough was made by mistake.

SCHIZOPHRENIA

The characterization of **schizophrenia** is difficult, for the diagnostic criteria used by psychiatrists are maddeningly inconsistent. The name is Greek for "split mind," a description that implies disordered thinking, although schizophrenia has nothing to do with the corpus callosum. Schizophrenia includes auditory hallucinations, disordered affect, and often a sense of being controlled by alien forces (Flekkøy, 1981).

Types of Schizophrenia

The American Psychiatric Association's "Diagnostic and Statistical Manual of Mental Disorders" (DSM III) lists five kinds of schizophrenia: paranoid, disorganized, catatonic, undifferentiated, and residual. **Paranoid schizophrenics** have probably the most elaborate cognition: delusions of grandeur, persecution, or control. The cartoon mental patient who thinks he is Napoleon is a paranoid schizophrenic. **Disorganized schizophrenics** suffer from marked incoherence and flat or silly affect. They may have fragmentary delusions, but they cannot sustain systematized ones. Associated features include grimaces, other mannerisms, and extreme social withdrawal.

Catatonic schizophrenics show very little activity, withdrawing both mentally and physically. Sometimes there is rapid alternation between extreme excitement and stupor. Severe cases show **waxy flexibility;** the limbs resist being moved passively but tend to remain where they were placed. It is as if the limbs have a high viscosity, like warm wax. Patients who recover from this phase report that mental activity continues even while the body is effectively paralyzed. Waxy flexibility was common several decades ago but is now rare. **Undifferentiated schizophrenia** is a grab-bag for schizophrenias that don't fit into any other category, and **residual schizophrenia** defines patients who have had at least one episode of schizophrenia but show only mild symptoms at the time of diagnosis.

Some of these symptoms can be identified as positive—for example, delusions, hallucinations, and thought disorders. They are probably related to neurotransmitter abnormalities. Negative symptoms indicate the lack of behavior. They include flattened affect, poverty of speech, and social withdrawal; and they may be related to brain damage (Crow, et al., 1982).

Two variants of the disease have also been identified. **Acute schizophrenia** has a rapid onset and includes episodes of spontaneous remission (return to normalcy for no obvious reason). **Chronic schizophrenia** is a more slowly developing condition that is more difficult to treat and often is permanent.

About one-third of all schizophrenics make a stable recovery, even without treatment. This fact has contributed to a lot of false leads toward cures in poorly controlled research and case histories, for one can point to a few "cures" following any treatment whatever. The disease is disturbingly common, affecting about 1 percent of the population at one time or another.

Many colorful hypotheses have been proposed about environmental causes of the disorder: mothers who are too warm or cold, fathers who are too timid or too intimidating, conflicting messages from parents, and so on. The evidence is now overwhelming, however, that genetics plays an important role in the origin of the disease.

Genetics of Schizophrenia

Schizophrenia tends to run in families, but this could be due to either environmental or genetic influences, since families have both environment and heredity in common. Both nature and culture, however, provide natural experiments that allow us to separate the two factors.

Twin Studies. Nature provides a controlled experiment in the contrast between **monozygotic** (identical) **twins** and **dizygotic** (fraternal) **twins.** Since the monozygotic twins come from the same egg, they have identical genes. Any condition fully determined by heredity will be identical in both of them. If one twin is blond, for instance, the other is always blond, and both are of the same sex. The similarity of traits in a group of pairs of twins is measured in a **concordance rate**—the percentage of twin pairs who share the trait. Concordance rates for schizophrenia are higher among monozygotic than among dizygotic twins.

Even for monozygotic twins, however, the rate is less than 100 percent, suggesting that genes do not play the only role in the development of the disease. In some of the cases where only one twin became schizophrenic, that twin often had a lower birth weight, suffered more physiological distress during development, or was seen by the parents as more submissive, fearful, and sensitive than the other twin (Wahl, 1976). Further evidence for the presence of a genetic propensity to schizophrenia in monozygotic twins, even where only one twin has the illness, is a similar rate of schizophrenia in the children of the normal twin and the affected twin (Fischer, 1971). The normal twin seems to carry the genetic trigger for the disease and passes it on to his or her children.

Adoption Studies. Another way to separate genetic and environmental contributions is to study adopted children. Most of the best studies come from Scandinavia, where social records are particularly complete and the natural and adoptive parents of a schizophrenic adoptee can be compared. An environmental theory would predict that the adoptive parents of schizophrenics would more often show signs of mental illness than would the biological parents. A genetic theory would predict the opposite—more abnormalities in the biological parents. Again supporting the genetic theory, pathology was found to be far more common among the biological than the adoptive parents (Kety et al., 1975).

If a genetic factor is important in causing schizophrenia, some anatomical or biochemical abnormality in the brain might trigger the disease. The search for that trigger was aided from some unexpected directions.

Biochemistry of Schizophrenia

Until the 1950s there were no effective treatments for schizophrenia. The usual treatment was hospitalization until a spontaneous remission occurred. This resulted in a psychiatric patient population in the United States of about half a million. At this time, Henri Laborit, a French surgeon, was searching for a drug that would relax muscles for surgery. He discovered a drug that also reduced the patient's worrying and preoperative tension. Recognizing the potential usefulness of such a drug, Laborit then collaborated with psychiatrists in trying the new drug, chlorpromazine, on psychiatric patients.

Success was so dramatic that the drug and its relatives, the **phenothiazines,** became widely used. The mental hospitals have been emptied in the past 30 years not by better behavioral therapies but by the use of antipsychotic drugs. Thus help for behavioral problems came not from behavioral but from biochemical therapies.

The Dopamine Hypothesis. As soon as the antipsychotic effect of phenothiazines was discovered, research began on their mode of action. The drugs were found to block postsynaptic receptor sites for dopamine (Creese, Burt & Snyder, 1976), as Figure 15.6 shows. This action led directly to the dopamine hypothesis of schizophrenia.

If schizophrenia is related to excess dopaminergic activity, one ought to find increased dopamine concentrations or increased numbers of dopamine receptors in schizophrenic brains. In fact, both have been found. Dopamine concentrations increase, but only in the nucleus accumbens and the anterior perforate substance (Bird, Spokes & Iverson, 1979). These are among the major areas in which the mesolimbic dopamine system terminates. The specificity of the dopamine increase corresponds with older EEG data (Heath, 1954) showing that schizophrenics have random spike activity from the region of the nucleus accumbens, septal nuclei, head of the caudate nucleus, and amygdala. All of these structures are major targets of mesolimbic dopamine neurons.

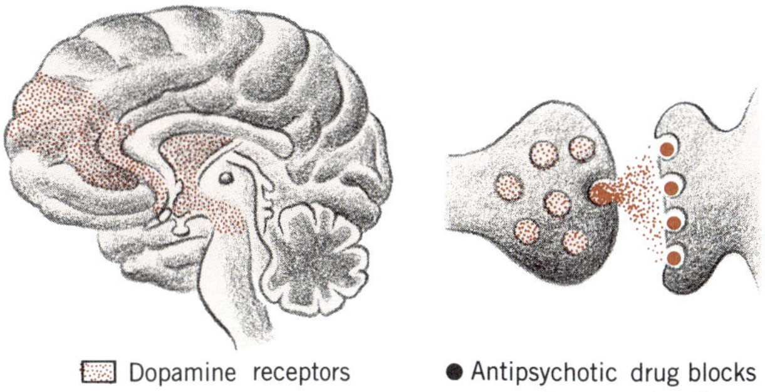

Figure 15.6 Distribution of dopamine receptor sites in the forebrain and midbrain. Other dopaminergic synapses in the retina are probably unrelated to schizophrenia. Most antischizophrenic drugs block postsynaptic dopamine receptor molecules.

A stronger conclusion would be possible if the biochemical tests could be done more easily in living schizophrenics. Researchers have attempted to measure concentrations of **homovanillic acid,** a product of dopamine metabolism. Early tests were inconsistent, but recent carefully controlled studies have shown higher concentrations in schizophrenics. Patients with stronger symptoms tend to have higher concentrations of the dopamine metabolite (Davis et al., 1985). Inexplicably, the correlations are better for blood plasma concentrations than for cerebrospinal fluid levels.

In postmortem examinations of brains, the number of dopamine receptors in schizophrenics has been found to be greater than that in normal controls (Lee & Seeman, 1980). This greater number would be expected for patients who had been taking phenothiazines, because the dopamine system might compensate for the drug-induced dopamine deprivation by increasing the number of receptors. But the number of receptors was also higher in 11 patients who had received very little or no long-term medication. A more recent study has found a bimodal distribution of the number of dopamine receptors; one group of patients had about 25 percent more dopamine receptors than controls did in the caudate, the putamen, and the nucleus accumbens. Another group had about 2.3 times more. This suggests that there may be two biochemically different kinds of schizophrenia (Seeman et al., 1984). The subjects came from clinics in four countries.

Other evidence for the dopamine hypothesis comes from treatments that make schizophrenia worse rather than better. If drugs that block dopamine receptors reduce the symptoms of schizophrenia, then drugs that increase brain dopamine might have the opposite effect. This experiment has been performed unintentionally in patients with Parkinson's disease, who are given the dopamine precursor L-dopa to compensate for their deficit in dopaminergic neurons (see Chapter 7). One side effect of this treatment in some Parkinson's patients is the appearance of schizophrenic symptoms. Conversely, a side effect of treating schizophrenics with phenothiazines is the appearance of Parkinson's symptoms. Furthermore, a particularly tragic side effect of prolonged treatment with phenothiazines is **tardive dyskinesia**—stereotyped involuntary movements, mostly of the face and arms. These symptoms suggest damage to the motor systems of the basal ganglia.

If the Parkinson's symptoms of the medicated schizophrenic are treated with L-dopa, the schizophrenia becomes worse (Yaryura-Tobias, Diamond & Merlis, 1970). It is as if everyone is walking a dopaminergic tightrope: too much dopamine leads to schizophrenia and too little to Parkinson's disease. In some patients the safe range seems to be particularly narrow. This is one of the problems now facing Parkinson patients who require the continued use of L-dopa (Flekkøy, 1981).

A treatment that seems to induce a condition indistinguishable from paranoid schizophrenia is the ingestion of large doses of amphetamine (Angrist et al., 1974). The similarity extends even to the types of disordered thought patterns characteristically found. The action of amphetamine on the brain is to release stored dopamine and noradrenaline and possibly to inhibit dopamine reuptake. Amphetamine psychosis can be reliably produced in normal individuals, showing that the drug does not bring out latent psychotic tendencies. Instead, it produces the psychosis by acting on otherwise normal brains. Nothing stands between us and psychosis but a biochemical feedback mechanism.

Other Biochemical Hypotheses. Several observations suggest that dopamine excess is not the only biochemical change in schizophrenia. One observation is that there is a discrepancy between the time courses of phenothiazine action and of behavioral improvement. Phenothiazines affect dopamine levels almost immediately. Yet improvement in the schizophrenic's behavioral symptoms comes only after a delay of days to weeks. Perhaps dopamine is only one of several agents involved in the psychosis.

A bewildering array of alternatives to the dopamine hypothesis is now being considered, each with its own suggestive but inconclusive evidence. One hypothesis stems from the existence of amphetamine psychosis; if a schizophrenialike state can be produced by amphetamine, perhaps natural schizophrenia is the result of a pathological production of some endogenous amphetaminelike substance. One suspect is phenylethylamine, normally produced in small quantities during the metabolism of norepinephrine.

Another hypothesis involving abnormal levels of endogenous substances is an endorphin theory. The idea was first proposed on the basis of elevated endorphin levels in the cerebrospinal fluid (CSF) of drugfree schizophrenics (Terenius et al., 1976). Supporting this theory is the relative insensitivity of schizophrenics to sensory stimulation. Their sensory evoked potentials are smaller than those of normals (Terenius, 1982). Elevated CSF endorphins are seen more frequently in some categories of schizophrenics than in others. Against the endorphin hypothesis is the fact that schizophrenia is unaffected by naloxone, an antagonist that affects all opiates. This result suggests that changed endorphin levels may be a consequence of the disease rather than a cause.

Still another hint about possible biochemical influences on schizophrenia comes from the observation that the malady generally has its onset after puberty. Could the increase of sex hormones at puberty somehow bring on the disease? The issue was studied in a particularly interesting schizophrenia-prone population.

About 350 years ago, a small number of families settled a remote area in the north of Sweden. They had numerous children and a high degree of intermarriage of relatives. By chance, the population, now numbering about 6000, has suffered from a high incidence of schizophrenia; the risk for children is about 10 percent. Another advantage of studying this population is that a good deal is known about it; large pedigrees have been assembled (see Figure 15.7), and the last three generations have been professionally examined.

Wetterberg (1982) has performed a large number of biochemical and hormonal assays on samples of the north Swedish population, finding lower levels of luteinizing hormone (LH) and

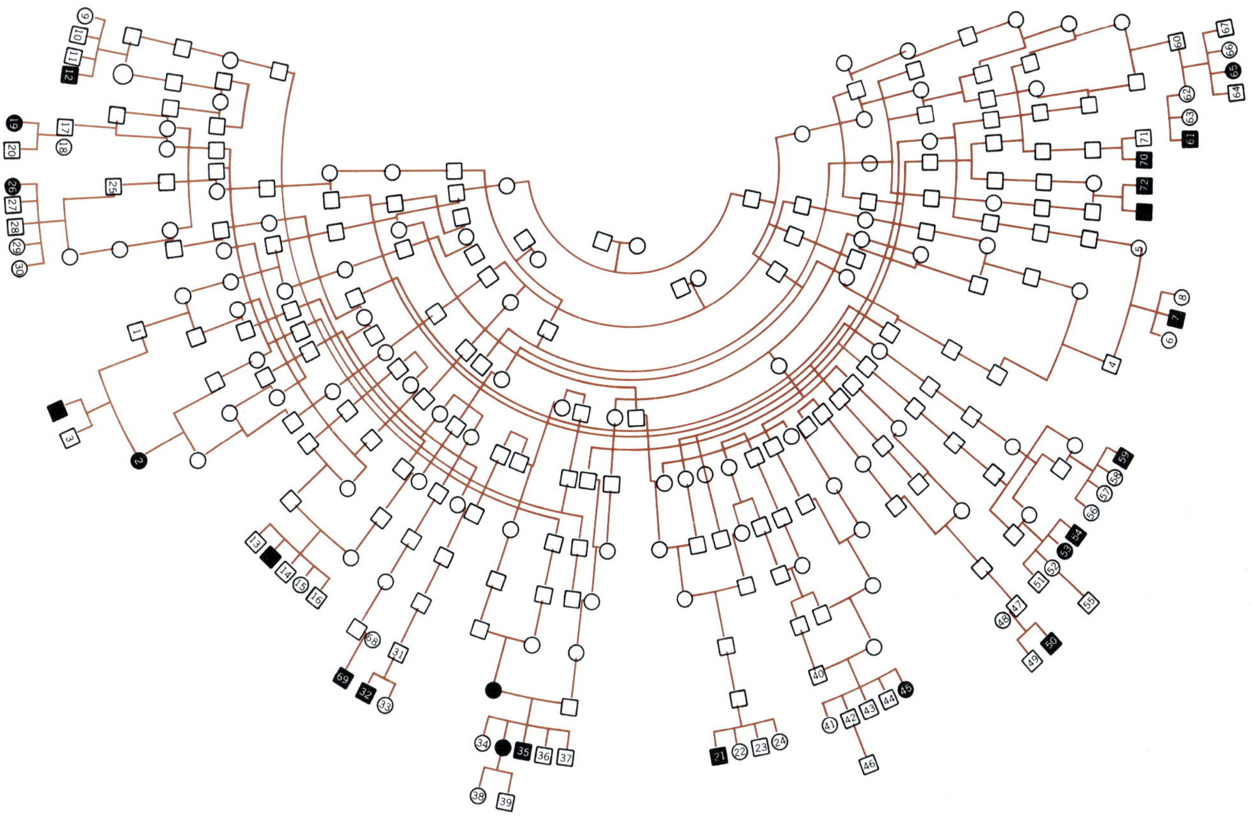

Squares = Males
Circles = Females
Black symbols = Patients with clinical manifest schizophrenia
White symbols = Patients with no clinical signs of schizophrenia

***Figure 15.7** A major pedigree showing genetic relationships among examined schizophrenic patients. The numbers in the symbols refer to individuals analyzed for catechol-O-methyltransferase.*

follicle-stimulating hormone (FSH) in schizophrenics than in their nonschizophrenic relatives. The levels of these hormones were compared with the levels of several hormones related to catecholamine metabolism. When the hormone levels were correlated with the catecholamine-related enzymes, the strongest relationship found for the population under 55 years of age was between dopamine-beta-hydroxylase (DBH)—an enzyme that breaks down dopamine—and FSH (see Figure 15.8).

This finding relates to still another theory of schizophrenia, a neurotoxin theory. Ordinarily, DBH converts dopamine into norepinephrine, so a deficiency in DBH activity should lead to the accumulation of dopamine. Excessive dopamine in turn would partly be hydroxylated into 6-hydroxydopamine, a substance that destroys dopaminergic and noradrenergic terminals (Stein & Wise, 1971). Evidence for this theory is still sketchy and contradictory, however, and more work will be required to settle the issue.

In conclusion, we have a wealth of theories, all relating in some way to catecholamine metabolism. Each theory has a plausible basis, and each explains some, but not all, of the data. The bio-

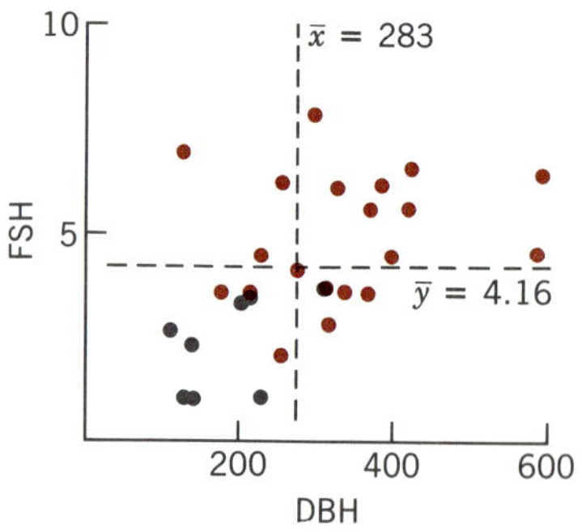

Figure 15.8 Serum follicle-stimulating hormone (FSH) plotted against plasma dopamine-beta-hydroxylase (DBH) for 28 patients. The black circles refer to schizophrenic patients, who characteristically have low levels of both hormones.

chemical trigger for schizophrenia may not be as simple as any of the current theories suggest. And there is an environmental influence on the disease as well.

AFFECTIVE ILLNESS

All of us become depressed at times, but in some people periods of severe depression alternate with periods of excessively expansive moods that are similar to the feelings of normal people taking cocaine or amphetamine. The manic mood includes overactivity, talkativeness, increased energy, and illusions of invincibility. The disease is also called **bipolar depression.** It is distinguished from ordinary depression, or **unipolar depression,** because the bipolar form usually strikes at a younger age and affects men and women about equally. Unipolar depression is most common in older women. Together the two forms are also called **affective illness:**

Both forms of depression show strong heritability, measured with the same kinds of studies that revealed heritability in schizophrenia—higher concordance in monozygotic twins than in dizygotic twins (Gershon et al., 1976). The concordance is similar whether the twins are reared apart or together (Price, 1968). Concordance rates are higher for bipolar than for unipolar forms, however. Adoption studies also show a genetic component; affective illness is correlated with biological parents rather than adoptive parents.

Unipolar Depression

Unipolar depression is usually treated with **monoamine oxidase (MAO) inhibitors** or with **trycyclic antidepressants;** the reason for the name of the latter family of antipsychotic drugs is clear from Figure 15.9. The effectiveness of MAO inhibitors implicates abnormally the low activity of norepinephrine and serotonin terminals as neurological concomitants of depression (Schildkraut & Kety, 1967). The discovery of the effectiveness of MAO inhibitors was again by accident, when the antituberculosis drug isoniazid was found to have a mood-elevating effect. A related drug, iproniazid, was found to be effective against unipolar depression (Crane, 1957).

MAO inhibitors slow the breakdown of the monoamine transmitters dopamine, norepinephrine, and serotonin, thus increasing their concentrations. Unfortunately, these drugs have toxic side effects. The "cheese effect" has also been a serious problem. Biogenic (naturally occurring) amines in foods such as cheese, wine, bread, chocolate, and some fruits and nuts are ordinarily metabolized by MAO in the blood. MAO inhibitors can prevent this action and cause severe reactions in the sympathetic subsystem.

The tricyclic antidepressants have been more satisfactory clinically, but they bring their own

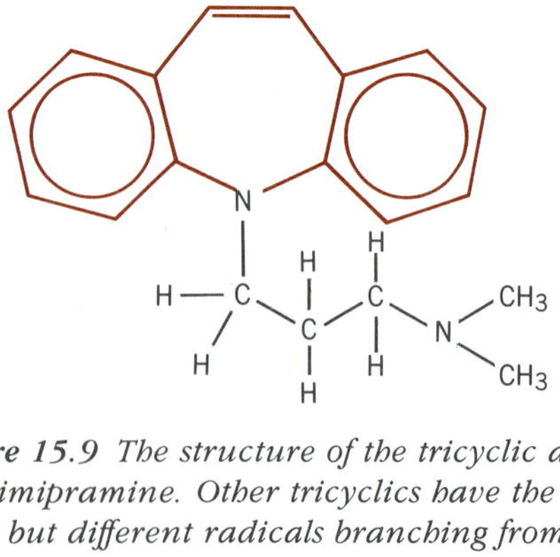

Figure 15.9 The structure of the tricyclic antidepressant imipramine. Other tricyclics have the same three rings but different radicals branching from the basic structure.

puzzles. Some of them block the reuptake of catecholamines, and others do not. The one property they have in common is that all of the clinically effective antidepressants block histamine receptors (Kanof & Greengard, 1978). **Histamine** is a probable neurotransmitter (Schwartz, 1977). A group of histamine fibers ascends in the medial forebrain bundle (a potent self-stimulation site examined in Chapter 9) to project to widespread forebrain regions. The MAO inhibitors do not affect histamine, however, so each set of drugs seems to carry its own theory. The link between the MAO inhibitors and the tricyclic depressants is still a mystery.

Panic. Everyone feels justified panic at times, such as right before an examination for which one isn't prepared. But some people suffer from severe attacks without warning and for no obvious reason. A victim can be just walking down the street and suddenly feel an overwhelming sense of dread or even of impending death. Though the attacks last only a few minutes, they are very stressful. The victims realize their lack of basis and seek help. Though the biochemical basis of the problem isn't completely worked out, antidepressants often reduce the frequency and severity of the attacks. Both tricyclics and MAO inhibitors seem to help. Large doses of caffeine (the equivalent of about eight cups of coffee) can induce panic attacks in people suffering from this disorder, though the drug does not have this effect in normal people.

Bipolar Depression

Manic-depressive psychosis—bipolar depression—is a very dangerous disease. If left untreated, about one-eighth of its victims die, not from the direct physical effects of the disease but from suicide. The psychosis is treated effectively with lithium, which, unlike the complex drugs used for other conditions, is an element, a metallic ion. Some other light metallic ions have similar effects, but lithium is by far the most potent. Treatment with lithium is sometimes difficult because lithium carbonate (Li_2CO_3), the salt commonly used, has a rather narrow range between therapeutic effectiveness and toxicity. Treatment requires constant monitoring by a physician. Other salts of lithium promise to ease this problem. Lithium affects catecholaminergic and cholinergic neurons and also influences amino acid neurotransmitters (Fieve, 1979). But there is still no satisfactory theory to explain why lithium is clinically effective.

Again we have practical answers followed by theoretical questions, but overall, progress in treating mental illness with biochemical interventions has been enormous. Continued research promises further improvements.

Like other drug treatments of psychotic disorders, lithium does not cure the disease. It only prevents the appearance of symptoms. Patients who stop taking the medicine risk more psychotic episodes. Patients must continue to take the drug for the rest of their lives, even if no symptoms remain. But when symptoms diminish, about half of all patients reduce or stop treatment, against medical advice. Psychotherapy is useful in helping patients to stay on medication and to cope with stresses that might precipitate psychotic episodes. We should not be deluded into thinking that drugs can solve all the problems even of biochemical disorders.

EATING DISORDERS

Some syndromes are related to both affective disorders and nutrition. Their victims' bizarre eating habits often cause secondary health problems from the resulting low weight or physiological stress. The diseases—**anorexia nervosa** and **bulimia**—usually affect women in their teens or 20s.

An adolescent girl weighs about 50 kg (110 lb) and appears healthy and normal; but a few months later her weight has declined to less than 35 kg. She looks like a walking skeleton, menstruation stops, and she is in danger of death from starvation. In fact, about 5 percent of anorectics (patients with anorexia nervosa) die of starvation, and another 5 percent commit suicide. At the same time, the victim has low self-esteem and feels herself to be too fat. A perfectionist, she continually diets and may check her weight several times a day. Many anorectics reduce their weight further with laxatives or diuretics.

Another young woman appears normal but secretly binges on huge amounts of calorie-rich foods. Feeling guilty, she then vomits; she repeats the cycle a few days later. Bulimic women usually are depressed after a binge, and, unlike anorectics, they worry about their condition. Many bulimics also have weight problems, suffering from low weight, obesity, or large fluctuations in weight.

Treatments of bulimia and anorexia are among the most unsatisfactory in clinical medicine (Herzog & Copeland, 1985). Psychotherapy is used without any clear indication that it is effective, and many drugs have shown mixed results. Depressive symptoms in many patients, especially bulimics, suggest a relationship between eating disorders and depression (Katz et al., 1984). Antidepressants—both MAO inhibitors and tricyclics—benefit some patients a little. Teams of nutritionists, psychologists, and physicians working together have had the most success.

The cause of these disorders remains unknown, but a recent proposal suggests that anorectics are addicted to the opioids that the body normally produces during starvation. Opioids are elevated in the cerebrospinal fluid of anorectics, and the victims show many characteristics of addiction—denial, compulsivity, persistence despite social and medical dangers, and a feeling of elation when dieting. More research on the relationship between eating disorders and neurotransmitters may help us design treatments. Nutrition research has already helped with some other disorders.

NUTRITION AND BRAIN FUNCTION

The brain always has first call on the body's energy resources (see Chapter 3). One would assume that it also has first call on the nutrients that are the starting points for the biosynthesis of neurotransmitters. The assumption is false: levels of several neurotransmitters depend on the composition of the diet.

CONTROL OF NEUROTRANSMITTER SYNTHESIS

The first hint of a relationship between nutrient levels and neurotransmitters came indirectly, from studies of human circadian rhythms of amino acids in the blood. The amino acid leucine, for instance, shows a daily fluctuation that depends on the amount of protein consumed. For subjects on a normal protein-rich diet, the amount of leucine in the blood plasma from 3 P.M. to 3 A.M. is double the amount during the rest of the day. The same subjects on a protein-free diet show a decrease in leucine concentrations at those times. The cause of the decrease appears to be insulin secreted in response to dietary carbohydrates. The insulin moves leucine (and other amino acids) from the blood into skeletal muscle (Wurtman, 1982).

Serotonin

If amino acid concentrations vary with the composition of the diet, what happens to the levels of the neurotransmitters synthesized from them? Researchers studied the question by giving rats doses of tryptophan, the amino acid that is a precursor to serotonin. The surprising result was that tryptophan doses that are within the normal daily variation can enhance serotonin synthesis (Fernstrom & Wurtman, 1971). The result is disturbing, for it means that serotonin, with all of its effects on mood, sleep, and appetite (described in Chapters 9 and 10), is at the mercy of dietary variation.

The next results made things even worse for the theorists. Insulin, which decreased the levels of leucine in the experiments with rats, actually increased tryptophan concentration in the brain, thus increasing serotonin synthesis in serotonergic neurons. And feeding large amounts of protein to animals reduced their brain tryptophan and serotonin levels. Tryptophan did not seem to follow the rules that describe the metabolism of other amino acids.

The paradoxes were resolved with a better understanding of the dynamics of how tryptophan and other amino acids cross the blood-brain barrier. Tryptophan is one of a group of amino acids that do not cross the barrier easily. These amino acids—large molecules without electric charges—must be actively helped across the blood-brain barrier by carrier molecules. Tryptophan shares one carrier molecule with five other amino acids, all of them generally present in higher concentrations than tryptophan in protein-rich foods. After a high-protein meal, the amino acids compete for access to the blood-brain transport system, and tryptophan loses out.

It is as if you were scooping marbles (amino acids) from a large bin (the blood) with a bucket (the brain) and finding a mixture of different marbles in the bucket. Following a high-protein meal, the bin is full; but the proportion of tryptophan marbles is small, so the bucket will contain few tryptophan marbles. After a high-carbohydrate meal, insulin will pick competing marbles out of the bin, allowing relatively more tryptophan marbles to enter the bucket even though the total number of marbles in the bin is smaller than before.

Further experiments showed how a feedback loop is closed, controlling the concentration of brain serotonin by influencing the relative amounts of protein and carbohydrate in the diet. We have seen that carbohydrate indirectly increases the amount of serotonin synthesized; serotonin in turn selectively reduces the amount of carbohydrate consumed (see Figure 15.10). There are several lines of evidence for this feedback. The drug fenfluramine, for instance, increases brain serotonin and selectively reduces carbohydrate consumption in rats. More relevant to human physiology, serotonin-increasing treatments reduce a craving for carbohydrates in obese people. Researchers measured the craving by allowing subjects to choose from a range of snack foods rich in either protein (peanuts) or carbohydrate (potato chips) over several weeks (Wurtman et al., 1981).

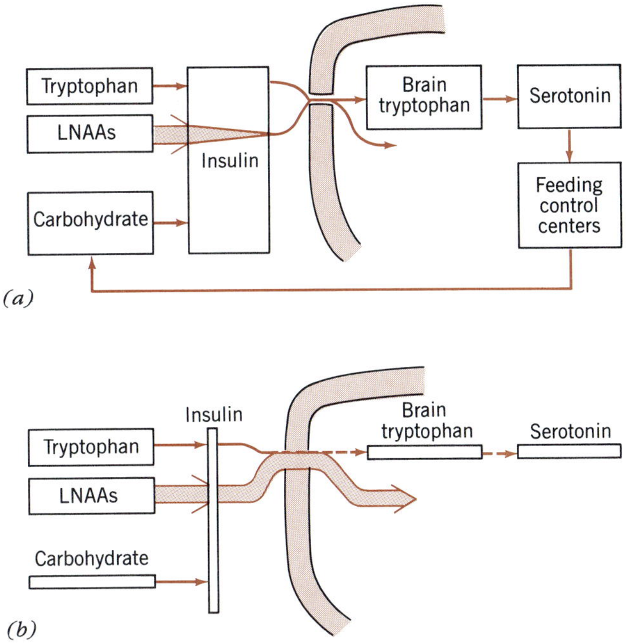

Figure 15.10 *Feedback control of brain serotonin levels.* (a) *High carbohydrate concentrations. In the presence of carbohydrates, insulin is produced. The insulin causes competing large neutral amino acids (LNAAs) to be absorbed from the bloodstream. Tryptophan does not have to compete with the LNAAs, so it crosses the blood-brain barrier to be converted in the brain to serotonin. The serotonin in turn reduces the amount of carbohydrate consumed, completing a negative feedback circuit.* (b) *Low carbohydrate concentrations. When carbohydrate concentrations in the bloodstream are low, little insulin is present and the LNAAs increase in concentration. They monopolize the transport system at the blood-brain barrier. Little tryptophan gets through, little serotonin is produced, and the negative feedback loop is not completed. The system regulates both serotonin and carbohydrate levels.*

Other Neurotransmitters

The regulation of acetylcholine and of the catecholamines proceeds by feedback mechanisms similar to that for serotonin. The mechanisms were discovered by experiments analogous to those just described. Acetylcholine, the catecholamines, and serotonin are synthesized by the actions of enzymes on dietary amino acids (see Figure 15.11), and they share a set of five biochemical characteristics necessary to let the feedbacks operate. First, some food must be able to elevate the plasma level of the nutrient. No local feedback mechanisms stabilizing the blood nutrient level are allowed. Second, the nutrient must cross the blood-brain barrier. Third, the transport system that brings the nutrient across the blood-brain barrier must be of the low-affinity type; that is, it must have some reserve capacity to carry more of the nutrient when that nutrient's concentration in the blood increases. Fourth, the enzyme that catalyzes the synthesis of the transmitter inside the neurons must also have a low affinity for the nutrient, so

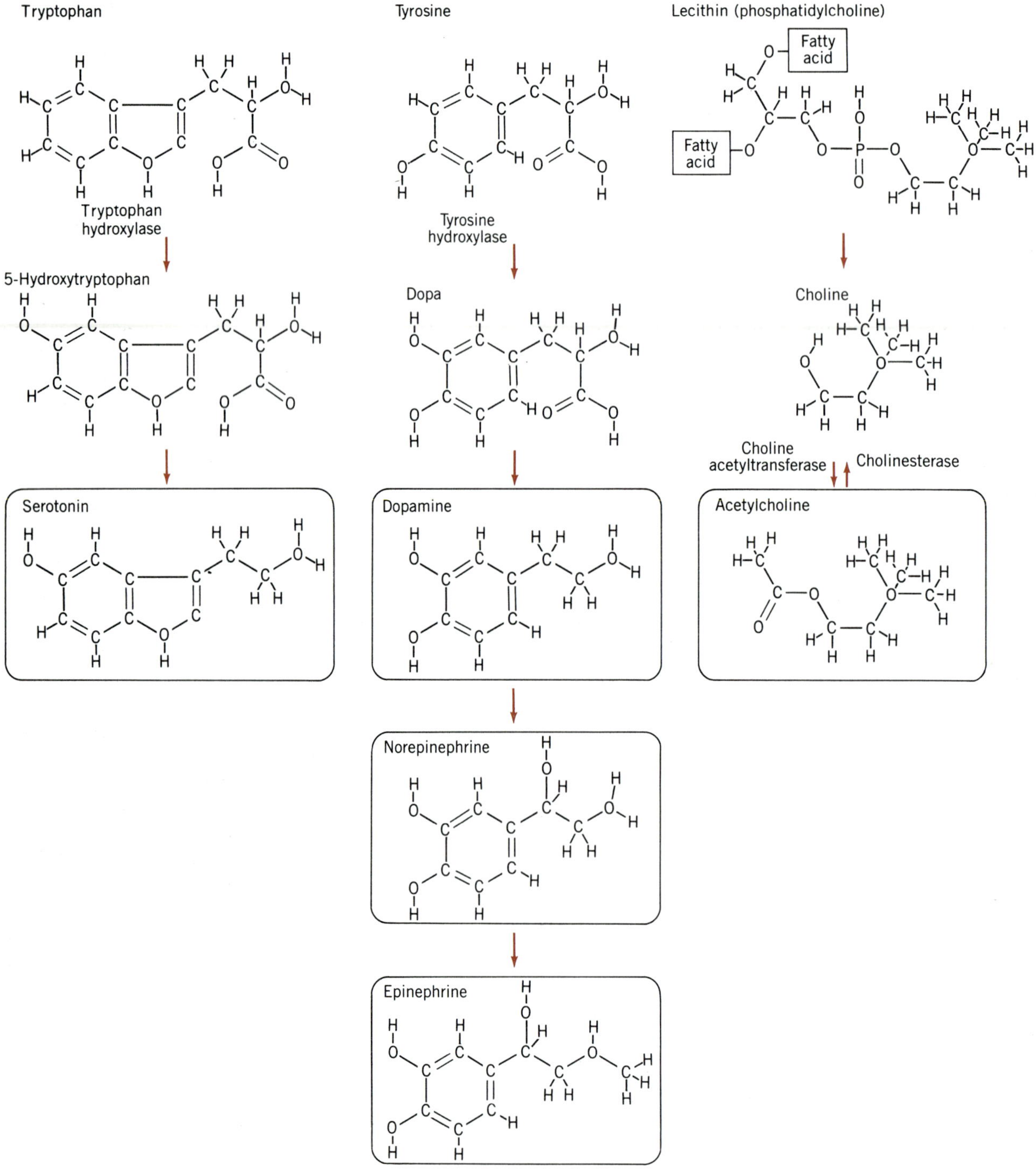

Figure 15.11 *Paths of synthesis for five neurotransmitters, beginning from three nutrients. Tryptophan and tyrosine are amino acids; they are produced by the splitting of dietary proteins into their components. Lecithin is present in much smaller quantities in the diet, but the choline synthesized from it is recycled. Synthesis in all three pathways is regulated by negative feedback mechanisms.*

synthesis can increase when the intracellular concentration of the precursor nutrient increases. Finally, the concentration of the neurotransmitter product of the synthesis cannot be controlled by an intracellular negative feedback. All of these conditions are met by serotonin, acetylcholine, and the catecholamines, and possibly by histamine and glycine as well.

Choline and Acetylcholine. The discovery of the dietary control of acetylcholine levels found a clinical application almost immediately. Dietary administration of choline or of phosphatidylcholine (one of the constituents of lecithin) relieved the involuntary movements of tardive dyskinesia in schizophrenic patients undergoing long-term treatment with antipsychotic drugs (Barbeau, 1979; Gelenberg, Wojcik & Growdon, 1979). Tardive dyskinesia is probably the severest side effect of antipsychotic medication. The treatment does not alter all cholinergic synapses; that result would have severe side effects of its own. Rather, the abnormally active neurons responsible for the dyskinesia seem to be more sensitive to dietary influences than are normal cholinergic neurons elsewhere in the brain.

Choline and lecithin may also be effective against Alzheimer's disease (senile dementia); reduced cholinergic functions may contribute to memory impairment. Chapter 11 reviewed the role of cholinergic systems in memory, including experiments in which younger people given scopolamine, a blocker of cholinergic transmission, suffer short-term memory defects similar to those seen in the aged. Thus it may be possible to reduce some of the effects of Alzheimer's disease with acetylcholine precursors in the diet. Results so far have been highly variable even if patients are flooded with 25 g or more of lecithin, a choline precursor, per day (Bartus et al., 1982). Most studies find no significant memory improvement. One possible explanation for the variability is that what is now called Alzheimer's disease will turn out to be several diseases, only some of which can be treated with choline therapy. Treatment seems to be more effective for mild cases, and it affects new learning ability rather than memory. In one study, this was true even for the youngest subject (age 42) (Etienne et al., 1979).

Tyrosine and the Catecholamines. The application of dietary tyrosine to the treatment of catecholamine deficiency diseases is another clinical possibility. One application is in the control of blood pressure. Tyrosine has the remarkable property of increasing dangerously low blood pressure and decreasing high blood pressure. The mechanism for this bit of biochemical magic depends on an increased sensitivity of abnormally firing neurons to increases in precursor availability. High blood pressure is associated with higher sustained levels of firing in norepinephrine neurons of the caudal brain stem; low pressure results in higher activity in the sympathetic ganglia and in the adrenal chromaffin cells (endocrine cells that secrete norepinephrine into the bloodstream). In each case, tyrosine selectively influences the abnormally active cells, restoring normal blood pressure.

Tyrosine is also being applied to clinical depression, with positive preliminary results, possibly through its action on catecholamine synthesis (Wurtman, 1982). The clinical effectiveness of the catecholamine precursor would suggest that a relatively simple neurotransmitter imbalance is responsible for depression.

CONCLUSION—NUTRITION OR THERAPY?

Often the same nutrients that are commonly consumed in foods have effects on everything from stress to psychosis. Most of the nutrients are clinically effective only if there is a disorder in normal function, however; tyrosine's effect on blood pressure is an example. The nutrients are not drugs, for they are metabolized by the normal biochemical routes that have evolved to utilize them; and they are quickly removed from the body. The conditions they treat are not due to nutrient deficiencies; tardive dyskinesia, for example, is not caused by choline deficiency. Thus the therapeutic role of amino acids is distinct from that of vitamins. (Scurvy, for instance, results from a deficiency of vitamin C.) Abnormally large amounts of the amino acids are used to compensate for an abnormality in function that is caused by something else.

Again we have found that the normal, healthy body and brain are set by nature at optimal levels for effective functioning. Just as one cannot improve memory or sex drive without paying a price somewhere else, amino acid therapy generally will not improve a system that is already performing normally. We are finely tuned machines, designed by evolutionary development to perceive, to think, to act effectively just as we are.

CHAPTER SUMMARY

1. Neuroscience has an important impact on society, both through changing our view of ourselves and through specific interventions relating to behavior. Psychosurgery—the effort to alter behavior through surgery—depends on three assumptions. First, a behavior must be controlled in an anatomically isolated brain center that has no other important functions. Second, a patient's symptoms must match the characteristics of the brain area. Both assumptions are questionable. Third, no other brain damage can result from surgery. Nevertheless, there have been repeated attempts to treat patients with psychosurgery.

2. Prefrontal lobotomy was instituted to make psychiatric patients calmer and more cooperative. But the patients suffered from interruption of planning ability and other deficits expected from prefrontal damage. With the arrival of antipsychotic drugs, the operation fell into disuse. Subcortical psychosurgery has included amygdalectomy aimed at relieving aggression. Success is difficult to evaluate because of the small number of patients and the lack of objective measures of the results. Psychosurgery in the hypothalamus was also attempted, to eliminate some forms of homosexuality. But the program had a poor theoretical backing, and the operation reduced sex drive rather than changing sexual preference.

3. Electrical self-stimulation in humans has shown that the effects, while sometimes quite pleasant or unpleasant, do not dominate a patient's behavior to the exclusion of other activities. Apparently, human behavior is driven by many systems, so simple activation of an anatomically restricted region cannot supersede other influences. Behavioral techniques of social control are technically more practical and just as powerful as physiological techniques.

4. Many mental disorders have a strong genetic component; these are the most susceptible to physiological analysis and treatment. PKU is a form of mental retardation caused by a defect in a single recessive gene. As a result, toxic products of phenylalanine accumulate in the blood. Mental retardation results unless phenylalanine in the diet is limited.

5. Schizophrenia is characterized by disordered thought, auditory hallucinations, and sometimes paranoid delusions. Hypotheses about environmentally based causes and cures have yielded little progress in treatment. The disease is inherited, but environment also plays a part, because not all of those genetically at risk become schizophrenic. The first effective treatments implicated excess dopamine as a cause of schizophrenia. There are increases in concentrations of dopamine in dopaminergic terminals and increases in the number of dopamine receptors. Amphetamine psychosis, indistinguishable from acute schizophrenia, also shows increased dopamine.

6. Other biochemical mechanisms may also play a role in schizophrenia. Dopamine is probably not the only chemical involved; antipsychotic drugs lower dopamine levels quickly, but behavioral change requires days or weeks. If schizophrenia is the same as amphetamine psychosis, perhaps an endogenous amphetaminelike substance causes the schizophrenia. Endorphins may also be related, though evidence is contradictory. Genetic studies find reduced LH and FSH in schizophrenics; lowered hormones correlate with lower levels of the enzyme DBH, which ordinarily breaks down dopamine. A related hypothesis considers schizophrenia to result from 6-hydroxy-dopamine, a toxic breakdown product that accumulates if DBH does not destroy excess dopamine.

7. Unipolar depression is treated with MAO inhibitors or with tricyclic antidepressents. MAO inhibitors implicate low norepinephrine and serotonin activity in the condition; tricyclics relate more consistently to histamine receptors. Manic-depressive psychosis is treated with lithium. This element affects a wide range of neurotransmitters, including the catecholamines, acetylcholine, and amino acids. Lithium prevents symptoms in most patients; but, like other biochemical interventions, it does not cure the underlying condition. both psychotherapy and drugs are necessary for effective management of psychoses.

8. Eating disorders can be severe threats to health and life. Anorexia nervosa involves severe weight loss along with distortions of the body image. Bulimia involves a binge-purge cycle of eating. Neither disorder has an effective treatment.

9. Many neurotransmitters, including serotonin, acetylcholine, the catecholamines, and perhaps histamine and glycine, are synthesized from amino acids in the diet. Concentrations of these neurotransmitters vary with the availability of the precursor amino acids. Tryptophan, the precursor of serotonin, is carried across the blood-brain barrier in competition with five other, more plentiful amino acids, so its availability is reduced after a protein-rich meal. Carbohydrate has the opposite effect, for the insulin secreted to digest carbohydrate also removes other amino acids from the blood, leaving a higher concentration of tryptophan relative to the other amino acids. Serotonin in turn reduces carbohydrate consumption, completing a feedback loop. Ordinarily, the feedback keeps brain serotonin levels stable and controls protein and carbohydrate balance in the diet.

10. Dietary regulation of neurotransmitter levels in the brain requires that five conditions be met. There must be a dietary precursor that can vary in concentration in the blood, and the precursor must cross the blood-brain barrier. A low-affinity transport system must bring the nutrient across the barrier, and another low-affinity enzyme must catalyze the synthesis itself. Finally, there must be no feedback control of neurotransmitter concentration within the brain.

11. Choline, the precursor of acetylcholine, reduces tardive dyskinesia in patients taking antipsychotic drugs. It corrects the condition without affecting other cholinergic systems. Choline and lecithin may also reduce the memory deficits of Alzheimer's disease in some patients. Tyrosine, the precursor of the catecholamines, has been used to treat catecholamine deficiency diseases. It returns blood pressure to normal if it is too high or too low, again affecting only abnormally firing neurons. Tyrosine has also been used in cases of depression. The amino acids that influence neurotransmitter concentrations are not drugs but normal nutrients. They are useful mainly in treating disease and generally do not enhance normal function. The healthy nervous system is already tuned to function optimally.

KEY TERMS

Neurosurgery
Psychosurgery
Prefrontal lobotomy
Aura
Phenylketonuria (PKU)
Heterozygous
Recessive
Schizophrenia
Paranoid schizophrenia
Disorganized schizophrenia
Catatonic schizophrenia
Waxy flexibility
Undifferentiated schizophrenia
Residual schizophrenia
Acute schizophrenia

Chronic schizophrenia
Monozygotic twins
Dizygotic twins
Concordance rate
Phenothiazines
Homovanillic acid
Tardive dyskinesia
Bipolar depression
Unipolar depression
Affective illness
Monoamine oxidase (MAO) inhibitor
Tricyclic antidepressant
Histamine
Anorexia nervosa
Bulimia

SUGGESTED READINGS

Buchsbaum, M. W., & Haier, R. J. (1984). Psychopathology: Biological approaches. *Annual Review of Psychology, 34,* 401–430.

This article introduces the biological model of mental disorders and reviews modern treatment alternatives.

Kety, S. S. (1979). Disorders of the human brain. In *The Brain* (A Scientific American Book) (pp. 120–127). San Francisco: Freeman.

A number of mental diseases are reviewed, including such unusual ones as kuru and Creutzfeldt-Jacob disease. Biochemical and physiological mechanisms are included.

Valenstein, E. S. (1973). *Brain control.* New York: Wiley.

Valenstein surveys the uses and abuses of psychosurgery, exposing some of the fallacies and misunderstandings that led to attempted psychosurgical treatments.

Wurtman, R. J. (1987). Circulating nutrients and neurotransmitter synthesis. *Journal of Applied Nutrition, 39,* 7-27.

This review article gives the latest on mechanisms governing nutrient effects on neurotransmitters and their behavioral implications.

Chapter 16

APPLICATIONS II: CLINICAL NEUROLOGY

New scientific ideas and techniques flow from research laboratories to practical applications. In the neurosciences the flow of ideas often benefits clinical medicine, but the influence goes both ways: basic research is applied in medicine, and clinical experience enriches basic knowledge. The past few years have seen an explosion of new techniques that can be applied to clinical medicine. Combined with older methods, these techniques are revolutionizing the diagnosis and treatment of brain disorders.

We have already had occasion to look at a number of important clinical problems because they are informative about normal brain function. Parkinson's disease, Alzheimer's disease, schizophrenia and other mental disorders, and the results of various brain injuries have been discussed in earlier chapters. This chapter begins with a look at some of the major diagnostic tools of clinical neurology and continues with their application to brain diseases.

TECHNIQUES

THE ELECTROENCEPHALOGRAM

The recording of brain electrical potentials directly from the scalp began with Hans Berger's (1929) discovery of the potentials now called the electroencephalogram (EEG). Because the recording electrodes are so distant from brain tissue, the EEG records the average activities of many neurons together. The resolution of the source of a wave is no better than 2 to 3 cm in clinical use. Events on the fraction of the cortex exposed to the skull are the most prominent. The EEG moved into clinical medicine on a large scale after World War II, when sensitive amplifiers became available. It was the first way to examine brain physiology without surgery, and it is still the most commonly used diagnostic tool in neurology.

As a noninvasive way of monitoring brain

states, the EEG is particularly useful in diagnosing functional brain damage. It is applied to sleep disorders and to seizure diseases such as epilepsy. The EEG's use in localizing tumors and brain trauma has been partially substituted by modern x-ray techniques (which will be reviewed shortly). A more recent use of the EEG is in the clinical definition of death, one of the most difficult determinations a physician must make. Now that respirators and pacemakers can maintain heart and lung function artificially, the legal definition of death in many states has become the recording of two flat EEGs (no brain activity) 24 hr apart.

One of the first discoveries about the EEG was that several characteristic brain wave patterns were related to states of arousal and attention. In general, high arousal correlates with a high-frequency, low-amplitude EEG (see Figure 16.1). Relaxation yields progressively larger and slower EEG waves. One wave, the alpha rhythm (at a frequency of about 10 Hz), presents a good example of a scientific controversy, with a radical interpretation challenging the established view.

Alpha Rhythm

When subjects have their eyes closed and are in an awake relaxed state, the EEG often has prominent waves at the alpha frequency. This is not an altered state of consciousness but a normal condition. Most subjects can increase the amount of alpha waves in their EEGs with biofeedback; if they are told when they are showing alpha waves, they can produce more of them. Some subjects are so highly motivated that they have difficulty relaxing enough to let the alpha waves appear; often they can be brought into the alpha state by being told, falsely, that their EEG is showing alpha activity. The subjects then relax and the rhythm appears.

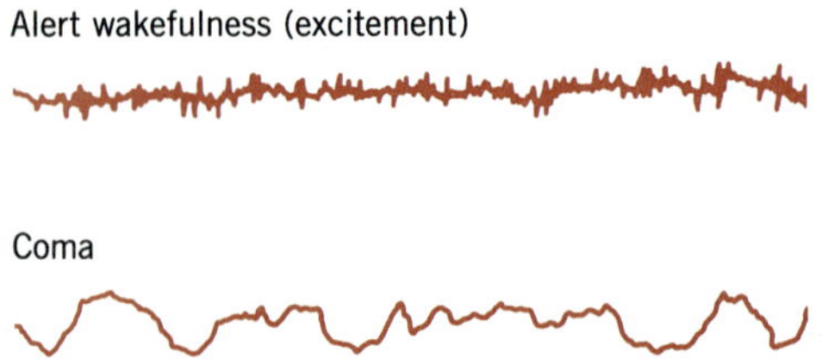

Figure 16.1 Characteristic EEG patterns for alert wakefulness (excitement) and coma. The coma pattern shown here indicates that the brain is alive even if the patient is unresponsive.

In clinical neurology the alpha rhythm indicates wakefulness. A reduced alpha frequency can aid in detecting brain damage and epilepsy.

Origins of Alpha Rhythm. The rules common to the other brain waves are not followed by the alpha rhythm. Alpha waves are over the occipital cortex, but they also are seen in patients with the occipital cortex removed on one side (Masland, Austin & Grant, 1949; Cobb & Sears, 1960).

Related to this puzzle is the failure to find a source for the current generating the alpha wave. When one drives depth electrodes into the cortex, one expects the electrical polarity of the signals to reverse. Positive voltages become negative, and negatives become positive as one passes the source of the current. The potential reversal is like climbing a hill. When you begin climbing the hill, a tree halfway up is above you. But as soon as you pass the tree, it is below you. The landscape has remained the same, but your position (or that of your electrode) is reversed relative to the tree. With the alpha rhythm, there is no phase reversal. Instead, the waves become larger when the electrode enters the white matter below the cortex. This observation had led to the hypothesis that the waves are generated in the thalamus. But there is no evidence for a 10 Hz generator there either.

Another anomaly of the alpha rhythm concerns the correspondence between the amplitude of the waves and their duration. Most brain waves increase in duration as they become larger, but the frequency of the alpha rhythm remains stable for a given subject at every amplitude, as Figure 16.2 shows. Furthermore, alpha waves are never seen in sleep, unlike the other EEG waves (see Chapter 10). They are not recorded from intracortical bipolar electrodes in animal studies either (Creutzfeldt, Watanabe & Lux, 1966).

Alpha Waves and Eye Tremors. These suspicious properties led to the startling hypothesis that the alpha rhythm was not a brain wave at all

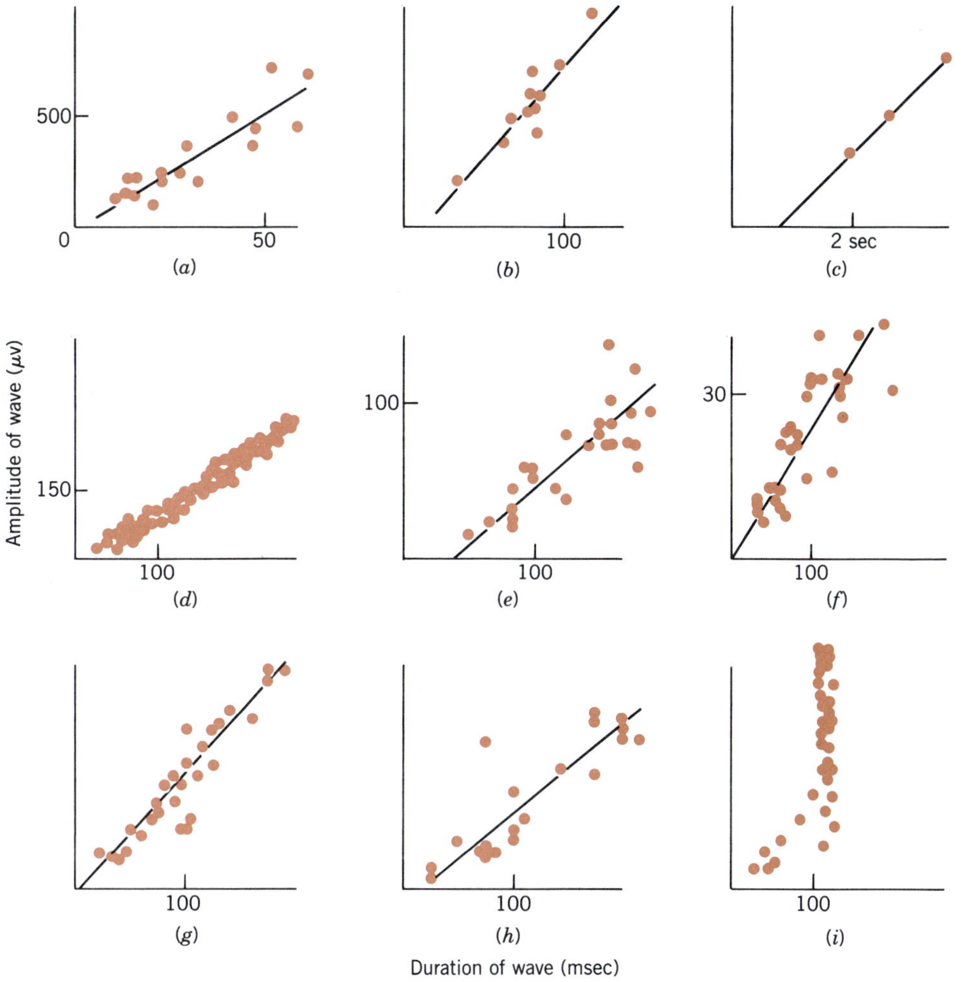

***Figure 16.2** Comparison of alpha and other brain waves.* (a) *through* (h). *Increase in duration of cortically recorded brainwaves with intensity.* (i) *Constancy of alpha duration with varying intensity. In this characteristic the rhythm is like that of a muscle tremor, changing its amplitude without changing its frequency. Most muscles show a tremor at about 10 Hz. From* (a) *Li & Jasper (1953);* (b) *Andersen (1966);* (c) *Adrian (1931);* (d) *Khristiansen & Courtois (1949);* (e) *Lindsley et al. (1950);* (f) *Goldenshoim et al. (1950);* (g) *Adrian (1950);* (h) *Berger (1929);* (i) *Adrian & Matthews (1934). Adapted from Lippold (1973).*

but originated in oscillations of the eyes forward and backward in their orbits (Lippold, 1973). Because the idea was controversial, more experimental evidence was necessary to back the idea. Evidence came from the dependence of the alpha rhythm on eye position (Mulholland & Evans, 1965; Lippold, 1973), as in Figure 16.3.

Furthermore, cooling or warming the orbits should slow or speed up the tremor, as it does for other muscle systems. Using baths of flowing water, Davidson (1970) and Lippold (1973) found the predicted changes in alpha frequency.

Objections and Replies. The tremor hypothesis has met with objections from electroenceph-

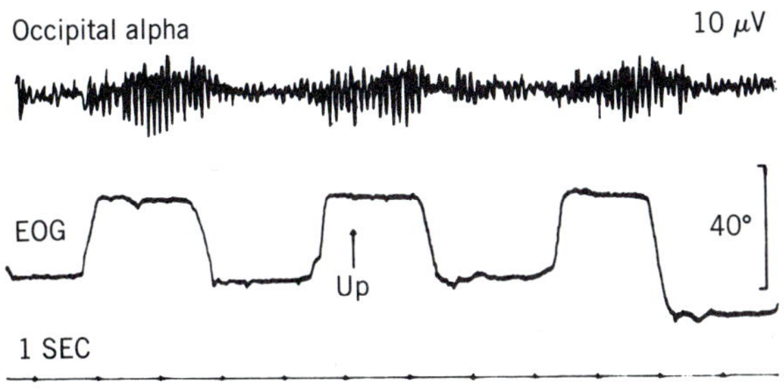

***Figure 16.3** Correlation of alpha amplitude and voluntary eye movements, with eyes closed and complete darkness. Adapted from Lippold (1973).*

alographers. First, alpha waves occur in the blind, even in those with both eyes enucleated (surgically removed). Lippold replies that the extraocular muscles are often spared in enucleation and the alpha waves usually are about a fifth of normal amplitude. Of course, blind subjects meet the criteria for the alpha state, for they are awake but not engaged in visual activity.

A second objection is that the potentials should be largest near the eyes rather than at the occipital cortex. The reply is that the movements are along the axis of the eye and therefore are not seen in the electrooculogram. When the alpha waves are recorded from a single active electrode rather than from paired electrodes, the rhythm is greatest at the front of the head. Movements of the eyes at 10 Hz can also be recorded directly (Coakley & Thomas, 1977). Lippold identifies a low-impedance pathway from the extraocular muscles through the base of the orbit to the lateral ventricles, which end just under the occipital cortex (see Figure 3.23).

Despite the evidence reviewed here, the alpha rhythm is not definitely an artifact of eye tremor. There may be both intracranial and ocular sources of 10 Hz rhythms, for example. But what if the idea is correct? Correlations between psychological state and alpha amplitude would not be altered, nor would any of the clinical uses of the alpha rhythm. The potential would still originate in the brain, coming ultimately from oculomotor rather than cortical centers.

IMAGING TECHNIQUES

Conventional x-rays give little information about brain structure because the x-rays must pass through the skull. X-rays powerful enough to do this are not impeded very much by the soft tissues of the brain. The situation can be improved by injecting a radio-opaque dye into the carotid artery while x-ray exposures are taken, so cerebral blood vessels become visible. Because an x-ray exposure requires only a fraction of a second, the dynamics of blood flow can be examined. The technique, called **angiography** (*angios* is Greek for "blood vessel," and *graph* is Greek for "write"), is particularly useful for identifying the locations of **strokes** (disruptions in brain function caused by blockage in cerebral blood vessels) and **aneurisms** (balloonings and thinnings of vessel walls that result in extensive damage if the bubbles burst).

The optical system used in x-rays and in angiography is like that of conventional photography. Indeed, the results are recorded on photographic plates. A newer technique uses x-rays in a radically different way to obtain a more detailed look into the structure of the living brain.

Computer Axial Tomography

X-ray probes combined with image-processing techniques to examine a single slice of living tissue are **computer axial tomography (CAT)** scans. Instead of having a photographic plate that receives the entire image all at once, tomography uses a small x-ray source that sends a sharp pencil of rays to a small detector. The source is mounted on one side of the head and the detector on the other. A pulse of x-rays is passed through the head to determine the tissue density along that path. Source and detector are then moved together to sample a location alongside the first, and the process is repeated (using the scheme of Figure 16.4) until the entire slice has been scanned at that angle.

The resulting set of densities carries information about only one dimension. An abnormally high x-ray density might be detected in one of the scans, for instance, but the clinician would not know where along that scan the abnormality was located. To transform this one-dimensional map of the slice into a two-dimensional map, identical sets of scans are made at different angles. The information from all of the scans together can give a surprisingly detailed look inside the living brain (as Figures 12.11 and 12.13 showed).

At this point a practical problem was encountered, for the job of translating the beam density values into a two-dimensional picture is enormously difficult. The technique became practical when efficient algorithms were developed, so computers could transform x-ray samples into pictures in a few minutes. The x-ray beam and detector technology had been available for a long time; the development of a practical brain-scanning device depended on advances in mathematics.

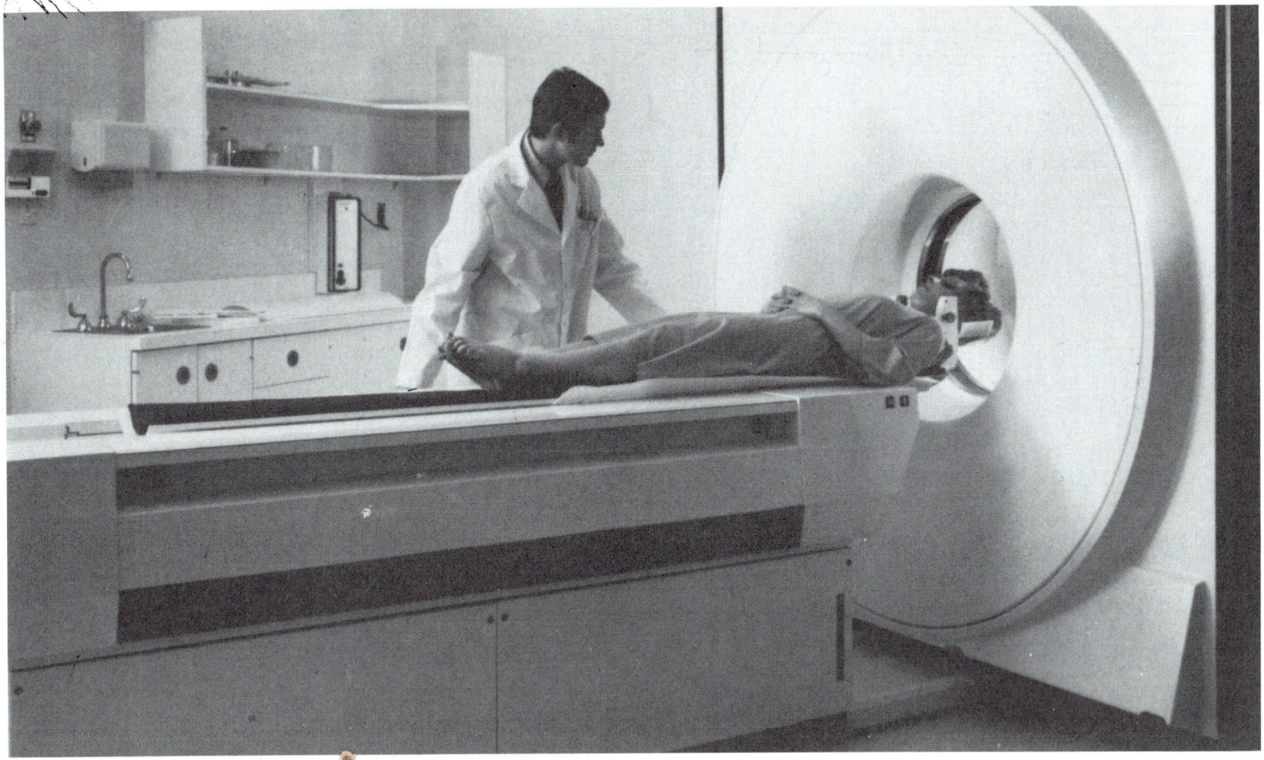

(a)

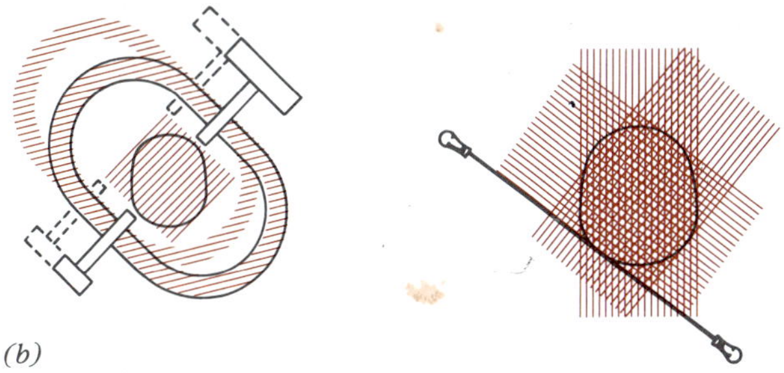

(b)

***Figure 16.4** CAT scan methods.* (a) *Patient in position. X-ray source and detector are located in the large box surrounding the head.* (b) *Scanning sequence. Each scan is a series of 180 parallel traverses, with a 1 deg rotation after each traverse. Readings are digitized and sent to a computer, which solves 28,000 simultaneous equations to derive the absorption values for each point in the slice.*

In clinical practice, a patient is gently restrained while the x-ray source and detector are moved around the head. Usually, several planes are scanned to find the expected tumor, blood accumulation, or other brain pathology. The information available to the physician is vastly improved, and risky operations can sometimes be avoided. Newer techniques, using multiple x-ray sources or electronic rather than mechanical scanning, promise scan times as short as 50 msec, so things can be seen in motion (Redington, 1981).

The CAT scan is limited to the display of anatomy; it does not indicate abnormal physiological processes. That limitation, however, is overcome with other imaging methods.

Positron Emission Tomography

A technique newer than CAT scans is **positron emission tomography (PET)** scans. This technique uses no x-rays; instead, the patient receives a dose of a radioactive substance that is carried in the bloodstream, and a detector moves around the patient to pick up the radiation. When more blood flows, more radioactivity is detected, so PET scans can measure cerebral blood flow without being invasive.

These scans take advantage of some unique properties of radioactive decay in unstable isotopes. Atoms of some unstable substances emit a single positron as they decay, but the positron doesn't last long. It is to antimatter what the electron is to ordinary matter: it has all of the properties of an electron except that its charge is positive instead of negative. A small fraction of a microsecond after it is produced, the positron collides with an electron (in dense matter, such as the brain, electrons are everywhere). The result is a spectacular, if tiny, mutual annihilation. The mass of both the positron and the electron is converted into energy, but in a peculiar way: two photons are emitted in exactly opposite directions. The photon is the particle that carries the energy of light, but these photons are much more energetic than those of visible light. They pass right through the brain tissue and skull to detectors mounted in the PET scan apparatus. Because all of the products of positron-electron annihilation have the same energy—511,000 electron volts—the detectors are tuned to accept only photons in that energy range.

When a PET scan detector senses a photon, there is no way of knowing the direction from which it came. But since the decay event ejects two photons at precisely the same time, two detectors placed on opposite sides of the head will detect the photons simultaneously. The decay event must have occurred somewhere on a straight line joining the two detectors. The detections of photon pairs can be stored in a computer and transformed into a two-dimensional image of cerebral blood flow in much the same way that the CAT scan's computer calculates tissue density.

To picture the geometry of the situation, imagine that you are standing in a room with a rifle. You fire a shot, putting a bullet hole in the wall, but the rifle is too powerful for you. It jumps backward to dent the wall in the direction exactly opposite the bullet hole. A detective will be able to determine where you were standing when you fired the rifle by drawing a line connecting the bullet hole and the dent in the wall. If you fire many pairs of shots in different directions, the intersections of the corresponding lines will determine your location.

One current PET scan technique begins when the patient inhales the inert but unstable gas krypton-79 (Yamamoto et al., 1981). The gas is dissolved in the bloodstream, passed from the lungs into the heart, and rapidly pumped to the brain. More blood flows in metabolically active regions, and thus more of the gas enters the tissues. In this way the photon density can indirectly measure the rate of metabolism in local regions of the brain. Resolution at present is about 3.6 mm, producing photos such as those in Figure 16.5; the detector array measures three brain slices simultaneously in a period of about 20 min. The technique has the disadvantage that the krypton-79 must be produced in a cyclotron, and its half-life is only 1.2 hr. This limits its use to major medical centers. Other, more convenient positron sources are now being developed.

PET scans give a glimpse of the activity of the whole brain, without surgical intervention. They are not yet in general clinical use, but they promise to offer an alternative to the EEG in measuring brain function. Their advantages are high resolution and the ability to image sections of the entire volume of the brain, not only the surface. An example of their potential application to the neural analysis of cognitive processes is shown in Figure 16.6, where xenon-133 is used to image cerebral blood flow (Ingvar, 1979).

Nuclear Magnetic Resonance

Radiographers (specialists in medical imaging techniques) are becoming excited about **nuclear magnetic resonance (NMR).** It promises a detailed look into the dynamic processes of living brains, showing both anatomy and physiology, and all without radiation. Physicians are now using the term *magnetic resonance imaging (MRI)* instead of NMR to assure patients that they are not being exposed to nuclear hazards (Fullerton & Cameron, 1985).

The Physics of NMR. You must be well grounded in physics to thoroughly understand how nuclear magnetic resonance works. The technique is applied to the nuclei of atoms that have a property called spin. It is as if each nucleus were a tiny top, spinning and wobbling a little in a ran-

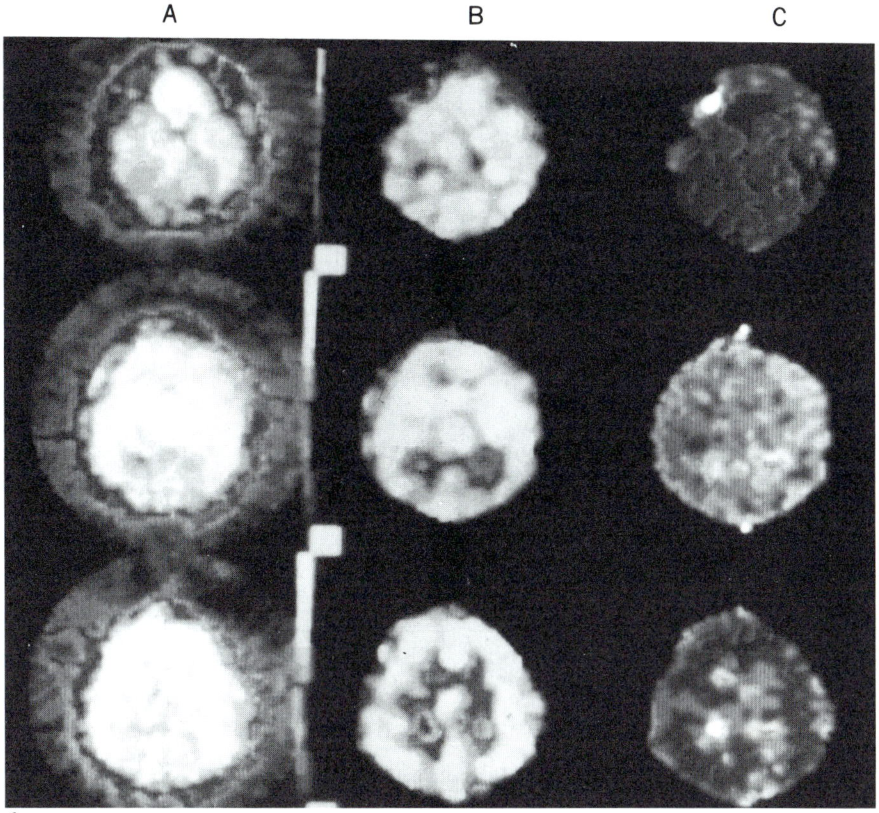

(a)

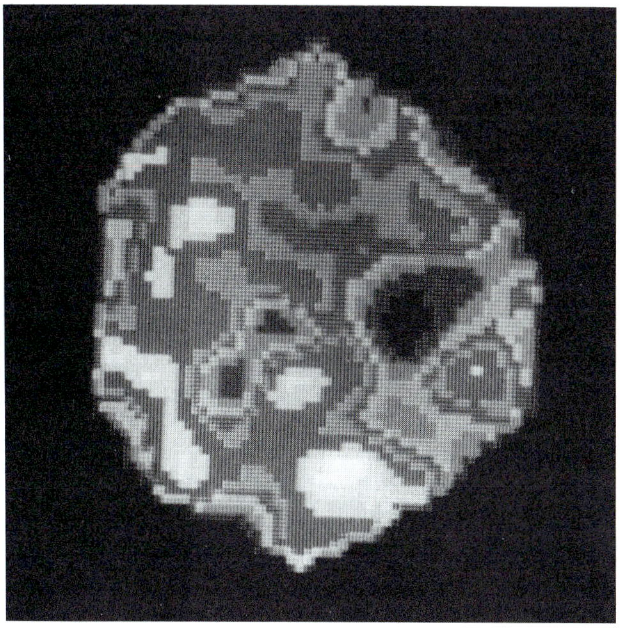

(b)

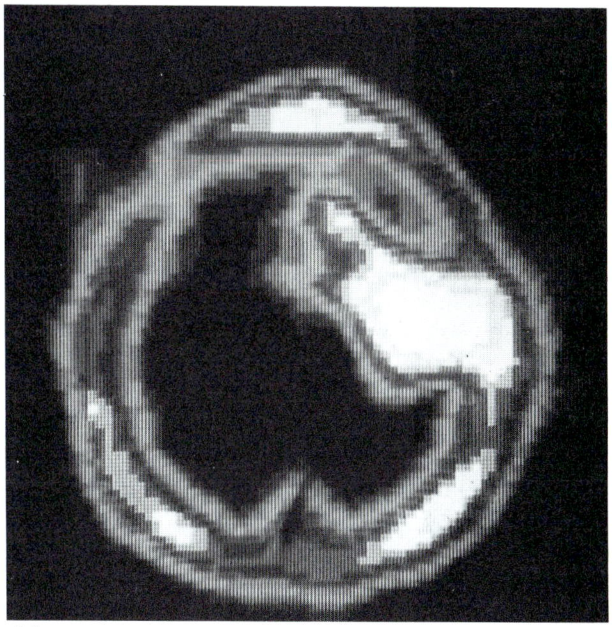

(c)

Figure 16.5 *PET scans of brain slices in the horizontal plane.* (a) *A: Tracer uptake. B: Statistically corrected values for regional cerebral blood flow. C: Error map for regional cerebral blood flow. 1, 2, and 3 are successively deeper levels in the brain.* (b) *Tracer uptake in a stroke patient.* (c) *Ga-EDTA PET scan indicating breakdown of the blood-brain barrier in the right posterior frontal region of the same patient.*

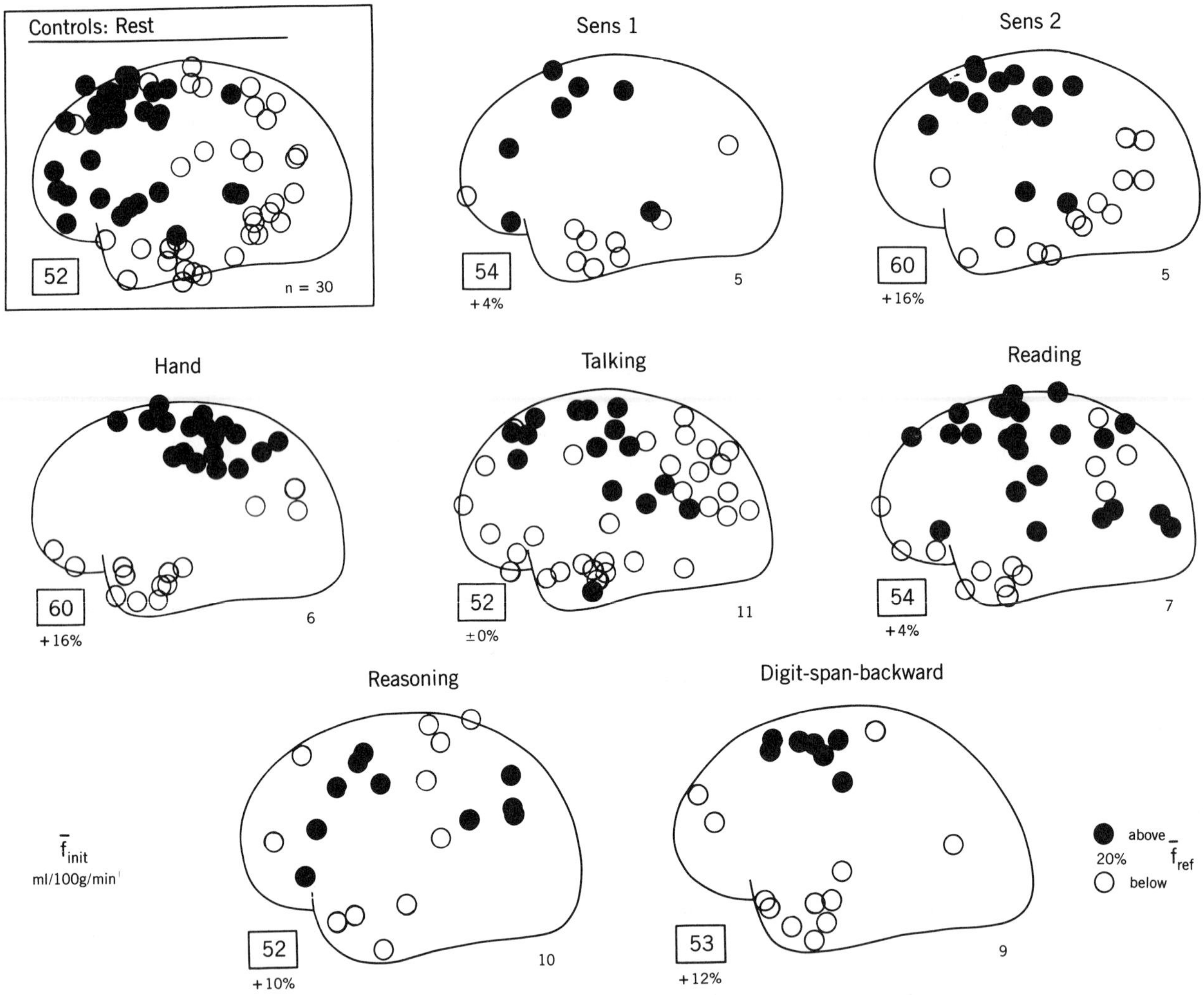

Figure 16.6 *Seven modes of brain activity, derived from studies of regional cerebral blood flow. The regions indicated have activities 20 percent higher (color) or 20 percent lower (open circles) than average for the hemisphere. The value in each box is the mean blood flow, and the percent increase above resting is indicated below each box. Anterior is left. Sens 1 and Sens 2 are low-intensity and high-intensity contralateral cutaneous stimulation, respectively. "Hand" is contralateral voluntary hand work. At rest the blood-flow pattern is distinctly hyperfrontal.*

domly oriented axis. The first step in obtaining an NMR image is to place the sample (in this case the whole head) in a constant, intense magnetic field. All of the spin axes line up along the field.

Then a burst of radio-frequency electromagnetic energy is passed through the head at right angles to the magnetic field. The spinning nuclei are forced to realign themselves along the axis of the electromagnetic pulse. The burst is very brief (20 μsec); and when it ends, the nuclei realign themselves in the original magnetic field. But they do so in a way that is characteristic of their physical properties, wobbling back into their original orientation with a characteristic "resonant" frequency.

Each nucleus generates a tiny current as it

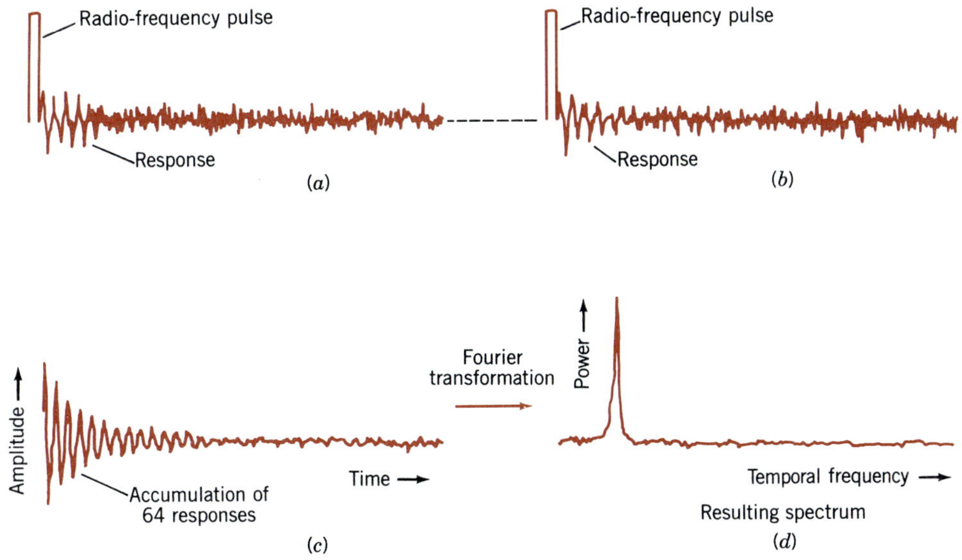

Figure 16.7 *Detection of signals from a sample using Fourier transform nuclear magnetic resonance.* (a) *and* (b). *Raw data—two consecutive responses to radio-frequency pulses.* (c) *The accumulation of 64 such responses. Amplitude is higher at the beginning of the response because the individual scans line up better there and sum together.* (d) *Fourier transform of* (c), *showing that most of the power is at a single frequency characteristic of the sampled molecule. The Fourier transform is the raw material from which scans are reconstructed.*

realigns, for it is a charged body moving through a magnetic field and generating current in the same way as a conventional electrical generator. Since all of the nuclei move in the same way at the same time, the currents add together and can be detected in the same coil of wire that sent the pulse through the sample. Figure 16.7 shows what the signal looks like. The nuclei might also be thought of as tiny tuning forks, which, when "struck" by the electromagnetic pulse, vibrate at a characteristic frequency. Each chemical element has its own characteristic resonant frequency. The magnetic field merely causes all of the vibrations to occur in the same physical orientation so their summed vibration can be detected.

In this way the presence of nuclei belonging to a particular element can be detected. The electromagnetic properties of the nuclei will be affected by the presence of other nearby atomic nuclei, so the resonance will be changed slightly if the element is part of a chemical compound. Thus the compound in which an element is combined can also be identified. The amplitude of the NMR signal indicates the concentration of the element in the sample.

Anatomical Imaging. This is fine for identifying what is present and in what amounts, but it does not indicate where the material is located within the head. For locating the material, a graded magnetic field is used instead of a homogeneous one. Because the frequency of the NMR signal depends on the strength of the magnetic field, signals arising at different distances from the detection apparatus will have slightly different frequencies. Thus one dimension, distance, can be ascertained. The other two dimensions are recovered by repeating the NMR scan in different orientations relative to the sample, and the resulting series of one-dimensional samples is combined in a way analogous to that of the CAT scan to create

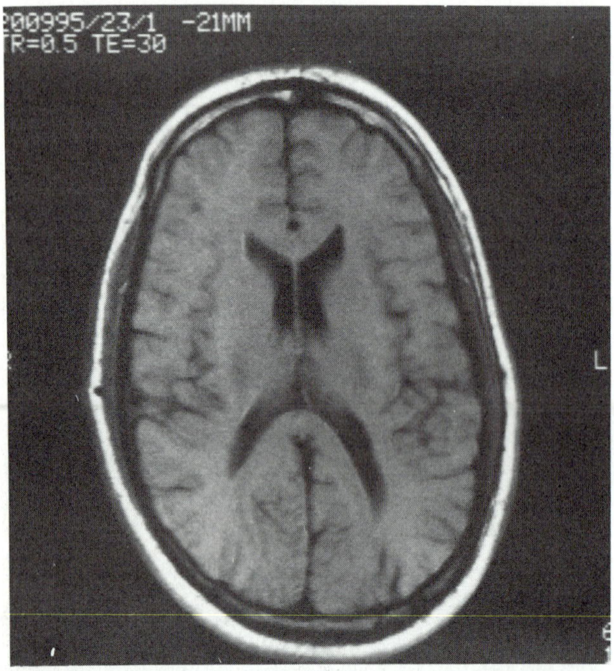

(a)

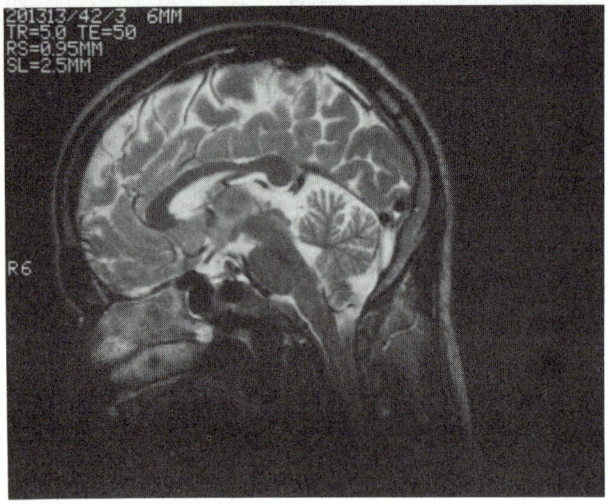

(b)

Figure 16.8 *Head scans from* ^{1}H *NMR spin imaging (detecting hydrogen atoms, mostly from water).* (a) *Axial transverse, the plane usually used for CAT scans.* (b) *Sagittal section.*

NMR images. Figure 16.8 shows a normal NMR scan (the sagittal section is impossible with current x-ray CAT scans). Figure 16.9 shows an indication of brain pathology. The magnetic field causes no apparent biological damage.

The most useful general technique for brain study is to tune the NMR probes to detect hydrogen ions as they are bound in water, for different tissues contain different concentrations of water (Lynch, 1983), and these concentrations can be used to image the brain. NMR promises the capability of seeing dynamic physiological processes such as blood flow in unparalleled detail and clarity, revealing disease states without risk to the patient.

NEUROLOGICAL DISEASES

TUMORS

After a normal and healthy childhood, a female university student began growing again. Her bones became heavier, especially in the facial region, her voice deepened, and hair began to grow on her chest and face. Menstruation, once normal, became irregular and then ceased altogether. The symptoms appeared slowly, over a period of years, and at first treatment was piecemeal. The facial hair was removed artificially, but the other symptoms caused more and more distress. The woman went from doctor to doctor. One doctor sent her home with a prescription for tranquilizers. Finally, a doctor referred her to a major medical center, where **acromegaly** was diagnosed and an operation was performed. The surgeons removed a pea-sized tumor from the pituitary gland, entering the skull at its base by a route through the back of the mouth. Following the operation the symptoms quickly disappeared, though the bone growth was permanent. The woman is now normal.

As it grew, this tumor had stimulated the secretion of androgens, gradually masculinizing the woman's body. Growth hormone was also secreted, and the continuous production of sex hormones stopped the menstrual cycle. If the tumor had been left in place, the symptoms would have become more and more severe, until the woman died—either of brain-stem damage from the pressure of the tumor growing on the brain or from the stress of the large amounts of hormones released.

This example shows that tumors in the cranial cavity do not always reveal themselves with such classic neurological signs as dizziness, vomiting,

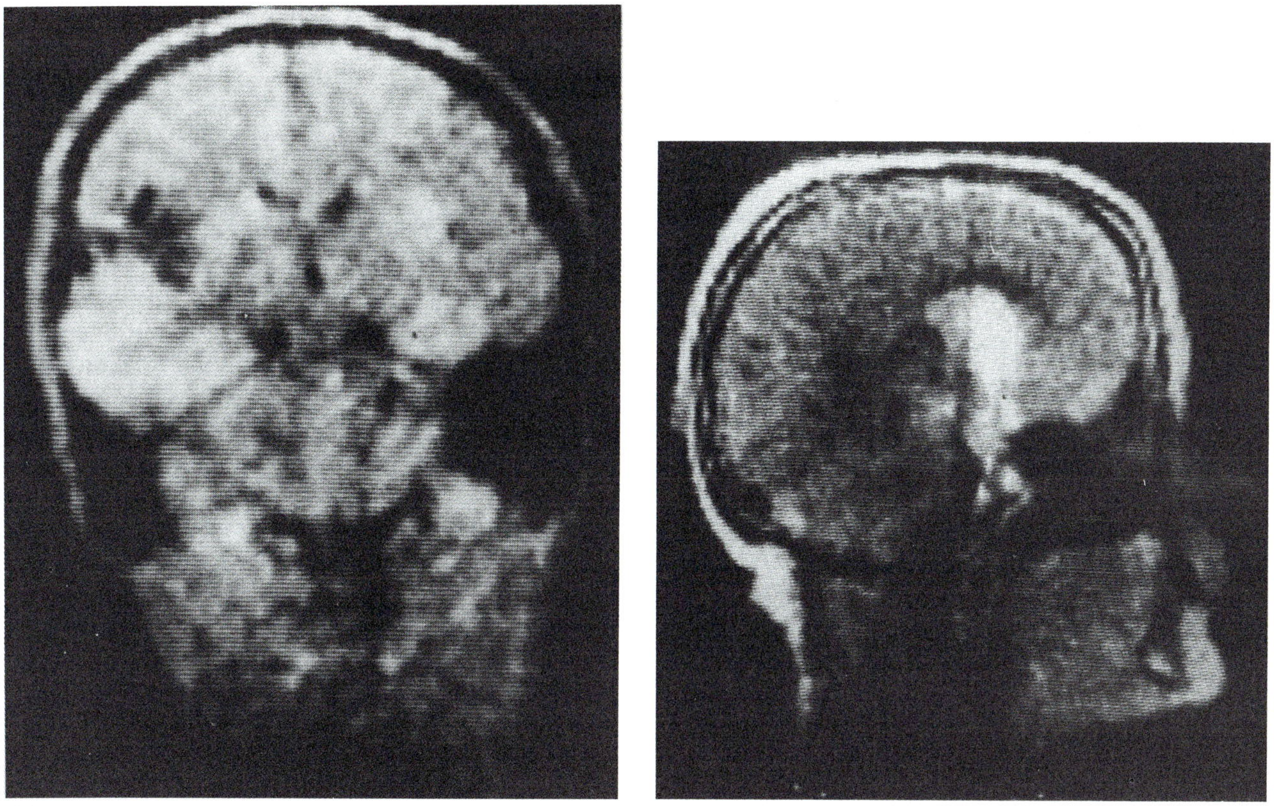

(a) *(b)*

Figure 16.9 *Pathology in ^1H NMR.* (a) *Spongework of contiguous black areas indicating arteriovenous malformation.* (b) *Large tumor appearing as region of high intensity.*

or sensory and motor deficits. Strictly speaking, neurons never develop tumors, for a **tumor** is an abnormal mass of cells dividing without control and mature neurons are incapable of dividing. Tumors can arise from glial cells or from the meninges surrounding the brain, however. Cancer can spread from malignant tumors that originate elsewhere in the body, as the malignant tumors shed abnormal cells that enter the brain through the circulatory system. Indeed, this is the most common form of intracranial tumor (Weisberg, Strub & Garcia, 1983). Figure 16.10 shows a CAT scan of tumors consisting of lung tissue that spread to the brain.

All intracranial tumors are dangerous to life because, as they grow, they occupy more and more volume. Elsewhere in the body this is not serious, but in the enclosed brain case the tumor eventually begins to force the funnel-shaped medulla through the **foramen magnum** (Latin for "large hole"), the spot where the brain stem passes through the skull. Diagnosis is often by neurological signs such as vomiting and dizziness. Exact localization of the tumor depends on CAT scans, EEG, or surgery. The recent improvements in brain imaging techniques are making it easier to find and treat intracranial cancers.

STROKES

In Western society strokes rank first among neurological diseases both in frequency and in seriousness. They are the third leading cause of death, following heart disease and cancer. The incidence

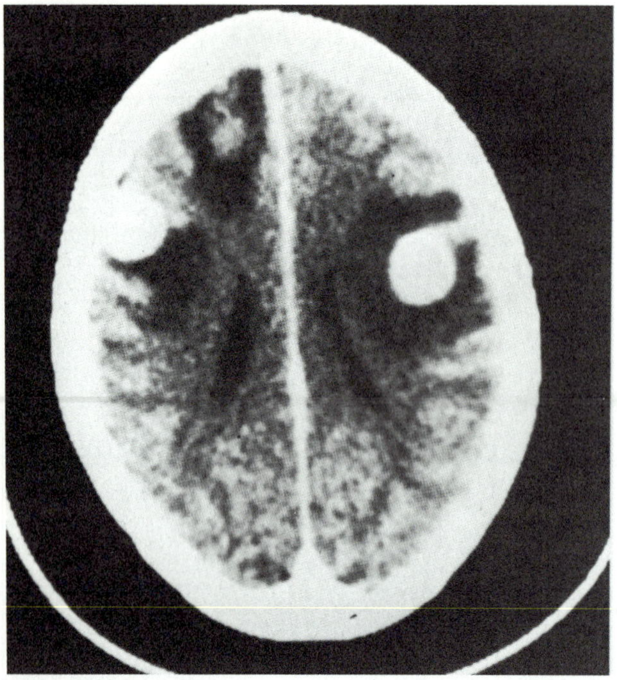

***Figure 16.10** CAT scan with image enhancement, maximizing contrast at densities near those of tumors. The dense areas are multiple bilateral round metastases surrounded by edema (tissue-swelling, low-density areas).*

of strokes has been declining, though, probably because of control of hypertension (high blood pressure), improved diet, exercise, and decreases in cigarette smoking (Weisberg, Strub & Garcia, 1983). Since strokes result from sudden interruption of the blood supply, they can be thought of as "heart attacks" of the brain. The blockage can come from a **thrombosis** (a blood clot that has broken loose from a damaged area elsewhere in the body) that lodges in a cerebral vessel, from **arteriosclerosis** (fat deposits constricting the vessels), or from spasms in weakened or damaged vessels. An aneurism can cause extensive damage if it bursts, because internal bleeding adds to the effects of the interruption of blood supply. Sometimes these problems can be detected and treated before a stroke occurs.

The mildest form of stroke is a transient ischemic attack, where a vessel is temporarily blocked. The victim may suddenly go speechless, only to recover 20 min later, or may temporarily become blind or partially paralyzed on one side. Though recovery is usually rapid, the attack is a sign that the intracranial circulatory system is in poor condition and medical attention should be sought immediately. The complete blockage of blood flow will begin killing neurons within 10 min (Kolb & Whishaw, 1980). If some blood is still flowing, the cells may survive even though they temporarily cease to function.

The extent of a stroke is governed by the anatomy of the arterial portion of the cerebrovascular system. The circle of Willis (see Figure 3.25) prevents a stroke from affecting the whole brain, for blood can find a route around the circle if it is blocked. Beyond this point a stroke can affect the anterior, middle, or posterior cerebral arteries or portions of the areas served by these major vessels.

In an example of a major stroke, a patient may suddenly suffer **hemiplegia** (*hemi* is Greek for "half," and *plegia* is Greek for "paralysis"), speech deficits, visual field defects, and agnosia (loss of the ability to perceive). The diagnosis from this combination of symptoms is a stroke of the middle cerebral artery on the left side. The lesioned area is called an **infarct** (see Figure 16.11). Recovery from the stroke depends entirely on the functions of the damaged region being taken over by other parts of the brain, a process in which rehabilitation therapy is becoming more and more important. Brain tissue transplants may someday be helpful, but the technique remains in the experimental stage.

EPILEPSY

Epilepsy is a neurological disease characterized by seizures that vary in severity from a momentary twitch to a violent series of convulsions, with loss of consciousness. Its origins are mysterious; sometimes it appears as a result of an identifiable brain injury, but usually there is no precipitating incident. The disease is not contagious, but about 35 percent of the close relatives of epileptics have EEG abnormalities similar to those seen in the affected person (Torres, 1980).

Not all brain seizures are due to epilepsy. In particular, over 10 percent of all children will have a seizure at one time or another, usually accompa-

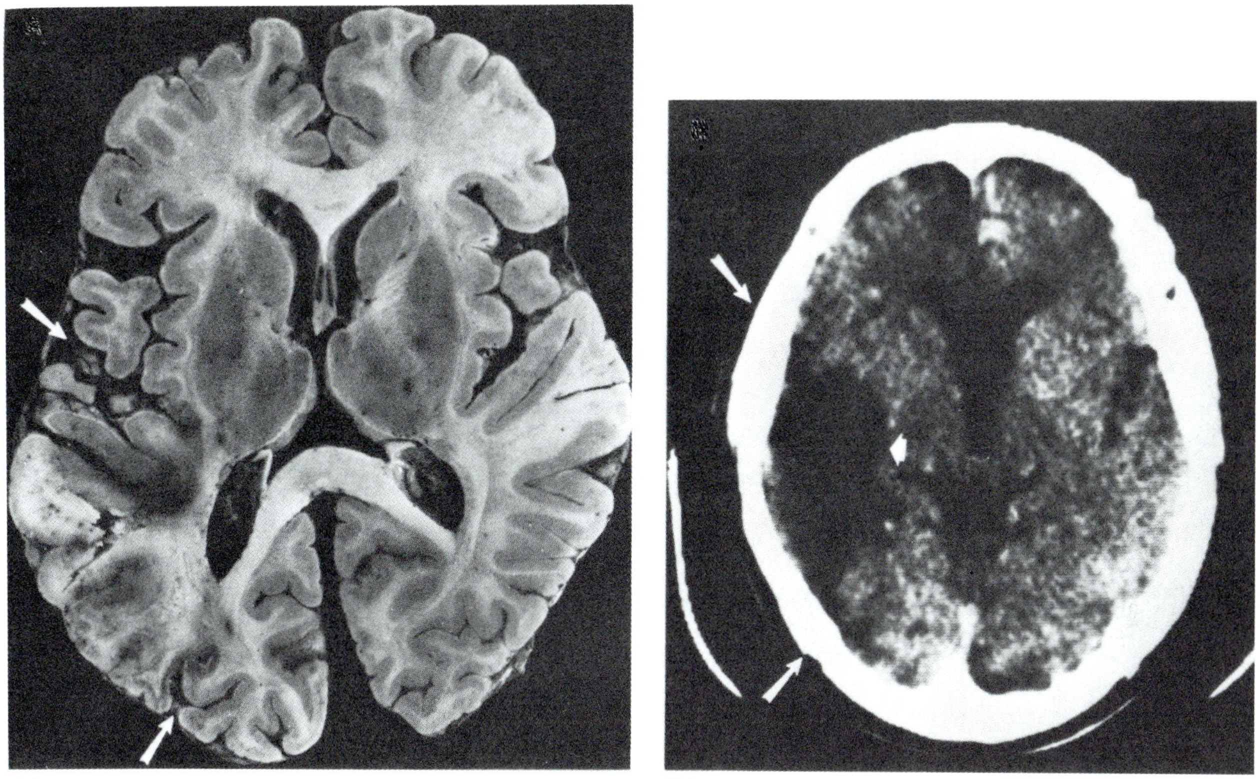

(a) *(b)*

Figure 16.11 *Horizontal sections of a brain showing an infarct in the posterior portion of the left middle cerebral artery (upper and lower arrows).* (a) *Anatomical section.* (b) *CAT scan.*

nying a high fever. A diagnosis of epilepsy requires a history of seizures. The EEG is an important tool in the diagnosis, though not all epileptics have recognizable epileptic brain activity. Also, about 1.8 percent of the population shows epilepticlike EEG signs without ever having seizures.

There are as many varieties of epilepsy as there are differentiated regions of the brain. Many cases have a focus—an area where abnormal activity begins. The location of the focus can determine the pattern of onset of a generalized seizure. Foci in the motor cortex, for instance, produce a Jacksonian seizure (after Hughlings Jackson, a 19th century neurologist). The seizure begins with twitching in one part of the body, say the neck, and progresses in a predictable order as the abnormal discharge moves along the cortical surface. A shoulder, arm, trunk, and leg become involved in sequence. Epilepsy of the temporal lobe, in contrast, might involve mostly disorientation. As noted in an earlier chapter, frequently there is an aura—a sensation that tells the epileptic that an attack is imminent. It might be a peculiar odor, such as the scent of burning rubber. Or it might be a sound—perhaps a whistling or grumbling—or a visual hallucination, or a vague feeling such as giddiness or dread.

Epileptic seizures can be petit mal (French for "small disease") or grand mal (French for "large disease") attacks. **Petit mal seizures** occur mostly in children of age 5 to 13 and may involve only a fluttering of the eyelids and a momentary unresponsiveness. *Grand mal seizures* (defined in Chapter 11) are the classic ones: intense oscillations of brain waves (see Figure 16.12) spread to the entire brain and send the patient into uncontrollable convulsions. Brain function is so disturbed that there is no memory of the episode.

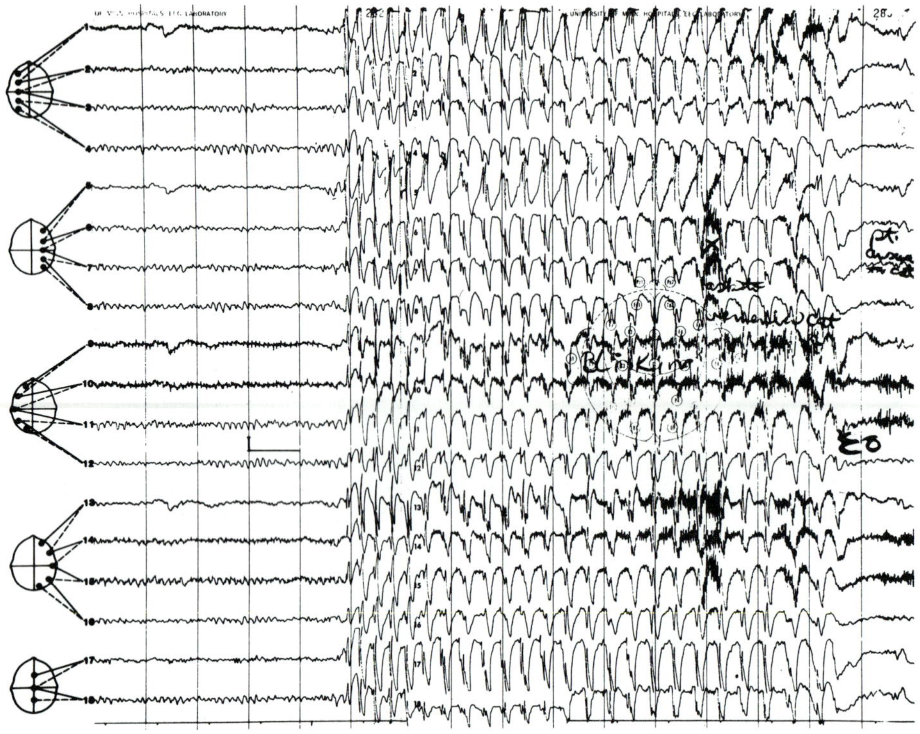

Figure 16.12 *Typical 3 Hz bilaterally synchronous spike-and-wave pattern of person with history of epileptic seizures (young adult with an 11 year history of absences and generalized tonic-clonic seizures—seizures that alternate movement and stiffness).*

Treatment of Epilepsy

Barbiturates and anticonvulsant drugs such as Dilantin can prevent seizures in about half of all epileptics and can reduce seizure frequency in another third. The drugs have severe side effects, though, so the patient and physician must decide whether the cure is worse than the disease. For the remaining epileptics, surgery is sometimes helpful if a focus can be found. An important step in the search for a focus is to record a seizure during an EEG, in order to localize the first or strongest abnormal activity. Because some attacks are brought on by flashing light, epileptics are routinely exposed to a strobe during the examination. The most effective strobe frequency is usually about 16 Hz. A common time for an attack is just after falling asleep. Thus a sleep study might be done (see Figure 16.13), depriving the patient of sleep the night before the recording session.

Sometimes the patient learns that a particular stimulus, such as a certain type of odor or sound, can bring on a seizure. In these cases the seizure-inducing stimulus is brought into the EEG laboratory, if possible. Stimuli that induce seizures can be surprisingly specific, as shown by the example in Figure 16.14. The episode was triggered in a 14 year old boy by the sight of his father's striped necktie (Klass, 1966).

If a well-defined focus is located, surgery can alleviate the symptoms by removing the diseased tissue; but of course there are side effects. The surgeon must weigh the disadvantage of continued attacks against the consequences of brain damage. Removing an important speech center, for example, might alleviate the epilepsy but leave the patient aphasic, in worse condition than before. It is in gaining information for making this decision that much of what we know about the neurology of language (see Chapter 12) has been discovered.

Some neurological problems require not removing the tissue but substituting for it with man-made devices. This is the realm of sensory substitution.

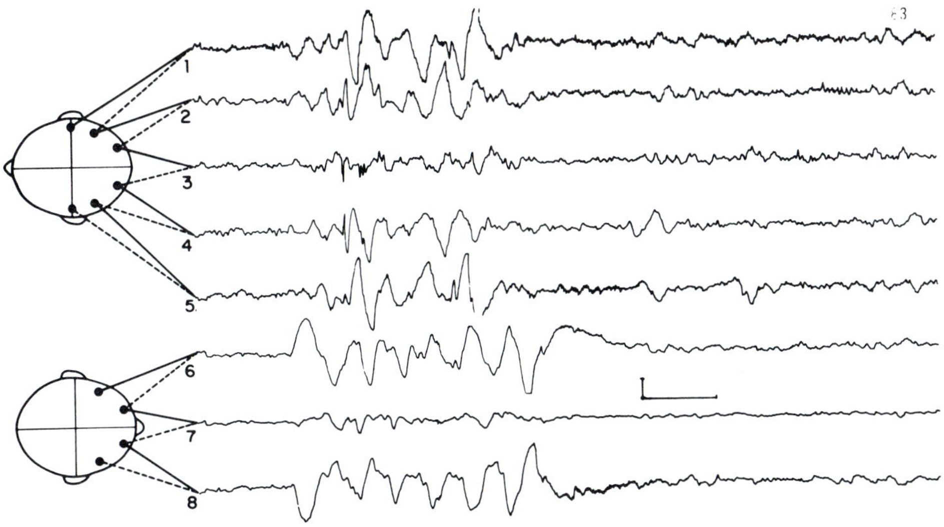

Figure 16.13 *Sleep record, showing occipital spikes, of 10 year old girl with generalized seizures. The waves here indicate brain abnormality even without a clinical seizure.*

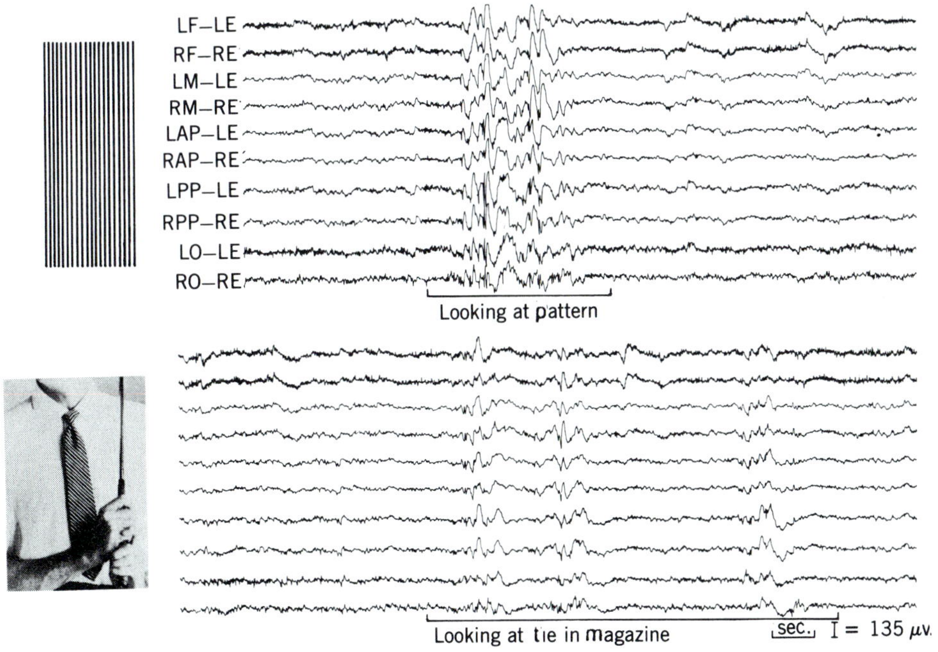

Figure 16.14 *Minor seizure triggered by the sight of stripes. LF-LE, RF-RE, and so on refer to electrode placements.*

SENSORY SUBSTITUTION

An area of neuroscience research that has not yet made its way into clinical practice is the provision of artificial sense organs for the blind and deaf. Eyeglasses and hearing aids can improve the quality of sensory signals before the transduction stage (see Chapter 4), but helping patients in whom the transducers no longer function has proved to be more difficult.

RETINAL SUBSTITUTION BY CORTICAL STIMULATION

Early efforts to restore vision in the blind were based on visual "phosphenes" (illusory spots) caused by direct electrical stimulation of the cortex. Electrical phosphenes from direct cortical stimulation had been known since the work of Frisch and Hitzig (1870). To make phosphenes usable in creating a substitute for the retina, electrodes were permanently implanted in the brains of blind human volunteers (Brindley & Lewin, 1968). The locations of the phosphenes could be predicted from the topographic map of the retina on the striate cortex. Stimulation of electrodes in the cortical projection of the fovea often yielded small spots of light like stars in the sky. Phosphenes from stimulating electrodes in more peripheral parts of the cortex were more cloudlike.

Transforming the phosphenes into meaningful visual information, however, has proved to be an insurmountable challenge. The problems are both technical and theoretical. On the technical side, a large number of electrodes is required to pass a meaningful amount of visual information. Many of the implanted electrodes fail to elicit a usable phosphene, and implanting too many electrodes may damage the cortex. There must be a way to pass the signals through the skin, and maintenance can be performed only with brain surgery.

Theoretical problems are based on the unnatural mode of cortical stimulation. The stimulation activates all neurons near an electrode, regardless of how the neurons normally interact with one another and regardless of the characteristics of the receptive fields. The problem is reduced by using bipolar electrodes, with current passing from one wire tip to another 1 or 2 mm away, but the activation is still nonselective. Furthermore, for many electrodes, the phosphene depends not only on the parameters of the electrical stimulation but also on the history of stimulation at that site in the past few minutes and even on the simultaneous activation of other electrodes. This problem becomes more severe as the electrodes are activated more frequently.

The most important shortcoming is that retinal and LGN preprocessing have been bypassed, so the cortex cannot code visual information in the usual way. The preprocessing cannot be duplicated artificially, for it involves important components of efferent control (see Chapter 5). As a result, not enough information can be presented to a subject to provide useful information about the world. When a group of electrodes are activated, the subject may see a swarm of dots; but there is never a naturalistic perception of an object in the world.

MOVING THE RETINA TO THE SKIN

A more successful approach to sensory substitution has been to stimulate an intact sensory surface instead of the missing retina. Reasoning that all of the senses are organized in a similar way after the transduction stage, Bach-y-Rita (1972) stimulated a patch of skin with an array of solenoids (mechanical stimulators activated electrically). The visual image came from a television camera and was transformed into signals for each of the solenoids by electronic circuits (see Figure 16.15). The first version used the back as a projection surface, but later models moved to the abdomen because the softer skin could contact the array of solenoids more easily.

Experience with this system has shed light on the organization of sensory systems, making the project valuable even if it never results in a substitute retina for the blind. First, subjects could "see" the patterns projected on the skin only if they had direct control of the camera. The camera had to be kept moving, and the experimenter could not move it for them. This compares to the necessity for self-generated image movements in the visual system. Second, the locus of perception changed with practice. At first, the sensation was of tickles on the skin. But after a few hours' practice, the images were seen in space—that is, they were referred to the outside world in the same way that retinal images are seen in the world rather than inside the eye, where the receptors are located. This implies that the projection of normal visual perception to the outside world does not depend on some unique property of the visual cortex. Rather, the projection results from the structure of the incoming information itself. Third, the "blind spot" at the subject's navel (the spot that the sole-

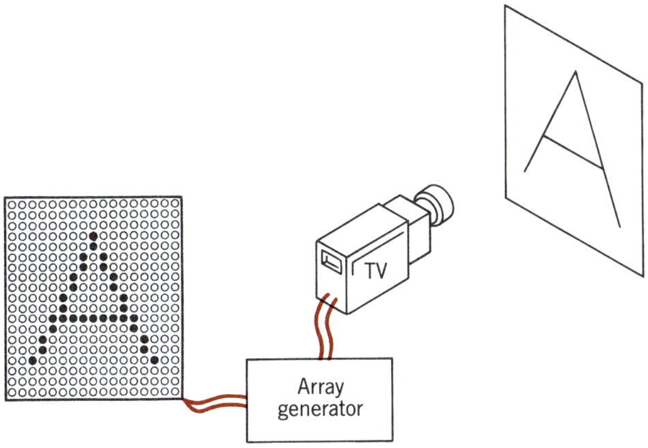

Figure 16.15 *A sensory substitution system picking up a visual record of the letter* A *and transforming it into a tactile array. The array generator is an electronic device that picks up the sequential scanning pattern of the TV camera and generates signals for each of the solenoids in the tactile stimulator.*

noids cannot reach) does not interfere with perception any more than the retinal blind spot interferes with normal vision.

With practice, subjects could learn to identify common objects in a laboratory environment, though it was necessary to keep the background uncluttered. Letters could be identified on a blackboard, making slow reading possible. One subject, a blind engineer employed by the project, mounted the TV camera directly on a microscope to examine integrated circuits.

Another version of the scanning device is mounted on the fingertip and enables a person to read, one letter at a time. Instead of a TV camera, the system uses an array of photocells aimed at the text and a similar array of tiny solenoids to stimulate the sensitive glabrous skin of the fingertip. The device is successful enough to be available commercially but can be used only for rather slow reading, and even that takes patience and practice.

Despite these successes, the skin imaging system has not resulted in a practical device for spatial vision in the blind. The equipment was not the problem; the electronics have been miniaturized to the size of a cigarette pack, and a TV camera no larger than a pen is mounted on a pair of eyeglasses. Rather, the limitation appears in the amount of information that can be passed to the subject. An array of 400 solenoids is pitifully small, compared to the 250 million visual receptors. Subjects can partially compensate for this limitation by using more time to scan an image, but this takes too long for the system to work in real time. Increasing the number of solenoids does not improve things, for the limitation is in the amount of information that the somatosensory nerves from the abdomen can carry. In short, the bandwidth of the biological part of the system is inadequate. In a normal environment, the rich texture that is almost everywhere in the visual field overwhelms the information-carrying capacity of the skin.

A Hybrid System

If the somatosensory system is inadequate, another sensory channel must be called into service. The only high-capacity sense left is the auditory system, but the blind already rely heavily on audition. In fact, many blind people use a primitive kind of sonar. They listen for the echoes of their footsteps, their own voices, and other sounds in the environment to locate large surfaces such as walls and doors. Could audition be used for more precise localization?

A prototype tactile-auditory guidance device has been developed by Carter Collins at the Smith-Kettlewell Institute of Visual Sciences in San Francisco. The device is based on the separation of the cognitive and ambient visual systems (reviewed in Chapter 5). In the artificial system, like the biological one, localization and identification are handled separately. The tactile-auditory device also takes advantage of another characteristic of the biological system: the apparent reduction of information as one moves centrally in a sensory system. The 250 million receptors reduce to about 2 million optic nerve axons, and from those we recognize only a handful of objects at any one time. If the first stages of processing and identification could be handled electronically, outside the body, the transfer of high-level information would require a much lower bandwidth.

The novel feature of the new device is a pattern-recognition system. Using AI techniques, a high-powered microprocessor identifies common objects found in a street environment and informs the wearer of the device about the objects with synthesized speech. The location of an object is given on a reduced array of solenoids, now mounted on the forehead. When the subject is walking down the street and nears a lamppost, for instance, the microprocessor will recognize the post in the TV image and send the words *lamppost ahead* to a set of earphones. The solenoid array will then locate the image, producing a buzz on the forehead in the direction of the lamppost.

At present, the device is still a prototype, with the electronics and power supplies housed in a cart that the experimenters wheel around behind the subject. The computer pattern recognition is limited to large objects likely to be found on a street, such as curbs and automobiles, and still cannot handle visual information outside this limited realm. The system is already fast enough to provide useful information in real time, though, so the major drawback of the earlier systems has been overcome. Miniaturizing the electronics should not be difficult. At present, there seems to be no reason why a practical sensory substitution system cannot be developed.

CHAPTER SUMMARY

1. Basic research and clinical medicine enrich each other. One contribution of basic research is to provide diagnostic tools for determining brain function in living patients. One of the first of these, and still among the most useful, is the EEG. It is important in diagnosing brain trauma, epilepsy, sleep disorders, and tumors. Two flat EEGs 24 hr apart define brain death, even though other organs may be functioning. Arousal is seen as low-amplitude, high-frequency EEG patterns.

2. The alpha rhythm, a 10 Hz EEG wave that is largest over the occipital cortex, does not follow the rules common to other brain waves. It is seen in patients without an occipital cortex, and there is no polarity reversal as an electrode moves to greater depths. The frequency of the alpha waves does not vary with duration, as is the case with other brain waves. The alpha rhythm may be an artifact of tremors in the extraocular muscles. The hypothesis is supported by a relationship between alpha amplitude and direction of gaze and from a slowing of alpha waves when the orbital muscles are cooled. Alpha waves in the blind are of small amplitude. The extraocular muscles are usually spared even after surgical enucleation of the eyes. If the alpha rhythm does turn out to be an extraocular muscle potential, it would still ultimately originate in the brain. Correlations of alpha waves with attention or cognitive functioning would remain valid.

3. X-ray techniques have recently been greatly improved. Angiography provides a way of imaging blood vessels, by injecting a radio-opaque dye just before a conventional x-ray. Computer axial tomography uses a different technique, sending narrow pencils of x-rays through the head at varying locations and angles to image a slice of brain in great detail, including soft tissues and abnormalities. Positron emission tomography measures blood flow by localizing the breakdown of a radioactive gas that is inhaled while photon emission is measured from the head. Computer image analysis similar to that used in computer axial tomography can then reconstruct patterns of blood flow and, by inference, the brain areas especially active in particular tasks. Nuclear magnetic resonance detects oscillations of nuclei in an intense magnetic field, providing a look at both the anatomy and chemistry of the living brain without introducing damaging radiation.

4. Neurons cannot become cancerous because they cannot divide. But cancers from glial cells, from meninges, or from cancer cells originating elsewhere in the body can grow in the cranial cavity. Intracranial cancers of glandular tissues can

cause hormonal symptoms that seem to have little to do with cancer. The usual effects of brain tumors stem from the brain squeezing through the foramen magnum as the tumor grows.

5. Strokes are interruptions of cerebral blood flow caused by blood clots, arteriosclerosis, spasms in vessels, or aneurisms. Transient ischemic attacks are the mildest form, with a temporary obstruction creating neurological symptoms for minutes or hours. Ten minutes of complete blockage will result in permanent damage to neural tissue. The pattern of symptoms depends on the anatomy of the region "downstream" of the blockage, and recovery depends on other brain regions taking over the functions of the damaged area.

6. Epilepsy is a disease of neurons whose intense and synchronized discharges result in seizures. A victim may experience only body twitches and brief loss of awareness or may be sent into prolonged convulsions. Some patients experience an aura, such as a particular sound or odor, that warns of an impending attack. Drugs can control or improve most cases, but surgery may be necessary if drugs fail and a focus of seizure activity can be found. The diagnosis of a focus often depends on inducing a seizure during an EEG recording session.

7. Sensory substitution—the construction of an artificial sensory input—has been attempted by direct cortical stimulation and by substituting tactile for visual input. Cortical stimulation results in phosphenes, but stimulating groups of electrodes gives the perception of groups of points rather than coherent objects in the world. Technical problems limit both the number of usable electrodes and the long-term practicality of the implant.

8. When a visual pattern is reproduced on the skin with mechanical stimulators, many properties of normal vision are re-created. The subject must move the camera generating the image in order to make sense of the input. After some practice, the subject perceives information in space rather than on the skin. The skin cannot transmit enough information, however, to allow the subject to recognize objects quickly, and textured backgrounds are confusing. An alternate system uses AI techniques to recognize common objects. It informs the subject with synthesized speech about the identity of an object while mechanical stimulators indicate its position.

KEY TERMS

Angiography
Stroke
Aneurism
Computer axial tomography (CAT)
Positron emission tomography (PET)
Nuclear magnetic resonance (NMR)
Acromegaly
Foramen magnum
Thrombosis
Arteriosclerosis
Hemiplegia
Infarct
Epilepsy
Petit mal epileptic seizure

SUGGESTED READINGS

Pincus, J. H., & Tucker, G. J. (1985). *Behavioral neurology.* New York: Oxford University Press.

Intended as a textbook for medical students, this book explores the border zone between neurological and psychiatric disorders.

Sacks, O. (1987). *The man who mistook his wife for a hat.* New York: Simon & Schuster.

This is a fascinating look behind neurological deficits to the humanistic side of medicine. Twenty-four case studies introduce us to the personalities of Sacks's patients and their adaptations to pathology.

Weisberg, L. A., Strub, R., & Garcia, C. A. (1983). *Essentials of clinical neurology.* Baltimore, MD: University Park Press.

Another medical textbook, this is a succinct review of major neurological diseases and their treatment.

GLOSSARY

The numbers that appear in parentheses after the terms indicate the chapters in which the terms are defined. Units of measure are defined elsewhere.

Absolute refractory period (2). A period of about 1 msec after an action potential when an axon cannot conduct another action potential.

Absorptive phase (8). The stage of digestion when nutrients are being absorbed from the gut into the bloodstream.

Accommodation (Piaget) (1). Reorganization of cognitive structures in response to challenges from the environment.

Acetoxycycloheximide (11). A protein synthesis inhibitor used in memory consolidation studies.

Acetylcholine (ACh) (2). A neurotransmitter at some synaptic junctions and at the neuromuscular junction.

Acetylcholinesterase (AChE) (2). The enzyme that breaks down the neurotransmitter acetylcholine.

Acromegaly (16). Abnormal growth caused by excess pituitary hormones.

Actin complex (7). A group of proteins that slide along myosin filaments in muscle contraction.

Action potentials (1). Traveling waves of instability in an axon membrane, caused by Na^+ channels that are opened by depolarization.

Active avoidance (11). A conditioning paradigm in which an animal must perform a behavior to avoid an aversive stimulus.

Acuity (5). The ability to resolve detail.

Adenosine triphosphate (ATP) (2). The molecule that energizes biological reactions by releasing a phosphate group to become adenosine diphosphate (ADP).

Adenyl cyclase (2). An intracellular molecule involved in metabotropic transmission.

Adrenocorticotropic hormone (ACTH) (9). A hormone released by the anterior pituitary in times of stress that acts on the adrenal glands.

Affective illness (15). Depression and manic-depressive psychosis.

Agranular frontal cortex (3). The part of the frontal lobe anterior to the motor areas and lacking the granular appearance of sensory or motor areas.

Algorithms (13). Recipes for solving a problem.

Alleles (12). Different forms of a particular gene.

Allocortex (3). Phylogenetically older three-layered cerebral cortex.

Alpha fibers (7). Large axons, such as those innervating extrafusal fibers in striated muscles.

Alpha rhythm (10). A rhythm at about 10 Hz recorded from scalp electrodes.

Alpha-methyl-p-tyrosine (alpha-MPT) (11). A drug that blocks dopamine synthesis.

Alzheimer's disease (11). A brain degeneration associated with memory loss and abnormality in acetylcholine metabolism, previously called senile dementia.

Amacrine cells (5). Retinal neurons that communicate between bipolar cells and ganglion cells in the inner plexiform layer.

Ambient visual system (5). A phylogenetically old visual system, largely subcortical, used in spatial orientation.

Amino acids (2). Organic acids containing an amine group, the building blocks of polypeptides and proteins.

Amnesia (11). Loss of memory.

Ampulla (4). A bulge in each semicircular canal where vestibular transduction of rotatory acceleration of the head takes place.

Amygdala (3). An almond-shaped nucleus beneath the temporal lobe, part of the limbic system.

Anaerobic metabolism (3). A metabolic pathway in muscles that does not use oxygen.

Analog (1). Continuously variable.

Androgens (9). Male sex hormones.

Aneurisms (16). Bulging arteries that will cause a stroke if they break in the brain.

Angiography (16). A method of visualizing blood vessels by injecting a radiopaque dye and viewing x-rays of the patient.

Angiotensin I (8). A hormone released by renin that helps regulate body fluid balance.

Anisomycin (11). A protein synthesis inhibitor used in studies of memory consolidation.

Anorexic (8). Absence of eating.

Anterior pituitary (3). The master endocrine gland, controlled by hypothalamic hormones through the portal system.

Anterograde amnesia (11). Loss of the ability to form new memories.

Anterograde degeneration (3). Axon degeneration between a point of injury and the axonal terminals.

Antidiuretic hormone (ADH) (8). A hormone that stimulates the kidneys to increase the reuptake of water, concentrating the urine and reducing water loss.

Antidromic (7). Reversing the normal physiological direction, as in the conduction of action potentials from the axon terminals toward the cell body.

Aphagia (8). Refusal to eat.

Aphasia (12). Inability to speak.

Apraxia (7). Inability to perform skilled motor acts.

Arachnoid trabeculae (3). The spongy middle layer of protective membranes covering the brain.

Archicerebellum (7). The oldest part of the cerebellum, concerned with coordinating movement with the vestibular system.

Archicortex (3). Phylogenetically older three-layered cortex.

Arcuate fasciculus (12). A band of fibers connecting posterior and anterior speech areas.

Arcuate sulcus (14). A sulcus in the lateral frontal cortex, in Brodmann's area 8 (the frontal eye fields).

Arecholine (11). A cholinergic agonist that improves long-term memory in some patients.

Arginine-vasopressin (8). A pituitary hormone involved in the regulation of fluid volume.

Arteriosclerosis (16). "Hardening of the arteries"—a buildup of fatty deposits in the arteries.

Artificial intelligence (AI) (13). The performance of intelligent tasks by machines.

Ascending reticular activating system (ARAS) (3). A series of centers in the brain-stem reticular formation involved in arousal.

Association cortex (3). The former name for all areas of the cortex that are not obviously either sensory or motor.

Astroglia (2). Glial cells that link the neurons with blood vessels.

Ataxia (7). Lack of muscle coordination.

Atonia (10). Lack of muscle tone, the constant low-level activation that aids in posture.

Atriopeptins (8). Hormones involved in volumetric thirst and fluid regulation.

Aura (15). An epileptic's warning that a seizure is about to begin, frequently a sensory hallucination.

Automata (13). Machines that perform specific logical functions.

Autonomic subsystems (3). Parts of the nervous system that control internal body functions, largely involuntary.

Autoradiography (3). The marking of cells or chemicals with radioactive tags and their identification with radioactivity.

Axon (2). A neuronal process that normally supports action potentials.

Axoplasmic transport (2). Transport of molecules or vesicles through the axoplasm, the internal medium of the axon.

Backward inhibition (2). Inhibition of cells at a lower layer in a chain of neurons.

Ballistic (6). Proceeding without feedback control once initiated, as in a saccadic eye movement.

Bandwidth (2). The information-carrying capacity of a communications channel.

Baroreceptors (8). Pressure receptors.

Basal ganglia (3). A group of subcortical forebrain nuclei involved in postural motor control.

Basilar membrane (4). A membrane stretching across the cochlea, holding the transduction apparatus for hearing.

Basket cells (3). Cerebellar inhibitory neurons that form a basketlike axonal arborization around a Purkinje cell.

Basolateral group (8). A functional division of the amygdala.

Behaviorism (1). A school of psychology admitting only stimuli and behavioral responses as legitimate data.

Bell and Magendie's law (3). The segregation of spinal afferents into the dorsal roots and of spinal efferents into the ventral roots.

Benzodiazepines (9). A class of tranquilizers that mimic neurotransmitter functions.

Bereitschaftspotential (14). A cortical potential appearing before a motor act.

Binaural interactions (5). Interactions of signals from both ears.

Binocular (4). Involving both eyes.

Biplexiform cell (5). A retinal neuron with arborizations in both the inner and outer plexiform layers.

Bipolar cell (5). A cell having two poles, as in retinal neurons that link receptors with ganglion cells.

Bipolar electrode (3). An electrode with two stimulating or recording surfaces.

Bipolar depression (15). Alternating phases of depression and mania (great energy, optimism, unrealistic goals), also called manic-depressive psychosis.

Bit (1). The amount of information contained in an equally probable two-alternative choice.

Bitemporal amnesia (11). Anterograde amnesia resulting from bilateral hippocampal damage, characterized by rapid forgetting.

Bleaching (4). Absorption of light by photopigments in the retina, after which the photopigments can no longer absorb light and therefore look bleached.

Blindsight (5). Visual capacity remaining after loss of visual cortex and absence of visual experience in the visual fields corresponding to the lost cortex.

Blood-brain barrier (2). A biochemical filter between the bloodstream and the neurons that passes some substances and blocks others.

Bottom-up (6). Information flowing from the outside world into the nervous system.

Brain models (13). Mathematically definable theories of brain function.

Brain stem (3). The core of the brain, a rostral continuation of the spinal cord.

Broca's aphasia (12). A language deficit characterized by good understanding but disturbed grammar and pronunciation; expressive aphasia.

Broca's area (12). The posterior inferior part of the lateral frontal cortex, part of the brain's machinery for speech production and organization.

Calpain (11). A calcium-dependent enzyme that splits proteins apart, thought to be involved in the memory-like process of long-term potentiation.

Canalized traits (12). Traits that are so important for a species that they are redundantly encoded in the genes and are shared by all members of the species.

Cannon-Bard theory (9). A theory of emotion that rejects a primary role for the viscera and places emotions in the thalamus.

Cannula (8). A tube through which fluid can be injected directly into the brain.

Capillaries (2). The smallest blood vessels, where exchange of oxygen and nutrients with body tissues takes place.

Cardiac muscle (7). The specialized muscle of the heart.

Caudal (3). Toward the tail, opposite of rostral.

Caudate nucleus (3). One of the basal ganglia, a long nucleus curving beneath the neocortex.

Cautery (3). Burning tissue, usually done in surgery to stop bleeding.

Central sulcus (3). A depression in the neocortex that separates the parietal and the temporal lobes.

Cerebellum (3). "Little brain," a highly organized hindbrain structure involved in coordinating movements.

Cerebrospinal fluid (3). A lymphlike fluid that bathes the brain and fills the cerebral ventricles.

Cerveau isolé preparation (10). A physiological preparation in which the brain is severed from the spinal cord.

Channels (2). Holes in a membrane; ion flow through the holes is controlled by specialized proteins guarding the openings.

Chemical synapses (2). Intercellular communication links consisting of a presynaptic terminal containing a neurotransmitter, a synaptic cleft between the cells, and a postsynaptic receptor membrane.

Cholecystokinin (CCK) (8). A hormone involved in the control of nutrient intake.

Choline acetyltransferase (11). An enzyme possibly involved in forming memory engrams.

Cholinergic (2). Using acetylcholine as an neurotransmitter.

Choroid plexus (3). Vascularized regions in the ventricles where cerebrospinal fluid is produced.

Chromatic gratings (5). Grating patterns made up of changes in color (chromaticity) without changes in brightness.

Cilia (4). Tiny whiplike appendages that give motility to many bacteria and other cells.

Ciliary muscles (4). The muscles that mediate accommodation in the lens of the eye.

Cingulate gyrus (3). A gyrus on the medial surface of the cortex, part of the limbic system.

Circadian rhythms (10). Biological rhythms having a period of about a day.

Cisterna magna (3). The major sinus draining blood from the brain.

Classical conditioning (11). Eliciting a conditioned response by providing a conditioned stimulus.

Climbing fibers (3). Inputs to the cerebellar cortex that climb a single Purkinje cell dendritic tree and synapse with it.

Cochlea (4). The inner ear, a coiled organ where the transduction of vibration to neuronal potentials takes place.

Cochlear microphonic (4). An electrical signal corresponding to the sound entering the cochlea, resulting from electrical gradients in the cochlea.

Cochlear nucleus (5). In the medulla, the site of the first synapse in the auditory pathway.

Columnar organization (3). The arrangement of the cortex into functional columns of cells extending from the top to the bottom of the cortex.

Complex cells (5). Neurons in the visual cortex that respond to an appropriate stimulus anywhere within their receptive fields.

Concentration gradient (2). A variation of concentration from high in one location to low in another.

Concordance rate (15). The fraction of individuals sharing a genetic trait who also share a behavioral or body trait.

Conditioned response (CR) (11). A response that occurs in classical conditioning after the presentation of a conditioned stimulus.

Conditioned stimulus (CS) (11). A stimulus that, by being presented repeatedly before an unconditioned stimulus, comes to elicit a conditioned response.

Conduction aphasia (12). A language deficit in which speech and language comprehension centers become disconnected.

Cones (4). High-threshold color-sensitive retinal receptors.

Contingent negative variation (CNV) (14). A slow potential recorded from the scalp, arising in the interval between a warning signal and a signal that triggers action.

Contralateral (5). On the other side of the left-right midline.

Convergence (2). Motion of both eyes toward the nose to fixate a close object.

Convergent evolution (10). The separate evolution of different species to have similar characteristics, such as the fins of fish and whales.

Cornea (4). The transparent covering of the front of the eye.

Corpora quadrigemina (3). The superior and inferior colliculi of the midbrain.

Corpus callosum (3). The tract of axons connecting corresponding regions of the occipital, parietal, and frontal lobes.

Corpus luteum (9). The remains of an egg follicle that secretes progesterone in the human female reproductive cycle.

Corpus striatum (3). The putamen and globus pallidus together.

Cortex (3). Neurons in a layered, sheetlike organization.

Corticomedial group (8). A functional division of the amygdala.

Corticosterone (9). A steroid hormone secreted by the adrenal cortex.

Cribiform plate (4). A plate of bone between the nasal cavity and the brain, with many small holes through which olfactory axons penetrate.

Crista (4). The receptive organ of the semicircular canals in the vestibular system, including the cupula and the hair cells.

Critical period (6). An interval during development when a particular environmental event or condition can influence the course of development.

Crossed-extensor reflex (7). A spinal reflex in which the excitation of flexors on one side results in the excitation of extensors on the other side.

Cupula (4). A gelatinous mass in the crista of the semicircular canals that moves as a result of fluid flow.

Cyclic adenosine monophosphate (cAMP) (2). A second messenger inside a neuron, involved in postsynaptic receptor systems for dopamine, norepinephrine, serotonin, and some other neurotransmitters.

Cycloheximide (11). A protein synthesis inhibitor used in studies of memory.

Dark adaptation (4). Increasing sensitivity to dim light following time spent in darkness.

Dark current (4). An electrical current that flows between the inner and outer segments of a photoreceptor in darkness, because of open channels in the outer segment membrane.

Declarative knowledge (11). Knowledge in memory that can be articulated in language.

Decussate (3). To cross the midline.

Deep structure (12). The logical structure of an utterance, distinct from the sequence of words used.

Delayed sleep phase syndrome (10). A sleep disorder in which going to sleep and waking are delayed in relation to the normal circadian rhythm.

Dendrites (2). Processes that extend the soma of a neuron.

Dendritic spines (11). Small protuberances on the dendrites of some neurons, possibly involved in synapses showing plasticity.

Deoxyribonucleic acid (DNA) (2). The biochemical molecule that contains the genes.

Depolarization (2). Reduction of the normal inside-negative electrical polarization of a cell.

Dermis (4). The inner layers of the skin.

Diagonal band of Broca (11). A nucleus in the diencephalon in the region where ACh neurons originate to innervate the cortex.

Dichotic listening (12). Hearing different sounds in the two ears.

Diencephalon (3). The posterior part of the forebrain, including the thalamus and hypothalamus.

Digital (1). Taking only two possible values, with no others allowed.

Divergence (2). Splitting of an axon to terminate in several locations.

Divergence movements (6). Motion of both eyes away from the nose to fixate a far object.

Dizygotic twins (15). Twins coming from two eggs, with different genes.

Dorsal root ganglia (3). Cell bodies of the afferent (sensory) nerves entering the dorsal part of the spinal cord.

Drives (9). Postulated mechanisms that activate behavior aimed at a particular goal.

Dualism (1). The philosophical idea that body and mind are separate entities.

Dura mater (3). The tough outer protective membrane surrounding the CNS.

Dynorphin (2). One family of endogenous opiate transmitters.

Dyskinesias (7). Nonfunctional, involuntary movements.

Dyslexia (12). Inability to read or difficulty in reading.

Ectoderm (3). The outermost of three layers of cells in an embryo, giving rise to the skin and nervous system.

Ectotherms (8). Animals whose body temperature is determined by the environment and regulated only by behavior.

Efferent (2). Exiting the nervous system or flowing to a more peripheral part of the nervous system.

Efferent control (2). Control of peripheral parts of a sensory system by more central parts, such as cortical influences on the lateral geniculate nucleus.

Electrical synapses (2). Junctions between neurons where presynaptic and postsynaptic membranes are so close together that electrical signals can jump from one neuron to the other.

Electroconvulsive shock (ECS) (11). A shock to the brain that causes convulsions and a period of unconsciousness.

Electroencephalogram (EEG) (5). A recording of brain electrical activity from electrodes on the scalp.

Electromyogram (EMG) (7). A recording of muscle activity from needle electrodes inserted into muscles in the intact organism.

Electrostatic gradient (2). A variation of electrical charge from high in one location to low in another.

Emergent phonemena (13). Properties of large groups of elements that are not evident in any of the elements individually or in small groups.

Encapsulated end organs (4). Somatosensory receptors surrounded by specialized cells.

Encephalization (3). Concentration of information-processing functions in the head during the course of evolution.

Endocrine glands (3). Tissues that secrete hormones directly into the bloodstream.

Endogenous (10). Originating from inside.

Endogenous rhythm (10). A biological rhythm originating from inside.

Endolymph (4). The fluid filling the inner ear and the vestibular system.

Endoplasmic reticulum (2). A cellular organelle that transports substances within the cell.

Endorphin (2). One class of endogenous opiate transmitters.

Endotherms (8). Animals that regulate their internal

temperature by changing their metabolic rate (in addition to behavioral thermoregulation).

Engram (11). The physical substrate of learning.

Enkephalins (2). A family of endogenous opiate transmitters—peptides with a length of five amino acids.

Entorhinal area (5). The secondary olfactory cortex, made of allocortex.

Enzyme (2). A protein that catalyzes a biochemical reaction.

Ephapse (2). A location where two neuronal processes are so close to each other that electrical influences can pass between them without specialized synaptic mechanisms.

Epidermis (4). The outer layer of skin.

Epilepsy (16). A brain disease characterized by seizures of uncontrolled neural firing.

Epileptic focus (3). A region of damaged neural tissue that generates epileptic seizures.

Episodic memory (11). Memory for particular past events (episodes).

Equilibrium (2). A stable state, with inputs matching outputs.

Equipotentiality (11). The ability of several brain tissues to perform the same function.

Estrogens (9). Female sex hormones involved in the menstrual cycle.

Evolution (1). The change in the genes of successive generations of animals response to pressures from the environment.

Excitatory postsynaptic potential (EPSP) (2). A depolarization of a postsynaptic membrane.

Exocrine glands (3). Glands that secrete their products through ducts to the site of action.

Exogenous rhythm (11). A brain rhythm driven by an outside stimulus.

Exponential (2). A quantity that changes by a fixed proportion of its current value in each time interval.

Extinction (9). In classical conditioning, the suppression of response after repeated presentation of the conditioned stimulus without the unconditioned stimulus.

Extracellular (3). Outside the cell, as in the space between cells.

Extrafusal fibers (7). The large muscle fibers that do the work of the muscle, distinguished from the intrafusal fibers.

Extraocular muscles (4). The muscles outside the eye that move the eyeball.

Extrapyramidal system (7). All of the motor system except for the segment that consists of corticospinal tracts that decussate in the pyramids of the medulla.

Extrinsic cortex (3). The cortex with direct connections to peripheral structures.

Extrinsic thalamic nuclei (3). The nuclei that connect the neocortex with peripheral structures, such as sensory and motor systems.

Factor S (10). A small molecule that induces sleep when introduced into the brain.

Fasting phase (8). A period between meals when the body lives on stored food reserves.

Feature detector theory (5). The theory that a neuron responds to the presence of a particular feature in the environment.

Fitness (1). In evolutionary theory, the success of an organism measured in the number of viable offspring produced.

Fixation (denaturing) (3). Changing proteins from their natural state to a biologically inactive state.

Flocculus (6). A part of the cerebellar cortex in which visual-vestibular interactions take place.

Fodrin (11). A structural protein inside the cell that may be involved in neuronal plasticity.

Follicle-stimulating hormone (FSH) (9). A sex hormone that controls the production of estrogen and progesterone.

Foramen magnum (16). The hole in the base of the skull through which the spinal cord passes.

Forebrain (3). The most rostral part of the brain, including the cerebral hemispheres, limbic system, thalamus, hypothalamus, and basal ganglia.

Formal systems (13). Sets of symbols generated and manipulated by explicit rules.

Formalin (3). A solution of formaldehyde (a denaturing agent) in water, used to fix and preserve tissues.

Forward inhibition (2). Inhibition of activity in a subsequent layer in a chain of neurons.

Fourier analysis (4). The process of describing a wave in terms of its sine-wave components.

Fovea (5). The rod-free center of the retina, which has the highest visual acuity.

Free nerve endings (4). Somatosensory endings without specialized structures in the skin.

Gain (7). The ratio of output to input.

Galvanic skin response (GSR) (9). A change in the

electrical resistance of the skin, part of the orienting response.

Gamete (9). A sex cell containing half of an organism's genes that fuses with another gamete in sexual reproduction.

Gamma fibers (7). Thin axons, including those that control the gamma-efferent system of muscle control.

Ganglion (2). A group of nerve cell bodies.

Ganglion cells (5). The neurons in the retina that give rise to the optic nerve.

Gap junctions (2). Electrical synapses in which two membranes lie about as closely together as the thickness of a single membrane.

Gas chromatograph (4). A device for separating gases according to their density.

Generator potentials (4). Graded potentials in receptors caused by sensory events.

Genes (1). Units of inheritance, carried on chromosomes and made of DNA.

Geniculostriate visual system (5). The branch of the visual system consisting of the retina, lateral geniculate nucleus, and striate cortex.

Ghost images (11). In holography, an image of one object elicited by reflection from another object.

Glabrous skin (4). Hairless, heavily innervated skin of the fingertips and other sensitive areas.

Glial cells (glia) (2). Cells that support neurons metabolically and structurally.

Gliosis (2). Proliferation of glial cells at a point of injury.

Globus pallidus (3). A subcortical forebrain nucleus, one of the basal ganglia.

Glycogen (7). Animal sugar, stored in the liver.

Golgi apparatus (2). A cellular organelle that manufactures membranes.

Golgi cells (3). Inhibitory neurons in the cerebellar cortex.

Golgi stain (3). A silver stain that affects only a small percentage of nerve cells.

Golgi tendon organs (7). Stretch receptors in the tendons that inhibit muscles under extreme tension.

Gonadotropin-releasing hormone (GnRH) (9). A hypothalamic hormone that causes the anterior pituitary to produce leutinizing hormone and follicle-stimulating hormone.

Graded potentials (2). Membrane potentials that can vary in magnitude and are conducted passively.

Grammar (12). A set of rules to organize words into meaningful utterances.

Grand mal epileptic seizure (11). A generalized epileptic seizure that involves loss of consciousness and convulsions of the entire body.

Granular layer (3). The deepest layer of the cerebellar cortex.

Granule cells (3). Cerebellar neurons in the granular layer, giving rise to parallel fibers, or small neurons elsewhere in the brain.

Growth cone (6). The expanded tip of a growing axon that guides its development.

Gustation (4). The sense of taste.

Habituation (9). A type of plasticity that results in reduced response following repeated presentations of a stimulus.

Hair cells (4). The receptors for the auditory and vestibular senses.

Hairy skin (4). The skin covering most of the body, with hairs that increase its sensitivity.

Helicotrema (4). The small hole that joins the two fluid chambers of the cochlea.

Hemianopic (12). Seeing on only one side of the visual field.

Hemiplegia (16). Paralysis of one side of the body.

Heterozygous (15). An organism having two versions of a particular gene.

Hindbrain (3). The most caudal part of the brain, including the cerebellum and the medulla.

Hippocampus (3). The part of the forebrain made of three-layered cortex curled under the temporal lobe, involved in memory and orienting.

Histamine (15). A probable neurotransmitter that may be involved in depression.

Histofluorescence (3). Techniques that cause appropriately stained cells to glow under ultraviolet light.

Histological techniques (3). Anatomical techniques related to cells.

Hologram (11). An interference pattern that stores wave fronts emanating from objects.

Holophrase (12). The earliest human utterances, combining word, gesture and context.

Homeostasis (3). The effort to keep the internal environment constant.

Homovanillic acid (15). A product of dopamine metabolism, sometimes found in elevated concentrations in schizophrenics.

Homunculus (7). A small image of the body projected onto the brain.

Horizontal cell (5). A retinal neuron without action potentials, linking receptors and bipolar cells.

Hormone (2). A substance carried in the bloodstream that affects target organs or tissues.

Horsley-Clarke system (3). A standardized system of brain coordinates that enables researchers to reach hidden brain areas without damaging overlying tissue.

Hydrocephalus (3). Increased intracranial pressure caused by closure of the normal drainage of cerebrospinal fluid.

Hydrophilic (2). Associating with water.

Hydrophobic (2). Avoiding association with water.

Hyperactivity (14). Overactivity and inability to concentrate in children, also called hyperkinesis.

Hyperacuity (5). Ability to distinguish structure in a visual stimulus at levels of detail finer than the distance between retinal cones.

Hypercomplex cells (5). Neurons in the visual cortex that respond to lines of a particular length and orientation anywhere in their receptive fields.

Hyperphagia (8). A condition of excessive food intake.

Hyperpolarization (2). Increase in nerve membrane potential tending to inhibit release of action potentials.

Hypertonic (8). A solution with a higher salt concentration than body fluids (about 0.9 percent salt).

Hypnotism (14). The act of inducing a state of increased suggestibility.

Hypopolarization (2). Decrease in nerve membrane potential tending to facilitate release of action potentials.

Hypothalamus (3). A control center in the diencephalon for many homeostatic functions.

Hypovolemia (8). A reduced volume of extracellular fluid.

Idealism (1). The philosophical idea of the existence of ideas as distinct from external physical objects.

Incus (4). One of the small bones in the middle ear that transfers sounds from air to a fluid medium.

Infarct (16). An interruption of blood supply, as in a heart attack.

Inferior colliculus (3). A cortically organized midbrain structure that processes auditory information.

Inferotemporal (IT) cortex (5). A region involved in higher-order visual processing.

Inhibitory postsynaptic potential (IPSP) (2). A hyperpolarization of a neuron's membrane caused by synaptic action, driving the neuron away from its firing threshold.

Inner ear (4). The fluid-filled part of the ear where transduction takes place.

Inner hair cells (4). Cochlear receptors for hearing.

Inner plexiform layer (5). The layer of the retina where ganglion cells, amacrine cells, and bipolar cells make synaptic contacts.

Innervation ratio (7). The ratio of muscle fibers to motor axons; a smaller ratio means finer control.

Instrumental conditioning (11). A form of associative learning in which a behavior increases in frequency if positive reinforcement follows it.

Insula (5). A part of the neocortex buried between the parietal and temporal lobes.

Insulin (8). A hormone released by the islets of Langerhans, in the pancreas, that lowers blood glucose.

Interface (1). A point of contact or communication.

Intracellular (3). Within the cell, as an intracellular electrode that records potentials from the inside of a cell.

Intrafusal fibers (7). Small muscle fibers that contain muscle spindle receptors.

Intrinsic cortex (3). Neocortex without direct connections to sensory or motor systems.

Intrinsic inhibitory neurons (3). Inhibitory neurons in a nucleus or cortical structure that have only local connections.

Intrinsic thalamic nuclei (3). Thalamic nuclei that are associated with intrinsic areas of the cortex.

Introspection (1). Learning about the mind by examining one's own thought process.

Invaginations (5). Hollows or indentations, as in the synaptic region of photoreceptors.

Invasive techniques (3). Techniques in brain research that require intervention in the brain.

Iodopsin (4). One of the visual pigments found in the cones of the retina.

Ion (2). A molecule with a net electric charge.

Iris (4). The muscle surrounding the pupil of the eye.

Isomer (2). A particular orientation of a molecule that can exist in two forms that are mirror images of each another.

James-Lange theory (9). The theory of emotion that

requires signals from the viscera together with sensory stimuli to evoke emotional reactions.

Juxtallocortex (3). Phylogenetically old cortex located next to the allocortex.

Kinesthetic sense (4). The sense of movement and position of parts of the body.

Korsakoff syndrome (11). A memory disorder including loss of some memories and impairment in forming new episodic memories, usually a result of chronic alcoholism.

Krause end bulbs (4). Specialized endings of somatosensory nerves.

Labia majora (9). The outer skin flaps covering the vagina.

Labyrinth (4). The chambers in the skull containing the vestibular organs.

Lateral frontal cortex (14). The part of the frontal cortex on the lateral sides of the frontal lobes, opposite the orbital frontal cortex, and probably involved in organizing long-term sequences of behavior.

Lateral geniculate nucleus (LGN) (3). The thalamic nucleus that sends visual signals to the cortex.

Lateral inhibition (2). Inhibition of each neuron in a parallel network by its neighbors, enhancing contrast and spreading information across the network.

L-dopa (7). A precursor of dopamine, given to some Parkinson's patients to reduce their symptoms.

Learning (11). The acquisition of new memories.

Lemniscal pathways (5). Direct, large-fiber somatosensory pathways in the spinal cord.

Lens (4). A flexible body of protein that helps focus light between the cornea and the retina of the eye.

Lexicon (12). The total of all words in a language.

Ligand (2). A molecule that binds selectively to a particular neurotransmitter.

Light adaptation (4). Reduction in retinal sensitivity following exposure to light.

Limbic system (3). A group of forebrain structures particularly concerned with homeostasis and fight-or-flight reactions.

Linear summation (5). Adding together several signals without distorting them.

Lipids (2). Fatlike molecules.

Local circuit neurons (2). A group of neurons in a small region that performs a particular function, often with graded potentials.

Locus coeruleus (10). A brain-stem cholinergic nucleus important in controlling sleep.

Long-term potentiation (LTP) (11). Lowered threshold of some neurons following stimulation, a model for memory.

Luteinizing hormone (LH) (9). A hormone released by the anterior pituitary in both sexes that influences hormonal secretions by the gonads.

Mach bands (5). Illusory light or dark bands seen at abrupt borders in rate of brightness change on a surface.

Malleus (4). A bone in the middle ear, connected to the eardrum, that transmits sound vibrations.

Mammillary bodies (3). A pair of nuclei at the base of the brain.

Martinotti cell (3). A type of cell found in the neocortex.

Mass action (11). The theory that the quality of information processing in a region depends on the number of functioning neurons.

Mechanism (1). The philosophical idea that all aspects of life have a physical basis.

Mechanoreceptors (4). Receptors sensitive to mechanical deformation, such as the receptors at the base of hairs in the skin.

Medial forebrain bundle (MFB) (9). A fiber tract in the subcortical forebrain, important in signals related to reward.

Medial geniculate nucleus (5). The thalamic nucleus that sends auditory signals to the cortex.

Medial septal nucleus (11). A limbic nucleus possibly involved in the formation of memories.

Medulla oblongata (3). The most caudal part of the hindbrain, also called the myelencephalon.

Meissner's corpuscles (4). Specialized sensory organs in the skin.

Memory (11). Information stored in the brain as a result of experience.

Meninges (3). Membranes that surround and protect the brain.

Merkel's disks (4). Specialized mechanoreceptor bundles in the skin.

Mesencephalon (3). The midbrain.

Mesopic range (4). An intermediate range of brightness where both rod and cone receptors are active.

Metabolism (2). The chemical processes of life.

Metabotropic transmitters (2). Neurotransmitters that

work indirectly, using an adenyl cyclase pathway within the postsynaptic neuron.

Metencephalon (3). The rostral part of the hindbrain, including the pons and cerebellum.

Microfilaments (2). Threadlike proteins important in the internal structure of a cell.

Microglia (2). Small free-ranging glial cells that remove cellular debris from dead or injured neurons.

Microsaccades (6). Small saccadic (jumping) eye movements made involuntarily during visual fixation.

Microtome (3). Specialized knife mounted on a stage to cut brain sections of precise thickness.

Microtubules (2). Cylindrical organelles in axons that aid in axoplasmic transport.

Midbrain (3). The middle part of the brain, including the corpora quadrigemina (superior and inferior colliculi) and tegmentum.

Middle ear (4). The air-filled chamber between the eardrum and the cochlea, containing the ossicles.

Mirror focus (3). A secondary epileptic focus caused by epileptic activity at a symmetrically opposite location.

Mitochondria (2). Cellular organelles that perform energy transfer reactions.

Mitral cell (5). A neuron in the olfactory bulb.

Molecular layer (3). The top layer of the cerebellar cortex.

Molecular weight (2). The weight of an atom or molecule expressed in units of the weight of a hydrogen atom.

Monoamine oxidase (MAO) inhibitors (15). A class of antidepressant drugs.

Monopolar (3). Referring to a neuron with a single branch leaving the cell body and then going in two directions, one the receptive zone and the other the output zone.

Monosynaptic (3). Transferring information in a single synaptic layer, such as the thalamic nuclei.

Monozygotic twins (15). Twins originating from a single egg, with identical genes.

Mossy fibers (3). Input fibers to the cerebellar cortex that synapse on granule cells.

Müllerian ducts (9). A system of ducts in the embryo that will develop into the female reproductive tract.

Multiplexing (5). Performing several functions in the same machinery at different times.

Muscarinic receptor (2). A type of ACh receptor.

Muscle unit (7). All of the muscle fibers innervated by a single axon.

Myelencephalon (3). The most caudal part of the hindbrain; the medulla.

Myelin (2). Fatty insulation surrounding an axon that is formed by glial cells and that improves the conduction speed of action potentials.

Myoglobin (7). A respiratory protein found in muscles.

Myosin (7). One of the two proteins, along with actin, that makes up the contractile part of muscle.

Naloxone (2). An opiate antagonist.

Narcolepsy (10). A sleep disorder marked by abruptly falling asleep, even in inappropriate circumstances.

Nativism (1). The philosophical idea that organisms have inborn mechanisms that structure their interactions with the world.

Natural selection (1). In evolution, the survival of animals that can best cope with their environments.

Negative feedback (2). A regulatory strategy in which output reduces the magnitude of input signals.

Neocerebellum (7). The phylogenetically newer part of the cerebellum, concerned principally with motor coordination.

Neocortex (3). The phylogenetically newer six-layered cortex of the forebrain.

Neostriatum (7). Phylogenetically newer basal ganglia, the putamen and caudate nucleus.

Nernst equation (2). The relationship between membrane potential, ion concentrations on both sides, and temperature.

Neural tube (3). A tube on the back of the embryo that develops into the brain and spinal cord.

Neuroembryology (6). Study of the prenatal development of the nervous system.

Neuromuscular junction (2). The large, specialized ACh synapse between a motor neuron and a muscle fiber.

Neuron (1). The cellular unit of the nervous system that is able to communicate with other neurons or with muscles through synapses.

Neuropil (3). Nervous tissue.

Neurosurgery (15). Brain surgery to repair trauma or treat disease.

Neurotransmitter (2). A chemical that is released at a presynaptic membrane and has a depolarizing or hyperpolarizing effect on the postsynaptic membrane.

Neutral zone (8). In a feedback system, such as thermoregulation, the range of input values that result in no change in output.

Nicotinic receptors (2). Type of ACh receptors.

Node of Ranvier (2). A gap between segments of myelin where ions are exchanged in saltatory axon conduction.

Norepinephrine (NE) (2). A neurotransmitter produced mostly in the brain stem.

Nuclear magnetic resonance (NMR) (16). A technique for imaging living tissues by detecting characteristic wobbles of atomic nuclei in strong magnetic fields.

Nucleolus (2). An organelle within a cell's nucleus.

Nucleus basalis of Meynert (11). A forebrain nucleus containing many of the brain's cholinergic neurons.

Nucleus circularis (8). A small hypothalamic nucleus that governs the secretion of antidiuretic hormone.

Nystagmus (7). Alternating slow drifts of the eye and quick returns in the opposite direction, elicited by visual or vestibular stimulation.

Object constancy (14). The tendency to perceive objects in their correct sizes regardless of their distance or the size of their retinal images.

Octave (5). A logarithmic unit; each octave indicates a doubling of the quantity.

Olfaction (4). The sense of smell.

Olfactory bulbs (3). The first processing station for olfactory signals.

Olfactory epithelium (5). The membrane in which the olfactory receptors are located.

Oligodendroglia (2). Glial cells that form myelin sheaths in the CNS, as Schwann cells do in the periphery.

Ontogeny (3). Development of an organism from birth to adulthood.

Opsin (4). A constituent of visual receptor pigment molecules.

Optic disc (5). The blind spot of the retina, where ganglion cell axons exit from the retina to form the optic nerve.

Optic radiations (5). Axons of lateral geniculate neurons that radiate out to the visual cortex.

Orbital frontal cortex (14). The part of the frontal cortex that lies behind the orbits of the eyes, associated with emotional and motivational systems.

Organelle (2). An assembly of membranes or molecules within a cell that performs a specific function in the life of the cell.

Organum vasculosum (8). A vascular part of the ventricular lining, possibly containing angiotensin receptors.

Orienting response (9). A set of behavioral and autonomic responses to a novel stimulus, including EEG activation and orienting of receptors.

Osmotic gradient (8). Change from a region of high concentration of particles in solution to a region of low concentration, or vice versa.

Osmotic pressure (8). Flow of water along an osmotic gradient across a semipermeable membrane, tending to equalize the concentrations of the solutions on the two sides of the membrane.

Ossicles (4). Tiny bones in the middle ear that reduce the amplitude and increase the power of sound vibrations while transmitting them from the eardrum to the oval window.

Otolith organs (4). The vestibular gravity organs—the utricle and the saccule.

Outer hair cells (4). Cochlear receptors for sound vibrations.

Outer plexiform layer (5). The retinal layer where bipolar cells, horizontal cells, and receptors make synaptic contacts.

Outer segment (4). The part of the photoreceptor cell that contains visual pigments and in which transduction takes place.

Pacemaker region (7). A region of the heart where cells spontaneously change their polarization, generating waves of activity that induce the heart to beat.

Pacinian corpuscles (4). Vibration receptors deep in the skin.

Paleocerebellum (7). A phylogenetically old part of the cerebellum where muscle tone is regulated.

Papez circuit (9). A group of forebrain nuclei concerned with the regulation of emotional behavior.

Papillae (4). Small bumps in the dermis that extend into the epidermis; in the mouth, specialized assemblies of cells on the tongue that contain taste receptors.

Parachlorophenylalanine (PCPA) (10). A drug that induces insomnia by reducing serotonin synthesis.

Paradoxical sleep (10). Stage of sleep characterized by an alert EEG pattern, movements of the eyes, and loss of muscle tone—also called REM (rapid eye movement) sleep.

Parallel fibers (3). Axons of cerebellar granule cells running parallel to each other and perpendicular to Purkinje cell dendritic trees.

Parasympathetic subsystem (3). A set of nerves originating in the cranial and sacral regions of the spinal cord, in general mediating homeostatic and restorative functions.

Parkinson's disease (7). A neurological disorder revealed by movement and posture difficulties and involving a loss of dopaminergic neurons.

Passive avoidance (11). Avoiding a shock by not performing a behavior.

Peduncles (3). Legs of nerve fibers connecting the brain stem to the cerebellum.

Perceptron (13). A pattern-recognition device consisting of a receptor array, linking lines with changeable weights, and an output element.

Perfuse (3). To introduce a fluid into a tissue via the circulation.

Periamygdaloid area (5). The region around the amygdala, under the temporal lobe.

Periglomerular cells (5). Cells surrounding a glomerulus, a bundle of highly organized synaptic contacts.

Peripheral nervous system (2). The part of the nervous system outside the brain and spinal cord, not covered by dura mater.

Periphery effect (5). Response of a visual neuron to appropriately organized stimuli outside its classical receptive field.

Permeable (2). Open to passage by fluids.

Perseverate (14). To continue a course of action after it ceases to be appropriate.

Perseveration-consolidation hypothesis (11). The idea that memories are stored in a vulnerable, temporary form while they are being transferred to a more permanent form.

Petit mal epileptic seizures (16). Epileptic seizures of short duration and few outward signs, such as fluttering of the eyelids.

Phagocytosis (2). Engulfing of one cell by another.

Phenothiazines (15). A class of antipsychotic drugs, affecting dopamine pathways.

Phenylketonuria (PKU) (15). A progressive form of mental retardation caused by inability to metabolize the amino acid phenylalanine.

Phonemes (12). Individual speech sounds.

Phosphorylation process (2). The chemical process of adding a phosphor group, important in biological energy-exchange reactions.

Photons (4). Elementary particles that carry electromagnetic energy such as light.

Photopic range (4). The higher range of brightness, where cone receptors are active.

Phototaxic (11). Tending to move or orient toward light.

Physostigmine (11). A cholinergic agonist that improves memory in humans.

Pia mater (3). The innermost of the meninges surrounding the brain.

Piezoelectric effect (4). The generating of electricity from the deformation of a crystal or other substance.

Pigment epithelium (4). A layer of cells that lines the inside surface of the eye and nourishes the photoreceptors.

Pineal organ (10). An endocrine gland that helps govern circadian rhythms.

Pinna (4). The visible outside portion of the ear, helpful in perceiving the direction of sound.

Pinocytosis (2). Pinching back a bit of plasma membrane to make an intracellular vesicle, used in recycling some neurotransmitters.

Place theory (4). The discrimination of sound frequencies by the location of largest amplitude of vibration in the cochlea.

Plasma membrane (2). The three-layered membrane surrounding all cells, consisting of two layers of phospholipid molecules lined up with their hydrophobic tails pointing inward and their hydrophilic heads outward.

Polymodal cells (3). Neurons responding to stimuli from more than one sensory modality.

Polysynaptic (2). Passing through several synaptic processing stages, as in the polysynaptic sensory pathway to the auditory cortex.

Pons (3). A band of fibers running laterally under the brain stem, part of the link between the brain stem and the cerebellum.

Portal system (3). A specialized set of blood vessels between the hypothalamus and the anterior pituitary carrying hypothalamic hormones.

Positron emission tomography (PET) scans (16). A method of localizing brain structure and function through radioactive tracers.

Postsynaptic (2). Receiving neurotransmitters on the "downstream" end of a synapse.

Potential (electrical) (2). Difference in electron concentration in two regions, measured in volts.

Prefrontal lobotomy (15). A surgical procedure to separate the prefrontal region of the neocortex from the rest of the brain.

Preganglionic axons (3). Axons situated on the presynaptic side of a ganglion.

Preoptic area (8). A nucleus of the hypothalamus, important in regulating sexual behavior.

Prepyriform cortex (5). A part of the archicortex, an olfactory center.

Presbyopia (4). Progressive loss of visual accommodation with age, caused by hardening of the lens.

Presynaptic (2). The part of the synaptic mechanism before the synaptic cleft, including the membrane that releases neurotransmitter.

Priming effect (9). Increase in conditioned behavior after an animal is given a "free" reward.

Principal cells (3). Thalamic neurons that send axons to the cortex.

Procedural knowledge (11). Memory for rules and procedures (things that are always the case), as opposed to particular incidents.

Processes (2). Axons and dendrites.

Progesterone (9). A female sex hormone, important in mantaining pregnancy.

Prosopagnosia (14). The inability to recognize faces because of neurological deficit.

Prosthesis (4). An artificial substitute for an organ or sense.

Protein kinase (2). A family of enzymes acting on proteins.

Proximal (3). Close to an organism; opposite of distal.

Psychosurgery (15). Brain surgery to change behaviors or attitudes.

Punctate pattern (4). A discontinuous pattern of points, as in regions of skin sensitive to particular stimuli.

Punctuated equilibrium (1). In evolutionary theory, the idea that species exist nearly unchanged until an environmental stress causes a brief period of rapid evolution.

Purkinje cells (3). The inhibitory output cells of the cerebellar cortex.

Purkinje layer (3). The layer of the cerebellar cortex that contains the Purkinje cell bodies.

Purkinje shift (4). The change in maximum light sensitivity to shorter wavelengths at low (scotopic) light levels.

Puromycin (11). A protein synthesis inhibitor used in early studies of memory consolidation.

Pursuit eye movements (6). Smooth eye movements made in tracking a moving object.

Putamen (3). One of the basal ganglia, part of the neostriatum.

Pyramidal cells (3). Cells of the cortex with a pyramid-shaped cell body and usually with an axon exiting from the cortex.

Pyramidal system (7). A set of large, fast axons coursing from the cortex directly to spinal motor neurons, through the pyramids of the medulla.

Pyrogens (8). Chemicals emitted by bacteria that induce fever in mammals.

Radioactive tracer (3). A compound containing unstable atoms that spontaneously decay, giving off detectable particles.

Raphe (10). A nucleus along the midline of the brain stem, important in controlling sleep.

Receptive field (5). The part of the world to which a neuron responds with increases or decreases in firing.

Receptors (2). Cells that transduce a form of energy, either chemical or mechanical, into membrane neural signals.

Recessive (15). In genetics, a trait that is not expressed unless it is inherited from both parents.

Reciprocal inhibition (7). Two neurons or nuclei, each inhibiting the other by an amount proportional to its own activity.

Reciprocal innervation (1). Inhibition of one muscle when its antagonist is stimulated.

Recovery function (10). A curve describing the increase in response to a stimulus as the interval between that stimulus and an earlier one is increased.

Rectify (2). To change so all positive and all negative voltages go in the same direction from zero.

Recurrent collateral (7). An axon branch that innervates, directly or indirectly, the neuron from which it came.

Red nucleus (7). A motor nucleus in the brain stem.

Reductionism (1). The philosophical idea that one can gain understanding of a whole by studying its parts.

Reflex (1). A stereotyped, unlearned response to a stimulus.

Relative refractory period (2). A time interval after an action potential when an axon can be triggered only with a stimulus that is stronger than normal.

Renin (8). A hormone that initiates body compensations for fluid loss.

Renshaw cells (7). Small spinal cord neurons that complete a negative feedback on motor neurons.

Resting potential (2). The negative potential shown by a neuron when it is not engaged in signal processing.

Reticular formation (3). A dense network of neurons and fibers at the core of the brain stem.

Retinal (4). A visual pigment molecule.

Retinohypothalamic tract (10). A small bundle of slowly conducting axons that provides a zeitgeber for circadian rhythms in the hypothalamus.

Retrograde amnesia (11). Forgetting of previous events, as in amnesia for events that occurred before a brain injury.

Retrograde degeneration (3). Destruction of a nerve cell body after injury to one of its processes.

Rhinencephalon (5). A part of the forebrain that includes the olfactory cortex.

Rhodopsin (4). The visual pigment (visual purple) found in rod photoreceptors.

Ribbon synapse (5). A specialized synapse, found in the retina, where the presynaptic terminal's vesicles are organized around a ribbon of membrane perpendicular to the synaptic membrane.

Ribonucleic acid (RNA) (2). The molecule that transfers genetic instructions to the machinery of the cell.

Ribosomes (2). Cellular organelles that manufacture proteins from RNA templates.

Rods (4). Retinal photoreceptors capable of detecting low levels of light.

Rostrally (3). Toward the head.

Round window (4). A membrane between the cochlea and the middle ear cavity.

Saccade (6). A rapid, ballistic movement of the eyes, the most common of all human behaviors.

Saccule (4). One of the otolith organs—gravity receptors of the vestibular system.

Saltatory conduction (2). In myelinated axons, propagation of nerve impulses by fast, graded potential conduction from one node of Ranvier to another.

Sarcomere (7). The smallest unit that contains all of the contractile components of a muscle.

Savings (11). Reduction in number of trials needed to relearn a task that had been learned previously.

Scanning electron microscope (3). A device that scans a sample with electrons in a pattern analogous to a TV camera.

Scanpath (11). A sequence of saccadic eye movements made in inspecting an image.

Schema (1). A plan for an action held in the brain.

Schizophrenia (15). A mental disorder characterized by loss of contact with reality and auditory hallucinations.

Schwann cells (2). Glial cells that form myelin in the peripheral nervous system.

Sclera (4). The tough outer coating of the eye.

Scoplamine (11). A drug used to investigate memory mechanisms.

Scotoma (5). A blind region in the visual field.

Scotopic range (4). Low light levels, where rod photoreceptors are used.

Selective pressure (1). Differential survival of a group of animals within a species having a particular trait, causing the spread of that trait within the population.

Semantic (12). Relating to meaning.

Semantic memory (11). Memory relating to rules and meaning, as in memory for the way through a maze.

Septum (3). A part of the limbic system in the medial forebrain.

Serotonin (10). 5-hydroxytryptamine, a neurotransmitter produced in the raphe nucleus that governs slow-wave sleep.

Set point (8). The value to which a feedback control system is tuned, as in the temperature set point in the hypothalamus.

Sham rage (9). Autonomic components of a rage response without a directed attack, seen in decorticate cats.

Shift effect (5). Response of a cortical neuron to the motion of a large texture outside its receptive field.

Simple cells (5). Neurons in the striate visual cortex that respond in a linear fashion, firing most strongly to a grating of a particular spatial frequency and orientation.

Simulate (13). To study the function of a system by designing a computer model of the system and testing the model under various conditions.

Sleep apnea (10). A sleep disorder in which the patient temporarily ceases to breathe while asleep.

Sleep spindles (10). Groups of spikes in the EEG present during stage 2 sleep.

Sleep stage 1 (10). The lightest stage of slow-wave sleep.

Sleep stage 2 (10). The second lightest stage of slow-wave sleep, characterized by sleep spindles in the EEG.

Sleep stage 3 (10). The third lightest stage of slow-wave sleep, with EEG sleep spindles and 1 to 2 Hz delta waves.

Sleep stage 4 (10). The deepest stage of slow-wave sleep, with the EEG dominated by 1 to 2 Hz delta waves.

Slot grammar (12). A two-word grammar used by young children before they acquire the grammar of their native language.

Slow-wave sleep (10). The four stages of non-REM sleep, characterized by slow waves in the EEG.

Smooth muscles (7). Muscles that tend to remain contracted for long periods and are usually involuntarily innervated.

Solitary nucleus (5). A sensory nucleus for the taste system in the brain stem.

Soma (2). The body of a cell, containing the nucleus.

Somatosensory system (4). The skin senses.

Spatial frequency (5). The number of cycles in one degree of visual angle in a grating pattern.

Sphincter muscles (3). Muscles that close a duct or vessel.

Spinal cord (1). The part of the CNS extending into the hollow spinal column of vertebrates.

Spinothalamic pathway (5). A phylogenetically newer, faster somatosensory pathway for fine-grained information.

Spiral ganglion (5). A group of cell bodies associated with the cochlea, containing the somas of the auditory nerve cells.

Stages of sleep (*see* sleep stage 1; sleep stage 2; sleep stage 3; sleep stage 4).

Stapedius muscle (4). A muscle attached to the stapes that modifies sound transmission through the middle ear.

Stapes (4). One of the ossicles, the small muscles that transmit sound vibrations through the middle ear.

Stellate cells (3). Small neurons with mostly local connections in a roughly spherical region surrounding the soma.

Stem cells (4). Embryonic neurons that guide the development of other neurons.

Stereochemical theory (4). A theory of olfaction stating that the shapes of molecules determine their odors by fitting into receptors of the appropriate shapes.

Stereotaxic (3). Reaching a particular brain region with a standardized system of three-dimensional coordinates.

Stimulus-response psychology (1). A psychology such as behaviorism that considers only the relationship between stimuli and responses, without considering internal processes.

Strabismus (6). A visual disorder in which the two eyes point in different directions.

Stretch reflex (7). The active contraction of a muscle when it is stretched, caused by excitation of spinal motor neurons by stretch receptors in the muscles.

Striate cortex (5). Primary visual cortex (area 17 of the cortex), where visual information from the lateral geniculate of the thalamus is arrayed in a topographic map of the retinas.

Striated muscles (7). Fast-contracting muscles in which contractile elements are aligned to form striations, including most voluntary muscles.

Stroke (16). Interruption of cerebral blood supply, causing death of part of the brain.

Subfornical organ (8). A region of the ventricle wall just below the fornix, a possible site of angiotensin receptors.

Substantia gelatinosa (9). A region of small neurons in the spinal cord that mediates pain processing.

Substantia nigra (3). A midbrain nucleus, part of the extrapyramidal motor system.

Sulcus principalis (14). A sulcus (groove) in the lateral frontal cortex.

Superior colliculus (3). A cortically organized midbrain structure concerned with eye movements and visually guided behavior.

Superior olive (5). A nucleus in the medulla involved in combining signals from the two ears.

Suprachiasmatic nucleus (10). A hypothalamic nucleus controlling circadian rhythms.

Suspensory ligaments (4). Connective tissue inside the eye linking the lens with the eyeball and with the accommodation muscles.

Symbiosis (2). Cooperation of two organisms for their mutual benefit.

Sympathetic ganglia (3). A chain of ganglia on either side of the spinal cord, part of the sympathetic nervous subsystem.

Sympathetic subsystem (3). A set of cholinergic nerves innervating many internal organs, generally preparing the body for activity.

Synapse (2). A structure mediating chemical or electrical communication between two neurons.

Synaptic cleft (2). The region between two neuronal membranes in a synapse.

Synaptic glomeruli (3). Specialized bundles of synapses linking processes from several neurons.

Syrinx (12). Part of the vocal apparatus of birds.

Tardive dyskinesia (15). Involuntary movements associated with prolonged use of antipsychotic drugs.

Tectorial membrane (4). A structure within the cochlea that undergoes a shearing motion relative to the basilar membrane as a result of sound vibrations.

Tectum (3). A visual processing center in the midbrain of primitive vertebrates, analogous to the superior colliculus of mammals.

Tegmentum (3). The dorsal part of the midbrain, below the superior and inferior colliculi.

Telencephalon (3). The rostral part of the forebrain, including the cerebral hemispheres.

Telephone theory (4). The theory that auditory frequencies are coded by the frequency of firing of neurons in the auditory pathway.

Tensor tympani (4). A small muscle attached to the malleus, stiffening the linkage between the eardrum and the oval window when it is contracted.

Testosterone (9). A male sex hormone.

Tetanus (7). Continuous contraction of a muscle.

Thalamus (3). A subcortical structure in the diencephalon that processes signals sent to and from the neocortex.

Thrombosis (16). Blockage of an artery by a blood clot, one cause of strokes.

Tight junctions (2). Electrical synapses in which the membranes are partially fused.

Time constant (2). The time that it takes for a momentarily stimulated neural membrane to return to the mathematical constant 1/e (0.368) times as much voltage as its level during stimulation.

Tonotopic map (5). An arrangement of the auditory cortex and some auditory nuclei where different tones are mapped onto different parts of the structure.

Top-down (6). Internally stored information that is used to interpret sensory messages.

Topographic map (3). Map that preserves order relationships but that does not necessarily maintain geometric proportion, as in the topographic map of the retina on the cortex that magnifies the foveal projection.

Torpor (8). Forced inactivity due to low body temperature.

Transduction (2). Change of one form of energy to another, as in auditory receptors that transduce motion into graded potentials.

Transfer RNA (11). RNA that functions to move genetic information from the nucleus of a cell to the cytoplasm, where the information is used to manufacture proteins.

Transmission electron microscope (3). A device that focuses a stream of electrons on a sample with optics analogous to that of a light microscope.

Treppe (7). The increase in force of muscle contraction as an unused muscle fiber is repeatedly stimulated.

Tricyclic antidepressants (15). A chemical family of drugs that treat depression by presynaptic reuptake of some neurotransmitters.

Tuning curve (5). Expression of the relationship between a sensory quantity and a neural response, as in the relationship between sound frequency and firing in some auditory neurons.

Turing test (13). A hypothetical test for artificial intelligence in which a human attempts to determine whether a terminal is connected to a computer or to another human.

Unconditioned response (UR) (11). A response to a stimulus that takes place without learning, such as the salivation of dogs in response to meat powder in the mouth.

Unconditioned stimulus (US) (11). The stimulus that elicits an unconditioned response.

Unilateral (10). On one side only.

Unipolar depression (15). A form of depression that alternates with periods of normal moods, without mania.

Utricle (4). An organ in the inner ear that senses static balance.

Vasopressin (*see* antidiuretic hormone [ADH]).

Vegetative body functions (3). Homeostatic functions that do not require overt activity, such as adjustments in blood chemistry.

Ventral nonadrenergic bundle (8). A principal source of adrenergic input to the cortex.

Ventricles (3). Four cavities within the brain, filled with cerebrospinal fluid.

Vermis (7). A part of the cerebellar cortex straddling the midline.

Vertex potential (14). An electrical potential recorded from the highest part of the head.

Vesicles (2). Small intracellular spheres made of unit membrane, sometimes storing neurotransmitter in a neuron.

Vestibule (4). The region in the labyrinth where the semicircular canals meet; origin of the term *vestibular system* for the detectors of head position and acceleration.

Visual capture (4). The tendency of visual information to dominate information from other sense modalities when the two come into conflict.

Vitalism (1). The philosophical idea that some aspects of living things are qualitatively different from nonliving matter and need not obey physical laws.

Volley principle (4). A theory in audition that extends the telephone theory by not requiring any single neuron to respond to every peak of a pressure wave, as long as one neuron or another responds to each peak.

Voltage clamp (2). A technique of holding transmembrane voltage constant with a feedback circuit so ionic currents can be studied.

Wada test (12). Injection of sodium amytal into a cerebral artery on one side to measure brain function when only the other side is active.

Waxy flexibility (15). A neurological symptom in which the patient will hold any posture that is imposed.

W-cells (5). Visual neurons with large receptive fields and small, very slow-conducting axons.

Wernicke's aphasia (12). Receptive aphasia, with inability to understand language and lack of meaning in speech.

Wolffian ducts (9). A set of ducts in the embryo that develop into the male reproductive tract.

X-cells (5). Visual neurons with small receptive fields, slow-conducting axons, and nonlinear summation within their receptive fields.

Y-cells (5). Visual neurons with large receptive fields, fast-conducting axons, and linear summation within their receptive fields.

Zeitgeber (10). A stimulus that resets a circadian rhythm.

Z-lines (7). Transverse lines visible in a striated muscle, where the ends of the sarcomeres line up.

REFERENCES

Abraham, S., Denton, D., & Weisinger, B. (1976). Effect of an angiotensin antagonist, Sar-Ala-Angiotensin II on physiological thirst. *Pharmacology, Biochemistry and Behavior, 4,* 243–247.

Adrian, E. D. (1931). Potential changes in the isolated nervous system of *Dytiscus marginalis. Journal of Physiology, 72,* 132–151.

Adrian, E. D. (1950). The electrical activity of the mammalian olfactory bulb. *Electroencephalography and Clinical Neurophysiology, 2,* 377–388.

Adrian, E. D., & Matthews, B. H. C. (1934). The Berger rhythm: Potential changes from the occipital lobes in man. *Brain, 57,* 355–385.

Agranoff, B. W., Davis, R. E., Casola, L., & Lim, R. (1967). Actinomycin-D blocks formation of memory of shock-avoidance in goldfish. *Science, 158,* 1600–1601.

Akert, K. (1964). Comparative anatomy of frontal cortex and thalamofrontal connections. In J. M. Warren & K. Akert (Eds.), *The frontal granular cortex and behavior.* New York: McGraw-Hill.

Akil, H., Watson, S. J., Young, E., Lewis, M. E., Khachaturian, H., & Walker, J. M. (1984). Endogenous opioids: Biology and function. *Annual Review of Neuroscience, 7,* 223–255.

Alberts, J. (1978). Huddling by rat pups: Multisensory control of contact behavior. *Journal of Comparative and Physiological Psychology, 92,* 220–230.

Albrecht, D., DeValois, R., & Thorell, L. (1980). Visual cortical neurons: Are bars or gratings the optimal stimuli? *Science, 207,* 88–90.

Alkon, D. (1983, July). Learning in a marine snail. *Scientific American,* pp. 70–84.

Alkon, D. (1984). Calcium-mediated reduction of ionic currents: A biophysical memory trace. *Science, 226,* 1037–1045.

Altar, C., O'Neil, S., Walter, R., & Marshall, J. F. (1985). Brain dopamine and serotonin receptor sites revealed by digital subtraction autoradiography. *Science, 228,* 597–600.

American Psychiatric Association. (1980). *Diagnostic and statistical manual of mental disorders* (3rd ed.). Washington, DC: Author.

Amoore, J. (1964). Current status of the steric theory of odor. *Annals of the New York Academy of Sciences, 116,* 457–476.

Anand, B. K., & Brobeck, J. (1951). Food intake and spontaneous activity of rats with lesions in the amygdaloid nuclei. *Journal of Neurophysiology, 15,* 421–430.

Andersen, P. (1966). Rhythmic X-section activity in the thalamus. In D. Purpura & M. Yahr (Eds.), *The thalamus.* New York: Columbia University Press.

Andersen, R. A., & Mountcastle, V. (1983). The influence of the angle of gaze upon the excitability of the light-sensitive neurons of the posterior parietal cortex. *Journal of Neurosciences, 3,* 532–548.

Anderson, R. M., Hunt, S. C., Vander Stoep, A., & Pribram, K. H. (1976). Object permanancy and delayed response as spatial context in monkeys with frontal lesions. *Neuropsychologia, 14,* 481–490.

Andrews, R. V. (1971). Circadian rhythms in adrenal organ cultures. *Gegenbaurs Morphologische Jahrbuch, 117,* 89–98.

Angrist, B., Sathananthan, G., Wilk, S., & Gershon, S. (1974). Amphetamine psychosis: Behavioural and biochemical aspects. *Journal of Psychiatric Research, 11,* 13–23.

Anisman, H. (1982). Anhedonia: Too much, too soon. *Behavioral and Brain Sciences, 5,* 53–54.

Arbib, M. (1972). *The metaphorical brain.* New York: Wiley.

Arbib, M., Kaplan, D., & Marshall, J. C. (Eds.) (1982). *Neural models of language processes.* New York: Academic Press.

Arthur, D. L., & Starr, A. (1984). Task-relevant late positive component of the auditory event related potential in monkeys resembles P300 in humans. *Science, 223,* 186–188.

Aschoff, J. (1979). Circadian rhythms: General features and endocrinological aspects. In D. T. Krieger (Ed.), *Endocrine rhythms.* New York: Raven Press.

Aserinsky, E., & Kleitman, N. (1955). Two types of ocular motility occurring in sleep. *Journal of Applied Physiology, 8,* 1–10.

Ashton-Jones, G., Ennis, M., Pieribone, V., Nickell, W., & Shipley, M. (1986). The brain nucleus locus coeruleus: Restricted afferent control of a broad efferent network. *Science, 234,* 734–737.

Athenstaedt, H., Claussen, H., & Schaper, D. (1982). Epidermis of human skin: Pyroelectric and piezoelectric sensor layer. *Science, 216,* 1018–1020.

Ayoub, D., Greenough, W., & Juraska, J. (1983). Sex differences in dendritic structure in the preoptic area of the juvenile macaque monkey brain. *Science, 219,* 197–198.

Bach-y-Rita, P. (1972). *Brain mechanisms in sensory substitution.* New York: Academic Press.

Bagshaw, M., & Coppock, H. (1968). Galvanic skin response conditioning deficit in amygdalectomized monkeys. *Experimental Neurology, 20,* 188–196.

Bagshaw, M., & Pribram, K. H. (1953). Cortical organization in gustation (Macaca mulatta). *Journal of Neurophysiology, 16,* 499–508.

Bahill, A. T., Ciuffreda, K., Kenyon, R., & Stark, L. (1975). Dynamic and static violations of Hering's law of equal innervation. *American Journal of Optometry & Physiological Optics, 53,* 786–796.

Bahill, A. T., Clark, M. R., & Stark, L. (1975). The main sequence, a tool for studying human eye movements. *Mathematical Biosciences, 24,* 191–204.

Bahill, A. T., & Stark, L. (1975). The high-frequency burst of motoneuronal activity lasts about half the duration of saccadic eye movements. *Mathematical Biosciences, 26,* 319–323.

Baker, M. (1979, May). A brain-cooling system in mammals. *Scientific American,* pp. 130–139.

Balasubramaniam, V., & Ramamurthi, B. (1970). Stereotaxic amygdalotomy in behavior disorders. *Confina Neurologica, 32,* 367–373.

Bancroft, J. (1978). The relationship between hormones and sexual behavior in humans. In J. Hutchinson (Ed.), *Biological determinants of sexual behavior.* New York: Wiley.

Bancroft, J., & Sakkebaek, J. (1979). Androgens and human sexual behavior. In R. Porter & O. Whelan (Eds.), *Sex, hormones and behavior.* Ciba Foundation Symposium 62. Amsterdam: Excerpta Medica.

Barbeau, A. (1979). Lecithin in movement disorders. In A. Barbeau, J. Growdon, & R. Wurtman (Eds.), *Nutrition and the brain* (Vol. 5). New York: Raven Press.

Bard, P. (1934). On emotional expression after decortication with some remarks on certain theoretical views. *Psychological Review, 41,* 309–329.

Barondes, S., & Cohen, H. D. (1967). Comparative effects of cyclohexamide and puromycin on cerebral proteinsynthesis and consolidation of memory in mice. *Brain Research, 4,* 44–51.

Bartlett, F., & John, E. R. (1973). Equipotentiality quantified: The anatomical distribution of the engram. *Science, 181,* 764–767.

Bartoshuk, L. (1978). Taste. In R. Masterson (Ed.), *Handbook of neurobiology* (Vol. 1). New York: Plenum Press.

Bartus, R., Dean, R., Beer, B., & Lippa, A. (1982). The cholinergic hypothesis of geriatric memory dysfunction. *Science, 217,* 408–417.

Beidler, L. M. (1963). Dynamics of taste cells. In Y. Zotterman (Ed.), *Olfaction and taste.* New York: Macmillan.

Békésy, G. von (1964). Sweetness produced electrically on the tongue and its relation to taste theories. *Journal of Applied Physiology, 19,* 1105–1113.

Békésy, G. von (1966). Taste theories and the chemical stimulation of single papillae. *Journal of Applied Physiology, 21,* 1–9.

Békésy, G. von (1967). *Sensory inhibition.* Princeton, NJ: Princeton University Press.

Békésy, G. von, & Rosenblith, W. A. (1951). The mechanical properties of the ear. In S. S. Stevens (Ed.), *Handbook of experimental psychology.* New York: Wiley.

Bennett, E. L., Rosenzweig, M., & Flood, J. F. (1979). Role of neurotransmitters and protein synthesis in short- and long-term memory. In J. Obiols, C. Ballus, E. Gonzales Monclus, & J. Pujol (Eds.), *Biological psychiatry today.* Amsterdam: Elsevier/North-Holland.

Bennett, M. V. L. (1973). Function of electronic junctions in embryonic and adult tissues. *Federation of Societies for Experimental Biology Proceedings, 32,* 65–75.

Berger, H. (1935). Über das elektrenkephalogramm des menschen. *Archives für Psychiatrie und Nervenkremkheiten, 103,* 527–570.

Berger, R. J. (1968). Characteristics of REM sleep following different conditioned rates of waking eye movement in the monkey. *Perceptual and Motor Skills, 27,* 99–117.

Berger, T. W. (1984). Long-term potentiation of hippocampal synaptic transmission affects rate of behavior learning. *Science, 224,* 627–630.

Berger, T. W., Laham, R. I., & Thompson, R. F. (1980). Hippocampal unit-behavior correlations during classical conditioning. *Brain Research, 193,* 229–248.

Berger, T. W., & Thompson, R. F. (1978). Neuronal plasticity in the limbic system during classical conditioning of the rabbit nictitating membrane response: 1. The hippocampus. *Brain Research, 145,* 323–346.

Bernheim, H., & Kluger, M. J. (1976). Fever and antipyresis in the lizard, *Dipsosaurus dorsalis. American Journal of Physiology, 231,* 198–203.

Bickerton, D. (1981). *Roots of language.* Ann Arbor, MI: Karoma Publishers.

Bickerton, D. (1983, July). Creole languages. *Scientific American,* pp. 116–122.

Bickerton, D. (1984). The language bioprogram hypothesis. *Behavioral and Brain Sciences, 7,* 173–221.

Binet, A., & Simon, T. (1909). Le développement de l'intelligence des enfants. *L'Annèe Psychologique, 14,* 1–94.

Bird, E. D., Spokes, E. G., & Iversen, L. L. (1979). Brain

norepinephrine and dopamine in schizophrenia. *Science, 204,* 93–94.

Birnholz, J. C. (1981). The development of human fetal eye movement patterns. *Science, 213,* 679–681.

Bishop, P. O., Coombs, J. S., & Henry, G. H. (1971). Interaction effects of visual contours on the discharge frequency of simple striate neurons. *Journal of Physiology, 219,* 659–687.

Bizzi, E. (1968). Discharge of frontal eye field neurons during saccadic and following eye movements in unanesthetized monkeys. *Experimental Brain Research, 6,* 69–80.

Bizzi, E., & Schiller, P. (1970). Single unit activity in the frontal eye fields of unanesthetized monkeys during eye and head movement. *Experimental Brain Research, 10,* 151–158.

Blakemore, C., & Cooper, G. F. (1970). Development of the brain depends on the visual environment. *Nature, 228,* 467–478.

Blakemore, C., & Sutton, P. (1969). Size adaptation: A new aftereffect. *Science, 166,* 245–247.

Blass, E., & Hall, W. G. (1976). Drinking termination: Interactions among hydrational, orogastric, and behavioral controls in rats. *Psychological Review, 83,* 356–374.

Bliss, T. V. P., & Lømo, T. (1973). Long-lasting potentiation of synaptic transmission in the dentate area of the anaesthetized rabbit following stimulation of the perforant path. *Journal of Physiology, 232,* 331–356.

Bloch, V. (1976). Brain activation and memory consolidation. In M. Rosenzweig & E. Bennett (Eds.), *Neural mechanisms of learning and memory.* Cambridge, MA: MIT Press.

Blumstein, S. E. (1981). Neurolinguistic disorders: Language-brain relationships. In S. B. Filskov & T. J. Boll (Eds.), *Handbook of clinical neuropsychology.* New York: Wiley.

Bohn, M., Cupit, L., Marciano, F., & Gash, D. (1987). Adrenal medulla grafts enhance recovery of striatal dopaminergic fibers. *Science, 237,* 913–916.

Borda, R. P. (1970). The effect of altered drive states on the contingent negative variation (CNV) in rhesus monkeys. *Electroencephalography and Clinical Neurophysiology, 29,* 173–180.

Boring, E. (1950). *A history of experimental psychology.* New York: Appleton-Century-Crofts.

Bower, G. H., & Miller, N. E. (1958). Rewarding and punishing effects from stimulating the same place in the rat's brain. *Journal of Comparative and Physiological Psychology, 51,* 669–674.

Boyd, I. (1966). The behaviour of isolated mammalian muscle spindles with intact innervation. *Journal of Physiology, 186,* 109P–110P.

Braitenberg, V. (1977). *On the texture of brains.* New York: Springer-Verlag.

Braitenberg, V., & Atwood, R. P. (1958). Morphological observations on the cerebellar cortex. *Journal of Comparative Neurology, 109,* 1–34.

Brebbia, D., & Altschuler, K. (1965). Oxygen consumption rate and electroencephalographic stages of sleep. *Science, 150,* 1621–1623.

Breitmeyer, B. G., & Valberg, A. (1979). Local, foveal inhibitory effects of global, peripheral excitation. *Science, 203,* 463–465.

Bremer, F. (1935). Cerveau isolé et physiologie du sommeil. *Compte Rendu Société Biologique, 118,* 1235–1241.

Bremer, F. (1970). Preoptic hypnogenic focus and mesencephalic reticular formation. *Brain Research, 21,* 132–134.

Bremer, F. (1975). A further study of the inhibitory processes induced by the activation of the preoptic hypnogenic structure. *Archives Italiennes de Biologie, 113,* 79–88.

Bridgeman, B. (1971). Metacontrast and lateral inhibition. *Psychological Review, 78,* 528–539.

Bridgeman, B. (1972). Lateral interactions and visual coding. *Dissertation Abstracts International* (University Microfilms No. 72-16694).

Bridgeman, B. (1973). Background activity in single cells of monkey visual cortex during visual tracking. *International Journal of Neuroscience, 6,* 153–158.

Bridgeman, B. (1978). Distributed sensory coding applied to simulations of iconic storage and metacontrast. *Bulletin of Mathematical Biology, 40,* 605–623.

Bridgeman, B. (1979a). Adaptation and the two-visual-systems hypothesis. *Behavioral and Brain Sciences, 2,* 64–65.

Bridgeman, B. (1979b). Neurologizing mental imagery: The physiological optics of the mind's eye. *Behavioral and Brain Sciences, 2,* 550.

Bridgeman, B. (1980a). Brains + programs = minds. *Behavioral and Brain Sciences, 3,* 427–428.

Bridgeman, B. (1980b). Temporal response characteristics of cells in monkey striate cortex measured with metacontrast masking and brightness discrimination. *Brain Research, 196,* 347–364.

Bridgeman, B. (1982). Multiplexing in single cells of the alert monkey's visual cortex during brightness discrimination. *Neuropsychologia, 20,* 33–42.

Bridgeman, B., & Artim, J. (1983). Information flow through single cells of cat striate cortex. *Neuroscience Abstracts, 9,* 619.

Bridgeman, B., Hendry, D., & Stark, L. (1975). Failure to detect displacement of the visual world during saccadic eye movements. *Vision Research, 15,* 719–722.

Bridgeman, B., & Palca, J. (1980). The role of microsaccades in high acuity observational tasks. *Vision Research, 20,* 813–817.

Bridgeman, B., & Staggs, D. (1982). Plasticity in human blindsight. *Vision Research, 22,* 1199–1203.

Brindley, G., & Lewin, W. (1968). the sensations produced by electrical stimulation of the visual cortex. *Journal of Physiology, 196,* 479–493.

Brodmann, K. (1912). Neue Ergebnisse über die vergleichende histologische Lokalisation der Grosshirnrinde mit besonderer Berücksichtigung des Stirnhirns. *Anatomische Anzeiger, 41* (Suppl.) 157–216.

Brooks, D., & Bizzi, E. (1963). Brain stem electrical activity during sleep. *Archives Italiennes de Biologie, 101,* 648–665.

Brown, J. E., Coles, J. A., & Pinto, L. H. (1977). Effect of injection of calcium and EGTA into the outer segments of retinal rods of *Bufo marinus. Journal of Physiology, 269,* 707–722.

Brown, R. (1965). *Social psychology.* New York: Free Press.

Brown, R. (1970). *Psycholinguistics.* New York: Free Press.

Brown, R. (1973). *A first language: The early stages.* Cambridge, MA: Harvard University Press.

Brown, R., & McNeill, D. (1966). The "tip of the tongue" phenomenon. *Journal of Verbal Learning and Verbal Behavior, 5,* 325–337.

Brownell, W., Bader, C., Bertrand, D., & De Ribaupierre, Y. (1985). Evoked mechanical responses of isolated cochlear outer hair cells. *Science, 227,* 194–196.

Butters, N., Butter, C., Rosen, J., & Stein, D. (1973). Behavioral effects of sequential and one-stage ablations of orbital prefrontal cortex in monkeys. *Experimental Neurology, 39,* 204–214.

Cabanac, M. (1971). Physiological role of pleasure. *Science, 173,* 1103–1107.

Cajal, S. Ramon Y. (1911). *Histologie du système nerveux de l'homme et des vertébrés.* Paris: Maloine.

Campbell, D. T. (1983). The two distinct routes beyond kin selection to ultrasociality: Implications for the humanities and social sciences. In D. L. Bridgeman (Ed.), *The nature of prosocial development.* New York: Academic Press.

Campbell, F. W., & Robson, J. G. (1968). Application of Fourier analysis to the visibility of gratings. *Journal of Physiology, 197,* 551–556.

Cannon, W. (1929). Organization for physiological homeostasis. *Psychological Review, 9,* 399–431.

Cauna, N. (1968). Light and electron microscopal structure of sensory end-organs in human skin. In D. R. Kenshalo (Ed.), *The skin senses.* Springfield, IL: Charles C Thomas.

Cecchi, G., Griffiths, P., & Taylor, S. (1982). Muscular contraction: Kinetics of crossbridge attachment studied by high-frequency stiffness measurements. *Science, 217,* 70–72.

Cerletti, U., & Bini, L. (1938). L'elettroshock [Electric shock]. *Bollettino ed Atti della Accademia Medica di Roma, 64,* 36.

Charness, M., Gordon, A. S., & Diamond, I. (1983). Ethanol modulation of opiate receptors in cultured neural cells. *Science, 222,* 1246–1248.

Chi, C. C., & Flynn, J. P. (1971). Neural pathways associated with hypothalamically elicited attack behavior in cats. *Science, 171,* 703–706.

Chomsky, N. (1965). *Aspects of the theory of syntax.* Cambridge, MA: MIT Press.

Chomsky, N. (1980). *Rules and representations.* New York: Columbia University Press.

Chorover, S., & Schiller, P. (1965). Short-term retrograde amnesia in rats. *Journal of Comparative and Physiological Psychology, 59,* 73–78.

Clark, M. R., & Stark, L. (1975). Time optimal behavior of human saccadic eye movement. *IEEE Transactions on Automatic Control, AC-20,* 345–348.

Clavier, R., Fibiger, H., & Phillips, A. (1976). Evidence that self-stimulation of the region of the locus coeruleus in rats does not depend upon noradrenergic projections to telencephalon. *Brain Research, 113,* 71–81.

Cleland, B. G., Dubin, M. W., & Levick, W. R. (1970a). Field suppression: A functional property of cat lateral geniculate cells. *Proceedings: Australian Physiological & Pharmacological Society, 1,* 26.

Cleland, B. G., Dubin, M. W., & Levick, W. R. (1970b). Simultaneous recording of cat geniculate cells and the retinal ganglion cells driving them. *Proceedings: Australian Physiological & Pharmacological Society, 1,* 27.

Cleland, C. L., Rymer, W., & Edwards, F. R. (1982). Force-sensitive interneurons in the spinal cord of the cat. *Science, 217,* 652–655.

Clemens, L. (1971). Influence of prenatal litter composition on mounting behavior of female rats. *American Zoologist, 11,* 617–618.

Clemente, C., Sterman, M., & Wyrwicka, W. (1963). Forebrain inhibitory mechanisms: Conditioning of basal forebrain induced EEG synchronization and sleep. *Experimental Neurology, 7,* 404–417.

Coakley, D., & Thomas, J. G. (1977). The ocular microtremor record and the prognosis of the unconscious patient. *Lancet, 1,* 512–515.

Cobb, W., & Sears, T. A. (1960). A study of the transmission of potentials after hemispherectomy. *Electroencephalography and Clincial Neurophysiology, 12,* 371–383.

Cohen, A. I. (1972). Rods and cones. In M. Fuortes (Ed.), *Handbook of sensory physiology: Vol. 7/1B. Physiology of photoreceptor organs.* Berlin: Springer-Verlag.

Cohen, H. D., Ervin, F., & Barondes, S. (1966). Puromycin and cyclohexamide: Different effects on hippocampal electrical activity. *Science, 154,* 1552–1558.

Cohen, N. J., & Squire, L. (1980). Preserved learning and retention of pattern analyzing skill in amnesia: Dissociation of knowing how and knowing that. *Science, 210,* 207–209.

Colquhoun, D., Henderson, R., & Ritchie, J. M. (1972). The binding of labelled tetrodotoxin to non-myelinated nerve fibers. *Journal of Physiology, 227,* 95–126.

Constantine-Paton, M., & Law, M. (1982, December). The development of maps and stripes in the brain. *Scientific American,* pp. 62–70.

Coombs, J. S., Eccles, J. C., & Fatt, P. (1955). Excitatory synaptic actions in motor neurons. *Journal of Physiology, 130,* 374–395.

Cooper, B. R., Konkol, R., & Breese, G. (1978). Effects of catecholamine depleting drugs and d-amphetamine on self-stimulation of the substantia nigra and locus coeruleus. *Journal of Pharmacology and Experimental Therapeutics, 204,* 592–605.

Corey, D., & Hudspeth, A. (1983). Kinetics of the receptor current in bullfrog saccular hair cells. *Journal of Neuroscience, 3,* 962–976.

Cowles, R. (1958). Possible origin of dermal temperature regulation. *Evolution, 12,* 347–357.

Coyle, J., Price, D. L., & DeLong, M. (1983). Alzheimer's disease: A disorder of cortical cholinergic innervation. *Science, 219,* 1184–1190.

Cragg, B. G. (1962). Centrifugal fibers to retina and olfactory bulb, and composition of supraoptic commissures in rabbit. *Experimental Neurology, 5,* 406–427.

Crane, G. E. (1957). Iproniazid (Marsilid) phosphate: A therapeutic agent for mental disorders and debilitating diseases. *Psychiatric Research Reports, 8,* 142–152.

Cranefield, P. (1957). The organic physics of 1847 and the biophysics of today. *Journal of the History of Medicine, 12,* 407–423.

Crawford, M. L. J., Smith, E. L., III, & von Noorden, G. (1984). Stereoblind monkeys have few binocular neurons. *Investigative Ophthalmology & Visual Science, 25,* 779–781.

Creese, I., Burt, D. R., & Snyder, S. H. (1976). Dopamine receptor binding predicts clinical and pharmacological potencies of antischizophrenic drugs. *Science, 192,* 481–483.

Creutzfeldt, O. D., Watanabe, S., & Lux, H. D. (1966). Relations between EEG phenomena and potentials of single cortical cells: 2. Spontaneous and convulsoid activity. *Electroencephalography and Clinical Neurophysiology, 20,* 19–37.

Crow, T., Cross, A., Johnstone, E., & Owen, F. (1982). Two syndromes in schizophrenia and their pathogenesis. In F. Henn & H. Nasrallah (Eds.), *Schizophrenia as a brain disease.* New York: Oxford University Press.

Czeisler, C., Allan, S., Strogatz, S., Ronda, J., Sanchez, R., Rios, C., Freitag, W., Richardson, G., & Kronauer, R. (1986). Bright light resets the human circadian pacemaker independent of the timing of the sleep-wake cycle. *Science, 233,* 667–671.

Czeisler, C., Richardson, G., Coleman, R., Zimmerman, J., Moore-Ede, M., Dement, W., & Weitzman, E. (1981). Chronotherapy: Resetting the circadian clocks of patients with delayed sleep phase insomnia. *Sleep, 4,* 1–21.

Darian-Smith, I., Sugitani, M., & Heywood, J. (1982). Touching textured surfaces: Cells in somatosensory cortex respond both to finger movement and to surface features. *Science, 218,* 906–909.

Darwin, C. (1950). *On the origin of species by means of natural selection.* London: Watts. (Original work published 1859)

Davidson, J. M., Camargo, C., & Smith, E. R. (1979). Effects of androgen on sexual behavior in hypogonadal men. *Journal of Clinical Endocrinology and Metabolism, 48,* 955–958.

Davidson, N. (1970). Alpha rhythm: An artefact? *Lancet, 1,* 1109–1110.

Davis, H. (1965). A model for transducer action in the cochlea. *Cold Spring Harbor Symposia on Quantitative Biology, 30,* 181–190.

Davis, K. L., Davidson, M., Mohs, R., Kendler, K., Davis, B. M., Johns, C., DeNigris, Y., & Horvath, T. (1985). Plasma homovanillic acid concentration and the severity of schizophrenic illness. *Science, 227,* 1601–1602.

Davis, K. L., Mohs, R., Tinklenberg, J. Pfefferbau, A., Hollister, L., & Kopell, B. (1978). Physostigmine: Improvement of long-term memory processes in normal humans. *Science, 201,* 272–274.

Davis, W. J., & Mpitsos, G. (1971). Behavioral choice and habituation in the marine mollusk *Pleurobranchaea californica MacFarland (Gastropoda, Opisthobranchia). Zeitschrift für Vergleichende Physiologie, 75,* 207–232.

Dawkins, R. (1976). *The selfish gene.* Oxford: Oxford University Press.

deLacoste-Utamsing, C., & Holloway, R. (1982). Sexual dimorphism in the human corpus callosum. *Science, 216,* 1431–1432.

Delgado, J. M. R. (1969a). Offensive-defensive behaviour in free monkeys and chimpanzees induced by radio stimulation of the brain. In S. Garattini & E. Sigg (Eds.), *Aggressive behaviour.* New York: Wiley.

Delgado, J. M. R. (1969b). *Physical control of the mind.* New York: Harper & Row.

DeLong, M. (1974). Motor functions of the basal ganglion: Single-unit activity during movement. In F. Schmitt & F. Worden (Eds.), *The neurosciences: Third study program.* Cambridge, MA: MIT Press.

Dement, W. (1960). The effect of dream deprivation. *Science, 131,* 1705–1707.

Dement, W. (1974). *Some must watch while some must sleep.* San Francisco: Freeman.

Dement, W., Ferguson, F., Cohen, H., & Barchas, J. (1969). Nonchemical methods and data using a biochemical model: The REM quanta. In A. Mandell & M. Mandell (Eds.), *Psychochemical research in man.* New York: Academic Press.

Dement, W., & Kleitman, N. (1957a). Cyclic variations in EEG during sleep and their relation to eye movements, body motility, and dreaming. *Electroencephalography and Clinical Neurophysiology, 9,* 673–690.

Dement, W., & Kleitman, N. (1957b). The relation of eye movements during sleep to dream activity: An objective method for the study of dreaming. *Journal of Experimental Psychology, 53* 339–346.

Descartes, R. (1972). *Treatise on man* (T. S. Hall, Ed. and Trans.). Cambridge, MA: Harvard University Press. (Original work published 1665)

Desimone, R., Albright, T. Gross, C. G., & Bruce, C. (1984). Stimulus-selective properties of inferior temporal neurons in the macaque. *Journal of Neuroscience, 4,* 2051–2062.

Desimone, R., Schwartz, E., Albright, T., & Gross, C. G. (1982). Inferior temporal neurons selective for stimulus shape. *Investigative Ophthalmology & Visual Science, 22* (Suppl.), 238.

Dethier, V. (1976). *The hungry fly: A physiological study of behavior associated with feeding.* Cambridge, MA: Harvard University Press.

Deutsch, J. A. (1973). The cholinergic synapse and the site of memory. In J. A. Deutsch (Ed.), *The psychological basis of memory.* New York: Academic Press.

Deutsch, J. A. (1978). The stomach in food satiation and the regulation of appetite. *Progress in Neurobiology, 10,* 135–153.

Deutsch, J. A., & Hardy, W. (1977). Cholecystokinin produces bait shyness in rats. *Nature, 266,* 196.

DeValois, K., & Tootell, R. (1982). Spatial frequency inhibition in cat striate cortex cells. *Investigative Ophthalmology & Visual Science, 22* (Suppl.), 206.

DeValois, R., Abramov, I., & Jacobs, G. H. (1966). Analysis of response patterns of LGN cells. *Journal of the Optical Society of America, 56,* 966–977.

DeValois, R., Albrecht, D., & Thorell, L. (1982). Spatial frequency selectivity of cells in macaque visual cortex. *Vision Research, 22,* 545–559.

Dewson, J., III (1968). Efferent olivocochlear bundle: Some relationships to stimulus discrimination in noise. *Journal of Neurophysiology, 31,* 122–130.

Diamond, I. T., & Neff, W. (1957). Ablation of temporal cortex and discrimination of auditory patterns. *Journal of Neurophysiology, 20,* 300–315.

Douglas, R. J. (1967). The hippocampus and behavior. *Psychological Bulletin, 67,* 416–422.

Dowling, J. E. (1979). Information processing by local circuits: The vertebrate retina as a model system. In F. O. Schmitt & F. G. Worden (Eds.), *The neurosciences: Fourth study program.* Cambridge, MA: MIT Press.

Drachman, D. A., & Arbit, J. (1966). Memory and the hippocampal complex: 2. Is memory a multiple process? *Archives of Neurology, 15,* 52–61.

Drachman, D. A., & Leavitt, J. (1974). Human memory and the cholinergic system. *Archives of Neurology, 30,* 113–121.

Duncan, C. P. (1949). The retroactive effect of electroshock on learning. *Journal of Comparative and Physiological Psychology, 42,* 32–44.

Dunn, A. J. (1980). Neurochemistry of learning and memory: An evaluation of recent data. *Annual Review of Psychology, 31,* 343–390.

Eccles, J. C. (1958, September). The physiology of imagination. *Scientific American,* pp. 135–146.

Eccles, J. C. (1964). *The physiology of synapses.* New York: Academic Press.

Eccles, J. C. (1973). *The understanding of the brain.* New York: McGraw-Hill.

Eccles, J. C. (1982). The synapse: From electrical to chemical transmission. *Annual Review of Neuroscience, 5,* 325–339.

Eccles, J. C., Ito, M., & Szentagothai, J. (1967). *The cerebellum as a neuronal machine.* New York: Springer-Verlag.

Eccles, J. C., Magni, F., & Willis, W. D. (1962). Depolarization of central terminals of Group I afferent fibers from muscle. *Journal of Physiology, 160,* 62–93.

Eccles, J. C., & Sherrington, C. (1930). Numbers and contraction-values of individual motor-units examined in some muscles of the limb. *Proceedings of the Royal Society of London, Series B, 106,* 326–357.

Eich, J. (1982). A composite holographic associative recall model. *Psychological Review, 89,* 627–661.

Ekstrand, B. R., Barrett, R. T., West, J. M., & Maier, W. G. (1977). The effect of human long-term memory. In R. R. Drucker-Colin & J. L. McGaugh (Eds.), *Neurobi-*

ology of sleep and memory. New York: Oxford University Press.

Enroth-Cugell, C., & Robson, J. G. (1966). The contrast sensitivity of retinal ganglion cells of the cat. *Journal of Physiology, 187,* 517–552.

Epstein, A., Fitzsimons, J., & Rolls, B. J. (1970). Drinking induced by injection of angiotensin into the brain of the rat. *Journal of Physiology, 210,* 457–474.

Erhardt, A. A., & Meyer-Bahlburg, H. (1979). *Psychosexual development: An examination of the role of prenatal hormones.* Ciba Foundation Symposium 62. Amsterdam: Excerpta Medica.

Etienne, P., Gauthier, S., Dastoor, D., Collier, B., & Ratner, J. (1979). Alzheimer's disease: Clinical effect of lecithin treatment. In A. Barbeau, J. Growdon, & R. Wurtman (Eds.), *Nutrition and the brain:* Vol 5. *Choline and lecithin in brain disorders.* New York: Raven Press.

Ettlinger, G., & Wegener, J. (1958). Somesthetic alternation, discrimination and orientation after frontal anparietal lesions in monkeys. *Quarterly Journal of Experimental Psychology, 10,* 177–186.

Evarts, E. V. (1968). Relation of pyramidal tract activity to force exerted during voluntary movement. *Journal of Neurophysiology, 31,* 14–27.

Evarts, E. V. (1974). Sensorimotor cortex activity associated with movements triggered by visual as compared to somesthetic inputs. In F. O. Schmitt & F. G. Worden (Eds.), *The neurosciences: Third study program.* Cambridge, MA: MIT Press.

Fanselow, M. (1979). Naloxone attenuates rat's preference for signaled shock. *Physiological Psychology, 7,* 70–74.

Faris, P., Komisaruk, B., Watkins, L. R., & Mayer, D. J. (1983). Evidence for the neuropeptide cholecystokinin as an antagonist of opiate analgesia. *Science, 219,* 310–312.

Fernstrom, J., & Wurtman, R. J. (1971). Brain serotonin content: Physiological dependence on plasma tryptophan levels. *Science, 173,* 149–152.

Fibiger, H. (1978). Drugs and reinforcement mechanisms: A critical review of the catecholamine theory. *Annual Review of Pharmacology and Toxicology, 18,* 37–56.

Fieve, R. (1979). The clinical effects of lithium treatment. *Trends in Neurosciences, 2,* 66–68.

Fifkova, E., & van Harreveld, A. (1977). Long lasting morphological changes in dendritic spines of dentate granular cells following stimulation of the entorhinal area. *Journal of Neurocytology, 6,* 211–230.

Fischer, B. (1973). Overlap of receptive field centers and representation of the visual field in the cat's optic tract. *Vision Research, 13,* 2113–2120.

Fischer, B., & Boch, R. (1982). Activation of prelunate cortex and saccadic reaction times of trained rhesus monkeys. *Investigative Ophthalmology & Visual Science, 22* (Suppl.), 237.

Fischer, B., & Kruger, J. (1974). Shift-effect in cats [*sic*] lateral geniculate neurons. *Experimental Brain Research, 21,* 225–227.

Fischer, M. (1971). Psychoses in the offspring of schizophrenic monozygotic twins and their normal co-twins. *British Journal of Psychiatry, 118,* 43–52.

Fitzsimons, J., & LeMagnen, J. (1969). Eating as a regulatory control of drinking in the rat. *Journal of Comparative and Physiological Psychology, 67,* 273–283.

Flekkøy, K. (1981). *Biological aspect of schizophrenia.* Oslo: Universitetsforlaget.

Flexner, J., Flexner, L., & Stellar, E. (1963). Memory in mice as affected by intracerebral puromycin. *Science, 141,* 57–59.

Flood, J. F., Bennett, E., Rosenzweig, M., & Orme, A. (1973). The influence of duration of protein synthesis inhibition on memory. *Physiology and Behavior, 10,* 555–562.

Flood, J. F., Jarvik, M. E., Bennett, E. L., Orme, A. E., & Rosenzweig, M. R. (1977). The effect of stimulants, depressants and protein synthesis inhibition on retention. *Behavioral Biology, 20,* 168–183.

Fouriezos, G., & Wise, R. A. (1976). Pimozide-induced extinction of intracranial self-stimulation: Response patterns rule out motor or performance deficits. *Brain Research, 103,* 377–380.

Freeman, W., & Watts, J. W. (1950). *Psychosurgery.* Springfield, IL: Charles C Thomas.

French, G., & Harlow, H. (1955). Locomotor reaction decrement in normal and brain-damaged monkeys. *Journal of Comparative and Physiological Psychology, 52,* 496–501.

Friedman, M., & Stricker, E. (1976). The physiological psychology of hunger: A physiological perspective. *Psychological Review, 83,* 409–431.

Fritsch, G., & Hitzig, E. (1969). On the electrical excitability of the cerebrum. In K. H. Pribram (Ed.), *Brain and behaviour: Vol. 2. Perception and action.* Harmondsworth, England, and Baltimore: Penguin. (Original work published 1870)

Frohman, L. (1971). The hypothalamus and metabolic control. In H. Ioachim (Ed.), *Pathobiology annual (Vol. 1).* New York: Appleton-Century-Crofts.

Fuchs, A. F., & Ron, S. (1968). An analysis of rapid eye movements of sleep in monkey. *Electroencephalography and Clinical Neurophysiology, 25,* 244–253.

Fulginiti, S., Molina, V., & Orsingher, O. (1976). Inhibition of catecholamine biosynthesis and memory processes. *Psychopharmacology, 51,* 65–69.

Fullerton, G., & Cameron, I. (1985). Nuclear magnetic

resonance imaging in biological systems. *BioTechniques, 3,* 458–465.

Funkenstein, H., Nelson, P., Winter, P., Wollberg, Z., & Newman, J. (1971). Unit responses in the auditory cortex of awake squirrel monkeys to vocal stimulation. In M. Sachs (Ed.), *Physiology of the auditory system.* Baltimore: National Educational Consultants.

Fuster, J. M. (1980). *The prefrontal cortex.* New York: Raven Press.

Fuster, J. M., & Alexander, G. (1971). Neuron activity related to short-term memory. *Science, 173,* 652–654.

Gabersek, V., & Ghiloni, H. (1970). Etude électro-oculographique des mouvements oculaires pendant la phase paradoxale du sommeil. *Revue Neurologique* (Paris), *123,* 251–255.

Gabor, D. (1949). Microscopy by reconstructed wave fronts. *Proceedings of the Royal Society of London, Series A, 197,* 454–487.

Gadian, D. (1983). *Nuclear magnetic resonance and its applications to living systems.* Oxford: Clarendon Press.

Gage, F., Björklund, A., Stenevi, U., Dunnett, S., & Kelly, P. A. T. (1984). Intrahippocampal septal grafts ameliorate learning impairments in aged rats. *Science, 225,* 533–536.

Gallagher, M., & Kapp, B. S. (1978). Opiate administration into the amygdala: Effects on memory processes. *Neuroscience Abstracts, 4,* 258.

Gardner, B. T., & Gardner, R. A. (1975). Evidence for sentence constituents in the early utterances of child and chimpanzee. *Journal of Experimental Psychology: General, 104,* 244–267.

Gardner, E. J. (1983). *Human heredity.* New York: Wiley.

Gardner, R. A., & Gardner, B. T. (1969). Teaching sign language to a chimpanzee. *Science, 165,* 664–672.

Gastaut, H., Lugaresi, E., Berti-Ceroni, G., & Coccagna, G. (1968). *The abnormalities of sleep in man.* Bologna: Aulo Gaggi.

Gazzaniga, M. (1970). *The bisected brain.* New York: Appleton-Century-Crofts.

Gazzaniga, M. (1983). Right hemisphere language following brain bisection: A 20-year perspective. *American Psychologist, 38,* 525–537.

Geddes, J., Monaghan, D., Cotman, C., Lott, I., Kim, R. C., & Chui, H. (1985). Plasticity of hippocampal circuitry in Alzheimer's disease. *Science, 230,* 1179–1181.

Geldard, F. A. (1972). *The human senses* (2nd ed.). New York: Wiley.

Gelenberg, A., Wojcik, J., & Growdon, J. (1979). Lecithin for the treatment of tardive dyskinesia. In A. Barbeau, J. Growdon, & R. Wurtman (Eds.), *Nutrition and the brain,* (Vol. 5). New York: Raven Press.

Georgopoulos, A., Schwartz, A., & Kettner, R. (1986). Neuronal population coding of movement direction. *Science, 233,* 1416–1419.

Gerard, R. W. (1949). Physiology and psychiatry. *American Journal of Psychiatry, 106,* 161–173.

Gerbrandt, L. K., Spinelli, D. N., & Pribram, R. H. (1970). The interaction of visual attention and temporal cortex stimulation on electrical recording in the striate cortex. *Electroencephalography and Clinical Neurophysiology, 29,* 146–155.

Gerrits, H. J. M., Stassen, H. P. W., & van Erning, L. J. Th. O. (1984). The role of drifts and saccades for the preservation of brightness perception. In L. Spillman & B. Wooten (Eds.), *Sensory experience, adaptation, and perception.* Hillsdale, NJ: Lawrence Erlbaum.

Gershon, E., Bunney, W., Leckman, J., Van Eerdewegh, M., & DeBauche, B. (1976). The inheritance of affective disorders: A review of data and hypotheses. *Behavior Genetics, 6,* 227–261.

Geschwind, N. (1965). Disconnexion syndromes in animals and man. *Brain, 88,* 237–294, 585–644.

Geschwind, N. (1970). The organization of language and the brain. *Science, 170,* 940–944.

Geschwind, N. (1975). The apraxias: Neural mechanisms of disorders of learned movement. *American Scientist, 63,* 188–195.

Gibbs, J., Young, R. C., & Smith, G. P. (1973). Cholecystokinin decreases food intake in rats. *Journal of Comparative and Physiological Psychology, 84,* 488–495.

Gibson, J. J. (1966). *The senses considered as perceptual systems.* Boston: Houghton Mifflin.

Gilman, A. (1937). The relation between blood osmotic pressure, fluid distribution and voluntary water intake. *American Journal of Physiology, 120,* 323–328.

Ginsburg, A. (1984). Visual form perception based on biological filtering. In L. Spillman & B. Wooten (Eds.), *Sensory experience, adaptation, and perception.* Hillsdale, NJ: Lawrence Erlbaum.

Gladue, B., Green, R., & Hellman, R. (1984). Neuroendocrine response to estrogen and sexual orientation. *Science, 225,* 1496–1499.

Glenn, L., Foutz, A., & Dement, W. (1978). Membrane potential of spinal motoneurons during natural sleep in cats. *Sleep, 1,* 199–204.

Glickman, S. E. (1977). Comparative psychology. In P. Mussen & M. Rosenzweig (Eds.), *Psychology: An introduction* (2nd ed.). Lexington, MA: D. C. Heath.

Gold, P. E., & van Buskirk, R. B. (1975). Facilitation of time-dependent memory processes with posttrial epinephrine injections. *Behavioral Biology, 13,* 145–153.

Gold, R. M. (1973). Hypothalamic obesity: The myth of the ventromedial nucleus. *Science, 182,* 488–490.

Goldberg, M. E., & Bushnell, M. C. (1979). Monkey frontal eye fields have a neuronal signal that precedes visually guided saccades. *Society for Neurosciences Abstracts, 5,* 779.

Goldensohn, E. S., Busse, E. W., Spencer, J. N., Draper, W. B., & Whitehead, R. W. (1950). Studies on diffusion respiration: 7. The cortical electrical activity of dogs. *Electroencephalography and Clinical Neurophysiology, 2,* 33–40.

Goldman, P., & Rosvold, H. (1970). Localization of function within the dorsolateral prefrontal cortex of the rhesus monkey. *Experimental Neurology, 27,* 291–304.

Goldstein, S. K. (1944). The mental changes due to frontal lobe damage. *Journal of Psychology, 17,* 187–208.

Goodglass, H. (1976). Agrammatism. In H. Whitaker & H. A. Whitaker (Eds.), *Studies in neurolinguistics.* New York: Academic Press.

Gorski, R., Gordon, J. H., Shryne, J., & Southam, A. (1978). Evidence for a morphological sex difference within the medial preoptic area of the rat brain. *Brain Research, 148,* 333–346.

Graf, P., Mandler, G., & Haden, P. (1982). Simulating amnesic symptoms in normal subjects. *Science, 218,* 1243–1244.

Granit, R. (1977). *The purposive brain.* Cambridge, MA: MIT Press.

Graubard, K., & Calvin, W. H. (1979). Presynaptic dendrites: Implications of spikeless synaptic transmission and dendritic geometry. In F. O. Schmitt & F. G. Worden (Eds.), *The neurosciences: Fourth study program.* Cambridge, MA: MIT Press.

Green, J. P., & Maayani, S. (1977). Tricyclic antidepressant drugs block histamine H2 receptor in brain. *Nature, 269,* 163–165.

Greenberg, M. E., Ziff, E., & Greene, L. (1986). Stimulation of neuronal acetylcholine receptors induces rapid gene transcription. *Science, 234,* 80–83.

Gross, C. G. (1963). Locomotor activity following lateral frontal lesions in rhesus monkeys. *Journal of Comparative and Physiological Psychology, 56,* 232–236.

Gross, C. G., Bender, D., & Rocha-Miranda, C. (1969). Visual receptive fields of neurons in inferotemporal cortex of the monkey. *Science, 166,* 1303–1306.

Grossman, S. P., Dacey, D., Halaris, A. Collier, T., & Routtenberg, A. (1978). Aphagia and adipsia after preferential destruction of nerve cell bodies in hypothalamus. *Science, 202,* 537–539.

Grueninger, W., & Pribram, K. H. (1969). Effects of spatial and nonspatial distractors on performance latency of monkeys with frontal lesions. *Journal of Comparative and Physiological Psychology, 68,* 203–209.

Grüsser, O.-J., Pause, M., & Schreiter, U. (1983). A new vestibular area in the primate cortex. *Neuroscience Abstracts, 9,* 749.

Guillery, R. (1969). The organization of synaptic interconnections in the laminae of the dorsal lateral geniculate nucleus of cat. *Zeitschrift für Zellforschung, 96,* 400–415.

Hagins, W., & Yoshikami, S. (1977). Intracellular transmission of visual excitation in photoreceptors: Electrical effects of chelating agents introduced into rods by vesicle fusion. In H. B. Barlow & P. Fatt (Eds.), *Vertebrate photoreception.* London: Academic Press.

Harding, C., & Leshner, A. (1972). The effects of adrenalectomy on the aggressiveness of differently housed mice. *Physiology & Behavior, 8,* 437–440.

Harlow, H. (1962). The heterosexual affectional system in monkeys. *American Psychologist, 17,* 1–9.

Harlow, H., & Dagnon, J. (1943). Problem solution by monkeys following bilateral removal of prefrontal areas: 1. Discrimination and discrimination reversal. *Journal of Experimental Psychology, 32,* 351–356.

Harlow, H., & Settlage, P. (1948). Effect of extirpation of frontal areas upon learning performance of monkeys. *Research Publication Association for Nervous and Mental Disease, 27,* 446–459.

Harlow, H., & Zimmerman, R. (1958). The development of affectional responses in infant monkeys. *Proceedings: American Philosophical Society, 102,* 501–509.

Harlow, J. (1868). Recovery from the passage of an iron bar through the head. *Publications of Massachusetts Medical Society* (Boston), *2,* 327–346.

Harris, L. J. (1978). Sex differences in spatial ability: Possible environmental, genetic, and neurological factors. In M. Kinsbourne (Ed.), *Asymmetrical function of the brain.* Cambridge: Cambridge University Press.

Harrison, J. M., & Howe, M. E. (1974). Anatomy of the afferent auditory nervous system of mammals. In W. D. Keidel & W. D. Neff (Eds.), *Handbook of sensory physiology: Vol. 1. Auditory system.* Berlin: Springer-Verlag.

Hart, B. L. (1973). Effects of testosterone propionate and dihydrotestosterone on penile morphology and sexual reflexes of spinal male rats. *Hormones and Behavior, 4,* 239–246.

Hart, B. L. (1974). Gonadal androgen and sociosexual behavior of male mammals: A comparative analysis. *Psychological Bulletin, 81,* 383–400.

Hart, B. L. (1978). Hormones, spinal reflexes, and sexual behaviour. In J. B. Hutchison (Ed.), *Biological determinants of sexual behaviour.* New York: Wiley.

Haskell, E., Palca, J., Walker, J., Berger, R., & Heller, H. (1981). Metabolism and thermoregulation during stages of sleep in humans exposed to heat and cold. *Journal of Applied Physiology, 51,* 948–954.

Hatton, G. (1976). Nucleus circularis: Is it an osmoreceptor in the brain? *Brain Research Bulletin, 1,* 123–131.

Hawke, C. (1950). Castration and sex crimes. *American Journal of Mental Deficiency, 55,* 220–226.

Hawkins, R. D., Abrams, T. W., Carew, T. J., & Kandel,

E. R. (1983). A cellular mechanism of classical conditioning in *Aplysia:* Activity-dependent amplification of pre-synaptic facilitation. *Science, 219,* 400–405.

Haycock, J., van Buskirk, R., & McGaugh, J. (1977). Effects of catecholaminergic drugs upon memory storage processes in mice. *Behavioral Biology, 20,* 281–310.

Hayes, C. (1951). *The ape in our house.* New York: Harper & Bros.

Heath, R. G. (1954). *Studies in Schizophrenia.* Cambridge, MA: Harvard University Press.

Heath, R. G. (1963). Electrical self-stimulation of the brain in man. *American Journal of Psychiatry, 120,* 571–577.

Hebb, D. O. (1949). *The organization of behavior.* New York: Wiley.

Hecht, S., Schlaer, A., & Pirenne, M. H. (1942). Energy, quanta, and vision. *Journal of General Physiology, 19,* 819–840.

Heffner, H. E., & Heffner, R. (1984). Temporal lobe lesions and perception of species-specific vocalizations by macaques. *Science, 226,* 75–76.

Heffner, R., & Masterson, B. (1975). Variation in form of the pyramidal tract and its relation to digital dexterity. *Brain, Behavior and Evolution, 12,* 161–200.

Heilman, K., & Valenstein, E. (1979). *Clinical neuropsychology.* New York: Oxford University Press.

Held, R., & Hein, A. (1963). Movement-produced stimulation in the development of visually guided behavior. *Journal of Comparative and Physiological Psychology, 56,* 872–876.

Heller, H. C., & Glotzbach, S. (1977). Thermoregulation during sleep and hibernation. *Environmental Physiology: 2. International Review of Physiology, 15,* 147–188.

Helmholtz, H. von (1867). *Handbuch der Physiologischen Optik* (Vol. 3). Leipzig: Voss.

Hendricks, J., Morrison, A. R., & Mann, G. (1982). Different behaviors during paradoxical sleep without atonia depend on pontine lesion site. *Brain Research, 239,* 81–105.

Hendriksen, S., Dement, W., & Barchas, J. (1974). The role of serotonin in the regulation of a phasic event of rapid eye movement sleep: The ponto-geniculo-occipital wave. *Advances in Biochemical Psychopharmacology, 11,* 169–179.

Hensel, H. (1968). Electrophysiology of cutaneous thermoreceptors. In D. R. Kenshalo (Ed.), *The skin senses.* Springfield, IL: Charles C Thomas.

Hering, E. (1977). *The theory of binocular vision* (B. Bridgeman, Trans.; B. Bridgeman & L. Stark, Eds.). New York: Plenum Publishing, 1977. (Original work published 1868)

Hering, E. (1964). *Outlines of a theory of the light sense* (L. Hurvich & D. Jameson, Trans.). Cambridge, MA: Harvard University Press. (Original work published 1920)

Herman, J., & Roffwarg, H. (1983). Modifying oculomotor activity in awake subjects increases the amplitude of eye movements during REM sleep. *Science, 220,* 1074–1076.

Herzog, D., & Copeland, P. (1985). Eating disorders. *New England Journal of Medicine, 313,* 295–303.

Hess, E. H. (1956, July). Space perception in the chick. *Scientific American,* pp. 71–80.

Hetherington, A., & Ranson, S. (1940). Hypothalamic lesions and adiposity in the rat. *Anatomical Record, 78,* 149–172.

Hilgard, E. R. (1969). Pain: A puzzle for psychology and physiology. *American Psychologist, 24,* 103–113.

Hilgard, E. R. (1973). A neodissociation interpretation of pain reduction in hypnosis. *Psychological Review, 80,* 396–411.

Hilgard, E. R., Atkinson, R. C., & Atkinson, R. L. (1979). *Introduction to Psychology* (7th ed). New York: Harcourt Brace Jovanovich.

Hillyard, S., & Picton, T. (1979). Event-related brain potentials and selective information processing in man. In J. Desmedt (Ed.), *Cognitive components in cerebral event-related potentials and selective attention.* Basel: S. Karger.

Hinton, G., & Anderson, J. A. (Eds.). (1981). *Parallel models of associative memory.* Hillsdale, NJ: Lawrence Erlbaum.

Hirsch, H. V. B. (1972). Visual perception in cats after environmental surgery. *Experimental Brain Research, 15,* 405–423.

Hirsch, H. V. B., & Spinelli, D. N. (1970). Visual experience modifies distribution of horizontally and vertically oriented receptive fields in cats. *Science, 168,* 869–871.

Hockett, C. F. (1972). Origin of speech. In R. F. Thompson (Ed.), *Physiological psychology.* San Francisco: Freeman.

Hodgkin, A. L., & Huxley, A. F. (1952a). The components of membrane conductance in the giant axon of *Loligo. Journal of Physiology, 116,* 473–496.

Hodgkin, A. L., & Huxley, A. F. (1952b). Currents carried by sodium and potassium ions through the membrane of the giant axon of *Loligo. Journal of Physiology, 116,* 449–472.

Hodgkin, A. L., & Huxley, A. F. (1952c). A quantitative description of membrane current and its application to conduction and excitation in nerve. *Journal of Physiology, 117,* 500–544.

Hodgkin, A. L., & Katz, B. (1949). The effect of sodium

ions on the electrical activity of the giant axon of the squid. *Journal of Physiology, 108,* 37–77.

Hoffman, K.-P., & Stone, J. (1971). Conduction velocity of afferents to cat visual cortex: Correlation with cortical receptive field properties. *Brain Research, 32,* 460–466.

Hofstadter, D. (1979). *Gödel, Escher, Bach: An eternal golden braid.* New York: Basic Books.

Holaday, J., Wei, E., Loh, H. H., & Li, C. H. (1978). Endorphins may function in heat adaptation. *Proceedings of the National Academy of Sciences, 75,* 2923–2927.

Horel, J. (1978). The neuroanatomy of amnesia: A critique of the hippocampal memory hypothesis. *Brain, 101,* 403–445.

Horovitz, A., Piala, J., High, J., Burke, J., & Leaf, R. (1966). Effects of drugs on the mouse-killing (muricide) test and its relationship to amygdaloid function. *International Journal of Neuropharmacology, 5,* 405–411.

Hosobuchi, Y., Rossier, J., Bloom, F., & Guillemin, R. (1979). Stimulation of human periaqueductal gray for pain relief increases immunoreactive beta-endorphin in ventricular fluid. *Science, 203,* 279–281.

Hoyle, G. (1983). *Muscles and their neural control.* New York: Wiley.

Hrushesky, W., Fader, D., Schmitt, O., & Gilbertson, V. (1984). The respiratory sinus arrhythmia: A measure of cardiac age. *Science, 224,* 1001–1004.

Hubel, D., & Wiesel, T. (1962). Receptive fields, binocular interaction and functional architecture in the cat's visual cortex. *Journal of Physiology, 160,* 106–154.

Hubel, D., & Wiesel, T. (1965a). Binocular interactions in striate cortex kittens reared with artificial squint. *Journal of Neurophysiology, 28,* 1041–1059.

Hubel, D., & Wiesel, T. (1965b). Receptive fields and functional architecture in two non-striate visual areas (18 and 19) of the cat. *Journal of Neurophysiology, 28,* 229–289.

Hubel, D., & Wiesel, T. (1968). Receptive fields and functional architecture of monkey striate cortex. *Journal of Physiology, 195,* 215–243.

Hubel, D. Wiesel, T., & Levay, S. (1977). Plasticity of ocular dominance columns in monkey striate cortex. *Philosophical Transactions: Royal Society of London, Series B, 278,* 377–409.

Hubel, D., Wiesel, T., & Stryker, M. (1978). Anatomical demonstration of orientation columns in macaque monkey. *Journal of Comparative Neurology, 177,* 361–380.

Hudspeth, A. J. (1982). Extracellular current flow and the site of transduction by vertebrate hair cells. *Journal of Neuroscience, 2,* 1–10.

Hudspeth, A. J. (1985). The cellular basis of hearing: The biophysics of hair cells. *Science, 230,* 745–752.

Hughes, J., Smith, T. W., Kosterlitz, H., Fothergill, L., Morgan, B., & Moris, H. (1975). Identification of two related pentapeptides from the brain with potent opiate agonist activity. *Nature, 258,* 577–579.

Huppert, F., & Piercy, M. (1978). Dissociation between learning and remembering in organic amnesia. *Nature, 275,* 317–318.

Huppert, F., & Piercy, M. (1979). Normal and abnormal forgetting in organic amnesia: Effect of locus of lesion. *Cortex, 15,* 385–390.

Huxley, H. E. (1973). Muscle contraction and cell motility. *Nature, 243,* 445–449.

Hydén, H. (1965). Activation of nuclear RNA in neurons and glia in learning. In D. P. Kimble (Ed.), *The anatomy of memory.* Palo Alto, CA: Science and Behavior Books.

Iggo, A., & Muir, A. (1969). The structure and function of a slowly adapting touch corpuscle in hairy skin. *Journal of Physiology, 200,* 763–796.

Iggo, A., & Andres, K. (1982). Morphology of cutaneous receptors. *Annual Review of Neuroscience, 5,* 1–32.

Ikeda, H., & Wright, M. J. (1972). The outer disinhibitory surround of the retinal ganglion cell receptive field. *Journal of Physiology, 226,* 511–544.

Ingvar, D. (1979). Brain activation patterns revealed by measurements of regional cerebral blood flow. In J. Desmedt (Ed.), *Cognitive components in cerebral event-related potentials and selective attention.* Basel: S. Karger.

Isaacson, R. (1972). Hippocampal destruction in man and other animals. *Neuropsychologia, 10,* 47–64.

Iurato, S. (1974). Efferent innervation of the cochlea. In W. D. Keidel & W. D. Neff (Eds.), *Handbook of sensory physiology: Vol. 1. Auditory system.* Berlin: Springer-Verlag.

Iverson, L. (1979). The chemistry of the brain. In *The brain* (a Scientific American book) (pp. 71–81). San Francisco: Freeman.

Iverson, S. D. (1967). Tactile learning and memory in baboons after temporal and frontal lesions. *Experimental Neurology, 18,* 228–238.

Iverson, S. D., & Bloom, F. E. (1972). Studies of the uptake of 3H-GABA and 3H glycine in slices and homogenates of rat brain and spinal cord by electron microscopic autoradiography. *Brain Research, 41,* 131–143.

Jacobs, B., & Trulson, M. (1979). Mechanisms of action of LSD. *American Scientist, 67,* 396–404.

Jacobsen, C. F. (1936). Studies of cerebral function in primates: 1. The functions of the frontal association areas in monkeys. *Comparative Psychology Monographs, 13,* 3–60.

Jacobsen, C. F., Wolfe, J., & Jackson, T. A. (1935). An experimental analysis of the functions of the frontal association areas in primates. *Journal of Nervous and Mental Disease, 82,* 1–14.

Jakobson, R., Fant, G., & Halle, M. (1952). *Preliminaries to speech analysis* (Technical Report No. 13). Cambridge, MA: Acoustics Laboratory, MIT.

James, W. (1893). *The principles of psychology.* New York: Henry Holt.

Järvilehto, T., & Fruhstorfer, H. (1970). Differentiation between slow cortical potentials associated with motor and mental acts in man. *Experimental Brain Research, 11,* 309–317.

Jensen, R., Martinez, J., Messing, R., Spiehler, V., Vasquez, B., Soumireu-Mourat, B., Liang, K., & McGaugh, J. (1978). Morphine and naloxone after memory in rats. *Neuroscience Abstracts, 4,* 260.

John, E. R. (1967). *Mechanisms of memory.* New York: Academic Press.

John, E. R. (1972). Switchboard versus statistical theories of learning and memory. *Science, 177,* 850–864.

John, E. R., Tang, Y., Brill, B., Young, R., & Ono, K. (1986). Double-labeled metabolic maps of memory. *Science, 233,* 1167–1175.

Johnson, A. K., & Buggy, J. (1977). A critical analysis of the site of action for the dipsogenic effect of angiotensin II. In J. P. Buckley & C. Ferrario (Eds.), *International symposium on the central actions of angiotensin and related hormones.* Oxford: Pergamon Press.

Jones, B. E., Bobillier, P., & Jouvet, M. (1969). Effets de la destruction des neurones contenant des catecholamines du mesencephale sur le cycle vielle-sommeils du chat. *Comptes Rendus des Séances de la Société de Biologie, 163,* 176–180.

Jones, E. G., & Powell, P. (1969). Electron microscopy of the somatic sensory cortex of the cat: 1. Cell types and synaptic organization. *Proceedings of the Royal Society of London, Series B, 972,* 153–171.

Jouvet, M. (1968). Insomnia and decrease of cerebral 5-hydroxytryptamine after destruction of the raphe system in the cat. *Advances in Pharmacology, 6,* 265–279.

Jouvet, M. (1972). The role of monoamines and acetylcholine-containing neurons in the regulation of the sleep-waking cycle. *Ergebnisse der Physiologie, 64,* 166–307.

Jouvet, M. (1974). Monoaminergic regulation of the sleep-waking cycle in the cat. In F. O. Schmitt & F. G. Worden (Eds.), *The neurosciences: Third study program.* Cambridge, MA: MIT Press.

Jouvet, M., & Renault, J. (1966). Insomnie persistante après lésions des noyaux du raphe chez le chat. *Comptes Rendus des Séances de la Société de Biologie, 160,* 1461–1465.

Kaada, B., Pribram, K. H., & Epstein, J. A. (1949). Respiratory and vascular responses in monkeys from temporal pole, insula, orbital surface and cingulate gyrus: A preliminary report. *Journal of Neurophysiology, 12,* 347–356.

Kaissling, K.-E. (1986). Chemo-electrical transduction in insect olfactory receptors. *Annual Review of Neuroscience, 9,* 121–145.

Kaissling, K.-E., Klein, U., de Kramer, J., Keil, T., Kanaujia, S., & Hemberger, J. (1985). Insect olfactory cells: Electrophysiological and biochemical studies. In J. Changeus, F. Hucho, A. Maelicke, & E. Neumann (Eds.), *Molecular basis of nerve activity.* Berlin: de Gruyter.

Kalil, R., & Chase, R. (1970). Corticofugal influence on activity of lateral geniculate neurons in the cat. *Journal of Neurophysiology, 33,* 459–474.

Kandel, E. R. (1976). *Cellular basis of behavior.* San Francisco: Freeman.

Kandel, E. R. (1979, September). Small systems of neurons. *Scientific American,* pp. 66–76.

Kandel, E. R., & Schwartz, J. (1982). *Principles of neural science.* New York: Elsevier/North Holland.

Kandel, E. R., & Spencer, W. A. (1961). Electrophysiology of hippocampal neurons: 2. Afterpotentials and repetitive firing. *Journal of Neurophysiology, 24,* 243–259.

Kanof, P., & Greengard, P. (1978). Brain histamine receptors as targets for antidepressant drugs. *Nature, 272,* 329–333.

Kapatos, G., & Gold, R. M. (1973). Evidence for ascending noradrenergic mediation of hypothalamic hyperphagia. *Pharmacology, Biochemistry and Behavior, 1,* 81–87.

Kasamatsu, T., & Pettigrew, J. (1979). Preservation of binocularity after monocular deprivation in the striate cortex of kittens treated with 6-hydroxydopamine. *Journal of Comparative Neurology, 185,* 139–162.

Kasamatsu, T., Watabe, K., Schöller, E., & Heggelund, P. (1983). Restoration of neuronal plasticity in cat visual cortex by electrical stimulation of the locus coeruleus. *Neuroscience Abstracts, 9,* 911.

Katsuki, Y. (1961). Neural mechanism of auditory sensation in cats. In W. A. Rosenblith (Ed.), *Sensory communication.* Cambridge, MA: MIT Press.

Katz, J., Kuperberg, A., Pollack, C., Walsh, B., Zumoff, B., & Weiner, H. (1984). Is there a relationship between eating disorder and affective disorder? New evidence from sleep recordings. *American Journal of Psychiatry, 141,* 753–759.

Kauer, J. S., & Moulton, D. G. (1974). Responses of olfactory bulb neurones to odour stimulation of small nasal areas in the salamander. *Journal of Physiology, 243,* 717–737.

Keesey, R. (1980). A set-point analysis of the regulation of body weight. In A. Stunkard (Ed.), *Obesity.* Philadelphia: Saunders.

Kennard, M. (1939). Alterations in response to visual stimuli following lesions of frontal lobe in monkeys. *Archives of Neurology and Psychiatry, 41,* 1153–1165.

Kertesz, A. (1982). Two case studies: Broca's and Wernicke's aphasia. In M. Arbib, D. Caplan, & J. C. Marshall (Eds.), *Neural models of language processes.* New York: Academic Press.

Kety, S. S., Rosenthal, D., Wender, P., Schulsinger, F., & Jacobsen, B. (1975). Mental illness in the biological and adoptive families of adopted individuals who have become schizophrenics: A preliminary report based on psychiatric interviews. In R. Fieve, D. Rosenthal, & H. Brill (Eds.), *Genetic research in psychiatry.* Baltimore: Johns Hopkins University Press.

Khachaturian, H., Lewis, M. E., Hollt, V., & Watson, S. J. (1983). Telencephalic enkephalinergic systems in the rat brain. *Journal of Neuroscience, 3,* 844–855.

Khanna, S., & Leonard, D. (1982). Basilar membrane tuning in the cat cochlea. *Science, 215,* 305–306.

Kimble, D. P. (1968). Hippocampus and internal inhibition. *Psychological Bulletin, 70,* 285–295.

Kimble, D. P., Bagshaw, M., & Pribram, K. H. (1965). The GSR of monkeys during orienting and habituation after selective partial ablations of the cingulate and frontal cortex. *Neuropsychologia, 3,* 121–128.

Klein, M., & Kandel, E. R. (1980). Mechanism of calcium modulation underlying presynaptic facilitation and behavioral sensitization in *Aplysia. Proceedings of the National Academy of Sciences, 77,* 6912.

Kleitman, N. (1963). *Sleep and wakefulness.* Chicago: University of Chicago Press.

Kluger, M., & Rothenburg, B. (1979). Fever and reduced iron: Their interaction as a host defense response to bacterial infection. *Science, 203,* 374–376.

Klüver, H. (1933). *Behavior mechanisms in monkeys.* Chicago: University of Chicago Press.

Klüver, H., & Bucy, P. (1939). Preliminary analysis of functions of the temporal lobes in monkeys. *Archives of Neurology and Psychiatry, 42,* 979–1000.

Koch, S. (1962). *Psychology: Study of a science.* New York: McGraw-Hill.

Kohlerman, N., Gibson, A. R., & Houk, J. (1982). Velocity signals related to hand movements recorded from red nucleus in monkeys. *Science, 217,* 857–880.

Kolb, B., & Whishaw, I. (1980). *Fundamentals of human neuropsychology.* San Francisco: Freeman.

Konorski, J., & Lawicka, W. (1964). Analysis of errors of prefrontal animals on the delayed-response test. In J. M. Warren & K. Akert (Eds.), *The frontal granular cortex and behavior.* New York: McGraw-Hill.

Korn, H., & Faber, D. S. (1979). Electrical interactions between vertebrate neurons: Field effects and electrotonic coupling. In F. O. Schmitt & F. G. Worden (Eds.), *The neurosciences: Fourth study program.* Cambridge, MA: MIT Press.

Kornhuber, H. (1974). Cerebral cortex, cerebellum, and basal ganglia: An introduction to their motor functions. In F. O. Schmitt & F. G. Worden (Eds.), *The neurosciences: Third study program.* Cambridge, MA: MIT Press.

Kornhuber, H., & Deecke, L. (1965). Hirnpotentialaenderungen bei Willkürbewegungen und passiven Bewegungen des Menschen: Bereitschaftspotential und reafferente Potentiale. *Pflügers Archiv für die Gesamte Physiologie, 284,* 1–17.

Krech, D. (1973). Discussion. In J. McGaugh (Ed.), *The chemistry of mood, motivation and memory.* New York: Plenum Publishing.

Krieger, D. T. (1983). Brain peptides: What, where and why? *Science, 222,* 975–985.

Kristiansen, K., & Courtois, G. (1949). Rhythmic electrical activity from isolated cerebral cortex. *Electroencephalography and Clinical Neurophysiology, 1,* 254–272.

Krueger, J. M., Pappenheimer, J., & Karnovsky, M. (1982). The composition of sleep-promoting factor isolated from human urine. *Journal of Biological Chemistry, 257,* 1164–1669.

Kruger, J., & Fischer, B. (1973). Strong periphery effect in cat retinal ganglion cells—excitatory responses in on-center and off-center neurons to single grating displacements. *Experimental Brain Research, 18,* 316–318.

Kuffler, S. W. (1953). Discharge patterns and functional organization of mammalian retina. *Journal of Neurophysiology, 16,* 37–68.

Kuhl, K., & Miller, J. D. (1975). Speech perception by chinchilla—phonetic boundaries for synthetic VOT stimuli. *Journal of the Acoustical Society, 57,* S49–S50.

Kulkosly, P., Breckenridge, C., Krinsky, R., & Woods, S. (1976). Satiety elicited by the C-terminal octapeptice of cholecystokinin-pancreozymin in normal and VMH-lesioned rats. *Behavioral Biology, 18,* 227–234.

Labbe, R., Firl, A., Mufson, E., & Stein, D. G. (1983). Fetal brain transplants: Reduction of cognitive deficits in rats with frontal cortex lesions. *Science, 221,* 470–472.

Land, L. J., & Shepherd, G. M. (1974). Autoradiographic analysis of olfactory receptor projections in the rabbit. *Brain Research, 70,* 506–510.

Langston, J., Ballard, P., Tetrud, J., & Irwin, I. (1983). Chronic parkinsonism in humans due to a product of meperidine-analog synthesis. *Science, 219,* 979–980.

Laschet, U. (1973). Antiandrogen in the treatment of sex offenders: Mode of action and therapeutic outcome.

In J. Zubin & J. Money (Eds.), *Contemporary sexual behavior: Critical issues in the 1970's.* Baltimore: Johns Hopkins University Press.

Lashley, K. (1929). *Brain mechanisms and intelligence.* Chicago: University of Chicago Press.

Lashley, K. (1950). In search of the engram. In Society for Experimental Biology (Great Britain) (Ed.), *Physiological mechanisms in animal behavior.* New York: Academic Press.

Lasiewski, R. (1964). Body temperature, heart and breathing rate and evaporative water loss in hummingbirds. *Physiological Zoology, 37,* 212–223.

Latto, R. (1978). The effects of bilateral frontal eye-field lesions on the learning of a visual search task by rhesus monkeys. *Brain Research, 147,* 370–376.

Latto, R., & Cowey, A. (1971). Fixation changes after frontal eye-field lesions in monkeys. *Brain Research, 30,* 25–36.

Laurent, J., Cespuglio, R., & Jouvet, M. (1974). Delimitation des voies ascendantes de l'activité ponto-geniculo-occipitale chez le chat. *Brain Research, 65,* 29–52.

Law, M., & Constantine-Paton, M. (1981). Anatomy and physiology of experimentally produced striped tecta. *Journal of Neuroscience, 1,* 741–759.

Lawrence, M. (1965). Dynamic range of the cochlear transducer. *Cold Spring Harbor Symposia on Quantitative Biology, 30,* 159–167.

Lee, T., & Seeman, P. (1980). Elevation of brain neuroleptic/dopamine receptors in schizophrenia. *American Journal of Psychiatry, 137,* 191–197.

Lenneberg, E. (1967). *Biological foundations of language.* New York: Wiley.

Leshner, A., Walker, W. A., Johnson, A. E., Kelling, J., Kreisler, S., & Svare, B. (1973). Pituitary adrenocortical activity and intermale aggressiveness in isolated mice. *Physiology & Behavior, 11,* 705–711.

Levine, S. (1966, April). Sex differences in the brain. *Scientific American,* pp. 84–90.

Levine, S., Gordon, N., Bornstein, J., & Fields, H. (1976). Role of pain in placebo analgesia. *Proceedings of the National Academy of Sciences, 76,* 337–339.

Levitt, P. (1984). A monoclonal antibody to limbic system neurons. *Science, 223,* 299–301.

Lewis, D. J., Misanin, J. R., & Miller R. R. (1968). Recovery of memory following amnesia. *Nature, 220,* 704–705.

Lhermitte, F., & Signoret, J.-L. (1972). Analyse neuropsychologique et différenciation des syndromes amnésiques. *Revue Neurologiue* (Paris), *126,* 161–178.

Li, C.-L., & Jaster, H. (1953). Microelectrode studies of the electrical activity of the cerebral cortex in the cat. *Journal of Physiology, 121,* 117–140.

Liberman, A. M. (1974). The specialization of the language hemisphere. In F. O. Schmitt & F. G. Worden (Eds.), *The neurosciences: Third study program.* Cambridge, MA: MIT Press.

Liberman, A. M. (1982). On finding that speech is special. *American Psychologist, 37,* 148–167.

Libet, B. (1973). Electrical stimulation of cortex in human subjects, and conscious sensory aspects. In A. Iggo (Ed.), *Handbook of sensory physiology: Vol. 2. Somatosensory system.* Berlin: Springer-Verlag.

Libet, B., Alberts, W. W., Wright, E. W., Jr., & Feinstein, B. (1967). Responses of human somatosensory cortex to stimuli below threshold for conscious sensation. *Science, 158,* 1597–1600.

Licklider, J. C. R. (1951). A duplex theory of pitch perception. *Experientia, 7,* 128–134.

Lieberman, P. (1979). Hominid evolution, supralaryngeal vocal-tract physiology and the fossil evidence for reconstructions. *Brain and Language, 7,* 101–126.

Liebeskind, J., & Paul, L. (1977). Psychological and physiological mechanisms of pain. *Annual Review of Psychology, 28,* 41–60.

Lindsley, D. B., Schriener, L. H., Knowles, W. B., & Magoun, H. W. (1950). Behavioral and EEG changes following chronic brain stem lesions in the cat. *Electroencephalography and Clinical Neurophysiology, 2,* 483–498.

Lippa, A., Antelman, S., Fisher, A., & Canfield, D. (1973). Neurochemical mediation of reward: A significant role for dopamine? *Pharmacology, Biochemistry and Behavior, 1,* 23–28.

Lippold, O. (1973). *The origin of the alpha rhythm.* Edinburgh: Churchill Livingstone.

Lipton, J. (1968). Effects of preoptic lesions in heat-escape responding and colonic temperature in the rat. *Physiology and Behavior, 3,* 165–169.

Lockhart, M., & Moore, J. W. (1975). Classical differential and operant conditioning in rabbits (*Orycytolagus culiculus*) with septal lesions. *Journal of Comparative and Physiological Psychology, 88,* 147–154.

Loeb, G. E. (1985, February). The functional replacement of the ear. *Scientific American,* pp. 104–111.

Loewenstein, W. R., & Mendelson, M. (1965). Components of receptor adaptation in a Pacinian corpuscle. *Journal of Physiology, 177,* 377–397.

Lorente de No, R. (1949). Cerebral cortex: Architecture, intracortical connections, motor projections. In J. F. Fulton (Ed.), *Physiology of the nervous system* (3rd ed.). New York: Oxford University Press.

Luchero, M. (1970). Lengthening of REM sleep duration consecutive to learning in the rat. *Brain Research, 20,* 319–322.

Luckhardt, A., & Carlson, A. J. (1915). Contributions to

the physiology of the stomach: 18. On the chemical control of the gastric hunger mechanism. *American Journal of Physiology, 36,* 37.

Luria, A. R. (1964). Factors and forms of aphasia. In A. V. S. de Reuch & M. O'Connor (Eds.), *Disorders of language.* Boston: Little, Brown.

Luria, A. R. (1966). *Higher cortical functions in man.* London: Tavistock.

Luria, A. R. (1970a, March). The functional organization of the brain. *Scientific American,* pp. 66–79.

Luria, A. R. (1970b). *Traumatic aphasia.* The Hague: Mouton.

Lynch, G., & Baudry, M. (1984). The biochemistry of memory: A new and specific hypothesis. *Science, 224,* 1057–1063.

Lynch, J. C. (1980). The functional organization of posterior parietal association cortex. *Behavioral and Brain Sciences, 3,* 485–534.

Lynch, J. C., & Graybiel, A. (1983). Comparison of afferents traced to the superior colliculus from the frontal eye fields and from two sub-regions of area 7 of the rhesus monkey. *Neuroscience Abstracts, 9,* 750.

Lynch, J. C., Mountcastle, V., Talbot, W. H., & Yin, T. (1977). Parietal lobe mechanisms for directed visual attention. *Journal of Neurophysiology, 40,* 362–389.

Lynch, L. J. (1983). Water relaxation in heterogeneous and biological systems. In J. S. Cohen (Ed.), *Magnetic resonance in biology* (Vol. 2). New York: Wiley.

Mack, A. (1970). An investigation of the relationship between eye and retinal image movement in the perception of movement. *Perception & Psychophysics, 8,* 291–298.

Maclean, P. D. (1949). Psychosomatic disease and the "visceral brain": Recent developments bearing on the Papez theory of emotion. *Psychosomatic Medicine, 11,* 338–353.

Maclean, P. D. (1958). Contrasting functions of limbic and neocortical systems of the brain and their relevance to psychophysiological aspects of medicine. *American Journal of Medicine, 25,* 611–626.

Maier, S., Drugan, R., & Grau, W. (1982). Controllability, coping behavior, and stress-induced analgesia in the rat. *Pain, 12,* 47–56.

Makowski, L., Caspar, W., Phillips, W., & Goodenough, D. (1977). Gap junction structure: 2. Analysis of the x-ray diffraction data. *Journal of Cell Biology, 74,* 629–645.

Mangiapane, M., & Simpson, J. B. (1980). Subfornical organ: Forebrain site of pressor and dipsogenic action of angiotensin II. *American Journal of Physiology, 239,* R382–R389.

Manning, P., Schwartz, D., Katsube, N., Holmberg, S., & Needleman, P. (1985). Vasopressin-stimulated release of atriopeptin: Endocrine antagonists in fluid homeostasis. *Science, 229,* 395–397.

Marianai, A. P. (1982). Biplexiform cells: Ganglion cells of the primate retina that contact photoreceptors. *Science, 216,* 1134–1136.

Mark, V. H., & Ervin, E. (1970). *Violence and the brain.* New York: Harper & Row.

Marks, W. B., Dobelle, W. H., & MacNichol, E. F. (1964). Visual pigments of single primate cones. *Science, 143,* 1181–1183.

Marler, Peter, & Tamura, M. (1964). Culturally transmitted patterns of vocal behavior in sparrows. *Science, 146,* 1483–1486.

Marrocco, R. (1986). The neurobiology of perception. In J. LeDoux & W. Hirst (Eds.), *Mind and brain: Dialogues in cognitive neuroscience.* Cambridge: Cambridge University Press.

Martin, G. E., & Bacino, C. (1978). Action of intrahypothalamically-injected beta-endorphin on the body temperature of the rat. *Society for Neuroscience Abstracts, 4,* 411.

Martres, P.-M., Bouthenet, M.-L., Sales, N., Sokoloff, P., & Schwartz, J.-C. (1985). Widespread distribution of brain dopamine receptors evidenced with [125 I] iodosulpride, a highly selective ligand. *Science, 228,* 752–755.

Masland, R., Austin, G., & Grant, F. C. (1949). The electroencephalogram following occipital lobectomy. *Electroencephalography and Clinical Neurophysiology, 1,* 273–282.

Massaro, D. (1979). Letter information and orthographic context in word perception. *Journal of Experimental Psychology: Human Perception and Performance, 5,* 595–609.

Massaro, D., & Cohen, M. M. (1983). Categorical or continuous speech perception: A new test. *Speech Communication, 2,* 15–35.

Masters, W. H., & Johnson, V. E. (1971). The sexual response cycles of the human male and female: Comparative anatomy and physiology. In B. Lieberman (Ed.), *Human sexual behavior.* New York: Wiley.

Mayer, D., Price, D., Rafii, A., & Barber, J. (1976). Acupuncture analgesia: Evidence for activation of a central control system as a mechanism of action. In J. Bonica & D. Albe-Fessard (Eds.), *Advances in pain research and therapy,* (Vol. 1). New York: Raven Press.

Mayer, J. (1953). Glucostatic mechanisms of regulation of food intake. *New England Journal of Medicine, 249,* 13–16.

McConnell, J. V. (1962). Memory transfer through cannibalism in planarians. *Journal of Neuropsychiatry, 3* (Suppl. 1), 542–548.

McCormick, D., & Thompson, R. F. (1984). Cerebellum: Essential involvement in the classically conditioned eyelid response. *Science, 223,* 296–299.

McCulloch, W. S., & Pitts, W. (1943). A logical calculus

of the ideas immanent in nervous activity. In W. McCulloch (Ed.), *Embodiments of mind.* Cambridge, MA: MIT Press.

McDougall, W. (1901). Facilitative and disruptive effects of strychnine sulphate on maze learning. *Psychological Reports, 8,* 99–104.

McGaugh, J. L. (1973). Drug facilitation of learning and memory. *Annual Review of Pharmacology, 13,* 229–241.

McGinty, D., & Sterman, M. (1968). Sleep suppression after basal forebrain lesions in the cat. *Science, 160,* 1253–1255.

McGrath, M., & Cohen, D. (1978). REM sleep facilitation of adaptive waking behavior: A review of the literature. *Psychological Bulletin, 85,* 24–57.

McIlwain, J. (1964). Receptive fields of optic tract axons and lateral geniculate cells: Peripheral extend and barbiturate sensitivity. *Journal of Neurophysiology, 27,* 1154–1173.

Meddis, R. (1979). The evolution and function of sleep. In D. A. Oakley & H. C. Plotkin (Eds.), *Brain, behavior and evolution.* London: Methuen.

Melzack, R., & Wall, P. D. (1965). Pain mechanisms: A new theory. *Science, 150,* 971–979.

Menaker, M. (1974). Aspects of the physiology of circadian rhythmicity in the vertebrate central nervous system. In F. O. Schmitt & F. G. Worden (Eds.), *The neurosciences: Third study program.* Cambridge, MA: MIT Press.

Mesulam, M., Van Hoesen, G., Pandya, D., & Geschwind, N. (1977). Limbic and sensory connections of the inferior parietal lobule (area PG) in the rhesus monkey: A study with a new method for horseradish peroxidase histochemistry. *Brain Research, 136,* 393–414.

Miczek, K., Thompson, M. L., & Shuster, L. (1982). Opioid-like amnesia in defeated mice. *Science, 215,* 1520–1522.

Miller, G. A. (1956). The magical number seven, plus or minus two. *Psychological Review, 63,* 81–97.

Miller, G. A., Galanter, E., & Pribram, K. H. (1960). *Plans and the structure of behavior.* New York: Holt, Rinehart & Winston.

Milner, B. (1965). Memory disturbance after bilateral hippocampal lesions. In P. M. Milner & S. Glickman (Eds.), *Cognitive processes and the brain.* Princeton, NJ: Van Nostrand, 1965.

Milner, B. (1970). Memory and the temporal regions of the brain. In K. H. Pribram & D. E. Broadbent (Eds.), *Biology of memory.* New York: Academic Press.

Minsky, M., & Papert, S. (1969). *Perceptrons.* Cambridge, MA: MIT Press.

Mishkin, M. (1964). Perseveration of central sets after frontal lesions in monkeys. In J. M. Warren & K. Akert (Eds.), *The frontal granular cortex and behavior.* New York: McGraw-Hill.

Mishkin, M., Ungerleider, L., & Macko, K. (1983). Object vision and spatial vision: Two cortical pathways. *Trends in Neurosciences, 6,* 414–417.

Mittelstaedt, H. (1985). Subjective vertical in weightlessness. In M. Igarashi (Ed.), *Proceedings of the 7th International Symposium on Posture and Equilibrium.* Basel: Karger.

Mize, R., & Murphy, E. H. (1973). Selective visual experience fails to modify receptive field properties of rabbit striate cortical neurones. *Science, 180,* 320–323.

Mohler, C., Goldberg, M. E., & Wurtz, R. (1973). Visual receptive fields of frontal eye field neurons. *Brain Research, 61,* 385–389.

Moller, A. R. (1974). Function of the middle ear. In W. E. Keidel & W. D. Neff (Eds.), *Handbook of sensory physiology: Vol. 1. Auditory system.* Berlin: Springer-Verlag.

Money, J., & Ehrhardt, A. (1972). *Man and woman, boy and girl.* Baltimore: Johns Hopkins University Press.

Moniz, E. (1936). *Tentatives operatoires dans le traitement de certaines psychoses.* Paris: Masson.

Moore, R. Y. (1974). Visual pathways and the central neural control of diurnal rhythms. In F. O. Schmitt & F. G. Worden (Eds.), *The neurosciences: Third study program.* Cambridge, MA: MIT Press.

Moore, R. Y., & Bloom, F. E. (1979). Central catecholamine neuron systems: Anatomy and physiology of the dopamine systems. *Annual Review of Neuroscience, 1,* 129–169.

Mora, F., Sanguinetti, A., Rolls, E. T., & Shaw, S. G. (1975). Differential effects of self-stimulation and motor behavior produced by microintracranial injections of a dopamine-receptor blocking agent. *Neuroscience Letters, 1,* 179–184.

Morgane, P., & Kosman, A. (1960). Relationship of the middle hypothalamus to amygdalar hyperphagia. *American Journal of Physiology, 198,* 1315–1318.

Morrell, F. (1972). Visual system's view of acoustic space. *Nature, 238,* 44–46.

Morrison, A. R. (1983, April). A window on the sleeping brain. *Scientific American,* pp. 94–102.

Moruzzi, G., & Magoun, H. (1949). Brain stem reticular formation and activation of the EEG. *Electroencephalography and Clinical Neurophysiology, 1,* 455–473.

Moskowitz, E., & Berger, R. (1969). Rapid eye movements and dream imagery—Are they related? *Nature, 224,* 613.

Mountcastle, V. B. (1957). Modality and topographic properties of single neurons of cat's somatic sensory cortex. *Journal of Neurophysiology, 20,* 408–434.

Mountcastle, V. B. (1967). The problem of sensing and the neural coding of sensory events. In G. Quarton, T.

Melnechuk, & F. O. Schmitt (Eds.), *The neurosciences.* New York: Rockefeller University Press.

Mountcastle, V. B., & Powell, T. P. S. (1959). Neural mechanisms subserving cutaneous sensibility, with special reference to the role of afferent inhibition in sensory perception and discrimination. *Bulletin of the Johns Hopkins Hospital, 105,* 201–232.

Moyer, K. E. (1976). *The psychobiology of aggression.* New York: Harper & Row.

Mozell, M. M. (1967). The effect of concentration upon the spatio-temporal coding of odorants. In T. Hayashi (Ed.), *International Symposium on Olfaction and Taste* (Vol. 2). Oxford: Pergamon Press.

Mozell, M. M. (1970). Evidence for a chromatographic model of olfaction. *Journal of General Physiology, 56,* 46–63.

Mueller, K., & Hsiaso, S. (1978). Current status of cholescystokinin as a short-term satiety hormone. *Neuroscience and Biobehavioral Reviews, 2,* 79–87.

Mulholland, T., & Evans, C. R. (1965). An unexpected artifact in the human electroencephalogram concerning the alpha rhythm and the orientation of the eyes. *Nature, 207,* 36–37.

Müller, G. E., & Pilzecker, A. (1900). Experimentale Beiträge zur Lehre vom Gedächtnis. *Zeitschrift für Psychologie* (Suppl.), 1–288.

Murdoch, B., Jr. (1982). A theory for the storage and retrieval of item and associative information. *Psychological Review, 89,* 609–626.

Naka, K. I. (1977). Functional organization of catfish retina. *Journal of Neurophysiology, 40,* 26–43.

Narabayashi, H. (1972). Stereotaxic amygdalectomy. In B. E. Eleftheriou (Ed.), *The neurobiology of the amygdala.* New York: Plenum Publishing.

Narabayashi, H., Nagao, T., Saito, Y., Yoshida, M., & Nagahata, M. (1963). Stereotaxic amygdalotomy for behavior disorders. *Archives of Neurology, 9,* 1–16.

Nathan, P., & Smith, M. C. (1951). The centripetal pathway from the bladder and urethra within the spinal cord. *Journal of Neurology, Neurosurgery, & Psychiatry, 14,* 262–280.

Nauta, W. J. H. (1946). Hypothalamic regulation of sleep in rats: Experimental study. *Journal of Neurophysiology, 9,* 285–316.

Nauta, W. J. H., & Gygax, P. (1954). Silver impregnation of degenerating axons in the central nervous system: A modified technic. *Stain Technology, 29,* 91–93.

Neisser, U. (1967). *Cognitive psychology.* New York: Appleton-Century-Crofts.

Nieuwenhuys, R. (1969). The cerebellum. In C. A. Fox (Ed.), *Progress in brain research* (Vol. 25). Amsterdam: Elsevier/North Holland.

Niijima, A. (1969). Afferent impulse discharges from glucoreceptors in the liver of the guinea pig. *Annals of the New York Academy of Sciences, 157,* 690–700.

Niki, H., & Watanabe, M. (1976a). Cingulate unit activity and delayed response. *Brain Research, 110,* 381–386.

Niki, H., & Watanabe, M. (1976b). Prefrontal unit activity and delayed response: Relation to cue location versus direction of response. *Brain Research, 105,* 79–88.

Ninan, P., Insel, T., Cohen, R. M., Cook, J. M., Skolnik, P., & Paul, S. (1982). Benzodiazepine receptor-mediated experimental "anxiety" in primates. *Science, 218,* 1332–1334.

Noble, D. (1966). Applications of Hodgkin-Huxley equations to excitable tissues. *Physiological Review, 46,* 1–46.

Norman, D. A., & Shallice, T. (1980). Attention to action: Willed and automatic control of behavior. In *Center for Human Information Processing Technical Report 8006.* La Jolla: University of California at San Diego.

Norris, K. (1967). Color adaptation in desert reptiles and its thermal relationships. In W. W. Milstead (Ed.), *Lizard ecology: A symposium.* Columbia: University of Missouri Press.

Noton, D., & Stark, L. (1971). Scanpaths in eye movements during pattern perception. *Science, 171,* 308–311.

Nottebohm, F. (1977). Asymmetries in neural control of vocalization in the canary. In S. Harnad, R. W. Doty, L. Goldstein, J. Jaynes, & G. Krauthamer (Eds.), *Lateralization in the nervous system.* New York: Academic Press.

Nottebohm, F. (1980). Brain pathways for vocal learning in birds: A review of the first 10 years. In J. Sprague & A. Epstein (Eds.), *Progress in psychobiology and physiological psychology* (Vol. 9). New York: Academic Press.

O'Brien, D. F. (1982). The chemistry of vision. *Science, 218,* 961–966.

Ojemann, G. (1983). The intrahemispheric organization of human language, derived with electrical stimulation techniques. *Trends in Neurosciences, 6,* 184–189.

Ojemann, G., & Mateer, C. (1979). Human language cortex: Localization of memory, syntax, and sequential motor-phoneme identification systems. *Science, 205,* 1401–1403.

Olds, J. (1973). Commentary. In E. S. Valenstein (Ed.), *Brain stimulation and motivation.* Glenview, IL: Scott, Foresman.

Olds, J., Allan, W., & Briese, E. (1971). Differentiation of hypothalamic drive and reward centers. *American Journal of Physiology, 221,* 672–674.

Olds, J., & Milner, P. (1954). Positive reinforcement produced by electrical stimulation of septal area and other regions of rat brain. *Journal of Comparative and Physiological Psychology, 47,* 419–427.

Olds, M. E., & Fobes, J. (1981). The central basis of motivation: Intracranial self-stimulation studies. *Annual Review of Psychology, 32,* 523–574.

Oomura, Y. (1976). Significance of glucose, insulin, and free fatty acid on the hypothalamic feeding and satiety neurons. In D. Novin, W. Wyrwricka, & G. Bray (Eds.), *Hunger: Basic mechanisms and clinical implications.* New York: Raven Press.

Owen, F., Cross, A. J., Crow, T., Longden, M., Poulter, M., & Riley, G. J. (1978). Increased dopamine-receptor sensitivity in schizophrenia. *Lancet, 2,* 223–226.

Pagano, R., Rose, R. M., Stivcers, R., & Warrenburg, S. (1976). Sleep during transcendental meditation. *Science, 191,* 308–310.

Palay, S. (1967). Principles of cellular organization in the nervous system. In G. Quarton, T. Melnechuk, & F. O. Schmitt (Eds.), *The neurosciences: A study program.* New York: Rockefeller University Press.

Panksepp, J. (1971). Drugs and stimulus-bound attack. *Physiology & Behavior, 6,* 317–320.

Panksepp, J. (1982). Toward a general psychobiological theory of emotions. *Behavioral and Brain Sciences, 5,* 407–467.

Panskepp, J., & Trowill, J. (1967). Intraoral self-injection: 2. The simulation of self-stimulation phenomena with a conventional reward. *Psychonomic Science, 9,* 407–408.

Papez, J. (1937). A proposed mechanism of emotion. *Archives of Neurology and Psychiatry* (Chicago), *38,* 725–743.

Parmeggiani, P., & Rabini, C. (1967). Shivering and panting during sleep. *Brain Research, 6,* 789–791.

Passingham, R. (1973). Anatomical differences between the neocortex of man and other primates. *Brain Behavior & Evolution, 7,* 337–359.

Paton, J., & Nottebohm, F. (1984). Neurons generated in the adult brain are recruited into functional circuits. *Science, 225,* 1046–1048.

Patterson, M. M., Berger, T. W., & Thompson, R. F. (1979). Neuronal plasticity recorded from cat hippocampus during classical conditioning. *Brain Research, 163,* 339–343.

Paul, S., Hulihan-Giblin, B., & Skolnick, P. (1982). Amphetamine binding to rat hypothalamus: Relation to anorexic potency of phenylethylamines. *Science, 218,* 487–490.

Pavlov, I. P. (1927). *Conditioned reflexes.* New York: Oxford University Press.

Peck, J., & Blass, E. (1975). Localization of thirst and antidiuretic osmoreceptors by intracranial injections in rats. *American Journal of Physiology, 5,* 1501–1509.

Penfield W., & Rasmussen, T. (1950). *The cerebral cortex of man: A clinical study of localization of function.* New York: Macmillan.

Penfield, W., & Roberts, L. (1959). *Speech and brain mechanisms.* Princeton, NJ: Princeton University Press.

Penfield, W., & Welch, K. (1951). The supplementary motor area of the cerebral cortex: A clinical and experimental study. *Archives of Neurology and Psychiatry, 66,* 289–317.

Pepperberg, S. (1983). Cognition in the African grey parrot—Preliminary evidence for auditory vocal comprehension of the class concept. *Animal Learning, Series B, 11,* 179–185.

Pert, C., & Snyder, S. (1973). Opiate receptor: Demonstration in nervous tissue. *Science, 179,* 1011–1014.

Pettigrew, J. D. & Freeman, R. (1973). Visual experience without lines: Effect on developing cortical neurons. *Science, 182,* 599–601.

Pettigrew, J. D., Nikara, T., & Bishop, P. O. (1968). Responses to moving slits by single units in cat striate cortex. *Experimental Brain Research, 6,* 373–390.

Phillips, A., Van der Kooy, D., & Fibiger, H. (1977). Maintenance of intracranial self-stimulation in hippocampus and olfactory bulb following regional depletion of noradrenalin. *Neuroscience Letters, 4,* 77–84.

Phillips, C. G. (1956). Intracellular records from Betz cells in the cat. *Quarterly Journal of Experimental Physiology, 41,* 58–69.

Piaget, J. (1973). *The child and reality.* New York: Penguin Books.

Picton, T., Hillyard, S., Krausz, H., & Galambos, R. (1974). Human auditory evoked potentials: 1. Evaluation of components. *Electrocephalography and Clinical Neurophysiology, 36,* 179–190.

Pike, R. (1984). Comparison of convolution and matrix distributed memory systems for associative recall and recognition. *Psychological Review, 91,* 281–294.

Pittendrigh, C. (1974). Circadian oscillations in cells and the circadian organization of multicellular systems. In F. O. Schmitt & F. G. Worden (Eds.), *The neurosciences: Third study program.* Cambridge, MA: MIT Press.

Ploog, D. (1981). Neurobiology of primate audio-vocal behavior. *Brain Research Reviews, 3,* 35–62.

Poggio, G. F., & Mountcastle, V. B. (1960). A study of the functional contributions of the lemniscal and spinothalamic systems to somatic sensibility: Central nervous mechanisms in pain. *Bulletin of the Johns Hopkins Hospital, 106,* 266–316.

Pons, T., Garraghty, P., Friedman, D., & Mishkin, M. (1987). Physiological evidence for serial processing in somatosensory cortex. *Science, 237,* 417–420.

Popper, K. (1968). *The logic of scientific discovery* (3rd ed.). London: Hutchinson.

Poritsky, R. (1969). Reconstruction from serial electron micrographs of a motoneuron. *Journal of Comparative Neurology, 135,* 423–452.

Porter, K. R., Byers, H. R., & Ellisman, M. H. (1979). The cytoskeleton. In F. O. Schmitt & F. G. Worden (Eds.), *The Neurosciences: Fourth study program.* Cambridge, MA: MIT Press.

Poschel, B., & Ninteman, F. (1966). Psychotrophic drug effects on self-stimulation of the brain: A control of motor output. *Psychological Reports, 19,* 79–82.

Premack, A. J., & Premack, D. (1972, October). Teaching language to an ape. *Scientific American,* pp. 92–99.

Premack, D. (1959). Toward empirical behavior laws: 1. Positive reinforcement. *Psychological Review, 66,* 219–233.

Pribram, K. H. (1960). The intrinsic systems of the forebrain. In J. Field, H. W. Magoun, & V. E. Hall (Eds.), *Handbook of physiology, neurophysiology* (Vol. 2). Washington, D.C.: American Physiological Society.

Pribram, K. H. (1962). Interrelations of psychology and the neurological disciplines. In S. Koch (Ed.), *Psychology: A study of a science* (Vol. 4). New York: McGraw-Hill.

Pribram, K. H. (1967). The limbic systems, efferent control of neural inhibition and behavior. In W. Adey & T. Tokizane (Eds.), *Progress in brain research* (Vol. 27). Amsterdam: Elsevier/North Holland.

Pribram, K. H. (1971). *Languages of the brain.* Englewood Cliffs, NJ: Prentice-Hall.

Pribram, K. H. (1981). Emotions. In S. Filskov & T. Boll (Eds.), *Handbook of clinical neuropsychology.* New York: Wiley.

Pribram, K. H., & Bagshaw, M. (1953). Further analysis of the temporal lobe syndrome utilizing frontotemporal ablations in monkeys. *Journal of Comparative Neurology, 99,* 347–375.

Pribram, K. H., Blehert, S. R., & Spinelli, D. N. (1966). Effects on visual discrimination of crosshatching and undercutting the inferotemporal cortex of monkeys. *Journal of Comparative and Physiological Psychology, 62,* 358–364.

Pribram, K. H., Douglas, R. J., & Pribram, B. J. (1969). The nature of nonlimbic learning. *Journal of Comparative and Physiological Psychology, 69,* 765–772.

Pribram, K. H., Nuwer, M., & Baron, R. (1974). The holographic hypothesis of memory structure in brain function and perception. In D. Krantz, R. C. Atkinson, R. Luce, & P. Suppes (Eds.), *Contemporary developments in mathematical psychology* (Vol. 2). San Francisco: Freeman.

Pribram, K. H., Plotkin, H. C., Anderson, R. M., & Leong, D. (1977). Information sources in the delayed alternation task for normal and "frontal" monkeys. *Neuropsychologia, 15,* 329–340.

Pribram, K. H., & Tubbs, W. E. (1967). Short-term memory, parsing and the primate frontal cortex. *Science, 156,* 1765–1767.

Price, J. (1968). The genetics of depressive behavior. *British Journal of Psychiatry, 2,* 37–45.

Pucetti, R., & Dykes, B. (1978). Sensory cortex and the mind-brain problem. *Behavioral and Brain Sciences, 3,* 337–375.

Purpura, D. P., & Cohen, B. (1962). Intracellular recording from thalamic neurons during recruiting responses. *Journal of Neurophysiology, 25,* 621–635.

Rakic, P. (1981). Overview. *Neurosciences Brain Research Bulletin, 202,* 435.

Rakic, P. (1985). Limits of neurogenesis in primates. *Science, 227,* 1054–1056.

Rall, W., Shepherd, G. M., Reese, T. S., & Brightman, M. W. (1966). Dendrodendritic synaptic pathway for inhibition in the olfactory bulb. *Experimental Neurology, 14,* 44–56.

Ralston, H. J., III (1971). Evidence for presynaptic dendrites and a proposal for their mechanism of action. *Nature, 230,* 585–587.

Ramsay, D., Rolls, B., & Wood, R. (1977). Thirst following water deprivation in dogs. *American Journal of Physiology, 232,* R93–R100.

Ratliff, F. (1965). *Mach bands: Quantitative studies on neural networks in the retina.* San Francisco: Holden-Day.

Redington, R. (1981). Medical imaging systems. *Physics Today, 34,* 36–44.

Redman, J., Armstrong, S., & Ng, K. T. (1983). Free-running activity rhythms in the rat: Entrainment by melatonin. *Science, 219,* 1089–1091.

Reed D., & Woodbury, D. (1962). Effects of hypertonic urea on cerebrospinal fluid pressure and brain volume. *Journal of Physiology, 164,* 252–264.

Reese, T. S., & Brightman, M. W. (1970). Olfactory surface and central olfactory connections in some vertebrates. In G. Pappas & D. Purpura (Eds.), *CIBA Foundation symposium on taste and smell in vertebrates.* New York: Raven Press.

Reis, D (1986). Regulation by brain of its own blood flow and metabolism: Intrinsic neural control of the cerebral circulation. *Society for Neuroscience Abstracts, 12,* 756.

Repp, B., Liberman, A. M., Eccardt, A., & Pesetsky, D. (1978). Perceptual integration of acoustic cues for stop, fricative, and affricate manner. *Journal of Experimental Psychology: Human Perception and Performance, 4,* 621–637.

Richardson, D. B., & Mogenson, G. (1981). Water intake elicited by injections of angiotensin II into the preoptic area of rats. *American Journal of Physiology, 240,* R70–R74.

Richardson, D. E., & Akil, H. (1974). Chronic self-administration of brain stimulation for pain relief in human patients. *Proceedings American Association of Neurological Surgeons,* St. Louis, Mo.

Richter, C. P. (1965). *Biological clocks in medicine and psychiatry.* Springfield, IL: Charles C Thomas.

Richter, C. P. (1970). Blood-clock barrier: Its penetration by heavy water. *Proceedings of the National Academy of Sciences, 66,* 244.

Richter, C. P. (1975). Deep hypothermia and its effect on the 24-hour clock of rats and hamsters. *Johns Hopkins Medical Journal, 136,* 1–10.

Rideout, B. (1979). Non-REM sleep as a source of learning deficits induced by REM sleep deprivation. *Physiology & Behavior, 22,* 1043–1047.

Ridgway, E., Gordon, A. M., & Martyn, D. (1983). Hysteresis in the force-calcium relation in muscle. *Science, 219,* 1075–1077.

Ritter, W., & Vaughan, H. (1969). Averaged evoked responses in vigilance and discrimination: A reassessment. *Science, 164,* 326–328.

Roberts, L. (1961). Activation and interference of cortical functions. In D. Sheer (Ed.), *Electrical stimulation of the brain.* Austin: University of Texas Press.

Roberts, W. W. (1958). Both rewarding and punishing effects from stimulation of posterior hypothalamus of cats with same electrode at same intensity. *Journal of Comparative and Physiological Psychology, 51,* 400–407.

Roberts, W. W., & Mooney, R. D. (1974). Brain areas controlling thermoregulatory grooming, prone extension, locomotion, and tail vasodilation in rats. *Journal of Comparative and Physiological Psychology, 86,* 470–480.

Roberts, W. W., & Robinson, T. C. (1969). Relaxation and sleep induced by warming of preoptic region and anterior hypothalamus in cats. *Experimental Neurology, 25,* 282–294.

Robinson, D. A. (1981). Control of eye movements. In V. B. Brooks (Ed.), *Handbook of physiology: Sec. 1. The nervous system: Vol. 2. Motor control, Pt. 2.* Bethesda, MD: American Physiological Society.

Rodin, J. (1981). Current status of the external-internal hypothesis for obesity. *American Psychologist, 36,* 361–372.

Rolls, B., & Rolls, E. (1982). *Thirst.* Cambridge: Cambridge University Press.

Rolls, B., Wood, R., & Rolls, E. (1980). Thirst: The initiation, maintenance, and termination of drinking. In J. Sprague & A. Epstein (Eds.), *Progress in psychobiology and physiological psychology* (Vol. 9). New York: Academic Press.

Rose, J. E., Brugge, J. F., Anderson, D. J., & Hind, J. E. (1967). Phase-locked response to low-frequency tones in single auditory nerve fibers of the squirrel monkey. *Journal of Neurophysiology, 30,* 769–793.

Rose, J. E., & Mountcastle, V. B. (1959). Touch and kinesthesis. In J. Field (Ed.), *Handbook of physiology, neurophysiology* (Vol. 1). Washington, DC: American Physiological Society.

Rosen, I., & Asanuma, H. (1972). Peripheral inputs to the forelimb area of the monkey motor cortex: Input-output relations. *Experimental Brain Research, 14,* 257–273.

Rosenblatt, F. (1960). Perception simulation experiments. *Proceedings of the Institute of Radio Engineers, 48,* 301–309.

Rosenkilde, C. (1979). Functional heterogeneity of the prefrontal cortex in the monkey: A review. *Behavioral and Neural Biology, 25,* 301–345.

Rosenkilde, C., Rosvold, H., & Mishkin, M. (1981). Time discrimination with positional responses after selective prefrontal lesions in monkeys. *Brain Research, 210,* 129–144.

Rosenzweig, M., & Bennett, E. L. (1978). Experimental influences on brain anatomy and brain chemistry in rodents. In G. Gottlieb (Ed.), *Studies on the development of behavior and the nervous system* (Vol. 4). New York: Academic Press.

Rosenzweig, M., Krech, D., & Bennett, E. L. (1961). Heredity, environment, brain biochemistry, and learning. In W. Dennis (Ed.), *Current trends in psychological theory.* Pittsburgh, PA: University of Pittsburgh Press.

Rosenzweig, M., Krech, D., Bennett, E. L., & Diamond, M. (1962). Effects of environmental complexity and training on brain chemistry and anatomy: A replication and extension. *Journal of Comparative and Physiological Psychology, 55,* 429–437.

Rosvold, H., Mirsky, A., & Pribram, K. H. (1954). Influence of amygdalectomy on social behavior in monkeys. *Journal of Comparative and Physiological Psychology, 47,* 173–178.

Rothblat, L., & Pribram, K. H. (1972). Selective attention: Input filter or response selection? An electrophysiological analysis. *Brain Research, 39,* 427–436.

Rowland, N., & Antelman, S. (1976). Stress-induced hyperphagia and obesity in rats: A possible model for understanding human obesity. *Science, 191,* 310–312.

Rozin, P., Poritsky, S., & Sotski, R. (1971). American children with reading problems can easily learn to read English represented by Chinese characters. *Science, 171,* 1264–1267.

Ruda, M. (1982). Opiates and pain pathways: Demonstration of enkephalin synapses on dorsal horn projection neurons. *Science, 215,* 1523–1525.

Rumbaugh, D. (Ed.). (1977). *Language learning by a chimpanzee: The Lana project.* New York: Academic Press.

Rumelhart, D. (1981). Schemata: The building blocks of cognition. In R. Spiro, B. Bruce, & W. Brewer (Eds.), *Theoretical issues in reading comprehension.* Hillsdale, NJ: Lawrence Erlbaum.

Russel, R., & Sellick, S. (1981). In J. Syka & L. Aitkin (Eds.), *Neuronal mechanisms of hearing.* New York: Plenum Publishing.

Ryle, G. (1949). *The concept of mind.* New York: Barnes & Noble.

Sackitt, B. (1972). Counting every quantum. *Journal of Physiology, 223,* 131–150.

Sacks, O. (1987). The Man Who Mistook His Wife for a Hat. New York: Harper & Row.

Sandrew, D. B., Stamm, J. S., & Rosen, S. C. (1977). Steady potential shifts and facilitated learning of delayed response in monkeys. *Experimental Neurology, 55,* 43–55.

Sasanuma, S. (1975). Kana and Kanji processing in Japanese aphasics. *Brain and Language, 2,* 369–383.

Satinoff, E. (1978). Neural organization and evolution of thermal regulation in mammals. *Science, 201,* 16–22.

Satinoff, E., & Henderson, R. (1977). In W. Honig & J. E. R. Staddon (Eds.), *Handbook of operant behavior.* Englewood Cliffs, NJ: Prentice-Hall.

Satinoff, E., & Shan, S. Y. (1971). Loss of behavioral thermoregulation after lateral hypothalamic lesions in rats. *Journal of Comparative and Physiological Psychology, 77,* 302–312.

Schank, R., & Abelson, R. (1977). *Scripts, plans, goals and understanding.* Hillsdale, NJ: Lawrence Erlbaum.

Scheibel, M., & Scheibel, A. (1961). On circuit patterns of the brain stem reticular core. *Annals of the New York Academy of Science, 89,* 857–865.

Schildkraut, J., & Kety, S. (1967). Biogenic amines and emotion. *Science, 156,* 21–30.

Schiller, P. H., Finlay, B., & Volman, S. (1976). Quantitative studies of single-cell properties in monkey striate cortex: 3. Spatial frequency. *Journal of Neurophysiology, 39,* 1334–1351.

Schiller, P. H., & Malpeli, J. (1977). Properties and tectal projections of monkey retinal ganglion cells. *Journal of Neurophysiology, 40,* 428–445.

Schiller, P. H., True, S., & Conway, J. (1980). Deficits in eye movements following frontal eye-field and superior colliculus ablations. *Journal of Neurophysiology, 44,* 1175–1189.

Schlag, J., & Schlag-Rey, M. (1985). Unit activity related to spontaneous saccades in dorsomedial cortex of monkey. *Experimental Brain Research, 58,* 208–211.

Schlag-Rey, M., & Lindsley, D. (1970). Effect of prefrontal lesions on trained anticipatory visual attending in cats. *Physiology and Behavior, 5,* 1033–1041.

Schmidt, R. F. (1978). *Fundamentals of neurophysiology.* New York: Springer-Verlag.

Schmidt-Nielson, K., Dawson, T., & Crawford, E. (1966). Temperature regulation in the echidna (*Tachyglossus aculeatus*). *Journal of Cellular Physiology, 67,* 63–72.

Schneider, G. E. (1969). Two visual systems. *Science, 163,* 895–902.

Schor, C., Bridgeman, B., & Tyler, C. W. (1983). Spatial characteristics of static and dynamic stereoacuity in strabismus. *Investigative Ophthalmology and Visual Science, 24,* 1572–1579.

Schreiner, L., & Kling, A. (1953). Behavioral changes following rhinencephalic injury in cat. *Journal of Neurophysiology, 16,* 643–658.

Schumann, M., & Kreulen, D. (1986). Evidence that cholecystokinin is a neurotransmitter in the inferior mesenteric ganglion of guinea pig. *Society for Neuroscience Abstracts, 12,* 1496.

Schwartz, J. (1977). Histaminergic mechanisms in brain. *Annual Review of Pharmacology and Toxicology, 17,* 325–339.

Schwartz, W. J., & Gainer, H. (1977). Suprachiasmatic nucleus: Use of 14C-labelled deoxyglucose uptake as a functional marker. *Science, 197,* 1089–1091.

Sclafani, A., Springer, D., & Kluge, L. (1976). Effects of quinine adulteration on the food intake and body weight of obese and non-obese hypothalamic hyperphagic rats. *Physiology and Behavior, 16,* 631–640.

Scoville, W., & Milner, B. (1957). Loss of recent memory after bilateral hippocampal lesions. *Journal of Neurology, Neurosurgery, & Psychiatry, 20,* 11–21.

Searle, J. (1980). Minds, brains, and programs. *Behavioral and Brain Sciences, 3,* 417–457.

Seeman, P., Ulpian, C., Bergeron, C., Riederer, P., Jellinger, K., Gabriel, E., Reynolds, G. P., & Tourtellotte, W. (1984). Bimodal distribution of dopamine receptor densities in brains of schizophrenics. *Science, 225,* 728–731.

Selhorst, J., Stark, L., Ochs, A., & Hoyt, W. (1976a). Disorders in cerebellar ocular motor control: 1. Saccadic overshoot dysmetria: An oculographic, control system and clinico-anatomical analysis. *Brain, 99,* 497–508.

Selhorst, J., Stark, L., Ochs, A., & Hoyt, W. (1976a). Disorders in cerebellar ocular motor control: 2. Macrosaccadic oscillation: An oculographic, control system and clinico-anatomical analysis. *Brain, 99,* 509–522.

Shagass, C., & Schwartz, M. (1961). Evoked cortical potentials and sensation in man. *Journal of Neuropsychiatry, 2,* 267–270.

Shallice, T. (1972). Dual functions of consciousness. *Psychological Review, 79,* 383–393.

Shallice, T. (1978). The dominant action system: An information-processing approach to consciousness. In K. Pope & J. E. Singer (Eds.), *The flow of conscious experience*. New York: Plenum Publishing.

Shannon, C., & Weaver, W. (1949). *The mathematical theory of communication*. Urbana: University of Illinois Press.

Shepherd, G. M. (1974). *The synaptic organization of the brain*. New York: Oxford University Press.

Shepherd, G. M. (1979). Functional analysis of local circuits in the olfactory bulb. In F. O. Schmitt & F. G. Worden (Eds.), *The neurosciences: Fourth study program*. Cambridge, MA: MIT Press.

Shepherd, G. M. (1983). *Neurobiology*. New York: Oxford University Press.

Sherrington, C. S. (1906). *The integrative action of the nervous system*. New Haven, CT: Yale University Press.

Shirokawa, T., & Kasamatsu, T. (1984). Beta-adrenergic receptor mediates neuronal plasticity in visual cortex. *Investigative Ophthalmology and Visual Science, 25* (Suppl.), 214.

Siegel, J. M., & McGinty, D. J. (1977). Pontine reticular formation neurons: Relationship of discharge to motor activity. *Science, 196,* 678–680.

Simpson, B. A., & Iversen, S. D. (1971). Effects of substantia nigra lesions on the locomotor and stereotyped responses to amphetamine. *Nature, 230,* 30–32.

Simpson, J., Epstein, A., & Camardo, J. (1978). The localization of dipsogenic receptors for angiotensin II in the subfornical organ. *Journal of Comparative and Physiological Psychology, 92,* 581–608.

Sinclair, D. C. (1967). *Cutaneous sensation*. London: Oxford University Press.

Singer, S. J., & Nicolson, G. L. (1972). The fluid mosaic model of the structure of cell membranes. *Science, 175,* 720–731.

Singer, W., & Creutzfeldt, O.-D. (1970). Reciprocal lateral inhibition of on- and off-center neurones in the lateral geniculate body of the cat. *Experimental Brain Research, 10,* 311–330.

Sitaram, N., Weingartner, H., & Gillin, J. (1978). Human serial learning: Enhancement with arecholine and choline and impairment with scopolamine. *Science, 201,* 274–276.

Skinner, B. F. (1957). *Verbal behavior*. New York: Appleton-Century-Crofts.

Slimp, J., Hart, B. L., & Goy, R. W. (1978). Heterosexual, autosexual and social behavior of adult male rhesus monkeys with medial preoptic-anterior hypothalamic lesions. *Brain Research, 142,* 105–122.

Smith, C. A., & Rasmussen, G. (1963). Recent observations on the olivo-cochlear bundle. *Annals of Otology, Rhinology, & Laryngology, 72,* 489–507.

Smith, C. C., O'Neill, J., Zipser, B., Shreeve, S., Fraser, C., Venter, J., Weber, J., & Pert, C. (1985). Isolation, purification, and characterization of rat brain opiate receptors. *Neuroscience Abstracts, 11,* 583.

Smith, G. P., Jerome, C., Cuslien, B., Eterno, R., & Simansky, K. (1981). Abdominal vagotomy blocks the satiety effect of cholecystokinin in the rat. *Science, 213,* 1036–1037.

Snyder, S. (1977, March). Opiate receptors and internal opiates. *Scientific American,* pp. 44–56.

Sokolov, E. N. (1960). Neuronal models and the orienting reflex. In M. A. B. Brazier (Ed.), *The central nervous system and behavior*. New York: Josiah Macy, Jr., Foundation.

Sparks, D., & Pollack, J. (1977). The neural control of saccadic eye movements: The role of the superior colliculus. In B. A. Brooks & F. Bajandas (Eds.), *Eye movements*. New York: Plenum Publishing.

Spear, P., Langsetmo, A., & Smith, D. C. (1980). Age-related changes in effects of monocular deprivation on cat striate cortex neurons. *Journal of Neurophysiology, 43,* 559–580.

Spear, P., & Tong, L. (1980). Effects of monocular deprivation on neurons in cat's lateral suprasylvian visual area: 1. Comparison of binocular and monocular segments. *Journal of Neurophysiology, 44,* 568–584.

Sperry, R. (1974). Lateral specialization in the surgically separated hemispheres. In F. O. Schmitt & F. G. Worden (Eds.), *The neurosciences: Third study program*. Cambridge, MA: MIT Press.

Sperry, R., Gazzaniga, M., & Bogen, J. (1969). Interhemispheric relationships: The neocortical commisures—Syndromes of hemisphere disconnection. In P. Vinken & G. Bruyn (Eds.), *Handbook of clinical neurology* (Vol. 4). Amsterdam: North-Holland.

Sperry, R., Stamm, J., & Miner, N. (1956). Relearning tests for interocular transfer following division of optic chiasma and corpus callosum in cats. *Journal of Comparative and Physiological Psychology, 49,* 529–533.

Spinelli, D. N., Bridgeman, B., & Phelps, R. (1970). Inhibitory interactions of principal cells in the lateral geniculate body of the cat. *Federation of Societies for Experimental Biology Proceedings, 29,* 3347.

Spinelli, D. N., Hirsch, H. V. B., Phelps, R., & Metzler, J. (1972). Visual experience as a determinant of the response characteristics of cortical receptive fields in cats. *Experimental Brain Research, 15,* 289–304.

Spinelli, D. N., & Jensen, F. (1979). Plasticity: The mirror of experience. *Science, 203,* 75–78.

Spinelli, D. N., Jensen, F., & DiPrisco, G. (1979). Early experience effect on dendritic branching in normally reared kittens. *Experimental Neurology, 62,* 1–11.

Spinelli, D. N., Jensen, F., & Standish, L. (1979). Induced plasticity in visual cortex of adult cats. *Neuroscience Abstracts, 5,* 684.

Spinelli, D. N., & Pribram, K. H. (1966). Changes in visual recovery functions produced by temporal lobe stimulation in monkeys. *Electroencephalography and Clinical Neurophysiology, 20,* 44–49.

Spinelli, D. N., & Pribram, K. H. (1967). Changes in visual recovery function and unit activity produced by frontal and temporal cortex stimulation. *Electroencephalography and Clinical Neurophysiology, 22,* 143–149.

Spinelli, D. N., Pribram, K. H., & Bridgeman, B. (1970). Visual receptive field organization of single units in the visual cortex of monkey. *International Journal of Neurosciences, 1,* 67–74.

Spinelli, D. N., Pribram, K. H., & Weingarten, M. (1965). Centrifugal optic nerve responses evoked by auditory and somatic stimulation. *Experimental Neurology, 12,* 303–319.

Spinelli, D. N., Starr, A., & Barrett, T. (1968). Auditory specificity in unit recordings from cat's visual cortex. *Experimental Neurology, 22,* 75–84.

Spinelli, D. N., & Weingarten, M. (1966). Afferent and efferent activity in single units of the cat's optic nerve. *Experimental Neurology, 13,* 347–361.

Spoendlin, H. (1972). Innervation densities of the cochlea. *Acta Oto-laryngologica* (Stockholm), *73,* 235–248.

Squire, L. (1982). The neuropsychology of human memory. *Annual Review of Neuroscience, 5,* 241–273.

Squire, L. (1986). Mechanisms of memory. *Science, 232,* 1612–1619.

Squire, L., Amaral, D., Zola-Morgan, S., Kritchevsky, M., & Press, G. (1987). New evidence of brain injury in the amnesic patient N. A. based on magnetic resonance imaging. *Society for Neuroscience Abstracts* in press.

Squire, L., & Moore, R. (1979). Dorsal thalamic lesion in a noted case of chronic memory dysfunction. *Annals of Neurology, 6,* 503–506.

Stamm, J., & Rosen, S. (1975). Dissociations within prefrontal cortex between intratrial cue-directional and mnemonic processes in delayed response. In S. Kondo, M. Kawai, A. Ehara, & S. Kawamura (Eds.), *Symposia of the Fifth Congress of the International Primatological Society.* Tokyo: Japan Science Press.

Stanley, S. M. (1981). *The new evolutionary timetable.* New York: Basic Books.

Stark, L. W. (1968). *Neurôlogical control systems.* New York: Plenum Publishing.

Stark, L. W., & Ellis, S. (1981). Scanpaths revisited: Cognitive models direct active looking. In D. Fisher, R. Monty, & J. Senders (Eds.), *Eye movements: Cognition and visual perception.* Hillsdale, NJ: Lawrence Erlbaum.

Stein, L. (1964). Self-stimulation of the brain and the central stimulant action of amphetamine. *Federation of Societies for Experimental Biology Proceedings, 23,* 836–850.

Stein, L. (1968). Chemistry of reward and punishment. In D. Efron (Ed.), *Psychopharmacology: A review of progress.* Washington, DC: Government Printing Office.

Stein, L., & Ray, O. (1960). Brain stimulation reward "thresholds" self-determined in the rat. *Psychopharmacologia, 1,* 251–256.

Stein, L., & Wise, C. D. (1971). Possible etiology of schizophrenia: Progressive damage to the noradrenergic reward system by 6-hydroxydopamine. *Science, 171,* 1032–1036.

Steinhausen, W. (1931). Über den experimentellen Nachweis der Ablenkung der Cupula terminalis in der intakten Bogengangsampulle des Labyrinths bei der thermischen and adaquäten rotatorischen Reizung. *Zeitschrift für Hals-, Nasen- und Orhenheilkunde, 29,* 211–216.

Sterman, M., & Clemente, C. (1962). Forebrain inhibitory mechanisms: Sleep patterns induced by basal forebrain stimulation in the behaving cat. *Experimental Neurology, 6,* 103–117.

Stevens, C. F. (1966). *Neurophysiology: A primer.* New York: Wiley.

Stevens, C. F. (1979). The neuron. In *The brain* (a Scientific American book). San Francisco: Freeman.

Stevens, J. K., Emerson, R., Gerstein, G., Kallos, T., Neufeld, G., Nichols, C., & Rosenquist, A. (1976). Paralysis of the awake human: Visual perceptions. *Vision Research, 16,* 93–98.

Stone, J., & Hoffman, K.-P. (1972). Very slow-conducting ganglion cells in the cat's retina: A major, new functional type? *Brain Research, 43,* 610–616.

Stratton, G. (1917). *Theophrastus and the Greek physiological psychology before Aristotle.* London: George Allen & Unwin.

Straus, E., & Yalow, R. (1979). Cholecystokinin in the brains of obese and nonobese mice. *Science, 203,* 68–69.

Stricker, E. (1977). The renin-angiotensin system and thirst: A re-evaluation: 2. Drinking elicited in rats by cavalligation or isoproterenol. *Journal of Comparative and Physiological Psychology, 91,* 1220–1231.

Stricker, E. (1978). The renin-angiotensin system and thirst: Some unanswered questions. *Federation of Societies for Experimental Biology Proceedings, 37,* 2704–2710.

Stryer, L. (1986). Cyclic GMP cascade of vision. *Annual Review of Neuroscience, 9,* 87–119.

Stryer, L. (1987, July). The molecules of visual excitation. *Scientific American,* pp. 42–50.

Stryker, M., & Sherk, H. (1975). Modification of cortical orientation of selectivity in the cat by restricted visual experience: A reexamination. *Science, 190,* 904–906.

Stryker, M., Sherk, H., Leventhal, A., & Hirsch, H. V. B. (1978). Physiological consequences for the cat's visual cortex of effectively restricting early visual experience with oriented contours. *Journal of Neurophysiology, 41,* 896–909.

Sturdevant, R., & Goetz, H. (1976). Cholecystokinin both stimulates and inhibits human food intake. *Nature, 261,* 713–715.

Sturup, G. (1961). Correctional treatment and the criminal sexual offender. *Canadian Journal of Correction, 3,* 250–265.

Swaab, D., & Fliers, E. (1985). A sexually dimorphic nucleus in the human brain. *Science, 228,* 1112–1115.

Swanson, L. W., Kucharczyk, J., & Mogenson, G. (1978). Autoradiographic evidence for pathways from the medial preoptic area to the midbrain involved in the drinking response to angiotensin II. *Journal of Comparative Neurology, 178,* 645–660.

Szentagothai, J., Hamori, J., & Tömböl, T. (1966). Degeneration and electron microscope analysis of the synaptic glomeruli in the lateral geniculate body. *Experimental Brain Research, 2,* 283–301.

Talbot, W. H., Darlan-Smith, I., Kornhuber, H. H., & Mountcastle, V. B. (1968). The sense of flutter-vibration: Comparison of the human capacity with response patterns of mechanoreceptive afferents from the monkey hand. *Journal of Neurophysiology, 31,* 301–334.

Tani, K., & Yoshii, N. (1970). Efficiency of verbal learning during sleep as related to EEG pattern. *Brain Research, 17,* 277–283.

Tasaki, I. (1953). *Nervous transmission.* Springfield, IL: Charles C Thomas.

Taub, E., & Berman, A. J. (1968). Movement and learning in the absence of sensory feedback. In S. J. Freedman (Ed.), *The neuropsychology of spatially oriented behavior.* Homewood, IL: Dorsey Press.

Taub, J. M., & Berger, R. J. (1969). Extended sleep and performance: The Rip Van Winkle effect. *Psychonomic Science, 16,* 204–205.

Teitelbaum, P., & Stellar, E. (1954). Recovery from failure to eat produced by hypothalamic lesions. *Science, 120,* 894–895.

Terenius, L. (1982). Endorphins, perception, and schizophrenia. In G. Hemmings (Ed.), *Biological aspects of schizophrenia and addiction.* New York: Wiley.

Terenius, L., & Walström, A., (1975). Morphine-like ligand for opiate receptors in human CSF. *Life Sciences, 16,* 1759–1764.

Terenius, L., Wahlström, A., Lindström, L., & Widerlöv, E. (1976). Increased CSF levels of endorphins in chronic psychosis. *Neuroscience Letters, 3,* 157–162.

Terrace, H. (1979). *Nim.* New York: Knopf.

Teuber, H. L. (1964). The riddle of frontal lobe function in man. In J. M. Warren & K. Akert (Eds.), *The frontal granular cortex and behavior.* New York: McGraw-Hill.

Teuber, H. L. (1972). Unity and diversity of frontal lobe functions. *Acta Neurobiologica Experimentia, 32,* 615–656.

Thatcher, R. W., Walter, R. A., & Giudice, S. (1987). Human cerebral hemispheres develop at different rates and ages. *Science, 236,* 1110–1113.

Thompson, C. I. (1980). *Controls of eating.* Jamaica, NY: Spectrum.

Thompson, R. F. (1986). The neurobiology of learning and memory. *Science, 233,* 941–947.

Thorell, L., DeValois, R., & Albrecht, D. (1984). Spatial mapping of monkey V1 cells with pure color and luminance stimuli. *Vision Research, 24,* 751–769.

Tombaugh, T. (1982). A discriminating case against anhedonia. *Behavioral and Brain Sciences, 5,* 77–78.

Tong, L., & Spear, P. (1980). Effects of monocular deprivation on neurons in cat's lateral suprasylvian visual area: 2. Role of visual cortex and thalamus in the abnormalities. *Journal of Neurophysiology, 44,* 585–604.

Tootell, R., Silverman, M. S., & DeValois, R. (1981). Spatial frequency columns in primary visual cortex. *Science, 214,* 813–815.

Tootell, R., Silverman, M. S., Switkes, E., & DeValois, R. (1982). Deoxyglucose analysis of retinotopic organization in primate striate cortex. *Science, 218,* 902–904.

Torres, F. (1980). Epilepsy—Electroclinical correlations as a function of age. In C. E. Henry (Ed.), *Current clinical neurophysiology.* New York: Elsevier/North-Holland.

Tranel, D., & Damasio, A. (1985). Knowledge without awareness: An autonomic index of facial recognition by prosopagnosics. *Science, 228,* 1453–1454.

Trevarthen, C. (1968). Two mechanisms of vision in primates. *Psychologische Forschung, 31,* 299–337.

Trivers, R. (1983). The evolution of cooperation. In D. L. Bridgeman (Ed.), *The nature of prosocial development.* New York: Academic Press.

Truex, R. C., & Carpenter, M. B. (1964). *Strong and Elwyn's human neuroanatomy* (5th ed.). Baltimore: Williams & Wilkins.

Tunturi, A. (1952). A difference in the representation of auditory signals for the left and right ears in the isofrequency contours of right middle ectosylvian auditory cortex in the dog. *American Journal of Physiology, 168,* 712–727.

Turing, A. (1936). On computable numbers with an application to the Entscheidungsproblem. *Proceedings of the London Mathematical Society, 42,* 230–235.

Turing, A. (1937). On computable numbers with an application to the Entscheidungsproblem. *Proceedings of the London Mathematical Society, 43,* 544–546.

Turing, A. (1950). Computing machinery and intelligence. *Mind, 59,* 433–460.

Turkel, J., Gijsders, K., & Pritchard, R. (1975). Environmental modification of oculomotor and neural function in cats. *Investigative Ophthalmology & Visual Science, 14,* (Suppl.), 63.

Uttal, W. R. (1973). *The psychobiology of sensory coding.* New York: Harper & Row.

Uttal, W. R. (1975). *An autocorrelation theory of form detection.* Hillsdale, NJ: Lawrence Erlbaum.

Valbo, A. B. (1971). Muscle spindle response at the onset of isometric voluntary contractions in man: Time differences between fusimotor and skeletomotor effects. *Journal of Physiology, 218,* 405–431.

Valenstein, E. S. (1973). *Brain control.* New York: Wiley.

Valenstein, E. S., & Valenstein, T. (1964). Interaction of positive and negative reinforcing neural systems. *Science, 145,* 1456–1458.

Van Essen, D. C. (1979). Visual areas of the mammalian cerebral cortex. *Annual Review of Neuroscience, 2,* 227–263.

Van Essen, D. C., Newsome, W. T., & Bixby, J. L. (1982). The pattern of interhemispheric connections and its relationship to extrastriate visual areas in the macaque monkey. *Journal of Neuroscience, 2,* 265–283.

Van Zoeren, J., & Stricker, E. (1977). Effects of preoptic, lateral hypothalamic, or dopamine-depleting lesions on behavioral thermoregulation in rats exposed to the cold. *Journal of Comparative and Physiological Psychology, 91,* 989–999.

Villablanca, J. (1965). The electrocorticogram in the chronic cerveau isolé cat. *Electroencephalography and Clinical Neurophysiology, 19,* 576–586.

Volcer, L., & Loew, C. (1971). Penetration of angiotensin II into the brain. *Neuropharmacology, 10,* 631–636.

Volman, F., Riggs, L., White, K., & Moore, R. (1978). Contrast sensitivity during saccadic eye movements. *Vision Research, 18,* 1193–1199.

Wada, J., & Rasmussen, T. (1960). Intracarotid injection of sodium amytal for the lateralization of cerebral speech dominance: Experimental and clinical observations. *Journal of Neurosurgery, 17,* 266–282.

Waddington, C. H. (1960). Genetic assimilation. In E. W. Caspari & J. W. Thoday (Eds.), *Advances in genetics.* New York: Academic Press.

Waddington, C. H. (1968). The theory of evolution today. In A. Koestler & J. R. Smythies (Eds.), *Beyond reductionism.* New York: Macmillan.

Wagman, I., & Mehler, W. (1972). Physiology and anatomy of the cortico-oculomotor mechanism. *Progress in Brain Research, 37,* 619–635.

Wagner, G., Beauving, L., & Hutchinson, R. (1980). The effects of gonadal hormone manipulations on aggressive target-biting in mice. *Aggressive Behavior, 6,* 1–7.

Wahl, O. (1976). Monozygotic twins discordant for schizophrenia: A review. *Psychological Bulletin, 83,* 91–106.

Wald, G. (1967). Blue-blindness in the normal fovea. *Journal of the Optical Society of America, 57,* 1289–1303.

Wald, G. (1968). The molecular basis of visual excitation. *Science, 162,* 230–239.

Walker, J. M., & Berger, R. (1980). The ontogenesis of sleep states, thermogenesis and thermoregulation in the Virginia opposum. *Developmental Psychobiology, 13,* 443–454.

Walker, J. M., Glotzbach, S., Berger, R., & Heller, H. C. (1977). Sleep and hibernation in ground squirrels (*Citellus spp.*): Electrophysiological observations. *American Journal of Physiology, 233,* R213–R221.

Walker, L. E., Walker, J. M., Palca, J. W., & Berger, R. J. (1983). A continuum of sleep and shallow torpor in fasting doves. *Science, 221,* 194–195.

Walker, W. A., & Leshner, A. (1972). The role of the adrenals in aggression. *American Zoologist, 12,* 652.

Wall, P. D. (1961). Two transmission systems for skin sensations. In W. A. Rosenblith (Ed.), *Sensory communication,* Cambridge, MA: MIT Press.

Wall, P. D., & Pribram, K. H. (1961). Trigeminal neurotomy and blood pressure responses from stimulation of lateral cortex of Macaca Mulatta. *Journal of Neurophysiology, 13,* 409–412.

Walter, W. G. (1964). Slow potential waves in the human brain associated with expectancy, attention and decision. *Archiv für Psychiatrie und Nervenkrankheiten, 206,* 309–322.

Waltz, D. (1982, October). Artificial Intelligence. *Scientific American,* pp. 118–133.

Ward, I. (1972). Prenatal stress feminizes and demasculinizes the behavior of males. *Science, 175,* 82–84.

Warren, J. M. (1964). The behavior of carnivores and primates with lesions in the prefrontal cortex. In J. M. Warren & K. Ackert (Eds.), *The frontal cortex and behavior.* New York: McGraw-Hill.

Warrington, E., & Weiskrantz, L. (1974). The effect of prior learning on subsequent retention in amnesic patients. *Neuropsychologia, 12,* 419–428.

Watanabe, T., & Katsuki, Y. (1974). Response patterns of

single auditory neurons of the cat to species-specific vocalization. *Japanese Journal of Physiology, 24,* 135–155.

Watson, J. B. (1920). *Psychology from the standpoint of a behaviorist.* Philadelphia: Lippincott.

Watson, R. T., Miller, B. D., & Heilman, K. (1978). Nonsensory neglect. *Annals of Neurology, 3,* 505–508.

Waxman, S., & Ritchie, J. (1985). Organization of ion channels in the myelinated nerve fiber. *Science, 228,* 1502–1507.

Webb, W. B., & Agnew, H. (1975). Sleep efficiency for sleep-wake cycles of varied length. *Psychophysiology, 12,* 637–641.

Weber, A., & Murray, J. (1973). Molecular control mechanisms in muscle contraction. *Physiologial Reviews, 53,* 612–673.

Webster, W., & Aitkin, L. (1975). Central auditory processing. In M. Gazzaniga & C. Blakemore (Eds.), *Handbook of psychobiology.* New York: Academic Press.

Weisberg, L. A., Strub, R., & Garcia, C. A. (1983). *Essentials of clinical neurology.* Baltimore: University Park Press.

Weiskrantz, L., Warrington, E., Sanders, M., & Marshall, J. (1974). Visual capacity in the hemianopic field following a restricted occipital ablation. *Brain, 97,* 709–728.

Weisz, K., Solomin, P. R., & Thompson, R. F. (1980). The hippocampus appears necessary for trace conditioning. *Bulletin of the Psychonomic Society, 16,* 164.

Weitzenbaum, N. (1976). *Computer power and human reason: From judgment to calculation.* San Francisco: Freeman.

Weitzman, E., Czeisler, C., Coleman, R., Spielman, A., Zimmerman, J., & Dement, W. (1981). Delayed sleep phase syndrome. *Archives of General Psychiatry, 38,* 737–746.

Welt, C., Aschoff, J., Kameda, K., & Brooks, V. B. (1967). Intracortical organization of cat's motorsensory neurons. In M. Yahr & D. Purpura (Eds.), *Neurophysiological basis of normal and abnormal motor activities.* Hewlett, NY: Raven Press.

Wenger, M., Bagchi, B., & Anand, B. (1961). Experiments in India on "voluntary" control of the heart and pulse. *Circulation, 24,* 1319–1325.

Werblin, F. S. (1979). Integrative pathways in local circuits between slow-potential cells in the retina. In F. O. Schmitt & F. G. Worden (Eds.), *The neurosciences: Fourth study program,* Cambridge, MA: MIT Press.

Westheimer, G. (1982). The spatial grain of the perifoveal visual field. *Vision Research, 22,* 157–162.

Westlake, P. (1970). The possibilities of neural holographic processes within the brain. *Kybernetik, 7,* 129–153.

Wetterberg, L. (1982). The genetic control of catecholamines and its possible implication in schizophrenia. In G. Hemmings (Ed.), *Biological aspects of schizophrenia and addiction.* New York: Wiley.

Wever, E. G. (1949). *Theory of hearing.* New York: Wiley.

Wever, E. G. (1974). The evolution of vertebrate hearing. In W. E. Keidel & W. D. Neff (Eds.), *Handbook of sensory physiology: Vol. 1. Auditory system.* Berlin: Springer-Verlag.

Wever, E. G., & Bray, C. W. (1930). Action currents in the auditory nerve in response to acoustical stimulation. *Proceedings: National Academy of Sciences, 16,* 344–350.

Whipple, B., & Komisaruk, B. (1985). Regional specificity of vaginal stimulation sites producing analgesia in women. *Neuroscience Abstracts, 11,* 123.

Whitfield, I., & Evans, E. (1965). Responses of auditory cortical neurons to stimuli of changing frequency. *Journal of Neurophysiology, 28,* 655–672.

Wiesel, T., & Hubel, D. (1965). Extent of recovery from the effects of visual deprivation in kittens. *Journal of Neurophysiology, 28,* 1060–1072.

Willshaw, D., Buneman, O., & Longuet-Higgins, H. (1969). Non-holographic associative memory. *Nature, 222,* 960–962.

Wilson, D. S. (1980). *The selection of populations and communities.* Menlo Park, CA: Benjamin Cummings.

Wilson, E. O. (1975). *Sociobiology: The new synthesis.* Cambridge, MA: Harvard University Press, Belknap Press.

Winkelmann, R. K. (1960). Similarities in cutaneous nerve end-organs. In W. Montagna (Ed.), *Advances in Biology of Skin: Vol. 1. Cutaneous innervation.* New York: Pergamon Press.

Winterson, B., & Collewijn, H. (1976). Microsaccades during finely guided visuomotor tasks. *Vision Research, 16,* 1387–1390.

Wise, R. A. (1982). Neuroleptics and operant behavior: The anhedonia hypothesis. *Behavioral and Brain Sciences, 5,* 39–87.

Wolstencroft, J. (1964). Reticulospinal neurones. *Journal of Physiology, 174,* 91–99.

Woods, S., Vasselli, J., Kaestner, E., Szakmary, G., Milburn, P., & Vitello, M. (1977). Conditioned insulin secretion and meal feeding in rats. *Journal of Comparative and Physiological Psychology, 91,* 128–133.

Wright, J., & Harding, J. (1982). Recovery of olfactory function after bilateral bulbectomy. *Science, 216,* 322–324.

Wundt, W. (1910). *Principles of physiological psychology.* London: Swan Sonnenschein.

Wurtman, J. J., Wurtman, R., Growdon, J., Henry, P., Lipscomb, A., & Zeisel, S. (1982). Carbohydrate craving in obese people: Suppression by treatments affecting serotonergic transmission. *International Journal of Eating Disorders, 1,* 2–15.

Wurtman, R. (1982, April). Nutrients that modify brain function. *Scientific American,* pp. 50–59.

Wurtz, R. H., & Mohler, C. W. (1976a). Enhancement of visual responses in monkey striate cortex and frontal eye fields. *Journal of Neurophysiology, 39,* 766–772.

Wurtz, R. H., & Mohler, C. W. (1976b). Organization of monkey superior colliculus: Enhanced visual response of superficial layer cells. *Journal of Neurophysiology, 39,* 745–765.

Yalon, I., Green, R., & Fisk, F. (1973). Prenatal exposure to female hormones: Effect on psychosexual development in boys. *Archives of General Psychiatry, 28,* 554–561.

Yamamoto, Y., Thompson, C., Meyer, E., & Feindel, W. (1981). Positron emission tomography for measurement of regional cerebral blood flow. In A. L. Carney & E. M. Anderson (Eds.), *Advances in neurology* (Vol. 30). New York: Raven Press.

Yarbus, A. L. (1967). *Eye movements and vision* (L. A. Riggs, Trans.). New York: Plenum Publishing.

Yaryura-Tobias, J., Diamond, B., & Merlis, S. (1970). The action of L-DOPA on schizophrenic patients (a preliminary report). *Current Therapy Research, 12,* 528–531.

Young, L. R., Oman, C., Watt, D., Money, K., & Lichtenberg, B. (1984). Spatial orientation in weightlessness and readaptation to earth's gravity. *Science, 225,* 205–208.

Young, R. W. (1967). The renewal of photoreceptor cell outer segments. *Journal of Cell Biology, 33,* 61–72.

Young, R. W. (1969). A difference between rods and cones in the renewal of outer segment protein. *Investigative Ophthalmology, 8,* 222–231.

Younger, J., Adriance, W., & Berger, R. (1975). Sleep during transcendental meditation. *Perceptual and Motor Skills, 40,* 953–954.

Zaidel, A. (1983). A response to Gazzaniga: Language in the right hemisphere, convergent perspectives. *American Psychologist, 38,* 542–546.

Zarbin, M., Innis, J., Wamsley, S., Snyder, S., & Kuhar, M. (1983). Autoradiographic localization of cholecystokinin receptors in rodent brain. *Journal of Neuroscience, 3,* 877–906.

Zeaman, D., & House, B. J. (1963). The role of attention in retardate discrimination learning. In N. R. Ellis (Ed.), *Handbook of mental deficiency.* New York: McGraw-Hill.

Zernicki, B. (1972). Orienting response hypernormality in frontal cats. *Acta Neurobiologica Experimentia, 32,* 431–438.

Zettler, F., & Weiler, R. (1981). Propogation of non-spike signals in retinal neurons. *Vision Research, 21,* 1589–1590.

Zihl, J. (1982). "Blindsight": Improvement of visually guided eye movements by systematic practice in patients with cerebral blindness. *Neuropsychologia, 18,* 71–77.

Zola-Morgan, S., Squire, L., & Mishkin, M. (1982). The neuroanatomy of amnesia: Amygdala-hippocampus versus temporay stem. *Science, 218,* 1337–1339.

ILLUSTRATION CREDITS

(The brief citations are fully cited in the References section of the book.)

Figure 2.9 Adapted from Shepherd (1974), fig. 14.

Figure 2.10 Adapted from Shepherd (1974), fig. 6.

Figure 2.11 Adapted from Makowski et al., *The Journal of Cell Biology,* 1977, *74,* 629–645, by copyright permission of The Rockefeller University Press.

Figure 2.15 Adapted from Shepherd (1983), fig. 5.9.

Figure 2.17 Adapted from Noble, *Physiological Review, 46,* 1, 1966.

Figure 2.19 Adapted from Hodgkin & Huxley (1952).

Figure 2.21 Adapted from Schmidt, R. F., *Fundamentals of Neurophysiology,* 2nd edition, p. 100, 1978. Heidelberg: Springer-Verlag.

Figure 3.8 Adapted from Truex & Carpenter (1964), the Williams & Wilkins Co., Baltimore.

Figure 3.16 Adapted from Braitenberg (1977).

Figure 3.19 Adapted from Rakic, P. (1981), *Neurosciences Research Program Bulletin, 20,* p. 435. Cambridge, MA: MIT Press.

Figure 3.21 Adapted from Pribram (1971), *Languages of the Brain,* fig. 15–12.

Figure 4.3 Adapted from Loewenstein & Mendelson (1965).

Figure 4.10 Adapted from Cotman, C., & McGaugh, J. (1980), *Behavioral Neuroscience,* p. 407. Orlando: Academic Press.

Figure 4.13 Adapted from Wald. Copyright 1968 The Nobel Foundation.

Figure 4.29 Adapted from J. Rose, J. Brugge, D. J. Anderson, & J. Hind (1967), Phase-locked response to low-frequency tones in single auditory nerve fibers of the squirrel monkey. *Journal of Neurophysiology, 30,* fig. 1, p. 772. Bethesda, Md.: The American Physiological Society.

Figure 5.4 By permission of Prof. F. Ratliff.

Figure 5.7*a* Adapted from Poggio & Mountcastle (1960).

Figure 5.7*b* Adapted from Talbot et al. (1968).

Figure 5.10 Adapted from Mountcastle & Powell (1959).

Figure 5.11 Adapted from Mountcastle (1967).

Figure 5.12 Adapted from Shepherd (1974), fig. 26.

Figure 5.22 Adapted from Werblin (1979).

Figure 5.23 Adapted from Werblin (1979).

Figure 5.30 Adapted from Blakemore & Campbell (1969), The Physiological Society.

Figure 5.31 Adapted from Blakemore & Sutton. Copyright 1969 by the AAAS.

Figure 5.32 Adapted from DeValois et al. (1982), fig. 2, Pergamon Press Ltd.

Figure 5.33 Adapted from DeValois (1982), fig. 9, Pergamon Press, Inc.

Figure 5.39 Adapted from DeValois & DeValois (1975), fig. 4, Orlando: Academic Press.

Figure 5.40 Adapted from U. Dortmann & L. Spillman, Facilitation and inhibition in the jerk effect depend upon test flash duration and delay. *Vision Research, 21.* Copyright 1981, Pergamon Press Ltd.

Figure 5.42 Adapted from Truex & Carpenter (1964), fig. 16–9, Williams & Wilkins.

Figure 5.43 Adapted from Katsuki (1961), p. 566, MIT Press.

Figure 6.2 Adapted from Bridgeman, Hendry, & Stark (1975), fig. 1, Pergamon Press Ltd.

Figure 6.3 Adapted from Cohen & Komatsuzaki (1972), fig. 1, Academic Press.

Figure 6.4 Adapted from Bahill et al. (1976), fig. 7, Williams & Wilkins.

Figure 6.5 Adapted from D. A. Robinson (1981), fig. 10, The American Physiological Society.

Figure 6.9 Adapted from Gibson, p. 161. Copyright 1966 by Houghton Mifflin Company. Used by permission.

Figure 6.11 Adapted from Hubel & Wiesel (1965), The American Physiological Society.

Figure 6.13 Adapted from Hubel & Wiesel (1965), The American Physiological Society.

Figure 7.4 Adapted from Daube (1986), fig. 12–18, Little, Brown and Company.

Figure 7.11 Adapted from Barker (1948), The Company of Biologists Ltd.

Figure 7.13 Adapted from Granit (1955), fig. 91, Yale University Press.

Figure 7.14*a* Adapted from Pribram (1971), fig. 5–2.

Figure 7.15 Adapted from Pribram (1971), fig. 5–6.

Figure 7.20 Adapted from J. F. Fulton, *Textbook of Physiology,* 17th ed. (1955). Philadelphia: W. B. Saunders.

Figure 7.22 Adapted from Kohlerman, Gibson, & Houk, fig. 1, Copyright 1982 by the AAAS.

Figure 7.24 Adapted from Cohen, J. (1969), Very slow brain potentials relating to expectancy: The CNV. In *Average Evoked Potentials.* Washington, DC: NASA, fig. 4–26.

Figure 7.25 Adapted from Evarts (1968), fig. 1, The American Physiological Society.

Figure 7.27 Adapted from Evarts (1968), fig. 7, The American Physiological Society.

Figure 7.30 Adapted from Pribram (1971), fig. 12–9.

Figure 8.3 Adapted from Satinoff, fig. 2. Copyright 1978 by the AAAS. Very slow brain potentials relating to expectancy: The CNV.

Figure 8.11 and 8.12 Adapted from Hoebel, B., and Teitelbaum, P. (1966), Weight regulation in normal and hypothalamic hyperphagic rats. *Journal of Comparative and Physiological Psychology, 61,* 189–193, fig. 3, American Psychological Association.

Figure 8.15 Adapted from Paul et al., fig. 2, Copyright 1982 by the AAAS.

Figure 9.2 Adapted from Sheer (1961), *Electrical Stimulation of the Brain,* fig. 24.2. Austin: University of Texas Press.

Figure 9.6 Adapted from Wagner et al. (1980), fig. 1. Alan R. Liss, Inc.

Figure 9.11 From Gorski (1978).

Figure 9.12 From DeLacoste-Utamsing et al. Copyright 1982 by the AAAS.

Figure 10.1 Adapted from Aschoff, J. (1969), *Aerospace Medicine, 40,* p. 845. Washington, DC: Aerospace Medical Society.

Figure 10.10 Adapted from Herman & Roffwarg. Copyright 1983 by the AAAS.

Figure 10.16 Adapted from Brazier, M. (1960), *The Electrical Activity of the Nervous System,* 2nd ed., fig. 102. Reprinted with permission of Macmillan Publishing Company.

Figure 10.19 Adapted from Heilman (1985), figs. 10–1 and 10–6. New York: Oxford University Press.

Figure 10.21 Adapted from D. Smith et al. (1970), *Electroencephalography and Clinical Neurophysiology, 28,* fig. 3. Amsterdam: Elsevier Biomedical Press.

Figure 10.22 Adapted from Pribram (1971), figs. 11–7, 18–9, and 17–3, respectively.

Figure 11.2 Adapted from Lashley (1929), fig. 17, University of Chicago Press.

Figure 11.6 Adapted from Bartlett & John (1973). Copyright by the AAAS.

Figure 11.12 and 11.13 Adapted from Klein & Kandel (1980), fig. 5.

Figure 11.6 Adapted from Cotman, C., & McGaugh, J. (1980), *Behavioral Neuroscience,* fig. 5–27. New York: Raven Press.

Figure 11.17 Adapted from Chorover & Schiller (1965), p. 73. American Psychological Association.

Figure 11.22 Adapted from Flood et al. (1973), p. 555. ANKHO International Inc.

Figure 11.24 Adapted from Gold & van Buskirk (1975), p. 149.

Figure 11.25 Adapted from Bennett et al. (1979).

Figure 11.26 Adapted from Rosenzweig & Bennett (1978). Academic Press.

Figure 11.27 Adapted from Spinelli et al. Copyright 1979 by the AAAS.

Figure 11.29 Adapted from Milner. Copyright 1965 by D. Van Nostrand Company, Inc. Reprinted by permission of Wadsworth, Inc.

Figure 11.30 Adapted from Pribram et al. (1969), fig. 1. American Psychological Association.

Figure 11.31 Adapted from Zola-Morgan et al. Copyright 1982 by the AAAS.

Figure 11.32 Adapted from Squire & Moore (1979), p. 504. Little, Brown and Company.

Figure 11.33 Adapted from Berger & Thompson (1978), fig. 2. Amsterdam: Elsevier Science Publishers.

Figure 11.34 Adapted from Berger & Thompson (1978), fig. 6. Amsterdam: Elsevier Science Publishers.

Figure 11.37 Adapted from Gage et al. Copyright 1984 by the AAAS.

Figure 12.2 Adapted from Brown. Reprinted with permission of The Free Press, a Division of Macmillan Inc. Copyright 1965 by The Free Press.

Figure 12.4 Adapted from Liberman (1974), fig. 1. Cambridge, MA: MIT Press.

Figure 12.6 Adapted from Repp et al. Copyright 1978 by the American Psychological Association.

Figure 12.7 Adapted from Brown. Reprinted with permission of The Free Press, a Division of Macmillan Inc. Copyright 1965 by The Free Press.

Figure 12.10 Adapted from Roberts (1961), fig. 37.10, University of Texas Press.

Figure 12.14 Adapted from Ojemann & Mateer. Copyright 1979 by the AAAS.

Table 12.1 Adapted from Brown. Reprinted with permission of The Free Press, a Division of Macmillan Inc. Copyright 1965 by The Free Press.

Table 12.2 Adapted from Brown (1970). Reprinted with permission of The Free Press, a Division of Macmillan Inc. Copyright 1965 by The Free Press.

Table 12.3 Adapted from Brown (1973).

Tables 12.3–12.7 Adapted from Bickerton (1983).

Tables 12.8 and 12.9 Adapted from Kertesz. Copyright 1982 by Academic Press.

Figure 13.8 Adapted from *Computer Power and Human Reason* by J. Weizenbaum, W. H. Freeman and Company. Copyright 1966.

Figure 14.2 Adapted from Fuster (1980), fig. 1. Raven Press, New York.

Figure 14.3 Adapted from Akert. Copyright 1964 by McGraw-Hill Book Company.

Figure 14.5 Adapted from Pribram (1974), fig. 6. Cambridge, MA: MIT Press.

Figure 14.6 Adapted from Pribram (1971), fig. 9–12.

Figure 14.7 Adapted from Fuster (1973), fig. 3. The American Physiological Society.

Figure 14.9 Adapted from Pribram (1971), fig. 18–2.

Figure 14.11 Adapted from Rosenkilde. Copyright 1979 by Academic Press.

Figure 14.12 Adapted from Hillyard & Picton (1979), fig. 6. S. Karger AG, Basel.

Figure 14.13 Adapted from Hillyard & Picton (1979), fig. 16. S. Karger AG, Basel.

Figure 14.14 Adapted from Hillyard & Picton (1979), fig. 17. S. Karger AG, Basel.

Figure 14.15 Adapted from Grey Walter et al. (1964), fig. 1. Macmillan Publishing Company.

Figure 14.16 Adapted from Libet et al., fig. 2. Copyright 1967 by the AAAS.

Figure 14.17 Adapted from Libet (1964), fig. 7.2. New York: Springer-Verlag.

Figure 14.18 Adapted from Anderson et al. (1976), Pergamon Press Ltd.

Figure 14.19 Adapted from Hilgard et al. (1975). Courtesy of Department of Psychology, Stanford University.

Figure 16.2 Adapted from Lippold (1973), fig. 7.18. Churchill Livingstone, Edinburgh.

PHOTO CREDITS

Chapter 2 *Figs. 2.12–2.14:* Micrographs produced by Dr. John E. Heuser of Washington University School of Medicine, St. Louis, Missouri.

Chapter 3 *Fig. 3.1:* Courtesy Mary Carlson. *Fig. 3.3:* Courtesy Dr. Katherine V. Fite. *Fig. 3.4:* Courtesy Dr. Keith Porter, University of Maryland, Dept. of Biological Sciences. *Fig. 3.5:* Courtesy Edwin R. Lewis, University of California, Berkeley. *Fig. 3.11:* From *Introduction to Physiological Psychology,* by T. L. Bennet. © 1982 by Wadsworth, Inc. Reprinted by permission of Brooks/Cole Publishing Company, Monterey, California.

Chapter 4 *Fig. 4.1:* Courtesy Nikolajs Cauna, M.D., Professor Emeritus, University of Pittsburgh School of Medicine. *Fig. 4.7a:* Beidler, 1969. *Fig. 4.7b:* Courtesy Dr. Lee V. Leak, Howard University College of Medicine. *Fig. 4.11a:* Courtesy Peter Satir, Albert Einstein College of Medicine, New York. *Fig. 4.11b:* Courtesy Steven K. Fisher, University of California at Santa Barbara. *Fig. 4.12:* Courtesy Roy H. Steinberg, Dept. of Physiology, University of California at San Francisco. *Fig. 4.17:* From *Investigative Ophthamology and Visual Science* by D. Farber et al., 1985, Vol. 26, pgs. 1560–66. Reprinted with permission of Lippincott/Harper & Row. *Fig. 4.22:* Reprinted with permission of Alf Axelsson, M.D. from *Handbook of Sensory Physiology,* Springer-Verlag. *Fig. 4.24:* Courtesy Dr. Ivan Hunter-Duvar, Hospital for Sick Children, Toronto. *Fig. 4.26a and b:* Courtesy Dr. A. J. Hudspeth, Dept. of Physiology, University of California School of Medicine, with permission of The Williams & Wilkins Company.

Chapter 5 *Fig. 5.15:* © School of Optometry, University of California, Berkeley. *Fig. 5.16:* Courtesy Dr. John E. Dowling, Dept. of Cellular and Developmental Biology, Harvard University. Reprinted by permission of MIT Press. *Fig. 5.17:* Courtesy Peter Gouras and Wolf Krebs, Dept. of Ophthamology, College of Physicians and Surgeons, Columbia University. *Fig. 5.18:* Reprinted with permission from *Vision Research,* Vol. 17, pgs. 89–93, Gerald Westheimer and Richmond Products, Boca Raton, Florida. *Fig. 5.19: Mme. Isabella Lemannier-Seated,* Édouard Manet, 1877, oil on canvas, Philadelphia Museum of Art, bequest of Chalotte Dorrane Wright. *Fig. 5.20:* Courtesy Dr. John E. Dowling, Dept. of Cellular and Developmental Biology, Harvard University. Reprinted by permission of MIT Press. *Fig. 5.24 and 25:* Courtesy David Hubel, Harvard Medical School, Dept. of Neurobiology. *Fig. 5.34:* From *Sensory Experience Adaptation and Perception,* by Spillman and Wooten, © 1984 Lawrence Earlbaum Associates, Inc. Publishers. *Fig. 5.36:* From "Spatial Frequency Columns in Primary Visual Cortex," by Tootel and Silverman, Vol. 214, Fig. 1, pg. 813, *Science,* November 13, 1981 by permission. © 1981 by the AAAS. *Fig. 5.37:* Courtesy David Hubel, Harvard Medical School, Dept. of Neurobiology. *Fig. 5.38a and b:* From "Dexyglucose of Tetinotopic Organization in Primate Strate Cortex," by R. B. Tootell, et al., Vol. 218, Fig. 1, pgs. 900–902, *Science,* November 26, 1982 by permission. © 1982 by the AAAS. *Fig. 5.41:* From B. Julesz, "Toward an Axiomatic Theory of Preattentive Vision," *Dynamic Aspects of Neocortical Function,* Eds. G. L. Edelman, W. E. Gall, W. M. Cowan, pgs. 585–612, 1984. *Fig. 5.44:* Watanabe, Takeshi, Katsuki, and Yasuji, "Response Patterns of Single Auditory Neurons of the Cat to Specific Vocalization," *Japanese Journal of Physiology,* Vol. 24, pgs. 134–155, 1974. By permission of Center for Academic Publications.

Chapter 6 *Fig. 6.6:* From *Eye Movements: Cognition and Visual Perception,* by D. F. Fisher. Lawrence Earlbaum Associates, Inc. Publishers © 1981. *Fig. 6.7:* From Alfred L. Yarbus, *Eye Movements and Vision,* Plenum Publishing Co. *Fig. 6.10:* Courtesy Dr. Alan Hein, MIT. *Fig. 6.12a and b:* Reprinted from *Nature,* Vol. 278. © 1977 Macmillan Journals Limited. *Figs. 6.14 and 6.15:* Helmut V. B. Hirsch, D. N. Spinelli, Springer-Verlag (1971) *Experimental Brain Research.* Vol. 12. *Fig. 6.16:* Courtesy Colin Blakemore. From Schmitt and Worden, *The Neurosciences: 3rd Study Program.* Reprinted by permission of MIT Press.

Chapter 7 *Fig. 7.1a–c:* From J. Rhodin, *Histology,* Oxford University Press 1974. *Figs. 7.2 and 7.3:* From Hoyle, *Muscles and Their Neural Control,* John Wiley & Sons Publishers, 1983. *Fig. 7.14:* From Eccles and Sherrington, Proc. Roy. Soc. B. © 1930.

Chapter 8 *Fig. 8.1:* Bill Belknap/Rapho/Photo Researchers. *Fig. 8.8:* From Hutton, *Brain Research Bulletin,* 1976, Vol. 1, © 1976 Pergamon Journals Ltd.

Chapter 9 *Fig. 9.1:* Reprinted with permission of Elliot S. Valenstein. *Fig. 9.5:* S. Koch, *Interrelations of Psychology: A Study of Science,* McGraw Hill Book Company. *Fig. 9.10:* Courtesy Dr. John Money, The Johns Hopkins Hospital, Baltimore. *Fig. 9.11:* Courtesy Dr. Roger Gorski. From *Brain Research* no. 148. By permission of Elsevier Science Publications. *Fig. 9.15:* Courtesy University of Wisconsin Primate Laboratory, Madison. *Fig. 9.16:* Courtesy Dr. Harry F. Harlow, Regional Primate Research Center, Madison, Wisconsin. *Fig. 9.19:* "Opidid-Like Analgesia in Defeated Mouse," by Klaus A. Miczek, *Science,* Vol. 215, March 1982. © 1982 by the AAAS.

Chapter 10 *Fig. 10.2:* Courtesy Dr. Curt P. Richter, Professor Emeritus Psychobiology. *Johns Hopkins Medical Journal,* Vol. 141, Fig. 7, pg. 51, 1977. Reprinted by permission of the Johns Hopkins University Press. *Fig. 10.4:* "Free-Running Activity Rhythms in the Rat: Entrainment by Melatonin," Dr. Jenny Redman, et al., *Science,* March 4, 1983, Vol. 219, pgs. 1089–91. © 1983 by the AAAS. *Fig. 10.5:* Courtesy Drs. Schwartz and Gainer, Dept. of Neurology, University of Massachusetts. *Fig. 10.14:* From J. Magnus, G. Moruzzi, and O. Pompeiano, *Archives Italiennes de Biologie,* 1961, Vol. 99, pgs. 33–67. *Fig. 10.15:* Courtesy Dr. M. B. Sterman, Veterans Administration Medical Center. Sepulveda, California, by permission of Academic Press. *Fig. 10.17:* From "Chronotherapy: Resetting to Circadian Clocks," by Charles A. Czeisler et al., *Sleep,* 1981, Vol. 4, no. 1. *Fig. 10.18:* Courtesy of Josiah Macy Jr. Foundation. *Fig. 10.23:* Courtesy Dr. Karl Pribram, Stanford University, California.

Chapter 11 *Figs. 11.4 and 11.5:* From "Switchboard vs. Statistical Theories of Learning and Memory," by Dr. E. Roy John, *Science,* December 8, 1972, Vol. 177, pgs. 850–864. © 1972 by the AAAS. *Fig. 11.15:* From Holger Hyden University of Gotenberg/W. B. Saunders. *Fig. 11.28:* From D. N. Spinelli, F. E. Jensen, and G. V. DiPrisco *Experimental Neurology,* 1980, Vol. 62, pgs. 1–11. *Fig. 11.32:* L. R. Squire, D. G. Amaral, S. Zola-Morgan, M. Kritchevsky, and G. Press, Veterans Administration Hospital, San Diego, California. New evidence of brain injury in the amnesia patient N. A. based on magnetic resonance imaging. *Social Neuroscience Abstracts,* 1987, in press. *Fig. 11.36:* From "Intrahippocampal Septal Grafts Ameliorate Learning Impairments in Aged Rats," by Dr. Fred H. Gage et al. *Science,* August 3, 1984, Vol. 225, pgs. 533–36. © 1984 by the AAAS.

Chapter 12 *Fig. 12.3:* Courtesy Dr. Alvin M. Liberman, Haskins Laboratory at University of Connecticut. *Fig. 12.5:* From "On Finding that Speech Is Special," *American Psychologist,* Vol. 37, pgs. 148–67. © 1982 American Psychological Association. Reprinted by permission of Alvin Liberman. *Figs. 12.11 and 12.13:* From Michael Arbib, *Neural Models of Language Processing,* 1982, Academic Press. Reprinted by permission from Dr. Andrew Kertesz, "Two Case Studies: Broca's and Wernicke's Aphasia."

Chapter 13 *Fig. 13.1:* Bruce Bridgeman.

Chapter 14 *Fig. 14.4:* From *The New England Journal of Medicine,* Vol. 2, pgs. 327–46, 1868. *Fig. 14.8:* Adapted from Fuster and Alexander, © copyright 1971, AAAS. *Fig. 14.20:* Courtesy Philip Daly.

Chapter 15 *Fig. 15.1:* Reprinted with permission of Elliot S. Valenstein. *Fig. 15.2:* From L. Schreimer and A. Kling, *Journal of Neurophysiology,* 1953, Vol. 16, pg. 653. By permission of the American Physiological Society. *Fig. 15.3:* From Jose M. R. Delgado, *Physical Control of the Mind: Toward a Psychocivilized Society,* Harper & Row Publishers, New York, 1969, Fig. 24, pgs. 170–1. *Fig. 15.5:* Courtesy Armed Forces Institute of Pathology Photography.

Chapter 16 *Fig. 16.3:* From Lippold, Olaf, *The Origin of the Alpha Rhythm,* Churchill, Livingstone, London, 1973, pg. 138. *Fig. 16.4:* Courtesy General Electric Medical Systems Division, Milwaukee, Wisconsin. *Fig. 16.5:* From Y. L. Yamamoto, *Advances in Neurology: 3rd Study,* Raven Press, 1981, pg. 47. *Fig. 16.6:* Courtesy Dr. D. Ingvar, University of Lund, Sweden. *Fig. 16.8:* Courtesy Dr. Lawrence Crooks, University of California, San Francisco. *Fig. 16.9:* From Hawkes, Holland, Moore and Worthington," NMR Tomography of the Brain," *Journal of Computer Assisted Tomography,* Vol. 4, #5, pgs. 577–86. © 1980 Raven Press, New York. *Figs. 16.10 and 16.11:* From Leona Weisburg, Richard L. Sturb, Carlos A. Garcia, *Essentials of Clinical Neurology.* Reprinted by permission of Aspen Publishers, Inc. © 1983. *Figs. 16.12 and 16.13:* Reprinted with permission from F. Torres, 1980. *Fig. 16.14:* From Donald W. Klass, *Medical Clinics of North America,* "The Electroencephalogram in Evaluation of Seizure," Vol. 52, #4, July 1968. Reprinted by permission of W. B. Saunders.

INDEX